RAND McNALLY

PREMIER
WORLD ATLAS

**Chairman, President & CEO,
Rand McNally and Company**
Henry J. Feinberg

**Vice President and General Manager,
Map & Atlas Publishing**
Jayne L. Fenton

Director, Reference Business
Kendra L. Ensor

Editors
Brett R. Gover
Ann T. Natunewicz

Art Direction and Design
John C. Nelson
Jamie O'Neal

Cartography (U.S.)
V. Patrick Healy
Jon M. Leverenz
Robert K. Argersinger
Barbara Benstead-Strassheim
Kerry B. Chambers
Marzee L. Eckhoff
Winifred V. Farbman
Susan K. Hudson
Gwynn A. Lloyd
Nina Lusterman
John M. McAvoy
Robert L. Merrill
Patty A. Porter
James A. Purvis
David R. Simmons
Thomas F. Vitacco

Cartography (U.K.)
Craig Asquith

Cartography (Italy)
Giovanni Baselli
Ubaldo Uberti

Manufacturing
Terry D. Rieger

Marketing
JoEllen A. Klein

Photo Research
Feldman and Associates, Inc.

Photo Credits

(l=left, r=right, c=center, t=top, b=bottom)

Jacket/cover

Tony Stone Images: © Sally Mayman (volcano); © Art Wolfe (penguin); © John Beatty (desert); © Michael Busselle (Masai warrior); © William J Hebert (mountain and field); © Demetrio Carrasco (geishas)

Contents

© North Wind Picture Archives, iv (figures 4, 6, and 7)

Tony Stone Images: © Nicholas Parfitt, x (background); © Christopher Arnesen, x (t r); © Johnny Johnson, x (b l); © Warren Jacobs, xi (background); © Nicholas DeVore, xi (t r), xv (background); © Stephen Studd, xi (b r); © Tony Stone Images, xii (background); © Kevin Schafer, xii (m); © Joel Bennett, xiii (background and t l); © Fred Felleman, xiii (b r); © Tony Stone Images, xiv (background); © Paul Harris, xiv (t r); © Keren Su, xiv (b l); © Sylvain Grandadam, xv (t l); © Anthony Cassidy, xv (b r); © Oliver Strewe, xvi (background); © Paul Chesley, xvi (t r); © Penny Tweedie, xvi (b l); © Stuart Westmorland, xvii (background); © Chad Ehlers, xvii (t l); © Fred Bavendam, xvii (b r); © Art Wolfe, xviii (background); © Joe Cornish, xviii (b l), xix (t l); © David Hiser, xviii (t r); © David Paterson, xix (background); © David Sutherland, xix (b r); © Richard During, xx (background); © John Running, xx (t r); © Tim Davis, xx (b l); © Darrell Gulin, xxi (background); © Robert Frerck, xxi (t l)

© 1997 PhotoDisc: iii (t), vi (figure 3), viii (background), ix (background and t l), xxi (b r), xxiv (Energy)

Copyright © Corel Corp.: xxii (background, t r, and b l), xxiii (background, t l, and b r), xxiv (Land, Population, and Growth)

Satellite photo, iv (figure 1), provided by Wally Jansen, WTJ Software Series

Premier World Atlas

Copyright © 1997 by Rand McNally and Company
1998 Revised Printing

www.randmcnally.com

Published and printed in the United States of America

Rand McNally and Company.
      Rand McNally premier world atlas.
         p.   cm.
      Includes index.
      ISBN 0-528-83893-8 (hardback). - - ISBN 0-528-83894-6 (paperback)
      1. Atlases. I. Title.   II. Title: Premier world atlas
G1021 .R45   1997 <G&M>
912- - DC21   97-11900
                                           CIP
                                         MAPS

Contents

INTRODUCTORY SECTION

Understanding Maps & Atlases . . . . iv - v
How to Use the Atlas . . . . vi-vii
The World & Its Seven Continents . viii - xxiv

MAPS

Index Map and Legend 1

World 2-5

World, Political 2-3
World, Physical 4-5

Europe 6-23

Europe, Political 6-7
Northern Europe 8-9
Scandinavia and the Baltic States 10-11
Northwest Europe 12-13
Mediterranean Lands 14-15
Southwest Europe 16-17
Southern Europe 18-19
Central and Eastern Europe 20-21
Eastern Europe 22-23

Asia 24-45

Asia, Political 24-25
Northern Eurasia 26-27
China, Mongolia, Korea, and Japan 28-29
Eastern China 30
Japan 31
Southeast Asia 32-33
Mainland Southeast Asia and the Philippines . . 34-35
Malaysia, Singapore, and Indonesia 36-37
Southwest Asia 38-39
India 40-41
The Middle East 42-43
Turkey and Transcaucasia 44-45

Africa 46-57

Africa, Political 46-47
Northern Africa 48-49

West Africa 50-51
Central and Southern Africa 52-53
Central Africa 54-55
Southern Africa and Madagascar 56-57

Australia and Oceania 58-63

Australia and Oceania, Political 58-59
Western Australia 60-61
Eastern Australia and New Zealand 62-63

Pacific and Indian Oceans 64-65
Atlantic Ocean 66

Antarctica 67

South America 68-74

South America, Political 68
Southern South America 69
Northern South America 70-71
Central South America 72-73
Northeast Brazil 74

North America 75-143

North America, Political 75
Mexico, Central America, and the Caribbean . . 76-77
Mexico 78-79
Central America and the Caribbean 80-81
Canada and Alaska 82-83
Canadian Province Maps 84-91
United States 92-93
U.S. State Maps 94-143

Arctic Region 144

INDEX

Index to the Reference Maps . . . . I•1-I•80

Understanding
Maps & Atlases

figure 1

figure 2

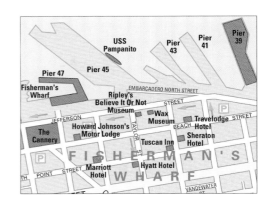

figure 3

What is a map?

A map is a representation, usually at a much-reduced size, of the location of things or places relative to one another. There are many different types of maps, including maps of the world, its regions or countries, cities, neighborhoods, and buildings. Figure 1 is a satellite image of California's San Francisco Bay area; figure 2 shows the same area represented on a road map; and figure 3 provides street-level detail of one of the city's neighborhoods.

figure 4

A set of maps bound together is called an atlas. Abraham Ortelius' *Theatrum orbis terrarum*, published in 1570, is considered to be the first modern "atlas," although it was not referred to as such for almost 20 years. In 1589, Gerardus Mercator (figure 4) coined the term when he named his collection of maps after the mythological titan Atlas, who carried the Earth on his shoulders as punishment for warring against Zeus. Since then, the definition of "atlas" has been expanded, and atlases often include additional geographic information in diagrams, tables, and text.

History of Cartography

Around 500 B.C., on a tiny clay tablet the size of a hand, the Babylonians inscribed the Earth as a flat disk (figure 5) with Babylon at the center. Geographic knowledge was also highly developed among the Egyptians, who drew maps on papyrus and carved them into temple walls. Ancient Greek philosophers and scientists debated endlessly the nature of the Earth and its place in the universe; Ptolemy, the influential geographer and astronomer, made an early attempt to map the known world (figure 6).

figure 5

Roman maps most often depicted boundaries, physical features, and the infrastructure of the Roman Empire. Over the following centuries, territorial expansion directly increased geographic knowledge, which in turn greatly enhanced the cartography, or map-making, of the time.

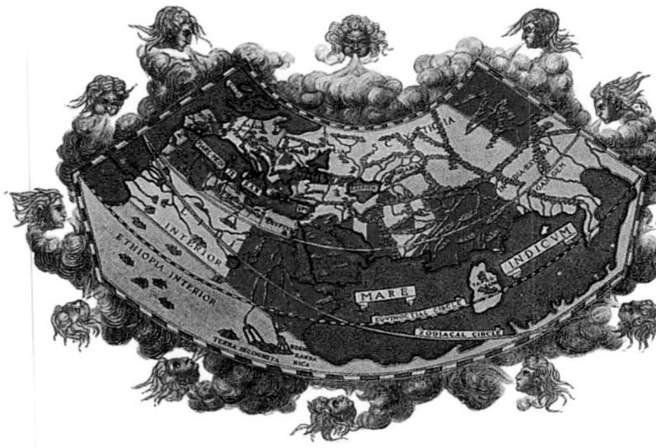

As trade and navigation grew, maps were developed to guide merchants and explorers. The Cantino map of 1502 (figure 7) is an example of a *portolan* (sea) chart used by mariners

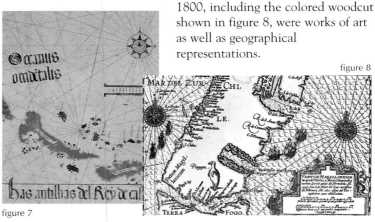

figure 6

traveling to the newly discovered Americas. Information gained from the past expeditions of John Cabot, Christopher Columbus, and Ferdinand Magellan led to great advances in the content and structure of world maps. As a result, many maps produced between 1600 and 1800, including the colored woodcut shown in figure 8, were works of art as well as geographical representations.

figure 8

figure 7

Over the past three centuries, cartography throughout the world has become extremely precise, aided most recently by satellites which provide images of the Earth and, within the last 25 years, have led to the development of global positioning systems. Sophisticated computers now manage large amounts of geographic information used to produce maps for a variety of purposes, including business, science, government, and education.

Latitude and Longitude

The imaginary horizontal line that circles the Earth exactly halfway between the North and South poles is called the Equator, which represents 0° latitude and lies 90° from either pole. The other lines of latitude, or parallels, measure the distance from the Equator, either north or south (figure 9). The imaginary vertical line that measures 0° longitude runs through the Greenwich Observatory in the United Kingdom, and is called the Prime Meridian. The other lines of longitude, or meridians, measure distances east and west of the Prime Meridian (figure 10), up to a maximum of 180°. Lines of latitude and longitude cross each other, forming a pattern called a grid system (figure 11). Any point on Earth can be located by its precise latitude and longitude coordinates.

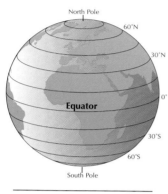

figure 9

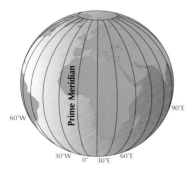

figure 10

figure 11

Map projections

Spherical representations of the Earth are called globes, while flat representations are called maps. Because globes are round and three-dimensional, they can show the continents and oceans undistorted and unbroken; therefore, they represent the Earth and its various features more correctly than do maps. Maps, however, generally feature larger scales and higher levels of detail.

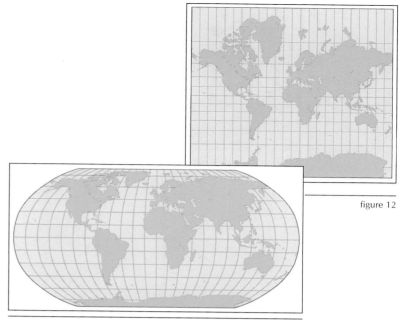

figure 12

figure 13

With the help of mathematics, cartographers are able to depict the curvature of the Earth on a two-dimensional surface. This process is called projecting a map, or creating a map projection. The size, shape, distance, area, and proportion of map features can be distorted, however, when the curves of a globe become the straight lines of a map. Distortion occurs because the Earth's spherical surface must be stretched and/or broken in places as it is flattened. Different map projections have specific properties that make them useful, and a cartographer must select the projection best-suited to the map's purpose.

The Mercator (figure 12) and the Robinson (figure 13) projections are commonly chosen for maps of the entire world. In this atlas, the Robinson is used along with four additional projections— the Lambert Azimuthal Equal Area, the Lambert Conformal Conic, the Sinusoidal, and the Azimuthal Equidisant.

Map scale

The scale of a map is the relationship between distances or areas shown on the map and the corresponding distances or areas on the Earth's surface. Large-scale maps generally show relatively small areas in greater detail than do small-scale maps, such as those of the world or the continents.

There are three different ways to express scale. Most often it is given as a fraction, such as 1:10,000,000, which means that the ratio of map distances to actual Earth distances is 1 to 10,000,000 (figure 14). Scale also can be expressed as a word phrase, such as, "One inch represents approximately 150 miles" (figure 15). Lastly, scale can be illustrated as a scale bar, labeled with miles on one side and kilometers on the other (figure 16). Any of these three scale expressions can be used to calculate distances on a map.

1:10 000 000

figure 14

One inch represents approximately 150 miles

figure 15

figure 16

How to Use the Atlas

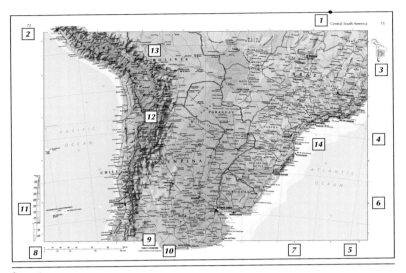

figure 1

[1] Map title
[2] Page number
[3] Locator map
[4] Latitude
[5] Longitude
[6] Index reference letter
[7] Index reference number
[8] Scale bar

[9] Scale ratio
[10] Map projection
[11] Hypsometric/bathymetric scale bar
[12] Shaded relief
[13] Hypsometric tints
      (to show elevation)
[14] Bathymetric tints
      (to show water depths)

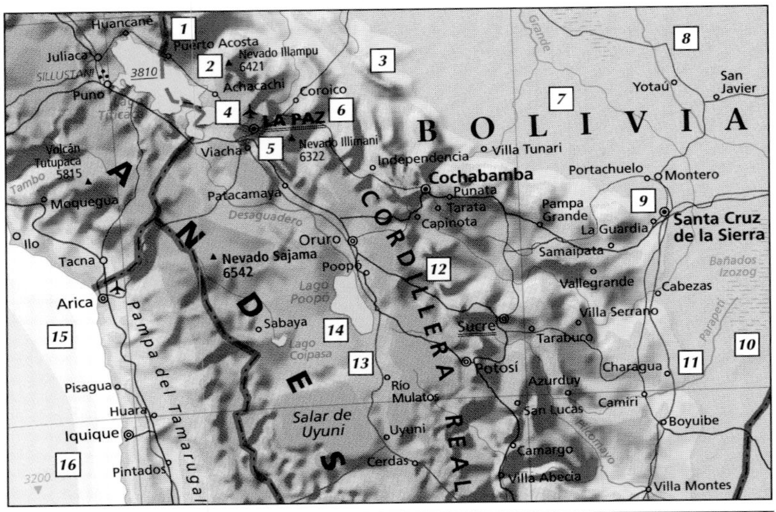

figure 2

[1] International boundary
[2] Mountain peak/elevation
[3] Hypsometric elevation tints
[4] International airport
[5] Urban area
[6] National capital
[7] Country name
[8] Road

[9] City/town
[10] Swamp
[11] River
[12] Mountain range
[13] Railroad
[14] Lake
[15] Bathymetric tints
[16] Depth of water (in meters)

What the *Premier World Atlas* includes

At the core of the *Premier World Atlas* is a collection of regional maps covering the entire world. The maps were designed to be as easy as possible to understand and use. Figure 1 is an example of a map spread contained in this atlas. The boxed numbers on this map, which correspond to items listed below it, highlight the features and information found on each map page—such as the map title, the locator map showing the area of the world depicted on the map, and the map scale.

Figure 2 is an enlarged section from the same map. As in figure 1, a few of the most common feature symbols have been highlighted. A more complete list of the map symbols used in this atlas can be found on page 1.

figure 4

Europe
Facts

Land area: 3.8 million square miles
   (9.9 million sq km)
Continental rank (in area): 6th
Estimated population: 712.1 million
Population density: 187/square mile (72/sq km)
Highest point: Gora El' Brus, Russia,
   18,510 feet (5,642 m)
Lowest point: Caspian Sea, Europe-Asia,
   92 feet (28 m) below sea level
Longest river: Volga, 2,194 miles (3,531 km)
Largest island: Great Britain, 88,795 square
   miles (229,978 sq km)
Largest lake: Caspian Sea, Europe-Asia,
   143,240 square miles (370,990 sq km)
Number of countries and dependencies: 49
Largest country: Russia, Europe-Asia,
   6.6 million square miles (17.1 million sq km)
Smallest country (excl. dependencies):
   Vatican City, 0.2 square miles (0.4 sq km)
Most populous country: Russia, Europe-Asia,
   150.5 million
Largest city: Moscow, metro. area pop.
   13.1 million

The atlas opens with a 17-page photographic essay devoted to the world and the continents (figure 3). Each of the seven continents is featured on two pages with photos and descriptive text. Fact blocks (figure 4) provide vital information about each continent's most notable characteristics and features.

figure 3

The World & its Seven Continents

Following the regional maps are individual maps of each of the United States, and the Canadian provinces (figure 5).

The last section of the *Premier World Atlas* is an 80-page index with entries for approximately 45,000 places and geographic features that appear on the maps.

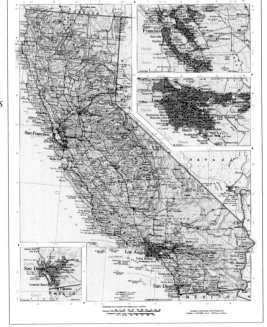

figure 5

Physical and Political Maps

The two main types of maps that appear in this atlas are physical maps and political maps. Physical maps, like the one shown in figure 6 (see next page), emphasize terrain, landforms, and elevation. Political maps, as in figure 7, emphasize countries and other political units over topography. The state and province maps found on pages 84-91 and pages 94-143 are both political and physical: they feature political coloration but also include shaded relief to depict landforms.

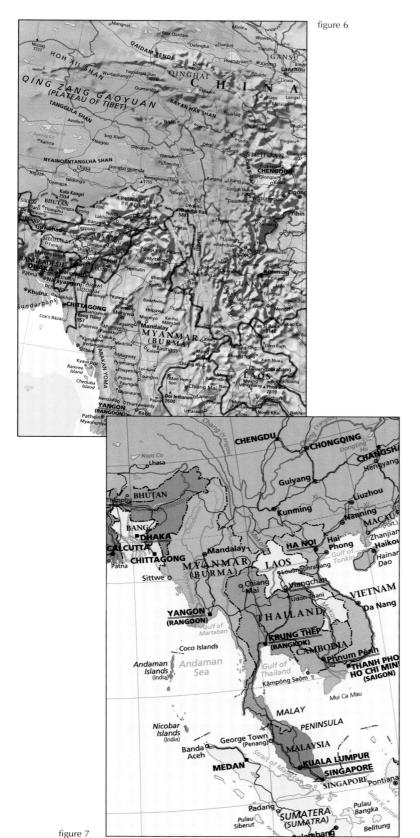

figure 6

figure 7

figure 8

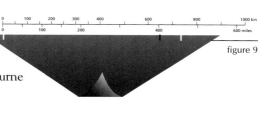

figure 9

between the 400-mile mark and the unlabeled 500-mile mark, indicating that the distance separating the two cities is approximately 450 miles (figure 9).

3) To confirm this measurement, make a third pencil mark (shown in red in figure 9) at the 400-mile mark. Slide the paper to the left so that the red mark lines up with 0. The white Sydney mark now falls very close to the 50-mile mark, which is unlabeled. Thus, Melbourne and Sydney are indeed approximately 450 (400 plus 50) miles apart.

Using the Index to Find Places

One of the most important purposes of an atlas is to help the reader locate places or features. In this atlas, each map is bordered by a letter and number grid. In the index, found in the back of the atlas on pages I•1 through I•80, every entry is assigned a map reference key, which consists of a letter and a number that correspond to a letter and a number on the grid. To locate places or features, follow the steps outlined in this example for Palembang, Indonesia:

P

Pālanpur, India	F5	40
Palaoa Point, C., Hi., U.S.	C4	104
Palapye, Bots.	F5	56
Palatine, Il., U.S.	A5	106
Palatka, Fl., U.S.	C5	102
Palau, ctry., Oc.	B8	37
Palawan, i., Phil.	B5	37
Pālayankottai, India	E8	41
Palembang, Indon.	D2	36
Palencia, Spain	G6	17
Palermo, Italy	D5	18
Palestine, Ar., U.S.	C5	97
Palestine, Il., U.S.	D6	106
Palestine, Tx., U.S.	D5	136

figure 10

1) Look up Palembang in the index. The entry (figure 10) contains the following information: the feature name (Palembang), an abbreviation for the country (Indon.) in which Palembang is located, the map reference key (D2) that corresponds to Palembang's location on the map, and the page number (36) of the map on which Palembang can be found.

2) Turn to page 36. Look along either the left or right margin for the letter "D" —the letter code given for Palembang. The "D" denotes a narrow horizontal band, roughly 1½" wide, in which Palembang is located. Then, look along either the top or bottom margin for the number "2" —the numerical part of the code given for Palembang. The "2" denotes a narrow vertical band, also roughly 1½" wide, in which Palembang is located.

3) Using your finger, follow the "D" band and the "2" band to the area where they meet (figure 11). Palembang can be found within the darker shaded square where the bands overlap.

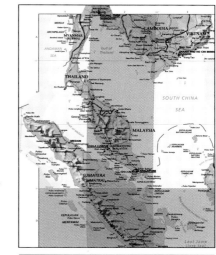

figure 11

Measuring Distances

Using a map scale bar, it is possible to calculate the distance between any two points on a map. To find the approximate distance between Melbourne and Sydney, Australia, for example, follow these steps:

1) Lay a piece of paper on the right-hand page of the "Eastern Australia and New Zealand" map found on pages 62-63, lining up its edge with the city dots for Melbourne and Sydney. Make a mark on the paper next to each dot (figure 8).

2) Place the paper along the scale bar found below the map, and position the first mark at 0. The second mark falls about halfway

Africa

Africa is a land of vast spaces and infinite variety. Across its great length and breadth are found tropical rain forests, savannas teeming with wildlife, sun-scorched deserts, sprawling modern cities, and a kaleidoscope of peoples and cultures.

The Sahara, largest of the world's deserts, dominates the northern half of the continent. Reaching from the Atlantic Ocean to the Red Sea, the Sahara covers an area nearly as large as the entire continent of Europe. Few people inhabit this inhospitable landscape of shifting sand dunes, gravel-covered plains, and bare mountains, where rain seldom falls and hot, dust-laden winds blow relentlessly.

Southern Africa also contains large arid regions, most notably the Namib and Kalahari deserts. Along the equator, however, rain falls in abundance. Verdant rain forests blanket much of this region, alive with monkeys, gorillas, wild pigs, and countless species of birds and insects. Between the deserts and the rain forests lie the broad swaths of grassland known as savannas. Herds of zebras, wildebeests, giraffes, elephants, and many other animals graze on the savannas, always on the alert for lions, hyenas, and other predators. Poaching and destruction of habitat have decimated animal populations in many parts of Africa, but enormous concentrations still exist in places such as northern Botswana and the Serengeti Plain of Tanzania.

Africa's greatest rivers are the Congo, the Zambezi, the Niger, and of course the Nile, the longest river in the world. From its headwaters in Burundi, the Nile flows northward more

Left page: Acacia trees on the Serengeti Plain, Tanzania; Samburu girls, Kenya; African elephant.

Right page: Sahara near Arak, Algeria; brightly painted hut and its occupants, Lesotho; avenue of sphinxes, Luxor, Egypt. .

than four thousand miles —through rugged mountains and highlands, the beautiful lake country of East Africa, and the wide marshy plain known as the Sudd—before spilling into the Mediterranean Sea.

Humans have farmed the fertile land of the Nile Delta from time immemorial, and it was here that the great civilization of the ancient Egyptians sprang up more than five thousand years ago. The marvelous archaeological legacies of this civilization include the Pyramids, the Sphinx, and the temples of Karnak and Luxor.

Among Africa's seven hundred million people there is tremendous ethnic and cultural diversity. More than eight hundred languages are spoken across the continent, and scores of distinct ethnic groups can be identified—groups such as the Tuareg and Berbers of Saharan Africa, the Masai and Kikuyu of the eastern savannas, the Fang and Bateke of the rain forests. Not surprisingly, few African countries are ethnically homogeneous.

Tremendous change has swept through Africa in the twentieth century. As recently as the 1940s, nearly the entire continent was controlled by colonial powers. In the wake of the Second World War, independence movements gathered strength, and by the end of the 1970s all of Africa's countries had shaken off their colonial shackles. For the first time in centuries, the continent was free to seek its own identity and destiny.

Africa Facts

Land area: 11.7 million square miles (30.3 million sq km)

Continental rank (in area): 2nd

Estimated population: 722.2 million

Population density: 62/square mile (24/sq km)

Highest point: Kilimanjaro, Tanzania, 19,340 feet (5,895 m)

Lowest point: Lac Assal, Djibouti, 515 feet (157 m) below sea level

Longest river: Nile, 4,145 miles (6,671 km)

Largest island: Madagascar, 226,658 square miles (587,041 sq km)

Largest lake: Lake Victoria, 26,820 square miles (69,463 sq km)

Number of countries and dependencies: 61

Largest country: Sudan, 967,500 square miles (2,505,813 sq km)

Smallest country (excl. dependencies): Seychelles, 175 square miles (453 sq km)

Most populous country: Nigeria, 102.9 million

Largest city: Cairo, metro. area pop. 13.4 million

Antarctica

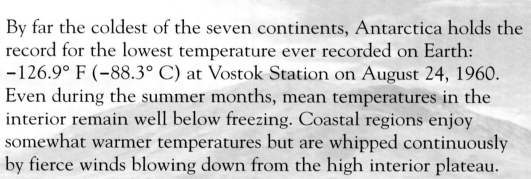

The frozen continent of Antarctica lies
at the very bottom of the world,
buried beneath a great sheet of ice and
encircled by frigid seas crowded with
towering icebergs.

By far the coldest of the seven continents, Antarctica holds the
record for the lowest temperature ever recorded on Earth:
–126.9° F (–88.3° C) at Vostok Station on August 24, 1960.
Even during the summer months, mean temperatures in the
interior remain well below freezing. Coastal regions enjoy
somewhat warmer temperatures but are whipped continuously
by fierce winds blowing down from the high interior plateau.

Because of the extreme cold, most of the snow that falls over
Antarctica's interior does not melt; instead, it accumulates and
gradually compacts. Over the course of millions of years,
this process has formed the ice sheet that now covers nearly the
entire continent. Almost inconceivably massive, the sheet has
an average thickness as great as the depth of the Grand Canyon;
its maximum thickness is three times greater. It holds some
ninety percent of all the ice on Earth, and seventy percent of
the fresh water.

As the ice sheet slowly spreads outward under its own
crushing weight, its edges spill into the surrounding seas,
forming immense shelves that in some places extend hundreds
of miles from the shore. The largest of these, the Ross Ice Shelf,
covers an area as large as the entire country of France.
Enormous pieces continuously break off, or "calve," from the
margins of the shelves and drift northward as icebergs.

If all of Antarctica's ice were to melt, the consequences would be disastrous. Ocean levels would rise dramatically, flooding coastal regions around the world. Florida, for example, would disappear under water, as would southeast Asia's Malay Peninsula and the Low Countries of Europe. More than half of the world's people would be forced to relocate.

Antarctica's coasts, islands, and seas are as full of life as its interior is barren. Clamorous penguin rookeries, some containing tens of thousands of individuals, dot the coastline. Petrels, albatrosses, and cormorants sail the coastal skies, searching the sea for fish and crustaceans. Seven species of seal, including leopard seals, elephant seals, and crabeaters, swim the nutrient-rich Antarctic waters along with squid, octopuses, killer whales, blue whales, and more than a dozen other whale species.

To whom does Antarctica belong? This question has provoked a great deal of controversy in the twentieth century, as numerous countries have explored the continent, made territorial claims, or established research stations. The possibility of rich mineral deposits adds urgency to the question.

In 1959, twelve countries drafted and signed the Antarctic Treaty, which declares Antarctica a natural reserve to be used only for peaceful purposes, especially scientific investigation. So far, the treaty has met with great success, and today Antarctica enjoys a spirit of international cooperation unknown elsewhere in the world.

Left page: Sled and dog team; Emperor penguins.
Right page: Iceberg and ice floes; research ship anchored along sea ice; killer whale.

Antarctica Facts

Land area: 5.4 million square miles (14 million sq km)

Continental rank (in area): 5th

Estimated population: No permanent population

Highest point: Vinson Massif, 16,066 feet (4,897 m)

Lowest point: Deep Lake, 184 feet (56 m) below sea level

Longest river: Antarctica has no true rivers

Largest island: Berkner Island, 20,005 square miles (51,829 sq km)

Number of countries with territorial claims: 7

Number of countries with research stations: 18

Asia

Three out of five people on Earth live in Asia, by far the world's largest and most heavily populated continent. With its myriad of landscapes, peoples, and historical treasures, and its swelling population, Asia represents a microcosm of the entire world.

Mountain systems—some ancient, some young and still rising—are the continent's signature landform. The Himalayas, which run through Pakistan, China, India, Nepal, and Bhutan, form the loftiest range in the world. Reaching more than five miles into the heavens, Mount Everest is the world's highest mountain, but nearby Kanchenjunga, Dhawalāgiri, Annapurna, and the peak known simply as K2 are hardly less formidable.

Seemingly endless expanses of semiarid grassland, or steppes, blanket much of the vast continental interior. Just north of the Himalayas lies the remote Tibetan Plateau, nicknamed the "Rooftop of the World": its average elevation is nearly half the height of Mount Everest.

The northern third of the continent is occupied by the region known as Siberia. Its name evokes images of a bitterly cold wasteland of snow and tundra, but visitors also discover vast, pristine forests, grassy plains, and extensive marshlands.

A long belt of desert stretches from the Arabian peninsula to eastern China. Most of this arid region is virtually uninhabited, and life is harsh for the few residents. The parched landscape of the Gobi, Asia's largest desert, contains little more than tough scrub vegetation and brackish lakes.

In the far west, the Arabian peninsula is a sea of sand dunes, punctuated by an occasional oasis where tall palm trees provide the desert's only shade.

In sharp contrast to these barren landscapes, the tropical lands and islands of Southeast Asia are awash in greenery. Crops and rain forests thrive in this wet region, where seasonal monsoon rains saturate the land for months at a time.

For centuries, rivers have been a lifeline for the people of the continent. Nestled between the Tigris and Euphrates rivers is the fertile land of Mesopotamia, which supported an advanced society that flourished as early as 4000 B.C. Ruins found in the lush Indus River valley of Pakistan tell of an advanced culture dating back to around 3000 B.C. And, almost 4,000 years ago, the ancient Chinese civilization developed along the banks of the Huang (Yellow) River.

Irrigation networks are vital to Asia because rocky terrain and minimal precipitation make much of the continent ill-suited for agriculture, and all arable land must be farmed intensively. The fertile valleys and coasts of eastern and southern Asia already strain to meet the demands of Asia's soaring population.

Recent economic and technological development has allowed Japan, Singapore, Indonesia, and Korea to rise to international prominence. It is likely that this trend will continue for these and other Asian countries into the 21st century, which many observers are already referring to as "the Asian Century." It will be a time for the countries of the continent to flex their collective muscle. Since Asia represents such a large percentage of the Earth's population, what happens there might dictate what the future brings to the rest of the world.

Left page: Mount Fuji and tea fields, Japan; Kazak man with hunting eagle, Mongolia; giant panda.

Right page: Mount Everest; Dome of the Rock, Omar Mosque, Jerusalem, Israel; schoolboys in Nāgaur, India.

Asia Facts

Land area: 17.3 million square miles (44.9 million sq km)

Continental rank (in area): 1st

Estimated population: 3.5 billion

Population density: 203/square mile (78/sq km)

Highest point: Mt. Everest, China (Tibet)-Nepal, 29,028 feet (8,848 m)

Lowest point: Dead Sea, Israel-Jordan, 1,339 feet (408 m) below sea level

Longest river: Yangtze (Chang), 3,900 miles (6,300 km)

Largest island: New Guinea, 309,000 square miles (800,000 sq km)

Largest lake: Caspian Sea, Asia-Europe, 143,240 square miles (370,990 sq km)

Number of countries and dependencies: 50

Largest country: Russia, Asia-Europe, 6.6 million square miles (17.1 million sq km)

Smallest country (excl. dependencies): Maldives, 115 square miles (298 sq km)

Most populous country: China, 1.2 billion

Largest city: Tokyo, metro. area pop. 31.3 million

Australia
& Oceania

The continent of Australia, along with its island neighbor New Zealand, is often classified as part of Oceania, a larger region that includes more than 25,000 islands, volcanic peaks, and coral atolls scattered across the southern Pacific Ocean.

The first European explorers to Australia came ashore near present-day Sydney and were so awed by the profusion of unfamiliar vegetation that they named the area Botany Bay. Today, eucalyptus and acacia trees, fuschias, and spear lilies thrive alongside exotic animal species such as kangaroos, wallabies, koala bears, kookaburras, and platypuses in Australia's warm climate.

Low, semiarid plateaus cover much of western Australia, taking in the Great Sandy Desert, the Gibson Desert, and the Great Victoria Desert. Here, scrubby grasses and spiky bushes break up stretches of pebble-covered land. This barren, largely uninhabited region is the Outback, whose harsh beauty and remoteness have come to epitomize "The Land Down Under" for many non-Australians.

Australia's indigenous people, called the Aborigines, arrived and settled the Outback and other parts of the continent perhaps 35,000 years prior to the Europeans. The complex Aboriginal society is based on kinship and the belief that humans, the environment, and time are intimately associated. Aborigines hold sacred numerous sites across Australia, including Uluru, or Ayers Rock, the world's largest monolith.

Among Australia's most valuable natural resources are its vast grasslands, dotted with woolly herds of grazing sheep and fenced in by the paddocks of great ranches, or stations. Australia is a major world producer and exporter of wool, veal, and mutton.
Sheep herding and grazing also dominate the economy of New Zealand, where sheep outnumber humans fourteen to one.

In this century, New Zealand has aggressively developed its own resources and now ranks among the world's most economically advanced countries. Cascading rivers provide water power for burgeoning industrial development, and rich reserves of minerals, natural gas, and timber drive a strong economy. With this wealth of resources, New Zealand has become a world leader in trade, much of which passes through the superb natural harbor of Wellington, the capital city.

New Zealand has two main islands, both of which are mountainous and ruggedly beautiful. On South Island, icy glaciers cut through the Southern Alps, and dazzling fjords such as Milford Sound indent the southwestern coast. The smaller North Island, home to three-quarters of the country's population, is dominated by a central volcanic plateau over which tower three impressive peaks: Ruapehu, Ngauruhoe, and Tongariro.

Papua New Guinea, on the eastern half of the island of New Guinea, is an uneven mixture of lush rain forests, swamplands, and steep volcanic mountains. Along with many of the smaller islands of Oceania, it lies on the southwestern section of the Ring of Fire—a band of active volcanoes that encircles the Pacific Ocean.

Every year, thousands of winter-weary tourists escape to Oceania's tropical island paradises, such as Tahiti, Fiji, and Guam. Here, they revel in the endless stretches of sandy beaches, secluded coves, and absolute isolation, half a world away from their homes.

Left page: Dirt road through Australia's Outback; Aboriginal man, northern Australia; koala bear, Australia.

Right page: Rock Islands, Palau; Mount Cook, New Zealand's highest peak; school of sweetips.

Australia & Oceania Facts

Land area: 3.3 million square miles (8.5 million sq km)
Continental rank (in area): 7th
Estimated population: 29.0 million
Population density: 8.8/square mile (3.4/sq km)
Highest point: Mt. Wilhelm, Papua New Guinea, 14,793 feet (4,509 m)
Lowest point: Lake Eyre, South Australia, 52 feet (16 m) below sea level
Longest river: Murray-Darling, 2,330 miles (3,750 km)
Largest island: New Guinea, Oceania-Asia, 309,000 square miles (800,000 sq km)
Largest lake: Lake Eyre, 3,700 square miles (9,500 sq km)
Number of countries and dependencies: 33
Largest country: Australia, 3 million square miles (7.7 million sq km)
Smallest country (excl. dependencies): Nauru, 8.1 square miles (21 sq km)
Most populous country: Australia, 18.4 million
Largest city: Sydney, metro. area pop. 3.5 million

Europe

Human settlements and civilizations have flourished in Europe for more than four thousand years, benefiting from the generally mild climate and the abundance of arable land, navigable rivers, and natural resources. The continent today ranks with East Asia and South Asia as one of the three greatest population centers in the world.

The northern half of Europe bears dramatic evidence of past ice ages. During the Pleistocene epoch, immense sheets and rivers of ice plowed across the region, rounding the mountains of Scandinavia and Scotland, scouring river valleys to create Norway's deep fjords, and depositing a thick layer of sand, gravel, and boulder-filled clay across the landscape. This glacial deposition played a major part in the formation of the Great European Plain, which stretches in an arc from western France to the Urals. The western part of the plain is Europe's most intensively farmed region as well as its most densely populated, home to such great cities as Paris, Amsterdam, Berlin, Stockholm, Warsaw, and Moscow.

Uplands and mountain systems dominate the southern half of the continent. The Pyrenees, Alps, and Carpathians together form a nearly unbroken band of mountains stretching from the Atlantic to central Romania. Until the advent of modern transportation, this formidable natural barrier impeded overland travel between the Mediterranean region and the rest of Europe, especially when winter snows fell on the mountain passes. As a result, a distinct Mediterranean culture evolved, and it remains strong today.

Thanks to a warm ocean current called the North Atlantic Drift, northwestern Europe enjoys a climate far milder than those of lands at similar latitudes in North America and Asia. The current warms and moistens offshore air masses, which then flow across the British Isles, the Low Countries, France, Denmark, Germany, and surrounding lands. As this maritime air moves into eastern Europe, its effects become weaker and weaker, and climates become increasingly extreme. Mountain systems block the air masses from the Mediterranean region, which has a hotter, drier climate.

Europe has been home to many great civilizations, including those of the Minoans, Mycenaeans, Greeks, and Romans. With the collapse of the Roman Empire, Europe plunged into a period of relative decline and darkness, but emerged roughly one thousand years later into the light of the Renaissance, a glorious rebirth that pervaded nearly every field of human endeavor but especially art and science.

The Renaissance also marked the beginning of an era of exploration and expansion. Great powers such as England, Spain, Portugal, and France explored, conquered, and colonized lands all over the world—Africa, the Americas, Australia, India, and other parts of Asia. As gold, silver, and other riches poured into Europe, emigrants poured out, spreading European ideas, languages, and cultures to nearly every part of the globe. The Industrial and Agricultural revolutions further increased the continent's wealth and dominance. Through the first part of the 20th century, Europe held sway over the world as no continent had ever done before or is likely to do in the future.

Left page: Ibexes on mountainside above lake, Interlaken, Switzerland; farmer picking grapes, Italy; Big Ben, London.

Right page: Highlands of Scotland; Cibeles Fountain, Madrid; St. Basil's Cathedral, Moscow.

Europe Facts

Land area: 3.8 million square miles (9.9 million sq km)
Continental rank (in area): 6th
Estimated population: 712.9 million
Population density: 188/square mile (72/sq km)
Highest point: Gora El'brus, Russia, 18,510 feet (5,642 m)
Lowest point: Caspian Sea, Europe-Asia, 92 feet (28 m) below sea level
Longest river: Volga, 2,194 miles (3,531 km)
Largest island: Great Britain, 88,795 square miles (229,978 sq km)
Largest lake: Caspian Sea, Europe-Asia, 143,240 square miles (370,990 sq km)
Number of countries and dependencies: 49
Largest country: Russia, Europe-Asia, 6.6 million square miles (17.1 million sq km)
Smallest country (excl. dependencies): Vatican City, 0.2 square miles (0.4 sq km)
Most populous country: Russia, Europe-Asia, 150.5 million
Largest city: Moscow, metro. area pop. 13.1 million

North America

Almost 30,000 years ago, the first North Americans arrived on the continent after crossing the Bering land bridge from Asia. Before them lay a rich land of dense forests, virgin streams and lakes, and prairies where great herds of bison roamed.

These same treasures beckoned the first European settlers to North America in the early 16th century. For nearly 500 years, emigrants from all corners of the globe have been pouring onto the continent in search of a better life. Many have realized their dreams, and along the way North America has become the world's wealthiest and most influential continent.

Among its richest resources are vast tracts of arable land. The farmland of the Great Plains is so productive that this region has been called "the Breadbasket of the World." The United States and Canada are world leaders in food production, harvesting so much wheat, corn, barley, soybeans, oats, sugar, and fruit each year that thousands of surplus tons can be exported.

Sweeping mountain systems frame the plains in the east and west. Eastern North America is traversed by the ancient, well-weathered Appalachian Mountains, which stretch from Newfoundland south through Georgia. The soaring Rockies extend from western Canada into New Mexico, showcasing some of

Left page: Jasper National Park, Canadian Rockies, Alberta; Tarahumara man, Mexico; red-eyed tree frog, Central America.

Right page: farmhouse and fields near Moscow, Idaho; El Tajin, a Mayan temple in Veracruz, Mexico; spikes of wheat.

North America Facts

Land area: 9.5 million square miles (24.7 million sq km)

Continental rank (in area): 3rd

Estimated population: 459.6 million

Population density: 48/square mile (19/sq km)

Highest point: Mt. McKinley, Alaska, U.S., 20,320 feet (6,194 m)

Lowest point: Death Valley, California, U.S., 282 feet (84 m) below sea level

Longest river: Mississippi-Missouri, 3,740 miles (6,019 km)

Largest island: Greenland, 840,000 square miles (2,175,600 sq km)

Largest lake: Lake Superior, Canada-U.S., 31,700 square miles (82,100 sq km)

Number of countries and dependencies: 38

Largest country: Canada, 3.8 million square miles (10 million sq km)

Smallest country (excl. dependencies): St. Kitts and Nevis, 104 square miles (269 sq km)

Most populous country: United States, 265.1 million

Largest city: Mexico City, metro. area pop. 18.4 million

the continent's most dramatic landscapes. Mexico's greatest mountain ranges, the Sierra Madres, collide to form a spiny, volcanic backbone that continues into Central America.

Fed by hundreds of tributaries, the Mississippi-Missouri river system—North America's longest—cuts a path through the center of the continent. The mighty river both embraces and disregards those who settle along its banks, providing fertile farmland and access to a vital transport corridor, but also periodically flooding adjacent farms and towns.

Canada, the United States, and Mexico comprise almost 90% of North America. The United States and Canada have diversified, service-oriented economies, and increasingly urban populations. Mexico, although poorer than its northern neighbors, has in recent decades become a key manufacturing center and a popular tourist destination.

Brilliant tropical vegetation and exotic wildlife abound in the seven countries of Central America, which occupy a slender isthmus connecting Mexico and South America. Unlike the rest of North America, Central America has a population that is both dispersed and predominantly rural.

Many people in Mexico and Central America are of mixed Spanish and Indian ancestry, a rich heritage defined by a proud culture. This blending is less evident in remote areas, where Indian villages have remained virtually unchanged for centuries. In the cities, however, a strong Indian influence intermingles with architectural remnants of the colonial era and dramatic evidence of modern development.

To the east lie the balmy islands of the Caribbean Sea, including Cuba, Hispaniola, the West Indies, Jamaica, and Puerto Rico. Each boasts a colorful culture that reflects the diverse mix of peoples—Europeans, Africans, and Indians—who found themselves thrown together during the colonial past.

South America

South America is a land of untamed beauty and tremendous diversity—in its landscapes, plant and animal life, and people.

Large parts of the continent remain as wild and pristine as they were when the first humans arrived more than eleven millennia ago. Human movement and settlement have been hindered by the rugged Andes mountains and the nearly impenetrable Amazonian rain forest.

The Andes, which curve along the continent's western edge from Venezuela in the north to Tierra del Fuego in the south, form the longest mountain system in the world. The loftiest Andean peaks reach greater heights than any others in the Western Hemisphere.

High in the Andes, clear, cold streams wander among moss-covered boulders, merge with one another, and eventually tumble out of the mountains as the Marañon and Ucayali rivers. These are the principal tributaries of the world's mightiest river, the Amazon. Crossing nearly the entire breadth of the continent, the Amazon carries one-fifth of all of the world's flowing water.

The rain forest that covers much of the Amazon's vast drainage basin holds an astonishing abundance and variety of life. Still largely unexplored, the rain forest is a torrid, watery realm of slow-moving rivers and sloughs, of colorful birds, insects, and flowers, and of trees growing so densely that little sunlight

Left page: Incan ruins, Machupicchu, Peru; Quechua woman and child, Peru; great blue heron, Galapagos Islands.

Right page: Iguassu Falls, Argentina-Brazil; colonial buildings, Bahia, Brazil; bird of paradise flower, Amazonia.

reaches the forest floor. Most of Amazonia's animals and insects live high up in the forest canopy and rarely descend to the ground.

Archaeologists believe that the first humans to reach South America were groups of hunters and gatherers migrating southward from North America some 11,000 to 14,000 years ago. Thousands of years later, the descendants of these first arrivals built several great civilizations on the continent, including the magnificent Inca Empire, which reached its maximum extent during the period AD 1100—1350. The city of Cusco, in present-day Peru, served as the Incas' capital, and today tourists are drawn to the many splendid ruins in and around the city.

The arrival of Europeans in the early 1500s, and their subsequent conquest and colonization of the continent, were disastrous to the indigenous peoples: it is estimated that three-quarters of the population died as a result of European diseases, warfare, and forced labor.

Although the colonial period came to an end in the 1800s, its architectural legacy endures in cathedrals, plazas, houses, and government buildings found in cities throughout the continent.

Nine out of ten South Americans live within 150 miles of the coast; much of the interior is only sparsely settled. For this reason, South America is sometimes spoken of as "the hollow continent." In recent decades, millions of people have abandoned their small farms and villages in search of a better life in the city.

This trend has greatly swollen the populations of many of the largest cities, including São Paulo, Rio de Janeiro, Buenos Aires, and Caracas. As a new millennium begins, the crowding and frenzy of such cities stand in sharp contrast to remote interior villages, where the people live just as they have for centuries and time seems to stand still.

South America Facts

Land area: 6.9 million square miles (17.8 million sq km)

Continental rank (in area): 4th

Estimated population: 319.5 million

Population density: 46/square mile (18/sq km)

Highest point: Cerro Aconcagua, Argentina, 22,831 feet (6,959 m)

Lowest point: Salinas Chicas, Argentina, 138 feet (42m) below sea level

Longest river: Amazon, 4,000 miles (6,400 km)

Largest island: Tierra del Fuego, 18,600 square miles (48,200 sq km)

Largest lake: Lake Titicaca, Bolivia-Peru, 3,200 square miles (8,300 sq km)

Number of countries and dependencies: 15

Largest country: Brazil, 3.3 million square miles (8.5 million sq km)

Smallest country (excl. dependencies): Suriname, 63,251 square miles (163,820 sq km)

Most populous country: Brazil, 161.7 million

Largest city: São Paulo, metro. area pop. 16.7 million

Land

The Earth has a total surface area of 197 million square miles (510.2 million sq km). Water, including oceans, seas, lakes, and rivers, covers nearly three-quarters of this area; land only one-quarter.

The largest landmass is Eurasia, shared by the continents of Europe and Asia. Eurasia represents 36.5% of the Earth's total land area (but only 10.7% of the total surface area). The largest continent is Asia, which accounts for 30% of the total land area. Africa ranks second, with 20% of the total land area.

The smallest continent by far is Australia, which holds only 5.1% of the world's land. When it is grouped with New Zealand and the other islands of Oceania, the figure rises only slightly, to 5.7%.

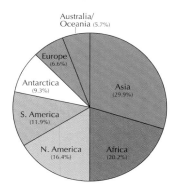

Australia/Oceania (5.7%)
Europe (6.6%)
Antarctica (9.3%)
Asia (29.9%)
S. America (11.9%)
N. America (16.4%)
Africa (20.2%)

Percentage of world land area

Energy

A large percentage of the world's energy is used for manufacturing. This fact helps explain the great variances among the continents in the consumption of energy. Highly developed North America, with only 8% of the world's population, consumes nearly 30% of the world's energy, and more than five times as much as Africa and South America combined.

For two continents, energy consumption exceeds production: North America produces roughly nine-tenths of the energy it consumes, and Europe only three-fifths. In contrast, Africa consumes less than two-fifths of the energy it produces.

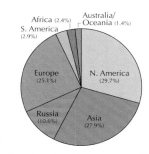

Africa (2.4%)
Australia/Oceania (1.4%)
S. America (2.9%)
Europe (25.1%)
N. America (29.7%)
Russia (10.6%)
Asia (27.9%)

Percentage of world energy consumption

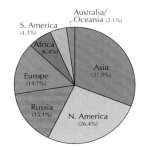

Australia/Oceania (2.1%)
S. America (4.3%)
Africa (6.4%)
Asia (31.0%)
Europe (14.7%)
Russia (15.1%)
N. America (26.4%)

Percentage of world energy production

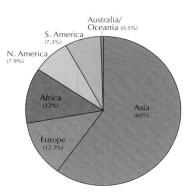

Population

Asia is the world's most populous continent, and has been for at least two millennia. Its current population of 3.5 billion represents an astonishing 60% of the world's people, nearly five times as much as any other continent. It is home to the world's two most populous countries: China, with nearly 1.2 billion people, and India, with 900 million. Four other Asian countries rank among the ten most populous in the world: Indonesia (4th), Pakistan (7th), Japan (8th), and Bangladesh (9th).

Europe and Africa each contain roughly 700 million people. Europe, however, has only one-third the land area of Africa, so its population density is three times greater. Antarctica has no permanent population and therefore does not appear on the graph.

Australia/Oceania (0.5%)
S. America (7.3%)
N. America (7.9%)
Africa (12%)
Asia (60%)
Europe (12.3%)

Percentage of world population

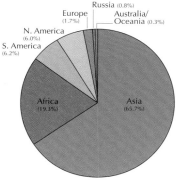

population Growth

The world's population is growing at a rapid pace: at present, the annual rate of natural increase (births minus deaths) is 1.5%. Today, the world holds 5.8 billion people; some experts predict that by the year 2050 this number will have increased by two-thirds, to 9.8 billion.

The largest part of the growth is taking place in Asia, which already is home to three-fifths of the world's people. Of every hundred people added to the Earth's population each year, 65 are Asian. Africa is also gaining a larger share of the world total: the continent's current population represents 12% of the world total, but its growth accounts for more than 19% of the annual world increase.

Europe, on the other hand, is seeing its share of the world population erode. Although Europe is the second most populous continent, its annual growth represents less than 2% of the world total.

Russia (0.8%)
Europe (1.7%)
Australia/Oceania (0.3%)
N. America (6.0%)
S. America (6.2%)
Africa (19.3%)
Asia (65.7%)

Percentage of world population growth

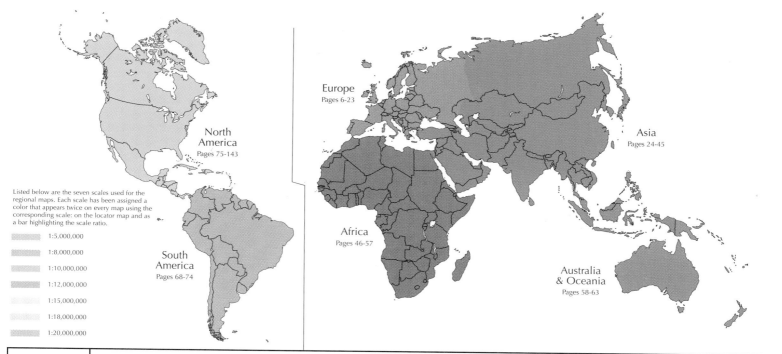

Europe
Pages 6-23

Asia
Pages 24-45

North
America
Pages 75-143

Africa
Pages 46-57

South
America
Pages 68-74

Australia
& Oceania
Pages 58-63

Listed below are the seven scales used for the
regional maps. Each scale has been assigned a
color that appears twice on every map using the
corresponding scale: on the locator map and as
a bar highlighting the scale ratio.

1:5,000,000
1:8,000,000
1:10,000,000
1:12,000,000
1:15,000,000
1:18,000,000
1:20,000,000

Legend

World and Regional Maps

Hydrographic Features

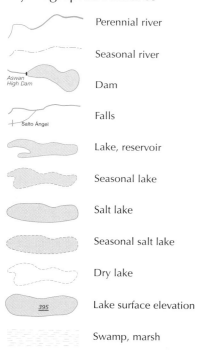

Perennial river

Seasonal river

Dam

Falls

Lake, reservoir

Seasonal lake

Salt lake

Seasonal salt lake

Dry lake

395   Lake surface elevation

Swamp, marsh

Reef

Glacier/ice sheet

Topographic Features

Elevations and depths are given in meters.

764   Depth of water
▼

2278   Elevation above sea level
▲

1700   Elevation below sea level
▼

≍   Mountain pass

Huo Shan   Mountain peak/elevation
1774

The highest elevation on each continent is underlined.
The highest elevation in each country is shown in boldface.

Transportation Features

Major road

Other road

Trail

Major railway

Other railway

Navigable canal

Tunnel

Ferry

✈ International airport

✈ Other airport

Political Features

International Boundaries (First-order political unit)

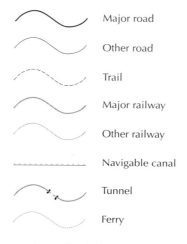

International

Disputed (de facto)

Disputed (de jure)

Indefinite/undefined

Demarcation line

Internal Boundaries

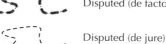

State/province

NORMANDIE   Cultural/historic region
(Denmark)   Administering country

Cities and Towns
The size of symbol and type indicates the relative importance of the locality.

■ **LONDON**
▣ **CHICAGO**
◉ **Milwaukee**
◎ Tacna
◉ Iquitos
○ Old Crow
∘ Mettawa
⬤ Urban area

Capitals

MEXICO CITY
Bonn   Country, dependency

RIO DE JANEIRO
Perth   State, province

MANCHESTER
Chester   County

Cultural Features

┌┄┐ or ▪   National park

▪   Point of interest

nnnnnn   Wall

∴   Ruins

State and Province Maps
Pages 84-91 and Pages 94-143

✪ Capital
○ County seat
▲ Military installation
△ Point of interest
+ Mountain peak

International boundary

State/province boundary

County boundary

Road

Railroad

 Urban area

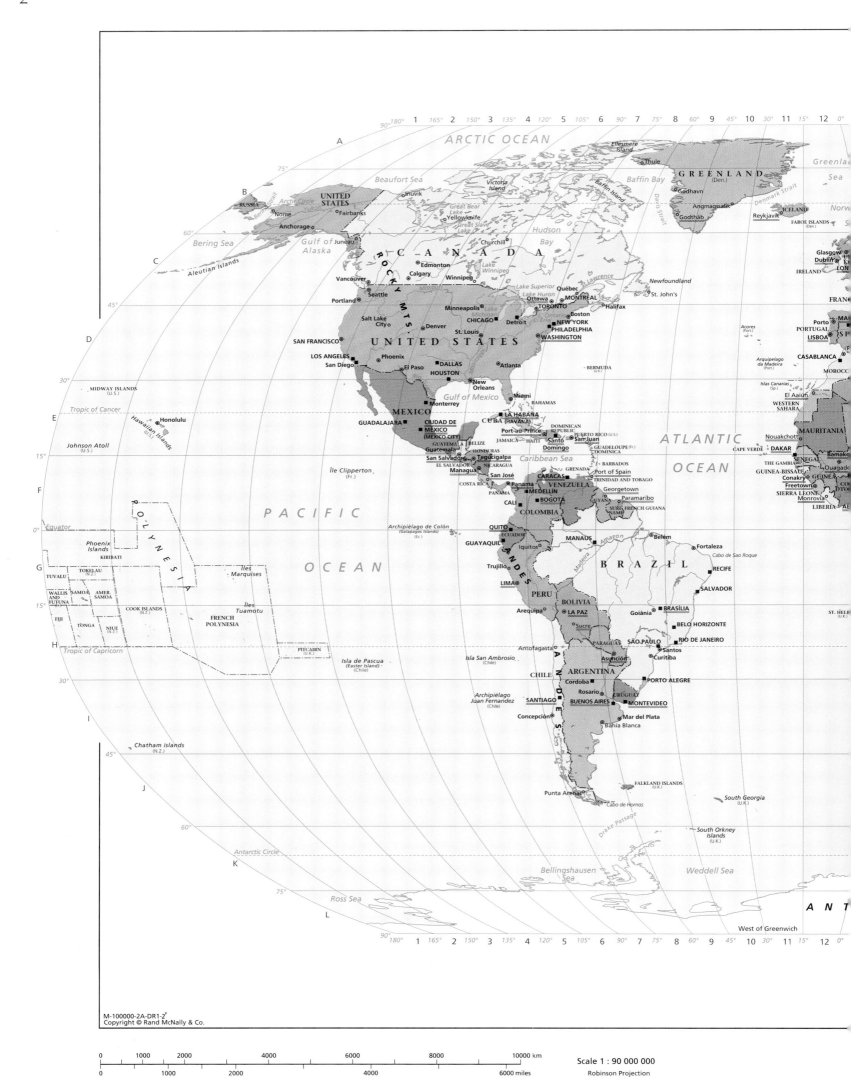

ARCTIC OCEAN

GREENLAND
(Den.)

Ellesmere Island

Thule

Godhavn

Angmagssalik

Godthåb

Reykjavik

ICELAND

FAROE ISLANDS
(Den.)

Baffin Bay

Davis Strait

Denmark Strait

Baffin Island

Victoria Island

Beaufort Sea

RUSSIA

Bering Strait

Arctic Circle

Inuvik

Great Bear Lake

Yellowknife

Great Slave Lake

UNITED STATES

Nome

Anchorage

Fairbanks

Yukon

Gulf of Alaska

Juneau

Aleutian Islands

Bering Sea

Glasgow

Dublin

IRELAND

LON

FRANC

C A N A D A

Churchill

Hudson Bay

ROCKY MTS.

Edmonton

Calgary

Vancouver

Seattle

Portland

Lake Winnipeg

Winnipeg

Lake Superior

Lake Michigan

Lake Huron

Minneapolis

CHICAGO

Québec

Ottawa

TORONTO

Lake Ontario

Lake Erie

St. Lawrence

MONTREAL

Boston

NEW YORK

Newfoundland

St. John's

Halifax

Salt Lake City

Denver

St. Louis

Detroit

PHILADELPHIA

WASHINGTON

UNITED STATES

Missouri

SAN FRANCISCO

LOS ANGELES

San Diego

Phoenix

El Paso

DALLAS

HOUSTON

Atlanta

New Orleans

BERMUDA

Acores
(Port.)

Porto

PORTUGAL

LISBOA

SP

Arquipelago da Madeira
(Port.)

CASABLANCA

MOROCC

MIDWAY ISLANDS
(U.S.)

Tropic of Cancer

Honolulu

Hawaiian Islands

Johnson Atoll
(U.S.)

Monterrey

MEXICO

GUADALAJARA

CIUDAD DE MÉXICO
(MEXICO CITY)

Gulf of Mexico

Miami

BAHAMAS

CUBA

LA HABANA
(HAVANA)

DOMINICAN REPUBLIC

Port-au-Prince

Santo Domingo

PUERTO RICO (U.S.)

San Juan

Islas Canarias
(Sp.)

El Aaiún

WESTERN SAHARA

Nouakchott

MAURITANIA

ATLANTIC OCEAN

CAPE VERDE

DAKAR

SENEGAL

THE GAMBIA

GUINEA-BISSAU

Conakry

Freetown

SIERRA LEONE

Monrovia

LIBERIA

Bamako

Ouagad

GUINEA

CO

IVO

GUATEMALA

BELIZE

HONDURAS

San Salvador

Tegucigalpa

EL SALVADOR

Managua

NICARAGUA

San José

COSTA RICA

PANAMA

Panamá

CARACAS

MEDELLÍN

CALI

BOGOTÁ

VENEZUELA

COLOMBIA

JAMAICA

HAITI

GUADELOUPE (Fr.)

DOMINICA

BARBADOS

GRENADA

Port of Spain

TRINIDAD AND TOBAGO

Georgetown

GUYANA

Paramaribo

SURI
NAMI

FRENCH GUIANA

Île Clipperton
(Fr.)

Caribbean Sea

PACIFIC

OCEAN

POLYNESIA

Equator

Archipiélago de Colón
(Galapagos Islands)
(Ec.)

QUITO

ECUADOR

GUAYAQUIL

Iquitos

Trujillo

LIMA

MANAUS

Amazon

Madeira

BRAZIL

Belém

Fortaleza

Cabo de São Roque

RECIFE

SALVADOR

Phoenix Islands

KIRIBATI

TUVALU

TOKELAU

Îles Marquises

WALLIS AND FUTUNA

SAMOA

AMER. SAMOA

COOK ISLANDS
(N.Z.)

Îles Tuamotu

FRENCH POLYNESIA

FIJI

TONGA

NIUE
(N.Z.)

PERU

BOLIVIA

Arequipa

LA PAZ

Sucre

Goiânia

BRASÍLIA

BELO HORIZONTE

RIO DE JANEIRO

ST. HELE

Tropic of Capricorn

PITCAIRN
(U.K.)

Isla de Pascua
(Easter Island)
(Chile)

Isla San Ambrosio
(Chile)

Antofagasta

PARAGUAY

SÃO PAULO

Santos

Curitiba

Asunción

PORTO ALEGRE

URUGUAY

Chatham Islands
(N.Z.)

Archipiélago Juan Fernandez
(Chile)

SANTIAGO

CHILE

Córdoba

Rosario

ARGENTINA

ANDES

BUENOS AIRES

MONTEVIDEO

Mar del Plata

Bahía Blanca

Concepción

FALKLAND ISLANDS
(U.K.)

South Georgia
(U.K.)

Punta Arenas

Cabo de Hornos

Drake Passage

South Orkney Islands
(U.K.)

Antarctic Circle

Bellingshausen Sea

Weddell Sea

Ross Sea

West of Greenwich

ANT

0	1000	2000	4000	6000	8000	10000 km

0	1000	2000	4000	6000 miles

Scale 1 : 90 000 000

Robinson Projection

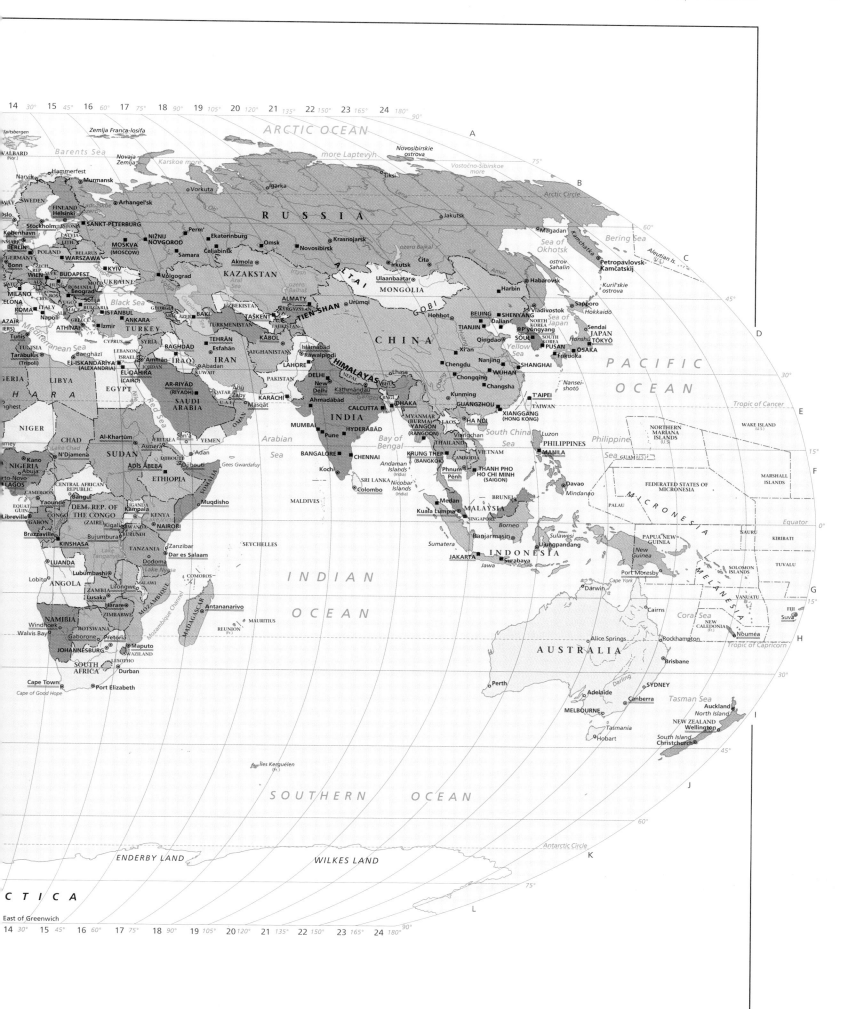

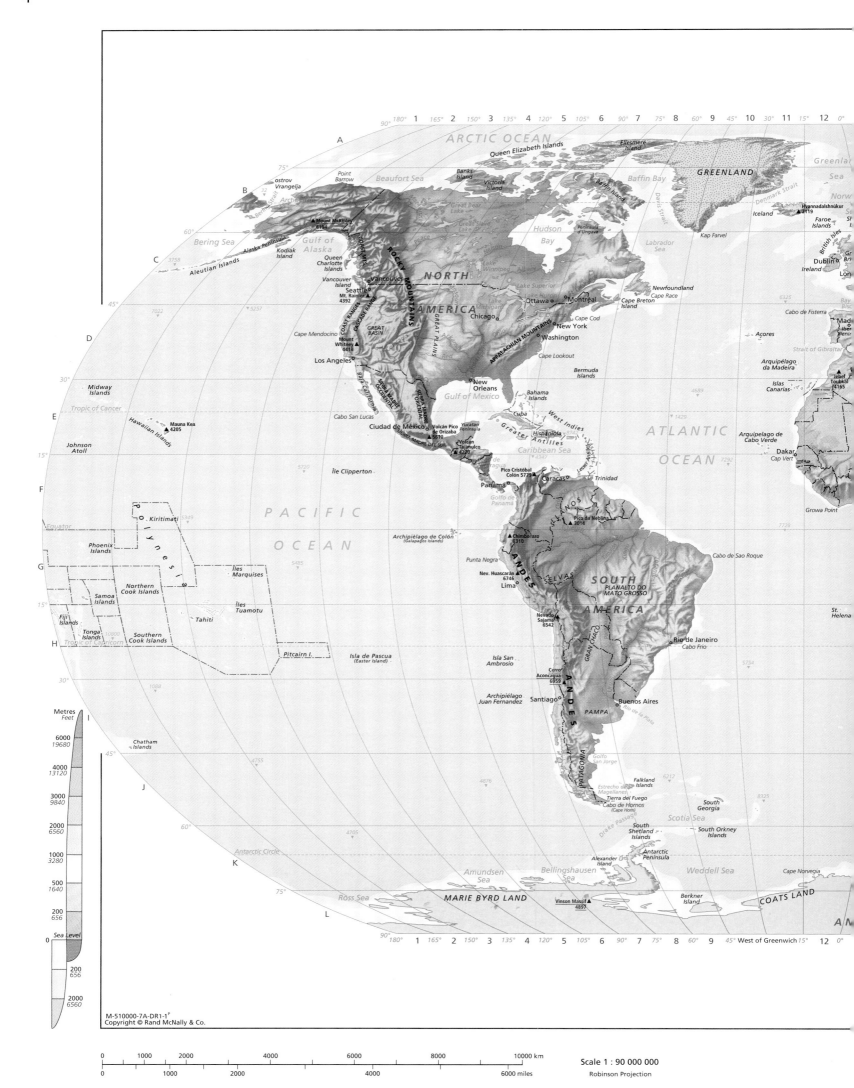

4

ARCTIC OCEAN

Queen Elizabeth Islands

Ellesmere Island

GREENLAND

Greenland Sea

Point Barrow

Banks Island

Baffin Bay

Norway

ostrov Vrangelja

Beaufort Sea

Victoria Island

Baffin Island

Denmark Strait

Arctic Circle

Great Bear Lake

Davis Strait

Hvannadalshnúkur ▲ 2119

Bering Strait

Mount McKinley ▲ 6194

Great Slave Lake

Iceland

Faroe Islands

Gulf of Alaska

NORTH

Hudson Bay

Peninsula d'Ungava

Kap Farvel

British Isles

Bering Sea

Alaska Peninsula

Kodiak Island

Queen Charlotte Islands

Lake Athabasca

Peace

Labrador Sea

Dublin Ireland

London

3758

Aleutian Islands

Vancouver Island

Vancouver Seattle

COAST MTS.

ROCKY MOUNTAINS

AMERICA

Lake Winnipeg

Nelson

Lake Superior

Newfoundland

Cape Race

Cape Breton Island

6325

Bay of Biscay

Mt. Rainier ▲ 4392

Ottawa

Montreal

7022

5257

CASCADE RANGE

GREAT PLAINS

Lake Michigan

Lake Huron

Chicago

Cape Cod

New York

Cabo de Fisterra

Madr

Iberi Penin

Cape Mendocino

Mount Whitney 4418

GREAT BASIN

Missouri

APPALACHIAN MOUNTAINS

Washington

Açores

Los Angeles

Cape Lookout

Strait of Gibraltar

Arquipélago da Madeira

Midway Islands

Baja California

SIERRA MADRE OCCIDENTAL

New Orleans

Gulf of Mexico

Bermuda Islands

4689

Islas Canarias

Jebel Toubkal ▲ 4165

Tropic of Cancer

Bahama Islands

SIERRA MADRE DEL SUR

Cabo San Lucas

Cuba

West Indies

1429

ATLANTIC

Hawaiian Islands

Mauna Kea ▲ 4205

Ciudad de México

Volcán Pico de Orizaba 5610

Yucatan Peninsula

Greater Antilles

Hispaniola

Arquipélago de Cabo Verde

Johnson Atoll

SIERRA MADRE DEL SUR

¡Volcán Tajumulco 4220

Caribbean Sea

4347

OCEAN

Dakar

Cap Vert

5720

Île Clipperton

de Nicaragua

Pico Cristóbal Colón 5775

7292

Kiritimati

Panamá

Caracas

Trinidad

5349

Golfo de Panamá

LLANOS

Pico da Neblina ▲ 3014

Growa Point

Equator

PACIFIC

Archipiélago de Colón (Galapagos Islands)

Chimborazo ▲ 6310

7728

Phoenix Islands

OCEAN

Punta Negra

ANDES

SOUTH

Cabo de Sao Roque

Îles Marquises

Polynesia

5185

Nev. Huascarán 6746

SELVAS

PLANALTO DO MATO GROSSO

AMERICA

St. Helena

Northern Cook Islands

Lima

Samoa Islands

Íles Tuamotu

Nevado Sajama 6542

Rio de Janeiro

Fiji Islands

Tahiti

Cabo Frio

Tonga Islands

10800

Southern Cook Islands

GRAN CHACO

5754

Tropic of Capricorn

Pitcairn I.

Isla de Pascua (Easter Island)

Isla San Ambrosio

Cerro Aconcagua 6959

ANDES

PAMPA

Buenos Aires

1088

Archipiélago Juan Fernandez

Santiago

Rio de la Plata

Chatham Islands

PATAGONIA

4755

Golfo San Jorge

6212

Falkland Islands

4876

Tierra del Fuego

South Georgia

Estrecho de Magallanes

Cabo de Hornos (Cape Horn)

Scotia Sea

8325

4705

Drake Passage

South Shetland Islands

South Orkney Islands

Antarctic Circle

Amundsen Sea

Bellingshausen Sea

Alexander Island

Antarctic Peninsula

Weddell Sea

Cape Norvegia

Ross Sea

MARIE BYRD LAND

Vinson Massif ▲ 4897

Berkner Island

COATS LAND

AM

Metres / Feet scale

Metres	Feet
6000	19680
4000	13120
3000	9840
2000	6560
1000	3280
500	1640
200	656
Sea Level	0
200	656
2000	6560

| 0 | 1000 | 2000 | 4000 | 6000 | 8000 | 10000 km |

| 0 | 1000 | 2000 | 4000 | 6000 miles |

Scale 1 : 90 000 000

Robinson Projection

Scale 1 : 15 000 000

Equidistant Conic Projection

| 0 | 200 | 400 | 800 | 1200 | 1600 km |

| 0 | 100 | 200 | 300 | 400 | 600 | 800 | 1000 miles |

West of Greenwich 0° East of Greenwich

D-550000-2A-DR1-1
Copyright © Rand McNally & Co.

8

Scale 1 : 10 000 000

Lambert Conformal Conic Projection

Metres	Feet
4000	13120
3000	9840
2000	6560
1000	3280
500	1640
200	656
Sea Level	
200	656
2000	6560

0 100 200 300 400 600 800 1000 km

0 100 200 400 600 miles

West of Greenwich 0° East of Greenwich

D-559100-7A-DR1-1°
Copyright © Rand McNally & Co.

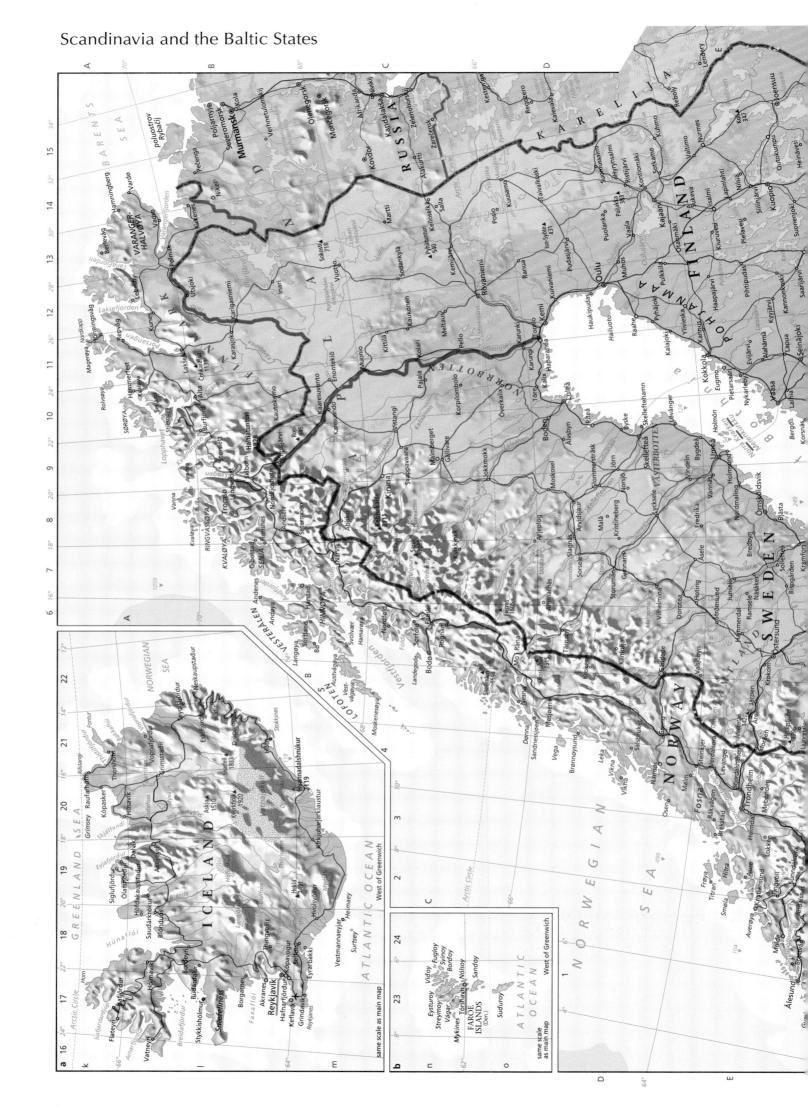

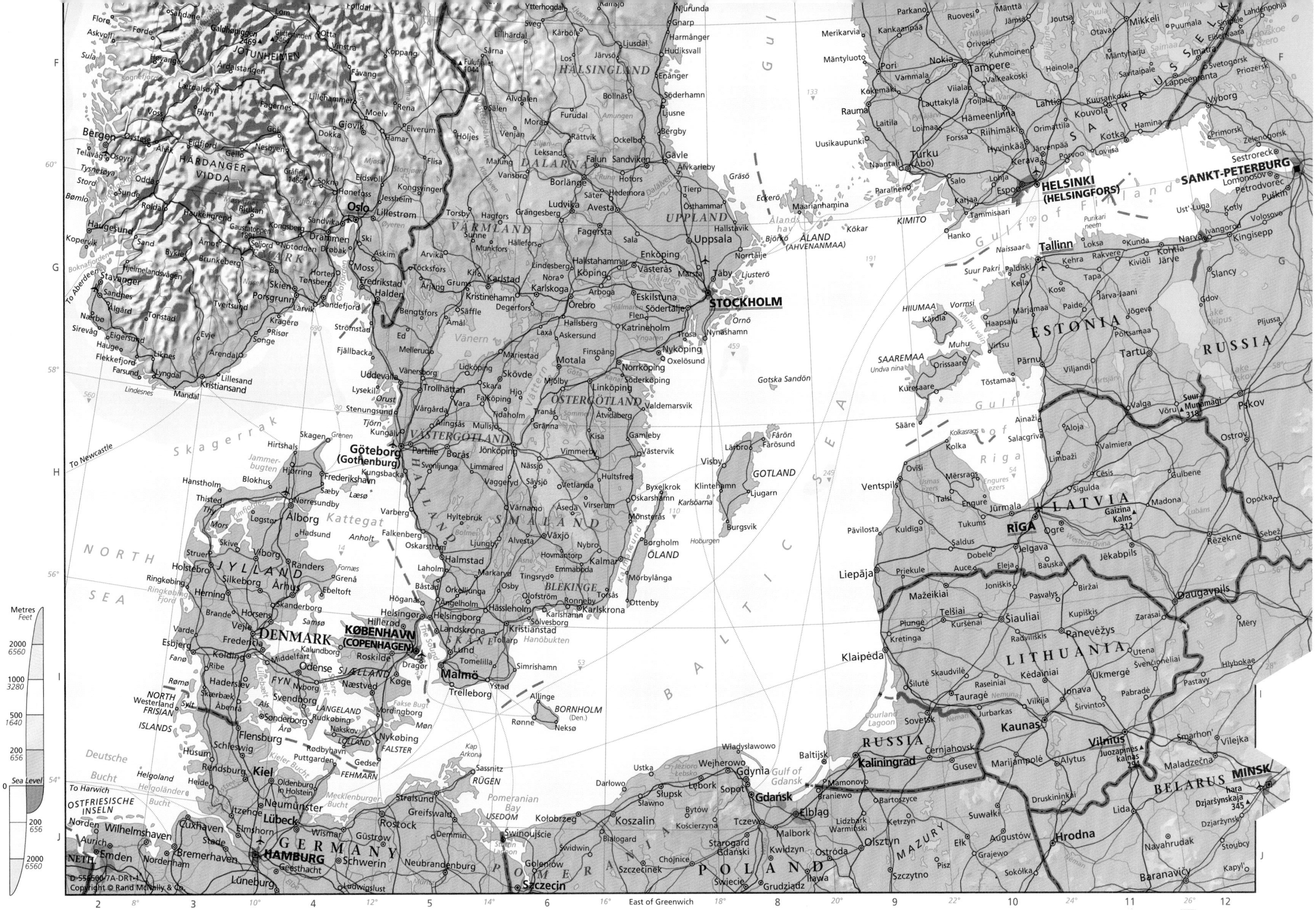

RUSSIA
BELARUS MINSK
ESTONIA
LATVIA
LITHUANIA
POLAND
GERMANY
DENMARK
SWEDEN
NORWAY
FINLAND
NETH.

SANKT-PETERBURG
HELSINKI (HELSINGFORS)
TALLINN
RIGA
VILNIUS
KAUNAS
Kaliningrad
RUSSIA
STOCKHOLM
OSLO
GÖTEBORG (Gothenburg)
KØBENHAVN (COPENHAGEN)
HAMBURG
Gdańsk
Szczecin
Lübeck
Kiel

BALTIC SEA
NORTH SEA
Gulf of Finland
Gulf of Riga
Gulf of Bothnia
Skagerrak
Kattegat
The Sound
Pomeranian Bay
Gulf of Gdańsk
Courland Lagoon

GOTLAND
ÖLAND
BORNHOLM (Den.)
ÅLAND (AHVENANMAA)
RÜGEN
FEHMARN
USEDOM
SJÆLLAND
FYN
JYLLAND
LOLLAND
FALSTER
LANGELAND
HIIUMAA
SAAREMAA

UPPLAND
DALARNA
HÄLSINGLAND
VÄRMLAND
HALLAND
SMÅLAND
VÄSTERGÖTLAND
ÖSTERGÖTLAND
BLEKINGE
JOTUNHEIMEN
HARDANGER-VIDDA
POMERANIA
MAZURY

Scale 1 : 5 000 000
Lambert Conformal Conic Projection
East of Greenwich

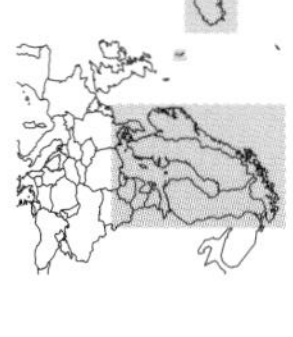

500 km
300 miles
0 50 100 150 200 300 400
0 100 200 300

Metres Feet
2000 6560
1000 3280
500 1640
200 656
Sea Level
200 656
2000 6560

Copyright © Rand McNally & Co.

12

Scale 1 : 5 000 000

Lambert Conformal Conic Projection

D-559594-7A-DR1-1°
Copyright © Rand McNally & Co.

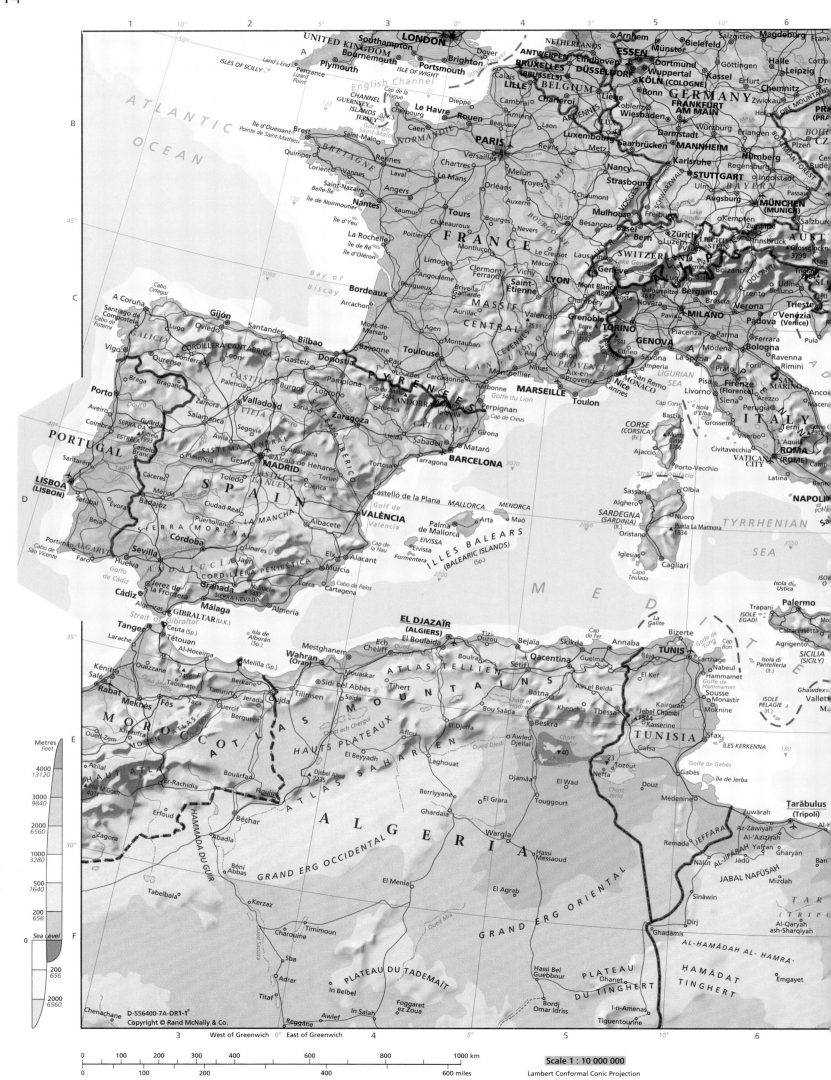

ATLANTIC OCEAN

English Channel

UNITED KINGDOM
LONDON
Southampton
Bournemouth
Plymouth
Penzance
Lizard Point
ISLES OF SCILLY
Land's End

Brighton
Portsmouth
ISLE OF WIGHT
Dover
CHANNEL
GUERNSEY
ISLANDS (U.K.)
JERSEY
Cherbourg
Caen
Le Havre
Rouen
Dieppe
Cap de la Hague
Calais

NETHERLANDS
Arnhem
Eindhoven
ANTWERPEN
BRUXELLES
(BRUSSELS)
BELGIUM
LILLE
Charleroi
Liège
Cambrai
Amiens
Beauvais
Laon
Reims

Bielefeld
Münster
Dortmund
ESSEN
DÜSSELDORF
Wuppertal
KÖLN (COLOGNE)
Bonn
Koblenz
Wiesbaden
FRANKFURT
AM MAIN
Darmstadt
Würzburg
LUXEMBOURG
Saarbrücken
Metz
Nancy
Karlsruhe
MANNHEIM
STUTTGART
Strasbourg
Mulhouse
Freiburg

Salzgitter
Magdeburg
Göttingen
Kassel
Erfurt
Halle
Leipzig
Chemnitz
Zwickau
Erlangen
Nürnberg
Regensburg
Ingolstadt
Ulm
Augsburg
MÜNCHEN
(MUNICH)
Kempten

GERMANY

ORE MOUNTAINS
BOHEMIAN FOREST

PARIS
Versailles
Chartres
Melun
Troyes
Chaumont
Orléans
Auxerre
Dijon
Besançon
Bern
ZÜRICH
SWITZERLAND
Luzern
LIECHTENSTEIN
Innsbruck
AUSTRIA
Zugspitze
2962
Grossglockner
3798

Brest
Quimper
Lorient
Saint-Nazaire
Belle-Île
Île d'Yeu
Île de Noirmoutier
Rennes
Laval
Vannes
Angers
NANTES
Le Mans
Tours
Saumur
Chateauroux
Poitiers
La Rochelle
Île de Ré
Île d'Oléron

FRANCE

Nevers
Le Creusot
Mâcon
Vichy
LYON
Saint-Étienne
Grenoble
Chambéry
Valence

Lausanne
Genève
Mont Blanc
4807
Barre des Écrins
4102

BRETAGNE
NORMANDIE
CHAMPAGNE
VOSGES
SCHWARZWALD
BAYERN

Bay of Biscay

Bordeaux
Arcachon
Mont-de-Marsan
Bayonne
Pau
Lourdes
PYRÉNÉES
Pic d'Aneto
3404
ANDORRA
Andorra la Vella

A Coruña
Cabo Ortegal
Santiago de Compostela
Cabo de Fisterra
Lugo
Gijón
Oviedo
Santander
Bilbao
Gasteiz
Donostia
Pamplona
Logroño
Huesca
Zaragoza
Soria
Burgos
Palencia
León
Vigo
Ourense
Ponferrada
CORDILLERA CANTÁBRICA
GALICIA

PORTUGAL
Braga
Bragança
Porto
Aveiro
Coimbra
Guarda
SERRA DA ESTRELA 1993
Castelo Branco
Douro
CASTILLA LA VIEJA
Valladolid
Zamora
Salamanca
Ávila
Segovia
SISTEMA CENTRAL
Guadalajara
MADRID
Alcalá de Henares
Getafe
SISTEMA IBÉRICO
Teruel
Cuenca
SPAIN

Santarém
LISBOA
(LISBON)
Setúbal
Évora
Beja
Cáceres
Plasencia
Toledo
CASTILLA LA NUEVA
Ciudad Real
Badajoz
Mérida
Guadiana
SERRA DO ALGARVE
Portimão
Cabo de São Vicente
Faro
Huelva
Sevilla
Córdoba
Puertollano
SIERRA MORENA
LA MANCHA
Albacete
Linares
ANDALUCÍA
Jaén
GUADALQUIVIR
Cádiz
Jerez de la Frontera
Granada
Mulhacén
3482
SIERRA NEVADA
Málaga
Almería
Lorca
Murcia
Cartagena
Cabo de Palos
Elx
Alacant

Tarragona
BARCELONA
Mataró
Sabadell
Lleida
Girona
Cap de Creus
CATALUNYA
Tortosa
Castelló de la Plana
VALÈNCIA
València
Golf de València
Cap de la Nau
Formentera
EIVISSA
Eivissa
ILLES BALEARS
(BALEARIC ISLANDS) (Sp.)
Palma de Mallorca
MALLORCA
Artà
MENORCA
Maó

Toulouse
Montauban
Agen
Périgueux
Brive-la-Gaillarde
Aurillac
MASSIF CENTRAL
Clermont-Ferrand
Limoges
Angoulême
Narbonne
Carcassonne
Perpignan
Montpellier
Nîmes
Avignon
Aix-en-Provence
MARSEILLE
Toulon
Cannes
Nice
MONACO
San Remo
Golfe du Lion
LANGUEDOC
PROVENCE
CÉVENNES

Novara
Cuneo
TORINO
GENOVA
Savona
Imperia
LIGURIAN SEA
Pavia
MILANO
Bergamo
Brescia
Verona
Pádova
VENÉZIA
(Venice)
Trento
Bolzano
DOLOMITI
Belluno
Udine
Trieste
Pula

Piacenza
Parma
Módena
Bologna
La Spézia
Pisa
Livorno
CORSE
(CORSICA) (Fr.)
Bastia
Ajaccio
Monte Cinto
2706
Porto-Vecchio
Strait of Bonifacio
Sassari
Olbia
Nuoro
Alghero
Oristano
SARDEGNA
(SARDINIA) (It.)
Punta La Marmora
1834
Iglésias
Cagliari
Capo Teulada

Ferrara
Ravenna
Forlì
Rimini
Prato
FIRENZE
(FLORENCE)
Siena
Arezzo
Grosseto
SAN MARINO
ITALY
Perúgia
L'Aquila
Terni
VITERBO
ROMA
(ROME)
VATICAN CITY
Latina
NÁPOLI

Cabo de Gata
Isla de Alborán (Sp.)
Cap Corse
Isola d'Elba
Cap de Fer

MEDITERRANEAN SEA

TYRRHENIAN SEA

Isola di Ustica
Trápani
ÍSOLE ÉGADI
Palermo
Caltanissetta
Agrigento
SICILIA (SICILY)
Isola di Pantelleria (It.)
ÍSOLE PELAGIE (It.)
Ghawdex
Valletta
MALTA

Tanger
Ceuta (Sp.)
Tétouan
Al-Hoceima
Larache
Kénitra
Salé
Rabat
Meknès
Fès
Taza
MOROCCO
MOYEN ATLAS
HAUT ATLAS
Taourirt
2456
Taounate
Ouezzane
Taouirt
Berkane
Melilla (Sp.)
Oujda
Sidi bel Abbès
Tilimsen
Saïda
Mestghanem
Wahran
(Oran)
Mouaskar
Tihert
GIBRALTAR (U.K.)
Strait of Gibraltar
Algeciras

EL DJAZAÏR
(ALGIERS)
El Boulaïda
Tizi Ouzou
Béjaïa
Skikda
Annaba
Bouïra
Sétif
Qacentina
Guelma
ATLAS TELLIEN
ATLAS MOUNTAINS
Batna
Aïn el Beïda
Ech Cheliff
Oued

Bizerte
TUNIS
Carthage
Nabeul
Béja
El Kef
Hammamet
Golfe de Tunis
Cap Bon
Golfe de Hammamet
Sousse
Monastir
Moknine
Kairouan
El Djem
Sfax
Gabès
ÍLES KERKENNA
TUNISIA

Oued Sebou
Oued Zem
Azilal
Er-Rachidia
Bouârfa
Béchar
Abadla
Béni Abbas
Kerzaz
Tabelbala
Zagora
Erfoud
HAMMADA DU GUIR
ANTI-ATLAS
Jbel M'Goun
4071
Aflou
Djelfa
Bou Saâda
Biskra
Laghouat
El Djelfa
El Beyyadh
Berriyane
El Grara
Ghardaïa
Wargla
Hassi Messaoud
Touggourt
El Wad
Nefta
Tozeur
23
Douz
40
Médenine
Gabès
Île de Jerba
Zuwārah
Az-Zāwiyah
Al-'Azīzīyah
Yaffan
Gharyān
JEFFARA
AL-JIFĀRAH
NAJŪT
JĀDU
JABAL NAFŪSAH
Mizdah
Ṭarābulus
(Tripoli)
Al-Qaryah ash-Sharqīyah
Ghadāmis

ALGERIA

HAUTS PLATEAUX
ATLAS SAHARIEN
GRAND ERG OCCIDENTAL
GRAND ERG ORIENTAL
Djebel Aïssa
2235
Djamâa
Oued Djedi
Awled Djellal
Oued Mia
Oued Soura
Chenachane
Chaouine
Timimoun
In Belbel
Titaf
Adrar
Reggane
Aoulef
Foggaret ez Zoua
In Salah
PLATEAU DU TADEMAÏT
Sba
Kerzaz
El Menia
El Agreb
Sinâwin
Dirj
Ghadāmis
Hassi Bel Guebbour
PLATEAU DU TINGHERT
HAMĀDAT TINGHERT
Ohanet
Bordj Omar Idriss
I-n-Amenas
Tiguentourine
TAR
(TRIPO
Al-Qaryah
ash-Sharqīyah
Emgayet
AL-ḤAMĀDAH AL-ḤAMRĀ'

Metres
Feet
4000
13120
3000
9840
2000
6560
1000
3280
500
1640
200
656
Sea Level
0
200
656
2000
6560

West of Greenwich 0° East of Greenwich

D-556400-7A-DR1-1°
Copyright © Rand McNally & Co.

0   100   200   300   400   600   800   1000 km
0   100   200   400   600 miles

Scale 1 : 10 000 000

Lambert Conformal Conic Projection

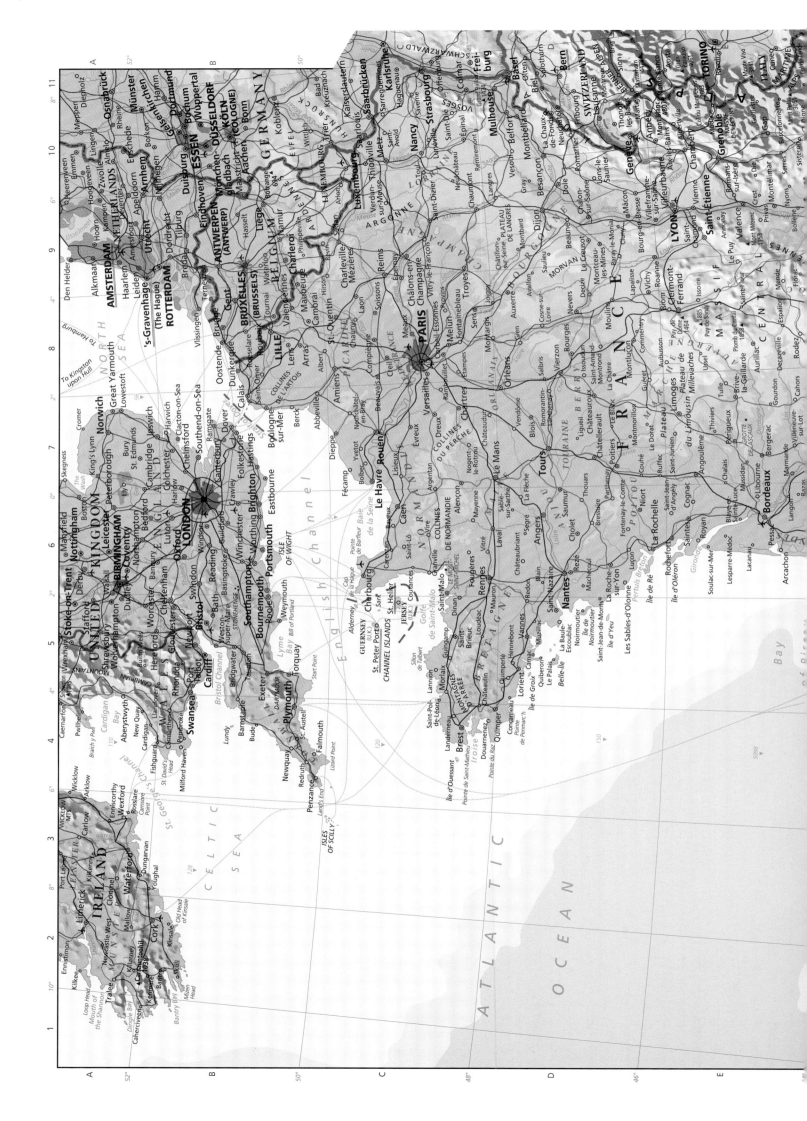

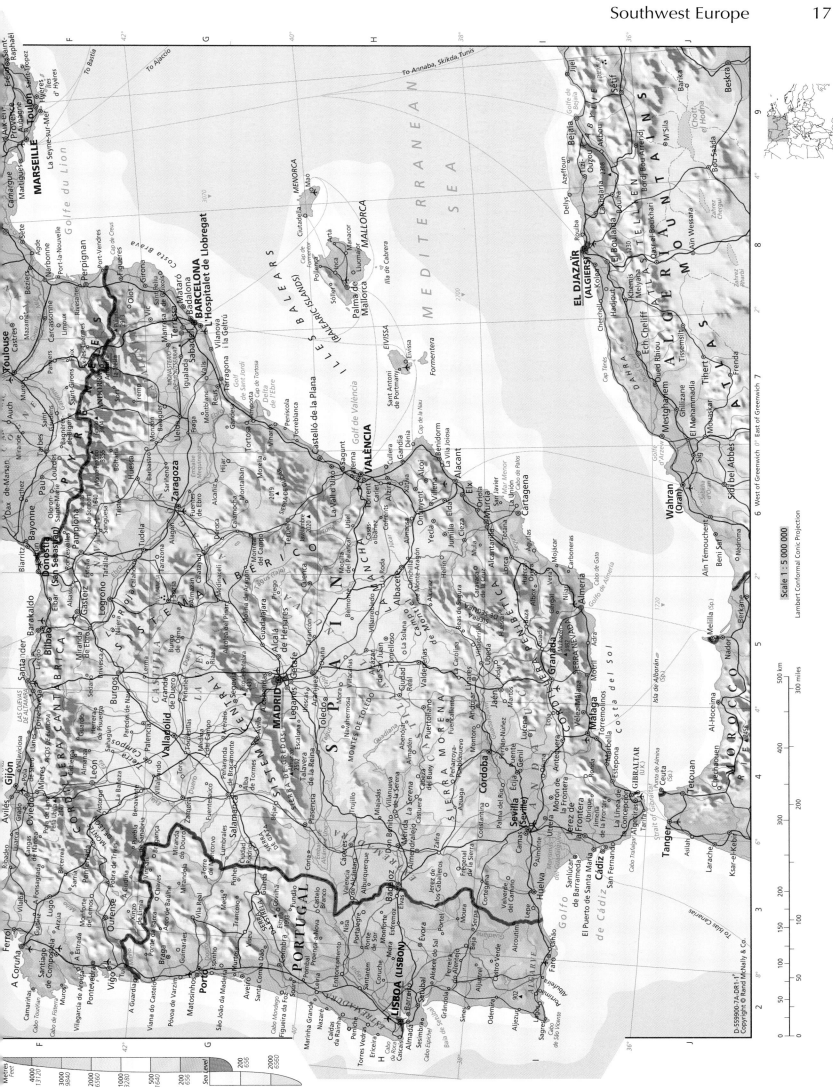

Metres
Feet

4000
13120

3000
9840

2000
6560

1000
3280

500
1640

200
656

0 Sea Level

200
656

2000
6560

Scale 1 : 5 000 000

Lambert Conformal Conic Projection

D-5560037A-DR1-1
Copyright © Rand McNally & Co.

0   50   100   150   200   300   400   500 km

0   50   100   200   300 miles

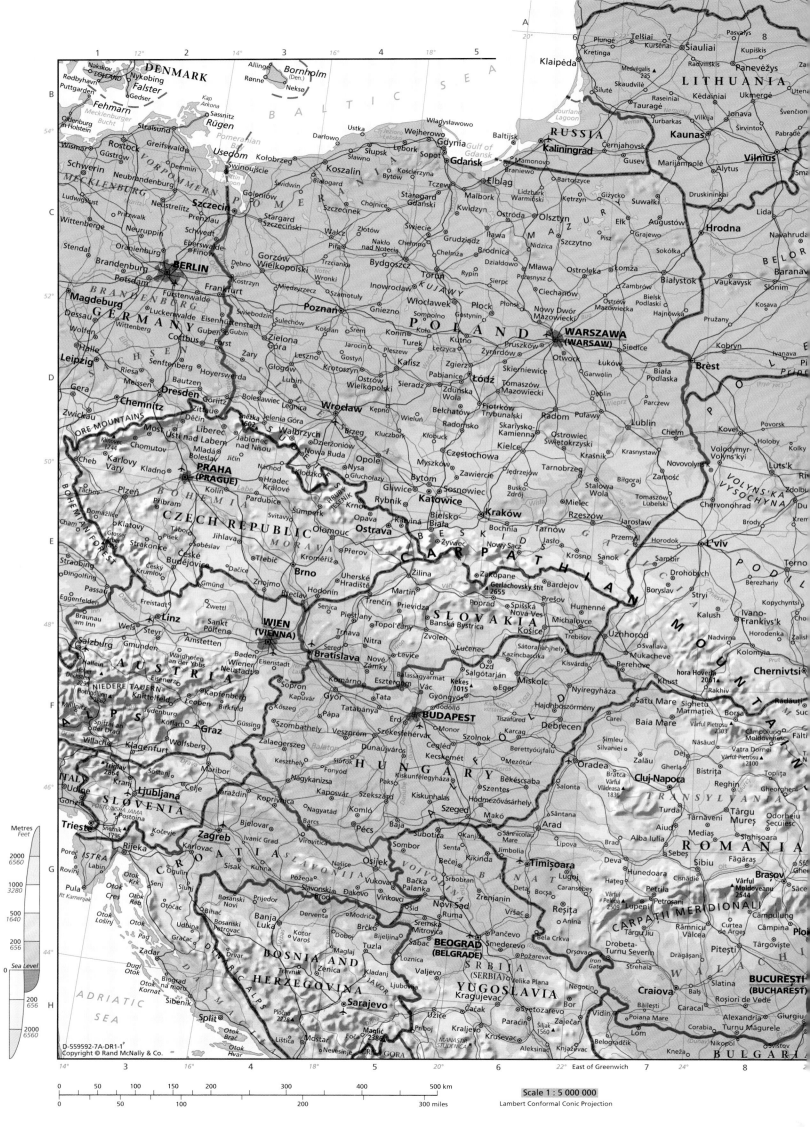

20

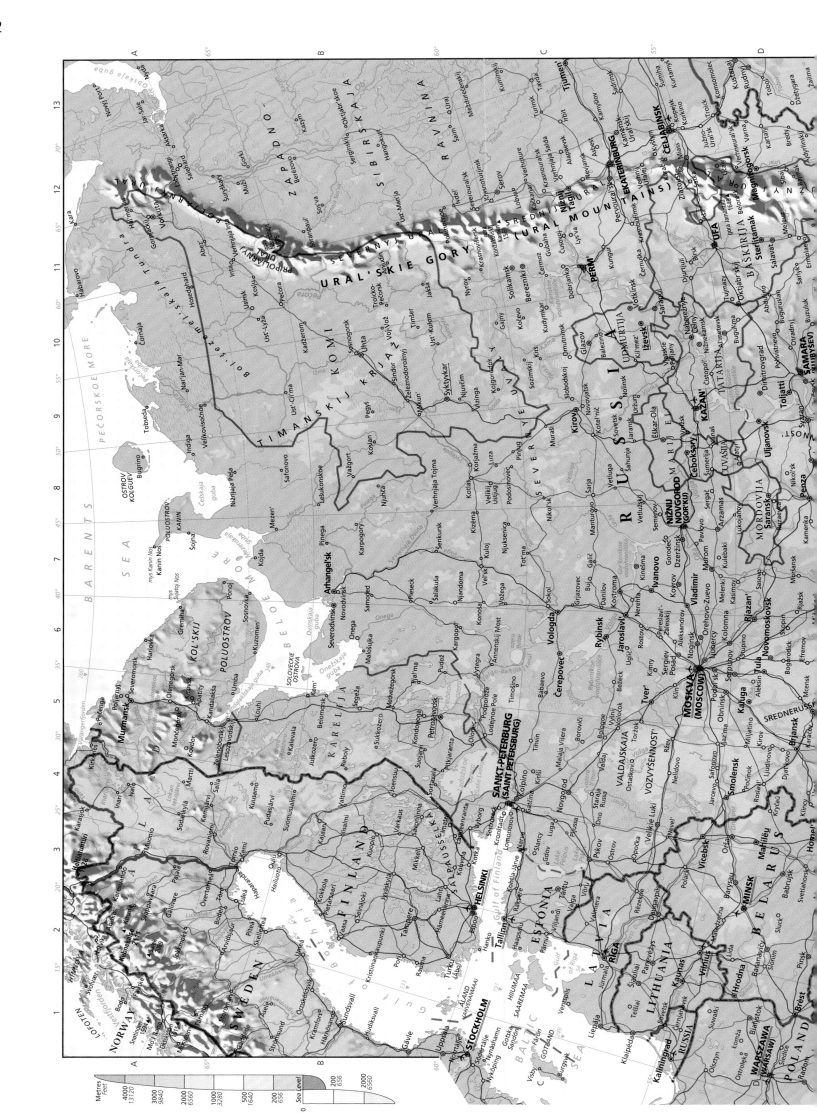

Metres	Feet
4000	13120
3000	9840
2000	6560
1000	3280
500	1640
200	656
Sea Level	0
200	656
2000	6560

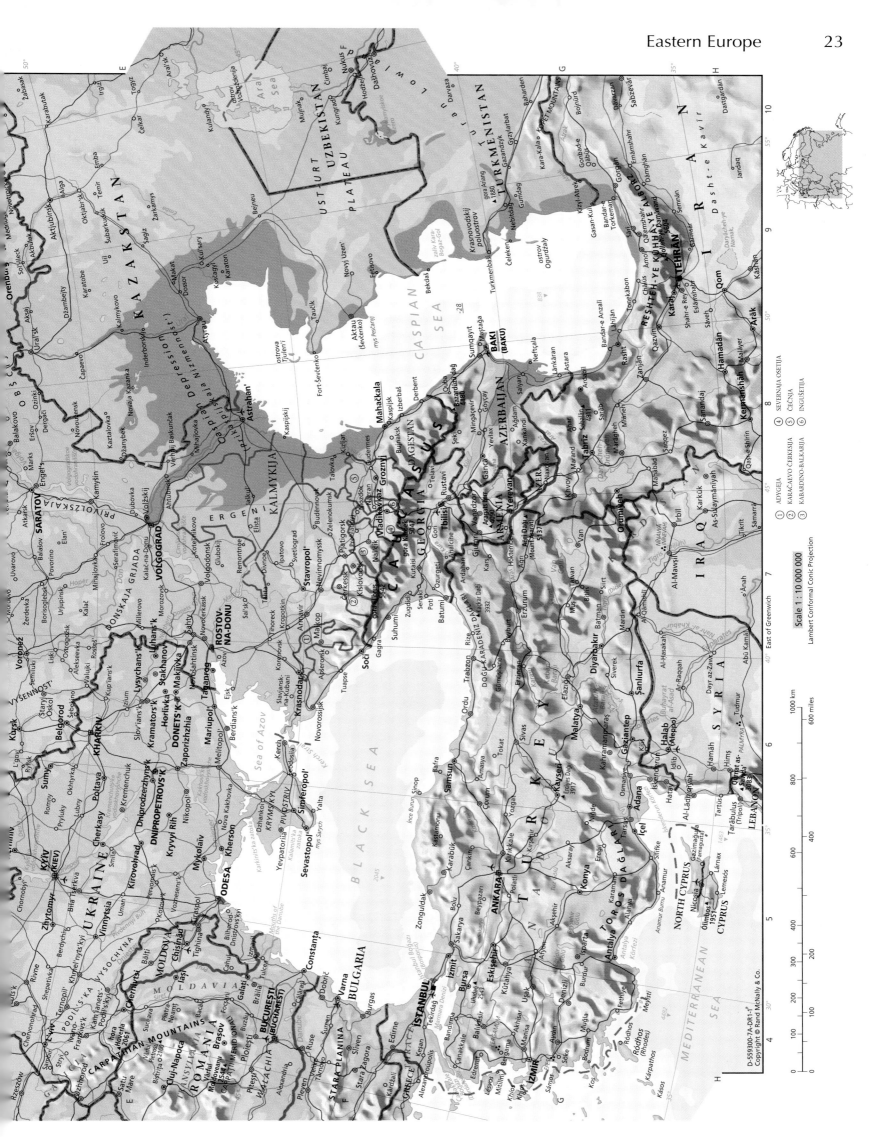

Scale 1 : 10 000 000

Lambert Conformal Conic Projection

① ADYGEJA
② KARAČAEVO ČERKESIJA
③ KABARDINO-BALKARIJA
④ SEVERNAJA OSETIJA
⑤ ČEČNJA
⑥ INGUŠETIJA

D-559300-7A-DR1-1°
Copyright © Rand McNally & Co.

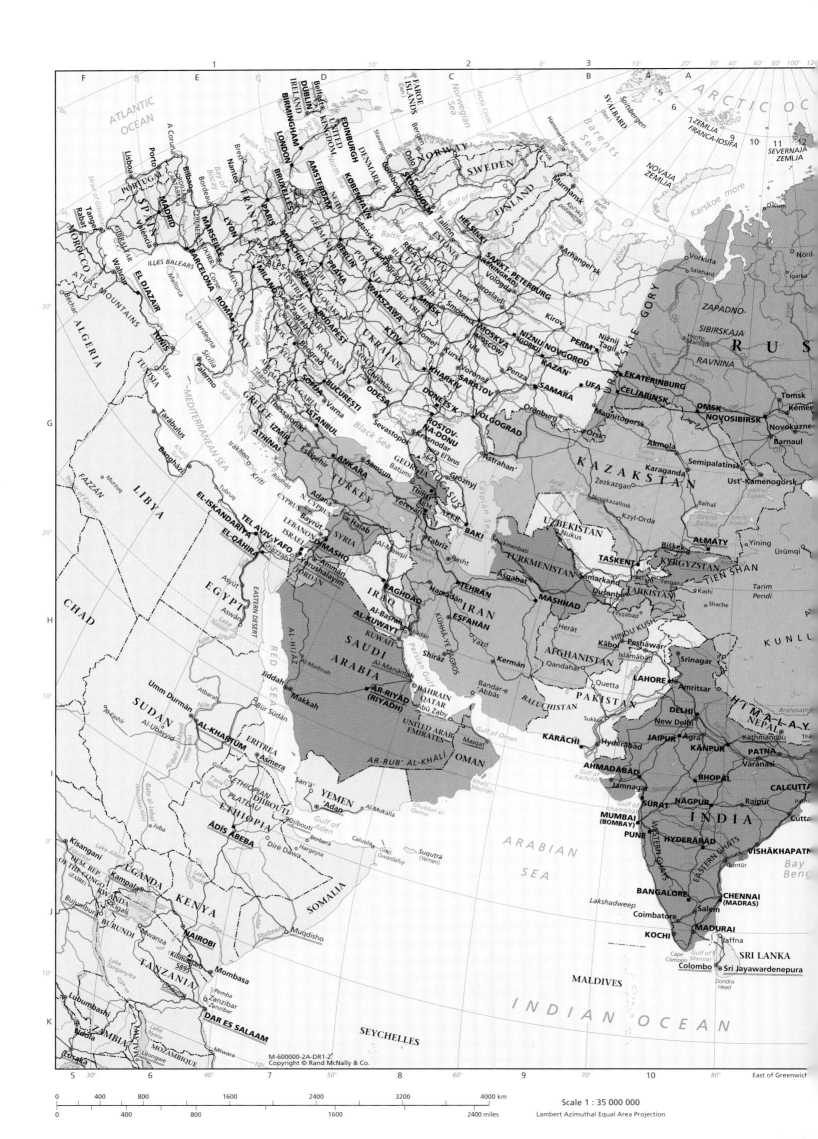

ARCTIC OC

ATLANTIC OCEAN

FAROE ISLANDS (Den.)

SVALBARD (Nor.)

Spitsbergen

1 ZEMLJA FRANCA-IOSIFA

NOVAJA ZEMLJA

SEVERNAJA ZEMLJA

Norwegian Sea

Barents Sea

Karskoe more

Dikson

Noril

IRELAND
DUBLIN
Belfast
Birmingham
UNITED KINGDOM
EDINBURGH
LONDON
AMSTERDAM
BRUXELLES
PARIS
FRANCE
DENMARK
KØBENHAVN
NORWAY
Oslo
Bergen
SWEDEN
STOCKHOLM
FINLAND
HELSINKI
ESTONIA
TALLINN
Murmansk
Hammerfest
Arhangel'sk

Lisboa
Porto
PORTUGAL
MADRID
SPAIN
Barcelona
MARSEILLE
LYON
MILANO
ROMA
ITALY
München
BERLIN
PRAHA
WIEN
BUDAPEST
WARSZAWA
RIGA
LATVIA
LITH.
Vilnius
BELARUS'
MINSK
KYÏV
UKRAINE
MOSKVA
Moscow
NIŽNIJ NOVGOROD
GORKIJ
KAZAN'
SANKT-PETERBURG
KALININGRAD
Smolensk
Tver'
Jaroslavl'
Vologda
Kirov
PERM'
EKATERINBURG
ČELJABINSK
Vorkuta
Salehard
Igarka

RUSSIA

MOROCCO
Rabat
Tanger
ATLAS MOUNTAINS
EL DJAZAÏR
ALGERIA
TUNIS
TUNISIA
Sfax
Tarābulus
LIBYA
FAZZAN
Murzuq
Banghāzī

Valencia
ILLES BALEARS
Mallorca
Sardegna
Sicilia
Palermo
MEDITERRANEAN SEA
Ionian Sea
Adriatic Sea
GREECE
SOFIA
BULGARIA
SKOPJE
BUCUREŞTI
ROMANIA
Beograd
Zagreb
ATHINA
IZMIR
ISTANBUL
ANKARA
TURKEY
Thessaloniki
CYPRUS
N. CYPRUS
Adana
Samsun
GEORGIA
Tbilisi
ARMENIA
Yerevan
AZER.
BAKI
CAUCASUS
5642
Groznyj
Astrahan'
VOLGOGRAD
ROSTOV-NA-DONU
DONE'CK
KHARKIV
Voronež
SARATOV
SAMARA
UFA
Oranburg
Magnitogorsk
OMSK
NOVOSIBIRSK
Tomsk
Novokuzne
Barnaul
Akmola
Karaganda
Semipalatinsk
Ust'-Kamenogorsk
Zajsan
KAZAKSTAN
Žezkazgan
Balhaš
ozero Balhaš
ozero Alakol'
Kzyl-Orda
Novokazalinsk
Aral'sk
Aral Sea

KAZAKSTAN

ZAPADNO-SIBIRSKAJA RAVNINA

GORY

Black Sea
Sevastopol'
Krasnodar
Batumi
ODESA
KIŠINĀU
Varna

EGYPT
EL-QAHIRA
EL-ISKANDARIYA
Aswān
Lake Nasser
EASTERN DESERT
Nile
Asyūt
RED SEA
CHAD
SUDAN
Al-Fashir
Umm Durmān
AL-KHARTUM
Al-Ubayyid
Atbarah
Bür Sūdān
Al-Bahr al-Abyad
ERITREA
Asmera
ETHIOPIA
ETHIOPIAN PLATEAU
ĀDĪS ĀBEBA
Gonder
DJIBOUTI
DJIBOUTI
Hāyk
SOMALIA
Berbera
Hargeysa
Dirē Dawa
Juba

LEBANON
Bayrūt
TEL AVIV-YAFO
ISRAEL
DIMASHQ
SYRIA
Halab
Al-Mawsil
Amman
Yerushalayim
JORDAN
IRAQ
BAGHDAD
Al-Basrah
AL-KUWAYT
KUWAIT
SAUDI ARABIA
AL-HIJAZ
Al-Madinah
Jiddah
Makkah
AR-RIYAD (RIYADH)
BAHRAIN
QATAR
Al-Manāmah
Abū Zaby
UNITED ARAB EMIRATES
Masqat
OMAN
AR-RUB' AL-KHĀLĪ
YEMEN
'Adan
Al-Mukallā
San'ā'

TÈHRAN
MASHHAD
ESFAHAN
IRAN
Tabrīz
Rasht
Hamadān
KŪHHĀ-YE ZAGROS
Shīrāz
Yazd
Kermān
Bandar-e Abbās
Ašgabat
TURKMENISTAN
Türkmenbati
UZBEKISTAN
Nukus
TAŠKENT
Samarkand
Dušanbe
TAJIKISTAN
KYRGYZSTAN
Biškek
ALMATY
TIEN SHAN
Kashi
Tarim Pendi
Ürümqi
Yining
Shache
AFGHANISTAN
Kābol
Qandahar
Herāt
HINDU KUSH
Peshāwar
Islāmābād
Quetta
BALUCHISTAN
PAKISTAN
Srinagar
Amritsar
LAHORE
DELHI
New Delhi
KUNLU
HIMALAY

KUWAIT
KUTHA-YE
Persian Gulf
Gulf of Oman

Caspian Sea

Aral Sea

NEPAL
Kathmandau
JAIPUR
AGRA
KĀNPUR
PATNA
Vārānasi
BHOPĀL
CALCUTTA
AHMADĀBĀD
Jāmnagar
SŪRAT
NĀGPUR
Raipur
Cutta
MUMBAI (BOMBAY)
PUNE
HYDERĀBĀD
INDIA
WESTERN GHATS
EASTERN GHATS
VISHĀKHAPATN
Guntūr
BANGALORE
Coimbatore
CHENNAI (MADRAS)
Salem
MADURAI
KOCHI
Jaffna
SRI LANKA
Cape Comorin
Colombo
Sri Jayawardenepura
Gulf of Mannar
Dondra Head
Lakshadweep
MALDIVES

Karāchi

Gulf of Kachchh

Bay of Bengal

ARABIAN SEA

KENYA
UGANDA
Kampala
NAIROBI
Kisangani
DEM. REP. OF THE CONGO (ZAIRE)
Lake Albert
Lake Edward
RWANDA
Kigali
BURUNDI
Bujumbura
TANZANIA
Mwanza
Lake Victoria
Lake Tanganyika
Kilimanjaro 5895
Mombasa
Zanzibar
Pemba
DAR ES SALAAM
Dodoma
ZAMBIA
Ndola
Lusaka
Lubumbashi
MOZAMBIQUE
Lilongwe
Lake Nyasa
Mtwara

SEYCHELLES

Suquträ (Yemen)
Gwardafuy
Muqdisho
Gulf of Aden
Calula

INDIAN OCEAN

M-600000-2A-DR1-2
Copyright © Rand McNally & Co.

Scale 1 : 35 000 000

Lambert Azimuthal Equal Area Projection

East of Greenwich

| 0 | 400 | 800 | 1600 | 2400 | 3200 | 4000 km |

| 0 | 400 | 800 | 1600 | 2400 miles |

A   B   C   D   E   F   G   H   I   J   K

NOVOSIBIRSKIE OSTROVA
more Laptevyh
Tiksi
Kazač'e
HREBET ČERSKOGO
Verhojansk
VERHOJANSKIJ HREBET
Žigansk
Anadyr'
Markovo
POLUOSTROV KAMČATKA
SREDINNYJ HREBET
Petropavlovsk-Kamčatskij
Bering Sea
ALEUTIAN ISLANDS (U.S.)
Attu Island
Arctic Circle

SIBIR' (SIBERIA)
nisej
ojarsk
Irkutsk
Ulan-Ude
Čita
ozero Bajkal
Hövsgöl nuur
ANGAYN NURUU
Ulaanbaatar
MONGOLIA
GOBI
Yinchuan
Lanzhou
Qinghai Hu

Lensk
Aldan
Tommot
Skovorodino
Komsomol'sk-na-Amure
Habarovsk
STANOVOJ HREBET
Ajan
Ohotsk
Sea of Okhotsk
mys Elizavety
Aleksandrovsk-Sahalinskij
OSTROV SAHALIN (SAKHALIN)
mys Terpenija
Južno-Sahalinsk
Tatarskij proliv
SIHOTE-ALIN'
Vladivostok

KURIL'SKIE OSTROVA (KURIL ISLANDS)

HOKKAIDŌ
Asahikawa
Sapporo
Hakodate
Aomori
HONSHŪ
Niigata
Sendai
Kanazawa
TŌKYŌ
YOKOHAMA
KYOTO NAGOYA
OSAKA
HIROSHIMA
FUKUOKA Shikoku
KYŪSHŪ
Kagoshima
JAPAN

PACIFIC OCEAN
Tropic of Cancer

Qiqihar
HARBIN
Jilin
CHANGCHUN
FUSHUN
SHENYANG
Dandong
NORTH KOREA
P'yongyang
Zhangjiakou
BEIJING
DALIAN
Hohhot
TIANJIN
Bo Hai
SOUTH KOREA
SŎUL (SEOUL)
Taejŏn
Taegu
PUSAN
Mokp'o
Cheju-do
Korea Strait
Yellow Sea

CHINA
TAIYUAN
Shijiazhuang
JINAN
Qingdao
Xuzhou
Zhengzhou
NANJING
XI'AN
WUHAN
SHANGHAI
Hangzhou
Ningbo
East China Sea
Amami-o-shima
NANSEI-SHOTŌ (RYUKYU ISLANDS)
Okinawa-jima
Naha

Farallon de Pajaros
Agrihan
Anatahan
NORTHERN MARIANA ISLANDS (U.S.)
Saipan
Rota
Agana
GUAM (U.S.)

CHENGDU
CHONGQING
Dongting Hu
CHANGSHA
Nanchang
Hengyang
Wenzhou
Fuzhou
T'AIPEI
TAIWAN
Tainan
KAOHSIUNG
Xiamen
GUANGZHOU
Liuzhou
Guiyang
Kunming
Nanning
XIANGGANG (HONG KONG)
MACAU (Port.)
Zhanjiang
Luzon Strait

Philippine Sea

FEDERATED STATES OF MICRONESIA

Mandalay
MYANMAR (BURMA)
LAOS
Chiang Mai
Louangphrabang
Nongchan
Udon Thani
VIETNAM
Da Nang
YANGON (RANGOON)
Gulf of Martaban
THAILAND
KRUNG THEP (BANGKOK)
CAMBODIA
Phnum Pénh
THANH PHO HO CHI MINH (SAIGON)
HA NOI
Hai Phong
Haikou
Hainan Dao
Gulf of Tonkin
South China Sea
LUZON
Baguio
PHILIPPINES
Quezon City
Naga
MANILA
Mindoro
Masbate Samar
Panay Cebu
Iloilo
Negros
Palawan
Zamboanga
MINDANAO
Davao
Cape San Agustin
Tinaca Point
Sulu Sea
Moro Gulf

Koror
PALAU

New Ireland
Kavieng
Rabaul
New Britain
Bismarck Sea

Coco Islands
Andaman Sea
Kâmpóng Saôm
Mui Ca Mau
Gulf of Thailand
MALAY PENINSULA
Gunong Kinabalu 4101
BRUNEI
Bandar Seri Begawan
Celebes Sea
Manado
HALMAHERA
Morotai
Biak
Jayapura
Wewak Madang
NEW GUINEA
PAPUA NEW GUINEA
Lae
Port Moresby
Gulf of Papua

Nicobar Islands (India)
Banda Aceh
George Town (Penang)
MEDAN
MALAYSIA
KUALA LUMPUR
SINGAPORE
Kuching
BORNEO (KALIMANTAN)
Pontianak
Balikpapan
SULAWESI (CELEBES)
Teluk Tomini
Pulau Taliabu
Buru
Pulau Seram (Ceram)
Laut Seram
Laut Maluku
Pulau Buton
Pulau Yos Sudarso

Torres Strait
Cape York
Cape Wessel
Gulf of Carpentaria
CAPE YORK PENINSULA
Cairns
Coral Sea

Padang
Pulau Siberut
SUMATERA (SUMATRA)
Palembang
Tanjungkarang Telukbetung
Pulau Bangka
Belitung
Banjarmasin
Tanjung Puting
Tanjung Selatan
Ujungpandang
Teluk Bone
Pulau Buton
INDONESIA
Laut Banda
Laut Flores
Laut Sawu
Dili
Timor
Kupang
Timor Sea
Melville Island
Darwin
AUSTRALIA
Arafura Sea

JAKARTA
BANDUNG
JAWA (JAVA)
Madura
SURABAYA
Bali
Lombok
Sumbawa
Sumba
Flores
Laut Jawa
Laut Bali
Selat Sunda

Scale 1 : 20 000 000

Lambert Conformal Conic Projection

M-700000-7A-DR1-2"
Copyright © Rand McNally & Co.

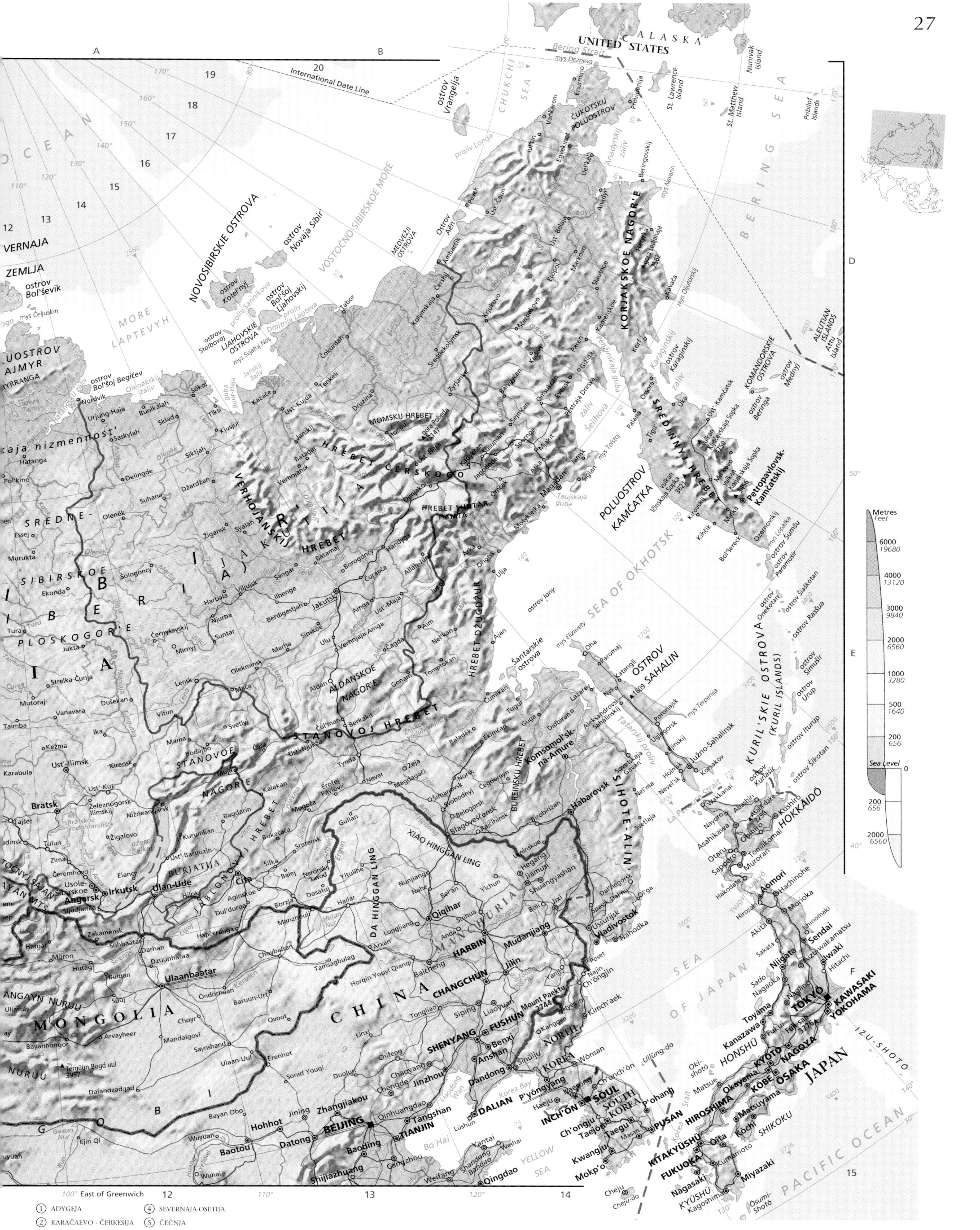

ALASKA
UNITED STATES
Bering Strait
mys Dežneva

CHUKCHI SEA
BERING SEA

ostrov Vrangelja

SREDNE-SIBIRSKOE PLOSKOGORE
SIBIRIJA
VERHOJANSKIJ HREBET
HREBET ČERSKOGO
ALDANSKOE NAGOR'E
STANOVOJ HREBET
STANOVOE NAGORE
BURIATHA
JABLONOVIJ HREBET
VITIM

KORJAKSKOE NAGOR'E
SREDINNYJ HREBET
POLUOSTROV KAMČATKA
Petropavlovsk-Kamčatskij

SEA OF OKHOTSK
OSTROV SAHALIN
KURIL'SKIE OSTROVA (KURIL ISLANDS)

Bratsk
Angarsk
Irkutsk
Ulan-Ude
Čita

ALEUTIAN ISLANDS

HOKKAIDO
Sapporo
Hakodate
Aomori
Akita
Sendai

SEA OF JAPAN
HONSHU
TOKYO
KAWASAKI
YOKOHAMA
NAGOYA
KYOTO
OSAKA
KOBE
HIROSHIMA
JAPAN
SHIKOKU
KITAKYŪSHŪ
FUKUOKA
KYŪSHŪ
Nagasaki
IZU-SHOTO

MONGOLIA
Ulaanbaatar
CHINA
Hohhot
BEIJING
TIANJIN
Baotou
Datong
Shijiazhuang
Qingdao

MANCHURIA
HARBIN
CHANGCHUN
SHENYANG
Anshan
FUSHUN
DALIAN
Mount Paektu
XIAO HINGGAN LING
DA HINGGAN LING
Qiqihar
Jilin
Mudanjiang

SIHOTE-ALIN'
Vladivostok
Komsomolsk-na-Amure
Habarovsk
Blagoveščensk

NORTH KOREA
P'yŏngyang
SOUTH KOREA
SŎUL
INCH'ŏN
PUSAN
Taegu

PACIFIC OCEAN
YELLOW SEA
Bo Hai

Metres / Feet
6000 / 19680
4000 / 13120
3000 / 9840
2000 / 6560
1000 / 3280
500 / 1640
200 / 656
Sea Level / 0

① ADYGEJA
② KARAČAEVO - ČERKESIJA
③ KABARDINO-BALKARIJA
④ SEVERNAJA OSETIJA
⑤ ČEČNJA
⑥ INGUŠETIJA

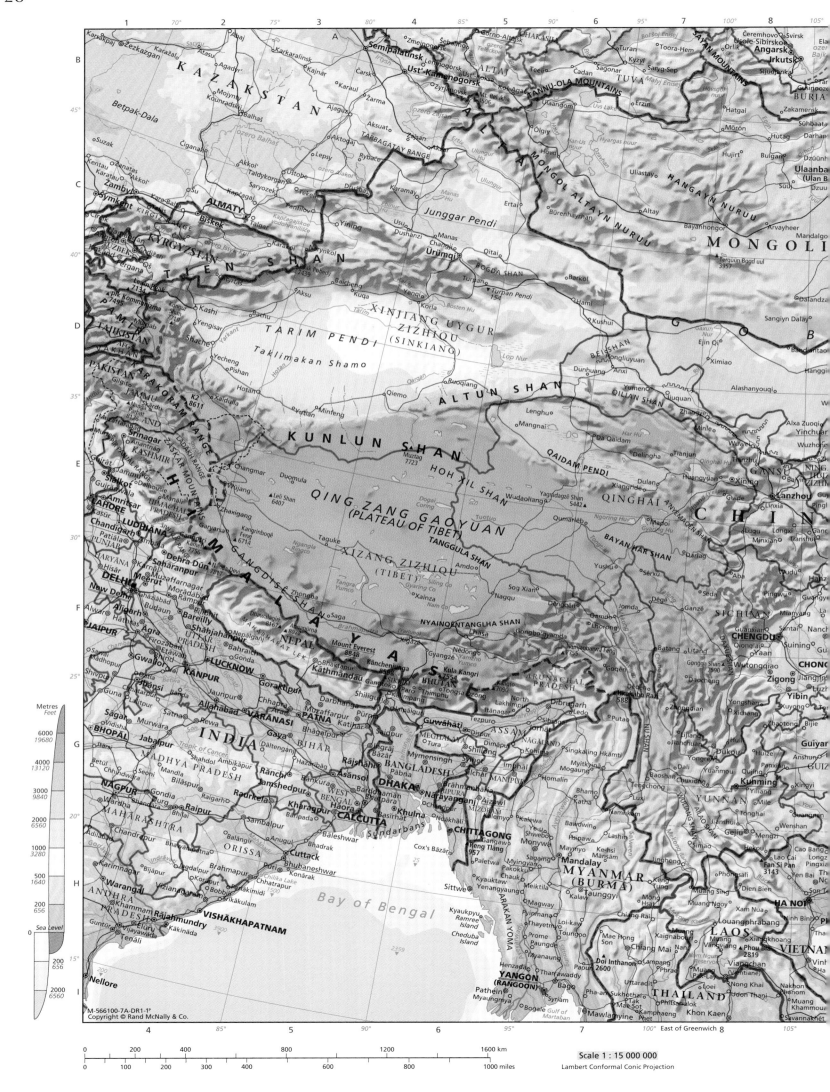

Scale 1 : 15 000 000

Lambert Conformal Conic Projection

M-566100-7A-DR1-1"
Copyright © Rand McNally & Co.

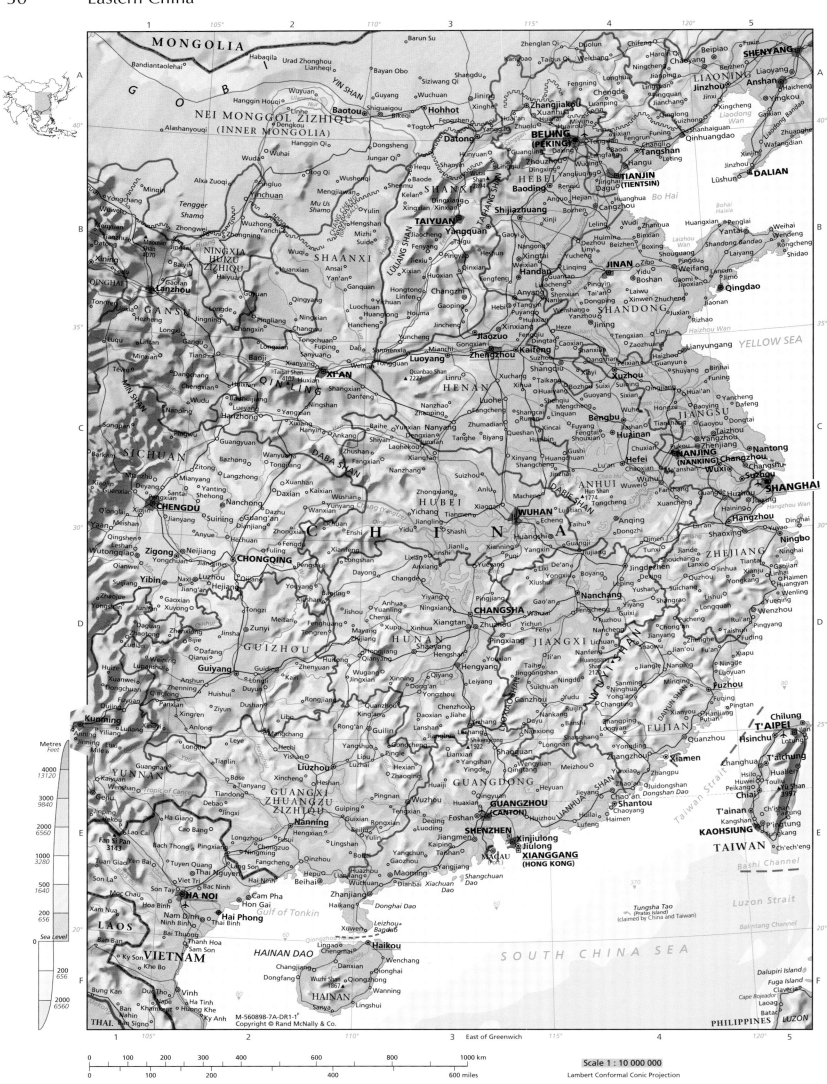

Metres
Feet

4000
13120

3000
9840

2000
6560

1000
3280

500
1640

200
656

Sea Level
0

200
656

2000
6560

Scale 1 : 10 000 000

Lambert Conformal Conic Projection

| 0 | 100 | 200 | 300 | 400 | 600 | 800 | 1000 km |

| 0 | 100 | 200 | 400 | 600 miles |

SEA OF JAPAN

(EAST SEA)

JAPAN

PACIFIC OCEAN

RUSSIA

CHINA

NORTH KOREA

SOUTH KOREA

Formerly part of Japan, Malaja Kuril'skaja, Šikotan, Kunašir, and Iturup, occupied by Russia since 1945, are claimed by Japan pending a final peace treaty.

HOKKAIDŌ

HONSHŪ

SHIKOKU

KYŪSHŪ

PACIFIC OCEAN

a same scale as main map

EAST CHINA SEA (DONG HAI)

NANSEI-SHOTŌ (RYUKYU ISLANDS)

JAPAN

PACIFIC OCEAN

Metres	Feet
3000	9840
2000	6560
1000	3280
500	1640
200	656
Sea Level	0
200	656
2000	6560

W-561500-7A-DR1-2
Copyright © Rand McNally & Co.

Scale 1 : 8 000 000
Lambert Conformal Conic Projection

0 100 200 300 400 600 800 km
0 50 100 150 200 300 500 miles

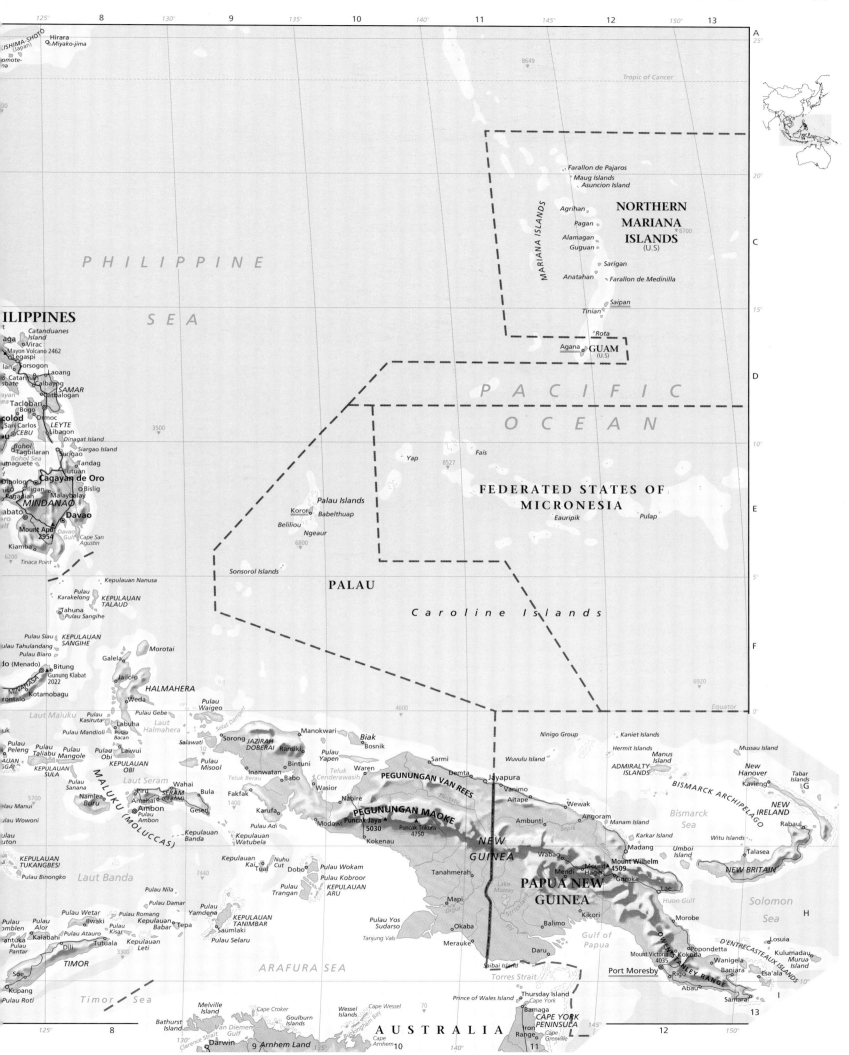

KISHIMA-SHOTO (Japan)
Hirara
Miyako-jima
omote-

8649

Tropic of Cancer

Farallon de Pajaros
Maug Islands
Asuncion Island

NORTHERN
MARIANA
ISLANDS
(U.S)

Agrihan

Pagan

MARIANA ISLANDS

Alamagan

Guguan

8700

Sarigan

Anatahan   Farallon de Medinilla

Saipan

Tinian

Rota

Agana   GUAM
(U.S)

PHILIPPINE

SEA

ILIPPINES
aga
t
Catanduanes
Island
Virac
Mayon Volcano 2462
Legaspi
lang
orsogon
Catanduan
Laoang
sbate   Calbayog
ayan
SAMAR
atbalogan
Tacloban
Bogo
colod   Ormoc   LEYTE
San Carlos   Libagon
CEBU
Dinagat Island
Bohol
Tagbilaran   Siargao Island
umaguete   Surigao   Tandag
Dinolog   Gutuan
Cagayan de Oro
niso   Iligan
abato   Malaybalay
MINDANAO
Davao
aro   Davao
Mount Apo   Gulf
2954   Cape San
Agustin
Kiamba
uf
6200
Tinaca Point

PACIFIC

OCEAN

3500

Yap

Fais

8527

FEDERATED STATES OF
MICRONESIA

Palau Islands

Koror   Babelthuap
Beliliou   Ngeaur
Ngeaur
6800

Eauripik   Pulap

Sonsorol Islands

PALAU

Caroline   Islands

Kepulauan Nanusa

Pulau
Karakelong   KEPULAUAN
TALAUD
Tahuna
Pulau Sangihe

Pulau Siau   KEPULAUAN
SANGIHE
ulau Tahulandang
Pulau Biaro
do (Menado)   Bitung
MINAHASA   Gunung Klabat
2022
rontalo   Kotamobagu

Morotai

Galela
Jailolo

HALMAHERA

Weda

6920

Equator

Laut Maluku   Pulau
Kasiruta
uk   Labuha
Pulau Mandioli   Pulau
Bacan
Pulau
Pulau   Peleng
Taliabu   Pulau
Mangole   Pulau
Obi   Pulau Gebe
Pulau Waigeo
AUAN   KEPULAUAN
GGAI   OBI   Selat Dampier
KEPULAUAN
SULA   Pulau
Sanana   Salawati
Manokwari
Biak
Sorong   JAZIRAH   Bosnik
DOBERAI   Ransiki
Pulau
Misool   Bintuni
Pulau
Inanwatan   Yapen
Teluk
Babo   Cenderawasih
Wasior
ulau Manui   5700   Wahai   Bula
Namlea   SERAM   Fakfak   Nabire
Buru   (CERAM)   Karufa   PEGUNUNGAN MAOKE
Amahai   1400
ulau Wowoni   Ambon   Geser   Puncak Jaya
Pulau   Modowi   5030   Puncak Trikora
uton   Banda   Pulau Adi   4750
Kepulauan   Kokenau
Watubela
Kepulauan   Kepulauan
Banda   Nuhu
KEPULAUAN   Kai   Cut   Dobo
TUKANGBESI   Tual   Pulau Wokam
Pulau Binongko   Laut Banda   Pulau   Pulau Kobroor
7440   Trangan   KEPULAUAN
Pulau Nila   ARU
Pulau Damar   Pulau
Yamdena
Pulau Wetar   Pulau Romang   KEPULAUAN
Pulau   Ilwaki   Pulau Kisar   TANIMBAR
omblen   Alor   Kepulauan   Saumlaki
antuka   Kalabahi   Babar   Pulau Selaru
Pulau   Tutuala   Tepa
Pantar   Dili   Kepulauan
Leti
3300
TIMOR
Soe
Kupang
Pulau Roti

Ninigo Group   Kaniet Islands
Hermit Islands   Mussau Island
Wuvulu Island   Manus
Sarmi   Island
Demta   ADMIRALTY   New
Jayapura   ISLANDS   Hanover
Vanimo   Kavieng
Waren   Aitape   Wewak
PEGUNUNGAN VAN REES   Angoram
Ambunti   Manam Island
Karkar Island
NEW   Sepik   Madang   Umboi
GUINEA   Wabag   Island
Mount
Mendi   Hagen
Goroka   Lae
PAPUA NEW   Mount Wilhelm
Tanahmerah   GUINEA   4509
Mapi   Lake
Murray   Kikori   Morobe
Okaba   Huon Gulf
Balimo   Gulf of
Merauke   Daru   Papua
Mount Victoria
Tanjung Vals   4035
Sibai Island   Port Moresby

BISMARCK ARCHIPELAGO

NEW
IRELAND

Bismarck
Sea   Rabaul

Witu Islands   Talasea

NEW BRITAIN

Solomon
Sea

Tabar
Islands

Kokoda   D'ENTRECASTEAUX ISLANDS
Popondetta   Losuia
Wanigela   Kulumadau
Murua
Banaira   Esa'ala
Rigo
Abau   Samarai

ARAFURA SEA

Torres Strait

Thursday Island
Cape York

Prince of Wales Island

Bamaga
CAPE YORK
PENINSULA
Iron
Range
Cape
Grenville

Timor   Sea

Melville
Island   Cape Croker   Wessel
Goulburn   Wessel Island   70
Islands   Islands   Cape Wessel

AUSTRALIA

Bathurst
Island   Van Diemen
Gulf
Darwin   Arnhem Land
Clarence Strait   Cape
Arnhem

Metres / Feet

6000 / 19680
4000 / 13120
3000 / 9840
2000 / 6560
1000 / 3280
500 / 1640
200 / 656
Sea Level
200 / 656
2000 / 6560

M-569891-7A-DR1-1°
Copyright © Rand McNally & Co.

Scale 1 : 10 000 000
Lambert Conformal Conic Projection

East of Greenwich

110°   6   115°   7   120°   8   125°   9

Baoqing   Pingjiang   Nanchang   Shangrao   Lishui   Yueqing   Wenling   Tokuno-shima
Jishou   Yuanling   Yiyang   Fengcheng   Shangrao   Suichang   Longquan   Wenzhou   Okino-Erabu-shima
Mayang   Xupu   Xinhua   Ningxiang   Wanzai   Yichun   Guixi   Pucheng   Pingyang   EAST CHINA SEA   Okinawa-jima   Nago   A
Zhijiang   CHANGSHA   Nanfeng   Jianou   Ngde   Naha   Ishikawa
HUNAN   Shaoyang   Xiangtan   Zhuzhou   Yongfeng   Lichuan   Sanming   Jiangle   Fu'an   NANSEI-SHOTO (RYUKYU ISLANDS)   Hirara   Miyako-jima
Hengyang   Huanggang   2158   Minqing   Fuzhou   (Japan)   25°
Jingxian   Wugang   Qiyang   JIANGXI   Ningdu   Shicheng   Nanping   Pingtan
Xinning   Dong'an   Leiyang   WUYI   Shanghang   Yong'an   FUJIAN   Fuqing   Taoyuan   T'AIPEI   Chilung
Quanzhou   Xing'an   Daoxian   Jiahe   Yizhang   SHAN   Longnan   Ruijin   Liancheng   DAIYUN SHAN   Putian   Hsinchu   Ilan
Rong'an   Guilin   Lanshan   Chenzhou   Ganzhou   Yudu   Changting   Yong'an   Zhangping   Hanjiang   Miaoli   Lotung
Yangshuo   Gongcheng   Jianghua   Yongding   Longyan   Quanzhou   T'aichung   Hualien
Lipu   Pingle   Yanghang   Nanxiong   Dayu   Nankang   Banshi   Zhangzhou   Xiamen   Changhua   Hsilo   Tropic of Cancer
Liuzhou   Hexian   Yangshan   Shikengkong   1902   Meizhou   Yunxiao   Zhangpu   Chao'an   Peikang   Huwei   Touliu   Yaeyama-rettō   Ishigaki
Zhaoqing   Huaiji   Qingyuan   Shaoguan   Chaozhou   Zhao'an   Dongshan Dao   Chiai   Yü Shan   Iriomote-jima
Pingnan   GUANGDONG   Heyuan   Jieyang   Juidongshan   3997   TAIWAN
Guiping   Tengxian   Deqing   Foshan   Shantou   Ch'ishan   B
Yulin   Beiliu   Luoding   Shunde   Panyu   GUANGZHOU   Huizhou   T'ainan   T'aitung
Lingshan   Gaozhou   Yangchun   Jiangmen   (CANTON)   Huilai   Kangshan   P'ingtung
Bobai   Zhongshan   Shenzhen   Haimen   KAOHSIUNG   Tungkang
Dianbai   Maoming   Yangjiang   Xinjiulong (New Kowloon)   ch'ech'eng
Huazhou   XIANGGANG   6500
Zhanjiang   Wuchuan   Xiachuan   Dao   MACAU   (HONG KONG)
Donghai Dao   Shangchuan Dao   (Port.)   Bashi Channel   PACIFIC
Leizhou   370   BATAN   OCEAN
Xuwen   Bandao   60   Luzon Strait   ISLANDS
Haikou   Tungsha Tao   Balintang Channel   20°
Wenchang   (Pratas Island)   BABUYAN   Babuyan Island
Qionghai   (claimed by   ISLANDS   Calayan Island
Qiongzhong   China and Taiwan)   Dalupiri Island   Camiguin Island
867   Wanning   Fuga Island   Babuyan Channel
Baoting   Lingshui   Claveria   Escarpada Point
HAINAN DAO   Cape Bojeador   Laoag   Aparri
Batac   Tuguegarao City   C
Vigan   Bontoc   Palanan Point
San Fernando   CORDILLERA CENTRAL   Ilagan   SIERRA   PHILIPPINE
Pattle Island   Lagawe   MADRE   SEA
Xisha Qundao   Rena Point   Solano
(Paracel Islands)   Bolinao   Baguio   Bayombong   Casiguran
(claimed by China,   Lingayen   San Carlos   Gapan
Taiwan, and Vietnam)   Caiman Point   Lingayen   Dagupan   Baler   15°
Gulf   LUZON   PHILIPPINES
Ngai   Iba   Cabanatuan
Quan   Angeles   San Fernando
uynh   Olongapo   Malolos   Polillo
Quan   Bacoor   Quezon City   Calagua Islands
Nhon   MANILA   Lamon   Daet
uy Nhon   SOUTH CHINA SEA   Cavite   Bay   Caramoan   Catanduanes
ong Cau   San Pablo   Island   Virac
uy Hoa   Tagaytay   Lipa   Lucena   Naga   Lagonoy
Lubang   Batangas   Calapan   Mayon   Gulf
Islands   Mount Halcon   Marinduque   Volcano   Legaspi
2800   2585   Calapan   2462   Sorsogon   D
a Trang   Mamburao   Santa Cruz   Bulan   Irosin   Laoang
MINDORO   Sibuyan   Burias   Masbate   Catarman
m Ranh   Bongabong   Sea   Island   Calbayog
n Rang   Central   Masbate   SAMAR
Calamian   Mandaon   Samar Sea   Naval   Tacloban
Group   Busuanga   Tablas   Sibuyan   Placer   Catbalogan
Island   Island   Island   Borongan
4424   Kalibo   Visayan   Ormoc   Guiuan
Linapacan Strait   10   Roxas   Sea   Bogo   LEYTE
Libro Point   PANAY   Cadiz   Sogod
5100   El Nido   Cuyo   Victorias   Camotes   Dinagat Island   10°
Islands   Iloilo   Sagay   Sea
Taytay   Bacolod   San   Cebu
Roxas   Dumaran   Guimaras   La Carlota   Carlos   CEBU   Libagon
Island   Island   NEGROS   Bohol   Surigao   Siargao Island
Bacungan   Cagayan Islands   Sipalay   Tagbilaran   Camiguin   Cabadbaran
wick   Puerto Princesa   Cavili Island   Hinoba-an   Bais   Santander   Island   Tandag
Inagahuan   Arena   Dumaguete   Siquijor   Bohol   Gingoog   Butuan   Prosperidad
PALAWAN   Island   Island   Sea   Cagayan de Oro   Bislig
SPRATLY ISLANDS   5576   Dipolog   Oroquieta   Iligan   Kalatungan Mountain   Lianga
(claimed by Brunei, China, Malaysia,   Mount Mantalingajan   Liloy   Ozamis   Bay   Malaybalay   2865   Cateel
Philippines, Taiwan and Vietnam)   2085   Brooke's Point   Kabasalan   Marawi   MINDANAO   Bagangan
Bugsuk Island   Siocon   Pagadian   Illana   Tagum   Davao
Balabac Island   Balabac   Sulu Sea   Zamboanga   Bay   Cotabato   Mount Apo   Mati
San Miguel Islands   Peninsula   Sibuguey   2954   Digos
3200   Pulau   Cagayan Sulu   Zamboanga   Bay   Moro Gulf   Tacurong   Davao
Balambangan   Pulau Banggi   Island   Koronadal   Gulf   Cape San
Kudat   Basilan Island   Kiamba   Agustin
Kota Belud   Senaja   Pulau
Gunong Kinabalu   Sandakan   Pangutaran Group   Jolo   Jolo Island   6200   Tinaca Point   Karakaralong
4101   Ranau   Tawitawi   Sarangani Island   KEPULAUAN
Kota Kinabalu   Sukau   Group   Tapul Group   TALAUD
Papar   MALAYSIA   SULU ARCHIPELAGO   INDONESIA   F
Pulau Labuan   Beaufort   Lahad Datu   4900
Bandar Seri Begawan   Labuan   SABAH   Sibutu
BRUNEI   Lawas   Tenom   Telukan   Sibutu Island   CELEBES SEA   Pulau Sangihe   Tahuna
Seria   Limbang   Kalabakan   Datu   Island
Miri   Gunong Mulu   BORNEO   Tawau   Semporna   Sebatik Island   Pulau Sangihe
2377

110°   6   115°   7   120°   8   125°   9

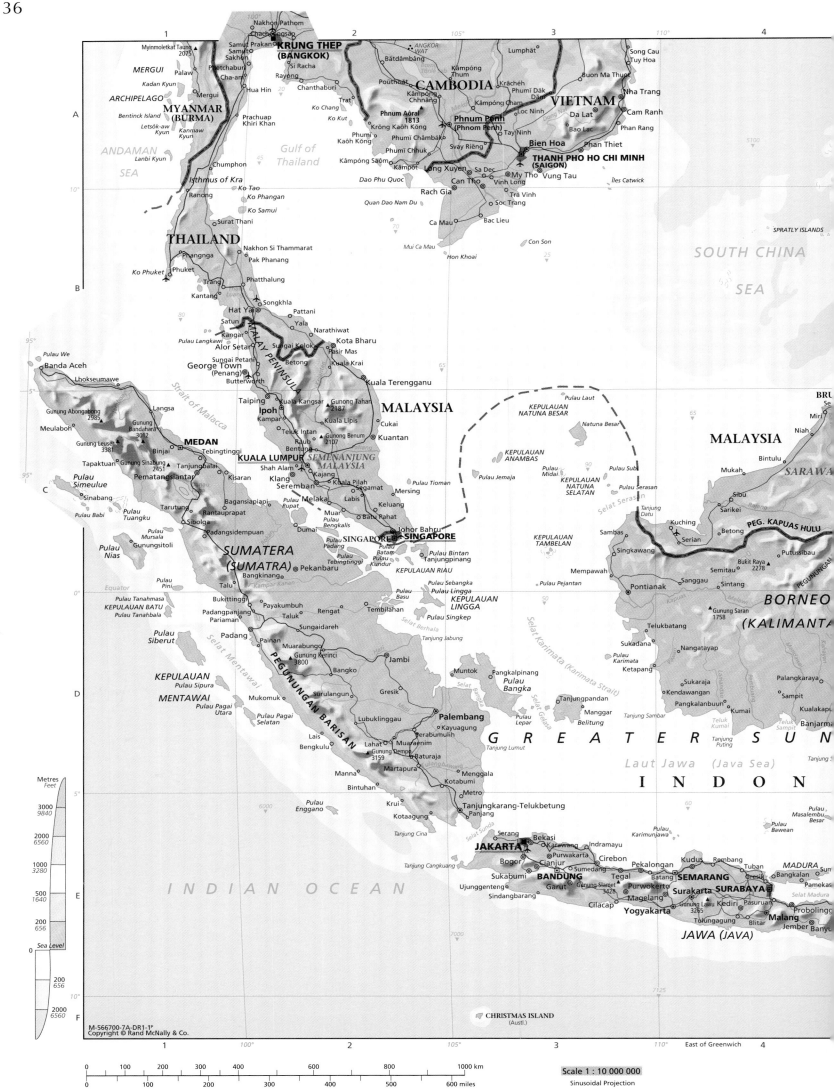

MYANMAR
(BURMA)

MERGUI

ARCHIPELAGO

Bentinck Island

Letsôk-aw
Kyun

Lanbi Kyun

Kadan Kyun

Myinmoletkat Taung
2075

Samut Prakan
Samut
Sakhon

Nakhon Pathom
Chachoengsao

KRUNG THEP
(BANGKOK)

Phetchaburi

Cha-am

Hua Hin

Prachuap
Khiri Khan

Chumphon

Isthmus of Kra

Ranong

Ko Tao

Ko Phangan

Ko Samui

Surat Thani

THAILAND

Phangnga

Nakhon Si Thammarat

Pak Phanang

Ko Phuket

Phuket

Trang

Kantang

Phatthalung

Si Racha

Rayong

Chanthaburi

Trat

Ko Chang

Ko Kut

ANDAMAN

SEA

Gulf of
Thailand

ANGKOR
WAT

Bătdâmbâng

Pouthisăt

Kâmpóng
Chhnăng

Phumĭ
Kaôh Kông

Krông Kaôh Kông

Phumĭ Chhlông

Kâmpóng Saôm

Kâmpôt

Phumĭ Chhuk

Svay Riĕng

Hat Yai

Satun

Kangar

Pulau Langkawi

Alor Setar

Sungai Petani

George Town
(Penang)

Butterworth

Taiping

Ipoh

Kampar

Teluk Intan

Raub

Bentung

Songkhla

Pattani

Yala

Narathiwat

Betong

Sungai Kolok

Kota Bharu

Pasir Mas

Kuala Krai

Kuala Terengganu

Kuala Kangsar

Kuala Lipis

Gunong Tahan
2187

MALAYSIA

Cukai

Gunong Benum
2107

Kuantan

CAMBODIA

Lumphăt

Krâchéh

Phumĭ Dâk
Dâm

Kâmpóng
Thum

Phnum Aôral
1813

Phnum Pénh
(Phnom Penh)

Kâmpóng Cham

Loc Ninh

Tay Ninh

Long Xuyen

Sa Dec

Song Cau

Tuy Hoa

Buon Ma Thuot

VIETNAM

Da Lat

Bao Loc

Da Lac

Bien Hoa

THANH PHO HO CHI MINH
(SAIGON)

My Tho
Can Tho

Vinh Long

Vung Tau

Trà Vinh

Soc Trang

Ca Mau

Bac Lieu

Mui Ca Mau

Rach Gia

Quan Dao Nam Du

Dao Phu Quoc

Hon Khoai

Con Son

Nha Trang

Cam Ranh

Phan Rang

Phan Thiet

Îles Catwick

SPRATLY ISLANDS

SOUTH CHINA

SEA

MALAY PENINSULA

Banda Aceh

Pulau We

Lhokseumawe

Langsa

Gunung Abongabong
2985

Gunung
Bandahara
3012

Meulaboh

Gunung Leuser
3381

Binjai

MEDAN

Tebingtinggi

Tapaktuan

Gunung Sinabung
2451

Pematangsiantar

Tanjungbalai

Kisaran

KUALA LUMPUR

Shah Alam

Klang

Seremban

Kajang

Kuala Pilah

Jegamat

Labis

Keluang

Muar

Pulau
Rupat

Batu Pahat

Dumai

Pulau
Bengkalis

Semenanjung
MALAYSIA

Mersing

Pulau Tioman

MALAYSIA

KEPULAUAN
NATUNA BESAR

Pulau Laut

Natuna Besar

KEPULAUAN
ANAMBAS

Pulau
Midai

Pulau Jemaja

KEPULAUAN
NATUNA
SELATAN

Pulau Subi

Pulau Serasan

Selat Serasan

BRU

Miri

Niah

Mukah

Bintulu

SARAWAK

PEG. KAPUAS HULU

Betong

Kuching

Serian

Sibu

Sarikei

Singkawang

Tanjung
Datu

Sambas

Putussibau

Bukit Raya
2278

Semitau

Sanggau

Sintang

Strait of Malacca

Pulau
Simeulue

Sinabang

Pulau Babi

Pulau Nias

Pulau
Mursala

Gunungsitoli

Pulau
Tuangku

Tarutung

Sibolga

Rantauprapat

Bagansiapiapi

Padangsidempuan

Bukittinggi

Talu

Bangkinang

Kampar Kanan

Pekanbaru

SUMATERA
(SUMATRA)

SINGAPORE

SINGAPORE

Johor Bahru

Pulau
Padang

Pulau
Tebingtinggi

Pulau
Kundur

Pulau
Batam

Pulau Bintan

Tanjungpinang

KEPULAUAN RIAU

KEPULAUAN
TAMBELAN

Pulau Pejantan

Mempawah

Pontianak

Singkawang

BORNEO
(KALIMANTAN)

Gunung Saran
1758

PEGUNUNGAN

Equator

Pulau
Pini

KEPULAUAN BATU

Pulau Tanahmasa

Pulau Tanahbala

Payakumbuh

Padangpanjang

Pariaman

Taluk

Rengat

Tembilahan

Pulau Sebangka

KEPULAUAN
LINGGA

Pulau Lingga

Pulau Singkep

Selat Berhala

Pulau
Basu

Tanjung Jabung

Telukbatang

Sukadana

Nangatayap

Pulau
Karimata

Ketapang

Sanggau

Sintang

Palangkaraya

Sampit

Pulau
Siberut

Padang

Painan

Muarabungo

Sungaidareh

Surulangun

Mukomuk

Jambi

Bangko

Lubuklinggau

Gresik

PEGUNUNGAN BARISAN

Gunung Kerinci
3800

KEPULAUAN

MENTAWAI

Pulau Sipura

Pulau Pagai
Utara

Pulau Pagai
Selatan

Lais

Bengkulu

Manna

Bintuhan

Gunung Dempo
3159

Lahat

Muaraenim

Martapura

Baturaja

PALEMBANG

Kayuagung

Menggala

Kotabumi

Metro

Krui

Kotaagung

Tanjungkarang-Telukbetung
Panjang

Pulau
Enggano

Tanjung Cina

Selat Berhala

Selat
Bangka

Muntok

Pangkalpinang

Pulau
Bangka

Tanjungpandan

Manggar

Belitung

Pulau
Lepar

Tanjung Lumut

GREATER SUN

Selat Gelasa

Tanjung Sambar

Kumai

Pangkalanbuun

Kualakapu

Kuala

Banjarma

Teluk
Kumai

Tanjung
Puting

Teluk
Sampit

Tanjung

Laut Jawa (Java Sea)

INDON

Selat Karimata (Karimata Strait)

INDIAN OCEAN

Pulau
Masalembu
Besar

Pulau
Bawean

Serang

Bekasi

Karawang

Indramayu

JAKARTA

Bogor

Purwakarta

Cianjur

Cirebon

Pekalongan

Kudus

Rembang

Tuban

MADURA

Bangkalan

Pamekas

Sukabumi

BANDUNG

Sumedang

Tegal

Garut

Gunung Slamet
3428

Purwokerto

SEMARANG

Surakarta

SURABAYA

Gresik

Selat Madura

Ujunggenteng

Sindangbarang

Cilacap

Magelang

Yogyakarta

Gunung Lawu
3265

Kediri

Pasuruan

Malang

Probolinggo

Banyu

Tulungagung

Blitar

Jember

JAWA (JAVA)

Pulau
Karimunjawa

CHRISTMAS ISLAND
(Austl.)

Metres
Feet

3000
9840

2000
6560

1000
3280

500
1640

200
656

Sea Level

200
656

2000
6560

0   100   200   300   400   600   800   1000 km

0   100   200   300   400   500   600 miles

Scale 1 : 10 000 000

Sinusoidal Projection

East of Greenwich

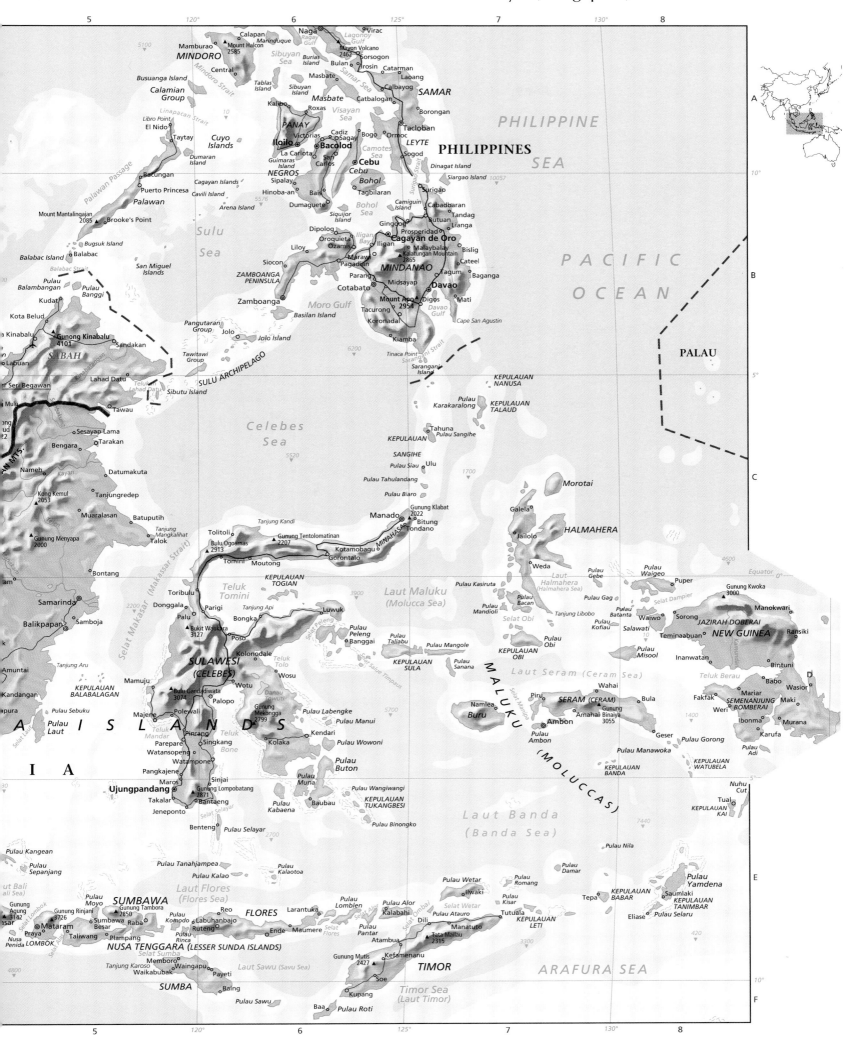

38

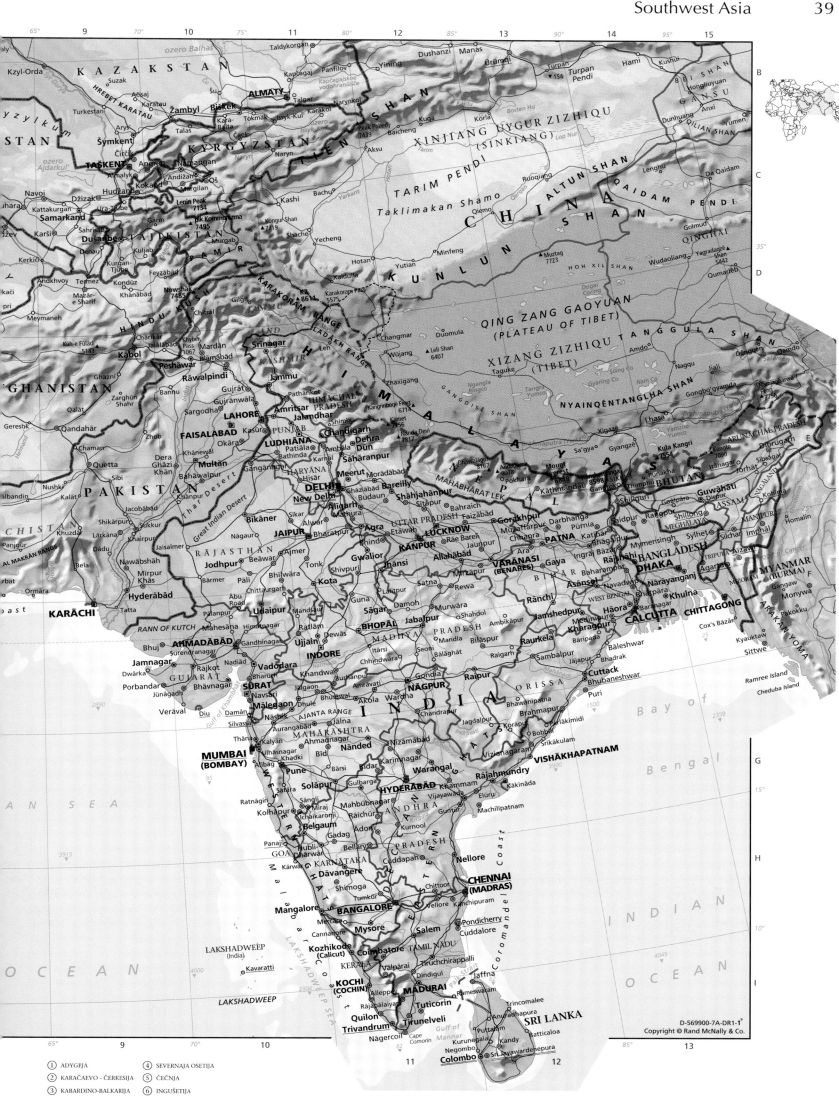

① ADYGEJA   ④ SEVERNAJA OSETIJA
② KARAČAEVO - ČERKESIJA   ⑤ ČEČNJA
③ KABARDINO-BALKARIJA   ⑥ INGUŠETIJA

D-569900-7A-DR1-1°
Copyright © Rand McNally & Co.

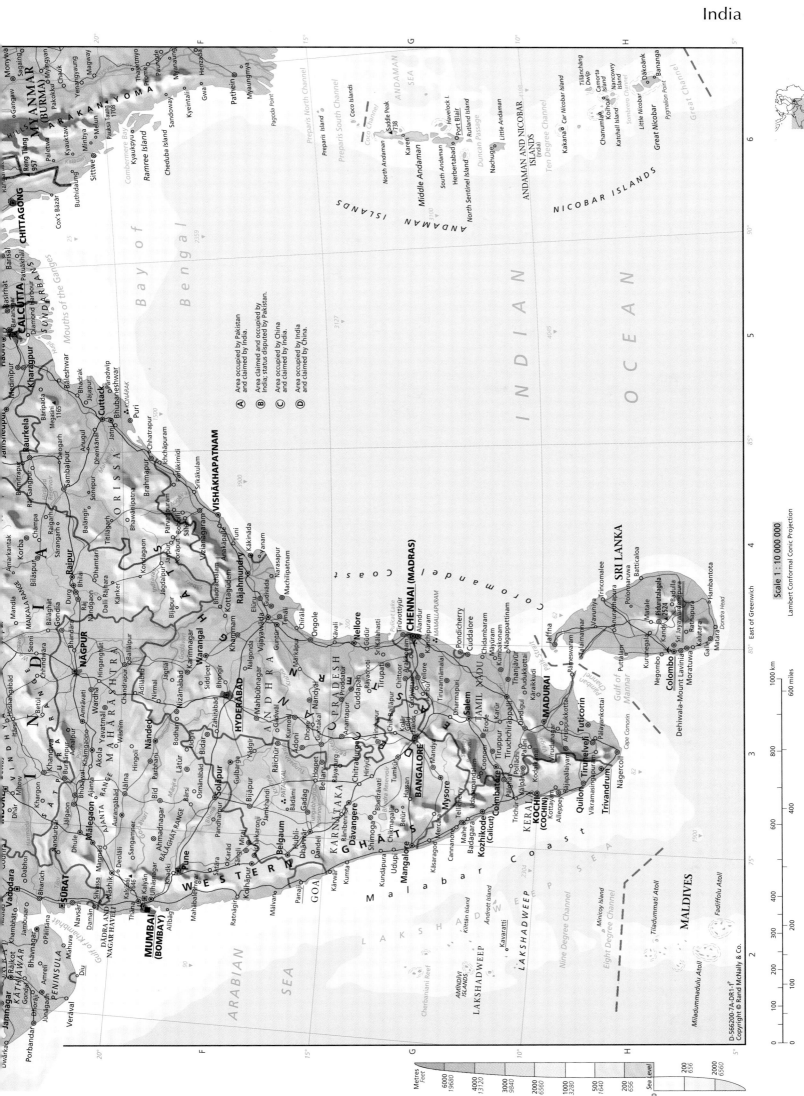

Ⓐ Area occupied by Pakistan
   and claimed by India.

Ⓑ Area claimed and occupied by
   India; status disputed by Pakistan.

Ⓒ Area occupied by China
   and claimed by India.

Ⓓ Area occupied by India
   and claimed by China.

Scale 1 : 10 000 000

Lambert Conformal Conic Projection

D-566200-7A-DR1-1ᵉ
Copyright © Rand McNally & Co.

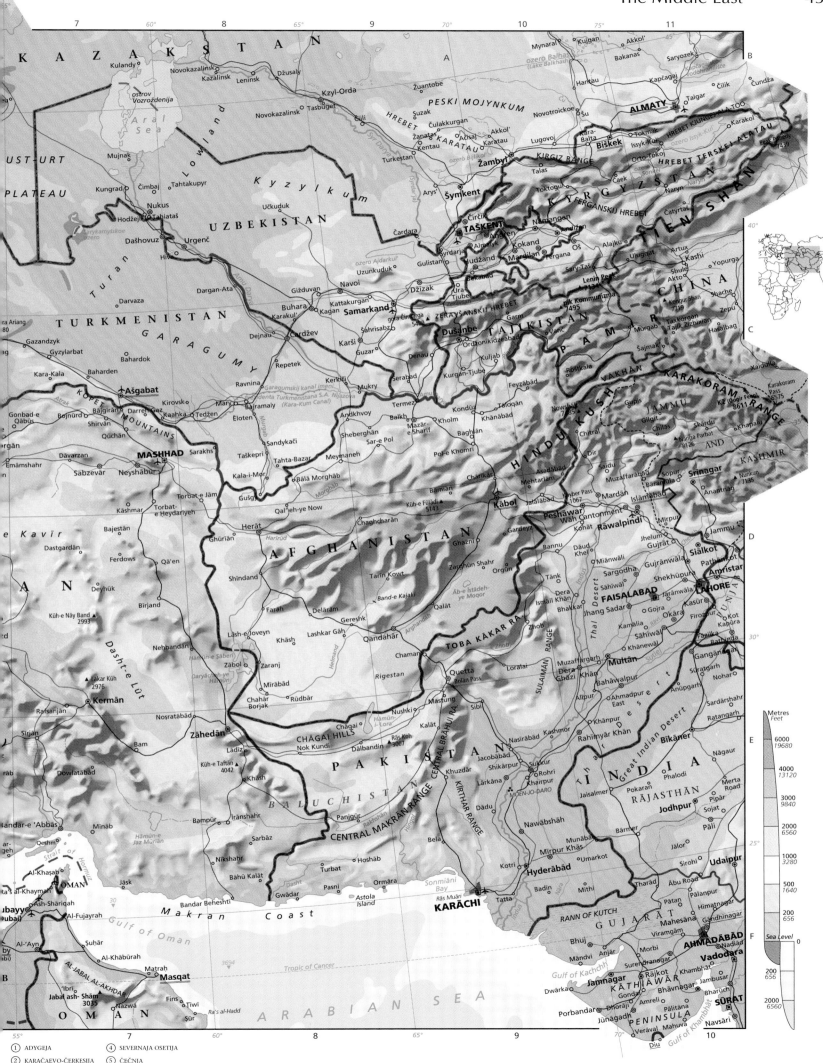

① ADYGEJA
② KARAČAEVO-ČERKESIJA
③ KABARDINO-BALKARIJA
④ SEVERNAJA OSETIJA
⑤ ČEČNJA
⑥ INGUŠETIJA

In November 1983 Turkish Cypriots unilaterally declared their independence as the Turkish Republic of Northern Cyprus. A United Nations buffer zone now runs across the island.

Area occupied by Israel since June 1967
Ⓐ Golan Heights: occupied by Israel
Ⓑ West Bank: parts occupied by Israel

Scale 1 : 5 000 000

Lambert Conformal Conic Projection

D-563700-7A-DR1-1°
Copyright © Rand McNally & Co.

Metres / Feet
4000 / 13120
3000 / 9840
2000 / 6560
1000 / 3280
500 / 1640
200 / 656
0 / Sea Level
200 / 656
2000 / 6560

8 10 12 13 14

Soči
Adler
Gagra
Gudauta
Suhumi
Očamčira
Gali
Zugdidi
Senaki
Poti
Samtredia
Ozurgeti
Batumi
Hopa
Kobuleti

KARAČAEVO ČERKESIJA
gora El'brus 5642
gora Psiš 3789
KABARDINO-BALKARIJA
Nal'čik
Terek
INGUŠETIJA
Nazran'
Beslan
Alagiro
SEVERNAJA OSETIJA
Vladikavkaz
ČEČNJA
Itum-Kale
perevál Mamisonski 2829
perevál Krestovyj 2379
gora Šara 5068
gora Kazbek 5047
gora Tebulosmta 4492

RUSSIA
Botlih
Bujnaksk
Mahačkala
Kaspijsk
Izberbaš
Levaši
Gunib
Bežta
DAGESTAN
Madžalis
Derbent
Kasumkent
Rutul
Vači
Sergokala

CASPIAN SEA
788
-28
42°

Tkvarčeli
Kutaisi
 Čiatura
Gori
Chinvali
Duševi
Kaspi
Telavi
Kvareli
Gurdžaani
Zaqatala
Bazardüzü dag 4480
Qusar
Xaçmaz
Quba
Qonaqkänd
Siyäzän

GEORGIA
Zestafoni
Bakuriani
Boržomi
Hašuri
Calka
Tbilisi
Rustavi
Dedoplis Ckaro
Zemo-Kedi
Šeki
Oğuz
Mingäçevir
Göyçay
İsmayıllı
Altıağac
Šamaxı
Märäzä
Sumqayıt
Maştağa

Posof
Ahalcihe
Ahalkalaki
Bolnisi
Dmanisi
Tovuz
Ğänçä
Ağdaş
Tärtär
Bärdä
Kürdämir
Sabirabad
Qobustan
Turkmenbaši
BAKI (BAKU)
Suiti burnu 40°

Ardahan
Çıldır
Ardešen
Artvin
Yusufeli
Oldu Gölü
Ardanuç
Arpaçay
Gjumri
Vanadzor
Šämkir
Yevlax
Uçar
Saatlı
Äli Bayramlı
Salyan

Trabzon
Rize
Pazar
Akçaabat
Of
Maçka
Kaçkar Dağı 3932
DOĞU KARADENIZ DAĞLARI
ALLAHÜEKBER DAĞLARI
Kars
ARMENIA
Artik
Aragats Lerr 4090
Ashtarak
Sevan
Sevana Lich 1900
Ğämiş dağ 3724
AZERBAIJAN
Xankändi
Fūzuli
Biläsuvar
Neftçala

Tirebolu
Giresun
DOĞU KARADENIZ DAĞLARI
Gümüşhane
Aluçra
Bayburt
Kelkit
Mescit Tepe 3230
Göle
Sarıkamış
Kağızman
Hoktemberjan
Yerevan
Vanadzor
Ğänçä
Martuni
Ağdam
İmişli

karahisar
Refahiye
Kemah
Erzincan
KEŞIŞ DAĞLARI
Çayırlı
Kop Geçidi 2430
Aşkale
Erzurum
Tercan
Tekman
Narman
Oltu
Pasinler
Horasan
Ağrı
Tutak
Aras
Aşağı Dağı 3275
Iğdır
Ağrı Dağı (Mount Ararat) 5137
Doğubayazıt
Ararat
Artashat
Vike
Sürur
Naxçıvan
Qazangöldağ 3829
Culfa
Meğri
Kapan
AZER.
Bälän Šafar 'Ali
Garmi
Masallı

Elazığ
Hankendi
Palu
Maden
Genç
Muş
HACREŞ DAĞLARI
Bulanık
Malazgirt
Tendürek Dağı 3533
Patnos
Ercis
Zurabad
Māku
Khvoy
Ahar
Marand
Meshgin Shahr
Sabalān 4814
Namin
Āstārā
Ardabil
Haviq
Lankäran
Astara
KŪHHA-YE TAVÁLEŠ

MUNZUR DAĞLARI
Ovacık
Nazimiye
Tunceli
Kiğı
Karlıova
BINGÖL DAĞLARI
Hınıs
Varto
Bingöl
Süphan Dağı 4058
Ahlat
Tatvan
Van Gölü 1646
Gevaş
Van
Gürpınar
Qotur
Salmās
Sūfiān
Talkheh
Oskū
Tabrīz
Sabalān
Sarāb

atya
Sivrice
Ergani
Diyarbakır
Bismil
Batman
Hazro
Silvan
Líce
Kulp
Muradiye
Başkale
Daryācheh-ye Orūmīyeh 1275
Azar Shahr
Kūh-e Sahand 3712
Marāgheh

Karaca Dağ 1957
Siverek
Hilvan
Çınar
Midyat
Mardin
Savur
Derik
Kurtalan
Siirt
Pervari
Çatak
Hakkâri
Cilo Dağı 4168
Çukurca
Silvāneh
Orūmīyeh
'Ajab Shīr
Benāb
Mālek Kandi
Mīāndoāb

Atatürk Barajı
Karakeçi
Viranşehir
Kızıltepe
Nusaybin
İdil
Cizre
Zakho
Al-'Amādīyah
Dahūk
'Aqrah
Rawanduz
3607
Osnovīyeh
Naqadeh
Šā'in Dezh
Miāneh
Bandar-e Anzalī
Fowman

Şanlıurfa
Süruç
Akçakale
Ceylanpınar
Ra's al-'Ayn
Tall Tamir
'Āmūdah
Al-Qāmishlī
Tall Küjik
NĪNAWĀ (NINEVEH)
Piran Shahr
Mahābād
Būkān
Saqqez
Takāb
Zanjan
Saïdiyeh
Abhar

JABAL 'ABD AL-'AZĪZ
Al-Hasakah
JABAL SINJAR
Sinjār
Tall 'Afar
Al-Mawşil (Mosul)
Irbīl
Sar Dasht
Rāniyah
Baneh
Divāndarreh
Bijār
Qeydar
Zanjan

Ash Shaddādah
Ar-Raqqah
Suwaydah
As-Suwar
Dayr az-Zawr
Ash-Sharqāt
Karkūk
Altun Kupri
As-Sulaymānīyah
Halabjah
Pāveh
Sanandaj
Hoseynābād
Qorveh
Kabūdarāhang
Razan

JABAL BISHRĪ
Al-Mayādin
Buşayrah
MESOPOTAMIA
Tāwūq
Tuz
Kifrī
Khānaqīn
Jalūlā'
Qasr-e Shīrīn
Sūmār
Kermānshāh (Bākhtarān)
Harsin
Songor
Asadābād
Kangāvar
Sahneh
Bahār
Hamadān
Tūysärkān
Malāyer

Abū Kamāl
Al Qā'im
Hadīthah
Khān al-Baghdādī
Hīt
'Ānah
Sāmarrā'
Tikrit
Balad
Al-Miqdādiyah
Mandali
Īlam
Eslāmābād
Mehrān
Kūhdasht
Nahāvand
Oshtorinān
Borūjerd
Khorramābād

'Akāshāt
Ar-Ramādī
Al-Fallūjah
BAGHDĀD
Ba'qūbah
Al-Khāliş
KABĪR KŪH
Abdānān
KŪHHA-YE ZAGROS

Wādī Hawrān
Buhayrat al-Habbānīyah
Ar-Ruṭbah
An-Nukhayb
Karbalā'
Al-Musayyib
ATLĀL BĀBIL (BABYLON)
Al-Hindīyah
Al-Hillah
Al-Kūt
Shaykh Sa'd
'Alī al-Gharbī
Dehlorān
Andimeshk
Dezful

Jabal 'Unayzah 940
Al-Jalāmīd
SAUDI ARABIA
Ash-Shināfīyah
Ar-Rumaythah
An-Najaf
Al-Kūfah
Al-Kifl
Ad-Dīwānīyah
Ash-Shāmīyah
Qal'at Sukkar
Ash-Shatrah
Al-Hayy
Al-'Amārah
Al-Halfāyah
Bostān
Sūsangerd
Hūzgān
Ahvāz

As-Samāwah
An-Nāşirīyah
Al-Qurnah
IRAQ
SYRIAN DESERT

8 40° 9 42° 10 44° 11 46° 12 48° 13

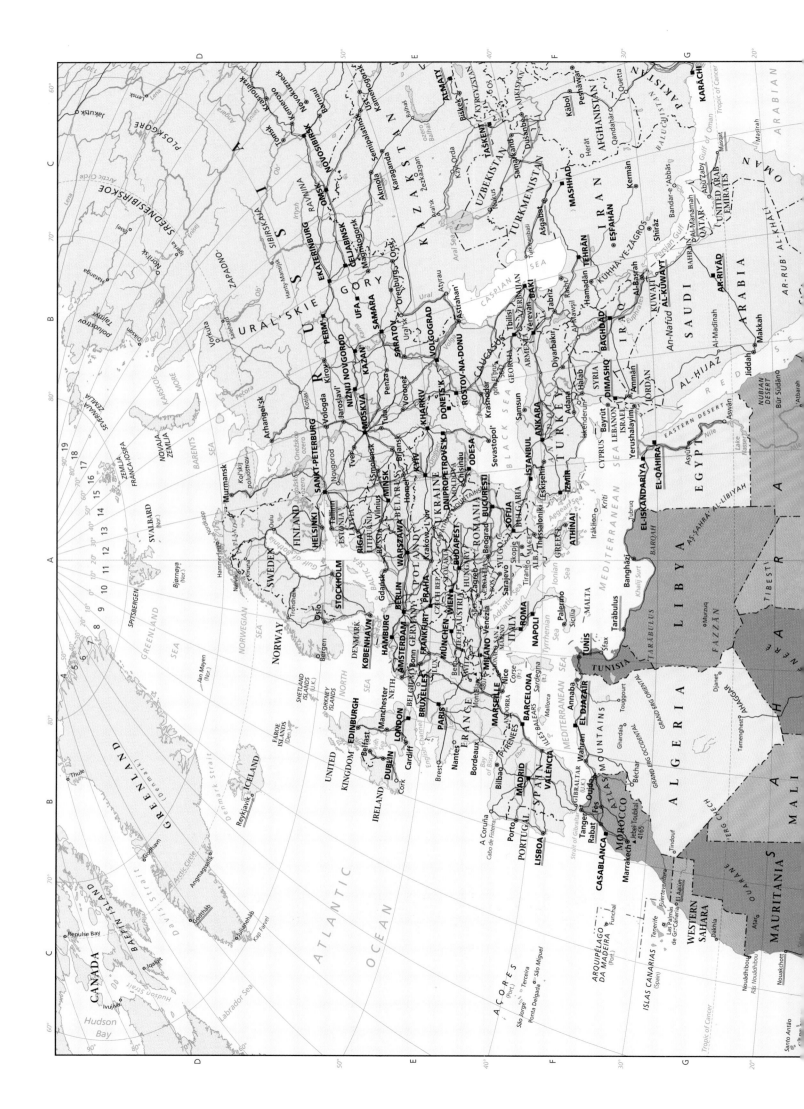

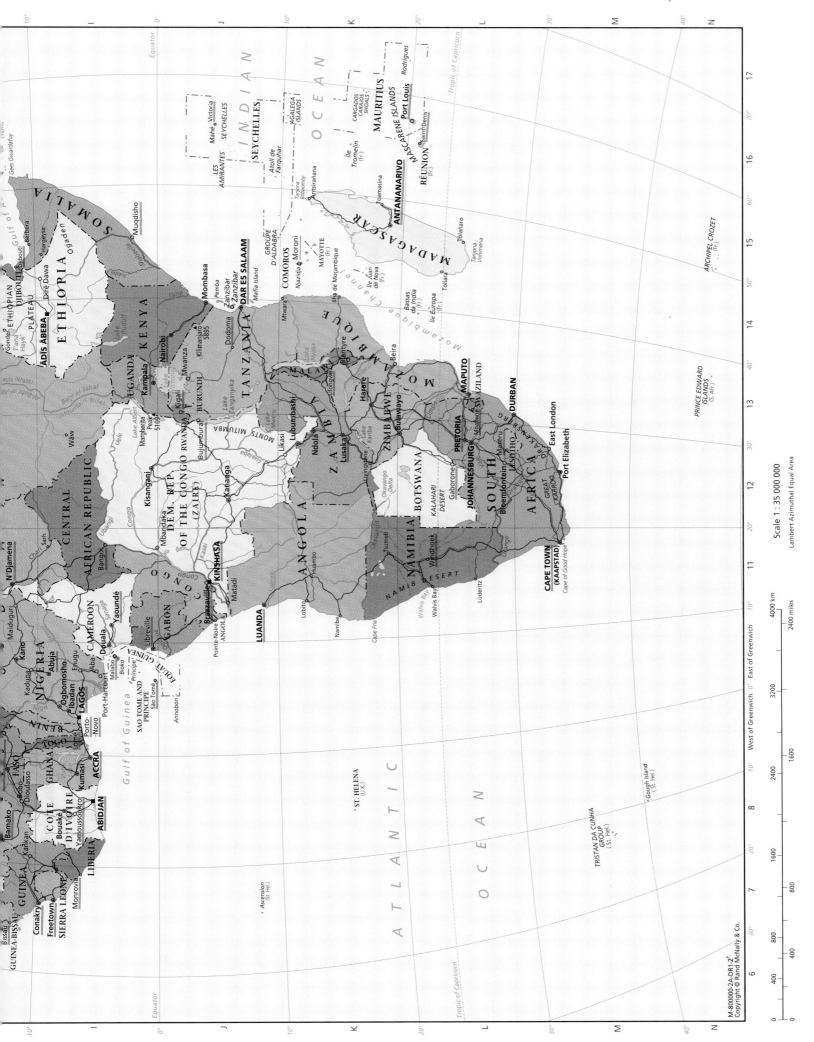

Scale 1 : 35 000 000

Lambert Azimuthal Equal Area

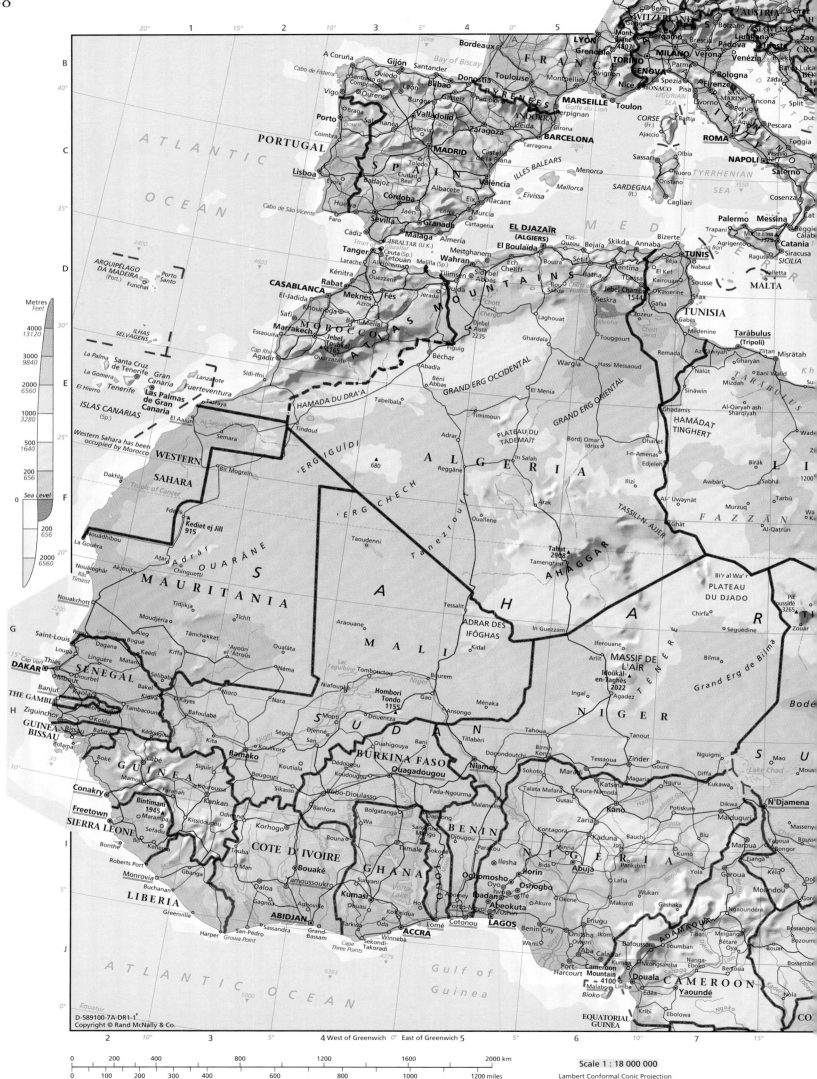

Scale 1 : 18 000 000

Lambert Conformal Conic Projection

D-589100-7A-DR1-1°
Copyright © Rand McNally & Co.

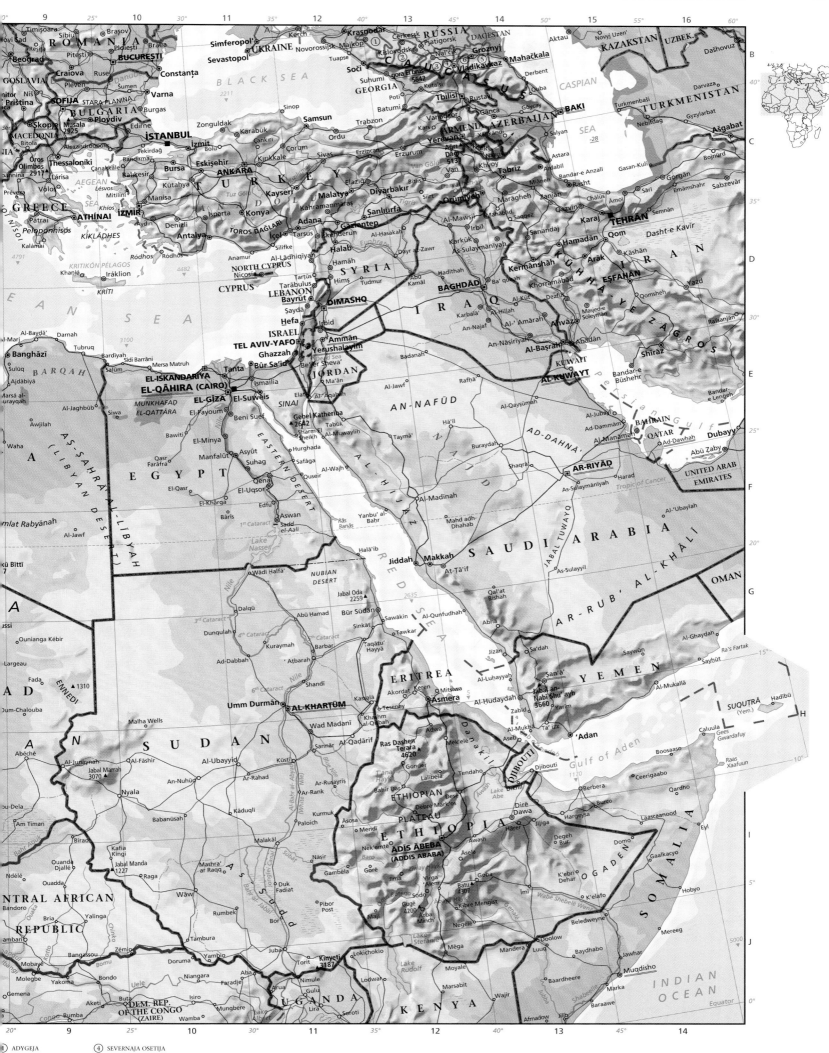

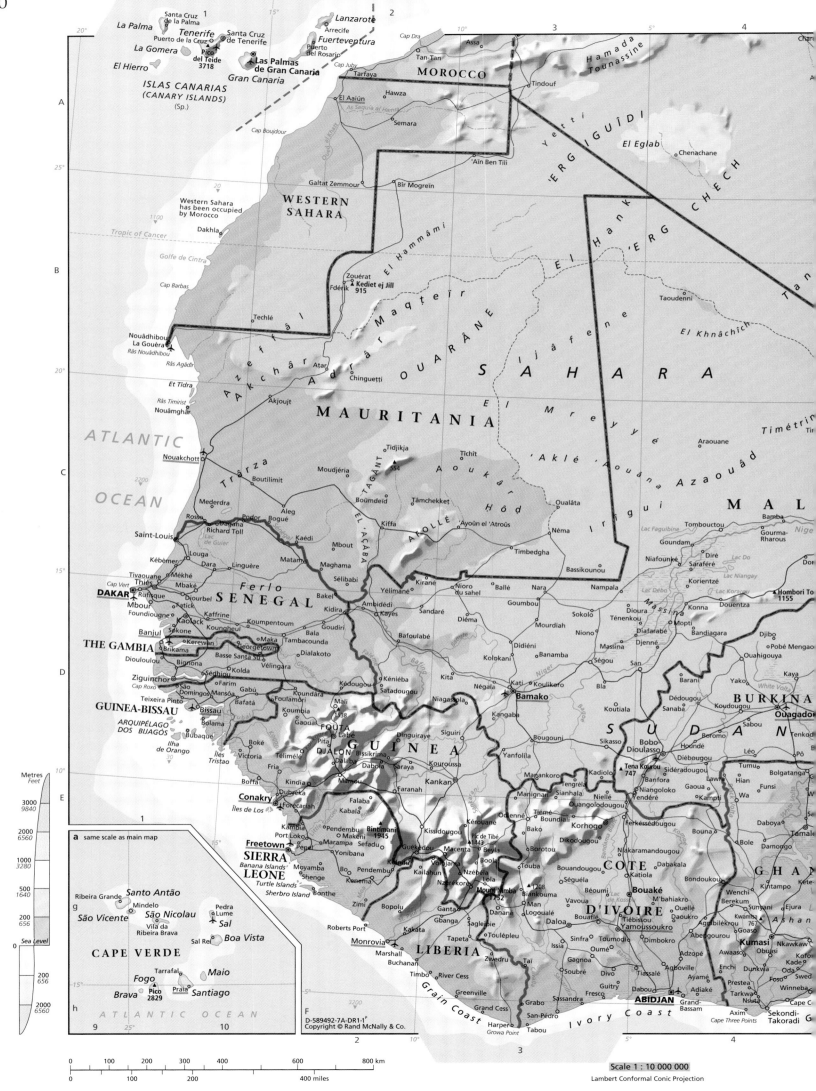

ISLAS CANARIAS
(CANARY ISLANDS)
(Sp.)

La Palma
Santa Cruz
de la Palma
Puerto de la Cruz
Tenerife
Santa Cruz
de Tenerife
La Gomera
Pico
del Teide
3718
El Hierro
Las Palmas
de Gran Canaria
Gran Canaria

Lanzarote
Arrecife
Fuerteventura
Puerto
del Rosario

Cap Dra

MOROCCO

Hamada
Tounassine

Assa
Tan-Tan

'ERG IGUÎDI

Yetti

El Eglab
Chenachane

'ERG CHECH

Tarfaya
Cap Juby

El Aaiún
As Saquia al Hamra
Hawza

WESTERN
SAHARA

Semara

'Aïn Ben Tili

Tindouf

Cap Boujdour

Western Sahara
has been occupied
by Morocco

Galtat Zemmour

Bîr Mogreïn

El Hank

Taoudenni

Tropic of Cancer

Dakhla

Golfe de Cintra

Cap Barbas

Zouérat
Fdérik
Kediet ej Jill
915

El Hammâmi

El Khnâchich

Maqteïr

Techlé

OUARÂNE

Ijâfene

SAHARA

Nouâdhibou
La Goûèra
Râs Nouâdhibou

Atâr
Chinguetti

Adrâr

El
Mreyyé

Araouane

Timétri

Akjoujt

MAURITANIA

'Aklé 'Aouâna

Azaouâd

Râs Agâdîr
Et Tîdra
Râs Timirist
Nouâmghâr

Tidjikja

Tîchît

Aoukâr

Oualâta

Irigui

MAL

ATLANTIC

Nouakchott

Moudjéria

554

Hôd

Néma

Bamba

Tombouctou

Gourma-
Rharous

Nige

OCEAN

Boutilimit

Tâmchekket

'Aklé

Ayoûn el 'Atroûs

Lac Faguibine

Goundam
Diré
Lac Do

Mederdra
Aleg
Bogué

Rosso
Richard Toll
Dagana

Podor
Kiffa

Timbedgha

Niafounké
Saraféré

Lac Débo
Lac Niangay

Saint-Louis
Lac
de Guier

Kaédi

Mbout

Maghama

Bassikounou

Korientzé

Lac Korarou

Hombori To
1155

Kébèmer
Louga
Dara
Linguère

Matam

Sélibabi
Kirané
Nioro
du sahel

Ballé

Nara

Nampala

Dioura

Konna

Douentza

Tivaouane
Mékhé
Cap Vert
Thiès

FERLO

Bakel
Yélimané

Goumbou

Sokolo

Ténenkou

Mopti

Djibo

DAKAR
Rufisque

SENEGAL

Kidira

Ambidédi
Kayes

Sandaré

Dièma

Mourdiah

Niono

Diafarabé

Bandiagara

Mbour
Fatick
Diourbel

Kaffrine
Koumpentoum
Goudiri

Bafoulabé

Didiéni

Massina

Djenné

Pobé Mengao

Ouahigouya

Foundiougne
Kaolack

Koungheul
Bala
Tambacounda

Banamba

Ségou

San

Kaya

THE GAMBIA
Banjul
Sokone
Kerewan

Maka
Georgetown
Dialakoto

Kita

Négala
Kati
Koulikoro

Bla

Barani

Yako

White Volta

BURKINA

Brikama

Basse Santa Su
Vélingara

Kédougou

Kéniéba

Koutiala

Sanaba
Koudougou

Dioulou lou
Bignona

Kolda

Satadougou

Niagassola

Kangaba

Sabou

Bafatá

Koundára
Foulamôri

Mali
1538

Ouagado

Ziguinchor
Cap Roxo
São
Domingos Mansôa
Farim

Gabú

Koumbia

Gaoual

FOUTA

Dinguiraye

Siguiri

Bougouni

Sikasso

Bobo
Dioulasso

Boromo

Léo

Tenko

Pô

GUINEA-BISSAU
Teixeira
Pinto
Bissau

Bolama

Boké
Victoria

Pita
Labé
DJALON

Bissikrima
Kouroussa

Yanfolila

Houndé

Diébougou

ARQUIPÉLAGO
DOS BIJAGÓS
Ilha
de Orango

Bubaque

Télimélé

Daraya

Kankan

Mankono

Tengréla

Tena Kourou
747

Sidéradougou

Tumu

Bolgatanga

Fria

GUINEA

Banfora

Gaoua

Lawra

Hian

Funsi

Boffa
Kindia

Mamou

Faranah

Kadiolo

Niangoloko
Vendéré

Wa

Îles
Tristao

Dubréka
Forécariah

Falaba
Kabala

Odienné

Boundiali

Ouangolodougou

Niellé

Kampti

Conakry
Îles de Los

Kambia
Port Loko

Pendembu
Makeni
Sefadu

Kissidougou

Kérouane

Tiémé
Bako

Korhogo

Ferkéssédougou

Bouna

Bole

Daboya

Tamale

Freetown
Banana Islands
SIERRA
LEONE

Bintimani
1945

Pic de Tibé
1443

Guékédou

Macenta

Beyla

Borotou

Dikodougou

Niakaramandougou

COTE

Dabakala

GHAN

Marampa
Yonibana

Moyamba
Shenge

Bo

Pendembu

Koïdu
Voïnjama

Nzébéla

Touba

Bouandougou

Séguéla

Kong

Katiola

Bondoukou

Wenchi
Kintampo

Ashan

Turtle Islands
Sherbro Island

Bonthe

Kenema

Kailahun

Nzérékoré
Lola

Mount Nimba
1752

1208

Biankouma
Man

Bouaflé
Vavoua

Bouaké
M'bahiakro

Béoumi

Berekum

Sunyani

Ejura

Kumasi

Zimi

Bopolu

Ganta
Gbanga

Danané
Logoualé

Daloa

D'IVOIRE

Yamoussoukro

Agnibilékrou
Daoukro
Ouellé

Obuasi

Roberts Port

Kakata

Saglepie
Tapeta

Toulépleu
Guiglo

Issia
Sinfra
Oumé

Toumodi

Gagnoa
Sassandra

Dimbokro

Abengourou

Adzopé

Awaaso

Kade
Enchi

Oda
Dunkwa

Foso

Monrovia
Marshall
Buchanan

LIBERIA

Taï

Zwedru

River Cess

Timbo
Greenville

Grand Cess

Harper
Growa Point

Tabou

Grain Coast

Sassandra
Fresco

Soubré
Divo

Grabo
San-Pédro

Tiassalé
Ayamé

Guitry
Dabou

Abidjan
Grand-
Bassam

Axim
Cape Three Points

Agboville

Prestea
Tarkwa

Sekondi-
Takoradi

Winneba

Cape C

Nkaw

Kwame

Goaso

Ivory Coast

CAPE VERDE

Ribeira Grande
Mindelo
São Vicente

Santo Antão

São Nicolau

Pedra
Lume
Sal

Vila da
Ribeira Brava

Sal Rei
Boa Vista

Tarrafal
Fogo
Brava

Pico
2829

Maio

Praia
Santiago

ATLANTIC OCEAN

a same scale as main map

g

h

9 10

Metres
Feet

3000
9840

2000
6560

1000
3280

500
1640

200
656

Sea Level
0

200
656

2000
6560

0 100 200 300 400 600 800 km
0 100 200 400 miles

Scale 1 : 10 000 000
Lambert Conformal Conic Projection

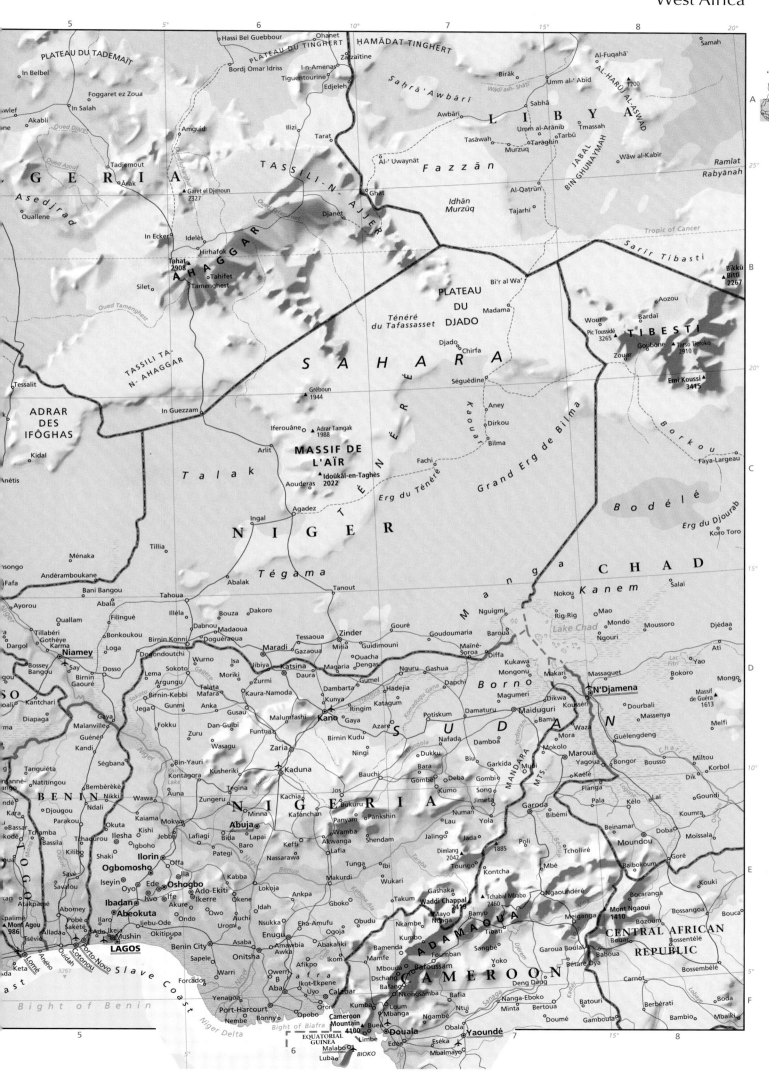

PLATEAU DU TADEMAÏT

In Belbel
wlef
Akabli
In Salah
Foggaret ez Zoua
In Salah
Oued Djaret

G E R I A

Asedirad

Ouallene

Hassi Bel Guebbour
Ohanet
PLATEAU DU TINGHERT   HAMĀDAT TINGHERT
Zarzaïtine
Bordj Omar Idriss
In-Amenas
Tiguentourine
Edjeleh
Ilizi
Tarat

Sahrā' Awbārī

Birāk
Umm al-'Abid
Sabhā
Awbārī

L I B Y A

Umm al-Arānib
Tasāwah
Tarāghin
Murzuq

Wādī ash-Shāti'

Al-Fuqahā'
AL-HARŪJ AL-ASWAD
1200

Samah

Amguid
Ārak
Tadjemout
In Ecker
Idelès
Hirhafok
Tahat
2908
Tahifet
Tamenghest
Silet

A H A G G A R

Garet el Djenoun
2327
Al-'Uwaynāt
Ghat

Idhān
Murzūq

Tajarhī

Al-Qatrūn

JABAL
BIN GHUNAYMAH

Ramlat
Rabyānah

Tropic of Cancer

Oued Tamenghest

TASSILI-N-AJJER
Djanet

Oued Tafassasset

Sarīr Tibasti

Bi'r al Wa'
Madama

Wour
Pic Toussidé
3265

Goubone
Bardaï
Zouar

Aozou

Bikkū
Bittî
2267

TIBESTI
Tarso Tieroko
2910

B

TASSILI TA-
N-AHAGGAR

Tessalit

ADRAR
DES
IFÔGHAS

Kidal

Anétis

k
a

In Guezzam

Gréboun
1944

Iferouâne
Arlit

Aoudéras

Adrar Tamgak
1988

MASSIF DE
L'AÏR

Idoûkâl-en-Taghès
2022

PLATEAU
DU
DJADO

Ténéré
du Tafassasset

Djado
Chirfa

Séguédine

S A H A R A

T É N É R É

Kaouar

Aney
Dirkou
Bilma

Erg du Ténéré

Fachi

Grand Erg de Bilma

Emi Koussi
3415

Borkou

Faya-Largeau

B o d é l é

Erg du Djourab

Koro Toro

C

Talak

Ménaka

Andéramboukane

Tillia

Ingal
Agadez

N I G E R

Abalak

T é g a m a

Tahoua

M a n g a

Nguigmi

C H A D

Nokou   Kanem
Rig-Rig
Baroua
Maïné-
Soroa

Salal

Mao
Mondo

Moussoro
Ngouri

Djédaa

Ati

Lac
Fitri
Yao

15°

Ayorou
Ouallam
Tillabéri
Gothèye
Karma
Niamey
Bossey
Bangou
Say

Bani Bangou
Abala

Filingué
Bonkoukou
Loga
Dosso

Dabnou
Birnin Konni
Dogondoutchi

Bouza   Dakoro
Illéla
Madaoua
Doguêraoua

Tanout

Gouré
Goudoumaria

Lake Chad

Kukawa
Diffa
Mongonu

Nguru   Gashua
Dapchi

Makari   N'Djamena

Ngouri

Bokoro

Mongo

Massif
de Guéra
1613

D

Ayorou
Dargol
Ayorou

Tessaoua
Zinder
Gazaoua
Miria
Maradi
Jibiya   Katsina
Magaria
Daura
Kunya
Dambarta
Hadejia

Guidimouni
Dengas

Ouacha

Borno
Magumeri
Dikwa
Bama

Kousséri
Dourbali
Massaguet

Massenya

Melfi

O
O
SO

Birnin
Gaouré
Kantchari
Diapaga

Sokoto
Lema   Isa   Moriki
Argungu   Zurmi
Wurno
Birnin-Kebbi   Mafara   Anka
Jega   Gunmi   Gusau
Fokku   Talata
Malumfashi
Kano
Ringim
Katagum
Potiskum
Damaturu   Maiduguri

Azare
Nafada
Dukku
Bara   Biu

Damboa

Garkida   Mubi
Mokolo
Wum   Mora

Maroua
Yagoua   Bongor

Guélengdeng

Bousso

Miltou   Korbol

Dik

Goundi

E

Gaya
Malanville
Guéné
Kandi

Birnin
Gaouré

Funtua
Dan-Gulbi

Birnin Kudu
Zuru
Wasagu   Zaria
Kaduna
Kachia
Kusheriki
Tegina

Bauchi

Gombe
Deba   Gombi
Kumo   Song

Jos
Bukuru
Panyam   Pankshin
Kafanchan
Minna

Numan
Lau   Jimeta
Garkida
Garoua
Bibémi

Kaélé

Fianga

Pala
Kélo
Lai

Beinamar
Moundou

Koumra
Goré

Doba   Moïssala

CENTRAL AFRICAN

BENIN   Nikki   Wawa
Djougou
Parakou   Okuta
Bassila
Kilibo
Shaki

Kontagora
Äuna   Zungeru
Kaiama   Mokwa
Biu   Lafiagi   Lapai
Jebba   Patigi   Baro
Bida

N I G E R I A

Abuja
Keffi
Nassarawa
Lafia

Wamba
Akwanga
Shendam

Tunga   Ibi

Jalingo
Jada
Poli

Dimlang
2042   1885
Toungo

Kontcha

Mbé

Ngaoundéré

Baïbokoum

Goundi

Bocaranga
Kouki

Bossangoa

Bozoum

Bouar

Bossembélé

E

T
O
G
O

Tchaourou
Bassari
Bassar
kodé
Tchamba
Kara
Bafilo

Bembèrèkè
Ndali

Iseyin
Savé   Oyo
Abomey
Ilaro
Kétou

Ibadan
Abeokuta

Mont Agou
986
Tsévié

Ilorin
Ogbomosho
Ede
Ife
Iwo
Oshogbo
Ado-Ekiti
Akure
Ikerre
Owo

Offa
Kabba
Lokoja
Okene

Makurdi
Wukari

Takum

Gashaka
Waddi Chappal
2419

Tchabal Mbabo
2460

Meiganga

Mont Ngaoui
1410

Bétaré Oya

Garoua Boulaï   Baboua

CENTRAL AFRICAN
REPUBLIC

Bétaré Oya
Bouca

Lomé
Aného
Keta
Ouidah
Cotonou
Porto-Novo
LAGOS
Mushin
Ikeja
Allada
Sakété
Badagry

Ilaro

Jebba
Ilesha
Iseyin

Ijebu-Ode
Ondo
Okitipupa

Benin City
Sapele
Warri
Forcados

Asaba
Onitsha
Agbor
Uromi
Auchi
Idah

Nsukka
Enugu
Awka
Abakaliki
Amawbia
Afikpo
Owerri

Obudu

Nkambe
Ndaga
Kumbo
Bamenda
Mamfe
Mbouda
Foumban
Dschang

Tibati

A D A M A O U A
Ngambe

Banyo
Yoko

Deng Deng

Carnot

Berbérati

Boda

Mbaiki

F

Mont Agou
986

Slave Coast

Bight of Benin

Niger Delta

Yenagoa
Port-Harcourt
Nembe
Bonny

EQUATORIAL
GUINEA
Malabo
Lubà

Opobo
Oron
Calabar

Ikot-Ekpene
Uyo

Kumba
Mbanga

Cameroon
Mountain
4100
Buéa
Limbe
Douala

BIOKO

Batang
Nkongsamba
Bafia

Yaoundé
Eséka

Bafia
Ntui
Minta
Obala
Mbalmayo

Bertoua
Doumé
Gambcula

Abong-Mbang

F

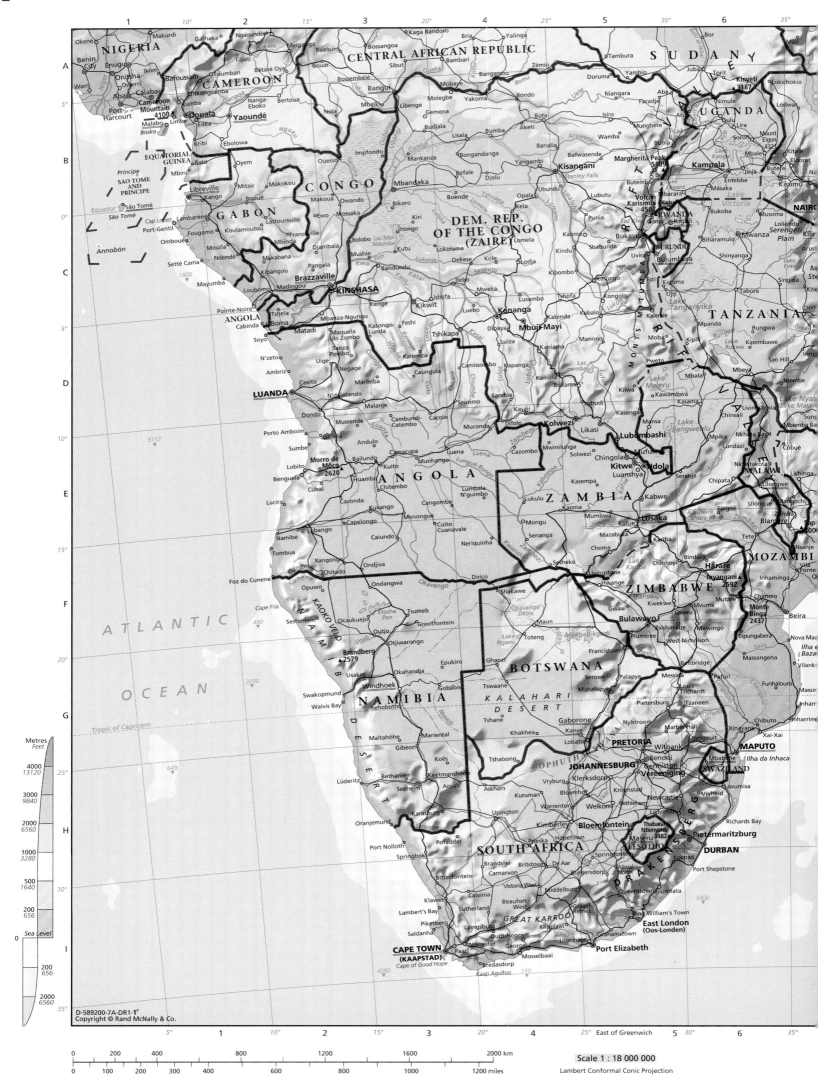

52

ETHIOPIA

Kibre Mengist
Ilmi
Gaalkacyo
Negele
K'elafo
Mēga
Doolow
Beledweyne
Mandera
Luuq
Moyale
Hobyo
Mandera
arsabit
Wajir
Baydhabo
Mereeg
Mado Gashi
Afmadow
Baardheere
Jawhar
Muqdisho
t Kenya)
Garissa
Jilib
Marka
Tana
Kismaayo
Jamaame
Baraawe

SOMALIA

Buur Gaabo

Equator

Lamu

Voi
Malindi
Mombasa
Tanga
Chake Chake
angani
Pemba
Zanzibar
Zanzibar
goro
DAR ES SALAAM
Mafia Island
Kilindoni
Kilwa Kivinje
wale
Lindi
ngwea
Masasi
Palma
ntandu
Mocímboa da Praia
puez
Pemba
Namapa
Lhrio
Nacala-a-Velha
mpula
Ilha de Moçambique
Mogincual
Moma
Angoche
bane
993

INDIAN

OCEAN

SEYCHELLES
Praslin
Victoria   Mahé
Poivre
Atoll
LES
AMIRANTES
Île Plate

Alphonse
Coëtivy

5340

6402

SEYCHELLES

GROUPE
D'ALDABRA
Île au Cerf
ATOLL DE
COSMOLEDO
Atoll de
Farquhar

4406

Njazidja   COMOROS
Moroni
Nzwani
Mwali   Mutsamudu
Dzaoudzi
MAYOTTE
(Fr.)
ARCHIPEL DES COMORES

ÎLES GLORIEUSES
(Fr.)
Tanjona
Bobaomby
Antsiranana
Ambilobe
Ambanja   Maromokotro
▲ 2876
Analalava   Bealanana
Sambava
Antsohihy   Antalaha
Mahajanga   Maroantsetra
Mampikony   Manara Avaratra
5300   Soalala   Tsaratanana
Besalampy   Maevatanana   Nosy
Sainte Marie
Île Juan
de Nova
(Fr.)
Morafenobe   Ambatondrazaka
Maintirano   Toamasina
Tsiroanomandidy
MADAGASCAR
Miandrivazo   ANTANANARIVO
Morondava   Ambatolampy
Antsirabe   Vatomandry
Mahanoro
Ambositra
Manja   Mandabe
Fianarantsoa
assas da India   Moromb e   Ambalavao   Mananjary
(Fr.)
Ihosy   Manakara
Île Europa   Ankazoabo
(Fr.)   Toliara   Farafangana
Betroka
Bekily
Ampanihy   Tôlañaro
Tsiombe   Ambovombe
Tanjona
Vohimena

AGALEGA
ISLANDS

Île Tromelin
(Fr.)

CARGADOS
CARAJOS
SHOALS

MAURITIUS

MASCARENE   ISLANDS
Rodrigues
MASCA
Port Louis
Mauritius
RÉUNION   Saint-Denis
(Fr.)   Saint-Pierre
4200

Mozambique Channel

4300

Tropic of Capricorn

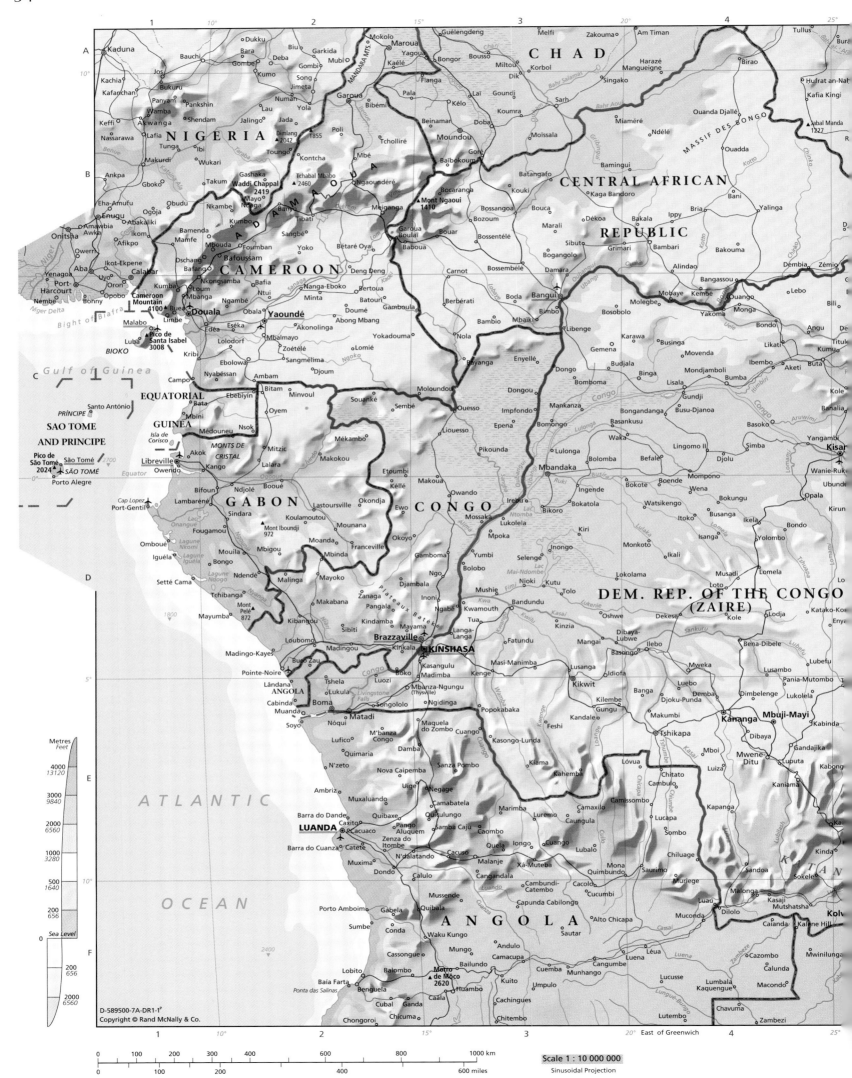

Scale 1 : 10 000 000

Sinusoidal Projection

D-589500-7A-DR1-1°
Copyright © Rand McNally & Co.

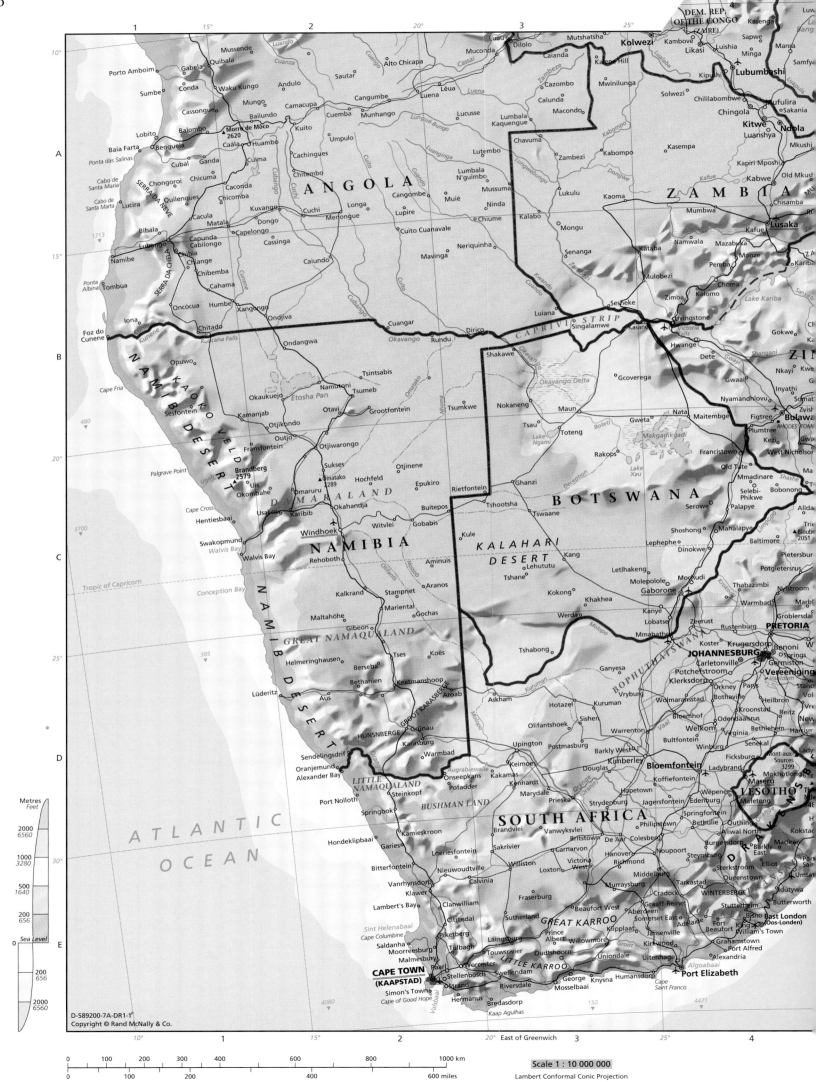

56

ATLANTIC OCEAN

Scale 1 : 10 000 000

Lambert Conformal Conic Projection

D-589200-7A-DR1-1"
Copyright © Rand McNally & Co.

Metres	Feet
2000	6560
1000	3280
500	1640
200	656
Sea Level	0
200	656
2000	6560

Main Map

TANZANIA

Kasama • Isoka • Chilumba
Chinsali • NYIKA PLATEAU 2607 ▲ Livingstone
Manda
Nyamtumbo
Lindi
Songea
Nachingwea
Mbinga
Mtama • Mikindani
Mtwara
Rumphi
Mzuzu
Nkhata Bay
Mbamba Bay
Tunduru
Masasi
Newala
Cabo Delgado
Palma
Mpika
Lundazi
474
Olivença
Rovuma
Chamba
Diaca
Mueda
Quiterajo
Mucojo
Quissanga
Nkhotakota
Cóbué
Metangula
Mecula
Macomia
Chipata
Katete
Lichinga
Catur
Belém
Nantulo
Montepuez
Ancuabe
Pemba
Nyimba
Lilongwe
MALAWI
Mchinji
Salima
Balama
Maúa
Lúrio
Namapa
Memba
Vila Gamito
Mandimba
Mangochi
Muite
Nacala-a-Velha
Furancungo
Ulóngue
Cuamba
Malema
Ribauè
Mecúburi
Momapa
Nacala
Zómbuè
Fíngoè
Kazula
Liwonde
Zomba
Lake Chilwa
SERRA NAMULI
Murrupula
Nampula
Lumbo
Ilha do Moçambique
Moatize
Tete
Blantyre
Sapitwa 3002
Thyolo
Milange
Namarrói
Erego
Mulevala
Mocuba
Mogincual
Chioco
Tambara
Doa
Chiromo
Chiperone 2054 ▲
Lugela
Mocubela
Moma
MAVURADONHA MTS.
Mazowe
Changara
Chemba
Mutarara
Morrumbala
Namacurra
Pebane
993
Shamva
ESCARPMENT
Inyangani 2592 ▲
Serra da Gorongosa 1856
Vila Fontes
Inhaminga
Mopeia
Quelimane
Bindura
Mutoko
Murewa
MOZAMBIQUE
Vila de Sena
Marromeu
Chinde
Harare
Rusape
Macheke
Chioco
Manica
Dondo
Beira
Chitungwiza
Marondera
Mvuma
Mutare
Chimoio
Monte Binga 2437 ▲
Sofala
ZIMBABWE
Chivhu
Chipinge
Chibabava
Espungabera
Mwenezi
Massangena
Nova Mambone
Mvuma
Mabote
Inhassoro
3000
Mwenezi
Massangena
Mapinhane
Vilankulo
bridge
Malvérnia
Mabote
4038
Punda Milia
Pafuri
Funhalouro
Massinga
Mapai
Morrumbene
Maxixe
Ponta da Barra
Inhambane
Phalaborwa
Mabalane
Panda
Inharrime
Chigubo
Quissico
Chicualacuala
Chókwè
Chibuto
Chidenguele
Xinavane
Macia
Xai-Xai
denburg
Komatipoort
Moamba
Nelspruit
MAPUTO
Ilha da Inhaca
Barberton
Mbabane
Bela Vista
Baía de Maputo
Manzini
Zitundo
SWAZILAND
Piet Retief
Lavumisa
Vryheid
Nongoma
Lake Saint Lucia
Ulundi
Mtubatuba
Cape Saint Lucia 1306
Empangeni
Richards Bay
eytown
etermaritzburg
Pinetown
DURBAN
Umzinto
ort Shepstone

INDIAN OCEAN

Île Juan de Nova (Fr.)

Bassas da India (Fr.)

Île Europa (Fr.)

Tropic of Capricorn

Comoros (inset area)

ATOLL DE COSMOLEDO (Sey.)
ÎLES GLORIEUSES (Fr.)
Njazidja
Moroni ▲ Kartala 2361
COMOROS
Nzwani
Mwali
Fomboni
Mutsamudu
MAYOTTE (Fr.)
Mamoudzou
ARCHIPEL DES COMORES

Madagascar

Tanjona Bobaomby
Antsiranana
Nosy Be
Andoany
Ambilobe
Iharana
Ambanja
Maromokotro 2876 ▲ TSARATANANA
Sambava
Analalava
Antsohihy
Andapa
Antalaha
Maroantsetra
Mahajanga
Soalala
Marovoay
Mandritsara
Rantabe
Helodrano Antongila
Besalampy
Madirovalo
Tsaratanana
Cap Masoala
Bekodoka
Mahabe
Maevatanana
Andilamena
Maintirano
Nosy Barren
Antsalova
Ankavandra
Ankazobe
Tsiroanomandidy
Arivonimamo
Soavinandriana
Andriamena
Mananara Avaratra
Nosy Sainte Marie
Ambodifototra
Fenoarivo Atsinanana
Belo Tsiribihina
Miandrivazo
ANTANANARIVO
Moramanga
Toamasina
Morondava
Tsiafajavona 2642
Ambatolampy
Manjakandriana
Ampasimanolotra
Mahabo
Betafo
Antsirabe
Ambositra
Mahanoro
Belo sur Mer
Malaimbandy
Ambatofinandrahana
Vatomandry
Mandabe
Ambohimahasoa
5322
Andranopasy
Mania
Fianarantsoa
Nosy-Varika
Morombe
Beroroha
Ifanadiana
Befandriana Atsimo
Ambalavao
Manakara
Ankazoabo
Ihosy
Pic Boby 2658 ▲
Vohipeno
Manombo Atsimo
Ranohira
Ivohibe
Farafangana
Sakaraha
Betroka
Vondrozo
Toliara
Bezaha
Vangaindrano
Onilahy
Mangoky
Midongy Atsimo
Ejeda
Bekily
Beraketa
Manantenina
Itampolo
Ampanihy
Amboasary
Androka
Ambovombe
Tsiombe
Tôlañaro
Tanjona Vohimena

Inset a

same scale as main map
INDIAN OCEAN
5300
2300
Port Louis
MAURITIUS
Piton de la Petite Rivière Noire 828 ▲
Curepipe
Mahébourg
Saint-Denis
Saint-Paul
Piton des Neiges 3070 ▲
Saint-Pierre
RÉUNION (Fr.)
4200
MASCARENE ISLANDS
55° East of Greenwich
10

Inset b

same scale as main map
INDIAN OCEAN
SEYCHELLES
Saint Pierre
4495
GROUP D'ALDABRA
ATOLL DE COSMOLEDO
Astove
4030
ATOLL DE FARQUHAR
4406
AGALEGA ISLANDS (Maur.)
50° East of Greenwich

Inset (Seychelles top right)

Praslin
La Digue
Silhouette
Victoria
Mahé
SEYCHELLES
Poivre Atoll
Desroches
Île Plate
LES AMIRANTES
Alphonse
Coëtivy Island

| 0 | 400 | 800 | 1600 | 2400 | 3200 | 4000 km |

| 0 | 400 | 800 | 1600 | 2400 miles |

Scale 1 : 35 000 000

Lambert Azimuthal Equal Area Projection

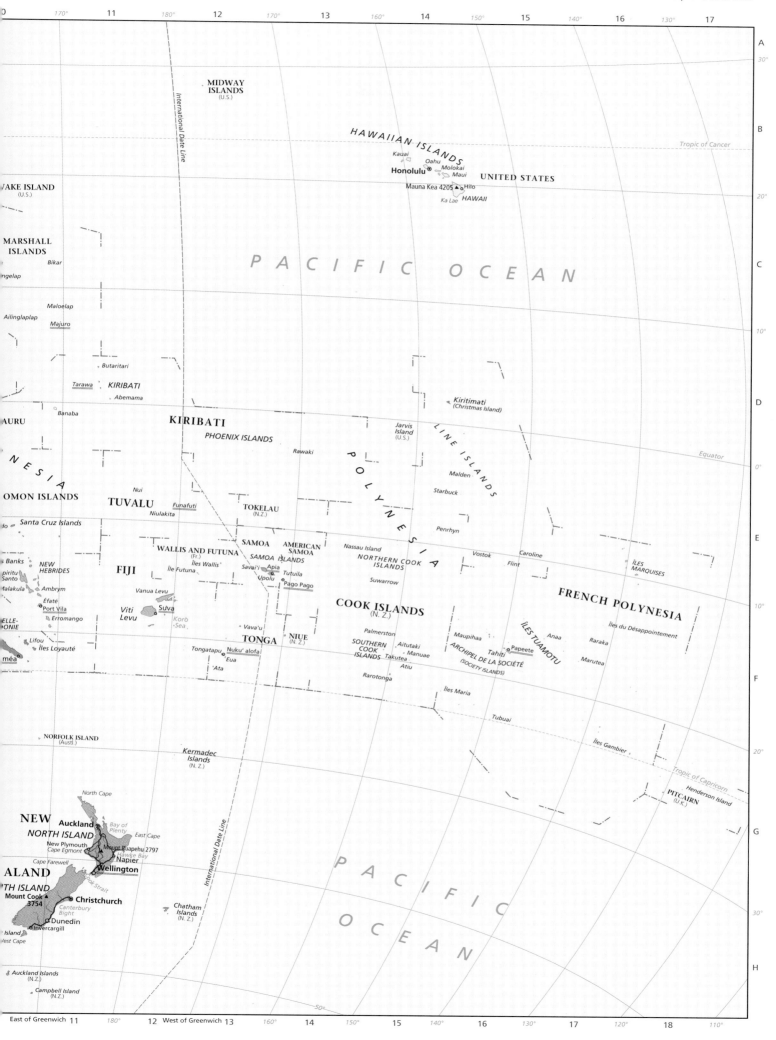

MIDWAY
ISLANDS
(U.S.)

HAWAIIAN ISLANDS

Kauai
Oahu Molokai
Honolulu Maui
Mauna Kea 4205 ▲ Hilo   UNITED STATES
Ka Lae HAWAII

WAKE ISLAND
(U.S.)

MARSHALL
ISLANDS

Bikar

PACIFIC OCEAN

ngelap

Maloelap

Ailinglaplap
Majuro

Butaritari

Tarawa KIRIBATI
Abemama

AURU
Banaba

KIRIBATI

PHOENIX ISLANDS

Kiritimati
(Christmas Island)

Jarvis
Island
(U.S.)

LINE ISLANDS

Rawaki

Malden

P
O
L
Y
N
E
S
I
A

Starbuck

Equator

NESIA

OMON ISLANDS

Nui

TUVALU *Funafuti*
Niulakita

TOKELAU
(N.Z.)

Penrhyn

Santa Cruz Islands

o

s Banks

NEW
HEBRIDES

piritu
Santo

Malakula Ambrym

Éfaté
Port Vila

Erromango

ELLE-
ONIE

Lifou

Îles Loyauté

méa

WALLIS AND FUTUNA
(Fr.)
Îles Wallis

FIJI Île Futuna

Vanua Levu

Viti
Levu Suva

Korb
Sea

SAMOA AMERICAN
SAMOA
SAMOA ISLANDS
Savai'i Apia
Upolu Tutuila
Pago Pago

Nassau Island

NORTHERN COOK
ISLANDS

Suwarrow

COOK ISLANDS
(N.Z.)

Vostok

Flint

Caroline

Maupihaa

Anaa

ÎLES TUAMOTU

Îles du Désappointement

Raraka

ÎLES
MARQUISES

FRENCH POLYNESIA

TONGA Vava'u NIUE
(N.Z.)

Tongatapu Nuku' alofa
'Eua

'Ata

Palmerston

SOUTHERN
COOK
ISLANDS

Aitutaki
Takutea Manuae
Atiu

Rarotonga

Maupihaa Tahiti Papeete
ARCHIPEL DE LA SOCIÉTÉ
(SOCIETY ISLANDS)

Marutea

Îles Maria

Tubuai

Îles Gambier

NORFOLK ISLAND
(Austl.)

Kermadec
Islands
(N.Z.)

Tropic of Capricorn

Henderson Island

PITCAIRN
(U.K.)

North Cape

NEW
NORTH ISLAND **Auckland**

Bay of
Plenty East Cape

New Plymouth
Cape Egmont Mount Ruapehu 2797
Hawke Bay
Napier
Cape Farewell **Wellington**

ALAND
TH ISLAND Cook Strait

Mount Cook ▲
3754 **Christchurch**
Canterbury
Bight

o Dunedin
Invercargill

Island

West Cape

International Date Line

Chatham
Islands
(N.Z.)

PACIFIC

OCEAN

Auckland Islands
(N.Z.)

Campbell Island
(N.Z.)

Tropic of Cancer

International Date Line

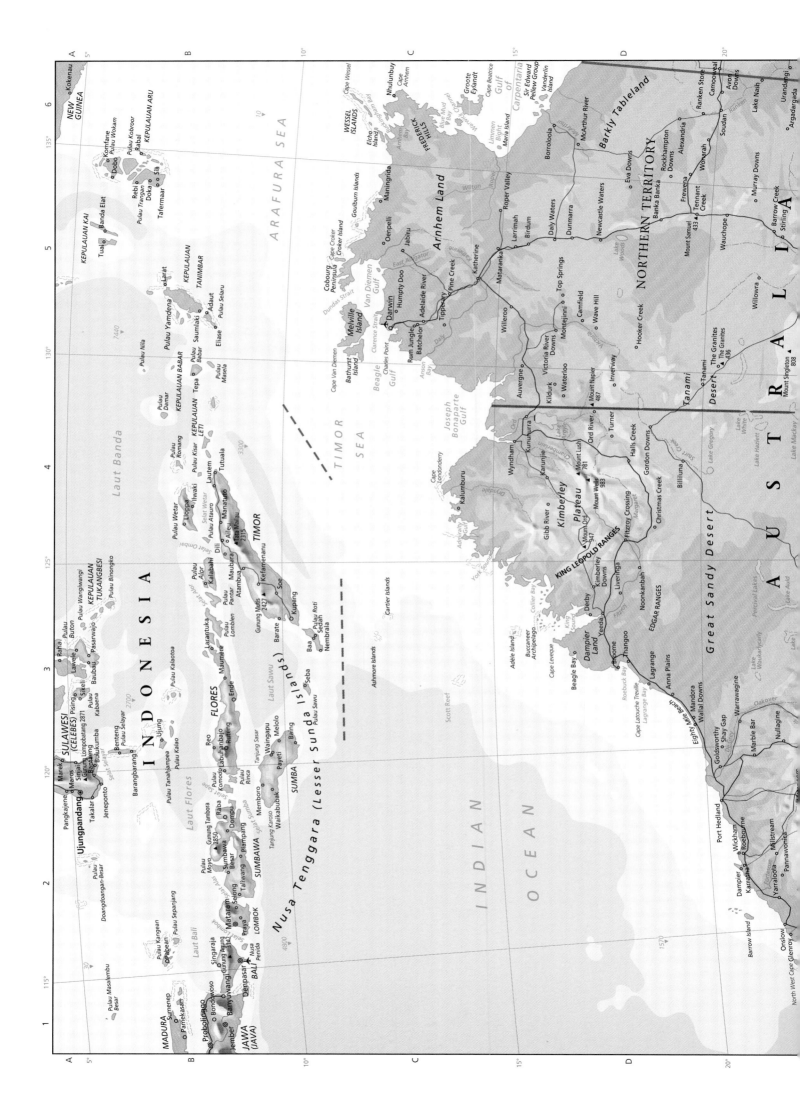

Simpson Desert

MACDONNELL RANGES

WESTERN AUSTRALIA

Gibson Desert

GREAT VICTORIA DESERT

SOUTH AUSTRALIA

Nullarbor Plain

HAMPTON TABLELAND

EYRE PENINSULA

YORKE PENINSULA

ADELAIDE

Great Australian Bight

SOUTHERN OCEAN

DARLING RANGE

PERTH

Scale 1 : 10 000 000
Lambert Conformal Conic Projection

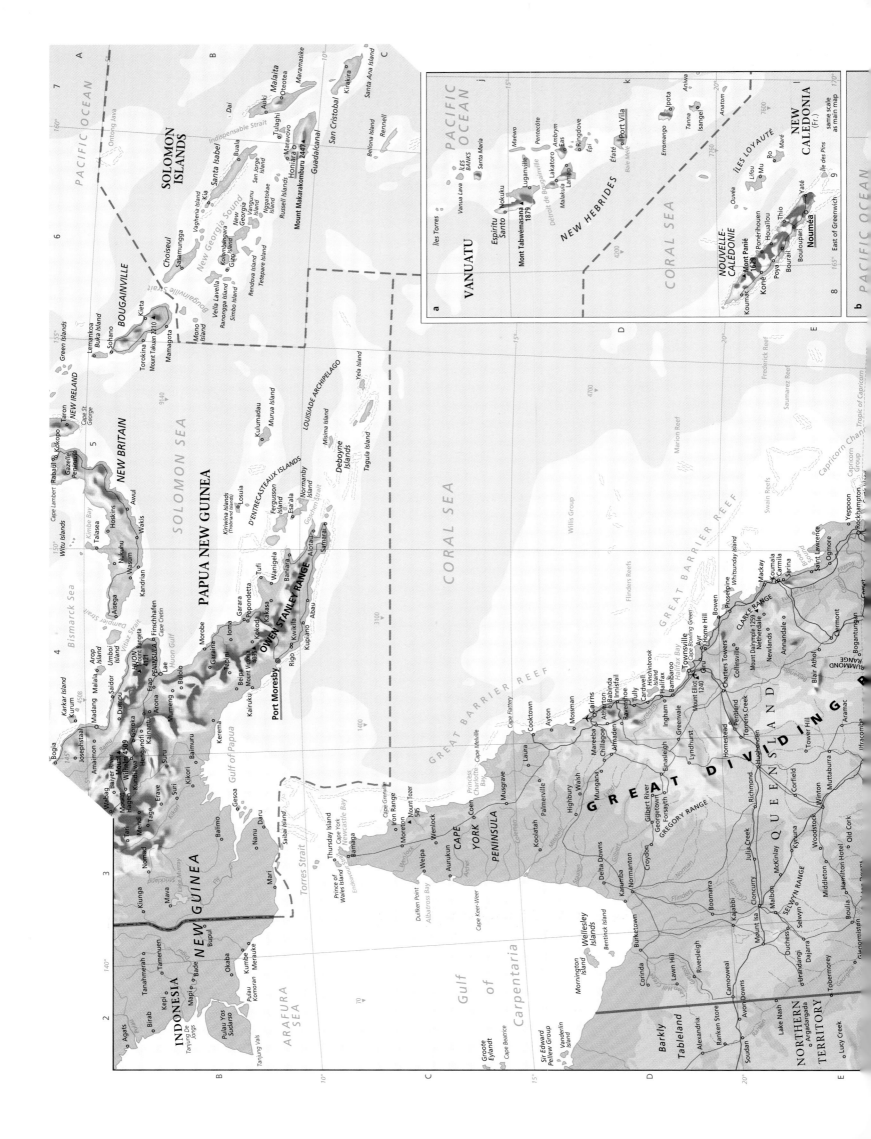

PACIFIC OCEAN

SOLOMON ISLANDS

Ontong Java

Malaita
Maramasike
Kirakira
Santa Ana Island
Dai
Auki
Oteotea

Kia
Santa Isabel
Buala
Vaghena Island

Tulaghi
Maravovo
Honiara
Guadalcanal
Mount Makarakomburu 2447

San Cristobal

Bellona Island
Rennell

Indispensable Strait

Kolombangara Island
New Georgia
Gizo
Vella Lavella
Ranongga Island
Vangunu Island
Rendova Island
Simbo Island
Nggatokae Island
Russell Islands

New Georgia Sound

Choiseul
Sasamungga

Lemankoa
Buka Island
Torokina
Sohano
Kieta
Mount Takuan 2210
Mamagota

BOUGAINVILLE

Mono Island

Bougainville Strait

Green Islands

Cape St. George
Kokopo
Rabaul
Taron
NEW IRELAND
Gazelle Peninsula
Cape Lambert
Kimbe Bay
Hoskins
Talasea
Awul

NEW BRITAIN

SOLOMON SEA

Bismarck Sea

Witu Islands
Dampier Strait
Umboi Island
Arop Island
Nukuhu
Wasum
Kandrian

Karkar Island
Kurum
Madang
Dumpu
Saidor
Malala
Aisega
Arop

Bogia
Amaimon
Josephstaal

Bupul
Tamenuen

NEW GUINEA

INDONESIA

Agats
Birab
Kepi
Mapi
Okaba
Pulau Yos Sudarso
Tanahmerah
Tanjung De Jorgs
Tanjung Vals
Pulau Komoran
Bade
Kumbe
Merauke

PAPUA NEW GUINEA

Mount Wilhelm 4509
Balyer River
Mount Hagen
Wabag
Kundiawa
Goroka
Kainantu
Henganofi
Tari
Mendi
Tage
Erave
Suru
Baimuru
Kikori
Kerema
Gesoa
Balimo
Nomad
Kunga
Mava
Mari
Daru
Nanu

HUON PENINSULA
Mount Bangeta 4121
Finschhafen
Cape Cretin
Lae
Bulolo
Mumeng
Wau
Huon Gulf

Ramu
Markham

OWEN STANLEY RANGE
Mount Victoria 4035

Morobe
Garaina
Tapini
Belpa
Iomu
Garara
Popondetta
Kokoda
Tufi
Wanigela
Baniara
Alotau
Samarai

Kairuku
Port Moresby
Rigo
Kupiano
Abau
Kwikila

Gulf of Papua

Torres Strait
Thursday Island
Prince of Wales Island
Salbai Island
Moreton
Bamaga
Cape York

LOUISIADE ARCHIPELAGO

Kiriwina Islands (Trobriand Islands)
D'ENTRECASTEAUX ISLANDS
Losuia
Kulumadau
Murua Island
Fergusson Island
Normanby Island
Esa'ala
Goschen Strait

Deboyne Islands
Tagula Island

Misima Island

Yela Island

CORAL SEA

Willis Group

Marion Reef

Frederick Reef

Saumarez Reef

GREAT BARRIER REEF

Flinders Reefs

Swain Reefs

Tropic of Capricorn

Capricorn Channel

Inset a — VANUATU

Îles Torres

PACIFIC OCEAN

Vanua Lava
ÎLES BANKS
Santa Maria
Maéwo
Pentecôte
Ambrym
Espiritu Santo
Mont Tabwémasana 1879
Luganville
Nokuku
détroit de Bougainville
Malakula
Lamap
Épi
Lakatoro
Ringdove
Eas

Port Vila
Éfaté
Baie Mélé

NEW HEBRIDES

Jpota
Tanna
Aniwa
Isangel

Erromango
Anatom

CORAL SEA

Inset b — NEW CALEDONIA (Fr.)

NOUVELLE-CALÉDONIE

same scale as main map

Koumac
Poum
Ouvéa
ÎLES LOYAUTÉ
Lifou
Ro
Mu
Maré

Koné
Poya
Ponérihouen
Houaïlou
Bourail
Bouloupari
Thio
Mont Panié 1628
Nouméa
Yaté
Île des Pins

PACIFIC OCEAN

East of Greenwich

AUSTRALIA

Yeppoon
Rockhampton
Mackay
Proserpine
Bowen
Home Hill
Ayr
Townsville
Ingham
Cardwell
Tully
Innisfail
Babinda
Cairns
Mareeba
Atherton
Ravenshoe
Mossman
Cooktown
Ayton
Cape Flattery

CLARK RANGE
Koumala
Carmila
Sarina
Saint Lawrence
Ogmore

Whitsunday Island
Cape Bowling Green
Halifax Bay
Hinchinbrook Island

Koumala
Nebo
Collinsville
Mount Dalrymple 1259
Netherdale
Newlands
Annandale
Blair Athol
Clermont

Charters Towers
Hughenden
Pentland
Torrens Creek
Homestead
Aramac

GREAT DIVIDING RANGE

QUEENSLAND

Chillagoe
Almaden
Lyndhurst
Einasleigh
Forsayth
Georgetown
Croydon
Normanton
Karumba

Mungana
Highbury
Walsh
Palmerville
Laura
Coen
Musgrave
Iron Range
Mount Tozer 545
Wenlock
Aurukun
Weipa

CAPE YORK PENINSULA

Koolatah
Delta Downs

GREGORY RANGE

SELWYN RANGE
Mount Isa
Cloncurry
Duchess
Selwyn
Malbon
Kajabbi
Gilbert River
Richmond
Maxwelton
Julia Creek
McKinlay
Kynuna
Winton
Corfield
Muttaburra

Burketown
Gregory Downs
Camooweal
Lawn Hill
Riversleigh
Lake Nash
Avon Downs
Ranken Store
Soudan

Gilberton

Corinda
Kamileroi

Boomarra

Duchess
Kajabbi

Dajarra
Boulia
Urandangi
Brandangi
Hamilton Hotel
Middleton
Old Cork
Glenormiston
Tobermorey

Cape Keer-Weer
Albatross Bay
Duifken Point

GREAT BARRIER REEF

BOGANTUNGAN
DRUMMOND RANGE

Gulf of Carpentaria

Wellesley Islands
Mornington Island
Bentinck Island

Groote Eylandt
Cape Beatrice
Sir Edward Pellew Group
Vanderlin Island

NORTHERN TERRITORY

Barkly Tableland
Alexandria
Argadargada
Anthony Lagoon
Brunette Downs
Lucy Creek

ARAFURA SEA

Endeavour Strait
Princess Charlotte Bay
Cape Melville

Flinders
Norman
Gilbert
Mitchell
Staaten
Coleman
Holroyd
Archer
Wenlock
Embley

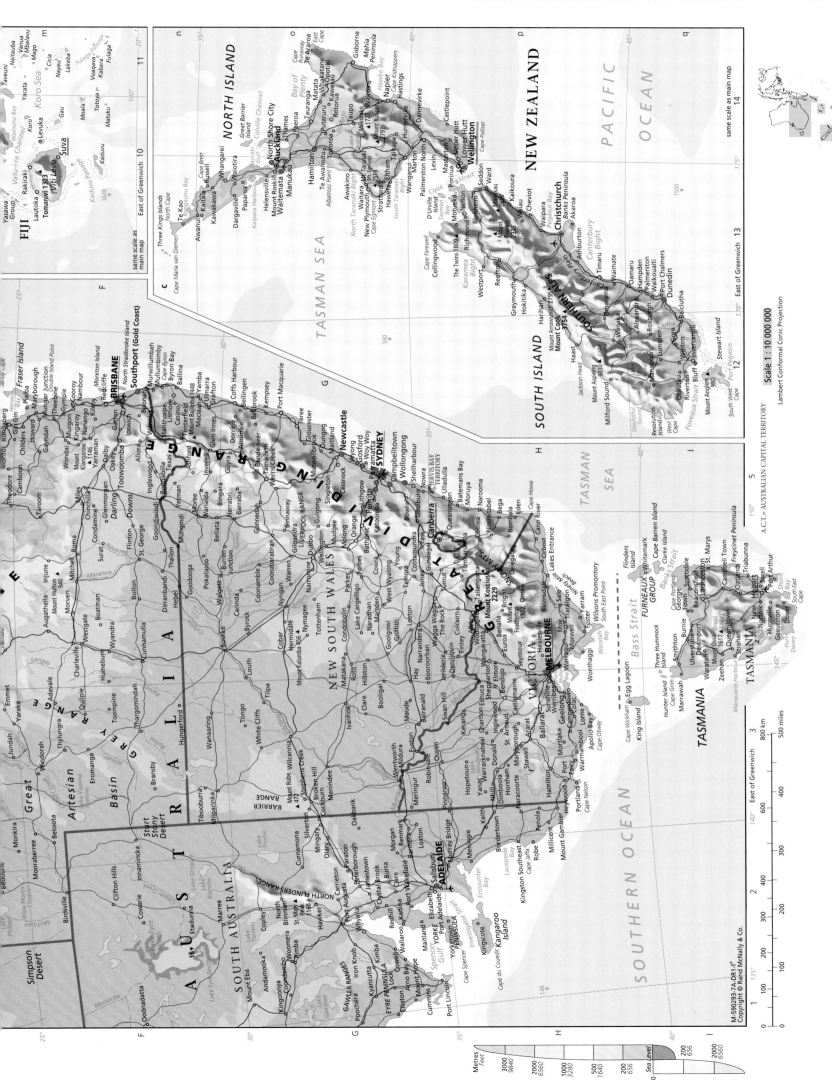

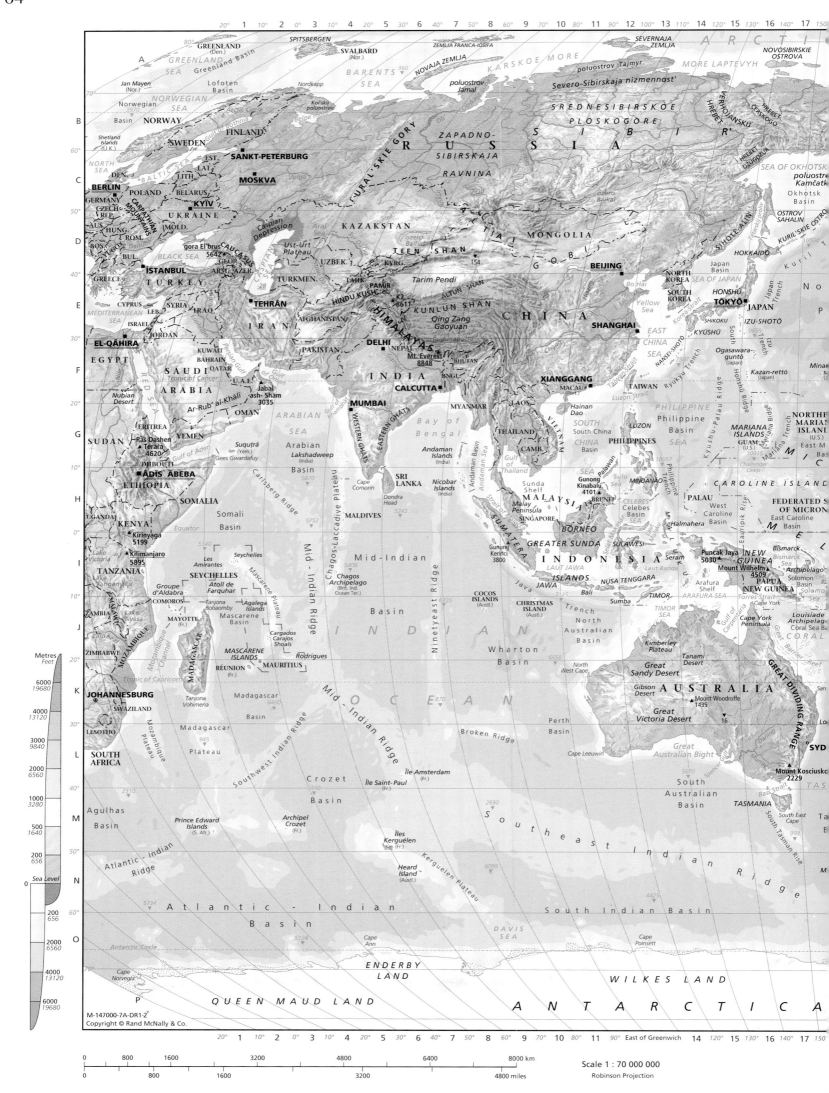

Metres / Feet

6000 / 19680
4000 / 13120
3000 / 9840
2000 / 6560
1000 / 3280
500 / 1640
200 / 656
0 / Sea Level
200 / 656
2000 / 6560
4000 / 13120
6000 / 19680

M-147000-7A-DR1-2°
Copyright © Rand McNally & Co.

0   800   1600   3200   4800   6400   8000 km
0   800   1600   3200   4800 miles

Scale 1 : 70 000 000
Robinson Projection

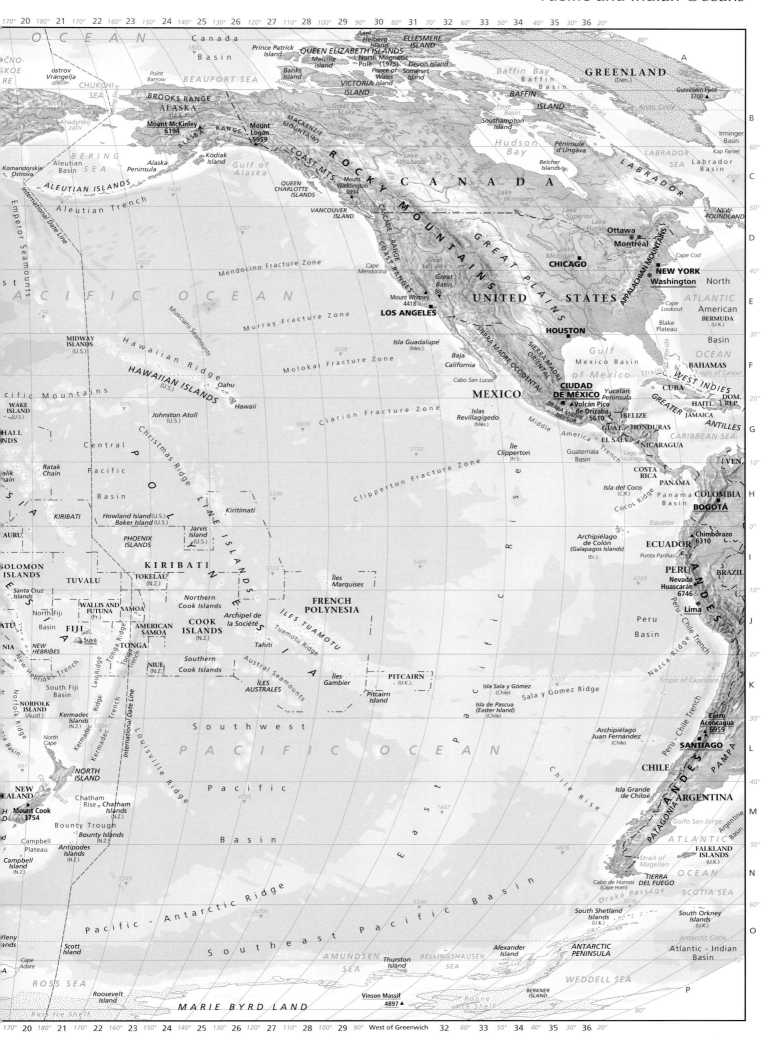

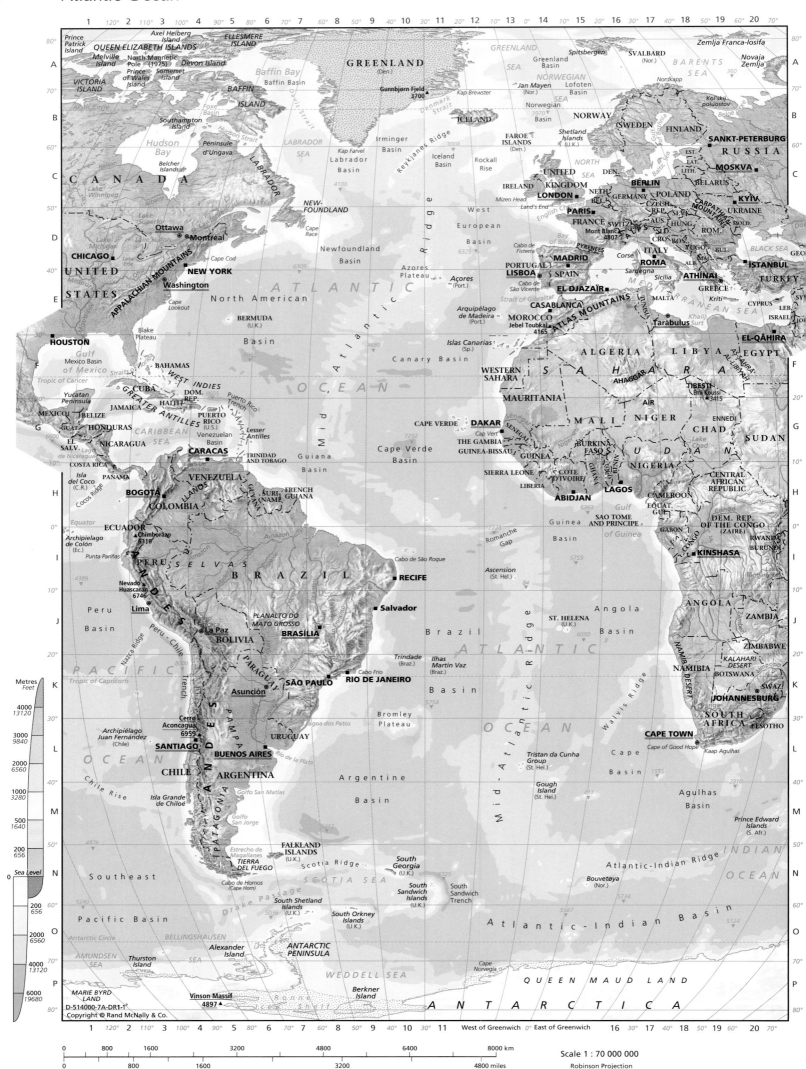

Scale 1 : 70 000 000

Robinson Projection

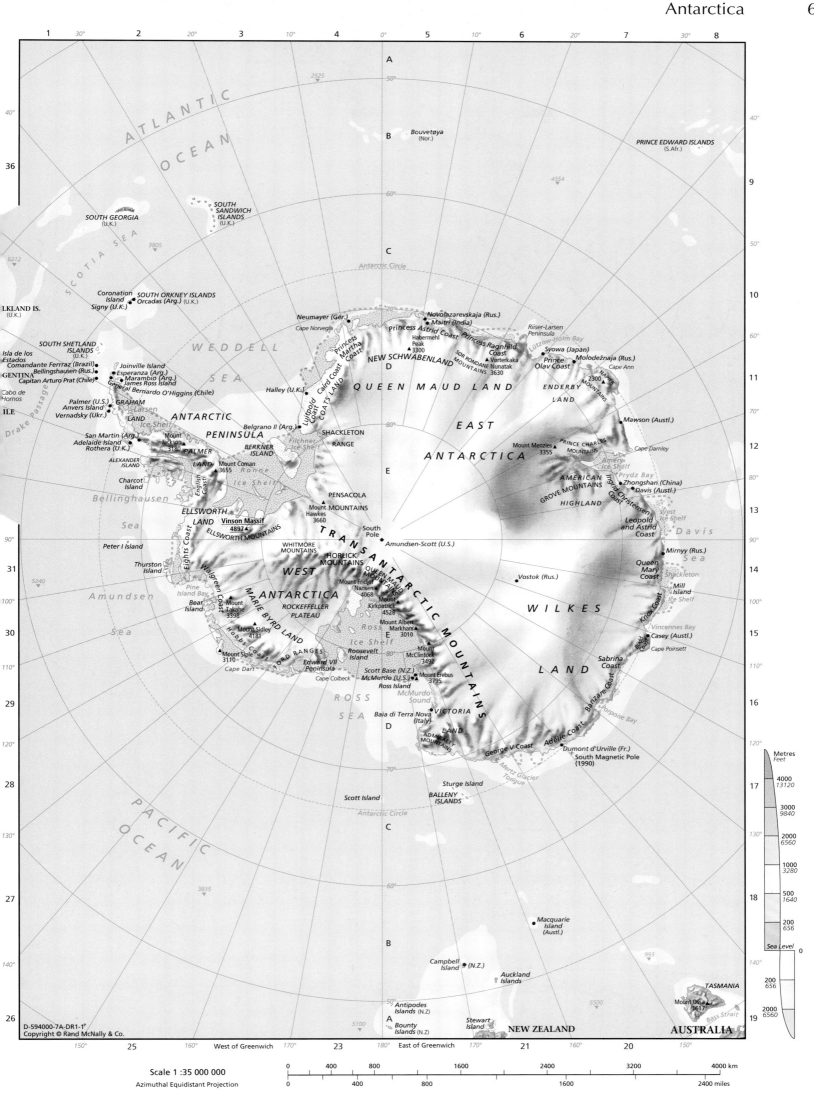

ATLANTIC OCEAN

SCOTIA SEA

WEDDELL SEA

Bouvetøya (Nor.)

PRINCE EDWARD ISLANDS (S.Afr.)

SOUTH GEORGIA (U.K.)

SOUTH SANDWICH ISLANDS (U.K.)

Antarctic Circle

Coronation Island
Signy (U.K.)   South Orkney Islands
Orcadas (Arg.) (U.K.)

LKLAND IS. (U.K.)

SOUTH SHETLAND ISLANDS (U.K.)

Isla de los Estados
Comandante Ferrraz (Brazil)
Bellingshausen (Rus.)
Capitan Arturo Prat (Chile)

GENTINA

Cabo de Hornos

ILE

Neumayer (Ger.)
Cape Norvegia

Novolazarevskaja (Rus.)
Maitri (India)

Princess Astrid Coast
Habermehl Peak 3300
Princess Ragnhild Coast

Riiser-Larsen Peninsula
Lützow-Holm Bay

Syowa (Japan)
Molodežnaja (Rus.)

Prince Olav Coast
Cape Ann

Joinville Island
Esperanza (Arg.)
Marambio (Arg.)
James Ross Island
General Bernardo O'Higgins (Chile)

Halley (U.K.)

Princess Martha Coast
Luitpold Coast
Caird Coast

NEW SCHWABENLAND

SØR RONDANE MOUNTAINS
Vorterkaka Nunatak 3630

ENDERBY LAND

2300
NAPIER MOUNTAINS

QUEEN MAUD LAND

Palmer (U.S.)
Anvers Island
Vernadsky (Ukr.)

GRAHAM LAND

ANTARCTIC PENINSULA

Belgrano II (Arg.)

OATS LAND

SHACKLETON RANGE

EAST ANTARCTICA

Mawson (Austl.)

San Martin (Arg.)
Adelaide Island
Rothera (U.K.)

Mount Jackson 3180

PALMER LAND

BERKNER ISLAND

Filchner Ice Shelf

Mount Menzies 3355

PRINCE CHARLES MOUNTAINS

Cape Darnley

ALEXANDER ISLAND

Mount Coman 3655

Ronne Ice Shelf

PENSACOLA MOUNTAINS

AMERICAN HIGHLAND

Amery Ice Shelf

Prydz Bay

Zhongshan (China)
Davis (Austl.)

Charcot Island

English Coast

GROVE MOUNTAINS

Ingrid Christensen Coast

Bellingshausen Sea

ELLSWORTH LAND

Vinson Massif 4897

Mount Hawkes 3660

TRANSANTARCTIC MOUNTAINS

South Pole
Amundsen-Scott (U.S.)

Leopold and Astrid Coast

West Ice Shelf

Davis Sea

Peter I Island

Eights Coast

ELLSWORTH MOUNTAINS

WHITMORE MOUNTAINS

HORLICK MOUNTAINS

QUEEN MAUD MOUNTAINS

Mirnyy (Rus.)

Queen Mary Coast

Shackleton Ice Shelf

Thurston Island

Pine Island Bay

WEST ANTARCTICA

Vostok (Rus.)

WILKES LAND

Mill Island Ice Shelf

Amundsen Sea

Walgreen Coast

Mount Takahe 3398

MARIE BYRD LAND

Bear Island

ROCKEFFELLER PLATEAU

Mount Fridtjof Nansen 4068

Mount Kirkpatrick 4528

Casey (Austl.)
Cape Poinsett

Vincennes Bay

Mount Sidley 4181

Hobbs Coast

FORD RANGES

Mount Siple 3110

Edward VII Peninsula

Cape Dart

Roosevelt Island

Ross Ice Shelf

Mount Albert Markham 3010

Mount McClintock 3492

Knox Coast

Sabrina Coast

Cape Colbeck

Scott Base (N.Z.)
McMurdo (U.S.)
Ross Island
Mount Erebus 3795

McMurdo Sound

Banzare Coast

ROSS SEA

Baia di Terra Nova (Italy)

VICTORIA LAND

George V Coast

Adélie Coast

Porpoise Bay

ADMIRALTY MOUNTAINS

Dumont d'Urville (Fr.)
South Magnetic Pole (1990)

Mertz Glacier Tongue

Sturge Island

Scott Island

BALLENY ISLANDS

Antarctic Circle

PACIFIC OCEAN

Macquarie Island (Austl.)

Campbell Island (N.Z.)

Auckland Islands

TASMANIA

Mount Ossa 1617

Bass Strait

Antipodes Islands (N.Z.)

Bounty Islands (N.Z.)

Stewart Island

NEW ZEALAND

AUSTRALIA

West of Greenwich   East of Greenwich

Scale 1 : 35 000 000
Azimuthal Equidistant Projection

0   400   800   1600   2400   3200   4000 km
0   400   800   1600   2400 miles

Metres / Feet
4000 / 13120
3000 / 9840
2000 / 6560
1000 / 3280
500 / 1640
200 / 656
Sea Level / 0
200 / 656
2000 / 6560

| 0 | 400 | 800 | 1600 | 2400 | 3200 | 4000 km |

| 0 | 400 | 800 | 1600 | 2400 miles |

Scale 1 : 35 000 000
Lambert Azimuthal Equal Area Projection

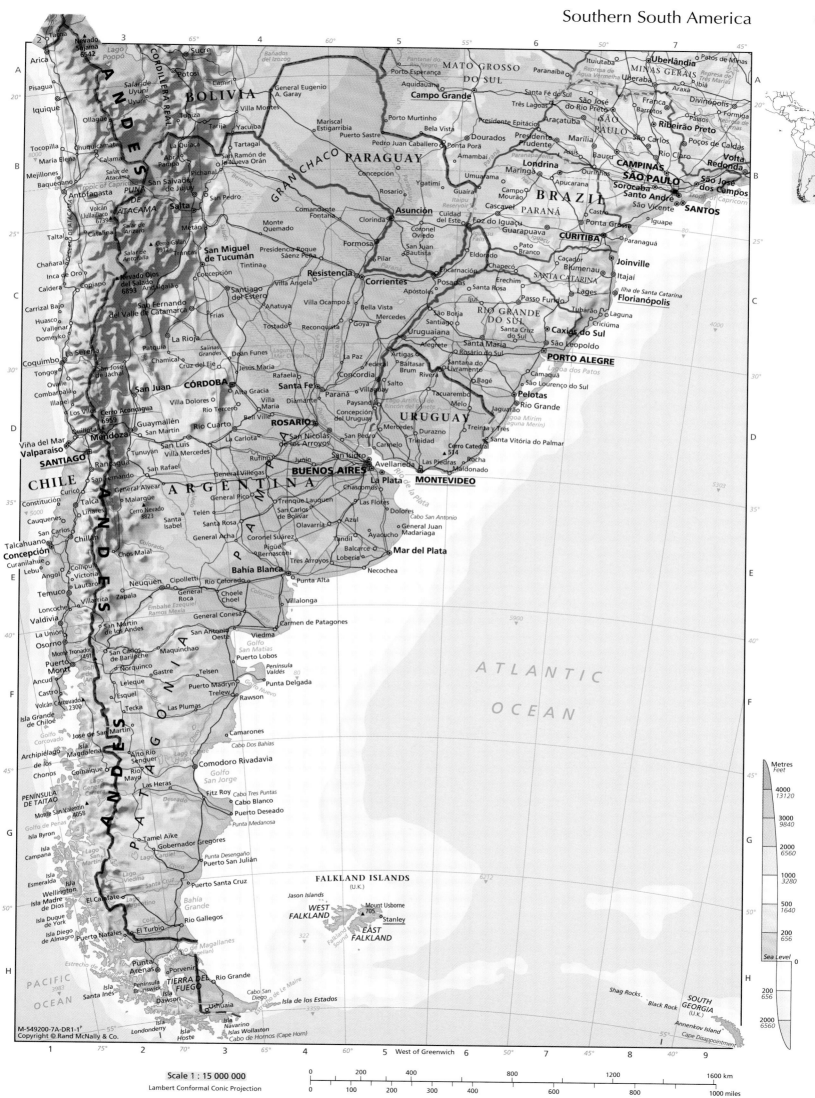

Scale 1 : 15 000 000
Lambert Conformal Conic Projection

M-549200-7A-DR1-1"
Copyright © Rand McNally & Co.

CARIBBEAN SEA

NICARAGUA

Chinandega
León
Managua
Granada
Rivas
Boaco
Bluefields
San Juan del Sur
Liberia
San Juan del Norte

COSTA RICA
Puntarenas
SAN JOSÉ
Cartago
Cerro Chirripó 3819
Volcán Irazú 3432
Puerto Limón
Bocas del Toro
Colón
Portobelo
PANAMA
Panamá
David
Volcán Barú 3475
Santiago
Chitré
La Chorrera
Penonomé
Las Tablas
La Palma

Península de Osa
Puerto Armuelles
Golfito
Golfo de Chiriquí
Isla de Coiba
Punta Mariato
Península de Azuero
Golfo de Panamá
Isla del Rey

Isla de San Andrés (Col.)
San Andrés

Punta Gallinas
Península de La Guajira
Riohacha
Uribia
Santa Marta
Barranquilla
Soledad
Cartagena
Sabanalarga
Valledupar
Plato
Magangué
El Carmen de Bolívar
Sincelejo
Lorica
Montería
Turbo
Simití
Puerto Wilches
Barrancabermeja
Yarumal
Puerto Berrío
Bello
MEDELLÍN
Itagüí
Chiguinhuirá
Quibdó
Manizales
Pereira
Armenia
Buga
Palmira
CALI
Neiva
Popayán
Buenaventura
Mosquera
Guapí
Tumaco
Barbacoas
Pasto
San Lorenzo
Ipiales
Tulcán
Ibarra
Esmeraldas

ARUBA (Neth.)
Oranjestad
Curaçao
Willemstad
NETHERLANDS ANTILLES
Bonaire
Punto Fijo
Coro
Puerto Cumarebo
Tucacas
Puerto Cabello
Maiquetía
CARACAS
Isla de Margarita
Porlam
Cumaná
Puerto la C

Golfo de Venezuela
MARACAIBO
Cabimas
San Felipe
Valencia
Maracay
Barcelona
Aragua de Barcelona
Machiques
BARQUISIMETO
Acarigua
Valera
Guanare
CORD. DE MÉRIDA
Mérida
Pico Bolívar 5007
Barinas
San Fernando de Apure
Calabozo
Valle de la Pascua
El Tigre
Cúcuta
San Cristóbal
Guasdualito
Apure
Ciudad Guaya
Ciudad Bolívar

Pico Cristóbal Colón 5775

Trujillo
San Carlos del Zulia
Ocaña
Gamarra
Pamplona
Bucaramanga
Socorro
Tame
Cerro Bolívar 802
Cerro Mato 1863

LLANOS
Puerto Carreño
Puerto Páez
Duitama
Tunja
Miraflores
Trinidad
Orocué
Cerro Nevado 4560
VILLAVICENCIO
Meta
San Fernando de Atabapo
VENEZUELA
Salto Ángel
Auyán
Cerro Yaví 2441

BOGOTÁ
Nevado del Tolima 5215
Honda
Ibagué
Villavicencio

COLOMBIA
San José del Guaviare
Guaviare
San Vicente del Caguán
Florencia
Tres Esquinas
Puerto Asís
Mitú
Vaupés
Apaporis
Taraira
Guainía
San Felipe
Maroa
Cerro Marahuaca 2579
San Carlos de Río Negro
PAKAR
Içana
Pico da Neblina 3014

Guapí

ARCHIPIÉLAGO DE COLÓN (GALAPAGOS ISLANDS) (Ec.)

Isla Pinta
Isla Marchena
Volcán Wolf 1646
Isla Santiago
Isla Santa Cruz
Puerto Villamil
Isla San Cristóbal
Isla Isabela
Isla Santa María
Puerto Baquerizo Moreno

Equator

ECUADOR
QUITO
Manta
Chone
Quevedo
Ambato
Chimborazo 6310
Riobamba
Portoviejo
Salinas
Milagro
GUAYAQUIL
Cuenca
Azogues
Isla Puná
Machala
Santa Rosa
Loja
Tumbes
Macará
Golfo de Guayaquil
Cotopaxi 5897
Cayambe 5790

Talara
Negritos
Piura
Sullana
Chulucanas
Castilla
Bahía de Sechura
Bayóvar
Punta Negra
Reventazón
Olmos
Lambayeque
Chiclayo
Pacasmayo
Puerto Chicama
Chocope
Trujillo
Chimbote

Paita
Jaén
Moyobamba
Chachapoyas
Cajamarca
Bellavista
Juanjuí
Nevado Huascarán 6746
Huánuco
Nevado Yerupajá 6634
Barranca
Huacho
Huaral
La Oroya

Iquitos
Puerto Leguízamo
La Chorrera
El Encanto
Arica
Napo
Leticia
Benjamin Constant
Esperança
Carauari
Tabatinga
Tapuruquara
Barcelos
Fonte Boa
Santo Antônio do Içá
São Paulo de Olivença
Tefé
Coari
Cama

AMAZONAS
SELV
Cruzeiro do Sul
Tarauacá
Feijó
ACRE
Boca do Acre
Sena Madureira
Rio Branco
Abunã
Ariquemes
Porto
RONDÔ

PERU
Yurimaguas
Tarapoto
Uchiza
Pucallpa
Tingo María
Cerro de Pasco
Puerto Bermúdez
Tarma
LIMA
Callao
Vitarte
Huancayo
Huancavelica
Ayacucho
Machupicchu
Abancay
Cusco
San Vicente de Cañete
Chincha Alta
Pisco
Ica
Puquio
Nasca
Camaná
Arequipa
Mollendo
Moquegua
Ilo

CORD. ORIENTAL
CORDILLERA OCCIDENTAL
CORDILLERA ORIENTAL
CORDILLERA CENTRAL
ANDES

Puerto Maldonado
Quince Mil
Nevado Auzangate 6384
Sicuani
Ayaviri
Juliaca
Puno
Lake Titicaca
Nevado Coropuna 6425
Nevado Chachani 6075
Volcán Misti
Volcán Putupaca 5815
Tacna
Arica

PACIFIC OCEAN

Punta Carreta

Rurrenabaque
San Borja
Santa Ana
Trinidad
San Ignacio de Moxo
Cobija
Riberalta
Villa Bella
Guajará-Mirim
Puerto Rico
Cochabamba
LA PAZ
Viacha
BOLIVIA
Coroico
Tarata
Santa de la Si
Oruro
Nevado Sajama 6542
Sucre
Potosí
Nevado Illimani 6421
Cordillera Real
Lago Poopó

Tocopilla
María Elena
Mejillones
Antofagasta
CHILE
El Toco
Calama
Chuquicamata
Salar de Atacama
Baquedano
ARGENTINA
La Quiaca
Tupiza
Tarija
San Ramón de Nueva Orán
Pichana

Iquique
Pisagua
Salar de Uyuni
Uyuni
Ollagüe

Metres Feet

6000 / 19680
4000 / 13120
3000 / 9840
2000 / 6560
1000 / 3280
500 / 1640
200 / 656
Sea Level / 0
200 / 656
2000 / 6560

M-549100-7A-DR1-1
Copyright © Rand McNally & Co.

West of Greenwich

0 200 400 800 1200 1600 km
0 100 200 300 400 600 800 1000 miles

Scale 1 : 15 000 000
Sinusoidal Projection

ATLANTIC

OCEAN

GRENADA
George's
Scarborough
Tobago
Port of Spain
Fernando
TRINIDAD AND TOBAGO
Trinidad

Morawhanna
Charity
Spring Garden
Georgetown
Parika
Bartica
New Amsterdam
Corriverton
Rockstone
Linden
Nieuw Amsterdam
Nickerie
Paramaribo
Nieuw Amsterdam
Kwakoegron
Saint-Laurent
du Maroni Île du Diable
Mount Roraima
2875
Brokopondo
Saint-Élie
Kourou
GUYANA
Brokopondo Stuwmeer
Cayenne
Lethem
SURINAME
FRENCH
GUIANA
Régina
Cabo Orange
Saint-Georges
Juliana Top
1230
Saül
Oiapoque

Vista
Cunani
Calçoene
Amapá
Caracaraí
AMAPÁ
Ilha de Maracá
ACARAÍ MTS.
TUMUCUMAC MTS.
Serra do
Navio
Ilha Janaucu
Ilha Caviana de Fora
Macapá
Ilha Mexiana
Equator

ATLANTIC
OCEAN

Represa
Balbina
ANAUS
Oriximiná
Alenquer
Amazon Porto
de Moz
Ilha
Grande
do Gurupá
ILHA DE
MARAJÓ
Bragança
Carutapera
Faro
Óbidos
Monte Alegre
Portel
Breves
BELÉM
Abaetetuba
Cururupu
Itacoatiara
Maués
Santarém
Cametá
Camiranga
São Luís
Careiro
Altamira
Pinheiro
Rosário
Parnaíba
Acaraú
Borba
Itaituba
Tucuruí
Viana
Monção
Itapecuru-Mirim
Brejo
Camocim
Sobral
FORTALEZA
Novo Aripuanã
PARÁ
Bacabal
Codó
Barras
Ipu
Maranguape
Baturité
Aracati
Manicoré
Marabá
Imperatriz
Barra do Corda
Caxias
Campo
Maior
Crateús
Quixadá
Areia Branca
Macau Cabo de São Roque
Ceará-Mirim
São João do
Araguaia
Grajaú
Colinas
Amarante
MARANHÃO
CEARÁ
Senador
Pompeu
Mossoró
RIO GRANDE
DO NORTE
Natal
Prainha Nova
SERRA DOS CARAJÁS
Carajás
Araguatins
Tocantinópolis
Mirador
Floriano
Picos
Juazeiro
do Norte
Iguatu
Pau dos
Ferros
Caicó
Currais Novos
Rio Tinto
SERRA DO CACHIMBO
Gradaús
BRAZIL
Conceição do Araguaia
Carolina
Loreto
Oeiras
PIAUÍ
PARAÍBA
Sertânia
João Pessoa
Campina Grande
Olinda
SERRA DOS APIACÁS
Araguacema
Pedro Afonso
Alto Parnaíba
Balsas
Benedito Leite
Santa Filomena
São Raimundo
Nonato
Paulistana
PERNAMBUCO
Serra
Talhada
Caruaru
Garanhuns
RECIFE
Barreiros

Tocantinópolis
Pium
Cristalândia
Palmas
Porto Nacional
Gilbués
Parnaguá
Remanso
Juazeiro
Petrolina
Paulo Afonso
Jeremoabo
ALAGOAS
Arapiraca
Maceió
Propriá
Vilhena
MATO GROSSO
PLANALTO DO
MATO GROSSO
Diamantino
Utiariti
SERRA FORMOSA
Ilha do
Bananal
TOCANTINS
Gurupi
Dianópolis
Natividade
Xique-Xique
Barra
Represa de
Sobradinho
Senhor do Bonfim
Tucano
Jacobina
Serrinha
SERGIPE
Itabaiana
Estância
Inhambupe
Alagoinhas
Aracaju

Rosário Oeste
Paranã
Arraias
Barreiras
BAHIA
Morro do Chapéu
Santo Antônio
de Jesus
Feira de Santana
Santo Amaro
Candeias
SALVADOR
Porto Esperidião
Cuiabá
Cáceres
São Miguel
do Araguaia
Porangatu
Posse
Bom Jesus
da Lapa
Paramirim
Caetité
Valença
San Ignacio
de Velasco
GOIÁS
Aruanã
Guanambi
Jequié
Itabuna
Ibicaraí
Ilhéus
Roboré
Diamantino
San José de Chiquitos
Aragarças
Goiás
Anápolis
DISTRITO
FEDERAL
BRASÍLIA
Luziânia
Formosa
Januária
São Francisco
Pedra Azul
Vitória da
Conquista
Monte Azul
Itapetinga
Canavieiras
Belmonte
Puerto Suárez
Corumbá
Rondonópolis
Alto Araguaia
Jataí
Iporá
GOIÂNIA
Pires do Rio
Montes Claros
Araçuaí
Almenara
Porto Seguro
Prado
Alcobaça
Caravelas
Porto
Esperança
MATO GROSSO
DO SUL
Coxim
Rio Verde
Morrinhos
Catalão
Araguari
Picapora
MINAS GERAIS
Diamantina
Governador
Valadares
SERRA DO ESPINHAÇO
Nanuque
São Mateus
Aquidauana
Santa Fé do Sul
Ituiutaba
Uberlândia
Araxá
Ibiá
Curvelo
Sete Lagoas
Caratinga
ESPÍRITO
SANTO
Campo Grande
Três Lagoas
Uberaba
Araçatuba
Paranaíba
Represa de
Água Vermelha
São José
do Rio Preto
Barretos
Franca
Represa de
Três Marias
Corinto
Araguari
Ipatinga
BELO
HORIZONTE
Ponte Nova
Conselheiro
Lafaiete
Cachoeiro de Itapemirim
Colatina
Aracruz
Vitória
Vila Velha
Porto Murtinho
Bela Vista
Dourados
Presidente
Prudente
Marília
Bauru
Rio Claro
SÃO PAULO
Poços de
Caldas
Guaxupé
Divinópolis
Formiga
Passos
Represa de
Furnas
Juiz de
Fora
Itaúna
Campos
Cabo de São Tomé
PARAGUAY
GRAN CHACO
Ponta Porã
Amambaí
Umuarama
Maringá
Apucarana
Londrina
Sorocaba
SÃO PAULO
PARANÁ
CAMPINAS
Ribeirão
Preto
Volta Redonda
São José dos
Campos
Nova Iguaçu
RIO DE JANEIRO
Niterói
RIO DE JANEIRO
Tropic of Capricorn
Pedro Juan
Caballero
Concepción

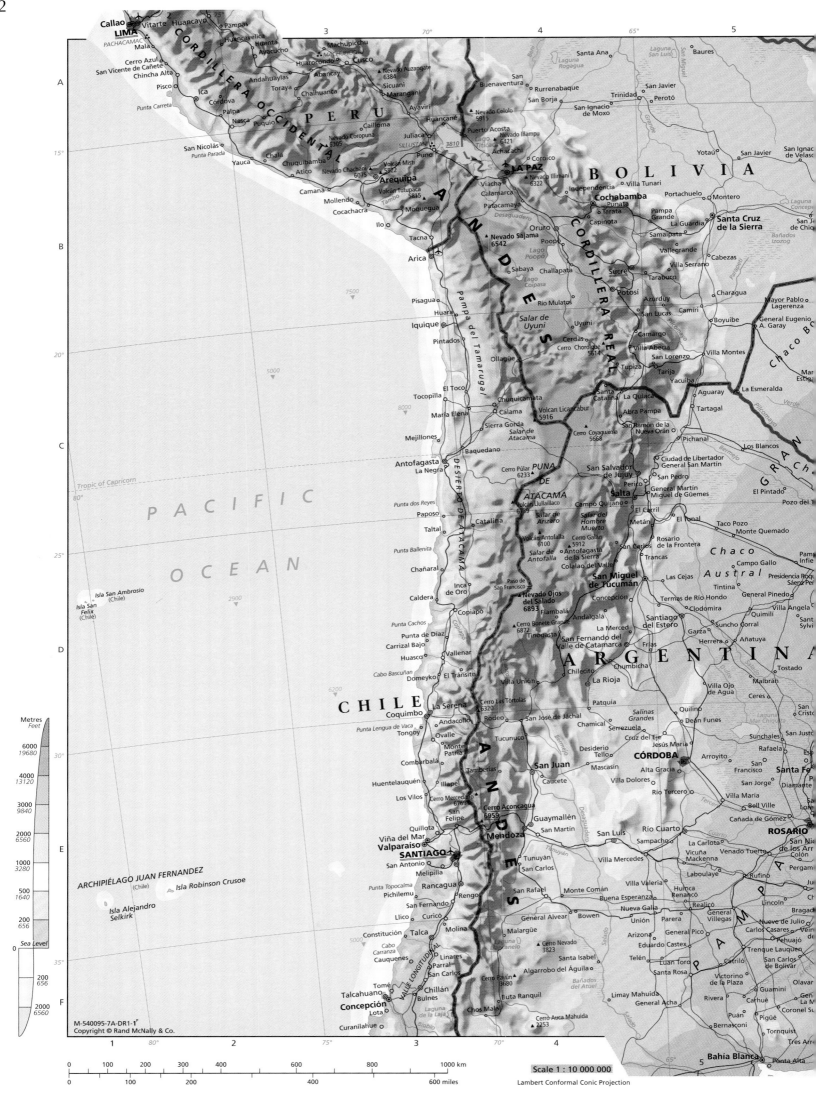

Metres / Feet

6000	19680
4000	13120
3000	9840
2000	6560
1000	3280
500	1640
200	656
0	Sea Level
200	656
2000	6560

M-540095-7A-DR1-1°
Copyright © Rand McNally & Co.

PERU · CORDILLERA OCCIDENTAL · BOLIVIA · CORDILLERA REAL · CHILE · ARGENTINA

PACIFIC OCEAN

ANDES

Tropic of Capricorn

ARCHIPIÉLAGO JUAN FERNANDEZ (Chile)
Isla Robinson Crusoe
Isla Alejandro Selkirk

Scale 1 : 10 000 000
Lambert Conformal Conic Projection

| 0 | 100 | 200 | 300 | 400 | 600 | 800 | 1000 km |
| 0 | 100 | 200 | 400 | 600 miles |

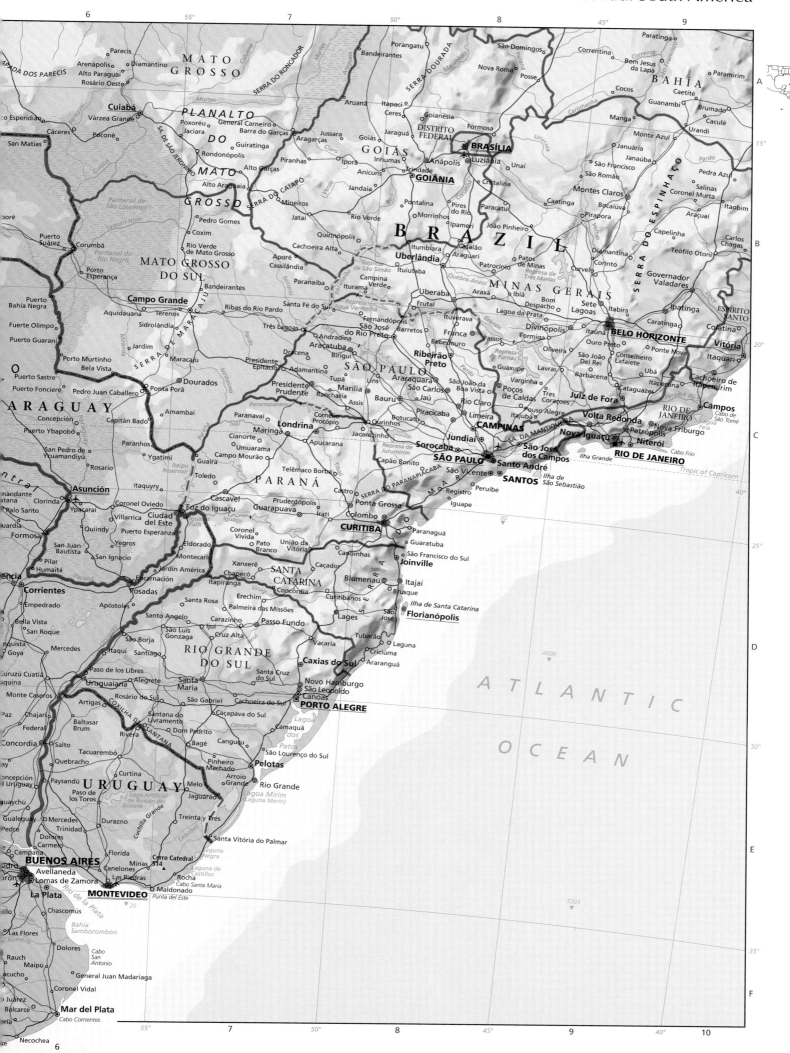

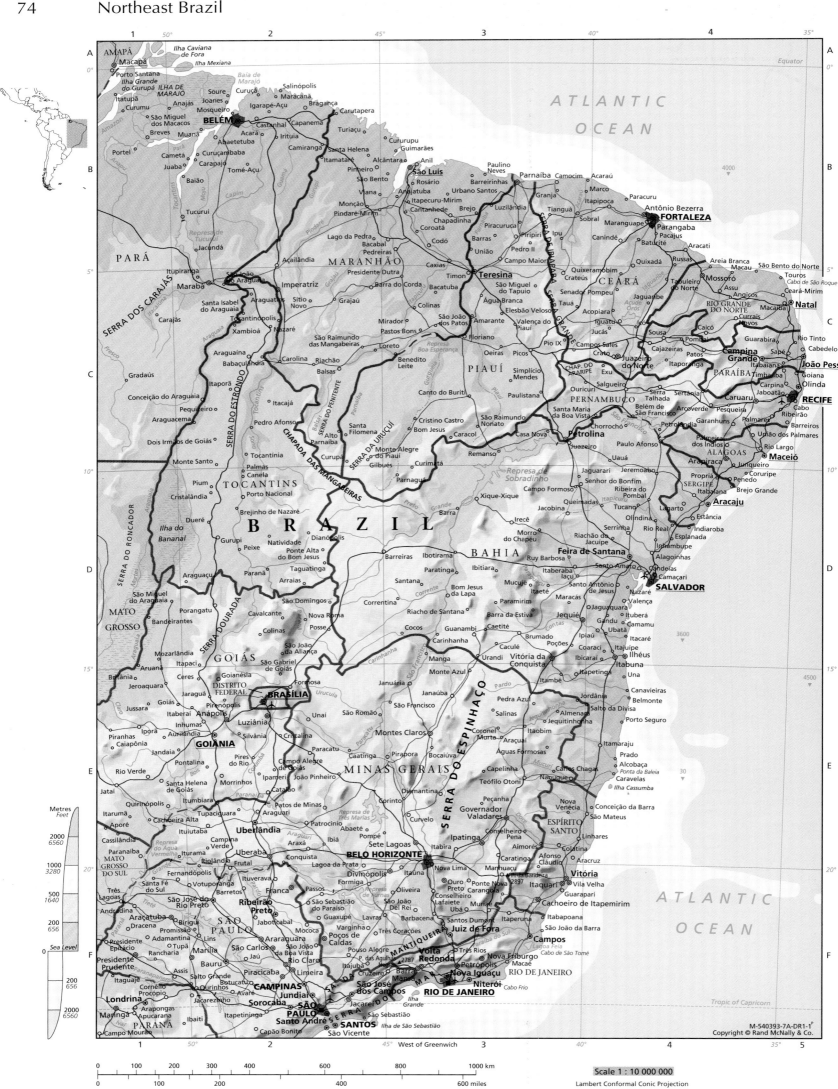

Scale 1 : 10 000 000

M-540393-7A-DR1-1
Copyright © Rand McNally & Co.

Lambert Conformal Conic Projection

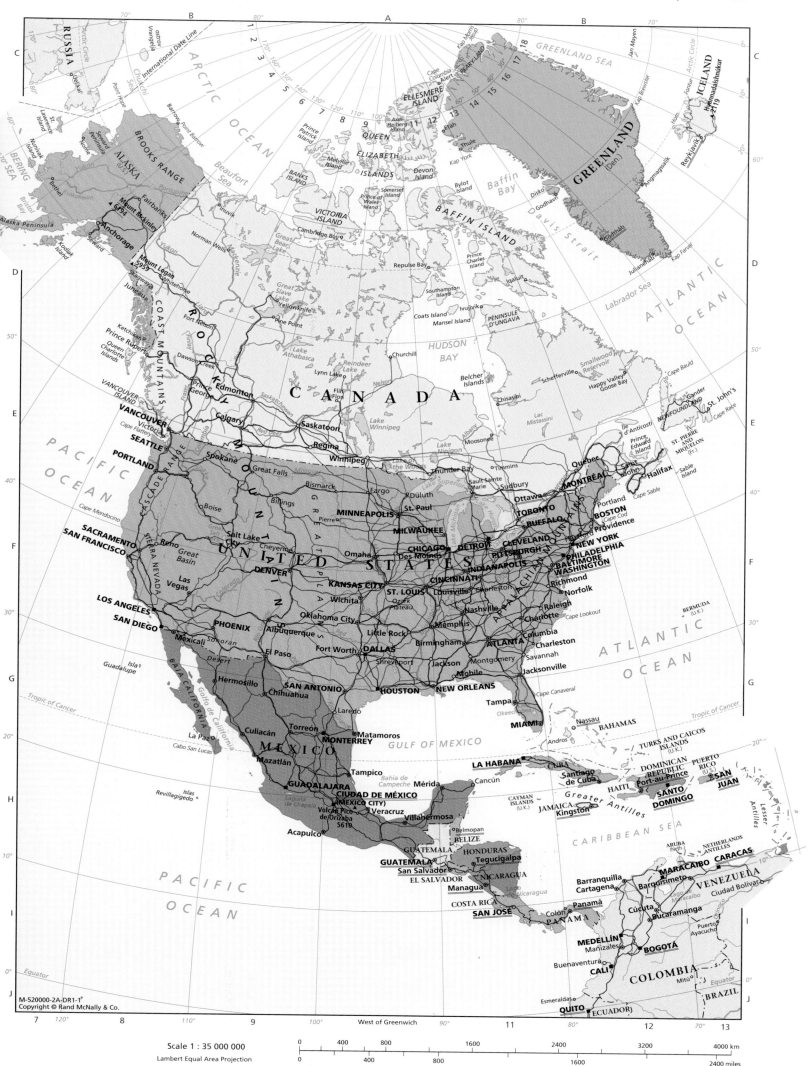

Scale 1 : 35 000 000

Lambert Equal Area Projection

0	400	800	1600	2400	3200	4000 km	
0	400	800	1600			2400 miles	

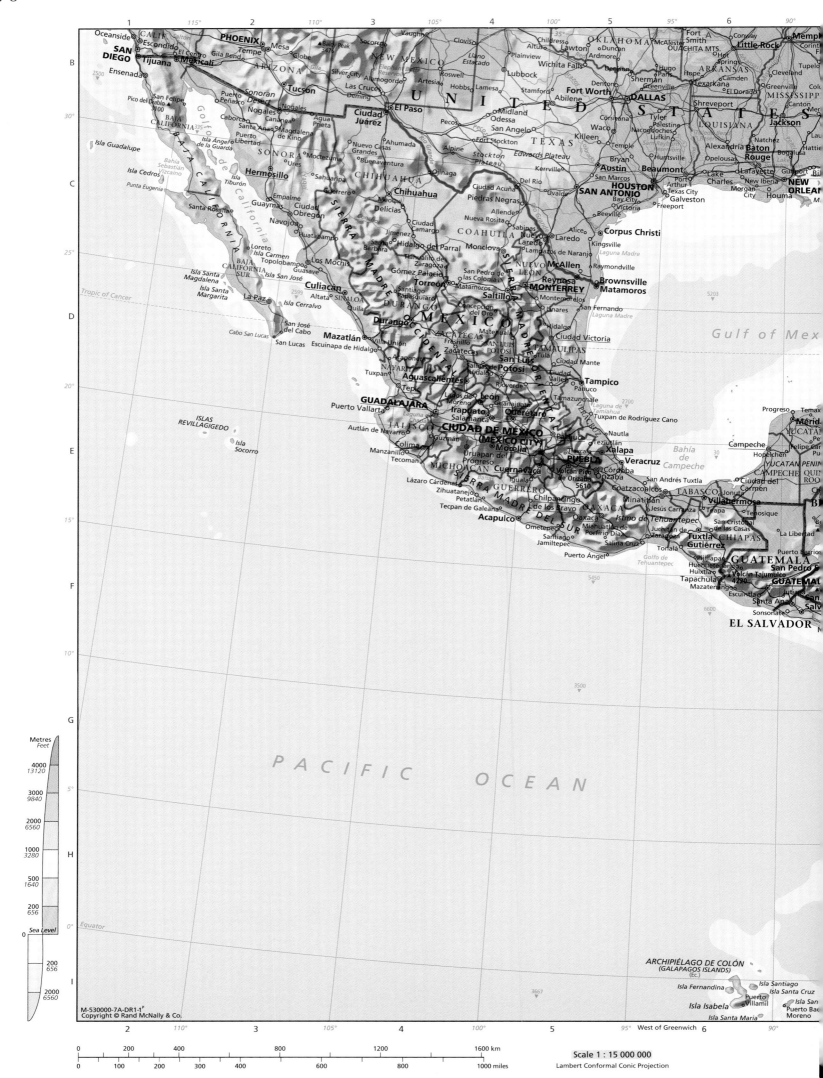

PACIFIC OCEAN

BAJA CALIFORNIA

BAJA CALIFORNIA SUR

SONORA

ARIZONA

NEW MEXICO

CHIHUAHUA

SINALOA

DURANGO

ZACATECAS

NAYARIT

JALISCO

COLIMA

ISLAS REVILLAGIGEDO (Mex.)

ISLAS TRES MARIAS

SAN DIEGO
Tijuana
Mexicali
Tucson
El Paso
Ciudad Juárez
Hermosillo
Chihuahua
Culiacán
Mazatlán
Durango
Torreón
Tepic
Puerto Vallarta
La Paz

Metres
Feet

4000
13120

3000
9840

2000
6560

1000
3280

500
1640

200
656

0
Sea Level

200
656

2000
6560

W-532000-7A-DR1-Z
Copyright © Rand McNally & Co.

| 0 | 100 | 200 | 300 | 400 | 600 | 800 km |

| 0 | 50 | 100 | 150 | 200 | 300 | 400 | 500 miles |

Scale 1 : 8 000 000

Lambert Conformal Conic Projection

West of Greenwich

Mexican State Abbreviations
AGS = AGUASCALIENTES
TLAX = TLAXCALA
D.F. = DISTRITO FEDERAL

GULF OF MEXICO

Tropic of Cancer

LA HABANA (HAVANA)

San José de las Lajas

San Antonio de los Baños

Consolación del Sur

Artemisa

Güira de Melena

Matanzas

Cárdenas

Jovellanos

Güines

Colón

Pinar del Río

Guane

Península de Zapata

Sagua la Grande

Santa Clara

Caibarién

Placetas

CUBA

Cruces

Cienfuegos

Cabaiguán

Morón

Nueva Gerona

Archipiélago de los Canarreos

Pico San Juan 1140

Sancti Spíritus

Ciego de Ávila

Trinidad

Florida

Camagüey

Puerto Padre

Gibara

Isla de la Juventud

Golfo de Ana María

Santa Cruz del Sur

Nuevitas

Las Tunas

Holguín

Golfo de Guacanayabo

Bayamo

Manzanillo

Palma Soriano

Niquero

Pico Turquino 1972

Santiago de Cuba

SIERRA MAESTRA

Cabo Cruz

Cabo Catoche

Progreso

Hunucmá

Temax

Tizimín

Mérida

Izamal

Umán

Muna

CHICHÉN ITZÁ

Cancún

Puerto Juárez

Ticul

Tekax

Valladolid

Peto

YUCATÁN

Halachó

Hecelchakán

Campeche

Punta Morro

Hopelchén

Cozumel

Isla Cozumel

YUCATAN PENINSULA

Champotón

CAMPECHE

QUINTANA ROO

Felipe Carrillo Puerto

MEXICO

Laguna de Términos

Escárcega

Chetumal

Corozal

Orange Walk

Banco Chinchorro

San Pedro Tabasco

CHIAPAS

Tenosique

Piedras Negras

La Libertad

TABASCO

Chuntuquí

Belize City

Belmopan

BELIZE

Dangriga

Victoria Peak 1120

Turneffe Islands

TIKAL

Flores

La Florida

San Benito

San Luis

Punta Gorda

Gulf of Honduras

ISLAS DE LA BAHÍA

Isla de Roatán

Isla de Guanaja

Islas Santanilla (Hon.)

Barillas

GUATEMALA

Lago de Izabal

Huehuetenango

Cobán

Santa Cruz del Quiché

Zacapa

Chiquimula

Cerro San Ildefonso 2228

Livingston

Puerto Barrios

Puerto Cortés

Isla de Utila

La Ceiba

Balfate

Trujillo

Cabo de Honduras

Cabo Camarón

Limón

Punta Patuca

San Pedro Sula

El Progreso

Santa Rita

Yoro

Olanchito

Cerro Payas 1128

Laguna de Caratasca

GUATEMALA

Escuintla

Jutiapa

Cerro El Pital 2730

Santa Bárbara

Pico Pijol 2282

Cerro Las Minas 2849

Siguatepeque

Comayagua

HONDURAS

Juticalpa

La Paz

La Esperanza

Montaña El Chile 2256

Cabo Gracias a Dios

Puerto San José

Santa Ana

Sonsonate

Chalatenango

Metapán

Tegucigalpa

Danlí

Waspam

Mogotón 2107

Cerro Saslaya 1650

Bonanza

Cayos Miskitos

San Salvador

San Vicente

San Miguel

Usulután

La Unión

Choluteca

Ocotal

Estelí

Puerto Cabezas

Punta Gorda

EL SALVADOR

Golfo de Fonseca

Punta Cosigüina

Volcán Cosigüina 859

Puerto Morazán

Matagalpa

Prinzapolka

NICARAGUA

Chinandega

Volcán San Cristóbal 1745

Boaco

León

Lago de Managua

Tipitapa

Isla de Providencia (Col.)

Managua

Masaya

Granada

San Andrés

Isla de San Andrés (Col.)

Volcán Concepción 1610

Rivas

Bluefields

Islas del Maíz

Cayos del Este Sudeste (Col.)

Isla de Ometepe

Lago de Nicaragua

San Juan del Sur

Cayos de Albuquerque (Col.)

Cabo Santa Elena

San Juan del Norte

Bahía de Punta Gorda

Volcán Miravalles 2028

Golfo de Papagayo

Liberia

Bagaces

Cabo Velas

Cañas

Nicoya

Río San Carlos

Guápiles

Volcán Irazú 3432

Puntarenas

Alajuela

San José

Puerto Limón

SAN JOSÉ

Cartago

Cerro Azul 1018

Península de Nicoya

COSTA RICA

Cabo Blanco

Golfo de Nicoya

Cerro La Muerte 3491

San Isidro del General

Cerro Chirripó 3819

Bocas del Toro

Península Valiente

Golfo de los Mosquitos

Istmo de Panamá

Portobelo

Colón

Niatupo

Cartagena

Golfo de Morrosquillo

El Carmen de B

San

Arjona

Sincelejo

Lorica

Sahagú

Montería

Planeta Rica

Alto de Quimarí

Turbo 2000

Apartadó

Chigorodó

Volcán Barú 3475

Golfito

Amatitlán

Boquete

La Concepción

David

Natá

Penonomé

La Chorrera

Panamá

Río Hato

Bahía de Panamá

Golfo de Panamá

Península de Osa

Puerto Armuelles

Punta Burica

Golfo de Chiriquí

Aguadulce

Santiago

Cerro Santiago 2121

Las Tablas

Chitré

Archipiélago de las Perlas

Isla del Rey

La Palma

SERRANÍA DEL DARIÉN

Alto de Tres Morros 3400

Dabeiba

Bahía de Parita

PENÍNSULA DE AZUERO

Punta Mariato

Punta Mala

Isla de Coiba

PANAMÁ

Golfo de Cupica

MEDELLÍN

Urrao

Bello

PACIFIC

OCEAN

Ensenada de Tribugá

Nuquí

Quibdó

Condoto

Isla del Coco (C.R.)

Isla de Malpelo (Col.)

Pereira

Armenia

Tuluá

Buga

Buenaventura

Yumbo

CALI

Palmira

Punta Magdalena

GREAT

Cistern Point

Great Exuma

Ragged Island Range

Archipiélago de Sabana

Nicholas Channel

Cay Lobos

Cayo Sabinal

Cay Sal

Old Bahama Channel

Cayo Romano

Cayo Coco

Grand Cayman

George Town

Little Cayman

Cayman Brac

CAYMAN ISLANDS (U.K.)

GREATER

Falmouth

Montego Bay

Savanna-la-Mar

South Negril Point

Mandeville

Mount Denham 986

Ocho Ríos

Spanish Town

Kingston

Blue Mountain 2256

Port Antonio

Morant Point

Portland Point

JAMAICA

Morant Cays

Pedro Cays

CARI

West of Greenwich

CORDILLERA OCCIDENTAL

Metres Feet

4000 / 13120

3000 / 9840

2000 / 6560

1000 / 3280

500 / 1640

200 / 656

0 / Sea Level

200 / 656

2000 / 6560

W-530093-7A-DR1-2

Copyright © Rand McNally & Co.

Lambert Conformal Conic Projection

Scale 1 : 8 000 000

| 0 | 100 | 200 | 300 | 400 | | 600 | | 800 km |

| 0 | 50 | 100 | 150 | 200 | 300 | 400 | 500 miles |

ATLANTIC OCEAN

Tropic of Cancer

BAHAMAS
Samana Cay
Crooked Island
Acklins
Mayaguana
Matthew Town
Great Inagua
Little Inagua

North Caicos
Middle Caicos
East Caicos
Caicos Islands
Grand Turk
Turks Islands
TURKS AND CAICOS ISLANDS
(U.K.)

HISPANIOLA
Manzanillo Bay
Cabo Isabela
Limbé
Cap-Haïtien
Puerto Plata
Cabo Francés Viejo
Mao
Santiago de los Caballeros
San Francisco de Macorís
Moca
Cabo Samaná
HAITI
Gonaïves
LA CITADELLE
La Vega
Sánchez
Pico Duarte 3175
Saint-Marc
Alto Bandera 2630
Golfe de la Gonâve
Higüey
Cabo Engaño
PUERTO RICO (U.S.)
Port-au-Prince
Pétion-Ville
SANTO DOMINGO
San Juan de la Maguana
San Cristóbal
Bani
San Pedro de Macorís
Morne La Selle 2674
Barahona
Azua
La Romana
Isla Saona
Arecibo
SAN JUAN
Bayamón
Caguas
Enriquillo
DOMINICAN REPUBLIC
Isla Beata
Cabo Beata
Mayagüez
Ponce
Cerro de Punta 1338
Isla de Mona
Cabo Rojo
Isla de Vieques

BRITISH VIRGIN ISLANDS
Anegada
Charlotte Amalie
Road Town
Virgin Gorda
St. John
St. Thomas
VIRGIN ISLANDS (U.S.)
Virgin Islands
St. Croix
ANGUILLA (U.K.)
The Valley
Saint Martin (Fr.-Neth.)
Saba (Neth.)
St. Christopher (St. Kitts)
Basseterre
ST. KITTS AND NEVIS
Nevis
MONTSERRAT (U.K.)
Plymouth
ANTIGUA AND BARBUDA
St. John's
Antigua
Barbuda

LESSER ANTILLES
LEEWARD ISLANDS

Basse-Terre
Soufrière 1467
Pointe-à-Pitre (Fr.)
GUADELOUPE
Grande-Terre
Marie Galante
Morne Diablotins 1447
Roseau
DOMINICA
Montagne Pelée 1397
Fort-de-France
MARTINIQUE (Fr.)
Mount Gimie 950
Castries
ST. LUCIA
Soufrière 1234
St. Vincent
ST. VINCENT AND THE GRENADINES
Kingstown
Grenadines
Bridgetown
Mount Hillaby 340
BARBADOS

WINDWARD ISLANDS

GREATER ANTILLES

CARIBBEAN SEA

ARUBA (Neth.)
Oranjestad
NETHERLANDS ANTILLES
Curaçao
Bonaire
Kralendijk
Willemstad
Islas de Aves

Isla La Orchila
Isla Blanquilla
St. George's
GRENADA
Tobago
Scarborough

LESSER ANTILLES

Punta Gallinas
Cabo de La Vela
Puerto Bolívar
Península de La Guajira
Punta Espada
Uribia
Riohacha
Maicao
Golfo de Venezuela
Punto Fijo
Coro
Puerto Cumarebo
Isla La Tortuga
Islas Los Roques
Isla de Margarita
La Asunción
Porlamar
Pen. de Paria
Punta Piedras
Port of Spain
Arima
TRINIDAD AND TOBAGO
Trinidad
Santa Marta
quilla
dad
Pico Cristóbal Colón 5775
MARACAIBO
La Concepción
Santa Rita
Dabajuro
Churuguara
Tucacas
Maiquetía
CARACAS
Guarenas
Cumaná
Carúpano
Güiria
San Fernando
Río Claro
Point Fortin
Valledupar
Agustín Codazzi
Cabimas
Ciudad Ojeda
Altagracia
San Rafael
San Felipe
Puerto Cabello
La Victoria
Guárico
Barcelona
Pozuelos
Carúpano
Caripito
Pedernales
Machiques
Cerro 1990
Carora
Chivacoa
Tinaquillo
MARACAY
VALENCIA
Cúa
Ocumare del Tuy
Puerto la Cruz
Cerro Turimiquire 2596
Maturín
Barquisimeto
Mene Grande
San Carlos
Tinaco
San Juan de los Morros
El Sombrero
Chaguaramas
Aragua de Barcelona
Anaco
Cantaura
Tucupita
DELTA DEL ORINOCO
Isla Tobejuba
Valera
Trujillo
Boconó
Acarigua
Calabozo
Valle de la Pascua
Pariaguán
El Tigre
San José de Guanipa
Temblador
Barrancas
Corocoro Island
Cerro Mu 2610
Mérida
Barinas
Guanare
Morawhanna
Pico Bolívar 5007
Guárico
Ciudad de Nutrias
Ciudad Guayana
Upata
Gamarra
Aguachica
Ocaña
San Juan de Colón
Santa Bárbara
VENEZUELA
Ciudad Bolívar
Guasipati
Simití
Cúcuta
San Cristóbal
Caicara de Orinoco
Cerro Bolívar 802
Ciudad Piar
El Callao
Tumeremo
Matthews Ridge
Puerto Wilches
Pamplona
Guasdualito
Elorza
Santa Rosa
Cabruta
Cerro 1863
La Paragua
El Dorado
GUYANA
COLOMBIA
Bucaramanga
Floridablanca
Arauquita
Arauca
La Urbana
Canaima
Piedecuesta
Tame
Salto Ángel
Auyán Tepuy 2950
cabermeja
San Gil
Socorro
Boavita
Cravo Norte
Casanare
Puerto Rondón
La Gran Sabana
Iru Tepuy 2620
Málaga
Puerto Páez
Cerro Yaví 2441
Mount Roraima 2875
iquinquirá
Barbosa
Duitama
Guadualito
Nueva Antioquia
Puerto Carreño
da
rada
Tunja
Sogamoso
Yopal
Trinidad
Puerto Ayacucho
yacá
Miraflores
Orocué
LLANOS
Arabelo
Cerro Uquía 2500
Cerro Nevado 4560
San Martín
BOGOTÁ
Villavicencio
Puerto López
Granada
Acacías
Puerto Inírida
RORAIMA
BRAZIL
San Fernando de Atabapo
PAKARAIMA MOUNTAINS

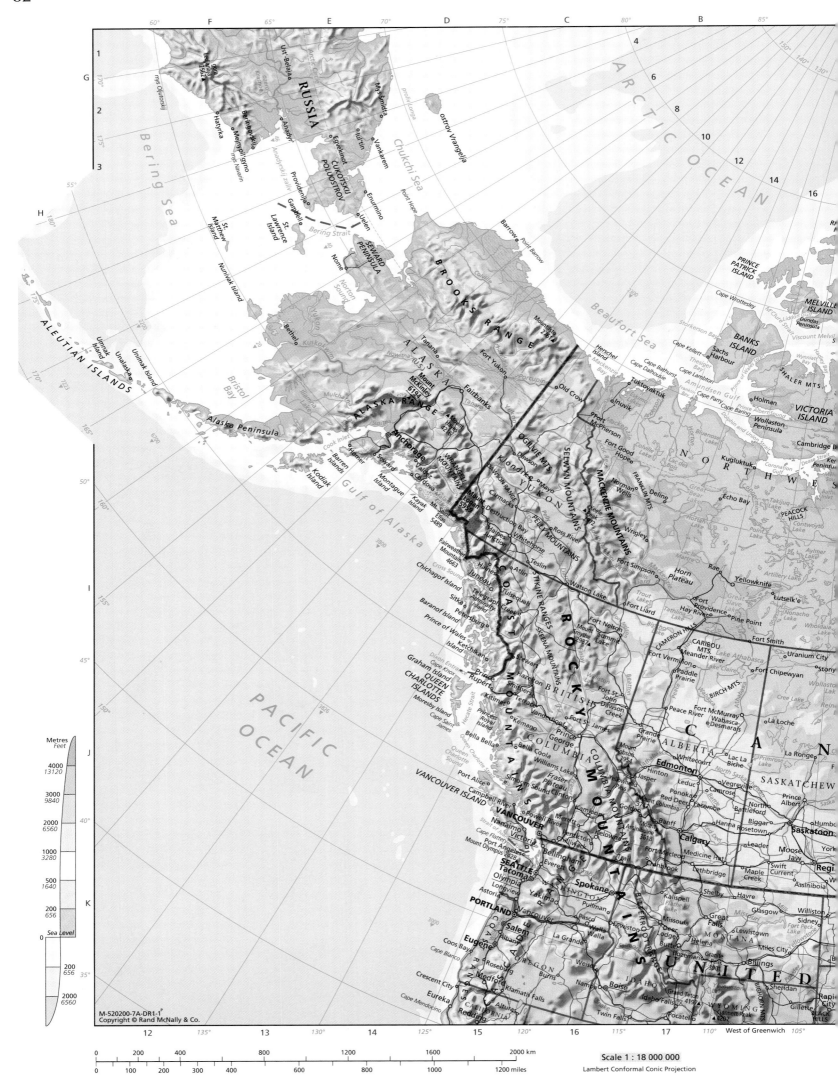

82

Scale 1 : 18 000 000

Lambert Conformal Conic Projection

M-520200-7A-DR1-1
Copyright © Rand McNally & Co.

B 36
34
32
30
28
26
24
22

C 75° D 70° E 65° F 60°

Torshavn
FAROE ISLANDS (Den.)
38

Greenland Sea

Arctic Circle
ICELAND
Ísafjörður
Siglufjörður
Akureyri
Seydisfjördur
Neskaupstadur
Hnappadalshnúkur 2119
Reykjavík
Vestmannaeyjar

Kap Morris Jesup
Peary Land
Kap York

Lincoln Sea
Cape Columbia
Alert
Barbeau Peak 2616
ELLESMERE ISLAND

AXEL HEIBERG ISLAND

Etah

Thule (Qaanaaq)

G

GREENLAND (Den.)

Gunnbjørn Field 3700

Mont Forel 3360

Kap Brewster

Kap Gustav Holm

Angmagssalik

Denmark Strait

Coburg Island
Cape Parker
Philpots Island
Cape Sherard
DEVON ISLAND

Cornwallis Island
Lancaster Sound
Barrow Strait
SOMERSET ISLAND

Upernavik
Umanak
Qutdligssat
Disko
Godhavn
Jakobshavn

Baffin Bay

Arctic Bay
Eclipse Sound
Borden Peninsula
BRODEUR PENINSULA
Prince Regent Inlet
Gulf of Boothia
BOOTHIA PENINSULA

Bylot Island
Pond Inlet
Cape Adair

Clyde River
McBeth Field
2100

Davis Strait

BAFFIN ISLAND

Egedesminde
Holsteinsborg
Søndre Strømfjord

Jens Munks Ø
Gydenløves Fjord
Kap Meeting

H

Cumberland Peninsula
Pangnirtung
Cumberland Sound
Cape Mercy
Exeter Sound
Cape Dyer

Sukkertoppen

Godthåb (Nuuk)

Frederikshåb
Ivigtut
Julianehåb

Kap Cort Adeler

Labrador Sea

Taloyoak
Cape Chapman
Prince Charles Island
Air Force Island
MELVILLE PENINSULA
Parry Bay
Cape Wilson

Igloolik
Hall Peninsula
Lemieux Islands
Brevoort Island

Kap Farvel

TERRITORIES
FOXE BASIN

Repulse Bay
Lyon Inlet
Vansittart Island
Cape Dorchester
FOXE PENINSULA
CAPE DORSET
Foxe Channel

Cape Dominion
Plain of the Koukdjuak
Netfilling
Amadjuak

Frobisher Bay
Loks Land
Resolution Island

Iqaluit
META INCOGNITA PENINSULA
Cap de Nouvelle-France
Hudson Strait

Cape Hopes Advance

Killiniq Island

Mount Caubvick 1652
Saglek Bay
Hebron

N E W

South Aulatsivik Island
Tunungayualok Island

Nain
Hopedale

Wager Bay
SOUTHAMPTON ISLAND
Coral Harbour
Seahorse Point
Nottingham Island
Cape Pembroke
Salluit
Kangiqsujuaq
Cratère du Nouveau-Québec
PÉNINSULE D'UNGAVA
Ivujivik
Kangirsuk

Cape Kendall
Cape Low
Coats Island
Mansel Island
Southampton

Ungava Bay
Kangiqsualujjuaq

Cape Harrison
Growater Bay
Sandwich Bay
Cartwright

I

Rankin Inlet
Arviat

Povungnituk

Povungnituk
Ottawa Islands
Hopewell Islands
Inukjuak

Kuujjuaq
Lac des Loups Marins
Lac Minto

F O U N D L A N D
Labrador
Happy Valley
Goose Bay
Lac Melville

Battle Harbour
Belle Isle
Cape Bauld
St. Anthony
Grey Islands
Fogo Island
Gander
Bonavista

Churchill
Cape Churchill

King George Islands
Belcher Islands

Whapmagoostui

Hudson Bay

Schefferville

Labrador City
Gagnon

Spingdale
St. John's
Carbonear
Grand Bank
Cape Race

NEWFOUNDLAND

J

Cape Tatnam
York Factory
Fort Severn
Winisk
Cape Henrietta Maria
Pointe Louis-XIV

D A
Wabowden
Norway House
Lake Winnipeg
Big Trout Lake

Chisasibi
Eastmain
Akimiski Island
James Bay

MONTS OTISH
QUÉBEC
Lac Mistassini

Sept-Îles
Îles de Mingan
Havre-Saint-Pierre
Détroit de Jacques-Cartier
ÎLE D'ANTICOSTI
Pointe de l'Est
Gaspé

Corner Brook
Stephenville
Channel-Port aux Basques
LONG RANGE MOUNTAINS

Grand Rapids
Berens River
Pickle Lake
Attawapiskat
Fort Albany
Moosonee

Waskaganish
Matagami
Chibougamau
Val-d'Or

Baie Comeau
Matane
Rimouski
Gulf of St. Lawrence

Îles de la Madeleine
CAPE BRETON
Glace Bay
Sydney
Charlottetown
New Glasgow

SAINT PIERRE AND MIQUELON (Fr.)

ONTARIO

Red Lake
Sioux Lookout
Armstrong
Hearst
Kapuskasing
Cochrane
Timmins
La Sarre
Rouyn-Noranda
La Tuque

Saint-Félicien
Alma
Jonquière
Chicoutimi
Saint-Georges

Edmundston
Bathurst
NEW BRUNSWICK
Fredericton
Moncton
Saint John

NOVA SCOTIA
Dartmouth
Halifax
Liverpool

K

Winnipeg
Altona
Kenora
Dryden
Atikokan
Thunder Bay
Isle Royale
Nipigon

Geraldton
Hornepayne
Marathon
Wawa
Chapleau
Sault Sainte Marie

New Liskeard
North Bay
Sudbury
Elliot Lake
Pembroke
Bancroft

Shawinigan
Trois-Rivières
Maniwaki
Joliette
MONTREAL
Hull
Ottawa

Québec
Sherbrooke
Drummondville

Portland
Portsmouth
BOSTON
Providence

Gulf of Maine

ATLANTIC OCEAN

Gimli
Selkirk
Lac Seul

Winnipeg

Kenora

Lake Superior

Sudbury
Barrie
Oshawa
TORONTO
Kitchener
Hamilton
London
Windsor

Peterborough
Belleville
Watertown
Rochester
Syracuse
Albany
Hartford
New Haven

Augusta
Lewiston
Concord

Bangor

Cape Cod

MINNESOTA
St. Cloud
St. Paul
MINNEAPOLIS
Madison
Milwaukee
Rockford
CHICAGO
Gary

WISCONSIN
Eau Claire
Green Bay
Appleton
Sheboygan

MICHIGAN
Grand Rapids
Flint
Lansing
DETROIT

Buffalo
Erie
Scranton
Binghamton
NEW YORK
Newark
NEW JERSEY
Trenton
PHILADELPHIA
2600

PENNSYLVANIA

U N I T E D   S T A T E S

Fargo
Aberdeen
Brookings
Sioux Falls

SOUTH DAKOTA

Rochester
La Crosse

ATLANTIC OCEAN

20 95° 21 23 80° 24 75° 25 70° 26 65° 27

Note: Map colors do not reflect elevation.

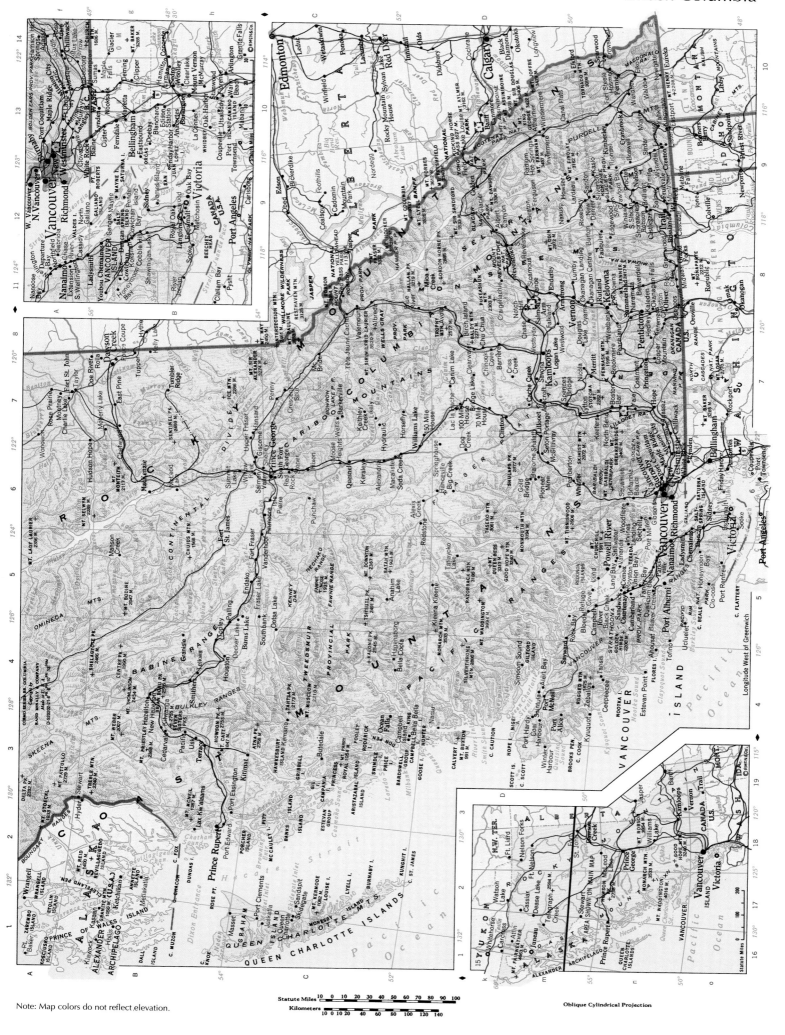

Note: Map colors do not reflect elevation.

Statute Miles 10 0 10 20 30 40 50 60 70 80 90 100

Kilometers 10 0 10 20 40 60 80 100 120 140

Oblique Cylindrical Projection

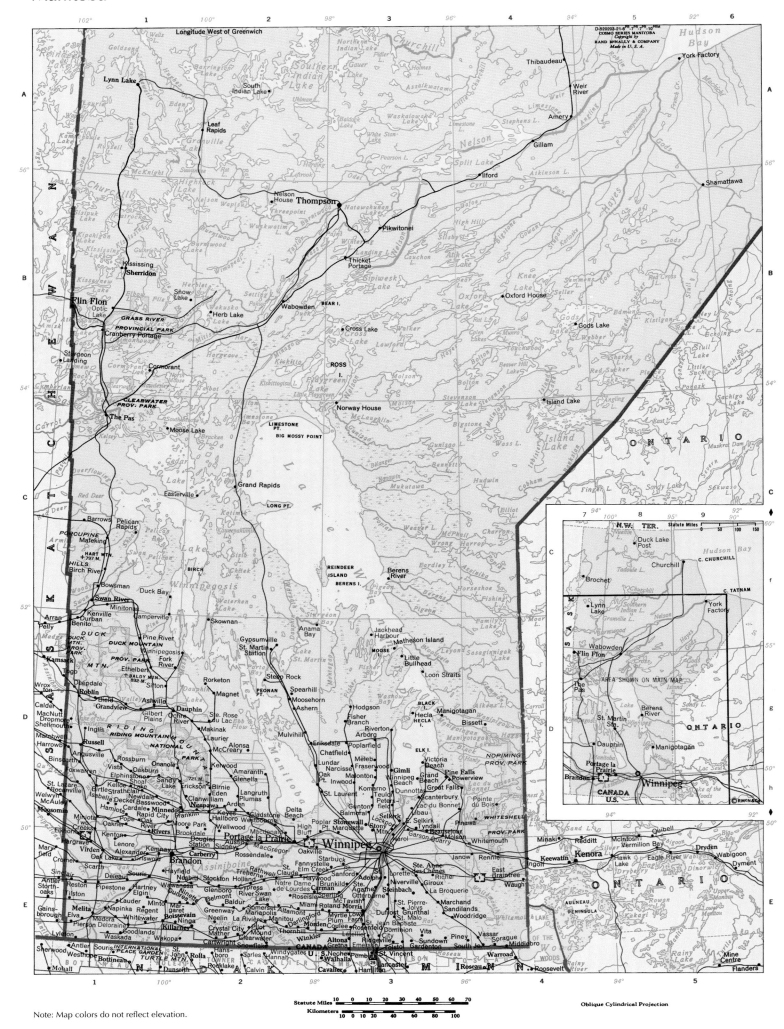

Note: Map colors do not reflect elevation.

Statute Miles 10 0 10 20 30 40 50 60 70

Kilometers 10 0 10 20 40 60 80 100

Oblique Cylindrical Projection

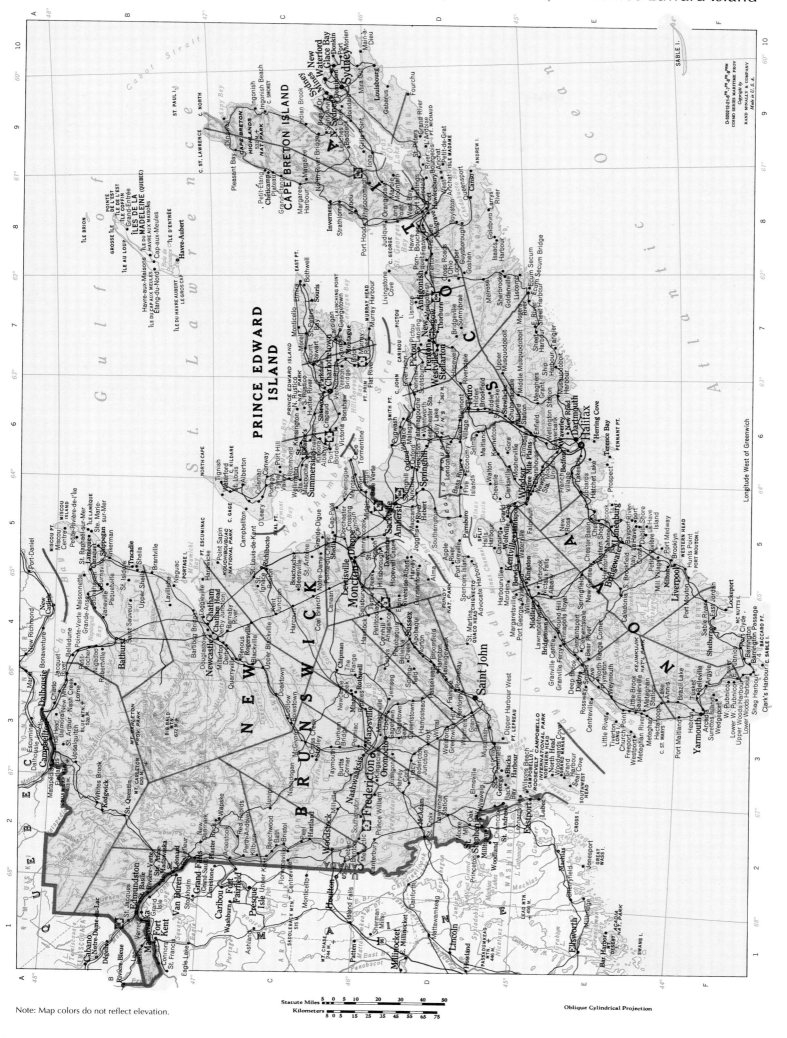

Note: Map colors do not reflect elevation.

Statute Miles   5 0 5   10   20   30   40   50
Kilometers   5 0 5   15   25   35   45   55   65   75

Oblique Cylindrical Projection

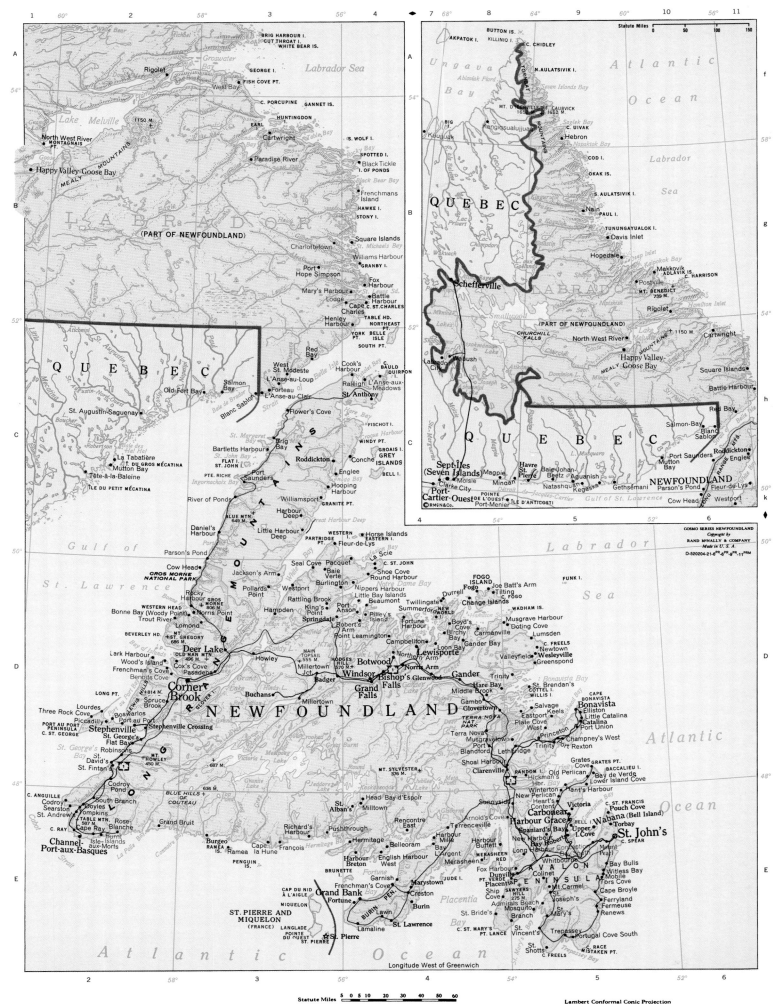

Note: Map colors do not reflect elevation.

Statute Miles
Kilometers

Lambert Conformal Conic Projection

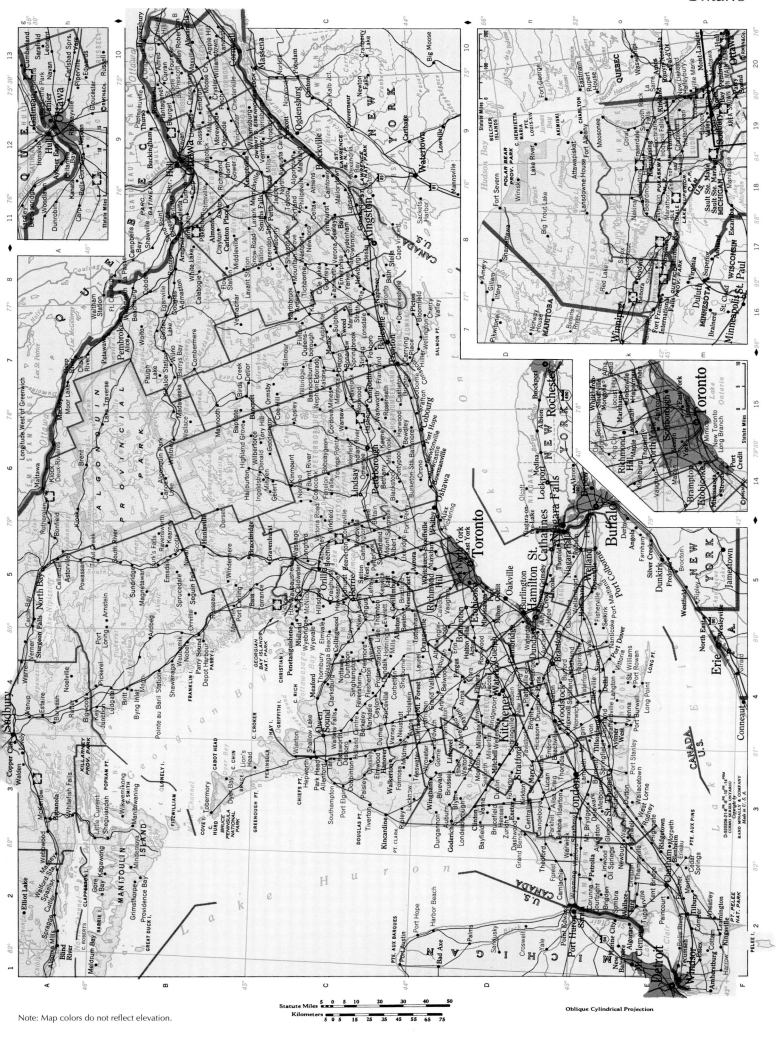

Note: Map colors do not reflect elevation.

Statute Miles
Kilometers

Oblique Cylindrical Projection

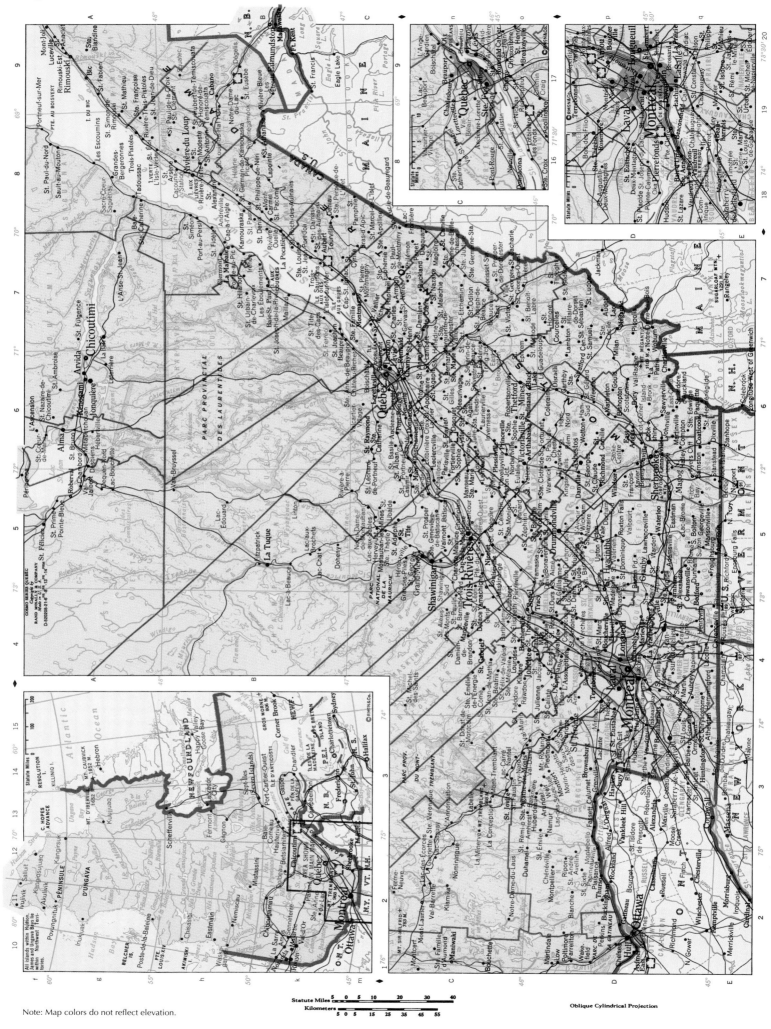

Note: Map colors do not reflect elevation.

Statute Miles 5 0 5 10 20 30 40
Kilometers 5 0 5 15 25 35 45 55

Oblique Cylindrical Projection

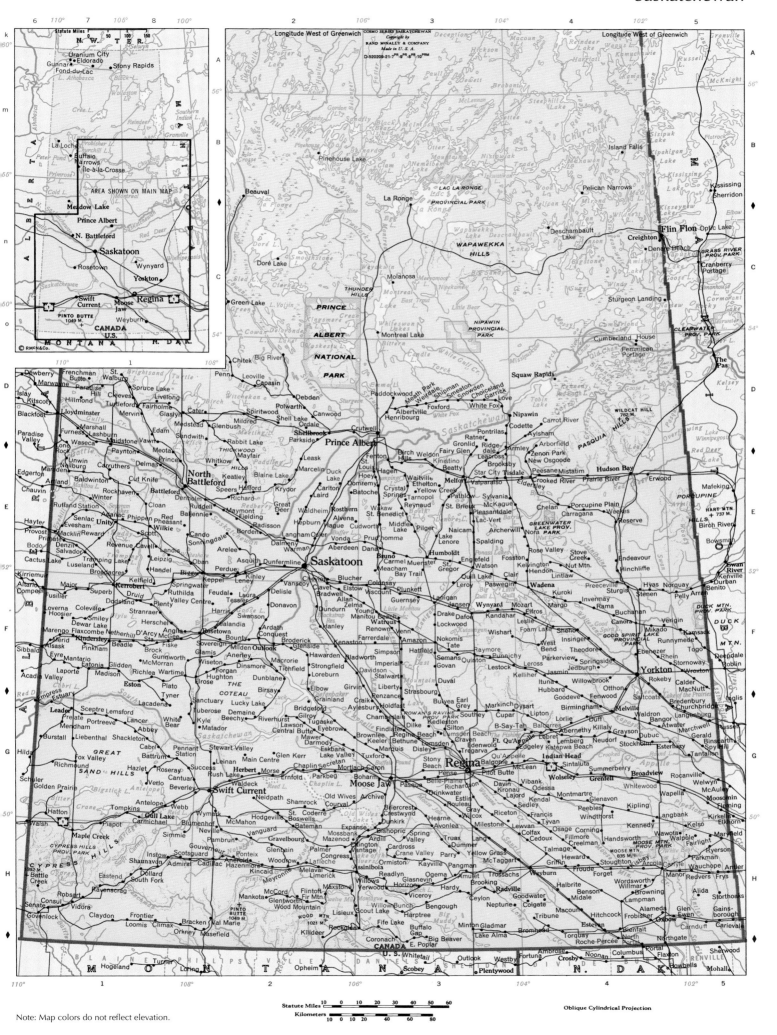

Note: Map colors do not reflect elevation.

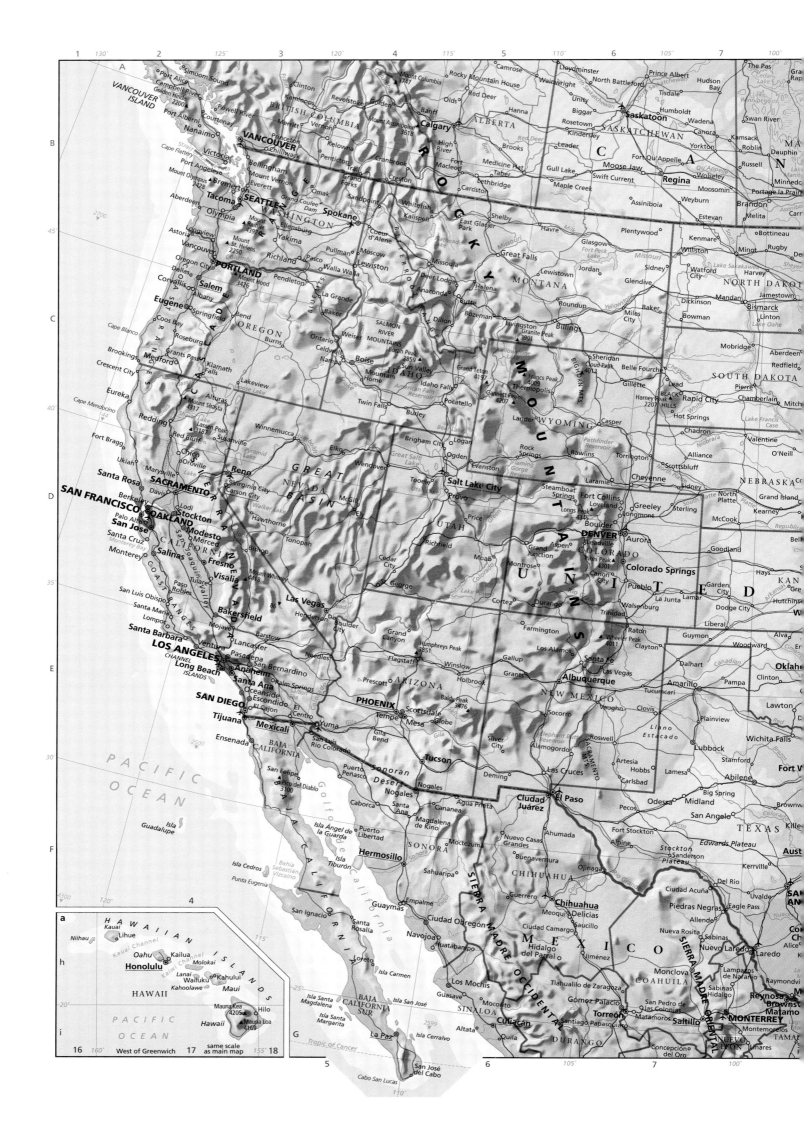

Scale 1 : 12 000 000
Lambert Conformal Conic Projection

95° West of Greenwich

Metres
Feet

4000
13120

3000
9840

2000
6560

1000
3280

500
1640

200
656

Sea Level
0

200
656

2000
6560

0   200   400   600   800   1200 km

0   100   200   300   400   500   600   800 miles

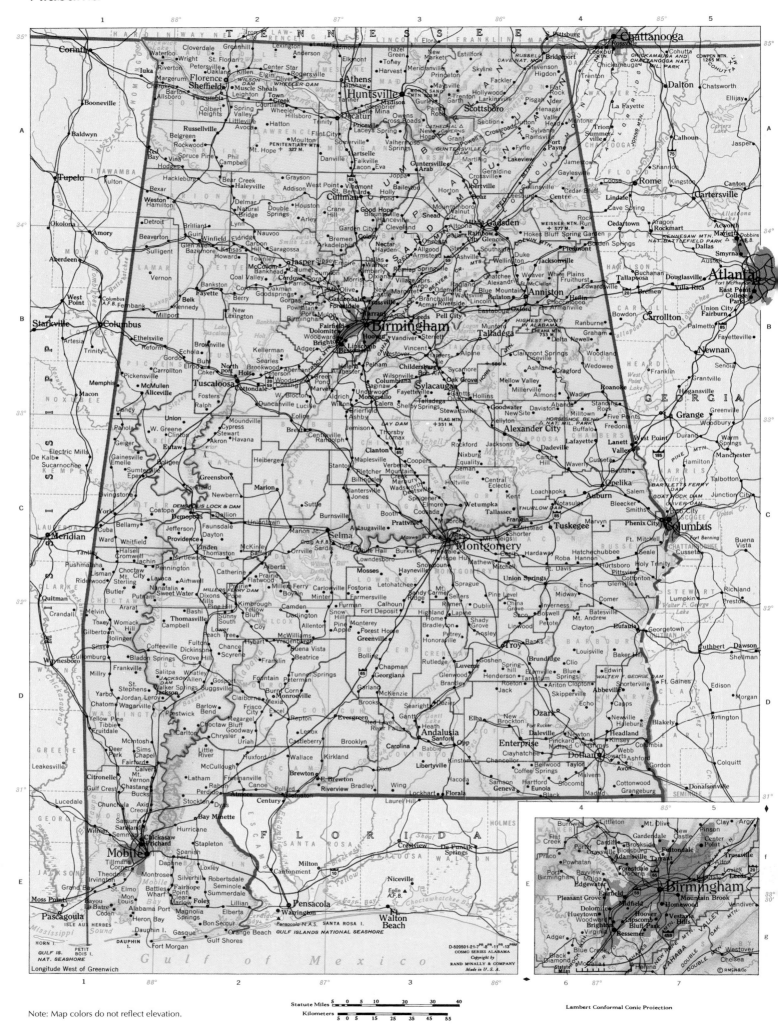

Note: Map colors do not reflect elevation.

Statute Miles
Kilometers

Lambert Conformal Conic Projection

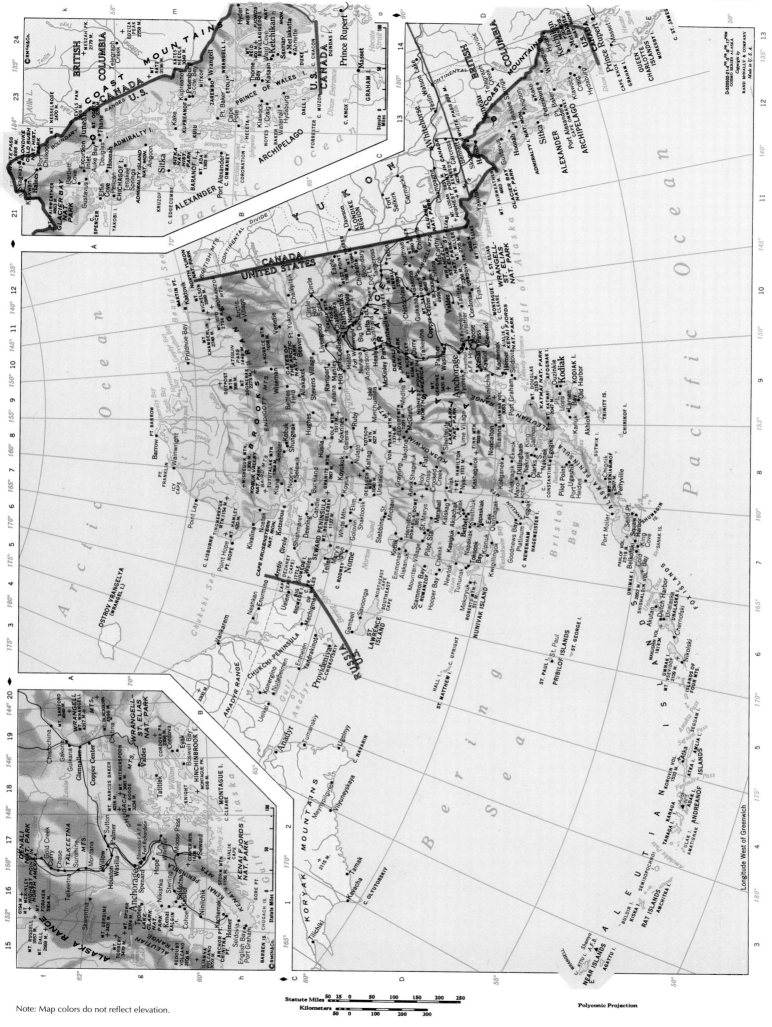

Note: Map colors do not reflect elevation.

Statute Miles 50 25 0 50 100 150 200 250
Kilometers 50 0 100 200 300

Polyconic Projection

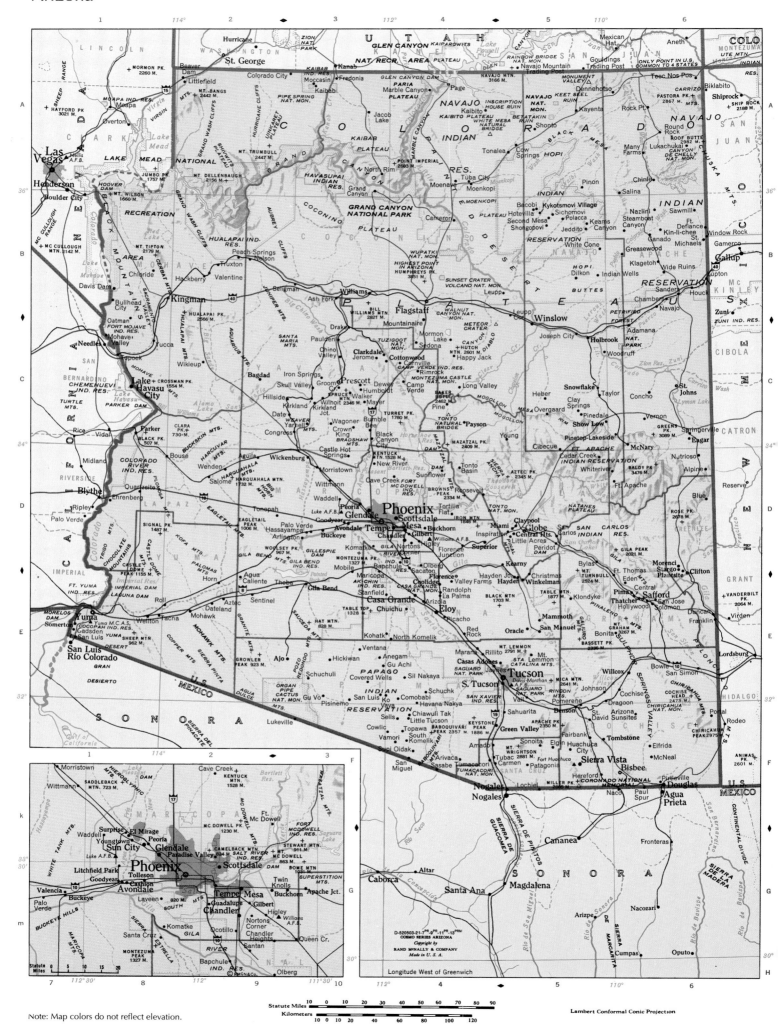

Note: Map colors do not reflect elevation.

Statute Miles
Kilometers

Lambert Conformal Conic Projection

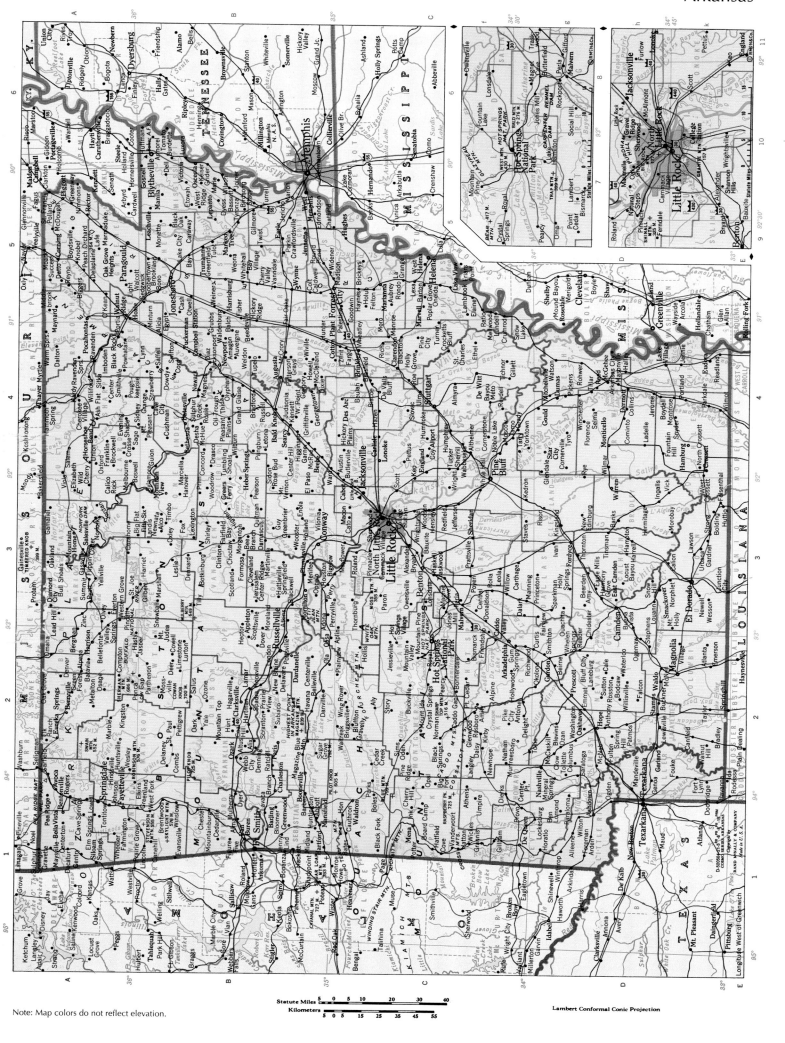

Note: Map colors do not reflect elevation.

Statute Miles
5 0 5 10   20   30   40
Kilometers
5 0 5 15   25   35   45   55

Lambert Conformal Conic Projection

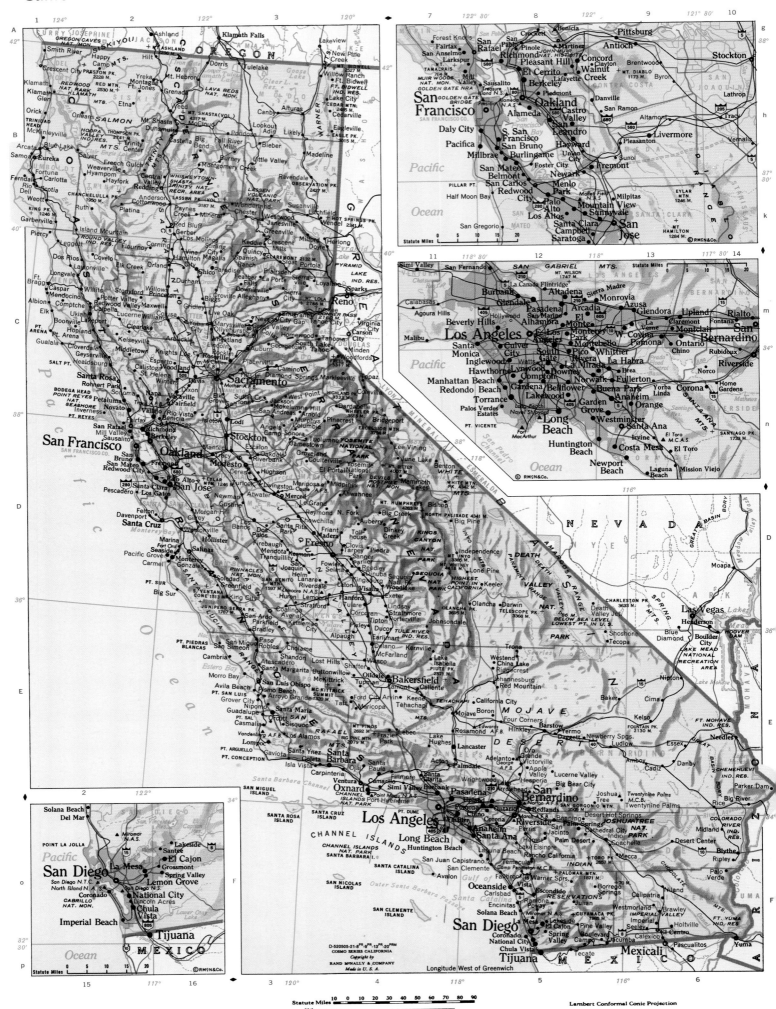

Note: Map colors do not reflect elevation.

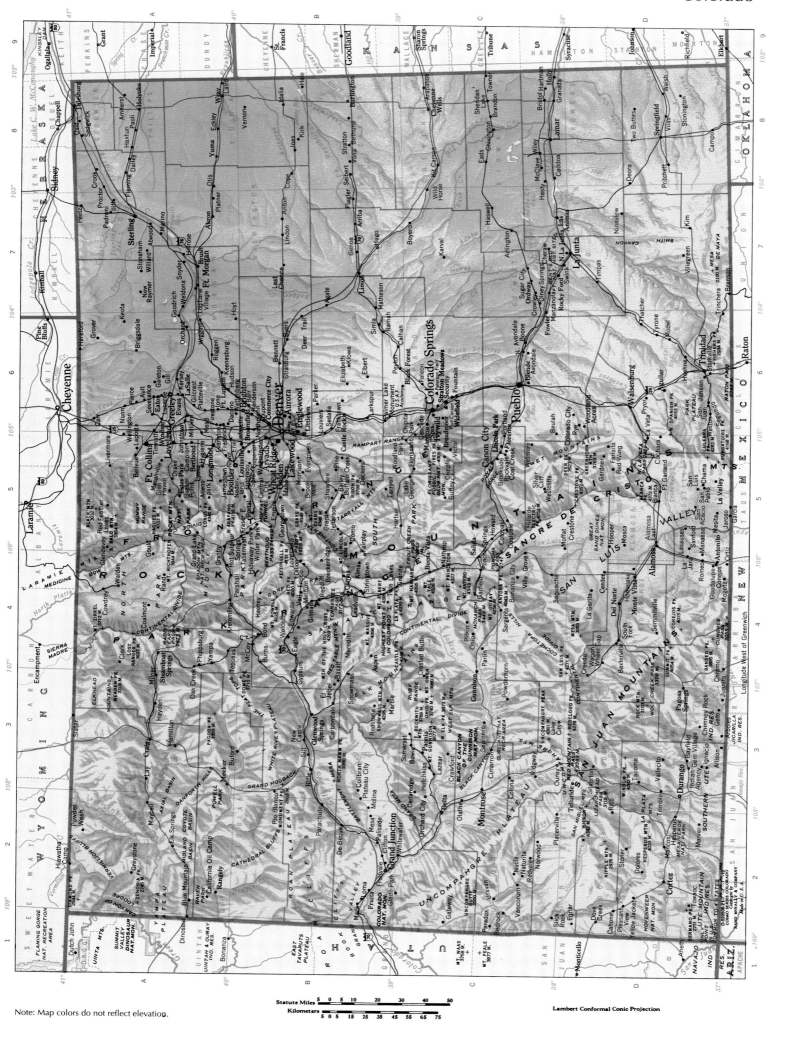

Note: Map colors do not reflect elevation.

Statute Miles 5 0 5 10 20 30 40 50
Kilometers 5 0 5 15 25 35 45 55 65 75

Lambert Conformal Conic Projection

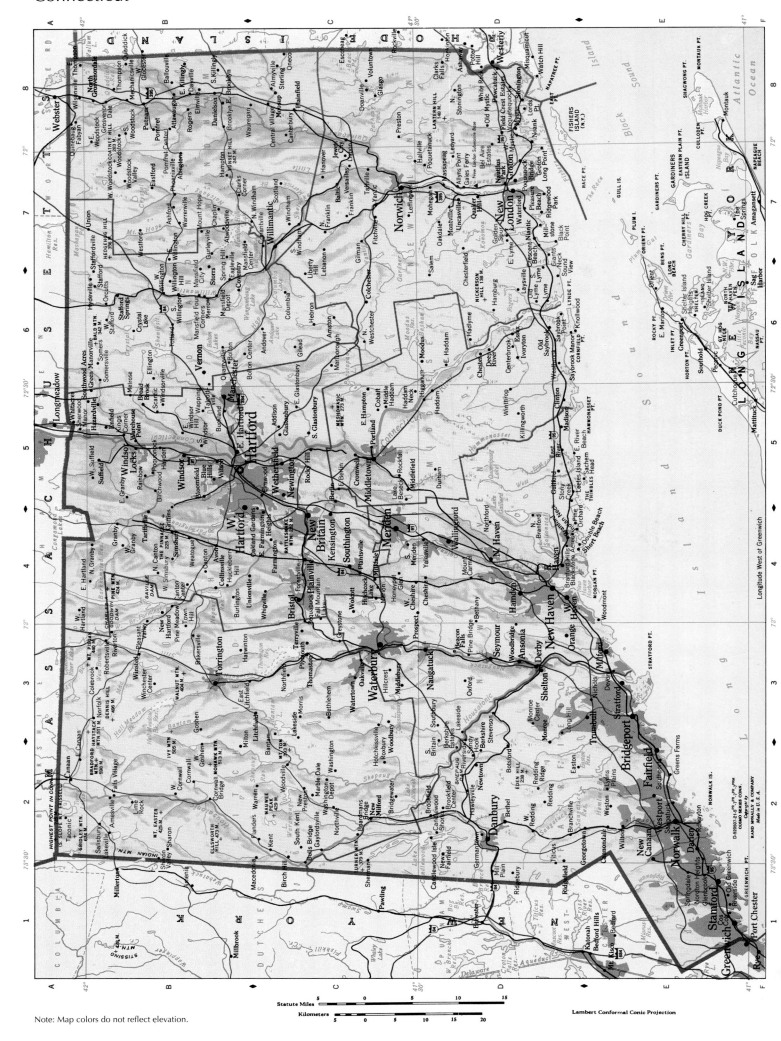

Note: Map colors do not reflect elevation.

Statute Miles

Kilometers

Lambert Conformal Conic Projection

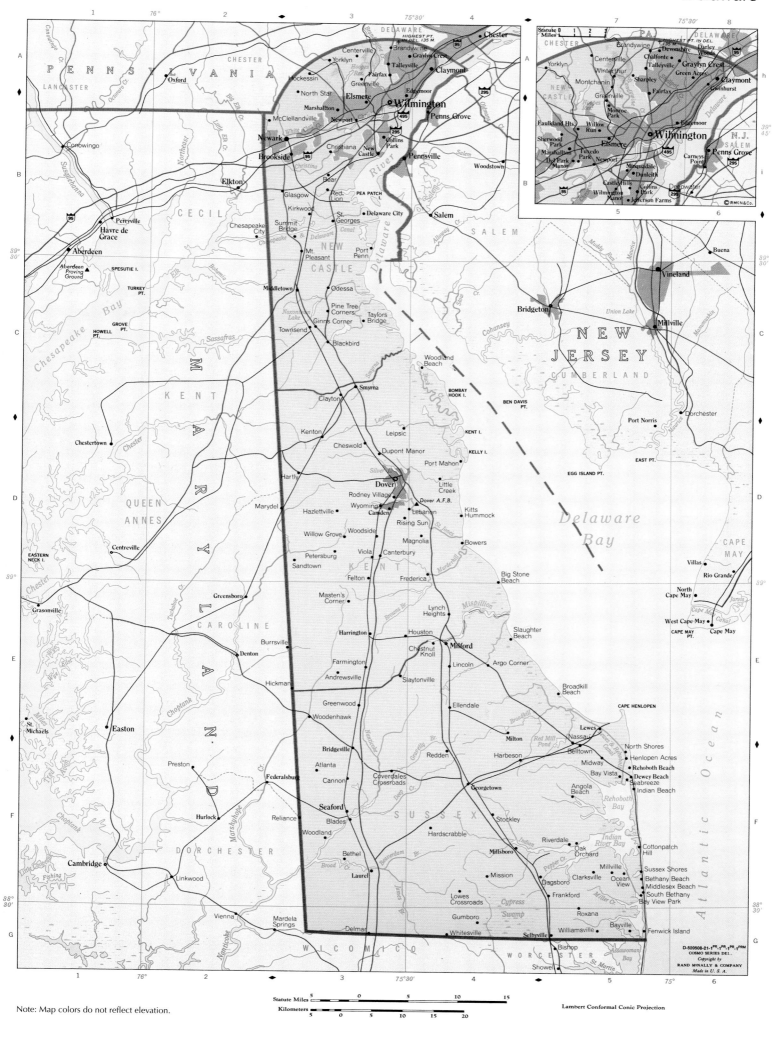

Note: Map colors do not reflect elevation.

Statute Miles

Kilometers

Lambert Conformal Conic Projection

D-520508-21-1PR-1PR-1PRM
COSMO SERIES DEL.
Copyright by
RAND McNALLY & COMPANY
Made in U.S.A.

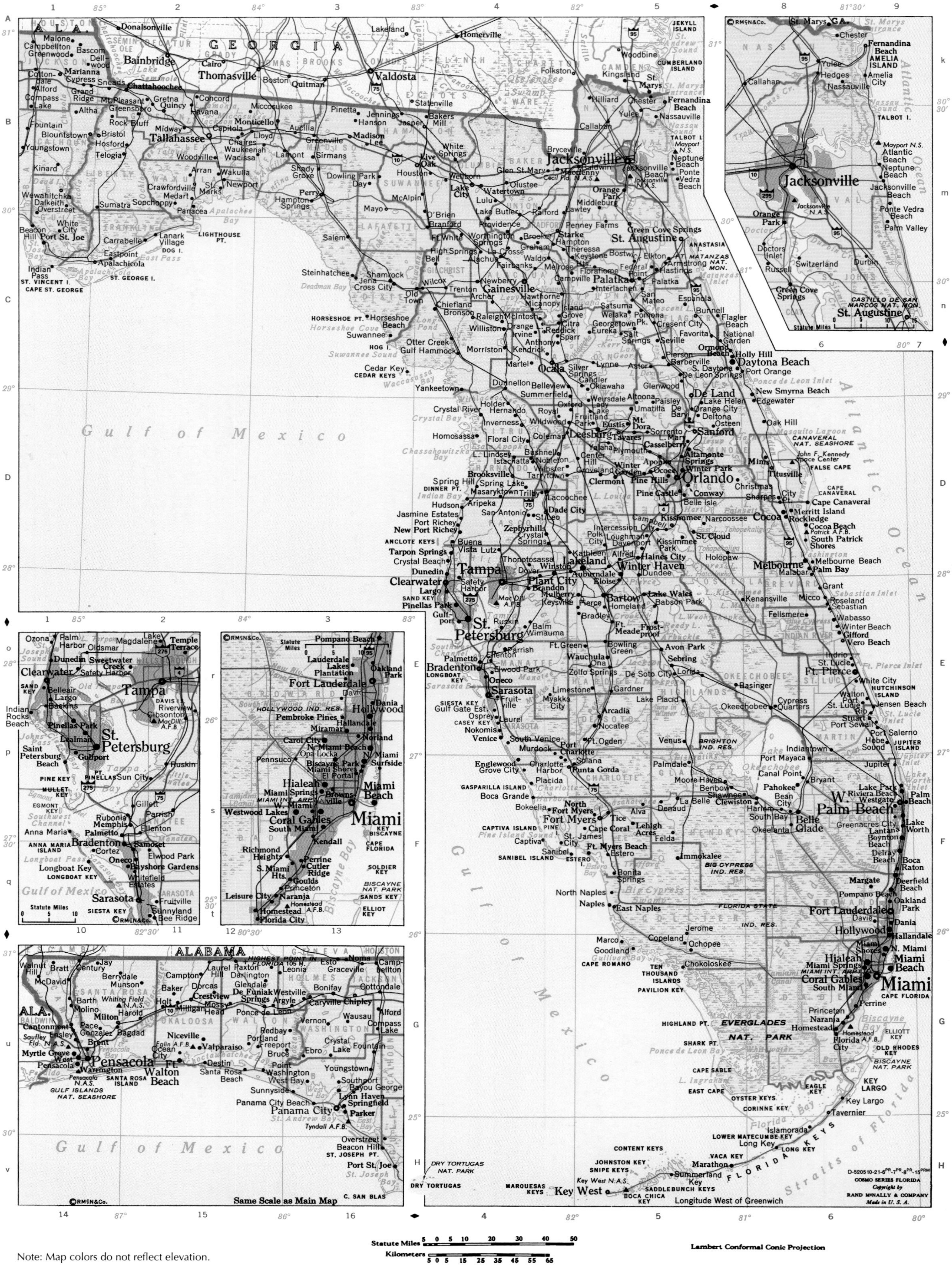

GEORGIA

ALABAMA

Gulf of Mexico

Atlantic Ocean

Straits of Florida

Jacksonville

St. Augustine

Tallahassee

Pensacola

Panama City

Tampa

St. Petersburg

Sarasota

Bradenton

Miami

Miami Beach

Fort Lauderdale

Hollywood

Hialeah

Coral Gables

W. Palm Beach

Orlando

Daytona Beach

Ocala

Gainesville

Palatka

Leesburg

Sanford

De Land

Melbourne

Cape Canaveral

Cocoa

Ft. Pierce

Lakeland

Winter Haven

Bartow

Clearwater

Plant City

Fort Myers

Naples

Key West

Key Largo

EVERGLADES NAT. PARK

DRY TORTUGAS NAT. PARK

Note: Map colors do not reflect elevation.

Statute Miles 5 0 5 10 20 30 40 50

Kilometers 5 0 5 15 25 35 45 55 65

Lambert Conformal Conic Projection

COSMO SERIES FLORIDA
Copyright by
RAND McNALLY & COMPANY
Made in U.S.A.

Same Scale as Main Map

Longitude West of Greenwich

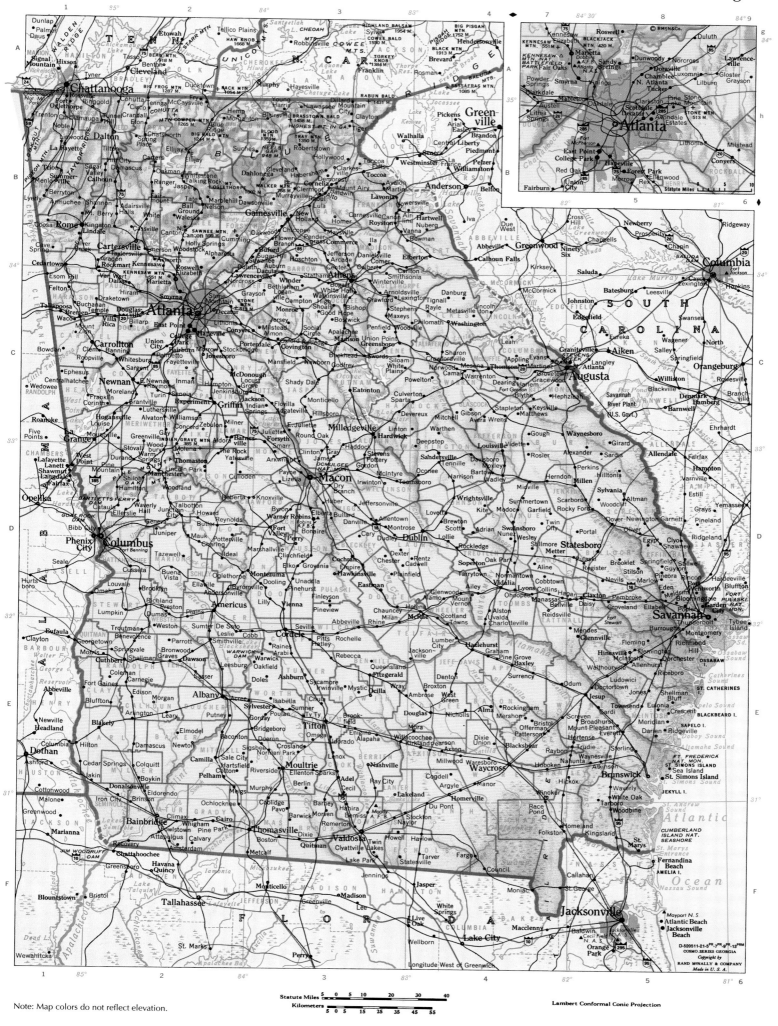

Note: Map colors do not reflect elevation.

Statute Miles
Kilometers

Lambert Conformal Conic Projection

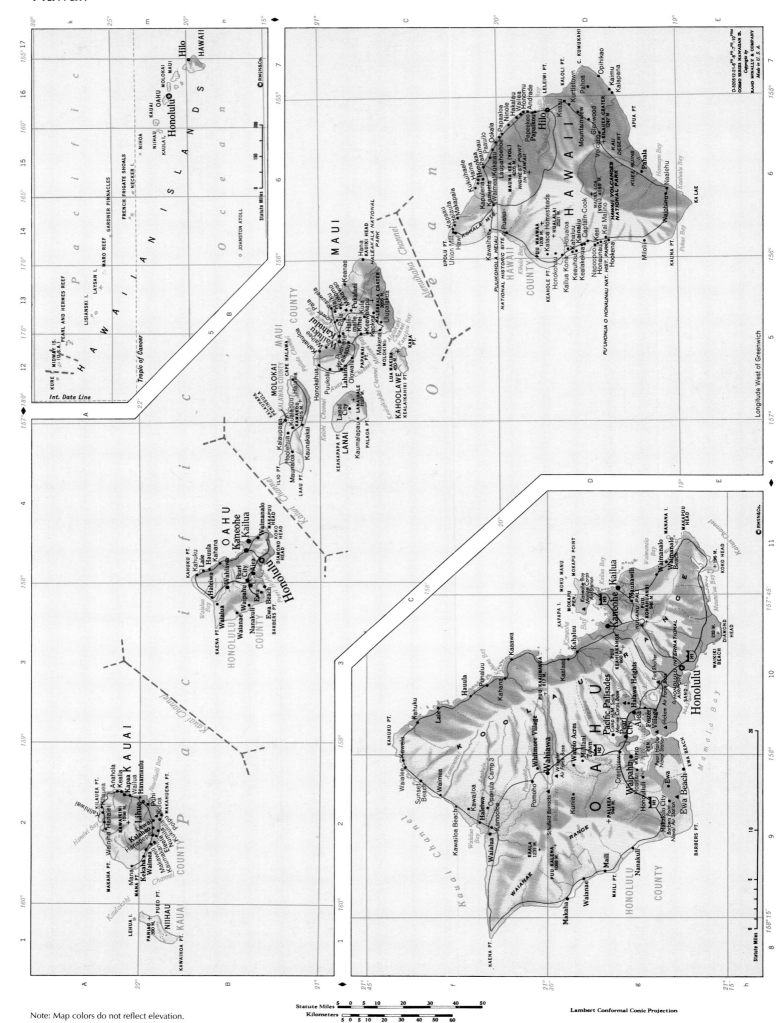

Note: Map colors do not reflect elevation.

Statute Miles 5 0 5 10   20   30   40   50
Kilometers 5 0 5 10 20 30 40 50 60

Lambert Conformal Conic Projection

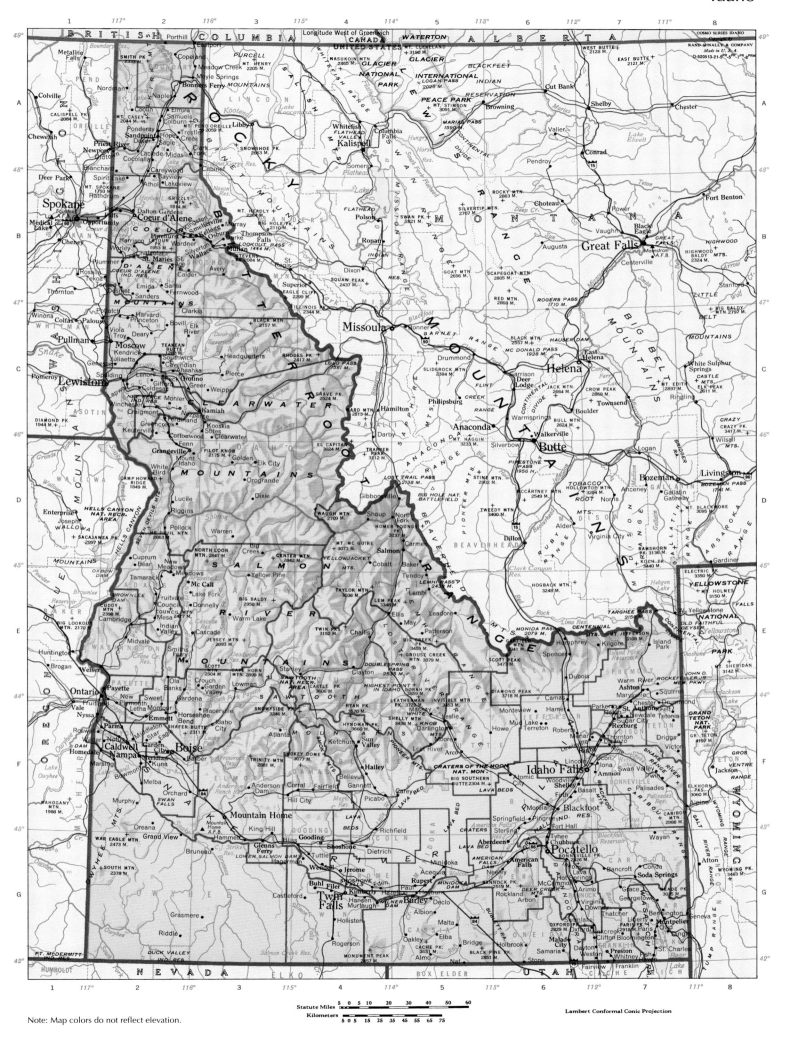

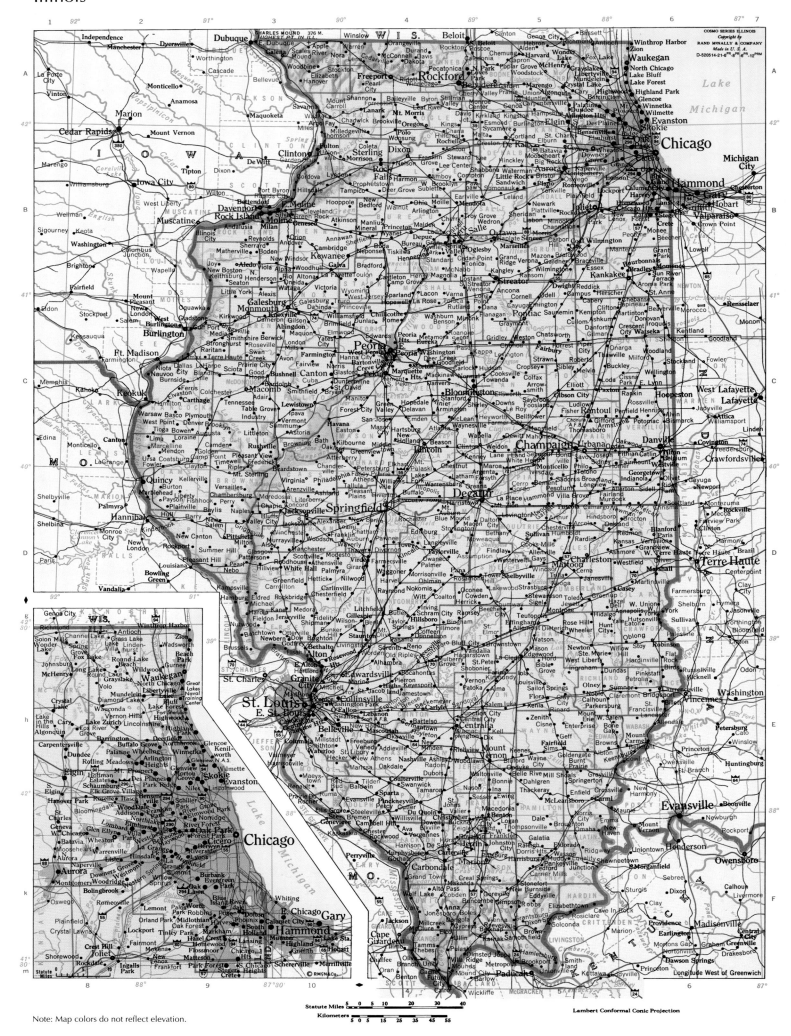

Note: Map colors do not reflect elevation.

Statute Miles

Kilometers

Lambert Conformal Conic Projection

Longitude West of Greenwich

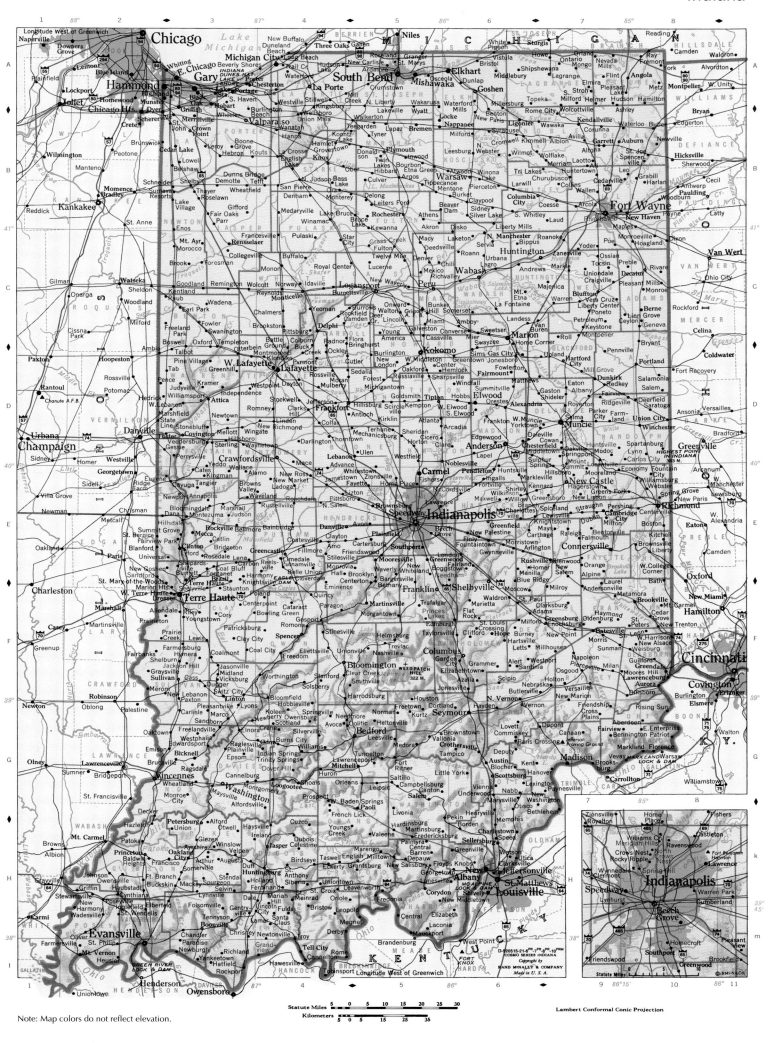

Note: Map colors do not reflect elevation.

Statute Miles
5 0 5 10 15 20 25 30
Kilometers
5 0 5   15   25   35

Lambert Conformal Conic Projection

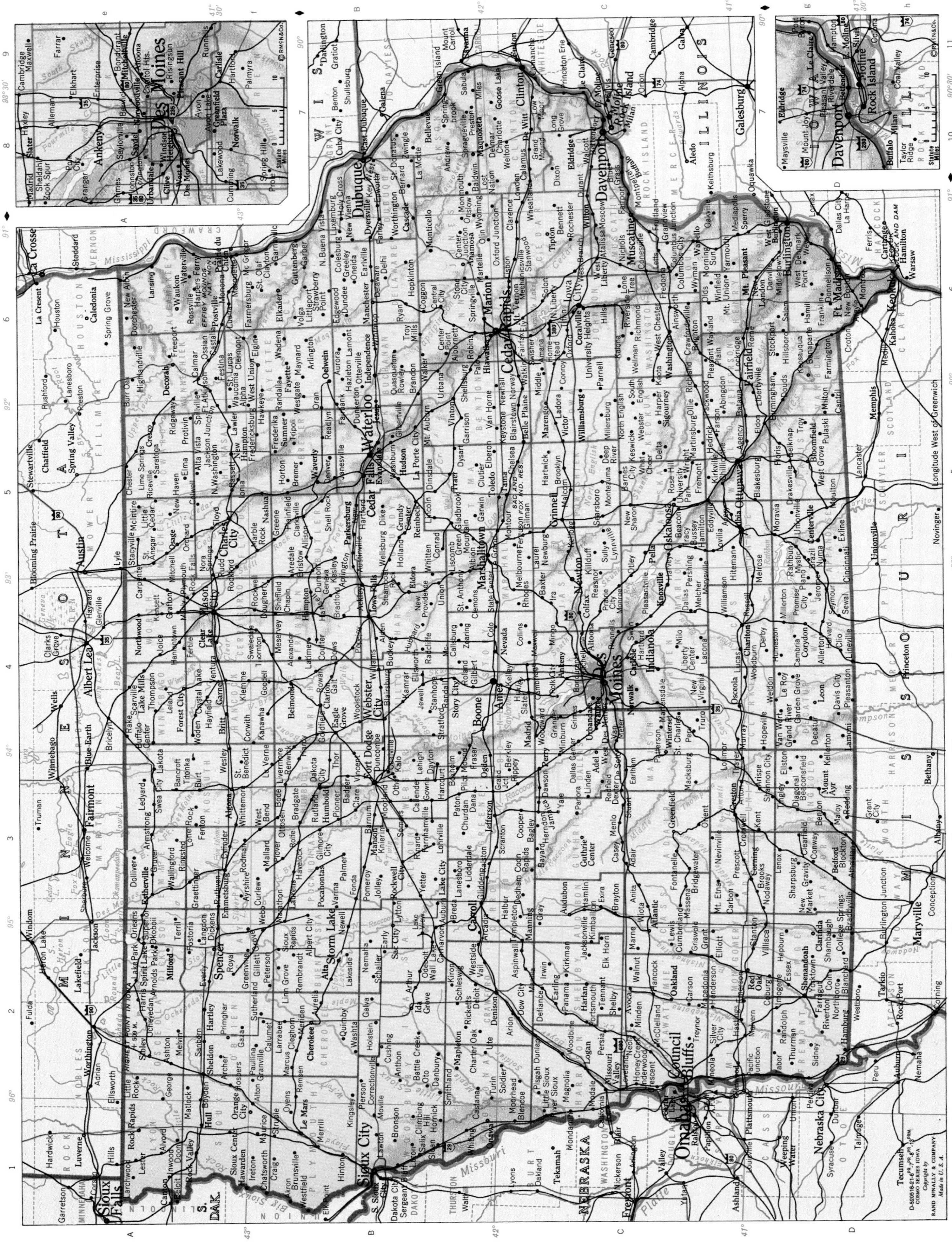

DES MOINES (inset map)

DAVENPORT (inset map)

Major cities and features: Sioux City, Council Bluffs, Omaha, Des Moines, Cedar Rapids, Waterloo, Cedar Falls, Dubuque, Davenport, Rock Island, Clinton, Muscatine, Burlington, Ft. Madison, Keokuk, Mason City, Charles City, Fort Dodge, Marshalltown, Ames, Boone, Oskaloosa, Ottumwa, Fairfield, Mt. Pleasant, Indianola, Storm Lake, Spencer, Fairmont, Albert Lea, Winterset, Newton, Grinnell, Marion, Galesburg, Decorah, Oelwein, La Crosse

Surrounding states: MINNESOTA, WISCONSIN, ILLINOIS, MISSOURI, NEBRASKA, S. DAK.

Rivers: Mississippi, Missouri, Des Moines, Cedar, Iowa, Skunk, Big Sioux

Note: Map colors do not reflect elevation.

Statute Miles 5 0 5 10 20 30 40

Kilometers 5 0 5 15 25 35 45 55

Lambert Conformal Conic Projection

RAND M9NALLY & COMPANY

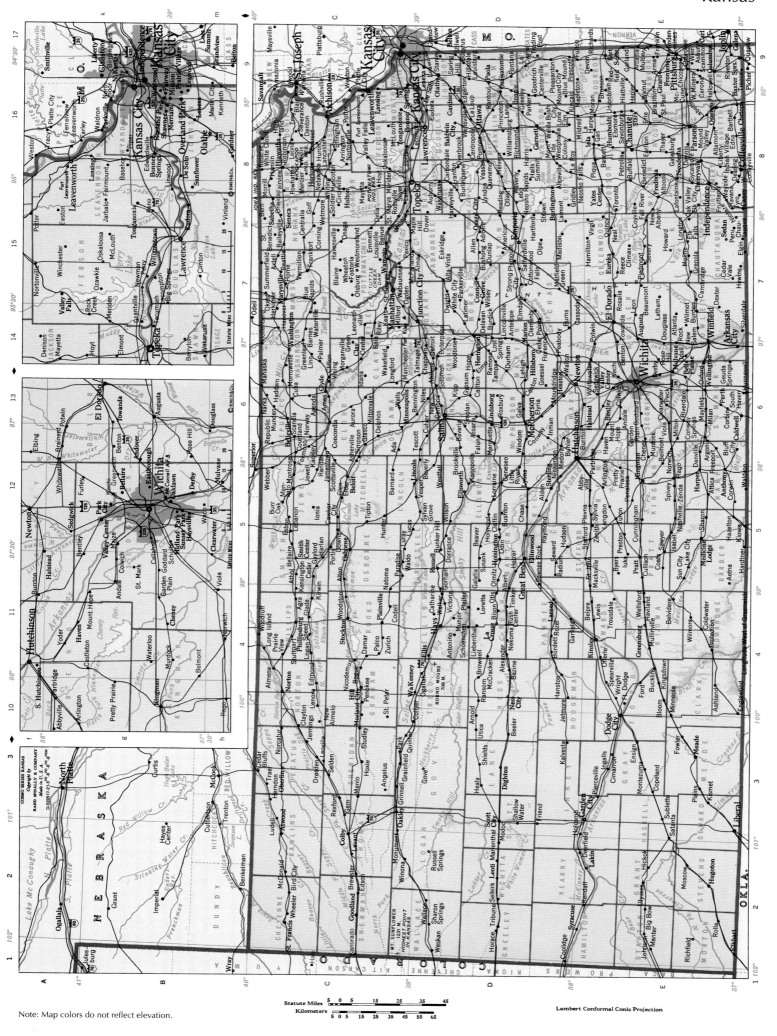

Note: Map colors do not reflect elevation.

Statute Miles
Kilometers

Lambert Conformal Conic Projection

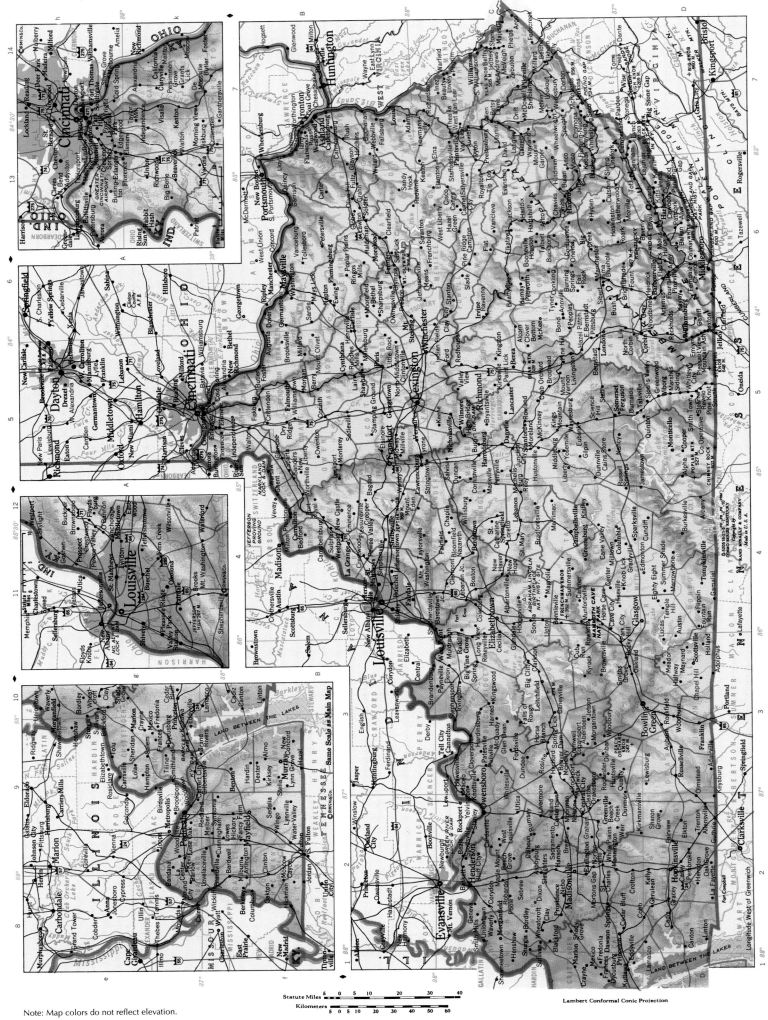

Note: Map colors do not reflect elevation.

Statute Miles
Kilometers

Lambert Conformal Conic Projection

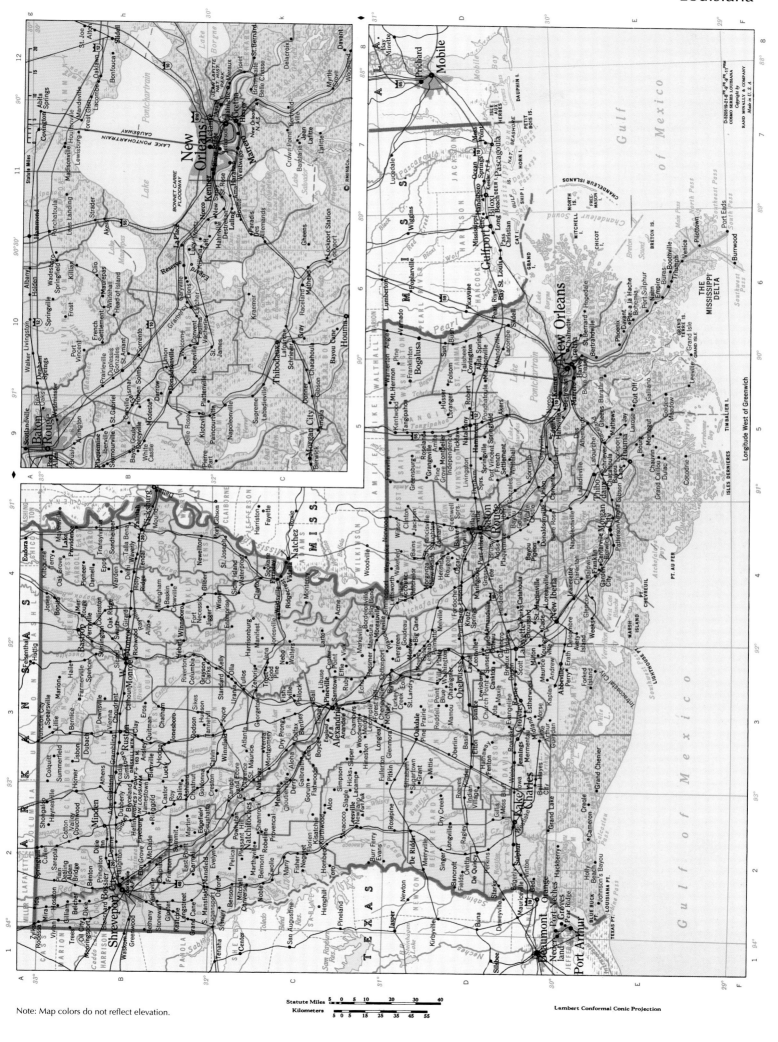

Note: Map colors do not reflect elevation.

Statute Miles
Kilometers

Lambert Conformal Conic Projection

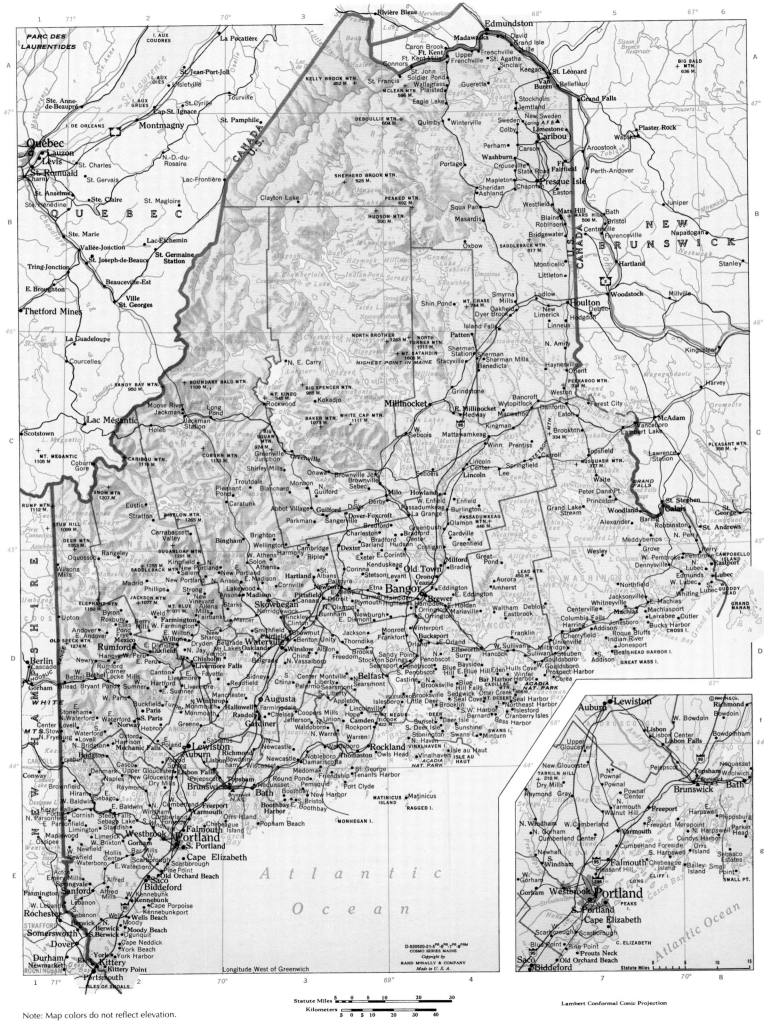

Note: Map colors do not reflect elevation.

D-520520-21-5 PR-8 PR-7 PR-9 PPM
COSMO SERIES MAINE
Copyright by
RAND MCNALLY & COMPANY
Made in U.S.A.

Statute Miles
Kilometers

Longitude West of Greenwich

Lambert Conformal Conic Projection

Statute Miles

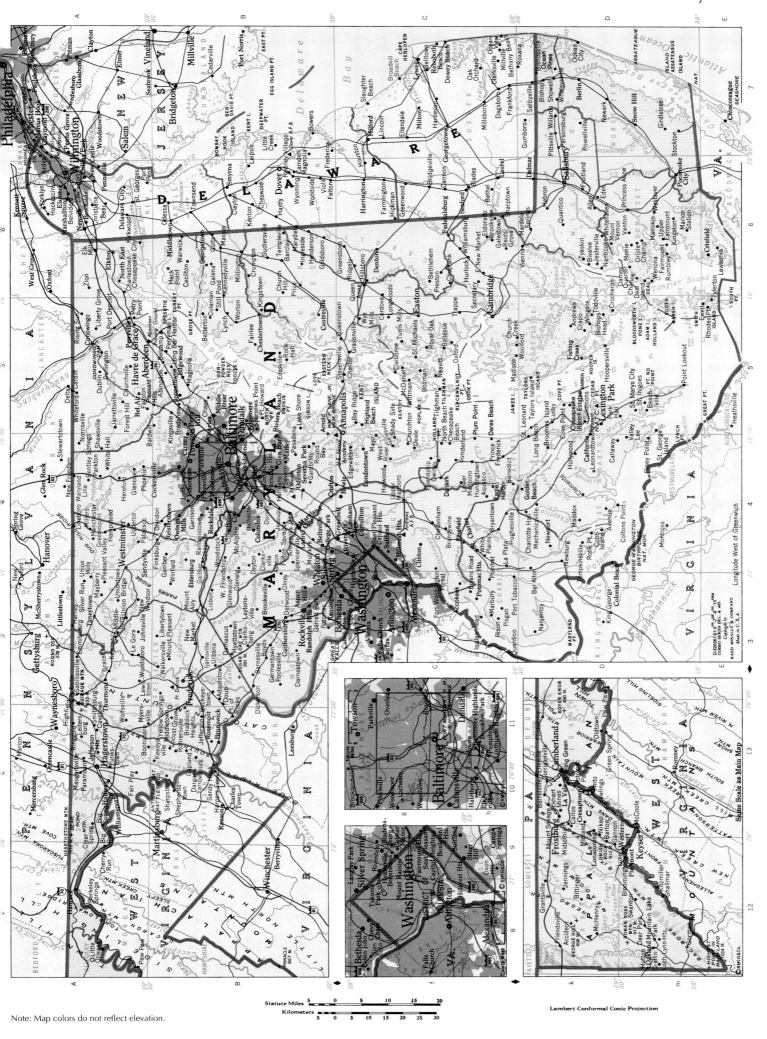

Note: Map colors do not reflect elevation.

Statute Miles   5   0   5   10   15   20
Kilometers   5   0   5   10   15   20   25   30

Lambert Conformal Conic Projection

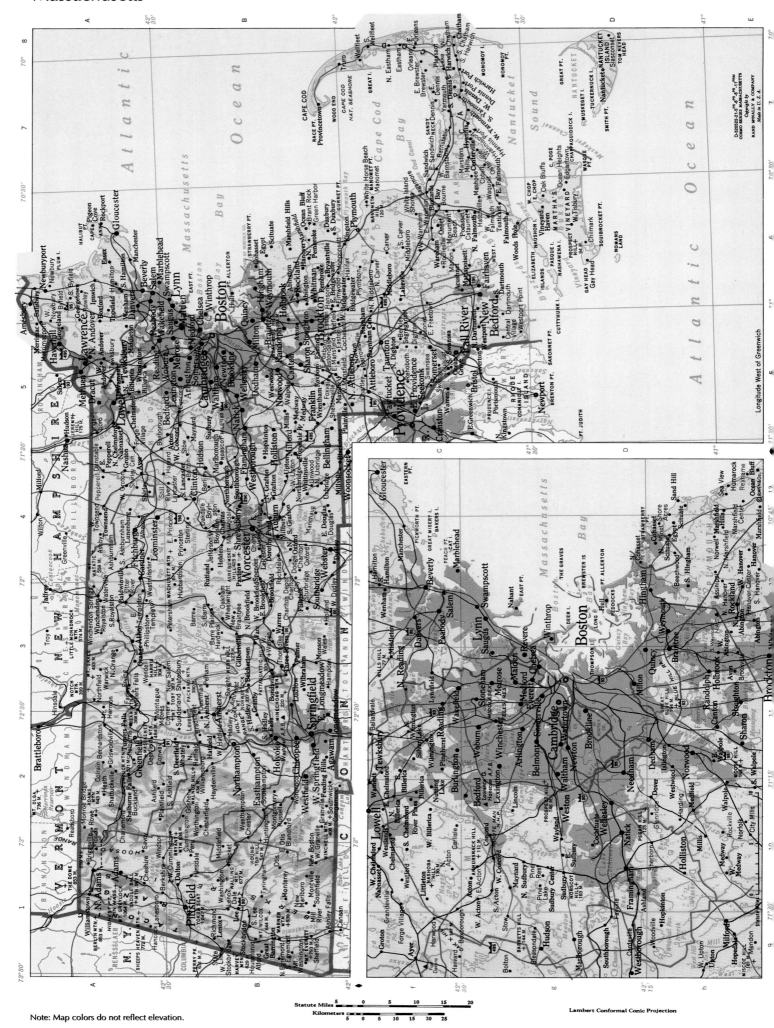

Note: Map colors do not reflect elevation.

Statute Miles

Kilometers

Lambert Conformal Conic Projection

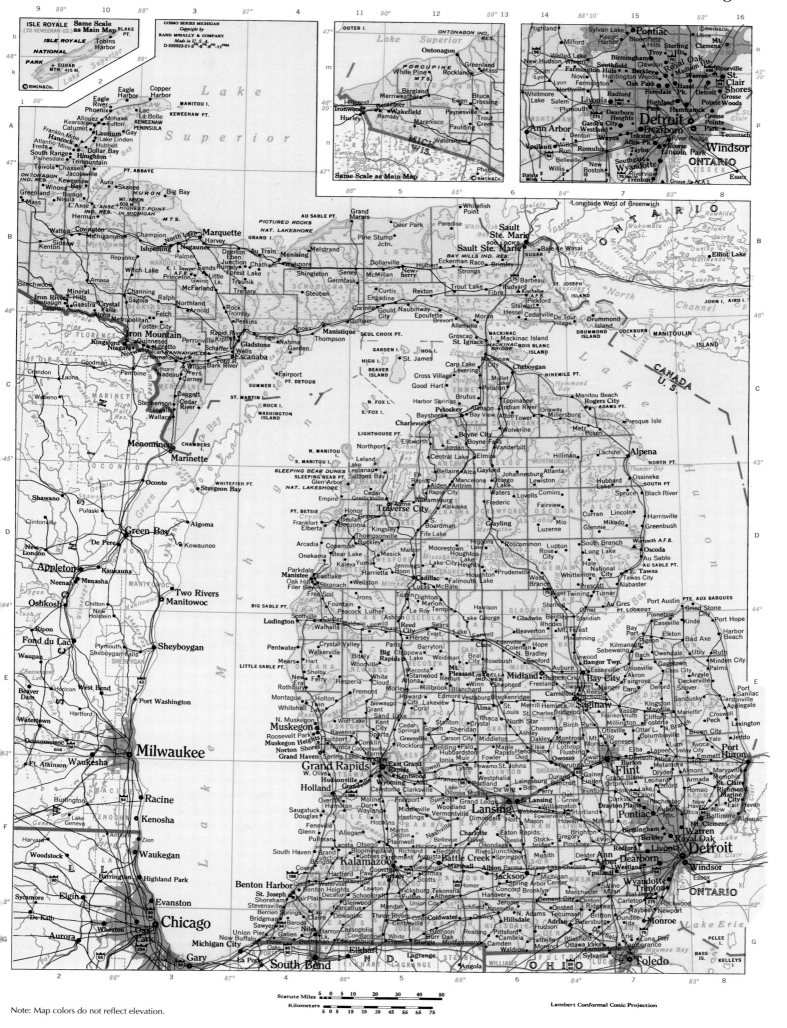

Statute Miles 5 0 5 10 20 30 40 50

Kilometers 5 0 5 15 25 35 45 55 65 75

Lambert Conformal Conic Projection

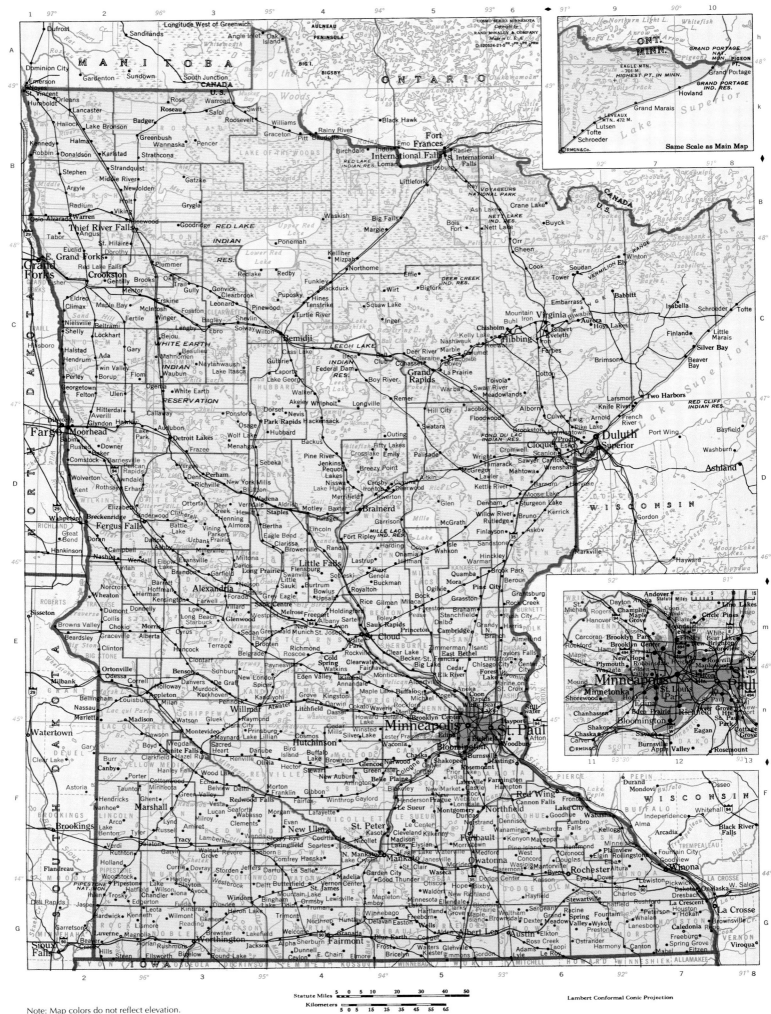

Note: Map colors do not reflect elevation.

Statute Miles

Kilometers

Lambert Conformal Conic Projection

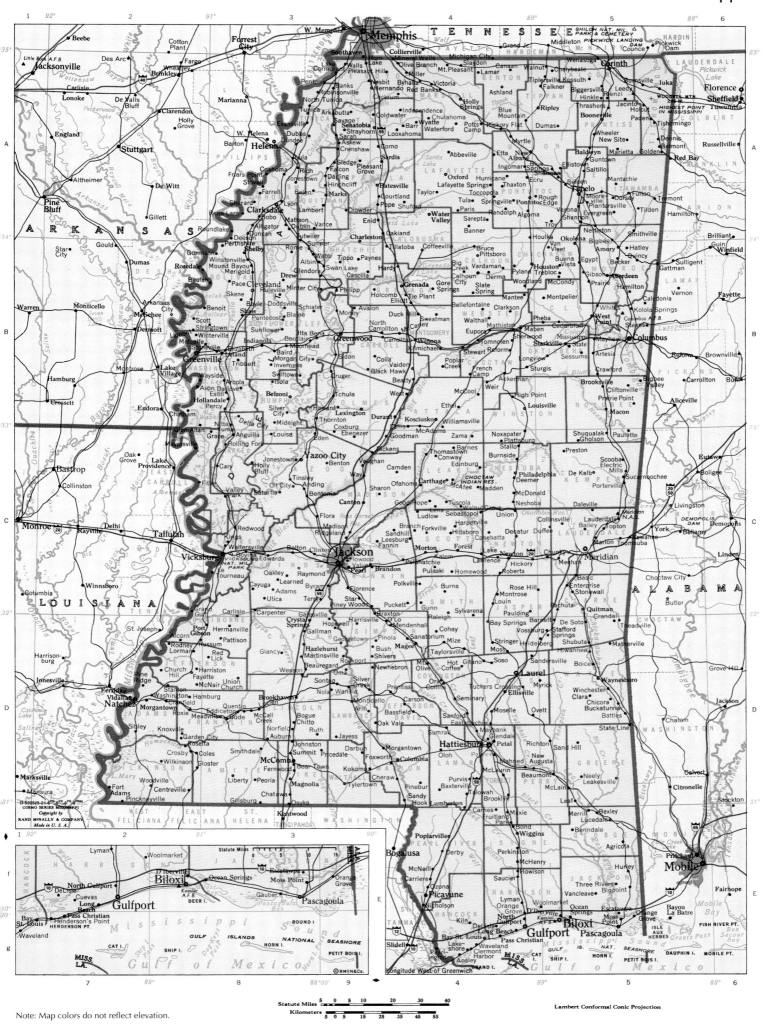

Note: Map colors do not reflect elevation.

Statute Miles
Kilometers

Lambert Conformal Conic Projection

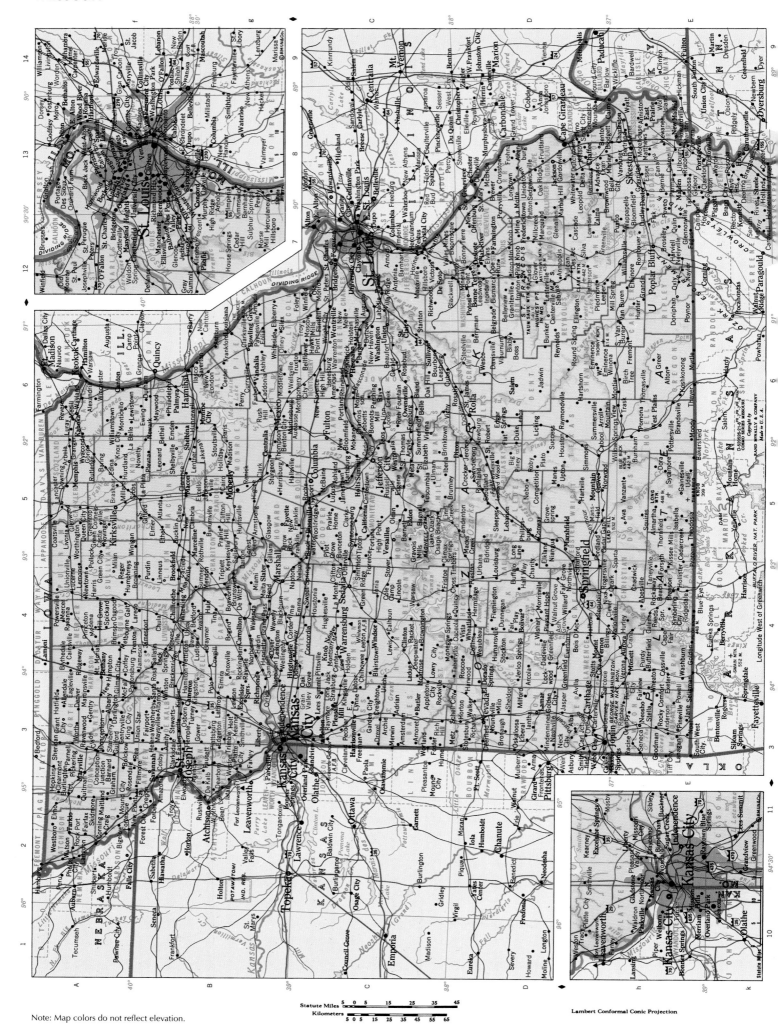

Note: Map colors do not reflect elevation.

Statute Miles 5 0 5 15 25 35 45
Kilometers 5 0 5 15 25 35 45 55 65

Lambert Conformal Conic Projection

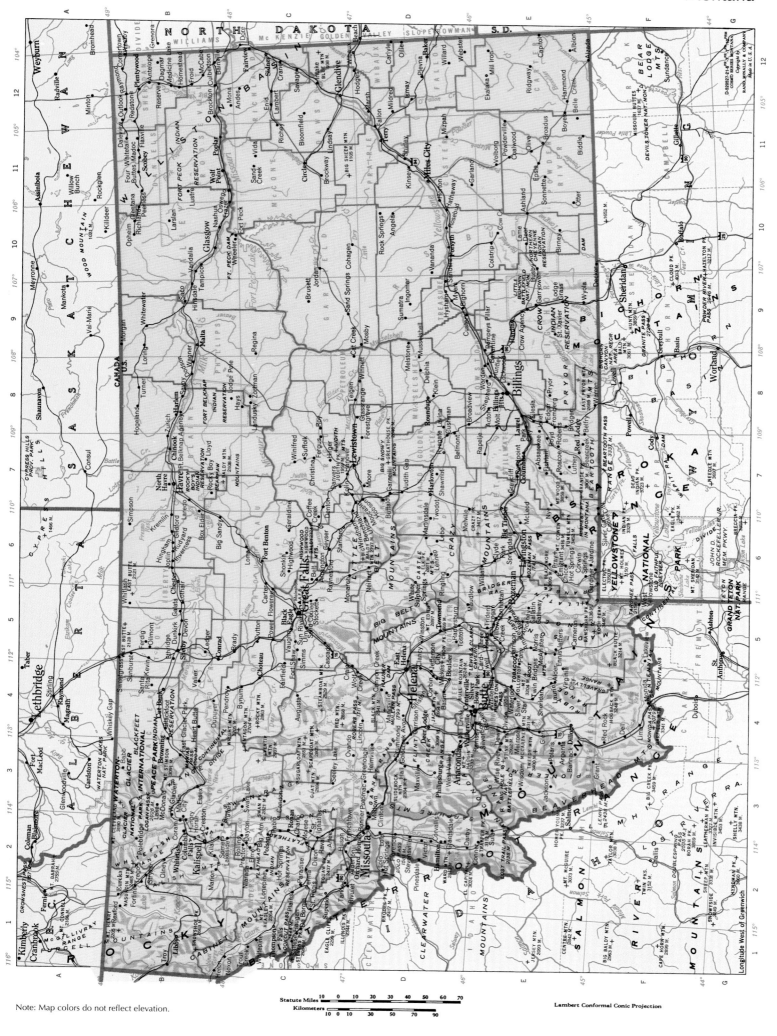

Note: Map colors do not reflect elevation.

Statute Miles 10 0 10 20 30 40 50 60 70

Kilometers 10 0 10 30 50 70 90

Lambert Conformal Conic Projection

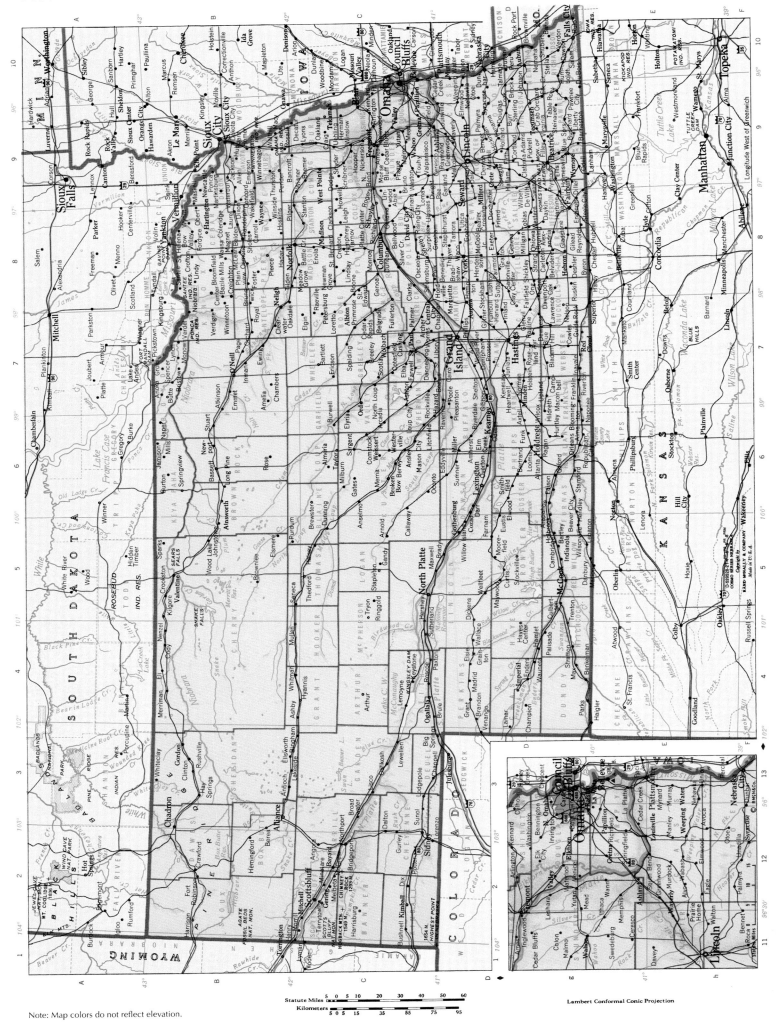

Note: Map colors do not reflect elevation.

Statute Miles   5 0 5 10   20   30   40   50   60
Kilometers   5 0 5   15   35   55   75   95

Lambert Conformal Conic Projection

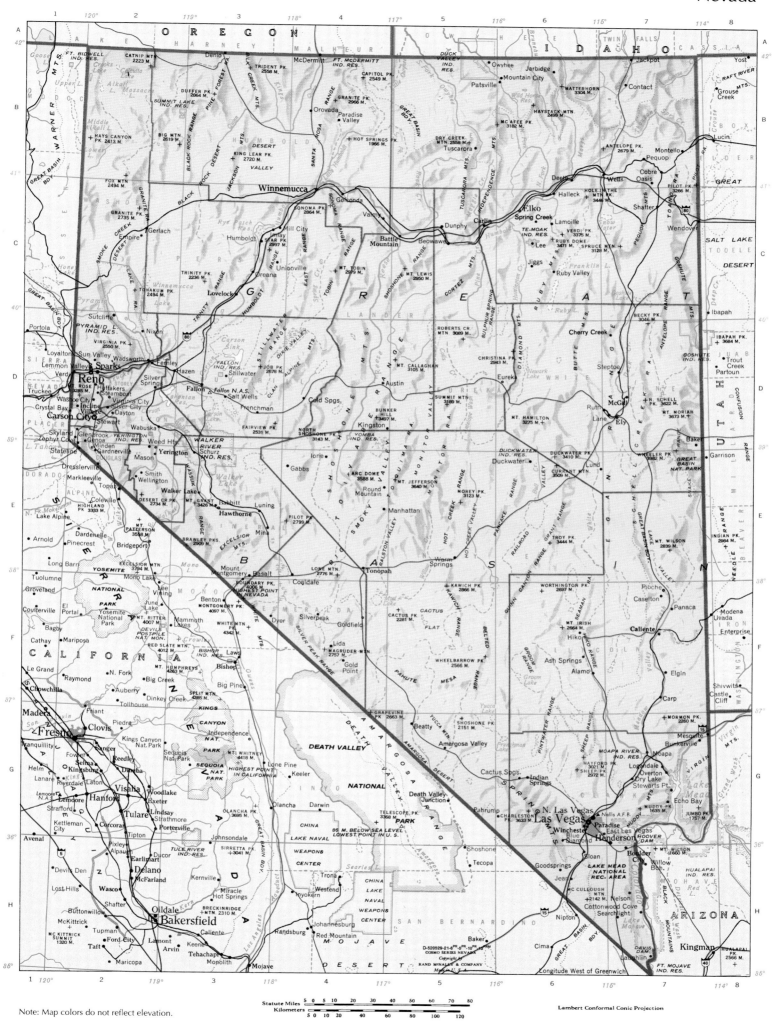

Note: Map colors do not reflect elevation.

Statute Miles
Kilometers

Lambert Conformal Conic Projection

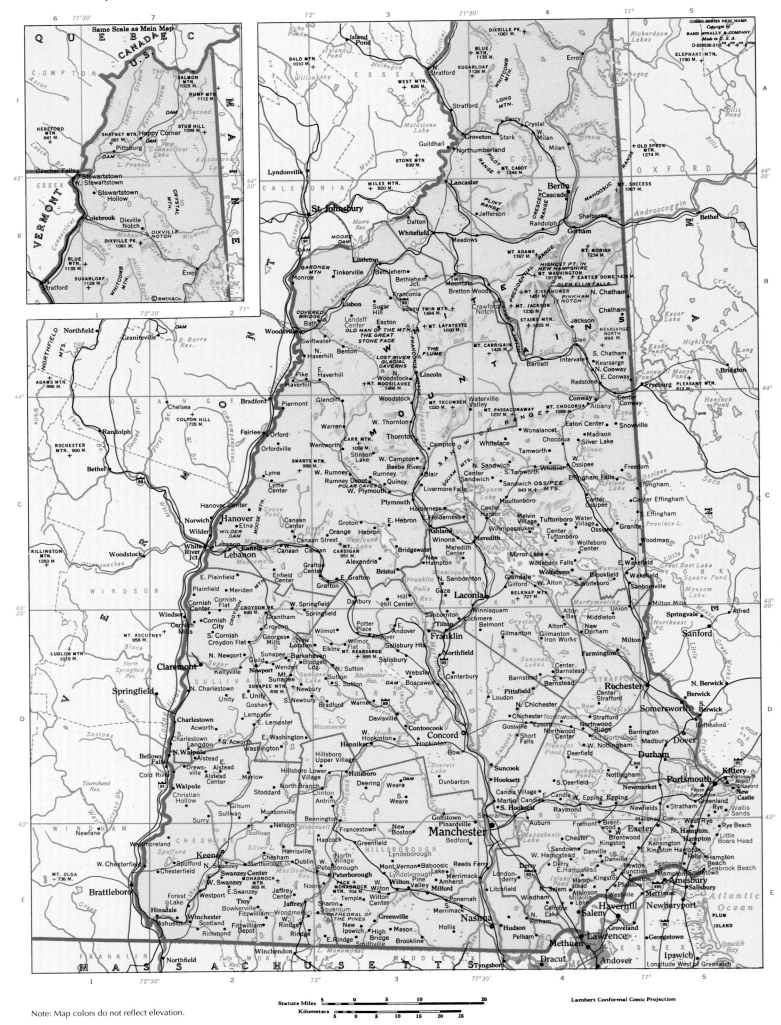

Note: Map colors do not reflect elevation.

Statute Miles
Kilometers

Lambert Conformal Conic Projection

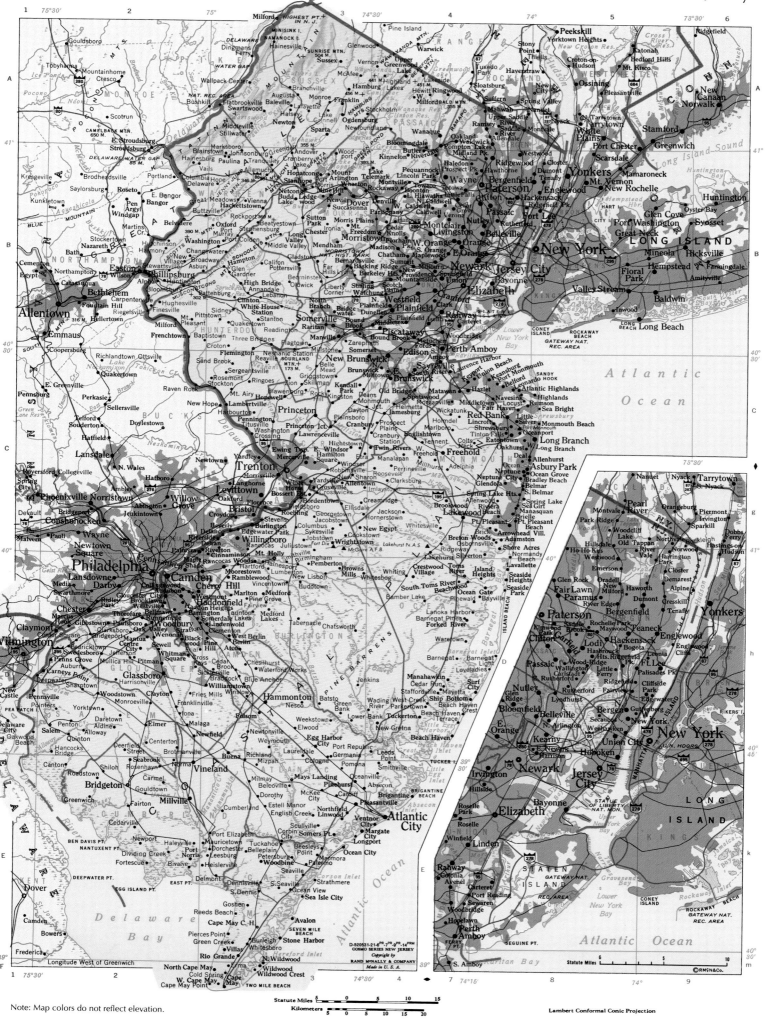

Note: Map colors do not reflect elevation.

Statute Miles

Kilometers

Lambert Conformal Conic Projection

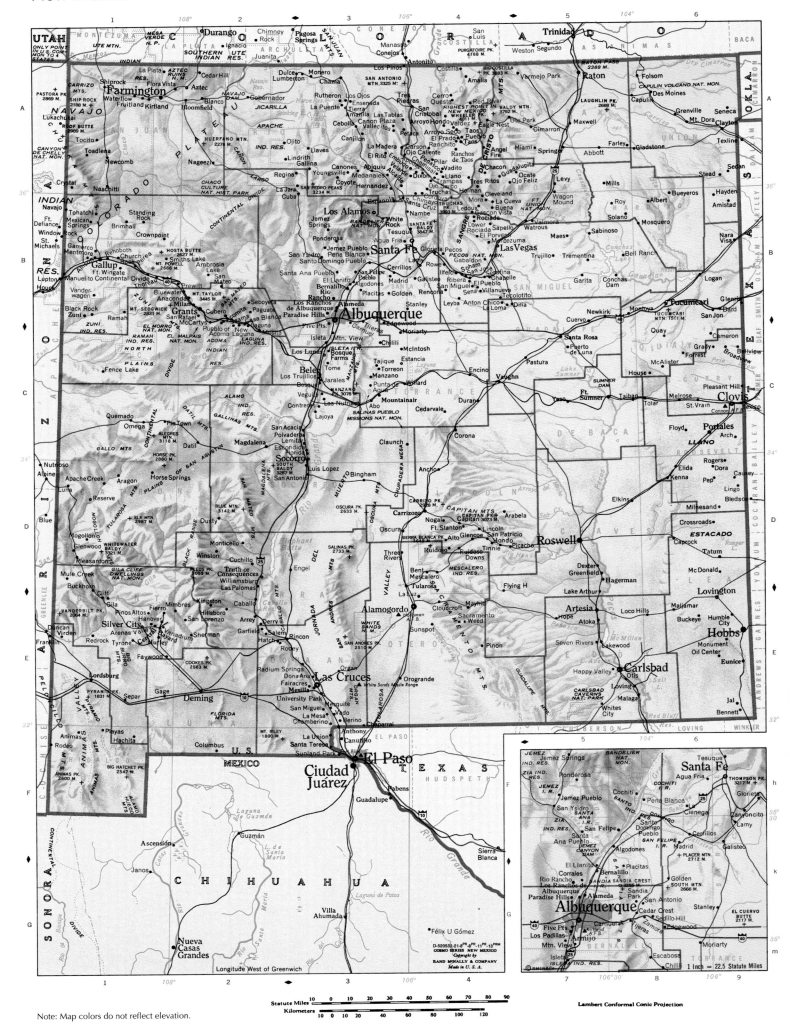

Note: Map colors do not reflect elevation.

Statute Miles 10 0 10 20 30 40 50 60 70 80 90
Kilometers 10 0 10 20 40 60 80 100 120

Lambert Conformal Conic Projection

1 Inch = 22.5 Statute Miles

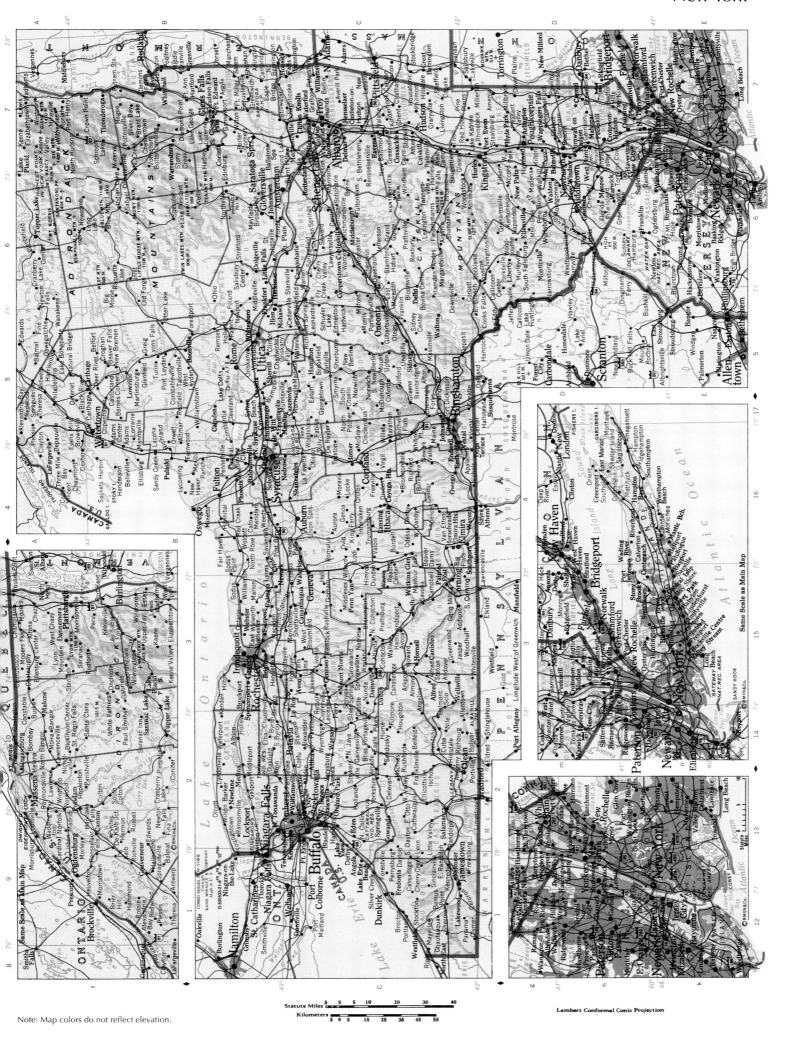

Note: Map colors do not reflect elevation.

Statute Miles 5 0 5 10 20 30 40
Kilometers 5 0 5 15 25 35 45 55

Lambert Conformal Conic Projection

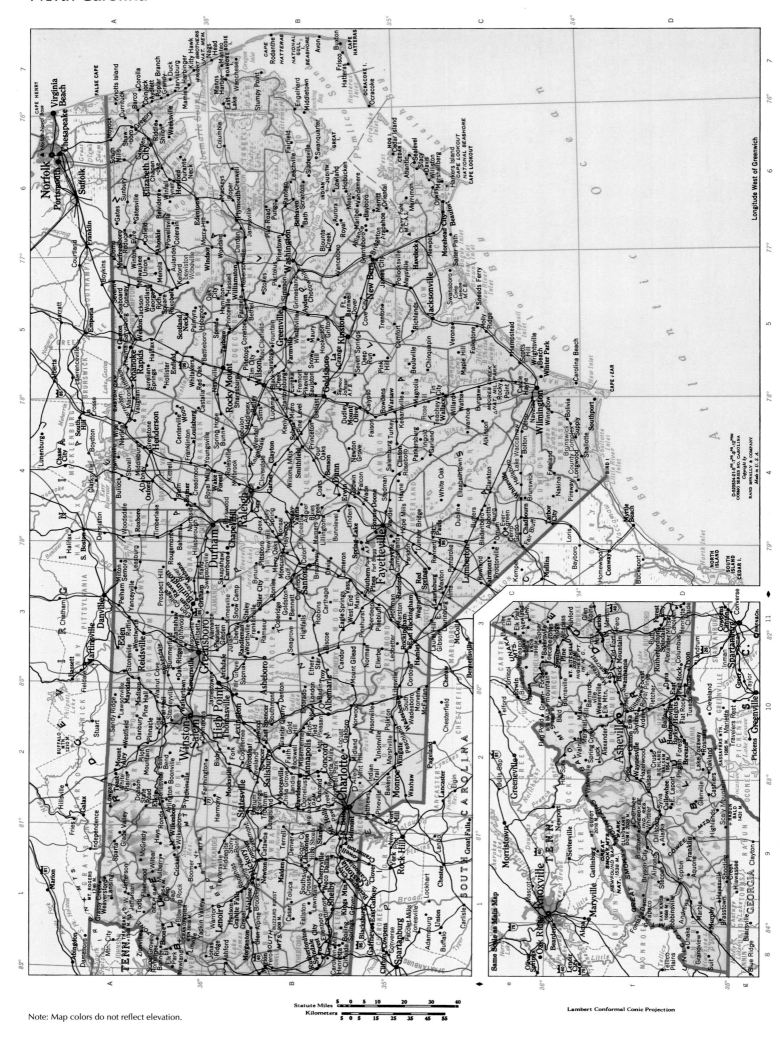

Note: Map colors do not reflect elevation.

Statute Miles
5 0 5 10 20 30 40
Kilometers
5 0 5 15 25 35 45 55

Lambert Conformal Conic Projection

Same Scale as Main Map

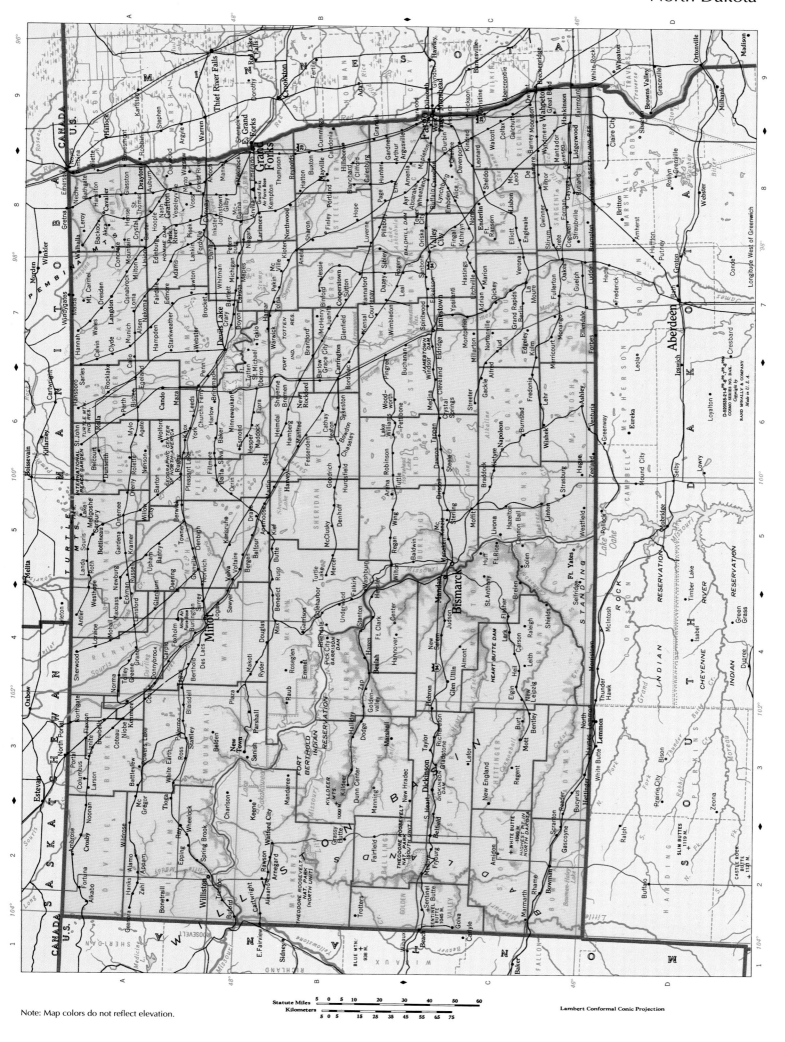

Note: Map colors do not reflect elevation.

Statute Miles 5 0 5 10   20   30   40   50   60
Kilometers 5 0 5   15   25   35   45   55 65 75

Lambert Conformal Conic Projection

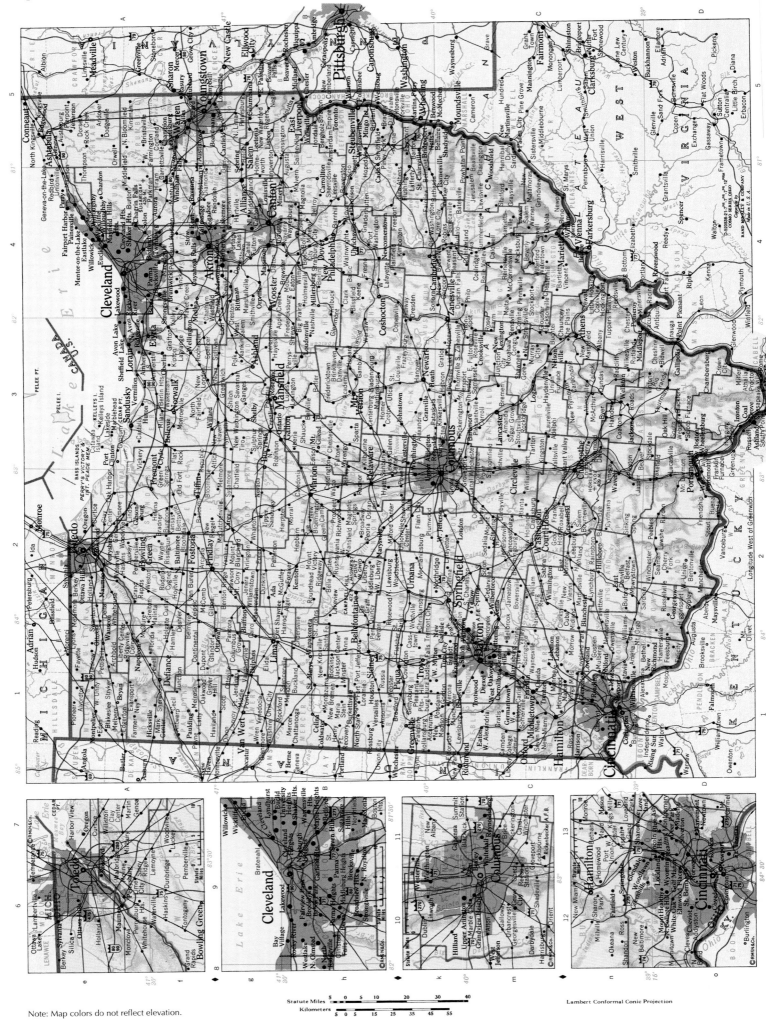

Note: Map colors do not reflect elevation.

Statute Miles
5 0 5 10 20 30 40

Kilometers
5 0 5 15 25 35 45 55

Lambert Conformal Conic Projection

Note: Map colors do not reflect elevation.

Statute Miles
Kilometers

Lambert Conformal Conic Projection

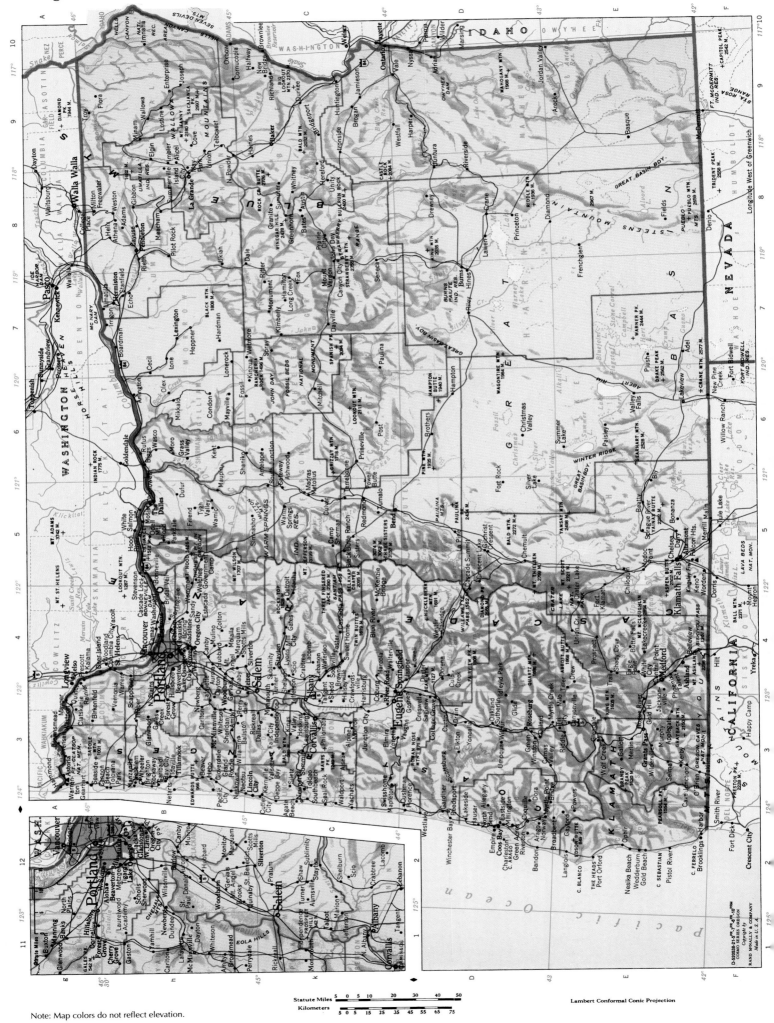

Statute Miles
Kilometers

Lambert Conformal Conic Projection

Note: Map colors do not reflect elevation.

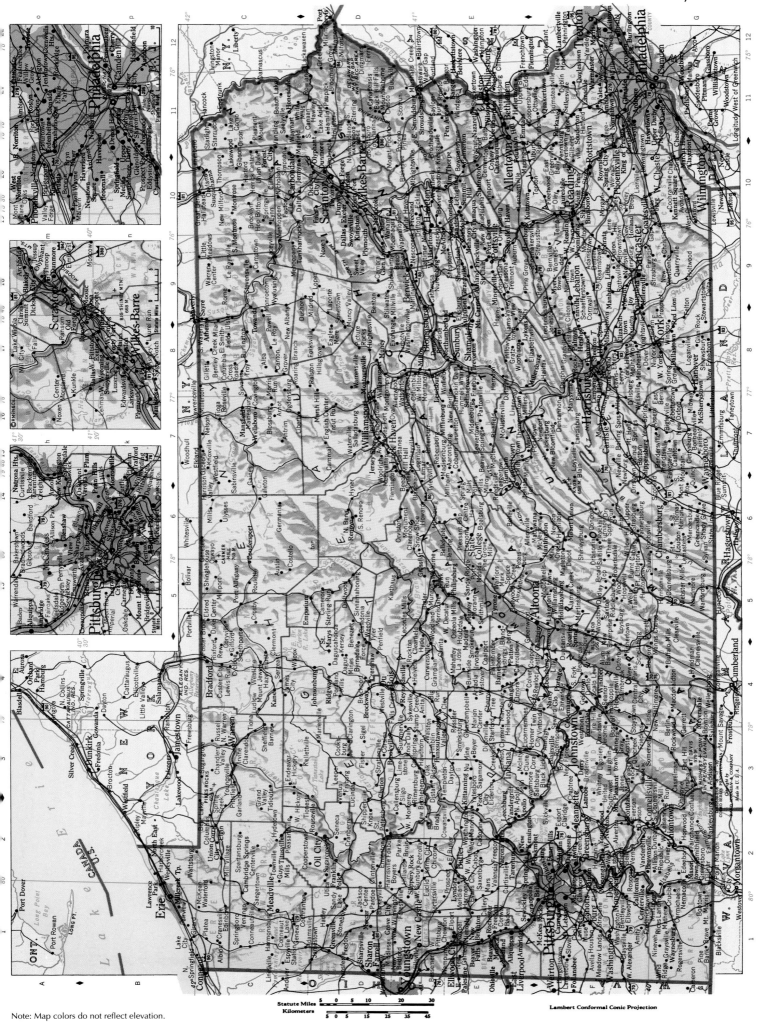

Note: Map colors do not reflect elevation.

Statute Miles
Kilometers

Lambert Conformal Conic Projection

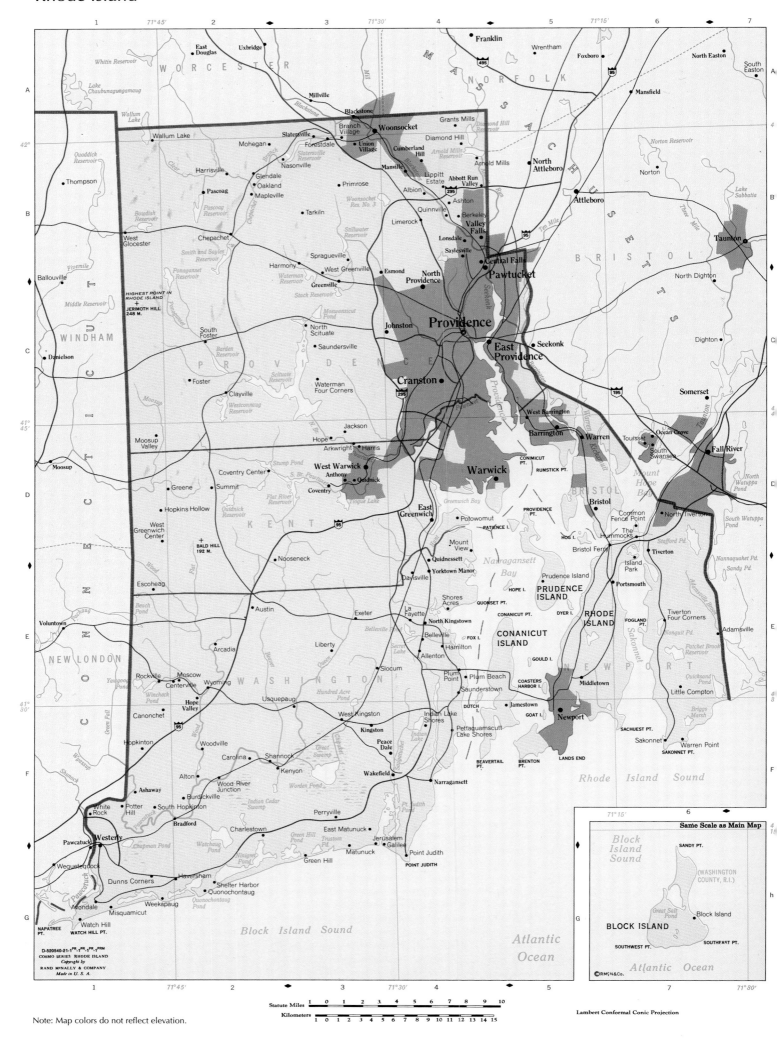

Note: Map colors do not reflect elevation.

Statute Miles 1 0 1 2 3 4 5 6 7 8 9 10
Kilometers 1 0 1 2 3 4 5 6 7 8 9 10 11 12 13 14 15

Lambert Conformal Conic Projection

Same Scale as Main Map

Block Island Sound

(WASHINGTON COUNTY, R.I.)

SANDY PT.

BLOCK ISLAND

Block Island

SOUTHWEST PT.   SOUTHEAST PT.

Atlantic Ocean

©RMcN&Co.

D-520540-21-1ᴾᴿ-1ᴾᴿ-1ᴾᴿ-1ᴾᴿᴹ
COSMO SERIES RHODE ISLAND
Copyright by
RAND MℂNALLY & COMPANY
Made in U.S.A.

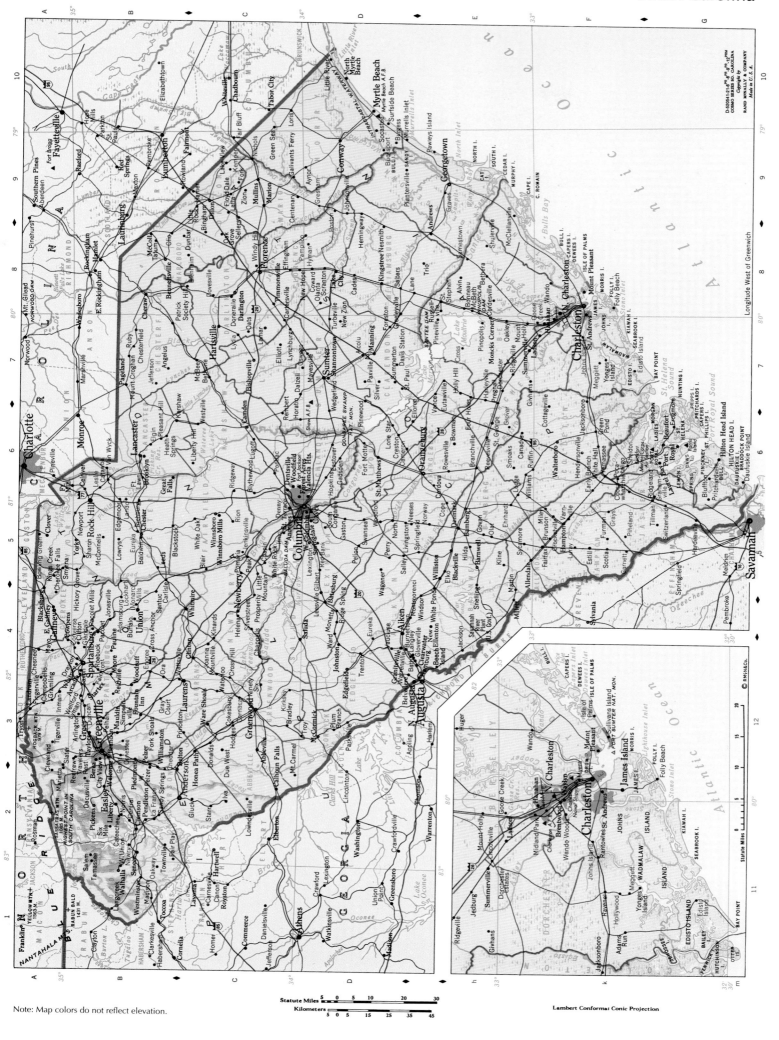

Note: Map colors do not reflect elevation.

Statute Miles
Kilometers

Lambert Conformal Conic Projection

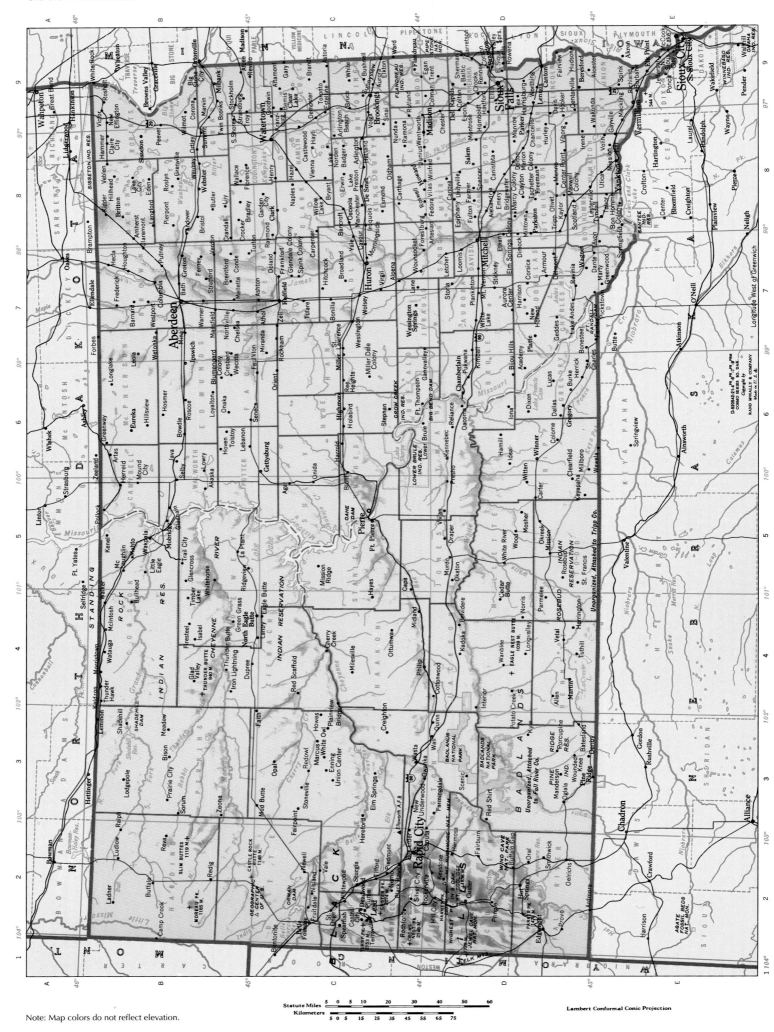

Note: Map colors do not reflect elevation.

Statute Miles 5 0 5 10 20 30 40 50 60
Kilometers 5 0 5 15 25 35 45 55 65 75

Lambert Conformal Conic Projection

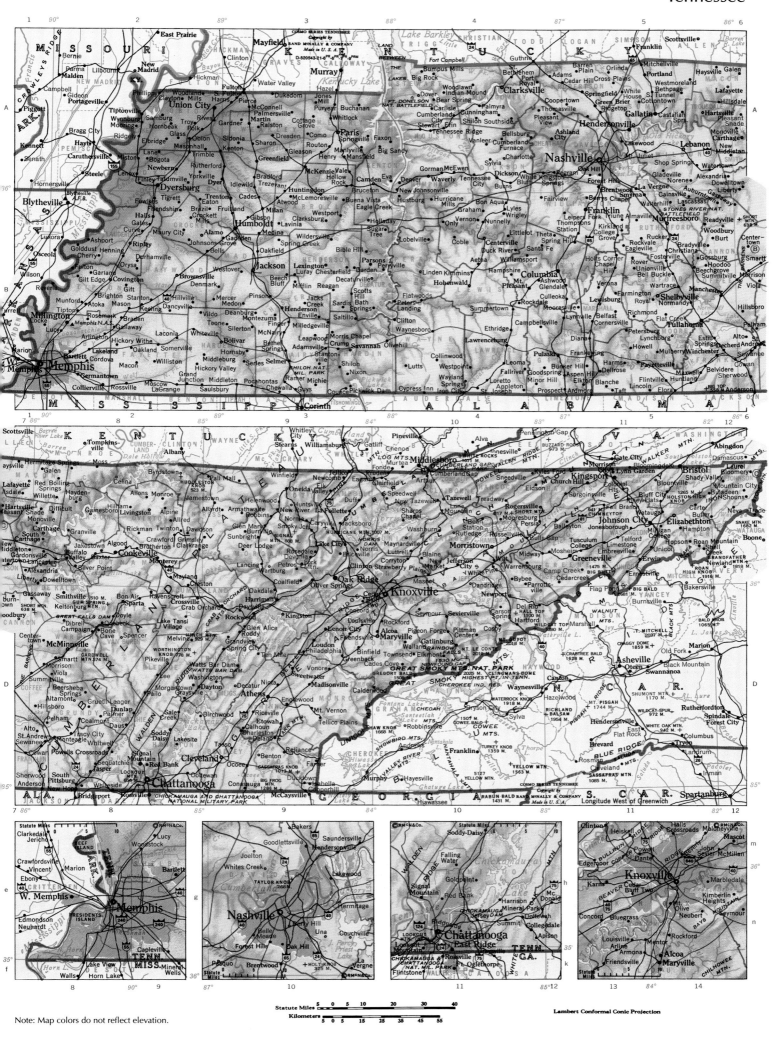

Note: Map colors do not reflect elevation.

Statute Miles 5 0 5 10 20 30 40
Kilometers 5 0 5 15 25 35 45 55

Lambert Conformal Conic Projection

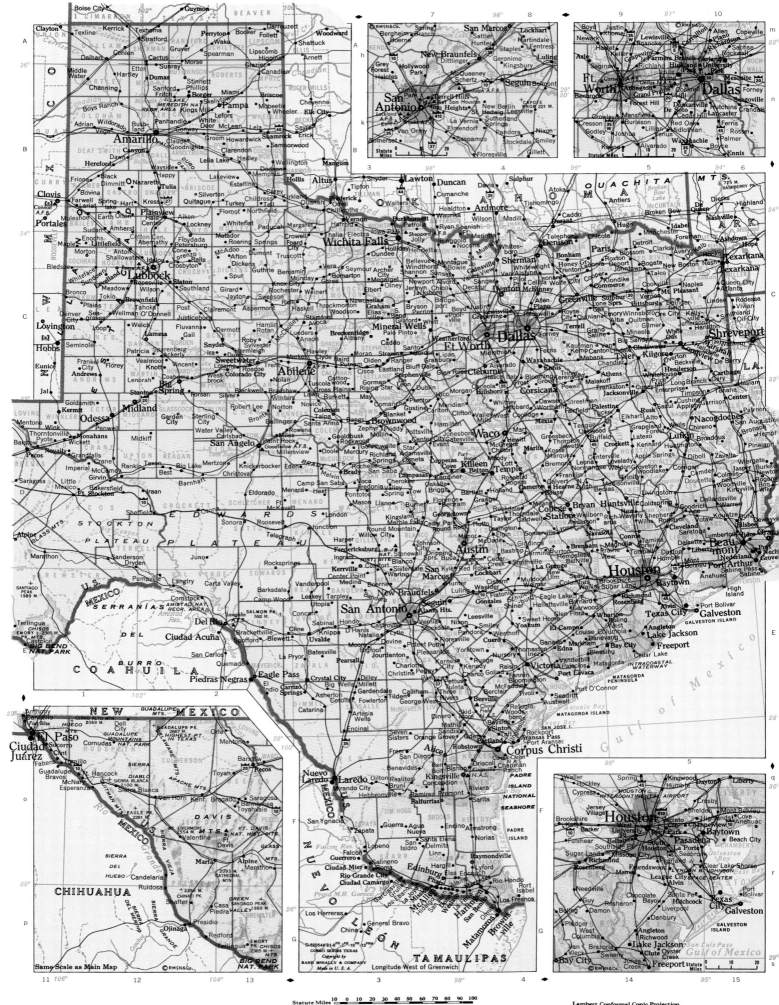

Note: Map colors do not reflect elevation.

Statute Miles 10 0 10 20 30 40 50 60 70 80 90 100
Kilometers 10 0 10 20 40 60 80 100 120 140

Lambert Conformal Conic Projection

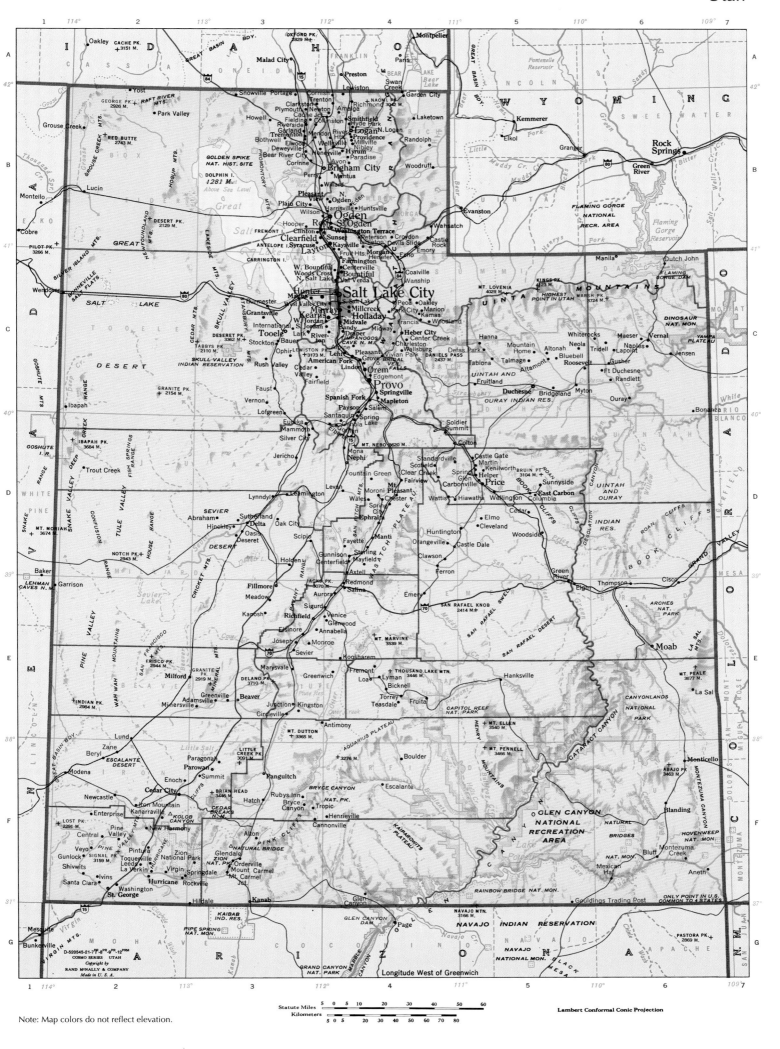

Note: Map colors do not reflect elevation.

Statute Miles 5 0 5 10   20   30   40   50   60
Kilometers 5 0 5   20   30 40   50 60 70 80

Lambert Conformal Conic Projection

Longitude West of Greenwich

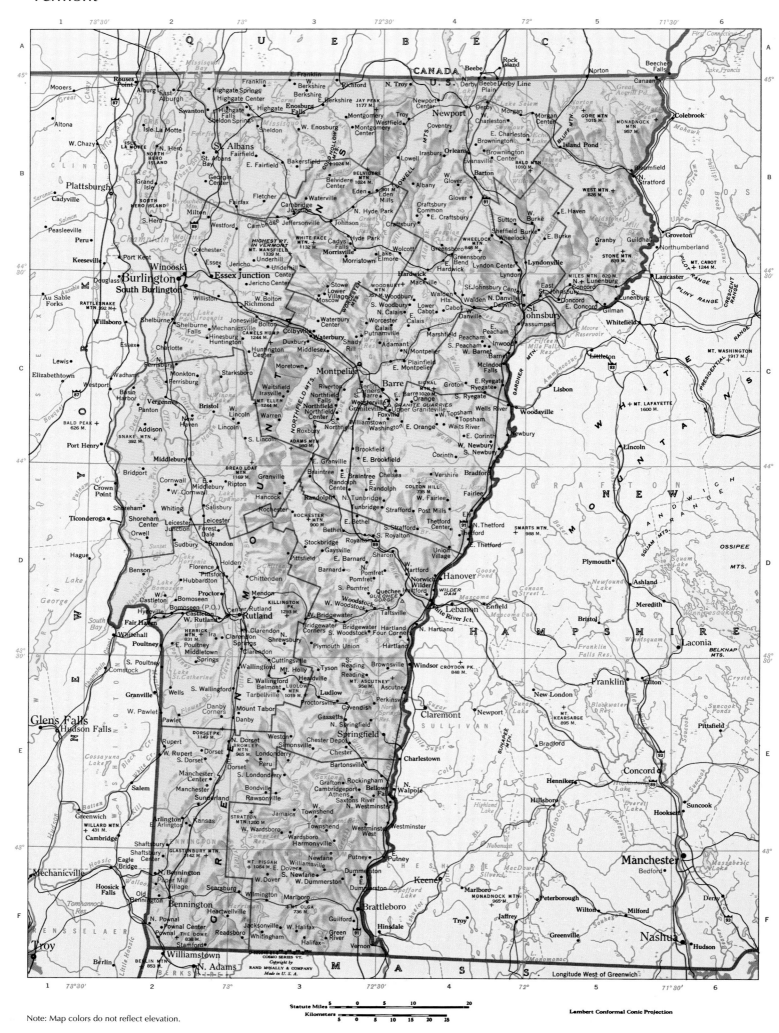

Note: Map colors do not reflect elevation.

Statute Miles
Kilometers

Lambert Conformal Conic Projection

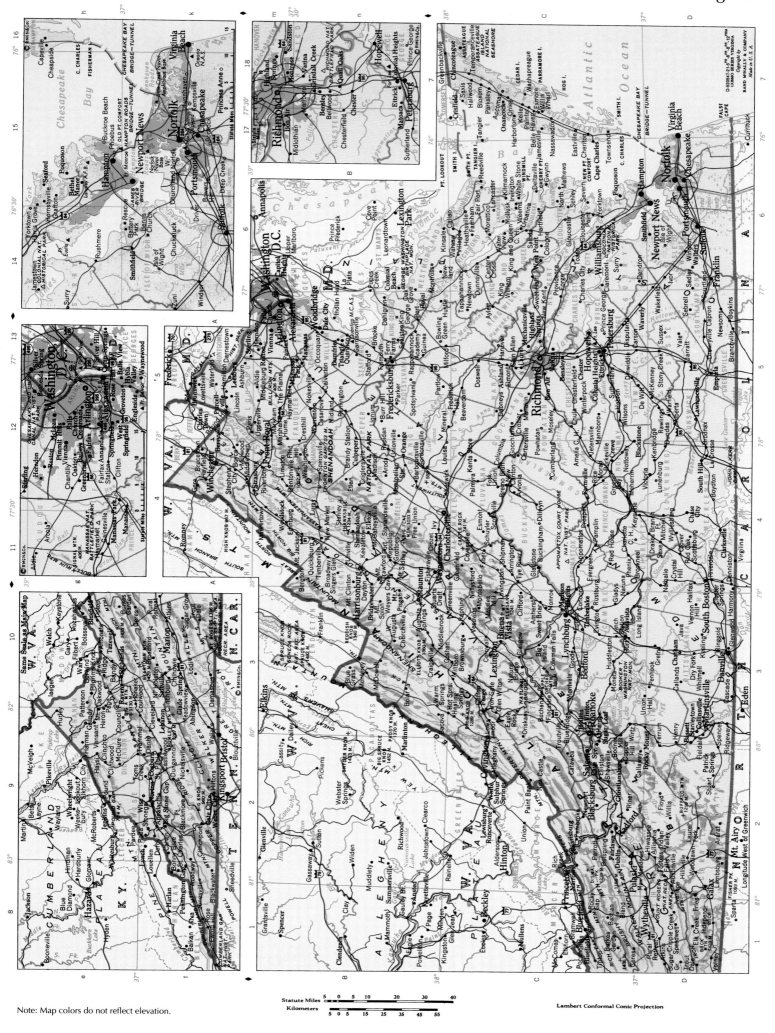

Note: Map colors do not reflect elevation.

Statute Miles
Kilometers

Lambert Conformal Conic Projection

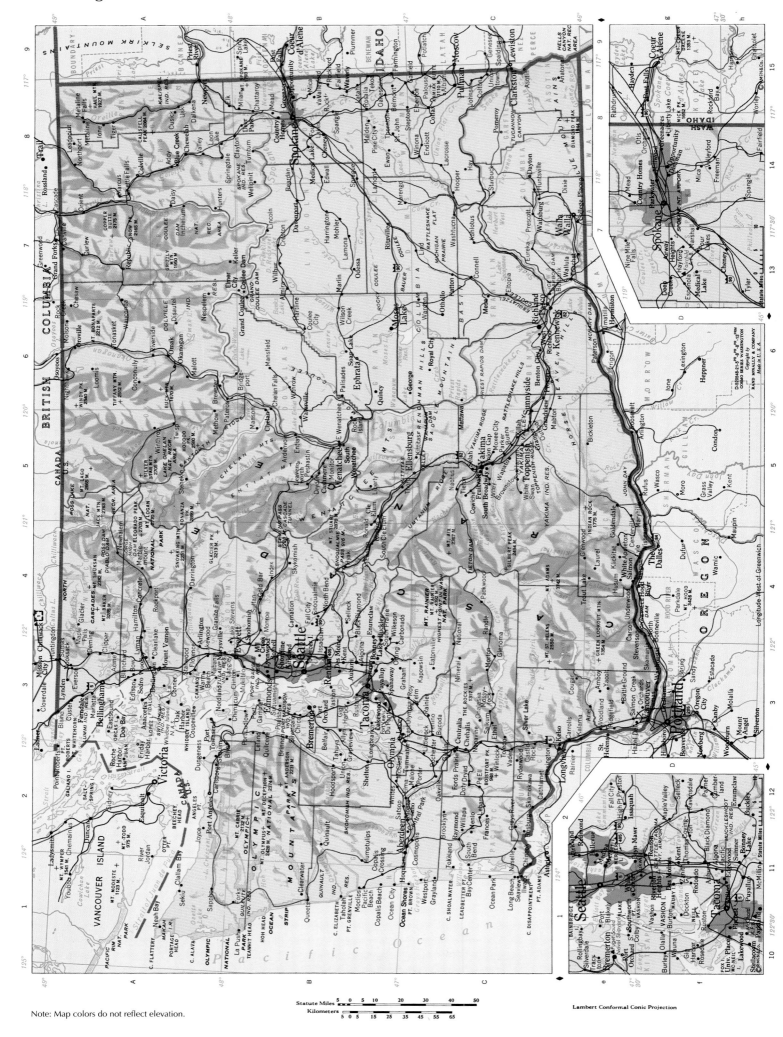

Note: Map colors do not reflect elevation.

Statute Miles 5 0 5 10   20   30   40   50
Kilometers 5 0 5 15 25 35 45 55 65

Lambert Conformal Conic Projection

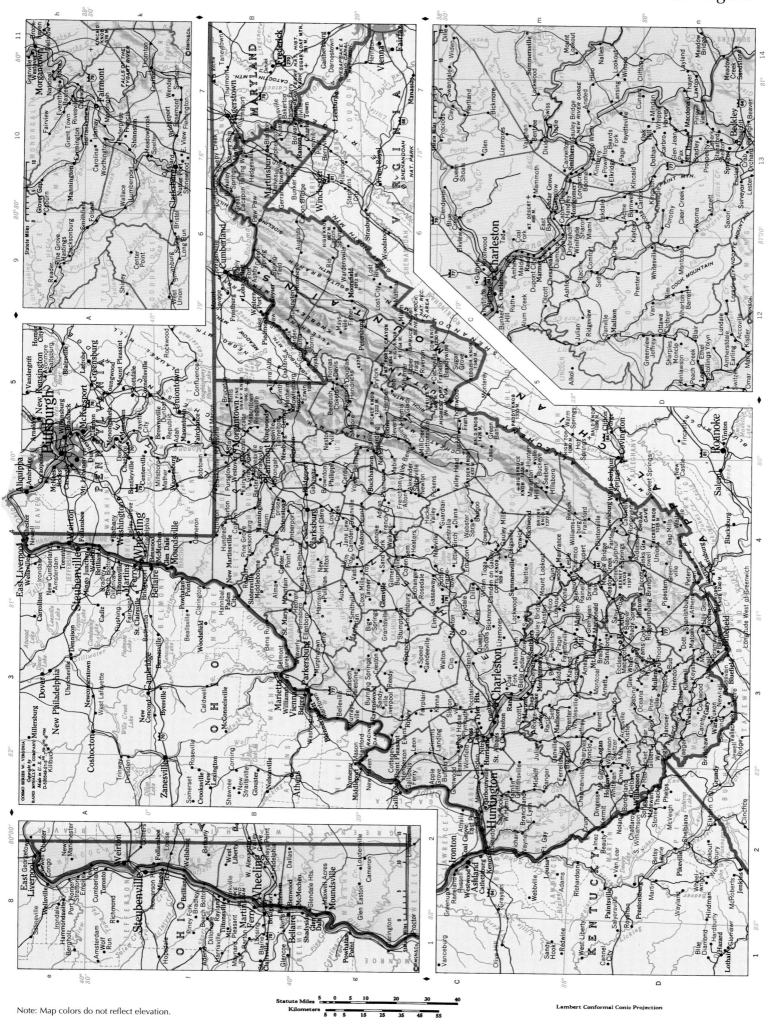

Note: Map colors do not reflect elevation.

Statute Miles

Kilometers

Lambert Conformal Conic Projection

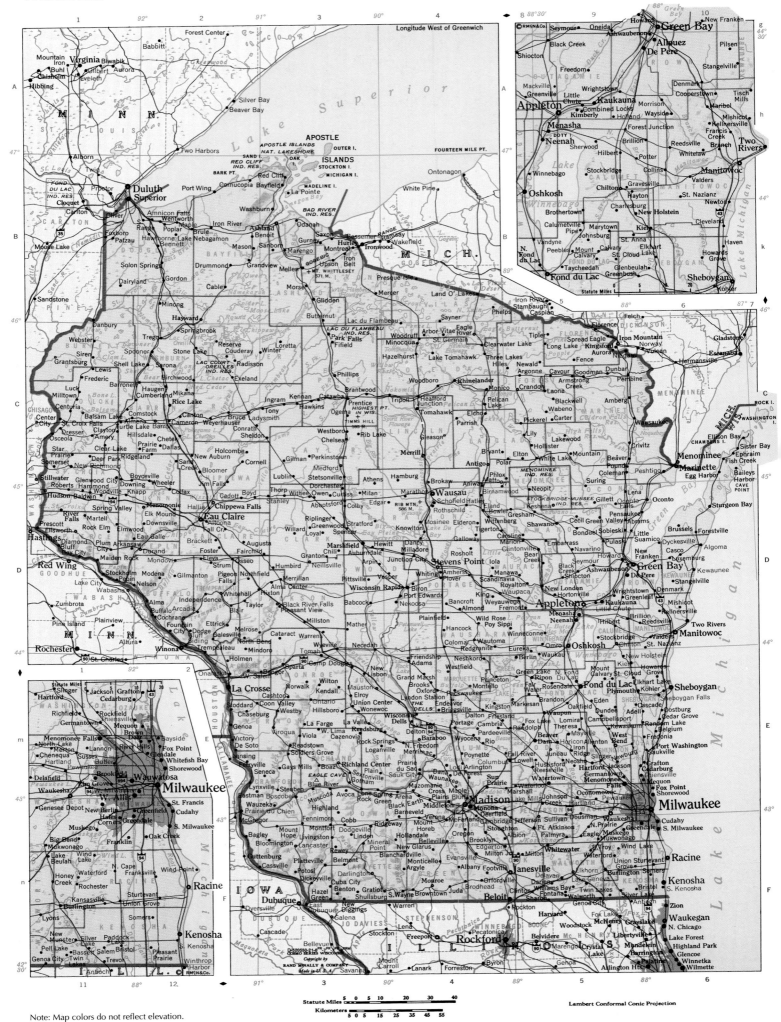

Note: Map colors do not reflect elevation.

Statute Miles
5 0 5 10   20   30   40

Kilometers
5 0 5 15 25 35 45 55

Lambert Conformal Conic Projection

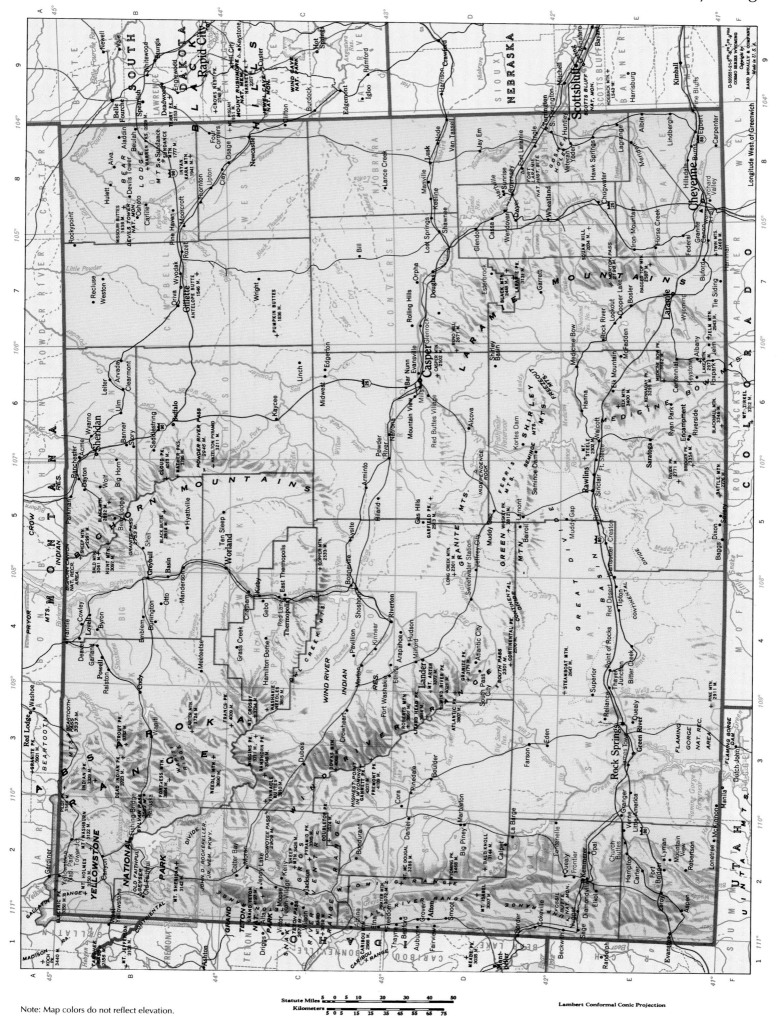

Note: Map colors do not reflect elevation.

Statute Miles 5 0 5 10   20   30   40   50

Kilometers 5 0 5 15 25 35 45 55 65 75

Lambert Conformal Conic Projection

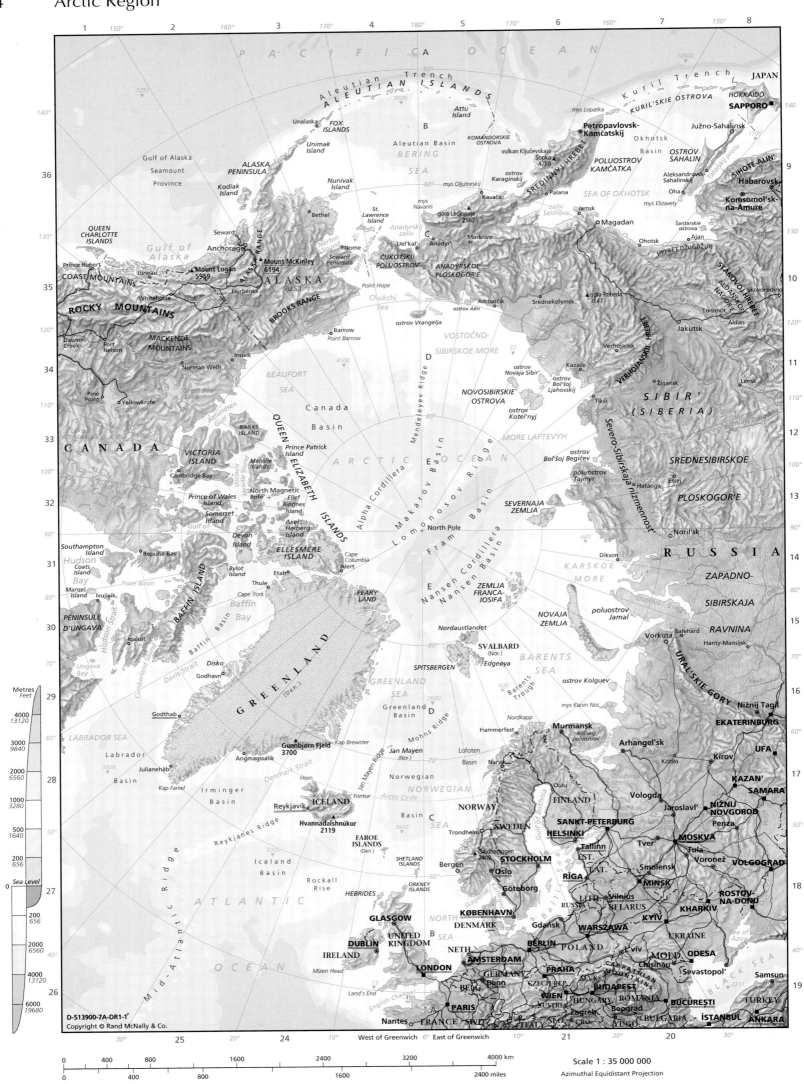

Scale 1 : 35 000 000
Azimuthal Equidistant Projection

D-513900-7A-DR1-1°
Copyright © Rand McNally & Co.

Index to World Reference Maps

Introduction to the Index

This index includes in a single alphabetical list approximately 45,000 names of features that appear on the reference maps. Each name is followed by the name of the country or continent in which it is located, a map reference key, and a page reference.

Names The names of cities appear in the index in regular type. The names of all other features appear in *italics*, followed by descriptive terms (hill, mtn., state) to indicate their nature.

Abbreviations of names on the maps have been standardized as much as possible. Names that are abbreviated on the maps are generally spelled out in full in the index.

Country names and names of features that extend beyond the boundaries of one country are followed by the name of the continent in which each is located. Country designations follow the names of all other places in the index. The locations of places in the United States, Canada, and the United Kingdom are further defined by abbreviations that indicate the state, province, or political division in which each is located.

All abbreviations used in the index are defined in the List of Abbreviations below.

Alphabetization Names are alphabetized in the order of the letters of the English alphabet. Spanish *ll* and *ch*, for example, are not treated as distinct letters. Furthermore, diacritical marks are disregarded in alphabetization—German or Scandinavian *ä* or *ö* are treated as *a* or *o*.

The names of physical features may appear inverted, since they are always alphabetized under the proper, not the generic, part of the name, thus: "Gibraltar, Strait of". Otherwise every entry, whether consisting of one word or more, is alphabetized as a single continuous entity. "Lakeland", for example, appears after "La Crosse" and before "La Salle". Names beginning with articles (Le Havre, Den Helder, Al-Manāmah) are not inverted. Names beginning "St.", "Ste." and "Sainte" are alphabetized as though spelled "Saint".

In the case of identical names, towns are listed first, then political divisions, then physical features. Entries that are completely identical are listed alphabetically by country name.

Map Reference Keys and Page References The map reference keys and page references are found in the last two columns of each entry.

Each map reference key consists of a letter and number. The letters appear along the sides of the maps. Lowercase letters indicate reference to inset maps. Numbers appear across the tops and bottoms of the maps.

Map reference keys for point features, such as cities and mountain peaks, indicate the locations of the symbols. For other features, such as countries, mountain ranges, or rivers, locations are given for the names.

The page number generally refers to the main map for the country in which the feature is located. Page references to two-page maps always refer to the left-hand page.

List of Abbreviations

Ab., Can.	Alberta, Can.	*ctry.*	independent country	*is.*	islands	N.H., U.S.	New Hampshire, U.S.	Som.	Somalia
Afg.	Afghanistan	Cuba	Cuba	Italy	Italy			Spain	Spain
Afr.	Africa	C.V.	Cape Verde	Jam.	Jamaica	Nic.	Nicaragua	Sp. N. Afr.	Spanish North Africa
Ak., U.S.	Alaska, U.S.	Cyp.	Cyprus	Japan	Japan	Nig.	Nigeria	Sri L.	Sri Lanka
Al., U.S.	Alabama, U.S.	Czech Rep.	Czech Republic	Jersey	Jersey	Niger	Niger	*state*	state, republic, canton
Alb.	Albania	D.C., U.S.	District of Columbia, U.S.	Jer.	Jericho Area	N. Ire., U.K.	Northern Ireland, U.K.	St. Hel.	St. Helena
Alg.	Algeria			Jord.	Jordan			St. K./N.	St. Kitts and Nevis
Am. Sam.	American Samoa	De., U.S.	Delaware, U.S.	Kaz.	Kazakstan	Niue	Niue	St. Luc.	St. Lucia
And.	Andorra	Den.	Denmark	Kenya	Kenya	N.J., U.S.	New Jersey, U.S.	*stm.*	stream (river, creek)
Ang.	Angola	*dep.*	dependency, colony	Kir.	Kiribati	N. Kor.	Korea, North	St. P./M.	St. Pierre and Miquelon
Anguilla	Anguilla	*depr.*	depression	Ks., U.S.	Kansas, U.S.	N.M., U.S.	New Mexico, U.S.		
Ant.	Antarctica	*dept.*	department, district	Kuw.	Kuwait	N. Mar. Is.	Northern Mariana Islands	*strt.*	strait
Antig.	Antigua and Barbuda	*des.*	desert	Ky., U.S.	Kentucky, U.S.			S. Tom./P.	Sao Tome and Principe
Ar., U.S.	Arkansas, U.S.	Dji.	Djibouti	Kyrg.	Kyrgyzstan	Nmb.	Namibia		
Arg.	Argentina	Dom.	Dominica	*l.*	lake, pond	Nor.	Norway	St. Vin.	St. Vincent and the Grenadines
Arm.	Armenia	Dom. Rep.	Dominican Republic	La., U.S.	Louisiana, U.S.	Norf. I.	Norfolk Island		
Aruba	Aruba	D.R.C.	Democratic Republic of the Congo	Laos	Laos	N.S., Can.	Nova Scotia, Can.	Sudan	Sudan
Asia	Asia			Lat.	Latvia	N.T., Can.	Northwest Territories, Can.	Sur.	Suriname
Aus.	Austria	Ec.	Ecuador	Leb.	Lebanon			Swaz.	Swaziland
Austl.	Australia	Egypt	Egypt	Leso.	Lesotho	Nv., U.S.	Nevada, U.S.	*sw.*	swamp, marsh
Az., U.S.	Arizona, U.S.	El Sal.	El Salvador	Lib.	Liberia	N.Y., U.S.	New York, U.S.	Swe.	Sweden
Azer.	Azerbaijan	Eng., U.K.	England, U.K.	Libya	Libya	N.Z.	New Zealand	Switz.	Switzerland
b.	bay, gulf, inlet, lagoon	Eq. Gui.	Equatorial Guinea	Liech.	Liechtenstein	Oc.	Oceania	Syria	Syria
		Erit.	Eritrea	Lith.	Lithuania	Oh., U.S.	Ohio, U.S.	Tai.	Taiwan
Bah.	Bahamas	Est.	Estonia	Lux.	Luxembourg	Ok., U.S.	Oklahoma, U.S.	Taj.	Tajikistan
Bahr.	Bahrain	*est.*	estuary	Ma., U.S.	Massachusetts, U.S.	Oman	Oman	Tan.	Tanzania
Barb.	Barbados	Eth.	Ethiopia	Macau	Macau	On., Can.	Ontario, Can.	T./C. Is.	Turks and Caicos Islands
B.C., Can.	British Columbia, Can.	Eur.	Europe	Mac.	Macedonia	Or., U.S.	Oregon, U.S.		
		Falk. Is.	Falkland Islands	Madag.	Madagascar	Pa., U.S.	Pennsylvania, U.S.	*ter.*	territory
Bdi.	Burundi	Far. Is.	Faroe Islands	Malay.	Malaysia	Pak.	Pakistan	Thai.	Thailand
Bel.	Belgium	Fiji	Fiji	Mald.	Maldives	Palau	Palau	Tn., U.S.	Tennessee, U.S.
Belize	Belize	Fin.	Finland	Mali	Mali	Pan.	Panama	Togo	Togo
Bela.	Belarus	Fl., U.S.	Florida, U.S.	Malta	Malta	Pap. N. Gui.	Papua New Guinea	Tok.	Tokelau
Benin	Benin	*for.*	forest, moor	Marsh. Is.	Marshall Islands	Para.	Paraguay	Tonga	Tonga
Ber.	Bermuda	Fr.	France	Mart.	Martinique	P.E., Can.	Prince Edward Island, Can.	Trin.	Trinidad and Tobago
Bhu.	Bhutan	Fr. Gu.	French Guiana	Maur.	Mauritania			Tun.	Tunisia
B.I.O.T.	British Indian Ocean Territory	Fr. Poly.	French Polynesia	May.	Mayotte	*pen.*	peninsula	Tur.	Turkey
		Ga., U.S.	Georgia, U.S.	Mb., Can.	Manitoba, Can.	Peru	Peru	Turk.	Turkmenistan
Bngl.	Bangladesh	Gabon	Gabon	Md., U.S.	Maryland, U.S.	Phil.	Philippines	Tuvalu	Tuvalu
Bol.	Bolivia	Gam.	Gambia	Me., U.S.	Maine, U.S.	Pit.	Pitcairn	Tx., U.S.	Texas, U.S.
Bos.	Bosnia and Herzegovina	Gaza Str.	Gaza Strip	Mex.	Mexico	*pl.*	plain, flat	U.A.E.	United Arab Emirates
		Geor.	Georgia	Mi., U.S.	Michigan, U.S.	*plat.*	plateau, highland	Ug.	Uganda
Bots.	Botswana	Ger.	Germany	Micron.	Micronesia, Federated States of	Pol.	Poland	U.K.	United Kingdom
Braz.	Brazil	Ghana	Ghana			Port.	Portugal	Ukr.	Ukraine
Br. Vir. Is.	British Virgin Islands	Gib.	Gibraltar	Mid. Is.	Midway Islands	P.Q., Can.	Quebec, Can.	Ur.	Uruguay
Bru.	Brunei	Golan Hts.	Golan Heights	*mil.*	military installation	P.R.	Puerto Rico	U.S.	United States
Bul.	Bulgaria	Grc.	Greece	Mn., U.S.	Minnesota, U.S.	*prov.*	province, region	Ut., U.S.	Utah, U.S.
Burkina	Burkina Faso	Gren.	Grenada	Mo., U.S.	Missouri, U.S.	Qatar	Qatar	Uzb.	Uzbekistan
c.	cape, point	Grnld.	Greenland	Mol.	Moldova	Reu.	Reunion	Va., U.S.	Virginia, U.S.
Ca., U.S.	California, U.S.	Guad.	Guadeloupe	Mon.	Monaco	*reg.*	physical region	*val.*	valley, watercourse
Camb.	Cambodia	Guam	Guam	Mong.	Mongolia	*res.*	reservoir	Vanuatu	Vanuatu
Cam.	Cameroon	Guat.	Guatemala	Monts.	Montserrat	*rf.*	reef, shoal	Vat.	Vatican City
Can.	Canada	Guernsey	Guernsey	Mor.	Morocco	R.I., U.S.	Rhode Island, U.S.	Ven.	Venezuela
C.A.R.	Central African Republic	Gui.	Guinea	Moz.	Mozambique	Rom.	Romania	Viet.	Vietnam
		Gui.-B.	Guinea-Bissau	Mrts.	Mauritius	Russia	Russia	V.I.U.S.	Virgin Islands (U.S.)
Cay. Is.	Cayman Islands	Guy.	Guyana	Ms., U.S.	Mississippi, U.S.	Rw.	Rwanda	*vol.*	volcano
Chad	Chad	Haiti	Haiti	Mt., U.S.	Montana, U.S.	S.A.	South America	Vt., U.S.	Vermont, U.S.
Chile	Chile	Hi., U.S.	Hawaii, U.S.	*mth.*	river mouth or channel	S. Afr.	South Africa	Wa., U.S.	Washington, U.S.
China	China	*hist.*	historic site, ruins			Sau. Ar.	Saudi Arabia	Wake I.	Wake Island
Christ. I.	Christmas Island	*hist. reg.*	historic region	*mtn.*	mountain	S.C., U.S.	South Carolina, U.S.	Wales, U.K.	Wales, U.K.
C. Iv.	Cote d'Ivoire	Hond.	Honduras	*mts.*	mountains	*sci.*	scientific station	S.D., U.S.	South Dakota, U.S.
clf.	cliff, escarpment	Hung.	Hungary	Mwi.	Malawi	S.D., U.S.	South Dakota, U.S.	Wal./F.	Wallis and Futuna
Co., U.S.	Colorado, U.S.	*i.*	island	Myan.	Myanmar	Sen.	Senegal	W.B.	West Bank
co.	county, parish	Ia., U.S.	Iowa, U.S.	N.A.	North America	Sey.	Seychelles	Wi., U.S.	Wisconsin, U.S.
Cocos Is.	Cocos (Keeling) Islands	Ice.	Iceland	Nauru	Nauru	S. Geor.	South Georgia and the South Sandwich Islands	W. Sah.	Western Sahara
		ice	ice feature, glacier	N.B., Can.	New Brunswick, Can.			W. Sam.	Western Samoa
Col.	Colombia	Id., U.S.	Idaho, U.S.					*wtfl.*	waterfall
Com.	Comoros	Il., U.S.	Illinois, U.S.	N.C., U.S.	North Carolina, U.S.	Sing.	Singapore	W.V., U.S.	West Virginia, U.S.
Congo	Congo	In., U.S.	Indiana, U.S.	N. Cal.	New Caledonia	Sk., Can.	Saskatchewan, Can.	Wy., U.S.	Wyoming, U.S.
cont.	continent	India	India	N. Cyp.	Cyprus, North	S. Kor.	Korea, South	Yemen	Yemen
Cook Is.	Cook Islands	Indon.	Indonesia	N.D., U.S.	North Dakota, U.S.	S.L.	Sierra Leone	Yk., Can.	Yukon Territory, Can.
C.R.	Costa Rica	I. of Man	Isle of Man	Ne., U.S.	Nebraska, U.S.	Slvk.	Slovakia		
crat.	crater	Iran	Iran	Nepal	Nepal	Slvn.	Slovenia	Yugo.	Yugoslavia
Cro.	Croatia	Iraq	Iraq	Neth.	Netherlands	S. Mar.	San Marino	Zam.	Zambia
Ct., U.S.	Connecticut, U.S.	Ire.	Ireland	Neth. Ant.	Netherlands Antilles	Sol. Is.	Solomon Islands	Zimb.	Zimbabwe
		Isr.	Israel	Nf., Can.	Newfoundland, Can.				

Name	Map Ref.	Page

A

Name	Map Ref.	Page
Aachen, Ger.	E10	12
Aali, Sadd el-, Egypt	F11	48
Äänekoski, Fin.	E11	10
Aba, China	E8	28
Aba, Nig.	E6	50
Abaco, i., Bah.	C9	76
Ābādān, Iran	D5	42
Ābādeh, Iran	D6	42
Abadla, Alg.	D4	48
Abaeté, Braz.	E2	74
Abaetetuba, Braz.	B2	74
Abag Qi, China	C10	28
Abaj, Kaz.	B2	28
Abajo Peak, mtn., Ut., U.S.	F6	137
Abakaliki, Nig.	E6	50
Abakan, Russia	D11	26
Abala, Niger	D5	50
Abancay, Peru	F5	70
Abashiri, Japan	B4	31
Abau, Pap. N. Gui.	I12	32
Ābay see Blue Nile, stm., Afr.	H11	48
Ābaya Hāyk', l., Eth.	B7	54
Abaza, Russia	D11	26
Abbeville, Point, c., Mi., U.S.	B2	115
Abbeville, Fr.	B7	16
Abbeville, Al., U.S.	D4	94
Abbeville, Ga., U.S.	E3	103
Abbeville, La., U.S.	E3	111
Abbeville, S.C., U.S.	C3	133
Abbeville, co., S.C., U.S.	C2	133
Abbotsford, Wi., U.S.	D3	142
Abbott Butte, mtn., Or., U.S.	E4	130
Abbott Run, stm., U.S.	B4	132
Abbott Run Valley, R.I., U.S.	B4	132
Ābdānān, Iran	F12	44
Abdulino, Russia	D9	22
Abe, Lake, l., Afr.	H13	48
Abéché, Chad	H9	48
Abengourou, C. Iv.	E4	50
Åbenrå, Den.	I3	10
Abeokuta, Nig.	E5	50
Aberdeen, Scot., U.K.	B5	12
Aberdeen, Id., U.S.	G6	105
Aberdeen, Md., U.S.	A5	113
Aberdeen, Ms., U.S.	B5	117
Aberdeen, N.C., U.S.	B3	126
Aberdeen, Oh., U.S.	D2	128
Aberdeen, S.D., U.S.	B7	134
Aberdeen, Wa., U.S.	C2	140
Aberdeen Lake, l., N.T., Can.	E20	82
Abernathy, Tx., U.S.	C2	136
Abert, Lake, l., Or., U.S.	E6	130
Abert Rim, clf., Or., U.S.	E6	130
Aberystwyth, Wales, U.K.	A11	22
Abez', Russia	A11	22
Abhā, Sau. Ar.	G4	38
Abhar, Iran	D13	44
Abidjan, C. Iv.	E4	50
Abilene, Ks., U.S.	D6	109
Abilene, Tx., U.S.	C3	136
Abingdon, Il., U.S.	C3	106
Abingdon, Md., U.S.	B5	113
Abingdon, Va., U.S.	f10	139
Abington, Ma., U.S.	B6	114
Abington [Township], Pa., U.S.	o21	131
Abinsk, Russia	G15	20
Abisko, Swe.	B8	10
Abita Springs, La., U.S.	D5	111
Abitibi, stm., On., Can.	H23	82
Åbo see Turku, Fin.	F10	10
Abomey, Benin	E5	50
Abongabong, Gunung, mtn., Indon.	C1	36
Abong Mbang, Cam.	C2	54
Abou-Deïa, Chad	H8	48
Abraham Lake, res., Ab., Can.	C2	84
Abraham Lincoln Birthplace National Historic Site, hist., Ky., U.S.	C4	110
Abra Pampa, Arg.	C4	72
Absaroka Range, mts., U.S.	F7	143
Absarokee, Mt., U.S.	E7	119
Absecon, N.J., U.S.	E4	123
Absecon Inlet, b., N.J., U.S.	E4	123
Abu Dhabi see Abū Ẓaby, U.A.E.	F6	42
Abū Ḥamad, Sudan	G11	48
Abuja, Nig.	E6	50
Abū Kamāl, Syria	E9	44
Abū Madd, Ra's, c., Sau. Ar.	F3	42
Abū Maṭāriq, Sudan	A5	54
Abunã, Braz.	E6	70
Ābu Road, India	E2	40
Abū Ẓaby (Abu Dhabi), U.A.E.	F6	42
Abu Zenîma, Egypt	F10	14
Abyaḍ, Al-Baḥr al- (White Nile), stm., Sudan	H11	48
Abyei, Sudan	B5	54
Academia, Oh., U.S.	B3	128
Acadia, co., La., U.S.	D3	111
Acadia National Park, Me., U.S.	D4	112
Açailândia, Braz.	B2	74
Acámbaro, Mex.	C4	78
Acaponeta, Mex.	C3	78
Acapulco, Mex.	D5	78
Acarai Mountains, mts., S.A.	C8	70
Acaraú, Braz.	B3	74
Acarigua, Ven.	B6	70
Acayucan, Mex.	D6	78
Accomack, co., Va., U.S.	C7	139
Accoville, W.V., U.S.	D3	141
Accra, Ghana	E4	50
Achacachi, Bol.	B4	72
Achalpur, India	E3	40
Acheng, China	B13	28
Achinsk, Russia	D11	26
Acireale, Italy	F5	18
Ačisaj, Kaz.	B9	42
Ackerman, Ms., U.S.	B4	117
Ackley, Ia., U.S.	B4	108
Acklins, i., Bah.	D10	76
Acoma Indian Reservation, N.M., U.S.	C2	124
Aconcagua, Cerro, mtn., Arg.	E4	72
Acopiara, Braz.	C4	74
Açores, is., Port.	F7	46
A Coruña, Spain	F2	16
Acre, state, Braz.	E5	70
Acton, Ma., U.S.	B5	114
Acton Vale, P.Q., Can.	D5	90
Acushnet, Ma., U.S.	C6	114
Acworth, Ga., U.S.	B2	103
Ada, Ghana	E5	50
Ada, Mn., U.S.	C2	116
Ada, Oh., U.S.	B2	128
Ada, Ok., U.S.	C5	129
Ada, co., Id., U.S.	F2	105
Ada, Mount, mtn., Ak., U.S.	m22	95
Adair, Ia., U.S.	C3	108
Adair, Ok., U.S.	A6	129
Adair, co., Ia., U.S.	C3	108
Adair, co., Ky., U.S.	C4	110
Adair, co., Mo., U.S.	A5	118
Adair, co., Ok., U.S.	B7	129
Adairsville, Ga., U.S.	B2	103
Adairville, Ky., U.S.	D3	110
Adak Island, i., Ak., U.S.	E4	95
Adak Naval Station, mil., Ak., U.S.	E4	95
Adam, Oman	F7	38
Adamantina, Braz.	F1	74
Adamaoua, prov., Cam.	E7	50
Adamaoua, mts., Afr.	B2	54
Adamawa see Adamaoua, mts., Afr.	B2	54
Adam Island, i., Md., U.S.	D5	113
Adams, Ma., U.S.	A1	114
Adams, Mn., U.S.	G6	116
Adams, N.Y., U.S.	B4	125
Adams, Wi., U.S.	E4	142
Adams, co., Co., U.S.	B6	99
Adams, co., Ia., U.S.	C3	108
Adams, co., Id., U.S.	E2	105
Adams, co., Il., U.S.	D2	106
Adams, co., In., U.S.	C8	107
Adams, co., Ms., U.S.	D2	117
Adams, co., N.D., U.S.	C3	127
Adams, co., Ne., U.S.	D7	120
Adams, co., Oh., U.S.	D2	128
Adams, co., Pa., U.S.	G7	131
Adams, co., Wa., U.S.	B7	140
Adams, co., Wi., U.S.	D4	142
Adams, Mount, mtn., N.H., U.S.	B4	122
Adams, Mount, mtn., Wa., U.S.	C4	140
Adams Point, c., Mi., U.S.	C7	115
Adams Run, S.C., U.S.	k11	133
Adamstown, Pa., U.S.	F9	131
Adamsville, Al., U.S.	f7	94
Adamsville, R.I., U.S.	E6	132
Adamsville, Tn., U.S.	B3	135
Adamsville Brook, stm., R.I., U.S.	E6	132
'Adan (Aden), Yemen	H5	38
Adana, Tur.	D6	44
Adare, Cape, c., Ant.	D22	67
Adda, stm., Italy	B2	18
Ad-Dabbah, Sudan	G11	48
Ad-Dahnā', des., Sau. Ar.	E5	38
Ad-Dāmir, Sudan	G2	38
Ad-Dammām, Sau. Ar.	E5	38
Ad-Dawhah (Doha), Qatar	E6	42
Ad-Diffah (Libyan Plateau), plat., Afr.	E9	14
Addis, La., U.S.	D4	111
Addis Ababa see Ādīs Ābeba, Eth.	B7	54
Addison, Al., U.S.	A2	94
Addison, Ct., U.S.	C5	100
Addison, Il., U.S.	k8	106
Addison, N.Y., U.S.	C3	125
Addison, co., Vt., U.S.	C2	138
Ad-Dīwānīyah, Iraq	D5	42
Addyston, Oh., U.S.	o12	128
Adel, Ga., U.S.	E3	103
Adel, Ia., U.S.	C3	108
Adelaide, Austl.	G2	62
Adelaide, S. Afr.	E4	56
Adelaide Island, i., Ant.	C33	67
Adelaide River, Austl.	C5	60
Adelanto, Ca., U.S.	E5	98
Adèle Island, i., Austl.	D3	60
Adelie Coast, Ant.	C19	67
Aden see 'Adan, Yemen	H5	38
Aden, Gulf of, b.	H5	38
Adi, Pulau, i., Indon.	D8	36
Adiaké, C. Iv.	E4	50
Adige, stm., Italy	D3	18
Ādīgrat, Eth.	H3	38
Ādilābād, India	F3	40
Adimi, Russia	B15	28
Adirondack Mountains, mts., N.Y., U.S.	A6	125
Ādīs Ābeba (Addis Ababa), Eth.	B7	54
Adıyaman, Tur.	D8	44
Adjuntas, Presa de las see Vicente Guerrero, Presa, res., Mex.	C5	78
Adler, Russia	A8	44
Admiralty Bay, b., Ak., U.S.	A9	95
Admiralty Gulf, b., Austl.	C4	60
Admiralty Inlet, b., N.T., Can.	D22	82
Admiralty Island, i., Ak., U.S.	m22	95
Admiralty Islands, is., Pap. N. Gui.	G12	32
Admiralty Mountains, mts., Ant.	D21	67
Ado, Nig.	E5	50
Adobe Creek Reservoir, res., Co., U.S.	C7	99
Ado-Ekiti, Nig.	E6	50
Ādoni, India	F3	40
Adour, stm., Fr.	F6	16
Adra, Spain	I5	16
Adrar, Alg.	E4	48
Adrâr, reg., Maur.	B2	50
Adrian, Ga., U.S.	D4	103
Adrian, Mi., U.S.	G6	115
Adrian, Mn., U.S.	G3	116
Adrian, Mo., U.S.	C3	118
Adrianople see Edirne, Tur.	B2	44
Adriatic Sea, Eur.	C5	18
Adusa, D.R.C.	C5	54
Advance, Mo., U.S.	D8	118
Ādwa, Eth.	H12	48
Adygeja, state, Russia	E5	26
Adzopé, C. Iv.	E4	50
Aegean Sea	E10	18
Aën, ostrov, i., Russia	C18	26
A Estrada, Spain	F2	16
Afadjoto, mtn., Ghana	E5	50
Afars and Issas see Djibouti, ctry., Afr.	H13	48
Afghanistan, ctry., Asia	D8	42
Afgooye, Som.	C9	54
Afikpo, Nig.	E6	50
Aflou, Alg.	E4	14
Afmadow, Som.	J13	48
Afognak Island, i., Ak., U.S.	D9	95
Africa	E14	4
Afşin, Tur.	C7	44
Afton, Ia., U.S.	C3	108
Afton, Mn., U.S.	F6	116
Afton, Ok., U.S.	A7	129
Afton, Wy., U.S.	D2	143
Afyon, Tur.	C4	44
Agadez, Niger	C6	50
Agadir, Mor.	D2	48
Agadyr', Kaz.	E9	26
Agalak, Sudan	A6	54
Agalega Islands, is., Mrts.	E11	52
Agana, Guam	D11	32
Agartala, India	E6	40
Agate Fossil Beds National Monument, Ne., U.S.	B2	120
Agattu Island, i., Ak., U.S.	E2	95
Agawam, Ma., U.S.	B2	114
Agboville, C. Iv.	E4	50
Ağdam, Azer.	C12	44
Agde, Fr.	F8	16
Agen, Fr.	E7	16
Agency, Ia., U.S.	D5	108
Agency, Mo., U.S.	B3	118
Āghā Jārī, Iran	D5	42
Aginskoe, Russia	D13	26
Agnew, Austl.	F3	60
Agnibilékrou, C. Iv.	E4	50
Agou, mort, mtn., Togo	E5	50
Agoura Hills, Ca., U.S.	m11	98
Āgra, India	D3	40
Ağrı, Tur.	C10	44
Ağrı Dağı, mtn., Tur.	C11	44
Agrigento, Italy	F4	18
Agrihan, i., N. Mar. Is.	C12	32
Agrínion, Grc.	E8	18
Agrópoli, Italy	D5	18
Água Branca, Braz.	C3	74
Aguachica, Col.	D5	80
Aguadas, Col.	D4	80
Aguadulce, Pan.	D3	80
Agua Fria, N.M., U.S.	B3	124
Agua Fria, stm., Az., U.S.	D3	96
Aguán, stm., Hond.	B2	80
Agua Prieta, Mex.	A3	78
A Guardia, Spain	G2	16
Aguarico, stm., S.A.	D4	70
Aguascalientes, Mex.	C4	78
Aguascalientes, state, Mex.	C4	78
Águas Formosas, Braz.	E3	74
Água Vermelha, Represa de, res., Braz.	G9	70
Aguelhok, Mali	C5	50
Aguila, Az., U.S.	D2	96
Águilas, Spain	I6	16
Agulhas, Kaap, c., S. Afr.	J3	56
Agulhas Basin	M15	66
Agustín Codazzi, Col.	B5	80
Ahaggar, mts., Alg.	F6	48
Ahaggar, Tassili ta-n-, plat., Alg.	B5	50
Ahalcihe, Geor.	B10	44
Ahalkalaki, Geor.	B10	44
Ahar, Iran	C5	42
Ahklun Mountains, mts., Ak., U.S.	D7	95
Ahlat, Tur.	C10	44
Ahmadābād, India	F2	40
Ahmadnagar, India	F2	40
Ahmadpur East, Pak.	E10	42
Ahmar Mountains, mts., Eth.	B8	54
Ahoskie, N.C., U.S.	A6	126
Ahtanum Creek, stm., Wa., U.S.	C5	140
Ahtubinsk, Russia	E6	26
Ahuacatlán, Mex.	C4	78
Ahumada, Mex.	A3	78
Ahvāz, Iran	D5	42
Ahvenanmaa see Åland, is., Fin.	G9	10
Aialik, Cape, c., Ak., U.S.	D10	95
Aiea, Hi., U.S.	B4	104
Aiken, S.C., U.S.	D4	133
Aiken, co., S.C., U.S.	D4	133
Ailao Shan, mts., China	G8	28
Aileron, Austl.	E5	60
Ailinglaplap, atoll, Marsh. Is.	D10	58
Ailsa Craig, On., Can.	D3	89
Aim, Russia	D15	26
Aimorés, Braz.	E3	74
Aïn el Beïda, Alg.	D5	48
Aïn Sefra, Alg.	J6	16
Aïn Témouchent, Alg.	J6	16
Aïn Wessara, Alg.	J8	16
Aïr, Massif de l', mts., Niger	C6	50
Airdrie, Ab., Can.	D3	84
Aïssa, Djebel, mtn., Alg.	D4	48
Aitape, Pap. N. Gui.	G11	32
Aitkin, Mn., U.S.	D5	116
Aitkin, co., Mn., U.S.	D5	116
Aitutaki, atoll, Cook Is.	F14	58
Aiud, Rom.	F7	20
Aix, Mount, mtn., Wa., U.S.	C4	140
Aix-en-Provence, Fr.	F9	16
Aix-les-Bains, Fr.	F9	16
Aíyina, i., Grc.	F9	18
Aíyion, Grc.	E9	18
Āīzawl, India	E6	40
Aizu-wakamatsu, Japan	D16	28
'Ajab Shīr, Iran	D11	44
Ajaccio, Fr.	D2	18
Ajaguz, Kaz.	E9	26
Ajan, Russia	D15	26
Ajanta, India	E3	40
Ajanta Range, mts., India	E3	40
Ajax, On., Can.	D6	89
Ajdābiyā, Libya	D9	48
Ajdarkul', ozero, l., Uzb.	B9	42
Ajdyrlinskij, Russia	D10	22
Ajjer, Tassili-n-, plat., Alg.	E6	48
Ajmer, India	D2	40
Ajo, Az., U.S.	E3	96
Āk'ak'Ī Besek'a, Eth.	B7	54
'Akāshāt, Iraq	F8	44
Akbou, Alg.	I9	16
Akbulak, Russia	D10	22
Akçaabat, Tur.	B8	44
Akçadağ, Tur.	C7	44
Akçakale, Tur.	D8	44
Akçakoca, Tur.	B4	44
Akchâr, reg., Maur.	C1	50
Ak-Chin Indian Reservation, Az., U.S.	E3	96
Akdağmadeni, Tur.	C6	44
Aketi, D.R.C.	C4	54
Akhḍar, Al-Jabal al-, mts., Oman	F7	42
Akhisar, Tur.	C2	44
Akiachak, Ak., U.S.	C7	95
Akita, Japan	D16	28
Akjoujt, Maur.	C2	50
Akkajaure, l., Swe.	C7	10
Akkol', Kaz.	E9	26
Akkol', Kaz.	B10	42
Akmola, Kaz.	D9	26
Akok, Gabon	C1	54
Akola, India	E3	40
Akonolinga, Cam.	C2	54
Akordat, Erit.	G12	48
Akranes, Ice.	I17	10a
Akron, Co., U.S.	A7	99
Akron, Ia., U.S.	B1	108
Akron, In., U.S.	B5	107
Akron, N.Y., U.S.	B2	125
Akron, Oh., U.S.	A4	128
Akron, Pa., U.S.	F9	131
Aksaj, Kaz.	D9	22
Aksaray, Tur.	C6	44
Aksarka, Russia	A12	22
Akşehir, Tur.	C4	44
Akşehir Gölü, l., Tur.	C4	44
Akseki, Tur.	D4	44
Aksu, China	A3	28
Aksuat, Kaz.	E10	26
Āksum, Eth.	H3	38
Aktau, Kaz.	E7	26
Aktjubinsk, Kaz.	D7	26
Akto, China	B3	40
Aktogaj, Kaz.	E9	26
Akune, Japan	D1	31
Akure, Nig.	E6	50
Akureyri, Ice.	I19	10a
Akwanga, Nig.	E6	50
Akžar, Kaz.	B4	28
Alabama, state, U.S.	C3	94
Alabama, stm., Al., U.S.	D2	94
Alabaster, Al., U.S.	B3	94
Alaca, Tur.	B6	44
Alaçam, Tur.	B6	44
Alacant, Spain	H6	16
Alachua, Fl., U.S.	C4	102
Alachua, co., Fl., U.S.	C4	102
Aladža manastir, Bul.	C12	18
Alagir, Russia	A11	44
Alagoas, state, Braz.	C4	74
Alagoinhas, Braz.	D4	74
Alagón, Spain	G6	16
Alahärmä, Fin.	E10	10
Alajuela, C.R.	C3	80
Alakanuk, Ak., U.S.	C7	95
Alakol', ozero, l., Kaz.	E10	26
Alalakeiki Channel, strt., Hi., U.S.	C5	104
Al-'Amādīyah, Iraq	D10	44
Alamagan, i., N. Mar. Is.	C12	32
Alamance, co., N.C., U.S.	B3	126
Al-'Amārah, Iraq	D5	42
Alameda, Ca., U.S.	h8	98
Alameda, N.M., U.S.	B3	124
Alameda, co., Ca., U.S.	D3	98
Alameda Naval Air Station, mil., Ca., U.S.	h8	98
Alamito Creek, stm., Tx., U.S.	p12	136
Alamo, Ga., U.S.	D4	103
Alamo, Nv., U.S.	F6	121
Alamo, Tn., U.S.	B2	135
Alamo, Tx., U.S.	F3	136
Alamogordo, N.M., U.S.	E4	124
Alamo Heights, Tx., U.S.	E3	136
Alamo Hueco Mountains, mts., N.M., U.S.	F1	124
Alamo Indian Reservation, N.M., U.S.	C2	124
Alamo Lake, res., Az., U.S.	C2	96
Alamosa, Co., U.S.	D5	99
Alamosa, co., Co., U.S.	D5	99
Alamosa, stm., Co., U.S.	D4	99
Alamosa Creek, stm., N.M., U.S.	D2	124
Alamosa East, Co., U.S.	D5	99
Åland, is., Fin.	G9	10
Ålands hav, Eur.	F8	10
Alandur, India	G4	40
Alanya, Tur.	D4	44
Alapaevsk, Russia	C11	22
Alapaha, Ga., U.S.	E3	103
Alapaha, stm., U.S.	E3	103
Al-'Aqabah, Jord.	E3	42
Alas, Selat, strt., Indon.	E5	36
Alaşehir, Tur.	C3	44
Alashanyouqi, China	C8	28
Alaska, state, U.S.	C9	95
Alaska, Gulf of, b., Ak., U.S.	D10	95
Alaska Peninsula, pen., Ak., U.S.	D8	95
Alaska Range, mts., Ak., U.S.	C9	95
Alatna, stm., Ak., U.S.	B9	95
Alatyr', Russia	D8	22
Alava, Cape, c., Wa., U.S.	A1	140
Alavus, Fin.	E10	10
Al-'Ayn, U.A.E.	F7	42
Al-'Azīzīyah, Libya	E6	14
Alba, Italy	B2	18
Al-Bāb, Syria	D7	44
Albacete, Spain	H6	16
Alba Iulia, Rom.	F7	20
Albania, ctry., Eur.	D7	18
Albano Laziale, Italy	D4	18
Albany, Austl.	G2	60
Albany, Ga., U.S.	E2	103
Albany, Il., U.S.	B3	106
Albany, In., U.S.	D7	107
Albany, Ky., U.S.	D4	110
Albany, La., U.S.	g10	111
Albany, Mn., U.S.	E4	116
Albany, Mo., U.S.	A3	118
Albany, N.Y., U.S.	C7	125
Albany, Or., U.S.	C3	130
Albany, Tx., U.S.	C3	136
Albany, Wi., U.S.	F4	142
Albany, co., N.Y., U.S.	C6	125
Albany, co., Wy., U.S.	E7	143
Albany, stm., On., Can.	o18	89
Al-Baṣrah, Iraq	D5	42
Al-Batrā' (Petra), hist., Jord.	D3	42
Al-Batrūn, Leb.	E6	44
Al-Bayḍā', Libya	D9	48
Albemarle, N.C., U.S.	B2	126
Albemarle, co., Va., U.S.	C4	139
Albemarle Island see Isabela, Isla, i., Ec.	D1	70
Albemarle Lake, l., Ms., U.S.	C2	117
Albemarle Sound, strt., N.C., U.S.	A6	126
Albert, Fr.	B8	16
Albert, Lake, l., Afr.	C6	54
Alberta, prov., Can.	C4	84
Alberta, Mount, mtn., Ab., Can.	C2	84
Albert City, Ia., U.S.	B3	108
Albert Lea, Mn., U.S.	G5	116
Albert Markham, Mount, mtn., Ant.	E22	67
Albert Nile, stm., Ug.	C6	54
Alberton, P.E., Can.	C5	87
Albertson, N.Y., U.S.	k13	125
Albertville see Kalemie, D.R.C.	E5	54
Albertville, Fr.	E10	16
Albertville, Al., U.S.	A3	94
Albertville, Mn., U.S.	E5	116
Albi, Fr.	F8	16
Albia, Ia., U.S.	C5	108
Albion, Il., U.S.	E5	106
Albion, In., U.S.	B7	107
Albion, Mi., U.S.	F6	115
Albion, Ne., U.S.	C7	120
Albion, N.Y., U.S.	B2	125
Albion, Pa., U.S.	C1	131
Albion, R.I., U.S.	B4	132
Albion, Wa., U.S.	C8	140
Al-Biqā', val., Leb.	F6	44
Alborán, Isla de, i., Spain	J5	16
Ålborg, Den.	H3	10
Alborz, Reshteh-ye Kūhhā-ye, mts., Iran	C6	42
Albox, Spain	I5	16

Name	Map Ref.	Page

Ālbū Gharz, Sabkhat, pl., Asia . . . . E9 . . 44
Albuquerque, N.M., U.S. . . B3 . 124
Alburquerque, Spain . . . . . H3 . 16
Alburtis, Pa., U.S. . . . . . . F10 . 131
Albury, Austl. . . . . H4 . 62
Alcalá de Henares, Spain . . G5 . 16
Alcalde, N.M., U.S. . . . . . . A3 . 124
Alcamo, Italy . . . . F4 . 18
Alcañiz, Spain . . . . G6 . 16
Alcántara Uno, Embalse de, res., Spain . . . . H3 . 16
Alcantarilla, Spain . . . . . . I6 . 16
Alcázar de San Juan, Spain . H5 . 16
Alcazarquivir see Er-Rachidia, Mor. . . . . E3 . 14
Alcester, S.D., U.S. . . . . . D9 . 134
Alchevs'k, Ukr. . . . . E15 . 20
Alcoa, Tn., U.S. . . . . D10 . 135
Alcobaça, Braz. . . . . G12 . 70
Alcobendas, Spain . . . . . . G5 . 16
Alcoi, Spain . . . . H6 . 16
Alcolu, S.C., U.S. . . . . . . D7 . 133
Alcona, co., Mi., U.S. . . . . D7 . 115
Alcorn, co., Ms., U.S. . . . . A5 . 117
Aldabra, Groupe d', i., Sey. . i11 . 57b
Aldama, Mex. . . . . B3 . 78
Aldan, Russia . . . . D14 . 26
Aldan, stm., Russia . . . . . C15 . 26
Aldan Plateau see Aldanskoe nagor'e, plat., Russia . . . . D14 . 26
Aldanskoe nagor'e, plat., Russia . . . . D14 . 26
Alden, Ia., U.S. . . . . B4 . 108
Alden, Mn., U.S. . . . . G5 . 116
Alden, N.Y., U.S. . . . . C2 . 125
Alder Brook, stm., Vt., U.S. B4 . 138
Alderney, i., Guernsey . . . . F5 . 12
Alderson, W.V., U.S. . . . . . D4 . 141
Aldrich, Al., U.S. . . . . B3 . 94
Aledo, Il., U.S. . . . . B3 . 106
Aleg, Maur. . . . . C2 . 50
Alegres Mountain, mtn., N.M., U.S. . . . . C2 . 124
Alegrete, Braz. . . . . D6 . 72
Alejandro Selkirk, Isla, i., Chile . . . . E1 . 74
Alejsk, Russia . . . . D10 . 26
Aleksandrov, Russia . . . . . C6 . 22
Aleksandrovsk-Sahalinskij, Russia . . . . D16 . 26
Alekseevka, Russia . . . . . . D15 . 20
Aleksin, Russia . . . . B14 . 20
Aleksinac, Yugo. . . . . C8 . 18
Alençon, Fr. . . . . C7 . 16
Alenquer, Braz. . . . . D9 . 70
Alenuihaha Channel, strt., Hi., U.S. . . . . C5 . 104
Aleppo see Ḥalab, Syria . . D7 . 44
Alert Bay, B.C., Can. . . . . D4 . 85
Alès, Fr. . . . . E9 . 16
Alessándria, Italy . . . . B2 . 18
Ålesund, Nor. . . . . E2 . 10
Aleutian Basin . . . . B4 . 144
Aleutian Islands, is., Ak., U.S. . . . . E3 . 95
Aleutian Range, mts., Ak., U.S. . . . . D9 . 95
Aleutian Trench . . . . B4 . 144
Aleutka, Russia . . . . B18 . 28
Alex, Ok., U.S. . . . . C4 . 129
Alexander, co., Il., U.S. . . . F4 . 106
Alexander, co., N.C., U.S. . . B1 . 126
Alexander, Lake, l., Mn., U.S. . . . . D4 . 116
Alexander Archipelago, is., Ak., U.S. . . . . D12 . 95
Alexander Bay, S. Afr. . . . . D2 . 56
Alexander City, Al., U.S. . . C4 . 94
Alexander Island, i., Ant. . . C33 . 67
Alexandra, N.Z. . . . . q12 . 63c
Alexandretta see İskenderun, Tur. . . . . D7 . 44
Alexandria, On., Can. . . . . B10 . 89
Alexandria see El-Iskandarīya, Egypt . . . E9 . 48
Alexandria, Rom. . . . . H8 . 20
Alexandria, S. Afr. . . . . . . E4 . 56
Alexandria, In., U.S. . . . . . D6 . 107
Alexandria, Ky., U.S. . . . . . B5 . 110
Alexandria, La., U.S. . . . . . C3 . 111
Alexandria, Mn., U.S. . . . . E3 . 116
Alexandria, Tn., U.S. . . . . . A5 . 135
Alexandria, Va., U.S. . . . . . B5 . 139
Alexandroúpolis, Grc. . . . . D10 . 18
Alexis, Il., U.S. . . . . B3 . 106
Alfalfa, co., Ok., U.S. . . . . A3 . 129
Al-Fallūjah, Iraq . . . . F10 . 44
Al-Fāshir, Sudan . . . . H10 . 48
Alföld, pl., Hung. . . . . F6 . 20
Alfred, On., Can. . . . . B10 . 89
Alfred, N.Y., U.S. . . . . C3 . 125
Al-Fujayrah, U.A.E. . . . . . E7 . 42
Al-Furāt see Euphrates, stm., Asia . . . . D4 . 42
Alga, Kaz. . . . . E10 . 22
Algarrobo del Águila, Arg. . F4 . 72
Algarve, hist. reg., Port. . . . I2 . 16
Algeciras, Spain . . . . I4 . 16
Alger, Oh., U.S. . . . . B2 . 128
Alger, co., Mi., U.S. . . . . . B4 . 115
Algeria, ctry., Afr. . . . . . . E5 . 48
Al-Ghaydah, Yemen . . . . . G6 . 38
Al-Ghazālah, Sau. Ar. . . . . E4 . 42

Alghero, Italy . . . . D2 . 18
Algiers see El Djazaïr, Alg. . C5 . 48
Algoabaai, b., S. Afr. . . . . E4 . 56
Algoma, Wi., U.S. . . . . . . D6 . 142
Algona, Ia., U.S. . . . . A3 . 108
Algona, Wa., U.S. . . . . B3 . 140
Algonac, Mi., U.S. . . . . . . F8 . 115
Algonquin, Il., U.S. . . . . . . A5 . 106
Algonquin Provincial Park, On., Can. . . . . B6 . 89
Algood, Tn., U.S. . . . . C8 . 135
Al-Ḥajarah, reg., Asia . . . . E5 . 42
Al-Ḥalfāyah, Iraq . . . . G12 . 44
Al-Ḥamād, pl., Sau. Ar. . . . G8 . 44
Alhambra, Ca., U.S. . . . . . m12 . 98
Al-Ḥarrah, Sau. Ar. . . . . . D3 . 42
Al-Ḥarūj al-Aswad, hills, Libya . . . . A8 . 50
Al-Ḥasakah, Syria . . . . D9 . 44
Al-Ḥawrah, Yemen . . . . . H5 . 38
Al-Ḥayy, Iraq . . . . F12 . 44
Al-Ḥijāz, reg., Sau. Ar. . . . E3 . 38
Al-Ḥillah, Iraq . . . . D4 . 42
Al-Hoceima, Mor. . . . . C4 . 48
Al-Ḥudaydah, Yemen . . . . H4 . 38
Al-Ḥufrah, reg., Sau. Ar. . . E3 . 42
Al-Ḥufūf, Sau. Ar. . . . . . . E5 . 38
Al-Ḥulwah, Sau. Ar. . . . . . F5 . 38
Aliağo, Tur. . . . . C2 . 44
'Alī al-Gharbī, Iraq . . . . . . F12 . 44
Alībāg, India . . . . F2 . 40
Āli Bayramlı, Azer. . . . . . . C13 . 44
Alicante see Alacant, Spain H6 . 16
Alice, Tx., U.S. . . . . F3 . 136
Alice Lake, l., Mn., U.S. . . . C7 . 116
Alice Springs, Austl. . . . . . E5 . 60
Aliceville, Al., U.S. . . . . . . B1 . 94
Alīgarh, India . . . . D3 . 40
Alīgūdarz, Iran . . . . D5 . 42
Alingsås, Swe. . . . . H5 . 10
Alīpur, Pak. . . . . E10 . 42
Aliquippa, Pa., U.S. . . . . . . E1 . 131
Aliwal North, S. Afr. . . . . . E4 . 56
Alix, Ab., Can. . . . . C4 . 84
Al-Jaghbūb, Libya . . . . . . E9 . 48
Al-Jahrah, Kuw. . . . . E5 . 42
Al-Jalāmīd, Sau. Ar. . . . . . G9 . 44
Al-Jawārah, Oman . . . . . . G7 . 38
Al-Jawf, Libya . . . . F9 . 48
Al-Jawf, Sau. Ar. . . . . E3 . 38
Al-Jubayl, Sau. Ar. . . . . . . E5 . 38
Al-Junaynah, Sudan . . . . . H9 . 48
Aljustrel, Port. . . . . I2 . 16
Alkali Lake, l., Nv., U.S. . . . B2 . 121
Alkali Lake, l., Or., U.S. . . . E6 . 130
Alkaline Lake, l., N.D., U.S. C6 . 127
Al-Khābūrah, Oman . . . . . F7 . 38
Al-Khalīl (Hebron), W.B. . . G6 . 44
Al-Kharṭūm, Sudan . . . . . G11 . 48
Al-Khaṣab, Oman . . . . E7 . 42
Al-Khums, Libya . . . . E6 . 14
Al-Kifl, Iraq . . . . F11 . 44
Alkmaar, Neth. . . . . D9 . 12
Al-Kūfah, Iraq . . . . D4 . 42
Al-Kūt, Iraq . . . . D5 . 42
Al-Kuwayt (Kuwait), Kuw. . E5 . 42
Al-Lādhiqīyah, Syria . . . . . E6 . 44
Allagash, stm., Me., U.S. . . B3 . 112
Allagash Lake, l., Me., U.S. . B3 . 112
Allahābād, India . . . . D4 . 40
Allah-Jun', Russia . . . . . . C15 . 26
Allamakee, co., Ia., U.S. . . A6 . 108
Allan, Sk., Can. . . . . F2 . 91
Allannyo, Myan. . . . . C3 . 34
Allardt, Tn., U.S. . . . . C9 . 135
Allatoona Lake, res., Ga., U.S. . . . . B2 . 103
Alldays, S. Afr. . . . . C4 . 56
Allegan, Mi., U.S. . . . . F5 . 115
Allegan, co., Mi., U.S. . . . . F5 . 115
Allegany, N.Y., U.S. . . . . . C2 . 125
Allegany, co., Md., U.S. . . . k13 . 113
Allegany, co., N.Y., U.S. . . . C2 . 125
Allegany Indian Reservation, N.Y., U.S. . . . . C2 . 125
Alleghany, co., N.C., U.S. . . A1 . 126
Alleghany, co., Va., U.S. . . . C2 . 139
Allegheny, co., Pa., U.S. . . . E2 . 131
Allegheny, stm., U.S. . . . . . E2 . 131
Allegheny Reservoir, res., U.S. . . . . B4 . 131
Allemands, Lac Des, l., La., U.S. . . . . E5 . 111
Allen, Ok., U.S. . . . . C5 . 129
Allen, co., In., U.S. . . . . . . B7 . 107
Allen, co., Ks., U.S. . . . . . E8 . 109
Allen, co., Ky., U.S. . . . . . D3 . 110
Allen, co., La., U.S. . . . . . . D3 . 111
Allen, co., Oh., U.S. . . . . . B1 . 128
Allen, Mount, mtn., Ak., U.S. . . . . C11 . 95
Allendale, N.J., U.S. . . . . . A4 . 123
Allendale, S.C., U.S. . . . . . E5 . 133
Allendale, co., S.C., U.S. . . F5 . 133
Allende, Mex. . . . . B4 . 78
Allen Park, Mi., U.S. . . . . . p15 . 115
Allenton, R.I., U.S. . . . . . . E4 . 132
Allenton, Wi., U.S. . . . . . . E5 . 142
Allentown, Pa., U.S. . . . . . E11 . 131
Alleppey, India . . . . H3 . 40
Allerton, Point, c., Ma., U.S. B6 . 114
Alliance, Ne., U.S. . . . . . . B3 . 120
Alliance, Oh., U.S. . . . . . . B4 . 128
Allier, stm., Fr. . . . . D8 . 16

Alligator, stm., N.C., U.S. . . B6 . 126
Alligator Lake, l., Me., U.S. . D4 . 112
Allison, Ia., U.S. . . . . B5 . 108
Allison, Pa., U.S. . . . . G2 . 131
Allison Park, Pa., U.S. . . . . h14 . 131
Alliston [Beeton Tecumseth and Tottenham], On., Can. . . . . C5 . 89
Allood, Tn., U.S. . . . . C8 . 135
Allouez, Wi., U.S. . . . . h9 . 142
Alloway Creek, stm., N.J., U.S. . . . . D2 . 123
Al-Luḥayyah, Yemen . . . . G4 . 38
Allumette Lake, l., Can. . . . B7 . 89
Allyn, Wa., U.S. . . . . B3 . 140
Alma, P.Q., Can. . . . . A6 . 90
Alma, Ar., U.S. . . . . B1 . 97
Alma, Ga., U.S. . . . . E4 . 103
Alma, Ks., U.S. . . . . C7 . 109
Alma, Mi., U.S. . . . . E6 . 115
Alma, Ne., U.S. . . . . D6 . 120
Alma, Wi., U.S. . . . . D2 . 142
Alma-Ata see Almaty, Kaz. . E9 . 26
Almada, Port. . . . . H2 . 16
Almadén, Spain . . . . H4 . 16
Al-Madīnah (Medina), Sau. Ar. . . . . F3 . 38
Al-Mafraq, Jord. . . . . F7 . 44
Almalyk, Uzb. . . . . E8 . 26
Al-Manāmah (Manama), Bahr. . . . . E6 . 42
Almanor, Lake, l., Ca., U.S. B3 . 98
Almansa, Spain . . . . H6 . 16
Al-Marj, Libya . . . . D9 . 48
Almaty, Kaz. . . . . E9 . 26
Al-Mawṣil, Iraq . . . . C4 . 42
Al-Mayādīn, Syria . . . . . . E9 . 44
Almelo, Neth. . . . . D10 . 12
Almenara, Braz. . . . . E8 . 74
Almendralejo, Spain . . . . . H3 . 16
Almería, Spain . . . . I5 . 16
Almería, Golfo de, b., Spain I5 . 16
Al'metevsk, Russia . . . . . . D7 . 26
Al-Mijlad, Sudan . . . . A5 . 54
Al-Miqdādīyah, Iraq . . . . . F11 . 44
Almirante, Pan. . . . . D3 . 80
Almont, Mi., U.S. . . . . F7 . 115
Almonte, On., Can. . . . . . . B8 . 89
Almonte, Spain . . . . I3 . 16
Al-Mubarraz, Sau. Ar. . . . . F5 . 38
Al-Mubarraz, Sau. Ar. . . . . F5 . 42
Al-Muḥarraq, Bahr. . . . . . . E6 . 42
Al-Mukallā, Yemen . . . . . H5 . 38
Al-Mukhā, Yemen . . . . . . H4 . 38
Al-Muwaylih, Sau. Ar. . . . . E3 . 38
Alnön, i., Swe. . . . . E7 . 10
Alnwick, Eng., U.K. . . . . . C6 . 12
Aloha, Or., U.S. . . . . h12 . 130
Alor, Pulau, i., Indon. . . . . E6 . 36
Alor Setar, Malay. . . . . . . B2 . 36
Alpena, Mi., U.S. . . . . C7 . 115
Alpena, co., Mi., U.S. . . . . D7 . 115
Alpha Cordillera . . . . E33 . 144
Alpharetta, Ga., U.S. . . . . . B2 . 103
Alphonse, i., Sey. . . . . i12 . 57b
Alpine, Az., U.S. . . . . D6 . 96
Alpine, Tx., U.S. . . . . D1 . 136
Alpine, Ut., U.S. . . . . C4 . 137
Alpine, co., Ca., U.S. . . . . . C4 . 98
Alps, mts., Eur. . . . . B5 . 14
Al-Qadārif, Sudan . . . . . . H12 . 48
Al-Qā'im, Iraq . . . . E9 . 44
Al-Qāmishlī, Syria . . . . . . D9 . 44
Al-Qaryah ash-Sharqīyah, Libya . . . . D7 . 48
Al-Qaryatayn, Syria . . . . . F7 . 44
Al-Qaṭīf, Sau. Ar. . . . . E6 . 38
Al-Qaṭrūn, Libya . . . . F7 . 48
Al-Qayṣūmah, Sau. Ar. . . . E5 . 38
Al-Quds see Jerusalem, Isr. G6 . 44
Al-Qunayṭirah, Syria . . . . . F6 . 44
Al-Qunfudhah, Sau. Ar. . . . G4 . 38
Al-Qurnah, Iraq . . . . G12 . 44
Al-Quṭayfah, Syria . . . . . . F7 . 44
Als, i., Den. . . . . I3 . 10
Alsace, hist. reg., Fr. . . . . . C10 . 16
Alsasua, Spain . . . . F5 . 16
Alta, Nor. . . . . B10 . 10
Alta, Ia., U.S. . . . . B2 . 108
Altadena, Ca., U.S. . . . . . . m12 . 98
Alta Gracia, Arg. . . . . C4 . 72
Altagracia, Ven. . . . . C5 . 80
Altai, mts., Asia . . . . A5 . 28
Altaj, state, Russia . . . . . . A5 . 28
Altamaha, stm., Ga., U.S. . . E4 . 103
Altamira, Braz. . . . . D9 . 70
Altamont, Il., U.S. . . . . D5 . 106
Altamont, Ks., U.S. . . . . . . E8 . 109
Altamont, Or., U.S. . . . . . . E5 . 130
Altamont, Tn., U.S. . . . . . . D8 . 135
Altamonte Springs, Fl., U.S. D5 . 102
Altamura, Italy . . . . D6 . 18
Altata, Mex. . . . . C4 . 78
Altavista, Va., U.S. . . . . . . C3 . 139
Altay, Mong. . . . . B7 . 28
Altay Mountains see Altai, mts., Asia . . . . B5 . 28
Altevatnet, l., Nor. . . . . . . B8 . 10
Alto, Ga., U.S. . . . . B3 . 103
Alto, N.M., U.S. . . . . D4 . 124
Alto Araguaia, Braz. . . . . . G9 . 70
Alto Garças, Braz. . . . . . . B7 . 72
Alton, Ia., U.S. . . . . B2 . 108
Alton, Il., U.S. . . . . E3 . 106

Alton, Mo., U.S. . . . . E6 . 118
Alton, N.H., U.S. . . . . D4 . 122
Altona, Mb., Can. . . . . E3 . 86
Alton Bay, N.H., U.S. . . . . D4 . 122
Altoona, Al., U.S. . . . . A3 . 94
Altoona, Fl., U.S. . . . . D5 . 102
Altoona, Ia., U.S. . . . . C4 . 108
Altoona, Pa., U.S. . . . . E5 . 131
Altoona, Wi., U.S. . . . . D2 . 142
Al-'Ubaylah, Sau. Ar. . . . . F6 . 38
Al-Ubayyiḍ, Sudan . . . . . . H10 . 48
Alucra, Tur. . . . . B8 . 44
Alum Bank, Pa., U.S. . . . . F4 . 131
Alum Creek, stm., Oh., U.S. k11 . 128
Alupka, Ukr. . . . . G13 . 20
Al-'Uqaylah, Libya . . . . . . E7 . 14
Alushta, Ukr. . . . . G13 . 20
Al-'Uwaynāt, Libya . . . . . . E7 . 48
Alva, Fl., U.S. . . . . F5 . 102
Alva, Ok., U.S. . . . . A3 . 129
Alvarado, Mex. . . . . D5 . 78
Alvarado, Tx., U.S. . . . . . . C4 . 136
Álvaro Obregón, Presa, res., Mex. . . . . B3 . 78
Älvdalen, Swe. . . . . F6 . 10
Alvin, Tx., U.S. . . . . E5 . 136
Alvinston, On., Can. . . . . . E3 . 89
Älvkarleby, Swe. . . . . F7 . 10
Alvord Lake, l., Or., U.S. . . E8 . 130
Al-Wajh, Sau. Ar. . . . . E3 . 38
Alwar, India . . . . D3 . 40
Alxa Zuoqi, China . . . . D9 . 28
Alzira, Spain . . . . H6 . 16
Ama, La., U.S. . . . . k11 . 111
Amacuro, stm., S.A. . . . . . D7 . 80
Amadeus, Lake, l., Austl. . . E5 . 60
Amador, co., Ca., U.S. . . . . C3 . 98
Amagansett, N.Y., U.S. . . . n16 . 125
Amahai, Indon. . . . . D7 . 36
Amakusa-nada, Japan . . . . D1 . 31
Amakusa Sea see Amakusa-nada, Japan . . . . D1 . 31
Åmål, Swe. . . . . G5 . 10
Amalfi, Col. . . . . D4 . 80
Amalfi, Italy . . . . D5 . 18
Amaliás, Grc. . . . . F8 . 18
Amambaí, Braz. . . . . H8 . 70
Amami-Ō-shima, i., Japan . . E1 . 31
Amami-shotō, is., Japan . . g6 . 31a
Amana, Ia., U.S. . . . . C6 . 108
Amapá, Braz. . . . . C9 . 70
Amapá, state, Braz. . . . . . C9 . 70
Amarante, Braz. . . . . E11 . 70
Amarapura, Myan. . . . . . . B3 . 34
Amargosa, stm., U.S. . . . . D5 . 98
Amargosa Desert, des., U.S. G5 . 121
Amargosa Range, mts., U.S. G5 . 121
Amargosa Valley, Nv., U.S. . G5 . 121
Amarillo, Tx., U.S. . . . . . . B2 . 136
Amarkantak, India . . . . . . E4 . 40
Amasya, Tur. . . . . B6 . 44
Amatignak Island, i., Ak., U.S. . . . . E4 . 95
Amawbia Awka, Nig. . . . . E6 . 50
Amazon (Solimões) (Amazonas), stm., S.A. . D9 . 70
Amazonas see Amazon, stm., S.A. . . . . D9 . 70
Ambāla, India . . . . C3 . 40
Ambalavao, Madag. . . . . . C8 . 56
Ambanja, Madag. . . . . A8 . 56
Ambarčik, Russia . . . . C18 . 26
Ambato, Ec. . . . . D4 . 70
Ambatofinandrahana, Madag. . . . . C8 . 56
Ambatolampy, Madag. . . . . B8 . 56
Ambatondrazaka, Madag. . . B8 . 56
Amberg, Ger. . . . . F12 . 12
Ambikāpur, India . . . . E4 . 40
Ambilobe, Madag. . . . . . . A8 . 56
Amble, Pa., U.S. . . . . F11 . 131
Amboasary, Madag. . . . . . C8 . 56
Ambodifototra, Madag. . . . B8 . 56
Ambon, Indon. . . . . D7 . 36
Ambon, Pulau, i., Indon. . . D7 . 36
Ambositra, Madag. . . . . . . C8 . 56
Ambovombe, Madag. . . . . D8 . 56
Amboy, Il., U.S. . . . . B4 . 106
Ambridge, Pa., U.S. . . . . . E1 . 131
Ambriz, Ang. . . . . E2 . 54
Ambrym, i., Vanuatu . . . . . k9 . 62a
Ambunti, Pap. N. Gui. . . . . G11 . 32
Ambūr, India . . . . G3 . 40
Ameca, Mex. . . . . G7 . 78
Amelia, La., U.S. . . . . E4 . 111
Amelia, Oh., U.S. . . . . C1 . 128
Amelia, co., Va., U.S. . . . . C4 . 139
Amelia Court House, Va., U.S. . . . . C5 . 139

Amelia Island, i., Fl., U.S. . . k9 . 102
American, stm., Ca., U.S. . . C3 . 98
American Falls, Id., U.S. . . . G6 . 105
American Falls Dam, Id., U.S. . . . . G6 . 105
American Falls Reservoir, res., Id., U.S. . . . . . . F5 . 105
American Fork, Ut., U.S. . . . C4 . 137
American Highland, plat., Ant. . . . . D12 . 67
American Samoa, dep., Oc. F12 . 58
Americus, Ga., U.S. . . . . . . D2 . 103
Americus, Ks., U.S. . . . . . . D7 . 109
Amersfoort, Neth. . . . . D9 . 12
Amery, Wi., U.S. . . . . C1 . 142
Amery Ice Shelf, Ant. . . . . C12 . 67
Ames, Ia., U.S. . . . . B4 . 108
Amesbury, Ma., U.S. . . . . . A6 . 114
Amfilokhía, Grc. . . . . E8 . 18
Amga, Russia . . . . C15 . 26
Amga, stm., Russia . . . . . . C14 . 26
Amgun', stm., Russia . . . . D15 . 26
Amherst, Ma., U.S. . . . . . . B2 . 114
Amherst, N.H., U.S. . . . . . E3 . 122
Amherst, N.Y., U.S. . . . . . . C2 . 125
Amherst, Oh., U.S. . . . . . . A3 . 128
Amherst, Va., U.S. . . . . . . C3 . 139
Amherst, Wi., U.S. . . . . . . D4 . 142
Amherst, co., Va., U.S. . . . . C3 . 139
Amherstburg, On., Can. . . . E1 . 89
Amherstdale, W.V., U.S. . . . n12 . 141
Amiens, Fr. . . . . C8 . 16
Aminuis, Nmb. . . . . C2 . 56
Amirantes, Les, is., Sey. . . . i12 . 57b
Amisk Lake, l., Sk., Can. . . C4 . 91
Amistad, Presa de la (Amistad Reservoir), res., N.A. . . . . B4 . 78
Amistad National Recreation Area, Tx., U.S. . . . . . . E2 . 136
Amistad Reservoir (Amistad, Presa de la), res., N.A. . B4 . 78
Amite, La., U.S. . . . . D5 . 111
Amite, co., Ms., U.S. . . . . . D3 . 117
Amite, stm., La., U.S. . . . . . D5 . 111
Amity, Ar., U.S. . . . . B3 . 130
Amityville, N.Y., U.S. . . . . E7 . 125
Amlia Island, i., Ak., U.S. . . E5 . 95
'Ammān, Jord. . . . . D3 . 42
Ammon, Id., U.S. . . . . F7 . 105
Ammonoosuc, stm., N.H., U.S. . . . . B3 . 122
Āmol, Iran . . . . C6 . 42
Amorgós, i., Grc. . . . . F10 . 18
Amory, Ms., U.S. . . . . B5 . 117
Amos, P.Q., Can. . . . . k11 . 90
Åmot, Nor. . . . . G2 . 10
Amoy see Xiamen, China . . G11 . 28
Ampanihy, Madag. . . . . . . C7 . 56
Ampasimanolotra, Madag. . B8 . 56
Amposta, Spain . . . . G7 . 16
Amrāvati, India . . . . E3 . 40
Amreli, India . . . . E2 . 40
Amritsar, India . . . . C2 . 40
Amroha, India . . . . D3 . 40
Amsterdam, Neth. . . . . D9 . 12
Amsterdam, N.Y., U.S. . . . . C6 . 125
Amstetten, Aus. . . . . F14 . 12
Am Timan, Chad . . . . A4 . 54
Amu Darya, stm., Asia . . . . B8 . 42
Amukta Pass, strt., Ak., U.S. E5 . 95
Amundsen Gulf, b., N.T., Can. . . . . D15 . 82
Amundsen Sea, Ant. . . . . . C30 . 67
Amuntai, Indon. . . . . D5 . 36
Amur (Heilong), stm., Asia . D16 . 26
Amurang, Indon. . . . . D6 . 36
Amvrakikós Kólpos, b., Grc. E8 . 18
Anaa, atoll, Fr. Poly. . . . . . F15 . 58
Anaco, Ven. . . . . D7 . 80
Anacoco, La., U.S. . . . . . . C2 . 111
Anaconda, Mt., U.S. . . . . . D4 . 119
Anaconda Range, mts., Mt., U.S. . . . . E3 . 119
Anacortes, Wa., U.S. . . . . . A3 . 140
Anacostia, stm., U.S. . . . . . C4 . 113
Anacostia, Northwest Branch, stm., Md., U.S. B3 . 113
Anadarko, Ok., U.S. . . . . . B3 . 129
Anadolu, hist. reg., Tur. . . . C6 . 44
Anadyr', Russia . . . . C19 . 26
Anadyr', stm., Russia . . . . . C19 . 26
Anadyr, Gulf of see Anadyrskij zaliv, b., Russia . . . . C20 . 26
Anadyrskij zaliv, b., Russia . C20 . 26
'Ānah, Iraq . . . . E9 . 44
Anaheim, Ca., U.S. . . . . . . F5 . 98
Anahola, Hi., U.S. . . . . A2 . 104
Anahuac, Tx., U.S. . . . . . . E5 . 136
Anakāpalle, India . . . . F4 . 40
Analalava, Madag. . . . . . . A8 . 56
Ana María, Golfo de, b., Cuba . . . . A4 . 80
Anambas, Kepulauan, is., Indon. . . . . C3 . 36
Anamosa, Ia., U.S. . . . . . . B6 . 108
Anamur, Tur. . . . . D5 . 44
Anan, Japan . . . . D2 . 31
Anan'iv, Ukr. . . . . F11 . 20
Anantapur, India . . . . G3 . 40
Anantnāg, India . . . . C3 . 40
Anapa, Russia . . . . G14 . 20
Anápolis, Braz. . . . . E2 . 74
Anastasia Island, i., Fl., U.S. C5 . 102
Anatahan, i., N. Mar. Is. . . C12 . 32

Name	Map Ref.	Page

Anatolia see Anadolu, hist. reg., Tur. ... **C6** 44
Anatom, i., Vanuatu ... **I9** 62a
Añatuya, Arg. ... **D5** 72
Anbei, China ... **A7** 40
Ancaster, On., Can. ... **D4** 89
Ancha, Sierra, mts., Az., U.S. ... **D4** 96
Anchorage, Ak., U.S. ... **C10** 95
Anchorage, Ky., U.S. ... **g11** 110
Anchor Point, Ak., U.S. ... **D9** 95
Anchor Point, c., Ak., U.S. ... **h15** 95
Ancienne-Lorette, P.Q., Can. ... **C6** 90
Anclote Keys, is., Fl., U.S. ... **D4** 102
Ancona, Italy ... **C4** 18
Ancud, Chile ... **F2** 69
Anda, China ... **B13** 28
Andacollo, Chile ... **E3** 72
Andalgalá, Arg. ... **D4** 72
Andalsnes, Nor. ... **E2** 10
Andalucía, hist. reg., Spain ... **I4** 16
Andalusia, Al., U.S. ... **D3** 94
Andalusia, Il., U.S. ... **B3** 106
Andaman and Nicobar Islands, ter., India ... **G6** 40
Andaman Basin ... **H12** 64
Andaman Islands, is., India ... **G6** 40
Andaman Sea, Asia ... **E3** 34
Andamooka, Austl. ... **G2** 62
Andapa, Madag. ... **A8** 56
Andéramboukane, Mali ... **C5** 50
Anderson, Ak., U.S. ... **C10** 95
Anderson, Ca., U.S. ... **B2** 98
Anderson, In., U.S. ... **D6** 107
Anderson, Mo., U.S. ... **E3** 118
Anderson, S.C., U.S. ... **B2** 133
Anderson, co., Ks., U.S. ... **D8** 109
Anderson, co., Ky., U.S. ... **C4** 110
Anderson, co., S.C., U.S. ... **B2** 133
Anderson, co., Tn., U.S. ... **C9** 135
Anderson, co., Tx., U.S. ... **D5** 136
Anderson, stm., N.T., Can. ... **E14** 82
Anderson, stm., In., U.S. ... **H4** 107
Anderson, Mount, mtn., Wa., U.S. ... **B2** 140
Anderson Ranch Reservoir, res., Id., U.S. ... **F3** 105
Andes, mts., S.A. ... **B4** 72
Andes, Lake, l., S.D., U.S. ... **D7** 134
Andfjorden, strt., Nor. ... **B7** 10
Andhra Pradesh, prov., India ... **F3** 40
Andīmeshk, Iran ... **F13** 44
Andirlang, China ... **B4** 40
Andižan, Uzb. ... **E9** 26
Andkhvoy, Afg. ... **C9** 42
Andoany, Madag. ... **A8** 56
Andong, S. Kor. ... **D13** 28
Andorra, ctry., Eur. ... **F7** 16
Andorra-la-Vella, And. ... **F7** 16
Andover, Ks., U.S. ... **g12** 109
Andover, Ma., U.S. ... **A5** 114
Andover, Mn., U.S. ... **m12** 116
Andover, Oh., U.S. ... **A5** 128
Andover Lake, res., Ct., U.S. ... **C6** 100
Andøya, i., Nor. ... **B6** 10
Andradina, Braz. ... **F1** 74
Andreanof Islands, is., Ak., U.S. ... **E4** 95
Andrew, co., Mo., U.S. ... **B3** 118
Andrew Island, i., N.S., Can. ... **D9** 87
Andrews, In., U.S. ... **C6** 107
Andrews, N.C., U.S. ... **f9** 126
Andrews, S.C., U.S. ... **E8** 133
Andrews, Tx., U.S. ... **C1** 136
Andrews, co., Tx., U.S. ... **C1** 136
Andrews Air Force Base, mil., Md., U.S. ... **C4** 113
Andria, Italy ... **D6** 18
Andriamena, Madag. ... **B8** 56
Androka, Madag. ... **D7** 56
Andropov see Rybinsk, Russia ... **D5** 26
Andros, i., Bah. ... **D9** 76
Ándros, i., Grc. ... **F10** 18
Androscoggin, co., Me., U.S. ... **D2** 112
Androscoggin, stm., Me., U.S. ... **D2** 112
Androscoggin Lake, l., Me., U.S. ... **D2** 112
Āndrott Island, i., India ... **G2** 40
Andudu, D.R.C. ... **C5** 54
Andújar, Spain ... **H4** 16
Andulo, Ang. ... **F3** 54
Anegada, i., Br. Vir. Is. ... **B7** 80
Anegada Passage, strt., N.A. ... **B7** 80
Aného, Togo ... **H5** 52
Aneto, mtn., Spain ... **F7** 16
Aney, Niger ... **C8** 50
Ang'angxi, China ... **B12** 28
Angara, stm., Russia ... **D11** 26
Angarsk, Russia ... **D12** 26
Änge, Swe. ... **E6** 10
Ángel, Salto (Angel Falls), wtfl., Ven. ... **B7** 70
Ángel de la Guarda, Isla, i., Mex. ... **B2** 78
Angeles, Phil. ... **C8** 34
Angeles Point, c., Wa., U.S. ... **A2** 140
Angel Falls see Ángel, Salto, wtfl., Ven. ... **B7** 70
Ängelholm, Swe. ... **H5** 10
Angelina, co., Tx., U.S. ... **D5** 136

Angels Camp, Ca., U.S. ... **C3** 98
Ångermanälven, stm., Swe. ... **E7** 10
Angers, Fr. ... **D6** 16
Angier, N.C., U.S. ... **B4** 126
Angkor Wat, hist., Camb. ... **D4** 34
Anglesey, i., Wales, U.K. ... **D4** 12
Angleton, Tx., U.S. ... **E5** 136
Angmagssalik, Grnld. ... **E32** 82
Ango, D.R.C. ... **C5** 54
Angoche, Moz. ... **B6** 56
Angol, Chile ... **E2** 69
Angola, In., U.S. ... **A8** 107
Angola, N.Y., U.S. ... **C1** 125
Angola, ctry., Afr. ... **F3** 54
Angola Basin ... **J14** 66
Angola Swamp, sw., N.C., U.S. ... **C5** 126
Angoon, Ak., U.S. ... **D13** 95
Angora see Ankara, Tur. ... **C5** 44
Angoram, Pap. N. Gui. ... **G11** 32
Angostura see Ciudad Bolívar, Ven. ... **B7** 70
Angostura, Presa de la, res., Mex. ... **D6** 78
Angostura Reservoir, res., S.D., U.S. ... **D2** 134
Angoulême, Fr. ... **E7** 16
Angren, Uzb. ... **E9** 26
Angu, D.R.C. ... **C4** 54
Anguilla, Ms., U.S. ... **C3** 117
Anguilla, dep., N.A. ... **E12** 76
Anguille, Cape, c., Nf., Can. ... **E2** 88
Anguo, China ... **B4** 30
Anholt, i., Den. ... **H4** 10
Anhua, China ... **D3** 30
Anhui, state, China ... **E11** 28
Aniak, Ak., U.S. ... **C8** 95
Anil, Braz. ... **B3** 74
Animas, stm., U.S. ... **D3** 99
Animas Mountains, mts., N.M., U.S. ... **F1** 124
Animas Peak, mtn., N.M., U.S. ... **F2** 124
Animas Valley, val., N.M., U.S. ... **F1** 124
Anina, Rom. ... **G6** 20
Anita, Ia., U.S. ... **C3** 108
Aniva, zaliv, b., Russia ... **B16** 28
Aniwa, i., Vanuatu ... **I9** 62a
Anjār, India ... **I2** 40
Anjou, P.Q., Can. ... **p19** 90
Anjou, hist. reg., Fr. ... **D6** 16
Anjouan see Nzwani, i., Com. ... **A7** 56
Anjudin, Russia ... **B10** 22
Ankang, China ... **E9** 28
Ankara, Tur. ... **C5** 44
Ankavandra, Madag. ... **B8** 56
Ankazoabo, Madag. ... **C7** 56
Ankazobe, Madag. ... **B8** 56
Ankeny, Ia., U.S. ... **C4** 108
Anking see Anqing, China ... **E11** 28
Ankoro, D.R.C. ... **E5** 54
Anlong, China ... **D2** 30
Anlu, China ... **E10** 28
Ann, Cape, c., Ma., U.S. ... **A6** 114
Anna, Russia ... **D16** 20
Anna, Il., U.S. ... **F4** 106
Anna, Oh., U.S. ... **B1** 128
Anna, Lake, res., Va., U.S. ... **B5** 139
Annaba, Alg. ... **C6** 48
An-Nabk, Syria ... **E7** 44
An-Nafūd, des., Sau. Ar. ... **E4** 38
An-Najaf, Iraq ... **D4** 42
An-Najaf, state, Iraq ... **G11** 44
Anna Maria, Fl., U.S. ... **p10** 102
Anna Maria Island, i., Fl., U.S. ... **q10** 102
Annandale, Mn., U.S. ... **E4** 116
Annandale, Va., U.S. ... **g12** 139
Anna Plains, Austl. ... **D3** 60
Annapolis, Md., U.S. ... **C5** 113
Annapolis, stm., N.S., Can. ... **E4** 87
Annapolis Junction, Md., U.S. ... **B4** 113
Annapolis Royal, N.S., Can. ... **E4** 87
Annapūrna, mtn., Nepal ... **D4** 40
Ann Arbor, Mi., U.S. ... **F7** 115
Annawan, Il., U.S. ... **B4** 106
Anne Arundel, co., Md., U.S. ... **B4** 113
Annecy, Fr. ... **E10** 16
Annette, Ak., U.S. ... **n24** 95
An Nhon, Viet. ... **D5** 34
Anning, China ... **E1** 30
Anniston, Al., U.S. ... **B4** 94
Annobón, i., Eq. Gui. ... **C1** 52
An-Nuhūd, Sudan ... **H10** 48
An Nukhayb, Iraq ... **F10** 44
An-Nu'mānīyah, Iraq ... **D5** 42
Annville, Pa., U.S. ... **F8** 131
Anoka, Mn., U.S. ... **E5** 116
Anoka, co., Mn., U.S. ... **E5** 116
Anori, Braz. ... **D7** 70
Anqing, China ... **E11** 28
Anshan, China ... **C12** 28
Anshun, China ... **F9** 28
Anson, Me., U.S. ... **D3** 112
Anson, Tx., U.S. ... **C3** 136
Anson, co., N.C., U.S. ... **B2** 126

Ansongo, Mali ... **C5** 50
Ansonia, Ct., U.S. ... **D3** 100
Ansonia, Oh., U.S. ... **B1** 128
Ansted, W.V., U.S. ... **C3** 141
Antalaha, Madag. ... **A9** 56
Antalya, Tur. ... **D4** 44
Antalya, Gulf of see Antalya Körfezi, b., Tur. ... **D4** 44
Antalya Körfezi, b., Tur. ... **D4** 44
Antananarivo, Madag. ... **B8** 56
Antarctica ... **L13** 4
Antarctic Peninsula, pen., Ant. ... **D35** 67
Antelope, co., Ne., U.S. ... **B7** 120
Antelope Creek, stm., Wy., U.S. ... **C7** 143
Antelope Island, i., Ut., U.S. ... **B3** 137
Antelope Peak, mtn., Nv., U.S. ... **B7** 121
Antelope Range, mts., Nv., U.S. ... **D7** 121
Antelope Reservoir, res., Or., U.S. ... **E9** 130
Antelope Wash, val., Nv., U.S. ... **D5** 121
Antequera, Spain ... **I4** 16
Antero, Mount, mtn., Co., U.S. ... **C4** 99
Antero Reservoir, res., Co., U.S. ... **C5** 99
Anthon, Ia., U.S. ... **B2** 108
Anthony, Fl., U.S. ... **C4** 102
Anthony, Ks., U.S. ... **E5** 109
Anthony, N.M., U.S. ... **F3** 124
Anthony, R.I., U.S. ... **D3** 132
Anthony, Tx., U.S. ... **o11** 136
Anthony Creek, stm., W.V., U.S. ... **D4** 141
Antibes, Fr. ... **F10** 16
Anticosti, Île d', i., P.Q., Can. ... **k14** 90
Antietam National Battlefield, hist., Md., U.S. ... **B2** 113
Antigo, Wi., U.S. ... **C4** 142
Antigua, i., Antig. ... **B7** 80
Antigua and Barbuda, ctry., N.A. ... **E12** 76
Antioch see Hatay, Tur. ... **D7** 44
Antioch, Ca., U.S. ... **h9** 98
Antioch, Il., U.S. ... **A5** 106
Antioquia, Col. ... **D4** 80
Antipodes Islands, is., N.Z. ... **N20** 64
Antlers, Ok., U.S. ... **C6** 129
Antofagasta, Chile ... **B2** 69
Antofalla, Salar de, pl., Arg. ... **D4** 72
Anton, Tx., U.S. ... **C1** 136
Antongila, Helodrano, b., Madag. ... **B8** 56
Antônio Bezerra, Braz. ... **B4** 74
Antonito, Co., U.S. ... **D5** 99
Antora Peak, mtn., Co., U.S. ... **C4** 99
Antrim, N.H., U.S. ... **D3** 122
Antrim, co., Mi., U.S. ... **C5** 115
Antsalova, Madag. ... **B7** 56
Antsirabe, Madag. ... **B8** 56
Antsirañana, Madag. ... **A8** 56
Antsohihy, Madag. ... **A8** 56
Antwerp see Antwerpen, Bel. ... **E9** 12
Antwerp, Oh., U.S. ... **A1** 128
Antwerpen (Antwerp), Bel. ... **E9** 12
Anugul, India ... **E5** 40
Anūpgarh, India ... **D2** 40
Anuradhapura, Sri L. ... **H4** 40
Anxi, China ... **C7** 28
Anxiang, China ... **D3** 30
Anyang, China ... **D10** 28
A'nyêmaqên Shan, mts., China ... **D7** 28
Anyue, China ... **C2** 30
Anžero-Sudžensk, Russia ... **D10** 26
Anzio, Italy ... **D4** 18
Aoga-shima, i., Japan ... **E15** 28
Aoji-ri, N. Kor. ... **B2** 31
Aomori, Japan ... **C16** 28
Aoral, Mount see Aôral, Phnum, mtn., Camb. ... **D4** 34
Aôral, Phnum, mtn., Camb. ... **D4** 34
Aosta, Italy ... **B1** 18
'Aouâna ('Aklé), reg., Afr. ... **C3** 50
Aouderas, Niger ... **C6** 50
Aouk, Bahr, stm., Afr. ... **I9** 48
Aoukâr, reg., Maur. ... **C3** 50
Aozou, Chad ... **B8** 50
Apache, Ok., U.S. ... **C3** 129
Apache, co., Az., U.S. ... **B6** 96
Apache Junction, Az., U.S. ... **m9** 96
Apache Peak, mtn., Az., U.S. ... **F5** 96
Apalachee Bay, b., Fl., U.S. ... **B2** 102
Apalachicola, Fl., U.S. ... **C2** 102
Apalachicola, stm., Fl., U.S. ... **B1** 102
Apalachicola Bay, b., Fl., U.S. ... **C2** 102
Apaporis, stm., S.A. ... **C5** 70
Aparri, Phil. ... **C8** 34
Apatity, Russia ... **C5** 26
Apatzingán de la Constitución, Mex. ... **D4** 78
Apeldoorn, Neth. ... **D9** 12
Apennines see Appennino, mts., Italy ... **C4** 18
Apex, N.C., U.S. ... **B4** 126

Apia, Samoa ... **F12** 58
Apiacás, Serra dos, plat., Braz. ... **E8** 70
Apishapa, stm., Co., U.S. ... **D6** 99
Aplington, Ia., U.S. ... **B5** 108
Apo, Mount, mtn., Phil. ... **E9** 34
Apollo, Pa., U.S. ... **E2** 131
Apopka, Fl., U.S. ... **D5** 102
Apopka, Lake, l., Fl., U.S. ... **D5** 102
Apostle Islands, is., Wi., U.S. ... **A3** 142
Apostle Islands National Lakeshore, Wi., U.S. ... **A3** 142
Apóstoles, Arg. ... **D6** 72
Apostolove, Ukr. ... **F12** 20
Appalachia, Va., U.S. ... **f9** 139
Appalachian Mountains, mts., N.A. ... **D11** 92
Appanoose, co., Ia., U.S. ... **D5** 108
Appennino, mts., Italy ... **C4** 18
Appennino Ligure, mts., Italy ... **B2** 18
Apple, stm., Wi., U.S. ... **C1** 142
Apple Creek, Oh., U.S. ... **B4** 128
Applegate, Or., U.S. ... **E3** 130
Applegate, stm., Or., U.S. ... **E3** 130
Appleton, Mn., U.S. ... **E2** 116
Appleton, Wi., U.S. ... **D5** 142
Appleton City, Mo., U.S. ... **C3** 118
Apple Valley, Ca., U.S. ... **E5** 98
Apple Valley, Mn., U.S. ... **n12** 116
Appling, co., Ga., U.S. ... **E4** 103
Appomattox, Va., U.S. ... **C4** 139
Appomattox, co., Va., U.S. ... **C4** 139
Appomattox, stm., Va., U.S. ... **C4** 139
Appomattox Court House National Historical Park, Va., U.S. ... **C4** 139
Apua Point, c., Hi., U.S. ... **D6** 104
Apucarana, Braz. ... **F1** 74
Apure, stm., Ven. ... **B6** 70
Apurímac, stm., Peru ... **F5** 70
Aqaba, Gulf of, b. ... **E2** 42
'Aqrah, Iraq ... **D10** 44
Aquarius Mountains, mts., Az., U.S. ... **C2** 96
Aquidauana, Braz. ... **H8** 70
Ara, India ... **D4** 40
Arab, Al., U.S. ... **A3** 94
'Arab, Bahr al-, stm., Sudan ... **A4** 54
Arabi, La., U.S. ... **k11** 111
Arabian Basin ... **G9** 64
Arabian Desert see Eastern Desert, des., Egypt ... **E11** 48
Arabian Gulf see Persian Gulf, b., Asia ... **E6** 42
Arabian Sea, Asia ... **G8** 38
Aracaju, Braz. ... **D4** 74
Aracati, Braz. ... **B4** 74
Araçatuba, Braz. ... **F1** 74
Aracruz, Braz. ... **E3** 74
Araçuaí, Braz. ... **E3** 74
Arad, Rom. ... **F6** 20
Arafura Sea ... **E7** 58
Arafura Shelf ... **I16** 64
Aragac, gora see Aragats Lerr, mtn., Arm. ... **B11** 44
Aragarças, Braz. ... **C7** 70
Aragats Lerr, mtn., Arm. ... **B11** 44
Arago, Cape, c., Or., U.S. ... **D2** 130
Aragon, Ga., U.S. ... **B1** 103
Aragón, hist. reg., Spain ... **G6** 16
Araguacema, Braz. ... **E10** 70
Araguaia, stm., Braz. ... **E10** 70
Araguaína, Braz. ... **C2** 74
Araguari, Braz. ... **E2** 74
Araguatins, Braz. ... **C2** 74
Ārāk, Alg. ... **E5** 48
Arāk, Iran ... **B2** 42
Arakan Yoma, mts., Myan. ... **B2** 34
Arakkonam, India ... **G3** 40
Araks (Aras) (Araz), stm., Asia ... **B10** 44
Aral see Aral'sk, Kaz. ... **B7** 42
Aral Sea, Asia ... **B7** 42
Aral'sk, Kaz. ... **B7** 42
Aranda de Duero, Spain ... **G5** 16
Aranjuez, Spain ... **G5** 16
Aranos, Nmb. ... **C2** 56
Aransas, co., Tx., U.S. ... **E4** 136
Aransas Bay, b., Tx., U.S. ... **E4** 136
Aransas Pass, Tx., U.S. ... **F4** 136
Aranyaprathet, Thai. ... **D4** 34
Araouane, Mali ... **B3** 50
Arapaho, Ok., U.S. ... **B3** 129
Arapahoe, Ne., U.S. ... **D6** 120
Arapahoe, co., Co., U.S. ... **B6** 99
Arapiraca, Braz. ... **C4** 74
Arapkir, Tur. ... **C8** 44
Arapongas, Braz. ... **F1** 74
Araranguá, Braz. ... **D8** 72
Araraquara, Braz. ... **F2** 74
Ararat, Arm. ... **C11** 44
Ararat, Austl. ... **H3** 62
Ararat, Mount see Ağrı Dağı, mtn., Tur. ... **C11** 44
Aras (Araks) (Araz), stm., Asia ... **C12** 44
Arauca, Col. ... **D5** 80
Arauquita, Col. ... **D5** 80
Araxá, Braz. ... **E2** 74
Araz (Araks) (Aras), stm., Asia ... **C12** 44

Ārba Minch', Eth. ... **B7** 54
Arboga, Swe. ... **G6** 10
Arborg, Mb., Can. ... **D3** 86
Arbroath, Scot., U.K. ... **B5** 12
Arbuckle, Lake, l., Fl., U.S. ... **E5** 102
Arbuckle Mountains, mts., Ok., U.S. ... **C4** 129
Arbuckle, Lake of the, res., Ok., U.S. ... **C5** 129
Arcachon, Fr. ... **E6** 16
Arcade, Ca., U.S. ... **B3** 103
Arcade, N.Y., U.S. ... **C2** 125
Arcadia, Ca., U.S. ... **m12** 98
Arcadia, Fl., U.S. ... **E5** 102
Arcadia, In., U.S. ... **D5** 107
Arcadia, La., U.S. ... **B3** 111
Arcadia, Mo., U.S. ... **D7** 118
Arcadia, S.C., U.S. ... **B4** 133
Arcadia, Wi., U.S. ... **D2** 142
Arcanum, Oh., U.S. ... **C1** 128
Arcata, Ca., U.S. ... **B1** 98
Arc Dome, mtn., Nv., U.S. ... **E4** 121
Archangel see Arhangel'sk, Russia ... **C6** 26
Archbald, Pa., U.S. ... **m18** 131
Archbold, Oh., U.S. ... **A1** 128
Archdale, N.C., U.S. ... **B3** 126
Archer, Fl., U.S. ... **C4** 102
Archer, co., Tx., U.S. ... **C3** 136
Archer City, Tx., U.S. ... **C3** 136
Arches National Park, Ut., U.S. ... **E6** 137
Archie, Mo., U.S. ... **C3** 118
Archuleta, co., Co., U.S. ... **D3** 99
Arco, Id., U.S. ... **F5** 105
Arcola, Il., U.S. ... **D5** 106
Arcoverde, Braz. ... **C4** 74
Arctic Ocean ... **E36** 144
Ardabīl, Iran ... **C5** 42
Ardahan, Tur. ... **B10** 44
Ardakān, Iran ... **D6** 42
Ardalstangen, Nor. ... **F2** 10
Ardennes, reg., Eur. ... **B9** 16
Ardeşen, Tur. ... **B9** 44
Ardmore, Al., U.S. ... **A3** 94
Ardmore, In., U.S. ... **A5** 107
Ardmore, Ok., U.S. ... **C4** 129
Ardmore, Tn., U.S. ... **B5** 135
Ardsley, N.Y., U.S. ... **g13** 125
Arecibo, P.R. ... **B6** 80
Areia Branca, Braz. ... **B4** 74
Arena, Point, c., Ca., U.S. ... **C2** 98
Arena, Punta, c., Mex. ... **C3** 78
Arenac, co., Mi., U.S. ... **D7** 115
Arenápolis, Braz. ... **A6** 72
Arenas, Cayo, i., Mex. ... **C6** 78
Arendal, Nor. ... **G3** 10
Arequipa, Peru ... **G5** 70
Arévalo, Spain ... **G4** 16
Arezzo, Italy ... **C3** 18
Argenta, Il., U.S. ... **D5** 106
Argentan, Fr. ... **C6** 16
Argentina, ctry., S.A. ... **E3** 69
Argentino, Lago, l., Arg. ... **H2** 69
Argentnie Basin ... **L9** 66
Argeş, stm., Rom. ... **G8** 20
Arghandāb, stm., Afg. ... **D9** 42
Argolikós Kólpos, b., Grc. ... **F9** 18
Argonne, reg., Fr. ... **C9** 16
Árgos, Grc. ... **F9** 18
Argos, In., U.S. ... **B5** 107
Argostólion, Grc. ... **E8** 18
Argun' (Ergun), stm., Asia ... **A12** 28
Argungu, Nig. ... **D5** 50
Argyle, Mn., U.S. ... **B2** 116
Argyle, Wi., U.S. ... **F4** 142
Arhangel'sk, Russia ... **C6** 26
Arhangel'skoe, Russia ... **C14** 20
Arhéa Epídavros, hist., Grc. ... **F9** 18
Århus, Den. ... **H4** 10
Arica, Chile ... **A2** 69
Arica, Col. ... **D5** 70
Arichat, N.S., Can. ... **D8** 87
Arid, Cape, c., Austl. ... **G3** 60
Arīḥā (Jericho), Gaza Str. ... **G6** 44
Arikaree, stm., U.S. ... **B8** 99
Arima, Trin. ... **C7** 80
Arinos, stm., Braz. ... **F8** 70
Ariquemes, Braz. ... **E7** 70
Aristazabal Island, i., B.C., Can. ... **C3** 85
Ariton, Al., U.S. ... **D4** 94
Arivonimamo, Madag. ... **B8** 56
Arizaro, Salar de, pl., Arg. ... **D4** 72
Arizona, Arg. ... **F4** 72
Arizona, state, U.S. ... **C4** 96
Arizona Sunsites, Az., U.S. ... **F6** 96
Arjay, Ky., U.S. ... **D6** 110
Arjeplog, Swe. ... **C7** 10
Arjona, Col. ... **C4** 80
Arka, Russia ... **C16** 22
Arkabutla Lake, res., Ms., U.S. ... **A4** 117
Arkadelphia, Ar., U.S. ... **C2** 97
Arkalyk, Kaz. ... **D8** 26
Arkansas, co., Ar., U.S. ... **C4** 97
Arkansas, state, U.S. ... **C3** 97
Arkansas, stm., U.S. ... **E9** 92
Arkansas City, Ks., U.S. ... **E6** 109
Arkoma, Ok., U.S. ... **B7** 129
Arktičeskogo Instituta, ostrova, is., Russia ... **B10** 26
Arles, Fr. ... **F9** 16
Arlington, Ga., U.S. ... **E2** 103
Arlington, Ma., U.S. ... **B5** 114

Name	Map Ref.	Page
Arlington, Mn., U.S.	F4	116
Arlington, N.C., U.S.	A2	126
Arlington, Ne., U.S.	C9	120
Arlington, N.Y., U.S.	D7	125
Arlington, Oh., U.S.	B2	128
Arlington, S.C., U.S.	B3	133
Arlington, S.D., U.S.	C8	134
Arlington, Tn., U.S.	B2	135
Arlington, Tx., U.S.	n9	136
Arlington, Va., U.S.	B5	139
Arlington, Vt., U.S.	E2	138
Arlington, Wa., U.S.	A3	140
Arlington, co., Va., U.S.	g12	139
Arlington, Lake, res., Tx., U.S.	n9	136
Arlington Heights, Il., U.S.	A5	106
Arlit, Niger	C6	50
Arlon, Bel.	F9	12
Arma, Ks., U.S.	E9	109
Armada, Mi., U.S.	F8	115
Armadale, Austl.	G2	60
Armagh, P.Q., Can.	C7	90
Armagnac, hist. reg., Fr.	F7	16
Armavir, Russia	B4	42
Armenia, Col.	C4	70
Armenia, ctry., Asia	B11	44
Armians'k, Ukr.	F12	20
Armidale, Austl.	G5	62
Armijo, N.M., U.S.	k7	124
Armour, S.D., U.S.	D7	134
Armstrong, B.C., Can.	D8	85
Armstrong, Ia., U.S.	A3	108
Armstrong, co., Pa., U.S.	E2	131
Armstrong, co., Tx., U.S.	B2	136
Armstrong Creek, stm., W.V., U.S.	m13	141
Arnaudville, La., U.S.	D4	111
Arnett, W.V., U.S.	D3	141
Arnhem, Neth.	E10	12
Arnhem, Cape, c., Austl.	C6	60
Arnhem Bay, b., Austl.	C6	60
Arnhem Land, reg., Austl.	C6	60
Arno, stm., Italy	C3	18
Arnold, Mn., U.S.	D6	116
Arnold, Mo., U.S.	C7	118
Arnold, Ne., U.S.	C5	120
Arnold, Pa., U.S.	h14	131
Arnold Mills, R.I., U.S.	B4	132
Arnold Mills Reservoir, res., R.I., U.S.	B4	132
Arnold's Cove, Nf., Can.	E4	88
Arnolds Park, Ia., U.S.	A2	108
Arnøya, Nor.	A9	10
Arnprior, On., Can.	B8	89
Aroab, Nmb.	D2	56
Aroostook, co., Me., U.S.	B4	112
Ar-Rahad, Sudan	H11	48
Arraias, Braz.	F10	70
Ar-Ramādī, Iraq	D4	42
Arran, Island of, i., Scot., U.K.	C4	12
Ar-Rank, Sudan	H11	48
Ar-Raqqah, Syria	E8	44
Arras, Fr.	B8	16
Arrecife, Spain	A2	50
Arriaga, Mex.	D6	78
Ar-Riyāḍ (Riyadh), Sau. Ar.	F5	38
Arroio Grande, Braz.	E7	72
Arrowhead Mountain Lake, res., Vt., U.S.	B2	138
Arrowrock Reservoir, res., Id., U.S.	F3	105
Arrowwood Lake, res., N.D., U.S.	B7	127
Arroyito, Arg.	E5	72
Arroyo Grande, Ca., U.S.	E3	98
Ar-Rub' al-Khālī, des., Asia	G6	38
Ar-Rumaythah, Iraq	D4	42
Ar-Ruṣayriṣ, Sudan	H11	48
Ar-Ruṭbah, Iraq	D4	42
Arsenev, Russia	C14	28
Árta, Grc.	E8	18
Artà, Spain	H8	16
Artašat (Artashat), Arm.	C11	44
Artashat (Artašat), Arm.	C11	44
Art'em, Russia	C14	28
Artemisa, Cuba	A3	80
Artemivs'k, Ukr.	E14	20
Artëmovsk, Russia	D11	26
Artemus, Ky., U.S.	D6	110
Arter, Mount, mtn., Wy., U.S.	D4	143
Artesia, N.M., U.S.	E5	124
Arthabaska, P.Q., Can.	C6	90
Arthur, On., Can.	D4	89
Arthur, Il., U.S.	D5	106
Arthur, co., Ne., U.S.	C4	120
Arthur, Lake, l., La., U.S.	D3	111
Arthur, Lake, res., Pa., U.S.	E1	131
Arthur Kill, stm., N.J., U.S.	k8	123
Artigas, Ur.	E6	72
Artik, Arm.	B10	44
Artsyz, Ukr.	F10	20
Artvin, Tur.	B9	44
Aru, Kepulauan, is., Indon.	H10	32
Aru, Tanjung, c., Indon.	D5	36
Arua, Ug.	C6	54
Aruanã, Braz.	G9	70
Aruba, dep., N.A.	C6	80
Arunāchal Pradesh, prov., India	D6	40
Aruppukkottai, India	H3	40
Arusha, Tan.	D7	54
Aruwimi, stm., D.R.C.	C4	54
Arvada, Co., U.S.	B5	99
Arvayheer, Mong.	B8	28
Arvidsjaur, Swe.	D8	10
Arvika, Swe.	G5	10
Arvin, Ca., U.S.	E4	98
Arvon, Mount, mtn., Mi., U.S.	B2	115
Arvonia, Va., U.S.	C4	139
Arxan, China	B11	28
Arys', Kaz.	E8	26
Arzamas, Russia	C7	22
Arzew, Golfe d', b., Alg.	J6	16
Aša, Russia	D10	22
Asaba, Nig.	E6	50
Asad, Buḥayrat al-, res., Syria	D8	44
Asad, Lake see Asad, Buḥayrat al-, res., Syria	D8	44
Asadābād, Afg.	C10	42
Asadābād, Iran	E13	44
Asahi-dake, vol., Japan	B4	31
Asahikawa, Japan	C16	28
Āsānsol, India	E5	40
Asbest, Russia	C11	22
Asbestos, P.Q., Can.	D6	90
Asbury Park, N.J., U.S.	C4	123
Ascensión, Mex.	A3	78
Ascension, co., La., U.S.	D5	111
Ascension, i., St. Hel.	J8	46
Ascoli Piceno, Italy	C4	18
Aseb, Erit.	H13	48
Åseda, Swe.	H6	10
Āsela, Eth.	B7	54
Åsele, Swe.	D7	10
Aşgabat, Turk.	F7	26
Ashanti, prov., Ghana	E4	50
Ashaway, R.I., U.S.	F1	132
Ashburn, Ga., U.S.	E3	103
Ashburton, N.Z.	p13	63c
Ashburton, stm., Austl.	E2	60
Ashcroft, B.C., Can.	D7	85
Ashdod, Isr.	G6	44
Ashdown, Ar., U.S.	D1	97
Ashe, co., N.C., U.S.	A1	126
Asheboro, N.C., U.S.	B3	126
Ashepoo, stm., S.C., U.S.	F6	133
Ashern, Mb., Can.	D2	86
Asherton, Tx., U.S.	E3	136
Asheville, N.C., U.S.	f10	126
Ash Flat, Ar., U.S.	A4	97
Ashford, Al., U.S.	D4	94
Ashford, W.V., U.S.	m12	141
Ash Grove, Mo., U.S.	D4	118
Ashikaga, Japan	C3	31
Ashkhabad see Aşgabat, Turk.	F7	26
Ashland, Al., U.S.	B4	94
Ashland, Il., U.S.	D3	106
Ashland, Ks., U.S.	E4	109
Ashland, Ky., U.S.	B7	110
Ashland, Ma., U.S.	g10	114
Ashland, Me., U.S.	B4	112
Ashland, Mo., U.S.	C5	118
Ashland, Ne., U.S.	C9	120
Ashland, N.H., U.S.	C3	122
Ashland, Oh., U.S.	B3	128
Ashland, Or., U.S.	E4	130
Ashland, Pa., U.S.	E9	131
Ashland, Va., U.S.	C5	139
Ashland, Wi., U.S.	B3	142
Ashland, co., Oh., U.S.	B3	128
Ashland, co., Wi., U.S.	B3	142
Ashland, Mount, mtn., Or., U.S.	E4	130
Ashland City, Tn., U.S.	A4	135
Ashland Reservoir, res., Ma., U.S.	h10	114
Ashley, In., U.S.	A7	107
Ashley, N.D., U.S.	C6	127
Ashley, Oh., U.S.	B3	128
Ashley, Pa., U.S.	n17	131
Ashley, co., Ar., U.S.	D4	97
Ashley, stm., S.C., U.S.	F7	133
Ashley Creek, stm., Ut., U.S.	C6	137
Ashmore, Il., U.S.	D5	106
Ashmore Islands, is., Austl.	C3	60
Ashokan Reservoir, res., N.Y., U.S.	D6	125
Ash-Shaddādah, Syria	D9	44
Ash-Shāmīyah, Iraq	F11	44
Ash-Shāriqah, U.A.E.	E7	42
Ash-Sharqāṭ, Iraq	E10	44
Ash-Shaṭrah, Iraq	G12	44
Ash-Shiḥr, Yemen	H5	38
Ash-Shināfīyah, Iraq	G11	44
Ashtabula, Oh., U.S.	A5	128
Ashtabula, co., Oh., U.S.	A5	128
Ashtabula, Lake, res., N.D., U.S.	B8	127
Ashtarak, Arm.	B11	44
Ashton, Id., U.S.	E7	105
Ashton, Il., U.S.	B4	106
Ashton, Md., U.S.	B3	113
Ashton, R.I., U.S.	B4	132
Ashuanipi Lake, l., Nf., Can.	h8	88
Ashuelot, stm., N.H., U.S.	E2	122
Ashville, Al., U.S.	B3	94
Ashville, Oh., U.S.	C3	128
Ashwaubenon, Wi., U.S.	D5	142
Asi, stm., Asia	D7	44
Asia	C19	4
Asilah, Mor.	J3	16
Asinara, Golfo dell', b., Italy	D2	18
Asinara, Isola, i., Italy	D2	18
Asino, Russia	D5	98
Asino, Russia	D10	26
Asipovičy, Bela.	C10	20
'Asīr, reg., Sau. Ar.	G4	38
Aşkale, Tur.	C9	44
Askersund, Swe.	G6	10
Askham, S. Afr.	D3	56
Asmara see Asmera, Erit.	G12	48
Asmera, Erit.	G12	48
Āsosa, Eth.	A6	54
Asotin, Wa., U.S.	C8	140
Asotin, co., Wa., U.S.	C8	140
Asotin Creek, stm., Wa., U.S.	C8	140
Aspen, Co., U.S.	B4	99
Aspen Butte, mtn., Or., U.S.	E4	130
Aspendos, hist., Tur.	D4	44
Aspermont, Tx., U.S.	C2	136
Aspinwall, Pa., U.S.	k14	131
Aspy Bay, b., N.S., Can.	C9	87
Assa, Mor.	A3	50
Assabet, stm., Ma., U.S.	g9	114
Aš-Šafirah, Syria	D7	44
As-Salt, Jord.	F6	44
Assam, prov., India	D6	40
As-Samāwah, Iraq	D5	42
Assateague Island, i., U.S.	D7	113
Assateague Island National Seashore, U.S.	D7	113
Assawoman Bay, b., Md., U.S.	D7	113
Assiniboine, co., Mn., U.S.	E2	86
Assiniboine, Mount, mtn., Can.	D3	84
Assis, Braz.	F1	74
Assu, Braz.	C4	74
As-Sudd, reg., Sudan	I11	48
As-Sulaymānīyah, Iraq	C5	42
As-Sulaymānīyah, Sau. Ar.	F5	38
As-Sulayyil, Sau. Ar.	F5	38
As-Sumayḥ, Sudan	B5	54
As-Suwaydā', Syria	F7	44
Astara, Azer.	C13	44
Āstārā, Iran	C13	44
Asti, Italy	B2	18
Astipálaia, i., Grc.	F11	18
Astorga, Spain	F3	16
Astoria, Il., U.S.	C3	106
Astoria, Or., U.S.	A3	130
Astove, i., Sey.	j11	57b
Astrahan', Russia	E6	26
Asunción, Par.	D6	72
Asuncion Island, i., N. Mar. Is.	C12	32
Aswân, Egypt	F11	48
Aswan High Dam see Aali, Sadd el-, Egypt	F11	48
Asyûṭ, Egypt	E11	48
'Ata, i., Tonga	G12	58
Atacama, Desierto de, des., Chile	C2	69
Atacama, Puna de, plat., S.A.	C4	72
Atacama, Salar de, pl., Chile	B3	69
Atakpamé, Togo	E5	50
Atambua, Indon.	E6	36
Atar, Maur.	B2	50
Atascadero, Ca., U.S.	E3	98
Atascosa, co., Tx., U.S.	E3	136
Atasu, Kaz.	E9	26
Atatürk Baraji, res., Tur.	D8	44
Atauro, Pulau, i., Indon.	E7	36
Atbara, Sudan	G11	48
Atbasar, Kaz.	D8	26
Atchafalaya, stm., La., U.S.	D4	111
Atchafalaya Bay, b., La., U.S.	E4	111
Atchison, Ks., U.S.	C8	109
Atchison, co., Ks., U.S.	C8	109
Atchison, co., Mo., U.S.	A2	118
Athabasca, Ab., Can.	B4	84
Athabasca, stm., Ab., Can.	G17	82
Athabasca, Lake, l., Can.	G17	82
Athena, Or., U.S.	B8	130
Athens, On., Can.	C9	89
Athens see Athínai, Grc.	E9	18
Athens, Al., U.S.	A3	94
Athens, Ga., U.S.	C3	103
Athens, Il., U.S.	D4	106
Athens, Mi., U.S.	F5	115
Athens, N.Y., U.S.	C7	125
Athens, Oh., U.S.	C3	128
Athens, Pa., U.S.	C8	131
Athens, Tn., U.S.	D9	135
Athens, Tx., U.S.	C5	136
Athens, W.V., U.S.	D3	141
Athens, Wi., U.S.	D3	142
Athens, co., Oh., U.S.	C3	128
Atherton, Austl.	D4	62
Athi, stm., Kenya	D7	54
Athínai (Athens), Grc.	E9	18
Athol, Ma., U.S.	A3	114
Áthos, mtn., Grc.	D10	18
Ati, Chad	D8	50
Atiak, Ug.	C6	54
Atik Lake, l., Mb., Can.	B4	86
Atikokan, On., Can.	o17	89
Atikonak Lake, l., Nf., Can.	h8	88
Atiu, i., Cook Is.	G14	58
Atka, Russia	E17	26
Atka Island, i., Ak., U.S.	E5	95
Atkarsk, Russia	D8	22
Atkins, Ar., U.S.	B3	97
Atkins, Va., U.S.	D1	139
Atkinson, Il., U.S.	B3	106
Atkinson, Ne., U.S.	B7	120
Atkinson, N.H., U.S.	E4	122
Atkinson, co., Ga., U.S.	E4	103
Atlanta, Ga., U.S.	C2	103
Atlanta, Il., U.S.	C4	106
Atlanta, In., U.S.	D5	107
Atlanta, Mi., U.S.	C6	115
Atlanta, Tx., U.S.	C5	136
Atlantic, Ia., U.S.	C2	108
Atlantic, N.C., U.S.	C6	126
Atlantic, co., N.J., U.S.	E3	123
Atlantic Beach, Fl., U.S.	m9	102
Atlantic City, N.J., U.S.	E4	123
Atlantic Highlands, N.J., U.S.	C4	123
Atlantic-Indian Basin	O12	66
Atlantic-Indian Ridge	N14	66
Atlantic Ocean	E9	66
Atlantic Peak, mtn., Wy., U.S.	D3	143
Atlas Mountains, mts., Afr.	D4	48
Atlas Saharien, mts., Alg.	E3	14
Atlas Tellien, mts., Alg.	D4	14
Atlin Lake, l., Can.	G13	82
Atmore, Al., U.S.	D2	94
Atna Peak, mtn., B.C., Can.	C3	85
Atoka, Ok., U.S.	C5	129
Atoka, Tn., U.S.	B2	135
Atoka, co., Ok., U.S.	C5	129
Atoka Reservoir, res., Ok., U.S.	C5	129
Atrak (Atrek), stm., Asia	C7	42
Atrato, stm., Col.	B4	70
Atrek (Atrak), stm., Asia	C6	42
Aṭ-Ṭā'if, Sau. Ar.	F4	38
Attala, co., Ms., U.S.	B4	117
Attalla, Al., U.S.	A3	94
Attapu, Laos	D5	34
Attawapiskat, stm., On., Can.	n18	89
Attica, In., U.S.	D3	107
Attica, Ks., U.S.	E5	109
Attica, N.Y., U.S.	C2	125
Attica, Oh., U.S.	A3	128
Attleboro, Ma., U.S.	C5	114
Attu Island, i., Ak., U.S.	E2	95
Atuel, Bañados del, sw., Arg.	F4	72
Atwater, Ca., U.S.	D3	98
Atwater, Mn., U.S.	E4	116
Atwood, On., Can.	D3	89
Atwood, Il., U.S.	D5	106
Atwood, Ks., U.S.	C2	109
Atwood, Tn., U.S.	B3	135
Atwood Lake, res., Oh., U.S.	B4	128
Atyrau, Kaz.	E7	26
Auau Channel, strt., Hi., U.S.	C5	104
Aubagne, Fr.	F9	16
Auberry, Ca., U.S.	D4	98
Auburn, Al., U.S.	C4	94
Auburn, Ca., U.S.	C3	98
Auburn, Ga., U.S.	B3	103
Auburn, Il., U.S.	D4	106
Auburn, In., U.S.	B7	107
Auburn, Ks., U.S.	D8	109
Auburn, Ky., U.S.	D3	110
Auburn, Ma., U.S.	B4	114
Auburn, Me., U.S.	D2	112
Auburn, Mi., U.S.	E6	115
Auburn, N.Y., U.S.	C4	125
Auburn, Wa., U.S.	B3	140
Auburndale, Fl., U.S.	D5	102
Auburn Heights, Mi., U.S.	F7	115
Aubusson, Fr.	E8	16
Auch, Fr.	F7	16
Auchi, Nig.	E6	50
Aucilla, stm., Fl., U.S.	B3	102
Auckland, N.Z.	o13	63c
Auckland Islands, is., N.Z.	J10	58
Audrain, co., Mo., U.S.	B6	118
Audubon, Ia., U.S.	C3	108
Audubon, N.J., U.S.	D2	123
Audubon, co., Ia., U.S.	C2	108
Augathella, Austl.	F4	62
Auglaize, co., Oh., U.S.	B1	128
Auglaize, stm., Oh., U.S.	A1	128
Augrabiesvalle, wtfl, S. Afr.	D3	56
Au Gres, Mi., U.S.	D7	115
Augsburg, Ger.	F12	12
Augusta, Austl.	G1	60
Augusta, Italy	F5	18
Augusta, Ar., U.S.	B4	97
Augusta, Ga., U.S.	C5	103
Augusta, Ks., U.S.	E7	109
Augusta, Ky., U.S.	B6	110
Augusta, Me., U.S.	D3	112
Augusta, Mi., U.S.	F5	115
Augusta, Va., U.S.	B3	139
Augusta, Wi., U.S.	D2	142
Augusta, co., Va., U.S.	B3	139
Augustów, Pol.	C7	20
Augustus, Mount, mtn., Austl.	E2	60
Aulander, N.C., U.S.	A5	126
Aulneau Peninsula, pen., On., Can.	E4	86
Ault, Co., U.S.	A6	99
Aumsville, Or., U.S.	k12	130
Aurangābād, India	F3	40
Aurangābād, India	E4	40
Aure, Nor.	E3	10
Aurelia, Ia., U.S.	B2	108
Aurich, Ger.	D10	12
Aurillac, Fr.	E8	16
Aurora, On., Can.	C5	89
Aurora, Co., U.S.	B6	99
Aurora, Il., U.S.	B5	106
Aurora, In., U.S.	F8	107
Aurora, Mn., U.S.	C6	116
Aurora, Mo., U.S.	E4	118
Aurora, Ne., U.S.	D7	120
Aurora, Oh., U.S.	A4	128
Aurora, S.D., U.S.	C9	134
Aurora, Ut., U.S.	E4	137
Aurora, co., S.D., U.S.	D7	134
Aus, Nmb.	D2	56
Au Sable, Mi., U.S.	D7	115
Au Sable, stm., Mi., U.S.	D6	115
Ausable, stm., N.Y., U.S.	f11	125
Au Sable Forks, N.Y., U.S.	f11	125
Au Sable Point, c., Mi., U.S.	D7	115
Au Sable Point, c., Mi., U.S.	B4	115
Austell, Ga., U.S.	h7	103
Austin, In., U.S.	G6	107
Austin, Mn., U.S.	G6	116
Austin, Nv., U.S.	D4	121
Austin, Tx., U.S.	D4	136
Austin, co., Tx., U.S.	E4	136
Austintown, Oh., U.S.	A5	128
Austinville, Va., U.S.	D2	139
Australia, ctry., Oc.	G7	58
Australia, i., Austl.	H21	4
Australian Capital Territory, ter., Austl.	H4	62
Austral Seamounts	K23	64
Austria, ctry., Eur.	G14	12
Autauga, co., Al., U.S.	C3	94
Autaugaville, Al., U.S.	C3	94
Autlán de Navarro, Mex.	D4	78
Auvergne, hist. reg., Fr.	E8	16
Auxerre, Fr.	D8	16
Auxier, Ky., U.S.	C7	110
Auxvasse, Mo., U.S.	B6	118
Auyán Tepuy, mtn., Ven.	B7	70
Auzangate, Nevado, mtn., Peru	F5	70
Ava, Mo., U.S.	E5	118
Avallon, Fr.	D8	16
Avalon, Ca., U.S.	F4	98
Avalon, Pa., U.S.	h13	131
Avalon, Lake, res., N.M., U.S.	E5	124
Avalon Peninsula, pen., Nf., Can.	E5	88
Avaré, Braz.	F2	74
Aveiro, Port.	G2	16
Avella, Pa., U.S.	F1	131
Avellaneda, Arg.	E6	72
Avellino, Italy	D5	18
Avenal, Ca., U.S.	E3	98
Avery, co., N.C., U.S.	e11	126
Avesta, Swe.	F7	10
Aves, Islas de, is., Ven.	C6	80
Avezzano, Italy	C4	18
Avignon, Fr.	F9	16
Ávila, Spain	G4	16
Avilés, Spain	F4	16
Avilla, In., U.S.	B7	107
Avis, Pa., U.S.	D7	131
Aviston, Il., U.S.	E4	106
Avoca, Ia., U.S.	C2	108
Avoca, Pa., U.S.	m18	131
Avola, Italy	F5	18
Avon, Ct., U.S.	B4	100
Avon, Il., U.S.	C3	106
Avon, Ma., U.S.	B5	114
Avon, Mn., U.S.	E4	116
Avon, N.Y., U.S.	C3	125
Avon, Oh., U.S.	A3	128
Avondale, Az., U.S.	D3	96
Avondale, Co., U.S.	C6	99
Avondale, Pa., U.S.	G10	131
Avondale Estates, Ga., U.S.	h8	103
Avon Lake, Oh., U.S.	e8	108
Avon Lake, Oh., U.S.	A3	128
Avonmore, Pa., U.S.	E3	131
Avon Park, Fl., U.S.	E5	102
Avoyelles, co., La., U.S.	C3	111
Awaaso, Ghana	E4	50
Āwarē, Eth.	B8	54
Āwasa, Eth.	B7	54
Āwash, Eth.	B8	54
Āwash, stm., Eth.	H13	48
Awbārī, Libya	E7	48
Awbārī, Şaḥrā', reg., Libya	A7	50
Awjilah, Libya	E9	48
Awled Djellal, Alg.	E5	14
Awlef, Alg.	F4	14
Axim, Ghana	F4	50
Axiós (Vardar), stm., Eur.	D9	18
Axis, Al., U.S.	E1	94
Axtell, Ne., U.S.	D6	120
Ayacucho, Arg.	F6	72
Ayacucho, Peru	F4	70
Ayamé, C. Iv.	E4	50
Ayancık, Tur.	B6	44
Ayapel, Col.	D4	80
Ayaviri, Peru	F5	70
Ayden, N.C., U.S.	B5	126
Aydın, Tur.	D2	44
Ayer, Ma., U.S.	A4	114
Ayers Cliff, P.Q., Can.	D5	90
Ayeyarwady, stm., Myan.	C3	34
Áyios Nikólaos, Grc.	G10	18
Ayíou Órous, Kólpos, b., Grc.	D10	18
Aylesford, N.S., Can.	D5	87

Name	Map Ref.	Page

Aylmer, Mount, mtn., Ab., Can. **D3** 84
Aylmer East, P.Q., Can. . . . **D2** 90
Aylmer West, On., Can. . . . **E4** 89
'Ayn Dār, Sau. Ar. **E5** 42
Ayorou, Niger **D5** 50
'Ayoûn el 'Atroûs, Maur. . . **C3** 50
Ayr, Austl. **D4** 62
Ayr, Scot., U.K. **C4** 12
Ayvalık, Tur. **C2** 44
Āzamgarh, India **D4** 40
Azaouâd, reg., Mali **C4** 50
Azare, Nig. **D7** 50
Āžar Shahr, Iran **D11** 44
Azdavay, Tur. **B5** 44
Azeffâl, reg., Afr. **B2** 50
Azerbaijan, ctry., Asia **B12** 44
Azilal, Mor. **E2** 14
Aziscohos Lake, l., Me., U.S. **C1** 112
Azle, Tx., U.S. **n9** 136
Azogues, Ec. **D4** 70
Azores see Açores, is., Port. **F7**
Azores Plateau **D10** 66
Azov, Russia **F15** 20
Azov, Sea of, Eur. **F14** 20
Azraq, Al-Baḥr al- see Blue Nile, stm., Afr. **H11** 48
Azrou, Mor. **D3** 48
Aztec, N.M., U.S. **A2** 124
Aztec Peak, mtn., Az., U.S. **D5** 96
Aztec Ruins National Monument, N.M., U.S. . **A1** 124
Azua, Dom. Rep. **B5** 80
Azuaga, Spain **H4** 16
Azuero, Península de, pen., Pan. **D3** 80
Azul, Arg. **F6** 72
Azurduy, Bol. **B5** 72
Azusa, Ca., U.S. **m13** 98
Az-Ẓahrān, Sau. Ar. **E5** 42
Az-Zarqā', Jord. **D3** 42
Az-Zāwiyah, Libya **D7** 48

B

Baa, Indon. **F6** 36
Baardheere, Som. **J13** 48
Babadag, Rom. **G10** 20
Babaeski, Tur. **B2** 44
Babaevo, Russia **C6** 22
Babanūsah, Sudan **H10** 48
Babar, Kepulauan, is., Indon. **E7** 36
Babb Creek, stm., Pa., U.S. **C7** 131
Babbitt, Mn., U.S. **C7** 116
Babbitt, Nv., U.S. **E3** 121
Bab el Mandeb see Mandeb, Bab el, strt. . . **H4** 38
Babelthuap, i., Palau **E9** 32
Bābil, Aṭlāl (Babylon), hist., Iraq **F11** 44
Babine, stm., B.C., Can. . . **B4** 85
Babine Lake, l., B.C., Can. . **B5** 85
Babine Range, mts., B.C., Can. **B4** 85
Babo, Indon. **D8** 36
Baboquivari Mountains, mts., Az., U.S. **F4** 96
Baboquivari Peak, mtn., Az., U.S. **F4** 96
Babrujsk, Bela. **C10** 20
Babuškin, Russia **B4** 28
Babuyan Channel, strt., Phil. **C8** 34
Babuyan Island, i., Phil. . . **C8** 34
Babuyan Islands, is., Phil. . **C8** 34
Babylon, N.Y., U.S. **n15** 125
Babylon see Bābil, Aṭlāl, hist., Iraq **F11** 44
Baca, Co., Co., U.S. **D8** 99
Bacabal, Braz. **B3** 74
Bacan, Pulau, i., Indon. . . . **D7** 36
Bacău, Rom. **F9** 20
Bachu, China **D3** 28
Back, stm., S.C., U.S. **h12** 133
Bačka Palanka, Yugo. **B7** 18
Backbone Mountain, mtn., U.S. **m12** 113
Bac Lieu, Viet. **E5** 34
Bac Ninh, Viet. **B5** 34
Bacolod, Phil. **D8** 34
Bacon, co., Ga., U.S. **E4** 103
Baconton, Ga., U.S. **E2** 103
Bacoor, Phil. **D8** 34
Bād, Iran **D6** 42
Bad, stm., S.D., U.S. **C5** 134
Bad, stm., Wi., U.S. **B3** 142
Badagara, India **G3** 40
Badajoz, Spain **H3** 16
Badalona, Spain **G8** 16
Bādāmi, India **F3** 40
Badanah, Sau. Ar. **D4** 38
Bad Axe, Mi., U.S. **E8** 115
Baddeck, N.S., Can. **C9** 87
Baden, Aus. **G14** 12
Baden, On., Can. **D4** 89
Baden, Pa., U.S. **E1** 131
Baden-Baden, Ger. **F11** 12
Badger, Nf., Can. **D3** 88
Bad Hersfeld, Ger. **E11** 12
Baḍīn, Pak. **F9** 42
Badin, N.C., U.S. **B2** 126
Badin Lake, res., N.C., U.S. **B2** 126
Bad Kreuznach, Ger. **F10** 12
Badlands, hills, S.D., U.S. . . **D3** 134

Badlands, reg., U.S. **C2** 127
Badlands National Park, S.D., U.S. **D3** 134
Bad Reichenhall, Ger. **G13** 12
Bad River Indian Reservation, Wi., U.S. . . **B3** 142
Bad Tölz, Ger. **G12** 12
Badulla, Sri L. **H4** 40
Badwater Creek, stm., Wy., U.S. **C5** 143
Bafang, Cam. **B2** 54
Bafatá, Gui.-B. **D2** 50
Baffin Basin **C29** 144
Baffin Bay, b., N.A. **D26** 82
Baffin Bay, b., Tx., U.S. . . . **E4** 136
Baffin Bugt see Baffin Bay, b., N.A. **D26** 82
Baffin Island, i., N.T., Can. **D24** 82
Bafia, Cam. **C2** 54
Bafing, stm., Afr. **D2** 50
Bafoulabé, Mali **D2** 50
Bafoussam, Cam. **B2** 54
Bafra, Tur. **B6** 44
Bafwasende, D.R.C. **C5** 54
Bagaces, C.R. **C2** 80
Bagamoyo, Tan. **E7** 54
Baganga, Phil. **E9** 34
Bagansiapiapi, Indon. **C2** 36
Bagdad see Baghdād, Iraq **D4** 42
Bagdad, Az., U.S. **C2** 96
Bagdad, Fl., U.S. **u14** 102
Bagdarin, Russia **D13** 26
Bagé, Braz. **E7** 72
Baggs, Wy., U.S. **E5** 143
Baghdād, Iraq **D4** 42
Bagheria, Italy **E4** 18
Baghlān, Afg. **C9** 42
Bagley, Mn., U.S. **C3** 116
Bagnères-de-Bigorre, Fr. . . **F7** 16
Bago, Myan. **C3** 34
Baguio, Phil. **C8** 34
Bahamas, ctry., N.A. **C9** 76
Bahār, Iran **E13** 44
Baharampur, India **E5** 40
Baharden, Turk. **C7** 42
Bahardok, Turk. **C7** 42
Bahāwalpur, Pak. **E10** 42
Bahçe, Tur. **D7** 44
Bahia, state, Braz. **D3** 74
Bahía, Islas de la, is., Hond. **B2** 80
Bahía Blanca, Arg. **F5** 72
Bahir Dar, Eth. **H12** 48
Bahraich, India **D4** 40
Bahrain, ctry., Asia **E6** 42
Bahta, Russia **C10** 26
Bāhū Kalāt, Iran **E8** 42
Baía Farta, Ang. **F2** 54
Baia Mare, Rom. **F7** 20
Baicheng, China **B12** 28
Baicheng, China **C4** 28
Baidoa see Baydhabo, Som. **J13** 48
Baie-Comeau, P.Q., Can. . **k13** 90
Baie-d'Urfé, P.Q., Can. . . **q19** 90
Baie-Saint-Paul, P.Q., Can. **B7** 90
Baie Verte, Nf., Can. **D3** 88
Baihe, China **C3** 30
Baikal, Lake see Bajkal, ozero, l., Russia **D12** 26
Baile Átha Cliath see Dublin, Ire. **D3** 12
Băileşti, Rom. **G7** 20
Bailey, co., Tx., U.S. **B1** 136
Bailey Island, Me., U.S. . . **g8** 112
Bailey Island, i., S.C., U.S. **k11** 133
Baileys Crossroads, Va., U.S. **g12** 139
Bailundo, Ang. **D3** 54
Bainbridge, Ga., U.S. **F2** 103
Bainbridge, In., U.S. **E4** 107
Bainbridge, Oh., U.S. **C2** 128
Bainbridge Island, i., Wa., U.S. **e10** 140
Baing, Indon. **F6** 36
Baird, Tx., U.S. **C3** 136
Bairdford, Pa., U.S. **h14** 131
Baird Inlet, b., Ak., U.S. . . **C7** 95
Baird Mountains, mts., Ak., U.S. **B7** 95
Bairin Zuoqi, China **C11** 28
Bairnsdale, Austl. **H4** 62
Bais, Phil. **E8** 34
Baishuijiang, China **C2** 30
Baitou Shan see Paektu, Mount, mtn., Asia **C13** 28
Baiyin, China **D8** 28
Baja, Hung. **F5** 20
Baja California, state, Mex. **A1** 78
Baja California, pen., Mex. **B2** 78
Baja California Norte see Baja California, state, Mex. **A1** 78
Baja California Sur, state, Mex. **B2** 78
Bajeştan, Iran **D7** 42
Bajkal, ozero, l., Russia . . . **D12** 26
Bajkit, Russia **C11** 26
Bajkonur, Kaz. **E8** 26
Bajmak, Russia **D10** 22
Bajo Boquete, Pan. **D3** 80
Bajramaly, Turk. **C8** 42
Bakala, C.A.R. **B4** 54
Bakanas, Kaz. **B11** 26
Bakel, Sen. **D2** 50
Baker, La., U.S. **D4** 111
Baker, Mt., U.S. **D12** 119
Baker, Or., U.S. **C9** 130

Baker, co., Fl., U.S. **B4** 102
Baker, co., Ga., U.S. **E2** 103
Baker, co., Or., U.S. **C9** 130
Baker, stm., N.H., U.S. **C3** 122
Baker, Mount, mtn., Wa., U.S. **A4** 140
Baker Air Force Base, mil., Ar., U.S. **B6** 97
Baker Butte, mtn., Az., U.S. **C4** 96
Baker Island, i., Oc. **H21** 64
Baker Island, i., Ak., U.S. . . **n22** 95
Baker Lake, l., Austl. **F4** 60
Baker Lake, l., Me., U.S. . . . **B3** 112
Baker Lake, res., Wa., U.S. **A4** 140
Bakersfield, Ca., U.S. **E4** 98
Bakers Island, i., Ma., U.S. **f12** 114
Bakerstown, Pa., U.S. **h14** 131
Bakhmach, Ukr. **D12** 20
Bakı (Baku), Azer. **B13** 44
Bako, Eth. **B7** 54
Bakouma, C.A.R. **B4** 54
Baku see Bakı, Azer. **B13** 44
Bala, Sen. **D2** 50
Balabac Island, i., Phil. . . . **E7** 34
Balabac Strait, strt., Asia . . **E7** 34
Ba'labakk, Leb. **F7** 44
Baladēk, Russia **D15** 26
Bālāghāt, India **E4** 40
Balaguer, Spain **G7** 16
Balakliia, Ukr. **E14** 20
Balakovo, Russia **D6** 26
Balama, Moz. **A6** 56
Balambangan, Pulau, i., Malay. **B5** 36
Bālā Morghāb, Afg. **C8** 42
Balāngīr, India **E4** 40
Balašov, Russia **D6** 26
Balassagyarmat, Hung. . . . **F5** 20
Balaton, Mn., U.S. **F3** 116
Balaton, l., Hung. **F4** 20
Balbina, Represa, res., Braz. **D8** 70
Balcad, Som. **C9** 54
Balcarce, Arg. **F6** 72
Balcarres, Sk., Can. **G4** 91
Balclutha, N.Z. **p12** 63c
Bald Eagle Lake, l., Mn., U.S. **C7** 116
Bald Eagle Lake, l., Mn., U.S. **m12** 116
Baldhill Dam, N.D., U.S. . . **B7** 127
Bald Knob, Ar., U.S. **B4** 97
Bald Knoll, mtn., Wy., U.S. **D2** 143
Bald Mountain, mtn., Or., U.S. **C9** 130
Bald Mountain, mtn., Or., U.S. **D5** 130
Bald Mountain, mtn., Wy., U.S. **B5** 143
Bald Mountains, mts., N.C., U.S. **f10** 126
Baldwin, Fl., U.S. **B5** 102
Baldwin, Ga., U.S. **B3** 103
Baldwin, La., U.S. **E4** 111
Baldwin, Mi., U.S. **E5** 115
Baldwin, Pa., U.S. **k14** 131
Baldwin, S.C., U.S. **B5** 133
Baldwin, Wi., U.S. **D1** 142
Baldwin, co., Al., U.S. **E2** 94
Baldwin, co., Ga., U.S. **C3** 103
Baldwin City, Ks., U.S. **D8** 109
Baldwinsville, N.Y., U.S. . . . **B4** 125
Baldwinville, Ma., U.S. . . . **A3** 114
Baldwyn, Ms., U.S. **A5** 117
Baldy Mountain, mtn., B.C., Can. **D7** 85
Baldy Mountain, mtn., Mb., Can. **D1** 86
Baldy Mountain, mtn., Mt., U.S. **B7** 119
Baldy Mountain, mtn., N.M., U.S. **A4** 124
Baldy Peak, mtn., Az., U.S. **D6** 96
Balearic Islands see Balears, Illes, is., Spain **H7** 16
Balears, Illes (Balearic Islands), is., Spain **H7** 16
Baleia, Ponta da, c., Braz. **E4** 74
Baleine, Rivière à la, stm., P.Q., Can. **g13** 90
Balej, Russia **D13** 26
Baler, Phil. **C8** 34
Bāleshwar, India **E5** 40
Balezino, Russia **C9** 22
Balfate, Hond. **B2** 80
Balfour, N.C., U.S. **f10** 126
Balhaš, Kaz. **E9** 26
Balhaš, ozero, l., Kaz. **E9** 26
Bali, i., Indon. **E5** 36
Bali, Laut (Bali Sea), Indon. **E5** 36
Bali Sea see Bali, Laut, Indon. **E5** 36
Balikesir, Tur. **C2** 44
Balikpapan, Indon. **D5** 36
Balimo, Pap. N. Gui. **H11** 62
Balintang Channel, strt., Phil. **C8** 34
Balkan Mountains see Stara Planina, mts., Eur. **C9** 18
Balkaria see Kabardino-Balkaria, state, Russia . . **E6** 26
Balkh, Afg. **C9** 42
Balkhash, Lake see Balhaš, ozero, l., Kaz. **E9** 26
Ball, La., U.S. **C3** 111
Balladonia, Austl. **G3** 60

Ballālpur, India **F3** 40
Ballarat, Austl. **H3** 62
Ballard, co., Ky., U.S. **e8** 110
Ball Club Lake, l., Mn., U.S. **C5** 116
Balleny Islands, is., Ant. . . **C21** 67
Ball Ground, Ga., U.S. **B2** 103
Ballina, Austl. **F5** 62
Ballina, Ire. **C2** 12
Ballinger, Tx., U.S. **D3** 136
Ball Mountain Lake, res., Vt., U.S. **E3** 138
Ballston Spa, N.Y., U.S. . . . **B7** 125
Ballwin, Mo., U.S. **f12** 118
Bally, Pa., U.S. **F10** 131
Ballymena, N. Ire., U.K. . . . **C3** 12
Balmoral, N.B., Can. **B3** 87
Balmoral Castle, hist., Scot., U.K. **B5** 12
Balmville, N.Y., U.S. **D6** 125
Balombo, Ang. **F2** 54
Balqash Köli see Balhaš, ozero, l., Kaz. **E9** 26
Balsam Lake, Wi., U.S. . . . **C1** 142
Balsam Lake, l., Wi., U.S. . . **C1** 142
Balsas, Braz. **E10** 70
Balsas, stm., Mex. **D4** 78
Balta, Ukr. **F10** 20
Baltasar Brum, Ur. **E6** 72
Balti, Mol. **F9** 20
Baltic, Ct., U.S. **C7** 100
Baltic, S.D., U.S. **D9** 134
Baltic Sea, Eur. **I7** 10
Baltijsk, Russia **B5** 20
Baltim, Egypt **E10** 14
Baltimore, Md., U.S. **B4** 113
Baltimore, Oh., U.S. **C3** 128
Baltimore, co., Md., U.S. . . **B4** 113
Baltimore Highlands, Md., U.S. **h11** 113
Baluchistan, hist. reg., Asia **E8** 42
Bālurghāt, India **D5** 40
Balygyčan, Russia **C17** 26
Bam, Iran **E7** 42
Bama, Nig. **D7** 50
Bamako, Mali **D3** 50
Bamba, Mali **C4** 50
Bambari, C.A.R. **B4** 54
Bamberg, Ger. **F12** 12
Bamberg, S.C., U.S. **E5** 133
Bamberg, co., S.C., U.S. . . **E5** 133
Bambesi, Eth. **B6** 54
Bamenda, Cam. **B2** 54
Bāmiān, Afg. **D9** 42
Bamingui, C.A.R. **B4** 54
Bampūr, Iran **E8** 42
Banaba, i., Kir. **E10** 58
Banalia, D.R.C. **C5** 54
Banamba, Mali **D3** 50
Banana River, b., Fl., U.S. . . **D6** 102
Bananal, Ilha do, i., Braz. . . **D1** 74
Bananga, India **H6** 40
Banas, Rās, c., Egypt **F12** 48
Banat, hist. reg., Eur. **G6** 20
Banaz, Tur. **C3** 44
Banbury, Eng., U.K. **D6** 12
Bancroft, On., Can. **B7** 89
Bancroft, Ia., U.S. **A3** 108
Bancroft see Chililabombwe, Zam. **A4** 56
Bānda, India **D4** 40
Banda, Kepulauan, is., Indon. **D7** 36
Banda, Laut (Banda Sea), Indon. **E7** 36
Banda Aceh, Indon. **B1** 36
Bandama, stm., C. Iv. **E4** 50
Bandar Beheshtī, Iran **E8** 42
Bandar-e 'Abbās, Iran **E7** 42
Bandar-e Anzalī, Iran **C5** 42
Bandar-e Būshehr, Iran . . . **E6** 42
Bandar-e Deylam, Iran . . . **E6** 42
Bandar-e Khomeynī, Iran . **D5** 42
Bandar-e Lengeh, Iran **E6** 42
Bandar-e Torkeman, Iran . . **C6** 42
Bandar Seri Begawan, Bru. **C4** 36
Banda Sea see Banda, Laut, Indon. **E7** 36
Banded Peak, mtn., Co., U.S. **D4** 99
Bandeira, Pico da, mtn., Braz. **F3** 74
Bandeirantes, Braz. **B7** 72
Bandelier National Monument, N.M., U.S. **B3** 124
Bandera, co., Tx., U.S. **E3** 136
Bandiagara, Mali **D4** 50
Bandiantaolehai, China . . . **C8** 28
Bandırma, Tur. **B2** 44
Bandon, Or., U.S. **D2** 130
Bandundu, D.R.C. **B3** 54
Bandung, Indon. **E3** 36
Bāneh, Iran **E11** 44
Banes, Cuba **A4** 80
Banff National Park, Ab., Can. **D2** 84
Banfora, Burkina **D4** 50
Bangalore, India **G3** 40
Bangassou, C.A.R. **C4** 54
Banggai, Indon. **D6** 36
Banggai, Kepulauan, is., Indon. **G7** 32
Banggi, Pulau, i., Malay. . . **B5** 36
Banghāzī, Libya **D9** 48

Bangka, Pulau, i., Indon. . . **D3** 36
Bangka, Selat, strt., Indon. **D3** 36
Bangkalan, Indon. **E4** 36
Bangkinang, Indon. **C2** 36
Bangko, Indon. **D2** 36
Bangkok see Krung Thep, Thai. **C3** 34
Bangladesh, ctry., Asia . . . **B2** 34
Bang Mun Nak, Thai. **C4** 34
Ban Gnômmarat Kèo, Laos **C5** 34
Bangor, N. Ire., U.K. **C4** 12
Bangor, Wales, U.K. **D4** 12
Bangor, Me., U.S. **D4** 112
Bangor, Mi., U.S. **F4** 115
Bangor, Pa., U.S. **E11** 131
Bangor, Wi., U.S. **E3** 142
Bangor Township, Mi., U.S. **E7** 115
Bangs, Tx., U.S. **D3** 136
Bangs, Mount, mtn., Az., U.S. **A2** 96
Bangui, C.A.R. **C3** 54
Bangweulu, Lake, l., Zam. **A4** 56
Ban Houayxay, Laos **B4** 34
Bani, Burkina **D4** 50
Bani, Dom. Rep. **B5** 80
Baniara, Pap. N. Gui. **B4** 62
Banister, stm., Va., U.S. . . . **D4** 139
Banī Walīd, Libya **D7** 48
Bāniyās, Syria **E6** 44
Banja Luka, Bos. **B6** 18
Banjarmasin, Indon. **D4** 36
Banjul, Gam. **D1** 50
Banka Banka, Austl. **D5** 60
Bankhead Lake, res., Al., U.S. **B2** 94
Banks, co., Ga., U.S. **B3** 103
Banks, Îles, is., Vanuatu . . . **j9** 62a
Banks Island, i., B.C., Can. **C2** 85
Banks Lake, res., Wa., U.S. **B6** 140
Banks Strait, strt., Austl. . . . **I4** 62
Bānkura, India **E5** 40
Ban Nalè, Laos **C4** 34
Banner, co., Ne., U.S. **C2** 120
Banner Elk, N.C., U.S. **A1** 126
Banning, Ca., U.S. **F5** 98
Bannock, co., Id., U.S. **G6** 105
Bannock Peak, mtn., Id., U.S. **F6** 105
Bannock Range, mts., Id., U.S. **G6** 105
Bannu, Pak. **D10** 42
Ban Pong, Thai. **D3** 34
Ban Signo, Laos **C5** 34
Banská Bystrica, Slvk. **F5** 20
Bānswāra, India **D2** 40
Bantaeng, Indon. **E6** 36
Bantam, stm., Ct., U.S. . . . **B3** 100
Bantam Lake, l., Ct., U.S. . . **C3** 100
Banyo, Cam. **B2** 54
Banyuwangi, Indon. **E4** 36
Banzare Coast, Ant. **C17** 67
Baode, China **D10** 28
Baodi, China **B4** 30
Baoding, China **D11** 28
Bao Ha, Viet. **B4** 34
Baoji, China **E9** 28
Baojing, China **D2** 30
Bao Lac, Viet. **D5** 34
Baoqing, China **A2** 31
Baoshan, China **F7** 28
Baoting, China **H9** 28
Baotou, China **C9** 28
Baoying, China **E11** 28
Ba'qūbah, Iraq **D4** 42
Baquedano, Chile **B2** 69
Bara, Nig. **D7** 50
Baraawe, Som. **J13** 48
Baraboo, Wi., U.S. **E4** 142
Baraboo, stm., Wi., U.S. . . **E3** 142
Baracoa, Cuba **A5** 80
Baraga, Mi., U.S. **B2** 115
Baraga, co., Mi., U.S. **B2** 115
Barahona, Dom. Rep. **B5** 80
Barakaldo, Spain **F5** 16
Baram, stm., Malay. **C4** 36
Bāramūla, India **C2** 40
Baranagar, India **E5** 40
Baranavičy, Bela. **C9** 20
Barani, Burkina **D4** 50
Baranof Island, i., Ak., U.S. **m22** 95
Barataria, La., U.S. **E5** 111
Barataria Bay, b., La., U.S. . **E6** 111
Barauni, India **D5** 40
Barbacena, Braz. **F3** 74
Barbacoas, Col. **C4** 70
Barbados, ctry., N.A. **F12** 76
Barbar, Sudan **G11** 48
Barbas, Cap, c., W. Sah. . . **B1** 50
Barbastro, Spain **F7** 16
Barber, co., Ks., U.S. **E5** 109
Barbers Point, c., Hi., U.S. . **B3** 104
Barbers Point Naval Air Station, mil., Hi., U.S. . . **g9** 104
Barberton, S. Afr. **D5** 56
Barberton, Oh., U.S. **A4** 128
Barbour, co., Al., U.S. **D4** 94
Barbour, co., W.V., U.S. . . **B4** 141
Barboursville, W.V., U.S. . . **C2** 141
Barbourville, Ky., U.S. **D6** 110
Barbuda, i., Antig. **B7** 80
Barcaldine, Austl. **D8** 62
Barcelona, Spain **G8** 16
Barcelona, Ven. **B6** 70
Barcelos, Braz. **D7** 70

Name	Map Ref.	Page
Barcroft, Lake, res., Va., U.S.	g12	139
Bärdä, Azer.	B12	44
Bardaï, Chad	B8	50
Bardawīl, Sabkhet el-, b., Egypt	G5	44
Bardejov, Slvk.	E6	20
Barden Reservoir, res., R.I., U.S.	C2	132
Bardīyah, Libya	D10	48
Bardstown, Ky., U.S.	C4	110
Bardwell, Ky., U.S.	f9	110
Bardwell Lake, res., Tx., U.S.	C4	136
Bareilly, India	D3	40
Barents Sea, Eur.	B6	26
Barents Trough	D20	144
Bargersville, In., U.S.	E5	107
Bar Harbor, Me., U.S.	D4	112
Bari, Italy	D6	18
Barika, Alg.	J9	16
Barillas, Guat.	B1	80
Barīm, i., Yemen	H4	38
Barinas, Ven.	B6	70
Bāripada, India	E5	40
Bârîs, Egypt	F11	48
Barisāl, Bngl.	E6	40
Barisan, Pegunungan, mts., Indon.	D2	36
Barkam, China	C1	30
Barker Heights, N.C., U.S.	f10	126
Barkhamsted Reservoir, res., Ct., U.S.	B3	100
Barkley, Lake, res., U.S.	f10	110
Barkley Sound, strt., B.C., Can.	E5	85
Barkly East, S. Afr.	E4	56
Barkly Tableland, plat., Austl.	D6	60
Barkol, China	C6	28
Bark Point, c., Wi., U.S.	B2	142
Barksdale Air Force Base, mil., La., U.S.	B2	111
Bârlad, Rom.	F9	20
Barlee, Lake, l., Austl.	F2	60
Barletta, Italy	D6	18
Barling, Ar., U.S.	B1	97
Barlow, Ky., U.S.	e8	110
Bärmer, India	D2	40
Barmera, Austl.	G3	62
Barnaul, Russia	D10	26
Barnegat Bay, b., N.J., U.S.	D4	123
Barnegat Inlet, b., N.J., U.S.	D4	123
Barnes, co., N.D., U.S.	B7	127
Barnesboro, Pa., U.S.	E4	131
Barnes Sound, strt., Fl., U.S.	G6	102
Barnesville, Ga., U.S.	C2	103
Barnesville, Mn., U.S.	D2	116
Barnesville, Oh., U.S.	C4	128
Barnhart, Mo., U.S.	C7	118
Barnsdall, Ok., U.S.	A5	129
Barnstable, Ma., U.S.	C7	114
Barnstable, co., Ma., U.S.	C7	114
Barnstaple, Eng., U.K.	E4	12
Barnwell, S.C., U.S.	E5	133
Barnwell, co., S.C., U.S.	E5	133
Baro, Nig.	E6	50
Barpeta, India	D6	40
Barqah (Cyrenaica), hist. reg., Libya	E8	14
Barques, Pointe aux, c., Mi., U.S.	D8	115
Barquisimeto, Ven.	A6	70
Barra, Braz.	D3	74
Barra, i., Scot., U.K.	B3	12
Barra, Ponta da, c., Moz.	C6	56
Barrackville, W.V., U.S.	B4	141
Barra do Corda, Braz.	C2	74
Barra do Cuanza, Ang.	E2	54
Barra do Dande, Ang.	E2	54
Barra do Garças, Braz.	B7	72
Barra Mansa, Braz.	F3	74
Barranca, Peru	F4	70
Barrancabermeja, Col.	B5	70
Barrancas, Ven.	D7	80
Barranquilla, Col.	A5	70
Barras, Braz.	B3	74
Barre, Vt., U.S.	C4	138
Barre, Lake, l., La., U.S.	E5	111
Barre Falls Reservoir, res., Ma., U.S.	B4	114
Barreiras, Braz.	D3	74
Barreiro, Port.	H2	16
Barreiros, Braz.	C4	74
Barren, co., Ky., U.S.	D4	110
Barren, stm., Ky., U.S.	C3	110
Barren, Nosy, is., Madag.	B7	56
Barren Islands, i., Md., U.S.	D5	113
Barren Islands, is., Ak., U.S.	h15	95
Barren River Lake, res., Ky., U.S.	D3	110
Barretos, Braz.	F2	74
Barrett, W.V., U.S.	D3	141
Barrhead, Ab., Can.	B3	84
Barrie, On., Can.	C5	89
Barrie Island, i., On., Can.	B2	89
Barrière, B.C., Can.	D7	85
Barrier Range, mts., Austl.	G3	62
Barrington, Il., U.S.	A5	106
Barrington, N.J., U.S.	D2	123
Barrington, R.I., U.S.	D5	132
Barrington, stm., R.I., U.S.	C5	132
Barron, Wi., U.S.	C2	142
Barron, co., Wi., U.S.	C2	142
Barron Lake, Mi., U.S.	G4	115
Barrow, Ak., U.S.	A8	95
Barrow, co., Ga., U.S.	B3	103
Barrow, Point, c., Ak., U.S.	A8	95
Barrow Creek, Austl.	E5	60
Barrow-in-Furness, Eng., U.K.	C5	12
Barrow Island, i., Austl.	E2	60
Barry, Il., U.S.	D2	106
Barry, co., Mi., U.S.	F5	115
Barry, co., Mo., U.S.	E4	118
Barrys Bay, On., Can.	B7	89
Bārsi, India	F3	40
Barstow, Ca., U.S.	E5	98
Bartholomew, co., In., U.S.	F6	107
Bartholomew, Bayou, stm., U.S.	D4	97
Bartica, Guy.	B8	70
Bartın, Tur.	B5	44
Bartlesville, Ok., U.S.	A6	129
Bartlett, N.H., U.S.	B4	122
Bartlett, Tn., U.S.	B2	135
Bartlett, Tx., U.S.	D4	136
Bartlett Reservoir, res., Az., U.S.	D4	96
Bartletts Ferry Dam, U.S.	C4	94
Barton, Oh., U.S.	B5	128
Barton, Vt., U.S.	B4	138
Barton, co., Ks., U.S.	D5	109
Barton, co., Mo., U.S.	D3	118
Barton, stm., Vt., U.S.	B4	138
Bartonville, Il., U.S.	C4	106
Bartow, Fl., U.S.	E5	102
Bartow, co., Ga., U.S.	B2	103
Barú, Volcán, vol., Pan.	D3	80
Barun Su, China	A3	30
Baruun-Urt, Mong.	B10	28
Barysau, Bela.	B10	20
Basalt, Co., U.S.	B3	99
Basankusu, D.R.C.	C3	54
Bascuñán, Cabo, c., Chile	D3	72
Basehor, Ks., U.S.	k16	109
Basel, Switz.	G10	12
Bashan Lake, l., Ct., U.S.	D6	100
Bashaw, Ab., Can.	C4	84
Bashi Channel, strt., Asia	B8	34
Basilan Island, i., Phil.	E8	34
Basile, La., U.S.	D3	111
Basin, Wy., U.S.	B5	143
Basingstoke, Eng., U.K.	E6	12
Basīrhāt, India	E5	40
Baskahegan Lake, l., Me., U.S.	C5	112
Başkale, Tur.	C10	44
Basking Ridge, N.J., U.S.	B3	123
Baškirija, state, Russia	D7	26
Basoko, D.R.C.	C4	54
Basra see Al-Başrah, Iraq	D5	42
Bassano, Ab., Can.	D4	84
Bassar, Togo	E5	50
Bassein see Pathein, Myan.	C2	34
Basse Santa Su, Gam.	D2	50
Basse-Terre, Guad.	B7	80
Basseterre, St. K./N.	B7	80
Basse-Terre, i., Guad.	B7	80
Bassett, Ne., U.S.	B6	120
Bassett, Va., U.S.	D3	139
Bassett Peak, mtn., Az., U.S.	E5	96
Bassikounou, Maur.	C3	50
Bass Islands, is., Oh., U.S.	A3	128
Bass Lake, In., U.S.	B4	107
Bass Strait, strt., Austl.	H4	62
Basswood Lake, l., Mn., U.S.	B7	116
Båstad, Swe.	H5	10
Bastia, Fr.	C2	18
Bastrop, La., U.S.	B4	111
Bastrop, Tx., U.S.	D4	136
Bastrop, co., Tx., U.S.	D4	136
Basu, Pulau, i., Indon.	D2	36
Basutoland see Lesotho, ctry., Afr.	D4	56
Bata, Eq. Gui.	C1	54
Batabanó, Golfo de, b., Cuba	A3	80
Batac, Phil.	C8	34
Batagaj, Russia	C15	26
Batala, India	C3	40
Batamaj, Russia	C14	26
Batang, China	E7	28
Batang, Indon.	E3	36
Batangafo, C.A.R.	B3	54
Batangas, Phil.	D8	34
Batan Islands, is., Phil.	B8	34
Batanta, Pulau, i., Indon.	D8	36
Batavia see Jakarta, Indon.	k13	36
Batavia, Il., U.S.	B5	106
Batavia, N.Y., U.S.	C2	125
Batavia, Oh., U.S.	C1	128
Batchelor, La., U.S.	C5	60
Batchelor Bay, b., N.C., U.S.	B6	126
Bātdâmbâng, Camb.	D4	34
Batemans Bay, Austl.	H5	62
Bates, co., Mo., U.S.	C3	118
Batesburg, S.C., U.S.	D4	133
Batesville, Ar., U.S.	B4	97
Batesville, In., U.S.	F7	107
Batesville, Ms., U.S.	A4	117
Bath, N.B., Can.	C2	87
Bath, On., Can.	C8	89
Bath, Eng., U.K.	E5	12
Bath, Me., U.S.	E3	112
Bath, N.Y., U.S.	C3	125
Bath, Pa., U.S.	E11	131
Bath, S.C., U.S.	D4	133
Bath, co., Ky., U.S.	B6	110
Bath, co., Va., U.S.	B3	139
Bathinda, India	C3	40
Bathurst, Austl.	G4	62
Bathurst, N.B., Can.	B4	87
Bathurst see Banjul, Gam.	D1	50
Bathurst Island, i., Austl.	C5	60
Batiscan, stm., P.Q., Can.	B5	90
Batman, Tur.	D9	44
Batna, Alg.	C6	48
Baton Rouge, La., U.S.	D4	111
Batouri, Cam.	C2	54
Batsto, stm., N.J., U.S.	D3	123
Batten Kill, stm., U.S.	E2	138
Batticaloa, Sri L.	H4	40
Battle, stm., Can.	H17	82
Battle Creek, Ia., U.S.	B2	108
Battle Creek, Mi., U.S.	F5	115
Battle Creek, Ne., U.S.	C8	120
Battle Ground, In., U.S.	C4	107
Battle Ground, Wa., U.S.	D3	140
Battle Lake, Mn., U.S.	D3	116
Battle Mountain, Nv., U.S.	C5	121
Battle Mountain, mtn., Wy., U.S.	E5	143
Batu, mtn., Eth.	B7	54
Batu, Kepulauan, is., Indon.	D1	36
Batumi, Geor.	B9	44
Batu Pahat, Malay.	C2	36
Baturaja, Indon.	D2	36
Baturité, Braz.	B4	74
Baubau, Indon.	E6	36
Bauchi, Nig.	D6	50
Baudette, Mn., U.S.	B4	116
Bauld, Cape, c., Nf., Can.	C4	88
Baures, Bol.	A5	72
Bauru, Braz.	F2	74
Bauska, Lat.	H11	10
Bautzen, Ger.	E14	12
Bavispe, stm., Mex.	A3	78
Bawdwin, Myan.	B3	34
Bawean, Pulau, i., Indon.	E4	36
Bawiti, Egypt	E10	48
Baxley, Ga., U.S.	E4	103
Baxter, Ia., U.S.	C4	108
Baxter, Mn., U.S.	D4	116
Baxter, Tn., U.S.	C8	135
Baxter, co., Ar., U.S.	A3	97
Baxter Springs, Ks., U.S.	E9	109
Bay, Ar., U.S.	B5	97
Bay, co., Fl., U.S.	u16	102
Bay, co., Mi., U.S.	E6	115
Bayamo, Cuba	A4	80
Bayamón, P.R.	B6	80
Bayan Har Shan, mts., China	E7	28
Bayanhongor, Mong.	B8	28
Bayano, Lago, res., Pan.	D4	80
Bayan Obo, China	C10	28
Bayard, Ne., U.S.	C2	120
Bayard, N.M., U.S.	E1	124
Bayboro, N.C., U.S.	B6	126
Bay Bulls, Nf., Can.	E5	88
Bayburt, Tur.	B9	44
Bay City, Mi., U.S.	E7	115
Bay City, Or., U.S.	B3	130
Bay City, Tx., U.S.	E5	136
Bay de Verde, Nf., Can.	D5	88
Baydhabo, Som.	J13	48
Bayeux, Fr.	C6	16
Bayfield, On., Can.	D3	89
Bayfield, Co., U.S.	D3	99
Bayfield, Wi., U.S.	B3	142
Bayfield, co., Wi., U.S.	B2	142
Baylor, co., Tx., U.S.	C3	136
Bay Mills Indian Reservation, Mi., U.S.	B6	115
Bay Minette, Al., U.S.	E2	94
Bayombong, Phil.	C8	34
Bayonne, Fr.	F6	16
Bayonne, N.J., U.S.	B4	123
Bayou Bodcau Reservoir, res., La., U.S.	B2	111
Bayou D'Arbonne Lake, res., La., U.S.	B3	111
Bayou George, Fl., U.S.	u16	102
Bayou Goula, La., U.S.	D4	111
Bayou La Batre, Al., U.S.	E1	94
Bayovar, Peru	E3	70
Bay Point, c., S.C., U.S.	G7	133
Bayport, Mn., U.S.	E6	116
Bayport, N.Y., U.S.	n15	125
Bayreuth, Ger.	F12	12
Bay Ridge, Md., U.S.	C5	113
Bay Roberts, Nf., Can.	E5	88
Bayrūt (Beirut), Leb.	F6	44
Bays, Lake of, l., On., Can.	B5	89
Bay Saint Louis, Ms., U.S.	E4	117
Bay Shore, N.Y., U.S.	E7	125
Bay Springs, Ms., U.S.	D4	117
Bayt Laḥm, W.B.	G6	44
Baytown, Tx., U.S.	E5	136
Bayview, Al., U.S.	f7	94
Bay Village, Oh., U.S.	h9	128
Baza, Spain	I5	16
Bazardjuzju, gora see Bazardüzü dağ, mtn., Azer.	B12	44
Bazardüzü dağ, mtn., Azer.	B12	44
Bazaruto, Ilha do, i., Moz.	C6	56
Bazhong, China	C2	30
Be, Nosy, i., Madag.	A8	56
Beach, Il., U.S.	h9	106
Beach, N.D., U.S.	C1	127
Beachburg, On., Can.	B8	89
Beach City, Oh., U.S.	B4	128
Beach Haven Inlet, b., N.J., U.S.	D4	123
Beach Pond, res., U.S.	C8	100
Beachville, On., Can.	D4	89
Beachwood, N.J., U.S.	D4	123
Beacon, Austl.	G2	60
Beacon, N.Y., U.S.	D7	125
Beacon Falls, Ct., U.S.	D3	100
Beaconsfield, P.Q., Can.	q19	90
Beadle, co., S.D., U.S.	C7	134
Beagle Gulf, b., Austl.	C6	60
Bealanana, Madag.	A8	56
Beale, Cape, c., B.C., Can.	E5	85
Beale Air Force Base, mil., Ca., U.S.	C3	98
Bear, De., U.S.	B3	101
Bear, stm., U.S.	B3	137
Bear Creek, Al., U.S.	A2	94
Bear Creek, stm., Or., U.S.	E4	130
Bear Creek, stm., Wy., U.S.	E8	143
Bear Creek, stm., U.S.	E2	109
Bearden, Ar., U.S.	D3	97
Bear Inlet, b., N.C., U.S.	C5	126
Bear Island see Bjørnøya, i., Nor.	B3	26
Bear Lake, co., Id., U.S.	G7	105
Bear Lake, l., Wi., U.S.	C2	142
Bear Lake, l., U.S.	C5	92
Bear Lake, l., U.S.	A4	137
Bear Lodge Mountains, mts., Wy., U.S.	B8	143
Bear Mountain, mtn., Or., U.S.	D4	130
Bearpaw Mountains, mts., Mt., U.S.	B7	119
Bear River, N.S., Can.	E4	87
Bear River City, Ut., U.S.	B3	137
Beartooth Pass, Wy., U.S.	B3	143
Beartooth Range, mts., U.S.	E7	119
Bear Town, Ms., U.S.	D3	117
Beas, stm., India	C3	40
Beata, Isla, i., Dom. Rep.	B5	80
Beatrice, Ne., U.S.	D9	120
Beatrice, Cape, c., Austl.	C2	62
Beatty, Nv., U.S.	G5	121
Beattyville, Ky., U.S.	C6	110
Beaufort, N.C., U.S.	C6	126
Beaufort, S.C., U.S.	G6	133
Beaufort, co., N.C., U.S.	B5	126
Beaufort, co., S.C., U.S.	G6	133
Beaufort Marine Corps Air Station, mil., S.C., U.S.	F6	133
Beaufort Sea, N.A.	D12	82
Beaufort West, S. Afr.	E3	56
Beauharnois, P.Q., Can.	D4	90
Beau Lake, l., Me., U.S.	A3	112
Beaumont, Ab., Can.	C4	84
Beaumont, Ms., U.S.	D5	117
Beaumont, Tx., U.S.	D5	136
Beaune, Fr.	D9	16
Beauport, P.Q., Can.	n17	90
Beaupré, P.Q., Can.	B7	90
Beauregard, co., La., U.S.	D2	111
Beausejour, Mb., Can.	D3	86
Beauvais, Fr.	C8	16
Beauval, Sk., Can.	B2	91
Beaver, Ok., U.S.	A1	129
Beaver, Pa., U.S.	E1	131
Beaver, Ut., U.S.	E3	137
Beaver, W.V., U.S.	D3	141
Beaver, co., Ok., U.S.	e10	129
Beaver, co., Pa., U.S.	E1	131
Beaver, co., Ut., U.S.	E2	137
Beaver, stm., Can.	B2	91
Beaver, stm., N.Y., U.S.	B6	125
Beaver, stm., R.I., U.S.	E2	132
Beaver, stm., Ut., U.S.	E2	137
Beaver, stm., U.S.	A2	129
Beaverbank, N.S., Can.	E6	87
Beaver Brook, stm., U.S.	E4	122
Beaver City, Ne., U.S.	D6	120
Beavercreek, Oh., U.S.	C1	128
Beaver Creek, stm., N.D., U.S.	C1	127
Beaver Creek, stm., N.D., U.S.	C5	127
Beaver Creek, stm., Ok., U.S.	C3	129
Beaver Creek, stm., Tn., U.S.	m13	135
Beaver Creek, stm., Wy., U.S.	D4	143
Beaver Creek, stm., U.S.	E4	120
Beaver Creek, stm., U.S.	C8	143
Beaver Dam, Ky., U.S.	C3	110
Beaver Dam, Wi., U.S.	E5	142
Beaverdam Branch, stm., De., U.S.	F3	101
Beaverdam Lake, res., Wi., U.S.	E5	142
Beaver Falls, Pa., U.S.	E1	131
Beaverhead, co., Mt., U.S.	E3	119
Beaverhead, stm., Mt., U.S.	E4	119
Beaverhead Mountains, mts., U.S.	D5	105
Beaverhill Lake, l., Ab., Can.	C4	84
Beaver Island, i., Mi., U.S.	C5	115
Beaver Lake, res., Ar., U.S.	A2	97
Beaverlodge, Ab., Can.	B1	84
Beaver Meadows, Pa., U.S.	E10	131
Beaver Run Reservoir, res., Pa., U.S.	F2	131
Beavertail Point, c., R.I., U.S.	F4	132
Beaverton, Mi., U.S.	E6	115
Beaverton, Or., U.S.	B4	130
Beāwar, India	D2	40
Bebedouro, Braz.	C8	72
Bécancour, P.Q., Can.	C5	90
Bečej, Yugo.	B8	18
Béchar, Alg.	D4	48
Becharof Lake, l., Ak., U.S.	D8	95
Bechuanaland see Botswana, ctry., Afr.	C3	56
Beckemeyer, Il., U.S.	E4	106
Becker, Mn., U.S.	E5	116
Becker, co., Mn., U.S.	D3	116
Beckham, co., Ok., U.S.	B2	129
Beckley, W.V., U.S.	D3	141
Becky Peak, mtn., Nv., U.S.	D7	121
Bedelē, Eth.	B7	54
Bedford, P.Q., Can.	D5	90
Bedford, Eng., U.K.	D6	12
Bedford, Ia., U.S.	D3	108
Bedford, In., U.S.	G5	107
Bedford, Ky., U.S.	B4	110
Bedford, Ma., U.S.	B5	114
Bedford, N.H., U.S.	E3	122
Bedford, Oh., U.S.	A4	128
Bedford, Pa., U.S.	F4	131
Bedford, Va., U.S.	C3	139
Bedford, co., Pa., U.S.	G4	131
Bedford, co., Tn., U.S.	B5	135
Bedford, co., Va., U.S.	C3	139
Bedford Hills, N.Y., U.S.	D7	125
Bee, co., Tx., U.S.	E4	136
Beebe, P.Q., Can.	D5	90
Beebe, Ar., U.S.	B4	97
Beecher, Il., U.S.	B6	106
Beech Fork, stm., Ky., U.S.	C4	110
Beech Grove, In., U.S.	E5	107
Beech Island, S.C., U.S.	E4	133
Beemer, Ne., U.S.	C9	120
Bee Ridge, Fl., U.S.	q11	102
Beersheba see Be'ér Sheva', Isr.	D2	42
Be'ér Sheva', Isr.	D2	42
Beeton (part of Alliston Beeton Tecumseth and Tottenham), On., Can.	C5	89
Beeville, Tx., U.S.	E4	136
Befale, D.R.C.	C4	54
Befandriana Atsimo, Madag.	C7	56
Bega, Austl.	H4	62
Beggs, Ok., U.S.	B5	129
Behbahān, Iran	D6	42
Behm Canal, strt., Ak., U.S.	n24	95
Bei'an, China	B13	28
Beigi, Eth.	B6	54
Beihai, China	G9	28
Beijing, China	D11	28
Beiliu, China	I3	30
Beipiao, China	C12	28
Beira, Moz.	B5	56
Beirut see Bayrūt, Leb.	F6	44
Bei Shan, mts., China	C7	28
Beitbridge, Zimb.	C5	56
Beizhen, China	A5	30
Beizhen, China	B4	30
Beja, Port.	I3	16
Béja, Tun.	C6	48
Bejaïa, Alg.	C6	48
Bejaïa, Golfe de, b., Alg.	I9	16
Béjar, Spain	E5	16
Bejneu, Kaz.	E7	26
Bekaa Valley see Al-Biqā', val., Leb.	F6	44
Bekabad, Uzb.	B9	42
Bekasi, Indon.	E3	36
Bekdaş, Turk.	B6	42
Békéscsaba, Hung.	C8	20
Bekily, Madag.	C8	56
Bekodoka, Madag.	B8	56
Bela, India	D4	40
Bela, Pak.	E9	42
Bela Crkva, Yugo.	B8	18
Bel Air, Md., U.S.	A5	113
Bel Alton, Md., U.S.	D4	113
Belarus, ctry., Eur.	C9	20
Belau see Palau, ctry., Oc.	F10	32
Bela Vista, Braz.	H8	70
Bela Vista, Moz.	D5	56
Belcamp, Md., U.S.	B5	113
Bełchatów, Pol.	D5	20
Belchertown, Ma., U.S.	B3	114
Belcourt, N.D., U.S.	A6	127
Belden, Ms., U.S.	A5	117
Belding, Mi., U.S.	E5	115
Beledweyne, Som.	J13	48
Belém, Braz.	B2	74
Belém, Moz.	A6	56
Belém de São Francisco, Braz.	C4	74
Belen, N.M., U.S.	C3	124
Belëv, Russia	C14	20
Belfair, Wa., U.S.	B3	140
Belfast, S. Afr.	D5	56
Belfast, N. Ire., U.K.	C4	12
Belfast, Me., U.S.	D3	112
Belfield, N.D., U.S.	C2	127
Belford, N.J., U.S.	C4	123
Belfort, Fr.	D10	16
Belfry, Ky., U.S.	C7	110
Belgaum, India	F2	40
Belgium, Wi., U.S.	E6	142

Name	Map Ref.	Page
Belgium, ctry., Eur.	B9	16
Belgorod, Russia	D5	26
Belgrade, Mn., U.S.	E3	116
Belgrade, Mt., U.S.	E5	119
Belgrade see Beograd, Yugo.	B8	18
Belhaven, N.C., U.S.	B6	126
Beliliou, i., Palau	E9	32
Belington, W.V., U.S.	B5	141
Belitung, i., Indon.	D3	36
Belize, ctry., N.A.	B2	80
Belize City, Belize	B2	80
Belknap, co., N.H., U.S.	C3	122
Belknap Crater, crat., Or., U.S.	C5	130
Bell, co., Ky., U.S.	D6	110
Bell, co., Tx., U.S.	D4	136
Bella Coola, stm., B.C., Can.	C4	85
Bellaire, Ks., U.S.	g12	109
Bellaire, Mi., U.S.	D5	115
Bellaire, Oh., U.S.	C5	128
Bellaire, Tx., U.S.	r14	136
Bellamy, Al., U.S.	C1	94
Bellary, India	F3	40
Bella Vista, Ar., U.S.	A1	97
Bellavista, Peru	E4	70
Bellbrook, Oh., U.S.	C1	128
Belle, Mo., U.S.	C6	118
Belle, W.V., U.S.	C3	141
Belle, stm., La., U.S.	k9	111
Belleair, Fl., U.S.	p10	102
Belle Bay, b., Nf., Can.	E4	88
Belle Chasse, La., U.S.	E5	111
Bellefontaine, Oh., U.S.	B2	128
Bellefonte, Pa., U.S.	E6	131
Belle Fourche, S.D., U.S.	C2	134
Belle Fourche, stm., U.S.	C3	134
Belle Fourche Reservoir, res., S.D., U.S.	C2	134
Belle Glade, Fl., U.S.	F6	102
Belle-Île, i., Fr.	D5	16
Belle Isle, Fl., U.S.	D5	102
Belle Isle, i., Nf., Can.	C4	88
Belle Isle, Strait of, strt., Nf., Can.	C3	88
Belle Meade, Tn., U.S.	g10	135
Belle Plaine, Ia., U.S.	C5	108
Belle Plaine, Ks., U.S.	E6	109
Belle Plaine, Mn., U.S.	F5	116
Belle River, On., Can.	E2	89
Belle Rose, La., U.S.	D4	111
Belle Vernon, Pa., U.S.	F2	131
Belleview, Fl., U.S.	C4	102
Belle View, Va., U.S.	g12	139
Belleville, On., Can.	C7	89
Belleville, Il., U.S.	E4	106
Belleville, Ks., U.S.	C6	109
Belleville, Mi., U.S.	p15	115
Belleville, N.J., U.S.	B4	123
Belleville, Pa., U.S.	E6	131
Belleville, Wi., U.S.	F4	142
Belleville Pond, l., R.I., U.S.	E4	132
Bellevue, Ia., U.S.	B7	108
Bellevue, Id., U.S.	F4	105
Bellevue, Ky., U.S.	h13	110
Bellevue, Mi., U.S.	F5	115
Bellevue, Ne., U.S.	C10	120
Bellevue, Oh., U.S.	A3	128
Bellevue, Pa., U.S.	F1	131
Bellevue, Wa., U.S.	e11	140
Bellflower, Ca., U.S.	n12	98
Bellingham, Ma., U.S.	B5	114
Bellingham, Wa., U.S.	A3	140
Bellingshausen Sea, Ant.	C32	67
Bellinzona, Switz.	A2	18
Bell Island, i., Nf., Can.	C4	88
Bellmawr, N.J., U.S.	D2	123
Bello, Col.	B4	70
Bellows Falls, Vt., U.S.	E4	138
Bellport, N.Y., U.S.	n16	125
Bells, Tn., U.S.	B2	135
Bells Creek, stm., W.V., U.S.	m13	141
Belluno, Italy	A4	18
Bell Ville, Arg.	E5	72
Bellville, Oh., U.S.	B3	128
Bellville, Tx., U.S.	E4	136
Bellwood, Il., U.S.	k9	106
Bellwood, Pa., U.S.	E5	131
Bellwood, Va., U.S.	n18	139
Belmar, N.J., U.S.	C4	123
Belmond, Ia., U.S.	B4	108
Belmont, On., Can.	E3	89
Belmont, Ca., U.S.	h8	98
Belmont, Ma., U.S.	g11	114
Belmont, Ms., U.S.	A5	117
Belmont, N.C., U.S.	B1	126
Belmont, N.H., U.S.	D4	122
Belmont, W.V., U.S.	B3	141
Belmont, Wi., U.S.	F3	142
Belmont, co., Oh., U.S.	C5	128
Belmonte, Braz.	G12	70
Belmopan, Belize	B2	80
Bel-Nor, Mo., U.S.	f13	118
Beloe, ozero, l., Russia	C5	26
Beloeil, P.Q., Can.	D4	90
Beloe more, Russia	C5	26
Belogorsk, Russia	D14	26
Belo Horizonte, Braz.	E3	74
Beloit, Ks., U.S.	C5	109
Beloit, Oh., U.S.	B5	128
Beloit, Wi., U.S.	F4	142
Belomorsk, Russia	C5	26
Beloreck, Russia	D10	22
Belorussia see Belarus, ctry., Eur.	C9	20
Belo Tsiribihina, Madag.	B7	56
Belpre, Oh., U.S.	C4	128
Belt, Mt., U.S.	C6	119
Belted Range, mts., Nv., U.S.	F5	121
Belton, Mo., U.S.	C3	118
Belton, S.C., U.S.	B3	133
Belton, Tx., U.S.	D4	136
Belton Lake, res., Tx., U.S.	D4	136
Beltrami, co., Mn., U.S.	B3	116
Beltsville, Md., U.S.	B4	113
Beluha, gora, mtn., Asia	B5	28
Belūr, India	G3	40
Belvedere, S.C., U.S.	D4	133
Belvidere, Il., U.S.	A5	106
Belvidere, N.J., U.S.	B2	123
Belyj, ostrov, i., Russia	B8	26
Belyj Jar, Russia	D10	26
Belzoni, Ms., U.S.	B3	117
Bembèrèkè, Benin	D5	50
Bement, Il., U.S.	D5	106
Bemidji, Mn., U.S.	C4	116
Bemidji, Lake, l., Mn., U.S.	C4	116
Benāb, Iran	D11	44
Bena-Dibele, D.R.C.	D4	54
Benalla, Austl.	H4	62
Benares see Vārānasi, India	D4	40
Benavente, Spain	F4	16
Benavides, Tx., U.S.	F3	136
Benbecula, i., Scot., U.K.	B3	12
Benbrook Lake, res., Tx., U.S.	n9	136
Bencubbin, Austl.	G2	60
Bend, Or., U.S.	C5	130
Ben Davis Point, c., N.J., U.S.	E2	123
Bendeleben, Mount, mtn., Ak., U.S.	B7	95
Bendigo, Austl.	H3	62
Benedict, Md., U.S.	C4	113
Benedito Leite, Braz.	E11	70
Benewah, co., Id., U.S.	B2	105
Bengal, Bay of, b., Asia	F5	40
Bengbu, China	E11	28
Benghazi see Banghāzī, Libya	D9	48
Bengkalis, Pulau, i., Indon.	C2	36
Bengkulu, Indon.	D2	36
Bengtsfors, Swe.	G5	10
Benguela, Ang.	F2	54
Bengweulu Swamps, sw., Zam.	A5	56
Benham, Ky., U.S.	D7	110
Ben Hill, co., Ga., U.S.	E3	103
Beni, D.R.C.	C5	54
Beni, stm., Bol.	F6	70
Béni Abbas, Alg.	D4	48
Benicia, Ca., U.S.	C2	98
Benidorm, Spain	H6	16
Beni-Mellal, Mor.	D3	48
Benin, ctry., Afr.	D5	50
Benin, Bight of, b., Afr.	E5	50
Benin City, Nig.	E6	50
Beni Saf, Alg.	J6	16
Beni Suef, Egypt	E11	48
Benito Juárez, Arg.	F6	72
Benjamin Constant, Braz.	D5	70
Benkelman, Ne., U.S.	D4	120
Benld, Il., U.S.	D4	106
Bennett, Co., U.S.	B6	99
Bennett, co., S.D., U.S.	D4	134
Bennettsville, S.C., U.S.	B8	133
Bennington, Ne., U.S.	g12	120
Bennington, N.H., U.S.	D3	122
Bennington, Vt., U.S.	F2	138
Bennington, co., Vt., U.S.	E2	138
Benoit, Ms., U.S.	B2	117
Benoni, S. Afr.	D4	56
Bénoué see Benue, stm., Afr.	E6	50
Bensenville, Il., U.S.	B6	106
Bensheim, Ger.	F11	12
Bensley, Va., U.S.	C5	139
Benson, Az., U.S.	F5	96
Benson, Mn., U.S.	E3	116
Benson, N.C., U.S.	B4	126
Benson, co., N.D., U.S.	A6	127
Bent, co., Co., U.S.	D7	99
Benteng, Indon.	E6	36
Bentinck Island, i., Austl.	D2	62
Bentinck Island, i., Myan.	C3	34
Bentley, Ab., Can.	C4	84
Bentleyville, Pa., U.S.	F1	131
Benton, Ar., U.S.	C3	97
Benton, Il., U.S.	E5	106
Benton, Ks., U.S.	E6	109
Benton, Ky., U.S.	f9	110
Benton, La., U.S.	B2	111
Benton, co., Ar., U.S.	A1	97
Benton, co., Ia., U.S.	B5	108
Benton, co., In., U.S.	C3	107
Benton, co., Mn., U.S.	E4	116
Benton, co., Mo., U.S.	C4	118
Benton, co., Ms., U.S.	A4	117
Benton, co., Or., U.S.	C3	130
Benton, co., Tn., U.S.	A3	135
Benton, co., Wa., U.S.	C6	140
Benton City, Wa., U.S.	C6	140
Benton Harbor, Mi., U.S.	F4	115
Benton Heights, Mi., U.S.	F4	115
Bentonville, Ar., U.S.	A1	97
Ben Tre, Viet.	D5	34
Bent's Old Fort National Historic Site, hist., Co., U.S.	C7	99
Bentung, Malay.	C2	36
Benue, stm., Afr.	E6	50
Benwood, W.V., U.S.	f8	141
Benxi, China	C12	28
Benzie, co., Mi., U.S.	D4	115
Beograd (Belgrade), Yugo.	B8	18
Béoumi, C. Iv.	E3	50
Beowawe, Nv., U.S.	C5	121
Beppu, Japan	D2	31
Beraketa, Madag.	C8	56
Berat, Alb.	D7	18
Berau, Teluk, b., Indon.	D8	36
Berazino, Bela.	C10	20
Berbera, Som.	H14	48
Berbérati, C.A.R.	C3	54
Berck, Fr.	B7	16
Berdians'k, Ukr.	F14	20
Berdigestjah, Russia	C14	26
Berdychiv, Ukr.	E10	20
Berea, Ky., U.S.	C5	110
Berea, Oh., U.S.	A4	128
Berea, S.C., U.S.	B3	133
Berehove, Ukr.	E7	20
Berekum, Ghana	E4	50
Berens, stm., Can.	C3	86
Beresford, S.D., U.S.	D9	134
Berettyóújfalu, Hung.	F6	20
Berezhany, Ukr.	E8	20
Berezivka, Ukr.	F11	20
Berezniki, Russia	D7	26
Berëzovo, Russia	C8	26
Berg, Swe.	F7	10
Bergama, Tur.	C2	44
Bergamo, Italy	B2	18
Bergen, Ger.	D12	12
Bergen, Nor.	F1	10
Bergen, co., N.J., U.S.	A4	123
Bergenfield, N.J., U.S.	B4	123
Bergerac, Fr.	E7	16
Bergland, Mi., U.S.	m12	115
Berguent, Mor.	E4	14
Berhala, Selat, strt., Indon.	D2	36
Beringa, ostrov, i., Russia	D18	26
Beringov proliv see Bering Strait, strt.	F6	82
Beringovskij, Russia	C19	26
Bering Sea	G3	82
Bering Strait, strt.	F6	82
Berkakit, Russia	D14	26
Berkane, Mor.	E3	14
Berkeley, Ca., U.S.	D2	98
Berkeley, Mo., U.S.	f13	118
Berkeley, R.I., U.S.	B4	132
Berkeley, co., S.C., U.S.	E8	133
Berkeley, co., W.V., U.S.	B6	141
Berkeley Heights, N.J., U.S.	B4	123
Berkeley Springs, W.V., U.S.	B6	141
Berkley, Mi., U.S.	F7	115
Berks, co., Pa., U.S.	F9	131
Berkshire, co., Ma., U.S.	B1	114
Berkshire Hills, hills, Ma., U.S.	B1	114
Berlevåg, Nor.	A13	10
Berlin, Ger.	D13	12
Berlin, Ct., U.S.	C5	100
Berlin, Md., U.S.	D7	113
Berlin, N.H., U.S.	B4	122
Berlin, N.J., U.S.	D3	123
Berlin, Pa., U.S.	G4	131
Berlin, Wi., U.S.	E5	142
Berlin Lake, res., Oh., U.S.	A4	128
Bermejo, stm., S.A.	C5	72
Bermuda, dep., N.A.	B12	76
Bern, Switz.	A1	18
Bernalillo, N.M., U.S.	B3	124
Bernalillo, co., N.M., U.S.	C3	124
Bernardsville, N.J., U.S.	B3	123
Bernasconi, Arg.	F5	72
Berne see Bern, Switz.	A1	18
Berne, In., U.S.	C8	107
Berner Alpen, mts., Switz.	A1	18
Bernese Alps see Berner Alpen, mts., Switz.	A1	18
Bernice, La., U.S.	B3	111
Bernie, Mo., U.S.	E8	118
Bernier Island, i., Austl.	E1	60
Bernina, Piz, mtn., Eur.	A2	18
Beroroha, Madag.	C8	56
Berrien, co., Ga., U.S.	E3	103
Berrien, co., Mi., U.S.	F4	115
Berrien Springs, Mi., U.S.	G4	115
Berry, Al., U.S.	B2	94
Berry, hist. reg., Fr.	D7	16
Berryessa, Lake, res., Ca., U.S.	C2	98
Berry Hill, Tn., U.S.	g10	135
Berryville, Ar., U.S.	A2	97
Berryville, Va., U.S.	A5	139
Berseba, Nmb.	D2	56
Bershad', Ukr.	E10	20
Berthierville, P.Q., Can.	C4	90
Berthoud, Co., U.S.	A5	99
Berthoud Pass, Co., U.S.	B5	99
Bertie, co., N.C., U.S.	A5	126
Bertoua, Cam.	C2	54
Bertrand, Mo., U.S.	E8	118
Bertrand, Ne., U.S.	D6	120
Berwick, Ia., U.S.	e8	108
Berwick, La., U.S.	E4	111
Berwick, Me., U.S.	E2	112
Berwick, Pa., U.S.	D9	131
Berwick-upon-Tweed, Eng., U.K.	C6	12
Berwyn, Ab., Can.	A2	84
Berwyn, Il., U.S.	k9	106
Berwyn, Pa., U.S.	o20	131
Besalampy, Madag.	B7	56
Besançon, Fr.	D7	16
Beskids, mts., Eur.	E5	20
Beskra, Alg.	D6	48
Beslan, Russia	A11	44
Besni, Tur.	D7	44
Bessemer, Al., U.S.	B3	94
Bessemer, Mi., U.S.	n11	115
Bessemer, Pa., U.S.	E1	131
Bessemer City, N.C., U.S.	B1	126
Bétaré Oya, Cam.	B2	54
Betatakin Ruin, hist., Az., U.S.	A5	96
Bethalto, Il., U.S.	E3	106
Bethanien, Nmb.	D2	56
Bethany, Ct., U.S.	D4	100
Bethany, Il., U.S.	D5	106
Bethany, Mo., U.S.	A3	118
Bethany, Ok., U.S.	B4	129
Bethany, W.V., U.S.	A4	141
Bethany Beach, De., U.S.	F5	101
Bethel, Ak., U.S.	C7	95
Bethel, Ct., U.S.	D2	100
Bethel, Me., U.S.	D2	112
Bethel, N.C., U.S.	B5	126
Bethel, Oh., U.S.	D1	128
Bethel, Vt., U.S.	D3	138
Bethel Park, Pa., U.S.	k14	131
Bethel Springs, Tn., U.S.	B3	135
Bethesda, Md., U.S.	C3	113
Bethesda, Oh., U.S.	B4	128
Bethlehem, S. Afr.	D4	56
Bethlehem, Ct., U.S.	C3	100
Bethlehem, N.H., U.S.	B3	122
Bethlehem, Pa., U.S.	E11	131
Bethlehem see Bayt Laḥm, W.B.	G6	44
Bethulie, S. Afr.	E4	56
Betong, Malay.	C4	36
Betong, Thai.	E4	34
Betoota, Austl.	F3	62
Betpak-Dala, des., Kaz.	E8	26
Betroka, Madag.	C8	56
Betsiboka, stm., Madag.	B8	56
Betsie, Point, c., Mi., U.S.	D4	115
Betsy Layne, Ky., U.S.	C7	110
Bettendorf, Ia., U.S.	C7	108
Bettiah, India	D4	40
Betūl, India	E3	40
Betwa, stm., India	D3	40
Betzdorf, Ger.	E10	12
Beulah, Co., U.S.	C6	99
Beulah, N.D., U.S.	B4	127
Beulah, Lake, l., Ms., U.S.	B3	117
Beulaville, N.C., U.S.	C5	126
Beuthen see Bytom, Pol.	D5	20
B. Everett Jordan Lake, res., N.C., U.S.	B3	126
Beverley Head, c., Nf., Can.	D2	88
Beverly, Ma., U.S.	A6	114
Beverly, N.J., U.S.	C3	123
Beverly, Oh., U.S.	C4	128
Beverly, W.V., U.S.	C5	141
Beverly Hills, Ca., U.S.	m12	98
Beverly Shores, In., U.S.	A4	107
Bexar, co., Tx., U.S.	E3	136
Bexley, Oh., U.S.	m11	128
Beyla, Gui.	E3	50
Beypazarı, Tur.	B4	44
Beyşehir, Tur.	D4	44
Beyşehir Gölü, l., Tur.	D4	44
Bezau, Russia	C6	22
Béziers, Fr.	F8	16
Bhadohi, India	D4	40
Bhadrachalam, India	F4	40
Bhadrak, India	E5	40
Bhadra Reservoir, res., India	G3	40
Bhadrāvati, India	G3	40
Bhāgalpur, India	D5	40
Bhāgīrathi see Ganges, stm., India	D5	40
Bhakkar, Pak.	D10	40
Bhaktapur, Nepal	D5	40
Bhamo, Myan.	B3	34
Bhandāra, India	E3	40
Bharatpur, India	D3	40
Bharūch, India	E2	40
Bhātpāra, India	E5	40
Bhāvnagar, India	E2	40
Bhawānipatna, India	F4	40
Bhilai, India	E4	40
Bhīlwāra, India	D2	40
Bhīma, stm., India	F3	40
Bhind, India	D3	40
Bhiwāni, India	D3	40
Bhongīr, India	F3	40
Bhopāl, India	E3	40
Bhubaneshwar, India	E5	40
Bhuj, India	E1	40
Bhusāwal, India	E3	40
Bhutan, ctry., Asia	D6	40
Bia, Mount see Bia, Phou, mtn., Laos	C4	34
Bia, Phou, mtn., Laos	C4	34
Biafra, Bight of, Afr.	C1	54
Biak, i., Indon.	G10	32
Biała Podlaska, Pol.	D7	20
Białogard, Pol.	B4	20
Białystok, Pol.	C7	20
Bianco, Monte (Blanc, Mont), mtn., Eur.	B1	18
Biankouma, C. Iv.	E3	50
Biaora, India	E3	40
Biaro, Pulau, i., Indon.	C7	36
Biarritz, Fr.	F6	16
Bibala, Ang.	A1	56
Bibb, co., Al., U.S.	C2	94
Bibb, co., Ga., U.S.	D3	103
Bibémi, Cam.	B2	54
Biberach an der Riss, Ger.	F11	12
Bic, P.Q., Can.	A9	90
Bic, Île du, i., P.Q., Can.	A9	90
Biche, Lac la, l., Ab., Can.	B4	84
Bicknell, In., U.S.	G3	107
Bīd, India	F3	40
Bida, Nig.	E6	50
Bīdar, India	F3	40
Biddeford, Me., U.S.	E2	112
Bidwell, Mount, mtn., U.S.	B3	98
Biel, Switz.	A1	18
Bielefeld, Ger.	E11	12
Biella, Italy	B2	18
Bielsko-Biała, Pol.	E5	20
Bielsk Podlaski, Pol.	C7	20
Bien Hoa, Viet.	D5	34
Bienville, co., La., U.S.	B2	111
Bienville, Lac, l., P.Q., Can.	g12	90
Big, stm., Mo., U.S.	c7	118
Biga, Tur.	B2	44
Big Bald, mtn., Ga., U.S.	B2	103
Big Bald Mountain, mtn., N.B., Can.	B3	87
Big Baldy, mtn., Id., U.S.	E3	105
Big Baldy Mountain, mtn., Mt., U.S.	D6	119
Big Bay De Noc, b., Mi., U.S.	C4	115
Big Bear City, Ca., U.S.	E5	98
Big Belt Mountains, mts., Mt., U.S.	D5	119
Big Bend, Wi., U.S.	n11	142
Big Bend Dam, S.D., U.S.	C6	134
Big Bend National Park, Tx., U.S.	E1	136
Big Birch Lake, l., Mn., U.S.	E4	116
Big Black, stm., Me., U.S.	B3	112
Big Black, stm., Ms., U.S.	C3	117
Big Blue, stm., In., U.S.	E6	107
Big Burro Mountains, mts., N.M., U.S.	E1	124
Big Cabin Creek, stm., Ok., U.S.	A6	129
Big Coal, stm., W.V., U.S.	C3	141
Big Costilla Peak, mtn., N.M., U.S.	A4	124
Big Creek, stm., Tn., U.S.	e8	135
Big Creek Lake, res., Al., U.S.	E1	94
Big Creek Peak, mtn., Id., U.S.	E5	105
Big Cypress Indian Reservation, Fl., U.S.	F5	102
Big Cypress Swamp, sw., Fl., U.S.	F5	102
Big Darby Creek, stm., Oh., U.S.	C2	128
Big Delta, Ak., U.S.	C10	95
Big Duke Dam, N.C., U.S.	B2	126
Big Eau Pleine, stm., Wi., U.S.	D3	142
Big Eau Pleine Reservoir, res., Wi., U.S.	D4	142
Big Escambia Creek, stm., U.S.	D2	94
Big Flats, N.Y., U.S.	C4	125
Bigfork, Mt., U.S.	B2	119
Big Fork, stm., Mn., U.S.	B5	116
Biggs, Ca., U.S.	C3	98
Big Hatchet Peak, mtn., N.M., U.S.	F1	124
Big Hole, stm., Mt., U.S.	E4	119
Big Hole National Battlefield, hist., Mt., U.S.	E3	119
Big Horn, co., Mt., U.S.	E9	119
Big Horn, co., Wy., U.S.	B4	143
Bighorn Canyon National Recreation Area, U.S.	F8	119
Bighorn Lake, res., U.S.	E8	119
Big Horn Mountains, mts., Az., U.S.	D2	96
Bighorn Mountains, mts., U.S.	C6	92
Bighorn Mountains, mts., U.S.	B5	143
Bight, Head of, b., Austl.	G5	60
Big Kandiyohi Lake, l., Mn., U.S.	E4	116
Big Lake, Mn., U.S.	E5	116
Big Lake, Tx., U.S.	D2	136
Big Lake, l., Me., U.S.	C5	112
Biglerville, Pa., U.S.	G7	131
Big Lookout Mountain, mtn., Or., U.S.	C9	130
Big Lost, stm., Id., U.S.	F5	105
Big Mossy Point, c., Mb., Can.	C2	86
Big Mountain, mtn., Nv., U.S.	B2	121
Big Muddy, stm., Il., U.S.	F4	106
Big Nemaha, stm., Ne., U.S.	D10	120
Bignona, Sen.	D1	50

Name	Map Ref.	Page
Big Otter, stm., Va., U.S.	C3	139
Big Pine Lake, l., Mn., U.S.	D3	116
Big Pine Mountain, mtn., Ca., U.S.	E4	98
Big Piney, Wy., U.S.	D2	143
Big Piney, stm., Mo., U.S.	D5	118
Bigpoint, Ms., U.S.	E5	117
Big Rapids, Mi., U.S.	E5	115
Big Rib, stm., Wi., U.S.	C3	142
Big River, Sk., Can.	D2	91
Big Sable Point, c., Mi., U.S.	D4	115
Big Sandy, Mt., U.S.	B6	119
Big Sandy, Tx., U.S.	C5	136
Big Sandy, stm., Az., U.S.	C2	96
Big Sandy, stm., Tn., U.S.	B3	135
Big Sandy, stm., Wy., U.S.	D3	143
Big Sandy, stm., U.S.	C2	141
Big Sandy Creek, stm., W.V., U.S.	C3	141
Big Sandy Lake, l., Mn., U.S.	D5	116
Big Sandy Reservoir, res., Wy., U.S.	D3	143
Big Sheep Mountain, mtn., Mt., U.S.	C11	119
Big Sioux, stm., U.S.	E9	134
Big Smoky Valley, val., Nv., U.S.	E4	121
Big Snowy Mountains, mts., Mt., U.S.	D7	119
Big Southern Butte, mtn., Id., U.S.	F5	105
Big South Fork, stm., Ky., U.S.	k13	110
Big Spring, Tx., U.S.	C2	136
Big Stone, co., Mn., U.S.	E2	116
Big Stone City, S.D., U.S.	B9	134
Big Stone Gap, Va., U.S.	f9	139
Big Stone Lake, l., U.S.	E2	116
Big Sunflower, stm., Ms., U.S.	B3	117
Big Thompson, stm., Co., U.S.	A5	99
Big Timber, Mt., U.S.	E7	119
Big Trout Lake, l., On., Can.	n17	89
Big Walnut Creek, stm., Oh., U.S.	m11	128
Big Wood, stm., Id., U.S.	F4	105
Bihać, Bos.	B5	18
Bīhar, India	D5	40
Bihār, prov., India	E5	40
Biharamulo, Tan.	D6	54
Bijagós, Arquipélago dos, is., Gui.-B.	D1	50
Bijāpur, India	F3	40
Bījār, Iran	E12	44
Bijeljina, Bos.	B7	18
Bijie, China	F9	28
Bijsk, Russia	D10	26
Bīkāner, India	D2	40
Bikar, atoll, Marsh. Is.	C10	58
Bikeqi, China	C10	28
Bikin, Russia	B14	28
Bikini, atoll, Marsh. Is.	C10	58
Bīkkū Bīttī, mtn., Libya	F8	48
Bikoro, D.R.C.	D3	54
Bilāspur, India	C3	40
Bilāspur, India	E4	40
Biläsuvar, Azer.	C13	44
Bila Tserkva, Ukr.	E11	20
Bilauktaung Range, mts., Asia	D3	34
Bilbao, Spain	F5	16
Bilecik, Tur.	B4	44
Biłgoraj, Pol.	D7	20
Bilhorod-Dnistrovs'kyi, Ukr.	F11	20
Bili, D.R.C.	C5	54
Bilk Creek Mountains, mts., Nv., U.S.	B3	121
Billerica, Ma., U.S.	A5	114
Billings, Mo., U.S.	D4	118
Billings, Mt., U.S.	E8	119
Billings, co., N.D., U.S.	B2	127
Billings Heights, Mt., U.S.	E8	119
Bill Williams, stm., Az., U.S.	C1	96
Bill Williams Mountain, mtn., Az., U.S.	B3	96
Bilma, Niger	C7	50
Bilohirs'k, Ukr.	G13	20
Bilopillia, Ukr.	D13	20
Biloxi, Ms., U.S.	E5	117
Biloxi, stm., Ms., U.S.	E4	117
Biloxi Bay, b., Ms., U.S.	f8	117
Biltmore Forest, N.C., U.S.	f10	126
Bimbo, C.A.R.	C3	54
Bimini Islands, is., Bah.	C9	76
Bīna-Etāwa, India	E3	40
Bindura, Zimb.	B5	56
Binga, D.R.C.	C4	54
Binga, Monte, mtn., Afr.	B5	56
Bingamon Creek, stm., W.V., U.S.	k10	141
Bingara, Austl.	F5	62
Bingen, Wa., U.S.	D4	140
Binger, Ok., U.S.	B3	129
Bingham, Me., U.S.	C3	112
Bingham, co., Id., U.S.	F6	105
Binghamton, N.Y., U.S.	C5	125
Bingöl, Tur.	C9	44
Binhai, China	E12	28
Binh Son, Viet.	C5	34
Binjai, Indon.	C1	36
Binongko, Pulau, i., Indon.	E6	36
Bintan, Pulau, i., Indon.	C1	36
Bintimani, mtn., S.L.	E2	50
Bintuhan, Indon.	D2	36
Bintulu, Malay.	C4	36
Bintuni, Indon.	D8	36
Binxian, China	B4	30
Binyang, China	B5	34
Bin-Yauri, Nig.	D5	50
Binzert see Bizerte, Tun.	C6	48
Biobío, stm., Chile	F3	72
Bioko, i., Eq. Gui.	C1	54
Birāk, Libya	E7	48
Bi'r al Wa'r, Libya	F7	48
Birao, C.A.R.	A4	54
Birch, stm., W.V., U.S.	C4	141
Birch Island, i., Mb., Can.	C2	86
Birch Lake, l., Mn., U.S.	C7	116
Birch River, Mb., Can.	C1	86
Birch Run, Mi., U.S.	E7	115
Birchy Bay, Nf., Can.	D4	88
Bird Creek, stm., Ok., U.S.	A6	129
Bird Island, Mn., U.S.	F4	116
Bird Island, i., N.C., U.S.	D4	126
Birdsboro, Pa., U.S.	F10	131
Birdum, Austl.	D5	60
Birecik, Tur.	D8	44
Birigui, Braz.	F1	74
Bīrjand, Iran	D7	42
Birmingham, Eng., U.K.	D6	12
Birmingham, Al., U.S.	B3	94
Birmingham, Mi., U.S.	F7	115
Birmitrapur, India	E4	40
Bîr Mogreïn, Maur.	A2	50
Birnin-Kebbi, Nig.	D5	50
Birnin Konni, Niger	D6	50
Birnin Kudu, Nig.	D6	50
Birobidžan, Russia	E15	26
Biron, Wi., U.S.	D4	142
Birsk, Russia	C10	22
Birtle, Mb., Can.	D1	86
Biržai, Lith.	H11	10
Bisbee, Az., U.S.	F6	96
Biscay, Bay of (Gascogne, Golfe de), b., Eur.	E5	16
Biscayne, Key, i., Fl., U.S.	s13	102
Biscayne Bay, b., Fl., U.S.	G6	102
Biscayne National Monument, Fl., U.S.	G6	102
Biscayne Park, Fl., U.S.	s13	102
Biscoe, N.C., U.S.	B3	126
Bishkek see Biškek, Kyrg.	E9	26
Bishop, Ca., U.S.	D4	98
Bishop, Tx., U.S.	F4	136
Bishop's Falls, Nf., Can.	D4	88
Bishopville, S.C., U.S.	C7	133
Biškek, Kyrg.	E9	26
Bislig, Phil.	E9	34
Bismarck, Il., U.S.	C6	106
Bismarck, Mo., U.S.	D7	118
Bismarck, N.D., U.S.	C5	127
Bismarck Archipelago, is., Pap. N. Gui.	G12	32
Bismarck Range, mts., Pap. N. Gui.	H11	32
Bismarck Sea, Pap. N. Gui.	G12	32
Bismil, Tur.	D9	44
Bison Peak, mtn., Co., U.S.	B5	99
Bissau, Gui.-B.	D1	50
Bissikrima, Gui.	D2	50
Bistineau, Lake, res., La., U.S.	B2	111
Bistrița, Rom.	F8	20
Bitam, Gabon	C2	54
Bitlis, Tur.	C10	44
Bitola, Mac.	D8	18
Bitou, Burkina	D4	50
Bitterfontein, S. Afr.	E2	56
Bitter Lake, l., S.D., U.S.	B8	134
Bitterroot, stm., Mt., U.S.	D2	119
Bitterroot Range, mts., U.S.	B4	92
Bitterroot Range, mts., U.S.	B3	105
Bitung, Indon.	C7	36
Biu, Nig.	D7	50
Biwabik, Mn., U.S.	C6	116
Biwa-ko, l., Japan	C3	31
Bixby, Ok., U.S.	B6	129
Biyang, China	C3	30
Bizerte, Tun.	C6	48
Bjala, Bul.	C10	18
Bjarežina, stm., Bela.	C10	20
Bjelovar, Cro.	B6	18
Bjørnøya, i., Nor.	B3	26
Bla, Mali	D3	50
Black, stm., Asia	B4	34
Black, stm., Ar., U.S.	B4	97
Black, stm., Az., U.S.	D5	96
Black, stm., La., U.S.	C4	111
Black, stm., Mi., U.S.	E8	115
Black, stm., N.C., U.S.	C4	126
Black, stm., N.Y., U.S.	B4	125
Black, stm., S.C., U.S.	D8	133
Black, stm., Vt., U.S.	E3	138
Black, stm., Wi., U.S.	D3	142
Blackall, Austl.	E4	62
Black Bear Creek, stm., Ok., U.S.	A4	129
Blackbeard Island, i., Ga., U.S.	E5	103
Blackburn, Mount, mtn., Ak., U.S.	C11	95
Black Butte, mtn., Mt., U.S.	F5	119
Black Butte Lake, res., Ca., U.S.	C2	98
Black Canyon, val., Co., U.S.	C3	99
Black Canyon City, Az., U.S.	C3	96
Black Canyon of the Gunnison National Monument, Co., U.S.	C3	99
Black Creek, B.C., Can.	E5	85
Black Creek, Wi., U.S.	D5	142
Black Creek, stm., S.C., U.S.	B7	133
Black Creek, stm., U.S.	B1	124
Black Diamond, Ab., Can.	D3	84
Black Diamond, Wa., U.S.	B4	140
Blackduck, Mn., U.S.	C4	116
Black Eagle, Mt., U.S.	C5	119
Black Earth, Wi., U.S.	E4	142
Blackfalds, Ab., Can.	C4	84
Blackfeet Indian Reservation, Mt., U.S.	B4	119
Blackfoot, Id., U.S.	F6	105
Blackfoot, stm., Mt., U.S.	C3	119
Blackfoot Mountains, mts., Id., U.S.	F7	105
Blackfoot Reservoir, res., Id., U.S.	G7	105
Blackford, co., In., U.S.	D7	107
Black Forest, Co., U.S.	C6	99
Black Forest see Schwarzwald, mts., Ger.	F11	12
Blackhall Mountain, mtn., Wy., U.S.	E6	143
Black Hawk, S.D., U.S.	C2	134
Black Hawk, co., Ia., U.S.	B5	108
Black Hills, mts., U.S.	C2	134
Blackjack Mountain, mtn., Ga., U.S.	h8	103
Black Lake, P.Q., Can.	C6	90
Black Lake, l., Mi., U.S.	C6	115
Black Lake, l., N.Y., U.S.	f9	125
Black Lick, Pa., U.S.	F3	131
Black Mesa, mtn., Ok., U.S.	e8	129
Black Mingo Creek, stm., S.C., U.S.	D9	133
Blackmore, Mount, mtn., Mt., U.S.	E6	119
Black Mountain, N.C., U.S.	f10	126
Black Mountain, mtn., Az., U.S.	E4	96
Black Mountain, mtn., Co., U.S.	A5	99
Black Mountain, mtn., Id., U.S.	C3	105
Black Mountain, mtn., Mt., U.S.	D4	119
Black Mountain, mtn., Or., U.S.	B7	130
Black Mountain, mtn., Wy., U.S.	B5	143
Black Mountain, mtn., Wy., U.S.	D7	143
Black Mountain, mtn., U.S.	D7	110
Black Mountains, mts., Az., U.S.	B1	96
Black Peak, mtn., Az., U.S.	C1	96
Black Pine Peak, mtn., Id., U.S.	G5	105
Blackpool, Eng., U.K.	D5	12
Black Range, mts., N.M., U.S.	D2	124
Black River Falls, Wi., U.S.	D3	142
Black Rock, Ar., U.S.	A4	97
Black Rock, N.M., U.S.	B1	124
Black Rock, rock, S. Geor.	H8	69
Black Rock Desert, des., Nv., U.S.	B3	121
Black Rock Range, mts., Nv., U.S.	B3	121
Blacks Fork, stm., U.S.	E3	143
Blacks Harbour, N.B., Can.	D3	87
Blackshear, Ga., U.S.	E4	103
Blackstone, Ma., U.S.	B4	114
Blackstone, Va., U.S.	C5	139
Blackstone, stm., R.I., U.S.	B4	132
Black Thunder Creek, stm., Wy., U.S.	C8	143
Blackville, N.B., Can.	C4	87
Blackville, S.C., U.S.	E5	133
Black Volta, stm., Afr.	D4	50
Blackwalnut Point, c., Md., U.S.	C5	113
Black Warrior, stm., Al., U.S.	C2	94
Blackwater, stm., Ire.	D2	12
Blackwater, stm., Fl., U.S.	u15	102
Blackwater, stm., Md., U.S.	D5	113
Blackwater, stm., N.H., U.S.	D3	122
Blackwater, stm., Va., U.S.	D6	139
Blackwater Reservoir, res., N.H., U.S.	D3	122
Blackwell, Ok., U.S.	A4	129
Blackwood, N.J., U.S.	D2	123
Bladen, co., N.C., U.S.	C4	126
Bladenboro, N.C., U.S.	C4	126
Bladensburg, Md., U.S.	f9	113
Blades, De., U.S.	F3	101
Blagoevgrad, Bul.	D9	18
Blagoveščensk, Russia	D14	26
Blaine, Me., U.S.	B5	112
Blaine, Mn., U.S.	m12	116
Blaine, Wa., U.S.	A3	140
Blaine, co., Id., U.S.	F4	105
Blaine, co., Mt., U.S.	B7	119
Blaine, co., Ne., U.S.	C6	120
Blaine, co., Ok., U.S.	B3	129
Blaine Lake, Sk., Can.	E2	91
Blair, Ne., U.S.	C9	120
Blair, Ok., U.S.	C2	129
Blair, W.V., U.S.	n12	141
Blair, Wi., U.S.	D2	142
Blair, co., Pa., U.S.	E5	131
Blairstown, Ia., U.S.	C5	108
Blairsville, Pa., U.S.	F3	131
Blake Island, i., Wa., U.S.	e11	140
Blakely, Ga., U.S.	E2	103
Blakely, Pa., U.S.	m18	131
Blake Plateau	E6	66
Blake Point, c., Mi., U.S.	h10	115
Blanc, Cap see Nouâdhibou, Râs, c., Afr.	B1	50
Blanc, Mont (Bianco, Monte), mtn., Eur.	B1	18
Blanca Peak, mtn., Co., U.S.	D5	99
Blanchard, La., U.S.	B2	111
Blanchard, Ok., U.S.	B4	129
Blanchard, stm., Oh., U.S.	A1	128
Blanchardville, Wi., U.S.	F4	142
Blanchester, Oh., U.S.	C2	128
Blanco, Tx., U.S.	D3	136
Blanco, co., Tx., U.S.	D3	136
Blanco, Cape, c., Or., U.S.	E2	130
Bland, Mo., U.S.	C6	118
Bland, co., Va., U.S.	C1	139
Blanding, Ut., U.S.	F6	137
Blandinsville, Il., U.S.	C3	106
Blanquilla, Isla, i., Ven.	C7	80
Blantyre, Mwi.	B5	56
Blasdell, N.Y., U.S.	C2	125
Blawnox, Pa., U.S.	k14	131
Bleckley, co., Ga., U.S.	D3	103
Bledsoe, co., Tn., U.S.	D8	135
Blekinge, hist. reg., Swe.	H6	10
Blende, Co., U.S.	C6	99
Blenheim, On., Can.	E3	89
Blenheim, N.Z.	p13	63c
Blennerhassett, W.V., U.S.	B3	141
Blind, stm., La., U.S.	h10	111
Blind River, On., Can.	A2	89
Blissfield, Mi., U.S.	G7	115
Blitar, Indon.	E4	36
Block Island, R.I., U.S.	h7	132
Block Island, i., R.I., U.S.	h7	132
Block Island Sound, strt., U.S.	G2	132
Bloemfontein, S. Afr.	D4	56
Bloemhof, S. Afr.	D4	56
Blois, Fr.	D7	16
Blommestein Meer see Brokopondo Stuwmeer, res., Sur.	C8	70
Blönduós, Ice.	l18	10a
Blood Mountain, mtn., Ga., U.S.	B3	103
Bloodsworth Island, i., Md., U.S.	D5	113
Bloodvein, stm., Can.	D3	86
Bloomer, Wi., U.S.	C2	142
Bloomfield, On., Can.	D7	89
Bloomfield, Ct., U.S.	B5	100
Bloomfield, Ia., U.S.	D5	108
Bloomfield, In., U.S.	F4	107
Bloomfield, Ky., U.S.	C4	110
Bloomfield, Mo., U.S.	E8	118
Bloomfield, Ne., U.S.	B8	120
Bloomfield, N.J., U.S.	h8	123
Bloomfield, N.M., U.S.	A2	124
Bloomfield Hills, Mi., U.S.	o15	115
Bloomingdale, Ga., U.S.	D5	103
Bloomingdale, Il., U.S.	k8	106
Bloomingdale, N.J., U.S.	A4	123
Bloomingdale, Tn., U.S.	C11	135
Blooming Prairie, Mn., U.S.	G5	116
Bloomington, Il., U.S.	C4	106
Bloomington, In., U.S.	F4	107
Bloomington, Mn., U.S.	F5	116
Bloomington, Tx., U.S.	E4	136
Bloomington, Wi., U.S.	F3	142
Bloomington, Lake, res., Il., U.S.	C5	106
Bloomsburg, Pa., U.S.	E9	131
Bloomville, Oh., U.S.	A2	128
Blossburg, Pa., U.S.	C7	131
Blossom, Tx., U.S.	C5	136
Blount, co., Al., U.S.	B3	94
Blount, co., Tn., U.S.	D10	135
Blountstown, Fl., U.S.	B1	102
Blountsville, Al., U.S.	A3	94
Blountville, Tn., U.S.	C11	135
Blowing Rock, N.C., U.S.	A1	126
Blue, stm., Co., U.S.	B4	99
Blue, stm., In., U.S.	H5	107
Blue, stm., Mo., U.S.	k10	118
Blue, stm., Ok., U.S.	C5	129
Blue Ash, Oh., U.S.	o13	128
Blue Buck Point, c., La., U.S.	E2	111
Blue Creek, W.V., U.S.	m13	141
Blue Creek, stm., W.V., U.S.	m13	141
Blue Cypress Lake, l., Fl., U.S.	E6	102
Blue Diamond, Nv., U.S.	G6	121
Blue Earth, Mn., U.S.	G4	116
Blue Earth, co., Mn., U.S.	G4	116
Blue Earth, stm., Mn., U.S.	G4	116
Bluefield, Va., U.S.	C1	139
Bluefield, W.V., U.S.	D3	141
Bluefields, Nic.	C3	80
Blue Grass, Ia., U.S.	C7	108
Blue Hill, Me., U.S.	D4	112
Blue Hill, Ne., U.S.	D7	120
Blue Hill Range, hills, Ma., U.S.	h11	114
Blue Hills, Ct., U.S.	B5	100
Blue Island, Il., U.S.	B6	106
Bluejoint Lake, l., Or., U.S.	E7	130
Blue Lake, Ca., U.S.	B2	98
Blue Mesa Reservoir, res., Co., U.S.	C3	99
Blue Mound, Il., U.S.	D4	106
Blue Mountain, Ms., U.S.	A4	117
Blue Mountain, mtn., Mt., U.S.	C12	119
Blue Mountain, mtn., N.M., U.S.	D2	124
Blue Mountain, mtn., Pa., U.S.	F6	131
Blue Mountain Lake, res., Ar., U.S.	B2	97
Blue Mountain Peak, mtn., Jam.	B4	80
Blue Mountains, mts., U.S.	B4	92
Blue Nile, stm., Afr.	H11	48
Blue Point, Me., U.S.	g7	112
Blue Rapids, Ks., U.S.	C7	109
Blue Ridge, Va., U.S.	C3	139
Blue Ridge, mts., U.S.	D11	92
Blue Ridge Summit, Pa., U.S.	G7	131
Blue Springs, Mo., U.S.	h11	118
Bluestone, stm., W.V., U.S.	D3	141
Bluestone Lake, res., U.S.	D4	141
Bluewell, W.V., U.S.	D3	141
Bluff, N.Z.	q12	63c
Bluff City, Tn., U.S.	C11	135
Bluff Creek, stm., Ok., U.S.	A4	129
Bluff Lake, res., Ms., U.S.	B5	117
Bluff Park, Al., U.S.	g7	94
Bluffs, Il., U.S.	D3	106
Bluffton, In., U.S.	C7	107
Bluffton, Oh., U.S.	B2	128
Bluffton, S.C., U.S.	G6	133
Blumenau, Braz.	D8	72
Bly, Or., U.S.	E5	130
Blying Sound, strt., Ak., U.S.	h17	95
Blyth, On., Can.	D3	89
Blythe, Ca., U.S.	F6	98
Blytheville, Ar., U.S.	B6	97
Bo, S.L.	E2	50
Boaco, Nic.	C2	80
Boa Esperança, Represa, res., Braz.	E11	70
Boalsburg, Pa., U.S.	E6	131
Boardman, Oh., U.S.	A5	128
Boardman, Or., U.S.	B7	130
Boa Vista, Braz.	C7	70
Boa Vista, i., C.V.	g10	50a
Boaz, Al., U.S.	A3	94
Bobai, China	E2	30
Bobaomby, Tanjona, c., Madag.	A8	56
Bobbili, India	F4	40
Bobcaygeon, On., Can.	C6	89
Bobo-Dioulasso, Burkina	D4	50
Bobonong, Bots.	C4	56
Bobrov, Russia	D16	20
Bobrynets', Ukr.	E12	20
Bobtown, Pa., U.S.	G2	131
Boby, mtn., Madag.	A8	56
Boca Chica Key, i., Fl., U.S.	H5	102
Boca Ciega Bay, b., Fl., U.S.	p10	102
Boca do Acre, Braz.	E6	70
Boca Grande, Fl., U.S.	F4	102
Bocaiúva, Braz.	E3	74
Bocaranga, C.A.R.	B3	54
Boca Raton, Fl., U.S.	F6	102
Bocas del Toro, Pan.	D3	80
Bochnia, Pol.	E6	20
Bochum, Ger.	E10	12
Boconó, Ven.	D5	80
Bocşa, Rom.	G6	20
Bodajbo, Russia	D13	26
Bodega Head, c., Ca., U.S.	C2	98
Bodélé, reg., Chad	C8	50
Boden, Swe.	D9	10
Bodhan, India	F3	40
Bodie Island, i., N.C., U.S.	B7	126
Bodkin Point, c., Md., U.S.	B5	113
Bodø, Nor.	C6	10
Bodrum, Tur.	D2	44
Boende, D.R.C.	D4	54
Boerne, Tx., U.S.	E3	136
Boeuf, stm., La., U.S.	C4	111
Boeuf, Lake, l., La., U.S.	k10	111
Boffa, Gui.	D2	50
Bogale, Myan.	C3	34
Bogalusa, La., U.S.	D6	111
Bogangolo, C.A.R.	B3	54
Bogart, Ga., U.S.	C3	103
Bogata, Tx., U.S.	C5	136
Boğazlıyan, Tur.	C6	44
Bogda Shan, mts., China	C5	28
Boger City, N.C., U.S.	B1	126
Bogo, Phil.	D8	34
Bogor, Indon.	E3	36
Bogorodick, Russia	C15	20
Bogotá, Col.	C5	70
Bogota, N.J., U.S.	h8	123
Bogué, Maur.	C2	50
Bogue Chitto, Ms., U.S.	D3	117
Bogue Chitto, stm., U.S.	D5	111
Bogue Inlet, b., N.C., U.S.	C5	126
Bogue Phalia, stm., Ms., U.S.	B3	117
Bo Hai, b., China	D11	28

Name	Map Ref.	Page
Bohai Haixia, strt., China	D12	28
Bohemia, hist. reg., Czech Rep.	E3	20
Bohodukhiv, Ukr.	D13	20
Bohol, i., Phil.	E8	34
Bohol Sea, Phil.	E8	34
Bohuslav, Ukr.	E11	20
Boiling Springs, N.C., U.S.	B1	126
Boiling Springs, Pa., U.S.	F7	131
Bois Blanc Island, i., Mi., U.S.	C6	115
Bois Brule, stm., Wi., U.S.	B2	142
Boischâtel, P.Q., Can.	C6	90
Bois-des-Filion, P.Q., Can.	p19	90
Bois de Sioux, stm., Mn., U.S.	E2	116
Boise, Id., U.S.	F2	105
Boise, co., Id., U.S.	F3	105
Boise City, Ok., U.S.	e8	129
Boissevain, Mb., Can.	E1	86
Boissevain, Va., U.S.	e10	139
Boistfort Peak, mtn., Wa., U.S.	C2	140
Bojeador, Cape, c., Phil.	C8	34
Bojnūrd, Iran	C7	42
Boké, Gui.	D2	50
Boknafjorden, strt., Nor.	G1	10
Boko, Congo	D2	54
Bokoro, Chad	D8	50
Bokungu, D.R.C.	D4	54
Bolama, Gui.-B.	D1	50
Bolbec, Fr.	C7	16
Bole, Ghana	E4	50
Bolesławiec, Pol.	D3	20
Boley, Ok., U.S.	B5	129
Bolgatanga, Ghana	D4	50
Bolhov, Russia	C14	22
Boli, China	B14	28
Bolingbrook, Il., U.S.	k8	106
Bolivar, Mo., U.S.	D4	118
Bolivar, Oh., U.S.	B4	128
Bolivar, Tn., U.S.	B3	135
Bolivar, W.V., U.S.	B7	141
Bolivar, co., Ms., U.S.	B3	117
Bolívar, Cerro, mtn., Ven.	B7	70
Bolivar, Lake, l., Ms., U.S.	B3	117
Bolívar, Pico, mtn., Ven.	B5	70
Bolivia, ctry., S.A.	G7	70
Bollinger, co., Mo., U.S.	D7	118
Bollnäs, Swe.	F7	10
Bolnisi, Geor.	B11	44
Bolobo, D.R.C.	D3	54
Bologna, Italy	B3	18
Bologoe, Russia	C5	22
Bolomba, D.R.C.	C3	54
Bol'šaja Murta, Russia	D11	26
Bolsena, Lago di, l., Italy	C3	18
Bol'šereck, Russia	D17	26
Bol'ševik, ostrov, i., Russia	B12	26
Bol'šezemel'skaja Tundra, reg., Russia	A9	22
Bol'šoj Begičev, ostrov, i., Russia	B13	26
Bol'šoj Enisej, stm., Russia	A7	28
Bol'šoj Kamen', Russia	B2	31
Bol'šoj Ljahovskij, ostrov, i., Russia	B16	26
Bolton, Eng., U.K.	D5	12
Bolton, Ms., U.S.	C3	117
Bolton Lakes, l., Ct., U.S.	B6	100
Bolton Landing, N.Y., U.S.	B7	125
Bolu, Tur.	B4	44
Bolvadin, Tur.	C4	44
Bolzano, Italy	A3	18
Boma, D.R.C.	E2	54
Bombay see Mumbai, India	F2	40
Bombay Hook Island, i., De., U.S.	C4	101
Bomberai, Semenanjung, pen., Indon.	D8	36
Bom Despacho, Braz.	B8	72
Bomdila, India	D6	40
Bom Jesus da Lapa, Braz.	D3	74
Bomongo, D.R.C.	C3	54
Bomoseen, Lake, l., Vt., U.S.	D2	138
Bomu, stm., Afr.	C4	54
Bon, Cap, c., Tun.	C7	48
Bon Accord, Ab., Can.	B4	84
Bon Air, Va., U.S.	C5	139
Bonaire, Ga., U.S.	D3	103
Bonaire, i., Neth. Ant.	C6	80
Bonanza Peak, mtn., Wa., U.S.	A5	140
Bonaparte, Mount, mtn., Wa., U.S.	A6	140
Bonasila Dome, mtn., Ak., U.S.	C7	95
Bonaventure, P.Q., Can.	A4	90
Bonavista, Nf., Can.	D5	88
Bonavista, Cape, c., Nf., Can.	D5	88
Bonavista Bay, b., Nf., Can.	D5	88
Bond, co., Il., U.S.	E4	106
Bondo, D.R.C.	C4	54
Bondo, D.R.C.	C3	54
Bondoukou, C. Iv.	E4	50
Bondsville, Ma., U.S.	B3	114
Bonduel, Wi., U.S.	D5	142
Bondurant, Ia., U.S.	C4	108
Bône see Annaba, Alg.	C6	48
Bone, Gulf of see Bone, Teluk, b., Indon.	D6	36
Bone, Teluk, b., Indon.	D6	36
Bone Lake, l., Wi., U.S.	C1	142
Bongandanga, D.R.C.	C4	54
Bongka, Indon.	D6	36
Bongo, Massif des, mts., C.A.R.	B4	54
Bongor, Chad	D8	50
Bonham, Tx., U.S.	C4	136
Bon Homme, co., S.D., U.S.	D8	134
Bonifacio, Strait of, strt., Eur.	D2	18
Bonifay, Fl., U.S.	u16	102
Bonin Islands see Ogasawara-guntō, is., Japan	F16	64
Bonita Springs, Fl., U.S.	F5	102
Bonkoukou, Niger	D5	50
Bonn, Ger.	E10	12
Bonneauville, Pa., U.S.	G7	131
Bonne Bay, b., Nf., Can.	D3	88
Bonner, co., Id., U.S.	A2	105
Bonners Ferry, Id., U.S.	A2	105
Bonner Springs, Ks., U.S.	C9	109
Bonnet Carre Floodway, La., U.S.	h11	111
Bonne Terre, Mo., U.S.	D7	118
Bonneville, co., Id., U.S.	F7	105
Bonneville Dam, U.S.	B4	130
Bonneville Peak, mtn., Id., U.S.	F6	105
Bonneville Salt Flats, pl., Ut., U.S.	C2	137
Bonney Lake, Wa., U.S.	B3	140
Bonnie Doone, N.C., U.S.	B4	126
Bonnie Rock, Austl.	G2	60
Bonny, Nig.	F6	50
Bonny Reservoir, res., Co., U.S.	B8	99
Bonnyville, Ab., Can.	B5	84
Bono, Ar., U.S.	B5	97
Bon Secour, Al., U.S.	E2	94
Bonthe, S.L.	E2	50
Bontoc, Phil.	C8	34
Booker, Tx., U.S.	A2	136
Booker T. Washington National Monument, Va., U.S.	C3	139
Boola, Gui.	E3	50
Boolaloo, Austl.	E2	60
Boomer, W.V., U.S.	C3	141
Boone, Ia., U.S.	B4	108
Boone, N.C., U.S.	A1	126
Boone, co., Ar., U.S.	A2	97
Boone, co., Ia., U.S.	B3	108
Boone, co., Il., U.S.	A5	106
Boone, co., In., U.S.	D4	107
Boone, co., Ky., U.S.	B5	110
Boone, co., Mo., U.S.	B5	118
Boone, co., Ne., U.S.	C7	120
Boone, co., W.V., U.S.	C3	141
Boone, stm., Ia., U.S.	B4	108
Boone Lake, res., Tn., U.S.	C11	135
Booneville, Ar., U.S.	B2	97
Booneville, Ms., U.S.	A5	117
Boonsboro, Md., U.S.	A2	113
Boonton, N.J., U.S.	B4	123
Boonville, In., U.S.	H3	107
Boonville, Mo., U.S.	C5	118
Boonville, N.C., U.S.	A2	126
Boonville, N.Y., U.S.	B5	125
Boosaaso, Som.	H14	48
Boothbay Harbor, Me., U.S.	E3	112
Boothia, Gulf of, b., N.T., Can.	D21	82
Booths Creek, stm., W.V., U.S.	h11	141
Boothville, La., U.S.	E6	111
Booué, Gabon	D2	54
Bophuthatswana, hist. reg., S. Afr.	D4	56
Bopolu, Lib.	E2	50
Bor, Sudan	I11	48
Bor, Tur.	D6	44
Bor, Yugo.	B9	18
Borah Peak, mtn., Id., U.S.	E5	105
Borås, Swe.	H5	10
Borba, Braz.	D8	70
Bordeaux, Fr.	E6	16
Borden, co., Tx., U.S.	C2	136
Bordentown, N.J., U.S.	C3	123
Bordj Bou Arreridj, Alg.	J9	16
Bordj Omar Idriss, Alg.	E6	48
Borðoy, i., Far. Is.	n23	10b
Borgarnes, Ice.	l17	10a
Borger, Tx., U.S.	B2	136
Borgholm, Swe.	H7	10
Borgne, Lake, b., La., U.S.	D6	111
Borisoglebsk, Russia	D7	22
Borken, Ger.	E10	12
Borkou, reg., Chad	C8	50
Borlänge, Swe.	F6	10
Borneo (Kalimantan), i., Asia	D4	36
Bornholm, i., Den.	I6	10
Borno, prov., Nig.	D7	50
Borogoncy, Russia	C15	26
Boromo, Burkina	D4	50
Boron, Ca., U.S.	E5	98
Borongan, Phil.	D9	34
Borovici, Russia	D5	26
Borrego Springs, Ca., U.S.	F5	98
Borroloola, Austl.	B6	60
Borșa, Rom.	B8	20
Borūjerd, Iran	D5	42
Boryslav, Ukr.	E7	20
Boryspil', Ukr.	D11	20
Borzja, Russia	D13	26
Boržomi, Geor.	B10	44
Bosanski Novi, Bos.	B6	18
Boscobel, Wi., U.S.	E3	142
Bose, China	G9	28
Boshan, China	D11	28
Bosna, stm., Bos.	B6	18
Bosnia and Herzegovina, ctry., Eur.	B6	18
Bosnik, Indon.	G10	32
Bosobolo, D.R.C.	C3	54
Bosporus see İstanbul Boğazı, strt., Tur.	B3	44
Bosque, co., Tx., U.S.	D4	136
Bossangoa, C.A.R.	B3	54
Bossembélé, C.A.R.	B3	54
Bossentélé, C.A.R.	B3	54
Bossier, co., La., U.S.	B2	111
Bossier City, La., U.S.	B2	111
Bostān, Iran	G13	44
Bosten Hu, l., China	C5	28
Boston, Eng., U.K.	D6	12
Boston, Ga., U.S.	F3	103
Boston, Ma., U.S.	B5	114
Boston Bay, b., Ma., U.S.	B6	114
Boston Mountains, mts., Ar., U.S.	B2	97
Boswell, In., U.S.	C3	107
Boswell, Ok., U.S.	C6	129
Boswell, Pa., U.S.	F3	131
Botetourt, co., Va., U.S.	C3	139
Bothell, Wa., U.S.	B3	140
Bothnia, Gulf of, b., Eur.	F8	10
Bothwell, On., Can.	E3	89
Botkins, Oh., U.S.	B1	128
Botlih, Russia	A12	44
Botoșani, Rom.	B9	20
Bo Trach, Viet.	C5	34
Botswana, ctry., Afr.	C3	56
Bottineau, N.D., U.S.	A5	127
Bottineau, co., N.D., U.S.	A4	127
Botucatu, Braz.	F2	74
Botwood, Nf., Can.	D4	88
Bouaflé, C. Iv.	E3	50
Bouaké, C. Iv.	E3	50
Bouar, C.A.R.	B3	54
Bouarfa, Mor.	E3	14
Bouca, C.A.R.	B3	54
Boucherville, P.Q., Can.	D4	90
Bouctouche, N.B., Can.	C5	87
Boudreaux, Lake, l., La., U.S.	E5	111
Bougainville, i., Pap. N. Gui.	B6	62
Bougainville, Détroit de, strt., Vanuatu	k9	62a
Bougie see Bejaïa, Alg.	C6	48
Bougouni, Mali	D3	50
Bouïra, Alg.	C5	48
Boujdour, Cap, c., W. Sah.	A2	50
Boulder, Co., U.S.	A5	99
Boulder, Mt., U.S.	D4	119
Boulder, co., Co., U.S.	A5	99
Boulder City, Nv., U.S.	H7	121
Boulevard Heights, Md., U.S.	f9	113
Boulia, Austl.	E2	62
Boulogne-sur-Mer, Fr.	B7	16
Boulsa, Burkina	D4	50
Bouna, C. Iv.	E4	50
Boundary, co., Id., U.S.	A2	105
Boundary Bay, b., Wa., U.S.	A3	140
Boundary Peak, mtn., Nv., U.S.	F3	121
Bound Brook, N.J., U.S.	B3	123
Boundiali, C. Iv.	E3	50
Bountiful, Ut., U.S.	C4	137
Bounty Islands, is., N.Z.	M21	64
Bounty Trough	M20	64
Bourail, N. Cal.	l9	62a
Bourbeuse, stm., Mo., U.S.	C6	118
Bourbon, In., U.S.	B5	107
Bourbon, Mo., U.S.	C6	118
Bourbon, co., Ks., U.S.	E9	109
Bourbon, co., Ky., U.S.	B5	110
Bourbonnais, Il., U.S.	B6	106
Bourem, Mali	C4	50
Bourg, La., U.S.	E5	111
Bourg-en-Bresse, Fr.	D9	16
Bourges, Fr.	D8	16
Bourgogne, hist. reg., Fr.	D9	16
Bourke, Austl.	G4	62
Bournemouth, Eng., U.K.	E5	12
Bou Saâda, Alg.	C5	48
Bousso, Chad	D8	50
Boutilimit, Maur.	C2	50
Boutte, La., U.S.	k11	111
Bouvetøya, i., Ant.	B5	67
Bouza, Niger	D6	50
Bovey, Mn., U.S.	C5	116
Bovina, Tx., U.S.	B1	136
Bow, N.H., U.S.	D3	122
Bow, stm., Ab., Can.	D4	84
Bowden, Ab., Can.	D4	84
Bowdish Reservoir, res., R.I., U.S.	B1	132
Bowdon, Ga., U.S.	C1	103
Bowen, Arg.	F4	72
Bowen, Austl.	D4	62
Bowie, Az., U.S.	E6	96
Bowie, Md., U.S.	C4	113
Bowie, Tx., U.S.	C4	136
Bowie, co., Tx., U.S.	C5	136
Bow Island, Ab., Can.	E5	84
Bow Lake, l., N.H., U.S.	D4	122
Bowling Green, Fl., U.S.	E5	102
Bowling Green, Ky., U.S.	D3	110
Bowling Green, Mo., U.S.	B6	118
Bowling Green, Oh., U.S.	A2	128
Bowling Green, S.C., U.S.	A5	133
Bowling Green, Va., U.S.	B5	139
Bowling Green, Cape, c., Austl.	D4	62
Bowman, Ga., U.S.	B3	103
Bowman, N.D., U.S.	C2	127
Bowman, S.C., U.S.	E6	133
Bowman, co., N.D., U.S.	C2	127
Bowman Creek, stm., Pa., U.S.	m16	131
Bowman-Haley Lake, res., N.D., U.S.	C2	127
Bowral, Austl.	G5	62
Bowron, stm., B.C., Can.	C7	85
Bowstring Lake, l., Mn., U.S.	C5	116
Box Butte, co., Ne., U.S.	B2	120
Box Butte Reservoir, res., Ne., U.S.	B2	120
Box Elder, S.D., U.S.	C2	134
Box Elder, co., Ut., U.S.	B2	137
Boxford, Ma., U.S.	A6	114
Boxing, China	B4	30
Boyabat, Tur.	B6	44
Boyang, China	D4	30
Boyce, La., U.S.	C3	111
Boyceville, Wi., U.S.	C1	142
Boyd, Tx., U.S.	C4	136
Boyd, co., Ky., U.S.	B7	110
Boyd, co., Ne., U.S.	B7	120
Boyden, Ia., U.S.	A2	108
Boyd Lake, l., Me., U.S.	C4	112
Boyer, stm., Ia., U.S.	C2	108
Boyertown, Pa., U.S.	F10	131
Boykins, Va., U.S.	D5	139
Boyle, Ab., Can.	B4	84
Boyle, Ms., U.S.	B3	117
Boyle, co., Ky., U.S.	C5	110
Boyne City, Mi., U.S.	C6	115
Boynton Beach, Fl., U.S.	F6	102
Boyoma Falls see Stanley Falls, wtfl, D.R.C.	C5	54
Boysen Reservoir, res., Wy., U.S.	C4	143
Boys Town, Ne., U.S.	g12	120
Bozeman, Mt., U.S.	E6	119
Bozeman Pass, Mt., U.S.	E6	119
Bozhen, China	D11	28
Bozhou, China	C4	30
Bozova, Tur.	D8	44
Bozoum, C.A.R.	B3	54
Bozüyük, Tur.	C3	44
Bra, Italy	B1	18
Bracebridge, On., Can.	B5	89
Bräcke, Swe.	E6	10
Bracken, co., Ky., U.S.	B5	110
Brackenridge, Pa., U.S.	h15	131
Brackettville, Tx., U.S.	E2	136
Brad, Rom.	F7	20
Braddock, Pa., U.S.	k14	131
Braddock Heights, Md., U.S.	B2	113
Braddock Point, c., S.C., U.S.	G6	133
Bradenton, Fl., U.S.	E4	102
Bradenville, Pa., U.S.	F3	131
Bradford, Eng., U.K.	D5	12
Bradford, Ar., U.S.	B4	97
Bradford, Oh., U.S.	B1	128
Bradford, Pa., U.S.	C4	131
Bradford, R.I., U.S.	F2	132
Bradford, Tn., U.S.	A3	135
Bradford, Vt., U.S.	D4	138
Bradford, co., Fl., U.S.	C4	102
Bradford, co., Pa., U.S.	C8	131
Bradford [West Gwillimbury], On., Can.	C5	89
Bradfordwoods, Pa., U.S.	h13	131
Bradley, Il., U.S.	B6	106
Bradley, Me., U.S.	D4	112
Bradley, W.V., U.S.	D3	141
Bradley, co., Ar., U.S.	D3	97
Bradley, co., Tn., U.S.	D9	135
Bradley Beach, N.J., U.S.	C4	123
Bradner, Oh., U.S.	A2	128
Bradshaw, Md., U.S.	B5	113
Bradshaw Mountains, mts., Az., U.S.	C3	96
Brady, Tx., U.S.	D3	136
Braga, Port.	D3	16
Bragado, Arg.	F5	72
Bragança, Braz.	B2	74
Bragança, Port.	G3	16
Braham, Mn., U.S.	E5	116
Brāhmanbāria, Bngl.	E6	40
Brahmapur, India	F4	40
Brahmaputra (Yarlung), stm., Asia	D6	40
Braidwood, Il., U.S.	B5	106
Brăila, Rom.	G9	20
Brainerd, Mn., U.S.	D4	116
Braintree, Ma., U.S.	B5	114
Brampton, On., Can.	D5	89
Bramwell, W.V., U.S.	D3	141
Branch, co., Mi., U.S.	G5	115
Branch, stm., R.I., U.S.	B3	132
Branch, stm., Wi., U.S.	h10	142
Branch Lake, l., Me., U.S.	D4	112
Branch Village, R.I., U.S.	B3	132
Branchville, S.C., U.S.	E6	133
Branco, stm., Braz.	C7	70
Brandberg, mtn., Nmb.	C1	56
Brandenburg, Ger.	C13	12
Brandenburg, Ky., U.S.	C3	110
Brandon, Mb., Can.	E2	86
Brandon, Fl., U.S.	E4	102
Brandon, Ms., U.S.	C4	117
Brandon, S.C., U.S.	B3	133
Brandon, S.D., U.S.	D9	134
Brandon, Vt., U.S.	D2	138
Brandon, Wi., U.S.	E5	142
Brandvlei, S. Afr.	E3	56
Brandy Peak, mtn., Or., U.S.	E3	130
Brandywine, Md., U.S.	C4	113
Brandywine Creek, stm.,	A3	101
Branford, Ct., U.S.	D4	100
Branford Hills, Ct., U.S.	D4	100
Branson, Mo., U.S.	E4	118
Brantford, On., Can.	D4	89
Brantley, Al., U.S.	D3	94
Brantley, co., Ga., U.S.	E4	103
Brant Rock, Ma., U.S.	B6	114
Brantville, N.B., Can.	B5	87
Bras d'Or Lake, l., N.S., Can.	D9	87
Brasil, ctry., S.A.	D2	74
Brasiléia, Braz.	F6	70
Brasília, Braz.	E2	74
Brașov, Rom.	G8	20
Brasstown Bald, mtn., Ga., U.S.	B3	103
Brassua Lake, res., Me., U.S.	C3	112
Bratenahl, Oh., U.S.	g9	128
Bratislava, Slvk.	G13	20
Bratsk, Russia	D12	26
Bratskoe vodohranilišče, res., Russia	D12	26
Bratsk Reservoir see Bratskoe vodohranilišče, res., Russia	D12	26
Brattleboro, Vt., U.S.	F3	138
Braunau am Inn, Aus.	F13	12
Braunschweig, Ger.	D12	12
Brava, i., C.V.	h10	50a
Bravo (Rio Grande), stm., N.A.	B5	78
Brawley, Ca., U.S.	F6	98
Brawley Peaks, mts., Nv., U.S.	E3	121
Braxton, co., W.V., U.S.	C4	141
Bray, Ok., U.S.	C4	129
Braymer, Mo., U.S.	B4	118
Brazeau, stm., Ab., Can.	C2	84
Brazil, In., U.S.	E3	107
Brazil, ctry., S.A.	D5	68
Brazil Basin	J11	66
Brazoria, Tx., U.S.	r14	136
Brazoria, co., Tx., U.S.	E5	136
Brazos, co., Tx., U.S.	D4	136
Brazos, stm., Tx., U.S.	D4	136
Brazzaville, Congo	D3	54
Brčko, Bos.	B7	18
Brea, Ca., U.S.	n13	98
Breakenridge, Mount, mtn., B.C., Can.	E7	85
Breathitt, co., Ky., U.S.	C6	110
Breaux Bridge, La., U.S.	D4	111
Breckenridge, Co., U.S.	B4	99
Breckenridge, Mi., U.S.	E6	115
Breckenridge, Mn., U.S.	D2	116
Breckenridge, Tx., U.S.	C3	136
Breckinridge, co., Ky., U.S.	C3	110
Brecksville, Oh., U.S.	A4	128
Břeclav, Czech Rep.	E4	20
Breda, Neth.	E9	12
Bredasdorp, S. Afr.	E3	56
Bredy, Russia	D11	22
Breese, Il., U.S.	E4	106
Breidafjörður, b., Ice.	I17	10a
Brejo, Braz.	D11	70
Bremen, Ger.	D11	12
Bremen, Ga., U.S.	C1	103
Bremen, In., U.S.	B5	107
Bremen, Oh., U.S.	C3	128
Bremer, co., Ia., U.S.	B5	108
Bremer Bay, Austl.	G2	60
Bremerhaven, Ger.	D11	12
Bremerton, Wa., U.S.	B3	140
Bremond, Tx., U.S.	D4	136
Brenham, Tx., U.S.	D4	136
Brenner Pass, Eur.	A3	18
Brent, Al., U.S.	C2	94
Brent, Fl., U.S.	u14	102
Brenton Point, c., R.I., U.S.	F5	132
Brentwood, Ca., U.S.	h9	98
Brentwood, Md., U.S.	f9	113
Brentwood, Mo., U.S.	f13	118
Brentwood, N.Y., U.S.	E7	125
Brentwood, Pa., U.S.	k14	131
Brentwood, S.C., U.S.	k11	133
Brentwood, Tn., U.S.	A5	135
Brescia, Italy	B3	18
Breslau see Wrocław, Pol.	D6	20
Bressuire, Fr.	D6	16
Brèst, Bela.	C7	20
Brest, Fr.	C4	16
Bretagne, hist. reg., Fr.	C5	16
Breton, Pertuis, strt., Fr.	D6	16
Breton Islands, is., La., U.S.	E6	111
Breton Sound, strt., La., U.S.	E6	111
Breueh, Pulau, i., Indon.	E1	32
Brevard, N.C., U.S.	f10	126
Brevard, co., Fl., U.S.	E6	102
Breves, Braz.	B1	74
Brevoort Lake, l., Mi., U.S.	B6	115
Brewer, Me., U.S.	D4	112
Brewster, Ma., U.S.	C7	114

Name	Map Ref.	Page
Brewster, N.Y., U.S.	D7	125
Brewster, Oh., U.S.	B4	128
Brewster, Wa., U.S.	A6	140
Brewster, co., Tx., U.S.	E1	136
Brewster, Kap, c., Grnld.	D35	82
Brewster Islands, is., Ma., U.S.	g12	114
Brewton, Al., U.S.	D2	94
Brezhnev see Naberežnye Čelny, Russia	D7	26
Bria, C.A.R.	B4	54
Brian Boru Peak, mtn., B.C., Can.	B4	85
Brian Head, mtn., Ut., U.S.	F3	137
Briceville, Tn., U.S.	C9	135
Brick [Township], N.J., U.S.	C4	123
Bridal Veil Falls, wtfl, Ut., U.S.	C4	137
Bridgehampton, N.Y., U.S.	n16	125
Bridgeport, Al., U.S.	A4	94
Bridgeport, Ct., U.S.	E3	100
Bridgeport, Il., U.S.	E6	106
Bridgeport, Mi., U.S.	E7	115
Bridgeport, Ne., U.S.	C2	120
Bridgeport, Oh., U.S.	B5	128
Bridgeport, Pa., U.S.	o20	131
Bridgeport, Tx., U.S.	C4	136
Bridgeport, W.V., U.S.	B4	141
Bridgeport, Wa., U.S.	B6	140
Bridger, Mt., U.S.	E8	119
Bridger Peak, mtn., Wy., U.S.	E5	143
Bridger Range, mts., Mt., U.S.	E6	119
Bridgeton, Mo., U.S.	C7	118
Bridgeton, N.J., U.S.	E2	123
Bridgetown, Austl.	G2	60
Bridgetown, Barb.	C7	80
Bridgetown, N.S., Can.	E4	87
Bridgeville, De., U.S.	F3	101
Bridgeville, Pa., U.S.	k13	131
Bridgewater, Ma., U.S.	C6	114
Bridgewater, N.J., U.S.	B3	123
Bridgewater, Va., U.S.	B4	139
Bridgman, Mi., U.S.	G4	115
Bridgton, Me., U.S.	D2	112
Bridgwater, Eng., U.K.	E5	12
Bridlington, Eng., U.K.	C6	12
Brielle, N.J., U.S.	C4	123
Brigantine, N.J., U.S.	E4	123
Brigantine Beach, N.J., U.S.	E4	123
Brigden, On., Can.	E2	89
Briggs Marsh, sw., R.I., U.S.	F6	132
Brigham City, Ut., U.S.	B3	137
Bright, Austl.	H4	62
Brighton, On., Can.	C7	89
Brighton, Eng., U.K.	E6	12
Brighton, Al., U.S.	B3	94
Brighton, Co., U.S.	B6	99
Brighton, Ia., U.S.	C6	108
Brighton, Il., U.S.	D3	106
Brighton, Mi., U.S.	F7	115
Brighton, N.Y., U.S.	B3	125
Brighton, Tn., U.S.	B2	135
Brighton Indian Reservation, Fl., U.S.	E5	102
Brikama, Gam.	D1	50
Brilliant, Al., U.S.	A2	94
Brilliant, Oh., U.S.	B5	128
Brillion, Wi., U.S.	D5	142
Brimfield, Il., U.S.	C4	106
Brindisi, Italy	D6	18
Brinkley, Ar., U.S.	C4	97
Brinnon, Wa., U.S.	B3	140
Brisbane, Austl.	F5	62
Briscoe, co., Tx., U.S.	B2	136
Bristol, N.B., Can.	C2	87
Bristol, Eng., U.K.	E5	12
Bristol, Ct., U.S.	C4	100
Bristol, In., U.S.	A6	107
Bristol, N.H., U.S.	C3	122
Bristol, R.I., U.S.	D5	132
Bristol, Tn., U.S.	C11	135
Bristol, Va., U.S.	f9	139
Bristol, Vt., U.S.	C2	138
Bristol, co., Ma., U.S.	C5	114
Bristol, co., R.I., U.S.	D5	132
Bristol Bay, b., Ak., U.S.	D7	95
Bristol Channel, strt., U.K.	E5	12
Bristol [Township], Pa., U.S.	F12	131
Bristow, Ok., U.S.	B5	129
British Columbia, prov., Can.	C6	85
British Guiana see Guyana, ctry., S.A.	B8	70
British Honduras see Belize, ctry., N.A.	B2	80
British Indian Ocean Territory, dep., Afr.	I10	64
British Isles, is., Eur.	C12	4
British Virgin Islands, dep., N.A.	E12	76
Britstown, S. Afr.	E3	56
Britt, Ia., U.S.	A4	108
Brittany see Bretagne, hist. reg., Fr.	C5	16
Britton, S.D., U.S.	B8	134
Brive-la-Gaillarde, Fr.	E7	16
Brjansk, Russia	D5	26
Brjuhoveckaja, Russia	G15	20
Brno, Czech Rep.	E4	20
Broad, stm., S.C., U.S.	C5	133
Broad Brook, Ct., U.S.	B5	100
Broadkill, stm., De., U.S.	E4	101
Broadkill Beach, De., U.S.	E5	101
Broad Run, stm., Va., U.S.	g11	139
Broad Sound, b., Austl.	E4	62
Broadus, Mt., U.S.	E11	119
Broadview Heights, Oh., U.S.	h9	128
Broadwater, co., Mt., U.S.	D5	119
Broadway, N.C., U.S.	B3	126
Broadway, Va., U.S.	B4	139
Brockman, Mount, mtn., Austl.	E2	60
Brockport, N.Y., U.S.	B3	125
Brockton, Ma., U.S.	B5	114
Brockton Reservoir, res., Ma., U.S.	h11	114
Brockville, On., Can.	C9	89
Brockway, Pa., U.S.	D4	131
Brodhead, Ky., U.S.	C5	110
Brodhead, Wi., U.S.	F4	142
Brodheadsville, Pa., U.S.	E11	131
Brodnica, Pol.	C5	20
Brody, Ukr.	D8	20
Broken Arrow, Ok., U.S.	A6	129
Broken Bow, Ne., U.S.	C6	120
Broken Bow, Ok., U.S.	C7	129
Broken Bow Lake, res., Ok., U.S.	C7	129
Broken Hill, Austl.	G3	62
Broken Hill see Kabwe, Zam.	A4	56
Broken Ridge	L12	64
Brokopondo, Sur.	C8	70
Brokopondo Stuwmeer, res., Sur.	C8	70
Brome, Lac, l., P.Q., Can.	D5	90
Bromley Plateau	K10	66
Bromptonville, P.Q., Can.	D6	90
Bronson, Mi., U.S.	G5	115
Bronx, co., N.Y., U.S.	E7	125
Bronxville, N.Y., U.S.	h13	125
Brook, In., U.S.	C3	107
Brooke, co., W.V., U.S.	A4	141
Brookfield, N.S., Can.	D6	87
Brookfield, Ct., U.S.	D2	100
Brookfield, Il., U.S.	k9	106
Brookfield, Mo., U.S.	B4	118
Brookfield, Wi., U.S.	m11	142
Brookfield Center, Ct., U.S.	D2	100
Brookhaven, Ms., U.S.	D3	117
Brookhaven, W.V., U.S.	h11	141
Brookings, Or., U.S.	E2	130
Brookings, S.D., U.S.	C9	134
Brookings, co., S.D., U.S.	C9	134
Brookland, Ar., U.S.	B5	97
Brooklandville, Md., U.S.	g10	113
Brooklet, Ga., U.S.	D5	103
Brookline, Ma., U.S.	B5	114
Brooklyn, N.S., Can.	E5	87
Brooklyn, Ct., U.S.	B8	100
Brooklyn, Ia., U.S.	C5	108
Brooklyn, In., U.S.	E5	107
Brooklyn, Mi., U.S.	F6	115
Brooklyn, Ms., U.S.	D4	117
Brooklyn, Oh., U.S.	h9	128
Brooklyn, S.C., U.S.	B6	133
Brooklyn, Wi., U.S.	F4	142
Brooklyn Center, Mn., U.S.	E5	116
Brooklyn Park, Md., U.S.	h11	113
Brooklyn Park, Mn., U.S.	m12	116
Brookneal, Va., U.S.	C4	139
Brook Park, Oh., U.S.	h9	128
Brookport, Il., U.S.	F5	106
Brooks, Ab., Can.	D5	84
Brooks, Ky., U.S.	g11	110
Brooks, co., Ga., U.S.	F3	103
Brooks, co., Tx., U.S.	F3	136
Brooks Air Force Base, mil., Tx., U.S.	k7	136
Brookshire, Tx., U.S.	E5	136
Brookside, Al., U.S.	f7	94
Brookside, De., U.S.	B3	101
Brooks Range, mts., Ak., U.S.	B9	95
Brookston, In., U.S.	C4	107
Brooksville, Fl., U.S.	D4	102
Brooksville, Ky., U.S.	B5	110
Brooksville, Ms., U.S.	B5	117
Brookville, In., U.S.	F8	107
Brookville, Oh., U.S.	C1	128
Brookville, Pa., U.S.	D3	131
Brookville Lake, res., In., U.S.	E7	107
Brookwood, Al., U.S.	B2	94
Brookwood, N.J., U.S.	C4	123
Broomall, Pa., U.S.	p20	131
Broome, Austl.	D3	60
Broome, co., N.Y., U.S.	C5	125
Broomfield, Co., U.S.	B5	99
Brossard, P.Q., Can.	q20	90
Broussard, La., U.S.	D4	111
Broward, co., Fl., U.S.	F6	102
Browerville, Mn., U.S.	D4	116
Brown, co., Il., U.S.	D3	106
Brown, co., In., U.S.	F5	107
Brown, co., Ks., U.S.	C8	109
Brown, co., Mn., U.S.	F4	116
Brown, co., Ne., U.S.	B6	120
Brown, co., Oh., U.S.	D2	128
Brown, co., S.D., U.S.	B7	134
Brown, co., Tx., U.S.	D3	136
Brown, co., Wi., U.S.	D6	142
Brown, Point, c., Wa., U.S.	C1	140
Brown City, Mi., U.S.	E8	115
Brown Deer, Wi., U.S.	m12	142
Brownfield, Tx., U.S.	C1	136
Browning, Mt., U.S.	B3	119
Brownlee Dam, U.S.	E2	105
Brownlee Reservoir, res., U.S.	C10	130
Browns, stm., Vt., U.S.	B2	138
Browns Branch, stm., De., U.S.	E3	101
Browns Inlet, b., N.C., U.S.	C5	126
Browns Mills, N.J., U.S.	D3	123
Browns Peak, mtn., Az., U.S.	D4	96
Brownstown, In., U.S.	G5	107
Browns Valley, Mn., U.S.	E2	116
Brownsville, Fl., U.S.	s13	102
Brownsville, Ky., U.S.	C3	110
Brownsville, Or., U.S.	C4	130
Brownsville, Pa., U.S.	F2	131
Brownsville, Tn., U.S.	B2	135
Brownsville, Tx., U.S.	G4	136
Brownton, Mn., U.S.	F4	116
Brownville Junction, Me., U.S.	C3	112
Brownwood, Tx., U.S.	D3	136
Brownwood, Lake, res., Tx., U.S.	D3	136
Broxton, Ga., U.S.	E4	103
Bruce, Ms., U.S.	B4	117
Bruce, Wi., U.S.	C2	142
Bruce, Mount, mtn., Austl.	E2	60
Bruce National Park, On., Can.	B3	89
Bruce Peninsula, pen., On., Can.	B3	89
Bruce Rock, Austl.	G2	60
Bruceton, Tn., U.S.	A3	135
Bruderheim, Ab., Can.	C4	84
Brugge, Bel.	E8	12
Bruin Point, mtn., Ut., U.S.	D5	137
Brule, co., S.D., U.S.	D6	134
Brule, stm., U.S.	C5	142
Brule Lake, l., Mn., U.S.	k9	116
Brumado, Braz.	D3	74
Brundidge, Al., U.S.	D4	94
Bruneau, stm., U.S.	G3	105
Brunei see Bandar Seri Begawan, Bru.	C4	36
Brunei, ctry., Asia	F6	34
Bruno, Sk., Can.	E3	91
Brunswick see Braunschweig, Ger.	D12	12
Brunswick, Ga., U.S.	E5	103
Brunswick, Md., U.S.	B2	113
Brunswick, Me., U.S.	E3	112
Brunswick, Mo., U.S.	B4	118
Brunswick, Oh., U.S.	A4	128
Brunswick, co., N.C., U.S.	C4	126
Brunswick, co., Va., U.S.	D5	139
Brunswick, Península, pen., Chile	H2	69
Brunswick Naval Air Station, mil., Me., U.S.	E3	112
Brush, Co., U.S.	A7	99
Brushy Mountains, mts., N.C., U.S.	B1	126
Brusly, La., U.S.	D4	111
Brusque, Braz.	D8	72
Brussels see Bruxelles, Bel.	E9	12
Brussels, On., Can.	D3	89
Bruxelles (Brussels), Bel.	E9	12
Bryan, Oh., U.S.	A1	128
Bryan, Tx., U.S.	D4	136
Bryan, co., Ga., U.S.	D5	103
Bryan, co., Ok., U.S.	D5	129
Bryans Road, Md., U.S.	C3	113
Bryant, Ar., U.S.	C3	97
Bryantville, Ma., U.S.	B6	114
Bryce Canyon National Park, Ut., U.S.	F3	137
Bryn Mawr, Wa., U.S.	e11	140
Bryson City, N.C., U.S.	f9	126
Brzeg, Pol.	D4	20
Bua Yai, Thai.	C4	34
Bu'ayrat al-Hasun, Libya	E7	14
Bubaque, Gui.-B.	D1	50
Bucak, Tur.	D4	44
Bucaramanga, Col.	B5	70
Buccaneer Archipelago, is., Austl.	D3	60
Buchanan, Lib.	E2	50
Buchanan, Ga., U.S.	C1	103
Buchanan, Mi., U.S.	G4	115
Buchanan, Va., U.S.	C3	139
Buchanan, co., Ia., U.S.	B6	108
Buchanan, co., Mo., U.S.	B3	118
Buchanan, co., Va., U.S.	e9	139
Buchans, Nf., Can.	D3	88
Bucharest see Bucureşti, Rom.	G9	20
Buckatunna, Ms., U.S.	D5	117
Buckeye, Az., U.S.	D3	96
Buckeye Lake, Oh., U.S.	C3	128
Buckhannon, W.V., U.S.	C4	141
Buck Hill Falls, Pa., U.S.	D11	131
Buckhorn Lake, res., Ky., U.S.	C6	110
Buckingham, P.Q., Can.	D2	90
Buckingham, co., Va., U.S.	C4	139
Buckley, Wa., U.S.	B3	140
Bucklin, Ks., U.S.	E4	109
Bucklin, Mo., U.S.	B5	118
Buck Mountain, mtn., Wa., U.S.	A6	140
Buckner, Mo., U.S.	h11	118
Bucks, co., Pa., U.S.	F11	131
Buckskin Mountains, mts., Az., U.S.	C2	96
Bucksport, Me., U.S.	D4	112
Bucksport, S.C., U.S.	D9	133
Buco Zau, Ang.	D2	54
Bucureşti (Bucharest), Rom.	G9	20
Bucyrus, Oh., U.S.	B3	128
Buda, Tx., U.S.	D4	136
Budapest, Hung.	F5	20
Budaun, India	D3	40
Budd Lake, l., N.J., U.S.	B3	123
Budënnovsk, Russia	B4	42
Būdir, Ice.	l21	10a
Budjala, D.R.C.	C3	54
Buea, Cam.	C1	54
Buechel, Ky., U.S.	B4	110
Buena, N.J., U.S.	D3	123
Buena, Wa., U.S.	C5	140
Buena Esperanza, Arg.	E4	72
Buena Park, Ca., U.S.	n12	98
Buena Vista, Co., U.S.	C4	99
Buena Vista, Fl., U.S.	D4	102
Buena Vista, Ga., U.S.	D2	103
Buena Vista, Va., U.S.	C3	139
Buena Vista, co., Ia., U.S.	B2	108
Buenaventura, Col.	C4	70
Buenaventura, Mex.	B3	78
Buenos Aires, Arg.	E6	72
Buffalo, Ia., U.S.	C7	108
Buffalo, Mn., U.S.	E5	116
Buffalo, Mo., U.S.	D4	118
Buffalo, N.Y., U.S.	C2	125
Buffalo, Ok., U.S.	A2	129
Buffalo, S.C., U.S.	B4	133
Buffalo, Tx., U.S.	D5	136
Buffalo, W.V., U.S.	C3	141
Buffalo, Wi., U.S.	D2	142
Buffalo, Wy., U.S.	B6	143
Buffalo, co., Ne., U.S.	D6	120
Buffalo, co., S.D., U.S.	C6	134
Buffalo, co., Wi., U.S.	D2	142
Buffalo, stm., Ar., U.S.	B3	97
Buffalo, stm., Tn., U.S.	B4	135
Buffalo, stm., Wi., U.S.	D2	142
Buffalo Bill Reservoir, res., Wy., U.S.	B3	143
Buffalo Center, Ia., U.S.	A4	108
Buffalo Creek, stm., W.V., U.S.	h10	141
Buffalo Creek, stm., W.V., U.S.	n12	141
Buffalo Creek, stm., U.S.	f8	141
Buffalo Grove, Il., U.S.	h9	106
Buffalo Lake, Mn., U.S.	F4	116
Buffalo Lake, l., Ab., Can.	C4	84
Buffalo Lake, res., Tx., U.S.	B1	136
Buffalo Lake, res., Wi., U.S.	E4	142
Buffumville Lake, res., Ma., U.S.	B4	114
Buford, Ga., U.S.	B2	103
Bug, stm., Eur.	C6	20
Buga, Col.	C4	70
Bugsuk Island, i., Phil.	E7	34
Bugt, China	B12	28
Bugul'ma, Russia	D9	22
Buguruslan, Russia	D9	22
Buhara, Uzb.	F8	26
Buhl, Id., U.S.	G4	105
Buhl, Mn., U.S.	C6	116
Buhler, Ks., U.S.	D6	109
Buies Creek, N.C., U.S.	B4	126
Buitepos, Nmb.	C2	56
Buj, Russia	C7	22
Bujnaksk, Russia	A12	44
Bujumbura, Bdi.	D5	54
Bukačača, Russia	D13	26
Bukama, D.R.C.	E5	54
Būkān, Iran	D12	44
Bukavu, D.R.C.	D5	54
Bukeya, D.R.C.	F5	54
Bukittinggi, Indon.	D2	36
Bukoba, Tan.	D6	54
Bula, Indon.	D8	36
Bulan, Phil.	D8	34
Bulan, Ky., U.S.	C6	110
Bulancak, Tur.	B8	44
Bulandshahr, India	D3	40
Bulanık, Tur.	C10	44
Bulawayo, Zimb.	C4	56
Buldan, Tur.	C3	44
Bulgan, Mong.	B8	28
Bulgaria, ctry., Eur.	C10	18
Bulkley, stm., B.C., Can.	B4	85
Bull Creek, stm., S.D., U.S.	B2	134
Bullfinch, Austl.	G2	60
Bullfrog Creek, stm., Ut., U.S.	F5	137
Bullhead City, Az., U.S.	B1	96
Bull Island, i., S.C., U.S.	D9	133
Bull Island, i., S.C., U.S.	F8	133
Bull Island, i., S.C., U.S.	G6	133
Bullitt, co., Ky., U.S.	C4	110
Bull Mountain, mtn., Mt., U.S.	D4	119
Bulloch, co., Ga., U.S.	D5	103
Bullock, co., Al., U.S.	C4	94
Bullock Creek, Mi., U.S.	E6	115
Bull Run, stm., Va., U.S.	g11	139
Bullrun Rock, mtn., Or., U.S.	C8	130
Bulls Bay, b., S.C., U.S.	F8	133
Bulls Gap, Tn., U.S.	C10	135
Bull Shoals, Ar., U.S.	A3	97
Bull Shoals Lake, res., U.S.	D9	92
Bull Shoals Lake, res., U.S.	A3	97
Bully Creek Reservoir, res., Or., U.S.	C9	130
Bultfontein, S. Afr.	D4	56
Bumba, D.R.C.	C4	54
Bumping, stm., Wa., U.S.	C4	140
Buna, Tx., U.S.	D6	136
Buncombe, co., N.C., U.S.	f10	126
Bundaberg, Austl.	E5	62
Būndi, India	D3	40
Bungoma, Kenya	C6	54
Bungo-suidō, strt., Japan	E14	28
Bunia, D.R.C.	C6	54
Bunker Hill, Il., U.S.	D4	106
Bunker Hill, In., U.S.	C5	107
Bunker Hill, W.V., U.S.	m12	141
Bunker Hill, W.V., U.S.	B6	141
Bunker Hill, mtn., Nv., U.S.	D4	121
Bunkerville, Nv., U.S.	G7	121
Bunkie, La., U.S.	D3	111
Bunnell, Fl., U.S.	C5	102
Buntok, Indon.	D4	36
Bünyan, Tur.	C6	44
Buolkalah, Russia	B13	26
Buon Ma Thuot, Viet.	D5	34
Buor-Haja, guba, b., Russia	B15	26
Buqayq, Sau. Ar.	C4	38
Bura, Kenya	D7	54
Burang, China	C4	40
Buras, La., U.S.	E6	111
Buraydah, Sau. Ar.	E4	38
Burbank, Ca., U.S.	E4	98
Burbank, Il., U.S.	k9	106
Burbank, Wa., U.S.	C7	140
Burco, Som.	I14	48
Burdickville, R.I., U.S.	F2	132
Burdur, Tur.	D4	44
Burdur Gölü, l., Tur.	D4	44
Bureinskij hrebet, mts., Russia	D15	26
Bürenhayrhan, Mong.	B6	28
Burfjord, Nor.	B10	10
Burgas, Bul.	C11	18
Burgaski Zaliv, b., Bul.	C11	18
Burgaw, N.C., U.S.	C5	126
Burgeo, Nf., Can.	E3	88
Burgersdorp, S. Afr.	E4	56
Burgettstown, Pa., U.S.	F1	131
Burgin, Ky., U.S.	C5	110
Burgo de Osma, Spain	C4	16
Burgos, Spain	F5	16
Burgundy see Bourgogne, hist. reg., Fr.	D9	16
Burhaniye, Tur.	C2	44
Burhānpur, India	E3	40
Burias Island, i., Phil.	D8	34
Burin, Nf., Can.	E4	88
Burin Peninsula, pen., Nf., Can.	E4	88
Burjatija, state, Russia	D13	26
Burkburnett, Tx., U.S.	B3	136
Burke, S.D., U.S.	D6	134
Burke, co., Ga., U.S.	C4	103
Burke, co., N.C., U.S.	B1	126
Burke, co., N.D., U.S.	A3	127
Burke Channel, strt., B.C., Can.	C4	85
Burkesville, Ky., U.S.	D4	110
Burketown, Austl.	D2	62
Burkina Faso, ctry., Afr.	D4	50
Burk's Falls, On., Can.	B5	89
Burleigh, co., N.D., U.S.	C5	127
Burleson, Tx., U.S.	n9	136
Burleson, co., Tx., U.S.	D4	136
Burley, Id., U.S.	G5	105
Burlingame, Ca., U.S.	h8	98
Burlingame, Ks., U.S.	D8	109
Burlington, On., Can.	D5	89
Burlington, Co., U.S.	B8	99
Burlington, Ia., U.S.	D6	108
Burlington, Ks., U.S.	D8	109
Burlington, Ky., U.S.	A5	110
Burlington, Ma., U.S.	f11	114
Burlington, N.C., U.S.	A3	126
Burlington, N.D., U.S.	A4	127
Burlington, N.J., U.S.	C3	123
Burlington, Vt., U.S.	C2	138
Burlington, Wa., U.S.	A3	140
Burlington, Wi., U.S.	F5	142
Burlington, co., N.J., U.S.	D3	123
Burlington Beach, In., U.S.	B3	107
Burlington Junction, Mo., U.S.	A2	118
Burlit, Russia	A2	31
Burma see Myanmar, ctry., Asia	B3	34
Burnaby, B.C., Can.	E6	85
Burnet, Tx., U.S.	D3	136
Burnet, co., Tx., U.S.	D3	136
Burnett, co., Wi., U.S.	C1	142
Burney, Ca., U.S.	B3	98
Burnham, Pa., U.S.	E6	131
Burnie, Austl.	I4	62
Burns, Or., U.S.	D7	130
Burns, Tn., U.S.	A4	135
Burns, Wy., U.S.	E8	143
Burns Flat, Ok., U.S.	B2	129
Burnside, Ky., U.S.	D5	110
Burns Lake, B.C., Can.	B5	85

Name	Map Ref.	Page

Burns Paiute Indian
Reservation, Or., U.S. . . D7   130
Burnsville, Mn., U.S. F5   116
Burnsville, Ms., U.S. A5   117
Burnsville, N.C., U.S. f10   126
Burntside Lake, res., W.V.,
U.S. C4   141
Burnt Islands, Nf., Can. . . . E2   88
Burnt Mills, Lake, l., Va.,
U.S. k14   139
Burntside Lake, l., Mn., U.S. C6   116
Burntwood, stm., Mb., Can. B2   86
Burra, Austl. G2   62
Burrel, Alb. D8   18
Burr Oak, Mi., U.S. G5   115
Burr Oak Reservoir, res.,
Oh., U.S. C3   128
Burrton, Ks., U.S. D6   109
Bursa, Tur. B3   44
Būr Saʿīd, Egypt D11   48
Būr Sūdān, Sudan G12   48
Burt, co., Ne., U.S. C9   120
Burt Lake, l., Mi., U.S. C6   115
Burton, Mi., U.S. F7   115
Burton, Oh., U.S. A4   128
Burtts Corner, N.B., Can. . . C3   87
Buru, i., Indon. D7   36
Burullus, Buheirat el-, l.,
Egypt G4   44
Burundi, ctry., Afr. D5   54
Burwell, Ne., U.S. C6   120
Bury Saint Edmunds, Eng.,
U.K. D7   12
Busanga, D.R.C. D4   54
Bushman Land, hist. reg., S.
Afr. D2   56
Bushnell, Fl., U.S. D4   102
Bushnell, Il., U.S. C3   106
Bushnell, Ne., U.S. C1   120
Bush River, b., Md., U.S. . . B5   113
Busia, Ug. C6   54
Businga, D.R.C. C4   54
Busira, stm., D.R.C. D3   54
Busko-Zdrój, Pol. D6   20
Busselton, Austl. G2   60
Busuanga Island, i., Phil. . . D8   34
Busu-Djanoa, D.R.C. C4   54
Buta, D.R.C. C4   54
Butare, Rw. D5   54
Butaritari, atoll, Kir. D11   58
Bute Inlet, b., B.C., Can. . . D5   85
Butembo, D.R.C. C5   54
Butere, Kenya C6   54
Buthidaung, Myan. B2   34
Butiaba, Ug. C6   54
Butler, Al., U.S. C1   94
Butler, Ga., U.S. D2   103
Butler, In., U.S. B8   107
Butler, Ky., U.S. B5   110
Butler, Mo., U.S. C3   118
Butler, N.J., U.S. B4   123
Butler, Oh., U.S. B3   128
Butler, Pa., U.S. E2   131
Butler, Wi., U.S. m11   142
Butler, co., Al., U.S. D3   94
Butler, co., Ia., U.S. B5   108
Butler, co., Ks., U.S. E7   109
Butler, co., Ky., U.S. C3   110
Butler, co., Mo., U.S. E7   118
Butler, co., Ne., U.S. C8   120
Butler, co., Oh., U.S. C1   128
Butler, co., Pa., U.S. E2   131
Butner, N.C., U.S. A4   126
Buton, Pulau, i., Indon. . . . D6   36
Butrint, hist., Alb. E8   18
Buttahatchee, stm., U.S. . . B5   117
Butte, Mt., U.S. E4   119
Butte, co., Ca., U.S. C3   98
Butte, co., Id., U.S. F5   105
Butte, co., S.D., U.S. C2   134
Butte des Morts, Lake, l.,
Wi., U.S. D5   142
Butte Mountains, mts., Nv.,
U.S. D6   121
Butternut Lake, l., Wi., U.S. C5   142
Butterworth, Malay. B2   36
Buttonwillow, Ca., U.S. . . . E4   98
Butts, co., Ga., U.S. C3   103
Butuan, Phil. E9   34
Buturlinovka, Russia D16   20
Buulobarde, Som. C9   54
Buur Gaabo, Som. D8   54
Buxton, N.C., U.S. B7   126
Büyük Ağrı Dağı see Ağrı
Dağı, mtn., Tur. C11   44
Büyükmenderes, stm., Tur. D2   44
Buzuluk, Russia D9   22
Buzzards Bay, Ma., U.S. . . . C6   114
Buzzards Bay, b., Ma., U.S. C6   114
Bwendi, D.R.C. C5   54
Bydgoszcz, Pol. C5   20
Byelorussia see Belarus,
ctry., Eur. C9   20
Byers, Co., U.S. B6   99
Byesville, Oh., U.S. C4   128
Byhalia, Ms., U.S. A4   117
Bybau, Bela. C11   20
Bylas, Az., U.S. D5   96
Byng, Ok., U.S. C5   129
Byrdstown, Tn., U.S. C8   135
Byro, Austl. F2   60
Byron, Ga., U.S. D3   103
Byron, Il., U.S. A4   106
Byron, Mn., U.S. F6   116
Byron, Wy., U.S. B4   143

Byron, Cape, c., Austl. F5   62
Byron Bay, Austl. F5   62
Byrranga, gory, mts., Russia B12   26
Bytom, Pol. D5   20
Bytów, Pol. B4   20
Byzantium see İstanbul, Tur.B3   44

C

Caála, Ang. F3   54
Caatinga, Braz. B8   72
Cabadbaran, Phil. E9   34
Cabaiguán, Cuba A4   80
Caballo Mountains, mts.,
N.M., U.S. E2   124
Caballo Reservoir, res.,
N.M., U.S. E2   124
Cabanatuan, Phil. C8   34
Cabano, P.Q., Can. B9   90
Cabarrus, co., N.C., U.S. . . B2   126
Cabbage Swamp, sw., Fl.,
U.S. m9   102
Cabedelo, Braz. C5   74
Cabell, co., W.V., U.S. C2   141
Cabeza del Buey, Spain . . . H4   16
Cabimas, Ven. A5   70
Cabin Creek, W.V., U.S. . . . m13   141
Cabin Creek, stm., W.V.,
U.S. m13   141
Cabinda, Ang. E2   54
Cabinet Gorge Reservoir,
res., U.S. B1   119
Cabinet Mountains, mts.,
Mt., U.S. B1   119
Cabin John, Md., U.S. C3   113
Cabo, Braz. C4   74
Cabo Blanco, Arg. G3   69
Cabonga, Réservoir, res.,
P.Q., Can. I24   82
Cabool, Mo., U.S. D5   118
Caborca, Mex. C2   78
Cabot, Ar., U.S. C3   97
Cabot, Mount, mtn., N.H.,
U.S. A4   122
Cabot Head, c., On., Can. . B3   89
Cabrayıl, Azer. C12   44
Cabri, Sk., Can. G1   91
Cabrillo National
Monument, Ca., U.S. . . o15   98
Caçador, Braz. D7   72
Čačak, Yugo. C8   18
Caçapava do Sul, Braz. . . . E7   72
Cacapon, stm., W.V., U.S. . B6   141
Cáceres, Braz. G8   70
Cáceres, Spain H3   16
Cache, Ok., U.S. C3   129
Cache, co., Ut., U.S. B4   137
Cache, stm., Ar., U.S. C4   97
Cache, stm., Il., U.S. F4   106
Cache Bay, On., Can. A5   89
Cache Creek, B.C., Can. . . D7   85
Cache la Poudre, stm., Co.,
U.S. A5   99
Cache Mountain, mtn., Ak.,
U.S. B10   95
Cache Peak, mtn., Id., U.S. G5   105
Cachimbo, Serra do, mts.,
Braz. E8   70
Cachingues, Ang. F3   54
Cachoeira do Sul, Braz. . . . E7   72
Cachoeiro de Itapemirim,
Braz. F3   74
Cacolo, Ang. F3   54
Caconda, Ang. A2   56
Cactus Flat, pl., Nv., U.S. . . F5   121
Cactus Peak, mtn., Nv., U.S.F5   121
Cacuaco, Ang. E2   54
Caculé, Braz. A9   72
Čadan, Russia D11   26
Caddo, Ok., U.S. C5   129
Caddo, co., La., U.S. B2   111
Caddo, co., Ok., U.S. B3   129
Caddo, stm., Ar., U.S. C2   97
Caddo Creek, stm., Ok.,
U.S. C4   129
Caddo Lake, res., U.S. B2   111
Cadillac, Mi., U.S. D5   115
Cadillac Mountain, mtn.,
Me., U.S. D4   112
Cadiz, Phil. D8   34
Cádiz, Spain I3   16
Cadiz, Ky., U.S. D2   110
Cadiz, Oh., U.S. B4   128
Cádiz, Golfo de, b., Eur. . . I3   16
Cadiz, Gulf of see Cádiz,
Golfo de, b., Eur. I3   16
Çadott, Wi., U.S. D2   142
Çaek, Kyrg. A2   40
Caen, Fr. C6   16
Caernarfon, Wales, U.K. . . D4   12
Caesar Creek Lake, res.,
Oh., U.S. C2   128
Caetité, Braz. D3   74
Cagayan de Oro, Phil. E8   34
Cagayan Islands, is., Phil. . . E8   34
Çagayan Sulu Island, i., Phil.E7   34
Çagda, Russia D15   26
Cagles Mill Lake, res., In.,
U.S. F4   107
Cagliari, Italy E2   18
Cagliari, Golfo di, b., Italy E2   18
Caguas, P.R. B6   80
Cahaba, stm., Al., U.S. . . . C2   94
Cahama, Ang. B1   56
Cahokia, Il., U.S. E3   106

Cahora Bassa, Albuíeira,
res., Moz. B5   56
Cahors, Fr. E7   16
Cahul, Mol. G10   20
Caiapó, Serra do, mts., Braz.B7   72
Caibarién, Cuba A4   80
Caicara de Orinoco, Ven. . . D6   80
Caicó, Braz. C4   74
Caicos Islands, is., T./C. Is. A5   80
Caicos Passage, strt., N.A. . A5   80
Cailloma, Peru B3   72
Caillou Bay, b., La., U.S. . . E5   111
Caillou Lake, l., La., U.S. . . E5   111
Caimanera, Cuba B4   80
Caimbambo, Ang. B2   56
Caiundo, Ang. B2   56
Cairnbrook, Pa., U.S. F4   131
Cairns, Austl. D4   62
Cairo see El-Qâhira, Egypt . D11   48
Cairo, Ga., U.S. F2   103
Cairo, Il., U.S. F4   106
Cairo, Ne., U.S. D7   120
Caiundo, Ang. B2   56
Cajamarca, Peru E4   70
Cajazeiras, Braz. C4   74
Calabar, Nig. F6   50
Calabozo, Ven. B6   70
Calagua Islands, is., Phil. . . D8   34
Calahorra, Spain F6   16
Calais, Fr. B7   16
Calais, Me., U.S. C5   112
Calama, Chile B3   69
Calamian Group, is., Phil. . D7   34
Calamus, stm., Ne., U.S. . . B6   120
Calapan, Phil. D8   34
Calapan, Wa., U.S. D3   140
Calamus, co., Id., U.S. F4   105
Ca Mau, Viet. E5   34
Ca Mau, Mui, c., Viet. E4   34
Cambodia, ctry., Asia D4   34
Cambrai, Fr. B8   16
Cambria, Ca., U.S. E3   98
Cambria, Wi., U.S. E4   142
Cambria, co., Pa., U.S. E4   131
Cambridge, On., Can. D4   89
Cambridge, Eng., U.K. D7   12
Cambridge, Ia., U.S. C4   108
Cambridge, Il., U.S. B3   106
Cambridge, Md., U.S. C5   113
Cambridge, Mn., U.S. E5   116
Cambridge, Ne., U.S. D5   120
Cambridge, N.Y., U.S. B7   125
Cambridge, Oh., U.S. B4   128
Cambridge, Wi., U.S. F4   142
Cambridge City, In., U.S. . . E7   107
Cambridge Reservoir, res.,
Ma., U.S. g10   114
Cambridge Springs, Pa.,
U.S. C1   131
Cambulo, Ang. E4   54
Cambundi-Catembo, Ang. . F3   54
Camden, Al., U.S. D2   94
Camden, Ar., U.S. D3   97
Camden, In., U.S. C4   107
Camden, Me., U.S. D3   112
Camden, N.J., U.S. D2   123
Camden, N.Y., U.S. B5   125
Camden, Oh., U.S. C1   128
Camden, S.C., U.S. C6   133
Camden, Tn., U.S. A3   135
Camden, co., Ga., U.S. . . . F5   103
Camden, co., Mo., U.S. . . . C5   118
Camden, co., N.C., U.S. . . . A6   126
Camden, co., N.J., U.S. . . . D3   123
Camdenton, Mo., U.S. D5   118
Camelback Mountain, mtn.,
Az., U.S. k9   96
Cameron, Az., U.S. B4   96
Cameron, La., U.S. E2   111
Cameron, Mo., U.S. B3   118
Cameron, Tx., U.S. D4   136
Cameron, W.V., U.S. B4   141
Cameron, Wi., U.S. C2   142
Cameron, co., La., U.S. . . . E2   111
Cameron, co., Pa., U.S. . . . D5   131
Cameron, co., Tx., U.S. . . . F4   136
Cameron Hills, hills, Can. . G16   82
Cameroon, ctry., Afr. J7   48
Cameroon Mountain, vol.,
Cam. C4   54
Cametá, Braz. B2   74
Çamiçi Gölü, l., Tur. D2   44
Camiguin Island, i., Phil. . . C8   34
Camiguin Island, i., Phil. . . E8   34
Camilla, Ga., U.S. E2   103
Camino, Ca., U.S. C3   98
Camiranga, Braz. D10   70
Camiri, Bol. G6   72
Camissombo, Ang. E4   54
Cammack Village, Ar., U.S. C3   97
Camocim, Braz. B3   74
Camooweal, Austl. D2   62
Camorta Island, i., India . . H6   40
Camotes Sea, Phil. D8   34
Camp, co., Tx., U.S. C5   136
Campana, Arg. E6   72
Campbell, Ca., U.S. k8   98
Campbell, Fl., U.S. D5   102
Campbell, Mo., U.S. E7   118
Campbell, Oh., U.S. A5   128
Campbell, co., Ky., U.S. . . . B5   110
Campbell, co., S.D., U.S. . . B5   134
Campbell, co., Tn., U.S. . . . C9   135
Campbell, co., Va., U.S. . . . C3   139
Campbell, co., Wy., U.S. . . B7   143

Calmar, Ia., U.S. A6   108
Caloosahatchee, stm., Fl.,
U.S. F5   102
Caltanissetta, Italy F4   18
Calulo, Ang. E2   54
Calumet, P.Q., Can. D3   90
Calumet, Mi., U.S. A2   115
Calumet, co., Wi., U.S. . . . D5   142
Calumet, Lake, l., Il., U.S. . k9   106
Calumet City, Il., U.S. B6   106
Calunda, Ang. F4   54
Caluula, Som. H15   48
Calvert, Tx., U.S. D4   136
Calvert, co., Md., U.S. C4   113
Calvert City, Ky., U.S. e9   110
Calverton Park, Mo., U.S. . f13   118
Calvillo, Mex. C4   78
Calvinia, S. Afr. E2   56
Camabatela, Ang. E3   54
Camaçari, Braz. D4   74
Camacupa, Ang. F3   54
Camaguán, Cuba A4   80
Camaná, Peru G5   70
Camano Island, i., Wa., U.S.A3   140
Camaquã, Braz. E7   72
Camará, Braz. D7   70
Camargo, Bol. C4   72
Camargue, reg., Fr. F9   16
Camarones, Arg. F3   69
Camas, Spain I3   16
Camas, Wa., U.S. D3   140
Camas, co., Id., U.S. F4   105
Cambará, Braz. C9   70
Cameta, Braz. B2   74

Calmar, Ab., Can. C4   84

Campbell Hill, hill, Oh.,
U.S. B2   128
Campbell Island, i., N.Z. . . J10   58
Campbell Lake, l., Or., U.S. E7   130
Campbell Plateau M20   64
Campbellsburg, In., U.S. . . G5   107
Campbellsburg, Ky., U.S. . . B4   110
Campbells Creek, stm.,
W.V., U.S. m13   141
Campbellsport, Wi., U.S. . . E5   142
Campbellsville, Ky., U.S. . . C4   110
Campbellton, Nf., Can. . . . D4   88
Campbelltown, Austl. G5   62
Campbeltown, Scot., U.K. . . C4   12
Campbellford, On., Can. . . C7   89
Campbellton, N.B., Can. . . A3   87
Campbello Island, i., N.B.,
Can. E3   87
Campo de la Cruz, Col. . . . C5   80
Campo Formoso, Braz. . . . D3   74
Campo Gallo, Arg. D5   72
Campo Grande, Braz. H9   70
Campo Maior, Braz. B3   74
Campo Mourão, Braz. F1   74
Campos, Braz. F3   74
Campos Sales, Braz. C3   74
Camp Pendleton Marine
Corps Base, mil., Ca.,
U.S. F5   98
Camp Point, Il., U.S. C2   106
Camp Springs, Md., U.S. . . f9   113
Campti, La., U.S. C2   111
Campton, N.H., U.S. C3   122
Câmpulung, Rom. G8   20
Câmpulung Moldovenesc,
Rom. F8   20
Camp Verde, Az., U.S. C4   96
Camp Verde Indian
Reservation, Az., U.S. . . C4   96
Cam Ranh, Viet. D5   34
Camrose, Ab., Can. C4   84
Çan, Tur. B2   44
Canaan, Ct., U.S. A2   100
Canaan, N.H., U.S. C2   122
Canaan, stm., N.B., Can. . . C4   87
Canada, ctry., N.A. G17   82
Canada Basin D1   144
Canada Bay, b., Nf., Can. . C3   88
Cañada de Gómez, Arg. . . . E5   72
Canada Falls Lake, res., Me.,
U.S. C2   112
Canadensis, Pa., U.S. D11   131
Canadian, Tx., U.S. B2   136
Canadian, co., Ok., U.S. . . B3   129
Canadian, stm., U.S. D7   92
Canaima, Ven. D7   80
Canajoharie, N.Y., U.S. . . . C6   125
Çanakkale, Tur. B2   44
Çanakkale Boğazı
(Dardanelles), strt., Tur. C1   44
Canal Flats, B.C., Can. D10   85
Canal Fulton, Oh., U.S. . . . B4   128
Canal Winchester, Oh., U.S.C3   128
Canandaigua, N.Y., U.S. . . C3   125
Canandaigua Lake, l., N.Y.,
U.S. C3   125
Cananea, Mex. A2   78
Canarias, Islas (Canary
Islands), is., Spain A1   50
Canary Basin F10   66
Canary Islands see Canarias,
Islas, is., Spain A1   50
Cañasgordas, Col. D4   80
Canastota, N.Y., U.S. B5   125
Canaveral, Cape, c., Fl.,
U.S. D6   102
Canaveral National
Seashore, Fl., U.S. D6   102
Canavieiras, Braz. E4   74
Canberra, Austl. H4   62
Canby, Mn., U.S. F2   116
Canby, Or., U.S. B4   130
Cancún, Mex. C7   78
Candeias, Braz. D4   74
Candia see Iráklion, Grc. . . G10   18
Candiac, P.Q., Can. q19   90
Candle Lake, l., Sk., Can. . . D3   91
Candler, co., Ga., U.S. D4   103
Candlewood, Lake, l., Ct.,
U.S. D1   100

Name	Map Ref.	Page

Candlewood Isle, Ct., U.S. . D2 — 100
Candlewood Shores, Ct., U.S. . . . . D2 — 100
Cando, N.D., U.S. . . . . . . A6 — 127
Candor, N.C., U.S. . . . . . B3 — 126
Cane, stm., La., U.S. . . . . C2 — 111
Canelones, Ur. . . . . E6 — 72
Caney, Ks., U.S. . . . . E8 — 109
Caney, stm., Ok., U.S. . . . A5 — 129
Caney Creek, stm., Tx., U.S.r14 — 136
Caney Fork, stm., Tn., U.S. C8 — 135
Canfield, Oh., U.S. . . . . . . A5 — 128
Cangas de Narcea, Spain . . F3 — 16
Cangkuang, Tanjung, c., Indon. . . . . E3 — 36
Cangombe, Ang. . . . . A2 — 56
Canguçu, Braz. . . . . E7 — 72
Cangumbe, Ang. . . . . F3 — 54
Cangyuan, China . . . . B3 — 34
Cangzhou, China . . . . D11 — 28
Caniapiscau, stm., P.Q., Can. . . . . g13 — 90
Canicattì, Italy . . . . F4 — 18
Canindé, Braz. . . . . E4 — 74
Canistear Reservoir, res., N.J., U.S. . . . . A4 — 123
Canisteo, N.Y., U.S. . . . . . C3 — 125
Canisteo, stm., N.Y., U.S. . C3 — 125
Canistota, S.D., U.S. . . . . D8 — 134
Çankırı, Tur. . . . . B5 — 44
Canmore, Ab., Can. . . . . . D3 — 84
Cannanore, India . . . . G3 — 40
Cannelton, In., U.S. . . . . . I4 — 107
Cannes, Fr. . . . . F10 — 16
Canning, N.S., Can. . . . . . D5 — 87
Cannon, co., Tn., U.S. . . . B5 — 135
Cannon, stm., Mn., U.S. . . F5 — 116
Cannon Air Force Base, mil., N.M., U.S. . . . . . C6 — 124
Cannonball, stm., N.D., U.S.C5 — 127
Cannon Beach, Or., U.S. . . B3 — 130
Cannondale, Ct., U.S. . . . . E2 — 100
Cannon Falls, Mn., U.S. . . F6 — 116
Cannonsburg, Ky., U.S. . . . B7 — 110
Cannonsville Reservoir, res., N.Y., U.S. . . . . C5 — 125
Canoas, Braz. . . . . D7 — 72
Canoinhas, Braz. . . . . D7 — 72
Canon, Ga., U.S. . . . . B3 — 103
Canon City, Co., U.S. . . . . C5 — 99
Canonsburg, Pa., U.S. . . . . F1 — 131
Cantabrian Mountains see Cantábrica, Cordillera, mts., Spain . . . . F4 — 16
Cantábrica, Cordillera, mts., Spain . . . . F4 — 16
Cantaura, Ven. . . . . B7 — 70
Canterbury, Eng., U.K. . . . E7 — 12
Canterbury, De., U.S. . . . . D3 — 101
Canterbury Bight, b., N.Z. . p13 — 63c
Can Tho, Viet. . . . . E5 — 34
Canton see Guangzhou, China . . . . E3 — 30
Canton, Ct., U.S. . . . . B4 — 100
Canton, Ga., U.S. . . . . B2 — 103
Canton, Il., U.S. . . . . C3 — 106
Canton, Ks., U.S. . . . . D6 — 109
Canton, Ma., U.S. . . . . . . B5 — 114
Canton, Mn., U.S. . . . . . . A6 — 118
Canton, Mo., U.S. . . . . . . C3 — 117
Canton, N.C., U.S. . . . . . . f10 — 126
Canton, N.Y., U.S. . . . . . . f9 — 125
Canton, Oh., U.S. . . . . B4 — 128
Canton, Ok., U.S. . . . . A3 — 129
Canton, S.D., U.S. . . . . . . D9 — 134
Canton, Tx., U.S. . . . . C5 — 136
Canton Lake, res., Ok., U.S. A3 — 129
Cantonment, Fl., U.S. . . . . u14 — 102
Canutama, Braz. . . . . E7 — 70
Canutillo, Tx., U.S. . . . . . . o11 — 136
Čany, ozero, l., Russia . . . D9 — 26
Canyon, Tx., U.S. . . . . B2 — 136
Canyon, co., Id., U.S. . . . . F2 — 105
Canyon City, Or., U.S. . . . C8 — 130
Canyon de Chelly National Monument, Az., U.S. . A6 — 96
Canyon Ferry Lake, res., Mt., U.S. . . . . D5 — 119
Canyon Lake, Tx., U.S. . . . E3 — 136
Canyon Lake, res., Tx., U.S. E3 — 136
Canyonlands National Park, Ut., U.S. . . . . E6 — 137
Canyonville, Or., U.S. . . . . E3 — 130
Cao Bang, Viet. . . . . B5 — 34
Caoxian, China . . . . C4 — 30
Capac, Mi., U.S. . . . . F8 — 115
Čapaevo, Kaz. . . . . D9 — 22
Cap-à-l'Aigle, P.Q., Can. . . B7 — 90
Capanema, Braz. . . . . B2 — 74
Capão Bonito, Braz. . . . . . F2 — 74
Cap-aux-Meules, P.Q., Can. B8 — 87
Cap-de-la-Madeleine, P.Q., Can. . . . . C5 — 90
Cape Barren Island, i., Austl.I4 — 62
Cape Basin . . . . L14 — 66
Cape Breton Highlands National Park, N.S., Can. . . . . C9 — 87
Cape Breton Island, i., N.S., Can. . . . . C9 — 87
Cape Broyle, Nf., Can. . . . . E5 — 88
Cape Canaveral, Fl., U.S. . . D6 — 102
Cape Charles, Va., U.S. . . . C6 — 139
Cape Coast, Ghana . . . . . E4 — 50

Cape Cod Bay, b., Ma., U.S.C7 — 114
Cape Cod Canal, Ma., U.S. C6 — 114
Cape Cod National Seashore, Ma., U.S. . . . C7 — 114
Cape Coral, Fl., U.S. . . . . . F5 — 102
Cape Elizabeth, Me., U.S. . E2 — 112
Cape Fear, stm., N.C., U.S. C4 — 126
Cape Girardeau, Mo., U.S. . D8 — 118
Cape Girardeau, co., Mo., U.S. . . . . D8 — 118
Cape Hatteras National Seashore, N.C., U.S. . . B7 — 126
Cape Horn Mountain, mtn., Id., U.S. . . . . E3 — 105
Cape Island, i., S.C., U.S. . E9 — 133
Capelinha, Braz. . . . . E3 — 74
Capelongo, Ang. . . . . A2 — 56
Cape Lookout National Seashore, N.C., U.S. . . C6 — 126
Cape May, N.J., U.S. . . . . . F3 — 123
Cape May, co., N.J., U.S. . . E3 — 123
Cape May Court House, N.J., U.S. . . . . E3 — 123
Capers Inlet, b., S.C., U.S. . k12 — 133
Capers Island, i., S.C., U.S. F8 — 133
Capers Island, i., S.C., U.S. G6 — 133
Cape Sable Island, i., N.S., Can. . . . . F4 — 87
Cape Town (Kaapstad), S. Afr. . . . . E2 — 56
Cape Verde Basin . . . . . . G10 — 66
Cape Verde, ctry., Afr. . . . g9 — 50a
Cape York Peninsula, pen., Austl. . . . . C3 — 62
Cap-Haïtien, Haiti . . . . B5 — 80
Capinota, Bol. . . . . B4 — 72
Capitan, N.M., U.S. . . . . . D4 — 124
Capitan Mountains, mts., N.M., U.S. . . . . D4 — 124
Capitan Peak, mtn., N.M., U.S. . . . . D4 — 124
Capitol Heights, Ia., U.S. . . e8 — 108
Capitol Heights, Md., U.S. . C4 — 113
Capitol Peak, mtn., Nv., U.S. . . . . B4 — 121
Capitol Reef National Park, Ut., U.S. . . . . E4 — 137
Čaplygin, Russia . . . . C15 — 20
Cap-Pelé, N.B., Can. . . . . . C5 — 87
Capreol, On., Can. . . . . . . p19 — 89
Capri, Isola di, i., Italy . . . D5 — 18
Capricorn Channel, strt., Austl. . . . . E5 — 62
Capricorn Group, is., Austl. E5 — 62
Caprivi Strip, hist. reg., Nmb. . . . . B3 — 56
Cap-Rouge, P.Q., Can. . . . n17 — 90
Cap-Saint-Ignace, P.Q., Can.B7 — 90
Captain Cook, Hi., U.S. . . . D6 — 104
Captiva, Fl., U.S. . . . . F4 — 102
Captiva Island, i., Fl., U.S. . F4 — 102
Capulin Volcano National Monument, N.M., U.S. A6 — 124
Capunda Cabilongo, Ang. . F2 — 54
Caquetá (Japurá), stm., S.A. D5 — 70
Čara, Russia . . . . D13 — 26
Caracal, Rom. . . . . G8 — 20
Caracaraí, Braz. . . . . C7 — 70
Caracas, Ven. . . . . A6 — 70
Carajás, Braz. . . . . E9 — 70
Carajás, Serra dos, hills, Braz. . . . . E9 — 70
Carangola, Braz. . . . . F3 — 74
Caransebeş, Rom. . . . . . . G7 — 20
Caraquet, N.B., Can. . . . . . B5 — 87
Caratasca, Laguna de, b., Hond. . . . . B3 — 80
Caratinga, Braz. . . . . E3 — 74
Carauari, Braz. . . . . D6 — 70
Caravaca de la Cruz, Spain . H6 — 16
Caravelas, Braz. . . . . G12 — 70
Caraway, Ar., U.S. . . . . . . B5 — 97
Carazinho, Braz. . . . . D7 — 72
Carberry, Mb., Can. . . . . . E2 — 86
Carbon, co., Mt., U.S. . . . . E7 — 119
Carbon, co., Pa., U.S. . . . . E10 — 131
Carbon, co., Ut., U.S. . . . . D5 — 137
Carbon, co., Wy., U.S. . . . . E5 — 143
Carbondale, Co., U.S. . . . . B3 — 99
Carbondale, Il., U.S. . . . . . F4 — 106
Carbondale, Ks., U.S. . . . . D8 — 109
Carbondale, Pa., U.S. . . . . C10 — 131
Carbonear, Nf., Can. . . . . . E5 — 88
Carbon Hill, Al., U.S. . . . . B2 — 94
Carbonia, Italy . . . . E2 — 18
Carcassonne, Fr. . . . . F8 — 16
Čardara, Kaz. . . . . B9 — 42
Cárdenas, Cuba . . . . A3 — 80
Cárdenas, Mex. . . . . D6 — 78
Cardiff, Wales, U.K. . . . . . E5 — 12
Cardigan, Wales, U.K. . . . . D4 — 12
Cardigan Bay, b., P.E., Can. C7 — 87
Cardigan Bay, b., Wales, U.K. . . . . D4 — 12
Cardinal, On., Can. . . . . . . C9 — 89
Cardington, Oh., U.S. . . . . B3 — 128
Cardston, Ab., Can. . . . . . E4 — 84
Cardwell, Mo., U.S. . . . . . E7 — 118
Čardžev, Turk. . . . . F8 — 26
Carei, Rom. . . . . F7 — 20
Careiro, Braz. . . . . D8 — 70
Carelia see Karelia, hist. reg., Eur. . . . . C12 — 6
Carencro, La., U.S. . . . . . . D3 — 111
Carentan, Fr. . . . . C6 — 16

Caretta, W.V., U.S. . . . . . . D3 — 141
Carey, Id., U.S. . . . . F5 — 105
Carey, Oh., U.S. . . . . B2 — 128
Carey Downs, Austl. . . . . . F2 — 60
Cargados Carajos Shoals, is., Mrts. . . . . F11 — 52
Caribbean Sea . . . . C4 — 80
Cariboo Mountains, mts., B.C., Can. . . . . C7 — 85
Caribou, Me., U.S. . . . . . . B5 — 112
Caribou, co., Id., U.S. . . . . G7 — 105
Caribou Island, i., N.S., Can.D7 — 87
Caribou Lake, l., Me., U.S. . C3 — 112
Caribou Mountain, mtn., Id., U.S. . . . . F7 — 105
Caribou Mountains, mts., Ab., Can. . . . . f7 — 84
Caribou Range, mts., Id., U.S. . . . . F7 — 105
Caripito, Ven. . . . . C7 — 80
Carl Blackwell, Lake, res., Ok., U.S. . . . . A4 — 129
Carlet, Spain . . . . H6 — 16
Carleton, Mi., U.S. . . . . . . F7 — 115
Carleton, Mount, mtn., N.B., Can. . . . . B3 — 87
Carleton Place, On., Can. . . B8 — 89
Carletonville, S. Afr. . . . . . D4 — 56
Carlin, Nv., U.S. . . . . C5 — 121
Carlinville, Il., U.S. . . . . . . D4 — 106
Carlisle, Eng., U.K. . . . . . . C5 — 12
Carlisle, Ar., U.S. . . . . C4 — 97
Carlisle, Ia., U.S. . . . . C4 — 108
Carlisle, In., U.S. . . . . G3 — 107
Carlisle, Ky., U.S. . . . . B5 — 110
Carlisle, Oh., U.S. . . . . C1 — 128
Carlisle, Pa., U.S. . . . . F7 — 131
Carlisle, co., Ky., U.S. . . . . f8 — 110
Carl Junction, Mo., U.S. . . D3 — 118
Carlos Casares, Arg. . . . . . F5 — 72
Carlos Chagas, Braz. . . . . . E3 — 74
Carlow, Ire. . . . . D3 — 12
Carlsbad see Karlovy Vary, Czech Rep. . . . . D2 — 20
Carlsbad, Ca., U.S. . . . . . . F5 — 98
Carlsbad, N.M., U.S. . . . . . E5 — 124
Carlsbad Caverns National Park, N.M., U.S. . . . . . E5 — 124
Carlsberg Ridge . . . . H8 — 64
Carlstadt, N.J., U.S. . . . . . h8 — 123
Carlton, Mn., U.S. . . . . . . D6 — 116
Carlton, Or., U.S. . . . . B3 — 130
Carlton, co., Mn., U.S. . . . D6 — 116
Carlyle, Il., U.S. . . . . E4 — 106
Carlyle Lake, res., Il., U.S. . E4 — 106
Carman, Mb., Can. . . . . . . E2 — 86
Carmanville, Nf., Can. . . . . D4 — 88
Carmarthen, Wales, U.K. . . E4 — 12
Carmaux, Fr. . . . . E9 — 16
Carmel, Ca., U.S. . . . . D3 — 98
Carmel, In., U.S. . . . . E5 — 107
Carmel, N.Y., U.S. . . . . . . D7 — 125
Carmelo, Ur. . . . . E6 — 72
Carmen, Isla, i., Mex. . . . . B2 — 78
Carmen, Isla del, i., Mex. . . D6 — 78
Carmen de Patagones, Arg. F4 — 69
Carmi, Il., U.S. . . . . E5 — 106
Carmi, Lake, l., Vt., U.S. . . . B3 — 138
Carnamah, Austl. . . . . F2 — 60
Carnarvon, Austl. . . . . E1 — 60
Carnarvon, S. Afr. . . . . E3 — 56
Carnation, Wa., U.S. . . . . . B4 — 140
Carnegie, Ok., U.S. . . . . . . B3 — 129
Carnegie, Pa., U.S. . . . . . . F1 — 131
Carnegie, Lake, l., Austl. . . E4 — 60
Carneys Point, N.J., U.S. . . D2 — 123
Carnic Alps, mts., Eur. . . . . A4 — 18
Car Nicobar Island, i., India H6 — 40
Carnot, C.A.R. . . . . C3 — 54
Caro, Mi., U.S. . . . . E7 — 115
Carol City, Fl., U.S. . . . . . . s13 — 102
Caroleen, N.C., U.S. . . . . . B1 — 126
Carolina, Braz. . . . . C2 — 74
Carolina, R.I., U.S. . . . . . . F2 — 132
Carolina, W.V., U.S. . . . . . k10 — 141
Carolina Beach, N.C., U.S. . C5 — 126
Caroline, co., Md., U.S. . . . C6 — 113
Caroline, co., Va., U.S. . . . C5 — 139
Caroline, atoll, Kir. . . . . . . E15 — 58
Caroline Islands, is., Oc. . . D8 — 58
Caroní, stm., Ven. . . . . . . C7 — 70
Carora, Ven. . . . . C5 — 80
Carpathian Mountains, mts., Eur. . . . . E6 — 20
Carpaţii Meridionali, mts., Rom. . . . . G7 — 20
Carpentaria, Gulf of, b., Austl. . . . . F7 — 58
Carpenter Dam, Ar., U.S. . . g7 — 97
Carpentersville, Il., U.S. . . . A5 — 106
Carpentras, Fr. . . . . E9 — 16
Carpina, Braz. . . . . C4 — 74
Carpinteria, Ca., U.S. . . . . E4 — 98
Carrabelle, Fl., U.S. . . . . . . C2 — 102
Carranza, Cabo, c., Chile . . F3 — 72
Carrara, Italy . . . . B3 — 18
Carrauntoohil, mtn., Ire. . . D2 — 12
Carrboro, N.C., U.S. . . . . . B3 — 126
Carreta, Punta, c., Peru . . . F4 — 70
Carrick on Shannon, Ire. . . C3 — 12
Carrie, Mount, mtn., Wa., U.S. . . . . B2 — 140
Carriere, Ms., U.S. . . . . . . E4 — 117
Carrier Mills, Il., U.S. . . . . . F5 — 106
Carrington, N.D., U.S. . . . . B6 — 127

Carrington Island, i., Ut., U.S. . . . . C3 — 137
Carrizal Bajo, Chile . . . . . . C2 — 69
Carrizo Creek, stm., U.S. . . A1 — 136
Carrizozo, N.M., U.S. . . . . D4 — 124
Carroll, Ia., U.S. . . . . B3 — 108
Carroll, co., Ar., U.S. . . . . . A2 — 97
Carroll, co., Ga., U.S. . . . . C1 — 103
Carroll, co., Ia., U.S. . . . . . B3 — 108
Carroll, co., Il., U.S. . . . . . A4 — 106
Carroll, co., In., U.S. . . . . . C4 — 107
Carroll, co., Ky., U.S. . . . . B4 — 110
Carroll, co., Md., U.S. . . . . A3 — 113
Carroll, co., Mo., U.S. . . . . B4 — 118
Carroll, co., Mo., U.S. . . . . B4 — 117
Carroll, co., N.H., U.S. . . . . C4 — 122
Carroll, co., Oh., U.S. . . . . B4 — 128
Carroll, co., Tn., U.S. . . . . . B3 — 135
Carroll, co., Va., U.S. . . . . . D2 — 139
Carrollton, Al., U.S. . . . . . . B1 — 94
Carrollton, Ga., U.S. . . . . . C1 — 103
Carrollton, Il., U.S. . . . . . . D3 — 106
Carrollton, Ky., U.S. . . . . . B4 — 110
Carrollton, Mi., U.S. . . . . . E7 — 115
Carrollton, Mo., U.S. . . . . . B4 — 118
Carrollton, Oh., U.S. . . . . . B4 — 128
Carrollton, Pa., U.S. . . . . . E4 — 131
Carrot, stm., Can. . . . . D4 — 91
Carry Falls Reservoir, res., N.Y., U.S. . . . . f10 — 125
Çarşamba, Tur. . . . . B7 — 44
Čarsk, Kaz. . . . . B4 — 28
Carson, Ia., U.S. . . . . C2 — 108
Carson, Wa., U.S. . . . . D4 — 140
Carson, co., Tx., U.S. . . . . . B2 — 136
Carson, stm., Nv., U.S. . . . D2 — 121
Carson City, Mi., U.S. . . . . E6 — 115
Carson City, Nv., U.S. . . . . D2 — 121
Carson Lake, l., Nv., U.S. . . D3 — 121
Carson Sink, l., Nv., U.S. . . D3 — 121
Carson Spring, Tn., U.S. . . D10 — 135
Carstairs, Ab., Can. . . . . . . D3 — 84
Cartagena, Col. . . . . A4 — 70
Cartagena, Spain . . . . I6 — 16
Cartago, Col. . . . . A4 — 70
Cartago, C.R. . . . . D3 — 80
Carter, co., Ky., U.S. . . . . . B6 — 110
Carter, co., Mo., U.S. . . . . . E7 — 118
Carter, co., Mt., U.S. . . . . . E12 — 119
Carter, co., Ok., U.S. . . . . . C4 — 129
Carter, co., Tn., U.S. . . . . . C11 — 135
Carter Lake, Ia., U.S. . . . . . C2 — 108
Carter Mountain, mtn., Wy., U.S. . . . . B3 — 143
Carters Lake, res., Ga., U.S. B2 — 103
Cartersville, Ga., U.S. . . . . B2 — 103
Carterville, Il., U.S. . . . . . . F4 — 106
Carterville, Mo., U.S. . . . . . D3 — 118
Carthage, Tun. . . . . F3 — 18
Carthage, Il., U.S. . . . . C2 — 106
Carthage, In., U.S. . . . . E6 — 107
Carthage, Mo., U.S. . . . . . . D3 — 118
Carthage, Ms., U.S. . . . . . . C4 — 117
Carthage, N.C., U.S. . . . . . B3 — 126
Carthage, N.Y., U.S. . . . . . B5 — 125
Carthage, Tn., U.S. . . . . . . C8 — 135
Carthage, Tx., U.S. . . . . . . C5 — 136
Carthage, hist., Tun. . . . . . F3 — 18
Cartier Islands, is., Austl. . . C3 — 60
Cartwright, Nf., Can. . . . . . B3 — 88
Cartwright, Ok., U.S. . . . . . D5 — 129
Caruaru, Braz. . . . . C4 — 74
Carúpano, Ven. . . . . A7 — 70
Carutapera, Braz. . . . . D10 — 70
Caruthersville, Mo., U.S. . . E8 — 118
Carver, Ma., U.S. . . . . C6 — 114
Carver, Mn., U.S. . . . . F5 — 116
Carver, co., Mn., U.S. . . . . F5 — 116
Carville, La., U.S. . . . . h9 — 111
Carvoeiro, Braz. . . . . D7 — 70
Cary, Il., U.S. . . . . A5 — 106
Cary, N.C., U.S. . . . . B4 — 126
Caryville, Tn., U.S. . . . . . . C9 — 135
Casablanca, Mor. . . . . D3 — 48
Casa Grande, Az., U.S. . . . E4 — 96
Casa Grande National Monument, Az., U.S. . E4 — 96
Casale Monferrato, Italy . . B2 — 18
Casa Nova, Braz. . . . . C3 — 74
Casas Adobes, Az., U.S. . . . E5 — 96
Cascade, Ia., U.S. . . . . B6 — 108
Cascade, Id., U.S. . . . . E2 — 105
Cascade, Mt., U.S. . . . . . . C5 — 119
Cascade, co., Mt., U.S. . . . C5 — 119
Cascade Locks, Or., U.S. . . B5 — 130
Cascade Range, mts., N.A. . C3 — 92
Cascade Reservoir, res., Id., U.S. . . . . E3 — 105
Cascade Tunnel, Wa., U.S. . B4 — 140
Cascais, Port. . . . . H2 — 16
Cascavel, Braz. . . . . D7 — 72
Casco Bay, b., Me., U.S. . . E3 — 112
Caserta, Italy . . . . D5 — 18
Caseville, Mi., U.S. . . . . . . E8 — 115
Casey, Il., U.S. . . . . D6 — 106
Casey, co., Ky., U.S. . . . . . C5 — 110
Casey, Mount, mtn., Id., U.S. . . . . A2 — 105
Casey Key, i., Fl., U.S. . . . . E4 — 102

Cashion, Az., U.S. . . . . m8 — 96
Cashmere, Wa., U.S. . . . . . B5 — 140
Cashton, Wi., U.S. . . . . . . E3 — 142
Casino, Austl. . . . . F5 — 62
Casper, Wy., U.S. . . . . D6 — 143
Casper Mountain, mtn., Wy., U.S. . . . . D6 — 143
Caspian, Mi., U.S. . . . . B2 — 115
Caspian Depression (Prikaspijskaja nizmennost'), pl. . . . . E8 — 22
Caspian Lake, l., Vt., U.S. . . B4 — 138
Caspian Sea . . . . F9 — 22
Cass, co., Ia., U.S. . . . . C3 — 108
Cass, co., Il., U.S. . . . . D3 — 106
Cass, co., In., U.S. . . . . C5 — 107
Cass, co., Mi., U.S. . . . . . . G4 — 115
Cass, co., Mn., U.S. . . . . . . D4 — 116
Cass, co., Mo., U.S. . . . . . . C3 — 118
Cass, co., N.D., U.S. . . . . . C8 — 127
Cass, co., Ne., U.S. . . . . . . D9 — 120
Cass, co., Tx., U.S. . . . . . . C5 — 136
Cass, stm., Mi., U.S. . . . . . E7 — 115
Cassai (Kasai), stm., Afr. . . F4 — 54
Cass City, Mi., U.S. . . . . . . E7 — 115
Casselberry, Fl., U.S. . . . . . D5 — 102
Casselman, On., Can. . . . . B9 — 89
Casselman, stm., U.S. . . . . k12 — 113
Casselton, N.D., U.S. . . . . . C8 — 127
Cassia, co., Id., U.S. . . . . . G5 — 105
Cassiar, B.C., Can. . . . . . . m17 — 85
Cassilândia, Braz. . . . . E1 — 74
Cassinga, Ang. . . . . B2 — 56
Cassino, Italy . . . . D4 — 18
Cass Lake, Mn., U.S. . . . . . C4 — 116
Cass Lake, l., Mn., U.S. . . . C4 — 116
Cassongue, Ang. . . . . F2 — 54
Cassopolis, Mi., U.S. . . . . . G4 — 115
Cassumba, Ilha, i., Braz. . . E4 — 74
Cassville, Ga., U.S. . . . . . . B2 — 103
Cassville, Mo., U.S. . . . . . . E4 — 118
Cassville, Wi., U.S. . . . . . . F3 — 142
Castalia, Oh., U.S. . . . . A3 — 128
Castanea, Pa., U.S. . . . . . . D7 — 131
Castanhal, Braz. . . . . B2 — 74
Castellammare, Golfo di, b., Italy . . . . E4 — 18
Castelló de la Plana, Spain . H6 — 16
Castelo Branco, Port. . . . . . H3 — 16
Castelsarrasin, Fr. . . . . F7 — 16
Castelvetrano, Italy . . . . . . F4 — 18
Castilla, Peru . . . . E3 — 70
Castilla la Nueva, hist. reg., Spain . . . . H4 — 16
Castilla la Vieja, hist. reg., Spain . . . . G5 — 16
Castillo de San Marcos National Monument, Fl., U.S. . . . . n9 — 102
Castine, Me., U.S. . . . . D4 — 112
Castlebar, Ire. . . . . D2 — 12
Castleberry, Al., U.S. . . . . . D2 — 94
Castle Dale, Ut., U.S. . . . . . D4 — 137
Castle Dome Mountains, mts., Az., U.S. . . . . . . D1 — 96
Castle Dome Peak, mtn., Az., U.S. . . . . D1 — 96
Castlegar, B.C., Can. . . . . . E9 — 85
Castle Hayne, N.C., U.S. . . C5 — 126
Castle Hills, De., U.S. . . . . . i7 — 101
Castlemaine, Austl. . . . . . . H3 — 62
Castle Mountains, mts., Mt., U.S. . . . . D6 — 119
Castle Peak, mtn., Co., U.S. B4 — 99
Castle Peak, mtn., Id., U.S. E4 — 105
Castle Point, Mo., U.S. . . . f13 — 118
Castle Rock, Co., U.S. . . . . B6 — 99
Castle Rock, Wa., U.S. . . . . C3 — 140
Castle Rock, mtn., Or., U.S. C8 — 130
Castle Rock Lake, res., Wi., U.S. . . . . E4 — 142
Castleton, Vt., U.S. . . . . . . D2 — 138
Castlewood, Va., U.S. . . . . f9 — 139
Castor, Ab., Can. . . . . C5 — 84
Castor, stm., Mo., U.S. . . . D7 — 118
Castres, Fr. . . . . F8 — 16
Castries, St. Luc. . . . . C7 — 80
Castro, Braz. . . . . C7 — 72
Castro, Chile . . . . E2 — 69
Castro, co., Tx., U.S. . . . . . B1 — 136
Castro Valley, Ca., U.S. . . . h8 — 98
Castroville, Tx., U.S. . . . . . E3 — 136
Castuera, Spain . . . . H4 — 16
Caswell, co., N.C., U.S. . . . A3 — 126
Cataguazes, Braz. . . . . C9 — 72
Catahoula, co., La., U.S. . . C4 — 111
Catahoula Lake, l., La., U.S. C3 — 111
Catalão, Braz. . . . . E2 — 74
Catalina, Nf., Can. . . . . . . D5 — 88
Catalina, Chile . . . . C3 — 69
Catalunya, hist. reg., Spain . F7 — 16
Catanduanes Island, i., Phil. D8 — 34
Catania, Italy . . . . F5 — 18
Catanzaro, Italy . . . . E6 — 18
Cataouatche, Lake, l., La., U.S. . . . . k11 — 111
Catarino Rodríguez, Mex. . C4 — 78
Catarman, Phil. . . . . D8 — 34
Cataumet, Ma., U.S. . . . . . C6 — 114
Catawba, co., N.C., U.S. . . B1 — 126
Catawba, stm., S.C., U.S. . . B6 — 133
Catawba, South Fork, stm., N.C., U.S. . . . . B1 — 126

Name	Map Ref.	Page

Catawissa, Pa., U.S. **E9** 131
Catbalogan, Phil. **D8** 34
Catete, Ang. **E2** 54
Cathance, Lake, l., Me.,
U.S. **D5** 112
Cathedral City, Ca., U.S. . **F5** 98
Cathedral of the Pines,
N.H., U.S. **E3** 122
Catherine, Lake, res., Ar.,
U.S. **C3** 97
Cat Island, i., Bah. **D9** 76
Cat Island, i., Ma., U.S. . **f12** 114
Cat Island, i., Ms., U.S. . . **E4** 117
Cat Island, i., S.C., U.S. . **E9** 133
Catlettsburg, Ky., U.S. . . . **B7** 110
Catlin, Il., U.S. **C6** 106
Catnip Mountain, mtn., Nv.,
U.S. **B2** 121
Catoche, Cabo, c., Mex. . . **C7** 78
Catonsville, Md., U.S. **B4** 113
Catoosa, Ok., U.S. **A6** 129
Catoosa, co., Ga., U.S. . . . **B1** 103
Catriló, Arg. **F5** 72
Catron, co., N.M., U.S. . . **D1** 124
Catskill, N.Y., U.S. **C7** 125
Catskill Mountains, mts.,
N.Y., U.S. **C6** 125
Catt, Mount, mtn., B.C.,
Can. **B3** 85
Cattaraugus, co., N.Y., U.S. **C2** 125
Cattaraugus Creek, stm.,
N.Y., U.S. **C2** 125
Cattaraugus Indian
Reservation, N.Y., U.S. **C3** 125
Čatyrtaš, Kyrg. **A3** 40
Caubvick, Mount (Iberville,
Mont d'), mtn., Can. . . . **f9** 88
Cauca, stm., Col. **B5** 70
Caucasia, Col. **D4** 80
Caucasus, mts. **A10** 44
Caucete, Arg. **E4** 72
Caucomgomoc Lake, l.,
Me., U.S. **B3** 112
Caungula, Ang. **E3** 54
Cauquenes, Chile **E2** 69
Caura, stm., Ven. **B7** 70
Cavalier, N.D., U.S. **A8** 127
Cavalier, co., N.D., U.S. . . **A7** 127
Cave City, Ar., U.S. **B4** 97
Cave City, Ky., U.S. **C4** 110
Cave Creek, Az., U.S. **D4** 96
Cave Junction, Or., U.S. . . **E3** 130
Cave Point, c., Wi., U.S. . . **D6** 142
Cave Run Lake, res., Ky.,
U.S. **B6** 110
Cave Spring, Ga., U.S. . . . **B1** 103
Cave Spring, Va., U.S. . . . **C2** 139
Cavetown, Md., U.S. **A2** 113
Caviana de Fora, Ilha, i.,
Braz. **A2** 74
Cavite, Phil. **D8** 34
Cawood, Ky., U.S. **D6** 110
Cawston, B.C., Can. **E8** 85
Caxias, Braz. **B3** 74
Caxias do Sul, Braz. **D7** 72
Caxito, Ang. **E2** 54
Cayambe, vol., Ec. **C4** 70
Cayce, S.C., U.S. **D5** 133
Cayenne, Fr. Gu. **C9** 70
Cayman Brac, i., Cay. Is. . **B4** 80
Cayman Islands, dep., N.A. **E8** 76
Cayuga, In., U.S. **E3** 107
Cayuga, co., N.Y., U.S. . . . **C4** 125
Cayuga Heights, N.Y., U.S. **C4** 125
Cayuga Lake, l., N.Y., U.S. **C4** 125
Cazenovia, N.Y., U.S. **C5** 125
Cazombo, Ang. **F4** 54
Ceará, state, Braz. **C4** 74
Ceará-Mirim, Braz. **C4** 74
Ceballos, Mex. **B4** 78
Čeboksary, Russia **D6** 26
Cebu, Phil. **D8** 34
Cebu, i., Phil. **D8** 34
Cecil, co., Md., U.S. **A6** 113
Cecil Field Naval Air
Station, mil., Fl., U.S. . **B5** 102
Cecilia, Ky., U.S. **C4** 110
Cecina, Italy **C3** 18
Čečnja, state, Russia **E6** 26
Cedar, co., Ia., U.S. **C6** 108
Cedar, co., Mo., U.S. **D4** 118
Cedar, co., Ne., U.S. **B8** 120
Cedar, stm., Ne., U.S. . . . **B7** 120
Cedar, stm., Wa., U.S. . . . **B4** 140
Cedar, stm., U.S. **C6** 108
Cedar Bluff, Al., U.S. **A4** 94
Cedar Bluff Reservoir, res.,
Ks., U.S. **D4** 109
Cedar Breaks National
Monument, Ut., U.S. . . **F3** 137
Cedarburg, Wi., U.S. **E6** 142
Cedar City, Ut., U.S. **F2** 137
Cedar Creek, stm., N.D.,
U.S. **C3** 127
Cedar Creek, stm., N.J.,
U.S. **D4** 123
Cedar Creek, stm., Oh.,
U.S. **e7** 128
Cedar Creek Lake, res., Tx.,
U.S. **C4** 136
Cedar Crest, N.M., U.S. . . **k8** 124
Cedaredge, Co., U.S. **C3** 99
Cedar Falls, Ia., U.S. **B5** 108
Cedar Grove, N.J., U.S. . . **B4** 123

Cedar Grove, W.V., U.S. . . **C3** 141
Cedar Grove, Wi., U.S. . . . **E6** 142
Cedar Hill, Mo., U.S. **g12** 118
Cedar Hill, Tx., U.S. **n10** 136
Cedarhurst, N.Y., U.S. . . **k13** 125
Cedar Island, i., N.C., U.S. **C6** 126
Cedar Island, i., S.C., U.S. **E9** 133
Cedar Island, i., Va., U.S. **C7** 139
Cedar Key, Fl., U.S. **C3** 102
Cedar Keys, is., Fl., U.S. . . **C3** 102
Cedar Lake, In., U.S. **B3** 107
Cedar Lake, res., Mb., Can. **C1** 86
Cedar Lake, res., Il., U.S. . **F4** 106
Cedar Mountain, mtn., Ca.,
U.S. **B3** 98
Cedar Point, c., Md., U.S. . **D5** 113
Cedar Point, c., Oh., U.S. . **A3** 128
Cedar Point, c., Oh., U.S. . **e7** 128
Cedar Rapids, Ia., U.S. . . . **C6** 108
Cedar Springs, Mi., U.S. . . **E5** 115
Cedartown, Ga., U.S. **B1** 103
Cedar Vale, Ks., U.S. **E7** 109
Cedarville, Oh., U.S. **C2** 128
Cedros, Isla, i., Mex. **B1** 78
Ceduna, Austl. **G5** 60
Ceeriigaabo, Som. **H14** 48
Cefalonia see Kefallinía, i.,
Grc. **E8** 18
Cefalù, Italy **F5** 18
Čegdomyn, Russia **D15** 26
Cegléd, Hung. **F5** 20
Čehov, Russia **B14** 20
Čehov, Russia **A4** 31
Çekerek, Tur. **B6** 44
Çekerek, stm., Tur. **C6** 44
Celaya, Mex. **C4** 78
Celebes see Sulawesi, i.,
Indon. **D6** 36
Celebes Basin **H15** 64
Celebes Sea, Asia **C6** 36
Čeleken, Turk. **C6** 42
Celina, Oh., U.S. **B1** 128
Celina, Tn., U.S. **C8** 135
Celina, Tx., U.S. **C4** 136
Čeljabinsk, Russia **D8** 26
Celje, Slvn. **A5** 18
Čeljuskin, mys, c., Russia **B12** 26
Čelkar, Kaz. **E7** 26
Celle, Ger. **D11** 12
Celtic Sea, Eur. **B3** 16
Cement, Ok., U.S. **C3** 129
Cementon, Pa., U.S. **E10** 131
Cenderawasih, Teluk, b.,
Indon. **G10** 32
Cenderawasih Bay see
Cenderawasih, Teluk,
b., Indon. **G10** 32
Centennial Mountains, mts.,
Id., U.S. **E7** 105
Center, Co., U.S. **D4** 99
Center, N.D., U.S. **B4** 127
Center, Tx., U.S. **D5** 136
Centerbrook, Ct., U.S. . . . **D6** 100
Centereach, N.Y., U.S. . . **n15** 125
Centerfield, Ut., U.S. **D4** 137
Center Hill Lake, res., Tn.,
U.S. **C8** 135
Center Moriches, N.Y., U.S. **n16** 125
Center Mountain, mtn., Id.,
U.S. **D3** 105
Center Point, Al., U.S. . . . **f7** 94
Center Point, Ia., U.S. . . . **B6** 108
Centerville, Ia., U.S. **D5** 108
Centerville, In., U.S. **E8** 107
Centerville, La., U.S. **E4** 111
Centerville, Ma., U.S. **C7** 114
Centerville, Oh., U.S. **C1** 128
Centerville, Pa., U.S. **F2** 131
Centerville, S.D., U.S. . . . **D9** 134
Centerville, Tn., U.S. **B4** 135
Centerville, Ut., U.S. **C4** 137
Central, Phil. **D8** 34
Central, N.M., U.S. **E1** 124
Central, S.C., U.S. **B2** 133
Central, Cordillera, mts.,
Col. **E4** 80
Central, Cordillera, mts.,
Peru **E4** 70
Central, Massif, mts., Fr. . **E8** 16
Central, Sistema, mts., Spain **G4** 16
Central African Republic,
ctry., Afr. **B3** 54
Central City, Co., U.S. . . . **B5** 99
Central City, Ia., U.S. **B6** 108
Central City, Il., U.S. **E4** 106
Central City, Ky., U.S. **C2** 110
Central City, Ne., U.S. . . . **C7** 120
Central City, Pa., U.S. **F4** 131
Central Falls, R.I., U.S. . . . **B4** 132
Central Heights, Az., U.S. . **D5** 96
Centralia, Il., U.S. **E4** 106
Centralia, Mo., U.S. **B5** 118
Centralia, Wa., U.S. **C3** 140
Central Islip, N.Y., U.S. . . **n15** 125
Central Lake, Mi., U.S. . . . **C5** 115
Central Makrān Range, mts.,
Pak. **E8** 42
Central Pacific Basin **G21** 64
Central Park, Wa., U.S. . . . **C2** 140
Central Point, Or., U.S. . . . **E4** 130
Central Siberian Uplands
see Srednesibirskoe
ploskogor'e, plat.,
Russia **C12** 26

Central Square, N.Y., U.S. . **B4** 125
Central Valley, Ca., U.S. . . **B2** 98
Central Valley, N.Y., U.S. . **D6** 125
Central Village, Ct., U.S. . . **C8** 100
Centre, Al., U.S. **A4** 94
Centre, co., Pa., U.S. **E6** 131
Centre Hall, Pa., U.S. **E6** 131
Centreville, Al., U.S. **C2** 94
Centreville, Il., U.S. **E3** 106
Centreville, Md., U.S. **B5** 113
Centreville, Mi., U.S. **G5** 115
Centreville, Ms., U.S. **D2** 117
Centuria, Wi., U.S. **C1** 142
Century, Fl., U.S. **u14** 102
Ceos see Kéa, i., Grc. . . . **F10** 18
Ceram see Seram, i., Indon. **D7** 36
Ceram Sea see Seram, Laut,
Indon. **D7** 36
Cerbat Mountains, mts., Az.,
U.S. **B1** 96
Cerdas, Bol. **C4** 72
Ceredo, W.V., U.S. **C2** 141
Čeremhovo, Russia **D12** 26
Čerepovec, Russia **D5** 26
Ceres, Arg. **D5** 72
Ceres, Braz. **E2** 74
Ceres, Ca., U.S. **D3** 98
Ceresco, Ne., U.S. **C9** 120
Cerignola, Italy **D5** 18
Čerkessk, Russia **E6** 26
Čerlak, Russia **D9** 26
Čermoz, Russia **C10** 26
Cernavodă, Rom. **G10** 20
Černjahovsk, Russia **B6** 20
Černjanka, Russia **D14** 20
Černobyl', Ukr. **D11** 20
Černuška, Russia **C10** 22
Černyševskij, Russia **C13** 26
Cerralvo, Isla, i., Mex. **C3** 78
Cerritos, Mex. **C4** 78
Cerro Azul, Peru **A2** 72
Cerro de Pasco, Peru **F4** 70
Cerro Gordo, Il., U.S. **D5** 106
Cerro Gordo, co., Ia., U.S. **A4** 108
Čerskij, Russia **C18** 26
Čerskogo, hrebet, mts.,
Russia **C15** 26
Červen', Bela. **C10** 20
Cervino see Matterhorn,
mtn., Eur. **A1** 18
Cesena, Italy **B4** 18
Cēsis, Lat. **H11** 10
České Budějovice, Czech
Rep. **E3** 20
Çeşme, Tur. **C2** 44
Češskaja guba, b., Russia **A8** 22
Cessnock, Austl. **G5** 62
Cetinje, Yugo. **C7** 18
Ceuta, Sp. N. Afr. **J4** 16
Cévennes, reg., Fr. **E8** 16
Ceyhan, Tur. **D6** 44
Ceyhan, stm., Tur. **D6** 44
Ceylanpınar, Tur. **D9** 44
Ceylon see Sri Lanka, ctry.,
Asia **H4** 40
Cha-am, Thai. **D3** 34
Chachani, Nevado, vol.,
Peru **G5** 70
Chachapoyas, Peru **E4** 70
Chachoengsao, Thai. **D4** 34
Chaco, stm., N.M., U.S. . . **A1** 124
Chaco Austral, reg., Arg. . **A5** 72
Chaco Boreal, reg., Para. . **C5** 72
Chaco Central, reg., Arg. . **C5** 72
Chaco Culture National
Historic Park, N.M.,
U.S. **A2** 124
Chacon, Cape, c., Ak., U.S. **n24** 95
Chad, ctry., Chad **G8** 48
Chad, Lake, l., Afr. **D7** 50
Chadbourn, N.C., U.S. . . . **C4** 126
Chadds Ford, Pa., U.S. . . **G10** 131
Chadron, Ne., U.S. **B3** 120
Chadwicks, N.Y., U.S. **B5** 125
Chaffee, Mo., U.S. **D8** 118
Chaffee, co., Co., U.S. . . . **C4** 99
Chaffin, Ma., U.S. **B4** 114
Chaghchārān, Afg. **D9** 42
Chagos Archipelago, is.,
B.I.O.T. **I10** 64
Chagos-Laccadive Plateau . **I10** 64
Chagrin Falls, Oh., U.S. . . **A4** 128
Chaguaramas, Ven. **D6** 80
Chahār Borjak, Afg. **D8** 42
Chai Nat, Thai. **C4** 34
Chaiyaphum, Thai. **C4** 34
Chajarí, Arg. **E6** 72
Chakachamna Lake, l., Ak.,
U.S. **g15** 95
Chakari, Zimb. **B4** 56
Chakasija, state, Russia . . **A5** 28
Chala, Peru **B3** 72
Chalatenango, El Sal. **C2** 80
Chalbi Desert, des., Kenya **C7** 54
Chalcidice see Khalkidhikí,
hist. reg., Grc. **C9** 18
Chalcis see Khalkís, Grc. . **E9** 18
Chaleur Bay, b., Can. **B4** 87
Chalfonte, De., U.S. **h7** 101
Chalk River, On., Can. . . . **A7** 89
Challapata, Bol. **B4** 72
Challenger Deep **G17** 64
Challis, Id., U.S. **E4** 105
Chalmette, La., U.S. **E6** 111
Châlons-en-Champagne, Fr. **C9** 16

Chalon-sur-Saône, Fr. **D9** 16
Chālūs, Iran **C6** 42
Chama, N.M., U.S. **A3** 124
Chama, Rio, stm., N.M.,
U.S. **A3** 124
Chaman, Pak. **D9** 42
Chambal, stm., India **D3** 40
Chamberlain, S.D., U.S. . . **D6** 134
Chamberlain Lake, l., Me.,
U.S. **B3** 112
Chamberlin, Mount, mtn.,
Ak., U.S. **B10** 95
Chambers, co., Al., U.S. . . **C4** 94
Chambers, co., Tx., U.S. . . **E5** 136
Chambersburg, Pa., U.S. . **G6** 131
Chambers Island, i., Wi.,
U.S. **C6** 142
Chambéry, Fr. **E9** 16
Chambi, Jebel, mtn., Tun. . **C6** 48
Chamblee, Ga., U.S. **h8** 103
Chambly, P.Q., Can. **D4** 90
Chamical, Arg. **E4** 72
Chamisal, N.M., U.S. **A4** 124
Chāmpa, India **E4** 40
Champagne, hist. reg., Fr. . **C9** 16
Champaign, Il., U.S. **C5** 106
Champaign, co., Il., U.S. . . **C5** 106
Champaign, co., Oh., U.S. **B2** 128
Champasak, Laos **D5** 34
Champlain, Lake, l., N.A. . **C13** 92
Champlin, Mn., U.S. **m12** 116
Champotón, Mex. **D6** 78
Chañaral, Chile **C2** 69
Chancelulla Peak, mtn.,
Ca., U.S. **B2** 98
Chandalar, stm., Ak., U.S. **B10** 95
Chandeleur Islands, is., La.,
U.S. **E7** 111
Chandeleur Sound, strt.,
La., U.S. **E6** 111
Chandīgarh, India **C3** 40
Chandler, P.Q., Can. **k14** 90
Chandler, Az., U.S. **D4** 96
Chandler, In., U.S. **H3** 107
Chandler, Ok., U.S. **B5** 129
Chandler, Tx., U.S. **C5** 136
Chandler Heights, Az., U.S. **m9** 96
Chāndpur, Bngl. **E6** 40
Chandrapur, India **F3** 40
Chang (Yangtze), stm.,
China **E9** 28
Chang, Ko, i., Thai. **D4** 34
Changane, stm., Moz. **C5** 56
Changara, Moz. **B5** 56
Chang Cheng (Great Wall),
China **B2** 30
Changchun, China **C13** 28
Changde, China **F10** 28
Changhua, Tai. **E5** 30
Changji, China **C6** 28
Changjiang, China **H9** 28
Changli, China **B4** 30
Changmar, China **E3** 28
Changning, China **B3** 34
Changsha, China **F10** 28
Changshu, China **C5** 30
Changting, China **F11** 28
Changwu, China **B2** 30
Changzhi, China **D10** 28
Changzhou, China **E12** 28
Chanhassen, Mn., U.S. . . **n11** 116
Channahon, Il., U.S. **B5** 106
Channel Islands, is., Eur. . . **C5** 16
Channel Islands National
Park, Ca., U.S. **F4** 98
Channel Lake, Il., U.S. . . . **H8** 106
Channel-Port-aux-Basques,
Nf., Can. **E2** 88
Channelview, Tx., U.S. . . **r14** 136
Chanthaburi, Thai. **D4** 34
Chantilly, Va., U.S. **g12** 139
Chanute, Ks., U.S. **E8** 109
Chao'an, China **G11** 28
Chao Hu, l., China **E11** 28
Chaoxian, China **C4** 30
Chaoyang, China **C12** 28
Chaoyang, China **E4** 30
Chapadinha, Braz. **B3** 74
Chapala, Laguna de, l.,
Mex. **C4** 78
Chaparral, Col. **E4** 80
Chapecó, Braz. **D7** 72
Chapel Hill, N.C., U.S. . . . **B3** 126
Chapel Hill, Tn., U.S. **B5** 135
Chaplin, stm., Ky., U.S. . . **C4** 110
Chaplin Lake, l., Sk., Can. . **G2** 91
Chaplynka, Ukr. **F12** 20
Chapman, Ks., U.S. **D6** 109
Chapman Pond, l., R.I., U.S. **F1** 132
Chapmanville, W.V., U.S. . **D2** 141
Chappaquiddick Island, i.,
Ma., U.S. **D7** 114
Chappell, Ne., U.S. **C3** 120
Chardon, Oh., U.S. **A4** 128
Charenton, La., U.S. **E4** 111
Chari, stm., Afr. **H8** 48
Chārīkār, Afg. **C4** 42
Chariton, Ia., U.S. **C4** 108
Chariton, co., Mo., U.S. . . **B4** 118
Chariton, stm., U.S. **A5** 118
Charity, Guy. **B8** 70

Charleroi, Bel. **E9** 12
Charleroi, Pa., U.S. **F2** 131
Charles, co., Md., U.S. . . . **C3** 113
Charles, stm., Ma., U.S. . . **B5** 114
Charles, Cape, c., Va., U.S. **C6** 139
Charles A. Goodwin Dam,
Ct., U.S. **B3** 100
Charlesbourg, P.Q., Can. **n17** 90
Charles City, Ia., U.S. **A5** 108
Charles City, co., Va., U.S. **C5** 139
Charles Mill Lake, res., Oh.,
U.S. **B3** 128
Charles Mix, co., S.D., U.S. **D7** 134
Charles Mound, hill, Il., U.S. **A3** 106
Charleston, Ar., U.S. **B1** 97
Charleston, Il., U.S. **D5** 106
Charleston, Mo., U.S. **E8** 118
Charleston, Ms., U.S. **A3** 117
Charleston, Or., U.S. **D2** 130
Charleston, S.C., U.S. **F8** 133
Charleston, Tn., U.S. **D9** 135
Charleston, W.V., U.S. . . . **C3** 141
Charleston, co., S.C., U.S. . **F8** 133
Charleston Air Force Base,
mil., S.C., U.S. **k11** 133
Charleston Naval Shipyard,
mil., S.C., U.S. **k12** 133
Charleston Peak, mtn., Nv.,
U.S. **G6** 121
Charlestown, In., U.S. **H6** 107
Charlestown, N.H., U.S. . . **D2** 122
Charlestown, R.I., U.S. . . . **F2** 132
Charles Town, W.V., U.S. . **B7** 141
Charlevoix, Mi., U.S. **C5** 115
Charlevoix, co., Mi., U.S. . **C5** 115
Charlevoix, Lake, l., Mi.,
U.S. **C5** 115
Charlo, N.B., Can. **B3** 87
Charlotte, Mi., U.S. **F6** 115
Charlotte, N.C., U.S. **B2** 126
Charlotte, Tn., U.S. **A4** 135
Charlotte, Tx., U.S. **E3** 136
Charlotte, co., Fl., U.S. . . . **F5** 102
Charlotte, co., Va., U.S. . . **C4** 139
Charlotte Amalie, V.I.U.S. . **B6** 80
Charlotte Hall, Md., U.S. . . **D4** 113
Charlotte Harbor, Fl., U.S. . **F4** 102
Charlotte Harbor, b., Fl.,
U.S. **F4** 102
Charlottesville, Va., U.S. . . **B4** 139
Charlottetown, P.E., Can. . **C6** 87
Charlton, co., Ga., U.S. . . **F4** 103
Charmco, W.V., U.S. **C4** 141
Charny, P.Q., Can. **C6** 90
Charters Towers, Austl. . . **E4** 62
Chartres, Fr. **C7** 16
Chascomús, Arg. **F6** 72
Chase, B.C., Can. **D8** 85
Chase, Md., U.S. **B5** 113
Chase, co., Ks., U.S. **D7** 109
Chase, co., Ne., U.S. **D4** 120
Chase City, Va., U.S. **D4** 139
Chaska, Mn., U.S. **F5** 116
Chassahowitzka Bay, b., Fl.,
U.S. **D4** 102
Chassell, Mi., U.S. **B2** 115
Châteaubriant, Fr. **D6** 16
Châteaudun, Fr. **C7** 16
Châteauguay, P.Q., Can. . **D4** 90
Château-Richer, P.Q., Can. **C6** 90
Châteauroux, Fr. **D7** 16
Châtellerault, Fr. **D7** 16
Chatfield, Mn., U.S. **G6** 116
Chatham, N.B., Can. **B4** 87
Chatham, On., Can. **E2** 89
Chatham, Il., U.S. **D4** 106
Chatham, La., U.S. **B3** 111
Chatham, Ma., U.S. **C8** 114
Chatham, N.J., U.S. **B4** 123
Chatham, N.Y., U.S. **C7** 125
Chatham, Va., U.S. **D3** 139
Chatham, co., Ga., U.S. . . **E5** 103
Chatham, co., N.C., U.S. . . **B3** 126
Chatham Islands, is., N.Z. . **I12** 58
Chatham Rise **M21** 64
Chatham Strait, strt., Ak.,
U.S. **m22** 95
Châtillon-sur-Seine, Fr. . . . **D9** 16
Chatom, Al., U.S. **D1** 94
Chatsworth, Ga., U.S. **B2** 103
Chatsworth, Il., U.S. **C5** 106
Chatsworth Reservoir, res.,
Ca., U.S. **m11** 98
Chattahoochee, Fl., U.S. . . **B2** 102
Chattahoochee, co., Ga.,
U.S. **D2** 103
Chattahoochee, stm., U.S. . **E1** 103
Chattanooga, Tn., U.S. . . . **D8** 135
Chattaroy, W.V., U.S. **D2** 141
Chattooga, co., Ga., U.S. . **B1** 103
Chattooga, stm., U.S. **B1** 133
Chatuge Lake, res., U.S. . . **g9** 126
Chaudière, stm., P.Q., Can. **C7** 90
Chauk, Myan. **B2** 34
Chaumont, Fr. **C9** 16
Chauncey, Oh., U.S. **C3** 128
Chauny, Fr. **C8** 16
Chautauqua, co., Ks., U.S. **E7** 109
Chautauqua, co., N.Y., U.S. **C1** 125
Chautauqua Lake, l., N.Y.,
U.S. **C1** 125
Chauvin, La., U.S. **E5** 111
Chaves, Port. **G3** 16

Name	Map Ref.	Page

Chaves, co., N.M., U.S. **D5** 124
Cheaha Mountain, mtn., Al.,
　U.S. **B4** 94
Cheat, Shavers Fork, stm.,
　W.V., U.S. **B5** 141
Cheatham, co., Tn., U.S. . . . **A4** 135
Cheb, Czech Rep. **D2** 20
Chebanse, Il., U.S. **C6** 106
Cheboygan, Mi., U.S. **C6** 115
Cheboygan, co., Mi., U.S. . . **C6** 115
Chech, 'Erg, des., Afr. **B4** 50
Chechaouen, Mor. **J4** 16
Chechnya see Čečnja, state,
　Russia **E6** 26
Checotah, Ok., U.S. **B6** 129
Chedabucto Bay, b., N.S.,
　Can. **D8** 87
Cheduba Island, i., Myan. . . **C2** 34
Cheektowaga, N.Y., U.S. . . . **C2** 125
Cheeseman Lake, res., Co.,
　U.S. **B5** 99
Chehalem Mountains, mts.,
　Or., U.S. **h12** 130
Chehalis, Wa., U.S. **C3** 140
Chehalis, stm., Wa., U.S. . . **C2** 140
Cheju, S. Kor. **E13** 28
Cheju-do, i., S. Kor. **E13** 28
Chekhov see Čehov, Russia **B14** 20
Chekhov see Čehov, Russia **A4** 31
Chelan, Wa., U.S. **B5** 140
Chelan, co., Wa., U.S. **B4** 140
Chelan, Lake, l., Wa., U.S. . **A5** 140
Chelan Mountains, mts.,
　Wa., U.S. **A5** 140
Chelif, Oued, stm., Alg. . . . **D4** 14
Chełm, Pol. **D7** 20
Chełmno, Pol. **C5** 20
Chelmsford, Eng., U.K. **E7** 12
Chelmsford, Ma., U.S. **A5** 114
Chelsea, P.Q., Can. **D2** 90
Chelsea, Al., U.S. **g7** 94
Chelsea, Ma., U.S. **B5** 114
Chelsea, Mi., U.S. **F6** 115
Chelsea, Ok., U.S. **A6** 129
Cheltenham, Eng., U.K. **E5** 12
Cheltenham, Md., U.S. **C4** 113
Chelyabinsk see Čeljabinsk,
　Russia **D8** 26
Chelyan, W.V., U.S. **C3** 141
Chemba, Moz. **B5** 56
Chemehuevi Indian
　Reservation, Ca., U.S. . . **E6** 98
Chemnitz, Ger. **E13** 12
Chemquasabamticook Lake
　(Ross Lake), l., Me.,
　U.S. **B3** 112
Chemung, co., N.Y., U.S. . . **C4** 125
Chemung, stm., Pa., U.S. . . **C8** 131
Chemung Lake, l., On.,
　Can. **C6** 89
Chenāb, stm., Asia **C2** 40
Chenango, co., N.Y., U.S. . . **C5** 125
Chenango, stm., N.Y., U.S. . **C5** 125
Chenango Bridge, N.Y., U.S. **C5** 125
Chenes, River Aux, b., La.,
　U.S. **k12** 111
Chénéville, P.Q., Can. **D2** 90
Cheney, Ks., U.S. **E6** 109
Cheney, Wa., U.S. **B8** 140
Cheney Reservoir, res., Ks.,
　U.S. **E6** 109
Cheneyville, La., U.S. **C3** 111
Chengde, China **C11** 28
Chengdu, China **E8** 28
Chengmai, China **F2** 30
Chengshan Jiao, c., China . **D12** 28
Chengxian, China **C2** 30
Chennai (Madras), India . . . **G4** 40
Chenoa, Il., U.S. **C5** 106
Chenoweth, Or., U.S. **B5** 130
Chenxi, China **D3** 30
Chenzhou, China **F10** 28
Chepachet, R.I., U.S. **B2** 132
Chepachet, stm., R.I., U.S. . **B2** 132
Chequamegon Bay, b., Wi.,
　U.S. **B3** 142
Cher, stm., Fr. **D7** 16
Cheraw, S.C., U.S. **B8** 133
Cherbaniani Reef, rf., India **G2** 40
Cherbourg, Fr. **C6** 16
Cherchell, Alg. **I8** 16
Chergui, Chott ech, l., Alg. . **D5** 14
Cherkasy, Ukr. **E11** 20
Cherkessia see Karačaevo-
　Čerkesija, state, Russia **E6** 26
Cherniakhiv, Ukr. **D10** 20
Chernihiv, Ukr. **D11** 20
Chernivtsi, Ukr. **E8** 20
Chernobyl see Černobyl',
　Ukr. **D11** 20
Cherokee, Al., U.S. **A2** 94
Cherokee, Ia., U.S. **B2** 108
Cherokee, Ks., U.S. **E9** 109
Cherokee, Ok., U.S. **A3** 129
Cherokee, co., Al., U.S. . . . **A4** 94
Cherokee, co., Ga., U.S. . . . **B2** 103
Cherokee, co., Ia., U.S. . . . **B2** 108
Cherokee, co., Ks., U.S. . . . **E9** 109
Cherokee, co., N.C., U.S. . . **f8** 126
Cherokee, co., Ok., U.S. . . . **B6** 129
Cherokee, co., S.C., U.S. . . **A4** 133
Cherokee, co., Tx., U.S. . . . **D5** 136
Cherokee Indian
　Reservation, N.C., U.S. **f9** 126

Cherokee Lake, res., Tn.,
　U.S. **C10** 135
Cherokees, Lake O' The,
　res., Ok., U.S. **A7** 129
Cherokee Village, Ar., U.S. **A4** 97
Cherry, co., Ne., U.S. **B4** 120
Cherry Creek, stm., S.D.,
　U.S. **C3** 134
Cherry Hill, N.J., U.S. **D2** 123
Cherry Point, c., Va., U.S. . **C6** 139
Cherry Point Marine Corps
　Air Station, mil., N.C.,
　U.S. **C6** 126
Cherryvale, Ks., U.S. **E8** 109
Cherry Valley, Ar., U.S. . . . **B5** 97
Cherry Valley, Il., U.S. **A5** 106
Cherryville, N.C., U.S. **B1** 126
Cherskiy Mountains see
　Čerskogo, hrebet, mts.,
　Russia **C15** 26
Chervonohrad, Ukr. **D8** 20
Chesaning, Mi., U.S. **E6** 115
Chesapeake, Oh., U.S. . . . **D3** 128
Chesapeake, Va., U.S. **D6** 139
Chesapeake, W.V., U.S. . . . **C3** 141
Chesapeake and Delaware
　Canal, U.S. **B3** 101
Chesapeake Bay, b., U.S. . **D12** 92
Chesapeake Bay Bridge-
　Tunnel, Va., U.S. **D7** 139
Chesapeake Beach, Md.,
　U.S. **C4** 113
Chesapeake City, Md., U.S. **A6** 113
Chesdin, Lake, res., Va.,
　U.S. **C5** 139
Chesha Bay see Česskaja
　guba, b., Russia **A8** 22
Cheshire, Ct., U.S. **D4** 100
Cheshire, co., N.H., U.S. . . **E2** 122
Cheshire Reservoir, res.,
　Ma., U.S. **A1** 114
Chesley, On., Can. **C3** 89
Chesnee, S.C., U.S. **A4** 133
Chester, Eng., U.K. **D5** 12
Chester, Ca., U.S. **B3** 98
Chester, Ct., U.S. **D6** 100
Chester, Ga., U.S. **D3** 103
Chester, Il., U.S. **F4** 106
Chester, Md., U.S. **C5** 113
Chester, Mt., U.S. **B6** 119
Chester, N.H., U.S. **E4** 122
Chester, N.Y., U.S. **D6** 125
Chester, Pa., U.S. **G11** 131
Chester, S.C., U.S. **B5** 133
Chester, Va., U.S. **C5** 139
Chester, Vt., U.S. **E3** 138
Chester, W.V., U.S. **A4** 141
Chester, co., Pa., U.S. **G10** 131
Chester, co., S.C., U.S. . . . **B5** 133
Chester, co., Tn., U.S. **B3** 135
Chester, co., Md., U.S. . . . **B5** 113
Chester Basin, N.S., Can. . **E5** 87
Chester Depot, Vt., U.S. . . **E3** 138
Chesterfield, In., U.S. **D6** 107
Chesterfield, S.C., U.S. . . . **B7** 133
Chesterfield, co., S.C., U.S. **B7** 133
Chesterfield, co., Va., U.S. **C5** 139
Chesterton, In., U.S. **A3** 107
Chestertown, Md., U.S. . . . **B5** 113
Chesterville, On., Can. **B9** 89
Chesuncook Lake, l., Me.,
　U.S. **C3** 112
Cheswick, Pa., U.S. **h14** 131
Cheswold, De., U.S. **D3** 101
Cheta see Heta, stm.,
　Russia **B11** 26
Chetac, Lake, l., Wi., U.S. . **C2** 142
Chetco, stm., Or., U.S. . . . **E2** 130
Chetek, Wi., U.S. **C2** 142
Chetek, Lake, l., Wi., U.S. . **C2** 142
Chetopa, Ks., U.S. **E8** 109
Chetumal, Mex. **D7** 78
Chetumal, Bahia, b., N.A. . **B2** 80
Chetwynd, B.C., Can. **B7** 85
Chevak, Ak., U.S. **C6** 95
Cheviot, Oh., U.S. **C1** 128
Chevreuil, Point, c., La.,
　U.S. **E4** 111
Chevy Chase, Md., U.S. . . **C3** 113
Chewack, stm., Wa., U.S. . **A5** 140
Chewelah, Wa., U.S. **A8** 140
Cheyenne, Ok., U.S. **B2** 129
Cheyenne, Wy., U.S. **E8** 143
Cheyenne, co., Co., U.S. . . **C8** 99
Cheyenne, co., Ks., U.S. . . **C2** 109
Cheyenne, co., Ne., U.S. . . **C2** 120
Cheyenne, stm., U.S. **C7** 92
Cheyenne, stm., U.S. **C4** 134
Cheyenne, Dry Fork, stm.,
　Wy., U.S. **C7** 143
Cheyenne River Indian
　Reservation, S.D., U.S. **B4** 134
Cheyenne Wells, Co., U.S. **C8** 99
Chhapra, India **D4** 40
Chhatarpur, India **E3** 40
Chhatrapur, India **F5** 40
Chhindwāra, India **E3** 40
Chi, stm., Thai. **C4** 34
Chiai, Tai. **E5** 30
Chiange, Ang. **B1** 56
Chiang Kham, Thai. **C4** 34
Chiang Khan, Thai. **C4** 34
Chiang Mai, Thai. **C3** 34
Chiang Rai, Thai. **C3** 34
Chiapas, state, Mex. **D6** 78

Chiba, Japan **C4** 31
Chiblow Lake, l., On., Can. **A1** 89
Chibougamau, P.Q., Can. . **k12** 90
Chibuto, Moz. **C5** 56
Chicago, Il., U.S. **B6** 106
Chicago Heights, Il., U.S. . **B6** 106
Chicago Sanitary and Ship
　Canal, Il., U.S. **k8** 106
Chicamacomico, stm., Md.,
　U.S. **D6** 113
Chicapa, stm., Afr. **E4** 54
Chichagof Island, i., Ak.,
　U.S. **m22** 95
Chichén Itzá, hist., Mex. . . **C7** 78
Chickahominy, stm., Va.,
　U.S. **C5** 139
Chickamauga, Ga., U.S. . . **B1** 103
Chickamauga and
　Chattanooga National
　Military Park, U.S. **k11** 135
Chickamauga Dam, Tn.,
　U.S. **h11** 135
Chickamauga Lake, res.,
　Tn., U.S. **D8** 135
Chickasaw, Al., U.S. **E1** 94
Chickasaw, co., Ia., U.S. . . **A5** 108
Chickasaw, co., Ms., U.S. . **B5** 117
Chickasawhay, stm., Ms.,
　U.S. **D5** 117
Chickasaw National
　Recreation Area, Ok.,
　U.S. **C5** 129
Chickasha, Ok., U.S. **B4** 129
Chickasha, Lake, res., Ok.,
　U.S. **B3** 129
Chickwolnepy Stream, stm.,
　N.H., U.S. **A4** 122
Chiclayo, Peru **E4** 70
Chico, Ca., U.S. **C3** 98
Chico, stm., Arg. **F3** 69
Chicomba, Ang. **A1** 56
Chicopee, Ga., U.S. **B3** 103
Chicopee, Ma., U.S. **B2** 114
Chicora, Pa., U.S. **E2** 131
Chicot, Lake, l., Ar., U.S. . . **D4** 97
Chicot Island, i., La., U.S. . **E6** 111
Chicoutimi, P.Q., Can. . . . **A6** 90
Chicoutimi, stm., P.Q., Can. **A6** 90
Chidambaram, India **G3** 40
Chiefland, Fl., U.S. **C4** 102
Chieti, Italy **C5** 18
Chiefeng, China **C11** 28
Chignecto, Cape, c., N.S.,
　Can. **D5** 87
Chignecto Bay, b., Can. . . **D5** 87
Chigubo, Moz. **C5** 56
Chihli, Gulf of see Bo Hai,
　b., China **D11** 28
Chihuahua, Mex. **B3** 78
Chihuahua, state, Mex. . . **B3** 78
Chihuahuan Desert, des.,
　N.A. **A3** 78
Chikaskia, stm., U.S. **A4** 129
Chik Ballāpur, India **G3** 40
Chikmagalūr, India **G3** 40
Chilās, Pak. **C10** 42
Childersburg, Al., U.S. . . . **B3** 94
Childress, Tx., U.S. **B2** 136
Childress, co., Tx., U.S. . . . **B2** 136
Chile, ctry., S.A. **D2** 69
Chile Rise **L29** 64
Chilecito, Arg. **D4** 72
Chilhowie, Va., U.S. **f10** 139
Chililabombwe, Zam. **A4** 56
Chilko, stm., B.C., Can. . . . **D6** 85
Chilko Lake, l., B.C., Can. . **D5** 85
Chillán, Chile **E2** 69
Chillicothe, Il., U.S. **C4** 106
Chillicothe, Mo., U.S. **B4** 118
Chillicothe, Oh., U.S. **C3** 128
Chilliwack, B.C., Can. **E7** 85
Chillum, Md., U.S. **f9** 113
Chiloé, Isla Grande de, i.,
　Chile **F2** 69
Chiloquin, Or., U.S. **E5** 130
Chilpancingo de los Bravo,
　Mex. **D5** 78
Chilton, Wi., U.S. **D5** 142
Chilton, co., Al., U.S. **C3** 94
Chiluage, Ang. **E4** 54
Chilung, Tai. **D5** 30
Chimacum, Wa., U.S. **A3** 140
Chimayo, N.M., U.S. **A4** 124
Chimborazo, vol., Ec. **D4** 70
Chimbote, Peru **E4** 70
Chimney Rock, mtn., Ne.,
　U.S. **C2** 120
Chimoio, Moz. **B5** 56
China, ctry., Asia **D8** 28
China Grove, N.C., U.S. . . **B2** 126
China Lake, l., Me., U.S. . . **D3** 112
Chinandega, Nic. **C2** 80
Chincha Alta, Peru **F4** 70
Chinchilla, Austl. **F5** 62
Chincoteague, Va., U.S. . . **C7** 139
Chincoteague Bay, b., U.S. **D7** 113
Chinde, Moz. **B6** 56
Chindwin, stm., Myan. . . . **A3** 34
Chingola, Zam. **A4** 56
Chinguetti, Maur. **B2** 50
Chin Hills, hills, Myan. . . . **A2** 34
Chinhoyi, Zimb. **B5** 56
Chinitna Point, c., Ak., U.S. **h15** 95
Chinju, S. Kor. **D13** 28
Chinle, Az., U.S. **A6** 96

Chino, Ca., U.S. **F5** 98
Chinook, Mt., U.S. **B7** 119
Chinook, Wa., U.S. **C2** 140
Chinook, Lake, res., Or.,
　U.S. **C5** 130
Chino Valley, Az., U.S. . . . **C3** 96
Chinsali, Zam. **A5** 56
Chioco, Moz. **B5** 56
Chioggia, Italy **B4** 18
Chios see Khíos, Grc. **E11** 18
Chipata, Zam. **A5** 56
Chipita Park, Co., U.S. . . . **C6** 99
Chipley, Fl., U.S. **u16** 102
Chipman, N.B., Can. **C4** 87
Chipola, stm., Fl., U.S. . . . **B1** 102
Chippewa, co., Mi., U.S. . . **B6** 115
Chippewa, co., Mn., U.S. . **E3** 116
Chippewa, co., Wi., U.S. . . **C2** 142
Chippewa, stm., Mn., U.S. **E3** 116
Chippewa, stm., Wi., U.S. . **D2** 142
Chippewa, Lake, l., Wi.,
　U.S. **C2** 142
Chippewa Falls, Wi., U.S. . **D2** 142
Chipuxet, stm., R.I., U.S. . **F3** 132
Chiquimula, Guat. **C2** 80
Chiquinquirá, Col. **B5** 70
Chīrāla, India **F4** 40
Chirfa, Niger **B7** 50
Chiricahua Mountains, mts.,
　Az., U.S. **E6** 96
Chiricahua National
　Monument, Az., U.S. . . . **F6** 96
Chiricahua Peak, mtn., Az.,
　U.S. **F6** 96
Chirikof Island, i., Ak., U.S. **D8** 95
Chiriquí, Golfo de, b., Pan. **D3** 80
Chiriquí, Laguna de, b.,
　Pan. **D3** 80
Chiromo, Mwi. **B6** 56
Chirripó, Cerro, mtn., C.R. **D3** 80
Chisago, co., Mn., U.S. . . . **E6** 116
Chisago City, Mn., U.S. . . **E6** 116
Ch'ishan, Tai. **E5** 30
Chisholm, Me., U.S. **D2** 112
Chisholm, Mn., U.S. **C6** 116
Chishui, stm., China **D2** 30
Chişinău, Mol. **F10** 20
Chisos Mountains, mts., Tx.,
　U.S. **E1** 136
Chita see Čita, Russia **D13** 26
Chitado, Ang. **B1** 56
Chitato, Ang. **E4** 54
Chitembo, Ang. **F3** 54
Chitina, stm., Ak., U.S. . . . **g19** 95
Chitose, Japan **B4** 31
Chitradurga, India **G3** 40
Chitrāl, Pak. **C10** 42
Chitré, Pan. **D3** 80
Chittagong, Bngl. **E6** 40
Chittaurgarh, India **E2** 40
Chittenden, N.Y., U.S. **B5** 125
Chittenden, co., Vt., U.S. . **C2** 138
Chittenden Reservoir, res.,
　Vt., U.S. **D3** 138
Chittoor, India **G3** 40
Chitungwiza, Zimb. **B5** 56
Chiumbe (Tshumbe), stm.,
　Afr. **E4** 54
Chiume, Ang. **B3** 56
Chivacoa, Ven. **C6** 80
Chivilcoy, Arg. **E5** 72
Chŏam Khsant, Camb. . . . **D4** 34
Chocolate Mountains, mts.,
　U.S. **F6** 98
Chocope, Peru **E4** 70
Choctaw, Ok., U.S. **B4** 129
Choctaw, co., Al., U.S. . . . **C1** 94
Choctaw, co., Ms., U.S. . . **B4** 117
Choctaw, co., Ok., U.S. . . **C6** 129
Choctawhatchee Bay, b.,
　Fl., U.S. **u15** 102
Choctaw Indian
　Reservation, Ms., U.S. . **C4** 117
Choele Choel, Arg. **E3** 69
Chojnice, Pol. **C4** 20
Chókwe, Moz. **C5** 56
Cholet, Fr. **D6** 16
Choluteca, Hond. **C2** 80
Choluteca, stm., Hond. . . . **C2** 80
Choma, Zam. **B4** 56
Chomutov, Czech Rep. . . . **D2** 20
Chon Buri, Thai. **D4** 34
Chone, Ec. **D3** 70
Chong'an, China **D4** 30
Ch'ŏngjin, N. Kor. **C13** 28
Ch'ŏngju, S. Kor. **D13** 28
Chongqing, China **F9** 28
Chongxin, China **D2** 30
Chongzuo, China **G9** 28
Chŏnju, S. Kor. **D13** 28
Chonos, Archipiélago de
　los, is., Chile **G2** 69
Choptank, stm., Md., U.S. **C6** 113
Chornomors'ke, Ukr. **G12** 20
Chortkiv, Ukr. **E8** 20
Chōshi, Japan **C4** 31
Chos Malal, Arg. **F3** 72
Choteau, Mt., U.S. **C4** 119
Chouteau, Ok., U.S. **A6** 129
Chouteau, co., Mt., U.S. . . **C6** 119
Chowan, co., N.C., U.S. . . **A6** 126
Chowan, stm., N.C., U.S. . **A6** 126
Chowchilla, Ca., U.S. **D3** 98
Choybalsan, Mong. **B10** 28

Choyr, Mong. **B9** 28
Chrisman, Il., U.S. **D6** 106
Christchurch, N.Z. **p13** 63c
Christian, co., Il., U.S. . . . **D4** 106
Christian, co., Ky., U.S. . . **D2** 110
Christian, co., Mo., U.S. . . **E4** 118
Christiana, De., U.S. **B3** 101
Christiana, Pa., U.S. **G9** 131
Christiansburg, Va., U.S. . **C2** 139
Christian Sound, strt., Ak.,
　U.S. **n22** 95
Christina, stm., Ab., Can. . **A5** 84
Christina, stm., De., U.S. . **B3** 101
Christina, Lake, l., Mn., U.S. **D3** 116
Christina Peak, mtn., Nv.,
　U.S. **D6** 121
Christmas, Fl., U.S. **D5** 102
Christmas Island, dep., Oc. **I4** 32
Christmas Island, i., Christ.
　I. **F4** 58
Christmas Island see
　Kiritimati, atoll, Kir. . . . **D14** 58
Christmas Lake, l., Or., U.S. **D6** 130
Christmas Ridge **G22** 64
Christopher, Il., U.S. **F4** 106
Chubbuck, Id., U.S. **G6** 105
Chubut, stm., Arg. **F3** 69
Chugach Islands, is., Ak.,
　U.S. **h16** 95
Chugach Mountains, mts.,
　Ak., U.S. **g18** 95
Chugwater, Wy., U.S. **E8** 143
Chugwater Creek, stm.,
　Wy., U.S. **E8** 143
Chuhuív, Ukr. **E14** 20
Chukchi Sea **E5** 82
Chukotsk Peninsula see
　Čukotskij poluostrov,
　pen., Russia **C20** 26
Chula Vista, Ca., U.S. . . . **F5** 98
Chulucanas, Peru **E3** 70
Chumbicha, Arg. **D4** 72
Chumphon, Thai. **D3** 34
Chum Saeng, Thai. **C4** 34
Chunchula, Al., U.S. **E1** 94
Chungking see Chongqing,
　China **F9** 28
Chuntuquí, Guat. **B1** 80
Chupadera Mesa, mtn.,
　N.M., U.S. **D3** 124
Chuquibamba, Peru **B3** 72
Chuquicamata, Chile **B3** 69
Chur, Switz. **A2** 18
Church Hill, Tn., U.S. **C11** 135
Churchill, Mb., Can. **f9** 86
Churchill, co., Nv., U.S. . . **D3** 121
Churchill, stm., Can. **G21** 82
Churchill, stm., Nf., Can. . **h9** 88
Churchill, Cape, c., Mb.,
　Can. **f9** 86
Churchill, Mount, mtn.,
　B.C., Can. **E6** 85
Churchill Falls, wtfl, Nf.,
　Can. **h8** 88
Churchill Lake, l., Sk., Can. **m7** 91
Churchill Lake, l., Me., U.S. **B3** 112
Church Point, La., U.S. . . . **D3** 111
Church Rock, N.M., U.S. . . **B1** 124
Churchton, Md., U.S. **C4** 113
Churchville, N.Y., U.S. . . . **B3** 125
Chūru, India **D2** 40
Churubusco, In., U.S. **B7** 107
Chuska Mountains, mts.,
　Az., U.S. **A6** 96
Chuuk Islands, is., Micron. **D9** 58
Chuvashia see Čuvašija,
　state, Russia **D6** 26
Chuxian, China **C4** 30
Chuxiong, China **F8** 28
Cianjur, Indon. **E3** 36
Cianorte, Braz. **C7** 72
Čiatura, Geor. **A10** 44
Cibecue, Az., U.S. **C5** 96
Cibola, co., N.M., U.S. . . . **C1** 124
Cibolo Creek, stm., Tx.,
　U.S. **h7** 136
Cicero, Il., U.S. **B6** 106
Cicero, In., U.S. **D5** 107
Cide, Tur. **B5** 44
Ciechanów, Pol. **C6** 20
Ciego de Ávila, Cuba **A4** 80
Cienfuegos, Cuba **A3** 80
Cieza, Spain **H6** 16
Çifteler, Tur. **C4** 44
Çiganak, Kaz. **E9** 26
Çihanbeyli, Tur. **C5** 44
Čiili, Kaz. **B9** 42
Čikoj, stm., Asia **D12** 26
Cilacap, Indon. **E3** 36
Çıldır Gölü, l., Tur. **B10** 44
Çilik, Tur. **B11** 42
Cimarron, Ks., U.S. **E3** 109
Cimarron, N.M., U.S. **A5** 124
Cimarron, co., Ok., U.S. . . **e8** 129
Cimarron, stm., U.S. **D8** 92
Čimbaj, Uzb. **B7** 42
Cimljanskoe vodohranilišče,
　res., Russia **E7** 22
Cina, Tanjung, c., Indon. . **E2** 36
Çınar, Tur. **D9** 44
Cincinnati, Oh., U.S. **C1** 128
Çine, Tur. **D3** 44
Cinnaminson, N.J., U.S. . . **D3** 123
Cintalapa, Mex. **D6** 78
Cinto, Monte, mtn., Fr. . . . **C2** 18

Name	Map Ref.	Page

Cintra, Golfe de, b., W. Sah. . . . B1 50
Cipolletti, Arg. . . . E3 69
Čirčik, Uzb. . . . E8 26
Circle, Ak., U.S. . . . B11 95
Circle, Mt., U.S. . . . C11 119
Circle Pines, Mn., U.S. . . . m12 116
Circleville, Oh., U.S. . . . C3 128
Cirebon, Indon. . . . E3 36
Cirò Marina, Italy . . . E6 18
Cisco, Tx., U.S. . . . C3 136
Ciskei, hist. reg., S. Afr. . . . E4 56
Cisnădie, Rom. . . . G8 20
Cispus, stm., Wa., U.S. . . . C4 140
Cissna Park, Il., U.S. . . . C6 106
Čistopol', Russia . . . C9 22
Čita, Russia . . . D13 26
Citlaltépetl, Volcán see Pico de Orizaba, Volcán, vol., Mex. . . . D5 78
Citra, Fl., U.S. . . . C4 102
Citronelle, Al., U.S. . . . D1 94
Citrus, co., Fl., U.S. . . . D4 102
City of Refuge National Historical Park, Hi., U.S. . . . D5 104
City View, S.C., U.S. . . . B3 133
Ciudad Acuña, Mex. . . . B4 78
Ciudad Anáhuac, Mex. . . . B4 78
Ciudad Bolívar, Ven. . . . B7 70
Ciudad Camargo, Mex. . . . B5 78
Ciudad Camargo, Mex. . . . B3 78
Ciudad Constitución, Mex. . . . C2 78
Ciudad del Carmen, Mex. . . . D6 78
Ciudad del Este, Para. . . . D7 72
Ciudad de Libertador General San Martín, Arg. . . . C5 72
Ciudad de México (Mexico City), Mex. . . . D5 78
Ciudad de Nutrias, Ven. . . . D6 80
Ciudad Guayana, Ven. . . . B7 70
Ciudad Juárez, Mex. . . . A3 78
Ciudad Madero, Mex. . . . C5 78
Ciudad Mante, Mex. . . . C5 78
Ciudad Miguel Alemán, Mex. . . . B5 78
Ciudad Netzahualcóyotl, Mex. . . . D5 78
Ciudad Obregón, Mex. . . . B3 78
Ciudad Ojeda, Ven. . . . C5 80
Ciudad Real, Spain . . . H5 16
Ciudad Rodrigo, Spain . . . G3 16
Ciudad Valles, Mex. . . . C5 78
Ciudad Victoria, Mex. . . . C5 78
Ciutadella, Spain . . . G8 16
Civitanova Marche, Italy . . . C4 18
Civitavecchia, Italy . . . C3 18
Çivril, Tur. . . . C3 44
Cizre, Tur. . . . D10 44
C.J. Strike Reservoir, res., Id., U.S. . . . G3 105
Clackamas, Or., U.S. . . . h12 130
Clackamas, co., Or., U.S. . . . B4 130
Clacton-on-Sea, Eng., U.K. . . . E7 12
Claflin, Ks., U.S. . . . D5 109
Claiborne, co., La., U.S. . . . B2 111
Claiborne, co., Ms., U.S. . . . D3 117
Claiborne, co., Tn., U.S. . . . C10 135
Claiborne, Lake, res., La., U.S. . . . B3 111
Clair, N.B., Can. . . . B1 87
Claire, Lake, l., Ab., Can. . . . f8 84
Clair Engle Lake, res., Ca., U.S. . . . B2 98
Clairton, Pa., U.S. . . . F2 131
Clallam, co., Wa., U.S. . . . B1 140
Clallam Bay, Wa., U.S. . . . A1 140
Clam Lake, l., Wi., U.S. . . . C1 142
Clan Alpine Mountains, mts., Nv., U.S. . . . D4 121
Clanton, Al., U.S. . . . C3 94
Clanwilliam, S. Afr. . . . E2 56
Clara City, Mn., U.S. . . . F3 116
Clara Peak, mtn., Az., U.S. . . . C2 96
Clare, Mi., U.S. . . . E6 115
Clare, co., Mi., U.S. . . . E6 115
Claremont, Ca., U.S. . . . m13 98
Claremont, N.C., U.S. . . . B1 126
Claremont, N.H., U.S. . . . D2 122
Claremont, mtn., Ca., U.S. . . . C3 98
Claremore, Ok., U.S. . . . A6 129
Clarence, Ia., U.S. . . . C6 108
Clarence, Mo., U.S. . . . B5 118
Clarence Strait, strt., Austl. . . . C5 60
Clarence Strait, strt., U.S. . . . n23 95
Clarendon, Ar., U.S. . . . C4 97
Clarendon, Tx., U.S. . . . B2 136
Clarendon, co., S.C., U.S. . . . D7 133
Clarendon, stm., Vt., U.S. . . . E2 138
Clarendon Hills, Il., U.S. . . . k9 106
Clarenville, Nf., Can. . . . D4 88
Claresholm, Ab., Can. . . . D4 84
Claridge, Pa., U.S. . . . F2 131
Clarinda, Ia., U.S. . . . D2 108
Clarion, Ia., U.S. . . . B4 108
Clarion, Pa., U.S. . . . D3 131
Clarion, co., Pa., U.S. . . . D3 131
Clarion, stm., Pa., U.S. . . . D3 131
Clarión, Isla, i., Mex. . . . D2 78
Clarion Fracture Zone . . . G25 64
Clarissa, Mn., U.S. . . . D4 116
Clark, N.J., U.S. . . . B4 123
Clark, S.D., U.S. . . . C8 134

Clark, co., Ar., U.S. . . . C2 97
Clark, co., Id., U.S. . . . E6 105
Clark, co., Il., U.S. . . . D6 106
Clark, co., In., U.S. . . . H6 107
Clark, co., Ks., U.S. . . . E4 109
Clark, co., Ky., U.S. . . . C5 110
Clark, co., Mo., U.S. . . . A6 118
Clark, co., Nv., U.S. . . . G6 121
Clark, co., Oh., U.S. . . . C2 128
Clark, co., S.D., U.S. . . . C8 134
Clark, co., Wa., U.S. . . . D3 140
Clark, co., Wi., U.S. . . . D3 142
Clark, Lake, l., Ak., U.S. . . . C9 95
Clark, Point, c., On., Can. . . . C3 89
Clarkdale, Az., U.S. . . . C3 96
Clarkdale, Ga., U.S. . . . h7 103
Clarke, co., Al., U.S. . . . D2 94
Clarke, co., Ga., U.S. . . . C3 103
Clarke, co., Ia., U.S. . . . D4 108
Clarke, co., Ms., U.S. . . . C5 117
Clarke, co., Va., U.S. . . . A4 139
Clarke Island, i., Austl. . . . l4 62
Clarkesville, Ga., U.S. . . . B3 103
Clarkfield, Mn., U.S. . . . F3 116
Clark Fork, stm., U.S. . . . C1 119
Clarks, La., U.S. . . . B3 111
Clarks, stm., Ky., U.S. . . . f9 110
Clarksburg, Md., U.S. . . . B3 113
Clarksburg, W.V., U.S. . . . B4 141
Clarksdale, Ms., U.S. . . . A3 117
Clarks Grove, Mn., U.S. . . . G5 116
Clark's Harbour, N.S., Can. . . . F4 87
Clarks Hill, In., U.S. . . . D4 107
Clarks Hill Lake, res., U.S. . . . E11 92
Clarkson, Ky., U.S. . . . C3 110
Clarkson, Ne., U.S. . . . C8 120
Clarks Summit, Pa., U.S. . . . m18 131
Clarkston, Ga., U.S. . . . h8 103
Clarkston, Mi., U.S. . . . F7 115
Clarkston, Ut., U.S. . . . B3 137
Clarkston, Wa., U.S. . . . C8 140
Clarksville, Ar., U.S. . . . B2 97
Clarksville, De., U.S. . . . F5 101
Clarksville, Ia., U.S. . . . B5 108
Clarksville, In., U.S. . . . H6 107
Clarksville, Tn., U.S. . . . A4 135
Clarksville, Tx., U.S. . . . C5 136
Clarksville, Va., U.S. . . . D4 139
Clarkton, Mo., U.S. . . . E8 118
Clarkton, N.C., U.S. . . . C4 126
Clatskanie, Or., U.S. . . . A3 130
Clatsop, co., Or., U.S. . . . A3 130
Claude, Tx., U.S. . . . B2 136
Clawson, Mi., U.S. . . . o15 115
Claxton, Ga., U.S. . . . D5 103
Clay, Ky., U.S. . . . C2 110
Clay, co., Al., U.S. . . . B4 94
Clay, co., Ar., U.S. . . . A5 97
Clay, co., Fl., U.S. . . . B5 102
Clay, co., Ga., U.S. . . . E2 103
Clay, co., Ia., U.S. . . . A2 108
Clay, co., Il., U.S. . . . E5 106
Clay, co., In., U.S. . . . F3 107
Clay, co., Ks., U.S. . . . C6 109
Clay, co., Ky., U.S. . . . C6 110
Clay, co., Mn., U.S. . . . D2 116
Clay, co., Mo., U.S. . . . B3 118
Clay, co., Ms., U.S. . . . B5 117
Clay, co., N.C., U.S. . . . f9 126
Clay, co., Ne., U.S. . . . D7 120
Clay, co., S.D., U.S. . . . E8 134
Clay, co., Tn., U.S. . . . C8 135
Clay, co., Tx., U.S. . . . C3 136
Clay, co., W.V., U.S. . . . C3 141
Clay Center, Ks., U.S. . . . C6 109
Clay Center, Ne., U.S. . . . D7 120
Clay City, Il., U.S. . . . E5 106
Clay City, In., U.S. . . . F3 107
Clay City, Ky., U.S. . . . C6 110
Clay Creek, stm., S.D., U.S. . . . D8 134
Claymont, De., U.S. . . . A4 101
Claypool, Az., U.S. . . . D5 96
Claysburg, Pa., U.S. . . . F5 131
Claysville, Pa., U.S. . . . F1 131
Clayton, Al., U.S. . . . D4 94
Clayton, De., U.S. . . . C3 101
Clayton, Ga., U.S. . . . B3 103
Clayton, In., U.S. . . . E4 107
Clayton, La., U.S. . . . C4 111
Clayton, Mo., U.S. . . . f13 118
Clayton, N.C., U.S. . . . B4 126
Clayton, N.J., U.S. . . . D2 123
Clayton, N.M., U.S. . . . A6 124
Clayton, N.Y., U.S. . . . A4 125
Clayton, Ok., U.S. . . . C6 129
Clayton, co., Ga., U.S. . . . C2 103
Clayton, co., Ia., U.S. . . . B6 108
Claytor Lake, res., Va., U.S. . . . C2 139
Clear, stm., R.I., U.S. . . . B2 132
Clear Boggy Creek, stm., Ok., U.S. . . . C5 129
Clear Creek, co., Co., U.S. . . . B5 99
Clear Creek, stm., Tn., U.S. . . . C9 135
Clear Creek, stm., Wy., U.S. . . . B6 143
Cleare, Cape, c., Ak., U.S. . . . D10 95
Clearfield, Ky., U.S. . . . B6 110
Clearfield, Pa., U.S. . . . D5 131
Clearfield, Ut., U.S. . . . B3 137
Clearfield, co., Pa., U.S. . . . D5 131
Clear Fork, stm., W.V., U.S. . . . n13 141
Clear Fork, stm., W.V., U.S. . . . D3 141
Clearlake, Ca., U.S. . . . C2 98
Clear Lake, Ia., U.S. . . . A4 108

Clear Lake, S.D., U.S. . . . C9 134
Clearlake, Wa., U.S. . . . A3 140
Clear Lake, Wi., U.S. . . . C1 142
Clear Lake, l., Ia., U.S. . . . A4 108
Clear Lake, l., Ut., U.S. . . . D3 137
Clear Lake, res., Ca., U.S. . . . C2 98
Clear Lake Reservoir, res., Ca., U.S. . . . B3 98
Clear Lake Shores, Tx., U.S. . . . r15 136
Clear Stream, stm., N.H., U.S. . . . g7 122
Clearwater, B.C., Can. . . . D7 85
Clearwater, Fl., U.S. . . . E4 102
Clearwater, Ks., U.S. . . . E6 109
Clearwater, S.C., U.S. . . . E4 133
Clearwater, co., Id., U.S. . . . C3 105
Clearwater, co., Mn., U.S. . . . C3 116
Clearwater, stm., Can. . . . A5 84
Clearwater, stm., Id., U.S. . . . C2 105
Clearwater, stm., Mn., U.S. . . . C3 116
Clearwater Lake, res., Mo., U.S. . . . D7 118
Clearwater Mountains, mts., Id., U.S. . . . C2 105
Cleburne, Tx., U.S. . . . C4 136
Cleburne, co., Al., U.S. . . . B4 94
Cleburne, co., Ar., U.S. . . . B3 97
Cle Elum, Wa., U.S. . . . B5 140
Cle Elum, stm., Wa., U.S. . . . B4 140
Cle Elum Lake, res., Wa., U.S. . . . B4 140
Clementon, N.J., U.S. . . . D3 123
Clemmons, N.C., U.S. . . . A2 126
Clemson, S.C., U.S. . . . B2 133
Clendenin, W.V., U.S. . . . C3 141
Cleona, Pa., U.S. . . . F9 131
Clermont, Austl. . . . E4 62
Clermont, P.Q., Can. . . . B7 90
Clermont, Fl., U.S. . . . D5 102
Clermont, co., Oh., U.S. . . . C1 128
Clermont-Ferrand, Fr. . . . E8 16
Cleveland, Al., U.S. . . . A3 94
Cleveland, Ga., U.S. . . . B3 103
Cleveland, Mn., U.S. . . . F5 116
Cleveland, Ms., U.S. . . . B3 117
Cleveland, N.C., U.S. . . . B2 126
Cleveland, Oh., U.S. . . . A4 128
Cleveland, Ok., U.S. . . . A5 129
Cleveland, Tn., U.S. . . . D9 135
Cleveland, Tx., U.S. . . . D5 136
Cleveland, Wi., U.S. . . . k10 142
Cleveland, co., Ar., U.S. . . . D3 97
Cleveland, co., N.C., U.S. . . . B1 126
Cleveland, co., Ok., U.S. . . . B4 129
Cleveland, Mount, mtn., Mt., U.S. . . . B3 119
Cleveland Heights, Oh., U.S. . . . A4 128
Cleves, Oh., U.S. . . . o12 128
Clew Bay, b., Ire. . . . D2 12
Clewiston, Fl., U.S. . . . F6 102
Cliff Island, i., Me., U.S. . . . g7 112
Clifford, On., Can. . . . D4 89
Cliffside, N.C., U.S. . . . B1 126
Cliffside Park, N.J., U.S. . . . h9 123
Clifton, Az., U.S. . . . D6 96
Clifton, Co., U.S. . . . B2 99
Clifton, Il., U.S. . . . C6 106
Clifton, N.J., U.S. . . . B4 123
Clifton, S.C., U.S. . . . B4 133
Clifton, Tn., U.S. . . . B4 135
Clifton, Tx., U.S. . . . D4 136
Clifton Forge, Va., U.S. . . . C3 139
Clifton Knolls, N.Y., U.S. . . . C7 125
Clifton Springs, N.Y., U.S. . . . C3 125
Clinch, co., Ga., U.S. . . . F4 103
Clinch, stm., U.S. . . . D9 135
Clinchco, Va., U.S. . . . e9 139
Clinch Mountain, mtn., U.S. . . . C10 135
Clingmans Dome, mtn., U.S. . . . D10 135
Clinton, B.C., Can. . . . D7 85
Clinton, On., Can. . . . D3 89
Clinton, Ar., U.S. . . . B3 97
Clinton, Ct., U.S. . . . D5 100
Clinton, Ia., U.S. . . . C7 108
Clinton, Il., U.S. . . . C5 106
Clinton, In., U.S. . . . E3 107
Clinton, Ky., U.S. . . . f9 110
Clinton, La., U.S. . . . D4 111
Clinton, Ma., U.S. . . . B4 114
Clinton, Md., U.S. . . . C4 113
Clinton, Me., U.S. . . . D3 112
Clinton, Mi., U.S. . . . F7 115
Clinton, Mo., U.S. . . . C4 118
Clinton, Ms., U.S. . . . C3 117
Clinton, N.C., U.S. . . . C4 126
Clinton, N.J., U.S. . . . B3 123
Clinton, N.Y., U.S. . . . B5 125
Clinton, Ok., U.S. . . . B3 129
Clinton, S.C., U.S. . . . C4 133
Clinton, Tn., U.S. . . . C9 135
Clinton, Ut., U.S. . . . B3 137
Clinton, Wa., U.S. . . . B3 140
Clinton, Wi., U.S. . . . F5 142
Clinton, co., Ia., U.S. . . . C7 108
Clinton, co., Il., U.S. . . . E4 106
Clinton, co., In., U.S. . . . D4 107
Clinton, co., Ky., U.S. . . . D4 110
Clinton, co., Mi., U.S. . . . F6 115
Clinton, co., Mo., U.S. . . . B3 118
Clinton, co., N.Y., U.S. . . . f11 125
Clinton, co., Oh., U.S. . . . C2 128
Clinton, co., Pa., U.S. . . . D6 131

Clinton, Lake, res., Il., U.S. . . . C5 106
Clinton Lake, res., Ks., U.S. . . . m15 109
Clinton Reservoir, res., N.J., U.S. . . . A4 123
Clintonville, Wi., U.S. . . . D5 142
Clintwood, Va., U.S. . . . e9 139
Clio, Al., U.S. . . . D4 94
Clio, Mi., U.S. . . . E7 115
Clio, S.C., U.S. . . . B8 133
Clipperton, Île, atoll, Oc. . . . G28 64
Clipperton Fracture Zone . . . H25 64
Clive, In., U.S. . . . e8 108
Clodomira, Arg. . . . D5 72
Cloncurry, Austl. . . . E3 62
Clonmel, Ire. . . . D3 12
Cloquet, Mn., U.S. . . . D6 116
Cloquet, stm., Mn., U.S. . . . C6 116
Clorinda, Arg. . . . D6 72
Closter, N.J., U.S. . . . B5 123
Clothier, W.V., U.S. . . . n12 141
Cloud, co., Ks., U.S. . . . C6 109
Cloudcroft, N.M., U.S. . . . E4 124
Cloud Peak, mtn., Wy., U.S. . . . B5 143
Clover, S.C., U.S. . . . A5 133
Cloverdale, Al., U.S. . . . A2 94
Cloverdale, Ca., U.S. . . . C2 98
Cloverdale, In., U.S. . . . E4 107
Cloverport, Ky., U.S. . . . C3 110
Clovis, Ca., U.S. . . . D4 98
Clovis, N.M., U.S. . . . C6 124
Cluj-Napoca, Rom. . . . F7 20
Clute, Tx., U.S. . . . r14 136
Clyde, Ks., U.S. . . . C6 109
Clyde, N.C., U.S. . . . f10 126
Clyde, N.Y., U.S. . . . B4 125
Clyde, Oh., U.S. . . . A3 128
Clyde, Tx., U.S. . . . C3 136
Clyde, Firth of, b., Scot., U.K. . . . C4 12
Clymer, N.Y., U.S. . . . C1 125
Clymer, Pa., U.S. . . . E3 131
Cnossus see Knossós, hist., Grc. . . . G10 18
Coachella, Ca., U.S. . . . F5 98
Coachella Canal, Ca., U.S. . . . F6 98
Coahoma, Tx., U.S. . . . C2 136
Coahoma, co., Ms., U.S. . . . A3 117
Coahuila, state, Mex. . . . B4 78
Coal, co., Ok., U.S. . . . C5 129
Coal, stm., W.V., U.S. . . . C3 141
Coal Branch, N.B., Can. . . . C4 87
Coal City, Il., U.S. . . . B5 106
Coal Creek, stm., Ok., U.S. . . . B6 129
Coaldale, Ab., Can. . . . E4 84
Coal Fork, W.V., U.S. . . . C3 141
Coal Fork, stm., W.V., U.S. . . . m13 141
Coalgate, Ok., U.S. . . . C5 129
Coal Grove, Oh., U.S. . . . D3 128
Coal Hill, Ar., U.S. . . . B2 97
Coalhurst, Ab., Can. . . . E4 84
Coalinga, Ca., U.S. . . . D3 98
Coalmont, Tn., U.S. . . . D8 135
Coalville, Ut., U.S. . . . C4 137
Coalwood, W.V., U.S. . . . D3 141
Coaraci, Braz. . . . D4 74
Coari, Braz. . . . D7 70
Coasters Harbor Island, i., R.I., U.S. . . . E5 132
Coast Mountains, mts., N.A. . . . G13 82
Coast Ranges, mts., U.S. . . . C3 92
Coatesville, Pa., U.S. . . . G10 131
Coaticook, P.Q., Can. . . . D6 90
Coats, N.C., U.S. . . . B4 126
Coats Land, reg., Ant. . . . D2 67
Coatzacoalcos, Mex. . . . D6 78
Cobalt, On., Can. . . . p19 89
Cobán, Guat. . . . B1 80
Cobar, Austl. . . . G4 62
Cobb, co., Ga., U.S. . . . C2 103
Cobb, stm., Mn., U.S. . . . G5 116
Cobble Mountain Reservoir, res., Ma., U.S. . . . B2 114
Cobbosseecontee Lake, l., Me., U.S. . . . D3 112
Cobden, On., Can. . . . B8 89
Cobden, Il., U.S. . . . F4 106
Cobequid Mountains, mts., N.S., Can. . . . D5 87
Cobham, stm., Can. . . . C4 86
Cobija, Bol. . . . F6 70
Cobleskill, N.Y., U.S. . . . C6 125
Cobourg, On., Can. . . . D6 89
Cobourg Peninsula, pen., Austl. . . . C5 60
Cóbuè, Moz. . . . A5 56
Cobun Creek, stm., W.V., U.S. . . . h11 141
Coburg, Ger. . . . E12 12
Coburg, Or., U.S. . . . C3 130
Cocachacra, Peru . . . B3 72
Cochabamba, Bol. . . . B4 72
Cocheco, stm., N.H., U.S. . . . D5 122
Cochin see Kochi, India . . . H3 40
Cochise, co., Az., U.S. . . . F5 96
Cochise Head, mtn., Az., U.S. . . . E6 96
Cochiti Indian Reservation, N.M., U.S. . . . h8 124
Cochiti Reservoir, res., N.M., U.S. . . . B3 124
Cochituate, Ma., U.S. . . . g10 114
Cochituate, Lake, l., Ma., U.S. . . . g10 114
Cochran, Ga., U.S. . . . D3 103
Cochran, co., Tx., U.S. . . . C1 136
Cochrane, Ab., Can. . . . D3 84

Cochrane, On., Can. . . . o19 89
Cochranton, Pa., U.S. . . . C1 131
Cocke, co., Tn., U.S. . . . D10 135
Cockeysville, Md., U.S. . . . B4 113
Cockrell Hill, Tx., U.S. . . . n10 136
Coco, stm., N.A. . . . F8 76
Coco, Cayo, i., Cuba . . . A4 80
Coco, Isla del, i., C.R. . . . D2 80
Cocoa, Fl., U.S. . . . D6 102
Cocoa Beach, Fl., U.S. . . . D6 102
Coco Channel, strt., Asia . . . D2 34
Coco Islands, is., Myan. . . . D2 34
Coconino, co., Az., U.S. . . . B3 96
Cocopah Indian Reservation, Az., U.S. . . . E1 96
Cocos Islands, dep., Oc. . . . F3 58
Cocos Ridge . . . H5 66
Cod, Cape, c., Ma., U.S. . . . C7 114
Codajás, Braz. . . . D7 70
Coden, Al., U.S. . . . E1 94
Codington, co., S.D., U.S. . . . C8 134
Codó, Braz. . . . B3 74
Cody, Wy., U.S. . . . B3 143
Coeburn, Va., U.S. . . . f9 139
Coen, Austl. . . . C3 62
Coeroeni (Corentyne), stm., S.A. . . . C8 70
Coëtivy, i., Sey. . . . i13 57b
Coeur d'Alene, Id., U.S. . . . B2 105
Coeur d'Alene, stm., Id., U.S. . . . B2 105
Coeur d'Alene Indian Reservation, Id., U.S. . . . B2 105
Coeur d'Alene Lake, res., Id., U.S. . . . B2 105
Coeur d'Alene Mountains, mts., Id., U.S. . . . B2 105
Coffee, co., Al., U.S. . . . D3 94
Coffee, co., Ga., U.S. . . . E4 103
Coffee, co., Tn., U.S. . . . B5 135
Coffeeville, Ms., U.S. . . . B4 117
Coffey, co., Ks., U.S. . . . D8 109
Coffeyville, Ks., U.S. . . . E8 109
Coffs Harbour, Austl. . . . G5 62
Coggon, Ia., U.S. . . . B6 108
Cognac, Fr. . . . E6 16
Cohansey, stm., N.J., U.S. . . . E2 123
Cohasset, Ma., U.S. . . . B6 114
Cohasset, Mn., U.S. . . . C5 116
Cohocton, stm., N.Y., U.S. . . . C3 125
Cohoes, N.Y., U.S. . . . C7 125
Cohoon, Lake, res., Va., U.S. . . . k14 139
Cohutta Mountain, mtn., Ga., U.S. . . . B2 103
Coiba, Isla de, i., Pan. . . . D3 80
Coihaique, Chile . . . G2 69
Coimbatore, India . . . G3 40
Coimbra, Port. . . . G2 16
Coipasa, Lago, l., Bol. . . . B4 72
Cojutepeque, El Sal. . . . C2 80
Cokato, Mn., U.S. . . . E4 116
Coke, co., Tx., U.S. . . . D2 136
Cokeville, Wy., U.S. . . . D2 143
Çokurdah, Russia . . . B16 26
Colac, Austl. . . . H3 62
Colatina, Braz. . . . E3 74
Colbeck, Cape, c., Ant. . . . D25 67
Colbert, Ok., U.S. . . . D5 129
Colbert, co., Al., U.S. . . . A2 94
Colborne, On., Can. . . . C7 89
Colby, Ks., U.S. . . . C2 109
Colby, Wi., U.S. . . . D3 142
Colchester, Eng., U.K. . . . E7 12
Colchester, Ct., U.S. . . . C6 100
Colchester, Il., U.S. . . . C3 106
Colcord, Ok., U.S. . . . A7 129
Cold, stm., N.H., U.S. . . . D2 122
Cold, stm., N.H., U.S. . . . C4 122
Cold Bay, Ak., U.S. . . . E7 95
Cold Lake, Ab., Can. . . . B5 84
Cold Spring, Ky., U.S. . . . A5 110
Cold Spring, Mn., U.S. . . . E4 116
Coldwater, On., Can. . . . C5 89
Coldwater, Ks., U.S. . . . E4 109
Coldwater, Mi., U.S. . . . G5 115
Coldwater, Ms., U.S. . . . A4 117
Coldwater, Oh., U.S. . . . B1 128
Coldwater, stm., Ms., U.S. . . . A3 117
Coldwater Creek, stm., U.S. . . . e9 117
Cole, co., Mo., U.S. . . . C5 118
Colebrook, N.H., U.S. . . . g7 122
Colebrook River Lake, res., Ct., U.S. . . . A3 100
Cole Camp, Mo., U.S. . . . C4 118
Coleen, stm., Ak., U.S. . . . B11 95
Coleman, Mi., U.S. . . . E6 115
Coleman, Tx., U.S. . . . D3 136
Coleman, Wi., U.S. . . . C5 142
Coleman, co., Tx., U.S. . . . D3 136
Coleraine, N. Ire., U.K. . . . C3 12
Coleraine, Mn., U.S. . . . C5 116
Coles, co., Il., U.S. . . . D5 106
Colesberg, S. Afr. . . . E4 56
Colfax, Ca., U.S. . . . C3 98
Colfax, Ia., U.S. . . . C4 108
Colfax, Il., U.S. . . . C5 106
Colfax, In., U.S. . . . D4 107
Colfax, La., U.S. . . . C3 111
Colfax, Wa., U.S. . . . C8 140
Colfax, Wi., U.S. . . . D2 142
Colfax, co., Ne., U.S. . . . C8 120
Colfax, co., N.M., U.S. . . . A5 124
Colhué Huapi, Lago, l., Arg. . . . G3 69
Colima, Mex. . . . D4 78

Name	Map Ref.	Page

Colima, state, Mex. D4 78
Colinas, Braz. C3 74
Coll, i., Scot., U.K. B3 12
College, Ak., U.S. B10 95
Collegedale, Tn., U.S. . . . h11 135
College Park, Ga., U.S. . . C2 103
College Park, Md., U.S. . . C4 113
College Place, Wa., U.S. . . C7 140
College Station, Ar., U.S. . C3 97
College Station, Tx., U.S. . D4 136
Collegeville, In., U.S. C3 107
Collegeville, Pa., U.S. . . F11 131
Colleton, co., S.C., U.S. . . F6 133
Collie, Austl. G2 60
Collier, co., Fl., U.S. F5 102
Colliers, W.V., U.S. f8 141
Collierville, Tn., U.S. B2 135
Collin, co., Tx., U.S. C4 136
Collingdale, Pa., U.S. . . . p20 131
Collingswood, N.J., U.S. . . D2 123
Collingsworth, co., Tx., U.S. B2 136
Collingwood, On., Can. . . . C4 89
Collins, Ms., U.S. D4 117
Collins Park, De., U.S. . . . B3 101
Collinsville, Al., U.S. A4 94
Collinsville, Ct., U.S. B4 100
Collinsville, Il., U.S. E4 106
Collinsville, Ms., U.S. C5 117
Collinsville, Ok., U.S. A6 129
Collinwood, Tn., U.S. B4 135
Collipulli, Chile E2 69
Colmar, Fr. C10 16
Colmar Manor, Md., U.S. . f9 113
Colo, i., U.S. B4 108
Cologne see Köln, Ger. . . E10 12
Coloma, Mi., U.S. F4 115
Colombia, ctry., S.A. C5 70
Colombo, Braz. D8 72
Colombo, Sri L. H3 40
Colón, Arg. E5 72
Colón, Cuba A3 80
Colón, Pan. D3 80
Colon, Mi., U.S. G5 115
Colón, Archipiélago de
(Galapagos Islands), is.,
Ec. C2 70
Colonial Beach, Va., U.S. . B6 139
Colonial Heights, Tn., U.S. C11 135
Colonial Heights, Va., U.S. C5 139
Colonial National Historical
Park, Va., U.S. C6 139
Colonie, N.Y., U.S. C7 125
Colorado, co., Tx., U.S. . . E4 136
Colorado, state, U.S. B5 99
Colorado, stm., Arg. E4 69
Colorado, stm., N.A. E5 92
Colorado, stm., Tx., U.S. . . D3 136
Colorado City, Az., U.S. . . A3 96
Colorado City, Co., U.S. . . D6 99
Colorado City, Tx., U.S. . . C2 136
Colorado City, Lake, res.,
Tx., U.S. C2 136
Colorado National
Monument, Co., U.S. . B2 99
Colorado River Aqueduct,
Ca., U.S. F6 98
Colorado River Indian
Reservation, U.S. D1 96
Colorado Springs, Co., U.S. C6 99
Colquitt, Ga., U.S. E2 103
Colquitt, co., Ga., U.S. . . . E3 103
Colstrip, Mt., U.S. E10 119
Colton, S.D., U.S. D9 134
Coltons Point, Md., U.S. . . D4 113
Columbia, Al., U.S. D4 94
Columbia, Il., U.S. E3 106
Columbia, Ky., U.S. C4 110
Columbia, Md., U.S. B4 113
Columbia, Mo., U.S. C5 118
Columbia, Ms., U.S. D4 117
Columbia, N.C., U.S. B6 126
Columbia, Pa., U.S. F9 131
Columbia, S.C., U.S. C5 133
Columbia, Tn., U.S. B4 135
Columbia, co., Ar., U.S. . . D2 97
Columbia, co., Fl., U.S. . . . B4 102
Columbia, co., Ga., U.S. . . C4 103
Columbia, co., N.Y., U.S. . C7 125
Columbia, co., Or., U.S. . . B3 130
Columbia, co., Pa., U.S. . . D9 131
Columbia, co., Wa., U.S. . . C7 140
Columbia, co., Wi., U.S. . . E4 142
Columbia, stm., N.A. B3 92
Columbia, Mount, mtn.,
Can. C2 84
Columbia City, In., U.S. . . B7 107
Columbia City, Or., U.S. . . B4 130
Columbia Falls, Mt., U.S. . B2 119
Columbia Heights, Mn.,
U.S. m12 116
Columbia Lake, res., Ct.,
U.S. C6 100
Columbia Mountains, mts.,
B.C., Can. C7 85
Columbia Mountains, mts.,
N.A. H15 82
Columbiana, Al., U.S. B3 94
Columbiana, Oh., U.S. . . . B5 128
Columbiana, co., Oh., U.S. B5 128
Columbiaville, Mi., U.S. . . E7 115
Columbus, Ga., U.S. D2 103
Columbus, In., U.S. F6 107
Columbus, Ks., U.S. E9 109
Columbus, Ms., U.S. B5 117
Columbus, Mt., U.S. E7 119

Columbus, N.C., U.S. f10 126
Columbus, Ne., U.S. C8 120
Columbus, N.M., U.S. F2 124
Columbus, Oh., U.S. C2 128
Columbus, Tx., U.S. E4 136
Columbus, Wi., U.S. E4 142
Columbus, co., N.C., U.S. . C4 126
Columbus Air Force Base,
mil., Ms., U.S. B5 117
Columbus Grove, Oh., U.S. B1 128
Columbus Junction, Ia., U.S. C6 108
Columbus Lake, res., Ms.,
U.S. B5 117
Colusa, Ca., U.S. C2 98
Colusa, co., Ca., U.S. C2 98
Colver, Pa., U.S. E4 131
Colville, Wa., U.S. A8 140
Colville, stm., Ak., U.S. . . B9 95
Colville, stm., Wa., U.S. . . A8 140
Colville Indian Reservation,
Wa., U.S. A6 140
Colvos Passage, strt., Wa.,
U.S. f10 140
Colwich, Ks., U.S. E6 109
Colwood, B.C., Can. h12 85
Comacchio, Italy B4 18
Comacchio, Valli di, l., Italy B4 18
Comal, co., Tx., U.S. E3 136
Comalcalco, Mex. D6 78
Coman, Mount, mtn., Ant. . D34 67
Comanche, Ok., U.S. C4 129
Comanche, Tx., U.S. D3 136
Comanche, co., Ks., U.S. . . E4 109
Comanche, co., Ok., U.S. . . C3 129
Comanche, co., Tx., U.S. . . D3 136
Comandante Fontana, Arg. . D6 72
Comayagua, Hond. C2 80
Combahee, stm., S.C., U.S. F6 133
Combarbalá, Chile D2 69
Comber, On., Can. E2 89
Combermere Bay, b., Myan. C2 34
Combined Locks, Wi., U.S. h9 142
Combs, Ky., U.S. C6 110
Comer, Ga., U.S. B3 103
Comfort, Tx., U.S. E3 136
Comilla, Bngl. E6 40
Comitán, Mex. D6 78
Comite, stm., La., U.S. . . . D4 111
Commerce, Ga., U.S. B3 103
Commerce, Ok., U.S. A7 129
Commerce, Tx., U.S. C5 136
Commerce City, Co., U.S. . B6 99
Committee Bay, b., N.T.,
Can. E22 82
Common Fence Point, R.I.,
U.S. D6 132
Communism Peak see
Kommunizma, pik,
mtn., Taj. F9 26
Como, Italy B2 18
Como, Ms., U.S. A4 117
Como, Lago di, l., Italy . . . B2 18
Comodoro Rivadavia, Arg. . G3 69
Comores, Archipel des, is.,
Afr. A7 56
Comorin, Cape, c., India . . H3 40
Comoros, ctry., Afr. A7 56
Comox, B.C., Can. E5 85
Compiègne, Fr. C8 16
Compostela, Mex. C4 78
Compton, P.Q., Can. D6 90
Compton, Ca., U.S. n12 98
Comrat, Mol. F10 20
Comstock, Mi., U.S. F5 115
Conakry, Gui. E2 50
Conanicut Island, i., R.I.,
U.S. E5 132
Conanicut Point, c., R.I.,
U.S. E5 132
Concarneau, Fr. D5 16
Conceição da Barra, Braz. . E4 74
Conceição do Araguaia,
Braz. C2 74
Concepción, Arg. D4 72
Concepción, Chile E2 69
Concepción, Para. C6 72
Concepción del Oro, Mex. . C4 78
Concepción del Uruguay,
Arg. E6 72
Conception, Point, c., Ca.,
U.S. E3 98
Conception Bay, b., Nf.,
Can. E5 88
Conception Bay South, Nf.,
Can. E5 88
Conchas Lake, res., N.M.,
U.S. B5 124
Concho, co., Tx., U.S. D3 136
Concho, stm., Tx., U.S. . . . D2 136
Conchos, stm., Mex. B3 78
Concord, Ca., U.S. h8 98
Concord, Ma., U.S. B5 114
Concord, Mi., U.S. F6 115
Concord, Mo., U.S. g13 118
Concord, N.C., U.S. B2 126
Concord, N.H., U.S. D3 122
Concord, stm., Ma., U.S. . . A5 114
Concordia, Arg. E6 72
Concórdia, Braz. D7 72
Concordia, Ks., U.S. C6 109
Concordia, Mo., U.S. C4 118
Concordia, co., La., U.S. . . C4 111
Concrete, Wa., U.S. A4 140
Conda, Ang. F2 54
Condobolin, Austl. G4 62

Condon, Or., U.S. B6 130
Condoto, Col. D4 80
Conecuh, co., Al., U.S. . . . D2 94
Conecuh, stm., U.S. D3 94
Conejos, co., Co., U.S. . . . D4 99
Conejos, stm., Co., U.S. . . D4 99
Conejos Peak, mtn., Co.,
U.S. D4 99
Conemaugh, Pa., U.S. F4 131
Conemaugh River Lake,
res., Pa., U.S. F3 131
Congamond Lakes, l., U.S. . A4 100
Congaree, stm., S.C., U.S. . D6 133
Congaree Swamp National
Monument, S.C., U.S. . D6 133
Congo, ctry., Afr. D3 54
Congo (Zaïre), stm., Afr. . . D2 54
Congo, Democratic
Republic of the, ctry.,
Afr. D4 54
Congress, Az., U.S. C3 96
Conimicut Point, c., R.I.,
U.S. D5 132
Conklin, N.Y., U.S. C5 125
Connaught, hist. reg., Ire. . D2 12
Conneaut, Oh., U.S. A5 128
Conneaut Creek, stm., Oh.,
U.S. A5 128
Conneaut Lake, l., Pa., U.S. C1 131
Connecticut, state, U.S. . . . C5 100
Connecticut, stm., U.S. . . . C5 100
Connell, Wa., U.S. C7 140
Connellsville, Pa., U.S. . . . F2 131
Connersville, In., U.S. E7 107
Conover, N.C., U.S. B1 126
Conowingo, Md., U.S. A5 113
Conrad, Ia., U.S. B5 108
Conrad, Mt., U.S. B5 119
Conroe, Tx., U.S. D5 136
Conselheiro Lafaiete, Braz. . F3 74
Conselheiro Pena, Braz. . . E3 74
Conshohocken, Pa., U.S. . . F11 131
Consolación del Sur, Cuba . A3 80
Con Son, is., Viet. E5 34
Consort, Ab., Can. C5 84
Constance see Konstanz,
Ger. G11 12
Constance, Lake, l., Eur. . . A2 18
Constanța, Rom. G10 20
Constantina, Spain I4 16
Constantine see Qacentina,
Alg. C6 48
Constantine, Mi., U.S. G5 115
Constantine, Cape, c., Ak.,
U.S. D8 95
Constantinople see İstanbul,
Tur. B3 44
Constitución, Chile E2 69
Contas, stm., Braz. D3 74
Content Keys, is., Fl., U.S. . H5 102
Continental, Oh., U.S. A1 128
Continental Peak, mtn.,
Wy., U.S. D4 143
Continental Reservoir, res.,
Co., U.S. D3 99
Contoocook, N.H., U.S. . . . D3 122
Contoocook, stm., N.H.,
U.S. D3 122
Contra Costa, co., Ca., U.S. D3 98
Contrecoeur, P.Q., Can. . . D4 90
Converse, In., U.S. C6 107
Converse, S.C., U.S. B4 133
Converse, co., Wy., U.S. . . C7 143
Convoy, Oh., U.S. B1 128
Conway, Ar., U.S. B3 97
Conway, Fl., U.S. D5 102
Conway, Mo., U.S. D5 118
Conway, N.C., U.S. A5 126
Conway, N.H., U.S. C4 122
Conway, Pa., U.S. E1 131
Conway, S.C., U.S. D9 133
Conway, co., Ar., U.S. B3 97
Conway, Lake, res., Ar.,
U.S. B3 97
Conway Lake, l., N.H., U.S. C4 122
Conway Springs, Ks., U.S. . E6 109
Conyers, Ga., U.S. C2 103
Coober Pedy, Austl. F5 60
Cook, Mn., U.S. C6 116
Cook, co., Ga., U.S. E3 103
Cook, co., Il., U.S. B6 106
Cook, co., Mn., U.S. k9 116
Cook, Cape, c., B.C., Can. . D4 85
Cook, Mount, mtn., N.Z. . . p12 63c
Cooke, co., Tx., U.S. C4 136
Cookes Peak, mtn., N.M.,
U.S. E2 124
Cookeville, Tn., U.S. C8 135
Cook Inlet, b., Ak., U.S. . . D9 95
Cook Islands, dep., Oc. . . . F13 58
Cook Point, c., Md., U.S. . . C5 113
Cookshire, P.Q., Can. D6 90
Cookson, Ok., U.S. B7 129
Cook Strait, strt., N.Z. . . . p13 63c
Cooktown, Austl. D4 62
Cooleemee, N.C., U.S. . . . B2 126
Coolgardie, Austl. G3 60
Coolidge, Az., U.S. E4 96
Coolidge, Ga., U.S. E3 103
Cooma, Austl. H4 62
Coonabarabran, Austl. . . . G4 62
Coonamble, Austl. G4 62
Coonoor, India G3 40
Coon Rapids, Ia., U.S. . . . C3 108
Coon Rapids, Mn., U.S. . . E5 116

Coon Valley, Wi., U.S. . . . E2 142
Cooper, Tx., U.S. C5 136
Cooper, co., Mo., U.S. C5 118
Cooper, stm., S.C., U.S. . . F8 133
Cooper Creek, stm., Austl. . F2 60
Cooper Mountain, mtn.,
Ak., U.S. g17 95
Coopersburg, Pa., U.S. . . . F11 131
Cooperstown, N.D., U.S. . . B7 127
Cooperstown, N.Y., U.S. . . C6 125
Coopersville, Mi., U.S. . . . E5 115
Coorow, Austl. F2 60
Coos, co., N.H., U.S. A4 122
Coos, co., Or., U.S. D2 130
Coos, stm., Or., U.S. D2 130
Coosa, co., Al., U.S. C3 94
Coosa, stm., U.S. C3 94
Coosada, Al., U.S. C3 94
Coosawhatchie, stm., S.C.,
U.S. F5 133
Coos Bay, Or., U.S. D2 130
Cootamundra, Austl. G4 62
Copalis Beach, Wa., U.S. . B1 140
Copan, Ok., U.S. A6 129
Copan Reservoir, res., Ok.,
U.S. A6 129
Copenhagen see
København, Den. I5 10
Copiah, co., Ms., U.S. D3 117
Copiapó, Chile C2 69
Coplay, Pa., U.S. E10 131
Copper, stm., Ak., U.S. . . . C11 95
Copperas Cove, Tx., U.S. . D4 136
Copper Butte, mtn., Wa.,
U.S. A7 140
Copper Mountain, mtn.,
Wy., U.S. C5 143
Copper Mountains, mts.,
Az., U.S. E2 96
Coquille, Or., U.S. D2 130
Coquimbo, Chile C2 69
Corabia, Rom. H8 20
Coral Gables, Fl., U.S. . . . G6 102
Coral Sea, Oc. F9 58
Coral Sea Basin J18 64
Coralville, Ia., U.S. C6 108
Coralville Lake, res., Ia.,
U.S. C5 108
Coraopolis, Pa., U.S. E1 131
Corbeil-Essonnes, Fr. C8 16
Corbin, Ky., U.S. D5 110
Corcoran, Ca., U.S. D4 98
Corcoran, Mn., U.S. m11 116
Corcovado, Golfo, b., Chile F2 69
Corcovado, Volcán, vol.,
Chile F2 69
Cordele, Ga., U.S. E3 103
Cordell, Ok., U.S. B3 129
Cordell Hull Lake, res., Tn.,
U.S. C8 135
Córdoba, Arg. E5 72
Córdoba, Mex. D5 78
Córdoba, Spain I4 16
Córdova, Peru A2 72
Cordova see Córdoba,
Spain I4 16
Cordova, Ak., U.S. C10 95
Cordova, Al., U.S. B2 94
Cordova, N.C., U.S. C3 126
Cordova, N.M., U.S. A4 124
Cordova Peak, mtn., Ak.,
U.S. C10 95
Corentyne (Coeroeni), stm.,
S.A. C8 70
Corfu see Kérkira, Grc. . . . E7 18
Corfu see Kérkira, i., Grc. . E7 18
Coria, Spain H3 16
Corinna, Me., U.S. D3 112
Corinne, Ut., U.S. B3 137
Corinne Key, i., Fl., U.S. . . G6 102
Corinth see Kórinthos, Grc. F9 18
Corinth, Ms., U.S. A5 117
Corinth, N.Y., U.S. B7 125
Corinth, Gulf of see
Korinthiakós Kólpos, b.,
Grc. E9 18
Corinto, Braz. E3 74
Corisco, Isla de, i., Eq. Gui. C1 54
Cork, Ire. E2 12
Çorlu, Tur. B2 44
Cormorant Lake, l., Mb.,
Can. B1 86
Cornelia, Ga., U.S. B3 103
Cornélio Procópio, Braz. . . F1 74
Cornelius, N.C., U.S. B2 126
Cornelius, Or., U.S. g11 130
Cornell, Wi., U.S. C2 142
Corner Brook, Nf., Can. . . D3 88
Cornersville, Tn., U.S. B5 135
Cornfield Point, c., Ct., U.S. D6 100
Cornie Bayou, stm., U.S. . . D3 97
Corning, Ar., U.S. A5 97
Corning, Ca., U.S. C2 98
Corning, Ia., U.S. D3 108
Corning, N.Y., U.S. C3 125
Cornish, Me., U.S. E2 112
Corno Grande, mtn., Italy . C4 18
Cornville, Az., U.S. C4 96
Cornwall, On., Can. B10 89
Cornwall, Pa., U.S. F9 131
Cornwall, hist. reg., Eng.,
U.K. E4 12
Cornwall on Hudson, N.Y.,
U.S. D6 125
Coro, Ven. A6 70

Coroatá, Braz. B3 74
Corocoro Island, i., S.A. . . D7 80
Čoroh, stm., Asia B9 44
Coroico, Bol. B4 72
Coromandel Coast, India . G4 40
Corona, Ca., U.S. F5 98
Coronado, Ca., U.S. F5 98
Coronado, Bahía de, b.,
C.R. D3 80
Coronado National
Memorial, Az., U.S. . . F5 96
Coronation, Ab., Can. C5 84
Coronation Gulf, b., N.T.,
Can. E17 82
Coronation Island, i., B.A. . B36 67
Coronation Island, i., Ak.,
U.S. n22 95
Coronel Murta, Braz. B9 72
Coronel Oviedo, Para. D6 72
Coronel Suárez, Arg. F5 72
Coronel Vivida, Braz. D7 72
Coropuna, Nevado, vol.,
Peru G5 70
Corozal, Belize B2 80
Corozal, Col. D4 80
Corpus Christi, Tx., U.S. . . F4 136
Corpus Christi Naval Air
Station, mil., Tx., U.S. . F4 136
Correctionville, Ia., U.S. . . B2 108
Correntina, Braz. A9 72
Corrib, Lough, l., Ire. D2 12
Corrientes, Arg. D6 72
Corrientes, Cabo, c., Col. . B4 80
Corrientes, Cabo, c., Mex. . C3 78
Corrigan, Tx., U.S. D5 136
Corriganville, Md., U.S. . . k13 113
Corrigin, Austl. G2 60
Corriverton, Guy. B8 70
Corry, Pa., U.S. C2 131
Corse (Corsica), i., Fr. C2 18
Corse, Cap, c., Fr. C2 18
Corsica, S.D., U.S. D7 134
Corsica see Corse, i., Fr. . . C2 18
Corsicana, Tx., U.S. C4 136
Corson, co., S.D., U.S. . . . B4 134
Corson Inlet, b., N.J., U.S. . E3 123
Cort Adelaer, Kap, c.,
Grnld. F31 82
Corte, Fr. C2 18
Cortés, Mar de see
California, Golfo de, b.,
Mex. B2 78
Cortez, Co., U.S. D2 99
Cortez, Fl., U.S. q10 102
Cortez, Sea of see
California, Golfo de, b.,
Mex. B2 78
Cortez Mountains, mts.,
Nv., U.S. C5 121
Cortland, Il., U.S. B5 106
Cortland, N.Y., U.S. C4 125
Cortland, Oh., U.S. A5 128
Cortland, co., N.Y., U.S. . . C4 125
Çorum, Tur. B6 44
Corumbá, Braz. G8 70
Corunna see A Coruña,
Spain F2 16
Corunna, Mi., U.S. F6 115
Coruripe, Braz. D4 74
Corvallis, Or., U.S. C3 130
Corydon, Ia., U.S. D4 108
Corydon, In., U.S. H5 107
Corydon, Ky., U.S. C2 110
Coryell, co., Tx., U.S. D4 136
Cos see Kos, i., Grc. F11 18
Cosenza, Italy E6 18
Coshocton, Oh., U.S. B4 128
Coshocton, co., Oh., U.S. . B4 128
Cosmoledo, Atoll de, i.,
Sey. i11 57b
Cosmopolis, Wa., U.S. . . . C2 140
Cosmos, Mn., U.S. F4 116
Cosne-sur-Loire, Fr. D8 16
Cossatot, stm., Ar., U.S. . . C1 97
Costa Mesa, Ca., U.S. n13 98
Costa Rica, Mex. C3 78
Costa Rica, ctry., N.A. . . . F8 76
Costilla, co., Co., U.S. D5 99
Coswig, Ger. E13 12
Cotabato, Phil. E8 34
Coteau-Landing, P.Q., Can. D3 90
Cote d'Ivoire, ctry., Afr. . . E3 50
Cotonou, Benin E5 50
Cotopaxi, vol., Ec. D4 70
Cottage Grove, Mn., U.S. . n13 116
Cottage Grove, Or., U.S. . . D3 130
Cottage Grove Reservoir,
res., Or., U.S. D3 130
Cottam, On., Can. E2 89
Cottbus, Ger. E14 12
Cotter, Ar., U.S. A3 97
Cottle, co., Tx., U.S. B2 136
Cottleville, Mo., U.S. f12 118
Cotton, co., Ok., U.S. C3 129
Cottondale, Al., U.S. B2 94
Cotton Plant, Ar., U.S. . . . B4 97
Cottonport, La., U.S. C3 111
Cotton Valley, La., U.S. . . . B2 111
Cottonwood, Al., U.S. D4 94
Cottonwood, Az., U.S. C3 96
Cottonwood, Ca., U.S. B2 98
Cottonwood, Id., U.S. C2 105
Cottonwood, Mn., U.S. . . . F3 116
Cottonwood, co., Mn., U.S. F3 116
Cottonwood, stm., Ks., U.S. D7 109

Name | Map Ref. | Page

Cottonwood, stm., Mn., U.S. F3 116
Cottonwood Creek, stm., Wy., U.S. C4 143
Cottonwood Falls, Ks., U.S. D7 109
Cotuit, Ma., U.S. C7 114
Cotulla, Tx., U.S. E3 136
Coudersport, Pa., U.S. C5 131
Cougar Reservoir, res., Or., U.S. C4 130
Coulee Creek, stm., Wa., U.S. g13 140
Coulee Dam, Wa., U.S. B7 140
Coulee Dam National Recreation Area, Wa., U.S. A7 140
Coulterville, Il., U.S. E4 106
Counce, Tn., U.S. B3 135
Council, Id., U.S. E2 105
Council Bluffs, Ia., U.S. C2 108
Council Grove, Ks., U.S. D7 109
Council Grove Lake, res., Ks., U.S. D7 109
Council Mountain, mtn., Id., U.S. E2 105
Country Homes, Wa., U.S. B8 140
Coupeville, Wa., U.S. A3 140
Courland Lagoon, b., Eur. B6 20
Courtenay, B.C., Can. E5 85
Courte Oreilles, Lac, l., Wi., U.S. C2 142
Courtland, On., Can. E4 89
Courtland, Al., U.S. A2 94
Courtland, Va., U.S. D5 139
Coushatta, La., U.S. B2 111
Cove Creek, stm., Ut., U.S. E3 137
Covedale, Oh., U.S. o12 128
Coventry, Eng., U.K. D6 12
Coventry, Ct., U.S. B6 100
Coventry, R.I., U.S. D3 132
Cove Point, c., Md., U.S. D5 113
Covilhã, Port. G3 16
Covina, Ca., U.S. m13 98
Covington, Ga., U.S. C3 103
Covington, In., U.S. D3 107
Covington, Ky., U.S. A5 110
Covington, La., U.S. D5 111
Covington, Oh., U.S. B1 128
Covington, Tn., U.S. B2 135
Covington, Va., U.S. C3 139
Covington, co., Al., U.S. D3 94
Covington, co., Ms., U.S. D4 117
Cowan, Tn., U.S. B5 135
Cowansville, P.Q., Can. D5 90
Cowarts, Al., U.S. D4 94
Cow Creek, stm., Wa., U.S. C7 140
Cowee Mountains, mts., N.C., U.S. f9 126
Cowell, Austl. G2 62
Cowen, Mount, mtn., Mt., U.S. E6 119
Coweta, Ok., U.S. B6 129
Coweta, co., Ga., U.S. C2 103
Cow Head, Nf., Can. D3 88
Cowichan Bay, B.C., Can. g12 85
Cow Lakes, l., Or., U.S. D9 130
Cowley, Wy., U.S. B4 143
Cowley, co., Ks., U.S. E7 109
Cowlington, Ok., U.S. B7 129
Cowlitz, co., Wa., U.S. C2 140
Cowlitz, stm., Wa., U.S. C3 140
Cowpasture, stm., Va., U.S. B3 139
Cowpen Mountain, mtn., Ga., U.S. B2 103
Cowpens, S.C., U.S. A4 133
Cowra, Austl. G4 62
Coxim, Braz. G9 70
Coxsackie, N.Y., U.S. C7 125
Cox's Bāzār, Bngl. E6 40
Cox's Cove, Nf., Can. D2 88
Coyuca de Catalán, Mex. D4 78
Cozad, Ne., U.S. D6 120
Cozumel, Mex. C7 78
Cozumel, Isla, i., Mex. C7 78
Crab Creek, stm., Wa., U.S. B7 140
Crab Creek, stm., Wa., U.S. C6 140
Crab Orchard, Ky., U.S. C5 110
Crab Orchard, Tn., U.S. D9 135
Crab Orchard, W.V., U.S. n13 141
Crab Orchard Lake, res., Il., U.S. F4 106
Crabtree, Pa., U.S. F3 131
Crabtree Mills, P.Q., Can. D4 90
Cracow see Kraków, Pol. D5 20
Cradock, S. Afr. E4 56
Crafton, Pa., U.S. k13 131
Craig, Ak., U.S. D13 95
Craig, Co., U.S. A3 99
Craig, co., Ok., U.S. A6 129
Craig, co., Va., U.S. C2 139
Craig Air Force Base, mil., Al., U.S. C3 94
Craig Creek, stm., Va., U.S. C2 139
Craighead, co., Ar., U.S. B5 97
Craigsville, Va., U.S. B3 139
Craigsville, W.V., U.S. C4 141
Craiova, Rom. G7 20
Cramerton, N.C., U.S. B1 126
Cranberry Lake, l., N.Y., U.S. A6 125
Cranberry Portage, Mb., Can. B1 86
Cranbrook, Austl. G2 60
Cranbrook, B.C., Can. E10 85
Crandall, Tx., U.S. n10 136
Crandon, Wi., U.S. C5 142
Crane, Mo., U.S. E4 118
Crane, Tx., U.S. D1 136
Crane, co., Tx., U.S. D1 136
Crane Creek, stm., Oh., U.S. e7 128
Crane Creek Reservoir, res., Id., U.S. E2 105
Crane Lake, l., Il., U.S. C3 106
Crane Lake, l., Mn., U.S. B6 116
Crane Mountain, mtn., Or., U.S. E6 130
Crane Prairie Reservoir, res., Or., U.S. D5 130
Cranford, N.J., U.S. B4 123
Cranston, R.I., U.S. C4 132
Crater Lake, l., Or., U.S. E4 130
Crater Lake National Park, Or., U.S. E4 130
Craters of the Moon National Monument, Id., U.S. F5 105
Crateús, Braz. C3 74
Crato, Braz. C4 74
Craven, co., N.C., U.S. B5 126
Crawford, Ga., U.S. C3 103
Crawford, Ms., U.S. B5 117
Crawford, Ne., U.S. B2 120
Crawford, co., Ar., U.S. B1 97
Crawford, co., Ga., U.S. D3 103
Crawford, co., Ia., U.S. B2 108
Crawford, co., Il., U.S. D6 106
Crawford, co., In., U.S. H4 107
Crawford, co., Ks., U.S. E9 109
Crawford, co., Mi., U.S. D6 115
Crawford, co., Mo., U.S. D6 118
Crawford, co., Oh., U.S. B3 128
Crawford, co., Pa., U.S. C1 131
Crawford, co., Wi., U.S. E3 142
Crawford Lake, l., Me., U.S. C5 112
Crawford Notch State Park, N.H., U.S. B4 122
Crawfordsville, Ar., U.S. B5 97
Crawfordsville, In., U.S. D4 107
Crawfordville, Fl., U.S. B2 102
Crawley, Eng., U.K. E6 12
Crazy Mountains, mts., Mt., U.S. D6 119
Crazy Peak, mtn., Mt., U.S. D6 119
Crazy Woman Creek, stm., Wy., U.S. B6 143
Creal Springs, Il., U.S. F5 106
Creedmoor, N.C., U.S. A4 126
Creek, co., Ok., U.S. B5 129
Cree Lake, l., Sk., Can. m7 91
Creemore, On., Can. C4 89
Creighton, Ne., U.S. B8 120
Creighton, Pa., U.S. h14 131
Creil, Fr. C8 16
Crema, Italy D4 18
Cremona, Italy D5 18
Crenshaw, Ms., U.S. A3 117
Crenshaw, co., Al., U.S. D3 94
Creola, Al., U.S. E1 94
Cres, Otok, i., Cro. E9 18
Cresaptown, Md., U.S. k13 113
Crescent, Ok., U.S. B4 129
Crescent, Or., U.S. D5 130
Crescent, Lake, l., Wa., U.S. A2 140
Crescent City, Ca., U.S. B1 98
Crescent City, Fl., U.S. C5 102
Crescent Lake, l., Fl., U.S. C5 102
Crescent Lake, l., Or., U.S. D5 130
Crescent Springs, Ky., U.S. h13 110
Cresco, Ia., U.S. A5 108
Cresskill, N.J., U.S. h9 123
Cresson, Pa., U.S. F4 131
Cressona, Pa., U.S. E9 131
Crested Butte, Co., U.S. C4 99
Crest Hill, Il., U.S. k8 106
Crestline, Oh., U.S. B3 128
Creston, B.C., Can. E9 85
Creston, Ia., U.S. C3 108
Creston, Oh., U.S. B4 128
Crestone Peak, mtn., Co., U.S. D5 99
Crestview, Fl., U.S. u15 102
Crestview, Hi., U.S. g10 104
Crestwood, Ky., U.S. B4 110
Crestwood Village, N.J., U.S. D4 123
Creswell, Or., U.S. D3 130
Crete, Il., U.S. B6 106
Crete, Ne., U.S. D9 120
Crete see Kríti, i., Grc. N9 18
Crete, Sea of see Kritikón Pélagos, Grc. G10 18
Creve Coeur, Il., U.S. C4 106
Crewe, Va., U.S. C4 139
Criciúma, Braz. D8 72
Cricket, N.C., U.S. A1 126
Cridersville, Oh., U.S. B1 128
Crimean Mountains see Kryms'ki hory, mts., Ukr. G13 20
Crimean Peninsula see Kryms'kyi pivostriv, pen., Ukr. G12 20
Crisfield, Md., U.S. E6 113
Crisp, co., Ga., U.S. E3 103
Cristalândia, Braz. F10 70
Cristalina, Braz. E2 74
Cristóbal Colón, Pico, mtn., Col. A5 70
Crittenden, Ky., U.S. B5 110
Crittenden, co., Ar., U.S. B5 97
Crittenden, co., Ky., U.S. e9 110
Crivitz, Wi., U.S. C6 142
Crna Gora (Montenegro), prov., Yugo. C7 18
Croatia, ctry., Eur. B5 18
Crocker, Mo., U.S. D5 118
Crockett, Ca., U.S. g8 98
Crockett, Tx., U.S. D5 136
Crockett, co., Tn., U.S. B2 135
Crockett, co., Tx., U.S. D2 136
Crofton, Ky., U.S. C2 110
Crofton, Md., U.S. B4 113
Crofton, Ne., U.S. B8 120
Croix, Lac la, l., Mn., U.S. B6 116
Croker, Cape, c., Austl. C5 60
Croker, Cape, c., On., Can. C4 89
Croker Island, i., Austl. C5 60
Cromona, Ky., U.S. C7 110
Cromwell, Ct., U.S. C5 100
Crook, co., Or., U.S. C6 130
Crook, co., Wy., U.S. B8 143
Crooked, stm., Or., U.S. C6 130
Crooked Creek, stm., Pa., U.S. C7 131
Crooked Creek, stm., U.S. E3 109
Crooked Creek Lake, res., Pa., U.S. E3 131
Crooked Island, i., Bah. D10 76
Crooked Island Passage, strt., Bah. A5 80
Crooked Lake, l., Fl., U.S. E5 102
Crooked Lake, l., Mn., U.S. B7 116
Crooks, S.D., U.S. D9 134
Crooks Lake, l., Nv., U.S. B2 121
Crookston, Mn., U.S. C2 116
Crooksville, Oh., U.S. C3 128
Crosby, Mn., U.S. D5 116
Crosby, N.D., U.S. A2 127
Crosby, Tx., U.S. r14 136
Crosby, co., Tx., U.S. C2 136
Crosby, Mount, mtn., Wy., U.S. C3 143
Crosbyton, Tx., U.S. C2 136
Cross, co., Ar., U.S. B5 97
Cross Bay, b., Mb., Can. C2 86
Cross City, Fl., U.S. C3 102
Cross Creek, stm., W.V., U.S. f8 141
Crossett, Ar., U.S. D4 97
Crossfield, Ab., Can. D3 84
Cross Island, i., Me., U.S. D5 112
Cross Lake, Mb., Can. B3 86
Crosslake, Mn., U.S. D4 116
Cross Lake, l., Me., U.S. A4 112
Cross Lake, res., La., U.S. B2 111
Cross Lanes, W.V., U.S. C3 141
Crossman Peak, mtn., Az., U.S. C1 96
Cross Plains, Tn., U.S. A5 135
Cross Plains, Tx., U.S. C3 136
Cross Plains, Wi., U.S. E4 142
Cross Sound, strt., Ak., U.S. k21 95
Crossville, Al., U.S. A4 94
Crossville, Il., U.S. E5 106
Crossville, Tn., U.S. D8 135
Croswell, Mi., U.S. E8 115
Crothersville, In., U.S. G6 107
Crotone, Italy E6 18
Croton-on-Hudson, N.Y., U.S. D7 125
Crouse, N.C., U.S. B1 126
Crow, stm., Mn., U.S. F4 116
Crow Agency, Mt., U.S. E9 119
Crow Creek, stm., U.S. A6 99
Crow Creek Indian Reservation, S.D., U.S. C6 134
Crowder, Ms., U.S. A3 117
Crowell, Tx., U.S. C3 136
Crow Indian Reservation, Mt., U.S. E9 119
Crowley, La., U.S. D3 111
Crowley, Tx., U.S. n9 136
Crowley, co., Co., U.S. C7 99
Crowley, Lake, res., Ca., U.S. D4 98
Crowleys Ridge, mtn., U.S. B5 97
Crown Point, In., U.S. B3 107
Crown Point, La., U.S. k11 111
Crownpoint, N.M., U.S. B1 124
Crow Peak, mtn., Mt., U.S. D5 119
Crowsnest Pass, Ab., Can. E3 84
Crowsnest Pass, Can. E3 84
Crow Wing, co., Mn., U.S. D4 116
Crow Wing, stm., Mn., U.S. D4 116
Crozet, Va., U.S. B4 139
Crozet, Archipel, is., Afr. N15 46
Crozet Basin L9 64
Cruces, Cuba A3 80
Crump Lake, l., Or., U.S. E7 130
Cruz, Cabo, c., Cuba B4 80
Cruz Alta, Braz. D7 72
Cruz del Eje, Arg. E5 72
Cruzeiro, Braz. F2 74
Cruzeiro do Sul, Braz. E5 70
Crystal, Mn., U.S. m12 116
Crystal, stm., Co., U.S. B3 99
Crystal Bay, Nv., U.S. D1 121
Crystal Bay, b., Fl., U.S. D4 102
Crystal Beach, Fl., U.S. D4 102
Crystal City, Mb., Can. E2 86
Crystal City, Mo., U.S. C7 118
Crystal City, Tx., U.S. E3 136
Crystal Falls, Mi., U.S. B2 115
Crystal Lake, Ct., U.S. B6 100
Crystal Lake, Fl., U.S. u16 102
Crystal Lake, Il., U.S. A5 106
Crystal Lake, l., Ct., U.S. B6 100
Crystal Lake, l., Mi., U.S. D4 115
Crystal Lake, l., N.H., U.S. D4 122
Crystal Lake, l., Vt., U.S. B4 138
Crystal Lawns, Il., U.S. k8 106
Crystal Pond, res., Ct., U.S. B7 100
Crystal River, Fl., U.S. D4 102
Crystal Springs, Ms., U.S. D3 117
Ču, stm., Asia B10 42
Cúa, Ven. C6 80
Cuamba, Moz. A6 56
Cuando (Kwando), stm., Afr. B3 56
Cuangar, Ang. B2 56
Cuango, Ang. E3 54
Cuango, Ang. E3 54
Cuango (Kwango), stm., Afr. E3 54
Cuanza, stm., Ang. E3 52
Cuauhtémoc, Mex. B3 78
Cuba, Il., U.S. C3 106
Cuba, Mo., U.S. C6 118
Cuba, N.M., U.S. A3 124
Cuba, N.Y., U.S. C2 125
Cuba, ctry., N.A. D9 76
Cuba City, Wi., U.S. F3 142
Cubal, Ang. F2 54
Cubango (Okavango), stm., Afr. B2 56
Cubero, N.M., U.S. B2 124
Çubuk, Tur. B5 44
Cucharas, stm., Co., U.S. D6 99
Cúcuta, Col. B5 70
Cudahy, Wi., U.S. F6 142
Cuddalore, India G3 40
Cuddapah, India G3 40
Cuddy Mountain, mtn., Id., U.S. E2 105
Cue, Austl. F2 60
Cuenca, Ec. D4 70
Cuenca, Spain G5 16
Cuencamé de Ceniceros, Mex. C4 78
Cuernavaca, Mex. D5 78
Cuero, Tx., U.S. E4 136
Cuiabá, Braz. G8 70
Cuilo (Kwilu), stm., Afr. E3 54
Cuima, Ang. A2 56
Cuíto, stm., Ang. B2 56
Cuito Cuanavale, Ang. B2 56
Cuitzeo, Lago de, l., Mex. D4 78
Cuivre, West Fork, stm., Mo., U.S. B6 118
Cukai, Malay. C2 36
Čukotskij poluostrov, pen., Russia C20 26
Čulakkurgan, Kaz. B9 42
Culberson, co., Tx., U.S. o12 136
Culbertson, Mt., U.S. B12 119
Culbertson, Ne., U.S. D5 120
Culebra Peak, mtn., Co., U.S. D5 99
Culfa, Azer. C11 44
Culiacán, Mex. C3 78
Cullen, La., U.S. B2 111
Cullera, Spain H6 16
Cullman, Al., U.S. A3 94
Cullman, co., Al., U.S. A3 94
Culloden, W.V., U.S. C2 141
Cullowhee, N.C., U.S. f9 126
Čul'man, Russia D14 26
Culpeper, Va., U.S. B4 139
Culpeper, co., Va., U.S. B5 139
Culver, In., U.S. B5 107
Culver City, Ca., U.S. m12 98
Culvers Lake, l., N.J., U.S. A3 123
Čulym, Russia D10 26
Čulym, stm., Russia D10 26
Cumaná, Ven. A7 70
Cumberland, B.C., Can. E5 85
Cumberland, Ky., U.S. D7 110
Cumberland, Md., U.S. k13 113
Cumberland, Wi., U.S. C2 142
Cumberland, co., Il., U.S. D5 106
Cumberland, co., Ky., U.S. D4 110
Cumberland, co., Me., U.S. E2 112
Cumberland, co., N.C., U.S. C4 126
Cumberland, co., N.J., U.S. E2 123
Cumberland, co., Pa., U.S. F7 131
Cumberland, co., Tn., U.S. D8 135
Cumberland, co., Va., U.S. C4 139
Cumberland, stm., U.S. D4 110
Cumberland, Lake, res., Ky., U.S. D5 110
Cumberland Center, Me., U.S. g7 112
Cumberland Foreside, Me., U.S. E2 112
Cumberland Gap, U.S. D6 110
Cumberland Gap National Historical Park, U.S. D6 110
Cumberland Hill, R.I., U.S. B4 132
Cumberland Island National Seashore, Ga., U.S. F5 103
Cumberland Lake, l., Sk., Can. C4 91
Cumbres Pass, Co., U.S. D4 99
Čumikan, Russia D15 26
Cuming, co., Ne., U.S. C9 120
Cumming, Ga., U.S. B2 103
Çumra, Tur. D5 44
Cunani, Braz. C9 70
Čundža, Kaz. B11 42
Cunene (Kunene), stm., Afr. B1 56
Cuneo, Italy B1 18
Čunja, stm., Russia C11 26
Cunnamulla, Austl. F4 62
Cunningham, Ky., U.S. f9 110
Cupar, Sk., Can. G3 91
Curaçao, i., Neth. Ant. C6 80
Curanilahue, Chile E2 69
Čurapča, Russia C15 26
Curecanti National Recreation Area, Co., U.S. C3 99
Curepipe, Mrts. g10 57a
Curicó, Chile D2 69
Curitiba, Braz. D8 72
Curitibanos, Braz. D7 72
Curlew Creek, stm., Wa., U.S. A7 140
Curlew Lake, l., Wa., U.S. A7 140
Currais Novos, Braz. C4 74
Currant Mountain, mtn., Nv., U.S. E6 121
Current, stm., U.S. A5 97
Currituck, co., N.C., U.S. A6 126
Curry, co., N.M., U.S. C6 124
Curry, co., Or., U.S. E2 130
Curtea de Argeş, Rom. G8 20
Curtin Springs, Austl. F5 60
Curtis, Ne., U.S. D5 120
Curtis Island, i., Austl. E5 62
Curtisville, Pa., U.S. E2 131
Cururupu, Braz. B3 74
Curuzú Cuatiá, Arg. D6 72
Curvelo, Braz. E3 74
Curwensville, Pa., U.S. E4 131
Curwensville Lake, res., Pa., U.S. E4 131
Curwood, Mount, mtn., Mi., U.S. B2 115
Cusco, Peru F5 70
Cushing, Ok., U.S. B5 129
Cushman, Lake, res., Wa., U.S. B2 140
Čusovoj, Russia C10 22
Cusseta, Ga., U.S. D2 103
Custer, S.D., U.S. D2 134
Custer, co., Co., U.S. C5 99
Custer, co., Id., U.S. E4 105
Custer, co., Mt., U.S. D11 119
Custer, co., Ne., U.S. C6 120
Custer, co., Ok., U.S. B2 129
Custer, co., S.D., U.S. D2 134
Custer Battlefield National Monument, Mt., U.S. E9 119
Cut, Nuhu, i., Indon. E8 36
Cut Bank, Mt., U.S. B4 119
Cut Bank Creek, stm., N.D., U.S. A4 127
Cutchogue, N.Y., U.S. m16 125
Cuthbert, Ga., U.S. E2 103
Cutler Ridge, Fl., U.S. s13 102
Cut Off, La., U.S. E5 111
Cuttack, India E5 40
Cuttyhunk Island, i., Ma., U.S. D6 114
Čuvašija, state, Russia D6 26
Cuvier, Cape, c., Austl. E1 60
Cuxhaven, Ger. D11 12
Cuyahoga, co., Oh., U.S. A4 128
Cuyahoga, stm., Oh., U.S. A4 128
Cuyahoga Falls, Oh., U.S. A4 128
Cuyama, stm., Ca., U.S. E4 98
Cuyamaca Peak, mtn., Ca., U.S. F5 98
Cuyo Islands, is., Phil. D8 34
Cuyuni, stm., S.A. D7 80
C.W. McConaughy, Lake, res., Ne., U.S. C4 120
Cyclades see Kikládhes, is., Grc. F10 18
Cynthiana, In., U.S. H2 107
Cynthiana, Ky., U.S. B5 110
Cypress Creek, stm., Tx., U.S. r14 136
Cypress Hills Provincial Park, Sk., Can. H1 91
Cypress Lake, l., Fl., U.S. D5 102
Cypress Quarters, Fl., U.S. E6 102
Cypress Swamp, sw., U.S. F4 101
Cyprus, ctry., Asia E5 44
Cyprus, North see North Cyprus, ctry., Asia E5 44
Cyrenaica see Barqah, hist. reg., Libya E8 14
Cyril, Ok., U.S. C3 129
Cythera see Kíthira, i., Grc. F9 18
Cythnos see Kíthnos, i., Grc. F10 18
Czech Republic, ctry., Eur. E3 20
Częstochowa, Pol. D5 20

D

Dabajuro, Ven. C5 80
Dabeiba, Col. D4 80
Dabhoi, India E2 40
Dabie Shan, mts., China E11 28
Dabola, Gui. D2 50
Dabou, C. Iv. E4 50
Daboya, Ghana E4 50
Dacca see Dhaka, Bngl. E6 40
Dac Glei, Viet. C5 34
Dachau, Ger. F12 12
Dacono, Co., U.S. A6 99
Dacula, Ga., U.S. C3 103
Dade, co., Fl., U.S. G6 102
Dade, co., Ga., U.S. B1 103

Name	Map Ref.	Page
Dade, co., Mo., U.S.	D4	118
Dade City, Fl., U.S.	D4	102
Dadeville, Al., U.S.	C4	94
Dādra and Nagar Haveli, prov., India	E2	40
Dādu, Pak.	E9	42
Daet, Phil.	D8	34
Dafang, China	D2	30
Dafeng, China	C5	30
Daga Medo, Eth.	B8	54
Dagana, Sen.	C1	50
Dagestan, state, Russia	E6	26
Dagestan see Altaj, state, Russia	A5	28
Daggett, co., Ut., U.S.	C6	137
Dagsboro, De., U.S.	F5	101
Dagu, China	B4	30
Daguan, China	D1	30
Dagupan, Phil.	D8	34
Da Hinggan Ling, mts., China	B12	28
Dahlak Archipelago, is., Erit.	G4	38
Dahlonega, Ga., U.S.	B3	103
Dāhod, India	E2	40
Dahomey see Benin, ctry., Afr.	D5	50
Dahra, Libya	E8	48
Dahūk, Iraq	D10	44
Dailing, China	A1	31
Daingerfield, Tx., U.S.	C5	136
Dairen see Dalian, China	D12	28
Dakar, Sen.	D1	50
Dakhla, W. Sah.	B1	50
Dākoānk, India	H6	40
Dakoro, Niger	D6	50
Dakota, co., Mn., U.S.	F5	116
Dakota, co., Ne., U.S.	B9	120
Dakota City, Ia., U.S.	B3	108
Dakota City, Ne., U.S.	B9	120
Dalälven, stm., Swe.	F7	10
Dalandzadgad, Mong.	C8	28
Dalarna, hist. reg., Swe.	F6	10
Da Lat, Viet.	D5	34
Dālbandin, Pak.	E8	42
Dalby, Austl.	F5	62
Dale, In., U.S.	H4	107
Dale, co., Al., U.S.	D4	94
Dale City, Va., U.S.	B5	139
Dale Hollow Lake, res., U.S.	C8	135
Daleville, Al., U.S.	D4	94
Daleville, In., U.S.	D6	107
Dalhart, Tx., U.S.	A1	136
Dalhousie, N.B., Can.	A3	87
Dalhousie, India	C3	40
Dali, China	F8	28
Dali, China	C2	30
Dalian, China	D12	28
Dall, Mount, mtn., Ak., U.S.	f15	95
Dallam, co., Tx., U.S.	A1	136
Dallas, Ga., U.S.	C2	103
Dallas (part of Melcher), Ia., U.S.	C4	108
Dallas, N.C., U.S.	B1	126
Dallas, Or., U.S.	C3	130
Dallas, Pa., U.S.	D10	131
Dallas, Tx., U.S.	C4	136
Dallas, co., Al., U.S.	C2	94
Dallas, co., Ar., U.S.	D3	97
Dallas, co., Ia., U.S.	C3	108
Dallas, co., Mo., U.S.	D4	118
Dallas, co., Tx., U.S.	C4	136
Dallas Center, Ia., U.S.	C4	108
Dallas City, Il., U.S.	C2	106
Dallas Naval Air Station, mil., Tx., U.S.	n9	136
Dallastown, Pa., U.S.	G8	131
Dalli Rājhara, India	E4	40
Dall Island, i., Ak., U.S.	n23	95
Dalmacija, hist. reg., Eur.	C6	18
Dalmatia see Dalmacija, hist. reg., Eur.	C6	18
Dal'negorsk, Russia	E15	26
Dal'nerečensk, Russia	B14	143
Daloa, C. Iv.	E3	50
Dalqū, Sudan	F11	48
Dāltenganj, India	E4	40
Dalton, Ga., U.S.	B2	103
Dalton, Ma., U.S.	B1	114
Dalton, Oh., U.S.	B4	128
Dalton, Pa., U.S.	C10	131
Dalton Gardens, Id., U.S.	B2	105
Dalupiri Island, i., Phil.	C8	34
Dalvík, Ice.	I19	10a
Dalwallinu, Austl.	G2	60
Daly, stm., Austl.	D5	60
Daly City, Ca., U.S.	h8	98
Daly Waters, Austl.	D5	60
Damān, India	E2	40
Damanhūr, Egypt	E10	14
Damar, Pulau, i., Indon.	E7	36
Damaraland, hist. reg., Nmb.	C2	56
Damariscotta, Me., U.S.	D3	112
Damariscotta Lake, l., Me., U.S.	D3	112
Damascus see Dimashq, Syria	F7	44
Damascus, Md., U.S.	B3	113
Damascus, Va., U.S.	f10	139
Damaturu, Nig.	D7	50
Damāvand, Qolleh-ye, vol., Iran	C6	42
Damba, Ang.	E3	54
Dambarta, Nig.	D6	50
Dāmghān, Iran	C6	42
Damietta, Egypt	E10	14
Damoh, India	E3	40
Damongo, Ghana	E4	50
Dampier, Austl.	E2	60
Dampier, Selat, strt., Indon.	D8	36
Dan, stm., U.S.	D3	139
Dana, In., U.S.	E3	107
Danakil, reg., Afr.	H13	48
Danané, C. Iv.	E3	50
Da Nang, Viet.	C5	34
Danbury, Ct., U.S.	D2	100
Danbury, Tx., U.S.	r14	136
Dandeli, India	F2	40
Dandong, China	C12	28
Dandridge, Tn., U.S.	C10	135
Dane, co., Wi., U.S.	E4	142
Danfeng, China	C3	30
Dangchang, China	C1	30
Dangriga, Belize	B2	80
Dangshan, China	C4	30
Dania, Fl., U.S.	F6	102
Daniels, co., Mt., U.S.	B11	119
Danielson, Ct., U.S.	B8	100
Daniels Pass, Ut., U.S.	C4	137
Danilov, Russia	C7	22
Danlí, Hond.	C2	80
Dannemora, N.Y., U.S.	f11	125
Dannevirke, N.Z.	p14	63c
Dansville, N.Y., U.S.	C3	125
Dante, Va., U.S.	f9	139
Danube, stm., Eur.	C9	14
Danube, Mouths of the, mth., Eur.	G10	20
Danvers, Il., U.S.	C4	106
Danvers, Ma., U.S.	A6	114
Danville, P.Q., Can.	D5	90
Danville, Ar., U.S.	B2	97
Danville, Ca., U.S.	h9	98
Danville, Ia., U.S.	D6	108
Danville, Il., U.S.	C6	106
Danville, In., U.S.	E4	107
Danville, Ky., U.S.	C5	110
Danville, Oh., U.S.	B3	128
Danville, Pa., U.S.	E8	131
Danville, Va., U.S.	D3	139
Danxian, China	F2	30
Danzig see Gdańsk, Pol.	B5	20
Daocheng, China	F8	28
Daoukro, C. Iv.	E4	50
Daoxian, China	D3	30
Dapaong, Togo	D5	50
Dapchi, Nig.	D7	50
Daphne, Al., U.S.	E2	94
Da Qaidam, China	D7	28
Dar'ā, Syria	F7	44
Dārāb, Iran	E6	42
Darabani, Rom.	E9	20
Dārayyā, Syria	F7	44
Darbhanga, India	D5	40
Darby, Mt., U.S.	D2	119
Darby, Pa., U.S.	G11	131
Dardanelle, Ar., U.S.	B2	97
Dardanelle Lake, res., Ar., U.S.	B2	97
Dardanelles see Çanakkale Boğazı, strt., Tur.	C1	44
Dare, co., N.C., U.S.	B7	126
Darende, Tur.	C7	44
Dar es Salaam, Tan.	E7	54
Dargan-Ata, Turk.	B8	42
Dargaville, N.Z.	o13	63c
Darhan, Mong.	B9	28
Darien, Ct., U.S.	E2	100
Darien, Ga., U.S.	E5	103
Darien, Wi., U.S.	F5	142
Dārjiling, India	D5	40
Darke, co., Oh., U.S.	B1	128
Darlag, China	E7	28
Darley Woods, De., U.S.	h8	101
Darling, stm., Austl.	G3	62
Darling, Lake, res., N.D., U.S.	A4	127
Darling Range, mts., Austl.	G2	60
Darlington, Eng., U.K.	C6	12
Darlington, In., U.S.	D4	107
Darlington, Md., U.S.	A5	113
Darlington, S.C., U.S.	C8	133
Darlington, Wi., U.S.	F3	142
Darlington, co., S.C., U.S.	C8	133
Darłowo, Pol.	B4	20
Darmstadt, Ger.	F11	12
Darnah, Libya	D9	48
Darnley, Cape, c., Ant.	C12	67
Darrah, Mount, mtn., Can.	E3	84
Darreh Gaz, Iran	C7	42
Darrington, Wa., U.S.	A4	140
Dart, Cape, c., Ant.	D27	67
Daru, Pap. N. Gui.	H11	32
Darvaza, Turk.	E7	26
Darwin, Austl.	C5	60
Daşhovuz, Turk.	E7	26
Dassel, Mn., U.S.	E4	116
Dastgardān, Iran	D7	42
Date, Japan	B4	31
Datia, India	D3	40
Datil Mountains, mts., N.M., U.S.	C2	124
Datong, China	C10	28
Datong, China	B1	30
Datu, Tanjung, c., Asia	C3	36
Daufuskie Island, i., S.C., U.S.	G6	133
Daung Kyun, i., Myan.	D3	34
Dauphin, Mb., Can.	D1	86
Dauphin, co., Pa., U.S.	F8	131
Dauphin, stm., Mb., Can.	D2	86
Dauphin Island, Al., U.S.	E1	94
Dauphin Island, Al., U.S.	E1	94
Dauphin Lake, l., Mb., Can.	D2	86
Dāvangere, India	G3	40
Davao, Phil.	E9	34
Davao Gulf, b., Phil.	E9	34
Dāvarzan, Iran	C7	42
Daveluyville, P.Q., Can.	C5	90
Davenport, Fl., U.S.	D5	102
Davenport, Ia., U.S.	C7	108
Davenport, Ok., U.S.	B5	129
Davenport, Wa., U.S.	B7	140
David, Pan.	D3	80
David City, Ne., U.S.	C8	120
Davidson, N.C., U.S.	B2	126
Davidson, co., N.C., U.S.	B2	126
Davidson, co., Tn., U.S.	A5	135
Davidsville, Pa., U.S.	F4	131
Davie, Fl., U.S.	F6	102
Davie, co., N.C., U.S.	B2	126
Daviess, co., In., U.S.	G3	107
Daviess, co., Ky., U.S.	C2	110
Daviess, co., Mo., U.S.	B3	118
Davis, Ca., U.S.	C3	98
Davis, Ok., U.S.	C4	129
Davis, W.V., U.S.	B5	141
Davis, co., Ia., U.S.	D5	108
Davis, co., Ut., U.S.	C4	137
Davis, Mount, mtn., Pa., U.S.	G3	131
Davis Creek, stm., W.V., U.S.	m12	141
Davis Dam, U.S.	H7	121
Davis Islands, is., Fl., U.S.	p11	102
Davis Lake, l., Or., U.S.	E5	130
Davis-Monthan Air Force Base, mil., Az., U.S.	E5	96
Davison, Mi., U.S.	E7	115
Davison, co., S.D., U.S.	D7	134
Davis Sea, Ant.	C13	67
Davisstraedet see Davis Strait, strt., N.A.	E28	82
Davis Strait, strt., N.A.	E28	82
Davisville, R.I., U.S.	E4	132
Dawa, stm., Afr.	C7	54
Dawei, Myan.	D3	34
Dawes, co., Ne., U.S.	B2	120
Dawna Range, mts., Myan.	C3	34
Daws Island, i., S.C., U.S.	G6	133
Dawson, Ga., U.S.	E2	103
Dawson, Mn., U.S.	F2	116
Dawson, co., Ga., U.S.	B2	103
Dawson, co., Mt., U.S.	C11	119
Dawson, co., Ne., U.S.	D6	120
Dawson, co., Tx., U.S.	C1	136
Dawson, Isla, i., Chile	H2	69
Dawson, Mount, mtn., B.C., Can.	D9	85
Dawson Creek, B.C., Can.	B7	85
Dawson Springs, Ky., U.S.	C2	110
Dax, Fr.	F6	16
Daxian, China	E9	28
Daxing, China	B4	30
Daxue Shan, mts., China	E8	28
Day, co., S.D., U.S.	B8	134
Dayao, China	A4	34
Dayong, China	D3	30
Dayr az-Zawr, Syria	E9	44
Daysland, Ab., Can.	C4	84
Dayton, Ia., U.S.	B3	108
Dayton, In., U.S.	D4	107
Dayton, Ky., U.S.	h14	110
Dayton, Md., U.S.	B4	113
Dayton, Mn., U.S.	m12	116
Dayton, Nv., U.S.	D2	121
Dayton, Oh., U.S.	C1	128
Dayton, Or., U.S.	B3	130
Dayton, Tn., U.S.	D8	135
Dayton, Tx., U.S.	D5	136
Dayton, Va., U.S.	B4	139
Dayton, Wa., U.S.	C8	140
Daytona Beach, Fl., U.S.	C5	102
Dayu, China	F10	28
Da Yunhe (Grand Canal), China	D11	28
Dayville, Ct., U.S.	B8	100
Dazhu, China	C2	30
De Aar, S. Afr.	E3	56
Dead, North Branch, stm., Me., U.S.	C2	112
Dead, South Branch, stm., Me., U.S.	C2	112
Dead Creek, stm., Vt., U.S.	C2	138
Dead Diamond, stm., N.H., U.S.	g7	122
Dead Indian Peak, mtn., Wy., U.S.	B3	143
Dead Lake, l., Mn., U.S.	D3	116
Dead Lakes, l., Fl., U.S.	B1	102
Deadman Bay, b., Fl., U.S.	C3	102
Deadman Creek, stm., Wa., U.S.	g14	140
Dead Sea, l., Asia	G6	44
Deadwood, S.D., U.S.	C2	134
Deadwood Reservoir, res., Id., U.S.	E3	105
Deaf Smith, co., Tx., U.S.	B1	136
Deakin, Austl.	G4	60
Deale, Md., U.S.	C4	113
Deal Island, Md., U.S.	D6	113
Deal Island, i., Md., U.S.	D6	113
De'an, China	D4	30
Deán Funes, Arg.	E5	72
Dearborn, Mi., U.S.	F7	115
Dearborn, co., In., U.S.	F7	107
Dearborn Heights, Mi., U.S.	p15	115
Death Valley, val., Ca., U.S.	D5	98
Death Valley National Park, U.S.	D5	98
Deba, Nig.	D7	50
De Baca, co., N.M., U.S.	C5	124
Debao, China	E2	30
De Bary, Fl., U.S.	D5	102
Debauch Mountain, mtn., Ak., U.S.	C8	95
Deblin, Pol.	D6	20
Debre Birhan, Eth.	B7	54
Debrecen, Hung.	F6	20
Debre Mark'os, Eth.	A7	54
Debre Tabor, Eth.	H3	38
Debre Zeyit, Eth.	B7	54
De Cade, Lake, l., La., U.S.	E5	111
Decatur, Al., U.S.	A3	94
Decatur, Ar., U.S.	A1	97
Decatur, Ga., U.S.	C2	103
Decatur, Il., U.S.	D5	106
Decatur, In., U.S.	C8	107
Decatur, Mi., U.S.	F5	115
Decatur, Ms., U.S.	C4	117
Decatur, Ne., U.S.	B9	120
Decatur, Tn., U.S.	D9	135
Decatur, Tx., U.S.	C4	136
Decatur, co., Ga., U.S.	F2	103
Decatur, co., Ia., U.S.	D4	108
Decatur, co., In., U.S.	F6	107
Decatur, co., Ks., U.S.	C3	109
Decatur, co., Tn., U.S.	B3	135
Decatur, Lake, res., Il., U.S.	D5	106
Decaturville, Tn., U.S.	B3	135
Decazeville, Fr.	E8	16
Decherd, Tn., U.S.	B5	135
Děčín, Czech Rep.	D3	20
Deckerville, Mi., U.S.	E8	115
Decorah, Ia., U.S.	A6	108
Dedham, Ma., U.S.	B5	114
Dedoplis Ckaro, Geor.	B12	44
Dédougou, Burkina	D4	50
Deep, stm., N.C., U.S.	B3	126
Deep Creek, stm., Ut., U.S.	F3	137
Deep Creek, stm., Ut., U.S.	B3	137
Deep Creek, stm., Ut., U.S.	C2	137
Deep Creek, stm., Wa., U.S.	g13	140
Deep Creek Lake, res., Md., U.S.	K12	113
Deep Creek Mountains, mts., Id., U.S.	G6	105
Deep Fork, stm., Ok., U.S.	B5	129
Deep Inlet, b., Nf., Can.	g10	88
Deep Red Creek, stm., Ok., U.S.	C3	129
Deep River, On., Can.	A7	89
Deep River, Ct., U.S.	D6	100
Deer Creek, stm., Oh., U.S.	C2	128
Deer Creek Indian Reservation, Mn., U.S.	C5	116
Deerfield, Il., U.S.	h9	106
Deerfield, Ks., U.S.	E2	109
Deerfield, Ma., U.S.	A2	114
Deerfield, Mi., U.S.	G7	115
Deerfield, Wi., U.S.	E4	142
Deerfield, stm., U.S.	A2	114
Deerfield Beach, Fl., U.S.	F6	102
Deer Island, pen., Ma., U.S.	g12	114
Deer Island, i., Ms., U.S.	f8	117
Deer Isle, i., Me., U.S.	D4	112
Deer Lake, Nf., Can.	D3	88
Deer Lake, l., Nf., Can.	D3	88
Deer Lake, l., Mn., U.S.	C5	116
Deer Lodge, Mt., U.S.	D4	119
Deer Lodge, co., Mt., U.S.	E3	119
Deer Park, N.Y., U.S.	n15	125
Deer Park, Oh., U.S.	o13	128
Deer Park, Wa., U.S.	B8	140
Deer Peak, mtn., Co., U.S.	C5	99
Deer River, Mn., U.S.	C5	116
Defiance, Oh., U.S.	A1	128
Defiance, co., Oh., U.S.	A1	128
Defiance, Mount, mtn., Or., U.S.	B5	130
De Forest, Wi., U.S.	E4	142
De Funiak Springs, Fl., U.S.	u15	102
Dêgê, China	E7	28
Degeh Bur, Eth.	B8	54
Dégelis, P.Q., Can.	B9	90
Degerfors, Swe.	G10	10
De Graff, Oh., U.S.	B2	128
De Gray Lake, res., Ar., U.S.	C2	97
Dehiwala-Mount Lavinia, Sri L.	H3	40
Dehlorān, Iran	F12	44
Dehra Dūn, India	C3	40
Dehui, China	C13	28
Dej, Rom.	F7	20
Dejnau, Turk.	C8	42
De Kalb, Il., U.S.	B5	106
De Kalb, Ms., U.S.	C5	117
De Kalb, Tx., U.S.	C5	136
De Kalb, co., Al., U.S.	A4	94
De Kalb, co., Ga., U.S.	C2	103
De Kalb, co., Il., U.S.	B5	106
De Kalb, co., In., U.S.	B7	107
De Kalb, co., Mo., U.S.	B3	118
De Kalb, co., Tn., U.S.	D8	135
Dekese, D.R.C.	D4	54
Delafield, Wi., U.S.	m11	142
Delanco, N.J., U.S.	C3	123
De Land, Fl., U.S.	C5	102
Delano, Ca., U.S.	E4	98
Delano, Mn., U.S.	E5	116
Delano Peak, mtn., Ut., U.S.	E3	137
Delārām, Afg.	D8	42
Delaronde Lake, l., Sk., Can.	C2	91
Delavan, Il., U.S.	C4	106
Delavan, Wi., U.S.	F5	142
Delaware, co., Ia., U.S.	B6	108
Delaware, co., In., U.S.	D7	107
Delaware, co., N.Y., U.S.	C5	125
Delaware, co., Oh., U.S.	B2	128
Delaware, co., Ok., U.S.	A7	129
Delaware, co., Pa., U.S.	G11	131
Delaware, state, U.S.	D3	101
Delaware, stm., Ks., U.S.	C8	109
Delaware, stm., U.S.	G11	131
Delaware, East Branch, stm., N.Y., U.S.	C5	125
Delaware Bay, b., U.S.	D13	92
Delaware City, De., U.S.	B3	101
Delaware Lake, res., Oh., U.S.	B3	128
Delaware Water Gap, N.J., U.S.	B2	123
Delaware Water Gap National Recreation Area, U.S.	B2	123
Delbarton, W.V., U.S.	D2	141
Delcambre, La., U.S.	E4	111
Del City, Ok., U.S.	B4	129
De Leon, Tx., U.S.	C3	136
De Leon Springs, Fl., U.S.	C5	102
Delfzijl, Neth.	D10	12
Delgado, Cabo, c., Moz.	A7	56
Delhi, India	C3	40
Delhi, La., U.S.	B4	111
Delhi, N.Y., U.S.	C6	125
Delice, stm., Tur.	B6	44
Delicias, Mex.	B3	78
Delingde, Russia	B13	26
Delingha, China	D7	28
De Lisle, Ms., U.S.	E4	117
Dellenbaugh, Mount, mtn., Az., U.S.	A2	96
Dell Rapids, S.D., U.S.	D9	134
Dellys, Alg.	I8	16
Del Mar, Ca., U.S.	o15	98
Delmar, De., U.S.	G3	101
Delmar, Md., U.S.	D6	113
Delmar, N.Y., U.S.	C7	125
Delmenhorst, Ger.	D11	12
Del Norte, Co., U.S.	D4	99
Del Norte, co., Ca., U.S.	B2	98
Deloraine, Mb., Can.	E1	86
Delos see Dhílos, hist., Grc.	F10	18
Del Park Manor, De., U.S.	i7	101
Delphi, In., U.S.	C4	107
Delphi see Dhelfoí, hist., Grc.	E9	18
Delphos, Oh., U.S.	B1	128
Delran, N.J., U.S.	C3	123
Delray Beach, Fl., U.S.	F6	102
Del Rio, Tx., U.S.	E2	136
Delson, P.Q., Can.	q19	90
Delta, Co., U.S.	C2	99
Delta, Oh., U.S.	A2	128
Delta, Ut., U.S.	D3	137
Delta, co., Co., U.S.	C3	99
Delta, co., Mi., U.S.	C3	115
Delta, co., Tx., U.S.	C5	136
Delta, reg., India	B3	117
Delta Junction, Ak., U.S.	C10	95
Delta Peak, mtn., B.C., Can.	A3	85
Delta Reservoir, res., N.Y., U.S.	B5	125
Deltaville, Va., U.S.	C6	139
Deltona, Fl., U.S.	D5	102
Del Verme Falls, wtfl, Eth.	B8	54
Demarest, N.J., U.S.	h9	123
Demba, D.R.C.	E4	54
Dembia, C.A.R.	B4	54
Dembī Dolo, Eth.	B6	54
Demidov, Russia	B11	20
Deming, N.M., U.S.	E2	124
Demirci, Tur.	C3	44
Demjanskoe, Russia	D8	26
Demmin, Ger.	D13	12
Democratic Republic of the Congo see Congo, Democratic Republic of the, ctry., Afr.	D4	52
Demopolis, Al., U.S.	C2	94
Demorest, Ga., U.S.	B3	103
Demotte, In., U.S.	B3	107
Dempo, Gunung, vol., Indon.	D2	36
Demta, Indon.	G11	32
Denakil see Danakil, reg., Afr.	H13	48
Denali National Park, Ak., U.S.	C9	95
Denan, Eth.	B8	54
Denare Beach, Sk., Can.	C4	91

Name	Map Ref.	Page

Denau, Uzb. **F8** 26
Dengas, Niger **D6** 50
Dengkou, China **A2** 30
Dêngqên, China **E7** 28
Dengxian, China **C3** 30
Denham, Austl. **F1** 60
Denham, Mount, mtn. **B4** 80
Denham Springs, La., U.S. **D5** 111
Den Helder, Neth. **D9** 12
Dénia, Spain **H7** 16
Deniliquin, Austl. **H4** 62
Denison, Ia., U.S. **B2** 108
Denison, Tx., U.S. **C4** 136
Denison Dam, U.S. **D5** 129
Denizli, Tur. **D3** 44
Denmark, Austl. **G2** 60
Denmark, S.C., U.S. . . . **E5** 133
Denmark, Wi., U.S. **D6** 142
Denmark, ctry., Eur. **I4** 10
Denmark Strait, strt. . . . **E34** 82
Dennehotso, Az., U.S. . . **A6** 96
Dennis, Ma., U.S. **C7** 114
Dennison, Oh., U.S. **B4** 128
Dennis Port, Ma., U.S. . . **C7** 114
Denny Terrace, S.C., U.S. . **C5** 133
Dent, co., Mo., U.S. **D6** 118
Denton, Md., U.S. **C6** 113
Denton, N.C., U.S. **B2** 126
Denton, Tx., U.S. **C4** 136
Denton, co., Tx., U.S. . . . **C4** 136
D'Entrecasteaux, Point, c.,
Austl. **G2** 60
D'Entrecasteaux Islands, is.,
Pap. N. Gui. **H13** 32
Dentsville, S.C., U.S. . . **C6** 133
Denver, Co., U.S. **B6** 99
Denver, Ia., U.S. **B5** 108
Denver, Pa., U.S. **F9** 131
Denver, co., Co., U.S. . . . **B6** 99
Denver City, Tx., U.S. . . **C1** 136
Denville, N.J., U.S. **B4** 123
Deoghar, India **E5** 40
Deolāli, India **F2** 40
De Pere, Wi., U.S. **D5** 142
Depew, N.Y., U.S. **C2** 125
Depoe Bay, Or., U.S. . . . **C2** 130
Deposit, N.Y., U.S. **C5** 125
Depue, Il., U.S. **B4** 106
Dêqên, China **F7** 28
Deqing, China **E3** 30
De Queen, Ar., U.S. **C1** 97
De Queen Reservoir, res.,
Ar., U.S. **C1** 97
De Quincy, La., U.S. **D2** 111
Dera Ghāzi Khān, Pak. . . **E10** 42
Dera Ismāīl Khān, Pak. . **D10** 42
Derbent, Russia **E6** 26
Derby, Austl. **D3** 60
Derby, Eng., U.K. **D6** 12
Derby, Ct., U.S. **D3** 100
Derby, Ks., U.S. **E6** 109
Derby, Vt., U.S. **B4** 138
Derby Line, Vt., U.S. . . . **A4** 138
Derg, Lough, l., Ire. **D2** 12
Dergači, Russia **D8** 22
De Ridder, La., U.S. **D2** 111
Derik, Tur. **D9** 44
Derma, Ms., U.S. **B4** 117
Dermott, Ar., U.S. **D4** 97
Dernieres, Isles, is., La., U.S. **E5** 111
Derry see Londonderry, N.
Ire. **C3** 12
Derry, N.H., U.S. **E4** 122
Derry, Pa., U.S. **F3** 131
Derventa, Bos. **B6** 18
Derwood, Md., U.S. **B3** 113
Des Allemands, La., U.S. . **E5** 111
Désappointement, Îles du,
is., Fr. Poly. **F15** 58
Des Arc, Ar., U.S. **C4** 97
Desbiens, P.Q., Can. . . . **A6** 90
Descanso, Mex. **A1** 78
Deschaillons [-sur-Saint-
Laurent], P.Q., Can. . . **C5** 90
Deschambault, P.Q., Can. . **C6** 90
Deschambault Lake, l., Sk.,
Can. **C4** 91
Deschutes, co., Or., U.S. . **D5** 130
Deschutes, stm., Or., U.S. . **B6** 130
Desē, Eth. **H12** 48
Deseado, stm., Arg. **G3** 69
Desengaño, Punta, c., Arg. . **G3** 69
Deseret Peak, mtn., Ut.,
U.S. **C3** 137
Deseronto, On., Can. . . . **C7** 89
Desert Creek Peak, mtn.,
Nv., U.S. **E2** 121
Desert Hot Springs, Ca.,
U.S. **F5** 98
Desert Peak, mtn., Ut., U.S. **B2** 137
Desert Valley, val., Nv., U.S. **B3** 121
Desha, Ar., U.S. **B4** 97
Desha, co., Ar., U.S. **D4** 97
Deshler, Ne., U.S. **D8** 120
Deshler, Oh., U.S. **A2** 128
Des Lacs, stm., N.D., U.S. **A4** 127
Desloge, Mo., U.S. **D7** 118
De Smet, S.D., U.S. **C8** 134
Des Moines, Ia., U.S. . . . **C4** 108
Des Moines, Wa., U.S. . . **B3** 140
Des Moines, co., Ia., U.S. . **D6** 108
Des Moines, stm., U.S. . . **D5** 108
Desna, stm., Eur. **D11** 20
De Soto, Ia., U.S. **C3** 108

De Soto, Il., U.S. **F4** 106
De Soto, Ks., U.S. **D9** 109
De Soto, Mo., U.S. **C7** 118
De Soto, co., Fl., U.S. . . . **E5** 102
De Soto, co., La., U.S. . . . **B2** 111
De Soto, co., Ms., U.S. . . . **A3** 117
Despard, W.V., U.S. **k10** 141
Des Peres, Mo., U.S. . . . **f13** 118
Des Plaines, Il., U.S. **A6** 106
Des Plaines, stm., U.S. . . **k8** 106
Desroches, i., Sey. **i12** 57b
Dessau, Ger. **E13** 12
Destin, Fl., U.S. **u15** 102
Destrehan, La., U.S. **E5** 111
Detour, Point, c., Mi., U.S. **C4** 115
Detroit, Mi., U.S. **F7** 115
Detroit Lake, res., Or., U.S. **C4** 130
Detroit Lakes, Mn., U.S. . **D3** 116
Dettifoss, wtfl., Ice. **l20** 10a
Deuel, co., Ne., U.S. **C3** 120
Deuel, co., S.D., U.S. . . . **C9** 134
Deutsche Bucht, b., Ger. . **C10** 12
Deux-Montagnes, P.Q.,
Can. **p19** 90
Deux Montagnes, Lac des,
l., P.Q., Can. **q19** 90
Deva, Rom. **G7** 20
De Valls Bluff, Ar., U.S. . . **C4** 97
Develi, Tur. **C6** 44
Deventer, Neth. **D10** 12
DeView, Bayou, stm., Ar.,
U.S. **B4** 97
Devils Island see Diable, Île
du, i., Fr. Gu. **B9** 70
Devils Lake, N.D., U.S. . . **A7** 127
Devils Lake, l., N.D., U.S. . **A6** 127
Devils Paw, mtn., Ak., U.S. **k23** 95
Devils Postpile National
Monument, Ca., U.S. . . **D4** 98
Devils Tower National
Monument, Wy., U.S. . . **B8** 143
Devil Track Lake, l., Mn.,
U.S. **k9** 116
Devine, Tx., U.S. **E3** 136
DeVola, Oh., U.S. **C4** 128
Devon, Ab., Can. **C4** 84
Devonport, Austl. **I4** 62
Devonshire, De., U.S. . . . **h7** 101
Devrek, Tur. **B4** 44
Dewar, Ok., U.S. **B6** 129
Dewās, India **E3** 40
Dewees Inlet, b., S.C., U.S. **k12** 133
Dewees Island, i., S.C., U.S. **F8** 133
Dewey, Az., U.S. **C3** 96
Dewey, Ok., U.S. **A6** 129
Dewey, co., Ok., U.S. . . . **B2** 129
Dewey, co., S.D., U.S. . . **B4** 134
Dewey Beach, De., U.S. . . **F5** 101
Dewey Lake, res., Ky., U.S. **C7** 110
Deweyville, Tx., U.S. . . . **D6** 136
De Witt, Ar., U.S. **C4** 97
De Witt, Ia., U.S. **C7** 108
De Witt, Mi., U.S. **F6** 115
De Witt, N.Y., U.S. **B4** 125
De Witt, co., Il., U.S. . . . **C4** 106
De Witt, co., Tx., U.S. . . . **E4** 136
Dexing, China **D4** 30
Dexter, Ia., U.S. **C3** 108
Dexter, Me., U.S. **C3** 112
Dexter, Mi., U.S. **F7** 115
Dexter, Mo., U.S. **E8** 118
Dexter, N.M., U.S. **D5** 124
Dexter, Lake, l., Fl., U.S. . **C5** 102
Dezfūl, Iran **D5** 42
Dezhou, China **D11** 28
Dežneva, mys, c., Russia . **C21** 26
Dhahran see Az̧-Z̧ahrān,
Sau. Ar. **E5** 42
Dhaka, Bngl. **E6** 40
Dhamtari, India **E4** 40
Dhanbād, India **E5** 40
Dhār, India **E3** 40
Dharān, Nepal **D5** 40
Dharmapuri, India **G3** 40
Dhawalāgiri, mtn., Nepal . **D4** 40
Dhelfoí, hist., Grc. **E9** 18
Dhenkānāl, India **E5** 40
Dhílos, hist., Grc. **F10** 18
Dhodhekánisos, is., Grc. . **F11** 18
Dhone, India **F3** 40
Dhoomadheere, Som. . . . **C8** 54
Dhorāji, India **E2** 40
Dhuburi, India **D5** 40
Dhule, India **E2** 40
Diable, Île du, i., Fr. Gu. . **B9** 70
Diablo, Canyon, val., Az.,
U.S. **C4** 96
Diablo, Mount, mtn., Ca.,
U.S. **h9** 98
Diablo, Pico del, mtn., Mex. **A1** 78
Diablo Dam, Wa., U.S. . . **A4** 140
Diablo Lake, res., Wa., U.S. **A4** 140
Diablo Range, mts., Ca.,
U.S. **D3** 98
Diablotins, Morne, vol.,
Dom. **B7** 80
Diaca, Moz. **A6** 56
Dialakoto, Sen. **D2** 50
Diamante, Arg. **E5** 72
Diamantina, Braz. **E3** 74
Diamantina, stm., Austl. . **E3** 62
Diamantino, Braz. **F8** 70
Diamond Harbour, India . **E5** 40
Diamond Head, crat., Hi.,
U.S. **B4** 104

Diamond Hill, R.I., U.S. . . **B4** 132
Diamond Hill Reservoir,
res., R.I., U.S. **A4** 132
Diamond Lake, Il., U.S. . . **h9** 106
Diamond Lake, l., Or., U.S. **D4** 130
Diamond Mountains, mts.,
Nv., U.S. **D6** 121
Diamond Peak, mtn., Co.,
U.S. **A2** 99
Diamond Peak, mtn., Id.,
U.S. **E5** 105
Diamond Peak, mtn., Or.,
U.S. **D4** 130
Diamond Peak, mtn., Wa.,
U.S. **C8** 140
Diamondville, Wy., U.S. . . **E2** 143
Dianbai, China **E3** 30
Dianjiang, China **C2** 30
Dianópolis, Braz. **F10** 70
Diapaga, Burkina **D5** 50
Diaz, Ar., U.S. **B4** 97
Dibaya, D.R.C. **C4** 54
D'Iberville, Ms., U.S. . . . **E5** 117
Diboll, Tx., U.S. **D5** 136
Dibrugarh, India **D6** 40
Dickens, co., Tx., U.S. . . . **C2** 136
Dickenson, co., Va., U.S. . **e9** 139
Dickerson, Md., U.S. . . . **B3** 113
Dickey, co., N.D., U.S. . . **C7** 127
Dickeyville, Wi., U.S. . . . **F3** 142
Dickinson, N.D., U.S. . . . **C3** 127
Dickinson, co., Ia., U.S. . . **A2** 108
Dickinson, co., Ks., U.S. . . **D6** 109
Dickinson, co., Mi., U.S. . . **B3** 115
Dickinson Dam, N.D., U.S. **C3** 127
Dickson, Ok., U.S. **C5** 129
Dickson, Tn., U.S. **A4** 135
Dickson, co., Tn., U.S. . . **A4** 135
Dickson City, Pa., U.S. . . **D10** 131
Dicle see Tigris, stm., Asia **D5** 42
Didao, China **A2** 31
Didiaran, Russia **D15** 26
Didsbury, Ab., Can. **D3** 84
Dīdwāna, India **D2** 40
Diefenbaker, Lake, res., Sk.,
Can. **F2** 91
Diego de Almagro, Isla, i.,
Chile **H1** 69
Diégo-Suarez see
Antsiranana, Madag. . . **A8** 56
Diéma, Mali **D3** 50
Dien Bien, Viet. **B4** 34
Diepholz, Ger. **D11** 12
Dieppe, N.B., Can. **C5** 87
Dieppe, Fr. **C7** 16
Dierks, Ar., U.S. **C1** 97
Di'er Songhua see Songhua,
stm., China **B14** 28
Dif, Kenya **C8** 54
Diffa, Niger **D7** 50
Dighton, Ks., U.S. **D3** 109
Digne, Fr. **E10** 16
Digos, Phil. **E9** 34
Digul, stm., Indon. **H10** 32
Diinsor, Som. **C8** 54
Dijlah see Tigris, stm., Asia **D5** 42
Dijon, Fr. **D9** 16
Dike, Ia., U.S. **B5** 108
Dikhil, Dji. **H13** 48
Dikili, Tur. **C2** 44
Dikson, Russia **B10** 26
Dikwa, Nig. **D7** 50
Dīla, Eth. **B7** 54
Dili, Indon. **E7** 36
Dillard, Or., U.S. **D3** 130
Dill City, Ok., U.S. **B2** 129
Dilley, Tx., U.S. **E3** 136
Dillingham, Ak., U.S. . . . **D8** 95
Dillon, Mt., U.S. **E4** 119
Dillon, S.C., U.S. **C9** 133
Dillon, co., S.C., U.S. . . . **C9** 133
Dillon Lake, res., Oh., U.S. **B3** 128
Dillon Reservoir, res., Co.,
U.S. **B4** 99
Dillonvale, Oh., U.S. **B5** 128
Dillsboro, In., U.S. **F7** 107
Dillsburg, Pa., U.S. **F7** 131
Dilolo, D.R.C. **F4** 54
Dilworth, Mn., U.S. **D2** 116
Dimāpur, India **D6** 40
Dimashq (Damascus), Syria **F7** 44
Dimbokro, C. Iv. **E4** 50
Dimitrovgrad, Bul. **C10** 18
Dimitrovgrad, Russia **D6** 26
Dimlang, mtn., Nig. **E7** 50
Dimmit, co., Tx., U.S. . . . **E3** 136
Dimmitt, Tx., U.S. **B1** 136
Dimondale, Mi., U.S. . . . **F6** 115
Dinagat Island, i., Phil. . . **D9** 34
Dinājpur, Bngl. **D5** 40
Dinan, Fr. **C5** 16
Dinar, Tur. **C4** 44
Dinaric Alps, mts., Eur. . . **G4** 20
Dindigul, India **G3** 40
Dinghai, China **E12** 28
Dingle Bay, b., Ire. **D1** 12
Dingmans Ferry, Pa., U.S. . **D12** 131
Dingolfing, Ger. **F13** 12
Dingtao, China **B4** 30
Dinguiraye, Gui. **D2** 50
Dingxiang, China **B3** 30
Dingxing, China **B4** 30
Dinner Point, c., Fl., U.S. . **D4** 102
Dinokwe, Bots. **C4** 56

Dinosaur National
Monument, U.S. **C6** 137
Dinuba, Ca., U.S. **D4** 98
Dinwiddie, co., Va., U.S. . **C5** 139
Dioura, Mali **D3** 50
Diourbel, Sen. **D1** 50
Dipolog, Phil. **E8** 34
Dīr, Pak. **C10** 42
Diré, Mali **C4** 50
Dirē Dawa, Eth. **B8** 54
Dirico, Ang. **B3** 56
Dirj, Libya **E6** 14
Dirk Hartog Island, i., Austl. **F1** 60
Dirkou, Niger **C7** 50
Dirty Devil, stm., Ut., U.S. **E5** 137
Disappointment, Cape, c.,
S. Geor. **H9** 69
Disappointment, Cape, c.,
Wa., U.S. **C1** 140
Disappointment, Lake, l.,
Austl. **E3** 60
Dishman, Wa., U.S. **g14** 140
Disko, i., Grnld. **E28** 82
Dismal, stm., Ne., U.S. . . **C5** 120
Dispur, India **D6** 40
Disraëli, P.Q., Can. **D6** 90
District of Columbia, dept.,
U.S. **f8** 113
Distrito Federal, state, Braz. **E2** 74
Distrito Federal, state, Mex. **D5** 78
Diu, India **E2** 40
Dīvāndarreh, Iran **E12** 44
Divernon, Il., U.S. **D4** 106
Divide, co., N.D., U.S. . . . **A2** 127
Divide Peak, mtn., Wy.,
U.S. **E5** 143
Divinópolis, Braz. **F3** 74
Divisor, Serra do, plat., S.A. **E5** 70
Divnoe, Russia **A4** 42
Divo, C. Iv. **E3** 50
Diviği, Tur. **C8** 44
Dix, stm., Ky., U.S. **C5** 110
Dixfield, Me., U.S. **D2** 112
Dixie, co., Fl., U.S. **C3** 102
Dixie Valley, val., Nv., U.S. **D4** 121
Dixon, Ca., U.S. **C3** 98
Dixon, Il., U.S. **B4** 106
Dixon, Mo., U.S. **D5** 118
Dixon, N.M., U.S. **A4** 124
Dixon, co., Ne., U.S. **B9** 120
Dixon Entrance, strt., N.A. **H13** 82
Dixonville, Pa., U.S. **E3** 131
Diyarbakır, Tur. **D9** 44
Djado, Plateau du, plat.,
Niger **B7** 50
Djamâa, Alg. **E5** 14
Djambala, Congo **D2** 54
Djanet, Alg. **B6** 50
Djat'kovo, Russia **C13** 20
Djelmila, hist., Alg. **I9** 16
Djenné, Mali **D4** 50
Djibo, Burkina **D4** 50
Djibouti, Dji. **H13** 48
Djibouti, ctry., Afr. **H13** 48
Djoku-Punda, D.R.C. **E4** 54
Djougou, Benin **E5** 50
Djoum, Cam. **C2** 54
Djugu, D.R.C. **C6** 54
Djurtjuli, Russia **C9** 22
Dmitrija Lapteva, proliv,
strt., Russia **B16** 26
Dmitrijev-L'govskij, Russia . **C13** 20
Dnepropetrovsk see
Dnipropetrovs'k, Ukr. . . **E13** 20
Dnepr see Dnieper, stm.,
Eur. **F12** 20
Dnestr see Dniester, stm.,
Eur. **F11** 20
Dnieper (Dnepr) (Dnipro),
stm., Eur. **F12** 20
Dniester (Nistru) (Dnister),
stm., Eur. **F11** 20
Dniprodzerzhyns'k, Ukr. . . **E13** 20
Dniprodzerzhyns'ke
vodoskhovyshche, res.,
Ukr. **E13** 20
Dnipropetrovs'k, Ukr. . . . **E13** 20
Dnister see Dniester, stm.,
Eur. **F11** 20
Dno, Russia **C5** 22
Dôa, Moz. **B5** 56
Doaktown, N.B., Can. . . . **C3** 87
Doba, Chad **E8** 50
Dobbs Ferry, N.Y., U.S. . . **g13** 125
Dobele, Lat. **H10** 10
Doberai, Jazirah, pen.,
Indon. **D8** 36
Dobo, Indon. **H9** 32
Doboj, Bos. **B7** 18
Dobrič, Bul. **C11** 18
Dobrjanka, Russia **C10** 22
Dobruja, hist. reg., Eur. . . **H9** 20
Dobson, N.C., U.S. **A2** 126
Docena, Al., U.S. **f7** 94
Doce, stm., Braz. **E3** 74
Docena, Al., U.S. **f7** 94
Doctors Lake, l., Fl., U.S. . **m8** 102
Doddridge, co., W.V., U.S. **B4** 141
Dodecanese see
Dhodhekánisos, is.,
Grc. **F11** 18
Dodge, Ne., U.S. **C9** 120
Dodge, co., Ga., U.S. . . . **D3** 103
Dodge, co., Mn., U.S. . . . **G6** 116
Dodge, co., Ne., U.S. . . . **C9** 120
Dodge, co., Wi., U.S. . . . **E5** 142
Dodge Center, Mn., U.S. . **F6** 116
Dodge City, Ks., U.S. . . . **E3** 109

Dodgeville, Wi., U.S. . . . **F3** 142
Dodoma, Tan. **E7** 54
Doerun, Ga., U.S. **E3** 103
Doe Run, Mo., U.S. **D7** 118
Dog, stm., Vt., U.S. **C3** 138
Dog Island, i., Fl., U.S. . . **C2** 102
Dog Keys Pass, strt., Ms.,
U.S. **g8** 117
Dog Lake, l., Mb., Can. . . **D2** 86
Do Gonbadān, Iran **D6** 42
Dogondoutchi, Niger **D5** 50
Doğubayazıt, Tur. **C11** 44
Doğu Karadeniz Dağları,
mts., Tur. **B8** 44
Doha see Ad-Dawḩah,
Qatar **E6** 42
Dokka, Nor. **F4** 10
Dokuchaievs'k, Ukr. **F14** 20
Dolbeau, P.Q., Can. **k12** 90
Dole, Fr. **D9** 16
Dolgeville, N.Y., U.S. . . . **B6** 125
Dolinsk, Russia **B16** 28
Dollar Bay, Mi., U.S. . . . **A2** 115
Dolomite, Al., U.S. **B3** 94
Dolomites see Dolomiti,
mts., Italy **A3** 18
Dolomiti, mts., Italy **A3** 18
Dolores, Arg. **E6** 72
Dolores, Co., U.S. **D2** 99
Dolores, Ur. **F6** 72
Dolores, co., Co., U.S. . . . **D2** 99
Dolores, stm., U.S. **E7** 137
Dolphin Island, i., Ut., U.S. **B3** 137
Dolton, Il., U.S. **k9** 106
Dolyns'ka, Ukr. **E12** 20
Dombås, Nor. **E3** 10
Dome Mountain, mtn., Az.,
U.S. **k9** 96
Dome Peak, mtn., Co., U.S. **B3** 99
Domeyko, Chile **C2** 69
Dominica, ctry., N.A. . . . **E12** 76
Dominican Republic, ctry.,
N.A. **H12** 75
Dominique, Canal de la see
Martinique Passage,
strt., N.A. **B7** 80
Domo, Eth. **I14** 48
Dom Pedrito, Braz. **E7** 72
Don, stm., Russia **E6** 26
Dona Ana, N.M., U.S. . . . **E3** 124
Dona Ana, co., N.M., U.S. **E2** 124
Donaldsonville, La., U.S. . **D4** 111
Donalsonville, Ga., U.S. . . **E2** 103
Donau see Danube, stm.,
Eur. **C9** 14
Donauwörth, Ger. **F12** 12
Don Benito, Spain **H4** 16
Dondo, Ang. **E2** 54
Dondo, Moz. **B5** 56
Dondra Head, c., Sri L. . . **H4** 40
Donegal, Ire. **C2** 12
Donegal Bay, b., Ire. . . . **C2** 12
Doneraile, S.C., U.S. **C8** 133
Donets'k, Ukr. **F14** 20
Dong, stm., China **B7** 34
Dong'an, China **D3** 30
Dongara, Austl. **F1** 60
Dongchuan, China **D1** 30
Dongfang, China **H9** 28
Donggala, Indon. **D5** 36
Donghai Dao, i., China . . **G10** 28
Dong Hoi, Viet. **C5** 34
Dongjingcheng, China . . . **B1** 31
Dongo, Ang. **A2** 56
Dongping, China **B4** 30
Dongsheng, China **B3** 30
Dongtai, China **C5** 30
Dongting Hu, l., China . . **F10** 28
Dongzhi, China **C4** 30
Doniphan, Mo., U.S. **E7** 118
Doniphan, Ne., U.S. **D7** 120
Doniphan, co., Ks., U.S. . . **C8** 109
Donkey Creek, stm., Wy.,
U.S. **B7** 143
Donkin, N.S., Can. **C10** 87
Donley, co., Tx., U.S. . . . **B2** 136
Dønna, Nor. **C5** 10
Donna, Tx., U.S. **F3** 136
Donnacona, P.Q., Can. . . **C6** 90
Donnellson, Ia., U.S. **D6** 108
Donner Pass, Ca., U.S. . . **C3** 98
Donnybrook, Austl. **G2** 60
Donora, Pa., U.S. **F2** 131
Donostia (San Sebastián),
Spain **F6** 16
Donskaja grjada, hills, Eur. **E7** 22
Don Upland see Donskaja
grjada, hills, Eur. **E7** 22
Doolow, Som. **J13** 48
Dooly, co., Ga., U.S. **D3** 103
Doonerak, Mount, mtn.,
Ak., U.S. **B9** 95
Door, co., Wi., U.S. **D6** 142
Dora, Al., U.S. **B2** 94
Doraville, Ga., U.S. **h8** 103
Dorcheat, Bayou, stm., U.S. **B2** 111
Dorchester, N.B., Can. . . **D5** 87
Dorchester, Eng., U.K. . . **E5** 12
Dorchester, Ne., U.S. . . . **D8** 120
Dorchester, co., Md., U.S. **D5** 113
Dorchester, co., S.C., U.S. **E7** 133
Dordogne, stm., Fr. **E7** 16
Dordrecht, Neth. **E9** 12
Doré Lake, l., Sk., Can. . . **C2** 91

Name	Map Ref.	Page
Dorena Lake, res., Or., U.S.	D3	130
Dori, Burkina	D4	50
Dorion-Vaudreuil, P.Q., Can.	q18	90
Dormont, Pa., U.S.	k13	131
Dornbirn, Aus.	G11	12
Dorogobuž, Russia	B12	20
Dorohoi, Rom.	F9	20
Dorothy Pond, Ma., U.S.	B4	114
Dorre Island, i., Austl.	F1	60
Dorset, Vt., U.S.	E2	138
Dorsey, Md., U.S.	B4	113
Dortmund, Ger.	E10	12
Dorton, Ky., U.S.	C7	110
Dörtyol, Tur.	D7	44
Do Rūd, Iran	D5	42
Doruma, D.R.C.	C5	54
Dorval, P.Q., Can.	q19	90
Dosatuj, Russia	D13	26
Dos Bahías, Cabo, c., Arg.	G3	69
Dosso, Niger	D5	50
Dossor, Kaz.	E9	22
Dothan, Al., U.S.	D4	94
Douala, Cam.	C1	54
Douarnenez, Fr.	C4	16
Double Beach, Ct., U.S.	D4	100
Double Island Point, c., Austl.	F5	62
Doublespring Pass, Id., U.S.	E5	105
Double Springs, Al., U.S.	A2	94
Doubletop Peak, mtn., Wy., U.S.	C2	143
Doubs, stm., Eur.	D9	16
Douentza, Mali	C4	50
Dougherty, co., Ga., U.S.	E2	103
Douglas, I. of Man	C4	12
Douglas, S. Afr.	D3	56
Douglas, Az., U.S.	F6	96
Douglas, Ga., U.S.	E4	103
Douglas, Mi., U.S.	F4	115
Douglas, Wy., U.S.	D7	143
Douglas, co., Co., U.S.	B6	99
Douglas, co., Ga., U.S.	C2	103
Douglas, co., Il., U.S.	D5	106
Douglas, co., Ks., U.S.	D8	109
Douglas, co., Mn., U.S.	E3	116
Douglas, co., Mo., U.S.	E5	118
Douglas, co., Ne., U.S.	C9	120
Douglas, co., Nv., U.S.	E2	121
Douglas, co., Or., U.S.	D3	130
Douglas, co., S.D., U.S.	D7	134
Douglas, co., Wa., U.S.	B6	140
Douglas, co., Wi., U.S.	B2	142
Douglas, Mount, mtn., Ak., U.S.	D9	95
Douglas Channel, strt., B.C., Can.	C3	85
Douglas Lake, l., Mi., U.S.	C6	115
Douglas Lake, res., Tn., U.S.	D10	135
Douglass, Ks., U.S.	E7	109
Douglastown, N.B., Can.	B4	87
Douglasville, Ga., U.S.	C2	103
Dourados, Braz.	H9	70
Dourbali, Chad	D8	50
Douro (Duero), stm., Eur.	G2	16
Dousman, Wi., U.S.	E5	142
Dove Creek, Co., U.S.	D2	99
Dover, Eng., U.K.	E7	12
Dover, Ar., U.S.	B2	97
Dover, De., U.S.	D3	101
Dover, Fl., U.S.	D4	102
Dover, Ma., U.S.	h10	114
Dover, N.H., U.S.	D5	122
Dover, N.J., U.S.	B3	123
Dover, Oh., U.S.	B4	128
Dover, Pa., U.S.	F8	131
Dover, Tn., U.S.	A4	135
Dover, Strait of, strt., Eur.	B7	16
Dover Air Force Base, mil., De., U.S.	D4	101
Dover-Foxcroft, Me., U.S.	C3	112
Dover Plains, N.Y., U.S.	D7	125
Dowagiac, Mi., U.S.	G4	115
Dowlatābād, Iran	E7	42
Downers Grove, Il., U.S.	B5	106
Downey, Ca., U.S.	n12	98
Downey, Id., U.S.	G6	105
Downingtown, Pa., U.S.	F10	131
Downpatrick, N. Ire., U.K.	C4	12
Downs, Ks., U.S.	C5	109
Downs Mountain, mtn., Wy., U.S.	C3	143
Downton, Mount, mtn., B.C., Can.	C5	85
Dows, Ia., U.S.	B4	108
Doylestown, Oh., U.S.	B4	128
Doylestown, Pa., U.S.	F11	131
Doyline, La., U.S.	B2	111
Dra'a, Hamada du, des., Alg.	E3	48
Dracena, Braz.	F1	74
Dracut, Ma., U.S.	A5	114
Drăgăşani, Rom.	G8	20
Dragør, Den.	I5	10
Drain, Or., U.S.	D3	130
Drakensberg, mts., Afr.	D4	56
Drake Passage, strt.	B33	67
Drake Peak, mtn., Or., U.S.	E6	130
Dráma, Grc.	D10	18
Drammen, Nor.	G4	10
Draper, Ut., U.S.	C4	137
Drau (Dráva), stm., Eur.	F2	20
Dráva (Drau), stm., Eur.	G4	20
Drayton, On., Can.	D4	89

Name	Map Ref.	Page
Drayton, N.D., U.S.	A8	127
Drayton, S.C., U.S.	B4	133
Drayton Plains, Mi., U.S.	F7	115
Drayton Valley, Ab., Can.	C3	84
Dresden, On., Can.	E2	89
Dresden, Ger.	E13	12
Dresden, Oh., U.S.	B3	128
Dresden, Tn., U.S.	A3	135
Dresslerville, Nv., U.S.	E2	121
Dreux, Fr.	C7	16
Drew, Ms., U.S.	B3	117
Drew, co., Ar., U.S.	D4	97
Drews Reservoir, res., Or., U.S.	E6	130
Drexel, Mo., U.S.	C3	118
Drexel, N.C., U.S.	B1	126
Drexel, Oh., U.S.	C1	128
Drift, Ky., U.S.	C7	110
Driggs, Id., U.S.	F7	105
Drinit, Gjiri i, b., Alb.	D7	18
Driskill Mountain, hill, La., U.S.	B3	111
Drobeta-Turnu Severin, Rom.	G7	20
Drogheda, Ire.	D3	12
Drohobych, Ukr.	E7	20
Drumheller, Ab., Can.	D4	84
Drum Island, i., S.C., U.S.	k12	133
Drummond, Lake, l., Va., U.S.	D6	139
Drummond Island, i., Mi., U.S.	C7	115
Drummondville, P.Q., Can.	D5	90
Drumright, Ok., U.S.	B5	129
Druskininkai, Lith.	I11	10
Družba, Kaz.	B4	28
Družina, Russia	C16	26
Drybranch, W.V., U.S.	m13	141
Dry Cimarron, stm., U.S.	A6	124
Dry Creek Mountain, mtn., Nv., U.S.	B5	121
Dryden, On., Can.	o16	89
Dryden, N.Y., U.S.	C4	125
Dry Fork, stm., Mo., U.S.	D6	118
Dry Fork, stm., W.V., U.S.	D3	141
Dry Fork, stm., W.V., U.S.	B5	141
Dry Ridge, Ky., U.S.	B5	110
Dry Tortugas, is., Fl., U.S.	H5	102
Dschang, Cam.	B1	54
Duarte, Pico, mtn., Dom. Rep.	B5	80
Dubach, La., U.S.	B3	111
Dubai see Dubayy, U.A.E.	E7	42
Dubăsari, Mol.	F10	20
Du Bay, Lake, res., Wi., U.S.	D4	142
Dubayy (Dubai), U.A.E.	E7	42
Dubbo, Austl.	G4	62
Dublin (Baile Átha Cliath), Ire.	D3	12
Dublin, Ga., U.S.	D4	103
Dublin, In., U.S.	E7	107
Dublin, N.H., U.S.	E2	122
Dublin, Oh., U.S.	k10	128
Dublin, Pa., U.S.	F11	131
Dublin, Tx., U.S.	C3	136
Dublin, Va., U.S.	C2	139
Dubno, Ukr.	D8	20
Dubois, In., U.S.	H4	107
Du Bois, Pa., U.S.	D4	131
Dubois, Wy., U.S.	C3	143
Dubois, co., In., U.S.	H4	107
Duboistown, Pa., U.S.	D7	131
Dubovka, Russia	E7	22
Dubréka, Gui.	E2	50
Dubrovnik, Cro.	C7	18
Dubrovytsia, Ukr.	D9	20
Dubuque, Ia., U.S.	B7	108
Dubuque, co., Ia., U.S.	B7	108
Duchesne, Ut., U.S.	C5	137
Duchesne, co., Ut., U.S.	C5	137
Duchesne, stm., Ut., U.S.	C5	137
Duck, stm., Tn., U.S.	B4	135
Duck Bay, Mb., Can.	C1	86
Duck Creek, stm., Oh., U.S.	C4	128
Duck Creek, stm., Wi., U.S.	h9	142
Duck Lake, Sk., Can.	E2	91
Duck Lake, l., Me., U.S.	C4	112
Duck Mountain Provincial Park, Sk., Can.	F5	91
Duck Valley Indian Reservation, U.S.	B5	121
Duckwater Indian Reservation, Nv., U.S.	E6	121
Duckwater Peak, mtn., Nv., U.S.	E6	121
Du Couedic, Cape, c., Austl.	H2	62
Dudinka, Russia	C10	26
Dudley, Eng., U.K.	D5	12
Dudley, Ma., U.S.	B4	114
Duenweg, Mo., U.S.	D3	118
Duero (Douro), stm., Eur.	G4	16
Due West, S.C., U.S.	C3	133
Duffer Peak, mtn., Nv., U.S.	B3	121
Dufourspitze, mtn., Eur.	B1	18
Dugdemona, stm., La., U.S.	B3	111
Dugger, In., U.S.	F3	107
Dugi Otok, i., Cro.	C5	18
Duifken Point, c., Austl.	C3	62
Duisburg, Ger.	E10	12
Duitama, Col.	B5	70
Duke Island, i., Ak., U.S.	n24	95
Dukes, co., Ma., U.S.	D6	114
Duk Fadiat, Sudan	I11	48

Name	Map Ref.	Page
Dukhān, Qatar	E6	42
Dukku, Nig.	D7	50
Dukou, China	F8	28
Dulan, China	D7	28
Dulce, N.M., U.S.	A2	124
Dulce, stm., Arg.	E5	72
Duľdurga, Russia	D13	26
Duluth, Ga., U.S.	B2	103
Duluth, Mn., U.S.	D6	116
Dūmā, Syria	F7	44
Dumaguete, Phil.	E8	34
Dumai, Indon.	C2	36
Dumaran Island, i., Phil.	D7	34
Dumas, Ar., U.S.	D4	97
Dumas, Tx., U.S.	B2	136
Dumfries, Scot., U.K.	C5	12
Dumfries, Va., U.S.	B5	139
Dumont, Ia., U.S.	B5	108
Dumont, N.J., U.S.	B5	123
Dumraon, India	D4	40
Duna see Danube, stm., Eur.	C9	14
Dunai see Danube, stm., Eur.	C9	14
Dunaïvtsi, Ukr.	E9	20
Dunaj see Danube, stm., Eur.	C9	14
Dunărea see Danube, stm., Eur.	C9	14
Dunaújváros, Hung.	F5	20
Dunav see Danube, stm., Eur.	C9	14
Dunay see Danube, stm., Eur.	C9	14
Dunbar, Pa., U.S.	G2	131
Dunbar, W.V., U.S.	C3	141
Duncan, B.C., Can.	E6	85
Duncan, Az., U.S.	E6	96
Duncan, Ok., U.S.	C4	129
Duncan, S.C., U.S.	B3	133
Duncan Falls, Oh., U.S.	C4	128
Duncan Lake, res., B.C., Can.	D9	85
Duncannon, Pa., U.S.	F7	131
Duncan Passage, strt., India	G6	40
Duncansville, Pa., U.S.	F5	131
Duncanville, Tx., U.S.	n10	136
Dundalk, On., Can.	C4	89
Dundalk, Ire.	C3	12
Dundalk, Md., U.S.	B4	113
Dundalk Bay, b., Ire.	D3	12
Dundas, On., Can.	D5	89
Dundee, S. Afr.	D5	56
Dundee, Scot., U.K.	B5	12
Dundee, Fl., U.S.	D5	102
Dundee, Il., U.S.	A5	106
Dundee, Mi., U.S.	G7	115
Dundee, N.Y., U.S.	C4	125
Dundee, Or., U.S.	h11	130
Dundy, co., Ne., U.S.	D4	120
Dunedin, N.Z.	q13	63c
Dunedin, Fl., U.S.	D4	102
Dunellen, N.J., U.S.	B4	123
Dunfermline, Scot., U.K.	B5	12
Dūngarpur, India	E2	40
Dungarvan, Ire.	D3	12
Dungeness, stm., Wa., U.S.	A2	140
Dungu, D.R.C.	C5	54
Dunham, P.Q., Can.	D5	90
Dunhuang, China	C6	28
Dunkard Creek, stm., U.S.	B4	141
Dunkerque, Fr.	B8	16
Dunkerton, Ia., U.S.	B5	108
Dunkirk see Dunkerque, Fr.	B8	16
Dunkirk, In., U.S.	D7	107
Dunkirk, N.Y., U.S.	C1	125
Dunkirk, Oh., U.S.	B2	128
Dunklin, co., Mo., U.S.	E7	118
Dunkwa, Ghana	E4	50
Dún Laoghaire, Ire.	D3	12
Dunlap, Ia., U.S.	C2	108
Dunlap, Il., U.S.	C4	106
Dunlap, Tn., U.S.	A6	107
Dunlap, Tn., U.S.	D8	135
Dunleary see Dún Laoghaire, Ire.	D3	12
Dunleith, De., U.S.	i7	101
Dunloup Creek, stm., W.V., U.S.	n13	141
Dunmore, Pa., U.S.	D10	131
Dunmore, Lake, l., Vt., U.S.	D2	138
Dunn, N.C., U.S.	B4	126
Dunn, co., N.D., U.S.	B3	127
Dunn, co., Wi., U.S.	D2	142
Dunnellon, Fl., U.S.	C4	102
Dunnville, On., Can.	E5	89
Dunqulah, Sudan	G11	48
Dunseith, N.D., U.S.	A5	127
Dunsmuir, Ca., U.S.	B2	98
Dunville, Nf., Can.	E5	88
Dunwoody, Ga., U.S.	h8	103
Duolun, China	C11	28
Duomula, China	E4	28
Du Page, co., Il., U.S.	B5	106
Du Page, stm., Il., U.S.	k8	106
Duplin, co., N.C., U.S.	C5	126
Dupont, Co., U.S.	B6	99
Dupont, Pa., U.S.	n18	131
Dupont City, W.V., U.S.	m12	141
Dupont Manor, De., U.S.	D3	101
Du Quoin, Il., U.S.	E4	106

Name	Map Ref.	Page
Durand, Il., U.S.	A4	106
Durand, Mi., U.S.	F6	115
Durand, Wi., U.S.	D2	142
Durango, Mex.	E8	78
Durango, Co., U.S.	D3	99
Durango, state, Mex.	E8	78
Durant, Ia., U.S.	C7	108
Durant, Ms., U.S.	B4	117
Durant, Ok., U.S.	D5	129
Durazno, Ur.	E6	72
Durban, S. Afr.	D5	56
Durg, India	E4	40
Durgāpur, India	E5	40
Durham, On., Can.	C4	89
Durham, Eng., U.K.	C6	12
Durham, Ca., U.S.	C3	98
Durham, Ct., U.S.	D5	100
Durham, N.C., U.S.	B4	126
Durham, N.H., U.S.	D5	122
Durham, co., N.C., U.S.	A4	126
Durmitor, mtn., Yugo.	C7	18
Durrell, Nf., Can.	D4	88
Durrës, Alb.	D7	18
Dursunbey, Tur.	C3	44
D'Urville Island, i., N.Z.	p13	63c
Duryea, Pa., U.S.	D10	131
Dušanbe, Taj.	F8	26
Dušekan, Russia	C12	26
Dushan, China	F9	28
Dushanbe see Dušanbe, Taj.	F8	26
Dushanzi, China	C4	28
Duson, La., U.S.	D3	111
Düsseldorf, Ger.	E10	12
Dutchess, co., N.Y., U.S.	D7	125
Dutch Island, i., R.I., U.S.	F4	132
Dutton, On., Can.	E3	89
Dutton, Mount, mtn., Ut., U.S.	E3	137
Duval, co., Fl., U.S.	B5	102
Duval, co., Tx., U.S.	F3	136
Duxbury, Ma., U.S.	B6	114
Duyun, China	F9	28
Düzce, Tur.	B4	44
Dvina Bay see Dvinskaja guba, b., Russia	A6	22
Dvinskaja guba, b., Russia	A6	22
Dwārka, India	E1	40
Dwight, Il., U.S.	B5	106
Dwight D. Eisenhower Lock, N.Y., U.S.	f9	125
Dworshak Reservoir, res., Id., U.S.	C3	105
Dyer, In., U.S.	A2	107
Dyer, Tn., U.S.	A3	135
Dyer, co., Tn., U.S.	A2	135
Dyer Island, i., R.I., U.S.	E5	132
Dyersburg, Tn., U.S.	A2	135
Dyersville, Ia., U.S.	B6	108
Dyess Air Force Base, mil., Tx., U.S.	C3	136
Dysart, Ia., U.S.	B5	108
Džalinda, Russia	A12	28
Džambejty, Kaz.	D9	22
Džanybek, Kaz.	E8	22
Džardžan, Russia	C14	26
Dzaudzhikau see Vladikavkaz, Russia	E6	26
Dzerzhinsk see Dzjaržynsk, Bela.	C9	20
Dzerzhinsk see Dzeržinsk, Russia	C7	22
Dzeržinsk, Russia	C7	22
Džetygara, Kaz.	D8	26
Dzhambul see Žambyl, Kaz.		
Dzhankoi, Ukr.	G13	20
Dzierżoniów, Pol.	D4	20
Džizak, Uzb.	E8	26
Dzjaržynsk, Bela.	C9	20
Džugdžur, hrebet, mts., Russia	D15	26
Dzungarian Basin see Junggar Pendi, China	B5	28
Džusaly, Kaz.	A8	42
Dzüünharaa, Mong.	B9	28
Dzuunmod, Mong.	B9	28

E

Name	Map Ref.	Page
Eads, Co., U.S.	C8	99
Eagan, Mn., U.S.	n12	116
Eagar, Az., U.S.	C6	96
Eagle, Co., U.S.	B4	99
Eagle, Id., U.S.	F2	105
Eagle, Ne., U.S.	h12	120
Eagle, Wi., U.S.	F5	142
Eagle, co., Co., U.S.	B4	99
Eagle, stm., Nf., Can.	B2	88
Eagle Creek Reservoir, res., In., U.S.	E5	107
Eagle Grove, Ia., U.S.	B4	108
Eagle Key, i., Fl., U.S.	G6	102
Eagle Lake, Mn., U.S.	F5	116
Eagle Lake, Tx., U.S.	E4	136
Eagle Lake, l., Ca., U.S.	B3	98
Eagle Lake, l., Me., U.S.	B3	112
Eagle Lake, l., Me., U.S.	A4	112
Eagle Lake, l., Ms., U.S.	C3	117
Eagle Lake, l., Wi., U.S.	C4	142
Eagle Mountain, mtn., Mn., U.S.	k9	116
Eagle Mountain Lake, res., Tx., U.S.	m9	136

Name	Map Ref.	Page
Eagle Nest Lake, l., N.M., U.S.	A4	124
Eagle Pass, Tx., U.S.	E2	136
Eagle Peak, mtn., Ca., U.S.	B3	98
Eagle Point, Or., U.S.	E4	130
Eagle River, Wi., U.S.	C4	142
Eagletail Mountains, mts., Az., U.S.	D2	96
Eagletail Peak, mtn., Az., U.S.	D2	96
Eagletown, Ok., U.S.	C7	129
Earle, Ar., U.S.	B5	97
Earlham, Ia., U.S.	C3	108
Earlimart, Ca., U.S.	E4	98
Earlington, Ky., U.S.	C2	110
Earlville, Ia., U.S.	B6	108
Earlville, Il., U.S.	B5	106
Early, Ia., U.S.	B2	108
Early, co., Ga., U.S.	E2	103
Earth, Tx., U.S.	B1	136
Easley, S.C., U.S.	B2	133
East, stm., Ct., U.S.	D5	100
East, stm., N.Y., U.S.	k13	125
East, stm., Wi., U.S.	h9	142
East Alton, Il., U.S.	E3	106
East Angus, P.Q., Can.	D6	90
East Arlington, Vt., U.S.	E2	138
East Aurora, N.Y., U.S.	C2	125
East Bangor, Pa., U.S.	E11	131
East Bank, W.V., U.S.	m13	141
East Barre, Vt., U.S.	C4	138
East Baton Rouge, co., La., U.S.	D4	111
East Bay, b., Fl., U.S.	u16	102
East Bay, b., Tx., U.S.	R15	136
East Beckwith Mountain, mtn., Co., U.S.	C3	99
East Berlin, Ct., U.S.	C5	100
East Berlin, Pa., U.S.	G8	131
East Bernard, Tx., U.S.	E4	136
East Bernstadt, Ky., U.S.	C5	110
East Bethel, Mn., U.S.	E5	116
East Billerica, Ma., U.S.	f11	114
Eastborough, Ks., U.S.	g12	109
Eastbourne, Eng., U.K.	E7	12
East Brady, Pa., U.S.	E2	131
East Branch Clarion River Lake, res., Pa., U.S.	C4	131
East Brewton, Al., U.S.	D2	94
East Bridgewater, Ma., U.S.	B6	114
East Brimfield Lake, res., Ma., U.S.	B3	114
East Brooklyn, Ct., U.S.	B8	100
East Broughton, P.Q., Can.	C6	90
East Brunswick, N.J., U.S.	C4	123
East Butte, mtn., Mt., U.S.	B5	119
East Cache Creek, stm., Ok., U.S.	C3	129
East Caicos, i., T./C. Is.	A5	80
East Cape, c., N.Z.	o14	63c
East Cape, c., Fl., U.S.	G5	102
East Carbon, Ut., U.S.	D5	137
East Caroline Basin	H17	64
East Carroll, co., La., U.S.	B4	111
East Chicago, In., U.S.	A3	107
East China Sea, Asia	F12	28
East Chop, c., Ma., U.S.	D6	114
East Cleveland, Oh., U.S.	g9	128
East Cote Blanche Bay, b., La., U.S.	E4	111
East Dennis, Ma., U.S.	C7	114
East Derry, N.H., U.S.	E4	122
East Detroit, Mi., U.S.	p16	115
East Douglas, Ma., U.S.	B4	114
East Dubuque, Il., U.S.	A3	106
Eastend, Sk., Can.	H1	91
Easter Island see Pascua, Isla de, i., Chile	K28	64
Eastern Bay, b., Md., U.S.	C5	113
Eastern Desert, des., Egypt	E11	48
Eastern Ghāts, mts., India	G3	40
Eastern Neck Island, i., Md., U.S.	B5	113
Eastern Point, c., Ma., U.S.	f13	114
Eastern Sayans see Vostočnyj Sajan, mts., Russia	D11	26
Easterville, Mb., Can.	C2	86
East Falkland, i., Falk. Is.	H5	69
East Falmouth, Ma., U.S.	C6	114
East Feliciana, co., La., U.S.	D4	111
East Flat Rock, N.C., U.S.	f10	126
East Fork, stm., Wy., U.S.	D3	143
East Fork Lake, res., Oh., U.S.	C1	128
East Frisian Islands see Ostfriesische Inseln, is., Ger.	D10	12
East Gaffney, S.C., U.S.	A4	133
East Galesburg, Il., U.S.	C3	106
East Granby, Ct., U.S.	B5	100
East Grand Forks, Mn., U.S.	C2	116
East Grand Rapids, Mi., U.S.	F5	115
East Greenville, Pa., U.S.	F11	131
East Greenwich, R.I., U.S.	D4	132
East Gwillimbury, On., Can.	C5	89
East Hampstead, N.H., U.S.	E4	122
East Hampton, Ct., U.S.	C5	100
Easthampton, Ma., U.S.	B2	114
East Hartford, Ct., U.S.	B5	100
East Hartland, Ct., U.S.	B4	100
East Haven, Ct., U.S.	D4	100
East Helena, Mt., U.S.	D5	119
East Jordan, Mi., U.S.	C5	115
Eastlake, Oh., U.S.	A4	128

Name	Map Ref.	Page

East Lake Tohopekaliga, l., Fl., U.S. D5 102
Eastland, Tx., U.S. C3 136
Eastland, co., Tx., U.S. C3 136
East Lansing, Mi., U.S. F6 115
East Las Vegas, Nv., U.S. G6 121
East Liverpool, Oh., U.S. B5 128
East London (Oos-Londen), S. Afr. E4 56
East Longmeadow, Ma., U.S. B2 114
East Los Angeles, Ca., U.S. m12 98
East Lyme, Ct., U.S. D7 100
East Lynn Lake, res., W.V., U.S. C2 141
Eastmain-Opinaca, Réservoir, res., P.Q., Can. h11 90
Eastman, P.Q., Can. D5 90
Eastman, Ga., U.S. D3 103
East Mariana Basin G18 64
East Matunuck, R.I., U.S. . . F3 132
East Middlebury, Vt., U.S. . . D2 138
East Millinocket, Me., U.S. . . C4 112
East Moline, Il., U.S. B3 106
East Montpelier, Vt., U.S. . . C4 138
East Naples, Fl., U.S. F5 102
East Newnan, Ga., U.S. C2 103
East Nishnabotna, stm., Ia., U.S. C2 108
East Norriton, Pa., U.S. o20 131
East Olympia, Wa., U.S. C3 140
Easton, Md., U.S. C5 113
Easton, Pa., U.S. E11 131
Easton Reservoir, res., Ct., U.S. E2 100
East Orange, N.J., U.S. . . B4 123
East Orleans, Ma., U.S. C8 114
Eastover, S.C., U.S. D6 133
East Pacific Rise M27 64
East Pakistan see Bangladesh, ctry., Asia . B2 34
East Palatka, Fl., U.S. C5 102
East Palestine, Oh., U.S. . . B5 128
East Pass, strt., Fl., U.S. . . u15 102
East Pea Ridge, W.V., U.S. . C2 141
East Peoria, Il., U.S. C4 106
East Pepperell, Ma., U.S. . . A4 114
East Petersburg, Pa., U.S. . . F9 131
East Pittsburgh, Pa., U.S. . . k14 131
Eastpoint, Fl., U.S. C2 102
East Point, Ga., U.S. C2 103
East Point, c., P.E., Can. . . C8 87
East Point, c., Ma., U.S. . . B6 114
East Point, c., N.J., U.S. . . E2 123
Eastport, Nf., Can. D5 88
Eastport, Me., U.S. D6 112
East Prairie, Mo., U.S. E8 118
East Providence, R.I., U.S. . C4 132
East Pryor Mountain, mtn., Mt., U.S. E8 119
East Quogue, N.Y., U.S. n16 125
East Range, mts., Nv., U.S. . C4 121
East Ridge, Tn., U.S. h11 135
East River, Ct., U.S. D5 100
East Rochester, N.Y., U.S. . . B3 125
East Rockingham, N.C., U.S. C3 126
East Rutherford, N.J., U.S. . h8 123
East Saint Louis, Il., U.S. . . E3 106
East Sea see Japan, Sea of, Asia C14 28
East Selkirk, Mb., Can. . . D3 86
East Siberian Sea see Vostočno-Sibirskoe more, Russia . . B17 26
Eastsound, Wa., U.S. A3 140
East Spencer, N.C., U.S. . . B2 126
East Stroudsburg, Pa., U.S. D11 131
East Tawas, Mi., U.S. D7 115
East Troy, Wi., U.S. F5 142
East Vestal, N.Y., U.S. C4 125
East View, W.V., U.S. k10 141
East Walker, stm., U.S. E2 121
East Walpole, Ma., U.S. . . h11 114
East Wareham, Ma., U.S. . . C6 114
East Washington, Pa., U.S. . F1 131
East Wenatchee, Wa., U.S. B5 140
East Windsor, N.J., U.S. . . C3 123
East York, On., Can. D5 89
Eaton, Co., U.S. A6 99
Eaton, In., U.S. D7 107
Eaton, Oh., U.S. C1 128
Eaton, co., Mi., U.S. F6 115
Eaton Rapids, Mi., U.S. . . F6 115
Eatonton, Ga., U.S. C3 103
Eatontown, N.J., U.S. C4 123
Eatonville, Wa., U.S. C3 140
Eau Claire, Wi., U.S. D2 142
Eau Claire, co., Wi., U.S. . . D2 142
Eau Claire, stm., Wi., U.S. . D2 142
Eau Claire, Lac à l', l., P.Q., Can. g11 90
Eauripik Rise H17 64
Ebano, Mex. C5 78
Ebebiyín, Eq. Gui. C2 54
Ebensburg, Pa., U.S. F4 131
Eber Gölü, l., Tur. C4 44
Eberswalde-Finow, Ger. . . D13 12
Ebetsu, Japan B4 31
Ebinur Hu, l., China B4 28
Ebolowa, Cam. C2 54
Ebre see Ebro, stm., Spain . G7 16
Ebre, Delta de l', Spain . . G7 16
Ebro, stm., Spain G7 16
Eccles, W.V., U.S. n13 141

Ech Cheliff, Alg. C5 48
Echeng, China C3 30
Echo Bay, Nv., U.S. G7 121
Echo Lake, l., Me., U.S. . . D3 112
Echo Lake, l., Vt., U.S. . . B5 138
Echols, co., Ga., U.S. F4 103
Echuca, Austl. H3 62
Écija, Spain I4 16
Eckerö, i., Fin. F8 10
Eckhart Mines, Md., U.S. . . k13 113
Eckville, Ab., Can. C3 84
Eclectic, Al., U.S. C3 94
Econfina, stm., Fl., U.S. . . B3 102
Écorces, Rivière aux, stm., P.Q., Can. A6 90
Ecorse, Mi., U.S. p15 115
Ecru, Ms., U.S. A4 117
Ector, co., Tx., U.S. D1 136
Ecuador, ctry., S.A. D4 70
Edcouch, Tx., U.S. F4 136
Eddy, co., N.D., U.S. B7 127
Eddy, co., N.M., U.S. E5 124
Eddystone, Pa., U.S. p20 131
Eddyville, Ia., U.S. C5 108
Eddyville, Ky., U.S. e9 110
Ede, Nig. E5 50
Edéa, Cam. C2 54
Eden, Ga., U.S. D5 103
Eden, Md., U.S. D6 113
Eden, N.C., U.S. A3 126
Eden, N.Y., U.S. C2 125
Eden, Tx., U.S. D3 136
Edenburg, S. Afr. G5 56
Edenton, N.C., U.S. A6 126
Eden Prairie, Mn., U.S. . . n12 116
Eden Valley, Mn., U.S. . . E4 116
Edfu, Egypt F11 48
Edgar, Ne., U.S. D8 120
Edgar, Wi., U.S. D3 142
Edgar, co., Il., U.S. D6 106
Edgard, La., U.S. D5 111
Edgartown, Ma., U.S. D6 114
Edgecombe, co., N.C., U.S. B5 126
Edgecumbe, Cape, c., Ak., U.S. m21 95
Edgefield, S.C., U.S. D4 133
Edgefield, co., S.C., U.S. . . D4 133
Edgeley, N.D., U.S. C7 127
Edgemere, Md., U.S. B5 113
Edgemont, S.D., U.S. D2 134
Edgemoor, De., U.S. A3 101
Edgeøya, i., Nor. B4 26
Edgerton, Ks., U.S. D8 109
Edgerton, Mn., U.S. G2 116
Edgerton, Oh., U.S. A1 128
Edgerton, Wi., U.S. F4 142
Edgerton, Wy., U.S. C6 143
Edgewater, Al., U.S. i7 94
Edgewater, Fl., U.S. D6 102
Edgewater, Md., U.S. C4 113
Edgewater, N.J., U.S. h9 123
Edgewater Park, N.J., U.S. . C3 123
Edgewood, Ia., U.S. B6 108
Edgewood, In., U.S. D6 107
Edgewood, Ky., U.S. h13 110
Edgewood, Md., U.S. B5 113
Edgewood, N.M., U.S. B3 124
Edgewood, Oh., U.S. A5 128
Edgewood, Pa., U.S. k14 131
Edgewood, Wa., U.S. f11 140
Edgeworth, Pa., U.S. h13 131
Édhessa, Grc. D9 18
Edina, Mn., U.S. F5 116
Edina, Mo., U.S. A5 118
Edinboro, Pa., U.S. C1 131
Edinburg, Il., U.S. D4 106
Edinburg, Tx., U.S. F3 136
Edinburg, Va., U.S. B4 139
Edinburgh, Scot., U.K. C5 12
Edinburgh, In., U.S. F6 107
Edinet, Mol. E9 20
Edirne, Tur. B2 44
Edison, Ga., U.S. E2 103
Edison, N.J., U.S. B4 123
Edisto, stm., S.C., U.S. E6 133
Edisto Island, i., S.C., U.S. . F7 133
Edith, Mount, mtn., Mt., U.S. D5 119
Edjeleh, Alg. E6 48
Edmond, Ok., U.S. B4 129
Edmonds, Wa., U.S. B3 140
Edmonson, co., Ky., U.S. . . C3 110
Edmonton, Ab., Can. C4 84
Edmonton, Ky., U.S. D4 110
Edmore, Mi., U.S. E5 115
Edmunds, co., S.D., U.S. . . B6 134
Edmundston, N.B., Can. . . B1 87
Edna, Tx., U.S. E4 136
Edon, Oh., U.S. A1 128
Édouard, Lac, l., P.Q., Can. B5 90
Edremit, Tur. C2 44
Edremit Körfezi, b., Tur. . . C2 44
Edson, Ab., Can. C2 84
Edson Butte, mtn., Or., U.S. E2 130
Eduardo Castex, Arg. F5 72
Edward, Lake, l., Afr. D5 54
Edwards, Ms., U.S. C3 117
Edwards, co., Il., U.S. E5 106
Edwards, co., Ks., U.S. E4 109
Edwards, co., Tx., U.S. E2 136
Edwards Air Force Base, mil., Ca., U.S. E5 98
Edwardsburg, Mi., U.S. . . G4 115
Edwards Butte, mtn., Or., U.S. B3 130

Edwardsville, Il., U.S. E4 106
Edwardsville, Ks., U.S. k16 109
Edwardsville, Pa., U.S. n17 131
Edward VII Peninsula, pen., Ant. D25 67
Eel, stm., Ca., U.S. B2 98
Eel, stm., In., U.S. C6 107
Eel, stm., In., U.S. F3 107
Éfaté, i., Vanuatu k9 62a
Efes (Ephesus), hist., Tur. . D2 44
Effigy Mounds National Monument, Ia., U.S. . . A6 108
Effingham, Il., U.S. D5 106
Effingham, co., Ga., U.S. . . D5 103
Effingham, co., Il., U.S. . . D5 106
Efland, N.C., U.S. A3 126
Efremov, Russia C15 20
Egadi, Isole, is., Italy E4 18
Egan Range, mts., Nv., U.S. E7 121
Egedesminde, Grnld. E29 82
Eger, Hung. F6 20
Egg Harbor City, N.J., U.S. . D3 123
Egg Island Point, c., N.J., U.S. E2 123
Egijn, stm., Mong. A8 28
Eglin Air Force Base, mil., Fl., U.S. u15 102
Egmont, Cape, c., N.Z. . . o13 63c
Egmont, Mount see Taranaki, Mount, vol., N.Z. o13 63c
Egmont Bay, b., P.E., Can. . C5 87
Egmont Channel, strt., Fl., U.S. p10 102
Egmont Key, i., Fl., U.S. . . p10 102
Eğirdir, Tur. D4 44
Eğridir Gölü, l., Tur. C4 44
Egvekinot, Russia C20 26
Egypt, ctry., Afr. E10 48
Egypt, Lake of, res., Il., U.S. F5 106
Eha-Amufu, Nig. E6 50
Ehrenberg, Az., U.S. D1 96
Eibar, Spain F5 16
Eielson Air Force Base, mil., Ak., U.S. C10 95
Eigersund, Nor. G2 10
Eight Degree Channel, strt., Asia H2 40
Eights Coast, Ant. D31 67
Eighty Mile Beach, Austl. . D3 60
Eindhoven, Neth. E9 12
Eirunepé, Braz. E6 70
Eisenach, Ger. E12 12
Eisenerz, Aus. G14 12
Eisenhower, Mount, mtn., N.H., U.S. B4 122
Eisenhüttenstadt, Ger. . . D14 12
Eisenstadt, Aus. G15 12
Eivissa, Spain H7 16
Eivissa (Ibiza), i., Spain . . H7 16
Ejin Qi, China C8 28
Ejsk, Russia F15 20
Ejura, Ghana E4 50
Ekaterinburg, Russia D8 26
Ekibastuz, Kaz. D9 26
Ekimčan, Russia D15 26
Ekonda, Russia C12 26
Ela, Myan. C3 34
El Aaiún, W. Sah. A2 50
Elaine, Ar., U.S. C5 97
El-Alamein, Egypt E9 14
Elan', Russia D7 22
Elancy, Russia D12 26
El-Arish, Egypt E10 14
Elat, Isr. E2 42
Elat, Gulf of see Aqaba, Gulf of, b. E2 42
Elath see Elat, Isr. E2 42
Elazığ, Tur. C8 44
Elba, Al., U.S. D3 94
Elba, Isola d', i., Italy C3 18
El Banco, Col. D5 80
Elbasan, Alb. D7 18
Elbe see Labe, stm., Eur. . E14 12
Elberfeld, In., U.S. H3 107
Elbert, co., Co., U.S. B6 99
Elbert, co., Ga., U.S. B4 103
Elbert, Mount, mtn., Co., U.S. B4 99
Elberta, Ga., U.S. D3 103
Elberton, Ga., U.S. B4 103
El Beyyadh, Alg. E4 14
Elbistan, Tur. C7 44
Elbląg, Pol. B5 20
El Boulaïda, Alg. C5 48
Elbow, stm., Ab., Can. D3 84
Elbow Lake, Mn., U.S. E3 116
El'brus, gora, mtn., Russia . E6 26
Elbrus, Mount see El'brus, gora, mtn., Russia . . E6 26
Elburn, Il., U.S. B5 106
Elburz Mountains see Alborz, Reshteh-ye Kūhhā-ye, mts., Iran . . C6 42
El Cajon, Ca., U.S. F5 98
El Calafate, Arg. H2 69
El Callao, Ven. D7 80
El Campo, Tx., U.S. E4 136
El Capitan, mtn., Mt., U.S. . D2 119
El Capitan Reservoir, res., Ca., U.S. o16 98
El Carmen de Bolívar, Col. . B4 70
El Centro, Ca., U.S. F6 98

El Cerrito, Ca., U.S. h8 98
Elcho Island, i., Austl. C6 60
El Cuervo Butte, mtn., N.M., U.S. k9 124
Elda, Spain H6 16
El-Dab'a, Egypt G3 44
El Djazaïr (Algiers), Alg. . . C5 48
El Djelfa, Alg. E4 14
Eldon, Ia., U.S. D5 108
Eldon, Mo., U.S. C5 118
Eldora, Ia., U.S. B4 108
Eldorado, Arg. D7 72
El Dorado, Ar., U.S. D3 97
Eldorado, Il., U.S. F5 106
El Dorado, Ks., U.S. E7 109
Eldorado, Tx., U.S. D2 136
El Dorado, Ven. D7 80
El Dorado, co., Ca., U.S. . . C3 98
Eldorado Peak, mtn., Wa., U.S. A4 140
Eldorado Springs, Co., U.S. B5 99
El Dorado Springs, Mo., U.S. D3 118
Eldoret, Kenya C7 54
Eldridge, Ia., U.S. C7 108
Eleanor, W.V., U.S. C3 141
Elec, Russia D5 26
Electra, Tx., U.S. C3 136
Electra Lake, res., Co., U.S. D3 99
Electric Peak, mtn., Co., U.S. C5 99
Electric Peak, mtn., Mt., U.S. E6 119
Elefantes (Olifants), stm., Afr. C5 56
El Encanto, Col. D5 70
Elephant Butte Reservoir, res., N.M., U.S. D2 124
Eleuthera, i., Bah. C9 76
Eleven Mile Canyon Reservoir, res., Co., U.S. C5 99
Eleven Point, stm., U.S. . . A4 97
El-Fayoum, Egypt E11 14
Elgin, Scot., U.K. B5 12
Elgin, Ia., U.S. B6 108
Elgin, Il., U.S. A5 106
Elgin, Mn., U.S. F6 116
Elgin, N.D., U.S. C4 127
Elgin, Ne., U.S. C7 120
Elgin, Ok., U.S. C3 129
Elgin, Or., U.S. B9 130
Elgin, S.C., U.S. B6 133
Elgin, Tx., U.S. D4 136
Elgon, Mount, mtn., Afr. . . C6 54
El Grara, Alg. E4 14
El Hammâmi, reg., Maur. . . B2 50
El Hank, clf, Afr. B3 50
El Hierro, i., Spain A1 50
Elhovo, Bul. C11 18
Eliase, Indon. E8 36
Elida, Oh., U.S. B1 128
El-Iskandarîya, Egypt D10 48
Elista, Russia E6 26
Elizabeth, Austl. G2 62
Elizabeth, Co., U.S. B6 99
Elizabeth, N.J., U.S. B4 123
Elizabeth, W.V., U.S. B3 141
Elizabeth, Cape, c., Wa., U.S. B1 140
Elizabeth City, N.C., U.S. . . A6 126
Elizabeth Islands, is., Ma., U.S. D6 114
Elizabethton, Tn., U.S. C11 135
Elizabethtown, Ky., U.S. . . C4 110
Elizabethtown, N.C., U.S. . . C4 126
Elizabethtown, Pa., U.S. . . F8 131
Elizabethville, Pa., U.S. . . E8 131
Elizavety, mys, c., Russia . D16 26
El-Jadida, Mor. D3 48
El Jebel, Co., U.S. B3 99
Etk, Pol. C7 20
Elk, co., Ks., U.S. E7 109
Elk, co., Pa., U.S. D4 131
Elk, stm., Co., U.S. A4 99
Elk, stm., Ks., U.S. E7 109
Elk, stm., W.V., U.S. C3 141
Elk, stm., Wi., U.S. C3 142
Elk, stm., U.S. A2 94
Elkader, Ia., U.S. B6 108
Elk City, Id., U.S. D3 105
Elk City, Ok., U.S. B2 129
Elk City Lake, res., Ks., U.S. E7 109
Elk Creek, stm., Ok., U.S. . B2 129
Elk Creek, stm., S.D., U.S. . C3 134
El Kef, Tun. C6 48
El Kerê, Eth. B8 54
Elkford, B.C., Can. D10 85
Elk Grove, Ca., U.S. C3 98
Elk Grove Village, Il., U.S. . h9 106
El-Khârga, Egypt E11 48
Elkhart, In., U.S. A6 107
Elkhart, Ks., U.S. E2 109
Elkhart, Tx., U.S. D5 136
Elkhart, co., In., U.S. A6 107
Elkhart, stm., In., U.S. A6 107
Elkhart Lake, Wi., U.S. E5 142
Elkhead Mountains, mts., Co., U.S. A3 99
Elkhorn, Mb., Can. E1 86
Elk Horn, Ia., U.S. C2 108
Elkhorn, Ne., U.S. g12 120
Elkhorn, Wi., U.S. F5 142
Elkhorn, stm., Ne., U.S. . . B7 120

Elkhorn City, Ky., U.S. C7 110
Elkhorn Peaks, mts., Id., U.S. F7 105
Elkin, N.C., U.S. A2 126
Elkins, Ar., U.S. A1 97
Elkins, W.V., U.S. C5 141
Elkland, Pa., U.S. C7 131
Elk Mills, Md., U.S. A6 113
Elk Mound, Wi., U.S. D2 142
Elk Mountain, Wy., U.S. . . E6 143
Elk Mountain, mtn., N.M., U.S. D1 124
Elk Mountain, mtn., Wy., U.S. E6 143
Elk Mountains, mts., Co., U.S. B3 99
Elk Mountains, mts., ... D1 134
Elko, Nv., U.S. C6 121
Elko, co., Nv., U.S. B6 121
Elk Peak, mtn., Mt., U.S. . . D6 119
Elk Point, Ab., Can. C5 84
Elk Point, S.D., U.S. E9 134
Elk Rapids, Mi., U.S. D5 115
Elkridge, Md., U.S. B4 113
Elk River, Mn., U.S. E5 116
Elkton, Ky., U.S. D2 110
Elkton, Md., U.S. A6 113
Elkton, Mi., U.S. E7 115
Elkton, S.D., U.S. C9 134
Elkton, Va., U.S. B4 139
Elkview, W.V., U.S. m13 141
Elkville, Il., U.S. F4 106
Ellaville, Ga., U.S. D2 103
Ellen, Mount, mtn., Ut., U.S. E5 137
Ellendale, De., U.S. E4 101
Ellendale, N.D., U.S. C7 127
Ellensburg, Wa., U.S. C5 140
Ellenton, Fl., U.S. E4 102
Ellenville, N.Y., U.S. D6 125
Ellerbe, N.C., U.S. B3 126
Ellerslie, Md., U.S. k13 113
Ellesmere Island, i., N.T., Can. B24 82
Ellettsville, In., U.S. F4 107
Ellice Islands see Tuvalu, ctry., Oc. E11 58
Ellicott City, Md., U.S. B4 113
Ellijay, Ga., U.S. B2 103
Ellington, Ct., U.S. B6 100
Ellington, Mo., U.S. D7 118
Ellinwood, Ks., U.S. D5 109
Elliot, S. Afr. E4 56
Elliot Lake, On., Can. A2 89
Elliott, Ms., U.S. B4 117
Elliott, co., Ky., U.S. B6 110
Elliott Bay, b., Wa., U.S. . . e11 140
Elliott Key, i., Fl., U.S. G6 102
Ellis, Ks., U.S. D4 109
Ellis, co., Ks., U.S. D4 109
Ellis, co., Ok., U.S. A2 129
Ellis, co., Tx., U.S. C4 136
Ellis, stm., N.H., U.S. B4 122
Elliston, Va., U.S. C2 139
Ellisville, Mo., U.S. f12 118
Ellisville, Ms., U.S. D4 117
Ellore see Elūru, India F4 40
Elloree, S.C., U.S. D6 133
Ellport, Pa., U.S. E1 131
Ellsworth, Ks., U.S. D5 109
Ellsworth, Me., U.S. D4 112
Ellsworth, Pa., U.S. F1 131
Ellsworth, Wi., U.S. D1 142
Ellsworth, co., Ks., U.S. . . . D5 109
Ellsworth Air Force Base, mil., S.D., U.S. C2 134
Ellsworth Land, reg., Ant. . D32 67
Ellsworth Mountains, mts., Ant. D32 67
Ellwood City, Pa., U.S. E1 131
Elm, stm., U.S. B8 127
Elma, Ia., U.S. A5 108
Elma, Wa., U.S. C2 140
Elmadağ, Tur. C5 44
El-Mahalla el-Kubra, Egypt G4 44
Elmalı, Tur. D3 44
El-Mansûra, Egypt E10 14
Elm City, N.C., U.S. B5 126
Elm Creek, Ne., U.S. D6 120
Elmendorf Air Force Base, mil., Ak., U.S. C10 95
El Menia, Alg. D5 48
Elm Grove, Wi., U.S. m11 142
Elmhurst, Il., U.S. B6 106
Elmhurst, Pa., U.S. D10 131
El-Minya, Egypt E11 48
Elmira, N.Y., U.S. C4 125
El Mirage, Az., U.S. k8 96
Elmira Heights, N.Y., U.S. . C4 125
El Mohammadia, Alg. J7 16
Elmont, N.Y., U.S. k13 125
Elmora, Pa., U.S. E4 131
Elmore, Mn., U.S. G4 116
Elmore, Oh., U.S. A2 128
Elmore, co., Al., U.S. C3 94
Elmore, co., Id., U.S. F3 105
El Morro National Monument, N.M., U.S. B1 124
El Mreyyé, reg., Maur. C3 50
Elmsdale, N.S., Can. E6 87
Elmshorn, Ger. D11 12
Elm Springs, Ar., U.S. A1 97
Elmvale, On., Can. C5 89
Elmwood, Il., U.S. C3 106
Elmwood, Wi., U.S. D1 142
Elmwood Park, Il., U.S. . . . k9 106

Name	Map Ref.	Page

Elmwood Park, N.J., U.S. **h8** 123
Elmwood Place, Oh., U.S. . . . **o13** 128
Elnora, In., U.S. **G3** 107
Eloise, Fl., U.S. **E5** 102
Elon College, N.C., U.S. **A3** 126
Elora, On., Can. **D4** 89
Elorza, Ven. **D6** 80
Éloten, Turk. **C8** 42
Eloy, Az., U.S. **E4** 96
El Paso, Il., U.S. **C4** 106
El Paso, Tx., U.S. **o11** 136
El Paso, co., Co., U.S. **C6** 99
El Paso, co., Tx., U.S. **o11** 136
El Pital, Cerro, mtn., N.A. . . **C2** 80
El Portal, Fl., U.S. **s13** 102
El Prado, N.M., U.S. **A4** 124
El Progreso, Hond. **B2** 80
El Puerto de Santa María,
  Spain **I3** 16
El-Qâhira (Cairo), Egypt . . . **D10** 48
El-Qasr, Egypt **E10** 48
El Reno, Ok., U.S. **B4** 129
Elrose, Sk., Can. **F1** 91
Elroy, Wi., U.S. **E3** 142
Elsa, Tx., U.S. **F3** 136
Elsah, Il., U.S. **E3** 106
El Salto, Mex. **C3** 78
El Salvador, ctry., N.A. **C2** 80
El Sauzal, Mex. **A1** 78
Elsberry, Mo., U.S. **B7** 118
Elsie, Mi., U.S. **E6** 115
Elsinore, Ut., U.S. **E3** 137
El'sk, Bela. **D10** 20
Elsmere, De., U.S. **B3** 101
Elsmere, Ky., U.S. **B5** 110
El Sueco, Mex. **B3** 78
El-Suweis, Egypt **E11** 48
Eltham, N.Z. **o13** 63c
El Tigre, Ven. **B7** 70
El Toco, Chile **C4** 72
Elton, La., U.S. **D3** 111
El Toro Marine Corps Air
  Station, mil., Ca., U.S. . . **n13** 98
El Turbio, Arg. **H2** 69
El-Uqsor, Egypt **E11** 48
Elūru, India **F4** 40
El Vado Reservoir, res.,
  N.M., U.S. **A3** 124
Elvas, Port. **H3** 16
Elvins, Mo., U.S. **D7** 118
El Wad, Alg. **E5** 14
El Wak, Kenya **E5** 54
Elwell, Lake, res., Mt., U.S. **B5** 119
Elwha, stm., Wa., U.S. **A2** 140
Elwood, In., U.S. **D6** 107
Elwood, Ks., U.S. **C9** 109
Elwood, Ne., U.S. **D6** 120
Elwood, N.J., U.S. **h8** 123
Elx, Spain **H6** 16
Ely, Eng., U.K. **D7** 12
Ely, Mn., U.S. **C7** 116
Ely, Nv., U.S. **D7** 121
Elyria, Oh., U.S. **A3** 128
Elysburg, Pa., U.S. **E8** 131
Emāmshahr, Iran **C7** 42
Emanuel, co., Ga., U.S. **D4** 103
Emba, Kaz. **E10** 22
Emba, stm., Kaz. **E7** 26
Embarras, stm., Il., U.S. . . . **E6** 106
Embarrass, stm., Wi., U.S. . . **D5** 142
Embro, On., Can. **D4** 89
Embu, Kenya **D7** 54
Emden, Ger. **D10** 12
Emerald, Austl. **E4** 62
Emerson, Mb., Can. **E3** 86
Emerson, Ga., U.S. **B2** 103
Emerson, Ne., U.S. **B9** 120
Emerson, N.J., U.S. **h8** 123
Emery, co., Ut., U.S. **E5** 137
Emet, Tur. **C4** 44
Emiliano Zapata, Mex. **D6** 78
Emily, Mn., U.S. **D5** 116
Emily, Lake, l., Mn., U.S. . . **E3** 116
Eminence, Ky., U.S. **B4** 110
Emirdağ, Tur. **C4** 44
Emmaus, Pa., U.S. **E11** 131
Emmen, Neth. **D10** 12
Emmet, co., Ia., U.S. **A3** 108
Emmet, co., Mi., U.S. **C6** 115
Emmetsburg, Ia., U.S. **A3** 108
Emmett, Id., U.S. **F2** 105
Emmitsburg, Md., U.S. **A3** 113
Emmonak, Ak., U.S. **C7** 95
Emmons, co., N.D., U.S. . . . **C5** 127
Emory Peak, mtn., Tx., U.S. **E1** 136
Empalme, Mex. **B2** 78
Empangeni, S. Afr. **D6** 56
Empedrado, Arg. **D6** 72
Emperor Seamounts **D19** 64
Empire, La., U.S. **E6** 111
Empire, Nv., U.S. **C2** 121
Empoli, Italy **F5** 18
Emporia, Ks., U.S. **D7** 109
Emporia, Va., U.S. **D5** 139
Emporium, Pa., U.S. **D5** 131
Empty Quarter see Ar-Rubʿ
  al-Khālī, des., Asia **G6** 38
Emsworth, Pa., U.S. **h13** 131
Encampment, Wy., U.S. **E6** 143
Encarnación, Para. **D6** 72
Enchilayas, Mex. **A2** 78
Encinitas, Ca., U.S. **F5** 98
Encontrados, Ven. **D5** 80
Encounter Bay, b., Austl. . . **H2** 62
Ende, Indon. **E6** 36
Enderby, B.C., Can. **D8** 85

Enderby Land, reg., Ant. . . . **D9** 67
Enderlin, N.D., U.S. **C8** 127
Enders Reservoir, res., Ne.,
  U.S. **D4** 120
Endicott, N.Y., U.S. **C4** 125
Endicott Mountains, mts.,
  Ak., U.S. **B9** 95
Endless Lake, l., Me., U.S. . . **C4** 112
Endwell, N.Y., U.S. **C4** 125
Enewetak, atoll, Marsh. Is. . **C10** 58
Enfield (Thompsonville), Ct.,
  U.S. **B5** 100
Enfield, N.C., U.S. **A5** 126
Enfield, N.H., U.S. **C2** 122
Engel's, Russia **D6** 26
Enggano, Pulau, i., Indon. . . **E2** 36
England, Ar., U.S. **C4** 97
England, prov., U.K. **D6** 12
Englee, Nf., Can. **C3** 88
Engleside, Va., U.S. **g12** 139
Englewood, Co., U.S. **B6** 99
Englewood, Fl., U.S. **F4** 102
Englewood, N.J., U.S. **B5** 123
Englewood, Oh., U.S. **C1** 128
Englewood, Tn., U.S. **D9** 135
Englewood Cliffs, N.J., U.S. . **h9** 123
English, In., U.S. **H5** 107
English Bāzār see Ingrāj
  Bāzār, India **E5** 40
English Channel, strt., Eur. . **C5** 16
English Coast, Ant. **D33** 67
Enid, Ok., U.S. **A4** 129
Enid Lake, res., Ms., U.S. . . **A4** 117
Enigma, Ga., U.S. **E3** 103
Enisej (Yenisey), stm., Russia **C10** 26
eNjesuthi, mtn., Afr. **D4** 56
Enka, N.C., U.S. **f10** 126
Enköping, Swe. **G7** 10
Enna, Italy **F5** 18
Ennedi, plat., Chad **G9** 48
Ennis, Mt., U.S. **E5** 119
Ennis, Tx., U.S. **C4** 136
Enoch, Ut., U.S. **F2** 137
Enola, Pa., U.S. **F8** 131
Enontekiö, Fin. **B10** 10
Enoree, S.C., U.S. **B4** 133
Enoree, stm., S.C., U.S. . . . **B3** 133
Enosburg Falls, Vt., U.S. . . . **B3** 138
Enriquillo, Lago, l., Dom.
  Rep. **B5** 80
Enschede, Neth. **D10** 12
Ensenada, Mex. **A1** 78
Enshi, China **E9** 28
Enshu Bay see Enshū-nada,
  Japan **D3** 31
Enshū-nada, Japan **D3** 31
Ensley, Fl., U.S. **u14** 102
Entebbe, Ug. **C6** 54
Enterprise, Al., U.S. **D4** 94
Enterprise, Ks., U.S. **D6** 109
Enterprise, Or., U.S. **B9** 130
Enterprise, Ut., U.S. **F2** 137
Enterprise, W.V., U.S. **B4** 141
Entiat, stm., Wa., U.S. **B5** 140
Entiat, Lake, l., Wa., U.S. . . **B5** 140
Entiat Mountains, mts., Wa.,
  U.S. **B5** 140
Entroncamento, Port. **H2** 16
Enugu, Nig. **E6** 50
Enumclaw, Wa., U.S. **B4** 140
Enurmino, Russia **C20** 26
Enyamba, D.R.C. **D5** 54
Eola Hills, hills, Or., U.S. . . **h11** 130
Epena, Congo **C3** 54
Épernay, Fr. **C8** 16
Ephesus see Efes, hist., Tur. **D2** 44
Ephraim, Ut., U.S. **D4** 137
Ephrata, Pa., U.S. **F9** 131
Ephrata, Wa., U.S. **B6** 140
Épi, i., Vanuatu **I9** 62a
Épinal, Fr. **C10** 16
Epirus see Ípeiros, hist. reg.,
  Grc. **E8** 18
Epping, N.H., U.S. **D4** 122
Epukiro, Nmb. **C2** 56
Epworth, Ia., U.S. **B7** 108
Eqlīd, Iran **D6** 42
Equatorial Guinea, ctry., Afr. **C1** 54
Erath, La., U.S. **E3** 111
Erath, co., Tx., U.S. **C3** 136
Erbaa, Tur. **B7** 44
Erciş, Tur. **C10** 44
Erciyes Dağı, vol., Tur. **C6** 44
Érd, Hung. **F5** 20
Erdek, Tur. **B2** 44
Erdemli, Tur. **D6** 44
Erdene see Ulaan-Uul,
  Mong. **C10** 28
Erebus, Mount, mtn., Ant. . **D21** 67
Erechim, Braz. **D7** 72
Ereğli, Tur. **D5** 44
Ereğli, Tur. **B4** 44
Erenhot, China **C10** 28
Erfoud, Mor. **E3** 14
Erfurt, Ger. **E12** 12
Ergani, Tur. **C8** 44
Ergel, Mong. **C9** 28
Ergene, stm., Tur. **B2** 44
Ergun see Argun', stm., Asia **D14** 26
Erick, Ok., U.S. **B2** 129
Erickson, Mb., Can. **D2** 86
Erie, Co., U.S. **A5** 99
Erie, Il., U.S. **B3** 106
Erie, Ks., U.S. **E8** 109

Erie, Mi., U.S. **G7** 115
Erie, Pa., U.S. **B1** 131
Erie, co., N.Y., U.S. **C2** 125
Erie, co., Oh., U.S. **A3** 128
Erie, co., Pa., U.S. **C1** 131
Erie, Lake, l., N.A. **C11** 92
Erie Canal, N.Y., U.S. **B5** 125
Erimo-misaki, c., Japan . . . **C16** 28
Erin, On., Can. **D4** 89
Erin, Tn., U.S. **A4** 135
Eritrea, ctry., Afr. **G12** 48
Erlangen, Ger. **F12** 12
Erlanger, Ky., U.S. **A5** 110
Erling, Lake, res., Ar., U.S. . **D2** 97
Ermelo, S. Afr. **D4** 56
Ermenek, Tur. **D5** 44
Ermolaevo, Russia **D10** 22
Ermoúpolis, Grc. **F10** 18
Erne, Lower Lough, l., N.
  Ire. **C3** 12
Erne, Upper Lough, l., Eur. . **C3** 12
Erode, India **G3** 40
Erofej Pavlovič, Russia . . . **D14** 26
Eropol, Russia **C18** 26
Er-Rachidia, Mor. **E3** 14
Errego, Moz. **B6** 56
Erromango, i., Vanuatu . . . **I9** 62a
Eršov, Russia **D8** 22
Ertai, China **B6** 28
Ertil', Russia **D16** 20
Ertis see Irtysh, stm., Asia . **D8** 26
Ertix see Irtysh, stm., Asia . **B6** 28
Erwin, N.C., U.S. **B4** 126
Erwin, Tn., U.S. **C11** 135
Eryuan, China **A3** 34
Erzgebirge, mts., Eur. **E9** 8
Erzin, Russia **D11** 26
Erzincan, Tur. **C8** 44
Erzurum, Tur. **C9** 44
Esa'ala, Pap. N. Gui. **H13** 32
Esbjerg, Den. **I3** 10
Escalante, Ut., U.S. **F4** 137
Escalante, stm., Ut., U.S. . . **F4** 137
Escalon, Ca., U.S. **D3** 98
Escambia, co., Al., U.S. . . . **D2** 94
Escambia, co., Fl., U.S. . . **u14** 102
Escambia, stm., Fl., U.S. . . **u14** 102
Escanaba, Mi., U.S. **C3** 115
Escanaba, stm., Mi., U.S. . . **B3** 115
Escárcega, Mex. **D6** 78
Escarpada Point, c., Phil. . . **C8** 34
Escatawpa, Ms., U.S. **E5** 117
Escatawpa, stm., U.S. **D5** 117
Escondido, Ca., U.S. **F5** 98
Escondido, stm., Nic. **C3** 80
Escoumins, Rivière des,
  stm., P.Q., Can. **A8** 90
Escuinapa de Hidalgo, Mex. **C3** 78
Escuintla, Guat. **C1** 80
Escuminac, Point, c., N.B.,
  Can. **B5** 87
Eséka, Cam. **C2** 54
Eşfahān, Iran **D6** 42
Esil', Kaz. **D8** 26
Eškar-Ola, Russia **D6** 26
Eskilstuna, Swe. **G7** 10
Eskimo Lakes, l., N.T., Can. **E13** 82
Eskişehir, Tur. **C4** 44
Esla, stm., Spain **G4** 16
Eslāmābād, Iran **E12** 44
Eslāmshahr, Iran **C6** 42
Eşme, Tur. **C3** 44
Esmeralda, co., Nv., U.S. . . **F4** 121
Esmeraldas, Ec. **C4** 70
Esmond, R.I., U.S. **B4** 132
Esmond, R.I., U.S. **B4** 132
Espanola, On., Can. **A3** 89
Espanola, N.M., U.S. **B3** 124
Esparto, Ca., U.S. **C2** 98
Esperança, Braz. **B3** 70
Esperance, Austl. **G3** 60
Esperance Bay, b., Austl. . . **G3** 60
Esperanza, Arg. **E5** 72
Esperanza, Mex. **B3** 78
Espinhaço, Serra do, mts.,
  Braz. **E3** 74
Espinho, Port. **G2** 16
Espírito Santo, state, Braz. . **E3** 74
Espíritu Santo, i., Vanuatu . **j9** 62a
Espíritu Santo, Isla del, i.,
  Mex. **C2** 78
Esplanada, Braz. **D4** 74
Espoo, Fin. **F11** 10
Espungabera, Moz. **C5** 56
Espy, Pa., U.S. **D9** 131
Esquel, Arg. **F2** 69
Esquimalt, B.C., Can. **E6** 85
Esquina, Arg. **D6** 72
Essaouira, Mor. **D3** 48
Essendon, Mount, mtn.,
  Austl. **E3** 60
Essequibo, stm., Guy. **C8** 70
Essex, On., Can. **E2** 89
Essex, Ct., U.S. **D6** 100
Essex, Ia., U.S. **D2** 108
Essex, Ma., U.S. **A6** 114
Essex, Md., U.S. **B5** 113
Essex, Vt., U.S. **B2** 138
Essex, co., Ma., U.S. **A5** 114
Essex, co., N.J., U.S. **B4** 123
Essex, co., N.Y., U.S. **B7** 125
Essex, co., Vt., U.S. **B5** 138
Essex Junction, Vt., U.S. . . . **C2** 138

Essexville, Mi., U.S. **E7** 115
Esslingen am Neckar, Ger. . **F11** 12
Estacada, Or., U.S. **B4** 130
Estacado, Llano, pl., U.S. . . **C1** 136
Estados, Isla de los, i., Arg. **H4** 69
Eṣṭahbān, Iran **E6** 42
Estância, Braz. **D4** 74
Estancia, N.M., U.S. **C3** 124
Estcourt, S. Afr. **D4** 56
Estelí, Nic. **C2** 80
Estella, Spain **F5** 16
Estelline, S.D., U.S. **C9** 134
Estepona, Spain **I4** 16
Estero Bay, b., Ca., U.S. . . **E3** 98
Estero Bay, b., Fl., U.S. . . . **F5** 102
Estero Island, i., Fl., U.S. . . **F5** 102
Estes Park, Co., U.S. **A5** 99
Estherville, Ia., U.S. **A3** 108
Estherwood, La., U.S. **D3** 111
Estill, S.C., U.S. **F5** 133
Estill, co., Ky., U.S. **C6** 110
Estill Springs, Tn., U.S. **B5** 135
Estonia, ctry., Eur. **G11** 10
Estremadura, hist. reg., Port. **H2** 16
Esztergom, Hung. **F5** 20
Etah, Grnld. **C25** 82
Étampes, Fr. **C8** 16
Étang-du-Nord, P.Q., Can. . **B8** 87
Etāwah, India **D3** 40
Ethel, W.V., U.S. **n12** 141
Ethel Creek, Austl. **E3** 60
Ethiopia, ctry., Afr. **I12** 48
Etna, Pa., U.S. **k14** 131
Etna, Monte, vol., Italy . . . **F5** 18
Etobicoke, On., Can. **D5** 89
Etolin Island, i., Ak., U.S. . **m23** 95
Etolin Strait, strt., Ak., U.S. **C6** 95
Etosha Pan, pl., Nmb. **B2** 56
Etowah, Tn., U.S. **D9** 135
Etowah, co., Al., U.S. **A3** 94
Etowah, stm., Ga., U.S. . . . **B2** 103
Et Tîdra, i., Maur. **C1** 50
Ettrick, Va., U.S. **C5** 139
Eua, i., Tonga **G12** 58
Euboea see Évvoia, i., Grc. . **E9** 18
Euboea, Gulf of see Vórios
  Evvoïkós Kólpos, b.,
  Grc. **E9** 18
Eucla, Austl. **G4** 60
Euclid, Oh., U.S. **A4** 128
Eudora, Ar., U.S. **D4** 97
Eudora, Ks., U.S. **D8** 109
Eufaula, Al., U.S. **D4** 94
Eufaula, Ok., U.S. **B6** 129
Eufaula Lake, res., Ok., U.S. **B6** 129
Eugene, Or., U.S. **C3** 130
Eugenia, Punta, c., Mex. . . **B1** 78
Eugmo, i., Fin. **E10** 10
Eunice, La., U.S. **D3** 111
Eunice, N.M., U.S. **E6** 124
Euphrates (Al-Furāt), stm.,
  Asia **D4** 42
Eupora, Ms., U.S. **B4** 117
Eureka, Ca., U.S. **B1** 98
Eureka, Il., U.S. **C4** 106
Eureka, Ks., U.S. **E7** 109
Eureka, Mo., U.S. **f12** 118
Eureka, Mt., U.S. **B1** 119
Eureka, Nv., U.S. **D5** 121
Eureka, S.C., U.S. **B5** 133
Eureka, S.D., U.S. **B6** 134
Eureka, co., Nv., U.S. **D5** 121
Eureka Springs, Ar., U.S. . . **A2** 97
Euroa, Austl. **H4** 62
Europe **C13** 4
Eustis, Fl., U.S. **D5** 102
Eutaw, Al., U.S. **C2** 94
Eutsuk Lake, l., B.C., Can. . **C4** 85
Evangeline, co., La., U.S. . . **D3** 111
Evans, Co., U.S. **A6** 99
Evans, Ga., U.S. **C4** 103
Evans, W.V., U.S. **C3** 141
Evans, co., Ga., U.S. **D5** 103
Evans, Mount, mtn., Co.,
  U.S. **B5** 99
Evansburg, Ab., Can. **C3** 84
Evans City, Pa., U.S. **E1** 131
Evansdale, Ia., U.S. **B5** 108
Evanston, Il., U.S. **A6** 106
Evanston, Wy., U.S. **E2** 143
Evansville, In., U.S. **I2** 107
Evansville, Wi., U.S. **F4** 142
Evansville, Wy., U.S. **D6** 143
Eva Perón see La Plata, Arg. **F6** 72
Evart, Mi., U.S. **E5** 115
Evarts, Ky., U.S. **D6** 110
Eveleth, Mn., U.S. **C6** 116
Evensk, Russia **C17** 26
Everest, Mount, mtn., Asia . **D5** 40
Everett, Ma., U.S. **g11** 114
Everett, Pa., U.S. **F5** 131
Everett, Wa., U.S. **B3** 140
Everett Lake, res., N.H.,
  U.S. **D3** 122
Everglades National Park,
  Fl., U.S. **G5** 102
Evergreen, Al., U.S. **D3** 94
Evergreen, Co., U.S. **B5** 99
Evergreen Park, Il., U.S. . . . **k9** 106
Everly, Ia., U.S. **A2** 108
Everson, Wa., U.S. **A3** 140
Evje, Nor. **G2** 10
Évora, Port. **H3** 16
Évreux, Fr. **C7** 16

Évros (Marica) (Meriç), stm.,
  Eur. **D11** 18
E.V. Spence Reservoir, res.,
  Tx., U.S. **D2** 136
Évvoia, i., Grc. **E9** 18
Ewa, Hi., U.S. **B3** 104
Ewa Beach, Hi., U.S. **B3** 104
Ewa Beach, Hi., U.S. **g9** 104
Ewing Township, N.J., U.S. . **C3** 123
Ewo, Congo **D2** 54
Excelsior Mountain, mtn.,
  Ca., U.S. **C4** 98
Excelsior Mountains, mts.,
  Nv., U.S. **E3** 121
Excelsior Springs, Mo., U.S. **B3** 118
Exeter, On., Can. **D3** 89
Exeter, Eng., U.K. **E5** 12
Exeter, Ca., U.S. **D4** 98
Exeter, Ne., U.S. **D8** 120
Exeter, N.H., U.S. **E5** 122
Exeter, Pa., U.S. **D10** 131
Exeter, stm., N.H., U.S. . . . **E5** 122
Exira, Ia., U.S. **C3** 108
Exmore, Va., U.S. **C7** 139
Exmouth, Austl. **E1** 60
Exmouth Gulf, b., Austl. . . . **E1** 60
Experiment, Ga., U.S. **C2** 103
Exploits, stm., Nf., Can. . . . **D3** 88
Exploits, Bay of, b., Nf.,
  Can. **D4** 88
Export, Pa., U.S. **F2** 131
Extremadura, hist. reg.,
  Spain **H3** 16
Exuma Cays, is., Bah. **A4** 80
Exuma Sound, strt., Bah. . . **D9** 76
Eyasi, Lake, l., Tan. **D7** 54
Eyl, Som. **I14** 48
Eylar Mountain, mtn., Ca.,
  U.S. **D3** 98
Eyota, Mn., U.S. **G6** 116
Eyre, Austl. **G4** 60
Eyre North, Lake, l., Austl. . **F2** 62
Eyre Peninsula, pen., Austl. **G6** 60
Ezequiel Ramos Mexía,
  Embalse, res., Arg. **E3** 69
Ezine, Tur. **C2** 44

F

Fabens, Tx., U.S. **o11** 136
Fabius, stm., Mo., U.S. **A6** 118
Fabriano, Italy **C4** 18
Fachi, Niger **C7** 50
Factoryville, Pa., U.S. . . . **C10** 131
Fada, Chad **G9** 48
Fada-Ngourma, Burkina . . . **D5** 50
Faenza, Italy **B3** 18
Faeroe Islands see Faroe
  Islands, is., Far. Is. . . . **B12** 4
Fǎgǎraș, Rom. **G8** 20
Fagernes, Nor. **F3** 10
Fagersta, Swe. **G6** 10
Fairacres, N.M., U.S. **E3** 124
Fairbank, Ia., U.S. **B5** 108
Fairbanks, Ak., U.S. **C10** 95
Fair Bluff, N.C., U.S. **C3** 126
Fairborn, Oh., U.S. **C1** 128
Fairburn, Ga., U.S. **C2** 103
Fairbury, Il., U.S. **C5** 106
Fairbury, Ne., U.S. **D8** 120
Fairchance, Pa., U.S. **G2** 131
Fairchild Air Force Base,
  mil., Wa., U.S. **g13** 140
Fairdale, Ky., U.S. **B4** 110
Fairfax, Ca., U.S. **C2** 98
Fairfax, De., U.S. **A3** 101
Fairfax, Ia., U.S. **C6** 108
Fairfax, Mn., U.S. **F4** 116
Fairfax, Mo., U.S. **A2** 118
Fairfax, Ok., U.S. **A5** 129
Fairfax, S.C., U.S. **F5** 133
Fairfax, Va., U.S. **B5** 139
Fairfax, co., Va., U.S. **B5** 139
Fairfield, Al., U.S. **B3** 94
Fairfield, Ca., U.S. **C2** 98
Fairfield, Ct., U.S. **E2** 100
Fairfield, Ia., U.S. **C6** 108
Fairfield, Il., U.S. **E5** 106
Fairfield, Me., U.S. **D3** 112
Fairfield, Mt., U.S. **C5** 119
Fairfield, Oh., U.S. **n12** 128
Fairfield, Tx., U.S. **D4** 136
Fairfield, co., Ct., U.S. **D2** 100
Fairfield, co., Oh., U.S. . . . **C3** 128
Fairfield, co., S.C., U.S. . . . **C5** 133
Fairfield Bay, Ar., U.S. **B3** 97
Fairfield Pond, l., Vt., U.S. . **B3** 138
Fair Grove, Mo., U.S. **D4** 118
Fair Grove, N.C., U.S. **B2** 126
Fairhaven, Ma., U.S. **C6** 114
Fair Haven, Mi., U.S. **F8** 115
Fair Haven, N.J., U.S. **C4** 123
Fair Haven, Vt., U.S. **D2** 138
Fairhope, Al., U.S. **E2** 94
Fair Isle, i., Scot., U.K. . . . **i19** 12a
Fairland, In., U.S. **E6** 107
Fairland, Ok., U.S. **A7** 129
Fair Lawn, N.J., U.S. **h8** 123
Fairlawn, Va., U.S. **C2** 139
Fairlea, W.V., U.S. **D4** 141
Fairmont, Il., U.S. **C6** 106
Fairmont, Mn., U.S. **G4** 116
Fairmont, N.C., U.S. **C3** 126
Fairmont, Ne., U.S. **D8** 120
Fairmont, W.V., U.S. **B4** 141

Name	Map Ref.	Page

Name	Map Ref.	Page
Fairmount, Ga., U.S.	B2	103
Fairmount, In., U.S.	D6	107
Fairmount Heights, Md., U.S.	f9	113
Fair Oaks, Ca., U.S.	h7	98
Fairoaks, Pa., U.S.	h13	131
Fair Plain, Mi., U.S.	F4	115
Fairport, N.Y., U.S.	B3	125
Fairport Harbor, Oh., U.S.	A4	128
Fairvale, N.B., Can.	D4	87
Fairview, Ab., Can.	A1	84
Fairview, Mt., U.S.	C12	119
Fairview, N.J., U.S.	h8	123
Fairview, Ok., U.S.	A3	129
Fairview, Pa., U.S.	B1	131
Fairview, Tn., U.S.	B4	135
Fairview, Ut., U.S.	D4	137
Fairview Heights, Il., U.S.	E3	106
Fairview Park, In., U.S.	E3	107
Fairview Park, Oh., U.S.	g9	128
Fairview Peak, mtn., Nv., U.S.	D3	121
Fairview Peak, mtn., Or., U.S.	D4	130
Fairway, Ks., U.S.	k16	109
Fairweather Mountain, mtn., N.A.	G12	82
Fais, i., Micron.	E11	32
Faisalabad, Pak.	D10	42
Faison, N.C., U.S.	B4	126
Faizābād, India	D4	40
Fakfak, Indon.	D8	36
Fakse Bugt, b., Den.	I5	10
Faku, China	C12	28
Falaba, S.L.	E2	50
Falam, Myan.	B2	34
Falconer, N.Y., U.S.	C1	125
Falcon Heights, Mn., U.S.	n12	116
Falcon Heights, Or., U.S.	E5	130
Fălești, Mol.	F9	20
Falfurrias, Tx., U.S.	F3	136
Falher, Ab., Can.	B2	84
Falkenberg, Swe.	H5	10
Falkland Islands, dep., S.A.	H4	69
Falkland Islands, is., Falk. Is.	J9	4
Falkland Sound, strt., Falk. Is.	H4	69
Falköping, Swe.	G5	10
Falkville, Al., U.S.	A3	94
Fall, stm., Ks., U.S.	E7	109
Fall Branch, Tn., U.S.	C11	135
Fallbrook, Ca., U.S.	F5	98
Fall City, Wa., U.S.	B4	140
Fall Creek, Wi., U.S.	D2	142
Falling Creek, stm., Va., U.S.	n17	139
Falling Rock Creek, stm., W.V., U.S.	m13	141
Fall Mountain Lake, Ct., U.S.	C4	100
Fallon, Nv., U.S.	D3	121
Fallon, co., Mt., U.S.	D12	119
Fallon Indian Reservation, Nv., U.S.	D3	121
Fallon Naval Air Station, mil., Nv., U.S.	D3	121
Fall River, Ma., U.S.	C5	114
Fall River, Wi., U.S.	E4	142
Fall River, co., S.D., U.S.	D2	134
Fall River Lake, res., Ks., U.S.	E7	109
Falls, co., Tx., U.S.	D4	136
Falls Church, Va., U.S.	g12	139
Falls City, Ne., U.S.	D10	120
Falls City, Or., U.S.	C3	130
Falls Creek, Pa., U.S.	D4	131
Fallston, Md., U.S.	A5	113
Falmouth, N.S., Can.	E5	87
Falmouth, Eng., U.K.	E4	12
Falmouth, Ky., U.S.	B5	110
Falmouth, Ma., U.S.	C6	114
Falmouth, Me., U.S.	E2	112
Falmouth, Va., U.S.	B5	139
False Bay see Valsbaai, b., S. Afr.	E2	56
False Cape, c., Fl., U.S.	D6	102
False Cape, c., Va., U.S.	D7	139
Falster, i., Den.	I5	10
Fălticeni, Rom.	F9	20
Falun, Swe.	F6	10
Fanchang, China	C4	30
Fancy Farm, Ky., U.S.	f9	110
Fangak, Sudan	B6	54
Fangcheng, China	E2	30
Fangcheng, China	C3	30
Fangxian, China	C3	30
Fangzheng, China	A1	31
Fannin, co., Ga., U.S.	B2	103
Fannin, co., Tx., U.S.	C4	136
Fanny, Mount, mtn., Or., U.S.	B9	130
Fano, Italy	C4	18
Fan Si Pan, mtn., Viet.	B4	34
Faradje, D.R.C.	C5	54
Faradofay see Tôlañaro, Madag.	D8	56
Farafangana, Madag.	C8	56
Farāh, Afg.	D8	42
Farallon de Medinilla, i., N. Mar. Is.	C12	32
Farallon de Pajaros, i., N. Mar. Is.	B12	32
Faranah, Gui.	D2	50
Farasān, Jazā'ir, is., Sau. Ar.	G4	38
Farewell, Cape, c., N.Z.	p13	63c
Fargo, Ga., U.S.	F4	103

Name	Map Ref.	Page
Fargo, N.D., U.S.	C9	127
Faribault, Mn., U.S.	F5	116
Faribault, co., Mn., U.S.	G4	116
Farīdābād, India	D3	40
Farley, Ia., U.S.	B6	108
Farmer City, Il., U.S.	C5	106
Farmers Branch, Tx., U.S.	n10	136
Farmersburg, In., U.S.	F3	107
Farmerville, La., U.S.	B3	111
Farmingdale, Me., U.S.	D3	112
Farmington, Ar., U.S.	A1	97
Farmington, Ct., U.S.	C4	100
Farmington, Ia., U.S.	D6	108
Farmington, Il., U.S.	C3	106
Farmington, Me., U.S.	D2	112
Farmington, Mi., U.S.	p15	115
Farmington, Mn., U.S.	F5	116
Farmington, Mo., U.S.	D7	118
Farmington, N.H., U.S.	D4	122
Farmington, N.M., U.S.	A1	124
Farmington, Ut., U.S.	C4	137
Farmington, stm., Ct., U.S.	B4	100
Farmington Hills, Mi., U.S.	o15	115
Farmland, In., U.S.	D7	107
Farmville, N.C., U.S.	B5	126
Farmville, Va., U.S.	C4	139
Farnham, P.Q., Can.	D5	90
Faro, Braz.	D8	70
Faro, Port.	I3	16
Faroe Islands, dep., Eur.	o23	10b
Faroe Islands, is., Far. Is.	B12	4
Fårön, i., Swe.	H8	10
Fårösund, Swe.	H8	10
Farquhar, Atoll de, is., Sey.	j12	57b
Farrell, Pa., U.S.	D1	131
Farrukhābād, India	D3	40
Fartak, Ra's, c., Yemen	G6	38
Farvel, Kap, c., Grnld.	G31	82
Farwell, Mi., U.S.	E6	115
Farwell, Tx., U.S.	B1	136
Fasā, Iran	E6	42
Fastiv, Ukr.	D10	20
Fatick, Sen.	D1	50
Fatsa, Tur.	B7	44
Faulk, co., S.D., U.S.	B6	134
Faulkland Heights, De., U.S.	i7	101
Faulkner, co., Ar., U.S.	B3	97
Faulkton, S.D., U.S.	B6	134
Fauquier, co., Va., U.S.	B5	139
Fauske, Nor.	C6	10
Fawnie Nose, mtn., B.C., Can.	C5	85
Faxaflói, b., Ice.	l17	10a
Faya-Largeau, Chad	C8	50
Fayd, Sau. Ar.	E4	42
Fayette, Al., U.S.	B2	94
Fayette, Ia., U.S.	B6	108
Fayette, Mo., U.S.	B5	118
Fayette, Ms., U.S.	D2	117
Fayette, Oh., U.S.	A1	128
Fayette, co., Al., U.S.	B3	94
Fayette, co., Ga., U.S.	C2	103
Fayette, co., Ia., U.S.	B6	108
Fayette, co., Il., U.S.	D5	106
Fayette, co., In., U.S.	E7	107
Fayette, co., Ky., U.S.	B5	110
Fayette, co., Oh., U.S.	C2	128
Fayette, co., Pa., U.S.	G2	131
Fayette, co., Tn., U.S.	B2	135
Fayette, co., Tx., U.S.	E4	136
Fayette, co., W.V., U.S.	C3	141
Fayetteville, Ar., U.S.	A1	97
Fayetteville, Ga., U.S.	C2	103
Fayetteville, N.C., U.S.	B4	126
Fayetteville, Pa., U.S.	G6	131
Fayetteville, Tn., U.S.	B5	135
Fayetteville, W.V., U.S.	C3	141
Fāzilka, India	C2	40
Fazzān, hist. reg., Libya	A7	50
Fdérik, Maur.	B2	50
Fear, Cape, c., N.C., U.S.	D5	126
Feather, stm., Ca., U.S.	C3	98
Fécamp, Fr.	C7	16
Federal, Arg.	E6	72
Federalsburg, Md., U.S.	C6	113
Federated States of Micronesia see Micronesia, Federated States of, ctry., Oc.	D8	58
Feeding Hills, Ma., U.S.	B2	114
Fehmarn, i., Ger.	C12	12
Feijó, Braz.	E5	70
Feira de Santana, Braz.	D4	74
Felipe Carrillo Puerto, Mex.	D7	78
Fellsmere, Fl., U.S.	E6	102
Felton, Ca., U.S.	D2	98
Felton, De., U.S.	D3	101
Femunden, l., Nor.	E4	10
Fence, stm., Mi., U.S.	B2	115
Fence Lake, l., Wi., U.S.	C4	142
Fenelon Falls, On., Can.	C6	89
Fengcheng, China	F11	28
Fengdu, China	F9	28
Fengfeng, China	B3	30
Fenghuang, China	D2	30
Fengning, China	A4	30
Fengqing, China	B3	34
Fengqiu, China	B3	30
Fengrun, China	B4	30
Fengtai, China	C4	30
Fengzhen, China	A3	30

Name	Map Ref.	Page
Fenoarivo Atsinanana, Madag.	B8	56
Fenton, Mi., U.S.	F7	115
Fentress, co., Tn., U.S.	C9	135
Fenwick Island, i., S.C., U.S.	k11	133
Fenyang, China	D10	28
Fenyi, China	D3	30
Feodosiia, Ukr.	G13	20
Fer, Point au, c., La., U.S.	E4	111
Ferdinand, In., U.S.	H4	107
Ferdows, Iran	D7	42
Fergana, Uzb.	E9	26
Fergana Mountains see Ferganskij hrebet, mts., Kyrg.	A2	40
Ferganskij hrebet, mts., Kyrg.	A2	40
Fergus, On., Can.	D4	89
Fergus, co., Mt., U.S.	C7	119
Fergus Falls, Mn., U.S.	D2	116
Ferguson, Ky., U.S.	C5	110
Ferguson, Mo., U.S.	C7	118
Ferkéssédougou, C. Iv.	E3	50
Ferlo, reg., Sen.	C2	50
Ferme-Neuve, P.Q., Can.	C2	90
Fermo, Italy	C4	18
Fermont, P.Q., Can.	h13	90
Fernandina Beach, Fl., U.S.	B5	102
Fernando Póo see Bioko, i., Eq. Gui.	C1	54
Fernandópolis, Braz.	F1	74
Fernán-Núñez, Spain	I4	16
Fern Creek, Ky., U.S.	g11	110
Ferndale, Ca., U.S.	B1	98
Ferndale, Md., U.S.	B4	113
Ferndale, Mi., U.S.	P15	115
Ferndale, Pa., U.S.	F4	131
Ferndale, Wa., U.S.	A3	140
Fernie, B.C., Can.	E10	85
Fernley, Nv., U.S.	D2	121
Fern Ridge Lake, res., Or., U.S.	C3	130
Fernwood, Id., U.S.	B2	105
Fernwood, Ms., U.S.	D3	117
Feroe Islands see Faroe Islands, dep., Far. Is.	C5	8
Ferrara, Italy	B3	18
Ferrelo, Cape, c., Or., U.S.	E2	130
Ferriday, La., U.S.	C4	111
Ferris, Tx., U.S.	C4	136
Ferris Mountains, mts., Wy., U.S.	D5	143
Ferro see El Hierro, i., Spain	A1	50
Ferrol, Spain	F2	16
Ferron, Ut., U.S.	D4	137
Ferrum, Va., U.S.	D2	139
Ferry, co., Wa., U.S.	A7	140
Ferry Farms, Va., U.S.	B5	139
Ferryland, Nf., Can.	E5	88
Ferry Point, c., N.J., U.S.	k7	123
Fertile, Mn., U.S.	C2	116
Fès, Mor.	D4	48
Feshi, D.R.C.	E3	54
Fessenden, N.D., U.S.	B6	127
Festus, Mo., U.S.	C7	118
Fetești, Rom.	G9	20
Fethiye, Tur.	D3	44
Fetisovo, Kaz.	B6	42
Feuilles, Rivière aux, stm., P.Q., Can.	g12	90
Feyẕābād, Afg.	C10	42
Fianarantsoa, Madag.	C8	56
Fianga, Chad	E8	50
Fichē, Eth.	B7	54
Ficksburg, S. Afr.	D4	56
Fidalgo Island, i., Wa., U.S.	A3	140
Fieldale, Va., U.S.	D3	139
Fields, Lake, l., Fl., U.S.	B3	102
Fields, Lake, l., La., U.S.	k10	111
Fier, Alb.	D7	18
Fifteenmile Creek, stm., Wy., U.S.	B4	143
Fifteen Mile Falls Reservoir, res., U.S.	C5	138
Fifth Cataract, wtfl, Sudan	G11	48
Figtree, Zimb.	C4	56
Figueira da Foz, Port.	G2	16
Figueres, Spain	F8	16
Figuig, Mor.	D4	48
Fiji, ctry., Oc.	m10	63b
Filchner Ice Shelf, Ant.	D1	67
Filer, Id., U.S.	G4	105
Filingué, Niger	D5	50
Filippoi, hist., Grc.	D10	18
Fillmore, Ca., U.S.	E4	98
Fillmore, Ut., U.S.	E3	137
Fillmore, co., Mn., U.S.	G6	116
Fillmore, co., Ne., U.S.	D8	120
Fimi, stm., D.R.C.	C3	54
Findlay, Il., U.S.	D5	106
Findlay, Oh., U.S.	A2	128
Fíngoè, Moz.	B5	56
Finike, Tur.	D4	44
Finke, Austl.	F5	60
Finland, ctry., Eur.	E12	10
Finland, Gulf of, b., Eur.	G10	10
Finley, N.D., U.S.	B8	127
Finley, Tn., U.S.	A2	135
Finney, co., Ks., U.S.	D3	109
Finnmark, prov., Nor.	B11	10
Finn Mountain, mtn., Ak., U.S.	C8	95
Fins, Oman	F7	42
Finspång, Swe.	G6	10
Fircrest, Wa., U.S.	f10	140

Name	Map Ref.	Page
Firebaugh, Ca., U.S.	D3	98
Firenze (Florence), Italy	C3	18
Firestone, Co., U.S.	A6	99
Firozābād, India	D3	40
Firozpur, India	C2	40
First Cataract, wtfl, Egypt	F11	48
First Connecticut Lake, l., N.H., U.S.	f7	122
Firūzābād, Iran	E6	42
Fish, stm., Al., U.S.	E2	94
Fish, stm., Me., U.S.	A4	112
Fish Creek, stm., W.V., U.S.	g8	141
Fisher, Il., U.S.	C5	106
Fisher, co., Tx., U.S.	C2	136
Fisher Bay, b., Mb., Can.	D3	86
Fishers, In., U.S.	E5	107
Fishers Island, i., N.Y., U.S.	m16	125
Fishers Peak, mtn., Co., U.S.	D6	99
Fishersville, Va., U.S.	B4	139
Fishing Bay, b., Md., U.S.	D5	113
Fishing Creek, Md., U.S.	D5	113
Fishing Creek, stm., N.C., U.S.	A5	126
Fishing Creek, stm., S.C., U.S.	B5	133
Fishing Creek, stm., W.V., U.S.	B4	141
Fishing Creek Reservoir, res., S.C., U.S.	B6	133
Fishkill, N.Y., U.S.	D7	125
Fish Lake, l., Ut., U.S.	E4	137
Fish River Lake, l., Me., U.S.	B4	112
Fishtrap Lake, res., Ky., U.S.	C7	110
Fiskdale, Ma., U.S.	B3	114
Fisterra, Cabo de, c., Spain	F2	16
Fitchburg, Ma., U.S.	A4	114
Fitri, Lac, l., Chad	D8	50
Fitzgerald, Ga., U.S.	E3	103
Fitz Roy, Arg.	G3	69
Fitzroy, stm., Austl.	D3	60
Fitzroy Crossing, Austl.	D4	60
Fitzwilliam, N.H., U.S.	E2	122
Fitzwilliam Island, i., On., Can.	B3	89
Fiume see Rijeka, Cro.	B5	18
Five Island Lake, l., Ia., U.S.	A3	108
Fivemile Creek, stm., Wy., U.S.	C4	143
Five Points, N.M., U.S.	B3	124
Fizi, D.R.C.	D5	54
Flagler, co., Fl., U.S.	C5	102
Flagler Beach, Fl., U.S.	C5	102
Flagstaff, Az., U.S.	B4	96
Flagstaff Lake, l., Or., U.S.	E7	130
Flambeau, stm., Wi., U.S.	C3	142
Flaming Gorge Dam, Ut., U.S.	C6	137
Flaming Gorge National Recreation Area, U.S.	E3	143
Flaming Gorge Reservoir, res., U.S.	C6	92
Flaming Gorge Reservoir, res., U.S.	E3	143
Flanagan, Il., U.S.	C5	106
Flandreau, S.D., U.S.	C9	134
Flandreau Indian Reservation, S.D., U.S.	C9	134
Flat, stm., Mi., U.S.	E5	115
Flat, stm., N.C., U.S.	A4	126
Flat, stm., R.I., U.S.	E2	132
Flat Brook, stm., N.J., U.S.	A3	123
Flathead, co., Mt., U.S.	B2	119
Flathead, South Fork, stm., Mt., U.S.	C3	119
Flathead Indian Reservation, Mt., U.S.	C2	119
Flathead Lake, l., Mt., U.S.	C2	119
Flathead Valley, val., Mt., U.S.	C2	119
Flat Lake, l., La., U.S.	k9	111
Flat Lick, Ky., U.S.	D6	110
Flatonia, Tx., U.S.	E4	136
Flat River, Mo., U.S.	D7	118
Flat River Reservoir, res., R.I., U.S.	D3	132
Flat Rock, Mi., U.S.	F7	115
Flat Rock, N.C., U.S.	f10	126
Flatrock, stm., In., U.S.	F6	107
Flattery, Cape, c., Austl.	C4	62
Flattery, Cape, c., Wa., U.S.	A1	140
Flatwoods, Ky., U.S.	B7	110
Fleetwood, Pa., U.S.	F10	131
Fleming, co., Ky., U.S.	B6	110
Fleming-Neon, Ky., U.S.	C7	110
Flemingsburg, Ky., U.S.	B6	110
Flemington, N.J., U.S.	B3	123
Flemington, Pa., U.S.	D7	131
Flen, Swe.	G7	10
Flensburg, Ger.	C11	12
Fletcher, N.C., U.S.	f10	126
Fletcher, Ok., U.S.	C3	129
Flinders, stm., Austl.	D3	62
Flinders Bay, b., Austl.	G2	60
Flinders Island, i., Austl.	H4	62
Flinders Reefs, rf., Austl.	D4	62
Flin Flon, Mb., Can.	B1	86
Flint, i., Kir.	F14	58
Flint, stm., Ga., U.S.	E2	103
Flint, Mi., U.S.	E7	115
Flint City, Al., U.S.	A3	94
Flint Creek Range, mts., Mt., U.S.	D3	119
Flint Run, stm., W.V., U.S.	k9	141

Name	Map Ref.	Page
Flippin, Ar., U.S.	A3	97
Flisa, Nor.	F5	10
Flomaton, Al., U.S.	D2	94
Flora, Il., U.S.	E5	106
Flora, In., U.S.	C4	107
Flora, Ms., U.S.	C3	117
Florala, Al., U.S.	D3	94
Floral City, Fl., U.S.	D4	102
Florence see Firenze, Italy	C3	18
Florence, Al., U.S.	A2	94
Florence, Az., U.S.	D4	96
Florence, Co., U.S.	C5	99
Florence, Ks., U.S.	D7	109
Florence, Ky., U.S.	A5	110
Florence, Ms., U.S.	C3	117
Florence, N.J., U.S.	C3	123
Florence, Or., U.S.	D2	130
Florence, S.C., U.S.	C8	133
Florence, co., S.C., U.S.	C8	133
Florence, co., Wi., U.S.	C5	142
Florenceville, N.B., Can.	C2	87
Florencia, Col.	C4	70
Florencio, Col.	C4	70
Flores, i., Indon.	E6	36
Flores, Laut (Flores Sea), Indon.	E6	36
Flores Sea see Flores, Laut, Indon.	E6	36
Florești, Mol.	F10	20
Floresville, Tx., U.S.	E3	136
Florham Park, N.J., U.S.	B4	123
Floriano, Braz.	C3	74
Florianópolis, Braz.	D8	72
Florida, Cuba	A4	80
Florida, N.Y., U.S.	D6	125
Florida, Ur.	C6	72
Florida, state, U.S.	E5	102
Florida, Cape, c., Fl., U.S.	G6	102
Florida, Straits of, strt., N.A.	G11	92
Florida Bay, b., Fl., U.S.	H6	102
Floridablanca, Col.	D5	80
Florida City, Fl., U.S.	G6	102
Florida Keys, is., Fl., U.S.	H6	102
Florida Mountains, mts., N.M., U.S.	E2	124
Florida State Indian Reservation, Fl., U.S.	F5	102
Florien, La., U.S.	C2	111
Flórina, Grc.	D8	18
Florissant, Mo., U.S.	f13	118
Florissant Fossil Beds National Monument, Co., U.S.	C5	99
Florø, Nor.	F1	10
Flossmoor, Il., U.S.	k9	106
Flovilla, Ga., U.S.	C3	103
Flower Brook, stm., Vt., U.S.	E2	138
Flowery Branch, Ga., U.S.	B3	103
Flowood, Ms., U.S.	C3	117
Floyd, co., Ga., U.S.	B1	103
Floyd, co., Ia., U.S.	A5	108
Floyd, co., In., U.S.	H6	107
Floyd, co., Ky., U.S.	C7	110
Floyd, co., Tx., U.S.	B2	136
Floyd, co., Va., U.S.	D2	139
Floyd, stm., Ia., U.S.	B2	108
Floydada, Tx., U.S.	C2	136
Floyds Fork, stm., Ky., U.S.	B4	110
Floyds Knobs, In., U.S.	H6	107
Flushing see Vlissingen, Neth.	E8	12
Flushing, Mi., U.S.	E7	115
Flushing, Oh., U.S.	B4	128
Fluvanna, co., Va., U.S.	C4	139
Foard, co., Tx., U.S.	B3	136
Foča, Bos.	C7	18
Focșani, Rom.	G9	20
Foggia, Italy	D9	18
Fogland Point, c., R.I., U.S.	E6	132
Fogo, Nf., Can.	D4	88
Fogo, i., C.V.	g10	50a
Fogo, Cape, c., Nf., Can.	D5	88
Fogo Island, i., Nf., Can.	D4	88
Foix, Fr.	F7	16
Fokku, Nig.	D5	50
Folda, b., Nor.	C6	10
Foley, Al., U.S.	E2	94
Foley, Mn., U.S.	E5	116
Foligno, Italy	C4	18
Folkestone, Eng., U.K.	E7	12
Folkston, Ga., U.S.	F4	103
Follansbee, W.V., U.S.	A4	141
Folly Beach, S.C., U.S.	F8	133
Folly Island, i., S.C., U.S.	F8	133
Folsom, Ca., U.S.	C3	98
Fomboni, Com.	A7	56
Fonda, Ia., U.S.	B3	108
Fond du Lac, Wi., U.S.	E5	142
Fond du Lac, co., Wi., U.S.	E5	142
Fond du Lac Indian Reservation, Mn., U.S.	D6	116
Fonseca, Golfo de, b., N.A.	C2	80
Fontainebleau, Fr.	C8	16
Fontana, Ca., U.S.	m14	98
Fontana, Wi., U.S.	F5	142
Fontana Lake, res., N.C., U.S.	f9	126
Fontanelle, Ia., U.S.	C3	108
Fonte Boa, Braz.	D6	70
Fontenay-le-Comte, Fr.	D6	16
Fontenelle Reservoir, res., Wy., U.S.	D2	143
Fontur, c., Ice.	k21	10a
Foochow see Fuzhou, China	F11	28
Footville, Wi., U.S.	F4	142

Name	Map Ref.	Page

Foraker, Mount, mtn., Ak., U.S. f16 95
Forbes, Austl. G4 62
Forbes, Mount, mtn., Ab., Can. D2 84
Forcados, Nig. E6 50
Forchheim, Ger. F12 12
Ford, co., Il., U.S. C5 106
Ford, co., Ks., U.S. E4 109
Ford, stm., Mn., U.S. C3 115
Ford City, Ca., U.S. E4 98
Ford City, Pa., U.S. E2 131
Fordoche, La., U.S. D4 111
Fords Prairie, Wa., U.S. C2 140
Fordyce, Ar., U.S. D3 97
Forécariah, Gui. E2 50
Forel, Mont, mtn., Grnld. . . E32 82
Foreman, Ar., U.S. D1 97
Forest, On., Can. D2 89
Forest, Ms., U.S. C4 117
Forest, Oh., U.S. B2 128
Forest, co., Pa., U.S. C3 131
Forest, co., Wi., U.S. C5 142
Forest, stm., N.D., U.S. A8 127
Forest Acres, S.C., U.S. C6 133
Forestburg, Ab., Can. C4 84
Forest City, Ia., U.S. A4 108
Forest City, N.C., U.S. B1 126
Forest City, Pa., U.S. C11 131
Forestdale, R.I., U.S. B3 132
Forest Dale, Vt., U.S. D2 138
Forest Glen, La., U.S. h12 111
Forest Grove, Or., U.S. B3 130
Forest Hill, Md., U.S. A5 113
Forest Hills, Pa., U.S. k14 131
Forest Knolls, Ca., U.S. g7 98
Forest Lake, Mn., U.S. E6 116
Forest Park, Ga., U.S. h8 103
Forest Park, Il., U.S. k9 106
Forillon, Parc National de, P.Q., Can. k14 90
Fork Creek, stm., W.V., U.S.m12 141
Forked Deer, stm., Tn., U.S.B2 135
Forkland, Al., U.S. C2 94
Forks, Wa., U.S. B1 140
Forlì, Italy B4 18
Formentera, i., Spain H7 16
Formia, Italy D4 18
Formiga, Braz. F2 74
Formosa, Arg. D6 72
Formosa, Braz. E2 74
Formosa see Taiwan, ctry., Asia B8 34
Formosa, Serra, plat., Braz. . F9 70
Formosa Strait see Taiwan Strait, strt., Asia E4 30
Forney, Tx., U.S. C4 136
Forrest, Austl. G4 60
Forrest, Il., U.S. C5 106
Forrest, co., Ms., U.S. D4 117
Forrest City, Ar., U.S. B5 97
Forrester Island, i., Ak., U.S.n23 95
Forreston, Il., U.S. A4 106
Forsayth, Austl. D3 62
Forst, Ger. E14 12
Forsyth, Ga., U.S. C3 103
Forsyth, Il., U.S. D5 106
Forsyth, Mo., U.S. E4 118
Forsyth, Mt., U.S. D10 119
Forsyth, co., Ga., U.S. B2 103
Forsyth, co., N.C., U.S. A2 126
Fortaleza, Braz. B4 74
Fort Apache Indian Reservation, Az., U.S. . . D5 96
Fort-Archambault see Sarh, Chad B3 54
Fort Ashby, W.V., U.S. B6 141
Fort Atkinson, Wi., U.S. F5 142
Fort Beaufort, S. Afr. E4 56
Fort Belknap Indian Reservation, Mt., U.S. . . B8 119
Fort Belvoir, mil., Va., U.S. . g12 139
Fort Bend, co., Tx., U.S. E5 136
Fort Benjamin Harrison, mil., In., U.S. k10 107
Fort Benning, mil., Ga., U.S.D2 103
Fort Benton, Mt., U.S. C6 119
Fort Berthold Indian Reservation, N.D., U.S. B3 127
Fort Bidwell Indian Reservation, Ca., U.S. . B3 98
Fort Bliss, mil., Tx., U.S. . . . o11 136
Fort Bragg, Ca., U.S. C2 98
Fort Bragg, mil., N.C., U.S. . B3 126
Fort Branch, In., U.S. H2 107
Fort Calhoun, Ne., U.S. C9 120
Fort Campbell, mil., U.S. . . . A4 135
Fort Carson, mil., Co., U.S. . . C6 99
Fort Chipewyan, Ab., Can. . . f8 84
Fort Clatsop National Memorial, hist., Or., U.S. A3 130
Fort Cobb, Ok., U.S. B3 129
Fort Cobb Reservoir, res., Ok., U.S. B3 129
Fort Collins, Co., U.S. A5 99
Fort Coulonge, P.Q., Can. . . B8 89
Fort-Dauphin see Tôlañaro, Madag. D8 56
Fort Davis, Tx., U.S. o13 136
Fort Davis National Historic Site, hist., Tx., U.S. . . . o13 136
Fort Defiance, Az., U.S. B6 96
Fort-de-France, Mart. C7 80
Fort Deposit, Al., U.S. D3 94

Fort Detrick, mil., Md., U.S.B3 113
Fort Dix, mil., N.J., U.S. C3 123
Fort Dodge, Ia., U.S. B3 108
Fort Donelson National Battlefield, Tn., U.S. . . . A4 135
Fort Edward, N.Y., U.S. B7 125
Fort Erie, On., Can. E6 89
Fort Eustis, mil., Va., U.S. . . h14 139
Fort Fairfield, Me., U.S. B5 112
Fort Frances, On., Can. o16 89
Fort Gaines, Ga., U.S. E1 103
Fort Gay, W.V., U.S. C2 141
Fort Gibson, Ok., U.S. B6 129
Fort Gibson Lake, res., Ok., U.S. A6 129
Fort Gordon, mil., Ga., U.S. . C4 103
Fort Greely, mil., Ak., U.S. . C10 95
Forth, Firth of, b., Scot., U.K. B5 12
Fort Hall, Id., U.S. F6 105
Fort Hall Indian Reservation, Id., U.S. . . F6 105
Fort Hood, mil., Tx., U.S. . . . D4 136
Fort Howard, Md., U.S. B5 113
Fort Huachuca, mil., Az., U.S. F5 96
Fort Jackson, mil., S.C., U.S. C6 133
Fort Jefferson National Monument, Fl., U.S. . . . H4 102
Fort Kent, Me., U.S. A4 112
Fort Knox, mil., Ky., U.S. . . . B4 110
Fort-Lamy see N'Djamena, Chad D8 50
Fort Laramie, Wy., U.S. D8 143
Fort Laramie National Historic Site, hist., Wy., U.S. D8 143
Fort Lauderdale, Fl., U.S. . . . F6 102
Fort Lawn, S.C., U.S. B6 133
Fort Leavenworth, mil., Ks., U.S. C9 109
Fort Lee, N.J., U.S. B5 123
Fort Lee, mil., Va., U.S. C5 139
Fort Leonard Wood, mil., Mo., U.S. D5 118
Fort Lewis, mil., Wa., U.S. . . B3 140
Fort Loramie, Oh., U.S. B1 128
Fort Loudon, Pa., U.S. G6 131
Fort Loudoun Lake, res., Tn., U.S. D9 135
Fort Lupton, Co., U.S. A6 99
Fort MacArthur, mil., Ca., U.S. n12 98
Fort Macleod, Ab., Can. E4 84
Fort Madison, Ia., U.S. D6 108
Fort Matanzas National Monument, Fl., U.S. . . . C5 102
Fort McClellan, mil., Al., U.S. B4 94
Fort McDermitt Indian Reservation, U.S. B4 121
Fort McDowell Indian Reservation, Az., U.S. . D4 96
Fort McHenry National Monument And Historic Shrine, Md., U.S. g11 113
Fort McMurray, Ab., Can. . A5 84
Fort Meade, Fl., U.S. E5 102
Fort Meade, mil., Md., U.S. B4 113
Fort Meadow Reservoir, res., Ma., U.S. g9 114
Fort Mill, S.C., U.S. A6 133
Fort Mitchell, Al., U.S. C4 94
Fort Mitchell, Ky., U.S. h13 110
Fort Mojave Indian Reservation, U.S. C1 96
Fort-Monmouth, mil., N.J., U.S. C4 123
Fort Monroe, mil., Va., U.S. h15 139
Fort Morgan, Co., U.S. A7 99
Fort Myer, mil., Va., U.S. . . . g12 139
Fort Myers, Fl., U.S. F5 102
Fort Myers Beach, Fl., U.S. . F5 102
Fort Nelson, B.C., Can. . . . m18 85
Fort Oglethorpe, Ga., U.S. . B1 103
Fort Payne, Al., U.S. A4 94
Fort Peck Indian Reservation, Mt., U.S. . B11 119
Fort Peck Lake, res., Mt., U.S. C9 119
Fort Pierce, Fl., U.S. E6 102
Fort Pierce Inlet, b., Fl., U.S.E6 102
Fort Pierre, S.D., U.S. C5 134
Fort Plain, N.Y., U.S. C6 125
Fort Polk, mil., La., U.S. C2 111
Fort Portal, Ug. C6 54
Fort Randall Dam, S.D., U.S.D7 134
Fort Recovery, Oh., U.S. . . . B1 128
Fortress Mountain, mtn., Wy., U.S. B3 143
Fort Richardson, mil., Ak., U.S. C10 95
Fort Riley, mil., Ks., U.S. . . . C7 109
Fort Ritchie, mil., Md., U.S. A3 113
Fort Rucker, mil., Al., U.S. . D4 94
Fort Saint James, B.C., Can. B5 85
Fort Saint John, B.C., Can. . A7 85
Fort Sam Houston, mil., Tx., U.S. k7 136
Fort Saskatchewan, Ab., Can. C4 84
Fort Scott, Ks., U.S. E9 109
Fort-Ševčenko, Kaz. E7 26
Fort Shafter, mil., Hi., U.S. . g10 104

Fort Shawnee, Oh., U.S. . . B1 128
Fort Sill, mil., Ok., U.S. . . . C3 129
Fort Smith, Ar., U.S. B1 97
Fort Stewart, mil., Ga., U.S.D5 103
Fort Stockton, Tx., U.S. . . . D1 136
Fort Sumner, N.M., U.S. . . . C5 124
Fort Sumter National Monument, S.C., U.S. . k12 133
Fort Supply Lake, res., Ok., U.S. A2 129
Fort Thomas, Ky., U.S. h14 110
Fort Totten, N.D., U.S. B7 127
Fort Totten Indian Reservation, N.D., U.S. B7 127
Fortuna, Ca., U.S. B1 98
Fortune, Nf., Can. E4 88
Fortune Bay, b., Nf., Can. . . E4 88
Fort Union National Monument, N.M., U.S. . B5 124
Fort Valley, Ga., U.S. D3 103
Fort Vermilion, Ab., Can. . . . f7 84
Fortville, In., U.S. E6 107
Fort Wainwright, mil., Ak., U.S. C10 95
Fort Walton Beach, Fl., U.S.u15 102
Fort Washington Forest, Md., U.S. C4 113
Fort Wayne, In., U.S. B7 107
Fort William, Scot., U.K. . . . B4 12
Fort Wingate, N.M., U.S. . . . B1 124
Fort Worth, Tx., U.S. C4 136
Fort Wright, Ky., U.S. h13 110
Forty Fort, Pa., U.S. D10 131
Fort Yukon, Ak., U.S. B10 95
Fort Yuma Indian Reservation, Ca., U.S. . F6 98
Foshan, China G10 28
Foso, Ghana E4 50
Fossano, Italy B1 18
Fossil Butte National Monument, Wy., U.S. . . E2 143
Fossil Lake, l., Or., U.S. D6 130
Foss Reservoir, res., Ok., U.S. B2 129
Fosston, Mn., U.S. C3 116
Foster, Or., U.S. C4 130
Foster, co., N.D., U.S. B6 127
Foster Village, Hi., U.S. g10 104
Fostoria, Oh., U.S. A2 128
Fougamou, Gabon D2 54
Fougères, Fr. C6 16
Fouke, Ar., U.S. D2 97
Foulamôri, Gui. D2 50
Foumban, Cam. B2 54
Foundiougne, Sen. D1 50
Fountain, Co., U.S. C6 99
Fountain, co., In., U.S. D3 107
Fountain City, In., U.S. E8 107
Fountain City, Wi., U.S. D2 142
Fountain Hill, Pa., U.S. E11 131
Fountain Inn, S.C., U.S. B3 133
Fountain Peak, mtn., Ca., U.S. E6 98
Fourche LaFave, stm., Ar., U.S. C2 97
Fourche Maline, stm., Ok., U.S. C6 129
Four Mountains, Islands of, is., Ak., U.S. E6 95
Four Oaks, N.C., U.S. B4 126
Fourth Cataract, wtfl, Sudan E12 48
Fouta Djalon, reg., Gui. D2 50
Foveaux Strait, strt., N.Z. . . q12 63c
Fowler, Co., U.S. C6 99
Fowler, In., U.S. C3 107
Fowler, Mi., U.S. E6 115
Fowlerville, Mi., U.S. F6 115
Fowman, Iran D13 44
Foxboro, On., Can. C7 89
Foxboro, Ma., U.S. B5 114
Fox Creek, Ab., Can. B2 84
Foxe Basin, b., N.T., Can. . . E24 82
Fox Island, i., R.I., U.S. E4 132
Fox Island, i., Wa., U.S. f10 140
Fox Islands, is., Ak., U.S. . . . E6 95
Fox Lake, Il., U.S. A5 106
Fox Lake, Wi., U.S. E5 142
Fox Lake, l., Il., U.S. h8 106
Fox Mountain, mtn., Nv., U.S. B2 121
Fox Point, Wi., U.S. E6 142
Fox River Grove, Il., U.S. . . . h8 106
Foxworth, Ms., U.S. D4 117
Foz do Cunene, Ang. B1 56
Foz do Iguaçu, Braz. D7 72
Frackville, Pa., U.S. E9 131
Fraga, Spain D12 16
Fram Basin E22 144
Framingham, Ma., U.S. B5 114
Franca, Braz. F2 74
Franca-Iosifa, Zemlja, is., Russia B7 26
France, ctry., Eur. D8 10
Francesville, In., U.S. C4 107
Franceville, Gabon D2 54
Francis, Lake, l., N.H., U.S. . f7 122
Francis Case, Lake, res., S.D., U.S. D6 134
Francistown, Bots. C4 56

Franconia, N.H., U.S. B3 122
Franconia Notch, N.H., U.S.B3 122
Francs Peak, mtn., Wy., U.S. C3 143
Franken, hist. reg., Ger. . . . E11 12
Frankenmuth, Mi., U.S. E7 115
Frankford, On., Can. C7 89
Frankford, De., U.S. F5 101
Frankfort, Il., U.S. m9 106
Frankfort, In., U.S. D4 107
Frankfort, Ks., U.S. C7 109
Frankfort, Ky., U.S. B5 110
Frankfort, Mi., U.S. D4 115
Frankfort, N.Y., U.S. B5 125
Frankfort, Oh., U.S. C2 128
Frankfurt, Ger. D14 12
Frankfurt am Main, Ger. . . . E11 12
Franklin, Ga., U.S. C1 103
Franklin, In., U.S. F5 107
Franklin, Ky., U.S. D3 110
Franklin, La., U.S. E4 111
Franklin, Ma., U.S. B5 114
Franklin, N.C., U.S. f9 126
Franklin, Ne., U.S. D7 120
Franklin, N.H., U.S. D3 122
Franklin, N.J., U.S. A3 123
Franklin, Oh., U.S. C1 128
Franklin, Pa., U.S. D2 131
Franklin, Tn., U.S. B5 135
Franklin, Tx., U.S. D4 136
Franklin, Va., U.S. D6 139
Franklin, W.V., U.S. C5 141
Franklin, Wi., U.S. n11 142
Franklin, co., Al., U.S. A2 94
Franklin, co., Ar., U.S. B2 97
Franklin, co., Fl., U.S. C2 102
Franklin, co., Ga., U.S. B3 103
Franklin, co., Ia., U.S. B4 108
Franklin, co., Id., U.S. G7 105
Franklin, co., Il., U.S. E4 106
Franklin, co., In., U.S. F7 107
Franklin, co., Ks., U.S. D8 109
Franklin, co., Ky., U.S. B5 110
Franklin, co., La., U.S. B4 111
Franklin, co., Ma., U.S. A2 114
Franklin, co., Me., U.S. C2 112
Franklin, co., Mo., U.S. C6 118
Franklin, co., Ms., U.S. D3 117
Franklin, co., N.C., U.S. A4 126
Franklin, co., Ne., U.S. D7 120
Franklin, co., N.Y., U.S. f10 125
Franklin, co., Oh., U.S. B2 128
Franklin, co., Pa., U.S. G6 131
Franklin, co., Tn., U.S. B5 135
Franklin, co., Tx., U.S. C5 136
Franklin, co., Va., U.S. D3 139
Franklin, co., Vt., U.S. B2 138
Franklin, co., Wa., U.S. C6 140
Franklin, Point, c., Ak., U.S. A8 95
Franklin D. Roosevelt Lake, res., Wa., U.S. B7 140
Franklin Falls Reservoir, res., N.H., U.S. C3 122
Franklin Grove, Il., U.S. B4 106
Franklin Lake, l., Nv., U.S. . . C6 121
Franklin Park, Il., U.S. k9 106
Franklinton, La., U.S. D5 111
Franklinton, N.C., U.S. A4 126
Franklinville, N.Y., U.S. C2 125
Frankston, Tx., U.S. C5 136
Frankton, In., U.S. D6 107
Fransfontein, Nmb. C2 56
Franz Josef Land see Franca-Iosifa, Zemlja, is., Russia B7 26
Fraser, stm., B.C., Can. E7 85
Fraser, stm., Nf., Can. g9 88
Fraser, Mount, mtn., Can. . C8 85
Fraserburg, S. Afr. E3 56
Fraserburgh, Scot., U.K. B5 12
Fraser Island, i., Austl. F5 62
Fraser Lake, B.C., Can. B5 85
Fraser Plateau, plat., B.C., Can. D6 85
Frazee, Mn., U.S. D3 116
Frazeysburg, Oh., U.S. B3 128
Frazier Park, Ca., U.S. E4 98
Frederic, Wi., U.S. C1 142
Fredericia, Den. I3 10
Frederick, Co., U.S. A6 99
Frederick, Md., U.S. B3 113
Frederick, Ok., U.S. C2 129
Frederick, co., Md., U.S. B3 113
Frederick, co., Va., U.S. A4 139
Fredericksburg, Ia., U.S. . . . B5 108
Fredericksburg, Tx., U.S. . . . D3 136
Fredericksburg, Va., U.S. . . . B5 139
Frederick Sound, strt., Ak., U.S. m23 95
Fredericktown, Mo., U.S. . . . D7 118
Fredericktown, Oh., U.S. . . . B3 128
Fredericktown, Pa., U.S. . . . F1 131
Fredericton, N.B., Can. D3 87
Fredericton Junction, N.B., Can. D3 87
Frederikshåb, Grnld. F29 82
Frederikshavn, Den. H4 10
Fredonia, Az., U.S. A3 96
Fredonia, Ks., U.S. E8 109
Fredonia, N.Y., U.S. C1 125
Fredonia, Wi., U.S. E6 142
Fredrikstad, Nor. G4 10
Freeborn, co., Mn., U.S. G5 116
Freeburg, Il., U.S. E4 106

Freedom, Pa., U.S. E1 131
Freedom, Wy., U.S. D2 143
Freehold, N.J., U.S. C4 123
Freeland, Mi., U.S. E6 115
Freeland, Pa., U.S. D10 131
Freelandville, In., U.S. G3 107
Freel Peak, mtn., Ca., U.S. . . C4 98
Freels, Cape, c., Nf., Can. . . E5 88
Freels, Cape, c., Nf., Can. . . D5 88
Freeman, S.D., U.S. D8 134
Freeman, Lake, l., In., U.S. . . C4 107
Freemansburg, Pa., U.S. . . . E11 131
Freemason Island, i., La., U.S. E7 111
Freeport, Bah. C9 76
Freeport, Il., U.S. A4 106
Freeport, Me., U.S. E2 112
Freeport, N.Y., U.S. n15 125
Freeport, Pa., U.S. E2 131
Freeport, Tx., U.S. E5 136
Freer, Tx., U.S. F3 136
Freestone, co., Tx., U.S. D4 136
Freetown, S.L. E2 50
Freetown, In., U.S. G5 107
Freezeout Mountains, mts., Wy., U.S. D6 143
Fregenal de la Sierra, Spain H3 16
Freiburg, Ger. G10 12
Freising, Ger. F12 12
Freistadt, Aus. F14 12
Fréjus, Fr. F10 16
Fremantle, Austl. G2 60
Fremont, Ca., U.S. D2 98
Fremont, Ia., U.S. C5 108
Fremont, In., U.S. A8 107
Fremont, Mi., U.S. E5 115
Fremont, N.C., U.S. B5 126
Fremont, Ne., U.S. C9 120
Fremont, Oh., U.S. A2 128
Fremont, co., Co., U.S. C5 99
Fremont, co., Ia., U.S. D2 108
Fremont, co., Id., U.S. E7 105
Fremont, co., Wy., U.S. C4 143
Fremont, stm., Ut., U.S. E4 137
Fremont Island, i., Ut., U.S. B3 137
Fremont Lake, l., Wy., U.S. D3 143
Fremont Peak, mtn., Wy., U.S. C3 143
French Broad, stm., U.S. . . D10 135
Frenchburg, Ky., U.S. C6 110
French Creek, stm., Pa., U.S. C2 131
French Frigate Shoals, rf., Hi., U.S. m14 104
French Guiana, dep., S.A. . . C9 70
French Lick, In., U.S. G4 107
Frenchman Bay, b., Me., U.S. D4 112
Frenchman Creek, stm., U.S. D4 120
Frenchman Hills, hills, Wa., U.S. C6 140
Frenchman Lake, l., Nv., U.S. G6 121
French Polynesia, dep., Oc. F15 58
French Settlement, La., U.S.D5 111
French Somaliland see Djibouti, ctry., Afr. . . . H13 48
Frenda, Alg. J7 16
Freshfield, Mount, mtn., Can. D2 84
Fresnillo, Mex. C4 78
Fresno, Ca., U.S. D4 98
Fresno, co., Ca., U.S. D4 98
Fresno Reservoir, res., Mt., U.S. B6 119
Frewsburg, N.Y., U.S. C1 125
Freycinet Peninsula, pen., Austl. I4 62
Fria, Gui. D2 50
Fria, Cape, c., Nmb. B1 56
Friars Point, Ms., U.S. A3 117
Frías, Arg. D4 72
Fribourg, Switz. A1 18
Friday Harbor, Wa., U.S. . . . A2 140
Fridley, Mn., U.S. m12 116
Fridtjof Nansen, Mount, mtn., Ant. E25 67
Friedrichshafen, Ger. G11 12
Friend, Ne., U.S. D8 120
Friendsville, Tn., U.S. D9 135
Fries, Va., U.S. D2 139
Frio, co., Tx., U.S. E3 136
Frio, stm., Tx., U.S. E3 136
Frio, Cabo, c., Braz. F3 74
Friona, Tx., U.S. B1 136
Fripps Island, i., S.C., U.S. . G7 133
Frisco, Co., U.S. B4 99
Frisco City, Al., U.S. D2 94
Frisco Peak, mtn., Ut., U.S. E2 137
Frisian Islands, is., Eur. D9 10
Frissell, Mount, mtn., U.S. . A2 100
Fritch, Tx., U.S. B2 136
Friza, proliv, strt., Russia . . B17 28
Frobisher Bay, b., N.T., Can.F26 82
Frobisher Lake, l., Sk., Can. m7 91
Frolovo, Russia E7 22
Frome, L., l., Austl. E9 62
Frontenac, Ks., U.S. E9 109
Frontera, Mex. D6 78
Frontera, Mex. B4 78
Frontier, co., Ne., U.S. D5 120
Front Range, mts., Co., U.S.A5 99
Front Royal, Va., U.S. B4 139
Frosinone, Italy D4 18

Name	Map Ref.	Page
Frostburg, Md., U.S.	k13	113
Frostproof, Fl., U.S.	E5	102
Frøya, i., Nor.	E3	10
Fruita, Co., U.S.	B2	99
Fruit Heights, Ut., U.S.	B4	137
Fruitland, Id., U.S.	F2	105
Fruitland, Md., U.S.	D6	113
Fruitland, N.M., U.S.	A1	124
Fruitland Park, Fl., U.S.	D5	102
Fruitport, Mi., U.S.	E4	115
Fruitvale, B.C., Can.	E9	85
Fruitvale, Co., U.S.	B2	99
Fruitvale, Wa., U.S.	C5	140
Fruitville, Fl., U.S.	E4	102
Frunze see Biškek, Kyrg.	E9	26
Frutal, Braz.	E2	74
Fryeburg, Me., U.S.	D2	112
Fu'an, China	D4	30
Fuding, China	D5	30
Fuerte, stm., Mex.	B3	78
Fuerte Olimpo, Para.	C6	72
Fuerteventura, i., Spain	A2	50
Fuga Island, i., Phil.	C8	34
Fuji, Japan	C3	31
Fuji, Mount see Fuji-san, vol., Japan	D15	28
Fujian, state, China	F11	28
Fujin, China	B14	28
Fuji-san, vol., Japan	D15	28
Fujiyama see Fuji-san, vol., Japan	D15	28
Fukui, Japan	D15	28
Fukuoka, Japan	E14	28
Fukushima, Japan	C4	31
Fukuyama, Japan	D2	31
Fūlādī, Kūh-e, mtn., Afg.	D9	42
Fulaga Passage, i., Fiji	m11	63b
Fulda, Ger.	E11	12
Fulda, Mn., U.S.	G3	116
Fuling, China	D2	30
Fullerton, Ca., U.S.	n13	98
Fullerton, Ne., U.S.	C8	120
Fulton, Il., U.S.	B3	106
Fulton, Ky., U.S.	f9	110
Fulton, Md., U.S.	B4	113
Fulton, Mo., U.S.	C6	118
Fulton, Ms., U.S.	A5	117
Fulton, N.Y., U.S.	B4	125
Fulton, co., Ar., U.S.	A4	97
Fulton, co., Ga., U.S.	C2	103
Fulton, co., Il., U.S.	C3	106
Fulton, co., In., U.S.	B5	107
Fulton, co., Ky., U.S.	f8	110
Fulton, co., N.Y., U.S.	B6	125
Fulton, co., Oh., U.S.	A1	128
Fulton, co., Pa., U.S.	G5	131
Fultondale, Al., U.S.	f7	94
Funafuti, i., Tuvalu	E11	58
Funchal, Port.	D1	48
Fundy, Bay of, b., Can.	D4	87
Fundy National Park, N.B., Can.	D4	87
Funhalouro, Moz.	C5	56
Funing, China	B4	30
Funing, China	C4	30
Funkstown, Md., U.S.	A2	113
Funsi, Ghana	D4	50
Funtua, Nig.	D6	50
Fuping, China	C2	30
Fuqing, China	D4	30
Fuquay-Varina, N.C., U.S.	B4	126
Furnace Brook, stm., Vt., U.S.	D3	138
Furnas, co., Ne., U.S.	D6	120
Furnas, Represa de, res., Braz.	F2	74
Furneaux Group, is., Austl.	I4	62
Fürstenwalde, Ger.	D14	12
Furudal, Swe.	F6	10
Fushun, China	C12	28
Fusui, China	G9	28
Futuna, Île, i., Wal./F.	F12	58
Fuxin, China	A5	30
Fuyang, China	E11	28
Fuyu, China	B12	28
Fuyuan, China	D1	30
Fuzhou, China	F11	28
Fuzhou, China	F11	28
Füzuli, Azer.	C12	44
Fyffe, Al., U.S.	A4	94
Fyn, i., Den.	I4	10

G

Gaalkacyo, Som.	I14	48
Gabbs, Nv., U.S.	E4	121
Gabela, Ang.	F2	54
Gaberones see Gaborone, Bots.	C4	56
Gabès, Tun.	D7	48
Gabon, ctry., Afr.	D2	54
Gaborone, Bots.	C4	56
Gabriola, B.C., Can.	f12	85
Gabrovo, Bul.	C10	18
Gabú, Gui.-B.	D2	50
Gachsārān, Iran	D6	42
Gadag, India	F3	40
Gäddede, Swe.	D6	10
Gadsden, Al., U.S.	A3	94
Gadsden, co., Fl., U.S.	B2	102
Gadwāl, India	F3	40
Gaeta, Italy	D4	18
Gaeta, Golfo di, b., Italy	D4	18
Gaffney, S.C., U.S.	A4	133
Gafsa, Tun.	D6	48
Gag, Pulau, i., Indon.	D7	36
Gagarin, Russia	B13	20
Gage, co., Ne., U.S.	D9	120
Gagetown, N.B., Can.	D3	87
Gagnoa, C. Iv.	E3	50
Gagra, Geor.	A9	44
Gahanna, Oh., U.S.	k11	128
Gaillard, Lake, l., Ct., U.S.	D5	100
Gaines, Co., Tx., U.S.	C1	136
Gainesboro, Tn., U.S.	C8	135
Gaines Creek, stm., Ok., U.S.	C6	129
Gainesville, Fl., U.S.	C4	102
Gainesville, Ga., U.S.	B3	103
Gainesville, Mo., U.S.	E5	118
Gainesville, Tx., U.S.	C4	136
Gainesville, Va., U.S.	g11	139
Gairdner, Lake, l., Austl.	G2	62
Gaithersburg, Md., U.S.	B3	113
Gaixian, China	C12	28
Gaizina Kalns, hill, Lat.	H11	10
Gajny, Russia	B9	22
Galán, Cerro, mtn., Arg.	D4	72
Galapagos Islands see Colón, Archipiélago de, is., Ec.	C2	70
Galashiels, Scot., U.K.	C5	12
Galati, Rom.	G9	20
Galatia, Il., U.S.	F5	106
Galax, Va., U.S.	D2	139
Galdhøpiggen, mtn., Nor.	F3	10
Galela, Indon.	C7	36
Galena, Ak., U.S.	C8	95
Galena, Il., U.S.	A3	106
Galena, Ks., U.S.	E9	109
Galesburg, Mi., U.S.	F5	115
Galesburg, Il., U.S.	C3	106
Gales Ferry, Ct., U.S.	D7	100
Galesville, Md., U.S.	C4	113
Galesville, Wi., U.S.	D2	142
Galeton, Pa., U.S.	C6	131
Gali, Geor.	A9	44
Galič, Russia	C7	22
Galicia, hist. reg., Eur.	E7	20
Galilee, Sea of, l., Isr.	F6	44
Galion, Oh., U.S.	B3	128
Galisteo Creek, stm., N.M., U.S.	k8	124
Galiuro Mountains, mts., Az., U.S.	E5	96
Gallant, Al., U.S.	B3	94
Gallatin, Mo., U.S.	B4	118
Gallatin, Tn., U.S.	A5	135
Gallatin, co., Il., U.S.	F5	106
Gallatin, co., Ky., U.S.	B5	110
Gallatin, co., Mt., U.S.	E5	119
Gallatin, co., Mo., U.S.	C3	118
Gallatin, stm., Mt., U.S.	E5	119
Gallatin Range, mts., Mt., U.S.	E5	119
Gallaway, Tn., U.S.	B2	135
Galle, Sri L.	H4	40
Gallia, co., Oh., U.S.	D3	128
Galliano, La., U.S.	E5	111
Gallinas, Punta, c., Col.	A5	70
Gallinas Mountains, mts., N.M., U.S.	C2	124
Gallipoli, Italy	D6	18
Gallipoli see Gelibolu, Tur.	B2	44
Gallipolis, Oh., U.S.	D3	128
Gallitzin, Pa., U.S.	F4	131
Gällivare, Swe.	C9	10
Gallo Mountains, mts., N.M., U.S.	C1	124
Galloo Island, i., N.Y., U.S.	B4	125
Gallup, N.M., U.S.	B1	124
Galt, Ca., U.S.	C3	98
Galtat Zemmour, W. Sah.	A2	50
Galva, Il., U.S.	B3	106
Galva, Ks., U.S.	D6	109
Galveston, In., U.S.	C5	107
Galveston, Tx., U.S.	E5	136
Galveston, co., Tx., U.S.	E5	136
Galveston Bay, b., Tx., U.S.	E5	136
Galveston Island, i., Tx., U.S.	E5	136
Galway, Ire.	D2	12
Galway Bay, b., Ire.	D2	12
Gamarra, Col.	B5	70
Gambēla, Eth.	B6	54
Gambell, Ak., U.S.	C5	95
Gambia, stm., Afr.	D2	50
Gambia, The, ctry., Afr.	D1	50
Gambier, Oh., U.S.	B3	128
Gambier, Îles, is., Fr. Poly.	G16	58
Gambo, Nf., Can.	D4	88
Gamboma, Congo	D3	54
Gamboula, C.A.R.	C3	54
Gambrills, Md., U.S.	B4	113
Gan, stm., China	D4	30
Ganado, Az., U.S.	B6	96
Ganado, Tx., U.S.	E4	136
Gananoque, On., Can.	C8	89
Gäncä, Azer.	B12	44
Gand see Gent, Bel.	E8	12
Ganda, Ang.	F2	54
Gandajika, D.R.C.	E4	54
Gandak, stm., Asia	D4	40
Gander, Nf., Can.	D4	88
Gander, stm., Nf., Can.	D4	88
Gander Lake, l., Nf., Can.	D4	88
Gandesa, Spain	G7	16
Gāndhidhām, India	I2	40
Gandhi Reservoir see Gāndhi Sāgar, res., India	E3	40
Gāndhi Sāgar, res., India	E3	40
Gandia, Spain	H6	16
Gandu, Braz.	D4	74
Ganga see Ganges, stm., Asia	D5	40
Gangānagar, India	D2	40
Gangaw, Myan.	B2	34
Gangdisê Shan, mts., China	E4	28
Ganges, B.C., Can.	g12	85
Ganges (Ganga), stm., Asia	D5	40
Ganges, Mouths of the, mth., Asia	B1	34
Gang Mills, N.Y., U.S.	C3	125
Gangotri, India	C3	40
Gangtok, India	D5	40
Gangu, China	E9	28
Gannett Peak, mtn., Wy., U.S.	C3	143
Ganquan, China	B2	30
Gansu, state, China	D8	28
Gantt, S.C., U.S.	B3	133
Gantt Lake, res., Al., U.S.	D3	94
Ganzê, China	E8	28
Ganzhou, China	F10	28
Gao, Mali	C4	50
Gao'an, China	D4	30
Gaolan, China	B1	30
Gaomi, China	B4	30
Gaoping, China	B3	30
Gaoua, Burkina	D4	50
Gaoual, Gui.	D2	50
Gaoxian, China	D1	30
Gaoyou, China	C4	30
Gaoyou Hu, l., China	C4	30
Gaozhou, China	D3	30
Gap, Fr.	E10	16
Gap, Pa., U.S.	G9	131
Gapan, Phil.	C8	34
Garagumskij kanal imeni Prezidenta Turkmenistana S.A. Nijazova (Kara-Kum Canal), Turk.	C8	42
Garagumy, des., Turk.	F7	26
Garanhuns, Braz.	C4	74
Garber, Ok., U.S.	A4	129
Garberville, Ca., U.S.	B2	98
Garda, Lago di, l., Italy	B3	18
Garden, co., Ne., U.S.	C3	120
Gardena, Ca., U.S.	n12	98
Garden City, Ga., U.S.	D5	103
Garden City, Id., U.S.	F2	105
Garden City, Ks., U.S.	E3	109
Garden City, Mi., U.S.	p15	115
Garden City, Mo., U.S.	C3	118
Gardendale, Al., U.S.	B3	94
Garden Grove, Ca., U.S.	n13	98
Garden Island, i., Mi., U.S.	C5	115
Garden Plain, Ks., U.S.	E6	109
Gardeyz, Afg.	D9	42
Gardiner, Me., U.S.	D3	112
Gardiner, Mt., U.S.	E6	119
Gardiner, Or., U.S.	D2	130
Gardiners Island, i., N.Y., U.S.	m16	125
Gardner, Il., U.S.	B5	106
Gardner, Ks., U.S.	D9	109
Gardner, Ma., U.S.	A4	114
Gardner Canal, strt., B.C., Can.	C3	85
Gardner Lake, l., Ct., U.S.	C6	100
Gardner Lake, l., Me., U.S.	D5	112
Gardner Pinnacles, Hi., U.S.	k14	104
Gardnerville, Nv., U.S.	E2	121
Garfield, N.J., U.S.	h8	123
Garfield, co., Co., U.S.	B2	99
Garfield, co., Mt., U.S.	C9	119
Garfield, co., Ne., U.S.	C6	120
Garfield, co., Ok., U.S.	A4	129
Garfield, co., Ut., U.S.	F4	137
Garfield, co., Wa., U.S.	C8	140
Garfield Heights, Oh., U.S.	h9	128
Garfield Mountain, mtn., Mt., U.S.	F4	119
Garfield Peak, mtn., Wy., U.S.	D5	143
Garibaldi, Or., U.S.	A3	130
Garibaldi, Mount, mtn., B.C., Can.	E6	85
Garies, S. Afr.	E2	56
Garissa, Kenya	D7	54
Garland, N.C., U.S.	C4	126
Garland, Tx., U.S.	n10	136
Garland, Ut., U.S.	B3	137
Garland, co., Ar., U.S.	C2	97
Garm, Taj.	C10	42
Garmī, Iran	C13	44
Garmisch-Partenkirchen, Ger.	G12	12
Garmsār, Iran	C6	42
Garnavillo, Ia., U.S.	B6	108
Garner, Ia., U.S.	A4	108
Garner, N.C., U.S.	B4	126
Garnet Range, mts., Mt., U.S.	D3	119
Garnett, Ks., U.S.	D8	109
Garnish, Nf., Can.	E4	88
Garonne, stm., Eur.	E6	16
Garou, C.A.R.	C3	54
Garoua, Cam.	B2	54
Garoua Boulaï, Cam.	B2	54
Garrard, co., Ky., U.S.	C5	110
Garretson, S.D., U.S.	D9	134
Garrett, In., U.S.	B7	107
Garrett, co., Md., U.S.	k12	113
Garrett Park, Md., U.S.	B3	113
Garrettsville, Oh., U.S.	A4	128
Garrison, Ky., U.S.	B6	110
Garrison, Md., U.S.	B4	113
Garrison, N.D., U.S.	B4	127
Garrison Dam, N.D., U.S.	B4	127
Garsen, Kenya	D8	54
Garut, Indon.	E3	36
Garvin, co., Ok., U.S.	C4	129
Garwolin, Pol.	D6	20
Gary, In., U.S.	A3	107
Gary, W.V., U.S.	D3	141
Garyarsa, China	E4	28
Garysburg, N.C., U.S.	A5	126
Garyville, La., U.S.	D5	111
Garza, co., Tx., U.S.	C2	136
Garza-Little Elm Reservoir, res., Tx., U.S.	C4	136
Gasan-Kuli, Turk.	C6	42
Gas City, In., U.S.	D6	107
Gascogne, hist. reg., Fr.	F7	16
Gasconade, co., Mo., U.S.	C6	118
Gasconade, stm., Mo., U.S.	C6	118
Gascony see Gascogne, hist. reg., Fr.	F7	16
Gascoyne, stm., Austl.	E1	60
Gascoyne Junction, Austl.	F2	60
Gashaka, Nig.	E7	50
Gashua, Nig.	D7	50
Gasparilla Island, i., Fl., U.S.	F4	102
Gaspé, P.Q., Can.	k14	90
Gaspésie, Péninsule de la, pen., P.Q., Can.	k13	90
Gassaway, W.V., U.S.	C4	141
Gassville, Ar., U.S.	A3	97
Gasteiz, Spain	F5	16
Gaston, In., U.S.	D7	107
Gaston, N.C., U.S.	A5	126
Gaston, S.C., U.S.	D5	133
Gaston, co., N.C., U.S.	B1	126
Gaston, Lake, res., U.S.	A5	126
Gaston Dam, N.C., U.S.	A5	126
Gastonia, N.C., U.S.	B1	126
Gastre, Arg.	F3	69
Gate City, Va., U.S.	f9	139
Gates, Tn., U.S.	B2	135
Gates, co., N.C., U.S.	A6	126
Gates of the Arctic National Park, Ak., U.S.	B9	95
Gatesville, Tx., U.S.	D4	136
Gatineau, P.Q., Can.	D2	90
Gatineau, stm., P.Q., Can.	D2	90
Gatineau, Parc de la, P.Q., Can.	D2	90
Gatlinburg, Tn., U.S.	D10	135
Gatton, Austl.	F5	62
Gauley, co., W.V., U.S.	C3	141
Gauley Bridge, W.V., U.S.	C3	141
Gaustatoppen, mtn., Nor.	G3	10
Gautier, Ms., U.S.	f8	117
Gávdhos, i., Grc.	G10	18
Gavins Point Dam, U.S.	B8	120
Gävle, Swe.	F7	10
Gawler Ranges, mts., Austl.	G2	62
Gaya, India	E5	40
Gaya, Nig.	D6	50
Gaya, Niger	D5	50
Gay Head, c., Ma., U.S.	D6	114
Gaylord, Mi., U.S.	C6	115
Gaylord, Mn., U.S.	F4	116
Gayndah, Austl.	F5	62
Gaza see Ghazzah, Gaza Str.	G6	44
Gazandzyk, Turk.	C7	42
Gazaoua, Niger	D6	50
Gaza Strip, Asia	G6	44
Gaziantep, Tur.	D7	44
Gazimağusa (Famagusta), N. Cyp.	E5	44
Gazimağusa Körfezi, b., N. Cyp.	E6	44
Gazipaşa, Tur.	D5	44
Gbanga, Lib.	E3	50
Gboko, Nig.	E6	50
Gdańsk, Pol.	B5	20
Gdov, Russia	G12	10
Gdynia, Pol.	B5	20
Gearhart, Or., U.S.	A3	130
Gearhart Mountain, mtn., Or., U.S.	E6	130
Geary, N.B., Can.	D3	87
Geary, Ok., U.S.	B3	129
Geary, co., Ks., U.S.	D7	109
Geauga, co., Oh., U.S.	A4	128
Gebze, Tur.	B3	44
Gebe, Pulau, i., Indon.	D7	36
Gediz, Tur.	C3	44
Geelong, Austl.	H3	62
Geesthacht, Ger.	D12	12
Geilo, Nor.	F3	10
Geistown, Pa., U.S.	F4	131
Geist Reservoir, res., In., U.S.	E6	107
Geita, Tan.	D6	54
Gejiu, China	G8	28
Gela, Italy	F5	18
Gelasa, Selat, strt., Indon.	D3	36
Gelendžik, Russia	G15	20
Gelibolu, Tur.	B2	44
Gelsenkirchen, Ger.	E10	12
Gem, co., Id., U.S.	E2	105
Gemena, D.R.C.	C3	54
Gemlik, Tur.	B3	44
Gemlik Körfezi, b., Tur.	B3	44
Genalē (Jubba), stm., Afr.	B8	54
Genç, Tur.	C9	44
General Acha, Arg.	F5	72
General Alvear, Arg.	F4	72
General Carneiro, Braz.	B7	72
General Carrera, Lago, l., S.A.	G2	69
General Conesa, Arg.	F4	69
General Eugenio A. Garay, Para.	C5	72
General Juan José Ríos, Mex.	B3	78
General Juan Madariaga, Arg.	F6	72
General La Madrid, Arg.	F5	72
General Pico, Arg.	F5	72
General Pinedo, Arg.	D5	72
General Roca, Arg.	E3	69
General Villegas, Arg.	F5	72
Genesee, Id., U.S.	C2	105
Genesee, Mi., U.S.	E7	115
Genesee, co., Mi., U.S.	E7	115
Genesee, co., N.Y., U.S.	B2	125
Genesee, stm., N.Y., U.S.	C2	125
Geneseo, Il., U.S.	B3	106
Geneseo, N.Y., U.S.	C3	125
Geneva see Genève, Switz.	A1	18
Geneva, Al., U.S.	D4	94
Geneva, Il., U.S.	B5	106
Geneva, In., U.S.	C8	107
Geneva, Ne., U.S.	D8	120
Geneva, N.Y., U.S.	C4	125
Geneva, Oh., U.S.	A5	128
Geneva, co., Al., U.S.	D4	94
Geneva, Lake, l., Eur.	A1	18
Geneva, Lake, l., Wi., U.S.	F5	142
Geneva-on-the-Lake, Oh., U.S.	A5	128
Genève (Geneva), Switz.	A1	18
Gengma, China	B3	34
Genoa see Genova, Italy	B2	18
Genoa, Il., U.S.	A5	106
Genoa, Ne., U.S.	C8	120
Genoa, Nv., U.S.	D2	121
Genoa, Oh., U.S.	A2	128
Genoa, Gulf of see Genova, Golfo di, b., Italy	B2	18
Genoa City, Wi., U.S.	F5	142
Genola, Ut., U.S.	D4	137
Genova, Italy	B2	18
Genova, Golfo di, b., Italy	B2	18
Gent, Bel.	E8	12
Gentry, Ar., U.S.	A1	97
Gentry, co., Mo., U.S.	A3	118
Geographe Bay, b., Austl.	G2	60
George, S. Afr.	E3	56
George, Ia., U.S.	A2	108
George, co., Ms., U.S.	E5	117
George, stm., P.Q., Can.	g13	90
George, Cape, c., N.S., Can.	D8	87
George, Lake, l., Fl., U.S.	C5	102
George, Lake, l., N.Y., U.S.	B7	125
George B. Stevenson Reservoir, res., Pa., U.S.	D6	131
George Peak, mtn., Ut., U.S.	B2	137
George Town, Austl.	I4	62
Georgetown, Austl.	D3	62
Georgetown, P.E., Can.	C7	87
George Town, Cay. Is.	B3	80
Georgetown, Gam.	D2	50
Georgetown, Guy.	B8	70
George Town (Penang), Malay.	B2	36
Georgetown, Ca., U.S.	C3	98
Georgetown, Co., U.S.	B5	99
Georgetown, Ct., U.S.	D2	100
Georgetown, De., U.S.	F4	101
Georgetown, Ga., U.S.	E1	103
Georgetown, Il., U.S.	D6	106
Georgetown, In., U.S.	H6	107
Georgetown, Ky., U.S.	B5	110
Georgetown, Ma., U.S.	A6	114
Georgetown, Oh., U.S.	D2	128
Georgetown, S.C., U.S.	E9	133
Georgetown, Tx., U.S.	D4	136
Georgetown, co., S.C., U.S.	E9	133
George V Coast, Ant.	C20	67
George Washington Birthplace National Monument, Va., U.S.	B6	139
George Washington Carver National Monument, Mo., U.S.	E3	118
George West, Tx., U.S.	E3	136
Georgia, ctry., Asia	A10	44
Georgia, state, U.S.	D3	103
Georgiana, Al., U.S.	D3	94
Georgian Bay, b., On., Can.	B3	89
Georgina, stm., Austl.	E2	62
Gera, Ger.	E13	12
Gerald, Mo., U.S.	C6	118
Geraldine, Al., U.S.	A4	94
Geraldton, Austl.	F1	60
Geraldton, On., Can.	o18	89
Gerber Reservoir, res., Or., U.S.	E5	130
Gerdine, Mount, mtn., Ak., U.S.	C9	95
Gerede, Tur.	B5	44
Gereshk, Afg.	D8	42
Gering, Ne., U.S.	C2	120
Gerlach, Nv., U.S.	C2	121
Gerlachovský štít, mtn., Slvk.	E6	20

Name	Map Ref.	Page

Germantown, Il., U.S. E4   106
Germantown, Md., U.S. ...B3   113
Germantown, Oh., U.S. ...C1   128
Germantown, Tn., U.S. ...B2   135
Germantown, Wi., U.S. ...E5   142
Germany, ctry., Eur. E12   12
Gerona see Girona, Spain .G8   16
Germiston, S. Afr. D4   56
Geronimo, Ok., U.S. C3   129
Gervais, Or., U.S. B4   130
Gêrzê, China C4   40
Geser, Indon. D8   36
Getafe, Spain G5   16
Gettysburg, Pa., U.S. ...G7   131
Gettysburg, S.D., U.S. ..C6   134
Geyve, Tur. B4   44
Ghadāmis, Libya E6   48
Ghāghara, stm., Asia ...D4   40
Ghana, ctry., Afr. E4   50
Ghanzi, Bots. C3   56
Ghardaïa, Alg. D5   48
Gharyān, Libya D7   48
Ghāt, Libya F7   48
Għawdex, i., Malta F5   18
Ghazāl, Bahr al-, stm., Sudan B5   54
Ghāziābād, India D3   40
Ghāzīpur, India D4   40
Ghaznī, Afg. D9   42
Ghazzah, Gaza Str. ...G6   44
Gheen, Mn., U.S. C6   116
Gheorgheni, Rom. F8   20
Gherla, Rom. F7   20
Ghilizane, Alg. J7   48
Ghūrīān, Afg. D8   42
Gianitsá, Grc. D9   18
Giant's Causeway, N. Ire., U.K. C3   12
Giants Neck, Ct., U.S. ..D7   100
Gibara, Cuba A4   80
Gibbon, Mn., U.S. F4   116
Gibbon, Ne., U.S. D7   120
Gibbons, Ab., Can. ...C4   84
Gibb River, Austl. D4   60
Gibbstown, N.J., U.S. ..D2   123
Gibeon, Nmb. D2   56
Gibraltar, dep., Eur. ..I4   16
Gibraltar, Strait of, strt. .J4   16
Gibsland, La., U.S. B2   111
Gibson, Ga., U.S. C4   103
Gibson, co., In., U.S. ..H2   107
Gibson, co., Tn., U.S. ..A3   135
Gibsonburg, Oh., U.S. ..A2   128
Gibson City, Il., U.S. ..C5   106
Gibson Desert, des., Austl. .E3   60
Gibsonia, Pa., U.S. h14   131
Gibson Island, i., Md., U.S. B5   113
Gibsons, B.C., Can. E6   85
Gibsonton, Fl., U.S. ...p11   102
Gibsonville, N.C., U.S. ..A3   126
Giddings, Tx., U.S. D4   136
Gideon, Mo., U.S. E8   118
Gien, Fr. D8   14
Giessen, Ger. E11   12
Gifford, Fl., U.S. E6   102
Gifford, Il., U.S. C5   106
Gifford Creek, Austl. ..E2   60
Gifu, Japan D15   28
Gig Harbor, Wa., U.S. ..B3   140
Giglio, Isola del, i., Italy .C3   18
Gihon, stm., Vt., U.S. ..B3   138
Gijón, Spain F4   16
Gila, co., Az., U.S. D5   96
Gila, stm., U.S. E5   92
Gila Bend, Az., U.S. ...E3   96
Gila Bend Indian Reservation, Az., U.S. .D3   96
Gila Bend Mountains, mts., Az., U.S. .D2   96
Gila Cliff Dwellings National Monument, N.M., U.S. D1   124
Gila Mountains, mts., Az., U.S. .D6   96
Gila Peak, mtn., Az., U.S. D6   96
Gila River Indian Reservation, Az., U.S. .D4   96
Gilbert, Az., U.S. D4   96
Gilbert, Ia., U.S. B4   108
Gilbert, La., U.S. B4   111
Gilbert, Mn., U.S. C6   116
Gilbert Islands see Kiribati, is., Kir. D11   58
Gilbert Peak, mtn., Wa., U.S. .C4   140
Gilbert Plains, Mb., Can. .D1   86
Gilbertsville, Ky., U.S. ..f9   110
Gilbertsville, Pa., U.S. ..F10   131
Gilbertville, Ia., U.S. ...B5   108
Gilbués, Braz. E10   70
Gilchrist, Or., U.S. D5   130
Gilchrist, co., Fl., U.S. ..C4   102
Gilcrest, Co., U.S. A6   99
Giles, co., Tn., U.S. ...B4   135
Giles, co., Va., U.S. ...C2   139
Gilford Island, i., B.C., Can. D4   85
Gilgandra, Austl. G4   62
Gilgil, Kenya D7   54
Gilgit, Pak. C10   42
Gillam, Mb., Can. A4   86
Gillespie, Il., U.S. D4   106
Gillespie, co., Tx., U.S. .D3   136
Gillespie Dam, Az., U.S. .D3   96
Gillett, Ar., U.S. C4   97
Gillett, Wi., U.S. D5   142
Gillette, Wy., U.S. B7   143

Gilliam, co., Or., U.S. ...B6   130
Gilman, Il., U.S. C5   106
Gilman, Vt., U.S. C5   138
Gilmanton, N.H., U.S. ..D4   122
Gilmer, Tx., U.S. C5   136
Gilmer, co., Ga., U.S. ..B2   103
Gilmer, co., W.V., U.S. .C4   141
Gilpin, co., Co., U.S. ..B5   99
Gilroy, Ca., U.S. D3   98
Gīmbī, Eth. B7   54
Gimie, Mount, vol., St. Luc. C7   80
Gimli, Mb., Can. D3   86
Gingoog, Phil. E9   34
Gīnīr, Eth. B8   54
Giralia, Austl. E1   60
Girard, Il., U.S. D4   106
Girard, Ks., U.S. E9   109
Girard, Oh., U.S. A5   128
Girard, Pa., U.S. B1   131
Girardot, Col. E5   80
Girardville, Pa., U.S. ..E9   131
Giresun, Tur. B8   44
Girona, Spain G8   16
Gironde, est., Fr. E6   16
Girvan, Scot., U.K. ...C4   12
Gisborne, N.Z. o14   63c
Gitarama, Rw. D5   54
Gitega, Bdi. D5   54
Giurgiu, Rom. H8   20
Giyon, Eth. B7   54
Giza see El-Gîza, Egypt .E11   48
Giza, Pyramids of, Egypt .F10   14
Gižduvan, Uzb. B8   42
Gižiga, Russia C18   26
Giżycko, Pol. B6   20
Gjirokastër, Alb. D3   18
Gjøvik, Nor. F4   10
Gjumri, Arm. B10   44
Glacier, co., Mt., U.S. ..B3   119
Glacier Bay, b., Ak., U.S. k21   95
Glacier Bay National Park, Ak., U.S. .D12   95
Glacier National Park, B.C., Can. D9   85
Glacier National Park, Mt., U.S. B2   119
Glacier Peak, mtn., Wa., U.S. A4   140
Gladbrook, Ia., U.S. ...B5   108
Glade Creek, stm., W.V., U.S. n13   141
Glade Creek, stm., W.V., U.S. n14   141
Glade Creek, stm., Wa., U.S. C6   140
Glades, co., Fl., U.S. ..F5   102
Glade Spring, Va., U.S. .f10   139
Gladewater, Tx., U.S. ..C5   136
Gladstone, Austl. E5   62
Gladstone, Mb., Can. ..D2   86
Gladstone, Mi., U.S. ..C4   115
Gladstone, Mo., U.S. ..h10   118
Gladstone, Or., U.S. ..B4   130
Gladwin, Mi., U.S. E6   115
Gladwin, co., Mi., U.S. .D6   115
Glâma, stm., Nor. F4   10
Glascock, co., Ga., U.S. .C4   103
Glasford, Il., U.S. C4   106
Glasgow, Scot., U.K. ..C4   12
Glasgow, Ky., U.S. C4   110
Glasgow, Mo., U.S. ...B5   118
Glasgow, Mt., U.S. ...B10   119
Glasgow, Va., U.S. ...C3   139
Glasgow, W.V., U.S. ..m13   141
Glassboro, N.J., U.S. ..D2   123
Glasscock, co., Tx., U.S. .D2   136
Glassport, Pa., U.S. ...F2   131
Glastonbury, Ct., U.S. .C5   100
Glazier Lake, l., Me., U.S. A3   112
Glazov, Russia D7   26
Gleason, Tn., U.S. A3   135
Glen Allan, Ms., U.S. ..B2   117
Glen Allen, Va., U.S. ..C5   139
Glenboro, Mb., Can. ..E2   86
Glenbrook, Nv., U.S. ..D2   121
Glen Burnie, Md., U.S. .B4   113
Glen Canyon Dam, Az., U.S. A4   96
Glen Canyon National Recreation Area, U.S. .F5   137
Glencoe, On., Can. E3   89
Glencoe, Al., U.S. B4   94
Glencoe, Il., U.S. A6   106
Glencoe, Mn., U.S. ...F4   116
Glen Cove, N.Y., U.S. ..h13   125
Glendale, Az., U.S. ...D3   96
Glendale, Ca., U.S. ...m12   98
Glendale, Ms., U.S. ...D4   117
Glendale, Oh., U.S. ...C1   128
Glendale, Or., U.S. ...E3   130
Glendale, R.I., U.S. ...B2   132
Glendale, S.C., U.S. ..B4   133
Glen Dale, W.V., U.S. ..B4   141
Glendale, Wi., U.S. ...m12   142
Glendale Heights, W.V., U.S. g8   141
Glendive, Mt., U.S. ...C12   119
Glendo, Wy., U.S. D7   143
Glendora, Ca., U.S. ...m13   98
Glendo Reservoir, res., Wy., U.S. D8   143
Glenelg, Md., U.S. B4   113
Glen Ellis Falls, wtfl, N.H., U.S. B4   122
Glen Ellyn, Il., U.S. ...k8   106

Glenham, N.Y., U.S. ...D7   125
Glen Innes, Austl. F5   62
Glen Jean, W.V., U.S. ..D3   141
Glen Lake, l., Mi., U.S. .D5   115
Glen Lyon, Pa., U.S. ..D9   131
Glenmora, La., U.S. ...D3   111
Glenn, co., Ca., U.S. ..C2   98
Glennallen, Ak., U.S. ..f19   95
Glenns Ferry, Id., U.S. .G3   105
Glennville, Ca., U.S. ..E5   103
Glenolden, Pa., U.S. ..p20   131
Glenpool, Ok., U.S. ...B5   129
Glen Raven, N.C., U.S. .A3   126
Glen Ridge, N.J., U.S. ..h8   123
Glen Rock, N.J., U.S. ..h8   123
Glen Rock, Pa., U.S. ...G8   131
Glenrock, Wy., U.S. ...D7   143
Glen Rose, Tx., U.S. ..C4   136
Glenrothes, Scot., U.K. .B5   12
Glen Ullin, N.D., U.S. ..C4   127
Glenview, Il., U.S. h9   106
Glenville, Mn., U.S. ...G5   116
Glenville, W.V., U.S. ..C4   141
Glenwood, Nf., Can. ..D4   88
Glenwood, Ar., U.S. ..C2   97
Glenwood, Ga., U.S. ..D4   103
Glenwood, Ia., U.S. ..C2   108
Glenwood, Mn., U.S. ..E3   116
Glenwood, Va., U.S. ..D3   139
Glenwood City, Wi., U.S. C1   142
Glenwood Springs, Co., U.S. B3   99
Glidden, Ia., U.S. B3   108
Glide, Or., U.S. D3   130
Glittertinden, mtn., Nor. .F3   10
Globe, Az., U.S. D5   96
Gloster, Ms., U.S. D2   117
Gloucester, Eng., U.K. .E5   12
Gloucester, Ma., U.S. .A6   114
Gloucester, Va., U.S. ..C6   139
Gloucester, co., N.J., U.S. D2   123
Gloucester, co., Va., U.S. C6   139
Gloucester City, N.J., U.S. D2   123
Gloucester Point, Va., U.S. C6   139
Glouster, Oh., U.S. ...C3   128
Glover Island, i., Nf., Can. D3   88
Gloversville, N.Y., U.S. .B6   125
Glovertown, Nf., Can. ..D4   88
Gloverville, S.C., U.S. ..E4   133
Glubokij, Russia E7   22
Głuchołazy, Pol. D4   20
Gluck, S.C., U.S. C2   133
Glyndon, Md., U.S. ...B4   113
Glyndon, Mn., U.S. ...D2   116
Glynn, co., Ga., U.S. ..E5   103
Gmünd, Aus. F14   12
Gmunden, Aus. G13   12
Gnadenhutten, Oh., U.S. B4   128
Gnarp, Swe. E7   10
Gniezno, Pol. C4   20
Gnowangerup, Austl. ..F3   60
Goa, prov., India F2   40
Goālpāra, India D6   40
Goat Island, i., R.I., U.S. F5   132
Goat Mountain, mtn., Mt., U.S. C3   119
Goat Rock Dam, U.S. ..C4   94
Goba, Eth. B7   54
Gobabis, Nmb. C2   56
Gobernador Gregores, Arg. G2   69
Gobi, des., Asia C7   28
Gobles, Mi., U.S. F5   115
Gobō, Japan D31   31
Godafoss, wtfl, Ice. ...l20   10a
Godāvari, stm., India ..F3   40
Goddard, Ks., U.S. ...E6   109
Goderich, On., Can. ..D3   89
Godfrey, Il., U.S. E3   106
Godhavn, Grnld. E29   82
Godhra, India E2   40
Gödöllő, Hung. G20   20
Gods, stm., Mb., Can. .A5   86
Gods Lake, l., Mb., Can. B4   86
Godthåb (Nuuk), Grnld. .F29   82
Goff Creek, stm., Ok., U.S. e9   129
Goffstown, N.H., U.S. ..D3   122
Gogebic, co., Mi., U.S. .n12   115
Gogebic, Lake, l., Mi., U.S. m12   115
Goiana, Braz. C5   74
Goianésia, Braz. E2   74
Goiânia, Braz. E2   74
Goiás, Braz. E1   74
Goiás, state, Braz. B3   70
Gojra, Pak. D10   42
Gök, stm., Tur. B6   44
Gökçeada, i., Tur. B1   44
Gökova Körfezi, b., Tur. .D2   44
Göksun, Tur. C4   44
Gokwe, Zimb. B4   56
Golāghāt, India D6   40
Golconda, Il., U.S. ...F5   106
Golconda, Nv., U.S. ..C4   121
Gölcük, Tur. B4   44
Gold Bar, Wa., U.S. ...B4   140
Gold Beach, Or., U.S. .E2   130
Gold Coast see Southport, Austl. F5   62
Golden, B.C., Can. D9   85
Golden, Co., U.S. B5   99
Golden City, Mo., U.S. .D3   118

Goldendale, Wa., U.S. ..D5   140
Golden Gate Bridge, Ca., U.S. h7   98
Golden Gate National Recreation Area, Ca., U.S. h7   98
Golden Hinde, mtn., B.C., Can. E5   85
Golden Meadow, La., U.S. E5   111
Golden Spike National Historic Site, hist., Ut., U.S. B3   137
Golden Valley, Mn., U.S. .n12   116
Golden Valley, co., Mt., U.S. D7   119
Golden Valley, co., N.D., U.S. B2   127
Goldfield, Ia., U.S. ...B4   108
Goldfield, Nv., U.S. ...F4   121
Gold Hill, Or., U.S. ...E3   130
Goldsboro, N.C., U.S. .B5   126
Goldsby, Ok., U.S. ...B4   129
Goldsworthy, Austl. ..E2   60
Goldthwaite, Tx., U.S. .D3   136
Goleniów, Pol. C3   20
Goleta, Ca., U.S. E4   98
Golfito, C.R. D3   80
Golf Manor, Oh., U.S. .o13   128
Gölhisar, Tur. D3   44
Goliad, Tx., U.S. E4   136
Goliad, co., Tx., U.S. ..E4   136
Gölköy, Tur. B7   44
Golmud, China B6   40
Golpāyegān, Iran D6   42
Goma, D.R.C. D5   54
Gomati, stm., India ...D4   40
Gombe, Nig. D7   50
Gombi, Nig. D7   50
Gomel see Homel', Bela. .C11   20
Gómez Palacio, Mex. ..B4   78
Gonaïves, Haiti B5   80
Gonam, Russia D15   26
Gonâve, Golfe de la, b., Haiti B5   80
Gonâve, Île de la, i., Haiti B5   80
Gonbad-e Qābūs, Iran ..C7   42
Gonda, India D4   40
Gondal, India E2   40
Gonder, Eth. H12   48
Gondia, India E4   40
Gönen, Tur. B2   44
Gongbo'gyamda, China .E6   28
Gongcheng, China E3   30
Gongga Shan, mtn., China F8   28
Gongxian, China C3   30
Gongzhuling, China ...C12   28
Gonzales, Ca., U.S. ..D3   98
Gonzales, La., U.S. ...D5   111
Gonzales, Tx., U.S. ...E4   136
Gonzales, co., Tx., U.S. .E4   136
González, Mex. C5   78
Gonzalez, Fl., U.S. ...u14   102
Goochland, co., Va., U.S. C5   139
Goode, Mount, mtn., Ak., U.S. g18   95
Goodfellow Air Force Base, mil., Tx., U.S. ...D2   136
Good Hope, Cape of, c., S. Afr. E2   56
Good Hope Mountain, mtn., B.C., Can. .D5   85
Goodhue, co., Mn., U.S. .F6   116
Gooding, Id., U.S. G4   105
Gooding, co., Id., U.S. .F4   105
Goodland, In., U.S. ...C3   107
Goodland, Ks., U.S. ..C2   109
Goodlettsville, Tn., U.S. g10   135
Goodman, Mo., U.S. ..E3   118
Goodman, Ms., U.S. ..C4   117
Good Pine, La., U.S. ..C3   111
Goodsprings, Nv., U.S. .H6   121
Goodview, Mn., U.S. ..F7   116
Goodwater, Al., U.S. ..B3   94
Goodwell, Ok., U.S. ..e9   129
Goodyear, Az., U.S. ...D3   96
Goondiwindi, Austl. ..F5   62
Goose, stm., N.D., U.S. .B8   127
Goose Bay, b., Nf., Can. .B1   88
Gooseberry Creek, stm., Wy., U.S. B4   143
Goose Creek, S.C., U.S. .F7   133
Goose Creek, stm., Va., U.S. C3   139
Goose Creek, stm., U.S. .G5   105
Goose Creek Reservoir, res., S.C., U.S. ...k11   133
Goose Lake, l., U.S. ..C3   92
Goose Pond, l., N.H., U.S. C2   122
Goqên, China F7   28
Gorakhpur, India D4   40
Gorda, Punta, c., Cuba .A3   80
Gordion, hist., Tur. ..C4   44
Gordo, Al., U.S. B2   94
Gordon, Ga., U.S. D3   103
Gordon, Ne., U.S. B3   120
Gordon, co., Ga., U.S. .B2   103
Gordon Downs, Austl. .D4   60
Gordonsville, Tn., U.S. .C8   135
Gordonsville, Va., U.S. .B4   139
Goré, Chad E8   50
Gorē, Eth. B7   54
Gore, N.Z. q12   63c
Gore, Ok., U.S. B6   129
Gore Bay, On., Can. ...B2   89

Gore Point, c., Ak., U.S. ..h16   95
Gore Range, mts., Co., U.S. B4   99
Goreville, Il., U.S. F5   106
Gorgān, Iran C6   42
Gorge High Dam, Wa., U.S. A4   140
Gorham, Me., U.S. E2   112
Gorham, N.H., U.S. ...B4   122
Gori, Geor. A11   44
Gorizia, Italy B4   18
Gorjačij Ključ, Russia ..G15   20
Gor'kij see Nižnij Novgorod, Russia ...D6   26
Gorkiy Reservoir see Gor'kovskoe vodohranilišče, res., Russia C7   22
Gor'kovskoe vodohranilišče, res., Russia C7   22
Görlitz, Ger. E14   12
Gorlovka see Horlivka, Ukr. E15   20
Gorman, Tx., U.S. C3   136
Gorna Orjahovica, Bul. .C10   18
Gornjackij, Russia A11   22
Gorno-Altajsk, Russia ..D10   26
Gornozavodsk, Russia ..B16   28
Gorodec, Russia C7   22
Goroka, Pap. N. Gui. ..H12   32
Gorong, Pulau, i., Indon. .D8   36
Gorontalo, Indon. C6   36
Gorzów Wielkopolski, Pol. .C3   20
Gosford, Austl. G5   62
Goshen, In., U.S. A6   107
Goshen, N.Y., U.S. ...D6   125
Goshen, Oh., U.S. C1   128
Goshen, co., Wy., U.S. .D8   143
Goshute Indian Reservation, U.S. D7   121
Goshute Lake, l., Nv., U.S. C7   121
Goshute Mountains, mts., Nv., U.S. C7   121
Goslar, Ger. E12   12
Gosnells, Austl. G2   60
Gosper, co., Ne., U.S. .D6   120
Gosport, In., U.S. F4   107
Gossinga, Sudan B5   54
Gostivar, Mac. D8   18
Gostyń, Pol. D4   20
Gostynin, Pol. C5   20
Göteborg (Gothenburg), Swe. H4   10
Gothenburg see Göteborg, Swe. H4   10
Gothenburg, Ne., U.S. .D5   120
Gotland, i., Swe. H8   10
Gotō-rettō, is., Japan ..E13   28
Gotska Sandön, i., Swe. .G8   10
Göttingen, Ger. E11   12
Goubone, Chad B8   50
Goudoumaria, Niger ..D7   50
Gough Island, i., St. Hel. .N9   46
Gouin, Réservoir, res., P.Q., Can. l25   72
Goulburn, Austl. G4   62
Goulburn Islands, is., Austl. C5   60
Gould, Ar., U.S. D4   97
Goulding, Fl., U.S. ...u14   102
Gould Island, i., R.I., U.S. E5   132
Goulds, Fl., U.S. s13   102
Goundam, Mali C4   50
Goundi, Chad E8   50
Gouré, Niger D7   50
Gouverneur, N.Y., U.S. .f9   125
Gove, co., Ks., U.S. ..D3   109
Governador Valadares, Braz. E3   74
Govind Ballabh Pant Reservoir see Govind Ballabh Pant Sāgar, res., India E4   40
Govind Ballabh Pant Sāgar, res., India E4   40
Gowanda, N.Y., U.S. ..C2   125
Gower, Mo., U.S. B3   118
Gowrie, Ia., U.S. B3   108
Goya, Arg. D6   72
Göyçay, Azer. B12   44
Gozo see Għawdex, i., Malta F5   18
Graaff-Reinet, S. Afr. ..E3   56
Grabill, In., U.S. B8   107
Grabo, C. Iv. F3   50
Grace, Id., U.S. G7   105
Graceville, Fl., U.S. ...u16   102
Graceville, Mn., U.S. ..E2   116
Gracewood, Ga., U.S. .C4   103
Gracias a Dios, Cabo, c., N.A. F8   76
Gradaús, Braz. E9   70
Grady, co., Ga., U.S. ..F2   103
Grady, co., Ok., U.S. ..C4   129
Graettinger, Ia., U.S. ..A3   108
Grafton, Austl. F5   62
Grafton, Il., U.S. E3   106
Grafton, Ma., U.S. ...B4   114
Grafton, N.D., U.S. ...A8   127
Grafton, Oh., U.S. A3   128
Grafton, Va., U.S. h15   139
Grafton, W.V., U.S. ...B4   141
Grafton, Wi., U.S. E6   142
Grafton, co., N.H., U.S. .C3   122
Graham, N.C., U.S. ...A3   126
Graham, Tx., U.S. C3   136
Graham, co., Az., U.S. .E5   96
Graham, co., Ks., U.S. .C4   109
Graham, co., N.C., U.S. .f9   126

Name	Map Ref.	Page

Graham, Lake, res., Tx., U.S. **C3** 136
Graham, Mount, mtn., Az., U.S. **E6** 96
Graham Island, i., B.C., Can.**C1** 85
Graham Lake, l., Me., U.S. . **D4** 112
Graham Land, reg., Ant. . . **C34** 67
Grahamstown, S. Afr. **E4** 56
Grahn, Ky., U.S. **B6** 110
Grainger, co., Tn., U.S. . . **C10** 135
Grain Valley, Mo., U.S. . . . **B3** 118
Grajaú, Braz. **C2** 74
Grajewo, Pol. **C7** 20
Grambling, La., U.S. **B3** 111
Gramercy, La., U.S. **h10** 111
Granada, Col. **E5** 80
Granada, Nic. **C2** 80
Granada, Spain **I5** 16
Granbury, Tx., U.S. **C4** 136
Granby, P.Q., Can. **D5** 90
Granby, Co., U.S. **A5** 99
Granby, Ct., U.S. **B4** 100
Granby, Mo., U.S. **E3** 118
Granby, Lake, res., Co., U.S.**A5** 99
Gran Canaria, i., Spain **A1** 50
Gran Chaco, reg., S.A. **C5** 72
Grand, co., Co., U.S. **A4** 99
Grand, co., Ut., U.S. **E6** 137
Grand, stm., On., Can. **D4** 89
Grand, stm., Mi., U.S. **E5** 115
Grand, stm., Mo., U.S. **A3** 118
Grand, stm., Oh., U.S. **A4** 128
Grand, stm., S.D., U.S. **B4** 134
Grand Bahama, i., Bah. . . . **C9** 76
Grand Bank, Nf., Can. **E4** 88
Grand-Bassam, C. Iv. **E4** 50
Grand Bay, N.B., Can. **D3** 87
Grand Bay, Al., U.S. **E1** 94
Grand Bend, On., Can. **D3** 89
Grand Blanc, Mi., U.S. **F7** 115
Grand Caillou, La., U.S. . . . **E5** 111
Grand Canal see Da Yunhe, China **D11** 28
Grand Canyon, Az., U.S. . . **A3** 96
Grand Canyon, val., Az., U.S. **A3** 96
Grand Canyon National Park, Az., U.S. **B3** 96
Grand Cayman, i., Cay. Is. . **B3** 80
Grand Centre, Ab., Can. . . . **B5** 84
Grand Cess, Lib. **F3** 50
Grand Coteau, La., U.S. . . . **D3** 111
Grand Coulee, Wa., U.S. . . **B6** 140
Grand Coulee Dam, Wa., U.S. **B6** 140
Grande, stm., Bol. **G7** 70
Grande, stm., Braz. **F1** 74
Grande, stm., Ven. **D7** 80
Grande, Bahía, b., Arg. . . . **H3** 69
Grande, Boca, mth., Ven. . . **D7** 80
Grande, Ilha, i., Braz. **F3** 74
Grande, Rio see Rio Grande, stm., N.A. **B5** 78
Grande-Anse, N.B., Can. . . **B4** 87
Grande Cache, Ab., Can. . . **C1** 84
Grande Comore see Njazidja, i., Com. **A7** 56
Grande de Matagalpa, stm., Nic. **C3** 80
Grande de Santiago, stm., Mex. **C4** 78
Grande do Gurupá, Ilha, i., Braz. **B1** 74
Grand-Entrée, P.Q., Can. . . **B8** 87
Grande Prairie, Ab., Can. . . **B1** 84
Grand Erg de Bilma, des., Niger **C7** 50
Grand Erg Occidental, des., Alg. **D5** 48
Grand Erg Oriental, des., Alg. **D6** 48
Grande rivière de la Baleine, stm., P.Q., Can. **g11** 90
Grande Ronde, stm., U.S. . **C8** 140
Grandes, Salinas, pl., Arg. . **E4** 72
Grandes-Bergeronnes, P.Q., Can. **A8** 90
Grande-Terre, i., Guad. . . . **B7** 80
Grand Falls (Grand-Sault), N.B., Can. **B2** 87
Grand Falls, wtfl, Me., U.S. **C5** 112
Grand Falls [-Windsor], Nf., Can. **D4** 88
Grandfather Mountain, mtn., N.C., U.S. **A1** 126
Grandfield, Ok., U.S. **C3** 129
Grand Forks, B.C., Can. . . . **E8** 85
Grand Forks, N.D., U.S. . . . **B8** 127
Grand Forks, co., N.D., U.S.**B8** 127
Grand Forks Air Force Base, mil., N.D., U.S. **B8** 127
Grand Harbour, N.B., Can. **E3** 87
Grand Haven, Mi., U.S. . . . **E4** 115
Grand Island, Ne., U.S. . . . **D7** 120
Grand Island, i., La., U.S. . **E6** 111
Grand Island, i., Mi., U.S. . **B4** 115
Grand Isle, La., U.S. **E6** 111
Grand Isle, co., Vt., U.S. . . . **B2** 138
Grand Isle, i., La., U.S. . . . **E6** 111
Grand Junction, Co., U.S. . **B2** 99
Grand Junction, Ia., U.S. . . **B3** 108
Grand Lake, l., N.B., Can. . **D3** 87
Grand Lake, l., Nf., Can. . . **D3** 88
Grand Lake, l., La., U.S. . . . **E6** 111

Grand Lake, l., La., U.S. . . . **E3** 111
Grand Lake, l., Mi., U.S. . . . **C7** 115
Grand Lake, l., Oh., U.S. . . **B1** 128
Grand Lake Matagamon, l., Me., U.S. **B4** 112
Grand Lake Seboeis, l., Me., U.S. **B4** 112
Grand Ledge, Mi., U.S. . . . **F6** 115
Grand Manan Island, i., N.B., Can. **E3** 87
Grand Marais, Mn., U.S. . . **k9** 116
Grand Meadow, Mn., U.S. . **G6** 116
Grand-Mère, P.Q., Can. . . . **C5** 90
Grand Mound, Ia., U.S. . . . **C7** 108
Grand Portage Indian Reservation, Mn., U.S..**k10** 116
Grand Portage National Monument, Mn., U.S. . **h10** 116
Grand Prairie, Tx., U.S. . . **n10** 136
Grand Rapids, Mi., U.S. . . . **F5** 115
Grand Rapids, Mn., U.S. . . **C5** 116
Grand Rapids, Oh., U.S. . . . **f6** 128
Grand Saline, Tx., U.S. . . . **C5** 136
Grand Terre Islands, is., La., U.S. **E6** 111
Grand Teton, mtn., Wy., U.S. **C2** 143
Grand Teton National Park, Wy., U.S. **C2** 143
Grand Tower, Il., U.S. **F4** 106
Grand Traverse, co., Mi., U.S. **D5** 115
Grand Traverse Bay, b., Mi., U.S. **C5** 115
Grand Turk, T./C. Is. **A5** 80
Grand Valley, On., Can. . . . **D4** 89
Grandview, Mb., Can. **D1** 86
Grandview, In., U.S. **I4** 107
Grandview, Mo., U.S. **C3** 118
Grandview, Wa., U.S. **C6** 140
Grandview Heights, Oh., U.S. **m10** 128
Grandville, Mi., U.S. **F5** 115
Grandy, N.C., U.S. **A7** 126
Granger, Ia., U.S. **C4** 108
Granger, In., U.S. **A5** 107
Granger, Tx., U.S. **D4** 136
Granger, Wa., U.S. **C5** 140
Grängesberg, Swe. **F6** 10
Grangeville, Id., U.S. **D2** 105
Gran Guardia, Arg. **D6** 72
Granisle, B.C., Can. **B4** 85
Granite, Ok., U.S. **C2** 129
Granite, co., Mt., U.S. **D3** 119
Granite City, Il., U.S. **E3** 106
Granite Falls, Mn., U.S. . . . **F3** 116
Granite Falls, N.C., U.S. . . **B1** 126
Granite Falls, Wa., U.S. . . . **A4** 140
Granite Lake, res., Nf., Can. **D3** 88
Granite Mountain, mtn., Ak., U.S. **B7** 95
Granite Mountains, mts., Az., U.S. **E2** 96
Granite Mountains, mts., Wy., U.S. **D5** 143
Granite Pass, Wy., U.S. . . . **B5** 143
Granite Peak, mtn., Mt., U.S. **E7** 119
Granite Peak, mtn., Nv., U.S. **C2** 121
Granite Peak, mtn., Nv., U.S. **B4** 121
Granite Peak, mtn., Ut., U.S. **E3** 137
Granite Peak, mtn., Ut., U.S. **C2** 137
Granite Peak, mtn., Wy., U.S. **D4** 143
Granite Quarry, N.C., U.S. . **B2** 126
Granite Range, mts., Nv., U.S. **C2** 121
Graniteville, S.C., U.S. **D4** 133
Graniteville, Vt., U.S. **C4** 138
Granja, Braz. **B3** 74
Grant, Al., U.S. **A3** 94
Grant, Mi., U.S. **E5** 115
Grant, Ne., U.S. **D4** 120
Grant, co., Ar., U.S. **C3** 97
Grant, co., In., U.S. **D6** 107
Grant, co., Ks., U.S. **E2** 109
Grant, co., Ky., U.S. **B5** 110
Grant, co., La., U.S. **C3** 111
Grant, co., Mn., U.S. **E2** 116
Grant, co., N.D., U.S. **C4** 127
Grant, co., Ne., U.S. **C4** 120
Grant, co., N.M., U.S. **E1** 124
Grant, co., Ok., U.S. **A4** 129
Grant, co., Or., U.S. **C7** 130
Grant, co., S.D., U.S. **B8** 134
Grant, co., W.V., U.S. **B5** 141
Grant, co., Wa., U.S. **B6** 140
Grant, co., Wi., U.S. **F3** 142
Grant, Mount, mtn., Nv., U.S. **E3** 121
Grant City, Mo., U.S. **A3** 118
Grant Park, Il., U.S. **B6** 106
Grant Range, mts., Nv., U.S.**E6** 121
Grants, N.M., U.S. **B2** 124
Grantsburg, Wi., U.S. **C1** 142
Grants Pass, Or., U.S. **E3** 130
Grantsville, Ut., U.S. **C3** 137
Grantsville, W.V., U.S. **C3** 141
Grant Town, W.V., U.S. . . . **B4** 141
Grantville, Ga., U.S. **C2** 103
Granville, Fr. **C6** 16

Granville, Il., U.S. **B4** 106
Granville, N.Y., U.S. **B7** 125
Granville, Oh., U.S. **B3** 128
Granville, W.V., U.S. **h11** 141
Granville, co., N.C., U.S. . . **A4** 126
Grapeland, Tx., U.S. **D5** 136
Grapeview, Wa., U.S. **B3** 140
Grapevine, Tx., U.S. **C4** 136
Grapevine Lake, res., Tx., U.S. **n9** 136
Grapevine Peak, mtn., Nv., U.S. **G4** 121
Grasonville, Md., U.S. **C5** 113
Grass, stm., Mb., Can. **B2** 86
Grass, stm., N.Y., U.S. **f9** 125
Grass Lake, Il., U.S. **h8** 106
Grass Lake, Mi., U.S. **F6** 115
Grass Lake, l., Il., U.S. . . . **h8** 106
Grass Ruaha, stm., Tan. . . **E7** 54
Grass Valley, Ca., U.S. . . . **C3** 98
Grassy Brook, stm., Vt., U.S.**E3** 138
Grassy Lake, l., La., U.S. . . **k9** 111
Grates Point, c., Nf., Can. . **D5** 88
Gratiot, co., Mi., U.S. **E6** 115
Gratis, Oh., U.S. **C1** 128
Grave Creek, stm., W.V., U.S. **g8** 141
Gravelly Branch, stm., De., U.S. **F4** 101
Gravelly Range, mts., Mt., U.S. **E4** 119
Gravenhage, 's- see 's-Gravenhage, Neth. . . . **D8** 12
Gravenhurst, On., Can. . . . **C5** 89
Grave Peak, mtn., Id., U.S. **C4** 105
Graves, co., Ky., U.S. **f9** 110
Gravette, Ar., U.S. **A1** 97
Gray, Fr. **D9** 16
Gray, Ga., U.S. **C3** 103
Gray, Ky., U.S. **D5** 110
Gray, La., U.S. **k10** 111
Gray, Me., U.S. **g7** 112
Gray, co., Ks., U.S. **E3** 109
Gray, co., Tx., U.S. **B2** 136
Grayback Mountain, mtn., Or., U.S. **E3** 130
Gray Court, S.C., U.S. **B3** 133
Grayland, Wa., U.S. **C1** 140
Grayling, Mi., U.S. **D6** 115
Graylyn Crest, De., U.S. . . . **A3** 101
Grays Harbor, co., Wa., U.S. **B2** 140
Grays Harbor, b., Wa., U.S. **C1** 140
Grayslake, Il., U.S. **A5** 106
Grays Lake, sw., Id., U.S. . **F7** 105
Grayson, Ky., U.S. **B7** 110
Grayson, co., Ky., U.S. . . . **C3** 110
Grayson, co., Tx., U.S. . . . **C4** 136
Grayson, co., Va., U.S. **D1** 139
Grayson Lake, res., Ky., U.S.**B7** 110
Grays Peak, mtn., Co., U.S. **B5** 99
Gray Summit, Mo., U.S. . **g12** 118
Graysville, Al., U.S. **f7** 94
Graysville, Tn., U.S. **D8** 135
Grayville, Il., U.S. **E5** 106
Graz, Aus. **G14** 12
Great Alfold see Alföld, pl., Hung. **F6** 20
Great Artesian Basin, Austl. **F3** 62
Great Australian Bight, b., Austl. **G4** 60
Great Averill Pond, l., Vt., U.S. **B5** 138
Great Barrier Island, i., N.Z.**o14** 63c
Great Barrier Reef, rf., Austl.**D4** 62
Great Barrington, Ma., U.S. **B1** 114
Great Basin, b., U.S. **C4** 92
Great Basin National Park, Nv., U.S. **E7** 121
Great Bay, b., N.H., U.S. . . **D5** 122
Great Bay, b., N.J., U.S. . . . **D4** 123
Great Bear Lake, l., N.T., Can. **E15** 82
Great Belt see Storebælt, strt., Den. **I4** 10
Great Bend, Ks., U.S. **D5** 109
Great Britain see United Kingdom, ctry., Eur. . . **C6** 12
Great Captain Island, i., Ct., U.S. **F1** 100
Great Channel, strt., Asia . **E2** 34
Great Dismal Swamp, sw., U.S. **D6** 139
Great Divide Basin, Wy., U.S. **E4** 143
Great Dividing Range, mts., Austl. **H4** 62
Great East Lake, l., U.S. . . **C5** 122
Great Egg Harbor, stm., N.J., U.S. **D3** 123
Greater Antilles, is., N.A. . . **E9** 76
Greater Khingan Range see Da Hinggan Ling, mts., China **B12** 28
Greater Sunda Islands, is., Asia **D3** 36
Great Exuma, i., Bah. **D9** 76
Great Falls, Mt., U.S. **C5** 119
Great Falls, S.C., U.S. **B6** 133
Great Falls, wtfl, Md., U.S. **B3** 113
Great Falls Dam, Tn., U.S. **D6** 135
Greathouse Peak, mtn., Mt., U.S. **D7** 119

Great Inagua, i., Bah. **D10** 76
Great Indian Desert (Thar Desert), des., Asia . . . **D2** 40
Great Island, spit, Ma., U.S. **C7** 114
Great Island, i., N.C., U.S. . **B6** 126
Great Karroo, plat., S. Afr. . **E3** 56
Great Lakes Naval Training Center, mil., Il., U.S. . . **h9** 106
Great Miami, stm., U.S. . . . **C1** 128
Great Misery Island, i., Ma., U.S. **f12** 114
Great Moose Lake, l., Me., U.S. **D3** 112
Great Namaqualand, hist. reg., Nmb. **D2** 56
Great Neck, N.Y., U.S. . . . **h13** 125
Great Nicobar, i., India . . . **H6** 40
Great Ouse, stm., Eng., U.K.**D7** 12
Great Pee Dee, stm., U.S. . **D9** 133
Great Plains, pl., N.A. **E9** 75
Great Point, c., Ma., U.S. . . **D7** 114
Great Ruaha, stm., Tan. . . **E7** 54
Great Sacandaga Lake, l., N.Y., U.S. **C6** 125
Great Salt Lake, l., Ut., U.S.**B3** 137
Great Salt Lake Desert, des., Ut., U.S. **C2** 137
Great Salt Plains Lake, res., Ok., U.S. **A3** 129
Great Salt Pond, b., R.I., U.S. **h7** 132
Great Sand Dunes National Monument, Co., U.S. . **D5** 99
Great Sandy Desert, des., Austl. **E3** 60
Great Slave Lake, l., N.T., Can. **F17** 82
Great Smoky Mountains, mts., U.S. **B8** 135
Great Smoky Mountains National Park, U.S. . . **B8** 135
Great Swamp, sw., R.I., U.S.**F3** 132
Great Victoria Desert, des., Austl. **F4** 60
Great Village, N.S., Can. . . **D6** 87
Great Wall see Chang Cheng, hist., China . . **B2** 30
Great Wass Island, i., Me., U.S. **D5** 112
Great Yarmouth, Eng., U.K. **D7** 12
Great Zab, stm., Asia . . . **D10** 44
Gréboun, mtn., Niger **C6** 50
Greece, N.Y., U.S. **B3** 125
Greece, ctry., Eur. **E8** 18
Greeley, Co., U.S. **A6** 99
Greeley, Pa., U.S. **D12** 131
Greeley, co., Ks., U.S. **D2** 109
Greeley, co., Ne., U.S. **C7** 120
Green, Or., U.S. **D3** 130
Green, co., Ky., U.S. **C4** 110
Green, co., Wi., U.S. **F4** 142
Green, stm., Il., U.S. **B4** 106
Green, stm., Ky., U.S. **C2** 110
Green, stm., Wa., U.S. **B3** 140
Green, stm., U.S. **D6** 92
Green, stm., U.S. **F3** 138
Green Acres, De., U.S. . . . **h8** 101
Greenacres, Wa., U.S. **B8** 140
Greenacres City, Fl., U.S. . **F6** 102
Greenback, Tn., U.S. **D9** 135
Green Bay, Wi., U.S. **D6** 142
Green Bay, b., U.S. **B10** 92
Green Bay, b., U.S. **D3** 115
Greenbelt, Md., U.S. **C4** 113
Greenbriar, Va., U.S. **g12** 139
Greenbrier, Ar., U.S. **B3** 97
Green Brier, Tn., U.S. **A5** 135
Greenbrier, co., W.V., U.S. **D4** 141
Greenbrier, stm., W.V., U.S. **D4** 141
Greenbush, Mn., U.S. **B2** 116
Greencastle, In., U.S. **E4** 107
Greencastle, Pa., U.S. **G6** 131
Green City, Mo., U.S. **A5** 118
Green Cove Springs, Fl., U.S. **C5** 102
Greendale, In., U.S. **F8** 107
Greendale, Wi., U.S. **F6** 142
Greene, Ia., U.S. **B5** 108
Greene, N.Y., U.S. **C5** 125
Greene, co., Al., U.S. **C1** 94
Greene, co., Ar., U.S. **A5** 97
Greene, co., Ga., U.S. **C3** 103
Greene, co., Ia., U.S. **B3** 108
Greene, co., Il., U.S. **D3** 106
Greene, co., In., U.S. **F4** 107
Greene, co., Mo., U.S. **D4** 118
Greene, co., Ms., U.S. **D5** 117
Greene, co., N.C., U.S. . . . **B5** 126
Greene, co., N.Y., U.S. . . . **C6** 125
Greene, co., Oh., U.S. **C2** 128
Greene, co., Pa., U.S. **G1** 131
Greene, co., Tn., U.S. . . . **C11** 135
Greene, co., Va., U.S. **B4** 139
Greeneville, Tn., U.S. . . . **C11** 135
Green Fall, stm., U.S. **F1** 132
Greenfield, Ca., U.S. **D3** 98
Greenfield, Ia., U.S. **C3** 108
Greenfield, Il., U.S. **D3** 106
Greenfield, In., U.S. **E6** 107
Greenfield, Ma., U.S. **A2** 114
Greenfield, Mo., U.S. **D4** 118
Greenfield, N.H., U.S. **E3** 122
Greenfield, Oh., U.S. **C2** 128
Greenfield, Tn., U.S. **A3** 135
Greenfield, Wi., U.S. **n12** 142

Greenfield Plaza, Ia., U.S. . **e8** 108
Green Forest, Ar., U.S. **A2** 97
Green Harbor, Ma., U.S. . . **B6** 114
Green Hill Pond, l., R.I., U.S. **G3** 132
Greenhills, Oh., U.S. **n12** 128
Green Lake, Wi., U.S. **E5** 142
Green Lake, co., Wi., U.S. . **E4** 142
Green Lake, l., Me., U.S. . . **D4** 112
Green Lake, l., Wi., U.S. . . **E5** 142
Greenland, Ar., U.S. **B1** 97
Greenland, N.H., U.S. **D5** 122
Greenland, dep., N.A. . . . **D30** 82
Greenland Basin **D23** 144
Greenland Sea **B9** 46
Greenlee, co., Az., U.S. . . . **D6** 96
Green Lookout Mountain, mtn., Wa., U.S. **D3** 140
Green Mountain, mtn., Wy., U.S. **D5** 143
Green Mountain Reservoir, res., Co., U.S. **B4** 99
Green Mountains, mts., Vt., U.S. **F2** 138
Greenock, Scot., U.K. **C4** 12
Greenock, Pa., U.S. **F2** 131
Green Peter Lake, res., Or., U.S. **C4** 130
Green Pond, Al., U.S. **B2** 94
Green Pond, l., N.J., U.S. . . **A4** 123
Greenport, N.Y., U.S. . . . **m16** 125
Green River, Ut., U.S. **E5** 137
Green River, Wy., U.S. . . . **E3** 143
Green River Lake, res., Ky., U.S. **C4** 110
Green River Lock and Dam, U.S. **I2** 107
Green River Reservoir, res., Vt., U.S. **B3** 138
Green Rock, Il., U.S. **B3** 106
Greensboro, Al., U.S. **C2** 94
Greensboro, Ga., U.S. **C3** 103
Greensboro, Md., U.S. **C6** 113
Greensboro, N.C., U.S. . . . **A3** 126
Greensburg, In., U.S. **F7** 107
Greensburg, Ks., U.S. **E4** 109
Greensburg, Ky., U.S. **C4** 110
Greensburg, Pa., U.S. **F2** 131
Greens Peak, mtn., Az., U.S.**C6** 96
Green Springs, Oh., U.S. . . **A2** 128
Greensville, co., Va., U.S. . **D5** 139
Green Swamp, sw., N.C., U.S. **C4** 126
Greentown, In., U.S. **D6** 107
Greenup, Il., U.S. **D5** 106
Greenup, Ky., U.S. **B7** 110
Greenup, co., Ky., U.S. . . . **B7** 110
Green Valley, Az., U.S. . . . **F5** 96
Greenview, Il., U.S. **C4** 106
Greenville, Lib. **E3** 50
Greenville, Al., U.S. **D3** 94
Greenville, Ca., U.S. **B3** 98
Greenville, De., U.S. **A3** 101
Greenville, Ga., U.S. **C2** 103
Greenville, Il., U.S. **E4** 106
Greenville, Ky., U.S. **C2** 110
Greenville, Me., U.S. **C3** 112
Greenville, Mi., U.S. **E5** 115
Greenville, Ms., U.S. **B2** 117
Greenville, N.C., U.S. **B5** 126
Greenville, N.H., U.S. **E3** 122
Greenville, Oh., U.S. **B1** 128
Greenville, Pa., U.S. **D1** 131
Greenville, R.I., U.S. **C3** 132
Greenville, S.C., U.S. **B3** 133
Greenville, Tx., U.S. **C4** 136
Greenville, co., S.C., U.S. . **B3** 133
Greenville Creek, stm., Oh., U.S. **B1** 128
Greenville Junction, Me., U.S. **C3** 112
Greenwich, Ct., U.S. **E1** 100
Greenwich, N.Y., U.S. **B7** 125
Greenwich, Oh., U.S. **A3** 128
Greenwich Bay, b., R.I., U.S. **D4** 132
Greenwich Point, c., Ct., U.S. **E1** 100
Greenwood, B.C., Can. . . . **E8** 85
Greenwood, Ar., U.S. **B1** 97
Greenwood, De., U.S. **E3** 101
Greenwood, In., U.S. **E5** 107
Greenwood, La., U.S. **B2** 111
Greenwood, Mo., U.S. . . **k11** 118
Greenwood, Ms., U.S. **B3** 117
Greenwood, Pa., U.S. **E5** 131
Greenwood, S.C., U.S. . . . **C3** 133
Greenwood, Wi., U.S. **D3** 142
Greenwood, co., Ks., U.S. . **E7** 109
Greenwood, co., S.C., U.S. **C3** 133
Greenwood, Lake, res., In., U.S. **G4** 107
Greenwood, Lake, res., S.C., U.S. **C4** 133
Greenwood Lake, N.Y., U.S.**D6** 125
Greenwood Lake, l., Mn., U.S. **C7** 116
Greenwood Lake, l., U.S. . . **A4** 123
Greer, S.C., U.S. **B3** 133
Greer, co., Ok., U.S. **C2** 129
Greers Ferry Lake, res., Ar., U.S. **B3** 97
Greeson, Lake, res., Ar., U.S. **C2** 97
Gregg, co., Tx., U.S. **C5** 136

Name	Map Ref.	Page

Gregory, S.D., U.S. D6 134
Gregory, co., S.D., U.S. . . . D6 134
Gregory Range, mts., Austl. D3 62
Greifswald, Ger. C13 12
Greilickville, Mi., U.S. . . . D5 115
Gremiha, Russia C5 26
Grenada, Ms., U.S. B4 117
Grenada, co., Ms., U.S. . . . B4 117
Grenada, ctry., N.A. F12 76
Grenada Lake, res., Ms.,
  U.S. B4 117
Grenadines, is., N.A. F12 76
Grenen, c., Den. H4 10
Grenoble, Fr. E9 16
Grenville, P.Q., Can. D3 90
Grenville, Cape, c., Austl. . C3 62
Grenville, Point, c., Wa.,
  U.S. B1 140
Gresham, Or., U.S. B4 130
Gresik, Indon. E4 36
Gresik, Indon. D2 36
Gretna, Mb., Can. E3 86
Gretna, Fl., U.S. B2 102
Gretna, La., U.S. E5 111
Gretna, Ne., U.S. C9 120
Gretna, Va., U.S. D3 139
Grevená, Grc. D8 18
Grey, stm., Nf., Can. E3 88
Greybull, Wy., U.S. B4 143
Greybull, stm., Wy., U.S. . B4 143
Greylock, Mount, mtn.,
  Ma., U.S. A1 114
Greymouth, N.Z. p13 63c
Grey Range, mts., Austl. . . F3 62
Greys, stm., Wy., U.S. . . . C2 143
Greytown, S. Afr. D5 56
Gridley, Ca., U.S. C3 98
Gridley, Il., U.S. C5 106
Griffin, Ga., U.S. C2 103
Griffiss Air Force Base, mil.,
  N.Y., U.S. B5 125
Griffith, Austl. G4 62
Griffith, In., U.S. A3 107
Grifton, N.C., U.S. B5 126
Griggs, co., N.D., U.S. . . . B7 127
Griggsville, Il., U.S. D3 106
Grim, Cape, c., Austl. I3 62
Grimes, Ia., U.S. C4 108
Grimes, co., Tx., U.S. D4 136
Grimsby, On., Can. D5 89
Grimsby, Eng., U.K. D7 12
Grímsey, i., Ice. k20 10a
Grimshaw, Ab., Can. A2 84
Grimsley, Tn., U.S. C9 135
Grímsstadir, Ice. l20 10a
Grindall Creek, Va., U.S. . . n18 139
Grinnell, Ia., U.S. C5 108
Griswold, Ia., U.S. C2 108
Grizzly Mountain, mtn., Id.,
  U.S. B2 105
Grizzly Mountain, mtn., Or.,
  U.S. C6 130
Grizzly Mountain, mtn.,
  Wa., U.S. A7 140
Grjazi, Russia C15 20
Grjazovec, Russia C7 22
Groais Island, i., Nf., Can. . C4 88
Groblersdal, S. Afr. D4 56
Grodno see Hrodno, Bela. C7 20
Groesbeck, Tx., U.S. D4 136
Groningen, Neth. D10 12
Groom Lake, l., Nv., U.S. . F6 121
Groom Range, mts., Nv.,
  U.S. F6 121
Groote Eylandt, i., Austl. . . C6 60
Grootfontein, Nmb. B2 56
Gros Morne National Park,
  Nf., Can. D3 88
Grosse Isle Naval Air
  Station, mil., Mi., U.S. . . p15 115
Grosse Pointe Park, Mi.,
  U.S. p16 115
Grosse Pointe Woods, Mi.,
  U.S. p16 115
Grosseto, Italy C3 18
Grossglockner, mtn., Aus. . C12 12
Grossmont, Ca., U.S. o16 98
Gros Ventre, stm., Wy.,
  U.S. C2 143
Gros Ventre Range, mts.,
  Wy., U.S. C2 143
Groswater Bay, b., Nf., Can. H28 82
Groton, Ct., U.S. D7 100
Groton, N.Y., U.S. C4 125
Groton, S.D., U.S. B7 134
Groton Long Point, Ct., U.S. D7 100
Grottoes, Va., U.S. B4 139
Grouse Creek, stm., Ut.,
  U.S. B2 137
Grouse Creek Mountain,
  mtn., Id., U.S. E5 105
Grove, Ok., U.S. A7 129
Grove City, Fl., U.S. F4 102
Grove City, Oh., U.S. C2 128
Grove City, Pa., U.S. D1 131
Grove Hill, Al., U.S. D2 94
Groveland, Fl., U.S. D5 102
Groveland, Ma., U.S. A5 114
Grove Mountains, mts., Ant. D12 67
Grove Point, c., Md., U.S. . B5 113
Groveport, Oh., U.S. C3 128
Grover City, Ca., U.S. E3 98
Groves, Tx., U.S. E6 136
Groveton, N.H., U.S. A3 122
Groveton, Tx., U.S. D5 136
Groveton, Va., U.S. g12 139

Grovetown, Ga., U.S. C4 103
Groveville, N.J., U.S. C3 123
Growa Point, c., Lib. F3 50
Growler Peak, mtn., Az.,
  U.S. E2 96
Groznyj, Russia E6 20
Grudziądz, Pol. C5 20
Gruetli-Laager, Tn., U.S. . . D8 135
Grulla, Tx., U.S. F3 136
Grünau, Nmb. D2 56
Grundy, Va., U.S. e9 139
Grundy, co., Ia., U.S. B5 108
Grundy, co., Il., U.S. B5 106
Grundy, co., Mo., U.S. . . . A4 118
Grundy, co., Tn., U.S. D8 135
Grundy Center, Ia., U.S. . . B5 108
Grunthal, Mb., Can. E3 86
Gruver, Tx., U.S. A2 136
Guacanayabo, Golfo de, b.,
  Cuba A4 80
Guadalajara, Mex. C4 78
Guadalajara, Spain G5 16
Guadalcanal, i., Sol. Is. . . . B6 62
Guadalquivir, stm., Spain . I4 16
Guadalquivir, Marismas del,
  sw., Spain I3 16
Guadalupe, Mex. C4 78
Guadalupe, Mex. B4 78
Guadalupe, Az., U.S. m9 96
Guadalupe, Ca., U.S. E3 98
Guadalupe, co., N.M., U.S. C5 124
Guadalupe, co., Tx., U.S. . E4 136
Guadalupe, Isla, i., Mex. . . B1 78
Guadalupe Mountains, mts.,
  U.S. E5 124
Guadalupe Mountains
  National Park, Tx., U.S. o12 136
Guadalupe Peak, mtn., Tx.,
  U.S. o12 136
Guadeloupe, dep., N.A. . . E12 76
Guadeloupe Passage, strt.,
  N.A. B7 80
Guadiana, stm., Eur. I3 16
Guadix, Spain I5 16
Guaíra, Braz. C7 72
Guajará-Mirim, Braz. F6 70
Guaje, Laguna del, l., Mex. B4 78
Gualeguay, Arg. E6 72
Gualeguaychú, Arg. E6 72
Guam, dep., Oc. D12 32
Guaminí, Arg. F5 72
Guamúchil, Mex. B3 78
Guanaja, Isla de, i., Hond. . B2 80
Guanajuato, Mex. C4 78
Guanajuato, state, Mex. . . C4 78
Guanambi, Braz. D3 74
Guanare, Ven. B6 70
Guane, Cuba A3 80
Guang'an, China E9 28
Guangde, China C4 30
Guangdong, state, China . G10 28
Guangji, China D4 30
Guangling, China B3 30
Guangnan, China G8 28
Guangxi Zhuangzu Zizhiqu,
  state, China G9 28
Guangyuan, China E9 28
Guangzhou (Canton), China E3 30
Guano Lake, l., Or., U.S. . . E7 130
Guantánamo, Cuba A4 80
Guantao, China B4 30
Guanxian, China E8 28
Guanyun, China C4 30
Guapí, Col. C4 70
Guápiles, C.R. C3 80
Guaporé, stm., S.A. F7 70
Guarabira, Braz. C4 74
Guarapari, Braz. F3 74
Guarapuava, Braz. D7 72
Guaratuba, Braz. D8 72
Guarda, Port. G3 16
Guardafui, Cape see
  Gwardafuy, Gees c.,
  Som. H15 48
Guardo, Spain F4 16
Guarenas, Ven. C6 80
Guárico, stm., Ven. D6 80
Guasave, Mex. B3 78
Guasdualito, Ven. B5 70
Guasipati, Ven. B7 70
Guatemala, Guat. C1 80
Guatemala, ctry., N.A. . . . D6 78
Guatemala Basin G29 64
Guaviare, stm., Col. C6 70
Guaxupé, Braz. F2 74
Guayana see Ciudad
  Guayana, Ven. B7 70
Guayana see Guyana, ctry.,
  S.A. B8 70
Guayape, stm., Hond. C2 80
Guayaquil, Ec. D3 70
Guayaquil, Golfo de, b.,
  S.A. D3 70
Guaymallén, Arg. E4 72
Guaymas, Mex. B2 78
Gubaha, Russia C10 22
Gubbio, Italy C4 18
Guben (Gubin), Pol. E14 12
Guben (Gubin), Pol. D3 20
Gubin (Guben), Pol. D3 20
Gubkin, Russia D14 20
Gudauta, Geor. A9 44
Gudermes, Russia B5 44
Gudivāda, India F4 40
Gudiyāttam, India G3 40
Gūdūr, India G3 40

Guékédou, Gui. E2 50
Guélengdeng, Chad D8 50
Guelma, Alg. D5 14
Guelph, On., Can. D4 89
Guercif, Mor. E3 14
Güere, stm., Ven. D7 80
Guéret, Fr. D7 16
Guernsey, Wy., U.S. D8 143
Guernsey, co., Oh., U.S. . . B4 128
Guernsey, dep., Eur. F5 12
Guerrero, Mex. B3 78
Guerrero, state, Mex. D4 78
Guerrero Negro, Mex. . . . B2 78
Gueydan, La., U.S. D3 111
Guga, Russia D15 26
Gugē, mtn., Eth. B7 54
Guguan, i., N. Mar. Is. . . . C12 32
Guiana Basin G9 66
Guide, China D8 28
Guiding, China D2 30
Guildford, Eng., U.K. E6 12
Guilford, Ct., U.S. D5 100
Guilford, Me., U.S. C3 112
Guilford, co., N.C., U.S. . . A3 126
Guilin, China F10 28
Guimarães, Port. G2 16
Guimaras Island, i., Phil. . . D8 34
Guin, Al., U.S. B2 94
Guinea, ctry., Afr. D2 50
Guinea, Gulf of, b., Afr. . . I10 46
Guinea Basin H13 66
Guinea-Bissau, ctry., Afr. . . D1 50
Güines, Cuba A3 80
Guingamp, Fr. C5 16
Guiping, China E3 30
Güira de Melena, Cuba . . . A3 80
Güiria, Ven. A7 70
Guitry, C. Iv. E3 50
Guiuan, Phil. D9 34
Guixi, China D4 30
Guixian, China G9 28
Guiyang, China F9 28
Guizhou, state, China F9 28
Gujarāt, prov., India E2 40
Gujrānwāla, Pak. D10 42
Gujrāt, Pak. D10 42
Gulbarga, India F3 40
Gulbene, Lat. H12 10
Gulf, co., Fl., U.S. C1 102
Gulf, The see Persian Gulf,
  b., Asia E6 42
Gulf Gate Estates, Fl., U.S. E4 102
Gulf Islands National
  Seashore, U.S. E5 117
Gulf of Alaska Seamount
  Province B1 144
Gulfport, Fl., U.S. E4 102
Gulfport, Ms., U.S. E4 117
Gulf Shores, Al., U.S. E2 94
Gulgong, Austl. G4 62
Gulian, China A12 28
Gulistan, Uzb. B9 42
Gullfoss, wtfl., Ice. I19 10a
Gull Island, i., N.C., U.S. . . B7 126
Gullivan Bay, b., Fl., U.S. . G5 102
Gull Lake, l., Ab., Can. . . . C4 84
Gull Lake, l., Mn., U.S. . . . D4 116
Güllük Körfezi, b., Tur. . . . D2 44
Gulong, China C4 30
Gulu, Ug. C6 54
Gumboro, De., U.S. G4 101
Gumdag, Turk. C6 42
Gumel, Nig. D6 50
Gumi, S. Kor. D13 28
Gumma, prov., Japan E15 28
Gümüşhane, Tur. B8 44
Guna, India E3 40
Gundagai, Austl. H4 62
Gundji, D.R.C. C4 54
Gundu, D.R.C. E3 54
Gunisao, stm., Mb., Can. . C3 86
Gunmi, Nig. D6 50
Gunnbjørn Fjeld, mtn.,
  Grnld. E34 82
Gunnedah, Austl. G5 62
Gunnison, Co., U.S. C4 99
Gunnison, Ms., U.S. B3 117
Gunnison, Ut., U.S. D4 137
Gunnison, co., Co., U.S. . . C3 99
Gunnison, stm., Co., U.S. . C2 99
Gunnison, Mount, mtn.,
  Co., U.S. C3 99
Gunpowder Neck, c., Md.,
  U.S. B5 113
Gunpowder River, b., Md.,
  U.S. B5 113
Guntakal, India F3 40
Gunter Air Force Base, mil.,
  Al., U.S. C3 94
Guntersville, Al., U.S. A3 94
Guntersville Lake, res., Al.,
  U.S. A3 94
Guntown, Ms., U.S. A5 117
Guntūr, India F4 40
Gunungsitoli, Indon. C1 36
Guoyang, China C4 30
Gupis, Pak. C10 42
Gurdon, Ar., U.S. D2 97
Gurdžaani, Geor. B11 44
Gurley, Al., U.S. A3 94
Gurnee, Il., U.S. h9 106
Gurnet Point, c., Ma., U.S. B6 114
Gurskøya, i., Nor. E1 10
Gürün, Tur. C7 44
Gurupi, Braz. D2 74
Gurupi, stm., Braz. B2 74

Gusau, Nig. D6 50
Gusev, Russia B7 20
Gușǧy, Turk. F8 26
Gushi, China C4 30
Gusinoozersk, Russia A9 28
Guspini, Italy E2 18
Gustav Holm, Kap, c.,
  Grnld. E33 82
Gustine, Ca., U.S. D3 98
Güstrow, Ger. D13 12
Guthrie, Ky., U.S. D2 110
Guthrie, Ok., U.S. B4 129
Guthrie, W.V., U.S. m12 141
Guthrie, co., Ia., U.S. C3 108
Guthrie Center, Ia., U.S. . . C3 108
Guttenberg, Ia., U.S. B6 108
Guttenberg, N.J., U.S. . . . h8 123
Guwāhāti, India D6 40
Guyana, ctry., S.A. B8 70
Guyandotte, stm., W.V.,
  U.S. C2 141
Guyang, China A3 30
Guymon, Ok., U.S. e9 129
Guysborough, N.S., Can. . D8 87
Guyton, Ga., U.S. D5 103
Guyuan, China D9 28
Guzar, Uzb. C9 42
Güzelyurt Körfezi, b., N.
  Cyp. E5 44
Guzmán, Mex. D4 78
Gwaai, Zimb. B4 56
Gwādar, Pak. E8 42
Gwalia, Austl. F3 60
Gwalior, India D3 40
Gwanda, Zimb. C4 56
Gwardafuy, Gees, c., Som. H15 48
Gwayi, stm., Zimb. B4 56
Gweru, Zimb. B4 56
Gweta, Bots. C4 56
Gwinhurst, De., U.S. h8 101
Gwinn, Mi., U.S. B3 115
Gwinner, N.D., U.S. C8 127
Gwinnett, co., Ga., U.S. . . C2 103
Gwydyr Bay, b., Ak., U.S. . A10 95
Gwynns Falls, stm., Md.,
  U.S. g10 113
Gyangzê, China F5 28
Gyaring Co, l., China E5 28
Gyaring Hu, l., China E7 28
Gyda, Russia B9 26
Gydanskij poluostrov, pen.,
  Russia B9 26
Gyldenløves Fjord, b.,
  Grnld. F31 82
Gympie, Austl. F5 62
Gyöngyös, Hung. F5 20
Győr, Hung. F4 20
Gypsum, Co., U.S. B4 99
Gyzylarbat, Turk. F7 26

H

Haakon, co., S.D., U.S. . . . C4 134
Haapsalu, Est. G10 10
Haarlem, Neth. D9 12
Haast, N.Z. p12 63c
Habarovo, Russia A11 22
Habarovsk, Russia E15 26
Habbānīyah, Buhayrat al-,
  res., Iraq F10 44
Habersham, co., Ga., U.S. . B3 103
Hachijō-jima, i., Japan . . . E15 28
Hachinohe, Japan C16 28
Hachiōji, Japan C3 31
Hackberry, La., U.S. E2 111
Hackensack, N.J., U.S. . . . B4 123
Hackensack, stm., N.J., U.S. h8 123
Hackettstown, N.J., U.S. . . B3 123
Hackleburg, Al., U.S. A2 94
Haddam, Ct., U.S. D5 100
Haddock, Ga., U.S. C3 103
Haddonfield, N.J., U.S. . . . D2 123
Haddon Heights, N.J., U.S. D2 123
Hadejia, Nig. D7 50
Hadejia, stm., Nig. D6 50
Hadera, Isr. F6 44
Haderslev, Den. I3 10
Hadībū, Yemen H6 38
Hadīthah, Iraq D4 42
Hadjout, Alg. I8 16
Hadley Lake, l., Me., U.S. . D5 112
Hadrian's Wall, Eng., U.K. . C5 12
Haeju, N. Kor. D13 28
Hafik, Tur. C7 44
Hafnarfjördur, Ice. I17 10a
Haft Gel, Iran D5 42
Hagan, Ga., U.S. D5 103
Hagemeister Island, i., Ak.,
  U.S. D7 95
Hagerman, Id., U.S. G4 105
Hagerman, N.M., U.S. . . . D5 124
Hagerstown, In., U.S. E7 107
Hagerstown, Md., U.S. . . . A2 113
Hagfors, Swe. F5 10
Hagi, Japan D2 31
Ha Giang, Viet. B5 34
Hague, Sk., Can. E2 91
Haguenau, Fr. C10 16
Hagues Peak, mtn., Co.,
  U.S. A5 99
Hai Hai, Baie des, b., P.Q.,
  Can. C2 88

Hahira, Ga., U.S. F3 103
Hahnville, La., U.S. E5 111
Haicheng, China A5 30
Hai Duong, Viet. B5 34
Haifa see Ḥefa, Isr. D2 42
Haig, Austl. G4 60
Haikang, China E3 30
Haikou, China G10 28
Haiku, Hi., U.S. C5 104
Ḥā'il, Sau. Ar. E4 38
Hailar, China B11 28
Hailey, Id., U.S. F4 105
Haileybury, On., Can. p20 89
Haileyville, Ok., U.S. C6 129
Hailin, China B1 31
Hailun, China B13 28
Haimen, China F12 28
Haimen, China E4 30
Hainan, prov., China H9 28
Hainan Dao, i., China H9 28
Hainan Island see Hainan
  Dao, i., China H9 28
Haines, Ak., U.S. D12 95
Haines City, Fl., U.S. D5 102
Haining, China C5 30
Hai Ninh, Viet. B5 34
Hai Phong, Viet. B5 34
Haisyn, Ukr. E10 20
Haiti, ctry., N.A. H12 75
Haitun, China B7 40
Haiyuan, China B2 30
Haizhou, China E11 28
Haizhou Wan, b., China . . B4 30
Hajdúböszörmény, Hung. . F6 20
Hajnówka, Pol. C7 20
Hakkâri, Tur. D10 44
Hakodate, Japan C16 28
Ḥalab (Aleppo), Syria D7 44
Halachó, Mex. C6 78
Halā'ib, Sudan F12 48
Halawa, Cape, c., Hi., U.S. B5 104
Halawa Heights, Hi., U.S. . g10 104
Halberstadt, Ger. E12 12
Halden, Nor. G4 10
Haldimand, On., Can. E5 89
Haldwāni, India D3 40
Hale, co., Al., U.S. C2 94
Hale, co., Tx., U.S. B2 136
Haleakala Crater, crat., Hi.,
  U.S. C5 104
Haleakala National Park,
  Hi., U.S. C6 104
Hale Center, Tx., U.S. B2 136
Haleiwa, Hi., U.S. B3 104
Hales Corners, Wi., U.S. . . n11 142
Halethorpe, Md., U.S. B4 113
Haleyville, Al., U.S. A2 94
Half Moon Bay, Ca., U.S. . k8 98
Halfway, Md., U.S. A2 113
Haliburton, On., Can. B6 89
Halibut Point, c., Ma., U.S. A6 114
Halicarnassus, hist., Tur. . . D2 44
Halifax, N.S., Can. E6 87
Halifax, Va., U.S. D4 139
Halifax, co., N.C., U.S. . . . A5 126
Halifax, co., Va., U.S. D4 139
Haliimaile, Hi., U.S. C5 104
Hall, co., Ga., U.S. B3 103
Hall, co., Ne., U.S. D7 120
Hall, co., Tx., U.S. B2 136
Halla, Mount see Halla-san,
  mtn., S. Kor. E13 28
Hallam Peak, mtn., B.C.,
  Can. C8 85
Hallandale, Fl., U.S. G6 102
Ḥallānīyah, Juzur al-, is.,
  Oman G7 38
Halla-san, mtn., S. Kor. . . . E13 28
Halle, Ger. E12 12
Hälleforsse, Swe. G6 10
Hallein, Aus. G13 12
Hallettsville, Tx., U.S. E4 136
Hallie, Wi., U.S. D2 142
Hall Island, i., Ak., U.S. . . C5 95
Hall Meadow Brook
  Reservoir, res., Ct., U.S. B3 100
Hall Mountain, mtn., Wa.,
  U.S. A8 140
Hallock, Mn., U.S. B2 116
Hallowell, Me., U.S. D3 112
Halls, Tn., U.S. B2 135
Hallsberg, Swe. G6 10
Halls Creek, Austl. D4 60
Halls Creek, stm., Ut., U.S. F5 137
Halls Crossroads, Tn., U.S. m14 135
Halls Stream, stm., N.H.,
  U.S. f7 122
Hallstahammar, Swe. G7 10
Hallstead, Pa., U.S. C10 131
Hallsville, Mo., U.S. B5 118
Hallsville, Tx., U.S. C5 136
Halmahera, i., Indon. C7 36
Halmahera, Laut
  (Halmahera Sea), Indon. D7 36
Halmahera Sea see
  Halmahera, Laut,
  Indon. D7 36
Hal'mer-Ju, Russia A11 22
Halmstad, Swe. H5 10
Halsey, Or., U.S. C3 130
Hälsingland, hist. reg., Swe. F7 10
Halstad, Mn., U.S. C2 116
Halstead, Ks., U.S. E6 109

Name	Map Ref.	Page

Haltiatunturi, mtn., Eur. **B9** 10
Halton Hills, On., Can. . . . **D5** 89
Hamada, Japan **D2** 31
Hamadān, Iran **D5** 42
Ḥamāh, Syria **E7** 44
Ḥamāh, state, Syria **E7** 44
Hamamatsu, Japan **E15** 28
Hamar, Nor. **F4** 10
Hamarøya, Nor. **B6** 10
Hambantota, Sri L. **H4** 40
Hamblen, co., Tn., U.S. . . . **C10** 135
Hamburg, Ger. **D12** 12
Hamburg, Ar., U.S. **D4** 97
Hamburg, Ia., U.S. **D2** 108
Hamburg, N.Y., U.S. **C2** 125
Hamburg, Pa., U.S. **E10** 131
Hamden, Ct., U.S. **D4** 100
Hamden, Oh., U.S. **C3** 128
Hämeenlinna, Fin. **F11** 10
Hamel, Mn., U.S. **m11** 116
Hameln, Ger. **D11** 12
Hamersley Range, mts.,
  Austl. **E2** 60
Hami, China **C6** 28
Hamilton, Austl. **H3** 62
Hamilton, Ber. **B12** 76
Hamilton, On., Can. **D5** 89
Hamilton, N.Z. **o14** 63c
Hamilton, Al., U.S. **A2** 94
Hamilton, Il., U.S. **C2** 106
Hamilton, In., U.S. **A8** 107
Hamilton, Mi., U.S. **F4** 115
Hamilton, Mo., U.S. **B3** 118
Hamilton, Ms., U.S. **B5** 117
Hamilton, Mt., U.S. **D2** 119
Hamilton, N.Y., U.S. **C5** 125
Hamilton, Oh., U.S. **C1** 128
Hamilton, Tx., U.S. **D3** 136
Hamilton, Va., U.S. **A5** 139
Hamilton, co., Fl., U.S. . . . **B3** 102
Hamilton, co., Ia., U.S. . . . **B4** 108
Hamilton, co., Il., U.S. **E5** 106
Hamilton, co., In., U.S. . . . **D5** 107
Hamilton, co., Ks., U.S. . . . **E2** 109
Hamilton, co., Ne., U.S. . . . **D7** 120
Hamilton, co., N.Y., U.S. . . **B6** 125
Hamilton, co., Oh., U.S. . . . **C1** 128
Hamilton, co., Tn., U.S. . . . **D8** 135
Hamilton, co., Tx., U.S. . . . **D3** 136
Hamilton, Lake, res., Ar.,
  U.S. **C2** 97
Hamilton, Mount, mtn., Ak.,
  U.S. **C8** 95
Hamilton, Mount, mtn., Ca.,
  U.S. **k9** 98
Hamilton, Mount, mtn., Nv.,
  U.S. **D6** 121
Hamilton Inlet, b., Nf., Can. **A2** 88
Hamilton Reservoir, res.,
  Ma., U.S. **B3** 114
Hamilton Sound, strt., Nf.,
  Can. **D4** 88
Hamilton Square, N.J., U.S. **C3** 123
Hamina, Fin. **F12** 10
Hamiota, Mb., Can. **D1** 86
Hamīrpur, India **D4** 40
Hamlet, In., U.S. **B4** 107
Hamlet, N.C., U.S. **C3** 126
Hamlet, Mount, mtn., Ak.,
  U.S. **B6** 95
Hamlin, Pa., U.S. **D11** 131
Hamlin, Tx., U.S. **C2** 136
Hamlin, W.V., U.S. **C2** 141
Hamlin, co., S.D., U.S. . . . **C8** 134
Hamlin Lake, l., Mi., U.S. . . **D4** 115
Hamm, Ger. **E10** 12
Hammamet, Tun. **F3** 18
Hammamet, Golfe de, b.,
  Tun. **F3** 18
Hammam Lif, Tun. **F3** 18
Ḥammār, Hawr al-, l., Iraq . **G12** 44
Hammerfest, Nor. **A10** 10
Hammon, Ok., U.S. **B2** 129
Hammonasset, stm., Ct.,
  U.S. **D5** 100
Hammonasset Point, c., Ct.,
  U.S. **E5** 100
Hammond, In., U.S. **A2** 107
Hammond, La., U.S. **D5** 111
Hammond, Wi., U.S. **D1** 142
Hammond Bay, b., Mi., U.S. **C6** 115
Hammonton, N.J., U.S. . . . **D3** 123
Hamningberg, Nor. **A14** 10
Hampden, Nf., Can. **D3** 88
Hampden, Me., U.S. **D4** 112
Hampden, co., Ma., U.S. . . **B2** 114
Hampden Highlands, Me.,
  U.S. **D4** 112
Hampshire, Il., U.S. **A5** 106
Hampshire, co., Ma., U.S. . **B2** 114
Hampshire, co., W.V., U.S. **B6** 141
Hampstead, Md., U.S. **A4** 113
Hampstead, N.C., U.S. . . . **C5** 126
Hampton, N.B., Can. **D4** 87
Hampton, Ar., U.S. **D3** 97
Hampton, Ga., U.S. **C2** 103
Hampton, Ia., U.S. **B4** 108
Hampton, N.H., U.S. **E5** 122
Hampton, S.C., U.S. **F5** 133
Hampton, Tn., U.S. **C11** 135
Hampton, Va., U.S. **C6** 139
Hampton, co., S.C., U.S. . . **F5** 133
Hampton Bays, N.Y., U.S. . **n16** 125
Hampton Beach, N.H., U.S. **E5** 122

Hampton Butte, mtn., Or.,
  U.S. **D6** 130
Hampton Roads, Va., U.S. . **k15** 139
Hampton Roads Bridge-
  Tunnel, Va., U.S. **k15** 139
Ḥamrā', Al-Ḥamādah al-,
  des., Libya **F6** 14
Hamra, As Saquia al, stm.,
  W. Sah. **A2** 50
Hamtramck, Mi., U.S. **p15** 115
Ḥāmūn, Daryācheh-ye, l.,
  Iran **D8** 42
Han, stm., China **E9** 28
Hana, Hi., U.S. **C6** 104
Hanahan, S.C., U.S. **F7** 133
Hanalei Bay, b., Hi., U.S. . . **A2** 104
Hanamaki, Japan **D16** 28
Hanamaulu, Hi., U.S. **B2** 104
Hanapepe, Hi., U.S. **B2** 104
Hânceşti, Mol. **F10** 20
Hanceville, Al., U.S. **A3** 94
Hancheng, China **D10** 28
Hancock, Md., U.S. **A1** 113
Hancock, Mi., U.S. **A2** 115
Hancock, Mn., U.S. **E3** 116
Hancock, co., Ga., U.S. . . . **C3** 103
Hancock, co., Ia., U.S. . . . **A4** 108
Hancock, co., Il., U.S. **C2** 106
Hancock, co., In., U.S. . . . **E6** 107
Hancock, co., Ky., U.S. . . . **C3** 110
Hancock, co., Me., U.S. . . . **D4** 112
Hancock, co., Ms., U.S. . . . **E4** 117
Hancock, co., Oh., U.S. . . . **A2** 128
Hancock, co., Tn., U.S. . . **C10** 135
Hancock, co., W.V., U.S. . . **A4** 141
Hand, co., S.D., U.S. **C6** 134
Handan, China **D10** 28
Handyga, Russia **C15** 26
Hanford, Ca., U.S. **D4** 98
Hangayn nuruu, mts.,
  Mong. **B7** 28
Hangchow see Hangzhou,
  China **E12** 28
Hanggin Houqi, China **C9** 28
Hanggin Qi, China **D9** 28
Hangman Creek, stm., Wa.,
  U.S. **B8** 140
Hangokurt, Russia **B11** 22
Hangu, China **B4** 30
Hangzhou, China **E12** 28
Hangzhou Wan, b., China . . **C5** 30
Hanjiang, China **F11** 28
Hankinson, N.D., U.S. **C9** 127
Hanko, Fin. **G10** 10
Hanna, Ab., Can. **D5** 84
Hanna, Wy., U.S. **E6** 143
Hanna City, Il., U.S. **C4** 106
Hannahville Indian
  Reservation, Mi., U.S. . . **C3** 115
Hannibal, Mo., U.S. **B6** 118
Hannover, Ger. **D11** 12
Hanöbukten, b., Swe. **I6** 10
Ha Noi, Viet. **B5** 34
Hanover, On., Can. **C3** 89
Hanover see Hannover,
  Ger. **D11** 12
Hanover, Il., U.S. **A3** 106
Hanover, In., U.S. **G7** 107
Hanover, Ks., U.S. **C7** 109
Hanover, Ma., U.S. **B6** 114
Hanover, Mn., U.S. **m11** 116
Hanover, N.H., U.S. **C2** 122
Hanover, Pa., U.S. **G8** 131
Hanover, co., Va., U.S. . . . **C5** 139
Hanover Park, Il., U.S. . . . **k8** 106
Hansen, Id., U.S. **G4** 105
Hansford, co., Tx., U.S. . . . **A2** 136
Hanson, Ma., U.S. **B6** 114
Hanson, co., S.D., U.S. . . . **D8** 134
Hanstholm, Den. **H3** 10
Hantsport, N.S., Can. **D5** 87
Hanty-Mansijsk, Russia . . . **C8** 26
Hanyin, China **C2** 30
Hanzhong, China **E9** 28
Hāora, India **E5** 40
Haparanda, Swe. **D11** 10
Hapčeranga, Russia **E13** 26
Hapeville, Ga., U.S. **C2** 103
Happy Valley, N.M., U.S. . . **E5** 124
Happy Valley-Goose Bay,
  Nf., Can. **B1** 88
Hāpur, India **D3** 40
Ḥaraḍ, Sau. Ar. **F5** 38
Harahan, La., U.S. **k11** 111
Haralson, co., Ga., U.S. . . . **C1** 103
Harare, Zimb. **B5** 56
Harazé Mangueigne, Chad . **B4** 54
Harbala, Russia **C14** 26
Harbeson, De., U.S. **F4** 101
Harbin, China **B13** 28
Harbor, Or., U.S. **E2** 130
Harbor Beach, Mi., U.S. . . . **E8** 115
Harborcreek, Pa., U.S. . . . **B2** 131
Harbor Springs, Mi., U.S. . . **C6** 115
Harbour Breton, Nf., Can. . . **E4** 88
Harbour Grace, Nf., Can. . . **E5** 88
Harcuvar Mountains, mts.,
  Az., U.S. **D2** 96
Hardee, co., Fl., U.S. **E5** 102
Hardeeville, S.C., U.S. . . . **G5** 133
Hardeman, co., Tn., U.S. . . **B2** 135
Hardeman, co., Tx., U.S. . . **B3** 136
Hardin, Il., U.S. **D3** 106

Hardin, Mt., U.S. **E9** 119
Hardin, co., Ia., U.S. **B4** 108
Hardin, co., Il., U.S. **F5** 106
Hardin, co., Ky., U.S. **C4** 110
Hardin, co., Oh., U.S. **B2** 128
Hardin, co., Tn., U.S. **B3** 135
Hardin, co., Tx., U.S. **D5** 136
Harding, S. Afr. **E4** 56
Harding, co., N.M., U.S. . . . **B5** 124
Harding, co., S.D., U.S. . . . **B2** 134
Harding, Lake, res., U.S. . . **C4** 94
Hardinsburg, Ky., U.S. . . . **C3** 110
Hardisty, Ab., Can. **C5** 84
Hardoi, India **D4** 40
Hardwick, Ga., U.S. **C3** 103
Hardwick, Vt., U.S. **B4** 138
Hardwood Ridge, mtn., Pa.,
  U.S. **D11** 131
Hardy, co., W.V., U.S. **B6** 141
Hardy Lake, res., In., U.S. . **G6** 107
Hare Bay, Nf., Can. **D4** 88
Hare Bay, b., Nf., Can. . . . **C4** 88
Hārer, Eth. **B8** 54
Hargeysa, Som. **I13** 48
Har Hu, l., China **D7** 28
Hari, stm., Indon. **D2** 36
Haridwār, India **D3** 40
Harīrūd, stm., Asia **D8** 42
Harkers Island, N.C., U.S. . **C6** 126
Harlan, Ia., U.S. **C2** 108
Harlan, In., U.S. **B8** 107
Harlan, Ky., U.S. **D6** 110
Harlan, co., Ky., U.S. **D6** 110
Harlan, co., Ne., U.S. **D6** 120
Harlan County Lake, res.,
  Ne., U.S. **E6** 120
Harlem, Fl., U.S. **F6** 102
Harlem, Ga., U.S. **C4** 103
Harlem, Mt., U.S. **B8** 119
Harleyville, S.C., U.S. **E7** 133
Harlingen, Tx., U.S. **F4** 136
Harlow, Eng., U.K. **E7** 12
Harlowton, Mt., U.S. **D7** 119
Harmånger, Swe. **F7** 10
Harmon, co., Ok., U.S. . . . **C2** 129
Harmon Creek, stm., W.V.,
  U.S. **f8** 141
Harmony, In., U.S. **E3** 107
Harmony, Mn., U.S. **G6** 116
Harmony, Pa., U.S. **E1** 131
Harmony, R.I., U.S. **B3** 132
Harnett, co., N.C., U.S. . . . **B4** 126
Harney, co., Or., U.S. **D7** 130
Harney, Lake, l., Fl., U.S. . . **D5** 102
Harney Lake, l., Or., U.S. . . **D7** 130
Harney Peak, mtn., S.D.,
  U.S. **D2** 134
Härnösand, Swe. **E7** 10
Haro Strait, strt., Wa., U.S. . **A2** 140
Harper, Lib. **F3** 50
Harper, Ks., U.S. **E5** 109
Harper, co., Ks., U.S. **E5** 109
Harper, co., Ok., U.S. **A2** 129
Harper, Mount, mtn., Ak.,
  U.S. **C11** 95
Harpers Ferry, W.V., U.S. . . **B7** 141
Harpers Ferry National
  Historical Park, W.V.,
  U.S. **B7** 141
Harpersville, Al., U.S. **B3** 94
Harpeth, stm., Tn., U.S. . . . **A5** 135
Harqin Qi, China **A4** 30
Harquahala Mountain, mtn.,
  Az., U.S. **D2** 96
Harquahala Mountains,
  mts., Az., U.S. **D2** 96
Harrah, Ok., U.S. **B4** 129
Harricana, stm., Can. **H24** 82
Harriman, Tn., U.S. **D9** 135
Harriman Reservoir, res.,
  Vt., U.S. **F3** 138
Harrington, De., U.S. **E3** 101
Harrington Park, N.J., U.S. . **h9** 123
Harris, Mn., U.S. **E6** 116
Harris, R.I., U.S. **D3** 132
Harris, co., Ga., U.S. **D2** 103
Harris, co., Tx., U.S. **E5** 136
Harris, Lake, l., Fl., U.S. . . . **D5** 102
Harrisburg, Ar., U.S. **B5** 97
Harrisburg, Il., U.S. **F5** 106
Harrisburg, Or., U.S. **C3** 130
Harrisburg, Pa., U.S. **F8** 131
Harrisburg, S.D., U.S. **D9** 134
Harrismith, S. Afr. **D4** 56
Harrison, Ar., U.S. **A2** 97
Harrison, Mi., U.S. **D6** 115
Harrison, N.J., U.S. **k8** 123
Harrison, N.Y., U.S. **h13** 125
Harrison, Oh., U.S. **C1** 128
Harrison, Tn., U.S. **h11** 135
Harrison, co., Ia., U.S. . . . **C2** 108
Harrison, co., In., U.S. . . . **H5** 107
Harrison, co., Ky., U.S. . . . **B5** 110
Harrison, co., Mo., U.S. . . . **A3** 118
Harrison, co., Ms., U.S. . . . **E4** 117
Harrison, co., Oh., U.S. . . . **B4** 128
Harrison, co., Tx., U.S. . . . **C5** 136
Harrison, co., W.V., U.S. . . **B4** 141
Harrison, Cape, c., Nf., Can. **g10** 88
Harrison Bay, b., Ak., U.S. . **A9** 95
Harrisonburg, Va., U.S. . . . **B4** 139
Harrison Hot Springs, B.C.,
  Can. **f14** 85

Harrison Lake, l., B.C., Can. **E7** 85
Harrisonville, Mo., U.S. . . . **C3** 118
Harriston, On., Can. **D4** 89
Harristown, Il., U.S. **D4** 106
Harrisville, R.I., U.S. **B2** 132
Harrisville, Ut., U.S. **B4** 137
Harrisville, W.V., U.S. **B3** 141
Harrodsburg, Ky., U.S. . . . **C5** 110
Harrow, On., Can. **E2** 89
Harry S. Truman Reservoir,
  res., Mo., U.S. **C4** 118
Harry Strunk Lake, res., Ne.,
  U.S. **D5** 120
Harsīn, Iran **E12** 44
Harstad, Nor. **B7** 10
Hart, Mi., U.S. **E4** 115
Hart, Tx., U.S. **B1** 136
Hart, co., Ga., U.S. **B4** 103
Hart, co., Ky., U.S. **C4** 110
Hart, Lake, l., Fl., U.S. **D5** 102
Hartford, Al., U.S. **D4** 94
Hartford, Ar., U.S. **B1** 97
Hartford, Ct., U.S. **B5** 100
Hartford, Ia., U.S. **C4** 108
Hartford, Il., U.S. **E3** 106
Hartford, Ky., U.S. **C3** 110
Hartford, Mi., U.S. **F4** 115
Hartford, S.D., U.S. **D9** 134
Hartford, Vt., U.S. **D4** 138
Hartford, Wi., U.S. **E5** 142
Hartford, co., Ct., U.S. . . . **B4** 100
Hartford City, In., U.S. **D7** 107
Hartington, Ne., U.S. **B8** 120
Hartland, N.B., Can. **C2** 87
Hartland, Me., U.S. **D3** 112
Hartland, Wi., U.S. **E5** 142
Hartlepool, Eng., U.K. **C6** 12
Hartley, Ia., U.S. **A2** 108
Hartley, co., Tx., U.S. **B1** 136
Hartney, Mb., Can. **E1** 86
Hartselle, Al., U.S. **A3** 94
Hartshorne, Ok., U.S. **C6** 129
Hartsville, S.C., U.S. **C7** 133
Hartsville, Tn., U.S. **A5** 135
Hartville, Oh., U.S. **B4** 128
Hartwell, Ga., U.S. **B4** 103
Hartwell Lake, res., U.S. . . **B1** 133
Harvard, Il., U.S. **A5** 106
Harvard, Ne., U.S. **D7** 120
Harvard, Mount, mtn., Co.,
  U.S. **C4** 99
Harvey, Il., U.S. **B6** 106
Harvey, La., U.S. **E5** 111
Harvey, Mi., U.S. **B3** 115
Harvey, N.D., U.S. **B6** 127
Harvey, co., Ks., U.S. **D6** 109
Harvey Lake, res., Pa., U.S. **m16** 131
Harveys Creek, stm., Pa.,
  U.S. **n16** 131
Harwich, Eng., U.K. **E7** 12
Harwich Port, Ma., U.S. . . . **C7** 114
Harwinton, Ct., U.S. **B3** 100
Hawza, W. Sah. **A2** 50
Haryāna, prov., India **D3** 40
Hasalbag, China **C2** 30
Hasbrouck Heights, N.J.,
  U.S. **h8** 123
Haskell, Ar., U.S. **C3** 97
Haskell, Ok., U.S. **B6** 129
Haskell, Tx., U.S. **C3** 136
Haskell, co., Ks., U.S. **E3** 109
Haskell, co., Ok., U.S. **B6** 129
Haskell, co., Tx., U.S. **C3** 136
Haskovo, Bul. **D10** 18
Hassan, India **G3** 40
Hassayampa, stm., Az., U.S. **D3** 96
Hasselt, Bel. **E9** 12
Hassi Messaoud, Alg. **D6** 48
Hässleholm, Swe. **H5** 10
Hastings, On., Can. **C7** 89
Hastings, N.Z. **o14** 63c
Hastings, Eng., U.K. **E7** 12
Hastings, Mi., U.S. **F5** 115
Hastings, Mn., U.S. **F6** 116
Hastings, Ne., U.S. **D7** 120
Hastings, Pa., U.S. **E4** 131
Hastings-on-Hudson, N.Y.,
  U.S. **h13** 125
Hašuri, Geor. **B10** 44
Hatanga, Russia **B12** 26
Hatanga, stm., Russia **B12** 26
Hatangskij zaliv, b., Russia **B12** 26
Hatay (Antioch), Tur. **D7** 44
Hatch, N.M., U.S. **E2** 124
Hatchet Lake, N.S., Can. . . **E6** 87
Hatchie, stm., Tn., U.S. . . . **B2** 135
Hatchineha, Lake, l., Fl.,
  U.S. **D5** 102
Hat Creek, stm., S.D., U.S. . **E2** 134
Hatfield, In., U.S. **I3** 107
Hatfield, Pa., U.S. **F11** 131
Hatgal, Mong. **A8** 28
Hāthras, India **D3** 40
Ha Tinh, Viet. **C5** 34
Hat Mountain, mtn., Az.,
  U.S. **E3** 96
Hatteras, Cape, c., N.C.,
  U.S. **B7** 126
Hatteras Inlet, b., N.C., U.S. **B7** 126
Hattiesburg, Ms., U.S. . . . **D4** 117
Hatton, N.D., U.S. **B8** 127
Hat Yai, Thai. **E4** 34
Hatyrka, Russia **C19** 26
Haubstadt, In., U.S. **H2** 107

Haugesund, Nor. **G1** 10
Haughton, La., U.S. **B2** 111
Haukeligrend, Nor. **G2** 10
Haukivesi, l., Fin. **E13** 10
Hauraki Gulf, b., N.Z. **o13** 63c
Hauser, Or., U.S. **D2** 130
Haut, Isle au, i., Me., U.S. . **D4** 112
Haut Atlas, mts., Mor. **E2** 14
Hauula, Hi., U.S. **B4** 104
Havana see La Habana,
  Cuba **A3** 80
Havana, Fl., U.S. **B2** 102
Havana, Il., U.S. **C3** 106
Havasu, Lake, res., U.S. . . **C1** 96
Havasupai Indian
  Reservation, Az., U.S. . . **A3** 96
Havelock, On., Can. **C7** 89
Havelock, N.C., U.S. **C6** 126
Havelock Island, i., India . . **G6** 40
Haven, Ks., U.S. **E6** 109
Haverford [Township], Pa.,
  U.S. **o20** 131
Haverhill, Ma., U.S. **A5** 114
Haverstraw, N.Y., U.S. . . . **D7** 125
Haviland, Ks., U.S. **E4** 109
Havre see Le Havre, Fr. . . . **C7** 16
Havre, Mt., U.S. **B7** 119
Havre de Grace, Md., U.S. . **A5** 113
Havre North, Mt., U.S. **B7** 119
Havza, Tur. **B6** 44
Haw, stm., N.C., U.S. **B3** 126
Hawaii, co., Hi., U.S. **D6** 104
Hawaii, state, U.S. **C5** 104
Hawaii, i., Hi., U.S. **D6** 104
Hawaii, i., Hi., U.S. **i17** 92a
Hawaiian Islands, is., Hi.,
  U.S. **m14** 104
Hawaiian Ridge **F22** 64
Hawaii Volcanoes National
  Park, Hi., U.S. **D6** 104
Hawarden, Ia., U.S. **A1** 108
Hawera, N.Z. **o13** 63c
Hawesville, Ky., U.S. **C3** 110
Hawi, Hi., U.S. **C6** 104
Hawke Bay, b., N.Z. **o14** 63c
Hawker, Austl. **G2** 62
Hawkes, Mount, mtn., Ant. **E34** 67
Hawkesbury, On., Can. . . **B10** 89
Hawkesbury Island, i., B.C.,
  Can. **C3** 85
Hawkins, co., Tn., U.S. . . **C11** 135
Hawkinsville, Ga., U.S. . . . **D3** 103
Hawley, Mn., U.S. **D2** 116
Hawley, Pa., U.S. **D11** 131
Haworth, N.J., U.S. **h9** 123
Haw River, N.C., U.S. **A3** 126
Hawthorne, Ca., U.S. **n12** 98
Hawthorne, Fl., U.S. **C4** 102
Hawthorne, N.J., U.S. **B4** 123
Hawthorne, Nv., U.S. **E3** 121
Hawthorne, N.Y., U.S. . . . **g13** 125
Hawza, W. Sah. **A2** 50
Haxtun, Co., U.S. **A8** 99
Hay, Austl. **G3** 62
Hayden, Az., U.S. **E5** 96
Hayden, Co., U.S. **A3** 99
Hayden Lake, l., Id., U.S. . . **B2** 105
Hayes, La., U.S. **D3** 111
Hayes, co., Ne., U.S. **D4** 120
Hayes, stm., Mb., Can. . . . **B5** 86
Hayes, Mount, mtn., Ak.,
  U.S. **C10** 95
Hayfield, Mn., U.S. **G6** 116
Hayford Peak, mtn., Nv.,
  U.S. **G6** 121
Haymock Lake, l., Me., U.S. **B3** 112
Haynesville, La., U.S. **B2** 111
Hayneville, Al., U.S. **C3** 94
Hayrabolu, Tur. **B2** 44
Hays, Ks., U.S. **D4** 109
Hays, N.C., U.S. **A1** 126
Hays, co., Tx., U.S. **D3** 136
Hays Canyon Peak, mtn.,
  Nv., U.S. **B6** 121
Haysville, Ks., U.S. **g12** 109
Hayti, Mo., U.S. **E8** 118
Hayti Heights, Mo., U.S. . . **E8** 118
Hayward, Ca., U.S. **h8** 98
Hayward, Wi., U.S. **B2** 142
Haywood, co., N.C., U.S. . . **f9** 126
Haywood, co., Tn., U.S. . . . **B2** 135
Hazard, Ky., U.S. **C6** 110
Hazardville, Ct., U.S. **B5** 100
Hazārībāg, India **E5** 40
Hazel Crest, Il., U.S. **k9** 106
Hazel Dell, Wa., U.S. **D3** 140
Hazel Green, Al., U.S. **A3** 94
Hazel Green, Wi., U.S. . . . **F3** 142
Hazel Park, Mi., U.S. **p15** 115
Hazelton Pyramid, mtn.,
  Wy., U.S. **B5** 143
Hazelwood, N.C., U.S. . . . **f10** 126
Hazen, Ar., U.S. **C4** 97
Hazen, N.D., U.S. **B4** 127
Hazen Bay, b., Ak., U.S. . . **C6** 95
Hazlehurst, Ga., U.S. **E4** 103
Hazlehurst, Ms., U.S. **D3** 117
Hazlet, N.J., U.S. **C4** 123
Hazleton, Ia., U.S. **B6** 108
Hazleton, Pa., U.S. **E10** 131
Head Harbor Island, i., Me.,
  U.S. **D5** 112

Name	Map Ref.	Page
Headland, Al., U.S.	D4	94
Headley, Mount, mtn., Mt., U.S.	C1	119
Healdsburg, Ca., U.S.	C2	98
Healdton, Ok., U.S.	C4	129
Healesville, Austl.	H4	62
Healy, Ak., U.S.	C10	95
Heard, co., Ga., U.S.	C1	103
Hearne, Tx., U.S.	D4	136
Hearst, On., Can.	o19	89
Heart, stm., N.D., U.S.	C3	127
Heart Butte Dam, N.D., U.S.	C4	127
Heart Lake, l., Wy., U.S.	B2	143
Heart's Content, Nf., Can.	E5	88
Heath, Oh., U.S.	B3	128
Heath Springs, S.C., U.S.	B6	133
Heavener, Ok., U.S.	C7	129
Hebbronville, Tx., U.S.	F3	136
Hebei, state, China	D11	28
Heber, Az., U.S.	C5	96
Heber City, Ut., U.S.	C4	137
Heber Springs, Ar., U.S.	B3	97
Hébertville, P.Q., Can.	A6	90
Hebgen Lake, res., Mt., U.S.	F5	119
Hebi, China	D10	28
Hebrides, is., Scot., U.K.	D4	6
Hebrides, Sea of the, Scot., U.K.	B3	12
Hebron, N.S., Can.	F3	87
Hebron, Il., U.S.	A5	106
Hebron, In., U.S.	B3	107
Hebron, Ky., U.S.	h13	110
Hebron, Md., U.S.	D6	113
Hebron, N.D., U.S.	C3	127
Hebron, Ne., U.S.	D8	120
Hebron, Oh., U.S.	C3	128
Hebron see Al-Khalīl, W.B.	G6	44
Hecate Strait, strt., B.C., Can.	C2	85
Hecelchakán, Mex.	C2	78
Hechi, China	G9	28
Hechuan, China	D2	30
Hecla Island, i., Mb., Can.	D3	86
Hector, Mn., U.S.	F4	116
Hedemora, Swe.	F6	10
He Devil, mtn., Id., U.S.	D2	105
Hedrick, Ia., U.S.	C5	108
Hefa (Haifa), Isr.	D2	42
Hefei, China	E11	28
Heflin, Al., U.S.	B4	94
Hefner, Lake, res., Ok., U.S.	B4	129
Hegang, China	B14	28
Hegins, Pa., U.S.	E9	131
Heide, Ger.	C11	12
Heidelberg, Ger.	F11	12
Heidelberg, Ms., U.S.	D5	117
Heidrick, Ky., U.S.	D6	110
Heilbron, S. Afr.	D4	56
Heilbronn, Ger.	F11	12
Heilong (Amur), stm., Asia	D14	26
Heilongjiang, state, China	B13	28
Heilongjiang see Heilong, stm., Asia	D16	26
Heilongjiang see Amur, stm., Asia	D16	26
Heinävesi, Fin.	E13	10
Hejaz see Al-Ḥijāz, reg., Sau. Ar.	E3	38
Hejian, China	B4	30
Hejiang, China	D2	30
Hekimhan, Tur.	C7	44
Hekla, vol., Ice.	I19	10a
Hekou, China	G8	28
Helagsfjället, mtn., Swe.	E5	10
Helena, Al., U.S.	B3	94
Helena, Ar., U.S.	C5	97
Helena, Ga., U.S.	D4	103
Helena, Mt., U.S.	D4	119
Helena, Ok., U.S.	A3	129
Helensville, N.Z.	o13	63c
Helgoländer Bucht, b., Ger.	C11	12
Heli, China	A2	31
Hellam, Pa., U.S.	G8	131
Hellertown, Pa., U.S.	E11	131
Hellín, Spain	H6	16
Hells Canyon, val., U.S.	B10	130
Hells Canyon National Recreation Area, U.S.	B10	130
Hell-Ville see Andoany, Madag.	A8	56
Helmand, stm., Asia	D8	42
Helmeringhausen, Nmb.	D2	56
Helmstedt, Ger.	D12	12
Helotes, Tx., U.S.	h7	136
Helper, Ut., U.S.	D5	137
Helsingborg, Swe.	H5	10
Helsingfors see Helsinki, Fin.	F11	10
Helsingør, Den.	H5	10
Helsinki (Helsingfors), Fin.	F11	10
Hematite, Mo., U.S.	C7	118
Hemet, Ca., U.S.	F5	98
Hemingford, Ne., U.S.	B2	120
Hemingway, S.C., U.S.	D9	133
Hemlock, Mi., U.S.	E6	115
Hemlock Reservoir, res., Ct., U.S.	E2	100
Hemphill, Tx., U.S.	D6	136
Hemphill, co., Tx., U.S.	B2	136
Hempstead, N.Y., U.S.	n15	125
Hempstead, Tx., U.S.	D4	136
Hempstead, co., Ar., U.S.	D2	97
Hemsön, i., Swe.	E8	10
Henagar, Al., U.S.	A4	94
Henan, state, China	E10	28
Hendek, Tur.	B4	44
Henderson, Ky., U.S.	C2	110
Henderson, La., U.S.	D4	111
Henderson, Mn., U.S.	F5	116
Henderson, N.C., U.S.	A4	126
Henderson, Ne., U.S.	D8	120
Henderson, Nv., U.S.	G7	121
Henderson, Tn., U.S.	B3	135
Henderson, Tx., U.S.	C5	136
Henderson, co., Il., U.S.	C3	106
Henderson, co., Ky., U.S.	C2	110
Henderson, co., N.C., U.S.	f10	126
Henderson, co., Tn., U.S.	B3	135
Henderson, co., Tx., U.S.	C5	136
Henderson Island, i., Pit.	G17	58
Henderson's Point, Ms., U.S.	g7	117
Hendersonville, N.C., U.S.	f10	126
Hendersonville, Tn., U.S.	A5	135
Hendricks, Mn., U.S.	F2	116
Hendricks, co., In., U.S.	E4	107
Hendry, co., Fl., U.S.	F5	102
Hengshan, China	D9	28
Hengshan, China	D3	30
Hengxian, China	E2	30
Hengyang, China	F10	28
Heniches'k, Ukr.	F13	20
Henlawson, W.V., U.S.	n12	141
Henlopen, Cape, c., De., U.S.	E5	101
Hennebont, Fr.	D5	16
Hennepin, co., Mn., U.S.	E5	116
Hennessey, Ok., U.S.	A4	129
Henniker, N.H., U.S.	D3	122
Henning, Mn., U.S.	D3	116
Henning, Tn., U.S.	B2	135
Henrico, co., Va., U.S.	C5	139
Henrietta, N.C., U.S.	B1	126
Henrietta, Tx., U.S.	C3	136
Henrietta Maria, Cape, c., On., Can.	n19	89
Henry, Il., U.S.	B4	106
Henry, co., Al., U.S.	D4	94
Henry, co., Ga., U.S.	C2	103
Henry, co., Ia., U.S.	C6	108
Henry, co., Il., U.S.	B3	106
Henry, co., In., U.S.	E7	107
Henry, co., Ky., U.S.	B4	110
Henry, co., Mo., U.S.	C4	118
Henry, co., Oh., U.S.	A1	128
Henry, co., Tn., U.S.	A3	135
Henry, co., Va., U.S.	D3	139
Henry, Mount, mtn., Mt., U.S.	B1	119
Henryetta, Ok., U.S.	B6	129
Henrys Fork, stm., U.S.	E2	143
Henryville, P.Q., Can.	D4	90
Henryville, In., U.S.	G6	107
Hensall, On., Can.	D3	89
Hentiesbaai, Nmb.	C1	56
Henzada, Myan.	C3	34
Hephzibah, Ga., U.S.	C4	103
Heppner, Or., U.S.	B7	130
Hepu, China	G9	28
Hequ, China	B3	30
Herāt, Afg.	D8	42
Herbert G. West, Lake, res., Wa., U.S.	C7	140
Herbes, Isle aux, i., Al., U.S.	E1	94
Herculaneum, Mo., U.S.	C7	118
Hereford, Eng., U.K.	D5	12
Hereford, Md., U.S.	A4	113
Hereford, Tx., U.S.	B1	136
Hereford Inlet, b., N.J., U.S.	E3	123
Herford, Ger.	D11	12
Herington, Ks., U.S.	D7	109
Herkimer, N.Y., U.S.	B6	125
Herkimer, co., N.Y., U.S.	B5	125
Hermann, Mo., U.S.	C6	118
Hermano Peak, mtn., Co., U.S.	D2	99
Hermantown, Mn., U.S.	D6	116
Hermanus, S. Afr.	E2	56
Herminie, Pa., U.S.	F2	131
Hermiston, Or., U.S.	B7	130
Hermitage, Nf., Can.	E4	88
Hermitage, Ar., U.S.	D3	97
Hermitage Bay, b., Nf., Can.	E3	88
Hermit Islands, is., Pap. N. Gui.	G12	32
Hermon, Mount, mtn., Asia	F6	44
Hermosillo, Mex.	B2	78
Hernando, Fl., U.S.	D4	102
Hernando, Ms., U.S.	A4	117
Hernando, co., Fl., U.S.	D4	102
Herndon, Va., U.S.	B5	139
Herning, Den.	H3	10
Heron Lake, Mn., U.S.	G3	116
Herrera, Arg.	D5	72
Herrin, Il., U.S.	F4	106
Herring Bay, b., Md., U.S.	C4	113
Herring Cove, N.S., Can.	E6	87
Herrington Lake, res., Ky., U.S.	C5	110
Herscher, Il., U.S.	B5	106
Hershey, Pa., U.S.	F8	131
Hertford, N.C., U.S.	A6	126
Hertford, co., N.C., U.S.	A6	126
Hervey Bay, b., Austl.	E5	62
Heshan, China	E2	30
Heshun, China	B3	30
Hesperia, Ca., U.S.	E5	98
Hesperia, Mi., U.S.	E4	115
Hesperus Mountain, mtn., Co., U.S.	D2	99
Hesston, Ks., U.S.	D6	109
Heta, stm., Russia	B11	26
Hettinger, N.D., U.S.	D3	127
Hettinger, co., N.D., U.S.	C3	127
Hexian, China	G10	28
Heyburn, Id., U.S.	G5	105
Heyuan, China	E3	30
Heyworth, Il., U.S.	C5	106
Heze, China	B4	30
Hialeah, Fl., U.S.	G6	102
Hiawatha, Ia., U.S.	B6	108
Hiawatha, Ks., U.S.	C8	109
Hibbing, Mn., U.S.	C6	116
Hickam Air Force Base, mil., Hi., U.S.	g10	104
Hickman, Ky., U.S.	f8	110
Hickman, Ne., U.S.	D9	120
Hickman, co., Ky., U.S.	f8	110
Hickman, co., Tn., U.S.	B4	135
Hickory, N.C., U.S.	B1	126
Hickory, co., Mo., U.S.	D4	118
Hicksville, N.Y., U.S.	E7	125
Hicksville, Oh., U.S.	A1	128
Hico, Tx., U.S.	D3	136
Hico, W.V., U.S.	C3	141
Hidalgo, Mex.	C5	78
Hidalgo, Tx., U.S.	F3	136
Hidalgo, state, Mex.	C5	78
Hidalgo, co., N.M., U.S.	F1	124
Hidalgo, co., Tx., U.S.	F3	136
Hidalgo del Parral, Mex.	B3	78
Hiddenite, N.C., U.S.	B1	126
Hieroglyphic Mountains, mts., Az., U.S.	k8	96
Higbee, Mo., U.S.	B5	118
Higganum, Ct., U.S.	D5	100
Higgins Lake, l., Mi., U.S.	D6	115
Higgins Millpond, res., Md., U.S.	C6	113
Higginsville, Mo., U.S.	B4	118
High Bridge, N.J., U.S.	B3	123
High Falls Reservoir, res., Wi., U.S.	C5	142
High Island, i., Mi., U.S.	C5	115
Highland, Il., U.S.	E4	106
Highland, In., U.S.	A3	107
Highland, Ks., U.S.	C8	109
Highland, Mi., U.S.	o14	115
Highland, N.Y., U.S.	D7	125
Highland, Wi., U.S.	E3	142
Highland, co., Oh., U.S.	C2	128
Highland, co., Va., U.S.	B3	139
Highland Lake, l., Me., U.S.	g7	112
Highland Lakes, N.J., U.S.	A4	123
Highland Park, Il., U.S.	A6	106
Highland Park, Mi., U.S.	p15	115
Highland Park, Tx., U.S.	n10	136
Highland Peak, mtn., Ca., U.S.	C4	98
Highland Point, c., Fl., U.S.	G5	102
Highlands, N.C., U.S.	f9	126
Highlands, N.J., U.S.	C5	123
Highlands, Tx., U.S.	r14	136
Highlands, co., Fl., U.S.	E5	102
Highland Springs, Va., U.S.	C5	139
High Level, Ab., Can.	F7	84
Highmore, S.D., U.S.	C6	134
High Point, N.C., U.S.	B2	126
High Prairie, Ab., Can.	B2	84
High Ridge, Mo., U.S.	g12	118
High River, Ab., Can.	D4	84
Highrock Lake, l., Mb., Can.	B1	86
High Rock Lake, res., N.C., U.S.	B2	126
High Spire, Pa., U.S.	F8	131
High Springs, Fl., U.S.	C4	102
Hightstown, N.J., U.S.	C3	123
Highwood, Il., U.S.	A6	106
Highwood Baldy, mtn., Mt., U.S.	C6	119
Highwood Mountains, mts., Mt., U.S.	C6	119
Higuera de Abuya, Mex.	C3	78
Higüey, Dom. Rep.	B6	80
Hiiumaa, i., Est.	G10	10
Hiko Range, mts., Nv., U.S.	F6	121
Hilbert, Wi., U.S.	D5	142
Hildale, Ut., U.S.	F3	137
Hilden, N.S., Can.	D6	87
Hildesheim, Ger.	D11	12
Hill, co., Mt., U.S.	B6	119
Hill, co., Tx., U.S.	D4	136
Hillaby, Mount, mtn., Barb.	C8	80
Hill City, Ks., U.S.	C4	109
Hill City, S.D., U.S.	D2	134
Hillcrest, Il., U.S.	B4	106
Hillcrest Heights, Md., U.S.	C4	113
Hilliard, Fl., U.S.	B5	102
Hilliard, Oh., U.S.	k10	128
Hill Lake, l., Ar., U.S.	h10	97
Hills, Ia., U.S.	C6	108
Hills, Mn., U.S.	G2	116
Hillsboro, Il., U.S.	D4	106
Hillsboro, Ks., U.S.	D6	109
Hillsboro, Mo., U.S.	C7	118
Hillsboro, N.D., U.S.	B8	127
Hillsboro, N.H., U.S.	D3	122
Hillsboro, Oh., U.S.	C2	128
Hillsboro, Or., U.S.	B4	130
Hillsboro, Tx., U.S.	C4	136
Hillsboro, Wi., U.S.	E3	142
Hillsboro Canal, Fl., U.S.	F6	102
Hillsborough, N.B., Can.	D5	87
Hillsborough, N.C., U.S.	A3	126
Hillsborough, co., Fl., U.S.	E4	102
Hillsborough, co., N.H., U.S.	E3	122
Hillsborough Bay, b., P.E., Can.	C6	87
Hillsburgh, On., Can.	D4	89
Hills Creek Lake, res., Or., U.S.	D4	130
Hillsdale, Mi., U.S.	G6	115
Hillsdale, N.J., U.S.	g8	123
Hillsdale, co., Mi., U.S.	G6	115
Hillside, N.J., U.S.	k8	123
Hillsville, Pa., U.S.	D1	131
Hillsville, Va., U.S.	D2	139
Hilo, Hi., U.S.	D6	104
Hilo Bay, b., Hi., U.S.	D6	104
Hilok, Russia	D13	26
Hilton, N.Y., U.S.	B3	125
Hilton Head Island, S.C., U.S.	G6	133
Hilton Head Island, i., S.C., U.S.	G6	133
Hilvan, Tur.	D8	44
Himāchal Pradesh, prov., India	C3	40
Himalayas, mts., Asia	C3	40
Himatnagar, India	E2	40
Himeji, Japan	D2	31
Hims, Syria	E7	44
Hinchinbrook Island, i., Austl.	D4	62
Hinchinbrook Island, i., Ak., U.S.	g18	95
Hinckley, Il., U.S.	B5	106
Hinckley, Mn., U.S.	D6	116
Hinckley, Ut., U.S.	D3	137
Hinckley Reservoir, res., N.Y., U.S.	B5	125
Hindman, Ky., U.S.	C7	110
Hinds, co., Ms., U.S.	C3	117
Hindu Kush, mts., Asia	C1	40
Hindupur, India	G3	40
Hines, Or., U.S.	D7	130
Hinesville, Ga., U.S.	E5	103
Hinganghāt, India	E3	40
Hingham, Ma., U.S.	B6	114
Hingham Bay, b., Ma., U.S.	g12	114
Hingol, stm., Pak.	E9	42
Hingoli, India	F3	40
Hınıs, Tur.	C9	44
Hinnøya, i., Nor.	B6	10
Hinsdale, Il., U.S.	k9	106
Hinsdale, N.H., U.S.	E2	122
Hinsdale, co., Co., U.S.	D3	99
Hinton, Ab., Can.	C2	84
Hinton, Ia., U.S.	B1	108
Hinton, Ok., U.S.	B3	129
Hinton, W.V., U.S.	D4	141
Hīrākud Reservoir, res., India	E4	40
Hiram, Ga., U.S.	C2	103
Hiram, Oh., U.S.	A4	128
Hirara, Japan	B9	34
Hirfanlı Baraji, res., Tur.	C5	44
Hiriyūr, India	G3	40
Hirosaki, Japan	C16	28
Hiroshima, Japan	E14	28
Hirson, Fr.	C9	16
Hirtshals, Den.	H3	10
Hisār, India	D3	40
Hispaniola, i., N.A.	A5	80
Hita, Japan	D2	31
Hitachi, Japan	D16	28
Hitchcock, Tx., U.S.	r14	136
Hitchcock, co., Ne., U.S.	D4	120
Hitchcock, co., Ct., U.S.	C4	100
Hitoyoshi, Japan	D2	31
Hitra, i., Nor.	E3	10
Hiva, Uzb.	B8	42
Hiwassee, stm., Tn., U.S.	D9	135
Hiwassee Lake, res., N.C., U.S.	f8	126
Hjälmaren, l., Swe.	G6	10
Hjelmelandsvågen, Nor.	G2	10
Hjørring, Den.	H3	10
Hkakabo Razi, mtn., Myan.	A3	34
Hlukhiv, Ukr.	D12	20
Hlusk, Bela.	C10	20
Hlybokae, Bela.	B9	20
Ho, Ghana	E5	50
Hoa Binh, Viet.	B5	34
Hoagland, In., U.S.	C8	107
Hoback, stm., Wy., U.S.	C2	143
Hobart, Austl.	I4	62
Hobart, In., U.S.	A3	107
Hobart, Ok., U.S.	B2	129
Hobbs, N.M., U.S.	E6	124
Hobbs Coast, Ant.	D28	67
Hobe Sound, Fl., U.S.	E6	102
Hoboken, N.J., U.S.	k8	123
Hobyo, Som.	I14	48
Ho Chi Minh City see Thanh Pho Ho Chi Minh, Viet.	D5	34
Hockessin, De., U.S.	A3	101
Hocking, co., Oh., U.S.	C3	128
Hocking, stm., Oh., U.S.	C3	128
Hockley, co., Tx., U.S.	C1	136
Ḥôd, reg., Maur.	C3	50
Hodeida see Al-Ḥudaydah, Yemen	H4	38
Hodgeman, co., Ks., U.S.	D4	109
Hodgenville, Ky., U.S.	C4	110
Hodges Village Reservoir, res., Ma., U.S.	B4	114
Hódmezővásárhely, Hung.	F6	20
Hodna, Chott el, l., Alg.	C5	48
Hodonín, Czech Rep.	E4	20
Hodžejli, Uzb.	B7	42
Hoeryŏng-ŭp, N. Kor.	B1	31
Hof, Ger.	E12	12
Höfdakaupstadur, Ice.	I18	10a
Hoffman Estates, Il., U.S.	h8	106
Hofors, Swe.	F7	10
Hofsjökull, Ice.	I19	10a
Hōfu, Japan	D2	31
Höganäs, Swe.	H5	10
Hogansville, Ga., U.S.	C2	103
Hogback Mountain, mtn., Mt., U.S.	F4	119
Hoggar see Ahaggar, mts., Alg.	F6	48
Hog Island, i., Fl., U.S.	C3	102
Hog Island, i., Mi., U.S.	C5	115
Hog Island, i., N.C., U.S.	B6	126
Hog Island, i., R.I., U.S.	D5	132
Hog Island, i., Va., U.S.	C7	139
Hoh, stm., Wa., U.S.	B1	140
Hohenwald, Tn., U.S.	B4	135
Hoh Head, c., Wa., U.S.	B1	140
Hohhot, China	C10	28
Hohoe, Ghana	E5	50
Ho-Ho-Kus, N.J., U.S.	h8	123
Hoh Xil Shan, mts., China	D5	28
Hoi An, Viet.	C5	34
Hoima, Ug.	C6	54
Hoisington, Ks., U.S.	D5	109
Hojniki, Bela.	D10	20
Hokah, Mn., U.S.	G7	116
Hoke, co., N.C., U.S.	B3	126
Hokes Bluff, Al., U.S.	B4	94
Hokitika, N.Z.	p13	63c
Hokkaidō, i., Japan	C16	28
Hoktemberjan, Arm.	B11	44
Hola Prystan', Ukr.	F12	20
Holbrook, Az., U.S.	C5	96
Holbrook, Ma., U.S.	B5	114
Holcomb, Ks., U.S.	E3	109
Holden, Ma., U.S.	B4	114
Holden, Mo., U.S.	C4	118
Holden, W.V., U.S.	D2	141
Holdenville, Ok., U.S.	B5	129
Holdrege, Ne., U.S.	D6	120
Hole in the Mountain Peak, mtn., Nv., U.S.	C6	121
Holgate, Oh., U.S.	A1	128
Holguín, Cuba	A4	80
Holladay, Ut., U.S.	C4	137
Holland, In., U.S.	H3	107
Holland, Mi., U.S.	F4	115
Holland, Tx., U.S.	D4	136
Hollandale, Ms., U.S.	B3	117
Hollandia see Jayapura, Indon.	G11	32
Holland Island, i., Md., U.S.	D5	113
Holland Point, c., Md., U.S.	C4	113
Holland Straits, strt., Md., U.S.	D5	113
Holley, N.Y., U.S.	B2	125
Holliday, Tx., U.S.	C3	136
Hollidaysburg, Pa., U.S.	F5	131
Hollins, Va., U.S.	C3	139
Hollis, Ok., U.S.	C2	129
Hollister, Ca., U.S.	D3	98
Hollister, Mo., U.S.	E4	118
Holliston, Ma., U.S.	B5	114
Holloman Air Force Base, mil., N.M., U.S.	E3	124
Hollow Rock, Tn., U.S.	A3	135
Hollowtop Mountain, mtn., Mt., U.S.	E4	119
Holly, Co., U.S.	C8	99
Holly, Mi., U.S.	F7	115
Holly Grove, Ar., U.S.	C4	97
Holly Hill, Fl., U.S.	C5	102
Holly Hill, S.C., U.S.	E7	133
Holly Pond, Al., U.S.	A3	94
Holly Ridge, N.C., U.S.	C5	126
Holly Shelter Swamp, sw., N.C., U.S.	C5	126
Holly Springs, Ga., U.S.	B2	103
Holly Springs, Ms., U.S.	A4	117
Holly Springs, N.C., U.S.	B4	126
Hollywood, Al., U.S.	A4	94
Hollywood, Fl., U.S.	F6	102
Hollywood, Md., U.S.	D4	113
Hollywood, S.C., U.S.	k11	133
Hollywood Indian Reservation, Fl., U.S.	r3	102
Holmen, Wi., U.S.	E2	142
Holmes, co., Fl., U.S.	u16	102
Holmes, co., Ms., U.S.	B3	117
Holmes, co., Oh., U.S.	B4	128
Holmes, Mount, mtn., Wy., U.S.	B2	143
Holmsk, Russia	E16	26
Holoby, Ukr.	D8	20
Holstebro, Den.	H3	10
Holstein, Ia., U.S.	B2	108
Holsteinsborg, Grnld.	E29	82
Holston, stm., Tn., U.S.	C11	135
Holston, Middle Fork, stm., Va., U.S.	f10	139
Holston High Knob, mtn., Tn., U.S.	C11	135
Holt, Al., U.S.	B2	94

Name	Map Ref.	Page

Holt, Mi., U.S. ... F6 115
Holt, co., Mo., U.S. ... A2 118
Holt, co., Ne., U.S. ... B7 120
Holt Lake, res., Al., U.S. . B2 94
Holton, Ks., U.S. ... C8 109
Holtville, Ca., U.S. ... F6 98
Holualoa, Hi., U.S. ... D6 104
Holy Cross, Mountain of the, mtn., Co., U.S. . B4 99
Holyhead, Wales, U.K. . . D4 12
Holyoke, Co., U.S. ... A8 99
Holyoke, Ma., U.S. ... B2 114
Holyoke Range, hills, Ma., U.S. ... B2 114
Homalin, Myan. ... B2 34
Hombori Tondo, mtn., Mali C4 50
Hombre Muerto, Salar del, pl., Arg. ... D4 72
Homecroft, In., U.S. ... m10 107
Homedale, Id., U.S. ... F2 105
Home Hill, Austl. ... D4 62
Homel', Bela. ... C11 20
Homeland, Ga., U.S. ... F4 103
Home Place, In., U.S. ... E5 107
Homer, Ak., U.S. ... D9 95
Homer, Ga., U.S. ... B3 103
Homer, Il., U.S. ... C6 106
Homer, La., U.S. ... B2 111
Homer, Mi., U.S. ... F6 115
Homer, N.Y., U.S. ... C4 125
Homer City, Pa., U.S. ... E3 131
Homerville, Ga., U.S. ... E4 103
Homer Youngs Peak, mtn., Mt., U.S. ... E3 119
Homestead, Fl., U.S. ... G6 102
Homestead, Pa., U.S. ... k14 131
Homestead National Monument of America, Ne., U.S. ... D9 120
Homewood, Al., U.S. ... g7 94
Homewood, Il., U.S. ... B6 106
Homewood, Oh., U.S. ... C1 128
Hominy, Ok., U.S. ... A5 129
Hominy Creek, stm., Ok., U.S. ... A5 129
Homme Dam, N.D., U.S. . A8 127
Homochitto, stm., Ms., U.S. D4 117
Homosassa, Fl., U.S. ... D4 102
Homs see Al-Khums, Libya E6 14
Homs see Ḥimṣ, Syria ... E7 44
Honaker, Va., U.S. ... e10 139
Honan see Henan, state, China ... E10 28
Honaunau, Hi., U.S. ... D6 104
Honda, Col. ... B5 70
Hondo, Tx., U.S. ... E3 136
Hondo, stm., N.A. ... B2 80
Hondo, Rio, stm., N.M., U.S. ... D4 124
Honduras, ctry., N.A. ... C2 80
Honduras, Gulf of, b., N.A. B2 80
Honea Path, S.C., U.S. ... C3 133
Hønefoss, Nor. ... F4 10
Honeoye Falls, N.Y., U.S. . C3 125
Honesdale, Pa., U.S. ... C11 131
Honey Brook, Pa., U.S. . F10 131
Honey Grove, Tx., U.S. . . C5 136
Honey Lake, l., Ca., U.S. . B3 98
Honeypot Glen, Ct., U.S. . C4 100
Honeyville, Ut., U.S. ... B3 137
Hong, Song see Red, stm., Asia ... B4 34
Hon Gai, Viet. ... B5 34
Honga River, b., Md., U.S. D5 113
Hongjiang, China ... F9 28
Hong Kong see Xianggang, China ... E3 30
Hongliuyuan, China ... C7 28
Hongshui, stm., China ... G9 28
Hongtong, China ... B3 30
Hongze, China ... C4 30
Hongze Hu, l., China ... E11 28
Honiara, Sol. Is. ... B6 62
Honjō, Japan ... C3 31
Honokaa, Hi., U.S. ... C6 104
Honolulu, Hi., U.S. ... B4 104
Honolulu, co., Hi., U.S. . B3 104
Honolulu International Airport, Hi., U.S. ... g10 104
Honomu, Hi., U.S. ... D6 104
Honouliuli, Hi., U.S. ... g9 104
Honshū, i., Japan ... D16 28
Honuapo Bay, b., Hi., U.S. D6 104
Honuu, Russia ... C16 26
Hood, co., Tx., U.S. ... C4 136
Hood, Mount, mtn., Or., U.S. ... B5 130
Hood Canal, b., Wa., U.S. B2 140
Hoodoo Peak, mtn., Wa., U.S. ... A5 140
Hood Point, c., Austl. ... G2 60
Hood River, Or., U.S. ... B5 130
Hood River, co., Or., U.S. B5 130
Hoodsport, Wa., U.S. ... B2 140
Hoogeveen, Neth. ... D10 12
Hooker, Ok., U.S. ... e9 129
Hooker, co., Ne., U.S. ... C4 120
Hooker Creek, Austl. ... D5 60
Hooksett, N.H., U.S. ... D4 122
Hoonah, Ak., U.S. ... D12 95
Hoopa Valley Indian Reservation, Ca., U.S. . B2 98
Hooper, Ne., U.S. ... C9 120
Hooper Bay, Ak., U.S. ... C6 95

Hooper Islands, is., Md., U.S. ... D5 113
Hooper Strait, strt., Md., U.S. ... D5 113
Hoopes Reservoir, res., De., U.S. ... A3 101
Hoopeston, Il., U.S. ... C6 106
Hoorn, Neth. ... D9 12
Hoosac Range, mts., U.S. . A1 114
Hoosic, stm., U.S. ... C7 125
Hoosick Falls, N.Y., U.S. . C7 125
Hoover Dam, U.S. ... G7 121
Hoover Reservoir, res., Oh., U.S. ... B3 128
Hooverson Heights, W.V., U.S. ... f8 141
Hopa, Tur. ... B9 44
Hopatcong, N.J., U.S. ... B3 123
Hopatcong, Lake, l., N.J., U.S. ... A3 123
Hope, B.C., Can. ... E7 85
Hope, Ar., U.S. ... D2 97
Hope, In., U.S. ... F6 107
Hope, R.I., U.S. ... D3 132
Hope, Point, c., Ak., U.S. . B6 95
Hopedale, Il., U.S. ... C4 106
Hopedale, Ma., U.S. ... B4 114
Hope Island, i., R.I., U.S. . E5 132
Hopelchén, Mex. ... D7 78
Hope Mills, N.C., U.S. ... C4 126
Hopër, stm., Russia ... D7 22
Hopes Advance, Cap, c., P.Q., Can. ... f13 90
Hopetoun, Austl. ... G3 60
Hopetown, S. Afr. ... D3 56
Hope Valley, R.I., U.S. ... E2 132
Hopewell, Va., U.S. ... C5 139
Hopewell Junction, N.Y., U.S. ... D7 125
Hopi Indian Reservation, Az., U.S. ... A5 96
Hopkins, Mn., U.S. ... n12 116
Hopkins, S.C., U.S. ... D6 133
Hopkins, co., Ky., U.S. ... C2 110
Hopkins, co., Tx., U.S. ... C5 136
Hopkinsville, Ky., U.S. ... D2 110
Hopkinton, Ia., U.S. ... B6 108
Hopkinton, Ma., U.S. ... B4 114
Hopkinton, R.I., U.S. ... F1 132
Hopkinton Lake, res., N.H., U.S. ... D3 122
Hopwood, Pa., U.S. ... G2 131
Hoquiam, Wa., U.S. ... C2 140
Hor, Russia ... A2 31
Horace, N.D., U.S. ... C9 127
Horace Mountain, mtn., Ak., U.S. ... B10 95
Horasan, Tur. ... B10 44
Horatio, Ar., U.S. ... D1 97
Horicon, Wi., U.S. ... E5 142
Horine, Mo., U.S. ... C7 118
Horlick Mountains, mts., Ant. ... E29 67
Horlivka, Ukr. ... E15 20
Hormuz, Strait of, strt., Asia E7 42
Horn, c., Ice. ... k17 10a
Horn, Cape see Hornos, Cabo de, c., Chile ... I3 69
Hornavan, l., Swe. ... C7 10
Hornell, N.Y., U.S. ... C3 125
Hornersville, Mo., U.S. ... E7 118
Horn Island, i., Ms., U.S. . E5 117
Horn Island Pass, strt., Ms., U.S. ... g8 117
Horn Lake, Ms., U.S. ... A3 117
Hornos, Cabo de (Horn, Cape), c., Chile ... I3 69
Horodenka, Ukr. ... E8 20
Horodnia, Ukr. ... D11 20
Horodok, Ukr. ... E7 20
Horqin Youyi Qianqi, China B12 28
Horry, co., S.C., U.S. ... D10 133
Horse, stm., Ct., U.S. ... C6 100
Horse Cave, Ky., U.S. ... C4 110
Horse Creek, stm., U.S. ... E8 143
Horse Creek Reservoir, res., Co., U.S. ... C7 99
Horsehead Lake, l., N.D., U.S. ... B6 127
Horseheads, N.Y., U.S. ... C4 125
Horse Heaven Hills, hills, Wa., U.S. ... C6 140
Horsens, Den. ... I3 10
Horse Peak, mtn., N.M., U.S. ... D1 124
Horseshoe Bend, Id., U.S. . F2 105
Horseshoe Bend National Military Park, Al., U.S. . C4 94
Horseshoe Cove, b., Fl., U.S. ... C3 102
Horseshoe Point, c., Fl., U.S. ... C3 102
Horseshoe Reservoir, res., Az., U.S. ... C4 96
Horsham, Austl. ... H3 62
Horten, Nor. ... G4 10
Horton, Ks., U.S. ... C8 109
Horton, stm., N.T., Can. . B15 82
Hortonia, Lake, l., Vt., U.S. D2 138
Hortonville, Wi., U.S. ... D5 142
Horyn', stm., Eur. ... D9 20
Hosa'ina, Eth. ... B7 54
Hoschton, Ga., U.S. ... B3 103
Hosedahard, Russia ... A10 22
Hoshāb, Pak. ... E8 42

Hoshangābād, India ... E3 40
Hoshiārpur, India ... C3 40
Hospers, Ia., U.S. ... A2 108
Hospet, India ... F3 40
Hosta Butte, mtn., N.M., U.S. ... B1 124
Hotan, China ... D3 28
Hotan, stm., China ... A4 40
Hotazel, S. Afr. ... D3 56
Hotchkiss, Co., U.S. ... C3 99
Hot Creek Range, mts., Nv., U.S. ... E5 121
Hot Creek Valley, val., Nv., U.S. ... E5 121
Hot Spring, co., Ar., U.S. . C2 97
Hot Springs, S.D., U.S. ... D2 134
Hot Springs, co., Wy., U.S. C4 143
Hot Springs National Park, Ar., U.S. ... C2 97
Hot Springs National Park, Ar., U.S. ... C2 97
Hot Springs Peak, mtn., Ca., U.S. ... B3 98
Hot Springs Peak, mtn., Nv., U.S. ... B4 121
Houaïlou, N. Cal. ... l9 62a
Houghton, Mi., U.S. ... A2 115
Houghton, N.Y., U.S. ... C2 125
Houghton, co., Mi., U.S. . B2 115
Houghton Lake, Mi., U.S. . D6 115
Houghton Lake, l., Mi., U.S. D6 115
Houghton Lake Heights, Mi., U.S. ... D6 115
Houlton, Me., U.S. ... B5 112
Houma, China ... D10 28
Houma, La., U.S. ... E5 111
Housatonic, stm., U.S. ... D3 100
House Springs, Mo., U.S. . g12 118
Houston, De., U.S. ... E3 101
Houston, Mn., U.S. ... G7 116
Houston, Mo., U.S. ... D6 118
Houston, Ms., U.S. ... B4 117
Houston, Pa., U.S. ... F1 131
Houston, Tx., U.S. ... E5 136
Houston, co., Al., U.S. ... D4 94
Houston, co., Ga., U.S. ... D3 103
Houston, co., Mn., U.S. ... G7 116
Houston, co., Tn., U.S. ... A4 135
Houston, co., Tx., U.S. ... D5 136
Houston, stm., La., U.S. ... D2 111
Houston, Lake, res., Tx., U.S. ... r14 136
Houston Intercontinental Airport, Tx., U.S. ... r14 136
Houtman Abrolhos, is., Austl. ... F1 60
Houtzdale, Pa., U.S. ... E5 131
Hovd, Mong. ... B6 28
Hovd, stm., Mong. ... B6 28
Hovenweep National Monument, Ut., U.S. . F6 137
Hoverla, hora, mtn., Ukr. . E8 20
Hovmantorp, Swe. ... H6 10
Hövsgöl nuur, l., Mong. . A8 28
Howard, Ks., U.S. ... E7 109
Howard, S.D., U.S. ... C8 134
Howard, Wi., U.S. ... D5 142
Howard, co., Ar., U.S. ... C2 97
Howard, co., Ia., U.S. ... A5 108
Howard, co., In., U.S. ... C5 107
Howard, co., Md., U.S. ... B4 113
Howard, co., Mo., U.S. ... B5 118
Howard, co., Ne., U.S. ... C7 120
Howard, co., Tx., U.S. ... C2 136
Howard City, Mi., U.S. ... E5 115
Howard Hanson Reservoir, res., Wa., U.S. ... B4 140
Howard Lake, Mn., U.S. . E4 116
Howard Prairie Lake, res., Or., U.S. ... E4 130
Howards Grove-Millersville, Wi., U.S. ... E6 142
Howe, Cape, c., Austl. ... H5 62
Howell, Mi., U.S. ... F7 115
Howell, co., Mo., U.S. ... E6 118
Howells, Ne., U.S. ... C8 120
Howe Sound, strt., B.C., Can. ... E6 85
Howick, P.Q., Can. ... D4 90
Howland, Me., U.S. ... C4 112
Howland Island, i., Oc. . . H21 64
Hoxie, Ar., U.S. ... A5 97
Hoxie, Ks., U.S. ... C3 109
Hoyerswerda, Ger. ... E14 12
Hoyt Lakes, Mn., U.S. ... C6 116
Hradec Králové, Czech Rep.D3 20
Hrodno, Bela. ... C7 20
Hron, stm., Slvk. ... E5 20
Hsilo, Tai. ... E5 30
Hsinchu, Tai. ... E5 30
Hsipaw, Myan. ... B3 34
Huacho, Peru ... F4 70
Huachuca City, Az., U.S. . F5 96
Hua Hin, Thai. ... D3 34
Huai'an, China ... E11 28
Huai'an, China ... A3 30
Huaibin, China ... C4 30
Huaiji, China ... E3 30
Huailai, China ... A4 30
Huainan, China ... E11 28
Huairou, China ... A4 30
Huaiyang, China ... E11 28
Huajuapan de León, Mex. . D5 78
Hualahai, vol., Hi., U.S. . . D6 104

Hualapai Indian Reservation, Az., U.S. . B2 96
Hualapai Mountains, mts., Az., U.S. ... C2 96
Hualapai Peak, mtn., Az., U.S. ... B2 96
Hualien, Tai. ... E5 30
Huallaga, stm., Peru ... E4 70
Huambo, Ang. ... F3 54
Huanan, China ... A2 31
Huancavelica, Peru ... F4 70
Huancayo, Peru ... F4 70
Huang (Yellow), stm., China D11 28
Huangchuan, China ... E11 28
Huangho see Huang, stm., China ... D11 28
Huanghua, China ... B4 30
Huanglong, China ... B2 30
Huangshi, China ... E11 28
Huangxian, China ... B5 30
Huangyan, China ... D5 30
Huangyuan, China ... D8 28
Huanta, Peru ... A3 72
Huánuco, Peru ... E4 70
Huanxian, China ... B2 30
Huaral, Peru ... F4 70
Huarocondo, Peru ... A3 72
Huascarán, Nevado, mtn., Peru ... E4 70
Huasco, Chile ... C2 69
Huatabampo, Mex. ... B3 78
Huauchinango, Mex. ... C5 78
Huaxian, China ... E3 30
Huaxian, China ... B3 30
Huazhou, China ... E3 30
Hubbard, Ia., U.S. ... B4 108
Hubbard, Oh., U.S. ... A5 128
Hubbard, Or., U.S. ... B4 130
Hubbard, Tx., U.S. ... D4 136
Hubbard, co., Mn., U.S. . . C4 116
Hubbard Creek Lake, res., Tx., U.S. ... C3 136
Hubbard Lake, l., Mi., U.S. D7 115
Hubbardton, stm., Vt., U.S. D2 138
Hubbell, Mi., U.S. ... A2 115
Hubei, state, China ... E10 28
Hubli-Dhārwār, India ... F3 40
Huckleberry Mountain, mtn., Or., U.S. ... D4 130
Huddersfield, Eng., U.K. . D6 12
Hudiksvall, Swe. ... F7 10
Hudson, P.Q., Can. ... D3 90
Hudson, Co., U.S. ... A6 99
Hudson, Fl., U.S. ... D4 102
Hudson, Ia., U.S. ... B5 108
Hudson, Il., U.S. ... C5 106
Hudson, Ma., U.S. ... B4 114
Hudson, Mi., U.S. ... G6 115
Hudson, N.C., U.S. ... B1 126
Hudson, N.H., U.S. ... E4 122
Hudson, N.Y., U.S. ... C7 125
Hudson, Oh., U.S. ... A4 128
Hudson, Wi., U.S. ... D1 142
Hudson, Wy., U.S. ... D4 143
Hudson, co., N.J., U.S. ... B4 123
Hudson, co., Tx., U.S. ... E7 125
Hudson, Lake, res., Ok., U.S. ... A6 129
Hudson Bay, b., Can. ... G24 82
Hudson Falls, N.Y., U.S. . B7 125
Hudson Hope, B.C., Can. . A6 85
Hudson Lake, In., U.S. ... A4 107
Hudson Strait, strt., Can. . F25 82
Hudsonville, Mi., U.S. ... F5 115
Hudspeth, co., Tx., U.S. . o12 136
Hudžand, Taj. ... E8 26
Hue, Viet. ... C5 34
Huehuetenango, Guat. . . B1 80
Huelva, Spain ... I3 16
Huércal-Overa, Spain ... I6 16
Huerfano, co., Co., U.S. . D5 99
Huerfano, stm., Co., U.S. . D6 99
Huerfano Mountain, mtn., N.M., U.S. ... A2 124
Huesca, Spain ... F6 16
Huéscar, Spain ... I5 16
Huetamo de Núñez, Mex. . D4 78
Hueytown, Al., U.S. ... g6 94
Huffakers, Nv., U.S. ... D2 121
Hufrat an-Naḥās, Sudan . . B4 54
Hugh Butler Lake, res., Ne., U.S. ... D5 120
Hughenden, Austl. ... E3 62
Hughes, Ar., U.S. ... C5 97
Hughes, co., Ok., U.S. ... B5 129
Hughes, co., S.D., U.S. ... C5 134
Hughes, North Fork, stm., W.V., U.S. ... B3 141
Hughes, South Fork, stm., W.V., U.S. ... B3 141
Hughesville, Md., U.S. ... C4 113
Hughesville, Pa., U.S. ... D8 131
Hugli, stm., India ... I13 40
Hugo, Co., U.S. ... B7 99
Hugo, Mn., U.S. ... m13 116
Hugo, Ok., U.S. ... C6 129
Hugo Lake, res., Ok., U.S. C6 129
Hugoton, Ks., U.S. ... E2 109
Hūich'ŏn, N. Kor. ... C13 28
Huila, China ... F8 28
Huili, China ... F8 28
Huimin, China ... B4 30
Huinca Renancó, Arg. ... E5 72
Huishui, China ... D2 30
Huitong, China ... D2 30

Huixian, China ... C2 30
Huixtla, Mex. ... D6 78
Huize, China ... F8 28
Huizhou, China ... E3 30
Hujirt, Mong. ... B8 28
Hulah Lake, res., Ok., U.S. A5 129
Hulett, Wy., U.S. ... B8 143
Hulin, China ... B14 28
Hull, P.Q., Can. ... D2 90
Hull, Ia., U.S. ... A1 108
Hull, Ma., U.S. ... B6 114
Huma, China ... A13 28
Humaitá, Braz. ... E7 70
Humaitá, Para. ... D6 72
Humansdorp, S. Afr. ... E3 56
Humansville, Mo., U.S. ... D4 118
Humbe, Ang. ... B1 56
Humble, Tx., U.S. ... E5 136
Humboldt, Az., U.S. ... C3 96
Humboldt, Ia., U.S. ... B3 108
Humboldt, Ks., U.S. ... E8 109
Humboldt, Ne., U.S. ... D10 120
Humboldt, Tn., U.S. ... B3 135
Humboldt, co., Ca., U.S. . B2 98
Humboldt, co., Ia., U.S. . . B3 108
Humboldt, co., Nv., U.S. . B3 121
Humboldt Range, mts., Nv., U.S. ... C3 121
Humenné, Slvk. ... E6 20
Hummels Wharf, Pa., U.S. E8 131
Humphrey, Ar., U.S. ... C4 97
Humphrey, Ne., U.S. ... C8 120
Humphreys, co., Ms., U.S. B3 117
Humphreys, co., Tn., U.S. A4 135
Humphreys, Mount, mtn., Ca., U.S. ... D4 98
Humphreys Peak, mtn., Az., U.S. ... B4 96
Humpty Doo, Austl. ... C5 60
Hūn, Libya ... F7 14
Hun, stm., China ... A5 31
Húnaflói, b., Ice. ... k18 10a
Hunan, state, China ... F10 28
Hunchun, China ... B2 31
Hundred Acre Pond, l., R.I., U.S. ... E3 132
Hunedoara, Rom. ... G7 20
Hungary, ctry., Eur. ... F5 20
Hūngdŏki-dong, N. Kor. . D13 28
Hungry Horse, Mt., U.S. . B2 119
Hungry Horse Reservoir, res., Mt., U.S. ... B3 119
Hunjiang, China ... C13 28
Hunsberge, mts., Nmb. . . D2 56
Hunt, co., Tx., U.S. ... C4 136
Hunt, stm., R.I., U.S. ... D4 132
Hunterdon, co., N.J., U.S. B3 123
Hunter Island, i., Austl. . . I3 62
Hunter Island, i., B.C., Can. D3 85
Huntertown, In., U.S. ... B7 107
Huntingburg, In., U.S. ... H4 107
Huntingdon, P.Q., Can. . . D3 90
Huntingdon, Pa., U.S. ... F6 131
Huntingdon, Tn., U.S. ... A3 135
Huntingdon, co., Pa., U.S. F5 131
Hunting Island, i., S.C., U.S. G7 133
Huntington, Ar., U.S. ... B1 97
Huntington, In., U.S. ... C7 107
Huntington, N.Y., U.S. ... E7 125
Huntington, Tx., U.S. ... D5 136
Huntington, Ut., U.S. ... D5 137
Huntington, W.V., U.S. ... C2 141
Huntington, co., In., U.S. . C6 107
Huntington Beach, Ca., U.S. F4 98
Huntington Lake, res., In., U.S. ... C7 107
Huntington Woods, Mi., U.S. ... p15 115
Huntingtown, Md., U.S. . . C4 113
Huntland, Tn., U.S. ... B5 135
Huntley, Il., U.S. ... A5 106
Hunt Mountain, mtn., Wy., U.S. ... B5 143
Huntsville, On., Can. ... B5 89
Huntsville, Al., U.S. ... A3 94
Huntsville, Ar., U.S. ... A2 97
Huntsville, Mo., U.S. ... B5 118
Huntsville, Tn., U.S. ... C9 135
Huntsville, Tx., U.S. ... D5 136
Hunucmá, Mex. ... C7 78
Hunyuan, China ... D10 28
Huon Gulf, b., Pap. N. Gui. H12 32
Huoxian, China ... B3 30
Hurd, Cape, c., On., Can. . B3 89
Hurghada, Egypt ... E11 48
Hurley, Ms., U.S. ... E5 117
Hurley, N.M., U.S. ... E1 124
Hurley, N.Y., U.S. ... D6 125
Hurley, Wi., U.S. ... B3 142
Hurlock, Md., U.S. ... C6 113
Hurock, Oh., U.S. ... A3 128
Huron, S.D., U.S. ... C7 134
Huron, co., Mi., U.S. ... E7 115
Huron, co., Oh., U.S. ... A3 128
Huron, stm., Mi., U.S. ... p14 115
Huron, Lake, l., N.A. ... C11 92
Huron Mountains, hills, Mi., U.S. ... B3 115
Hurricane, Ut., U.S. ... F2 137
Hurricane, W.V., U.S. ... C2 141
Hurst, Il., U.S. ... F4 106
Hurt, Va., U.S. ... C3 139
Hurtsboro, Al., U.S. ... C4 94
Húsavík, Ice. ... k20 10a

Name	Map Ref.	Page
Huşi, Rom.	F10	20
Hustisford, Wi., U.S.	E5	142
Husum, Ger.	C11	12
Hutag, Mong.	B8	28
Hutchins, Tx., U.S.	n10	136
Hutchinson, Ks., U.S.	D6	109
Hutchinson, Mn., U.S.	F4	116
Hutchinson, co., S.D., U.S.	D8	134
Hutchinson, co., Tx., U.S.	B2	136
Hutchinson Island, i., Fl., U.S.	E6	102
Hutchinson Island, i., S.C., U.S.	k11	133
Hutch Mountain, mtn., Az., U.S.	C4	96
Huttig, Ar., U.S.	D3	97
Huwei, Tai.	E5	30
Huxian, China	C2	30
Huxley, Ia., U.S.	C4	108
Hūzgān, Iran	G13	44
Huzhou, China	E12	28
Hužir, Russia	A9	28
Hvannadalshnúkur, mtn., Ice.	m20	10a
Hwange, Zimb.	B4	56
Hwang Ho see Huang, stm., China	D11	28
Hyannis, Ma., U.S.	C7	114
Hyannis Port, Ma., U.S.	C7	114
Hyargas nuur, l., Mong.	B6	28
Hyattsville, Md., U.S.	C4	113
Hybla Valley, Va., U.S.	g12	139
Hyco, stm., N.a., U.S.	D3	139
Hyco Lake, res., N.C., U.S.	A3	126
Hydaburg, Ak., U.S.	D13	95
Hyde, Pa., U.S.	D5	131
Hyde, co., N.C., U.S.	B6	126
Hyde, co., S.D., U.S.	C6	134
Hyden, Austl.	G2	60
Hyde Park, N.Y., U.S.	D7	125
Hyde Park, Ut., U.S.	B4	137
Hyder, Ak., U.S.	D13	95
Hyderābād, India	F3	40
Hyderābād, Pak.	E9	42
Hydeville, Vt., U.S.	D2	138
Hydra see Ídhra, i., Grc.	F9	18
Hydro, Ok., U.S.	B3	129
Hyères, Fr.	F10	16
Hyesan, N. Kor.	C13	28
Hymera, In., U.S.	F3	107
Hyndman, Pa., U.S.	G4	131
Hyndman Peak, mtn., Id., U.S.	F4	105
Hyrum, Ut., U.S.	B4	137
Hythe, Ab., Can.	B1	84
Hyvinkää, Fin.	F11	10

I

Iaçu, Braz.	D3	74
Ialomiţa, stm., Rom.	G9	20
Iamonia, Lake, l., Fl., U.S.	B2	102
Iaşi, Rom.	F9	20
Iatt, Lake, res., La., U.S.	C3	111
Iba, Phil.	C7	34
Ibadan, Nig.	E5	50
Ibagué, Col.	C4	70
Ibaiti, Braz.	F1	74
Ibapah Peak, mtn., Ut., U.S.	D2	137
Ibarra, Ec.	C4	70
Ibembo, D.R.C.	C4	54
Iberia, Mo., U.S.	C5	118
Iberia, co., La., U.S.	E4	111
Iberian Mountains see Ibérico, Sistema, mts., Spain	G5	16
Ibérico, Sistema, mts., Spain	G5	16
Iberville, P.Q., Can.	D4	90
Iberville, co., La., U.S.	D4	111
Iberville, Mont d' (Caubvick, Mount), mtn., Can.	g14	90
Ibiá, Braz.	E2	74
Ibicaraí, Braz.	D4	74
Ibiza see Eivissa, i., Spain	H7	16
Ibonma, Indon.	D8	36
Ibotirama, Braz.	D3	74
'Ibrī, Oman	F7	42
Ica, Peru	F4	70
Içá (Putumayo), stm., S.A.	D6	70
Içana, Col.	C6	70
Içana (Isana), stm., S.A.	C6	70
Ice Harbor Dam, Wa., U.S.	C7	140
İçel, Tur.	D6	44
Iceland, ctry., Eur.	l18	10a
Iceland Basin	B25	144
Ichaikaronji, India	F2	40
Ichchāpuram, India	F4	40
Ichnia, Ukr.	D12	20
Icicle Creek, stm., Wa., U.S.	B5	140
Ičinskaja Sopka, vulkan, vol., Russia	D17	26
Icó, Braz.	E4	74
Icy Cape, c., Ak., U.S.	A7	95
Icy Strait, strt., Ak., U.S.	k22	95
Ida, Mi., U.S.	G7	115
Ida, co., Ia., U.S.	B2	108
Ida, Lake, l., Mn., U.S.	D3	116
Ida Grove, Ia., U.S.	B2	108
Idah, Nig.	E6	50
Idaho, co., Id., U.S.	D3	105
Idaho, state, U.S.	E3	105
Idaho Falls, Id., U.S.	F6	105
Idaho Springs, Co., U.S.	B5	99

Idalou, Tx., U.S.	C2	136
Idamay, W.V., U.S.	k10	141
Idaville, In., U.S.	C4	107
Ider, Al., U.S.	A4	94
Ídhi Óros, mtn., Grc.	G10	18
Ídhra, i., Grc.	F9	18
İdil, Tur.	D9	44
Idiofa, D.R.C.	D3	54
Idlib, state, Syria	E7	44
Idoûkâl-en-Taghès, mtn., Niger	C6	50
Idutywa, S. Afr.	E4	56
Ifakara, Tan.	E7	54
Ife, Nig.	E5	50
Iferouâne, Niger	C6	50
Ifôghas, Adrar des, mts., Afr.	C5	50
Iganga, Ug.	C6	54
Igarapé-Açu, Braz.	B2	74
Igarka, Russia	C10	26
Igboho, Nig.	E5	50
Iğdir, Tur.	C11	44
Iglesias, Italy	E2	18
Ignacio, Co., U.S.	D3	99
Iguaçu, stm., S.A.	D7	72
Iguala, Mex.	D5	78
Igualada, Spain	G7	16
Iguassu Falls see Iguaçu, Cataratas do, wtfl, Braz.	D7	72
Iguatu, Braz.	C4	74
Iguazú see Iguaçu, stm., S.A.	D7	72
Iguéla, Gabon	D1	54
Iguîdi, 'Erg, dunes, Afr.	A3	50
Iharaña, Madag.	A8	56
Iheya-shima, i., Japan	g6	31a
Ihosy, Madag.	C8	56
Iisalmi, Fin.	E12	10
Iizuka, Japan	D2	31
Ijâfene, des., Maur.	B3	50
Ijebu-Ode, Nig.	E5	50
IJsselmeer, l., Neth.	D9	12
Ijuí, Braz.	D7	72
Ika, Russia	D12	26
Ikaría, i., Grc.	F11	18
Ikeja, Nig.	E5	50
Ikela, D.R.C.	D4	54
Ikerre, Nig.	E6	50
Ikom, Nig.	E6	50
Ikot-Ekpene, Nig.	E6	50
Ila, Nig.	E5	50
Ilagan, Phil.	C8	34
Īlām, Iran	D5	42
Ilan, Tai.	E5	30
Ilaro, Nig.	E5	50
Iława, Pol.	C5	20
Ilbenge, Russia	C14	26
Île-à-la-Crosse, Lac, l., Sk., Can.	B2	91
Ilebo, D.R.C.	D4	54
Île-de-France, hist. reg., Fr.	C8	16
Île-Perrot, P.Q., Can.	q19	90
Ilesha, Nig.	E5	50
Ilha de Moçambique, Moz.	B7	56
Ilhéus, Braz.	D4	74
Iliamna Lake, l., Ak., U.S.	D8	95
Iliamna Volcano, vol., Ak., U.S.	C9	95
Iligan, Phil.	E8	34
Iligan Bay, b., Phil.	E8	34
Ilion, N.Y., U.S.	B5	125
Ilio Point, c., Hi., U.S.	B4	104
Ilizi, Alg.	E6	48
Iljinskij, Russia	E16	26
Illampu, Nevado, mtn., Bol.	G6	70
Illana Bay, b., Phil.	E8	34
Illapel, Chile	D2	69
Illéla, Niger	D6	50
Illichivs'k, Ukr.	F11	20
Illimani, Nevado, mtn., Bol.	B4	72
Illinois, state, U.S.	C4	106
Illinois, stm., Il., U.S.	B5	106
Illinois, stm., Or., U.S.	E3	130
Illinois, stm., U.S.	A7	129
Illinois Peak, mtn., Id., U.S.	B3	105
Illiopolis, Il., U.S.	D4	106
Illmo, Mo., U.S.	D8	118
Il'men', ozero, l., Russia	C5	22
Ilo, Peru	G5	70
Iloilo, Phil.	D8	34
Ilorin, Nig.	E5	50
Ilovlja, Russia	F15	8
Ilwaco, Wa., U.S.	C1	140
Ilwaki, Indon.	E7	36
Imabari, Japan	D2	31
Imandra, ozero, l., Russia	C15	10
Imatra, Fin.	F13	10
Imboden, Ar., U.S.	A4	97
Īmī, Eth.	B8	54
İmişli, Azer.	C13	44
Imlay, Nv., U.S.	C3	121
Imlay City, Mi., U.S.	E7	115
Immokalee, Fl., U.S.	F5	102
Imnaha, stm., Or., U.S.	B10	130
Imola, Italy	B3	18
Imperatriz, Braz.	C2	74
Imperia, Italy	C2	18
Imperial, Ca., U.S.	F6	98
Imperial, Mo., U.S.	C7	118
Imperial, Ne., U.S.	D4	120
Imperial, Pa., U.S.	k13	131
Imperial, co., Ca., U.S.	F6	98
Imperial Beach, Ca., U.S.	o15	98
Imperial Dam, U.S.	E1	96
Imperial Reservoir, res., U.S.	E1	96

Imperial Valley, val., Ca., U.S.	F6	98
Impfondo, Congo	C3	54
Imphāl, India	E6	40
I-n-Amenas, Alg.	E6	48
Inanwatan, Indon.	D8	36
Inari, Fin.	B12	10
Inarijärvi, l., Fin.	B12	10
In Belbel, Alg.	F4	14
Inca, Spain	H8	16
Inca de Oro, Chile	C3	69
İnce Burun, c., Tur.	A6	44
Inch'ŏn, S. Kor.	D13	28
Incline Village, Nv., U.S.	D2	121
Indé, Mex.	B3	78
Independence, Ia., U.S.	B6	108
Independence, Ks., U.S.	E8	109
Independence, Ky., U.S.	B5	110
Independence, La., U.S.	D5	111
Independence, Mo., U.S.	B3	118
Independence, Or., U.S.	C3	130
Independence, Va., U.S.	D1	139
Independence, Wi., U.S.	D2	142
Independence, co., Ar., U.S.	B4	97
Independence, stm., N.Y., U.S.	B5	125
Independence Mountains, mts., Nv., U.S.	C5	121
Independence National Historical Park, Pa., U.S.	p21	131
Independence Rock, mtn., Wy., U.S.	D5	143
Inderborskij, Kaz.	E7	26
India, ctry., Asia	E3	40
Indian, stm., On., Can.	B7	89
Indian, stm., De., U.S.	F4	101
Indian, stm., Mi., U.S.	B4	115
Indian, stm., N.Y., U.S.	A5	125
Indiana, Pa., U.S.	E3	131
Indiana, co., Pa., U.S.	E3	131
Indiana, state, U.S.	E5	107
Indiana Dunes National Lakeshore, In., U.S.	A3	107
Indianapolis, In., U.S.	E5	107
Indian Bay, b., Fl., U.S.	D4	102
Indian Cedar Swamp, sw., R.I., U.S.	F2	132
Indian Creek, stm., Oh., U.S.	C1	128
Indian Creek, stm., S.D., U.S.	B2	134
Indian Creek, stm., Tn., U.S.	B3	135
Indian Creek, stm., W.V., U.S.	D4	141
Indian Creek, stm., W.V., U.S.	k9	141
Indian Head, Md., U.S.	C3	113
Indian Island, i., N.C., U.S.	B6	126
Indian Lake, l., Mi., U.S.	C4	115
Indian Lake, l., N.Y., U.S.	B6	125
Indian Lake, l., Oh., U.S.	B2	128
Indian Lake, l., R.I., U.S.	F4	132
Indian Neck, Ct., U.S.	D4	100
Indian Ocean	J11	64
Indianola, Ia., U.S.	C4	108
Indianola, Ms., U.S.	B3	117
Indianola, Ne., U.S.	D5	120
Indian Peak, mtn., Ut., U.S.	E2	137
Indian Peak, mtn., Wy., U.S.	B3	143
Indian Prairie Canal, Fl., U.S.	E5	102
Indian River, co., Fl., U.S.	E6	102
Indian River, b., Fl., U.S.	D6	102
Indian River Bay, b., De., U.S.	F5	101
Indian Rock, mtn., Wa., U.S.	D5	140
Indian Rocks Beach, Fl., U.S.	p10	102
Indian Springs, Nv., U.S.	G6	121
Indian Stream, stm., N.H., U.S.	f7	122
Indiantown, Fl., U.S.	E6	102
Indian Trail, N.C., U.S.	B2	126
Indiga, Russia	A8	22
Indigirka, stm., Russia	C16	26
Indio, Ca., U.S.	F5	98
Indochina, reg., Asia	C4	34
Indonesia, ctry., Asia	D4	36
Indore, India	E3	40
Indramayu, Indon.	E3	36
Indrāvati, stm., India	F4	40
Indus, stm., Asia	D1	40
İnegöl, Tur.	B3	44
Infiernillo, Presa del, res., Mex.	D4	78
Ingal, Niger	C6	50
Ingalls, In., U.S.	E6	107
Ingalls Park, Il., U.S.	B5	106
Ingende, D.R.C.	D3	54
Ingersoll, On., Can.	D4	89
Ingham, Austl.	D4	62
Ingham, co., Mi., U.S.	F6	115
Ingleside, Tx., U.S.	F4	136
Inglewood, Ca., U.S.	n12	98
Ingolstadt, Ger.	F12	12
Ingraham, Lake, l., Fl., U.S.	G5	102
Ingrāj Bāzār, India	E5	40
Ingram, Pa., U.S.	k13	131
Ingrid Christensen Coast, Ant.	D12	67
In Guezzam, Alg.	G6	48
Ingušetija, state, Russia	E6	26

Ingushetia see Ingušetija, state, Russia	E6	26
Inhaca, Ilha da, i., Moz.	D5	56
Inhambane, Moz.	C6	56
Inhambane, Moz.	C6	56
Inhambupe, Braz.	F12	70
Inhaminga, Moz.	B6	56
Inharrime, Moz.	C6	56
Inhassoro, Moz.	C6	56
Inhulets', Ukr.	F12	20
Inhumas, Braz.	E2	74
Inírida, stm., Col.	C6	70
Inkerman, N.B., Can.	B5	87
Inkom, Id., U.S.	G6	105
Inkster, Mi., U.S.	p15	115
Inland Sea see Seto-naikai, Japan	E14	28
Inman, Ks., U.S.	D6	109
Inman, S.C., U.S.	A3	133
Inn, stm., Eur.	G12	12
Inner Channel, strt., Belize	B2	80
Inner Hebrides, is., Scot., U.K.	B3	12
Inner Mongolia see Nei Monggol Zizhiqu, prov., China	C10	28
Innisfail, Austl.	D4	62
Innisfail, Ab., Can.	C4	84
Innsbruck, Aus.	G12	12
Inola, Ok., U.S.	A6	129
Inongo, D.R.C.	D3	54
Inowrocław, Pol.	C5	20
In Salah, Alg.	E5	48
Inscription House Ruin, hist., Az., U.S.	A5	96
Institute, W.V., U.S.	m12	141
Inta, Russia	C8	26
Interlachen, Fl., U.S.	C5	102
International Falls, Mn., U.S.	B5	116
Inthanon, Doi, mtn., Thai.	C3	34
Intracoastal Waterway, U.S.	E4	111
Inukjuak, P.Q., Can.	g11	90
Invercargill, N.Z.	q12	63c
Inverell, Austl.	F5	62
Inver Grove Heights, Mn., U.S.	n12	116
Invermere, B.C., Can.	D9	85
Inverness, Scot., U.K.	B4	12
Inverness, Ca., U.S.	C2	98
Inverness, Fl., U.S.	D4	102
Inverness, Ms., U.S.	B3	117
Inverway, Austl.	D4	60
Investigator Strait, strt., Austl.	H2	62
Invisible Mountain, mtn., Id., U.S.	F5	105
Inwood, Ia., U.S.	A1	108
Inwood, N.Y., U.S.	k13	125
Inwood, W.V., U.S.	B6	141
Inyangani, mtn., Zimb.	B5	56
Inyan Kara Creek, stm., Wy., U.S.	B8	143
Inyan Kara Mountain, mtn., Wy., U.S.	B8	143
Inyo, co., Ca., U.S.	D5	98
Inyo, Mount, mtn., Ca., U.S.	D5	98
Inyo Mountains, mts., Ca., U.S.	D4	98
Ioánnina, Grc.	E8	18
Iola, Ks., U.S.	E8	109
Iola, Wi., U.S.	D4	142
Iola, Id., U.S.	F7	105
Ione, Ca., U.S.	C3	98
Iongo, Ang.	E3	54
Ionia, Mi., U.S.	F5	115
Ionia, co., Mi., U.S.	F5	115
Ionian Islands see Iónioi Nísoi, is., Grc.	E7	18
Ionian Sea, Eur.	E7	18
Iónioi Nísoi (Ionian Islands), is., Grc.	E7	18
Iony, ostrov, i., Russia	D16	26
Íos, i., Grc.	F10	18
Iosco, co., Mi., U.S.	D7	115
Iota, La., U.S.	D3	111
Iowa, La., U.S.	D2	111
Iowa, co., Ia., U.S.	C5	108
Iowa, co., Wi., U.S.	E3	142
Iowa, state, U.S.	C4	108
Iowa, stm., Ia., U.S.	C6	108
Iowa, West Branch, stm., Ia., U.S.	B4	108
Iowa City, Ia., U.S.	C6	108
Iowa Falls, Ia., U.S.	B4	108
Iowa Indian Reservation, U.S.	C8	109
Iowa Lake, l., U.S.	A3	108
Iowa Park, Tx., U.S.	C3	136
Ipameri, Braz.	E2	74
Ipatinga, Braz.	E3	74
Ipatovo, Russia	A4	42
Ipeiros, hist. reg., Grc.	E8	18
Iphigenia Bay, b., Ak., U.S.	n22	95
Ipiales, Col.	C4	70
Ipiaú, Braz.	D4	74
Ipoh, Malay.	C2	36
Iporá, Braz.	E1	74
Ippy, C.A.R.	B4	54
Ipswich, Austl.	F5	62
Ipswich, Eng., U.K.	D7	12
Ipswich, Ma., U.S.	A6	114
Ipswich, S.D., U.S.	B6	134
Ipswich, stm., Ma., U.S.	A5	114
Ipu, Braz.	B3	74
Iquique, Chile	B2	69
Iquitos, Peru	D5	70

Iraan, Tx., U.S.	D2	136
Iráklion, Grc.	G10	18
Iran, ctry., Asia	D6	42
Iran Mountains, mts., Asia	C5	36
Trānshahr, Iran	E8	42
Irapuato, Mex.	C4	78
Iraq, ctry., Asia	D4	42
Irati, Braz.	D7	72
Irazú, Volcán, vol., C.R.	C3	80
Irbid, Jord.	D3	42
Irbīl, Iraq	C4	42
Irbit, Russia	C11	22
Irecê, Braz.	D3	74
Iredell, co., N.C., U.S.	B2	126
Ireland, ctry., Eur.	D2	12
Irgiz, Kaz.	E8	26
Irgui, reg., Afr.	C3	50
Iriklinskij, Russia	D10	22
Iringa, Tan.	E7	54
Iriomote-jima, i., Japan	B8	34
Irion, co., Tx., U.S.	D2	136
Iriri, stm., Braz.	D9	70
Irish Sea, Eur.	D4	12
Irkutsk, Russia	D12	26
Irminger Basin	C26	144
Irmo, S.C., U.S.	C5	133
Iroise, b., Fr.	C4	16
Iron, co., Mi., U.S.	B2	115
Iron, co., Mo., U.S.	D7	118
Iron, co., Ut., U.S.	F2	137
Iron, co., Wi., U.S.	B3	142
Irondale, Al., U.S.	f7	94
Irondequoit, N.Y., U.S.	B3	125
Iron Gate, val., Eur.	G7	20
Iron Gate Reservoir, res., Ca., U.S.	B2	98
Iron Knob, Austl.	G2	62
Iron Mountain, Mi., U.S.	C2	115
Iron Mountain, mtn., Az., U.S.	D4	96
Iron Mountains, mts., U.S.	D1	139
Iron Ridge, Wi., U.S.	E5	142
Iron River, Mi., U.S.	B2	115
Iron River, Wi., U.S.	B2	142
Ironton, Mo., U.S.	D7	118
Ironton, Oh., U.S.	D3	128
Ironwood, Mi., U.S.	n11	115
Iroquois, P.Q., Can.	C9	89
Iroquois, co., Il., U.S.	C6	106
Iroquois, stm., U.S.	C6	106
Iroquois, Lake, l., Vt., U.S.	B2	138
Iroquois Falls, On., Can.	o19	89
Irosin, Phil.	D8	34
Irpin', Ukr.	D11	20
Irrawaddy see Ayeyarwady, stm., Myan.	C3	34
Irricana, Ab., Can.	D4	84
Irrigon, Or., U.S.	B7	130
Irtyš see Irtysh, stm., Asia	D8	26
Irtysh, stm., Asia	D8	26
Irtysj see Irtysh, stm., Asia	D8	26
Irtyšsk, Kaz.	D9	26
Irumu, D.R.C.	C5	54
Irún, Spain	F6	16
Iruña see Pamplona, Spain	F6	16
Irvine, Ca., U.S.	n13	98
Irvine, Ky., U.S.	C6	110
Irving, Tx., U.S.	n10	136
Irvington, Al., U.S.	E1	94
Irvington, Il., U.S.	E4	106
Irvington, Ky., U.S.	C3	110
Irvington, N.J., U.S.	k8	123
Irvington, N.Y., U.S.	g13	125
Irwin, Pa., U.S.	F2	131
Irwin, co., Ga., U.S.	E3	103
Irwinton, Ga., U.S.	D3	103
Isa, Nig.	D6	50
Isabel, Mount, mtn., Wy., U.S.	D2	143
Isabela, Isla, i., Ec.	D1	70
Isabella, co., Mi., U.S.	E6	115
Isabella Indian Reservation, Mi., U.S.	E6	115
Isabella Lake, l., Mn., U.S.	C7	116
Ísafjardardjúp, Ice.	k17	10a
Ísafjördur, Ice.	k17	10a
Isana (Içana), stm., S.A.	C5	70
Isanga, D.R.C.	D4	54
Isangel, Vanuatu	k9	62a
Isanti, Mn., U.S.	E5	116
Isanti, co., Mn., U.S.	E5	116
Isar, stm., Eur.	F13	12
Ischia, Isola d', i., Italy	D4	18
Ise, Japan	D3	31
Isernia, Italy	D5	18
Iset', stm., Russia	D8	26
Iseyin, Nig.	E5	50
Isfahan see Eşfahān, Iran	D6	42
Ishigaki, Japan	B8	34
Ishikari, stm., Japan	B4	31
Ishikawa, Japan	A9	34
Ishinomaki, Japan	D16	26
Ishpeming, Mi., U.S.	B3	115
Išim, Russia	D8	26
Išim, stm., Asia	D9	26
Isinglass, stm., N.H., U.S.	D4	122
Isiolo, Kenya	C7	54
Isiro, D.R.C.	C5	54
Iskār, stm., Bul.	C10	18
İskenderun, Tur.	D7	44
İskenderun Körfezi, b., Tur.	D6	44
İskilip, Tur.	B6	44
Islāmābād, Pak.	D10	42
Islamorada, Fl., U.S.	H6	102

Name	Map Ref.	Page
Island, co., Wa., U.S.	A3	140
Island Beach, N.J., U.S.	D4	123
Island City, Or., U.S.	B8	130
Island Falls, Me., U.S.	B4	112
Island Lake, l., Mb., Can.	C4	86
Island Park, R.I., U.S.	E6	132
Island Park Reservoir, res., Id., U.S.	E7	105
Island Pond, Vt., U.S.	B5	138
Island Pond, l., N.H., U.S.	E4	122
Islands, Bay of, b., Nf., Can.	D2	88
Isla Vista, Ca., U.S.	E4	98
Islay, i., Scot., U.K.	C3	12
Isle-aux-Morts, Nf., Can.	E2	88
Isle of Man, dep., Eur.	C4	12
Isle of Palms, S.C., U.S.	k12	133
Isle of Wight, co., Va., U.S.	D6	139
Isle of Wight Bay, b., Md., U.S.	D7	113
Isle Royale National Park, Mi., U.S.	h9	115
Islesboro Island, i., Me., U.S.	D4	112
Isleta, N.M., U.S.	C3	124
Isleta Indian Reservation, N.M., U.S.	C3	124
Islington, Ma., U.S.	h11	114
Ismailia, Egypt	D11	48
İsmayıllı, Azer.	B13	44
Isoka, Zam.	A5	56
Isola, Ms., U.S.	B3	117
Isparta, Tur.	D4	44
İspir, Tur.	B9	44
Israel, ctry., Asia	D2	42
Israel, stm., N.H., U.S.	B3	122
Issaquah, Wa., U.S.	B3	140
Issaquena, co., Ms., U.S.	C2	117
Issia, C. Iv.	E3	50
Issoire, Fr.	E8	16
Issoudun, Fr.	D8	16
Issyk-Kul', Kyrg.	E9	26
Issyk-Kul', ozero, l., Kyrg.	E9	26
İstanbul, Tur.	B3	44
İstanbul Boğazı (Bosporus), strt., Tur.	B3	44
Isto, Mount, mtn., Ak., U.S.	B11	95
Istokpoga, Lake, l., Fl., U.S.	E5	102
Itabaiana, Braz.	D4	74
Itabaiana, Braz.	C4	74
Itaberaba, Braz.	D3	74
Itaberaí, Braz.	E2	74
Itabira, Braz.	E3	74
Itabuna, Braz.	D4	74
Itacoatiara, Braz.	D8	70
Itaguí, Col.	B4	70
Itaipu Reservoir, res., S.A.	C7	72
Itaituba, Braz.	D8	70
Itajaí, Braz.	D8	72
Itajubá, Braz.	F2	74
Itajuípe, Braz.	D4	74
Italy, Tx., U.S.	C4	136
Italy, ctry., Eur.	C4	18
Itamaraju, Braz.	E4	74
Itambé, Braz.	E3	74
Itānagar, India	D6	40
Itaobim, Braz.	E3	74
Itaperuna, Braz.	F3	74
Itapetinga, Braz.	E3	74
Itapetininga, Braz.	F2	74
Itapipoca, Braz.	B4	74
Itapiranga, Braz.	D7	72
Itaporanga, Braz.	C4	74
Itaquari, Braz.	F3	74
Itaqui, Braz.	D6	72
Itārsi, India	E3	40
Itasca, Il., U.S.	k8	106
Itasca, Tx., U.S.	C4	136
Itasca, co., Mn., U.S.	C5	116
Itasca, Lake, l., Mn., U.S.	C3	116
Itaúna, Braz.	F3	74
Itawamba, co., Ms., U.S.	A5	117
Itenes see Guaporé, stm., S.A.	F7	70
Iténez see Guaporé, stm., S.A.	F7	70
Ithaca, Mi., U.S.	E6	115
Ithaca, N.Y., U.S.	C4	125
Ithaca see Itháki, i., Grc.	E8	18
Itháki, i., Grc.	E8	18
Itimbiri, stm., D.R.C.	C4	54
Itoigawa, Japan	C3	31
Itoko, D.R.C.	D4	54
Itta Bena, Ms., U.S.	B3	117
Ituango, Col.	D4	80
Ituberá, Braz.	D4	74
Ituiutaba, Braz.	E2	74
Itumbiara, Braz.	E2	74
Iturama, Braz.	E1	74
Iturup, ostrov, i., Russia	E16	26
Ituverava, Braz.	F3	74
Itzehoe, Ger.	D11	12
Iuka, Ms., U.S.	A5	117
Iul'tin, Russia	C20	26
Iva, S.C., U.S.	C2	133
Ivanava, Bela.	C8	20
Ivangorod, Russia	G13	10
Ivanhoe, Mn., U.S.	F2	116
Ivankov, Ukr.	D10	20
Ivano-Frankivs'k, Ukr.	E8	20
Ivanovo, Russia	D6	26
Ivdel', Russia	C8	26
Ivigtut, Grnld.	F30	82
Ivins, Ut., U.S.	F2	137
Ivohibe, Madag.	C8	56
Ivory Coast see Cote d'Ivoire, ctry., Afr.	E3	50
Ivoryton, Ct., U.S.	D6	100
Ivrea, Italy	B1	18
Iwaki, Japan	D16	28
Iwo, Nig.	E5	50
Ixmiquilpan, Méx.	C5	78
Ixtapa, Mex.	D4	78
Ixtepec, Mex.	D5	78
Izabal, Lago de, l., Guat.	B2	80
Izamal, Mex.	C7	78
Izard, co., Ar., U.S.	A4	97
Izberbaš, Russia	A12	44
Iževsk, Russia	D7	26
Iziaslav, Ukr.	D9	20
Izium, Ukr.	E14	20
Ižma, stm., Russia	A9	22
Izmaïl, Ukr.	G10	20
İzmir, Tur.	C2	44
İzmir Körfezi, b., Tur.	C2	44
İzmit, Tur.	B3	44
İzmit Körfezi, b., Tur.	B3	44
İznik, Tur.	B3	44
İznik Gölü, l., Tur.	B3	44
Izucar de Matamoros, Mex.	D5	78
Izu-shotō, is., Japan	E15	28
Izu Trench	F17	64

J

Name	Map Ref.	Page
Jabal, Bahr al- (Mountain Nile), stm., Sudan	I11	48
Jabalpur, India	E3	40
Jabiru, Austl.	C5	60
Jablah, Syria	E6	44
Jablonec nad Nisou, Czech Rep.	D3	20
Jablonovyj hrebet, mts., Russia	D13	26
Jaboatão, Braz.	C4	74
Jaboticabal, Braz.	F2	74
Jacareí, Braz.	F2	74
Jacarezinho, Braz.	F2	74
Jaciara, Braz.	B7	72
Jacinto City, Tx., U.S.	r14	136
Jack, co., Tx., U.S.	C3	136
Jackfish Lake, l., Sk., Can.	D1	91
Jackman, Me., U.S.	C2	112
Jackman Station, Me., U.S.	C2	112
Jack Mountain, mtn., Mt., U.S.	D4	119
Jack Mountain, mtn., Wa., U.S.	A5	140
Jackpot, Nv., U.S.	B7	121
Jacksboro, Tn., U.S.	C9	135
Jacksboro, Tx., U.S.	C3	136
Jacks Mountain, mtn., Pa., U.S.	E6	131
Jackson, Al., U.S.	D2	94
Jackson, Ca., U.S.	C3	98
Jackson, Ga., U.S.	C3	103
Jackson, Ky., U.S.	C6	110
Jackson, La., U.S.	D4	111
Jackson, Mi., U.S.	F6	115
Jackson, Mn., U.S.	G4	116
Jackson, Mo., U.S.	D8	118
Jackson, Ms., U.S.	C3	117
Jackson, Oh., U.S.	C3	128
Jackson, S.C., U.S.	E4	133
Jackson, Tn., U.S.	B3	135
Jackson, Wi., U.S.	E5	142
Jackson, Wy., U.S.	C2	143
Jackson, co., Al., U.S.	A3	94
Jackson, co., Ar., U.S.	B4	97
Jackson, co., Co., U.S.	A4	99
Jackson, co., Fl., U.S.	B1	102
Jackson, co., Ga., U.S.	B3	103
Jackson, co., Ia., U.S.	B7	108
Jackson, co., Il., U.S.	F4	106
Jackson, co., In., U.S.	G5	107
Jackson, co., Ks., U.S.	C8	109
Jackson, co., Ky., U.S.	C5	110
Jackson, co., La., U.S.	B3	111
Jackson, co., Mi., U.S.	F6	115
Jackson, co., Mn., U.S.	G3	116
Jackson, co., Mo., U.S.	B3	118
Jackson, co., Ms., U.S.	E5	117
Jackson, co., N.C., U.S.	f9	126
Jackson, co., Oh., U.S.	C3	128
Jackson, co., Ok., U.S.	C2	129
Jackson, co., Or., U.S.	E4	130
Jackson, co., S.D., U.S.	D4	134
Jackson, co., Tn., U.S.	C8	135
Jackson, co., Tx., U.S.	E4	136
Jackson, co., W.V., U.S.	C3	141
Jackson, co., Wi., U.S.	D3	142
Jackson, stm., Va., U.S.	C3	139
Jackson, Lake, l., Fl., U.S.	E5	102
Jackson, Lake, l., Fl., U.S.	B2	102
Jackson, Mount, mtn., Ant.	D34	67
Jackson, Mount, mtn., N.H., U.S.	B4	122
Jackson Center, Oh., U.S.	B1	128
Jackson Lake, res., Wy., U.S.	C2	143
Jackson Mountains, mts., Nv., U.S.	B3	121
Jackson's Arm, Nf., Can.	D3	88
Jacksons Gap, Al., U.S.	C4	94
Jacksonville, Al., U.S.	B4	94
Jacksonville, Ar., U.S.	C3	97
Jacksonville, Fl., U.S.	B5	102
Jacksonville, Il., U.S.	D3	106
Jacksonville, N.C., U.S.	C5	126
Jacksonville, Or., U.S.	E4	130
Jacksonville, Tx., U.S.	D5	136
Jacksonville Beach, Fl., U.S.	B5	102
Jacksonville Naval Air Station, mil., Fl., U.S.	B5	102
Jacks Peak, mtn., Ut., U.S.	E3	137
Jacmel, Haiti	B5	80
Jacobābād, Pak.	E9	42
Jacobina, Braz.	D3	74
Jacques-Cartier, stm., P.Q., Can.	B6	90
Jacques-Cartier, Détroit de, strt., P.Q., Can.	I27	82
Jacquet River, N.B., Can.	B4	87
Jacundá, Braz.	B2	74
Jada, Nig.	E7	50
Jaén, Peru	E4	70
Jaén, Spain	I5	16
Jaffa, Cape, c., Austl.	H2	62
Jaffna, Sri L.	H4	40
Jaffrey, N.H., U.S.	E2	122
Jagādhri, India	C3	40
Jagdalpur, India	F4	40
Jagersfontein, S. Afr.	D4	56
Jagodnoe, Russia	C16	26
Jagtiāl, India	F3	40
Jaguaquara, Braz.	D4	74
Jaguarão, Braz.	E7	72
Jaguaribe, Braz.	C4	74
Jahrom, Iran	E6	42
Jailolo, Indon.	C7	36
Jaipur, India	D3	40
Jaisalmer, India	D2	40
Jājapur, India	E5	40
Jakarta, Indon.	E3	36
Jakobshavn, Grnld.	E29	82
Jakša, Russia	B10	22
Jakutija, state, Russia	C14	26
Jakutsk, Russia	C14	26
Jal, N.M., U.S.	E6	124
Jalālābād, Afg.	D10	42
Jalandhar, India	C3	40
Jalapa see Xalapa, Mex.	D5	78
Jalaun, India	D3	40
Jālgaon, India	E3	40
Jalingo, Nig.	E7	50
Jalisco, state, Mex.	C4	78
Jālna, India	F3	40
Jālor, India	D2	40
Jalostotitlán, Mex.	C4	78
Jalpāiguri, India	D5	40
Jalūlā', Iraq	E11	44
Jamaica, ctry., N.A.	E9	76
Jamaica Bay, b., N.Y., U.S.	k13	125
Jamaica Channel, strt., N.A.	B4	80
Jamal, poluostrov, pen., Russia	B8	26
Jamantau, gora, mtn., Russia	D7	26
Jambi, Indon.	D2	36
Jambol, Bul.	C11	18
Jambusar, India	E2	40
James, stm., Mo., U.S.	E4	118
James, stm., Va., U.S.	C5	139
James, stm., U.S.	C8	92
James, Lake, l., In., U.S.	A7	107
James, Lake, res., N.C., U.S.	B1	126
James Bay, b., Can.	H23	82
James Branch, stm., De., U.S.	F3	101
Jamesburg, N.J., U.S.	C4	123
James City, N.C., U.S.	B5	126
James City, co., Va., U.S.	C6	139
James Island, S.C., U.S.	k12	133
James Island, i., Md., U.S.	C5	113
James Island, i., S.C., U.S.	F8	133
James River Bridge, Va., U.S.	k15	139
Jamestown, Austl.	G2	62
Jamestown, In., U.S.	E4	107
Jamestown, Ky., U.S.	D4	110
Jamestown, N.C., U.S.	B3	126
Jamestown, N.D., U.S.	C7	127
Jamestown, N.Y., U.S.	C1	125
Jamestown, Oh., U.S.	C2	128
Jamestown, R.I., U.S.	F5	132
Jamestown, Tn., U.S.	C9	135
James Town, Wy., U.S.	E3	143
Jamestown Dam, N.D., U.S.	C7	127
Jamestown Reservoir, res., N.D., U.S.	C7	127
Jamkhandi, India	F3	40
Jammerbugten, b., Den.	H3	10
Jammu, India	C2	40
Jammu and Kashmir, hist. reg., Asia	C10	38
Jamnagar, India	E2	40
Jämsä, Fin.	F11	10
Jamshedpur, India	E5	40
Jamsk, Russia	D17	26
Jämtland, hist. reg., Swe.	E6	10
Jamuna, stm., Bngl.	D5	40
Jana, stm., Russia	C15	26
Janaúba, Braz.	E3	74
Janaucu, Ilha, i., Braz.	C10	70
Janesville, Ca., U.S.	B3	98
Janesville, Ia., U.S.	B5	108
Janesville, Mn., U.S.	F5	116
Janesville, Wi., U.S.	F4	142
Jan Mayen, i., Nor.	D23	144
Jan Mayen Ridge	C24	144
Jansenville, S. Afr.	E3	56
Janskij, Russia	C15	26
Janskij zaliv, b., Russia	B15	26
Januária, Braz.	E3	74
Jaora, India	E3	40
Japan, ctry., Asia	D15	28
Japan, Sea of (East Sea), Asia	C14	28
Japan Basin	D16	64
Japan Trench	E17	64
Japurá (Caquetá), stm., S.A.	D6	70
Jaraguá, Braz.	E2	74
Jaransk, Russia	C8	22
Jarānwāla, Pak.	D10	42
Jarcevo, Russia	B12	20
Jardim, Braz.	C6	72
Jardín América, Arg.	D6	72
Jari, stm., Braz.	C9	70
Jarocin, Pol.	D4	20
Jaroslavl', Russia	D6	26
Jarosław, Pol.	D7	20
Jarrettsville, Md., U.S.	A5	113
Jar-Sale, Russia	A13	22
Järva-Jaani, Est.	G11	10
Järvenpää, Fin.	F11	10
Jarvis Island, i., Oc.	E13	58
Jasikan, Ghana	E5	50
Jāsk, Iran	E7	42
Jaškul', Russia	A5	42
Jasło, Pol.	E6	20
Jasmine Estates, Fl., U.S.	D4	102
Jasnogorsk, Russia	B14	20
Jason Islands, is., Falk. Is.	H4	69
Jasonville, In., U.S.	F3	107
Jasper, Al., U.S.	B2	94
Jasper, Fl., U.S.	B4	102
Jasper, Ga., U.S.	B2	103
Jasper, In., U.S.	H4	107
Jasper, Mo., U.S.	D3	118
Jasper, Tn., U.S.	D8	135
Jasper, Tx., U.S.	D6	136
Jasper, co., Ga., U.S.	C3	103
Jasper, co., Ia., U.S.	C4	108
Jasper, co., Il., U.S.	D5	106
Jasper, co., In., U.S.	B3	107
Jasper, co., Mo., U.S.	D3	118
Jasper, co., Ms., U.S.	C4	117
Jasper, co., S.C., U.S.	G5	133
Jasper, co., Tx., U.S.	D5	136
Jasper National Park, Ab., Can.	C1	84
Jataí, Braz.	E1	74
Jatni, India	E5	40
Jaú, Braz.	F2	74
Jaunpur, India	D4	40
Java (Jawa), i., Indon.	E3	36
Java Sea see Jawa, Laut, Indon.	D3	36
Java Trench	I13	64
Javari (Yavarí), stm., S.A.	D5	70
Jawa (Java), i., Indon.	E3	36
Jawa, Laut (Java Sea), Indon.	D3	36
Jawhar, Som.	J14	48
Jay, Ok., U.S.	A7	129
Jay, co., In., U.S.	D7	107
Jaya, Puncak, mtn., Indon.	G10	32
Jayapura, Indon.	G11	32
Jaypur, India	F4	40
Jaz Mūriān, Hāmūn-e, l., Iran	E7	42
J. B. Thomas, Lake, res., Tx., U.S.	C2	136
Jean, Nv., U.S.	H6	121
Jeanerette, La., U.S.	E4	111
Jean Lafitte National Historical Park, La., U.S.	k12	111
Jeannette, Pa., U.S.	F2	131
Jebba, Nig.	E5	50
Jeddore Lake, res., Nf., Can.	D3	88
Jędrzejów, Pol.	D6	20
Jeff Davis, co., Ga., U.S.	E4	103
Jeff Davis, co., Tx., U.S.	o12	136
Jefferson, Ga., U.S.	B3	103
Jefferson, Ia., U.S.	B3	108
Jefferson, La., U.S.	k11	111
Jefferson, N.C., U.S.	A1	126
Jefferson, Oh., U.S.	A5	128
Jefferson, Or., U.S.	C3	130
Jefferson, S.C., U.S.	B7	133
Jefferson, Tx., U.S.	C5	136
Jefferson, Wi., U.S.	E5	142
Jefferson, co., Al., U.S.	B3	94
Jefferson, co., Ar., U.S.	C3	97
Jefferson, co., Co., U.S.	B5	99
Jefferson, co., Fl., U.S.	B3	102
Jefferson, co., Ga., U.S.	C4	103
Jefferson, co., Ia., U.S.	C5	108
Jefferson, co., Id., U.S.	F6	105
Jefferson, co., Il., U.S.	E5	106
Jefferson, co., In., U.S.	G6	107
Jefferson, co., Ks., U.S.	C8	109
Jefferson, co., Ky., U.S.	B4	110
Jefferson, co., La., U.S.	E5	111
Jefferson, co., Mo., U.S.	C7	118
Jefferson, co., Ms., U.S.	D2	117
Jefferson, co., Mt., U.S.	D5	119
Jefferson, co., Ne., U.S.	D8	120
Jefferson, co., N.Y., U.S.	A5	125
Jefferson, co., Oh., U.S.	B5	128
Jefferson, co., Ok., U.S.	C4	129
Jefferson, co., Or., U.S.	C5	130
Jefferson, co., Pa., U.S.	D3	131
Jefferson, co., Tn., U.S.	C10	135
Jefferson, co., Tx., U.S.	E5	136
Jefferson, co., Wa., U.S.	B3	140
Jefferson, co., Wi., U.S.	E5	142
Jefferson, co., W.V., U.S.	B7	141
Jefferson, stm., Mt., U.S.	E5	119
Jefferson, Mount, mtn., Id., U.S.	E7	105
Jefferson, Mount, mtn., Nv., U.S.	E5	121
Jefferson, Mount, mtn., Or., U.S.	C5	130
Jefferson City, Mo., U.S.	C5	118
Jefferson City, Tn., U.S.	C10	135
Jefferson Davis, co., La., U.S.	D3	111
Jefferson Davis, co., Ms., U.S.	D4	117
Jefferson Farms, De., U.S.	i7	101
Jefferson Proving Ground, mil., In., U.S.	G7	107
Jeffersontown, Ky., U.S.	B4	110
Jeffersonville, Ga., U.S.	D3	103
Jeffersonville, In., U.S.	H6	107
Jeffersonville, Ky., U.S.	C6	110
Jeffersonville, Oh., U.S.	C2	128
Jeffrey, W.V., U.S.	D3	141
Jeffrey City, Wy., U.S.	D5	143
Jeffries Creek, stm., S.C., U.S.	C8	133
Jega, Nig.	D5	50
Jehossee Island, i., S.C., U.S.	k11	133
Jēkabpils, Lat.	H11	10
Jekyll Island, i., Ga., U.S.	E5	103
Jelenia Góra, Pol.	D3	20
Jelgava, Lat.	H10	10
Jellico, Tn., U.S.	C9	135
Jelm Mountain, mtn., Wy., U.S.	E7	143
Jemaja, Pulau, i., Indon.	C3	36
Jember, Indon.	E4	36
Jemez, stm., N.M., U.S.	k7	124
Jemez Canyon Dam, N.M., U.S.	k7	124
Jemez Indian Reservation, N.M., U.S.	h7	124
Jemez Pueblo, N.M., U.S.	B3	124
Jemison, Al., U.S.	C3	94
Jena, Ger.	E12	12
Jena, La., U.S.	C3	111
Jeneponto, Indon.	E5	36
Jenkins, Ky., U.S.	C7	110
Jenkins, co., Ga., U.S.	D5	103
Jenkintown, Pa., U.S.	o21	131
Jenks, Ok., U.S.	A6	129
Jennings, La., U.S.	D3	111
Jennings, Mo., U.S.	f13	118
Jennings, co., In., U.S.	G6	107
Jensen Beach, Fl., U.S.	E6	102
Jens Munks Ø, i., Grnld.	F32	82
Jequié, Braz.	D3	74
Jequitinhonha, Braz.	E3	74
Jequitinhonha, stm., Braz.	E3	74
Jerada, Mor.	D4	48
Jerauld, co., S.D., U.S.	C7	134
Jérémie, Haiti	B5	80
Jeremoabo, Braz.	D4	74
Jerez de García Salinas, Mex.	C4	78
Jerez de la Frontera, Spain	I3	16
Jerez de los Caballeros, Spain	H3	16
Jericho see Arīhā, Gaza Str.	G6	44
Jericho, Vt., U.S.	B3	138
Jerid, Chott, l., Tun.	D6	48
Jerimoth Hill, hill, R.I., U.S.	C1	132
Jermyn, Pa., U.S.	C10	131
Jerome, Id., U.S.	G4	105
Jerome, Pa., U.S.	F4	131
Jerome, co., Id., U.S.	G4	105
Jersey, co., Il., U.S.	D3	106
Jersey, dep., Eur.	F5	12
Jersey City, N.J., U.S.	B4	123
Jersey Mountain, mtn., Id., U.S.	E3	105
Jersey Shore, Pa., U.S.	D7	131
Jerseyville, Il., U.S.	D3	106
Jerusalem see Yerushalayim, Isr.	G6	42
Jervis Inlet, b., B.C., Can.	D6	85
Jesi, Italy	C4	18
Jessamine, co., Ky., U.S.	C5	110
Jesselton see Kota Kinabalu, Malay.	B5	36
Jessore, Bngl.	E5	40
Jessup, Md., U.S.	B4	113
Jessup, Pa., U.S.	m18	131
Jesup, Ga., U.S.	E5	103
Jesup, Ia., U.S.	B5	108
Jesup, Lake, l., Fl., U.S.	D5	102
Jésus, Île, i., P.Q., Can.	p19	90
Jesús Carranza, Mex.	D5	78
Jesús María, Arg.	E5	72
Jetmore, Ks., U.S.	D4	109
Jewel Cave National Monument, S.D., U.S.	D2	134
Jewell, Ia., U.S.	B4	108
Jewell, co., Ks., U.S.	C5	109
Jewett City, Ct., U.S.	C8	100
Jhālāwār, India	E3	40
Jhang Sadar, Pak.	D10	42
Jhānsi, India	D3	40
Jhelum, Pak.	D10	42
Jhunjhunūn, India	D3	40
Jiahe, China	D3	30
Jiali, China	C6	40
Jialing, stm., China	E8	28
Jiamusi, China	B14	28
Ji'an, China	D3	30
Jianchang, China	A4	30
Jianchuan, China	F8	28
Jiande, China	D4	30

Name	Map Ref.	Page
Jiang'an, China	D2	30
Jiangcheng, China	B4	34
Jiangjin, China	F9	28
Jiangle, China	D4	30
Jiangling, China	C3	30
Jiangmen, China	G10	28
Jiangsu, state, China	E11	28
Jiangxi, state, China	F11	28
Jianli, China	D3	30
Jian'ou, China	F11	28
Jianping, China	A4	30
Jianshui, China	G8	28
Jianyang, China	D4	30
Jianyang, China	C1	30
Jiaocheng, China	B3	30
Jiaonan, China	B4	30
Jiaoxian, China	D12	28
Jiaozuo, China	D10	28
Jiashan, China	C4	30
Jibiya, Nig.	D6	50
Jicarilla Apache Indian Reservation, N.M., U.S.	A2	124
Jičín, Czech Rep.	D3	20
Jiddah, Sau. Ar.	F3	38
Jiexiu, China	B3	30
Jieyang, China	G11	28
Jihlava, Czech Rep.	E3	20
Jijel, Alg.	I9	16
Jijiga, Eth.	B8	54
Jilib, Som.	J13	48
Jilin, China	C13	28
Jilin, state, China	C13	28
Jill, Kediet ej, mtn., Maur.	B2	50
Jīma, Eth.	B7	54
Jimbolia, Rom.	G6	20
Jiménez (Ciudad Jiménez), Mex.	B4	78
Jimeta, Nig.	E7	50
Jim Hogg, co., Tx., U.S.	F3	136
Jim Lake, res., N.D., U.S.	B7	127
Jimo, China	B5	30
Jim Thorpe, Pa., U.S.	E10	131
Jim Wells, co., Tx., U.S.	F3	136
Jinan, China	D11	28
Jincheng, China	B3	30
Jīnd, India	D3	40
Jingdezhen, China	F11	28
Jinggangshan, China	F10	28
Jinghai, China	B4	30
Jinghong, China	G8	28
Jingning, China	B2	30
Jingxi, China	E2	30
Jingxian, China	D2	30
Jinhua, China	F11	28
Jining, China	D11	28
Jining, China	C10	28
Jinja, Ug.	C6	54
Jinning, China	E1	30
Jinsha, China	D2	30
Jinshi, China	F10	28
Jinzhai, China	C4	30
Jinzhou, China	C12	28
Jinzhou, China	D12	28
Ji-Paraná, Braz.	F7	70
Jishou, China	D2	30
Jisr ash-Shughūr, Syria	E7	44
Jiu, stm., Rom.	G7	20
Jiujiang, China	F11	28
Jiulong (Kowloon), China	E3	30
Jiuquan, China	D7	28
Jiutai, China	C13	28
Jixi, China	B14	28
Jixian, China	C11	28
Jīzān, Sau. Ar.	G4	38
Joanna, S.C., U.S.	C4	133
João Pessoa, Braz.	C5	74
João Pinheiro, Braz.	E2	74
Job Peak, mtn., Nv., U.S.	D3	121
Jocassee, Lake, res., U.S.	B1	133
Jódar, Spain	I5	16
Jo Daviess, co., Il., U.S.	A3	106
Jodhpur, India	D2	40
Joe Batt's Arm [-Barr'd Islands-Shoal Bay], Nf., Can.	D4	88
Joensuu, Fin.	E13	10
Joes Brook, stm., Vt., U.S.	C4	138
Joes Creek, stm., W.V., U.S.	m14	141
Joetsu, Japan	D15	28
Joffre, Mount, mtn., Can.	D3	84
Johannesburg, S. Afr.	D4	56
John, Cape, c., N.S., Can.	D6	87
John Day, Or., U.S.	C8	130
John Day, stm., Or., U.S.	B6	130
John Day Dam, U.S.	D5	140
John Day Fossil Beds National Monument, Or., U.S.	C6	130
John F. Kennedy Space Center, sci., Fl., U.S.	D6	102
John H. Kerr Dam, Va., U.S.	D4	139
John H. Kerr Reservoir, res., U.S.	D4	139
John Martin Reservoir, res., Co., U.S.	C7	99
John Muir National Historical Site, hist., Ca., U.S.	h8	98
John Redmond Reservoir, res., Ks., U.S.	D8	109
John Sevier, Tn., U.S.	m14	135
Johns Island, i., S.C., U.S.	F7	133
Johnson, Ks., U.S.	E2	109
Johnson, Vt., U.S.	B3	138
Johnson, co., Ar., U.S.	B2	97
Johnson, co., Ga., U.S.	D4	103
Johnson, co., Ia., U.S.	C6	108
Johnson, co., Il., U.S.	F5	106
Johnson, co., In., U.S.	F5	107
Johnson, co., Ks., U.S.	D9	109
Johnson, co., Ky., U.S.	C7	110
Johnson, co., Mo., U.S.	C4	118
Johnson, co., Ne., U.S.	D9	120
Johnson, co., Tn., U.S.	C12	135
Johnson, co., Tx., U.S.	C4	136
Johnson, co., Wy., U.S.	B6	143
Johnsonburg, Pa., U.S.	D4	131
Johnson City, N.Y., U.S.	C5	125
Johnson City, Tn., U.S.	C11	135
Johnson City, Tx., U.S.	D3	136
Johnson Creek, Wi., U.S.	E5	142
Johnsonville, S.C., U.S.	D9	133
Johns Pass, strt., Fl., U.S.	p10	102
Johnston, Ia., U.S.	e8	108
Johnston, R.I., U.S.	C4	132
Johnston, S.C., U.S.	D4	133
Johnston, co., N.C., U.S.	B4	126
Johnston, co., Ok., U.S.	C5	129
Johnston Atoll, atoll, Oc.	G22	64
Johnston City, Il., U.S.	F5	106
Johnston Key, i., Fl., U.S.	H5	102
Johnstown, Co., U.S.	A6	99
Johnstown, N.Y., U.S.	B6	125
Johnstown, Oh., U.S.	B3	128
Johnstown, Pa., U.S.	F4	131
John W. Flannagan Reservoir, res., Va., U.S.	e9	139
Johor Bahru, Malay.	C2	36
Joigny, Fr.	C8	16
Joinville, Braz.	D8	72
Jokkmokk, Swe.	C8	10
Jolfā, Iran	C11	44
Joliet, Il., U.S.	B5	106
Joliette, P.Q., Can.	C4	90
Jolo, Phil.	E8	34
Jolo Island, i., Phil.	E8	34
Jomda, China	E7	28
Jones, Ok., U.S.	B4	129
Jones, co., Ga., U.S.	C3	103
Jones, co., Ia., U.S.	B6	108
Jones, co., Ms., U.S.	D4	117
Jones, co., N.C., U.S.	B5	126
Jones, co., S.D., U.S.	D5	134
Jones, co., Tx., U.S.	C3	136
Jonesboro, Ar., U.S.	B5	97
Jonesboro, Ga., U.S.	C2	103
Jonesboro, Il., U.S.	F4	106
Jonesboro, In., U.S.	D6	107
Jonesboro, La., U.S.	B3	111
Jonesborough, Tn., U.S.	C11	135
Jonesburg, Mo., U.S.	C6	118
Jones Creek, Tx., U.S.	s14	136
Jones Mill, Ar., U.S.	C3	97
Jonesport, Me., U.S.	D5	112
Jonestown, Ms., U.S.	A3	117
Jonesville, La., U.S.	C4	111
Jonesville, Mi., U.S.	G6	115
Jonesville, N.C., U.S.	A2	126
Jonesville, S.C., U.S.	B4	133
Jonesville, Va., U.S.	f8	139
Joniškis, Lith.	H10	10
Jonquière, P.Q., Can.	A6	90
Jonuta, Mex.	D6	78
Joplin, Mo., U.S.	D3	118
Joppatowne, Md., U.S.	B5	113
Jordan, Mn., U.S.	F5	116
Jordan, ctry., Asia	D3	42
Jordan, stm., Asia	F6	44
Jordan, stm., Ut., U.S.	C4	137
Jordan Creek, stm., U.S.	E9	130
Jordan Lake, res., Al., U.S.	C3	94
Jorhāt, India	D6	40
Jornado del Muerto, des., N.M., U.S.	D3	124
Joroinen, Fin.	E12	10
Jos, Nig.	E6	50
José de San Martín, Arg.	F2	69
Joseph, Or., U.S.	B9	130
Joseph, Lac, l., Nf., Can.	h8	88
Joseph Bonaparte Gulf, b., Austl.	C4	60
Joseph City, Az., U.S.	C5	96
Josephine, co., Or., U.S.	E3	130
Joshua, Tx., U.S.	n9	136
Joshua Tree, Ca., U.S.	E5	98
Joshua Tree National Monument, Ca., U.S.	F6	98
Jostedalsbreen, Nor.	F2	10
Jourdanton, Tx., U.S.	E3	136
Jovellanos, Cuba	A3	80
J. Percy Priest Lake, res., Tn., U.S.	A5	135
Juab, co., Ut., U.S.	D2	137
Juan Aldama, Mex.	C4	78
Juan de Fuca, Strait of, strt., N.A.	B3	92
Juan Fernandez, Archipiélago, is., Chile	E1	72
Juanjui, Peru	E4	70
Juazeiro, Braz.	C3	74
Juazeiro do Norte, Braz.	C4	74
Juba, Sudan	J11	48
Jubba (Genalē), stm., Afr.	C8	54
Juby, Cap, c., Mor.	A2	50
Júcar, stm., Spain	H6	16
Juchitán de Zaragoza, Mex.	D5	78
Judenburg, Aus.	G14	12
Judith, stm., Mt., U.S.	C7	119
Judith, Point, c., R.I., U.S.	G4	101
Judith Basin, co., Mt., U.S.	C6	119
Judith Island, i., N.C., U.S.	B6	126
Judith Mountains, mts., Mt., U.S.	C7	119
Judith Peak, mtn., Mt., U.S.	C7	119
Judsonia, Ar., U.S.	B4	97
Juhnov, Russia	B13	20
Juidongshan, China	E4	30
Juiz de Fora, Braz.	F3	74
Jukta, Russia	C12	26
Julesburg, Co., U.S.	A8	99
Juliaca, Peru	G5	70
Julia Creek, Austl.	E3	62
Julian, Ca., U.S.	F5	98
Julian, W.V., U.S.	C3	141
Julian Alps, mts., Eur.	A4	18
Juliana Top, mtn., Sur.	C8	70
Julianehåb, Grnld.	F30	82
Jumba, Som.	D8	54
Jumbo Peak, mtn., Nv., U.S.	G7	121
Jumilla, Spain	H6	16
Jump, stm., Wi., U.S.	C3	142
Jūnāgadh, India	E2	40
Junction, Tx., U.S.	D3	136
Junction City, Ar., U.S.	D3	97
Junction City, Ks., U.S.	C7	109
Junction City, Ky., U.S.	C5	110
Junction City, La., U.S.	A3	111
Junction City, Or., U.S.	C3	130
Jundiaí, Braz.	F2	74
Juneau, Ak., U.S.	D13	95
Juneau, Wi., U.S.	E5	142
Juneau, co., Wi., U.S.	E3	142
Junee, Austl.	G4	62
June in Winter, Lake, l., Fl., U.S.	E5	102
Jungar Qi, China	D10	28
Junggar Pendi, China	B5	28
Juniata, Ne., U.S.	D7	120
Juniata, co., Pa., U.S.	F7	131
Juniata, stm., Pa., U.S.	F7	131
Junín, Arg.	E5	72
Junior Lake, l., Me., U.S.	C4	112
Juniper Mountains, mts., Az., U.S.	B2	96
Junipero Serra Peak, mtn., Ca., U.S.	D3	98
Jūniyah, Leb.	F6	44
Junlian, China	D1	30
Junxian, China	E10	28
Jupiter, Fl., U.S.	F6	102
Jupiter Inlet, b., Fl., U.S.	F6	102
Jupiter Island, i., Fl., U.S.	E6	102
Jur, Russia	D15	26
Jura, i., Scot., U.K.	C4	12
Jurga, Russia	D10	26
Jūrmala, Lat.	H10	10
Juruá, stm., S.A.	E6	70
Juruena, stm., Braz.	F8	70
Jurumirim, Represa, res., Braz.	C8	72
Juškozero, Russia	B5	22
Jussara, Braz.	B7	72
Justin, Tx., U.S.	C4	136
Jutaí, stm., Braz.	D6	70
Jutiapa, Guat.	C1	80
Juticalpa, Hond.	C2	80
Jutland see Jylland, reg., Den.	I3	10
Juventud, Isla de la, i., Cuba	A3	80
Juxian, China	B4	30
Južno-Sahalinsk, Russia	E16	26
Južno-Ural'sk, Russia	D11	22
Jylland, reg., Den.	I3	10
Jyväskylä, Fin.	E11	10

K

K2 (Qogir Feng), mtn., Asia	B3	40
Kaaawa, Hi., U.S.	f10	104
Kaahka, Turk.	C7	42
Kaala, mtn., Hi., U.S.	f9	104
Kaalualu Bay, b., Hi., U.S.	E6	104
Kaaumakua, Puu, mtn., Hi., U.S.	f10	104
Kabaena, Pulau, i., Indon.	E6	36
Kabala, S.L.	E2	50
Kabale, Ug.	D5	54
Kabalega Falls, wtfl, Ug.	C6	54
Kabalo, D.R.C.	E5	54
Kabambare, D.R.C.	D5	54
Kabardino-Balkarija, state, Russia	E6	26
Kabba, Nig.	E6	50
Kabetogama Lake, l., Mn., U.S.	B5	116
Kabinda, D.R.C.	E4	54
Kabīr Kūh, mts., Iran	D9	42
Kābol, Afg.	D9	42
Kabompo, stm., Zam.	A3	56
Kabongo, D.R.C.	E5	54
Kabūdārāhang, Iran	E13	44
Kābul see Kābol, Afg.	D9	42
Kabwe, Zam.	A4	56
Kabylie, reg., Alg.	I9	16
Kachchh, Gulf of, b., India	E1	40
Kachess Lake, res., Wa., U.S.	B4	140
Kačkanar, Russia	C10	22
Kadan Kyun, i., Myan.	D3	34
Kade, Ghana	E4	50
Kadınhanı, Tur.	C5	44
Kadiolo, Mali	D4	50
Kadirli, Tur.	D7	44
Kadoka, S.D., U.S.	D4	134
Kadoma, Zimb.	B4	56
Kaduna, Nig.	D6	50
Kaduna, stm., Nig.	D6	50
Kāduqlī, Sudan	H10	48
Kadykčan, Russia	C16	26
Kadžerom, Russia	B10	22
Kaédi, Maur.	C2	50
Kaélé, Cam.	A2	54
Kaena Point, c., Hi., U.S.	B3	104
Kafanchan, Nig.	E6	50
Kaffrine, Sen.	D1	50
Kafia Kingi, Sudan	I9	48
Kafue, Zam.	B4	56
Kafue, stm., Zam.	A4	56
Kaga, Japan	C3	31
Kaga Bandoro, C.A.R.	B3	54
Kagan, Uzb.	C8	42
Kagera, stm., Afr.	D6	54
Kağızman, Tur.	B10	44
Kagoshima, Japan	E14	28
Kagul see Cahul, Mol.	G10	20
Kahaluu, Hi., U.S.	D6	104
Kahaluu, Hi., U.S.	g10	104
Kahama, Tan.	D6	54
Kahana Bay, b., Hi., U.S.	f10	104
Kahemba, D.R.C.	E3	54
Kahoka, Mo., U.S.	A6	118
Kahoolawe, i., Hi., U.S.	C5	104
Kahramanmaraş, Tur.	D7	44
Kahuku, Hi., U.S.	B4	104
Kahuku Point, c., Hi., U.S.	B4	104
Kahului, Hi., U.S.	C5	104
Kahului Bay, b., Hi., U.S.	C5	104
Kai, Kepulauan, is., Indon.	E8	36
Kaibab Indian Reservation, Az., U.S.	A3	96
Kaifeng, China	E10	28
Kaikoura, N.Z.	p13	63c
Kailahun, S.L.	E2	50
Kailas see Kangrinboqê Feng, mtn., China	E4	28
Kailas Range see Gangdisê Shan, mts., China	E4	28
Kaili, China	D2	30
Kailu, China	C12	28
Kailua, Hi., U.S.	B4	104
Kailua Bay, b., Hi., U.S.	g11	104
Kailua Kona, Hi., U.S.	D6	104
Kainji Lake, res., Nig.	D5	50
Kaiping, China	E3	30
Kairouan, Tun.	C7	48
Kaiserslautern, Ger.	F10	12
Kaitaia, N.Z.	o13	63c
Kaithal, India	D3	40
Kaiwi Channel, strt., Hi., U.S.	h17	92a
Kaiwi Channel, strt., Hi., U.S.	B4	104
Kaixian, China	C2	30
Kaiyuan, China	C12	28
Kaiyuan, China	E1	30
Kajaani, Fin.	D12	10
Kajakī, Band-e, res., Afg.	D9	42
Kajang, Malay.	C2	36
Kajiado, Kenya	D7	54
Kajnar, Kaz.	E9	26
Kaka, Sudan	A6	54
Kakamas, S. Afr.	D3	56
Kakamega, Kenya	C6	54
Kaka Point, c., Hi., U.S.	C5	104
Kakata, Lib.	E2	50
Kake, Ak., U.S.	D13	95
Kakhovka Reservoir see Kakhovs'ke vodoskhovyshche, res., Ukr.	F13	20
Kakhovs'ke vodoskhovyshche, res., Ukr.	F13	20
Kākināda, India	F4	40
Kalaa Kebira, Tun.	G3	18
Kalaallit Nunaat see Greenland, dep., N.A.	D30	82
Kalabahi, Indon.	E6	36
Kalabo, Zam.	B3	56
Kalač, Russia	D7	22
Kalač-na-Donu, Russia	E7	22
Kaladan, stm., Asia	B2	34
Ka Lae, c., Hi., U.S.	E6	104
Kalahari Desert, des., Afr.	C3	56
Kalaheo, Hi., U.S.	B2	104
Kalajoki, Fin.	D10	10
Kalakan, Russia	D13	26
Kalama, Wa., U.S.	C3	140
Kalámai, Grc.	F8	18
Kalamazoo, Mi., U.S.	F5	115
Kalamazoo, co., Mi., U.S.	F5	115
Kalamazoo, stm., Mi., U.S.	F5	115
Kalamits'ka zatoka, b., Ukr.	G12	20
Kalanchak, Ukr.	F12	20
Kalao, Pulau, i., Indon.	E6	36
Kalaotoa, Pulau, i., Indon.	E6	36
Kalasin, Thai.	C4	34
Kalāt, Pak.	E9	42
Kalaupapa Peninsula, pen., Hi., U.S.	B5	104
Kalaw, Myan.	B3	34
Kalawao, co., Hi., U.S.	B5	104
Kalbarri, Austl.	F1	60
Kale, Tur.	D3	44
Kalecik, Tur.	B5	44
Kaleden, B.C., Can.	E8	85
Kalemie, D.R.C.	E5	54
Kalemyo, Myan.	B2	34
Kalena, Puu, mtn., Hi., U.S.	g9	104
Kalene Hill, Zam.	A3	56
Kalevala, Russia	D14	10
Kalewa, Myan.	B2	34
Kalgin Island, i., Ak., U.S.	g16	95
Kalgoorlie-Boulder, Austl.	G3	60
Kalibo, Phil.	D8	34
Kalima, D.R.C.	D5	54
Kalimantan see Borneo, i., Asia	D4	36
Kálimnos, Grc.	F11	18
Kálimnos, i., Grc.	F11	18
Kālimpang, India	D5	40
Kalinin see Tver', Russia	D5	26
Kaliningrad, Russia	D4	26
Kalinkavičy, Bela.	C10	20
Kalispel Indian Reservation, Wa., U.S.	A8	140
Kalispell, Mt., U.S.	B2	119
Kalisz, Pol.	D5	20
Kalkaska, Mi., U.S.	D5	115
Kalkaska, co., Mi., U.S.	D5	115
Kallavesi, l., Fin.	E12	10
Kalmar, Swe.	H7	10
Kalmarsund, strt., Swe.	H7	10
Kalmykija, state, Russia	E6	26
Kalohi Channel, strt., Hi., U.S.	C4	104
Kaloli Point, c., Hi., U.S.	D7	104
Kalomo, Zam.	B4	56
Kalona, Ia., U.S.	C6	108
Kalone Peak, mtn., B.C., Can.	C4	85
Kalpin, China	A3	40
Kalsūbai, mtn., India	F2	40
Kaluga, Russia	D5	26
Kalundborg, Den.	I4	10
Kalush, Ukr.	E8	20
Kalutara, Sri L.	H4	40
Kalyān, India	F2	40
Kama, D.R.C.	D5	54
Kama, stm., Russia	D7	26
Kamaishi, Japan	D16	28
Kamakou, mtn., Hi., U.S.	B5	104
Kamālia, Pak.	D10	42
Kaman, Tur.	C5	44
Kamarān, i., Yemen	G4	38
Kama Reservoir see Kamskoe vodohranilišče, res., Russia	C10	22
Kamas, Ut., U.S.	C4	137
Kambalda, Austl.	G3	60
Kambove, D.R.C.	F5	54
Kamčatka, poluostrov, pen., Russia	D17	26
Kamchatka Peninsula see Kamčatka, poluostrov, pen., Russia	D17	26
Kamen', gora, mtn., Russia	C11	26
Kamenka, Russia	D15	20
Kamenka, Russia	D7	22
Kamen'-na-Obi, Russia	D10	26
Kamenskoe, Russia	C18	26
Kamensk-Ural'skij, Russia	C11	22
Kāmet, mtn., Asia	C3	40
Kamiah, Id., U.S.	C2	105
Kamiak Butte, mtn., Wa., U.S.	B8	140
Kam'ianets'-Podil's'kyi, Ukr.	E9	20
Kamina, D.R.C.	E5	54
Kamloops, B.C., Can.	D7	85
Kamo, Arm.	B11	44
Kampala, Ug.	C6	54
Kampar, Malay.	C2	36
Kampen, Neth.	D9	12
Kampeska, Lake, l., S.D., U.S.	C8	134
Kamphaeng Phet, Thai.	C3	34
Kâmpóng Cham, Camb.	D5	34
Kâmpóng Chhnáng, Camb.	D4	34
Kâmpóng Saôm, Camb.	D4	34
Kâmpóng Thum, Camb.	D4	34
Kâmpôt, Camb.	D4	34
Kampti, Burkina	D4	50
Kampuchea see Cambodia, ctry., Asia	D4	34
Kamskoe vodohranilišče, res., Russia	C10	22
Kamuela (Waimea), Hi., U.S.	C6	104
Kamyšin, Russia	D6	26
Kamyšlov, Russia	C11	22
Kanab, Ut., U.S.	F3	137
Kanab Creek, stm., U.S.	A3	96
Kanabec, co., Mn., U.S.	E5	116
Kanaga Island, i., Ak., U.S.	E4	95
Kanairiktok, stm., Nf., Can.	g9	88
Kananga, D.R.C.	E4	54
Kanapou Bay, b., Hi., U.S.	C5	104
Kanaš, Russia	C8	22
Kanata, On., Can.	B9	89
Kanawha, Ia., U.S.	B4	108
Kanawha, co., W.V., U.S.	C3	141
Kanawha, stm., W.V., U.S.	C3	141
Kanazawa, Japan	D15	28
Kānchenjunga, mtn., Asia	D5	40
Kānchipuram, India	G3	40
Kandahar see Qandahār, Afg.	D9	42
Kandalaksa, Russia	C15	10
Kandalaksha Bay see Kandalakskaja guba, b., Russia	A5	22

Name	Map Ref.	Page

Kandalakšskaja guba, b., Russia **A5** 22
Kandale, D.R.C. **E3** 54
Kandangan, Indon. **D5** 36
Kandi, Benin **D5** 50
Kandıra, Tur. **B4** 44
Kandiyohi, co., Mn., U.S. . . **E3** 116
Kandy, Sri L. **H4** 40
Kane, Pa., U.S. **C4** 131
Kane, co., Il., U.S. **B5** 106
Kane, co., Ut., U.S. **F3** 137
Kanem, prov., Chad **D8** 50
Kaneohe, Hi., U.S. **B4** 104
Kaneohe Bay, b., Hi., U.S. . **g10** 104
Kaneohe Bay Marine Corps Air Station, mil., Hi., U.S. **g10** 104
Kangaba, Mali **D3** 50
Kangal, Tur. **C7** 44
Kangān, Iran **E6** 42
Kangaroo Island, i., Austl. . . **H2** 62
Kangāvar, Iran **E12** 44
Kangbao, China **A3** 30
Kangean, Pulau, i., Indon. . **E5** 36
Kanggye, N. Kor. **C13** 28
Kango, Gabon **C2** 54
Kangpu, China **A3** 34
Kangrinboqê Feng, mtn., China **E4** 28
Kangshan, Tai. **E5** 30
Kangto, mtn., Asia **A2** 34
Kaniama, D.R.C. **E4** 54
Kaniet Islands, is., Pap. N. Gui. **G12** 32
Kanin, poluostrov, pen., Russia **C6** 26
Kaningo, Kenya **D7** 54
Kanin Nos, Russia **A7** 22
Kanin Nos, mys, c., Russia **C6** 26
Kanjiža, Yugo. **A8** 18
Kankakee, Il., U.S. **B6** 106
Kankakee, co., Il., U.S. . . . **B6** 106
Kankakee, stm., U.S. **B5** 106
Kankan, Gui. **D3** 50
Kānker, India **E4** 40
Kanmaw Kyun, i., Myan. . . **D3** 34
Kannapolis, N.C., U.S. **B2** 126
Kannonkoski, Fin. **E11** 10
Kano, Nig. **D6** 50
Kanopolis, Ks., U.S. **D5** 109
Kanopolis Lake, res., Ks., U.S. **D5** 109
Kanoya, Japan **D2** 31
Kānpur, India **D4** 40
Kansas, Il., U.S. **D6** 106
Kansas, state, U.S. **D5** 109
Kansas, stm., Ks., U.S. . . . **C7** 109
Kansas City, Ks., U.S. **C9** 109
Kansas City, Mo., U.S. . . . **B3** 118
Kansk, Russia **D11** 26
Kantang, Thai. **E3** 34
Kantchari, Burkina **D5** 50
Kantemirovka, Russia **E15** 20
Kanye, Bots. **D4** 56
Kaohsiung, Tai. **E5** 30
Kaoko Veld, plat., Nmb. . . . **B1** 56
Kaolack, Sen. **D1** 50
Kaoma, Zam. **A3** 56
Kaouar, reg., Niger **C7** 50
Kapaa, Hi., U.S. **A2** 104
Kapaau, Hi., U.S. **C6** 104
Kapan, Arm. **C12** 44
Kapanga, D.R.C. **C4** 54
Kapapa Island, i., Hi., U.S. **g10** 104
Kapčagaj, Kaz. **B11** 42
Kapčagajskoe vodohranilišče, res., Kaz. **B11** 42
Kapchagay Reservoir see Kapčagajskoe vodohranilišče, res., Kaz. **B11** 42
Kapfenberg, Aus. **G14** 12
Kapiri Mposhi, Zam. **A4** 56
Kaplan, La., U.S. **D3** 111
Kapoeta, Sudan **C6** 54
Kaposvár, Hung. **F4** 20
Kaptai Lake see Karnaphuli Reservoir, res., Bngl. . **E6** 40
Kapuas, stm., Indon. **D3** 36
Kapuas, stm., Indon. **D4** 36
Kapuas Hulu, Pegunungan (Kapuas Hulu, Pergunungan), mts., Asia **C4** 36
Kapuas Hulu, Pergunungan (Kapuas Hulu, Pegunungan), mts., Asia **C4** 36
Kapuskasing, On., Can. . . . **o19** 89
Kapuvár, Hung. **F4** 20
Kapyl', Bela. **C9** 20
Kara, Russia **C8** 26
Kara-Balta, Kyrg. **A2** 40
Karabaš, Russia **C11** 22
Kara-Bogaz-Gol, zaliv, b., Turk. **E7** 26
Kara-Bogaz-Gol Gulf see Kara-Bogaz-Gol, zaliv, b., Turk. **E7** 26
Karabük, Tur. **B5** 44
Karabula, Russia **D11** 26
Karaburun, Tur. **C2** 44
Karabutak, Kaz. **E11** 22
Karacabey, Tur. **B3** 44

Karačaevo-Čerkesija, state, Russia **E6** 26
Karačev, Russia **C13** 20
Karāchi, Pak. **F9** 42
Karād, India **F2** 40
Karaganda, Kaz. **E9** 26
Karaginskij, ostrov, i., Russia **D18** 26
Karaginskij zaliv, b., Russia **D18** 26
Kāraikkudi, India **G3** 40
Karaj, Iran **C6** 42
Karakaya Barajı, res., Tur. . . **C8** 44
Karakelong, Pulau, i., Indon. **F8** 32
Karakol, Kyrg. **E9** 26
Karakoram Pass, Asia **B3** 40
Karakoram Range, mts., Asia **B3** 40
Karakul', Uzb. **C8** 42
Kara-Kum Canal see Garagumskij kanal imeni Prezidenta Turkmenistana S.A. Nijazova, Turk. **C8** 42
Karaman, Tur. **D5** 44
Karamay, China **B4** 28
Karamea Bight, b., N.Z. . . **p13** 63c
Karapınar, Tur. **D5** 44
Karasay, China **B4** 40
Karasburg, Nmb. **D2** 56
Kara Sea see Karskoe more, Russia **B8** 26
Karasu, Tur. **B4** 44
Karasu, stm., Tur. **C9** 44
Karasuk, Russia **D9** 26
Karatau, Kaz. **B10** 42
Karatau, hrebet, mts., Kaz. . **E8** 26
Karatobe, Kaz. **E9** 22
Karaton, Kaz. **A6** 42
Karatsu, Japan **D1** 31
Karaul, Kaz. **B3** 28
Karaul, Russia **B10** 26
Karawang, Indon. **E3** 36
Karažal, Kaz. **B2** 28
Karbalā', Iraq **D4** 42
Karbalā', state, Iraq **F10** 44
Kårböle, Swe. **F6** 10
Karcag, Hung. **F6** 20
Kardeljevo, Cro. **C6** 18
Kardhítsa, Grc. **E8** 18
Kărdžali, Bul. **D10** 18
Karelia see Karelija, state, Russia **C5** 26
Karelia, hist. reg., Eur. **C12** 6
Karelija, state, Russia **C5** 26
Karema, Tan. **E6** 54
Karesuando, Swe. **B10** 10
Kargopol', Russia **C5** 26
Kariba, Zimb. **B4** 56
Kariba, Lake, res., Afr. **B4** 56
Karibib, Nmb. **C2** 56
Karigasniemi, Fin. **B11** 10
Karimata, Selat (Karimata Strait), strt., Indon. . . . **D3** 36
Karimata Strait see Karimata, Selat, strt., Indon. **D3** 36
Karīmganj, India **E6** 40
Karīmnagar, India **F3** 40
Karimunjawa, Pulau, i., Indon. **E4** 36
Karisimbi, Volcan, vol., Afr. **D5** 54
Karkaralinsk, Kaz. **B3** 28
Karkar Island, i., Pap. N. Gui. **G12** 32
Karkheh, stm., Iran **G12** 44
Karkinits'ka zatoka, b., Ukr. **G12** 20
Karkūk, Iraq **C4** 42
Karlivka, Ukr. **E13** 20
Karl-Marx-Stadt see Chemnitz, Ger. **E13** 12
Karlovac, Cro. **B5** 18
Karlovy Vary, Czech Rep. . . **D2** 20
Karlshamn, Swe. **H6** 10
Karlskoga, Swe. **G6** 10
Karlskrona, Swe. **H6** 10
Karlsruhe, Ger. **F11** 12
Karlstad, Swe. **G5** 10
Karlstad, Mn., U.S. **B2** 116
Karma, Niger **D5** 50
Karnāl, India **D3** 40
Karnaphuli Reservoir, res., Bngl. **E6** 40
Karnātaka, prov., India . . . **G3** 40
Karnes, co., Tx., U.S. **E4** 136
Karnes City, Tx., U.S. **E4** 136
Karns, Tn., U.S. **n13** 135
Kárpathos, i., Grc. **G11** 18
Karpogory, Russia **B7** 22
Karratha, Austl. **E2** 60
Kars, Tur. **B10** 44
Karsakpaj, Kaz. **B1** 28
Karši, Uzb. **F8** 26
Karskie Vorota, proliv, strt., Russia **B7** 26
Karskoe more, Russia **B8** 26
Kartaly, Russia **D8** 26
Karufa, Indon. **D8** 36
Kārūn, stm., Iran **G13** 44
Karūr, India **G3** 40
Karvinà, Czech Rep. **E5** 20
Kārwār, India **G2** 40
Karymskoe, Russia **A10** 28
Kasai (Cassai), stm., Afr. . . **D3** 54
Kasaji, D.R.C. **F4** 54
Kasama, Zam. **A5** 56
Kasane, Bots. **B4** 56
Kasanga, Tan. **E6** 54

Kasangulu, D.R.C. **D3** 54
Kāsaragod, India **G3** 40
Kasempa, Zam. **A4** 56
Kasenga, D.R.C. **F5** 54
Kasenye, D.R.C. **C6** 54
Kasese, D.R.C. **D5** 54
Kasese, Ug. **C6** 54
Kāshān, Iran **D6** 42
Kashgar see Kashi, China . . **D3** 28
Kashi, China **D3** 28
Kāshmar, Iran **C7** 42
Kasimov, Russia **B16** 20
Kasiruta, Pulau, i., Indon. . . **D7** 36
Kaskaskia, stm., Il., U.S. . . **D5** 106
Kaslo, B.C., Can. **E9** 85
Kasongo, D.R.C. **D5** 54
Kasongo-Lunda, D.R.C. . . . **E3** 54
Kásos, i., Grc. **G11** 18
Kasota, Mn., U.S. **F5** 116
Kaspi, Geor. **B11** 44
Kaspijsk, Russia **A12** 44
Kaspijskij, Russia **E6** 26
Kassalā, Sudan **G12** 48
Kassandra, Gulf of see Kassándras, Kólpos, b., Grc. **D9** 18
Kassándras, Kólpos, b., Grc. **D9** 18
Kassel, Ger. **E11** 12
Kasserine, Tun. **C6** 48
Kasson, Mn., U.S. **F6** 116
Kastamonu, Tur. **B5** 44
Kastoría, Grc. **D8** 18
Kasulu, Tan. **D6** 54
Kasūr, Pak. **D10** 42
Kataba, Zam. **B4** 56
Katahdin, Mount, mtn., Me., U.S. **C4** 112
Katako-Kombe, D.R.C. . . . **D4** 54
Katanga, hist. reg., D.R.C. . **E4** 54
Katangli, Russia **D16** 26
Katanning, Austl. **G2** 60
Katchall Island, i., India . . . **H6** 40
Kateríni, Grc. **D9** 18
Kates Needle, mtn., Ak., U.S. **m24** 95
Katha, Myan. **B3** 34
Katherína, Gebel, mtn., Egypt **E11** 48
Katherine, Austl. **C5** 60
Kāthiāwār Peninsula, pen., India **E2** 40
Kathleen, Fl., U.S. **D4** 102
Kāthmāndau, Nepal **D5** 40
Kati, Mali **D3** 50
Katihār, India **D5** 40
Katiola, C. Iv. **E3** 50
Katmai, Mount, mtn., Ak., U.S. **D9** 95
Katmai National Park, Ak., U.S. **D9** 95
Kātmāndu see Kāthmāndau, Nepal . **D5** 40
Katompi, D.R.C. **E5** 54
Katoomba, Austl. **G5** 62
Katowice, Pol. **D5** 20
Katrineholm, Swe. **G7** 10
Katsina, Nig. **D6** 50
Kattakurgan, Uzb. **C9** 42
Kattegat, strt., Eur. **B12** 12
Katy, Tx., U.S. **r14** 136
Kauai, co., Hi., U.S. **B1** 104
Kauai, i., Hi., U.S. **A2** 104
Kauai Channel, strt., Hi., U.S. **h17** 92a
Kauai Channel, strt., Hi., U.S. **B3** 104
Kau Desert, des., Hi., U.S. . **D6** 104
Kaufbeuren, Ger. **G12** 12
Kaufman, Tx., U.S. **C4** 136
Kaufman, co., Tx., U.S. . . . **C4** 136
Kauiki Head, c., Hi., U.S. . . **C6** 104
Kaujuitoq see Resolute, N.T., Can. **D20** 82
Kaukauna, Wi., U.S. **D5** 142
Kaula Island, i., Hi., U.S. . . **m15** 104
Kaulakahi Channel, strt., Hi., U.S. **A2** 104
Kaumakani, Hi., U.S. **B2** 104
Kaunakakai, Hi., U.S. **B4** 104
Kauna Point, c., Hi., U.S. . . **D6** 104
Kaura-Namoda, Nig. **D6** 50
Kavača, Russia **C19** 26
Kavadarci, Mac. **D8** 18
Kavála, Grc. **D10** 18
Kavalerovo, Russia **C15** 28
Kāvali, India **G4** 40
Kavaratti, India **G2** 40
Kāveri, stm., India **G3** 40
Kavieng, Pap. N. Gui. **G13** 32
Kavīr, Dasht-e, des., Iran . . **D8** 42
Kawaihoa Point, c., Hi., U.S. **B1** 104
Kawaikini, mtn., Hi., U.S. . . **A2** 104
Kawambwa, Zam. **E5** 54
Kawasaki, Japan **D15** 28
Kawerau, N.Z. **o14** 63c
Kawich Peak, mtn., Nv., U.S. **F5** 121
Kawich Range, mts., Nv., U.S. **F5** 121
Kaw Lake, res., Ok., U.S. . . **A5** 129
Kaxgar, stm., China **B3** 40
Kay, co., Ok., U.S. **A4** 129
Kaya, Burkina **D4** 50
Kaycee, Wy., U.S. **C6** 143
Kayenta, Az., U.S. **A5** 96

Kayes, Mali **D2** 50
Kayseri, Tur. **C6** 44
Kaysville, Ut., U.S. **B4** 137
Kayuagung, Indon. **D2** 36
Kazače, Russia **B15** 26
Kazahskij melkosopočnik, hills, Kaz. **D9** 26
Kazakh Hills see Kazahskij melkosopočnik, hills, Kaz. **D9** 26
Kazakstan, ctry., Asia **E8** 26
Kazalinsk, Kaz. **A8** 42
Kazan', Russia **D6** 26
Kazanka, Ukr. **F12** 20
Kazanlâk, Bul. **C10** 18
Kazan-rettō, is., Japan **F17** 64
Kazbek, gora, vol. **A11** 44
Kāzerūn, Iran **E6** 42
Kazincbarcika, Hung. **E6** 20
Kaztalovka, Kaz. **E8** 22
Kazym, Russia **B12** 22
Kéa, i., Grc. **F10** 18
Keaau, Hi., U.S. **D6** 104
Keahiakahoe, Puu, mtn., Hi., U.S. **g10** 104
Keahole Point, c., Hi., U.S. **D5** 104
Kealaikahiki Channel, strt., Hi., U.S. **C5** 104
Kealaikahiki Point, c., Hi., U.S. **C5** 104
Kealakekua, Hi., U.S. **D6** 104
Kealia, Hi., U.S. **A2** 104
Keams Canyon, Az., U.S. . . **B5** 96
Keanapapa Point, c., Hi., U.S. **C4** 104
Keansburg, N.J., U.S. **C4** 123
Kearney, Mo., U.S. **B3** 118
Kearney, Ne., U.S. **D6** 120
Kearney, co., Ne., U.S. . . . **D7** 120
Kearns, Ut., U.S. **C4** 137
Kearny, Az., U.S. **D5** 96
Kearny, N.J., U.S. **h8** 123
Kearny, co., Ks., U.S. **D2** 109
Keban Barajı, res., Tur. . . . **C8** 44
Keban Reservoir see Keban Barajı, res., Tur. **C8** 44
Kébèmer, Sen. **C1** 50
Kebnekaise, mtn., Swe. . . . **C8** 10
K'ebrī Dehar, Eth. **B8** 54
Kecskemét, Hung. **F5** 20
Kedges Straits, strt., Md., U.S. **D5** 113
Kedgwick, N.B., Can. **B2** 87
Kediri, Indon. **E4** 36
Kedon, Russia **C17** 26
Kédougou, Sen. **D2** 50
Keego Harbor, Mi., U.S. . . **o15** 115
Keene, N.H., U.S. **E2** 122
Keene, Tx., U.S. **n9** 136
Keer-Weer, Cape, c., Austl. **C3** 62
Keeseville, N.Y., U.S. **f11** 125
Keesler Air Force Base, mil., Ms., U.S. **E5** 117
Keetmanshoop, Nmb. **D2** 56
Keet Seel Ruin, hist., Az., U.S. **A5** 96
Keewatin, On., Can. **E4** 86
Keewatin, Mn., U.S. **C5** 116
Kefallinía, i., Grc. **E8** 18
Kefamenanu, Indon. **E6** 36
Keffi, Nig. **E6** 50
Keflavík, Ice. **m17** 10a
Kegonsa, Lake, l., Wi., U.S. **F4** 142
Kehra, Est. **G11** 10
Ke-hsi Mānsām, Myan. . . . **B3** 34
Keila, Est. **G11** 10
Keiser, Ar., U.S. **B5** 97
Keith, co., Ne., U.S. **C4** 120
Keizer, Or., U.S. **C3** 130
Kejimkujik National Park, N.S., Can. **E4** 87
Kekaha, Hi., U.S. **B2** 104
Kékes, mtn., Hung. **F5** 20
K'elafo, Eth. **B8** 54
Kelan, China **B3** 30
Kelantan, stm., Malay. **L6** 36
Kelibia, Tun. **F3** 18
Kelkit, Tur. **B8** 44
Kelkit, stm., Tur. **B7** 44
Kelleys Island, i., Oh., U.S. **A3** 128
Kellogg, Id., U.S. **C5** 108
Kellogg, Id., U.S. **B2** 105
Kelloselkä, Fin. **C13** 10
Kelly Air Force Base, mil., Tx., U.S. **k7** 136
Kelly Island, i., De., U.S. . . **D4** 101
Kellyville, Ok., U.S. **B5** 129
Kélo, Chad **E8** 50
Kelowna, B.C., Can. **E8** 85
Kelso, Wa., U.S. **C3** 140
Keluang, Malay. **C2** 36
Kem', Russia **C5** 26
Kembé, C.A.R. **C4** 54
Kemerovo, Russia **D10** 26
Kemi, Fin. **D11** 10
Kemijärvi, Fin. **C12** 10
Kemijoki, stm., Fin. **C11** 10
Kemmerer, Wy., U.S. **E2** 143
Kemp, Tx., U.S. **C4** 136
Kemp, Lake, res., Tx., U.S. **C3** 136
Kemper, co., Ms., U.S. . . . **C5** 117
Kempsey, Austl. **G5** 62
Kempten, Ger. **G12** 12

Kemptville, On., Can. **B9** 89
Kemul, Kong, mtn., Indon. . **C5** 36
Kenai, Ak., U.S. **C9** 95
Kenai Fjords National Park, Ak., U.S. **D10** 95
Kenai Mountains, mts., Ak., U.S. **h16** 95
Kenai Peninsula, pen., Ak., U.S. **h16** 95
Kenansville, N.C., U.S. . . . **C5** 126
Kenbridge, Va., U.S. **D4** 139
Kendal, Eng., U.K. **C5** 12
Kendall, Fl., U.S. **s13** 102
Kendall, co., Il., U.S. **B5** 106
Kendall, co., Tx., U.S. **E3** 136
Kendall Park, N.J., U.S. . . . **C3** 123
Kendallville, In., U.S. **B7** 107
Kendari, Indon. **D6** 36
Kendawangan, Indon. **D4** 36
Kenedy, Tx., U.S. **E4** 136
Kenedy, co., Tx., U.S. **F4** 136
Kenema, S.L. **E2** 50
Kenge, D.R.C. **D3** 54
Kēng Tung, Myan. **B3** 34
Kenhardt, S. Afr. **D3** 56
Kenilworth, Il., U.S. **h9** 106
Kénitra, Mor. **D3** 48
Kenly, N.C., U.S. **B4** 126
Kenmare, N.D., U.S. **A3** 127
Kenmore, N.Y., U.S. **C2** 125
Kennaday Peak, mtn., Wy., U.S. **E6** 143
Kennebago Lake, l., Me., U.S. **C2** 112
Kennebec, co., Me., U.S. . . **D3** 112
Kennebec, stm., Me., U.S. . **D3** 112
Kennebunk, Me., U.S. **E2** 112
Kennebunkport, Me., U.S. . **E2** 112
Kennedy, Cape see Canaveral, Cape, c., Fl., U.S. **D6** 102
Kennedy Entrance, strt., Ak., U.S. **D9** 95
Kenner, La., U.S. **E5** 111
Kennesaw, Ga., U.S. **B2** 103
Kennesaw Mountain, mtn., Ga., U.S. **h7** 103
Kennett, Mo., U.S. **E7** 118
Kennett Square, Pa., U.S. . **G10** 131
Kennewick, Wa., U.S. **C6** 140
Keno, Or., U.S. **E5** 130
Kénogami, Lac, l., P.Q., Can. **A6** 90
Kenora, On., Can. **o16** 89
Kenosha, Wi., U.S. **F6** 142
Kenosha, co., Wi., U.S. . . . **F5** 142
Kenova, W.V., U.S. **C2** 141
Kensett, Ar., U.S. **B4** 97
Kensico Reservoir, res., N.Y., U.S. **g13** 125
Kensington, P.E., Can. . . . **C6** 87
Kensington, Ct., U.S. **C4** 100
Kensington, Md., U.S. **B3** 113
Kent, Oh., U.S. **A4** 128
Kent, Wa., U.S. **B3** 140
Kent, co., De., U.S. **D3** 101
Kent, co., Md., U.S. **B5** 113
Kent, co., Mi., U.S. **E5** 115
Kent, co., R.I., U.S. **D2** 132
Kent, co., Tx., U.S. **C2** 136
Kentau, Kaz. **B9** 42
Kent City, Mi., U.S. **E5** 115
Kent Island, i., De., U.S. . . **D4** 101
Kent Island, i., Md., U.S. . . **C5** 113
Kentland, In., U.S. **C3** 107
Kenton, De., U.S. **D3** 101
Kenton, Oh., U.S. **B2** 128
Kenton, Tn., U.S. **A2** 135
Kenton, co., Ky., U.S. **B5** 110
Kent Point, c., Md., U.S. . . **C5** 113
Kentucky, state, U.S. **C4** 110
Kentucky, stm., Ky., U.S. . . **B5** 110
Kentucky Lake, res., U.S. . . **D10** 92
Kentwood, La., U.S. **D5** 111
Kentwood, Mi., U.S. **F5** 115
Kenvil, N.J., U.S. **B3** 123
Kenvir, Ky., U.S. **D6** 110
Kenya, ctry., Afr. **C7** 54
Kenya, Mount see Kirinyaga, mtn., Kenya **D7** 54
Kenyon, Mn., U.S. **F6** 116
Kenyon, R.I., U.S. **F2** 132
Keokea, Hi., U.S. **C5** 104
Keokuk, Ia., U.S. **D6** 108
Keokuk, co., Ia., U.S. **C5** 108
Keokuk Lock and Dam, U.S. **D6** 108
Keosauqua, Ia., U.S. **D6** 108
Keota, Ia., U.S. **C6** 108
Keota, Ok., U.S. **B7** 129
Keowee, Lake, res., S.C., U.S. **B2** 133
Kępno, Pol. **D4** 20
Kerala, prov., India **G3** 40
Kerang, Austl. **H3** 62
Kerava, Fin. **F11** 10
Kerch, Ukr. **G14** 20
Kerch Strait, strt., Eur. **G14** 20
Keremeos, B.C., Can. **E8** 85
Keren, Erit. **G12** 48
Kerens, Tx., U.S. **C4** 136
Kerguélen, Îles, is., Afr. . . . **M10** 64
Kerguelen Plateau **N10** 64
Kerhonkson, N.Y., U.S. . . . **D6** 125
Kericho, Kenya **D7** 54

Name	Map Ref.	Page

Kerinci, Gunung, vol., Indon. D2 36
Kerkhoven, Mn., U.S. . . . E3 116
Kerki, Turk. C9 42
Kerkiči, Turk. F8 26
Kérkira, Grc. E7 18
Kérkira (Corfu), i., Grc. . E7 18
Kermadec Islands, is., N.Z. G12 58
Kermadec Ridge L20 64
Kermadec Trench L21 64
Kermān, Iran D7 42
Kermānshāh (Bākhtarān), Iran D5 42
Kermit, Tx., U.S. D1 136
Kermode, Mount, mtn., B.C., Can. C2 85
Kern, co., Ca., U.S. E4 98
Kern, stm., Ca., U.S. E4 98
Kernersville, N.C., U.S. . . A2 126
Kernville, Ca., U.S. E4 98
Kérouané, Gui. E3 50
Kerr, co., Tx., U.S. D3 136
Kerr, Lake, l., Fl., U.S. . . . C5 102
Kerrville, Tx., U.S. D3 136
Kersey, Co., U.S. A6 99
Kershaw, S.C., U.S. B6 133
Kershaw, co., S.C., U.S. . . C6 133
Kerulen, stm., Asia B10 28
Keşan, Tur. B2 44
Kesennuma, Japan D16 28
Keshena, Wi., U.S. D5 142
Keskin, Tur. C5 44
Kesten'ga, Russia D14 10
Keszthely, Hung. F4 20
Ket', stm., Russia D10 26
Keta, Ghana E5 50
Ketapang, Indon. D3 36
Ketchikan, Ak., U.S. D13 95
Ketchum, Id., U.S. F4 105
Kete-Krachi, Ghana E4 50
Kętrzyn, Pol. B6 20
Kettering, Oh., U.S. C1 128
Kettle, stm., Mn., U.S. . . D6 116
Kettle Creek, stm., Pa., U.S. D6 131
Kettle Creek Lake, res., Pa., U.S. D6 131
Kettle Falls, Wa., U.S. . . . A7 140
Keuka Lake, l., N.Y., U.S. . C3 125
Kewanee, Il., U.S. B4 106
Kewaskum, Wi., U.S. E5 142
Kewaunee, Wi., U.S. D6 142
Kewaunee, co., Wi., U.S. . D6 142
Keweenaw, co., Mi., U.S. . A2 115
Keweenaw Bay, b., Mi., U.S. B2 115
Keweenaw Peninsula, pen., Mi., U.S. A3 115
Keweenaw Point, c., Mi., U.S. A3 115
Keya Paha, co., Ne., U.S. . B6 120
Keya Paha, stm., U.S. . . . A5 120
Keyhole Reservoir, res., Wy., U.S. B8 143
Key Largo, Fl., U.S. G6 102
Keyport, N.J., U.S. C4 123
Keyser, W.V., U.S. B6 141
Keystone, W.V., U.S. D3 141
Keystone Heights, Fl., U.S. C4 102
Keystone Lake, res., Ok., U.S. A5 129
Keystone Peak, mtn., Az., U.S. F4 96
Keysville, Va., U.S. C4 139
Key West, Fl., U.S. H5 102
Key West Naval Air Station, mil., Fl., U.S. H5 102
Kezar Falls, Me., U.S. . . . E2 112
Kezar Lake, l., Me., U.S. . . D2 112
Kezi, Zimb. C4 56
Kežma, Russia D12 26
Khābūr, Nahr al-, stm., Asia E9 44
Khadki, India F2 40
Khairpur, Pak. E9 42
Khajrāho, India E4 40
Khakhea, Bots. C3 56
Khalkhāl, Iran D13 44
Khalkidhikí, hist. reg., Grc. D9 18
Khalkís, Grc. E9 18
Khambhāt, India E2 40
Khambhāt, Gulf of, b., India E2 40
Khāmgaon, India E3 40
Khammam, India F4 40
Khānābād, Afg. C9 42
Khān al-Baghdādī, Iraq . . F10 44
Khānaqīn, Iraq E11 44
Khandwa, India E3 40
Khānewāl, Pak. D10 42
Khaniá, Grc. G9 18
Khaníon, Kólpos, b., Grc. . G9 18
Khanka, Lake, l., Asia . . . C14 28
Khānpur, Pak. E10 42
Kharagpur, India E5 40
Khargon, India E3 40
Kharkiv, Ukr. E14 20
Khartoum see Al-Kharṭūm, Sudan G11 48
Khāsh, Afg. D8 42
Khāsh, Iran E8 42
Khashm al-Qirbah, Sudan H12 48
Khemis Melyana, Alg. . . . I8 14
Khenchla, Alg. D5 14
Khenifra, Mor. E2 14
Kherson, Ukr. F12 20
Khíos, Grc. E11 18
Khíos, i., Grc. E10 18

Khmel'nyts'kyi, Ukr. E9 20
Khmil'nyk, Ukr. E9 20
Kholm, Afg. C9 42
Khomeynīshahr, Iran D6 42
Khong see Mekong, stm., Asia C4 34
Khon Kaen, Thai. C4 34
Khorramābād, Iran D5 42
Khorramshahr, Iran D5 42
Khotyn, Ukr. E9 20
Khouribga, Mor. D3 48
Khrystynivka, Ukr. E10 20
Khulna, Bngl. E5 40
Khust, Ukr. E7 20
Khuzdār, Pak. E9 42
Khvoy, Iran C4 42
Khyber Pass, Asia C2 40
Kiama, D.R.C. E3 54
Kiamba, Phil. E8 34
Kiamichi, stm., Ok., U.S. . C6 129
Kiamika, stm., P.Q., Can. . C2 90
Kiana, Ak., U.S. B7 95
Kiangarow, Mount, mtn., Austl. F5 62
Kiawah Island, i., S.C., U.S. F7 133
Kibangou, Congo D2 54
Kibombo, D.R.C. D5 54
Kibondo, Tan. D6 54
Kibre Mengist, Eth. B7 54
Kičevo, Mac. D8 18
Kickamuit, stm., R.I., U.S. . D5 132
Kickapoo, stm., Wi., U.S. . E3 142
Kickapoo, Lake, res., Tx., U.S. C3 136
Kickapoo Indian Reservation, Ks., U.S. . C8 109
Kicking Horse Pass, Can. . D2 84
Kidal, Mali C5 50
Kidatu, Tan. E7 54
Kidder, co., N.D., U.S. . . . C6 127
Kidira, Sen. D2 50
Kiefer, Ok., U.S. B5 129
Kiel, Ger. C12 12
Kiel, Wi., U.S. E5 142
Kiel Bay see Kieler Bucht, b., Ger. C12 12
Kiel Canal see Nord-Ostsee-Kanal, Ger. C11 12
Kielce, Pol. D6 20
Kieler Bucht, b., Ger. . . . C12 12
Kiester, Mn., U.S. G5 116
Kiev see Kyïv, Ukr. D11 20
Kiev Reservoir see Kyïvs'ke vodoskhovyshche, res., Ukr. D11 20
Kiffa, Maur. C2 50
Kigali, Rw. D6 54
Kigoma, Tan. D5 54
Kihčik, Russia D17 26
Kihei, Hi., U.S. C5 104
Kiholo Bay, b., Hi., U.S. . . D5 104
Kii Strait see Kii-suidō, strt., Japan E15 28
Kii-suidō, strt., Japan E15 28
Kikinda, Yugo. B8 18
Kikládhes, is., Grc. F10 18
Kikori, Pap. N. Gui. H11 32
Kikwit, D.R.C. E3 54
Kil, Swe. G5 10
Kilauea, Hi., U.S. A2 104
Kilauea Crater, crat., Hi., U.S. D6 104
Kilauea Point, c., Hi., U.S. . A2 104
Kilchu-ŭp, N. Kor. B1 31
Kildurk, Austl. D4 60
Kilgore, Tx., U.S. C5 136
Kilibo, Benin E5 50
Kiliia, Ukr. G10 20
Kilimanjaro, mtn., Tan. . . D7 54
Kilimli, Tur. B4 44
Kilindoni, Tan. E7 54
Kilis, Tur. D7 44
Kilkenny, Ire. D3 12
Kilkís, Grc. D9 18
Killaloe Station, On., Can. . B7 89
Killam, Ab., Can. C5 84
Killarney, Mb., Can. E2 86
Killarney Provincial Park, On., Can. A3 89
Killdeer, N.D., U.S. B3 127
Killeen, Tx., U.S. D4 136
Killen, Al., U.S. A2 94
Killian, La., U.S. h10 111
Killik, stm., Ak., U.S. B9 95
Killiniq Island, i., Can. . . . F27 82
Killona, La., U.S. h11 111
Kilmarnock, Scot., U.K. . . C4 12
Kilmarnock, Va., U.S. . . . C6 139
Kilmichael, Ms., U.S. B4 117
Kiln, Ms., U.S. E4 117
Kilomines, D.R.C. C6 54
Kilosa, Tan. E7 54
Kilttān Island, i., India . . . G2 40
Kilwa, D.R.C. D5 54
Kilwa Kivinje, Tan. E7 54
Kimba, Austl. G2 62
Kimball, Mn., U.S. E4 116
Kimball, Ne., U.S. C2 120
Kimball, S.D., U.S. D7 134
Kimball, co., Ne., U.S. . . . C2 120
Kimball, Mount, mtn., Ak., U.S. C11 95
Kimberley, B.C., Can. . . . E9 85
Kimberley, S. Afr. D3 56

Kimberley Plateau, plat., Austl. D4 60
Kimberlin Heights, Tn., U.S. n14 135
Kimberly, Al., U.S. B3 94
Kimberly, Id., U.S. G4 105
Kimberly, W.V., U.S. m13 141
Kimberly, Wi., U.S. h9 142
Kimble, co., Tx., U.S. D3 136
Kimch'aek, N. Kor. C13 28
Kimito, i., Fin. G10 10
Kimry, Russia C6 22
Kinabalu, Gunong, mtn., Malay. B5 36
Kinabatangan, stm., Malay. B5 36
Kinbasket Lake, res., B.C., Can. D8 85
Kincaid, Il., U.S. D4 106
Kincaid, W.V., U.S. m13 141
Kincaid, Lake, res., Il., U.S. D4 106
Kincardine, On., Can. . . . C3 89
Kincheloe Air Force Base, mil., Mi., U.S. B6 115
Kinda, D.R.C. E5 54
Kinder, La., U.S. D3 111
Kindia, Gui. D2 50
Kindu, D.R.C. D5 54
Kinešma, Russia C7 22
King, N.C., U.S. A2 126
King, Wi., U.S. D4 142
King, co., Tx., U.S. C2 136
King, co., Wa., U.S. B3 140
King and Queen, co., Va., U.S. C6 139
Kingaroy, Austl. F5 62
King City, Ca., U.S. D3 98
King City, Mo., U.S. A3 118
King Cove, Ak., U.S. E7 95
Kingfield, Me., U.S. D2 112
Kingfisher, Ok., U.S. B4 129
Kingfisher, co., Ok., U.S. . B3 129
King George, co., Va., U.S. B5 139
Kingisepp, Russia G13 10
King Island, i., Austl. H3 62
King Island, i., B.C., Can. . C4 85
King Lear Peak, mtn., Nv., U.S. B3 121
King Leopold Ranges, mts., Austl. D3 60
Kingman, Az., U.S. B1 96
Kingman, Ks., U.S. E5 109
Kingman, co., Ks., U.S. . . E5 109
King Mountain, mtn., Or., U.S. D8 130
King Mountain, mtn., Or., U.S. E3 130
Kingombe, D.R.C. D5 54
King Peak, mtn., Ca., U.S. . B1 98
Kings, Ms., U.S. C3 117
Kings, co., Ca., U.S. D4 98
Kings, co., N.Y., U.S. E7 125
Kings, stm., Ar., U.S. A2 97
Kings, stm., Ca., U.S. D4 98
Kings, stm., Nv., U.S. B3 121
King Salmon, Ak., U.S. . . D8 95
Kingsburg, Ca., U.S. D4 98
Kingsbury, co., S.D., U.S. . C8 134
Kings Canyon National Park, Ca., U.S. D4 98
Kingsey-Falls, P.Q., Can. . D5 90
Kingsford, Mi., U.S. C2 115
Kingsland, Ga., U.S. F5 103
Kingsland, Tx., U.S. D3 136
Kingsley, Ia., U.S. B2 108
Kingsley, Mi., U.S. D5 115
King's Lynn, Eng., U.K. . . D7 12
Kings Mountain, N.C., U.S. B1 126
King Sound, strt., Austl. . . D3 60
Kings Peak, mtn., Ut., U.S. C5 137
King's Point, Nf., Can. . . . D3 88
Kingsport, Tn., U.S. C11 135
Kingston, On., Can. C8 89
Kingston, Jam. B4 80
Kingston, Ga., U.S. B2 103
Kingston, Id., U.S. B2 105
Kingston, Ma., U.S. C6 114
Kingston, N.H., U.S. E4 122
Kingston, N.Y., U.S. D6 125
Kingston, Oh., U.S. C3 128
Kingston, Ok., U.S. D5 129
Kingston, Pa., U.S. D10 131
Kingston, R.I., U.S. F3 132
Kingston, Tn., U.S. D9 135
Kingston Springs, Tn., U.S. A4 135
Kingston upon Hull, Eng., U.K. D6 12
Kingstown see Dún Laoghaire, Ire. D3 12
Kingstown, St. Vin. C7 80
Kingstown, Md., U.S. B5 113
Kingstree, S.C., U.S. D8 133
Kingsville, On., Can. E2 89
Kingsville, Md., U.S. B5 113
Kingsville (North Kingsville), Oh., U.S. A5 128
Kingsville, Tx., U.S. F4 136
Kingsville Naval Air Station, mil., Tx., U.S. F4 136
King William, co., Va., U.S. C5 139
King William's Town, S. Afr. E4 56
Kingwood, W.V., U.S. B5 141
Kinistino, Sk., Can. E3 91
Kinkaid Lake, res., Il., U.S. F4 106
Kinkala, Congo D2 54
Kinloch, Mo., U.S. f13 118
Kinmundy, Il., U.S. E5 106

Kinnaird Head, c., Scot., U.K. B6 12
Kinnelon, N.J., U.S. B4 123
Kinney, co., Tx., U.S. E2 136
Kinsey, Al., U.S. D4 94
Kinshasa, D.R.C. D3 54
Kinsley, Ks., U.S. E4 109
Kinston, N.C., U.S. B5 126
Kintampo, Ghana E4 50
Kintyre, pen., Scot., U.K. . C4 12
Kinyeti, mtn., Sudan J11 48
Kinzia, D.R.C. D3 54
Kiowa, Ks., U.S. E5 109
Kiowa, Ok., U.S. C6 129
Kiowa, co., Co., U.S. C8 99
Kiowa, co., Ks., U.S. E4 109
Kiowa, co., Ok., U.S. C2 129
Kiowa Creek, stm., Ok., U.S. A1 129
Kiparissiakós Kólpos, b., Grc. F8 18
Kipembawe, Tan. E6 54
Kipengere Range, mts., Tan. E6 54
Kipili, Tan. E6 54
Kipini, Kenya D8 54
Kipnuk, Ak., U.S. C7 95
Kipushi, D.R.C. F5 54
Kirbyville, Tx., U.S. D6 136
Kirensk, Russia D12 26
Kirgiz Range, mts., Asia . . A2 40
Kiri, D.R.C. D3 54
Kiribati, ctry., Oc. E12 58
Kiribati, i., Kir. D11 58
Kırıkhan, Tur. D7 44
Kırıkkale, Tur. C5 44
Kirinyaga (Kenya, Mount), mtn., Kenya D7 54
Kiriši, Russia C5 22
Kiritimati (Christmas Island), atoll, Kir. D14 58
Kırkağaç, Tur. C2 44
Kirkcaldy, Scot., U.K. B5 12
Kirkenes, Nor. B14 10
Kirkjubœjarklaustur, Ice. . m19 6
Kirkland, Il., U.S. A5 106
Kirkland, Wa., U.S. B3 140
Kirkland Lake, On., Can. . o19 89
Kırklareli, Tur. B2 44
Kirklin, In., U.S. D5 107
Kirkpatrick, Mount, mtn., Ant. E22 67
Kirksville, Mo., U.S. A5 118
Kirkwall, Scot., U.K. A5 12
Kirkwood, S. Afr. E4 56
Kirkwood, De., U.S. B3 101
Kirkwood, Il., U.S. C3 106
Kirkwood, Mo., U.S. f13 118
Kirov, Russia B13 20
Kirov, Russia D6 22
Kirovabad see Gäncä, Azer. B12 44
Kirovakan see Vanadzor, Arm. B11 44
Kirovohrad, Ukr. E12 20
Kirovsk, Russia A5 22
Kirovsk, Turk. C8 42
Kirovskij, Russia D17 26
Kirovskij, Russia A2 31
Kirs, Russia C9 22
Kirsanov, Russia D7 22
Kırşehir, Tur. C6 44
Kīrthar Range, mts., Pak. . E9 42
Kirtland, N.M., U.S. A1 124
Kirtland Air Force Base, mil., N.M., U.S. k7 124
Kiruna, Swe. C9 10
Kirwin Reservoir, res., Ks., U.S. C4 109
Kisangani, D.R.C. C5 54
Kisar, Pulau, i., Indon. . . . E7 36
Kisaran, Indon. C1 36
Kishangarh Bās, India . . . D2 40
Kishi, Nig. E5 50
Kishinev see Chişinău, Mol. F10 20
Kishiwada, Japan D3 31
Kishwaukee, stm., Il., U.S. A5 106
Kisii, Kenya D6 54
Kisiju, Tan. E7 54
Kiska Island, i., Ak., U.S. . E3 95
Kiskunfélegyháza, Hung. . F5 20
Kiskunhalas, Hung. F5 20
Kislovodsk, Russia B4 42
Kismaayo, Som. D8 54
Kissidougou, Gui. D2 50
Kissimmee, Fl., U.S. D5 102
Kissimmee, stm., Fl., U.S. . E5 102
Kissimmee, Lake, l., Fl., U.S. E5 102
Kississing Lake, l., Mb., Can. B1 86
Kistler, W.V., U.S. D3 141
Kisumu, Kenya D6 54
Kisvárda, Hung. E7 20
Kita, Mali D3 50
Kitaibaraki, Japan C4 31
Kitakyūshū, Japan E14 28
Kitale, Kenya C7 54
Kitami, Japan B4 31
Kit Carson, co., Co., U.S. . B8 99
Kitchener, On., Can. D4 89
Kíthira, i., Grc. F9 18
Kíthnos, i., Grc. F10 18
Kitimat, B.C., Can. B3 85
Kitsap, co., Wa., U.S. B3 140
Kitscoty, Ab., Can. C5 84
Kittanning, Pa., U.S. E2 131
Kittatinny Mountain, mtn., U.S. B2 123

Kittery, Me., U.S. E2 112
Kittery Point, Me., U.S. . . E2 112
Kittitas, Wa., U.S. C5 140
Kittitas, co., Wa., U.S. . . . B4 140
Kitts, Ky., U.S. D6 110
Kitty Hawk, N.C., U.S. . . . A7 126
Kitty Hawk Bay, b., N.C., U.S. A7 126
Kittson, co., Mn., U.S. . . . B2 116
Kitui, Kenya D7 54
Kitwe, Zam. A4 56
Kiunga, Kenya D8 54
Kiviõli, Est. G12 10
Kivu, Lac, l., Afr. D5 54
Kizëma, Russia B7 22
Kızılcahamam, Tur. B5 44
Kızılırmak, stm., Tur. B6 44
Kızıltepe, Tur. D9 44
Kizljar, Russia B5 42
Kizyl-Atrek, Turk. C6 42
Kjusjur, Russia B14 26
Kjustendil, Bul. C9 18
Klabat, Gunung, vol., Indon. C7 36
Kladno, Czech Rep. D3 20
Klagenfurt, Aus. G14 12
Klaipėda, Lith. I9 10
Klamath, co., Or., U.S. . . . E5 130
Klamath, stm., U.S. B2 98
Klamath Falls, Or., U.S. . . E5 130
Klamath Mountains, mts., U.S. E2 130
Klang, Malay. C2 36
Klatovy, Czech Rep. E2 20
Klawer, S. Afr. E2 56
Klawock, Ak., U.S. D13 95
Kleberg, co., Tx., U.S. . . . F4 136
Klerksdorp, S. Afr. D4 56
Kletna, Russia C12 22
Klickitat, Wa., U.S. D4 140
Klickitat, co., Wa., U.S. . . D4 140
Klickitat, stm., Wa., U.S. . . C4 140
Klimpfjäll, Swe. D6 10
Klin, Russia C6 22
Klincy, Russia C12 20
Klipplaat, S. Afr. E3 56
Ključevskaja Sopka, vulkan, vol., Russia D18 26
Kłobuck, Pol. D5 20
Kłodzko, Pol. D4 20
Klondike, hist. reg., Yk., Can. F12 82
Klondike Gold Rush National Historical Park, Ak., U.S. k22 95
Kluczbork, Pol. D5 20
Klutina Lake, l., Ak., U.S. . g19 95
Knapp Creek, stm., W.V., U.S. C5 141
Knee Lake, l., Mb., Can. . . B4 86
Kneža, Bul. C10 18
Knife, stm., N.D., U.S. . . . B3 127
Knightdale, N.C., U.S. . . . B4 126
Knight Inlet, b., B.C., Can. . D5 85
Knight Island, i., Ak., U.S. . g18 95
Knightstown, In., U.S. . . . E6 107
Knightsville, In., U.S. E3 107
Knightville Reservoir, res., Ma., U.S. B2 114
Knittelfeld, Aus. G14 12
Knob Noster, Mo., U.S. . . C4 118
Knollwood, W.V., U.S. . . . m12 141
Knossós, hist., Grc. G10 18
Knott, co., Ky., U.S. C6 110
Knox, In., U.S. B4 107
Knox, Pa., U.S. D2 131
Knox, co., Il., U.S. B3 106
Knox, co., In., U.S. G3 107
Knox, co., Ky., U.S. D6 110
Knox, co., Me., U.S. D3 112
Knox, co., Mo., U.S. A5 118
Knox, co., Ne., U.S. B8 120
Knox, co., Oh., U.S. B3 128
Knox, co., Tn., U.S. C10 135
Knox, co., Tx., U.S. C3 136
Knox, Cape, c., B.C., Can. . B1 85
Knox City, Tx., U.S. C3 136
Knox Coast, Ant. C15 67
Knoxville, Ia., U.S. C4 108
Knoxville, Il., U.S. B3 106
Knoxville, Tn., U.S. D10 135
Knysna, S. Afr. E3 56
Kōbe, Japan E15 28
København (Copenhagen), Den. I5 10
Koblenz, Ger. E10 12
Kobroor, Pulau, i., Indon. . H9 32
Kobryn, Bela. C8 20
Kobuk, stm., Ak., U.S. . . . B8 95
Kobuk Valley National Park, Ak., U.S. B8 95
Kočani, Mac. D9 18
Kočevo, Russia C9 22
Kochi (Cochin), India . . . H3 40
Kōchi, Japan E14 28
Koch Peak, mtn., Mt., U.S. E5 119
Kodaikānal, India G3 40
Kodiak, Ak., U.S. D9 95
Kodiak Island, i., Ak., U.S. . D9 95
Kodok, Sudan B6 54
Koës, Nmb. D2 56
Kofa Mountains, mts., Az., U.S. D2 96
Köflach, Aus. G14 12
Koforidua, Ghana E4 50
Kōfu, Japan D15 28

Name	Map Ref.	Page
Kogaluk, stm., Nf., Can.	g9	88
Køge, Den.	I5	10
Kohala Mountains, mts., Hi., U.S.	C6	104
Kohāt, Pak.	D10	42
Kohīma, India	D6	40
Kohler, Wi., U.S.	E6	142
Kohtla-Järve, Est.	G12	10
Koihoa, India	H6	40
Koindu, S.L.	E2	50
Kojgorodok, Russia	B9	22
Kojonup, Austl.	G2	60
Kokand, Uzb.	E9	26
Kokanee Glacier Provincial Park, B.C., Can.	E9	85
Kokčetav, Kaz.	D8	26
Kokemäki, Fin.	F10	10
Kokenau, Indon.	G10	32
Kokkola, Fin.	E10	10
Kokoda, Pap. N. Gui.	H12	32
Koko Head, c., Hi., U.S.	B4	104
Kokolik, stm., Ak., U.S.	B7	95
Kokomo, In., U.S.	D5	107
Koko Nor see Qinghai Hu, l., China	D8	28
Kokosing, stm., Oh., U.S.	B3	128
Kokstad, S. Afr.	E4	56
Kola, Russia	B15	10
Kolaka, Indon.	D6	36
Kola Peninsula see Kol'skij poluostrov, pen., Russia	C5	26
Kolār Gold Fields, India	G3	40
Kolbio, Kenya	D8	54
Kolda, Sen.	D2	50
Kolding, Den.	I3	10
Kole, D.R.C.	D4	54
Kolea, Alg.	I8	14
Kolguev, ostrov, i., Russia	C6	26
Kolhāpur, India	F2	40
Kolka, Lat.	H10	10
Kolmogorovo, Russia	D11	26
Köln (Cologne), Ger.	E10	12
Koło, Pol.	C5	20
Koloa, Hi., U.S.	B2	104
Kołobrzeg, Pol.	B3	20
Kolokani, Mali	D3	50
Kolomna, Russia	D5	26
Kolonia, Micron.	D9	58
Kolonodale, Indon.	D6	36
Kolpaševo, Russia	D10	26
Kolpino, Russia	C5	22
Kol'skij poluostrov, pen., Russia	C5	26
Kolwezi, D.R.C.	F5	54
Kolyma, stm., Russia	C17	26
Kolymskaja, Russia	C17	26
Komandorskie ostrova, is., Russia	D18	26
Komandorski Islands see Komandorskie ostrova, is., Russia	D18	26
Komárno, Slvk.	F5	20
Komatipoort, S. Afr.	D5	56
Kome Island, i., Ug.	D6	54
Komi, state, Russia	C7	26
Komló, Hung.	F5	20
Kommunarsk see Alchevs'k, Ukr.	E15	20
Kommunizma, pik, mtn., Taj.	F9	26
Komodo, Pulau, i., Indon.	E5	36
Komoé, stm., Afr.	E4	50
Komotiní, Grc.	D10	18
Komsomolec, Kaz.	D11	22
Komsomolec, ostrov, i., Russia	A11	26
Komsomol'sk-na-Amure, Russia	D15	26
Konahuanui, Puu, mtn., Hi., U.S.	g10	104
Konārak, hist., India	F5	40
Konawa, Ok., U.S.	C5	129
Kondagaon, India	F4	40
Kondinin, Austl.	G2	60
Kondoa, Tan.	D7	54
Kondopoga, Russia	C5	26
Kondūz, Afg.	C9	42
Koné, N. Cal.	I8	62a
Kong, stm., Asia	C5	34
Kongolo, D.R.C.	E5	54
Kongor, Sudan	B6	54
Kongsvinger, Nor.	F5	10
Kongur Shan, mtn., China	D3	28
Königsberg see Kaliningrad, Russia	D4	26
Konin, Pol.	C5	20
Konna, Mali	D4	50
Konomoc, Lake, res., Ct., U.S.	D7	100
Konoša, Russia	C6	26
Konotop, Ukr.	D12	20
Konstanz, Ger.	G11	12
Kontagora, Nig.	D6	50
Kontcha, Cam.	B2	54
Kon Tum, Viet.	D5	34
Konya, Tur.	D5	44
Konza, Kenya	D7	54
Konžakovskij Kamen', gora, mtn., Russia	C10	22
Koochiching, co., Mn., U.S.	B4	116
Kookynie, Austl.	F3	60
Koolau Range, mts., Hi., U.S.	f10	104
Koontz Lake, In., U.S.	B5	107
Kooskia, Id., U.S.	C3	105
Kootenai, co., Id., U.S.	B2	105
Kootenay Lake, l., B.C., Can.	E9	85
Kootenay National Park, B.C., Can.	D9	85
Kópasker, Ice.	k20	10a
Kópavogur, Ice.	l18	10a
Kopejsk, Russia	C11	22
Kopet Mountains, mts., Asia	C7	42
Köping, Swe.	G6	10
Koppang, Nor.	F4	10
Koppel, Pa., U.S.	E1	131
Koprivnica, Cro.	A6	18
Korab (Korabit, Maja e), mtn., Eur.	D8	18
Korabit, Maja e (Korab), mtn., Eur.	D8	18
Korāput, India	F4	40
Korba, India	E4	40
Korbol, Chad	D8	50
Korçë, Alb.	D8	18
Korea, North, ctry., Asia	C13	28
Korea, South, ctry., Asia	D10	28
Korea Bay, b., Asia	D12	28
Korea Strait, strt., Asia	E13	28
Korenovsk, Russia	A3	42
Korf, Russia	C18	26
Korfovskij, Russia	A3	31
Korhogo, C. Iv.	E3	50
Korinthiakós Kólpos, b., Grc.	E9	18
Kórinthos, Grc.	F9	18
Kōriyama, Japan	C4	31
Korjakskaja Sopka, vulkan, vol., Russia	D17	26
Korjakskoe nagor'e, mts., Russia	C18	26
Korjažma, Russia	B8	22
Korkino, Russia	D11	22
Korkuteli, Tur.	D4	44
Korla, China	C5	28
Korliki, Russia	C10	26
Kornat, Otok, i., Cro.	C5	18
Korogwe, Tan.	E7	54
Koronadal, Phil.	E8	34
Koronis, Lake, l., Mn., U.S.	E4	116
Koror, Palau	D9	32
Koro Sea, Fiji	F12	58
Korosten', Ukr.	D10	20
Korostyshiv, Ukr.	D10	20
Korovin Volcano, vol., Ak., U.S.	E5	95
Korsakov, Russia	E16	26
Korsnäs, Fin.	E9	10
Kos, i., Grc.	F11	18
Koš-Agač, Russia	D10	26
Koščagyl, Kaz.	A6	42
Kościan, Pol.	C4	20
Kościerzyna, Pol.	B4	20
Kosciusko, Ms., U.S.	B4	117
Kosciusko, co., In., U.S.	B6	107
Kosciusko, Mount, mtn., Austl.	H4	62
Koshkonong, Lake, l., Wi., U.S.	F5	142
Košice, Slvk.	E6	20
Kosju, Russia	A13	22
Koslan, Russia	B8	22
Kosovska Mitrovica, Yugo.	C8	18
Kossou, Lac de, res., C. Iv.	E3	50
Kossuth, co., Ia., U.S.	A3	108
Kostjantynivka, Ukr.	E14	·20
Kostopil', Ukr.	D9	20
Kostroma, Russia	C7	22
Kostrzyn, Pol.	C3	20
Koszalin, Pol.	B4	20
Kőszeg, Hung.	F4	20
Kota, India	D3	40
Kotaagung, Indon.	E2	36
Kotabaru see Jayapura, Indon.	G11	32
Kotabaru, Indon.	G6	32
Kota Belud, Malay.	B5	36
Kota Bharu, Malay.	B2	36
Kota Kinabalu, Malay.	B5	36
Kotamobagu, Indon.	C6	36
Kotel'nič, Russia	C8	22
Kotel'nikovo, Russia	E7	22
Kotel'nyj, ostrov, i., Russia	B15	26
Kotido, Ug.	C6	54
Kotka, Fin.	F12	10
Kot Kapūra, India	C2	40
Kotlas, Russia	C6	26
Kotlik, Ak., U.S.	C7	95
Kotovs'k, Ukr.	F10	20
Kotri, Pak.	E9	42
Kottagūdem, India	F4	40
Kottayam, India	H3	40
Kotte see Sri Jayawardenepura, Sri L.	H4	40
Kotto, stm., C.A.R.	B4	54
Kotuj, stm., Russia	C12	26
Kotzebue, Ak., U.S.	B7	95
Kotzebue Sound, strt., Ak., U.S.	B7	95
Kouchibouguac National Park, N.B., Can.	C5	87
Koudougou, Burkina	D4	50
Kouki, C.A.R.	B3	54
Koulamoutou, Gabon	D2	54
Koulikoro, Mali	D3	50
Koumac, N. Cal.	I8	62a
Koumbia, Gui.	D2	50
Koumra, Chad	E8	50
Koundâra, Gui.	D2	50
Kounradskij, Kaz.	B2	28
Kountze, Tx., U.S.	D5	136
Kourou, Fr. Gu.	B9	70
Kouroussa, Gui.	D3	50
Kousséri, Cam.	D8	50
Koussi, Emi, mtn., Chad	C8	50
Koutiala, Mali	D3	50
Kouts, In., U.S.	B3	107
Kouvola, Fin.	F12	10
Kovdozero, ozero, res., Russia	C15	10
Kovel', Ukr.	D8	20
Kovrov, Russia	C7	22
Kowloon see Jiulong, China	E3	30
Koyukuk, stm., Ak., U.S.	B8	95
Kozan, Tur.	D6	44
Kozáni, Grc.	D8	18
Kozhikode (Calicut), India	G3	40
Koziatyn, Ukr.	E10	20
Kozlu, Tur.	B4	44
Kpalimé, Togo	E5	50
Kra, Isthmus of, Asia	D3	34
Krâchéh, Camb.	D5	34
Kragerø, Nor.	G3	10
Kragujevac, Yugo.	B8	18
Kraków, Pol.	D5	20
Kralendijk, Neth. Ant.	C6	80
Kraljevo, Yugo.	C8	18
Kramators'k, Ukr.	E14	20
Kramfors, Swe.	E7	10
Kranj, Slvn.	A5	18
Kraśnik, Pol.	D7	20
Krasnoarmiis'k, Ukr.	E14	20
Krasnodar, Russia	E5	26
Krasnogorsk, Russia	B16	28
Krasnohrad, Ukr.	E13	20
Krasnojarsk, Russia	D11	26
Krasnoperekops'k, Ukr.	G12	20
Krasnosel'kup, Russia	C10	26
Krasnoturjinsk, Russia	C11	22
Krasnoufimsk, Russia	C10	22
Krasnoural'sk, Russia	D8	26
Krasnovišersk, Russia	B10	22
Krasnovodsk see Turkmenbaši, Turk.	E7	26
Krasnoyarsk see Krasnojarsk, Russia	D11	26
Krasnoznamenskoje, Kaz.	D8	26
Krasnyi Luch, Ukr.	E15	20
Krasnystaw, Pol.	D7	20
Krasyliv, Ukr.	E9	20
Krebs, Ok., U.S.	C6	129
Kremenchug Reservoir see Kremenchuts'ke vodoskhovyshche, res., Ukr.	E12	20
Kremenchuk, Ukr.	E12	20
Kremenchuts'ke vodoskhovyshche, res., Ukr.	E12	20
Kremenets', Ukr.	D8	20
Kremmling, Co., U.S.	A4	99
Kretinga, Lith.	I9	10
Kreuztal, Ger.	E11	12
Kribi, Cam.	C1	54
Krishna, stm., India	F3	40
Krishnanagar, India	E5	40
Kristiansand, Nor.	G3	10
Kristianstad, Swe.	I6	10
Kristiansund, Nor.	E2	10
Kristiinankaupunki, Fin.	E9	10
Kristineberg, Swe.	D8	10
Kristinehamn, Swe.	G6	10
Kríti (Crete), i., Grc.	G10	18
Kritikón Pélagos, Grc.	G10	18
Krjukovo, Russia	C17	26
Krk, Otok, i., Cro.	B5	18
Krnov, Czech Rep.	D4	20
Kroměříž, Czech Rep.	E4	20
Krŏng Kaôh Kŏng, Camb.	D4	34
Kronštadt, Russia	B4	22
Kroonstad, S. Afr.	D4	56
Kropotkin, Russia	A4	42
Krosno, Pol.	E6	20
Krotoszyn, Pol.	D4	20
Krotz Springs, La., U.S.	D4	111
Krugersdorp, S. Afr.	D4	56
Krui, Indon.	E2	36
Krung Thep (Bangkok), Thai.	D4	34
Kruševac, Yugo.	C8	18
Kruzof Island, i., Ak., U.S.	m21	95
Kryčaŭ, Bela.	C11	20
Krymsk, Russia	G14	20
Kryms'ki hory, mts., Ukr.	G13	20
Kryms'kyi pivostriv (Crimean Peninsula), pen., Ukr.	G12	20
Kryvyi Rih, Ukr.	F12	20
Ksar-el-Kebir, Mor.	J4	16
Ksenevka, Russia	A11	28
Kšenskij, Russia	D14	20
Kuala Kangsar, Malay.	C2	36
Kualakapuas, Indon.	D4	36
Kuala Krai, Malay.	B2	36
Kuala Lipis, Malay.	C2	36
Kuala Lumpur, Malay.	C2	36
Kuala Pilah, Malay.	C2	36
Kuala Terengganu, Malay.	B2	36
Kuantan, Malay.	C2	36
Kuban', stm., Russia	E6	26
Kuching, Malay.	C4	36
Kuçovë, Alb.	D8	18
Kudat, Malay.	B5	36
Kudus, Indon.	E4	36
Kudymkar, Russia	C9	22
Kuee Ruins, hist., Hi., U.S.	D6	104
Kufstein, Aus.	G13	12
Kūhdasht, Iran	F12	44
Kuito, Ang.	F3	54
Kuiu Island, i., Ak., U.S.	m23	95
Kujawy, reg., Pol.	C5	20
Kujbyšev see Samara, Russia	D7	26
Kujbyšev, Russia	D9	26
Kujbyševskoe vodohranilišče, res., Russia	D8	22
Kujgan, Kaz.	A10	42
Kujū-san, vol., Japan	D2	31
Kukawa, Nig.	D7	50
Kula, Tur.	C3	44
Kula, Hi., U.S.	C5	104
Kula Kangri, mtn., Bhu.	D6	40
Kulab see Kuljab, Taj.	F8	26
Kule, Bots.	C3	56
Kulebaki, Russia	C7	22
Kuljab, Taj.	F8	26
Kulmbach, Ger.	E12	12
Kuloj, Russia	B7	22
Kulpmont, Pa., U.S.	E9	131
Kul'sary, Kaz.	E7	26
Kulu, Tur.	C5	44
Kulumadau, Pap. N. Gui.	H13	32
Kumagaya, Japan	C3	31
Kumai, Indon.	D4	36
Kumai, Teluk, b., Indon.	D4	36
Kumamoto, Japan	E14	28
Kumanovo, Mac.	C8	18
Kumasi, Ghana	E4	50
Kumba, Cam.	C1	54
Kumbakonam, India	G3	40
Kume-jima, i., Japan	A9	34
Kuminskij, Russia	C12	22
Kumluca, Tur.	D4	44
Kumo, Nig.	E7	50
Kumta, India	G2	40
Kumukahi, Cape, c., Hi., U.S.	D7	104
Kuna, Id., U.S.	F2	105
Kunašir, ostrov, i., Russia	E16	26
Kunda, S.L.	G12	10
Kundāpura, India	G2	40
Kundur, Pulau, i., Indon.	C2	36
Kunene (Cunene), stm., Afr.	B1	56
Kunghit Island, i., B.C., Can.	C2	85
Kungrad, Uzb.	B7	42
Kungur, Russia	C10	22
Kunhing, Myan.	B3	34
Kunlun Shan, mts., China	D5	28
Kunming, China	F8	28
Kununurra, Austl.	D4	60
Kunya, Nig.	D6	50
Kuopio, Fin.	E12	10
Kupang, Indon.	F6	36
Kup'ians'k, Ukr.	E14	20
Kupreanof Island, i., Ak., U.S.	m23	95
Kuqa, China	C4	28
Kuqa, China	C4	28
Kūr, stm., Asia	C13	44
Kurashiki, Japan	D2	31
Kuraymah, Sudan	G11	48
Kurčatov, Russia	D13	20
Kürdämir, Azer.	B13	44
Kure, Japan	D2	31
Kure Island, i., Hi., U.S.	k12	104
Kureika, stm., Russia	C10	26
Kuressaare, Est.	G10	10
Kurgan, Russia	D8	26
Kurgan-Tjube, Taj.	C9	42
Kuril Islands see Kuril'skie ostrova, is., Russia	E16	26
Kuril'sk, Russia	B17	28
Kuril'skie ostrova (Kuril Islands), is., Russia	E16	26
Kuril Trench	A7	144
Kurmuk, Sudan	H11	48
Kurnool, India	F3	40
Kursk, Russia	D5	26
Kurtalan, Tur.	D9	44
Kurtamyš, Russia	D11	22
Kurtistown, Hi., U.S.	D6	104
Kuruman, S. Afr.	D3	56
Kuruman, stm., S. Afr.	D3	56
Kurume, Japan	D2	31
Kurumkan, Russia	D13	26
Kurunegala, Sri L.	H4	40
Kuşadasi, Tur.	D2	44
Kuşadası Körfezi, b., Tur.	D2	44
Kuševskaja, Russia	F15	20
Kuş Gölü, l., Tur.	B2	44
Kushiro, Japan	C16	28
Kushui, China	C6	28
Kuskokwim, stm., Ak., U.S.	C8	95
Kuskokwim Bay, b., Ak., U.S.	D7	95
Kuskokwim Mountains, mts., Ak., U.S.	C8	95
Kustanaj, Kaz.	D6	26
Kūstī, Sudan	H11	48
Kut, Ko, i., Thai.	D4	34
Kütahya, Tur.	C3	44
Kutaisi, Geor.	A10	44
Kutch, Gulf of see Kachchh, Gulf of, b., India	E1	40
Kutch, Gulf of see Kachchh, Gulf of, b., India	E1	40
Kutch, Rann of, reg., Asia	E1	40
Kutina, Cro.	B6	18
Kutno, Pol.	C5	20
Kutu, D.R.C.	D3	54
Kutztown, Pa., U.S.	E10	131
Kuujjuaq, P.Q., Can.	g13	90
Kuusamo, Fin.	D13	10
Kuusankoski, Fin.	F12	10
Kuvango, Ang.	A2	56
Kuwait see Al-Kuwayt, Kuw.	E5	42
Kuwait, ctry., Asia	E5	42
Kuybyshev see Kujbyšev, Russia	D9	26
Kuybyshev see Samara, Russia	D7	26
Kuybyshev Reservoir see Kujbyševskoe vodohranilišče, res., Russia	D8	22
Kuz'movka, Russia	C11	26
Kuzneck, Russia	D6	26
Kuzomen', Russia	A6	22
Kvænangen, b., Nor.	A9	10
Kvaløya, i., Nor.	B8	10
Kvareli, Geor.	B11	44
Kwa, stm., D.R.C.	D3	54
Kwakoegron, Sur.	B8	70
Kwamouth, D.R.C.	D3	54
Kwando (Cuando), stm., Afr.	B3	56
Kwangju, S. Kor.	D13	28
Kwango (Cuango), stm., Afr.	D3	54
Kwangsi Chuang see Guangxi Zhuangzu Zizhiqu, state, China	G9	28
Kwekwe, Zimb.	B4	56
Kwenge, stm., Afr.	E3	54
Kwethluk, Ak., U.S.	C7	95
Kwidzyn, Pol.	C5	20
Kwigillingok, Ak., U.S.	D7	95
Kwilu (Cuilo), stm., Afr.	D3	54
Kyaikto, Myan.	C3	34
Kyaikkyi, Myan.	C3	34
Kyaukme, Myan.	B3	34
Kyaukpyu, Myan.	C2	34
Kyaukse, Myan.	B3	34
Kyaunggon, Myan.	C3	34
Kyauktaw, Myan.	B2	34
Kyïv (Kiev), Ukr.	D11	20
Kyïv's'ke vodoskhovyshche, res., Ukr.	D11	20
Kyle, Tx., U.S.	E4	136
Kyoga, Lake, l., Ug.	C6	54
Kyŏngju, S. Kor.	C1	31
Kyŏngsŏng-ŭp, N. Kor.	B1	31
Kyōto, Japan	D15	28
Kyrgyzstan, ctry., Asia	A2	40
Kyštovka, Russia	D9	26
Kyštym, Russia	C11	22
Kyuquot Sound, strt., B.C., Can.	E4	85
Kyūshū, i., Japan	E14	28
Kyushu-Palau Ridge	G16	64
Kyyiv see Kyïv, Ukr.	D11	20
Kyyjärvi, Fin.	E11	10
Kyzyl, Russia	D11	26
Kyzylkum, des., Asia	B8	42
Kzyl-Orda, Kaz.	E8	26
Kzyltu, Kaz.	D9	26

L

Name	Map Ref.	Page
Laascaanood, Som.	I14	48
La Asunción, Ven.	C7	80
Laau Point, c., Hi., U.S.	B4	104
Laayoune see El Aaiún, W. Sah.	A2	50
Labadieville, La., U.S.	E5	111
La Bañeza, Spain	F4	16
La Barca, Mex.	C4	78
La Barge, Wy., U.S.	D2	143
La Barge Creek, stm., Wy., U.S.	D2	143
La Baule-Escoublac, Fr.	D5	16
Labé, Gui.	D2	50
Labe, stm., Eur.	E14	12
La Belle, Fl., U.S.	F5	102
La Belle, Mo., U.S.	A6	118
Labette, co., Ks., U.S.	E8	109
Labinsk, Russia	B4	42
Labis, Malay.	C2	36
Laboulaye, Arg.	E5	72
Labrador, reg., Nf., Can.	g9	88
Labrador Basin	B28	144
Labrador City, Nf., Can.	h8	88
Labrador Sea, N.A.	F29	57
Lábrea, Braz.	E7	70
Labuan, Malay.	B5	36
Labuan, Pulau, i., Malay.	B5	36
Labuha, Indon.	G8	32
Labuhanbajo, Indon.	E5	36
Labytnangi, Russia	A12	22
Laç, Alb.	D7	18
La Canada Flintridge, Ca., U.S.	m12	98
La Carlota, Arg.	E5	72
La Carlota, Phil.	D8	34
La Carolina, Spain	H5	16
Lac-Bouchette, P.Q., Can.	A5	90
Lac-Brome, P.Q., Can.	D5	90
Laccadive, Minicoy and Amīndīvi Islands see Lakshadweep, prov., India	G2	40
Laccadive Islands see Lakshadweep, is., India	G2	40
Lac-Carré, P.Q., Can.	C3	90

Name	Map Ref.	Page
Lac Courte Oreilles Indian Reservation, Wi., U.S.	C2	142
Lac du Bonnet, Mb., Can.	D3	86
Lac du Flambeau, Wi., U.S.	B4	142
Lac du Flambeau Indian Reservation, Wi., U.S.	C3	142
La Ceiba, Hond.	B2	80
La Center, Ky., U.S.	e9	110
Lac-Etchemin, P.Q., Can.	C7	90
Lacey, Wa., U.S.	B3	140
La Chaux-de-Fonds, Switz.	A1	18
Lachine, P.Q., Can.	D4	90
La Chorrera, Col.	D5	70
La Chorrera, Pan.	D3	80
Lachute, P.Q., Can.	D3	90
La Citadelle, hist., Haiti	B5	80
Lackawanna, N.Y., U.S.	C2	125
Lackawanna, co., Pa., U.S.	D10	131
Lackland Air Force Base, mil., Tx., U.S.	k7	136
Lac La Biche, Ab., Can.	B5	84
Lac la Hache, B.C., Can.	D7	85
Laclede, co., Mo., U.S.	D5	118
Lac-Mégantic, P.Q., Can.	D7	90
Lacolle, P.Q., Can.	D4	90
La Columna see Bolívar, Pico, mtn., Ven.	B5	70
Lacombe, Ab., Can.	C4	84
Lacombe, La., U.S.	D6	111
Lacon, Il., U.S.	B4	106
La Concepción, Pan.	D3	80
La Concepción, Ven.	C5	80
Laconia, N.H., U.S.	C4	122
Laconia, Gulf of 20 Lakonikós Kólpos, b., Grc.	F9	18
La Conner, Wa., U.S.	A3	140
Lacoochee, Fl., U.S.	D4	102
La Coruña see A Coruña, Spain	F2	16
Lac qui Parle, co., Mn., U.S.	F2	116
Lac qui Parle, stm., Mn., U.S.	F2	116
La Creek Lake, l., S.D., U.S.	D4	134
La Crescent, Mn., U.S.	G7	116
La Crete, Ab., Can.	f7	84
La Crosse, In., U.S.	B4	107
La Crosse, Ks., U.S.	D4	109
La Crosse, Wi., U.S.	E2	142
La Crosse, co., Wi., U.S.	E2	142
La Crosse, stm., Wi., U.S.	E3	142
La Cygne, Ks., U.S.	D9	109
Ladākh Range, mts., Asia	C3	40
Ladd, Il., U.S.	B4	106
Ladies Island, i., S.C., U.S.	G6	133
La Dique, i., Sey.	h13	57b
Lādīz, Iran	E8	42
Ladoga, In., U.S.	E4	107
Ladoga, Lake see Ladožskoe ozero, l., Russia	C5	26
La Dorada, Col.	D5	80
Ladožskoe ozero, l., Russia	C5	26
Ladson, S.C., U.S.	F7	133
Ladybrand, S. Afr.	D4	56
Lady Lake, Fl., U.S.	D5	102
Lady Laurier, Mount, mtn., B.C., Can.	A6	85
Ladysmith, B.C., Can.	E6	85
Ladysmith, S. Afr.	D4	56
Ladysmith, Wi., U.S.	C2	142
Lae, Pap. N. Gui.	H12	32
La Encantada, Mex.	B4	78
Læsø, i., Den.	H4	10
La Esperanza, Hond.	C2	80
La Estrada see A Estrada, Spain	F2	16
La Farge, Wi., U.S.	E3	142
Lafayette, Al., U.S.	C4	94
Lafayette, Co., U.S.	B5	99
Lafayette, Ga., U.S.	B1	103
Lafayette, In., U.S.	D4	107
Lafayette, La., U.S.	D3	111
Lafayette, N.C., U.S.	B3	126
Lafayette, Or., U.S.	B3	130
La Fayette, R.I., U.S.	E4	132
Lafayette, Tn., U.S.	A5	135
Lafayette, co., Ar., U.S.	D2	97
Lafayette, co., Fl., U.S.	C3	102
Lafayette, co., La., U.S.	D3	111
Lafayette, co., Mo., U.S.	B4	118
Lafayette, co., Ms., U.S.	A4	117
Lafayette, co., Wi., U.S.	F3	142
Lafayette, Mount, mtn., N.H., U.S.	B3	122
La Feria, Tx., U.S.	F4	136
Lafia, Nig.	E6	50
Lafiagi, Nig.	E6	50
Lafitte, La., U.S.	k11	111
La Flèche, Fr.	D6	16
La Follette, Tn., U.S.	C9	135
La Fontaine, In., U.S.	C6	107
Lafourche, La., U.S.	E5	111
Lafourche, co., La., U.S.	E5	111
La France, S.C., U.S.	B2	133
La Galite, i., Tun.	F2	18
Lagarto, Braz.	D4	74
Lagawe, Phil.	C8	34
Lågen, stm., Nor.	F3	10
Lages, Braz.	D7	72
Laghouat, Alg.	D5	48
Lago, Mount, mtn., Wa., U.S.	A5	140
Lagoa da Prata, Braz.	F2	74
Lago da Pedra, Braz.	B2	74
La Gomera, i., Spain	A1	50
Lagonoy Gulf, b., Phil.	D8	34
Lagos, Nig.	E5	50
Lagos, Port.	I2	16
Lagos de Moreno, Mex.	C4	78
La Gouëra, W. Sah.	B1	50
La Grande, Or., U.S.	B8	130
La Grande, stm., P.Q., Can.	h11	90
La Grande Deux, Réservoir, res., P.Q., Can.	h11	90
Lagrange, Austl.	D3	60
La Grange, Ga., U.S.	C1	103
La Grange, Il., U.S.	B6	106
Lagrange, In., U.S.	A7	107
La Grange, Ky., U.S.	B4	110
La Grange, Mo., U.S.	A6	118
La Grange, N.C., U.S.	B5	126
Lagrange, Oh., U.S.	A3	128
La Grange, Tx., U.S.	E4	136
Lagrange, co., In., U.S.	A7	107
La Grange Park, Il., U.S.	k9	106
La Gran Sabana, pl., Ven.	B7	70
La Guadeloupe (Saint-Evariste), P.Q., Can.	D7	90
La Guajira, Península de, pen., S.A.	A5	70
La Guardia, Bol.	B5	72
La Guardia see A Guardia, Spain	G2	16
Laguna, Braz.	D8	72
Laguna, N.M., U.S.	B2	124
Laguna Beach, Ca., U.S.	F5	98
Laguna Dam, U.S.	E1	96
Laguna Indian Reservation, N.M., U.S.	B2	124
La Habana (Havana), Cuba	A3	80
La Habra, Ca., U.S.	n13	98
Lahad Datu, Malay.	C5	36
Lahad Datu, Telukan, b., Malay.	C5	36
Lahaina, Hi., U.S.	C5	104
La Harpe, Il., U.S.	C3	106
La Harpe, Ks., U.S.	E8	109
Lahat, Indon.	D2	36
La Have, stm., N.S., Can.	E5	87
Lahdenpohja, Russia	F14	10
Lāhījān, Iran	C6	42
Lahnstein, S. Afr.	E3	56
La Homa, Ok., U.S.	A3	129
Lahontan Reservoir, res., Nv., U.S.	D2	121
Lahore, Pak.	D10	42
Lahti, Fin.	F11	10
Laï, Chad	E8	50
Lai Chau, Viet.	B4	34
Laie, Hi., U.S.	B4	104
Lai-hka, Myan.	B3	34
Laingsburg, S. Afr.	E3	56
Laingsburg, Mi., U.S.	F6	115
Lainioälven, stm., Swe.	B9	10
Lais, Indon.	D2	36
Laisamis, Kenya	C7	54
Laiwu, China	B4	30
Laiwui, Indon.	G8	32
Laiyang, China	B5	30
Laizhou Wan, b., China	D11	28
La Jara, Co., U.S.	D5	99
La Jolla, Point, c., Ca., U.S.	o15	98
La Junta, Co., U.S.	D7	99
Lakatoro, Vanuatu	k9	62a
Lake, co., Ca., U.S.	C2	98
Lake, co., Co., U.S.	B4	99
Lake, co., Fl., U.S.	D5	102
Lake, co., Il., U.S.	A6	106
Lake, co., In., U.S.	B3	107
Lake, co., Mi., U.S.	E5	115
Lake, co., Mn., U.S.	C7	116
Lake, co., Mt., U.S.	C2	119
Lake, co., Oh., U.S.	A4	128
Lake, co., Or., U.S.	E6	130
Lake, co., S.D., U.S.	C8	134
Lake, co., Tn., U.S.	A2	135
Lake Alfred, Fl., U.S.	D5	102
Lake Andes, S.D., U.S.	D7	134
Lake Ariel, Pa., U.S.	D11	131
Lake Arrowhead, Ca., U.S.	E5	98
Lake Arthur, La., U.S.	D3	111
Lakeba, i., Fiji	m11	63b
Lake Benton, Mn., U.S.	F2	116
Lake Bluff, Il., U.S.	A6	106
Lake Butler, Fl., U.S.	B4	102
Lake Cargelligo, Austl.	G4	62
Lake Charles, La., U.S.	D2	111
Lake Chelan National Recreation Area, Wa., U.S.	A5	140
Lake City, Ar., U.S.	B5	97
Lake City, Fl., U.S.	B4	102
Lake City, Ia., U.S.	B3	108
Lake City, Mi., U.S.	D5	115
Lake City, Mn., U.S.	F6	116
Lake City, Pa., U.S.	B1	131
Lake City, S.C., U.S.	D8	133
Lake City, Tn., U.S.	C9	135
Lake Clark National Park, Ak., U.S.	C9	95
Lake Cowichan, B.C., Can.	g11	85
Lake Creek, stm., Wa., U.S.	B7	140
Lake Crystal, Mn., U.S.	F4	116
Lake Delta, N.Y., U.S.	B5	125
Lake Delton, Wi., U.S.	E4	142
Lake District, reg., Eng., U.K.	C5	12
Lake Elsinore, Ca., U.S.	F5	98
Lake Erie Beach, N.Y., U.S.	C1	125
Lakefield, On., Can.	C6	89
Lakefield, Mn., U.S.	G3	116
Lake Forest, Il., U.S.	A6	106
Lake Fork, stm., Ut., U.S.	C5	137
Lake Geneva, Wi., U.S.	F5	142
Lake Hamilton, Ar., U.S.	g7	97
Lake Havasu City, Az., U.S.	C1	96
Lake Helen, Fl., U.S.	D5	102
Lakehurst, N.J., U.S.	C4	123
Lakehurst Naval Air Station, mil., N.J., U.S.	C4	123
Lake in the Hills, Il., U.S.	h8	106
Lake Jackson, Tx., U.S.	r14	136
Lake Katrine, N.Y., U.S.	D7	125
Lake King, Austl.	G2	60
Lakeland, Fl., U.S.	D5	102
Lakeland, Ga., U.S.	E3	103
Lake Linden, Mi., U.S.	A2	115
Lake Louise, Ab., Can.	D2	84
Lake Magdalene, Fl., U.S.	o11	102
Lake Mary, Fl., U.S.	D5	102
Lake Mead National Recreation Area, U.S.	H7	121
Lake Meredith National Recreation Area, Tx., U.S.	B2	136
Lake Mills, Ia., U.S.	A4	108
Lake Mills, Wi., U.S.	E5	142
Lakemore, Oh., U.S.	A4	128
Lake Mountain, mtn., Wy., U.S.	E6	143
Lake Nebagamon, Wi., U.S.	B2	142
Lake Odessa, Mi., U.S.	F5	115
Lake of the Woods, co., Mn., U.S.	B4	116
Lake Orion, Mi., U.S.	F7	115
Lake Oswego, Or., U.S.	B4	130
Lake Ozark, Mo., U.S.	C5	118
Lake Park, Fl., U.S.	F6	102
Lake Park, Ia., U.S.	A2	108
Lake Park, Mn., U.S.	D2	116
Lake Placid, Fl., U.S.	E5	102
Lake Placid, N.Y., U.S.	A7	125
Lake Pontchartrain Causeway, La., U.S.	h11	111
Lakeport, Ca., U.S.	C2	98
Lake Preston, S.D., U.S.	C8	134
Lake Providence, La., U.S.	B4	111
Lake Range, mts., Nv., U.S.	C2	121
Lakes Entrance, Austl.	H4	62
Lake Shore, Md., U.S.	B5	113
Lakeshore, Ms., U.S.	E4	117
Lakeside, Az., U.S.	C6	96
Lakeside, Ca., U.S.	F5	98
Lakeside, Ct., U.S.	D3	100
Lakeside, Mt., U.S.	C2	119
Lakeside, Oh., U.S.	A3	128
Lakeside, Or., U.S.	D2	130
Lakeside Park, Ky., U.S.	h13	110
Lake Station, In., U.S.	A3	107
Lake Station, Ok., U.S.	A5	129
Lake Stevens, Wa., U.S.	A3	140
Lake Superior Provincial Park, On., Can.	p18	89
Lake Swamp, stm., S.C., U.S.	D8	133
Lake Tansi Village, Tn., U.S.	D8	135
Lake Valley, val., Nv., U.S.	E7	121
Lake View, Ia., U.S.	B2	108
Lakeview, Mi., U.S.	E5	115
Lakeview, Oh., U.S.	B2	128
Lakeview, Or., U.S.	E6	130
Lake View, S.C., U.S.	C9	133
Lake Villa, Il., U.S.	h8	106
Lake Village, Ar., U.S.	D4	97
Lake Village, In., U.S.	B3	107
Lakeville, Ct., U.S.	B2	100
Lakeville, In., U.S.	A5	107
Lakeville, Ma., U.S.	C6	114
Lakeville, Mn., U.S.	F5	116
Lake Waccamaw, N.C., U.S.	C4	126
Lake Wales, Fl., U.S.	E5	102
Lakewood, Ca., U.S.	n12	98
Lakewood, Co., U.S.	B5	99
Lakewood, Ia., U.S.	f8	108
Lakewood, Il., U.S.	D5	106
Lakewood, N.J., U.S.	C4	123
Lakewood, N.Y., U.S.	C1	125
Lakewood, Oh., U.S.	A4	128
Lakewood, Wa., U.S.	B3	140
Lake Worth, Fl., U.S.	F6	102
Lake Worth Inlet, b., Fl., U.S.	F7	102
Lake Zurich, Il., U.S.	h8	106
Lakhdaria, Alg.	I8	16
Lakhīmpur, India	D4	40
Lakin, Ks., U.S.	E2	109
Lakonikós Kólpos, b., Grc.	F9	18
Lakota, N.D., U.S.	A7	127
Laksefjorden, b., Nor.	A12	10
Lakshadweep, prov., India	G2	40
Lakshadweep, is., India	G2	40
Lakshadweep Sea, Asia	G2	40
Lalara, Gabon	C2	54
Lālībela, Eth.	H12	54
La Libertad, Guat.	B1	80
La Línea de la Concepción, Spain	I4	16
Lalitpur, India	E3	40
La Loche see Churchill, stm., Can.	G21	82
La Luz, N.M., U.S.	E4	124
La Malbaie, P.Q., Can.	B7	90
La Mancha, reg., Spain	H5	16
La Manche see English Channel, strt., Eur.	C5	16
Lamap, Vanuatu	k9	62a
Lamar, Ar., U.S.	B2	97
Lamar, Co., U.S.	C8	99
Lamar, Mo., U.S.	D3	118
Lamar, Pa., U.S.	D7	131
Lamar, S.C., U.S.	C7	133
Lamar, co., Al., U.S.	B1	94
Lamar, co., Ga., U.S.	C2	103
Lamar, co., Ms., U.S.	D4	117
Lamar, co., Tx., U.S.	C5	136
Lamar, stm., Wy., U.S.	B2	143
La Mauricie, Parc National de, P.Q., Can.	C5	90
Lamb, co., Tx., U.S.	B1	136
Lambaréné, Gabon	D2	54
Lambayeque, Peru	E4	70
Lambert, Ms., U.S.	A3	117
Lambert Glacier, Ant.	D11	67
Lamberton, Mn., U.S.	F3	116
Lambertville, Mi., U.S.	G7	115
Lambertville, N.J., U.S.	C3	123
Lame Deer, Mt., U.S.	E10	119
Lamèque, N.B., Can.	B5	87
Lamèque, Île, i., N.B., Can.	B5	87
La Mesa, Ca., U.S.	F5	98
La Mesa, N.M., U.S.	E3	124
Lamesa, Tx., U.S.	C2	136
Lamía, Grc.	E9	18
Lamoille, Nv., U.S.	C6	121
Lamoille, co., Vt., U.S.	B3	138
Lamoille, stm., Vt., U.S.	B3	138
La Moine, stm., Il., U.S.	C3	106
Lamon Bay, b., Phil.	D8	34
Lamoni, Ia., U.S.	D4	108
Lamont, Ab., Can.	C4	84
Lamont, Ca., U.S.	E4	98
La Monte, Mo., U.S.	C4	118
La Moure, N.D., U.S.	C7	127
La Moure, co., N.D., U.S.	C7	127
Lampang, Thai.	C3	34
Lampasas, Tx., U.S.	D3	136
Lampasas, co., Tx., U.S.	D3	136
Lampazos de Naranjo, Mex.	B4	78
Lamphun, Thai.	C3	34
Lampman, Sk., Can.	H4	91
Lamprey, stm., N.H., U.S.	D4	122
Lamu, Kenya	D8	54
Lanai, i., Hi., U.S.	C4	104
Lanai City, Hi., U.S.	C5	104
Lanaihale, mtn., Hi., U.S.	C5	104
Lanark, On., Can.	C8	89
Lanark, Il., U.S.	A4	106
Lanark, W.V., U.S.	D3	141
Lanbi Kyun, i., Myan.	D3	34
Lancang see Mekong, stm., Asia	A3	34
Lancaster, On., Can.	B10	89
Lancaster, Eng., U.K.	C5	12
Lancaster, Ca., U.S.	E4	98
Lancaster, Ky., U.S.	C5	110
Lancaster, Mo., U.S.	A5	118
Lancaster, N.H., U.S.	B3	122
Lancaster, N.Y., U.S.	C2	125
Lancaster, Oh., U.S.	C3	128
Lancaster, Pa., U.S.	F9	131
Lancaster, S.C., U.S.	B6	133
Lancaster, Tx., U.S.	n10	136
Lancaster, Wi., U.S.	F3	142
Lancaster, co., Ne., U.S.	D9	120
Lancaster, co., Pa., U.S.	G9	131
Lancaster, co., S.C., U.S.	B6	133
Lancaster, co., Va., U.S.	C6	139
Lance Creek, stm., Wy., U.S.	C8	143
Lanchow see Lanzhou, China	D8	28
Lanciano, Italy	C5	18
Lancun, China	B5	30
Lândana, Ang.	E2	54
Land Between the Lakes, U.S.	f9	110
Landeck, Aus.	G12	12
Landegode, Nor.	C6	10
Lander, Wy., U.S.	D4	143
Lander, co., Nv., U.S.	C4	121
Landerneau, Fr.	C4	16
Landes, reg., Fr.	E6	16
Landess, In., U.S.	C6	107
Landis, N.C., U.S.	B2	126
Lando, S.C., U.S.	B5	133
Landrum, S.C., U.S.	A3	133
Land's End, c., Eng., U.K.	E4	12
Lands End, c., R.I., U.S.	F5	132
Landshut, Ger.	F13	12
Landskrona, Swe.	I5	10
Lane, co., Ks., U.S.	D3	109
Lane, co., Or., U.S.	C4	130
La Negra, Chile	C3	72
Lanesboro, Mn., U.S.	G7	116
Lanett, Al., U.S.	C4	94
Langdon, N.D., U.S.	A7	127
Langeland, i., Den.	I4	10
Langeloth, Pa., U.S.	F1	131
Langfang, China	B4	30
Langjökull, Ice.	I20	10a
Langkawi, Pulau, i., Malay.	B1	34
Langlade, co., Wi., U.S.	C4	142
Langley, B.C., Can.	f13	85
Langley, S.C., U.S.	E4	133
Langley, Wa., U.S.	A3	140
Langley Air Force Base, mil., Va., U.S.	h15	139
Langley Park, Md., U.S.	f9	113
Langøya, i., Nor.	B6	10
Langres, Fr.	D9	16
Langsa, Indon.	C1	36
Lang Son, Viet.	B5	34
Langston, Ok., U.S.	B4	129
Languedoc, hist. reg., Fr.	F8	16
L'Anguille, stm., Ar., U.S.	B5	97
Langzhong, China	E9	28
Lanham, Md., U.S.	C4	113
Lanier, co., Ga., U.S.	E3	103
Länkäran, Azer.	C13	44
Lannion, Fr.	C5	16
Lannon, Wi., U.S.	m11	142
L'Annonciation, P.Q., Can.	C3	90
Lanping, China	A3	34
Lansdale, Pa., U.S.	F11	131
Lansdowne, Md., U.S.	B4	113
L'Anse, Mi., U.S.	B2	115
L'Anse-au-Loup, Nf., Can.	C3	88
L'Anse Indian Reservation, Mi., U.S.	B2	115
Lansford, Pa., U.S.	E10	131
Lanshan, China	D3	30
Lansing, Ia., U.S.	A6	108
Lansing, Il., U.S.	B6	106
Lansing, Ks., U.S.	C9	109
Lansing, Mi., U.S.	F6	115
Lantana, Fl., U.S.	F6	102
Lanxi, China	F11	28
Lanzarote, i., Spain	A2	50
Lanzhou, China	D8	28
Laoag, Phil.	C8	34
Laoang, Phil.	D9	34
Lao Cai, Viet.	B4	34
Laoha, stm., China	C12	28
Laohekou, China	E10	28
Laon, Fr.	C8	16
La Orchila, Isla, i., Ven.	C6	80
La Oroya, Peru	F4	70
Laos, ctry., Asia	B3	32
La Palma, Pan.	D4	80
La Palma, i., Spain	A1	50
La Paragua, Ven.	B7	70
La Paz, Arg.	E6	72
La Paz, Bol.	B4	72
La Paz, Mex.	C2	78
La Paz, co., Az., U.S.	D2	96
La Paz, Mex.	C2	78
La Perouse Strait, strt., Asia	B16	28
La Pine, Or., U.S.	D5	130
Lapinlahti, Fin.	E12	10
Lapland (Lappland), hist. reg., Eur.	B8	10
La Plata, Arg.	F6	72
La Plata, Md., U.S.	C4	113
La Plata, Mo., U.S.	A5	118
La Plata, co., Co., U.S.	D3	99
La Plata Mountains, mts., Co., U.S.	D3	99
La Plata Peak, mtn., Co., U.S.	B4	99
La Platte, stm., Vt., U.S.	C2	138
La Pocatière, P.Q., Can.	B7	90
Laporte, In., U.S.	A5	99
La Porte, In., U.S.	A4	107
La Porte, Tx., U.S.	r14	136
La Porte, co., In., U.S.	A4	107
La Porte City, Ia., U.S.	B5	108
Lappeenranta, Fin.	F13	10
Lappland (Lapland), hist. reg., Eur.	B8	10
La Prairie, P.Q., Can.	D4	90
La Pryor, Tx., U.S.	E3	136
Laptev Sea see Laptevyh, more, Russia	B14	26
Laptevyh, more, Russia	B14	26
La Push, Wa., U.S.	B1	140
Lapwai, Id., U.S.	C2	105
La Quiaca, Arg.	C4	72
L'Aquila, Italy	C4	18
Lār, Iran	E6	42
Larache, Mor.	C3	48
Laramie, Wy., U.S.	E7	143
Laramie, co., Wy., U.S.	E8	143
Laramie, stm., U.S.	E7	143
Laramie Mountains, mts., Wy., U.S.	D7	143
Laramie Peak, mtn., Wy., U.S.	D7	143
Larantuka, Indon.	E6	36
Lärbro, Swe.	H8	10
Larchmont, N.Y., U.S.	h13	125
Larchwood, Ia., U.S.	A1	108
Laredo, Spain	F5	16
Laredo, Tx., U.S.	F3	136
Largo, Fl., U.S.	E4	102
Largo, Cañon, val., N.M., U.S.	A2	124
Largo, Key, i., Fl., U.S.	G6	102
Larimer, co., Co., U.S.	A5	99
Larimore, N.D., U.S.	B8	127
La Rioja, Arg.	D4	72
La Rioja, reg., Spain	F12	131
Lárisa, Grc.	E9	18
Lārkāna, Pak.	E9	42
Lark Harbour, Nf., Can.	D2	88
Larkspur, Ca., U.S.	h7	98
Larksville, Pa., U.S.	n17	131
Larnaca see Lárnax, Cyp.	E5	44
Lárnax, Cyp.	E5	44
Larne, N. Ire., U.K.	C4	12
Larned, Ks., U.S.	D4	109

Name	Map Ref.	Page
La Rochelle, Fr.	D6	16
La Roche-sur-Yon, Fr.	D6	16
La Roda, Spain	H5	16
La Romana, Dom. Rep.	B6	80
Larose, La., U.S.	E5	111
Larrimah, Austl.	D5	60
Larsen Ice Shelf, Ant.	C34	67
Larue, co., Ky., U.S.	C4	110
Larvik, Nor.	G4	10
LaSalle, P.Q., Can.	q19	90
La Salle, Co., U.S.	A6	99
La Salle, Il., U.S.	B4	106
La Salle, co., Il., U.S.	B4	106
La Salle, co., La., U.S.	C3	111
La Salle, co., Tx., U.S.	E3	136
Las Animas, Co., U.S.	C7	99
Las Animas, co., Co., U.S.	D6	99
La Sarre, P.Q., Can.	k11	90
Las Casitas, mtn., Mex.	C3	78
Las Choapas, Mex.	D6	78
La Scie, Nf., Can.	D4	88
Las Cruces, N.M., U.S.	E3	124
La Selle, Morne, mtn., Haiti	B5	80
La Serena, Chile	C2	69
La Serena, reg., Spain	H4	16
La Seyne-sur-Mer, Fr.	F9	16
Las Flores, Arg.	F6	72
Lāsh-e Joveyn, Afg.	D8	42
Las Heras, Arg.	G3	69
Lashio, Myan.	B3	34
Lashkar Gāh, Afg.	D8	42
Las Margaritas, Mex.	D6	78
Las Minas, Cerro, mtn., Hond.	C2	80
La Solana, Spain	H5	16
Las Palmas de Gran Canaria, Spain	A1	50
La Spezia, Italy	B2	18
Las Piedras, Ur.	E6	72
Las Plumas, Arg.	F3	69
Las Rosas, Mex.	D6	78
Lassen, co., Ca., U.S.	B3	98
Lassen Peak, vol., Ca., U.S.	B3	98
Lassen Volcanic National Park, Ca., U.S.	B3	98
L'Assomption, P.Q., Can.	D4	90
Las Tablas, Pan.	D3	80
Last Mountain Lake, l., Sk., Can.	F3	91
Lastoursville, Gabon	D2	54
Las Tunas, Cuba	A4	80
Las Varas, Mex.	B3	78
Las Varas, Mex.	C3	78
Las Vegas, N.M., U.S.	B4	124
Las Vegas, Nv., U.S.	G6	121
Latah, co., Id., U.S.	C2	105
Latakia see Al-Lādhiqīyah, Syria	E6	44
Lathrop, Mo., U.S.	B3	118
Latimer, co., Ok., U.S.	C6	129
Latina, Italy	D4	18
Laton, Ca., U.S.	D4	98
La Tortuga, Isla, i., Ven.	C6	80
Latouche Treville, Cape, c., Austl.	D3	60
Latour Peak, mtn., Id., U.S.	B2	105
Latrobe, Pa., U.S.	F3	131
Latta, S.C., U.S.	C9	133
La Tuque, P.Q., Can.	B5	90
Lātūr, India	F3	40
Latvia, ctry., Eur.	H11	10
Lauderdale, Ms., U.S.	C5	117
Lauderdale, co., Al., U.S.	A2	94
Lauderdale, co., Ms., U.S.	C5	117
Lauderdale, co., Tn., U.S.	B2	135
Lauderdale Lakes, Fl., U.S.	r13	102
Laughlin, Nv., U.S.	H7	121
Laughlin Air Force Base, mil., Tx., U.S.	E2	136
Laughlin Peak, mtn., N.M., U.S.	A5	124
Laughlintown, Pa., U.S.	F3	131
Launceston, Austl.	I4	62
Launching Point, c., P.E., Can.	C7	87
La Unión, Chile	F2	69
La Unión, El Sal.	C2	80
La Unión, Spain	I6	16
Laurel, De., U.S.	F3	101
Laurel, Fl., U.S.	E4	102
Laurel, Md., U.S.	B4	113
Laurel, Ms., U.S.	D4	117
Laurel, Mt., U.S.	E8	119
Laurel, Ne., U.S.	B8	120
Laurel, Va., U.S.	C5	139
Laurel, co., Ky., U.S.	C5	110
Laurel, stm., Ky., U.S.	D5	110
Laurel Bay, S.C., U.S.	G6	133
Laurel Creek, stm., W.V., U.S.	n14	141
Laurel Creek, stm., W.V., U.S.	m12	141
Laureldale, Pa., U.S.	F10	131
Laurel Fork, stm., W.V., U.S.	C5	141
Laurel Hill, N.C., U.S.	C3	126
Laurel River Lake, res., Ky., U.S.	D5	110
Laurence G. Hanscom Air Force Base, mil., Ma., U.S.	g10	114
Laurence Harbor, N.J., U.S.	C4	123
Laurens, Ia., U.S.	B3	108
Laurens, S.C., U.S.	C3	133
Laurens, co., Ga., U.S.	D4	103
Laurens, co., S.C., U.S.	C4	133
Laurentides, P.Q., Can.	D4	90
Laurentides, Parc Provincial des, P.Q., Can.	B6	90
Lau Ridge	K21	64
Laurier, P.Q., Can.	C6	90
Laurierville, P.Q., Can.	C6	90
Laurinburg, N.C., U.S.	C3	126
Laurium, Mi., U.S.	A2	115
Lausanne, Switz.	A1	18
Laut, Pulau, i., Indon.	C3	36
Laut, Pulau, i., Indon.	D5	36
Laut, Selat, strt., Indon.	D5	36
Lautaro, Chile	E2	69
Lauzon (part of Lévis-Lauzon), P.Q., Can.	C6	90
Lava Beds National Monument, Ca., U.S.	B3	98
Lavaca, Ar., U.S.	B1	97
Lavaca, co., Tx., U.S.	E4	136
Laval, P.Q., Can.	D4	90
Laval, Fr.	B1	30
La Vale, Md., U.S.	k13	113
La Vall d'Uixó, Spain	H6	16
Lavaltrie, P.Q., Can.	D4	90
Laveen, Az., U.S.	m8	96
La Vega, Dom. Rep.	B5	80
L'Avenir, P.Q., Can.	D5	90
La Vergne, Tn., U.S.	A5	135
La Verkin, Ut., U.S.	F2	137
La Verne, Ca., U.S.	m13	98
Laverne, Ok., U.S.	A2	129
Laverton, Austl.	F3	60
La Veta, Co., U.S.	D5	99
La Victoria, Ven.	C6	80
La Vila Joiosa, Spain	H6	16
La Vista, Ne., U.S.	g12	120
Lavonia, Ga., U.S.	B3	103
Lavon Lake, res., Tx., U.S.	m10	136
Lavras, Braz.	F2	74
Lavumisa, Swaz.	D5	56
Lawai, Hi., U.S.	B2	104
Lawn, Nf., Can.	E4	88
Lawra, Ghana	D4	50
Lawrence, In., U.S.	E5	107
Lawrence, Ks., U.S.	D8	109
Lawrence, Ma., U.S.	A5	114
Lawrence, Mi., U.S.	F4	115
Lawrence, N.Y., U.S.	k13	125
Lawrence, co., Al., U.S.	A2	94
Lawrence, co., Ar., U.S.	A4	97
Lawrence, co., Il., U.S.	E6	106
Lawrence, co., In., U.S.	G4	107
Lawrence, co., Ky., U.S.	B7	110
Lawrence, co., Mo., U.S.	D4	118
Lawrence, co., Ms., U.S.	D3	117
Lawrence, co., Oh., U.S.	D3	128
Lawrence, co., Pa., U.S.	E1	131
Lawrence, co., Tn., U.S.	B4	135
Lawrenceburg, In., U.S.	F8	107
Lawrenceburg, Ky., U.S.	B5	110
Lawrenceburg, Tn., U.S.	B4	135
Lawrence Park, Pa., U.S.	B1	131
Lawrenceville, Ga., U.S.	C3	103
Lawrenceville, Il., U.S.	E6	106
Lawrenceville, Va., U.S.	D5	139
Lawson, Mo., U.S.	B3	118
Lawsonia, Md., U.S.	E6	113
Lawtell, La., U.S.	D3	111
Lawton, Mi., U.S.	F5	115
Lawton, Ok., U.S.	C3	129
Lawz, Jabal al-, mtn., Sau. Ar.	E3	42
Laxå, Swe.	G6	10
Lay Lake, res., Al., U.S.	B3	94
Laysan Island, i., Hi., U.S.	k13	104
Layton, Ut., U.S.	B4	137
Lazarev, Russia	D16	26
Lázaro Cárdenas, Mex.	D4	78
Lazo, Russia	B2	31
Leachville, Ar., U.S.	B5	97
Lead, S.D., U.S.	C2	134
Leadbetter Point, c., Wa., U.S.	C1	140
Leadville, Co., U.S.	B4	99
Leadwood, Mo., U.S.	D7	118
Leaf, stm., Ms., U.S.	D5	117
Leaf Rapids, Mb., Can.	A1	86
Leake, co., Ms., U.S.	C4	117
Leakesville, Ms., U.S.	D5	117
Lealman, Fl., U.S.	p10	102
Leamington, On., Can.	E2	89
Leary, Ga., U.S.	E2	103
Leatherman Peak, mtn., Id., U.S.	E5	105
Leavenworth, Ks., U.S.	C9	109
Leavenworth, Wa., U.S.	B5	140
Leavenworth, co., Ks., U.S.	C8	109
Leavittsburg, Oh., U.S.	A5	128
Leawood, Ks., U.S.	D9	109
Lebanon, De., U.S.	D4	101
Lebanon, Il., U.S.	E4	106
Lebanon, In., U.S.	D5	107
Lebanon, Ky., U.S.	C4	110
Lebanon, Mo., U.S.	D5	118
Lebanon, N.H., U.S.	C2	122
Lebanon, Oh., U.S.	C1	128
Lebanon, Or., U.S.	C4	130
Lebanon, Pa., U.S.	F9	131
Lebanon, Tn., U.S.	A5	135
Lebanon, Va., U.S.	f9	139
Lebanon, co., Pa., U.S.	F8	131
Lebanon, ctry., Asia	E6	44
Lebanon Junction, Ky., U.S.	C4	110
Lebanon Mountains see Lubnān, Jabal, mts., Leb.	F6	44
Lebedjan', Russia	C15	20
Lebedyn, Ukr.	D13	20
Lebesby, Nor.	A12	10
Lebjaže, Kaz.	D9	26
Lebo, Ks., U.S.	D8	109
Lębork, Pol.	B4	20
Lebu, Chile	E2	69
Lecce, Italy	D7	18
Lecco, Italy	B2	18
Le Center, Mn., U.S.	F5	116
Lechang, China	D3	30
Le Claire, Ia., U.S.	C7	108
Lecompte, La., U.S.	C3	111
Lecompton, Ks., U.S.	C8	109
Le Creusot, Fr.	D9	16
Łęczyca, Pol.	C5	20
Ledjanaja, gora, mtn., Russia	C19	26
Ledo, India	D7	40
Ledu, China	B1	30
Leduc, Ab., Can.	C4	84
Lee, Ma., U.S.	B1	114
Lee, co., Al., U.S.	C4	94
Lee, co., Ar., U.S.	C5	97
Lee, co., Fl., U.S.	F5	102
Lee, co., Ga., U.S.	E2	103
Lee, co., Ia., U.S.	D6	108
Lee, co., Il., U.S.	B4	106
Lee, co., Ky., U.S.	C6	110
Lee, co., Ms., U.S.	A5	117
Lee, co., N.C., U.S.	B3	126
Lee, co., S.C., U.S.	C7	133
Lee, co., Tx., U.S.	D4	136
Lee, co., Va., U.S.	f8	139
Lee, Lake, l., Ms., U.S.	B3	117
Leechburg, Pa., U.S.	E2	131
Leech Lake, l., Mn., U.S.	C4	116
Leech Lake Indian Reservation, Mn., U.S.	C4	116
Lee Creek, stm., U.S.	B1	97
Leeds, Eng., U.K.	D6	12
Leeds, Al., U.S.	B3	94
Leelanau, co., Mi., U.S.	D5	115
Leelanau, Lake, l., Mi., U.S.	C5	115
Lee Park, Pa., U.S.	n17	131
Leer, Ger.	D10	12
Leesburg, Fl., U.S.	D5	102
Leesburg, Ga., U.S.	E2	103
Leesburg, Oh., U.S.	C2	128
Leesburg, Va., U.S.	A5	139
Lees Summit, Mo., U.S.	C3	118
Leesville, La., U.S.	C2	111
Leesville, S.C., U.S.	D4	133
Leesville Lake, res., Va., U.S.	C3	139
Leeton, Austl.	G4	62
Leeton, Mo., U.S.	C4	118
Leetonia, Oh., U.S.	B5	128
Leetsdale, Pa., U.S.	h13	131
Leeuwarden, Neth.	C8	12
Leeuwin, Cape, c., Austl.	G1	60
Leeward Islands, is., N.A.	E12	76
Leflore, co., Ms., U.S.	B3	117
Le Flore, co., Ok., U.S.	C7	129
Lega Hida, Eth.	B8	54
Legal, Ab., Can.	C4	84
Leganés, Spain	G5	16
Legaspi, Phil.	D8	34
Leghorn see Livorno, Italy	C3	18
Legnica, Pol.	D4	20
Le Grand, Ca., U.S.	D3	98
Le Grand, Ia., U.S.	B5	108
Leh, India	C3	40
Le Havre, Fr.	C7	16
Lehi, Ut., U.S.	C4	137
Lehigh, co., Pa., U.S.	E10	131
Lehigh, stm., Pa., U.S.	E10	131
Lehigh Acres, Fl., U.S.	F5	102
Lehighton, Pa., U.S.	E10	131
Lehua Island, i., Hi., U.S.	A1	104
Lehututu, Bots.	C3	56
Leicester, Eng., U.K.	D6	12
Leicester, Ma., U.S.	B4	114
Leiden, Neth.	D9	12
Leighton, Al., U.S.	A2	94
Leinster, hist. reg., Ire.	D3	12
Leipsic, De., U.S.	D3	101
Leipsic, Oh., U.S.	A2	128
Leipsic, stm., De., U.S.	C3	101
Leipzig, Ger.	E13	12
Leiria, Port.	H2	16
Leisler, Mount, mtn., Austl.	E4	60
Leisure City, Fl., U.S.	s13	102
Leitchfield, Ky., U.S.	C3	110
Leiyang, China	D3	30
Leizhou Bandao, pen., China	E3	30
Leka, Nor.	D4	10
Leland, Il., U.S.	B5	106
Leland, Ms., U.S.	B3	117
Leleiwi Point, c., Hi., U.S.	D7	104
Leleque, Arg.	F2	69
Leling, China	B4	30
Leli Shan, mtn., China	E4	28
Le Mans, Fr.	C7	16
Le Mars, Ia., U.S.	B1	108
Lema Shilindi, Eth.	C8	54
Lemesós, Cyp.	E5	44
Lemhi, co., Id., U.S.	E5	105
Lemhi, stm., Id., U.S.	E5	105
Lemhi Pass, Id., U.S.	E5	105
Lemhi Range, mts., Id., U.S.	E5	105
Lemmon, S.D., U.S.	B3	134
Lemmon, Mount, mtn., Az., U.S.	E5	96
Lemmon Valley, Nv., U.S.	D2	121
Lemnos see Límnos, i., Grc.	E10	18
Lemon, Lake, l., In., U.S.	F5	107
Lemon Fair, stm., Vt., U.S.	C2	138
Lemon Grove, Ca., U.S.	o15	98
Lemon Island, i., S.C., U.S.	G6	133
Lemont, Il., U.S.	B5	106
Lemont, Pa., U.S.	E6	131
Lemonweir, stm., Wi., U.S.	D3	142
Lempa, stm., N.A.	C2	80
Lem Peak, mtn., Id., U.S.	E5	105
Lena, Il., U.S.	A4	106
Lena, stm., Russia	B14	26
Lenawee, co., Mi., U.S.	G6	115
Lenexa, Ks., U.S.	D9	109
Lenghu, China	D6	28
Leninakan see Gjumri, Arm.	B10	44
Leningrad see Sankt-Peterburg, Russia	D5	26
Leninogorsk, Kaz.	A4	28
Lenin Peak, mtn., Asia	B2	40
Leninsk, Kaz.	E8	26
Leninsk-Kuzneckij, Russia	D10	26
Leninskoe, Russia	E15	26
Lennonville, Austl.	F2	60
Lennox, S.D., U.S.	D9	134
Lennoxville, P.Q., Can.	D6	90
Lenoir, N.C., U.S.	B1	126
Lenoir, co., N.C., U.S.	B5	126
Lenoir City, Tn., U.S.	D9	135
Lenore Lake, l., Sk., Can.	E3	91
Lenore Lake, l., Wa., U.S.	B6	140
Lenox, Ga., U.S.	E3	103
Lenox, Ia., U.S.	D3	108
Lenox, Ma., U.S.	B1	114
Lens, Fr.	B8	16
Lensk, Russia	C13	26
Lentini, Italy	F5	18
Léo, Burkina	D4	50
Leo, In., U.S.	B7	107
Leoben, Aus.	G14	12
Leominster, Ma., U.S.	A4	114
León, Mex.	C4	78
León, Nic.	C2	80
León, Spain	F4	16
Leon, Ia., U.S.	D4	108
Leon, Ks., U.S.	E7	109
Leon, co., Fl., U.S.	B2	102
Leon, co., Tx., U.S.	D4	136
Leonard, Tx., U.S.	C4	136
Leonardo, N.J., U.S.	C4	123
Leonardtown, Md., U.S.	D4	113
Leonia, N.J., U.S.	h9	123
Leonora, Austl.	F3	60
Leonville, La., U.S.	D4	111
Leopold and Astrid Coast, Ant.	C13	67
Léopoldville see Kinshasa, D.R.C.	D3	54
Leoti, Ks., U.S.	D2	109
Lepanto, Ar., U.S.	B5	97
Lepar, Pulau, i., Indon.	D3	36
Lepe, Spain	I3	16
Lepel', Bela.	B10	20
Leping, China	D4	30
L'Épiphanie, P.Q., Can.	D4	90
Lepsy, Kaz.	B3	28
Le Puy, Fr.	E8	16
Le Roy, Il., U.S.	C5	106
Le Roy, Mn., U.S.	G6	116
Le Roy, N.Y., U.S.	C3	125
Lerwick, Scot., U.K.	h19	12a
Léry, P.Q., Can.	q19	90
Léry, Lake, l., La., U.S.	k12	111
Lesbos see Lésvos, i., Grc.	E10	18
Les Cayes, Haiti	B5	80
Leskovac, Yugo.	C8	18
Leslie, Mi., U.S.	F6	115
Leslie, S.C., U.S.	B6	133
Leslie, co., Ky., U.S.	C6	110
Lesosibirsk, Russia	D11	26
Lesotho, ctry., Afr.	D4	56
Lesozavodsk, Russia	B14	28
Les Sables-d'Olonne, Fr.	D6	16
Lesser Antilles, is.	F12	76
Lesser Caucasus, mts., Asia	B11	44
Lesser Khingan Range see Xiao Hinggan Ling, mts., China	A1	31
Lesser Slave Lake, l., Ab., Can.	B3	84
Lesser Sunda Islands see Tenggara, Nusa, is., Indon.	E5	36
Lester Prairie, Mn., U.S.	F4	116
Le Sueur, Mn., U.S.	F5	116
Le Sueur, co., Mn., U.S.	F5	116
Lešukonskoe, Russia	B8	22
Lésvos, i., Grc.	E10	18
Leszno, Pol.	D4	20
Letcher, co., Ky., U.S.	C7	110
Lethbridge, Ab., Can.	E4	84
Lethbridge, Nf., Can.	D5	88
Lethem, Guy.	C8	70
Leti, Kepulauan, is., Indon.	E7	36
Leticia, Col.	D6	70
Leting, China	B4	30
Letlhakeng, Bots.	C3	56
Letsôk-aw Kyun, i., Myan.	D3	34
Levanger, Nor.	E4	10
Levelland, Tx., U.S.	C1	136
Leveque, Cape, c., Austl.	D3	60
Levice, Slvk.	E5	20
Levin, N.Z.	p14	63c
Lévis [-Lauzon], P.Q., Can.	C6	90
Levisa Fork, stm., U.S.	C7	110
Levittown, N.Y., U.S.	E7	125
Levittown, Pa., U.S.	F12	131
Levkás, i., Grc.	E8	18
Levy, co., Fl., U.S.	C4	102
Levy Lake, l., Fl., U.S.	C4	102
Lewes, De., U.S.	E5	101
Lewes and Rehoboth Canal, De., U.S.	F5	101
Lewis, co., Id., U.S.	C2	105
Lewis, co., Ky., U.S.	B6	110
Lewis, co., Mo., U.S.	A6	118
Lewis, co., N.Y., U.S.	B5	125
Lewis, co., Tn., U.S.	B4	135
Lewis, co., W.V., U.S.	C4	141
Lewis, co., Wa., U.S.	C3	140
Lewis, stm., Wa., U.S.	C4	140
Lewis, stm., Wy., U.S.	B2	143
Lewis, Isle of, i., Scot., U.K.	A3	12a
Lewis, Mount, mtn., Nv., U.S.	C5	121
Lewis and Clark, co., Mt., U.S.	C4	119
Lewis and Clark Cavern, Mt., U.S.	D5	119
Lewis and Clark Lake, res., U.S.	E8	134
Lewisburg, Ky., U.S.	D3	110
Lewisburg, Oh., U.S.	C1	128
Lewisburg, Pa., U.S.	E8	131
Lewisburg, Tn., U.S.	B5	135
Lewisburg, W.V., U.S.	D4	141
Lewis Creek, stm., Vt., U.S.	C2	138
Lewis Lake, l., Wy., U.S.	B2	143
Lewisport, Ky., U.S.	C3	110
Lewisporte, Nf., Can.	D4	88
Lewis Smith Lake, res., Al., U.S.	B2	94
Lewiston, Id., U.S.	C1	105
Lewiston, Me., U.S.	D2	112
Lewiston, Mn., U.S.	G7	116
Lewiston, N.Y., U.S.	B1	125
Lewiston, Ut., U.S.	B4	137
Lewiston Peak, mtn., Ut., U.S.	C3	137
Lewiston Woodville, N.C., U.S.	A5	126
Lewistown, Il., U.S.	C3	106
Lewistown, Mt., U.S.	C7	119
Lewistown, Pa., U.S.	E6	131
Lewisville, Ar., U.S.	D2	97
Lewisville, Tx., U.S.	C4	136
Lewisville Lake, res., Tx., U.S.	C4	136
Lexington, Al., U.S.	A2	94
Lexington, Il., U.S.	C5	106
Lexington, Ky., U.S.	B5	110
Lexington, Ma., U.S.	B5	114
Lexington, Mi., U.S.	E8	115
Lexington, Mo., U.S.	B4	118
Lexington, Ms., U.S.	B3	117
Lexington, N.C., U.S.	B2	126
Lexington, Ne., U.S.	D6	120
Lexington, Oh., U.S.	B3	128
Lexington, Ok., U.S.	B4	129
Lexington, S.C., U.S.	D5	133
Lexington, Tn., U.S.	B3	135
Lexington, Va., U.S.	C3	139
Lexington, co., S.C., U.S.	D5	133
Lexington Park, Md., U.S.	D5	113
Leye, China	E2	30
Leyte, i., Phil.	D9	34
Lezhë, Alb.	D7	18
L'gov, Russia	D13	20
Lhasa, China	F6	28
Lhazê, China	D5	40
Lhokseumawe, Indon.	B1	36
Lhorong, China	E7	28
L'Hospitalet de Llobregat, Spain	G8	16
Lhünzê, China	D6	40
Liancheng, China	A7	34
Lianga, Phil.	E9	34
Lianjiang, China	E3	30
Lianxian, China	G10	28
Lianyungang, China	E11	28
Liao, stm., China	C12	28
Liaocheng, China	B4	30
Liaodong Bandao, pen., China	D12	28
Liaodong Bay see Liaodong Wan, b., China	C12	28
Liaodong Wan, b., China	C12	28
Liaoning, state, China	C12	28
Liaotung, Gulf of see Liaodong Wan, b., China	C12	28
Liaotung Bay see Liaodong Wan, b., China	C12	28
Liaoyang, China	A5	30
Liaoyuan, China	C13	28
Liard, stm., Can.	F15	82
Libagon, Phil.	D9	34
Libby, Mt., U.S.	B1	119
Libenge, D.R.C.	C3	54
Liberal, Ks., U.S.	E3	109
Liberal, Mo., U.S.	D3	118
Liberec, Czech Rep.	D3	20
Liberia, C.R.	C2	80

Name	Map Ref.	Page

Liberia, ctry., Afr. . . . . E3 — 50
Liberty, In., U.S. . . . . E8 — 107
Liberty, Ky., U.S. . . . . C5 — 110
Liberty, Mo., U.S. . . . . B3 — 118
Liberty, Ms., U.S. . . . . D3 — 117
Liberty, N.C., U.S. . . . . . . B3 — 126
Liberty, N.Y., U.S. . . . . . . D6 — 125
Liberty, S.C., U.S. . . . . B2 — 133
Liberty, Tx., U.S. . . . . D5 — 136
Liberty, co., Fl., U.S. . . . . . B2 — 102
Liberty, co., Ga., U.S. . . . . E5 — 103
Liberty, co., Mt., U.S. . . . . B5 — 119
Liberty, co., Tx., U.S. . . . . D5 — 136
Liberty Center, Oh., U.S. . . A1 — 128
Liberty Lake, Wa., U.S. . . . g14 — 140
Liberty Lake, res., Md., U.S. B4 — 113
Libertyville, Il., U.S. . . . . A6 — 106
Lībīyah, Aṣ-Ṣaḥrā' al-
(Libyan Desert), des.,
Afr. . . . . E9 — 48
Libo, China . . . . D2 — 30
Libourne, Fr. . . . . E6 — 16
Libreville, Gabon . . . . C1 — 54
Libuse, La., U.S. . . . . C3 — 111
Libya, ctry., Afr. . . . . E8 — 48
Libyan Desert see Lībīyah,
Aṣ-Ṣaḥrā' al-, des., Afr. E9 — 48
Licancábur, Cerro, vol., S.A. C4 — 72
Licata, Italy . . . . F4 — 18
Lice, Tur. . . . . C9 — 44
Lichinga, Moz. . . . . A6 — 56
Lichuan, China . . . . C2 — 30
Lichuan, China . . . . D4 — 30
Lick Creek, stm., Tn., U.S. . C11 — 135
Licking, Mo., U.S. . . . . . . D6 — 118
Licking, co., Oh., U.S. . . . B3 — 128
Licking, stm., Ky., U.S. . . . B6 — 110
Lida, Bela. . . . . C8 — 20
Lida, Lake, l., Mn., U.S. . . . D3 — 116
Liden, Swe. . . . . E7 — 10
Lidgerwood, N.D., U.S. . . . C8 — 127
Lidköping, Swe. . . . . G5 — 10
Lido di Ostia, Italy . . . . . . D4 — 18
Lidzbark Warmiński, Pol. . . B6 — 20
Liebig, Mount, mtn., Austl. E5 — 60
Liechtenstein, ctry., Eur. . . A2 — 18
Liège, Bel. . . . . E9 — 12
Lienz, Aus. . . . . G13 — 12
Liepāja, Lat. . . . . H9 — 10
Lièvre, Rivière du, stm.,
P.Q., Can. . . . . D2 — 90
Lifou, i., N. Cal. . . . . I9 — 62a
Lighthouse Inlet, b., S.C.,
U.S. . . . . k12 — 133
Lighthouse Point, c., Fl.,
U.S. . . . . C2 — 102
Lighthouse Point, c., La.,
U.S. . . . . E3 — 111
Lighthouse Point, c., Mi.,
U.S. . . . . C5 — 115
Lightning Creek, stm., Wy.,
U.S. . . . . C8 — 143
Ligonier, In., U.S. . . . . . . B6 — 107
Ligonier, Pa., U.S. . . . . . . F3 — 131
Ligurian Apennines see
Appennino Ligure, mts.,
Italy . . . . B2 — 18
Ligurian Sea, Eur. . . . . . . C2 — 18
Lihue, Hi., U.S. . . . . B2 — 104
Lijiang, China . . . . F8 — 28
Likasi, D.R.C. . . . . F5 — 54
Likati, D.R.C. . . . . C4 — 54
Lilbourn, Mo., U.S. . . . . . E8 — 118
Lilburn, Ga., U.S. . . . . . . h8 — 103
Lille, Fr. . . . . B8 — 16
Lillebælt, strt., Den. . . . . . I3 — 10
Lillehammer, Nor. . . . . . . F4 — 10
Lillesand, Nor. . . . . G3 — 10
Lillestrøm, Nor. . . . . G4 — 10
Lillian, Al., U.S. . . . . E2 — 94
Lillington, N.C., U.S. . . . . B4 — 126
Lillinonah, Lake, l., Ct., U.S. C2 — 100
Lillooet, B.C., Can. . . . . . D7 — 85
Lillooet, stm., B.C., Can. . . D6 — 85
Lilly, Pa., U.S. . . . . F4 — 131
Lilly Fork, stm., W.V., U.S. m13 — 141
Lilly Grove, W.V., U.S. . . . D3 — 141
Lilongwe, Mwi. . . . . A5 — 56
Liloy, Phil. . . . . E8 — 34
Lily, Ky., U.S. . . . . C5 — 110
Lima, Peru . . . . F4 — 70
Lima, N.Y., U.S. . . . . C3 — 125
Lima, Oh., U.S. . . . . B1 — 128
Lima Reservoir, res., Mt.,
U.S. . . . . F4 — 119
Limay Mahuida, Arg. . . . . F4 — 72
Limbe, Cam. . . . . C1 — 54
Limbé, Haiti . . . . B5 — 80
Limeira, Braz. . . . . F2 — 74
Limerick, Ire. . . . . D2 — 12
Limestone, Me., U.S. . . . . B5 — 112
Limestone, co., Al., U.S. . . A2 — 94
Limestone, co., Tx., U.S. . . D4 — 136
Limestone Point, pen., Mb.,
Can. . . . . C2 — 86
Limfjorden, l., Den. . . . . . H3 — 10
Limingen, l., Nor. . . . . . . D5 — 10
Limmen Bight, b., Austl. . . C6 — 60
Límnos, i., Grc. . . . . E10 — 18
Limoges, On., Can. . . . . . B9 — 89
Limoges, Fr. . . . . E7 — 16
Limón, Hond. . . . . B2 — 80
Limon, Co., U.S. . . . . . . B7 — 99
Limoux, Fr. . . . . F8 — 16
Limpopo, stm., Afr. . . . . . C5 — 56

Lin'an, China . . . . C4 — 30
Linapacan Strait, strt., Phil. D7 — 34
Linares, Chile . . . . E2 — 69
Linares, Mex. . . . . C5 — 78
Linares, Spain . . . . H5 — 16
Lincoln, Arg. . . . . E5 — 72
Lincoln, On., Can. . . . . . D5 — 89
Lincoln, Eng., U.K. . . . . . D6 — 12
Lincoln, Al., U.S. . . . . . . B3 — 94
Lincoln, Ar., U.S. . . . . . . B1 — 97
Lincoln, Ca., U.S. . . . . . . C3 — 98
Lincoln, De., U.S. . . . . . . E4 — 101
Lincoln, Id., U.S. . . . . . . F6 — 105
Lincoln, Il., U.S. . . . . C4 — 106
Lincoln, Ks., U.S. . . . . . . C5 — 109
Lincoln, Ma., U.S. . . . . . g10 — 114
Lincoln, Me., U.S. . . . . . . C4 — 112
Lincoln, Mo., U.S. . . . . . C4 — 118
Lincoln, Ne., U.S. . . . . . . D9 — 120
Lincoln, N.H., U.S. . . . . . B3 — 122
Lincoln, co., Ar., U.S. . . . D4 — 97
Lincoln, co., Co., U.S. . . . C7 — 99
Lincoln, co., Ga., U.S. . . . C4 — 103
Lincoln, co., Id., U.S. . . . G4 — 105
Lincoln, co., Ks., U.S. . . . C5 — 109
Lincoln, co., Ky., U.S. . . . C5 — 110
Lincoln, co., La., U.S. . . . B3 — 111
Lincoln, co., Me., U.S. . . . D3 — 112
Lincoln, co., Mn., U.S. . . . F2 — 116
Lincoln, co., Mo., U.S. . . . B7 — 118
Lincoln, co., Ms., U.S. . . . D3 — 117
Lincoln, co., Mt., U.S. . . . B1 — 119
Lincoln, co., N.C., U.S. . . B1 — 126
Lincoln, co., Ne., U.S. . . . D5 — 120
Lincoln, co., N.M., U.S. . . D4 — 124
Lincoln, co., Nv., U.S. . . . F6 — 121
Lincoln, co., Ok., U.S. . . . B5 — 129
Lincoln, co., Or., U.S. . . . C3 — 130
Lincoln, co., S.D., U.S. . . D9 — 134
Lincoln, co., Tn., U.S. . . . B5 — 135
Lincoln, co., W.V., U.S. . . C2 — 141
Lincoln, co., Wa., U.S. . . . B7 — 140
Lincoln, co., Wi., U.S. . . . C4 — 142
Lincoln, co., Wy., U.S. . . . D2 — 143
Lincoln, Mount, mtn., Co.,
U.S. . . . . B4 — 99
Lincoln Acres, Ca., U.S. . . o15 — 98
Lincoln City, Or., U.S. . . . C3 — 130
Lincoln Hav see Lincoln
Sea, N.A. . . . . B28 — 82
Lincoln Heights, Oh., U.S. . o13 — 128
Lincoln Park, Co., U.S. . . . C5 — 99
Lincoln Park, Ga., U.S. . . . D2 — 103
Lincoln Park, Mi., U.S. . . . p15 — 115
Lincoln Park, N.J., U.S. . . B4 — 123
Lincoln Sea, N.A. . . . . . . B28 — 82
Lincolnshire, Il., U.S. . . . . h9 — 106
Lincoln Tomb State
Memorial, hist., Il., U.S. D4 — 106
Lincolnton, Ga., U.S. . . . . C4 — 103
Lincolnton, N.C., U.S. . . . B1 — 126
Lincolnville, S.C., U.S. . . . h11 — 133
Lincolnwood, Il., U.S. . . . h9 — 106
Lincroft, N.J., U.S. . . . . . C4 — 123
Lindale, Ga., U.S. . . . . . . B1 — 103
Lindale, Tx., U.S. . . . . . . C5 — 136
Linden, Guy. . . . . B8 — 70
Linden, Al., U.S. . . . . C2 — 94
Linden, In., U.S. . . . . D4 — 107
Linden, Mi., U.S. . . . . F7 — 115
Linden, N.J., U.S. . . . . . . k8 — 123
Linden, Tn., U.S. . . . . B4 — 135
Linden, Tx., U.S. . . . . C5 — 136
Lindenhurst, Il., U.S. . . . . h8 — 106
Lindenhurst, N.Y., U.S. . . . n15 — 125
Lindenwold, N.J., U.S. . . . D3 — 123
Lindesberg, Swe. . . . . G6 — 10
Lindesnes, c., Nor. . . . . . . H2 — 10
Lindi, Tan. . . . . E7 — 54
Lindon, Ut., U.S. . . . . C4 — 137
Lindsay, On., Can. . . . . . . C6 — 89
Lindsay, Ca., U.S. . . . . . . D4 — 98
Lindsay, Ok., U.S. . . . . . . C4 — 129
Lindsborg, Ks., U.S. . . . . . D6 — 109
Lindstrom, Mn., U.S. . . . . E6 — 116
Line Islands, is., Oc. . . . . . E14 — 58
Linesville, Pa., U.S. . . . . . C1 — 131
Lineville, Al., U.S. . . . . . . B4 — 94
Linfen, China . . . . D10 — 28
Lingao, China . . . . F2 — 30
Lingayen, Phil. . . . . C8 — 34
Lingayen Gulf, b., Phil. . . . C8 — 34
Lingen, Ger. . . . . D10 — 12
Lingga, Kepulauan, is.,
Indon. . . . . D3 — 36
Lingga, Pulau, i., Indon. . . D2 — 36
Lingle, Wy., U.S. . . . . D8 — 143
Linglestown, Pa., U.S. . . . F8 — 131
Lingqiu, China . . . . B3 — 30
Lingshan, China . . . . E2 — 30
Lingshui, China . . . . F3 — 30
Linguère, Sen. . . . . C1 — 50
Lingyuan, China . . . . A4 — 30
Linhai, China . . . . F12 — 28
Linhares, Braz. . . . . E3 — 74
Linhe, China . . . . C9 — 28
Linière, P.Q., Can. . . . . . . C7 — 90
Linköping, Swe. . . . . G6 — 10
Linkou, China . . . . B14 — 28
Linn, Mo., U.S. . . . . C6 — 118
Linn, co., Ia., U.S. . . . . . . B6 — 108
Linn, co., Ks., U.S. . . . . . D9 — 109
Linn, co., Mo., U.S. . . . . . B4 — 118
Linn, co., Or., U.S. . . . . . C4 — 130
Lino Lakes, Mn., U.S. . . . . m12 — 116

Linqing, China . . . . B4 — 30
Linquan, China . . . . C4 — 30
Linru, China . . . . E10 — 28
Lins, Braz. . . . . F2 — 74
Lintan, China . . . . C1 — 30
Linthicum Heights, Md.,
U.S. . . . . B4 — 113
Linton, In., U.S. . . . . F3 — 107
Linton, N.D., U.S. . . . . . . C5 — 127
Linwood, N.J., U.S. . . . . . E3 — 123
Linxi, China . . . . C11 — 28
Linxia, China . . . . D8 — 28
Linyi, China . . . . D11 — 28
Linyi, China . . . . B4 — 30
Linz, Aus. . . . . F14 — 12
Lion, Golfe du, b., Fr. . . . . F9 — 16
Lion, Gulf of see Lion,
Golfe du, b. . . . . F9 — 16
Lipa, Phil. . . . . D8 — 34
Lipeck, Russia . . . . D5 — 26
Lipova, Rom. . . . . F6 — 20
Lipscomb, Al., U.S. . . . . . B3 — 94
Lipscomb, co., Tx., U.S. . . A2 — 136
Lipu, China . . . . E3 — 30
Lira, Ug. . . . . C6 — 54
Lisala, D.R.C. . . . . C4 — 54
Lisboa (Lisbon), Port. . . . . H2 — 16
Lisbon see Lisboa, Port. . . . H2 — 16
Lisbon, Ia., U.S. . . . . C6 — 108
Lisbon, Md., U.S. . . . . . . B3 — 113
Lisbon, Me., U.S. . . . . . . D2 — 112
Lisbon, N.D., U.S. . . . . . . C8 — 127
Lisbon, N.H., U.S. . . . . . . B3 — 122
Lisbon, Oh., U.S. . . . . . . B5 — 128
Lisbon Center, Me., U.S. . . f7 — 112
Lisbon Falls, Me., U.S. . . . E2 — 112
Lisburne, Cape, c., Ak., U.S. B6 — 95
Lishui, China . . . . F11 — 28
Lisianski Island, i., Hi., U.S. k13 — 104
Lisieux, Fr. . . . . C7 — 16
Liski, Russia . . . . D5 — 26
Lisle, Il., U.S. . . . . k8 — 106
L'Islet-sur-Mer, P.Q., Can. . B7 — 90
L'Isle-Verte, P.Q., Can. . . . A8 — 90
Lismore, Austl. . . . . F5 — 62
Listowel, On., Can. . . . . . D4 — 89
Litang, China . . . . E8 — 28
Litang, China . . . . G9 — 28
Litchfield, Ct., U.S. . . . . . C3 — 100
Litchfield, Il., U.S. . . . . . . D4 — 106
Litchfield, Mi., U.S. . . . . . F6 — 115
Litchfield, Mn., U.S. . . . . E4 — 116
Litchfield, co., Ct., U.S. . . B2 — 100
Litchfield Park, Az., U.S. . . m8 — 96
Lithgow, Austl. . . . . G5 — 62
Lithia Springs, Ga., U.S. . . h7 — 103
Lithonia, Ga., U.S. . . . . . . C2 — 103
Lithuania, ctry., Eur. . . . . F7 — 20
Lititz, Pa., U.S. . . . . F9 — 131
Litovko, Russia . . . . B15 — 28
Little, stm., Ct., U.S. . . . . C7 — 100
Little, stm., Ky., U.S. . . . . D2 — 110
Little, stm., La., U.S. . . . . C3 — 111
Little, stm., N.C., U.S. . . . B3 — 126
Little, stm., Ok., U.S. . . . . B5 — 129
Little, stm., S.C., U.S. . . . C2 — 133
Little, stm., Tn., U.S. . . . . n14 — 135
Little, stm., Va., U.S. . . . . D7 — 139
Little, stm., Va., U.S. . . . . D2 — 139
Little, stm., Vt., U.S. . . . . C3 — 138
Little, stm., U.S. . . . . B5 — 97
Little Acres, Az., U.S. . . . . D5 — 96
Little Andaman, i., India . . G6 — 40
Little Arkansas, stm., Ks.,
U.S. . . . . D6 — 109
Little Belt see Lillebælt, strt.,
Den. . . . . I3 — 10
Little Belt Mountains, mts.,
Mt., U.S. . . . . D6 — 119
Little Bighorn, stm., U.S. . . E9 — 119
Little Black, stm., Me., U.S. A3 — 112
Little Blue, stm., In., U.S. . H5 — 107
Little Blue, stm., U.S. . . . . C6 — 109
Little Bow, stm., Ab., Can. . D4 — 84
Little Cacapon, stm., W.V.,
U.S. . . . . B6 — 141
Little Catalina, Nf., Can. . . D5 — 88
Little Cayman, i., Cay. Is. . . B3 — 80
Little Cedar, stm., Ia., U.S. . A5 — 108
Little Churchill, stm., Mb.,
Can. . . . . A4 — 86
Little Chute, Wi., U.S. . . . D5 — 142
Little Coal, stm., W.V., U.S. C3 — 141
Little Colorado, stm., Az.,
U.S. . . . . B4 — 96
Little Compton, R.I., U.S. . E6 — 132
Little Creek, De., U.S. . . . . D4 — 101
Little Creek Naval
Amphibious Base, mil.,
Va., U.S. . . . . k15 — 139
Little Creek Peak, mtn., Ut.,
U.S. . . . . F3 — 137
Little Current, On., Can. . . B3 — 89
Little Diomede Island, i.,
Ak., U.S. . . . . B6 — 95
Little Egg Harbor, b., N.J.,
U.S. . . . . D4 — 123
Little Egg Inlet, b., N.J., U.S. E4 — 123
Little Falls, Mn., U.S. . . . . E4 — 116
Little Falls, N.J., U.S. . . . . B4 — 123
Little Falls, N.Y., U.S. . . . . B6 — 125
Little Ferry, N.J., U.S. . . . . h8 — 123
Littlefield, Tx., U.S. . . . . . C1 — 136
Little Fishing Creek, stm.,
W.V., U.S. . . . . h9 — 141

Littlefork, Mn., U.S. . . . . . B5 — 116
Little Fork, stm., Mn., U.S. . B5 — 116
Little Goose Creek, stm.,
Wy., U.S. . . . . B6 — 143
Little Gunpowder Falls,
stm., Md., U.S. . . . . . . A4 — 113
Little Humboldt, stm., Nv.,
U.S. . . . . B4 — 121
Little Inagua, i., Bah. . . . . D10 — 76
Little Kanawha, stm., W.V.,
U.S. . . . . C4 — 141
Little Karroo, plat., S. Afr. . E3 — 56
Little Lake, Mi., U.S. . . . . B3 — 115
Little Lake, l., La., U.S. . . . E5 — 111
Little Lynches, stm., S.C.,
U.S. . . . . C7 — 133
Little Manatee, stm., Fl.,
U.S. . . . . p11 — 102
Little Mecatina, stm., Can. . h9 — 88
Little Miami, stm., Oh., U.S. C1 — 128
Little Minch, The, strt.,
Scot., U.K. . . . . B3 — 12
Little Missouri, stm., Ar.,
U.S. . . . . D2 — 97
Little Missouri, stm., U.S. . B7 — 92
Little Muddy, stm., Il., U.S. E4 — 106
Little Muddy, stm., N.D.,
U.S. . . . . A2 — 127
Little Namaqualand, hist.
reg., S. Afr. . . . . D2 — 56
Little Nicobar, i., India . . . H6 — 40
Little Osage, stm., U.S. . . . E9 — 109
Little Otter Creek, stm., Vt.,
U.S. . . . . C2 — 138
Little Owyhee, stm., U.S. . . B5 — 121
Little Pee Dee, stm., S.C.,
U.S. . . . . C9 — 133
Little Powder, stm., U.S. . . F11 — 119
Little Red, stm., Ar., U.S. . . B4 — 97
Little River, co., Ar., U.S. . D1 — 97
Little River Inlet, b., S.C.,
U.S. . . . . D10 — 133
Little Rock, Ar., U.S. . . . . C3 — 97
Little Rock, stm., U.S. . . . . A1 — 108
Little Rock Air Force Base,
mil., Ar., U.S. . . . . C3 — 97
Little Sable Point, c., Mi.,
U.S. . . . . E4 — 115
Little Salt Lake, l., Ut., U.S. F3 — 137
Little Sandy, stm., Ky., U.S. B6 — 110
Little Sandy Creek, stm.,
Wy., U.S. . . . . D3 — 143
Little Sebago Lake, l., Me.,
U.S. . . . . g7 — 112
Little Silver, N.J., U.S. . . . C4 — 123
Little Sioux, stm., U.S. . . . B2 — 108
Little Sioux, West Fork,
stm., Ia., U.S. . . . . B2 — 108
Little Smoky, stm., Ab., Can.B2 — 84
Little Snake, stm., U.S. . . . A2 — 99
Little Spokane, stm., Wa.,
U.S. . . . . B8 — 140
Littlestown, Pa., U.S. . . . . G7 — 131
Little Tallapoosa, stm., U.S. B4 — 94
Little Tenmile Creek, stm.,
W.V., U.S. . . . . k10 — 141
Little Tennessee, stm., U.S. D9 — 135
Littleton, Co., U.S. . . . . . B6 — 99
Littleton, Ma., U.S. . . . . . f10 — 114
Littleton, Me., U.S. . . . . . B5 — 112
Littleton, N.C., U.S. . . . . . A5 — 126
Littleton, N.H., U.S. . . . . . B3 — 122
Littleville, Al., U.S. . . . . . A2 — 94
Little Wabash, stm., Il., U.S. E5 — 106
Little Walnut, stm., Ks., U.S. g13 — 109
Little White, stm., S.D., U.S. D5 — 134
Little Wolf, stm., Wi., U.S. . D4 — 142
Little Wood, stm., Id., U.S. . F4 — 105
Little Zab, stm., Asia . . . . E10 — 44
Liucheng, China . . . . G9 — 28
Liuzhou, China . . . . G9 — 28
Live Oak, Ca., U.S. . . . . . C3 — 98
Live Oak, Fl., U.S. . . . . . . B4 — 102
Live Oak, co., Tx., U.S. . . . E3 — 136
Livermore, Ca., U.S. . . . . . h9 — 98
Livermore, Ky., U.S. . . . . . C2 — 110
Livermore, Mount, mtn.,
Tx., U.S. . . . . o12 — 136
Livermore Falls, Me., U.S. . D2 — 112
Liverpool, Eng., U.K. . . . . D5 — 12
Livingston, Guat. . . . . B2 — 80
Livingston, Al., U.S. . . . . . C1 — 94
Livingston, Ca., U.S. . . . . . D3 — 98
Livingston, Il., U.S. . . . . . E4 — 106
Livingston, La., U.S. . . . . . D5 — 111
Livingston, Mt., U.S. . . . . . E6 — 119
Livingston, N.J., U.S. . . . . B4 — 123
Livingston, Tn., U.S. . . . . . C8 — 135
Livingston, Tx., U.S. . . . . . D5 — 136
Livingston, co., Il., U.S. . . . C5 — 106
Livingston, co., Ky., U.S. . . e9 — 110
Livingston, co., La., U.S. . . D5 — 111
Livingston, co., Mi., U.S. . . F7 — 115
Livingston, co., Mo., U.S. . B4 — 118
Livingston, co., N.Y., U.S. . C3 — 125
Livingston, Lake, res., Tx.,
U.S. . . . . D5 — 136
Livingstone, Zam. . . . . . . B4 — 56
Livingstone Falls, wtfl., Afr. E2 — 54
Livingstonia, Mwi. . . . . . . A5 — 56
Livny, Russia . . . . C14 — 20
Livonia, La., U.S. . . . . D4 — 111
Livonia, Mi., U.S. . . . . . . F7 — 115
Livorno, Italy . . . . C3 — 18
Liwale, Tan. . . . . E7 — 54

Liwonde, Mwi. . . . . B6 — 56
Lixi, China . . . . F10 — 28
Lixian, China . . . . D3 — 30
Lizard Head Pass, Co., U.S. D3 — 99
Lizard Head Peak, mtn.,
Wy., U.S. . . . . D3 — 143
Lizella, Ga., U.S. . . . . D3 — 103
Ljahovskie ostrova, is.,
Russia . . . . B15 — 26
Ljubercy, Russia . . . . C6 — 22
Ljubljana, Slvn. . . . . A5 — 18
Ljudinovo, Russia . . . . . . C13 — 20
Ljungby, Swe. . . . . H5 — 10
Ljusdal, Swe. . . . . F7 — 10
Ljusnan, stm., Swe. . . . . . E6 — 10
Ljusterö, i., Swe. . . . . G8 — 10
Llancanelo, Laguna, l., Arg. F4 — 72
Llano, Tx., U.S. . . . . D3 — 136
Llano, co., Tx., U.S. . . . . . D3 — 136
Llano, stm., Tx., U.S. . . . . D3 — 136
Llano Estacado see
Estacado, Llano, pl.,
U.S. . . . . C1 — 136
Llanos, pl., S.A. . . . . B6 — 70
Lleida, Spain . . . . G7 — 16
Llera de Canales, Mex. . . . C5 — 78
Lloyd, Ky., U.S. . . . . B7 — 110
Lloydminster, Ab., Can. . . . C5 — 84
Lloyds, stm., Nf., Can. . . . D3 — 88
Llucmajor, Spain . . . . H8 — 16
Llullaillaco, Volcán, vol.,
S.A. . . . . C4 — 72
Loami, Il., U.S. . . . . D4 — 106
Loange, stm., Afr. . . . . . . E3 — 54
Lobamba, Swaz. . . . . D5 — 56
Lobatse, Bots. . . . . D4 — 56
Lobelville, Tn., U.S. . . . . . B4 — 135
Lobería, Arg. . . . . F6 — 72
Lobito, Ang. . . . . F2 — 54
Lobos, Cay, i., Bah. . . . . . A4 — 80
Lobster Lake, l., Me., U.S. . C3 — 112
Lobva, Russia . . . . C11 — 22
Locarno, Switz. . . . . A2 — 18
Loch Raven Reservoir, res.,
Md., U.S. . . . . B4 — 113
Lochsa, stm., Id., U.S. . . . . C3 — 105
Lockeport, N.S., Can. . . . . F4 — 87
Lockesburg, Ar., U.S. . . . . D1 — 97
Lockhart, Tx., U.S. . . . . . . E4 — 136
Lock Haven, Pa., U.S. . . . . D7 — 131
Lockland, Oh., U.S. . . . . . o13 — 128
Lockney, Tx., U.S. . . . . . . B2 — 136
Lockport, Il., U.S. . . . . . . B5 — 106
Lockport, La., U.S. . . . . . . E5 — 111
Lockport, N.Y., U.S. . . . . . B2 — 125
Lockwood, Mo., U.S. . . . . D4 — 118
Lockwood, Mt., U.S. . . . . . E8 — 119
Loc Ninh, Viet. . . . . D5 — 34
Locust, N.C., U.S. . . . . . . B2 — 126
Locust Fork, stm., Al., U.S. . B3 — 94
Locust Grove, Ga., U.S. . . . C2 — 103
Locust Grove, Ok., U.S. . . . A6 — 129
Lodejnoe Pole, Russia . . . . B5 — 22
Lodgepole Creek, stm., U.S. C3 — 120
Lodi, Italy . . . . B2 — 18
Lodi, Ca., U.S. . . . . C3 — 98
Lodi, N.J., U.S. . . . . h8 — 123
Lodi, Oh., U.S. . . . . A3 — 128
Lodi, Wi., U.S. . . . . E4 — 142
Lodja, D.R.C. . . . . D4 — 54
Lodore, Canyon of, val.,
Co., U.S. . . . . A2 — 99
Lodwar, Kenya . . . . C7 — 54
Łódź, Pol. . . . . D5 — 20
Loei, Thai. . . . . C4 — 34
Lofoten, is., Nor. . . . . B5 — 10
Lofoten Basin . . . . D21 — 144
Loga, Niger . . . . D5 — 50
Logan, Ia., U.S. . . . . C2 — 108
Logan, Ks., U.S. . . . . C4 — 109
Logan, N.M., U.S. . . . . . . B6 — 124
Logan, Oh., U.S. . . . . C3 — 128
Logan, Ut., U.S. . . . . B4 — 137
Logan, W.V., U.S. . . . . . . D3 — 141
Logan, co., Ar., U.S. . . . . . B2 — 97
Logan, co., Co., U.S. . . . . A7 — 99
Logan, co., Il., U.S. . . . . . C4 — 106
Logan, co., Ks., U.S. . . . . . D2 — 109
Logan, co., Ky., U.S. . . . . . D3 — 110
Logan, co., N.D., U.S. . . . . C6 — 127
Logan, co., Ne., U.S. . . . . . C5 — 120
Logan, co., Oh., U.S. . . . . B2 — 128
Logan, co., Ok., U.S. . . . . B4 — 129
Logan, co., W.V., U.S. . . . . D3 — 141
Logan, Mount, mtn., Yk.,
Can. . . . . F11 — 82
Logan, Mount, mtn., Wa.,
U.S. . . . . A5 — 140
Logandale, Nv., U.S. . . . . . G7 — 121
Logan Lake, B.C., Can. . . . D7 — 85
Logan Martin Lake, res., Al.,
U.S. . . . . B3 — 94
Logan Pass, Mt., U.S. . . . . B2 — 119
Logansport, In., U.S. . . . . C5 — 107
Logansport, La., U.S. . . . . C2 — 111
Loganville, Ga., U.S. . . . . . C3 — 103
Loganville, Pa., U.S. . . . . . G8 — 131
Loggieville, N.B., Can. . . . B4 — 87
Log Lane Village, Co., U.S. A7 — 99
Logone, stm., Afr. . . . . . . B3 — 54
Logroño, Spain . . . . F5 — 16
Løgstør, Den. . . . . H3 — 10
Loi-kaw, Myan. . . . . C3 — 34
Loimaa, Fin. . . . . F10 — 10
Loire, stm., Fr. . . . . D6 — 16

Name	Map Ref.	Page
Loja, Ec.	D4	70
Loja, Spain	I4	16
Lokandu, D.R.C.	D5	54
Lokan tekojärvi, res., Fin.	C12	10
Lokichokio, Kenya	C6	54
Lokoja, Nig.	E6	50
Lokolama, D.R.C.	D3	54
Lola, Gui.	E3	50
Lola, Mount, mtn., Ca., U.S.	C3	98
Loliondo, Tan.	D7	54
Lolland, i., Den.	I4	10
Lolo, Mt., U.S.	D2	119
Lolo Pass, U.S.	C4	105
Lom, Bul.	C9	18
Lomami, stm., D.R.C.	C4	54
Lomas de Zamora, Arg.	E6	72
Lombard, Il., U.S.	k8	106
Lomblen, Pulau, i., Indon.	E6	36
Lombok, i., Indon.	E5	36
Lombok, Selat, strt., Indon.	E5	36
Lomé, Togo	D4	50
Lomela, D.R.C.	D4	54
Lomié, Cam.	C2	54
Lomira, Wi., U.S.	E5	142
Lomonosov, Russia	G13	10
Lomonosov Ridge	E8	144
Lompoc, Ca., U.S.	E3	98
Lom Sak, Thai.	C4	34
Łomża, Pol.	C7	20
Lonaconing, Md., U.S.	k13	113
Loncoche, Chile	E2	69
London, On., Can.	E3	89
London, Eng., U.K.	E6	12
London, Ar., U.S.	B2	97
London, Ky., U.S.	C5	110
London, Oh., U.S.	C2	128
Londonderry, N. Ire., U.K.	C3	12
Londonderry, N.H., U.S.	E4	122
Londonderry, Cape, c., Austl.	C4	60
Londonderry, Isla, i., Chile	I2	69
Londontown, Md., U.S.	C4	113
Londrina, Braz.	F1	74
Lone Grove, Ok., U.S.	C4	129
Lone Mountain, mtn., Nv., U.S.	E4	121
Lone Pine, Ca., U.S.	D4	98
Lone Tree, Ia., U.S.	C6	108
Long, co., Ga., U.S.	E5	103
Long Bar Harbor, Md., U.S.	B5	113
Long Beach, Ca., U.S.	F4	98
Long Beach, In., U.S.	A4	107
Long Beach, Md., U.S.	D5	113
Long Beach, Ms., U.S.	g7	117
Long Beach, N.Y., U.S.	E7	125
Long Beach, Wa., U.S.	C1	140
Longboat Key, Fl., U.S.	q10	102
Longboat Key, i., Fl., U.S.	q10	102
Longboat Pass, strt., Fl., U.S.	q10	102
Long Branch, N.J., U.S.	C5	123
Longbranch, Wa., U.S.	B3	140
Long Creek Mountain, mtn., Wy., U.S.	D5	143
Longde, China	B2	30
Longford, Ire.	D3	12
Long Grove, Ia., U.S.	C7	108
Long Harbour [-Mount Arlington Heights], Nf., Can.	E5	88
Longhua, China	A4	30
Longiram, Indon.	D5	36
Long Island, i., Bah.	D10	76
Long Island, i., N.S., Can.	E3	87
Long Island, i., Ma., U.S.	g12	114
Long Island, i., Me., U.S.	g7	112
Long Island, i., N.Y., U.S.	E7	125
Long Island Sound, strt., U.S.	E7	125
Longjiang, China	B12	28
Long Key, i., Fl., U.S.	H6	102
Long Lake, Il., U.S.	h8	106
Long Lake, l., Me., U.S.	A4	112
Long Lake, l., Me., U.S.	D2	112
Long Lake, l., Mi., U.S.	D5	115
Long Lake, l., Mi., U.S.	C7	115
Long Lake, l., Mn., U.S.	D4	116
Long Lake, l., N.D., U.S.	C6	127
Long Lake, l., N.Y., U.S.	B6	125
Long Lake, l., Wa., U.S.	f10	140
Long Lake, l., Wi., U.S.	C2	142
Longli, China	F9	28
Longling, China	B3	34
Longmeadow, Ma., U.S.	B2	114
Longmen, China	B6	34
Longmont, Co., U.S.	A5	99
Longnan, China	E3	30
Long Point, c., Mb., Can.	C2	86
Long Point, pen., On., Can.	E4	89
Long Pond, res., Fl., U.S.	C4	102
Long Prairie, Mn., U.S.	E4	116
Longquan, China	D4	30
Long Range Mountains, mts., Nf., Can.	D3	88
Longreach, Austl.	E3	62
Longshan, China	D2	30
Longs Peak, mtn., Co., U.S.	A5	99
Long Strait see Longa, proliv, strt., Russia	B19	26
Longueuil, P.Q., Can.	D4	90
Long View, N.C., U.S.	B1	126
Longview, Tx., U.S.	C5	136
Longview, Wa., U.S.	C3	140
Longxi, China	E8	28
Longxian, China	C2	30

Name	Map Ref.	Page
Long Xuyen, Viet.	D5	34
Longyan, China	D4	30
Longzhou, China	G9	28
Lonoke, Ar., U.S.	C4	97
Lonoke, co., Ar., U.S.	C4	97
Lonsdale, Mn., U.S.	F5	116
Lonsdale, R.I., U.S.	B4	132
Lons-le-Saunier, Fr.	D9	16
Loogootee, In., U.S.	G4	107
Lookout, Ky., U.S.	C7	110
Lookout, Cape, c., N.C., U.S.	C6	126
Lookout, Point, c., Mi., U.S.	d7	115
Lookout Mountain, Tn., U.S.	h11	135
Lookout Mountain, mtn., Or., U.S.	C6	130
Lookout Mountain, mtn., U.S.	D8	135
Lookout Pass, U.S.	B3	105
Lookout Point Lake, res., Or., U.S.	D4	130
Loongana, Austl.	G4	60
Loon Lake, Wa., U.S.	A8	140
Loon Lake, l., Me., U.S.	B3	112
Loop Creek, stm., W.V., U.S.	m13	141
Loosahatchie, stm., Tn., U.S.	B2	135
Lop, China	A4	40
Lopatka, mys, c., Russia	D17	26
Lop Buri, Thai.	D4	34
Lopez, Cap, c., Gabon	D1	54
Lopez Island, i., Wa., U.S.	A3	140
Lop Nor (Lop Nur), l., China	C6	28
Lop Nur (Lop Nor), l., China	C6	28
Lopphavet, Nor.	A9	10
Lora, Hāmūn-i-, l., Asia	E8	42
Lorain, Oh., U.S.	A3	128
Lorain, co., Oh., U.S.	A3	128
Loramie, Lake, res., Oh., U.S.	B1	128
Lorca, Spain	I6	16
Lord Howe Rise	K19	64
Lordsburg, N.M., U.S.	E1	124
Loreauville, La., U.S.	D4	111
Lorenzo, Tx., U.S.	C2	136
Loreto, Braz.	E10	70
Loreto, Mex.	B2	78
Lorette, Mb., Can.	E3	86
Loretteville, P.Q., Can.	C6	90
Loretto, Ky., U.S.	C4	110
Loretto, Pa., U.S.	F4	131
Loretto, Tn., U.S.	B4	135
Lorica, Col.	B4	70
Lorient, Fr.	D5	16
L'Orignal, On., Can.	B10	89
Loris, S.C., U.S.	C10	133
Lorn, Firth of, b., Scot., U.K.	B4	12
Lorne, Austl.	H3	62
Lorne, N.B., Can.	B3	87
Lorraine, hist. reg., Fr.	C9	16
Los, Îles de, is., Gui.	E2	50
Los Alamos, N.M., U.S.	B3	124
Los Alamos, co., N.M., U.S.	B3	124
Los Altos, Ca., U.S.	k8	98
Los Angeles, Ca., U.S.	E4	98
Los Angeles, co., Ca., U.S.	E4	98
Los Angeles Aqueduct, Ca., U.S.	E4	98
Los Banos, Ca., U.S.	D3	98
Los Blancos, Arg.	C5	72
Los Fresnos, Tx., U.S.	F4	136
Los Gatos, Ca., U.S.	D2	98
Lošinj, Otok, i., Cro.	B5	18
Los Lunas, N.M., U.S.	C3	124
Los Mochis, Mex.	B3	78
Los Pinos, stm., Co., U.S.	D3	99
Los Ranchos de Albuquerque, N.M., U.S.	B3	124
Los Roques, Islas, is., Ven.	C6	80
Lost, stm., In., U.S.	G4	107
Lost, stm., W.V., U.S.	B6	141
Lost, stm., Wa., U.S.	A5	140
Lost Creek, stm., Wy., U.S.	D4	143
Lost Peak, mtn., Ut., U.S.	F2	137
Lost Ranger Peak, mtn., Co., U.S.	A4	99
Lost River Glacial Caverns, N.H., U.S.	B3	122
Lost River Range, mts., Id., U.S.	E5	105
Lost Trail Pass, U.S.	E5	105
Losuia, Pap. N. Gui.	H13	32
Los Vilos, Chile	D2	69
Lot, stm., Fr.	E7	16
Lota, Chile	F3	72
Lotawana, Lake, l., Mo., U.S.	k11	118
Lotbinière, P.Q., Can.	C6	90
Loto, D.R.C.	D4	54
Lotung, Tai.	E5	30
Louang Namtha, Laos	B4	34
Louangphrabang, Laos	C4	34
Loubomo, Congo	D2	54
Loudon, Tn., U.S.	D9	135
Loudon, co., Tn., U.S.	D9	135
Loudonville, Oh., U.S.	B3	128
Loudoun, co., Va., U.S.	A5	139
Louga, Sen.	E1	50
Louhi, Russia	A5	22
Louisa, Ky., U.S.	B7	110
Louisa, Va., U.S.	B4	139
Louisa, co., Ia., U.S.	C6	108
Louisa, co., Va., U.S.	C5	139

Name	Map Ref.	Page
Louisa, Lake, l., Fl., U.S.	D5	102
Louisbourg, N.S., Can.	D10	87
Louisburg, Ks., U.S.	D9	109
Louisburg, N.C., U.S.	A4	126
Louisdale, N.S., Can.	D8	87
Louise, Lake, l., Ak., U.S.	f18	95
Louise Island, i., B.C., Can.	C2	85
Louiseville, P.Q., Can.	C5	90
Louisiana, Mo., U.S.	B6	118
Louisiana, state, U.S.	C3	111
Louisiana Point, c., La., U.S.	E2	111
Louis Trichardt, S. Afr.	C4	56
Louisville, Al., U.S.	D4	94
Louisville, Co., U.S.	B5	99
Louisville, Ga., U.S.	C4	103
Louisville, Il., U.S.	E5	106
Louisville, Ky., U.S.	B4	110
Louisville, Ms., U.S.	B4	117
Louisville, Ne., U.S.	D9	120
Louisville, Oh., U.S.	B4	128
Louisville Ridge	L22	64
Louis-XIV, Pointe, c., P.Q., Can.	h11	90
Loum, Cam.	C1	54
Loup, co., Ne., U.S.	C6	120
Loup, stm., Ne., U.S.	C8	120
Loup City, Ne., U.S.	C7	120
Lourdes, Nf., Can.	D2	88
Lourdes, Fr.	F6	16
Lourenço Marques see Maputo, Moz.	D5	56
Louviers, Co., U.S.	B6	99
Love, co., Ok., U.S.	D4	129
Loveč, Bul.	C10	18
Loveland, Co., U.S.	A5	99
Loveland, Oh., U.S.	n13	128
Loveland Park, Oh., U.S.	C1	128
Loveland Pass, Co., U.S.	B5	99
Lovell, Wy., U.S.	B4	143
Lovelock, Nv., U.S.	C3	121
Lovely, Ky., U.S.	C7	110
Lovenia, Mount, mtn., Ut., U.S.	C5	137
Love Point, c., Md., U.S.	B5	113
Loves Park, Il., U.S.	A4	106
Lovettsville, Va., U.S.	A5	139
Loving, N.M., U.S.	E5	124
Loving, co., Tx., U.S.	D1	136
Lovington, Ia., U.S.	e8	108
Lovington, Il., U.S.	D5	106
Lovington, N.M., U.S.	E6	124
Lóvua, Ang.	F4	54
Lowden, Ia., U.S.	C7	108
Lowell, Ar., U.S.	A1	97
Lowell, In., U.S.	B3	107
Lowell, Ma., U.S.	A5	114
Lowell, Mi., U.S.	F5	115
Lowell, N.C., U.S.	B1	126
Lowell, Or., U.S.	D4	130
Lowell, Lake, res., Id., U.S.	F2	105
Lowellville, Oh., U.S.	A5	128
Lower Arrow Lake, res., B.C., Can.	E8	85
Lower Brule Indian Reservation, S.D., U.S.	C6	134
Lower California see Baja California, pen., Mex.	B2	78
Lower Hutt, N.Z.	p14	63c
Lower Klamath Lake, l., Ca., U.S.	B3	98
Lower Matecumbe Key, i., Fl., U.S.	H6	102
Lower New York Bay, b., N.J., U.S.	B4	123
Lower Otay Lake, res., Ca., U.S.	o16	98
Lower Paia, Hi., U.S.	C5	104
Lower Red Lake, l., Mn., U.S.	C3	116
Lower Rice Lake, l., Mn., U.S.	C3	116
Lower Salmon Dam, Id., U.S.	G4	105
Lower Trajan's Wall, hist., Eur.	G10	20
Lower West Pubnico, N.S., Can.	F4	87
Lowestoft, Eng., U.K.	D7	12
Lowndes, co., Al., U.S.	C3	94
Lowndes, co., Ga., U.S.	F3	103
Lowndes, co., Ms., U.S.	B5	117
Lowry City, Mo., U.S.	C4	118
Lowville, N.Y., U.S.	B5	125
Loxley, Al., U.S.	E2	94
Loxton, Austl.	G3	62
Loyal, Wi., U.S.	D3	142
Loyall, Ky., U.S.	D6	110
Loyalsock Creek, stm., Pa., U.S.	D8	131
Loyalty Islands see Loyauté, Îles, is., N. Cal.	I9	62a
Loyauté, Îles, is., N. Cal.	I9	62a
Loznica, Yugo.	B7	18
Lozova, Ukr.	E14	20
Lualaba, stm., Afr.	D5	54
Lua Makika, crat., Hi., U.S.	C5	104
Lu'an, China	C4	30
Luan, stm., China	C11	28
Luanda, Ang.	E2	54
Luang, Thale, l., Thai.	E4	34
Luanginga, stm., Afr.	A3	56
Luangwa, stm., Afr.	A5	56
Luanping, China	A4	30
Luanshya, Zam.	A4	56
Luan Toro, Arg.	F4	72

Name	Map Ref.	Page
Luapula, stm., Afr.	A4	56
Luau, Ang.	F4	54
Luba, Eq. Gui.	C1	54
Lubang Islands, is., Phil.	C6	34
Lubango, Ang.	A1	56
Lubbock, Tx., U.S.	C2	136
Lubbock, co., Tx., U.S.	C2	136
Lubec, Me., U.S.	D6	112
Lübeck, Ger.	D12	12
Lubefu, D.R.C.	D4	54
Lubin, Pol.	D4	20
Lublin, Pol.	D7	20
Lubnān, Jabal, mts., Leb.	F6	44
Lubny, Ukr.	D12	20
Lubudi, D.R.C.	F5	54
Lubuklinggau, Indon.	D2	36
Lubumbashi, D.R.C.	F5	54
Lubutu, D.R.C.	D5	54
Lucama, N.C., U.S.	B4	126
Lucan, On., Can.	D3	89
Lucapa, Ang.	E4	54
Lucas, co., Ia., U.S.	C4	108
Lucas, co., Oh., U.S.	A2	128
Lucasville, Oh., U.S.	D3	128
Lucca, Italy	C3	18
Luce, co., Mi., U.S.	B5	115
Lucedale, Ms., U.S.	E5	117
Lucena, Phil.	D8	34
Lucena, Spain	I4	16
Lučenec, Slvk.	E5	20
Lucera, Italy	D5	18
Lucerne see Luzern, Switz.	A2	18
Lucerne, Ca., U.S.	C2	98
Lucerne, Lake see Vierwaldstätter See, l., Switz.	A2	18
Lucernemines, Pa., U.S.	E3	131
Lucerne Valley, Ca., U.S.	E5	98
Luceville, P.Q., Can.	A9	90
Lucira, Ang.	A1	56
Luck, Wi., U.S.	C1	142
Luckenwalde, Ger.	E13	12
Lucknow, On., Can.	D3	89
Lucknow, India	D4	40
Lucky Peak Lake, res., Id., U.S.	F3	105
Luçon, Fr.	D6	16
Lucusse, Ang.	A3	56
Lüda see Dalian, China	D12	28
Ludell, Mi., U.S.	E4	115
Ludhiāna, India	C3	40
Ludington, Mi., U.S.	E4	115
Ludlow, Ky., U.S.	h13	110
Ludlow, Ma., U.S.	B3	114
Ludlow, Vt., U.S.	E3	138
Ludogorie, reg., Bul.	C11	18
Ludowici, Ga., U.S.	E5	103
Ludvika, Swe.	F6	10
Ludwigsburg, Ger.	F11	12
Ludwigslust, Ger.	D12	12
Luebo, D.R.C.	E4	54
Lueyang, China	C2	30
Lufeng, China	E4	30
Lufkin, Tx., U.S.	D5	136
Luga, Russia	C4	22
Lugano, Switz.	A2	18
Luganville, Vanuatu	k9	62a
Lugards Falls, wtfl, Kenya	D7	54
Lugela, Moz.	B6	56
Lugo, Italy	B3	18
Lugo, Spain	F3	16
Lugoff, S.C., U.S.	C6	133
Lugoj, Rom.	G6	20
Lugovoj, Kaz.	B10	42
Luhans'k, Ukr.	E15	20
Luishia, D.R.C.	F5	54
Luiza, D.R.C.	E4	54
Luke Air Force Base, mil., Az., U.S.	D3	96
Lukenie, stm., D.R.C.	D3	54
Lukojanov, Russia	D7	22
Lukolela, D.R.C.	D3	54
Lukolela, D.R.C.	E4	54
Lukula, D.R.C.	E2	54
Lukulu, Zam.	A3	56
Lula, Ga., U.S.	B3	103
Luleå, Swe.	D10	10
Luleälven, stm., Swe.	C9	10
Lüleburgaz, Tur.	B2	44
Luliang, China	D1	30
Lüliang Shan, mts., China	D10	28
Luling, La., U.S.	k11	111
Luling, Tx., U.S.	E4	136
Lulua, stm., D.R.C.	E4	54
Lumana, D.R.C.	D5	54
Lumbala N'guimbo, Ang.	A3	56
Lumber, stm., U.S.	C9	133
Lumber City, Ga., U.S.	E4	103
Lumberport, W.V., U.S.	B4	141
Lumberton, Ms., U.S.	D4	117
Lumberton, N.C., U.S.	C3	126
Lumbo, Moz.	B7	56
Lumby, B.C., Can.	D8	85
Lumding, India	D6	40
Lummi Indian Reservation, Wa., U.S.	A3	140
Lumpkin, Ga., U.S.	D2	103
Lumpkin, co., Ga., U.S.	B2	103
Lumsden, Nf., Can.	D5	88
Lumut, Tanjung, c., Indon.	D3	36
Luna, co., N.M., U.S.	E2	124
Luna Pier, Mi., U.S.	G7	115

Name	Map Ref.	Page
Lund, Swe.	I5	10
Lund, Nv., U.S.	E6	121
Lundar, Mb., Can.	D2	86
Lundazi, Zam.	A5	56
Lüneburg, Ger.	D12	12
Lunenburg, Ma., U.S.	A4	114
Lunenburg, co., Va., U.S.	D4	139
Lunéville, Fr.	C10	16
Lungué-Bungo (Lungwebungu), stm., Afr.	A2	56
Lungwebungu (Lungué-Bungo), stm., Afr.	A3	56
Luninec, Bela.	C9	20
Luobei, China	A2	31
Luochuan, China	B2	30
Luoding, China	E3	30
Luohe, China	E10	28
Luotian, China	C4	30
Luoyang, China	E10	28
Luoyuan, China	D4	30
Luozi, D.R.C.	E2	54
Lupanshui, China	D1	30
Lupeni, Rom.	G7	20
Luputa, D.R.C.	E4	54
Luqu, China	E8	28
Luray, Va., U.S.	B4	139
Lure, Lake, res., N.C., U.S.	f10	126
Luremo, Ang.	E3	54
Lúrio, Moz.	A7	56
Lúrio, stm., Moz.	A6	56
Lusaka, Zam.	B4	56
Lusambo, D.R.C.	D4	54
Lusanga, D.R.C.	D3	54
Lusangi, D.R.C.	D5	54
Lusby, Md., U.S.	D5	113
Luseland, Sk., Can.	E1	91
Lushnjë, Alb.	D7	18
Lushoto, Tan.	D7	54
Lüshun, China	D12	28
Lusk, Wy., U.S.	D8	143
Lūt, dasht-e, des., Iran	D7	42
Lutcher, La., U.S.	D5	111
Luther, Ok., U.S.	B4	129
Lutherstadt Eisleben, Ger.	E12	12
Lutherstsadt Wittenberg, Ger.	E13	12
Luthersville, Ga., U.S.	C2	103
Lutherville-Timonium, Md., U.S.	B4	113
Luton, Eng., U.K.	E6	12
Lutselk'e, N.T., Can.	F17	82
Luts'k, Ukr.	D8	20
Luttrell, Tn., U.S.	C10	135
Lutz, Fl., U.S.	D4	102
Lutzow-Holm Bay, b., Ant.	C8	67
Luuq, Som.	J13	48
Luverne, Al., U.S.	D3	94
Luverne, Mn., U.S.	G2	116
Luwingu, Zam.	A4	56
Luwuk, Indon.	D6	36
Luxapallila Creek, stm., U.S.	B5	117
Luxembourg, Lux.	F9	12
Luxembourg, ctry., Eur.	C10	16
Luxemburg, Wi., U.S.	D6	142
Luxi, China	G7	28
Luxomni, Ga., U.S.	h8	103
Luxor see El-Uqsor, Egypt	E11	48
Luxora, Ar., U.S.	B6	97
Luza, Russia	B8	22
Luzern, Switz.	A2	18
Luzerne, Pa., U.S.	n17	131
Luzerne, co., Pa., U.S.	D9	131
Luzhai, China		
Luzhou, China	F9	28
Luziânia, Braz.	E2	74
Luzilândia, Braz.	B3	74
Luzon, i., Phil.	C4	34
Luzon Strait, strt., Asia	B8	34
L'viv, Ukr.	E8	20
L'vov see L'viv, Ukr.	E8	20
Lyallpur see Faisalabad, Pak.	D10	42
Lycksele, Swe.	D8	10
Lycoming, co., Pa., U.S.	D7	131
Lycoming Creek, stm., Pa., U.S.	D7	131
Lydenburg, S. Afr.	D5	56
Lyell, Mount, mtn., Can.	D2	84
Lyford, Tx., U.S.	F4	136
Lykens, Pa., U.S.	E8	131
Lyle, Wa., U.S.	D4	140
Lyman, S.C., U.S.	B3	133
Lyman, Wy., U.S.	E2	143
Lyman, co., S.D., U.S.	D6	134
Lyman Lake, res., Az., U.S.	C6	96
Lyme Bay, b., Eng., U.K.	E5	12
Lynch, Ky., U.S.	D7	110
Lynchburg, Oh., U.S.	C2	128
Lynchburg, Tn., U.S.	B5	135
Lynchburg, Va., U.S.	C3	139
Lynches, stm., S.C., U.S.	D8	133
Lynden, Wa., U.S.	A3	140
Lynde Point, c., Ct., U.S.	D6	100
Lyndhurst, N.J., U.S.	h8	123
Lyndhurst, Oh., U.S.	g9	128
Lyndon, Ks., U.S.	D8	109
Lyndon, Ky., U.S.	g11	110
Lyndon B. Johnson National Historical Site, hist., Tx., U.S.	D3	136
Lyndon B. Johnson Space Center, sci., Tx., U.S.	r14	136
Lyndonville, Vt., U.S.	B4	138
Lyndora, Pa., U.S.	E2	131
Lyngen, b., Nor.	B9	10

Name	Map Ref.	Page

Lynn, Al., U.S. ... A2 94
Lynn, In., U.S. ... D8 107
Lynn, Ma., U.S. ... B6 114
Lynn, co., Tx., U.S. ... C2 136
Lynn, Lake, res., W.V., U.S. ... B5 141
Lynn Canal, b., Ak., U.S. ... k22 95
Lynnfield, Ma., U.S. ... f11 114
Lynn Garden, Tn., U.S. ... C11 135
Lynn Haven, Fl., U.S. ... u16 102
Lynnhaven Roads, b., Va., U.S. ... k15 139
Lynnville, In., U.S. ... H3 107
Lynnwood, Wa., U.S. ... B3 140
Lynwood, Ca., U.S. ... n12 98
Lyon, Fr. ... E9 16
Lyon, co., Ia., U.S. ... A1 108
Lyon, co., Ks., U.S. ... D7 109
Lyon, co., Ky., U.S. ... C1 110
Lyon, co., Mn., U.S. ... F3 116
Lyon, co., Nv., U.S. ... D2 121
Lyons, Co., U.S. ... A5 99
Lyons, Ga., U.S. ... D4 103
Lyons, Il., U.S. ... k9 106
Lyons, In., U.S. ... G3 107
Lyons, Ks., U.S. ... D5 109
Lyons, Mi., U.S. ... F6 115
Lyons, Ne., U.S. ... C9 120
Lyons, N.Y., U.S. ... B3 125
Lyons, Or., U.S. ... C4 130
Lysekil, Swe. ... G4 10
Lyster Station, P.Q., Can. ... C6 90
Lys'va, Russia ... D7 26
Lysychans'k, Ukr. ... E15 20
Lytle, Tx., U.S. ... E3 136
Lyubotyn, Ukr. ... E13 20

M

Maalaea Bay, b., Hi., U.S. ... C5 104
Ma'ān, Jord. ... D3 42
Ma'anshan, China ... C4 30
Maarianhamina, Fin. ... F8 10
Ma'arrat an-Nu'mān, Syria ... E7 44
Maas (Meuse), stm., Eur. ... B9 16
Maastricht, Neth. ... E9 12
Mabank, Tx., U.S. ... C4 136
Mabel, Mn., U.S. ... G7 116
Maben, Ms., U.S. ... B4 117
Mableton, Ga., U.S. ... h7 103
Mabote, Moz. ... C5 56
Mabscott, W.V., U.S. ... D3 141
Mabton, Wa., U.S. ... C5 140
Mača, Russia ... D13 26
Macaé, Braz. ... F3 74
Macaíba, Braz. ... C4 74
Macapá, Braz. ... A1 74
Macará, Ec. ... D4 70
Macau, Braz. ... C4 74
Macau, Macau ... B5 34
Macau, dep., Asia ... E3 30
MacClenny, Fl., U.S. ... B4 102
MacDill Air Force Base, mil., Fl., U.S. ... E4 102
MacDonnell Ranges, mts., Austl. ... E5 60
MacDowell Reservoir, res., N.H., U.S. ... E2 122
Macedonia, Oh., U.S. ... A4 128
Macedonia, hist. reg., Eur. ... D9 18
Macedonia, ctry., Eur. ... D8 18
Maceió, Braz. ... C4 74
Macenta, Gui. ... E3 50
Macerata, Italy ... C4 18
Maces Bay, b., N.B., Can. ... D3 87
MacGregor, Mb., Can. ... E2 86
Machado, stm., Braz. ... E7 70
Machakos, Kenya ... D7 54
Machala, Ec. ... D4 70
Macheke, Zimb. ... B5 56
Macheng, China ... C3 30
Machias, Me., U.S. ... D5 112
Machias, stm., Me., U.S. ... D5 112
Machias, stm., Me., U.S. ... B4 112
Machias Bay, b., Me., U.S. ... D5 112
Machias Lakes, l., Me., U.S. ... C5 112
Machilipatnam, India ... F4 40
Machiques, Ven. ... A5 70
Macho, Arroyo del, val., N.M., U.S. ... C4 124
Machupicchu, Peru ... F5 70
Machupicchu, hist., Peru ... A3 72
Mackay, Austl. ... E4 62
Mackay, Lake, l., Austl. ... E4 60
MacKenzie, B.C., Can. ... B6 85
Mackenzie, stm., N.T., Can. ... E13 82
Mackenzie Bay, b., Can. ... E12 82
Mackenzie Mountains, mts., Can. ... F14 82
Mackinac, co., Mi., U.S. ... B5 115
Mackinac, Straits of, strt., Mi., U.S. ... C6 115
Mackinac Bridge, Mi., U.S. ... C6 115
Mackinac Island, i., Mi., U.S. ... C6 115
Mackinaw, Il., U.S. ... C4 106
Mackinaw, stm., Il., U.S. ... C4 106
Mackinaw City, Mi., U.S. ... C6 115
Mackinnon Road, Kenya ... D7 54
Maclean, Austl. ... F5 62
Maclear, S. Afr. ... E4 56
Macleod, Lake, l., Austl. ... E1 60
Maclovio Herrera, Mex. ... B3 78
Macomb, Il., U.S. ... C3 106
Macomb, co., Mi., U.S. ... F8 115
Macomer, Italy ... D2 18

Mâcon, Fr. ... D9 16
Macon, Ga., U.S. ... D3 103
Macon, Il., U.S. ... D5 106
Macon, Mo., U.S. ... B5 118
Macon, Ms., U.S. ... B5 117
Macon, co., Al., U.S. ... C4 94
Macon, co., Ga., U.S. ... D2 103
Macon, co., Il., U.S. ... D4 106
Macon, co., Mo., U.S. ... B5 118
Macon, co., N.C., U.S. ... f9 126
Macon, co., Tn., U.S. ... A5 135
Macon, Bayou, stm., U.S. ... B4 111
Macoupin, co., Il., U.S. ... D4 106
Macquarie Island, i., Austl. ... J23 4
Macquarie Ridge ... N18 64
MacTier, On., Can. ... B5 89
Macungie, Pa., U.S. ... E10 131
Macuspana, Mex. ... D6 78
Mad, stm., Ca., U.S. ... B2 98
Mad, stm., Ct., U.S. ... B3 100
Mad, stm., N.H., U.S. ... C3 122
Mad, stm., Oh., U.S. ... C2 128
Mad, stm., Vt., U.S. ... C3 138
Madagascar, ctry., Afr. ... B8 56
Madagascar Basin ... K8 64
Madagascar Plateau ... L7 64
Madame, Isle, i., N.S., Can. ... D9 87
Madang, Pap. N. Gui. ... H12 32
Madaoua, Niger ... D6 50
Madawaska, Me., U.S. ... A4 112
Madawaska, stm., Can. ... B9 90
Madawaska, stm., On., Can. ... B7 89
Madawaska Lake, l., Me., U.S. ... A4 112
Madaya, Myan. ... B3 34
Madeira, Oh., U.S. ... o13 128
Madeira, stm., S.A. ... E7 70
Madeira, Arquipélago da, is., Port. ... D1 48
Madeira Islands see Madeira, Arquipélago da, is., Port. ... D1 48
Madeleine, Îles de la, is., P.Q., Can. ... B8 87
Madelia, Mn., U.S. ... F4 116
Madeline Island, i., Wi., U.S. ... B3 142
Maden, Tur. ... C8 44
Madera, Mex. ... B3 78
Madera, Ca., U.S. ... D3 98
Madera, co., Ca., U.S. ... D4 98
Madera see Madeira, stm., S.A. ... E7 70
Madhya Pradesh, prov., India ... E3 40
Madill, Ok., U.S. ... C5 129
Madimba, D.R.C. ... D3 54
Madingo-Kayes, Congo ... D2 54
Madingou, Congo ... D2 54
Madirovalo, Madag. ... B8 56
Madison, Al., U.S. ... A3 94
Madison, Ar., U.S. ... B5 97
Madison, Ct., U.S. ... D5 100
Madison, Fl., U.S. ... B3 102
Madison, Ga., U.S. ... C3 103
Madison, Il., U.S. ... E3 106
Madison, In., U.S. ... G7 107
Madison, Ks., U.S. ... D7 109
Madison, Me., U.S. ... D3 112
Madison, Mn., U.S. ... E2 116
Madison, Ms., U.S. ... C3 117
Madison, N.C., U.S. ... A3 126
Madison, Ne., U.S. ... C8 120
Madison, N.J., U.S. ... B4 123
Madison, Oh., U.S. ... A4 128
Madison, S.D., U.S. ... D8 134
Madison, W.V., U.S. ... C3 141
Madison, Wi., U.S. ... E4 142
Madison, co., Al., U.S. ... A3 94
Madison, co., Ar., U.S. ... B2 97
Madison, co., Fl., U.S. ... B3 102
Madison, co., Ga., U.S. ... B3 103
Madison, co., Ia., U.S. ... C3 108
Madison, co., Id., U.S. ... F7 105
Madison, co., Il., U.S. ... E4 106
Madison, co., In., U.S. ... D6 107
Madison, co., Ky., U.S. ... C5 110
Madison, co., La., U.S. ... B4 111
Madison, co., Mo., U.S. ... D7 118
Madison, co., Ms., U.S. ... C3 117
Madison, co., Mt., U.S. ... E5 119
Madison, co., N.C., U.S. ... f10 126
Madison, co., Ne., U.S. ... C8 120
Madison, co., N.Y., U.S. ... C5 125
Madison, co., Oh., U.S. ... C2 128
Madison, co., Tn., U.S. ... B3 135
Madison, co., Tx., U.S. ... D5 136
Madison, co., Va., U.S. ... B4 139
Madison, stm., Mt., U.S. ... E5 119
Madison Heights, Mi., U.S. ... o15 115
Madison Heights, Va., U.S. ... C3 139
Madison Lake, Mn., U.S. ... F5 116
Madison Range, mts., Mt., U.S. ... E5 119
Madisonville, Ky., U.S. ... C2 110
Madisonville, La., U.S. ... D5 111
Madisonville, Tn., U.S. ... D9 135
Madisonville, Tx., U.S. ... D5 136
Madoc, On., Can. ... C7 89
Mado Gashi, Kenya ... C7 54
Madoi, China ... E7 28
Madona, Lat. ... H12 10
Madrakah, Ra's al-, c., Oman ... G7 38
Madras see Chennai, India ... G4 40

Madras, Or., U.S. ... C5 130
Madras see Tamil Nādu, prov., India ... G3 40
Madre, Laguna, b., Tx., U.S. ... F4 136
Madre, Laguna, l., Mex. ... B5 78
Madre, Sierra, mts., Phil. ... C8 34
Madre de Dios, stm., S.A. ... F6 70
Madre de Dios, Isla, i., Chile ... H1 69
Madre del Sur, Sierra, mts., Mex. ... D5 78
Madre Occidental, Sierra, mts., Mex. ... B3 78
Madre Oriental, Sierra, mts., Mex. ... C4 78
Madrid, Spain ... G5 16
Madrid, Ia., U.S. ... C4 108
Madura, i., Indon. ... E4 36
Madura, Selat, strt., Indon. ... E4 36
Madurai, India ... H3 40
Maebashi, Japan ... D15 28
Mae Hong Son, Thai. ... C3 34
Mae Sariang, Thai. ... C3 34
Maeser, Ut., U.S. ... C6 137
Mae Sot, Thai. ... C3 34
Maestra, Sierra, mts., Cuba ... B4 80
Maevatanana, Madag. ... B8 56
Maéwo, i., Vanuatu ... k9 62a
Mafeteng, Leso. ... D4 56
Mafia Island, i., Tan. ... E7 54
Magadan, Russia ... D17 26
Magadi, Kenya ... D7 54
Magallanes, Estrecho de (Magellan, Strait of), strt., S.A. ... H2 69
Magangué, Col. ... B5 70
Magaria, Niger ... D6 50
Magazine, Ar., U.S. ... B2 97
Magazine Mountain, mtn., Ar., U.S. ... B2 97
Magdagači, Russia ... D14 26
Magdalena, Bol. ... F7 70
Magdalena, N.M., U.S. ... C2 124
Magdalena, stm., Col. ... D5 80
Magdalena, stm., Mex. ... A2 78
Magdalena, Isla, i., Chile ... F2 69
Magdalena de Kino, Mex. ... A2 78
Magdalena Mountains, mts., N.M., U.S. ... D2 124
Magdeburg, Ger. ... D12 12
Magee, Ms., U.S. ... D4 117
Magelang, Indon. ... E4 36
Magellan, Strait of see Magallanes, Estrecho de, strt., S.A. ... H2 69
Maggie Creek, stm., Nv., U.S. ... C5 121
Maggiore, Lago, l., Eur. ... B2 18
Maghâgha, Egypt ... F10 14
Maghama, Maur. ... C2 50
Magic Reservoir, res., Id., U.S. ... F4 105
Maglie, Italy ... D7 18
Magna, Ut., U.S. ... C3 137
Magnetawan, stm., On., Can. ... B4 89
Magnitogorsk, Russia ... D7 26
Magnolia, Ar., U.S. ... D2 97
Magnolia, Ky., U.S. ... C4 110
Magnolia, Ms., U.S. ... D3 117
Magnolia, N.C., U.S. ... C4 126
Magnolia, Oh., U.S. ... B4 128
Magoffin, co., Ky., U.S. ... C6 110
Magog, P.Q., Can. ... D5 90
Magothy River, b., Md., U.S. ... B4 113
Magrath, Ab., Can. ... E4 84
Magruder Mountain, mtn., Nv., U.S. ... F4 121
Magway, Myan. ... B2 34
Mahābād, Iran ... C5 42
Mahābaleshwar, India ... F2 40
Mahabe, Madag. ... B8 56
Mahābhārat Lek, mts., Nepal ... D4 40
Mahabo, Madag. ... C7 56
Mahačkala, Russia ... E6 26
Mahagi, D.R.C. ... D5 54
Mahajanga, Madag. ... B8 56
Mahakam, stm., Indon. ... C5 36
Mahalapye, Bots. ... C4 56
Mahānadi, stm., India ... E4 40
Mahanoro, Madag. ... B8 56
Mahanoy City, Pa., U.S. ... E9 131
Mahārāshtra, prov., India ... E3 40
Maha Sarakham, Thai. ... C4 34
Mahaska, co., Ia., U.S. ... C5 108
Mahbūbnagar, India ... F3 40
Mahd adh-Dhahab, Sau. Ar. ... F4 38
Mahdia, Tun. ... G3 18
Mahe, India ... G3 40
Mahé, i., Sey. ... h13 57b
Mahébourg, Mrts. ... g10 57a
Mahenge, Tan. ... E7 54
Mahesāna, India ... E2 40
Mahi, stm., India ... E2 40
Mahilëu, Bela. ... C11 20
Mahmenn, Mn., U.S. ... C3 116
Mahnomen, co., Mn., U.S. ... C3 116
Mahogany Mountain, mtn., Or., U.S. ... D9 130
Mahomet, Il., U.S. ... C5 106
Mahón see Maó, Spain ... H9 16
Mahone Bay, N.S., Can. ... E5 87
Mahoning, co., Oh., U.S. ... B5 128

Mahoning, stm., U.S. ... A5 128
Mahopac, N.Y., U.S. ... D7 125
Mahuva, India ... E2 40
Mahwah, N.J., U.S. ... A4 123
Maicao, Col. ... C5 80
Maiden, N.C., U.S. ... B1 126
Maidstone Lake, l., Vt., U.S. ... B5 138
Maiduguri, Nig. ... D7 50
Maili, Hi., U.S. ... g9 104
Maili Point, c., Hi., U.S. ... g9 104
Main, stm., Ger. ... F11 12
Main Channel, strt., On., Can. ... B3 89
Mai-Ndombe, Lac, l., D.R.C. ... D3 54
Maine, hist. reg., Fr. ... C6 16
Maine, state, U.S. ... C3 112
Maine, Gulf of, b., N.A. ... C14 92
Mainland, i., Scot., U.K. ... A5 12
Mainland, i., Scot., U.K. ... h19 12a
Main Pass, strt., La., U.S. ... E6 111
Maintirano, Madag. ... B7 56
Mainz, Ger. ... E11 12
Maio, i., C.V. ... g10 50a
Maipú, Arg. ... F6 72
Maiquetía, Ven. ... A6 70
Maisonnette, N.B., Can. ... B4 87
Maitland, Austl. ... G5 62
Maitland, On., Can. ... C9 89
Maíz, Islas del, is., Nic. ... C3 80
Maize, Ks., U.S. ... g12 109
Maizuru, Japan ... C3 31
Maja, stm., Russia ... C15 26
Majene, Indon. ... D5 36
Majī, Eth. ... B7 54
Majkop, Russia ... E6 26
Major, co., Ok., U.S. ... A3 129
Majorca see Mallorca, i., Spain ... H8 16
Majuro, atoll, Marsh. Is. ... D11 58
Maka, Sen. ... D2 50
Makabana, Congo ... D2 54
Makaha, Hi., U.S. ... g9 104
Makaha Point, c., Hi., U.S. ... A2 104
Makah Indian Reservation, Wa., U.S. ... A1 140
Makahuena Point, c., Hi., U.S. ... B2 104
Makakilo City, Hi., U.S. ... g9 104
Makapuu Head, c., Hi., U.S. ... B4 104
Makarakomburu, Mount, mtn., Sol. Is. ... B6 62
Makarov, Russia ... B16 28
Makarov Basin ... E34 144
Makasar see Ujungpandang, Indon. ... E5 36
Makasar, Selat (Makassar Strait), strt., Indon. ... D5 36
Makassar Strait see Makasar, Selat, strt., Indon. ... D5 36
Makat, Kaz. ... E7 26
Makawao, Hi., U.S. ... C5 104
Makaweli, Hi., U.S. ... B2 104
Makeni, S.L. ... E2 50
Makgadikgadi, pl., Bots. ... C4 56
Makiïvka, Ukr. ... E14 20
Makindu, Kenya ... D7 54
Makkah, Sau. Ar. ... F3 38
Makó, Hung. ... F6 20
Makokou, Gabon ... C2 54
Makoua, Congo ... D3 54
Makrān Coast, Asia ... E7 42
Mākū, Iran ... C11 44
Makumbi, D.R.C. ... E4 54
Makurdi, Nig. ... E6 50
Makushin Volcano, vol., Ak., U.S. ... E6 95
Mala, Peru ... A2 72
Malabar, Fl., U.S. ... D6 102
Malabar Coast, India ... G2 40
Malabo, Eq. Gui. ... C1 54
Malacca see Melaka, Malay. ... C2 36
Malacca, Strait of, strt., Asia ... C1 36
Malad City, Id., U.S. ... G6 105
Maladzečna, Bela. ... B9 20
Málaga, Col. ... D5 80
Málaga, Spain ... I4 16
Malagarasi, Tan. ... E6 54
Malaimbandy, Madag. ... C8 56
Malaja Kuril'skaja Grjada, is., Russia ... B5 31
Malajaroslavec, Russia ... B14 20
Malaja Višera, Russia ... C5 22
Malakal, Sudan ... I11 48
Malakoff, Tx., U.S. ... C4 136
Malakula, i., Vanuatu ... I9 62a
Malambo, Col. ... C5 80
Malang, Indon. ... E4 36
Malanje, Ang. ... E3 54
Malanville, Benin ... D5 50
Malāren, l., Swe. ... G11 10
Malargüe, Arg. ... F4 72
Malartic, P.Q., Can. ... k11 90
Malatya, Tur. ... C8 44
Mala Vyska, Ukr. ... E11 20
Malawi, ctry., Afr. ... A5 56
Malawi, Lake see Nyasa, Lake, l., Afr. ... F6 54
Malaya see Semenanjung Malaysia, hist. reg., Malay. ... C2 36
Malaybalay, Phil. ... E9 34
Malāyer, Iran ... D5 42
Malay Peninsula, pen., Asia ... B2 36

Malaysia, ctry., Asia ... C4 36
Malazgirt, Tur. ... C10 44
Malbaie, stm., P.Q., Can. ... B7 90
Malbork, Pol. ... C5 20
Malbrán, Arg. ... D5 72
Malcolm, Austl. ... F3 60
Malden, Ma., U.S. ... B5 114
Malden, Mo., U.S. ... E8 118
Malden, W.V., U.S. ... m12 141
Malden, i., Kir. ... E14 58
Maldives, ctry., Asia ... I10 24
Maldonado, Ur. ... E7 72
Mālegaon, India ... E2 40
Malek Kandī, Iran ... D12 44
Malema, Moz. ... A6 56
Malha Wells, Sudan ... G10 48
Malheur, co., Or., U.S. ... D9 130
Malheur, stm., Or., U.S. ... D9 130
Malheur Lake, l., Or., U.S. ... D8 130
Mali, Gui. ... D2 50
Mali, ctry., Afr. ... C4 50
Malibu, Ca., U.S. ... m11 98
Malin, Or., U.S. ... E5 130
Malindi, Kenya ... D8 54
Malinga, Congo ... D2 54
Malka, Russia ... D17 26
Malkara, Tur. ... B2 44
Mallaig, Egypt ... F10 14
Malletts Bay, b., Vt., U.S. ... B2 138
Mallorca (Majorca), i., Spain ... H8 16
Malmberget, Swe. ... C9 10
Malmesbury, S. Afr. ... E2 56
Malmö, Swe. ... I5 10
Malmstrom Air Force Base, mil., Mt., U.S. ... C5 119
Maloelap, atoll, Marsh. Is. ... D11 58
Malone, N.Y., U.S. ... f10 125
Maloney Reservoir, res., Ne., U.S. ... C5 120
Malonga, D.R.C. ... F4 54
Malošuyka, Russia ... B6 22
Målöy, Nor. ... F1 10
Malpelo, Isla de, i., Col. ... C3 70
Malpeque Bay, b., P.E., Can. ... C6 87
Malta, Il., U.S. ... B5 106
Malta, Mt., U.S. ... B9 119
Malta, ctry., Eur. ... G5 18
Maltahöhe, Nmb. ... C2 56
Maluku (Moluccas), is., Indon. ... D7 36
Maluku, Laut (Molucca Sea), Indon. ... C7 36
Malumfashi, Nig. ... D6 50
Mālvan, India ... F2 40
Malvern, Ar., U.S. ... C3 97
Malvern, Ia., U.S. ... D2 108
Malvern, Oh., U.S. ... B4 128
Malvern, Pa., U.S. ... o19 131
Malverne, N.Y., U.S. ... k13 125
Malyj Enisej, stm., Russia ... A7 28
Malyn, Ukr. ... D10 20
Mama, Russia ... D13 26
Mamala Bay, b., Hi., U.S. ... g10 104
Mamallapuram, hist., India ... G4 40
Mamaroneck, N.Y., U.S. ... h13 125
Mamburao, Phil. ... D8 34
Mamfe, Cam. ... B1 54
Mammoth, Az., U.S. ... E5 96
Mammoth Cave National Park, Ky., U.S. ... C4 110
Mammoth Lakes, Ca., U.S. ... D4 98
Mammoth Spring, Ar., U.S. ... A4 97
Mamoré, stm., S.A. ... F6 70
Mamou, Gui. ... D2 50
Mamou, La., U.S. ... D3 111
Mamoudzou, May. ... A8 56
Mampikony, Madag. ... B8 56
Mamuju, Indon. ... D5 36
Man, C. Iv. ... E3 50
Man, W.V., U.S. ... D3 141
Manacapuru, Braz. ... D7 70
Manacor, Spain ... H8 16
Manado, Indon. ... C6 36
Managua, Nic. ... C2 80
Managua, Lago de, l., Nic. ... C2 80
Manakara, Madag. ... C8 56
Manāli, India ... C3 40
Manama see Al-Manāmah, Bahr. ... E6 42
Manam Island, i., Pap. N. Gui. ... G12 32
Manana Island, i., Hi., U.S. ... g11 104
Mananara Avaratra, Madag. ... B8 56
Mananjary, Madag. ... C8 56
Manankoro, Mali ... D3 50
Manantico Creek, stm., N.J., U.S. ... E3 123
Mana Point, c., Hi., U.S. ... A2 104
Manas, China ... C5 28
Manas Hu, l., China ... B5 28
Manasquan, N.J., U.S. ... C4 123
Manasquan, stm., N.J., U.S. ... C4 123
Manassa, Co., U.S. ... D5 99
Manassas, Va., U.S. ... B5 139
Manassas National Battlefield Park, Va., U.S. ... g11 139
Manassas Park, Va., U.S. ... B5 139
Manatee, co., Fl., U.S. ... E4 102
Manatee, stm., Fl., U.S. ... E4 102
Manatuto, Indon. ... E7 36
Manaus, Braz. ... D7 70
Manavgat, Tur. ... D4 44

Name	Map Ref.	Page
Manawa, Wi., U.S.	D5	142
Manbij, Syria	D7	44
Mancelona, Mi., U.S.	D5	115
Manchester, Eng., U.K.	D5	12
Manchester, Ct., U.S.	B5	100
Manchester, Ga., U.S.	D2	103
Manchester, Ia., U.S.	B6	108
Manchester, Ky., U.S.	C6	110
Manchester, Ma., U.S.	A6	114
Manchester, Md., U.S.	A4	113
Manchester, Me., U.S.	D3	112
Manchester, Mi., U.S.	F6	115
Manchester, Mo., U.S.	f12	118
Manchester, N.H., U.S.	E4	122
Manchester, N.Y., U.S.	C3	125
Manchester, Oh., U.S.	D2	128
Manchester, Pa., U.S.	F8	131
Manchester, Tn., U.S.	B5	135
Manchester, Vt., U.S.	E2	138
Manchester Center, Vt., U.S.	E2	138
Manchuria, hist. reg., China	B13	28
Mancos, Co., U.S.	D2	99
Mancos, stm., U.S.	D2	99
Manda, Tan.	F6	54
Mandabe, Madag.	C7	56
Manda Island, i., Kenya	B8	54
Mandal, Nor.	G2	10
Mandalay, Myan.	B3	34
Mandalgovi, Mong.	B9	28
Mandalī, Iraq	D5	42
Mandalya, Gulf of see Güllük Körfezi, b., Tur.	D2	44
Mandan, N.D., U.S.	C5	127
Mandar, Teluk, b., Indon.	D5	36
Mandara Mountains, mts., Afr.	A2	54
Mandeb, Bab el, strt.	H4	38
Mandera, Kenya	C8	54
Mandeville, Jam.	B4	80
Mandeville, Ar., U.S.	D2	97
Mandeville, La., U.S.	D5	111
Mandimba, Moz.	A6	56
Mandioli, Pulau, i., Indon.	D7	36
Mandla, India	E4	40
Mandritsara, Madag.	B8	56
Mandsaur, India	E3	40
Manduria, Italy	D6	18
Māndvi, India	E1	40
Mandya, India	G3	40
Manendragarh, India	E4	40
Manfalūt, Egypt	E11	48
Manfredonia, Italy	D5	18
Manfredonia, Golfo di, b., Italy	D6	18
Manga, Braz.	D3	74
Manga, reg., Niger	D7	50
Mangabeiras, Chapada das, hills, Braz.	C2	74
Mangai, D.R.C.	D3	54
Mangalia, Rom.	H10	20
Mangalore, India	G2	40
Mangchang, China	F9	28
Mange, China	C4	40
Manggar, Indon.	D3	36
Mangkalihat, Tanjung, c., Indon.	C5	36
Mangnai, China	D6	28
Mangochi, Mwi.	A6	56
Mangoky, stm., Madag.	C7	56
Mangole, Pulau, i., Indon.	D7	36
Mangum, Ok., U.S.	C2	129
Manhattan, Ks., U.S.	C7	109
Manhattan, Mt., U.S.	E5	119
Manhattan Beach, Ca., U.S.	n12	98
Manhattan Island, i., N.Y., U.S.	h13	125
Manheim, Pa., U.S.	F9	131
Manhuaçu, Braz.	F3	74
Manica, Moz.	B5	56
Manicoré, Braz.	E7	70
Manicouagan, Réservoir, res., P.Q., Can.	h13	90
Manignan, C. Iv.	D3	50
Manila, Phil.	D8	34
Manila, Ar., U.S.	B5	97
Manilla, Ia., U.S.	C2	108
Manipur, prov., India	D6	40
Manisa, Tur.	C2	44
Manistee, Mi., U.S.	D4	115
Manistee, co., Mi., U.S.	D4	115
Manistee, stm., Mi., U.S.	D5	115
Manistique, Mi., U.S.	C4	115
Manistique, stm., Mi., U.S.	B4	115
Manistique Lake, l., Mi., U.S.	B5	115
Manito, Il., U.S.	C4	106
Manitoba, prov., Can.	C3	86
Manitoba, Lake, l., Mb., Can.	D2	86
Manitou, Mb., Can.	E2	86
Manitou, Lake, l., On., Can.	B3	89
Manitou Island, i., Mi., U.S.	A3	115
Manitou Lake, l., Sk., Can.	E1	91
Manitoulin Island, i., On., Can.	B2	89
Manitou Springs, Co., U.S.	C6	99
Manitowoc, Wi., U.S.	D6	142
Manitowoc, co., Wi., U.S.	D6	142
Manitowoc, stm., Wi., U.S.	h10	142
Maniwaki, P.Q., Can.	C2	90
Manizales, Col.	B4	70
Manja, Madag.	C7	56
Manjakandriana, Madag.	B8	56
Manjimup, Austl.	G2	60
Mānjra, stm., India	F3	40
Mankanza, D.R.C.	C3	54
Mankato, Ks., U.S.	C5	109
Mankato, Mn., U.S.	F5	116
Manlius, N.Y., U.S.	C5	125
Manly, Ia., U.S.	A4	108
Manmād, India	E2	40
Manna, Indon.	D2	36
Mannar, Gulf of, b., Asia	H3	40
Mannford, Ok., U.S.	A5	129
Mannheim, Ger.	F11	12
Manning, Ab., Can.	A2	84
Manning, Ia., U.S.	C2	108
Manning, S.C., U.S.	D7	133
Mannington, W.V., U.S.	B4	141
Manns Creek, stm., W.V., U.S.	n14	141
Mannville, Ab., Can.	C5	84
Manokin, stm., Md., U.S.	D6	113
Manokotak, Ak., U.S.	D8	95
Manokwari, Indon.	D8	36
Manomet, Ma., U.S.	C6	114
Manomet Point, c., Ma., U.S.	C6	114
Manono, D.R.C.	E5	54
Manor, Tx., U.S.	D4	136
Manouane, Lac, l., P.Q., Can.	h12	90
Manresa, Spain	G7	16
Mansa, Zam.	A4	56
Manseau, P.Q., Can.	C5	90
Mansfield, Eng., U.K.	D6	12
Mansfield, Ar., U.S.	B1	97
Mansfield, Il., U.S.	C5	106
Mansfield, La., U.S.	B2	111
Mansfield, Ma., U.S.	B5	114
Mansfield, Mo., U.S.	D5	118
Mansfield, Oh., U.S.	B3	128
Mansfield, Pa., U.S.	C7	131
Mansfield, Tx., U.S.	n9	136
Mansfield, Mount, mtn., Vt., U.S.	B3	138
Mansfield Center, Ct., U.S.	B7	100
Mansfield Hollow Lake, res., Ct., U.S.	B7	100
Mansôa, Gui.-B.	D1	50
Manson, Ia., U.S.	B3	108
Manson, Wa., U.S.	B5	140
Mansonville, P.Q., Can.	D5	90
Mansura, La., U.S.	C3	111
Manta, Ec.	D3	70
Mantachie, Ms., U.S.	A5	117
Manteca, Ca., U.S.	D3	98
Manteno, Il., U.S.	B6	106
Manteo, N.C., U.S.	B7	126
Manti, Ut., U.S.	D4	137
Mantiqueira, Serra da, mts., Braz.	F2	74
Manton, Mi., U.S.	D5	115
Mantorville, Mn., U.S.	F6	116
Mántova, Italy	B3	18
Mantua, Oh., U.S.	A4	128
Mantua, Ut., U.S.	B4	137
Manturovo, Russia	C7	22
Mäntyluoto, Fin.	F9	10
Manuae, atoll, Cook Is.	F14	58
Manui, Pulau, i., Indon.	D6	36
Manukau, N.Z.	o13	63c
Manumuskin, stm., N.J., U.S.	E3	123
Manus Island, i., Pap. N. Gui.	G12	32
Manvel, Tx., U.S.	r14	136
Manville, N.J., U.S.	B3	123
Manville, R.I., U.S.	B4	132
Many, La., U.S.	C2	111
Manyara, Lake, l., Tan.	D7	54
Many Farms, Az., U.S.	A6	96
Manyoni, Tan.	D6	54
Manzanillo, Cuba	A4	80
Manzanillo, Mex.	D4	78
Manzanillo Bay, b., N.A.	A5	80
Manzano Mountains, mts., N.M., U.S.	C3	124
Manzano Peak, mtn., N.M., U.S.	C3	124
Manzhouli, China	B11	28
Manzini, Swaz.	D5	56
Mao, Chad	D8	50
Mao, Dom. Rep.	B5	80
Maó, Spain	H9	16
Maoke, Pegunungan, mts., Indon.	G10	32
Maoming, China	G10	28
Mapastepec, Mex.	D6	78
Mapi, Indon.	H10	32
Mapinhane, Moz.	C6	56
Maple, stm., Ia., U.S.	B2	108
Maple, stm., N.D., U.S.	C8	127
Maple, stm., U.S.	A7	134
Maple Bluff, Wi., U.S.	E4	142
Maple Grove, Mn., U.S.	m12	116
Maple Heights, Oh., U.S.	h9	128
Maple Lake, Mn., U.S.	E5	116
Maple Plain, Mn., U.S.	m11	116
Maple Shade, N.J., U.S.	D2	123
Maplesville, Al., U.S.	C3	94
Mapleton, Ia., U.S.	B2	108
Mapleton, Mn., U.S.	G5	116
Mapleton, N.D., U.S.	C8	127
Mapleton, Or., U.S.	C3	130
Mapleton, Ut., U.S.	C4	137
Maple Valley, Wa., U.S.	f11	140
Mapleville, R.I., U.S.	B2	132
Maplewood, Mn., U.S.	n12	116
Maplewood, Mo., U.S.	f13	118
Maplewood, N.J., U.S.	B4	123
Maputo, Moz.	D5	56
Maqteïr, reg., Maur.	B2	50
Maquela do Zombo, Ang.	E3	54
Maquinchao, Arg.	F3	69
Maquoketa, Ia., U.S.	B7	108
Maquoketa, stm., Ia., U.S.	B6	108
Maquoketa, North Fork, stm., Ia., U.S.	B7	108
Marabá, Braz.	C2	74
Maracá, Ilha de, i., Braz.	C9	70
Maracaibo, Ven.	A5	70
Maracaibo, Lago de, l., Ven.	B5	70
Maracaju, Braz.	C6	72
Maracás, Braz.	D3	74
Maracay, Ven.	A6	70
Marādah, Libya	E8	48
Maradi, Niger	D6	50
Marāgheh, Iran	C5	42
Marahuaca, Cerro, mtn., Ven.	C6	70
Marais des Cygnes, stm., U.S.	D8	109
Marajó, Baía de b., Braz.	B2	74
Marajó, Ilha de, i., Braz.	B2	74
Maralal, Kenya	C7	54
Marampa, S.L.	E2	50
Marana, Az., U.S.	E4	96
Marand, Iran	C5	42
Maranguape, Braz.	B4	74
Maranhão, state, Braz.	B2	74
Maranhão, stm., Braz.	A8	72
Marañón, stm., Peru	D5	70
Marathon, Fl., U.S.	H5	102
Marathon, Wi., U.S.	D4	142
Marathon, co., Wi., U.S.	D4	142
Marawi, Phil.	E8	34
Marbella, Spain	I4	16
Marble, Mn., U.S.	C5	116
Marble, N.C., U.S.	f9	126
Marble Bar, Austl.	E2	60
Marble Canyon, val., Az., U.S.	A4	96
Marble Falls, Tx., U.S.	D3	136
Marble Hall, S. Afr.	C4	56
Marblehead, Ma., U.S.	B6	114
Marble Hill, Mo., U.S.	D8	118
Marbleton, Wy., U.S.	D2	143
Marburg, Ger.	E11	12
Marbury, Md., U.S.	C3	113
Marceline, Mo., U.S.	B5	118
Marcellus, Mi., U.S.	F5	115
March Air Force Base, mil., Ca., U.S.	F5	98
Marche, hist. reg., Fr.	D7	16
Mar Chiquita, Laguna, l., Arg.	E5	72
Marco, Fl., U.S.	G5	102
Marcus, Ia., U.S.	B2	108
Marcus Baker, Mount, mtn., Ak., U.S.	g18	95
Marcus Hook, Pa., U.S.	G11	131
Marcus Island see Minami-Tori-shima, i., Japan	F18	64
Marcy, Mount, mtn., N.Y., U.S.	A7	125
Mardān, Pak.	D10	42
Mar del Plata, Arg.	F6	72
Mardin, Tur.	D9	44
Maré, i., N. Cal.	I9	62a
Mareeba, Austl.	D4	62
Marengo, Ia., U.S.	C5	108
Marengo, Il., U.S.	A5	106
Marengo, In., U.S.	H5	107
Marengo, co., Al., U.S.	C2	94
Marfa, Tx., U.S.	o12	136
Margaret, Al., U.S.	B3	94
Margaret River, Austl.	G1	60
Margarita, Isla de, i., Ven.	A7	70
Margate, Fl., U.S.	F6	102
Margate City, N.J., U.S.	E3	123
Margherita Peak, mtn., Afr.	C5	54
Margilan, Uzb.	B10	42
Margrethe, Lake, l., Mi., U.S.	D6	115
Marha, Russia	C14	26
Marhanets', Ukr.	F13	20
Maria, Îles, is., Fr. Poly.	G14	58
María Elena, Chile	B3	69
Maria Island, i., Austl.	C6	60
Mariakani, Kenya	D7	54
Marian, Lake, l., Fl., U.S.	E5	102
Mariana Islands, is., Oc.	C11	32
Mariana Ridge	G17	64
Mariana Trench	G17	64
Marianna, Ar., U.S.	C5	97
Marianna, Fl., U.S.	B1	102
Marias, stm., Mt., U.S.	B4	119
Marias Pass, Mt., U.S.	B3	119
Mariato, Punta, c., Pan.	D3	80
Maribor, Slvn.	A5	18
Marica (Évros) (Meriç), stm., Eur.	C10	18
Maricopa, Az., U.S.	E3	96
Maricopa, Ca., U.S.	E4	98
Maricopa, co., Az., U.S.	D3	96
Maricopa Mountains, mts., Az., U.S.	m7	96
Marie Byrd Land, reg., Ant.	D29	67
Marie-Galante, i., Guad.	B7	80
Mariemont, Oh., U.S.	o13	128
Mariental, Nmb.	C2	56
Marienville, Pa., U.S.	D3	131
Maries, co., Mo., U.S.	C6	118
Mariestad, Swe.	G5	10
Marietta, Ga., U.S.	C2	103
Marietta, Oh., U.S.	C4	128
Marietta, Ok., U.S.	D4	129
Marietta, S.C., U.S.	A2	133
Marieville, P.Q., Can.	D4	90
Marijampolė, Lith.	I10	10
Marij El, state, Russia	D6	26
Marília, Braz.	F2	74
Marimba, Ang.	E3	54
Marin, co., Ca., U.S.	C2	98
Mar''ina Horka, Bela.	C10	20
Marinduque, i., Phil.	D8	34
Marine, Il., U.S.	E4	106
Marine City, Mi., U.S.	F8	115
Marine On St. Croix, Mn., U.S.	E6	116
Marinette, Wi., U.S.	C6	142
Marinette, co., Wi., U.S.	C5	142
Maringá, Braz.	F1	74
Maringouin, La., U.S.	D4	111
Marion, Al., U.S.	C2	94
Marion, Ar., U.S.	B5	97
Marion, Ia., U.S.	B6	108
Marion, Il., U.S.	F5	106
Marion, In., U.S.	C6	107
Marion, Ks., U.S.	D6	109
Marion, Ky., U.S.	e9	110
Marion, La., U.S.	B3	111
Marion, Ms., U.S.	C5	117
Marion, N.C., U.S.	B1	126
Marion, Oh., U.S.	B2	128
Marion, Pa., U.S.	G6	131
Marion, S.C., U.S.	C9	133
Marion, S.D., U.S.	D8	134
Marion, Va., U.S.	f10	139
Marion, Wi., U.S.	D5	142
Marion, co., Al., U.S.	A2	94
Marion, co., Ar., U.S.	A3	97
Marion, co., Fl., U.S.	C4	102
Marion, co., Ga., U.S.	D2	103
Marion, co., Ia., U.S.	C4	108
Marion, co., Il., U.S.	E4	106
Marion, co., In., U.S.	E5	107
Marion, co., Ks., U.S.	D6	109
Marion, co., Ky., U.S.	C4	110
Marion, co., Mo., U.S.	B6	118
Marion, co., Ms., U.S.	D4	117
Marion, co., Oh., U.S.	B2	128
Marion, co., Or., U.S.	C4	130
Marion, co., S.C., U.S.	C9	133
Marion, co., Tn., U.S.	D8	135
Marion, co., Tx., U.S.	C5	136
Marion, co., W.V., U.S.	B4	141
Marion, Lake, res., S.C., U.S.	E7	133
Marion Reef, rf., Austl.	D5	62
Marion Station, Md., U.S.	D6	113
Marionville, Mo., U.S.	D4	118
Mariposa, co., Ca., U.S.	D3	98
Mariscal Estigarribia, Para.	C5	72
Marissa, Il., U.S.	E4	106
Maritime Alps, mts., Eur.	B1	18
Maritime Atlas see Atlas Tellien, mts., Alg.	D4	14
Mariupol', Ukr.	F14	20
Märjamaa, Est.	G11	10
Marka, Som.	J13	48
Mārkāpur, India	F3	40
Markdale, On., Can.	C4	89
Marked Tree, Ar., U.S.	B5	97
Markesan, Wi., U.S.	E5	142
Markham, On., Can.	D5	89
Markham, Il., U.S.	k9	106
Markham, Tx., U.S.	E4	136
Markit, China	B3	40
Markland Lock and Dam, U.S.	B5	110
Markle, In., U.S.	C7	107
Markovo, Russia	C19	26
Marks, Russia	D8	22
Marks, Ms., U.S.	A3	117
Marksville, La., U.S.	C3	111
Mark Twain Lake, res., Mo., U.S.	B6	118
Marlboro, N.Y., U.S.	D6	125
Marlboro, Va., U.S.	n17	139
Marlboro, co., S.C., U.S.	B8	133
Marlborough, Ct., U.S.	C6	100
Marlborough, Ma., U.S.	B4	114
Marlborough, N.H., U.S.	E2	122
Marlette, Mi., U.S.	E7	115
Marley, Md., U.S.	B4	113
Marlin, Tx., U.S.	D4	136
Marlinton, W.V., U.S.	C4	141
Marlow, Ok., U.S.	C4	129
Marlowe, W.V., U.S.	B7	141
Marlton, N.J., U.S.	D3	123
Marmaduke, Ar., U.S.	A5	97
Marmande, Fr.	E7	16
Marmara, Sea of see Marmara Denizi, Tur.	B3	44
Marmara Denizi, Tur.	B3	44
Marmaris, Tur.	D3	44
Marmet, W.V., U.S.	C3	141
Marmora, On., Can.	C7	89
Marne, stm., Fr.	C8	16
Maroa, Il., U.S.	C5	106
Maroa, Ven.	C6	70
Maroantsetra, Madag.	B8	56
Maromandia, Madag.	A8	56
Maromokotro, mtn., Madag.	A8	56
Marondera, Zimb.	B5	56
Maroni, stm., S.A.	C9	70
Maros, Indon.	E5	36
Maroua, Cam.	A2	54
Marovoay, Madag.	B8	56
Marowijne see Maroni, stm., S.A.	C9	70
Marquesas Islands see Marquises, Îles, is., Fr. Poly.	E16	58
Marquesas Keys, is., Fl., U.S.	H4	102
Marquette, Mi., U.S.	B3	115
Marquette, co., Mi., U.S.	B3	115
Marquette, co., Wi., U.S.	E4	142
Marquette Heights, Il., U.S.	C4	106
Marquises, Îles, is., Fr. Poly.	E16	58
Marrah, Jabal, hill, Sudan	H9	48
Marrakech, Mor.	D3	48
Marrero, La., U.S.	E5	111
Marromeu, Moz.	B6	56
Mars, Pa., U.S.	E1	131
Marsá al-Burayqah, Libya	D8	48
Marsabit, Kenya	C7	54
Marsala, Italy	F4	18
Marseille, Fr.	F9	16
Marseilles, Il., U.S.	B5	106
Marshall, Sk., Can.	D1	91
Marshall, Lib.	E2	50
Marshall, Ar., U.S.	B3	97
Marshall, Il., U.S.	D6	106
Marshall, Mi., U.S.	F6	115
Marshall, Mn., U.S.	F3	116
Marshall, Mo., U.S.	B4	118
Marshall, N.C., U.S.	f10	126
Marshall, Tx., U.S.	C5	136
Marshall, Va., U.S.	B5	139
Marshall, Wi., U.S.	E4	142
Marshall, co., Al., U.S.	A3	94
Marshall, co., Ia., U.S.	C4	108
Marshall, co., Il., U.S.	B4	106
Marshall, co., In., U.S.	B5	107
Marshall, co., Ks., U.S.	C7	109
Marshall, co., Ky., U.S.	f9	110
Marshall, co., Mn., U.S.	B2	116
Marshall, co., Ms., U.S.	A4	117
Marshall, co., Ok., U.S.	C5	129
Marshall, co., S.D., U.S.	B8	134
Marshall, co., Tn., U.S.	B5	135
Marshall, co., W.V., U.S.	B4	141
Marshall Islands, ctry., Oc.	C10	58
Marshall Islands. is., Marsh. Is.	F24	4
Marshallton, De., U.S.	B3	101
Marshalltown, Ia., U.S.	B5	108
Marshallville, Ga., U.S.	D3	103
Marshes Siding, Ky., U.S.	D5	110
Marshfield, Ma., U.S.	B6	114
Marshfield, Mo., U.S.	D5	118
Marshfield, Wi., U.S.	D3	142
Marshfield Hills, Ma., U.S.	B6	114
Marsh Fork, stm., W.V., U.S.	n13	141
Mars Hill, Me., U.S.	B5	112
Mars Hill, N.C., U.S.	f10	126
Marsh Island, i., La., U.S.	E4	111
Marsh Lake, res., Mn., U.S.	E2	116
Marsh Peak, mtn., Ut., U.S.	C6	137
Marshville, N.C., U.S.	C2	126
Marsing, Id., U.S.	F2	105
Märsta, Swe.	G7	10
Marston, Mo., U.S.	E8	118
Mart, Tx., U.S.	D4	136
Martaban, Gulf of, b., Myan.	C3	34
Martapura, Indon.	D2	36
Martapura, Indon.	D4	36
Marthasville, Mo., U.S.	C6	118
Martha's Vineyard, i., Ma., U.S.	D6	114
Martí, Cuba	A4	80
Martigny, Switz.	A1	18
Martigues, Fr.	F9	16
Martin, Slvk.	E5	20
Martin, Ky., U.S.	C7	110
Martin, S.D., U.S.	D4	134
Martin, Tn., U.S.	A3	135
Martin, co., Fl., U.S.	E6	102
Martin, co., In., U.S.	G4	107
Martin, co., Ky., U.S.	C7	110
Martin, co., Mn., U.S.	G4	116
Martin, co., N.C., U.S.	B5	126
Martin, co., Tx., U.S.	C2	136
Martinez, Ca., U.S.	C2	98
Martinez, Ga., U.S.	C4	103
Martínez de la Torre, Mex.	C5	78
Martinique, dep., N.A.	F12	76
Martinique Passage, strt., N.A.	B7	80
Martin Lake, res., Al., U.S.	C4	94
Martin Point, c., Ak., U.S.	A11	95
Martinsburg, Pa., U.S.	F5	131
Martinsburg, W.V., U.S.	B7	141
Martins Ferry, Oh., U.S.	B5	128
Martinsville, Il., U.S.	D6	106
Martinsville, In., U.S.	F5	107
Martinsville, Va., U.S.	D3	139
Marton, N.Z.	p14	63c
Martos, Spain	I5	16
Martti, Fin.	C13	10
Martuni, Arm.	B11	44
Marutea, atoll, Fr. Poly.	F15	58
Marv Dasht, Iran	D6	42
Marvell, Ar., U.S.	C5	97
Marvine, Mount, mtn., Ut., U.S.	E4	137
Mary, Turk.	F8	26

Name	Map Ref.	Page
Mary, Lake, l., Mn., U.S.	E3	116
Mary, Lake, l., Ms., U.S.	D2	117
Maryborough, Austl.	F5	62
Maryborough, Austl.	H3	62
Maryland, state, U.S.	B4	113
Maryland City, Md., U.S.	B4	113
Maryland Heights, Mo., U.S.	f13	118
Maryland Point, c., Md., U.S.	D3	113
Marys, stm., Nv., U.S.	B6	121
Marys Peak, mtn., Or., U.S.	C3'	130
Marystown, Nf., Can.	E4	88
Marysville, Ca., U.S.	C3	98
Marysville, Ks., U.S.	C7	109
Marysville, Mi., U.S.	F8	115
Marysville, Oh., U.S.	B2	128
Marysville, Pa., U.S.	F8	131
Marysville, Wa., U.S.	A3	140
Maryville, Mo., U.S.	A3	118
Maryville, Tn., U.S.	D10	135
Masai Steppe, plat., Tan.	D7	54
Masaka, Ug.	D6	54
Masalembu Besar, Pulau, i., Indon.	E4	36
Masallı, Azer.	C13	44
Masan, S. Kor.	D13	28
Masaya, Nic.	C2	80
Masbate, Phil.	D8	34
Masbate, i., Phil.	D8	34
Mascarene Basin	J8	64
Mascarene Islands, is., Afr.	g10	57a
Mascarene Plateau	I8	64
Mascasín, Arg.	E4	72
Mascoma, stm., N.H., U.S.	C2	122
Mascoma Lake, l., N.H., U.S.	C2	122
Mascot, Tn., U.S.	C10	135
Mascouche, P.Q., Can.	D4	90
Mascoutah, Il., U.S.	E4	106
Maseru, Leso.	D4	56
Mashapaug Pond, l., Ct., U.S.	A7	100
Mashava, Zimb.	B5	56
Mashhad, Iran	C7	42
Mashra'ar Raqq, Sudan	I10	48
Masi-Manimba, D.R.C.	D3	54
Masindi, Ug.	C6	54
Maşīrah, i., Oman	F7	38
Maşīrah, Khalīj, b., Oman	G7	38
Masjed-e Soleymān, Iran	D5	42
Maskinongé, P.Q., Can.	C4	90
Mason, Mi., U.S.	F6	115
Mason, Nv., U.S.	E2	121
Mason, Oh., U.S.	C1	128
Mason, Tx., U.S.	D3	136
Mason, W.V., U.S.	B2	141
Mason, co., Il., U.S.	C4	106
Mason, co., Ky., U.S.	B6	110
Mason, co., Mi., U.S.	D4	115
Mason, co., Tx., U.S.	D3	136
Mason, co., W.V., U.S.	C3	141
Mason, co., Wa., U.S.	B2	140
Mason City, Ia., U.S.	A4	108
Mason City, Il., U.S.	C4	106
Masontown, Pa., U.S.	G2	131
Masontown, W.V., U.S.	B5	141
Masqaţ, Oman	F7	38
Massa, Italy	B2	18
Massabesic Lake, l., N.H., U.S.	E4	122
Massac, co., Il., U.S.	F5	106
Massachusetts, state, U.S.	B4	114
Massachusetts Bay, b., Ma., U.S.	B6	114
Massacre Lake, l., Nv., U.S.	B2	121
Massangena, Moz.	C5	56
Massapoag Lake, l., Ma., U.S.	h11	114
Massasecum, Lake, l., N.H., U.S.	D3	122
Massawa see Mitsiwa, Erit.	G12	48
Massena, N.Y., U.S.	f10	125
Massenya, Chad	D8	50
Masset, B.C., Can.	C1	85
Massey, On., Can.	A2	89
Massillon, Oh., U.S.	B4	128
Massina, reg., Mali	D4	50
Massinga, Moz.	C6	56
Massive, Mount, mtn., Co., U.S.	B4	99
Maştağa, Azer.	B14	44
Masterton, N.Z.	p14	63c
Mastic Beach, N.Y., U.S.	n16	125
Mastung, Pak.	E9	42
Masuda, Japan	D2	31
Masuria see Mazury, reg., Pol.	C6	20
Masury, Oh., U.S.	A5	128
Masvingo, Zimb.	C5	56
Matadi, D.R.C.	E2	54
Matagalpa, Nic.	C2	80
Matagorda, co., Tx., U.S.	E5	136
Matagorda Bay, b., Tx., U.S.	E4	136
Matagorda Island, i., Tx., U.S.	E4	136
Matagorda Peninsula, pen., Tx., U.S.	E5	136
Matala, Ang.	A2	56
Matale, Sri L.	H4	40
Matam, Sen.	C2	50
Matamoras, Pa., U.S.	D12	131
Matamoros, Mex.	B4	78
Matamoros, Mex.	B5	78
Matane, P.Q., Can.	k13	90
Matanuska, stm., Ak., U.S.	g18	95
Matanzas, Cuba	A3	80
Matanzas Inlet, b., Fl., U.S.	C5	102
Matapan, Cape see Taínaron, Ákra, c., Grc.	F9	18
Matara, Sri L.	H4	40
Mataram, Indon.	E5	36
Mataranka, Austl.	C5	60
Mataró, Spain	G8	16
Mātātīla Dam, India	D3	40
Matawan, N.J., U.S.	C4	123
Matehuala, Mex.	C4	78
Matera, Italy	D6	18
Matewan, W.V., U.S.	D2	141
Mather, Pa., U.S.	G1	131
Mather Peaks, mts., Wy., U.S.	B5	143
Mathews, La., U.S.	E5	111
Mathews, Va., U.S.	C6	139
Mathews, co., Va., U.S.	C6	139
Mathews, Lake, l., Ca., U.S.	n14	98
Mathis, Tx., U.S.	E4	136
Mathiston, Ms., U.S.	B4	117
Mathura, India	D3	40
Mati, Phil.	E9	34
Matinicus Island, i., Me., U.S.	E3	112
Mato, Cerro, mtn., Ven.	B6	70
Matoaca, Va., U.S.	n18	139
Mato Grosso, Braz.	E5	68
Mato Grosso, state, Braz.	F8	70
Mato Grosso, Planalto do, plat., Braz.	F8	70
Mato Grosso do Sul, state, Braz.	B6	72
Matosinhos, Port.	G2	16
Matrah, Oman	F7	42
Matsqui, B.C., Can.	f13	85
Matsue, Japan	D14	28
Matsumoto, Japan	C3	31
Matsuyama, Japan	E14	28
Mattamiscontis Lake, l., Me., U.S.	C4	112
Mattamuskeet, Lake, l., N.C., U.S.	B6	126
Mattapoisett, Ma., U.S.	C6	114
Mattaponi, stm., Va., U.S.	C5	139
Mattawa, On., Can.	A6	89
Mattawamkeag, Me., U.S.	C4	112
Mattawamkeag, stm., Me., U.S.	C4	112
Mattawamkeag Lake, l., Me., U.S.	C4	112
Matterhorn (Cervino), mtn., Eur.	A1	18
Matterhorn, mtn., Nv., U.S.	B6	121
Matteson, Il., U.S.	k9	106
Matthews, Mo., U.S.	E8	118
Matthews, N.C., U.S.	B2	126
Matthew Town, Bah.	A5	80
Mattituck, N.Y., U.S.	n16	125
Mattoon, Il., U.S.	D5	106
Mattoon, Lake, res., Il., U.S.	D5	106
Mattydale, N.Y., U.S.	B4	125
Matunuck, R.I., U.S.	G3	132
Maturín, Ven.	B7	70
Matveev Kurgan, Russia	F15	20
Maúa, Moz.	A6	56
Maubeuge, Fr.	B8	16
Maud, Ok., U.S.	B5	129
Maués, Braz.	D8	70
Mauganj, India	E4	40
Maugansville, Md., U.S.	A2	113
Maug Islands, is., N. Mar. Is.	C12	32
Maui, co., Hi., U.S.	B5	104
Maui, i., Hi., U.S.	C6	104
Mauldin, S.C., U.S.	B3	133
Maumee, Oh., U.S.	A2	128
Maumee, stm., U.S.	A2	128
Maumee Bay, b., U.S.	G7	115
Maumelle, Lake, res., Ar., U.S.	C3	97
Maumere, Indon.	E6	36
Maun, Bots.	B3	56
Mauna Kea, vol., Hi., U.S.	D6	104
Maunaloa, Hi., U.S.	B4	104
Mauna Loa, vol., Hi., U.S.	D6	104
Maunalua Bay, b., Hi., U.S.	g10	104
Maunawili, Hi., U.S.	g10	104
Maupihaa, atoll, Fr. Poly.	F14	58
Maurepas, Lake, l., La., U.S.	D5	111
Maurice, Ia., U.S.	B1	108
Maurice, stm., N.J., U.S.	E2	123
Mauritania, ctry., Afr.	C2	50
Mauritius, ctry., Afr.	f10	57a
Mauritius, i., Mrts.	G11	57a
Maury, co., Tn., U.S.	B4	135
Maury City, Tn., U.S.	B2	135
Maury Island, i., Wa., U.S.	f11	140
Mauston, Wi., U.S.	E3	142
Maverick, co., Tx., U.S.	E2	136
Mavinga, Ang.	B3	56
Mawlaik, Myan.	B2	34
Mawlamyine, Myan.	C3	34
Maxinkuckee, Lake, l., In., U.S.	B5	107
Maxixe, Moz.	C6	56
Max Meadows, Va., U.S.	D2	139
Maxton, N.C., U.S.	C3	126
Maxville, On., Can.	B10	89
Maxwell, Ia., U.S.	C4	108
Maxwell Acres, W.V., U.S.	g8	141
Maxwell Air Force Base, mil., Al., U.S.	C3	94
Mayaguana, i., Bah.	D10	76
Mayaguana Passage, strt., Bah.	A5	80
Mayagüez, P.R.	B6	80
Mayang, China	D2	30
Mayenne, Fr.	C6	16
Mayer, Az., U.S.	C3	96
Mayerthorpe, Ab., Can.	C3	84
Mayes, co., Ok., U.S.	A6	129
Mayesville, S.C., U.S.	D7	133
Mayfield, Ky., U.S.	f9	110
Mayfield, Pa., U.S.	C10	131
Mayfield Heights, Oh., U.S.	A4	128
Mayfield Lake, res., Wa., U.S.	C3	140
Mayflower, Ar., U.S.	C3	97
Mayking, Ky., U.S.	C7	110
Maymyo, Myan.	B3	34
Maynard, Ma., U.S.	B5	114
Maynardville, Tn., U.S.	C10	T35
Mayne, B.C., Can.	g12	85
Mayo, Md., U.S.	C4	113
Mayo, S.C., U.S.	A4	133
Mayo, stm., Mex.	B3	78
Mayodan, N.C., U.S.	A3	126
Mayo Ndaga, Nig.	E7	50
Mayon Volcano, vol., Phil.	D8	34
Mayotte, dep., Afr.	A8	56
May Park, Or., U.S.	B8	130
Mayport Naval Station, mil., Fl., U.S.	B5	102
Maysville, Ga., U.S.	B3	103
Maysville, Ky., U.S.	B6	110
Maysville, Mo., U.S.	B3	118
Maysville, N.C., U.S.	C5	126
Maysville, Ok., U.S.	C4	129
Mayumba, Gabon	D2	54
Māyūram, India	G3	40
Mayville, Mi., U.S.	E7	115
Mayville, N.D., U.S.	B8	127
Mayville, N.Y., U.S.	C1	125
Mayville, Wi., U.S.	E5	142
Maywood, Il., U.S.	k9	106
Maywood, N.J., U.S.	h8	123
Mazabuka, Zam.	B4	56
Mazamet, Fr.	F8	16
Mazara del Vallo, Italy	F4	18
Mazār-e Sharīf, Afg.	C9	42
Mazaruni, stm., Guy.	D7	80
Mazatlán, Mex.	C3	78
Mazatzal Mountains, mts., Az., U.S.	C4	96
Mazatzal Peak, mtn., Az., U.S.	C4	96
Mažeikiai, Lith.	H10	10
Mazeppa, Mn., U.S.	F6	116
Mazomanie, Wi., U.S.	E4	142
Mazon, Il., U.S.	B5	106
Mazury, reg., Pol.	C6	20
Mazyr, Bela.	C10	20
Mbabane, Swaz.	D5	56
M'bahiakro, C. Iv.	E4	50
Mbaïki, C.A.R.	C3	54
Mbakê, Sen.	D1	50
Mbala, Zam.	E6	54
Mbale, Ug.	C6	54
Mbalmayo, Cam.	C2	54
Mbamba Bay, Tan.	F6	54
Mbandaka, D.R.C.	C3	54
Mbanga, Cam.	C1	54
Mbanza-Ngungu (Thysville), D.R.C.	E2	54
Mbarara, Ug.	D6	54
Mbeya, Tan.	E6	54
Mbigou, Gabon	D2	54
Mbinda, Congo	D2	54
Mbini, Eq. Gui.	C1	54
Mboi, D.R.C.	E4	54
Mboki, C.A.R.	B5	54
Mbouda, Cam.	B2	54
Mbour, Sen.	D1	50
Mbout, Maur.	C2	50
Mbuji-Mayi, D.R.C.	E4	54
McAdam, N.B., Can.	D2	87
McAdoo, Pa., U.S.	E9	131
McAfee Peak, mtn., Nv., U.S.	B6	121
McAlester, Ok., U.S.	C6	129
McAlester, Lake, res., Ok., U.S.	B6	129
McAllen, Tx., U.S.	F3	136
McAlmont, Ar., U.S.	h10	97
McAlpine, Md., U.S.	B4	113
McAlpine Lock and Dam, U.S.	H6	107
McArthur, Oh., U.S.	C3	128
McBee, S.C., U.S.	C7	133
McCall, Id., U.S.	E2	105
McCalla, Al., U.S.	g6	94
McCamey, Tx., U.S.	D1	136
McCammon, Id., U.S.	G6	105
McCandless, Pa., U.S.	h13	131
McCartney Mountain, mtn., Mt., U.S.	E4	119
McCaysville, Ga., U.S.	B2	103
McChord Air Force Base, mil., Wa., U.S.	f11	140
McClain, co., Ok., U.S.	C4	129
McCleary, Wa., U.S.	B2	140
McClintock, Mount, mtn., Ant.	D20	67
McCloud, Ca., U.S.	B2	98
McClure, Pa., U.S.	E7	131
McColl, S.C., U.S.	B8	133
McComas, W.V., U.S.	D3	141
McComb, Ms., U.S.	D3	117
McComb, Oh., U.S.	A2	128
McCone, co., Mt., U.S.	C11	119
McConnell Air Force Base, mil., Ks., U.S.	g12	109
McConnellsburg, Pa., U.S.	G6	131
McConnelsville, Oh., U.S.	C4	128
McCook, Ne., U.S.	D5	120
McCook, co., S.D., U.S.	D8	134
McCordsville, In., U.S.	E6	107
McCormick, S.C., U.S.	D3	133
McCormick, co., S.C., U.S.	D3	133
McCracken, co., Ky., U.S.	e9	110
McCreary, Mb., Can.	D2	86
McCreary, co., Ky., U.S.	D5	110
McCrory, Ar., U.S.	B4	97
McCulloch, co., Tx., U.S.	D3	136
McCullough Mountain, mtn., Nv., U.S.	H6	121
McCurtain, co., Ok., U.S.	C7	129
McDermitt, Nv., U.S.	B4	121
McDonald, co., Mo., U.S.	E3	118
McDonough, Ga., U.S.	C2	103
McDonough, co., Il., U.S.	C3	106
McDougall, Mount, mtn., Wy., U.S.	D2	143
McDowell, Ky., U.S.	C7	110
McDowell, co., N.C., U.S.	f10	126
McDowell, co., W.V., U.S.	D3	141
McDowell Mountains, mts., Az., U.S.	k9	96
McDowell Peak, mtn., Az., U.S.	k9	96
McDuffie, co., Ga., U.S.	C4	103
McElroy Creek, stm., W.V., U.S.	k9	141
Mcensk, Russia	C14	20
McEwen, Tn., U.S.	A4	135
McFarland, Ca., U.S.	E4	98
McFarland, Wi., U.S.	E4	142
McGehee, Ar., U.S.	D4	97
McGill, Nv., U.S.	D7	121
McGrath, Ak., U.S.	C8	95
McGregor, Ia., U.S.	A6	108
McGregor, Tx., U.S.	D4	136
McGregor, stm., B.C., Can.	B7	85
McGregor Lake, l., Ab., Can.	D4	84
McGuire, Mount, mtn., Id., U.S.	D4	105
McGuire Air Force Base, mil., N.J., U.S.	C3	123
McHenry, Il., U.S.	A5	106
McHenry, Md., U.S.	k12	113
McHenry, co., Il., U.S.	A5	106
McHenry, co., N.D., U.S.	A5	127
Mchinji, Mwi.	A5	56
McIntosh, Mn., U.S.	C3	116
McIntosh, co., Ga., U.S.	E5	103
McIntosh, co., N.D., U.S.	C6	127
McIntosh, co., Ok., U.S.	B6	129
McKean, co., Pa., U.S.	C4	131
McKee, Ky., U.S.	C6	110
McKeesport, Pa., U.S.	F2	131
McKees Rocks, Pa., U.S.	F1	131
McKenzie, Tn., U.S.	A3	135
McKenzie, co., N.D., U.S.	B2	127
McKenzie, stm., Or., U.S.	C4	130
McKinley, co., N.M., U.S.	B1	124
McKinley, Mount, mtn., Ak., U.S.	C9	95
McKinleyville, Ca., U.S.	B1	98
McKinney, Tx., U.S.	C4	136
McKinney, Lake, l., Ks., U.S.	E2	109
McKittrick Summit, mtn., Ca., U.S.	E4	98
McLaughlin, S.D., U.S.	B5	134
McLean, Il., U.S.	C4	106
McLean, Va., U.S.	g12	139
McLean, co., Il., U.S.	C4	106
McLean, co., Ky., U.S.	C2	110
McLean, co., N.D., U.S.	B4	127
McLeansboro, Il., U.S.	E5	106
McLennan, Ab., Can.	B2	84
McLennan, co., Tx., U.S.	D4	136
McLeod, co., Mn., U.S.	F4	116
M'Clintock Channel, strt., N.T., Can.	D19	82
McLoud, Ok., U.S.	B4	129
McLoughlin, Mount, mtn., Or., U.S.	D4	130
McLouth, Ks., U.S.	C8	109
McMechen, W.V., U.S.	B4	141
McMillan, Lake, res., N.M., U.S.	E5	124
McMinn, co., Tn., U.S.	D9	135
McMinnville, Or., U.S.	B3	130
McMinnville, Tn., U.S.	D8	135
McMullen, co., Tx., U.S.	E3	136
McMurdo Sound, strt., Ant.	D21	67
McNairy, co., Tn., U.S.	B3	135
McNary, Az., U.S.	C6	96
McNary Dam, U.S.	B7	130
McNeil, Ar., U.S.	D2	97
McNeil, Mount, mtn., B.C., Can.	B2	85
McNeil Island, i., Wa., U.S.	f10	140
McNeill, Ms., U.S.	E4	117
McPherson, Ks., U.S.	D6	109
McPherson, co., Ks., U.S.	D6	109
McPherson, co., Ne., U.S.	C4	120
McPherson, co., S.D., U.S.	B6	134
McQueeney, Tx., U.S.	h7	136
McRae, Ar., U.S.	B4	97
McRae, Ga., U.S.	D4	103
McRoberts, Ky., U.S.	C7	110
McSherrystown, Pa., U.S.	G7	131
Mdandu, Tan.	E6	54
Mead, Wa., U.S.	B8	140
Mead, Lake, res., U.S.	A1	96
Meade, Ks., U.S.	E3	109
Meade, co., Ks., U.S.	E3	109
Meade, co., Ky., U.S.	C3	110
Meade, co., S.D., U.S.	C3	134
Meade, stm., Ak., U.S.	B8	95
Meaden Peak, mtn., Co., U.S.	A3	99
Meade Peak, mtn., Id., U.S.	G7	105
Meadow, stm., W.V., U.S.	C4	141
Meadow Creek, stm., W.V., U.S.	n14	141
Meadow Lands, Pa., U.S.	F1	131
Meadow Valley Wash, val., Nv., U.S.	F7	121
Meadowview, Va., U.S.	f10	139
Meadville, Pa., U.S.	C1	131
Meaford, On., Can.	C4	89
Meagher, co., Mt., U.S.	D6	119
Meander Creek Reservoir, res., Oh., U.S.	A5	128
Meaux, Fr.	C8	16
Mebane, N.C., U.S.	A3	126
Mecca see Makkah, Sau. Ar.	F3	38
Mecca, Ca., U.S.	F5	98
Mechanic Falls, Me., U.S.	D2	112
Mechanicsburg, Oh., U.S.	B2	128
Mechanicsburg, Pa., U.S.	F7	131
Mechanicsville, Ia., U.S.	C6	108
Mechanicsville, Md., U.S.	D4	113
Mechanicsville, Va., U.S.	C5	139
Mechanicville, N.Y., U.S.	C7	125
Mechant, Lake, l., La., U.S.	E4	111
Mecklenburg, co., N.C., U.S.	B2	126
Mecklenburg, co., Va., U.S.	D4	139
Mecklenburg, hist. reg., Ger.	D12	12
Mecklenburg Bay see Mecklenburger Bucht, b., Ger.	C12	12
Mecklenburger Bucht, b., Ger.	C12	12
Mecosta, co., Mi., U.S.	E5	115
Mecúfi, Moz.	A7	56
Medan, Indon.	C1	36
Medanosa, Punta, c., Arg.	G3	69
Medaryville, In., U.S.	B4	107
Meddybumps Lake, l., Me., U.S.	C5	112
Medellín, Col.	B4	70
Médenine, Tun.	D7	48
Mederdra, Maur.	C1	50
Medfield, Ma., U.S.	h10	114
Medford, Ma., U.S.	B5	114
Medford, Mn., U.S.	F5	116
Medford, Or., U.S.	E4	130
Medford, Wi., U.S.	C3	142
Medford Lakes, N.J., U.S.	D3	123
Medgidia, Rom.	G10	20
Media, Pa., U.S.	G11	131
Mediapolis, Ia., U.S.	C6	108
Mediaş, Rom.	F8	20
Medical Lake, Wa., U.S.	B8	140
Medicine Bow, Wy., U.S.	E6	143
Medicine Bow, stm., Wy., U.S.	E6	143
Medicine Bow Mountains, mts., U.S.	E6	143
Medicine Bow Peak, mtn., Wy., U.S.	E6	143
Medicine Hat, Ab., Can.	D5	84
Medicine Lodge, Ks., U.S.	E5	109
Medicine Lodge, stm., U.S.	E4	109
Medina see Al-Madīnah, Sau. Ar.	F3	38
Medina, N.Y., U.S.	B2	125
Medina, Oh., U.S.	A4	128
Medina, Tn., U.S.	B3	135
Medina, Wa., U.S.	e11	140
Medina, co., Oh., U.S.	A4	128
Medina, co., Tx., U.S.	E3	136
Medina, stm., Tx., U.S.	k7	136
Medina del Campo, Spain	G4	16
Medinīpur, India	E5	40
Mediterranean Sea	D5	14
Mediterraneo, Mar see Mediterranean Sea	D5	14
Mednogorsk, Russia	D10	22
Mednyj, ostrov, i., Russia	D18	26
Medora, In., U.S.	G5	107
Médouneu, Gabon	C2	54
Medvežegorsk, Russia	B5	22
Medvežji ostrova, is., Russia	B18	26
Medway, Ma., U.S.	B5	114
Medway, Me., U.S.	C4	112
Medway, stm., N.S., Can.	E5	87
Meekatharra, Austl.	F2	60
Meeker, Co., U.S.	A3	99
Meeker, Ok., U.S.	B5	129
Meeker, co., Mn., U.S.	E4	116
Meelpaeg Lake, res., Nf., Can.	D3	88
Meerut, India	D3	40
Meeteetse, Wy., U.S.	B4	143
Mēga, Eth.	C7	54
Mégantic, Lac, l., P.Q., Can.	D7	90
Mégantic, Mont, mtn., P.Q., Can.	D6	90
Meggett, S.C., U.S.	F7	133

Name	Map Ref.	Page

Meghālaya, prov., India . . . **D6** 40
Meghri, Arm. **C12** 44
Meharry, Mount, mtn.,
  Austl. **H20** 4
Meherrin, stm., U.S. **A4** 126
Mehlville, Mo., U.S. **f13** 118
Mehtarlām, Afg. **D10** 42
Meia Meia, Tan. **E7** 54
Meiganga, Cam. **B2** 54
Meigs, Ga., U.S. **E2** 103
Meigs, co., Oh., U.S. **C3** 128
Meigs, co., Tn., U.S. **D9** 135
Meiktila, Myan. **B3** 34
Meiningen, Ger. **E12** 12
Meishan, China **C1** 30
Meitan, China **D2** 30
Meizhou, China **G11** 28
Mejillones, Chile **B2** 69
Mékambo, Gabon **B2** 54
Mek'elē, Eth. **H12** 48
Mékhé, Sen. **C1** 50
Meknès, Mor. **D3** 48
Mekong, stm., Asia **D5** 34
Mékôngk see Mekong, stm.,
  Asia **D5** 34
Melaka, Malay. **C2** 36
Melanesia, is., Oc. **E10** 58
Melbourne, Austl. **H4** 62
Melbourne, Ar., U.S. **A4** 97
Melbourne, Fl., U.S. **D6** 102
Melbourne, Ia., U.S. **C4** 108
Melbourne, Ky., U.S. . . . **h14** 110
Melbourne Beach, Fl., U.S. **D6** 102
Melcher, Ia., U.S. **C4** 108
Melchor Múzquiz, Mex. . . . **B4** 78
Melenki, Russia **C7** 22
Meleuz, Russia **D10** 22
Mélèzes, Rivière aux, stm.,
  P.Q., Can. **g12** 90
Melfi, Chad **D8** 50
Melfi, Italy **D10** 18
Melilla, Sp. N. Afr. **J5** 16
Melipilla, Chile **E3** 72
Melita, Mb., Can. **E1** 86
Melitopol', Ukr. **F13** 20
Mellen, Wi., U.S. **B3** 142
Mellette, co., S.D., U.S. . . **D5** 134
Melo, Ur. **E7** 72
Melocheville, P.Q., Can. . . **q19** 90
Melos see Mílos, i., Grc. . **F10** 18
Melrhir, Chott, l., Alg. **D6** 48
Melrose, Austl. **F3** 60
Melrose, Fl., U.S. **C4** 102
Melrose, Ma., U.S. **B5** 114
Melrose, Mn., U.S. **E4** 116
Melrose, N.M., U.S. **C6** 124
Melton Hill Lake, res., Tn.,
  U.S. **D9** 135
Meluco, Moz. **A6** 56
Melun, Fr. **C8** 16
Melvern Lake, res., Ks., U.S. **D8** 109
Melville, La., U.S. **D4** 111
Melville, Cape, c., Austl. . . **C3** 62
Melville, Lake, l., Nf., Can. **B2** 88
Melville Island, i., Austl. . . **C5** 60
Melville Sound, strt., N.T.,
  Can. **E18** 82
Melvin, Ky., U.S. **C7** 110
Memboro, Indon. **E5** 36
Memel see Klaipėda, Lith. . . **D8** 10
Memmingen, Ger. **G11** 12
Mempawah, Indon. **C3** 36
Memphis, Fl., U.S. **p10** 102
Memphis, Mi., U.S. **F8** 115
Memphis, Mo., U.S. **A5** 118
Memphis, Tn., U.S. **B1** 135
Memphis, Tx., U.S. **B2** 136
Memphis Naval Air Station,
  mil., Tn., U.S. **B2** 135
Mena, Ukr. **D12** 20
Mena, Ar., U.S. **C1** 97
Menahga, Mn., U.S. **D3** 116
Ménaka, Mali **C5** 50
Menan, Id., U.S. **F7** 105
Menands, N.Y., U.S. **C7** 125
Menard, Tx., U.S. **D3** 136
Menard, co., Il., U.S. **C4** 106
Menard, co., Tx., U.S. **D3** 136
Menasha, Wi., U.S. **D5** 142
Mende, Fr. **E8** 16
Mendeleyev Ridge **E4** 144
Mendenhall, Ms., U.S. **D4** 117
Mendham, N.J., U.S. **B3** 123
Mendī, Eth. **B7** 54
Mendi, Pap. N. Gui. **H11** 32
Mendocino, co., Ca., U.S. . **C2** 98
Mendocino Fracture Zone . **E3** 64
Mendon, Il., U.S. **C2** 106
Mendon, Mi., U.S. **F5** 115
Mendon, Ut., U.S. **B4** 137
Mendota, Ca., U.S. **D3** 98
Mendota, Il., U.S. **B4** 106
Mendota, Lake, l., Wi., U.S. **E4** 142
Mendoza, Arg. **E4** 72
Mene Grande, Ven. **D5** 80
Menemen, Tur. **C2** 44
Mengcheng, China **C4** 30
Menggala, Indon. **D3** 36
Menghai, China **B4** 34
Mengjiawan, China **B2** 30
Mengzi, China **G8** 28
Menifee, co., Ky., U.S. . . . **C6** 110
Menindee, Austl. **G3** 62
Menlo Park, Ca., U.S. . . . **k8** 98
Menno, S.D., U.S. **D8** 134
Menominee, Mi., U.S. **C3** 115

Menominee, co., Mi., U.S. . **C3** 115
Menominee, co., Wi., U.S. . **C5** 142
Menominee, stm., U.S. . . . **C6** 142
Menominee Indian
  Reservation, Wi., U.S. . **C5** 142
Menomonee, stm., Wi.,
  U.S. **m11** 142
Menomonee Falls, Wi., U.S. **E5** 142
Menomonie, Wi., U.S. **D2** 142
Menongue, Ang. **A2** 56
Menor, Mar, b., Spain **I6** 16
Menorca (Minorca), i., Spain **G9** 16
Mentawai, Kepulauan, is.,
  Indon. **D1** 36
Mentawai, Selat, strt.,
  Indon. **D1** 36
Mentone, In., U.S. **B5** 107
Mentor, Oh., U.S. **A4** 128
Mentor-on-the-Lake, Oh.,
  U.S. **A4** 128
Menzel Bourguiba, Tun. . . **F2** 18
Menzies, Austl. **F3** 60
Meoqui, Mex. **B3** 78
Meppen, Ger. **D10** 12
Mequinenza, Embalse de,
  res., Spain **G6** 16
Mequon, Wi., U.S. **E6** 142
Merambéllou, Kólpos, b.,
  Grc. **G10** 18
Meramec, stm., Mo., U.S. . **C7** 118
Merano, Italy **A3** 18
Merasheen Island, i., Nf.,
  Can. **E4** 88
Merauke, Indon. **H11** 32
Meraux, La., U.S. **k12** 111
Mercāra, India **G3** 40
Merced, Ca., U.S. **D3** 98
Merced, co., Ca., U.S. **D3** 98
Merced, stm., Ca., U.S. . . . **D3** 98
Mercedes, Arg. **D6** 72
Mercedes, Tx., U.S. **F4** 136
Mercedes, Ur. **E6** 72
Mercer, Pa., U.S. **D1** 131
Mercer, Wi., U.S. **B3** 142
Mercer, co., Il., U.S. **B3** 106
Mercer, co., Ky., U.S. **C5** 110
Mercer, co.,Mo., U.S. **A4** 118
Mercer, co., N.D., U.S. . . . **B4** 127
Mercer, co., N.J., U.S. **C3** 123
Mercer, co., Oh., U.S. **B1** 128
Mercer, co., Pa., U.S. **D1** 131
Mercer, co., W.V., U.S. . . . **D3** 141
Mercer Island, Wa., U.S. . . **B3** 140
Mercer Island, i., Wa., U.S. **e11** 140
Mercersburg, Pa., U.S. **G6** 131
Mercerville, N.J., U.S. **C3** 123
Mercier, P.Q., Can. **D4** 90
Meredith, N.H., U.S. **C3** 122
Meredith, Lake, l., Co., U.S. **C7** 99
Meredith, Lake, res., Tx.,
  U.S. **B2** 136
Meredosia, Il., U.S. **D3** 106
Meredosia Lake, l., Il., U.S. **D3** 106
Mereeg, Som. **J14** 48
Merefa, Ukr. **E14** 20
Merenkurkku (Norra
  Kvarken), strt., Eur. . . . **E9** 10
Mergui, Myan. **D3** 34
Mergui Archipelago, is.,
  Myan. **D3** 34
Meriç (Évros) (Marica), stm.,
  Eur. **D11** 18
Mérida, Mex. **C7** 78
Mérida, Spain **H3** 16
Mérida, Ven. . . . . . . : **B5** 70
Mérida, Cordillera de, mts.,
  Ven. **B5** 70
Meriden, Ct., U.S. **C4** 100
Meriden, Ks., U.S. **C8** 109
Meridian, Id., U.S. **F2** 105
Meridian, Ms., U.S. **C5** 117
Meridian, Pa., U.S. **E2** 131
Meridian, Tx., U.S. **D4** 136
Meridian Hills, In., U.S. . . **k10** 107
Meridian Naval Air Station,
  mil., Ms., U.S. **C5** 117
Meridianville, Al., U.S. **A3** 94
Merikarvia, Fin. **F9** 10
Merín, Laguna see Mirim,
  Lagoa, b., S.A. **E7** 72
Meriwether, co., Ga., U.S. . **C2** 103
Merkel, Tx., U.S. **C2** 136
Merlin, On., Can. **E2** 89
Mermentau, La., U.S. **D3** 111
Mermentau, stm., La., U.S. **E3** 111
Meron, Har, mtn., Isr. **F6** 44
Meron, Mount see Meron,
  Har, mtn., Isr. **F6** 44
Merredin, Austl. **G2** 60
Merriam, Ks., U.S. **k16** 109
Merrick, co., Ne., U.S. **C7** 120
Merrickville, On., Can. **C9** 89
Merrill, Ia., U.S. **B1** 108
Merrill, Mi., U.S. **E6** 115
Merrill, Or., U.S. **E5** 130
Merrill, Wi., U.S. **C4** 142
Merrillville, In., U.S. **B3** 107
Merrimac, Ma., U.S. **A5** 114
Merrimack, N.H., U.S. **E4** 122
Merrimack, co., N.H., U.S. . **D3** 122
Merrimack, stm., U.S. **A5** 114
Merritt, B.C., Can. **D7** 85
Merritt Island, Fl., U.S. . . . **D6** 102
Merritt Reservoir, res., Ne.,
  U.S. **B5** 120

Merrymeeting Lake, l., N.H.,
  U.S. **D4** 122
Merryville, La., U.S. **D2** 111
Mersa Matruh, Egypt . . . **D10** 48
Mersing, Malay. **C2** 36
Merthyr Tydfil, Wales, U.K. **E5** 12
Merton, Wi., U.S. **m11** 142
Meru, Kenya **C7** 54
Merwin, Lake, res., Wa.,
  U.S. **C3** 140
Merzifon, Tur. **B6** 44
Mesa, Az., U.S. **D4** 96
Mesa, co., Co., U.S. **C2** 99
Mesabi Range, hills, Mn.,
  U.S. **C6** 116
Mesa Mountain, mtn., Co.,
  U.S. **D4** 99
Mesa Verde National Park,
  Co., U.S. **D2** 99
Mescalero, N.M., U.S. **D4** 124
Mescalero Indian
  Reservation, N.M., U.S. **D4** 124
Meschede, Ger. **E11** 12
Meshgīn Shahr, Iran **C12** 44
Mesilla, N.M., U.S. **E3** 124
Mesolóngion, Grc. **E8** 18
Mesopotamia, hist. reg.,
  Asia **D4** 42
Mesquite, N.M., U.S. **E3** 124
Mesquite, Nv., U.S. **G7** 121
Mesquite, Tx., U.S. **n10** 136
Messalonskee Lake, l., Me.,
  U.S. **D3** 112
Messina, Italy **E5** 18
Messina, S. Afr. **C5** 56
Messina, Stretto di, strt.,
  Italy **E5** 18
Messiniakós Kólpos, b., Grc. **F9** 18
Mestghanem, Alg. **C4** 48
Mestre, Italy **B4** 18
Meta, stm., S.A. **B5** 70
Métabetchouan, P.Q., Can. **A6** 90
Métabetchouane, stm.,
  P.Q., Can. **A5** 90
Metairie, La., U.S. **k11** 111
Metamora, Il., U.S. **C4** 106
Metán, Arg. **D5** 72
Metapán, El Sal. **C2** 80
Metapontum, hist., Italy . . **D6** 18
Metcalfe, On., Can. **B9** 89
Metcalfe, Ms., U.S. **B2** 117
Metcalfe, co., Ky., U.S. . . . **C4** 110
Metedeconk, North Branch,
  stm., N.J., U.S. **C4** 123
Metedeconk, South Branch,
  stm., N.J., U.S. **C3** 123
Meteghan, N.S., Can. **E3** 87
Meteghan River, N.S., Can. **E3** 87
Metéora, Grc. **E8** 18
Meteor Crater, crat., Az.,
  U.S. **C4** 96
Methow, stm., Wa., U.S. . . **A5** 140
Methuen, Ma., U.S. **A5** 114
Metlakatla, Ak., U.S. **D13** 95
Metonga, Lake, l., Wi., U.S. **C5** 142
Metro, Indon. **E3** 36
Metropolis, Il., U.S. **F5** 106
Mettawee, stm., U.S. **E2** 138
Metter, Ga., U.S. **D4** 103
Metuchen, N.J., U.S. **B4** 123
Metz, Fr. **C10** 16
Metzger, Or., U.S. **h12** 130
Meulaboh, Indon. **C1** 36
Meuse (Maas), stm., Eur. . **C9** 16
Mexia, Tx., U.S. **D4** 136
Mexia, Lake, res., Tx., U.S. **D4** 136
Mexiana, Ilha, i., Braz. **A2** 74
Mexicali, Mex. **A1** 78
Mexican Basin **F4** 66
Mexico, In., U.S. **C5** 107
Mexico, Me., U.S. **D2** 112
Mexico, Mo., U.S. **B6** 118
México, state, Mex. **D4** 78
Mexico, ctry., N.A. **C4** 78
Mexico, Gulf of, b., N.A. . **F10** 92
Mexico City see Ciudad de
  México, Mex. **D5** 78
Meyersdale, Pa., U.S. **G3** 131
Meyísti, i., Grc. **F12** 18
Meymaneh, Afg. **C8** 42
Mezcala, Mex. **D5** 78
Mezdurečenskij, Russia . . **C12** 22
Mezen', Russia **C6** 26
Mezen', stm., Russia **C6** 26
Mezenskaja guba, b., Russia **A7** 22
Mezőtúr, Hung. **F6** 20
Mfangano Island, i., Kenya **D6** 54
Mgeta, Tan. **E7** 54
M'Goun, Irhil, mtn., Mor. . **E3** 14
Mhow, India **E3** 40
Miahuatlán de Porfirio Díaz,
  Mex. **D5** 78
Miajadas, Spain **H4** 16
Miaméré, C.A.R. **B3** 54
Miami, Az., U.S. **D5** 96
Miami, Fl., U.S. **G6** 102
Miami, Ok., U.S. **A7** 129
Miami, co., In., U.S. **C5** 107
Miami, co., Ks., U.S. **D9** 109
Miami, co., Oh., U.S. **B1** 128
Miami Beach, Fl., U.S. . . . **G6** 102
Miami Canal, Fl., U.S. **F6** 102
Miami International Airport,
  Fl., U.S. **G6** 102
Miamisburg, Oh., U.S. **C1** 128

Miami Shores, Fl., U.S. **G6** 102
Miami Springs, Fl., U.S. . . . **G6** 102
Mianchi, China **C3** 30
Miāndoāb, Iran **D12** 44
Miandrivazo, Madag. **B8** 56
Miāneh, Iran **C5** 42
Mianning, China **A4** 30
Mianwāli, Pak. **D10** 42
Mianyang, China **E8** 28
Mianzhu, China **C1** 30
Mianus Reservoir, res., U.S. **E1** 100
Miass, Russia **D8** 26
Mica Mountain, mtn., Az.,
  U.S. **E5** 96
Micco, Fl., U.S. **E6** 102
Miccosukee, Lake, res., Fl.,
  U.S. **B2** 102
Michalovce, Slvk. **E6** 20
Michelson, Mount, mtn.,
  Ak., U.S. **B11** 95
Michie, Tn., U.S. **B3** 135
Michigamme, Lake, l., Mi.,
  U.S. **B2** 115
Michigamme Reservoir, res.,
  Mi., U.S. **B2** 115
Michigan, state, U.S. **E6** 115
Michigan, stm., Co., U.S. . . **A4** 99
Michigan, Lake, l., U.S. . . **C10** 92
Michigan Center, Mi., U.S. **F6** 115
Michigan City, In., U.S. . . . **A4** 107
Michigan Island, i., Wi.,
  U.S. **B3** 142
Michoacán, state, Mex. . . . **D4** 78
Micronesia, is., Oc. **C9** 58
Micronesia, Federated
  States of, ctry., Oc. **D8** 58
Mičurinsk, Russia **C16** 20
Mid-Atlantic Ridge **F9** 66
Middelburg, S. Afr. **E3** 56
Middelburg, S. Afr. **D4** 56
Middelfart, Den. **I3** 10
Middle, stm., Ia., U.S. **C3** 108
Middle, stm., Mn., U.S. . . . **B2** 116
Middle America Trench . . . **G28** 64
Middle Andaman, i., India . **G6** 40
Middleboro (Middleborough
  Center), Ma., U.S. **C6** 114
Middlebourne, W.V., U.S. . **B4** 141
Middleburg, Fl., U.S. **B5** 102
Middleburg, Pa., U.S. **E7** 131
Middleburg Heights, Oh.,
  U.S. **h9** 128
Middlebury, Ct., U.S. **C3** 100
Middlebury, In., U.S. **A6** 107
Middlebury, Vt., U.S. **C2** 138
Middle Caicos, i., T./C. Is. . **A5** 80
Middlefield, Ct., U.S. **C5** 100
Middlefield, Oh., U.S. **A4** 128
Middle Island Creek, stm.,
  W.V., U.S. **B3** 141
Middle Nodaway, stm., Ia.,
  U.S. **C3** 108
Middle Park, val., Co., U.S. **A4** 99
Middle Patuxent, stm., Md.,
  U.S. **B4** 113
Middle Raccoon, stm., Ia.,
  U.S. **C3** 108
Middle River, Md., U.S. . . . **B5** 113
Middlesboro, Ky., U.S. **D6** 110
Middlesbrough, Eng., U.K. **C6** 12
Middlesex, N.C., U.S. **B4** 126
Middlesex, N.J., U.S. **B4** 123
Middlesex, co., Ct., U.S. . . **D5** 100
Middlesex, co., Ma., U.S. . **A5** 114
Middlesex, co., N.J., U.S. . . **C4** 123
Middlesex, co., Va., U.S. . . **C6** 139
Middlesex Fells Reservation,
  Ma., U.S. **g11** 114
Middleton, N.S., Can. **E4** 87
Middleton, Id., U.S. **F2** 105
Middleton, Ma., U.S. **A5** 114
Middleton, Wi., U.S. **E4** 142
Middletown, Ca., U.S. **C2** 98
Middletown, Ct., U.S. **C5** 100
Middletown, De., U.S. **C3** 101
Middletown, In., U.S. **D6** 107
Middletown, Ky., U.S. . . . **g11** 110
Middletown, Md., U.S. **B2** 113
Middletown, N.Y., U.S. . . . **D6** 125
Middletown, Oh., U.S. **C1** 128
Middletown, Pa., U.S. **F8** 131
Middletown, R.I., U.S. **E5** 132
Middletown, Va., U.S. **A4** 139
Middleville, Mi., U.S. **F5** 115
Midfield, Al., U.S. **g7** 94
Mid-Indian Basin **I10** 64
Mid-Indian Ridge **I9** 64
Midland, On., Can. **C5** 89
Midland, Mi., U.S. **E6** 115
Midland, N.C., U.S. **B2** 126
Midland, Pa., U.S. **E1** 131
Midland, Tx., U.S. **D1** 136
Midland, co., Mi., U.S. **E6** 115
Midland, co., Tx., U.S. **D1** 136
Midland City, Al., U.S. **D4** 94
Midland Park, N.J., U.S. . . . **B4** 123
Midland Park, S.C., U.S. . . **k11** 133
Midlothian, Il., U.S. **k9** 106
Midlothian, Tx., U.S. **C4** 136
Midongy Atsimo, Madag. . . **F9** 56
Mid-Pacific Mountains **F18** 64

Midvale, Ut., U.S. **C4** 137
Midville, Ga., U.S. **D4** 103
Midway, B.C., Can. **E8** 85
Midway, De., U.S. **F5** 101
Midway, Ky., U.S. **B5** 110
Midway, Pa., U.S. **G7** 131
Midway, Wy., U.S. **C3** 143
Midway Islands, dep., Oc. **B12** 58
Midwest, Wy., U.S. **C6** 143
Midwest City, Ok., U.S. . . . **B4** 129
Midyat, Tur. **D9** 44
Międzyrzecz, Pol. **C3** 20
Miekojärvi, l., Fin. **C11** 10
Mielec, Pol. **D6** 20
Mieres, Spain **F4** 16
Mifflin, co., Pa., U.S. **E6** 131
Mifflinburg, Pa., U.S. **E7** 131
Mifflinville, Pa., U.S. **D9** 131
Miguel Alemán, Presa, res.,
  Mex. **D5** 78
Miguel Auza, Mex. **C4** 78
Mihajlovka, Russia **B15** 20
Mihajlovka, Russia **D6** 26
Mikasa, Japan **C16** 28
Mikínai, hist., Grc. **F9** 18
Mikindani, Tan. **F8** 54
Mikkeli, Fin. **F12** 10
Míkonos, i., Grc. **F10** 18
Mikumi, Tan. **E7** 54
Mikun', Russia **B9** 22
Milaca, Mn., U.S. **E5** 116
Milagro, Ec. **D4** 70
Milam, co., Tx., U.S. **D4** 136
Milan see Milano, Italy . . . **B2** 18
Milan, Ga., U.S. **D3** 103
Milan, Il., U.S. **B3** 106
Milan, In., U.S. **F7** 107
Milan, Mi., U.S. **F7** 115
Milan, Mo., U.S. **A4** 118
Milan, N.M., U.S. **B2** 124
Milan, Oh., U.S. **A3** 128
Milan, Tn., U.S. **B3** 135
Milange, Moz. **B6** 56
Milano (Milan), Italy **B2** 18
Milâs, Tur. **D2** 44
Milazzo, Italy **E5** 18
Milbank, S.D., U.S. **B9** 134
Mildmay, On., Can. **C3** 89
Mildura, Austl. **G3** 62
Mile, China **G8** 28
Milesburg, Pa., U.S. **E6** 131
Miles City, Mt., U.S. **D11** 119
Milestone, Sk., Can. **G3** 91
Milet (Miletus), hist., Tur. . **D2** 44
Miletus see Milet, hist., Tur. **D2** 44
Milford, Ct., U.S. **E3** 100
Milford, De., U.S. **E4** 101
Milford, Ia., U.S. **A2** 108
Milford, Il., U.S. **C6** 106
Milford, In., U.S. **B6** 107
Milford, Ma., U.S. **B4** 114
Milford, Me., U.S. **D4** 112
Milford, Mi., U.S. **F7** 115
Milford, Ne., U.S. **D8** 120
Milford, N.H., U.S. **E3** 122
Milford, Oh., U.S. **C1** 128
Milford, Pa., U.S. **D12** 131
Milford, Ut., U.S. **E2** 137
Milford Haven, Wales, U.K. **E4** 12
Milford Lake, res., Ks., U.S. **C6** 109
Milford Station, N.S., Can. . **D6** 87
Milḥ, Baḥr al-, res., Iraq . . **F10** 44
Mililani Town, Hi., U.S. . . . **g9** 104
Milk, stm., N.A. **B6** 92
Mil'kovo, Russia **D17** 28
Milk River, Ab., Can. **E4** 84
Mill, stm., Ma., U.S. **h9** 114
Millard, co., Ut., U.S. **D2** 137
Millau, Fr. **E8** 16
Millbrae, Ca., U.S. **h8** 98
Millbrook, On., Can. **C6** 89
Millbrook, Al., U.S. **C3** 94
Mill Brook, stm., Vt., U.S. . **B5** 138
Millburn, N.J., U.S. **B4** 123
Millbury, Ma., U.S. **B4** 114
Millbury, Oh., U.S. **e7** 128
Mill City, Or., U.S. **C4** 130
Millcreek, Ut., U.S. **C4** 137
Mill Creek, W.V., U.S. **C5** 141
Mill Creek, stm., N.J., U.S. **D4** 123
Mill Creek, stm., Oh., U.S. **B2** 128
Mill Creek, stm., Tn., U.S. **g10** 135
Mill Creek, stm., W.V., U.S. **m13** 141
Mill Creek, stm., W.V., U.S. **C3** 141
Millcreek Township, Pa.,
  U.S. **B1** 131
Milledgeville, Ga., U.S. . . . **C3** 103
Milledgeville, Il., U.S. **B4** 106
Mille Îles, Rivière des, stm.,
  P.Q., Can. **p19** 90
Mille Lacs, co., Mn., U.S. . **E5** 116
Mille Lacs Indian
  Reservation, Mn., U.S. . **D5** 116
Mille Lacs Lake, l., Mn.,
  U.S. **D5** 116
Millen, Ga., U.S. **D5** 103
Miller, S.D., U.S. **C7** 134
Miller, co., Ar., U.S. **D2** 97
Miller, co., Ga., U.S. **E2** 103
Miller, co., Mo., U.S. **C5** 118
Miller, Mount, mtn., Ak.,
  U.S. **C11** 95
Millerovo, Russia **E7** 22
Miller Peak, mtn., Az., U.S. **F5** 96
Miller Run, stm., Vt., U.S. . **B4** 138

Name	Map Ref.	Page

Millers, stm., Ma., U.S. A3   114
Millersburg, In., U.S. A6   107
Millersburg, Ky., U.S. B5   110
Millersburg, Oh., U.S. B4   128
Millersburg, Pa., U.S. E8   131
Millersport, Oh., U.S. C3   128
Millersville, Pa., U.S. F9   131
Millet, Ab., Can. C4   84
Mill Hall, Pa., U.S. D7   131
Millicent, Austl. H3   62
Milliken, Co., U.S. A6   99
Millington, Mi., U.S. E7   115
Millington, Tn., U.S. B2   135
Millinocket, Me., U.S. C4   112
Millinocket Lake, l., Me.,
    U.S. C4   112
Millinocket Lake, l., Me.,
    U.S. B4   112
Millis, Ma., U.S. B5   114
Millport, Al., U.S. B1   94
Millry, Al., U.S. D1   94
Mills, Wy., U.S. D6   143
Mills, co., Ia., U.S. C2   108
Mills, co., Tx., U.S. D3   136
Millsboro, De., U.S. F4   101
Millsboro, Pa., U.S. G1   131
Millstadt, Il., U.S. E3   106
Millstone, stm., N.J., U.S. . . C4   123
Milltown, In., U.S. H5   107
Milltown, N.J., U.S. C4   123
Milltown, Wi., U.S. C1   142
Milltown [-Head of Bay
    d'Espoir], Nf., Can. E4   88
Millvale, Pa., U.S. k14   131
Mill Valley, Ca., U.S. D2   98
Millville, Ma., U.S. B4   114
Millville, N.J., U.S. E2   123
Millville, Pa., U.S. D9   131
Millville, Ut., U.S. B4   137
Millville Lake, N.H., U.S. . . E4   122
Millwood, Wa., U.S. g14   140
Millwood Lake, res., Ar.,
    U.S. D1   97
Milner Dam, Id., U.S. G5   105
Milnor, N.D., U.S. C8   127
Milo, Ia., U.S. C4   108
Milo, Me., U.S. C4   112
Mílos, Grc. F10   18
Mílos, i., Grc. F10   18
Milparinka, Austl. F3   62
Milroy, In., U.S. F7   107
Milroy, Pa., U.S. E6   131
Milstead, Ga., U.S. C3   103
Milton, On., Can. D5   89
Milton, De., U.S. E4   101
Milton, Fl., U.S. u14   102
Milton, In., U.S. E7   107
Milton, Ma., U.S. B5   114
Milton, N.H., U.S. D5   122
Milton, Pa., U.S. D8   131
Milton, Vt., U.S. B2   138
Milton, W.V., U.S. C2   141
Milton, Wa., U.S. f11   140
Milton, Wi., U.S. F5   142
Milton, Lake, l., Oh., U.S. . A4   128
Miltona, Lake, l., Mn., U.S. . D3   116
Milton-Freewater, Or., U.S. . B8   130
Milton Keynes, Eng., U.K. . D6   12
Milton Reservoir, res., Co.,
    U.S. A6   99
Milverton, On., Can. D4   89
Milwaukee, Wi., U.S. E6   142
Milwaukee, co., Wi., U.S. . . E6   142
Milwaukee, stm., Wi., U.S. . m12   142
Milwaukie, Or., U.S. B4   130
Mims, Fl., U.S. D6   102
Min, stm., China F8   28
Min, stm., China D4   30
Mina, Nv., U.S. E3   121
Mīnā' al-Aḥmadī, Kuw. E5   42
Mīnāb, Iran E7   42
Minahasa, pen., Indon. . . . C6   36
Minami-Tori-shima, i., Japan F18   64
Minas, Ur. E6   72
Minas Basin, b., N.S., Can. . D5   87
Minas Channel, strt., N.S.,
    Can. D5   87
Minas Gerais, state, Braz. . . E2   74
Minatare, Ne., U.S. C2   120
Minatitlán, Mex. D6   78
Minbya, Myan. B2   34
Minco, Ok., U.S. B4   129
Mindanao, i., Phil. E8   34
Mindanao Sea see Bohol
    Sea, Phil. E8   34
Mindelo, C.V. g10   50a
Minden, Ger. D11   12
Minden, La., U.S. B2   111
Minden, Ne., U.S. D7   120
Minden, Nv., U.S. E2   121
Minden, W.V., U.S. D3   141
Mindoro, i., Phil. D8   34
Mindoro Strait, strt., Phil. . D8   34
Mine Hill, N.J., U.S. B3   123
Mineiros, Braz. B7   72
Mineola, N.Y., U.S. E7   125
Mineola, Tx., U.S. C5   136
Miner, Mo., U.S. E8   118
Miner, co., S.D., U.S. D8   134
Mineral, co., Co., U.S. D4   99
Mineral, co., Mt., U.S. C1   119
Mineral, co., Nv., U.S. E3   121
Mineral, co., W.V., U.S. . . . B6   141
Mineral Point, Wi., U.S. . . . F3   142
Mineral Springs, Ar., U.S. . . D2   97

Mineral Wells, Tx., U.S. . . . C3   136
Minersville, Pa., U.S. E9   131
Minersville, Ut., U.S. E3   137
Minerva, Oh., U.S. B4   128
Minetto, N.Y., U.S. B4   125
Minfeng, China D4   28
Mingäçevir, Azer. B12   44
Mingäçevir su anbarı, res.,
    Azer. B12   44
Mingechaur Reservoir see
    Mingäçevir su anbarı,
    res., Azer. B12   44
Mingenew, Austl. F2   60
Mingo, co., W.V., U.S. D2   141
Mingo Junction, Oh., U.S. . . B5   128
Minho (Miño), stm., Eur. . . . G2   16
Minicoy Island, i., India . . . H2   40
Minidoka, co., Id., U.S. . . . G5   105
Minidoka Dam, Id., U.S. . . . G5   105
Minier, Il., U.S. C4   106
Minisink Island, i., N.J., U.S. A3   123
Minitonas, Mb., Can. C1   86
Minle, China D8   28
Minna, Nig. E6   50
Minneapolis, Ks., U.S. C6   109
Minneapolis, Mn., U.S. F5   116
Minnedosa, Mb., Can. D2   86
Minnedosa, stm., Mb., Can. . D1   86
Minnehaha, co., S.D., U.S. . D9   134
Minneola, Ks., U.S. E3   109
Minneota, Mn., U.S. F3   116
Minnesota, state, U.S. E4   116
Minnesota, stm., Mn., U.S. . F2   116
Minnesota Lake, Mn., U.S. . G5   116
Minnetonka, Mn., U.S. n12   116
Minnetonka, Lake, l., Mn.,
    U.S. n11   116
Minnewaska, Lake, l., Mn.,
    U.S. E3   116
Miño (Minho), stm., Eur. . . . F3   16
Minocqua, Wi., U.S. C4   142
Minonk, Il., U.S. C4   106
Minooka, Il., U.S. B5   106
Minot, N.D., U.S. A4   127
Minot Air Force Base, mil.,
    N.D., U.S. A4   127
Minqin, China B1   30
Minqing, China D4   30
Minquadale, De., U.S. i7   101
Minsk, Bela. B9   20
Minster, Oh., U.S. B1   128
Mint Hill, N.C., U.S. B2   126
Minto, N.B., Can. C3   87
Minturn, Co., U.S. B4   99
Minusinsk, Russia D11   26
Minute Man National
    Historical Park, Ma.,
    U.S. g10   114
Minvoul, Gabon C2   54
Minxian, China E8   28
Minya see El-Minya, Egypt . E11   48
Mio, Mi., U.S. D6   115
Mīrābād, Afg. D8   42
Mirabel, P.Q., Can. D3   90
Mirabella, Gulf of see
    Merambéllou, Kólpos,
    b., Grc. G10   18
Mirador, Braz. E11   70
Miraflores, Col. B5   70
Miraj, India F2   40
Miramar, Fl., U.S. s13   102
Miramar Naval Air Station,
    mil., Ca., U.S. F5   98
Miramichi Bay, b., N.B.,
    Can. B5   87
Miranda, stm., Braz. B6   72
Miranda de Ebro, Spain . . . F5   16
Mirbāṭ, Oman G6   38
Miri, Malay. C4   36
Miria, Niger D6   50
Mirim, Lagoa (Merín,
    Laguna), b., S.A. E7   72
Mirnyj, Russia C13   26
Mírpur, Pak. D10   42
Mīrpur Khās, Pak. E9   42
Mirror Lake, l., N.H., U.S. . C4   122
Mirzāpur, India D4   40
Miscouche, P.E., Can. C6   87
Miscou Island, i., N.B., Can. A5   87
Miscou Point, c., N.B., Can. A5   87
Misenheimer, N.C., U.S. . . . B2   126
Mishan, China B14   28
Mishawaka, In., U.S. A5   107
Misheguk Mountain, mtn.,
    Ak., U.S. B7   95
Mishicot, Wi., U.S. D6   142
Mishmi, Russia C15   10
Misiones, Pa., U.S. C6   87
Misool, Pulau, i., Indon. . . . D8   36
Mispillion, stm., De., U.S. . E4   101
Miṣrātah, Libya D8   48
Missaukee, co., Mi., U.S. . . D5   115
Missaukee, Lake, l., Mi.,
    U.S. D5   115
Mission, Ks., U.S. m16   109
Mission, S.D., U.S. D5   134
Mission, Tx., U.S. F3   136
Mission Range, mts., Mt.,
    U.S. C3   119
Mission Viejo, Ca., U.S. . . . n13   98
Missisquoi, stm., Vt., U.S. . B3   138
Missisquoi Bay, b., Vt., U.S. A2   138
Mississauga, On., Can. D5   89
Mississinewa, stm., U.S. . . . D7   107

Mississinewa Lake, res., In.,
    U.S. C6   107
Mississippi, co., Ar., U.S. . . B5   97
Mississippi, co., Mo., U.S. . . E8   118
Mississippi, state, U.S. C4   117
Mississippi, stm., U.S. E9   92
Mississippi Delta, La., U.S. . E6   111
Mississippi Sound, strt., U.S. E5   117
Mississippi State, Ms., U.S. . B5   117
Missoula, Mt., U.S. D2   119
Missoula, co., Mt., U.S. . . . D2   119
Missouri, state, U.S. C5   118
Missouri, stm., U.S. D9   92
Missouri City, Tx., U.S. . . . r14   136
Missouri Valley, Ia., U.S. . . C2   108
Mistassini, P.Q., Can. h12   90
Mistassini, Lac, l., P.Q.,
    Can. h12   90
Misti, Volcán, vol., Peru . . . G5   70
Mita, Punta de, c., Mex. . . . C3   78
Mitchell, Austl. F4   62
Mitchell, On., Can. D3   89
Mitchell, Il., U.S. E3   106
Mitchell, In., U.S. G5   107
Mitchell, Ne., U.S. C2   120
Mitchell, S.D., U.S. D7   134
Mitchell, co., Ga., U.S. E2   103
Mitchell, co., Ia., U.S. A5   108
Mitchell, co., Ks., U.S. C5   109
Mitchell, co., N.C., U.S. . . . e10   126
Mitchell, co., Tx., U.S. C2   136
Mitchell, stm., Austl. D3   62
Mitchell, Lake, l., Mi., U.S. . D5   115
Mitchell, Lake, res., Al., U.S. C3   94
Mitchell, Mount, mtn., N.C.,
    U.S. f10   126
Mitchell Island, i., La., U.S. E6   111
Mitchellville, Ia., U.S. C4   108
Mitilíni, Grc. E11   18
Mitkof Island, i., Ak., U.S. . m23   95
Mito, Japan C14   31
Mitsiwa, Erit. G12   48
Mitú, Col. C5   70
Mitumba, Monts, mts.,
    D.R.C. E5   54
Mitwaba, D.R.C. C5   54
Mitzic, Gabon C2   54
Miyake-jima, i., Japan E15   28
Miyako, Japan D16   28
Miyako-jima, i., Japan B9   34
Miyakonojō, Japan E14   28
Miyazaki, Japan E14   28
Miyazu, Japan D15   28
Miyoshi, Japan D2   31
Miyun, China A4   30
Mīzan Teferī, Eth. B7   54
Mizdah, Libya D7   48
Mizen Head, c., Ire. E2   12
Mizhi, China B3   30
Mizoram, prov., India E6   40
Mizusawa, Japan C14   31
Mjakit, Russia C17   26
Mjölby, Swe. G6   10
Mjøsa, l., Nor. F4   10
Mkalama, Tan. D6   54
Mkokotoni, Tan. D7   54
Mladá Boleslav, Czech Rep. D3   20
Mlanje Peak see Sapitwa,
    mtn., Mwi. B6   56
Mława, Pol. C6   20
Mmabatho, S. Afr. D4   56
Moab, Ut., U.S. E6   137
Moala, i., Fiji m10   63b
Moamba, Moz. D5   56
Moanda, Gabon D2   54
Moapa River Indian
    Reservation, Nv., U.S. . G7   121
Moba, D.R.C. E5   54
Mobaye, C.A.R. C4   54
Moberly, Mo., U.S. B5   118
Mobile, Al., U.S. E1   94
Mobile, co., Al., U.S. E1   94
Mobile, stm., Al., U.S. E1   94
Mobile Bay, b., Al., U.S. . . E1   99
Mobridge, S.D., U.S. B5   134
Mobutu Sese Seko, Lac see
    Albert, Lake, l., Afr. . . . C6   54
Moca, Dom. Rep. B5   80
Mocanaqua, Pa., U.S. D9   131
Moc Chau, Viet. B4   34
Mocha see Al-Mukhā,
    Yemen H4   38
Mochudi, Bots. C4   56
Mocímboa da Praia, Moz. . . A7   56
Mocksville, N.C., U.S. B2   126
Moclips, Wa., U.S. B1   140
Môco, Morro de, mtn., Ang. F3   54
Mococa, Braz. F2   74
Moctezuma, Mex. B3   78
Mocuba, Moz. B6   56
Model Reservoir, res., Co.,
    U.S. D6   99
Módena, Italy B3   18
Modesto, Ca., U.S. D3   98
Modoc, co., Ca., U.S. B3   98
Modowi, Indon. G9   32
Moe, Austl. H4   62
Moen-jo-Daro, hist., Pak. . . E9   42
Moenkopi, Az., U.S. A4   96
Moffat, co., Co., U.S. A2   99
Moffat Tunnel, Co., U.S. . . B5   99
Mogadishu see Muqdisho,
    Som. J14   48
Mogadore, Oh., U.S. A4   128
Mogaung, Myan. A3   34

Mogincual, Moz. B7   56
Mogoča, Russia D13   26
Mogogh, Sudan B6   54
Mogok, Myan. B3   34
Mogollon Mountains, mts.,
    N.M., U.S. D1   124
Mogollon Rim, clf, Az., U.S. C5   96
Mogotón, mtn., N.A. F7   76
Mogzon, Russia A10   28
Mohall, N.D., U.S. A4   127
Mohammed, Râs, c., Egypt . F10   14
Mohave, co., Az., U.S. B1   96
Mohave, Lake, res., U.S. . . H7   121
Mohave Mountains, mts.,
    Az., U.S. C1   96
Mohave Valley, Az., U.S. . . C1   96
Mohawk, N.Y., U.S. C5   125
Mohawk, stm., N.H., U.S. . g7   122
Mohawk, stm., N.Y., U.S. . C5   125
Mohawk Lake, l., N.J., U.S. A3   123
Mohawk Mountains, mts.,
    Az., U.S. E2   96
Mohe, China A12   28
Mohican, stm., Oh., U.S. . . B3   128
Mohns Ridge D23   144
Mohnton, Pa., U.S. F10   131
Mohnyin, Myan. B3   34
Mohyliv-Podil's'kyi, Ukr. . . E9   20
Mo i Rana, Nor. C6   10
Moisie, P.Q., Can. h8   88
Mojave, Ca., U.S. E4   98
Mojave, stm., Ca., U.S. . . . E5   98
Mojave Desert, des., Ca.,
    U.S. E5   98
Mojo, Eth. B7   54
Mojynty, Kaz. E9   26
Mokapu Peninsula, pen.,
    Hi., U.S. g10   104
Mokapu Point, c., Hi., U.S. g11   104
Mokelumne, stm., Ca., U.S. C3   98
Mokena, Il., U.S. k9   106
Mokhotlong, Leso. D4   56
Mokine, Peru G5   70
Moknine, Tun. G3   18
Mokolo, Cam. A2   54
Mokp'o, S. Kor. E13   28
Moku Manu, i., Hi., U.S. . . g11   104
Mokulini, i., Hi., U.S. C5   104
Mola di Bari, Italy D6   18
Molalla, Or., U.S. B4   130
Moldavia, hist. reg., Rom. . F9   20
Moldavia see Moldova,
    ctry., Eur. F10   20
Molde, Nor. E2   10
Moldova, ctry., Eur. F10   20
Moldoveanu, Vârful, mtn.,
    Rom. G8   20
Molepolole, Bots. C4   56
Molfetta, Italy D6   18
Moline, Il., U.S. B3   106
Moline, Mi., U.S. F5   115
Molino, Fl., U.S. u14   102
Mollendo, Peru G5   70
Molokai, i., Hi., U.S. B5   104
Molokai Fracture Zone F24   64
Molokini, i., Hi., U.S. C5   104
Molopo, stm., Afr. D3   56
Molotov see Perm', Russia . D7   26
Moloundou, Cam. C3   54
Molson Lake, l., Mb., Can. . B3   86
Moluccas see Maluku, is.,
    Indon. D7   36
Molucca Sea see Maluku,
    Laut, Indon. C7   36
Moma, Moz. B6   56
Mombasa, Kenya D7   54
Mombetsu, Japan C16   28
Momence, Il., U.S. B6   106
Mompós, Col. D5   80
Momskij hrebet, mts.,
    Russia C16   26
Møn, i., Den. I5   10
Mona, Isla de, i., P.R. B6   80
Monaca, Pa., U.S. E1   131
Monaco, ctry., Eur. C1   18
Monadnock, Mount, mtn.,
    N.H., U.S. E2   122
Monadnock Mountain,
    mtn., Vt., U.S. B5   138
Monahans, Tx., U.S. D1   136
Mona Passage, strt., N.A. . . B6   80
Mona Quimbundo, Ang. . . . E3   54
Monarch Mills, S.C., U.S. . . B4   133
Monarch Pass, Co., U.S. . . C4   99
Monashee Mountains, mts.,
    B.C., Can. D8   85
Monastir, Tun. G3   18
Monção, Braz. D10   70
Monção, Port. G7   16
Monchegorsk, Russia C15   10
Mönchengladbach, Ger. . . . E10   12
Moncks Corner, S.C., U.S. . E7   133
Monclova, Mex. B4   78
Moncton, N.B., Can. C5   87
Mondjamboli, D.R.C. C4   54
Mondovì, Wi., U.S. D2   142
Monee, Il., U.S. B6   106
Monessen, Pa., U.S. F2   131
Monett, Mo., U.S. E4   118
Monette, Ar., U.S. B5   97
Monfalcone, Italy B4   18
Monforte de Lemos, Spain . F3   16
Mongalla, Sudan B6   54
Möng Hpäyak, Myan. B3   34
Möng Hsat, Myan. B3   34
Mongo, Chad D8   50
Mongol Altayn nuruu, mts.,
    Asia B6   28

Mongolia, ctry., Asia B8   28
Mongonu, Nig. D7   50
Mongu, Zam. B3   56
Monhegan Island, i., Me.,
    U.S. E3   112
Monida Pass, U.S. E6   105
Moniteau, co., Mo., U.S. . . C5   118
Monitor Range, mts., Nv.,
    U.S. E5   121
Monitor Valley, val., Nv.,
    U.S. D5   121
Monmouth, Il., U.S. C3   106
Monmouth, Or., U.S. C3   130
Monmouth, co., N.J., U.S. . C4   123
Monmouth Beach, N.J., U.S. C5   123
Monmouth Mountain, mtn.,
    B.C., Can. D6   85
Mono, co., Ca., U.S. D4   98
Monocacy, stm., Md., U.S. . B3   113
Mono Lake, l., Ca., U.S. . . D4   98
Monomonac, Lake, l., U.S. . E3   122
Monomoy Island, i., Ma.,
    U.S. C7   114
Monomoy Point, c., Ma.,
    U.S. C7   114
Monon, In., U.S. C4   107
Monona, Ia., U.S. A6   108
Monona, Wi., U.S. E4   142
Monona, co., Ia., U.S. B1   108
Monona, Lake, l., Wi., U.S. E4   142
Monongah, W.V., U.S. B4   141
Monongahela, Pa., U.S. . . . F2   131
Monongahela, stm., U.S. . . G2   131
Monongalia, co., W.V., U.S. B4   141
Monopoli, Italy D6   18
Monor, Hung. F5   20
Monroe, Ga., U.S. C3   103
Monroe, Ia., U.S. C4   108
Monroe, In., U.S. C8   107
Monroe, La., U.S. B3   111
Monroe, Mi., U.S. G7   115
Monroe, N.C., U.S. C2   126
Monroe, N.Y., U.S. D6   125
Monroe, Oh., U.S. C1   128
Monroe, Ut., U.S. E3   137
Monroe, Wa., U.S. B4   140
Monroe, Wi., U.S. F4   142
Monroe, co., Al., U.S. D2   94
Monroe, co., Ar., U.S. C4   97
Monroe, co., Fl., U.S. G5   102
Monroe, co., Ga., U.S. D3   103
Monroe, co., Ia., U.S. D5   108
Monroe, co., Il., U.S. E3   106
Monroe, co., In., U.S. F4   107
Monroe, co., Ky., U.S. D4   110
Monroe, co., Mi., U.S. G7   115
Monroe, co., Mo., U.S. . . . B5   118
Monroe, co., Ms., U.S. . . . B5   117
Monroe, co., N.Y., U.S. . . . B3   125
Monroe, co., Oh., U.S. . . . C4   128
Monroe, co., Pa., U.S. D11   131
Monroe, co., Tn., U.S. D9   135
Monroe, co., W.V., U.S. . . . D4   141
Monroe, co., Wi., U.S. E3   142
Monroe Center, Ct., U.S. . . D3   100
Monroe City, Mo., U.S. . . . B6   118
Monroe Lake, res., In., U.S. F5   107
Monroe Park, De., U.S. . . . h7   101
Monroeville, Al., U.S. D2   94
Monroeville, In., U.S. C8   107
Monroeville, Oh., U.S. A3   128
Monroeville, Pa., U.S. k14   131
Monrovia, Lib. E2   50
Monrovia, Ca., U.S. m13   98
Monrovia, In., U.S. E5   107
Monson, Ma., U.S. B3   114
Mönsterås, Swe. H7   10
Montague, P.E., Can. C7   87
Montague, Mi., U.S. E4   115
Montague, co., Tx., U.S. . . C4   136
Montague Island, i., Ak.,
    U.S. D10   95
Montague Peak, mtn., Ak.,
    U.S. g18   95
Montague Strait, strt., Ak.,
    U.S. h18   95
Mont Alto, Pa., U.S. G6   131
Montana, Bul. C9   18
Montana, state, U.S. D7   119
Montargis, Fr. E8   16
Montauban, Fr. E7   16
Montauk, N.Y., U.S. m17   125
Montbard, Fr. D9   16
Montbéliard, Fr. D10   16
Mont Belvieu, Tx., U.S. . . . E5   136
Montblanc, Spain G7   16
Montcalm, co., Mi., U.S. . . E5   115
Montceau-les-Mines, Fr. . . D9   16
Montchanin, De., U.S. h7   101
Montclair, Ca., U.S. m13   98
Montclair, N.J., U.S. B4   123
Mont Clare, Pa., U.S. o19   131
Mont-de-Marsan, Fr. F6   16
Monte Alegre, Braz. D9   70
Monte Azul, Braz. E3   74
Montebello, P.Q., Can. . . . D3   90
Montebello, Ca., U.S. m12   98
Montecarlo, Arg. D7   72
Monte Caseros, Arg. E6   72
Monte Comán, Arg. E4   72
Montecristo, Isola di i., Italy C3   18
Montego Bay, Jam. B4   80
Montegut, La., U.S. E5   111

Name	Map Ref.	Page
Montélimar, Fr.	E9	16
Montello, Nv., U.S.	B7	121
Montello, Wi., U.S.	E4	142
Montemorelos, Mex.	B5	78
Montenegro see Crna Gora, state, Yugo.	C7	18
Monte Patria, Chile	E3	72
Montepuez, Moz.	A6	56
Montepulciano, Italy	C3	18
Monte Quemado, Arg.	D5	72
Monterey, Ca., U.S.	D3	98
Monterey, Tn., U.S.	C8	135
Monterey, co., Ca., U.S.	D3	98
Monterey Bay, b., Ca., U.S.	D2	98
Monterey Park, Ca., U.S.	m12	98
Montería, Col.	B4	70
Montero, Bol.	B5	72
Monterrey, Mex.	B4	78
Montesano, Wa., U.S.	C2	140
Montes Claros, Braz.	E3	74
Montevallo, Al., U.S.	B3	94
Montevideo, Mn., U.S.	F5	116
Montevideo, Ur.	E6	72
Monte Vista, Co., U.S.	D4	99
Montezuma, Ga., U.S.	D2	103
Montezuma, Ia., U.S.	C5	108
Montezuma, In., U.S.	E3	107
Montezuma, Ks., U.S.	E3	109
Montezuma, co., Co., U.S.	D2	99
Montezuma Castle National Monument, Az., U.S.	C4	96
Montezuma Peak, mtn., Az., U.S.	D3	96
Montgomery see Sāhīwāl, Pak.	D10	42
Montgomery, Al., U.S.	C3	94
Montgomery, Il., U.S.	B5	106
Montgomery, La., U.S.	C3	111
Montgomery, Mn., U.S.	F5	116
Montgomery, N.Y., U.S.	D6	125
Montgomery, Oh., U.S.	o13	128
Montgomery, Pa., U.S.	D8	131
Montgomery, W.V., U.S.	C3	141
Montgomery, co., Al., U.S.	C3	94
Montgomery, co., Ar., U.S.	C2	97
Montgomery, co., Ga., U.S.	D4	103
Montgomery, co., Ia., U.S.	C2	108
Montgomery, co., Il., U.S.	D4	106
Montgomery, co., In., U.S.	D4	107
Montgomery, co., Ks., U.S.	E8	109
Montgomery, co., Ky., U.S.	B6	110
Montgomery, co., Md., U.S.	B3	113
Montgomery, co., Mo., U.S.	C6	118
Montgomery, co., Ms., U.S.	B4	117
Montgomery, co., N.C., U.S.	B3	126
Montgomery, co., N.Y., U.S.	C5	125
Montgomery, co., Oh., U.S.	C1	128
Montgomery, co., Pa., U.S.	F11	131
Montgomery, co., Tn., U.S.	A4	135
Montgomery, co., Tx., U.S.	D5	136
Montgomery, co., Va., U.S.	C2	139
Montgomery City, Mo., U.S.	C6	118
Monticello, Ar., U.S.	D4	97
Monticello, Fl., U.S.	B3	102
Monticello, Ga., U.S.	C3	103
Monticello, Ia., U.S.	B6	108
Monticello, Il., U.S.	C5	106
Monticello, In., U.S.	C4	107
Monticello, Ky., U.S.	D5	110
Monticello, Mn., U.S.	E5	116
Monticello, Ms., U.S.	D3	117
Monticello, N.Y., U.S.	D6	125
Monticello, Ut., U.S.	F6	137
Monticello, Wi., U.S.	F4	142
Mont-Joli, P.Q., Can.	A9	90
Mont-Laurier, P.Q., Can.	C2	90
Montluçon, Fr.	D8	16
Montmagny, P.Q., Can.	C7	90
Montmorenci, S.C., U.S.	D4	133
Montmorency, co., Mi., U.S.	C6	115
Monto, Austl.	E5	62
Montoro, Spain	H4	16
Montour, co., Pa., U.S.	D8	131
Montour Falls, N.Y., U.S.	C4	125
Montoursville, Pa., U.S.	D8	131
Montpelier, Id., U.S.	G7	105
Montpelier, In., U.S.	C7	107
Montpelier, Oh., U.S.	A1	128
Montpelier, Vt., U.S.	C3	138
Montpellier, Fr.	F8	16
Montréal, P.Q., Can.	D4	90
Montreal, Wi., U.S.	B3	142
Montréal, Île de, i., P.Q., Can.	q19	90
Montreal Lake, l., Sk., Can.	C3	91
Montréal-Nord, P.Q., Can.	p19	90
Montreat, N.C., U.S.	f10	126
Montreux, Switz.	A1	18
Mont-Rolland, P.Q., Can.	D3	90
Montrose, B.C., Can.	E9	85
Montrose, Scot., U.K.	B5	12
Montrose, Al., U.S.	E2	94
Montrose, Co., U.S.	C3	99
Montrose, Ia., U.S.	D6	108
Montrose, Mi., U.S.	E7	115
Montrose, Pa., U.S.	C10	131
Montrose, Va., U.S.	m18	139
Montrose, co., Co., U.S.	C2	99
Mont-Royal, P.Q., Can.	p19	90
Mont-Saint-Michel, Le, Fr.	C6	16
Montserrat, dep., N.A.	E12	76
Montserrat, Monasterio de, Spain	G7	16
Mont-Tremblant, Parc Provincial du, P.Q., Can.	C3	90
Montvale, N.J., U.S.	A4	123
Montville, Ct., U.S.	D7	100
Monument, Co., U.S.	B6	99
Monument Beach, Ma., U.S.	C6	114
Monument Peak, mtn., Co., U.S.	B3	99
Monument Peak, mtn., Id., U.S.	G4	105
Monument Valley, val., Az., U.S.	A5	96
Monywa, Myan.	B2	34
Monza, Italy	B2	18
Monze, Zam.	B4	56
Monzón, Spain	G7	16
Moodus, Ct., U.S.	D6	100
Moodus Reservoir, res., Ct., U.S.	C6	100
Moody, Tx., U.S.	D4	136
Moody, co., S.D., U.S.	C9	134
Moon Lake, l., Ms., U.S.	A3	117
Moora, Austl.	G2	60
Moorcroft, Wy., U.S.	B8	143
Moore, Ok., U.S.	B4	129
Moore, co., N.C., U.S.	B3	126
Moore, co., Tn., U.S.	B5	135
Moore, co., Tx., U.S.	B2	136
Moore, Lake, l., Austl.	F2	60
Moore Dam, U.S.	B3	122
Moorefield, W.V., U.S.	B6	141
Moore Haven, Fl., U.S.	F5	102
Mooreland, Ok., U.S.	A2	129
Moore Reservoir, res., U.S.	B3	122
Moores Creek National Military Park, N.C., U.S.	C4	126
Moores Hill, In., U.S.	F7	107
Moorestown, N.J., U.S.	D3	123
Mooresville, In., U.S.	E5	107
Mooresville, N.C., U.S.	B2	126
Moorhead, Mn., U.S.	D2	116
Moorhead, Ms., U.S.	B3	117
Mooringsport, La., U.S.	B2	111
Moorreesburg, S. Afr.	E2	56
Moose, stm., N.H., U.S.	B4	122
Moose, stm., N.Y., U.S.	B5	125
Moose, stm., Vt., U.S.	B5	138
Moosehead Lake, l., Me., U.S.	C3	112
Moose Jaw, stm., Sk., Can.	G3	91
Moose Lake, Mb., Can.	C1	86
Moose Lake, Mn., U.S.	D6	116
Moose Lake, l., Wi., U.S.	B2	142
Mooseleuk Stream, stm., Me., U.S.	B4	112
Mooselookmeguntic Lake, l., Me., U.S.	D2	112
Moose Mountain Creek, stm., Sk., Can.	H4	91
Moose Mountain Provincial Park, Sk., Can.	H4	91
Moosic, Pa., U.S.	m18	131
Moosup, Ct., U.S.	C8	100
Moosup, stm., U.S.	C1	132
Mopang Lake, l., Me., U.S.	D5	112
Mopti, Mali	D4	50
Moquegua, Peru	G5	70
Mora, Cam.	D7	50
Mora, Spain	H5	16
Mora, Swe.	F6	10
Mora, Mn., U.S.	E5	116
Mora, N.M., U.S.	B4	124
Mora, co., N.M., U.S.	A5	124
Mora, stm., N.M., U.S.	B5	124
Morādābād, India	D3	40
Morafenobe, Madag.	B7	56
Moramanga, Madag.	B8	56
Morant Cays, is., Jam.	B4	80
Moratuwa, Sri L.	H3	40
Morava, hist. reg., Czech Rep.	E4	20
Moravia, Ia., U.S.	D5	108
Morawa, Austl.	F2	60
Morawhanna, Guy.	B8	70
Moray Firth, b., Scot., U.K.	B5	12
Morbi, India	I2	40
Morden, Mb., Can.	E2	86
Mordovia see Mordovija, state, Russia	D6	26
Mordovija, state, Russia	D6	26
Mordvinia see Mordovija, state, Russia	D6	26
Moreau, stm., S.D., U.S.	B3	134
Moreauville, La., U.S.	C4	111
Morecambe Bay, b., Eng., U.K.	D5	12
Moree, Austl.	F4	62
Morehead, Ky., U.S.	B6	110
Morehead City, N.C., U.S.	C6	126
Morehouse, Mo., U.S.	E8	118
Morehouse, co., La., U.S.	B4	111
Morelia, Mex.	D4	78
Morelos, state, Mex.	D5	78
Morena, Sierra, mts., Spain	H4	16
Morenci, Az., U.S.	D6	96
Morenci, Mi., U.S.	G6	115
Moresby Island, i., B.C., Can.	C2	85
Moreton Island, i., Austl.	F5	62
Morey, Lake, l., Vt., U.S.	D4	138
Morey Peak, mtn., Nv., U.S.	E5	121
Morgan, Mn., U.S.	F4	116
Morgan, Ut., U.S.	B4	137
Morgan, co., Al., U.S.	A3	94
Morgan, co., Co., U.S.	A7	99
Morgan, co., Ga., U.S.	C3	103
Morgan, co., Il., U.S.	D3	106
Morgan, co., In., U.S.	F5	107
Morgan, co., Ky., U.S.	C6	110
Morgan, co., Mo., U.S.	C5	118
Morgan, co., Oh., U.S.	C4	128
Morgan, co., Tn., U.S.	C9	135
Morgan, co., Ut., U.S.	B4	137
Morgan, co., W.V., U.S.	B6	141
Morgan City, La., U.S.	E4	111
Morganfield, Ky., U.S.	C2	110
Morgan Hill, Ca., U.S.	D3	98
Morgan Island, i., S.C., U.S.	G6	133
Morgan Point, c., Ct., U.S.	E4	100
Morganton, N.C., U.S.	B1	126
Morgantown, In., U.S.	F5	107
Morgantown, Ky., U.S.	C3	110
Morgantown, Ms., U.S.	D2	117
Morgantown, Tn., U.S.	D8	135
Morgantown, W.V., U.S.	B5	141
Morganza, La., U.S.	D4	111
Morghāb (Murgab), stm., Asia	C8	42
Moriah, Mount, mtn., Nv., U.S.	D7	121
Moriarty, N.M., U.S.	C3	124
Moriki, Nig.	D6	50
Morinville, Ab., Can.	C4	84
Morioka, Japan	D16	28
Morlaix, Fr.	C5	16
Morley, Mo., U.S.	D8	118
Mormon Peak, mtn., Nv., U.S.	G7	121
Morning Sun, Ia., U.S.	C6	108
Mornington Island, i., Austl.	D2	62
Morobe, Pap. N. Gui.	H12	32
Morocco, In., U.S.	C3	107
Morocco, ctry., Afr.	D3	48
Morogoro, Tan.	E7	54
Moro Gulf, b., Phil.	E8	34
Morombe, Madag.	C7	56
Morón, Arg.	E6	72
Morón, Cuba	A4	80
Mörön, Mong.	B8	28
Morondava, Madag.	C7	56
Morón de la Frontera, Spain	I4	16
Moroni, Com.	A7	56
Moroni, Ut., U.S.	D4	137
Morotai, i., Indon.	C7	36
Moroto, Ug.	C6	54
Morozovsk, Russia	E7	22
Morrill, Ne., U.S.	C2	120
Morrill, co., Ne., U.S.	C2	120
Morrilton, Ar., U.S.	B3	97
Morrinhos, Braz.	E2	74
Morris, Mb., Can.	E3	86
Morris, Al., U.S.	B3	94
Morris, Il., U.S.	B5	106
Morris, Mn., U.S.	E3	116
Morris, Ok., U.S.	B6	129
Morris, co., Ks., U.S.	D7	109
Morris, co., N.J., U.S.	B3	123
Morris, co., Tx., U.S.	C5	136
Morrisburg, On., Can.	C9	89
Morris Island, i., S.C., U.S.	F8	133
Morris Jesup, Kap, c., Grnld.	B33	82
Morrison, Il., U.S.	B4	106
Morrison, Ok., U.S.	A4	129
Morrison, co., Mn., U.S.	D4	116
Morrison City, Tn., U.S.	C11	135
Morrisonville, Il., U.S.	D4	106
Morrisonville, N.Y., U.S.	f11	125
Morris Plains, N.J., U.S.	B4	123
Morristown, In., U.S.	E6	107
Morristown, Mn., U.S.	F5	116
Morristown, N.J., U.S.	B4	123
Morristown, Tn., U.S.	C10	135
Morristown National Historical Park, N.J., U.S.	B3	123
Morrisville, N.Y., U.S.	C5	125
Morrisville, Pa., U.S.	F12	131
Morrisville, Vt., U.S.	B3	138
Morro Bay, Ca., U.S.	E3	98
Morro do Chapéu, Braz.	D3	74
Morrow, Ga., U.S.	C2	103
Morrow, Oh., U.S.	C1	128
Morrow, co., Oh., U.S.	B3	128
Morrow, co., Or., U.S.	B7	130
Morrumbala, Moz.	B6	56
Morrumbene, Moz.	C6	56
Moršansk, Russia	D7	22
Morse, La., U.S.	D3	111
Morse Reservoir, res., In., U.S.	D5	107
Morses Creek, stm., N.J., U.S.	k8	123
Mortes, stm., Braz.	F9	70
Morton, Il., U.S.	C4	106
Morton, Ms., U.S.	C4	117
Morton, Tx., U.S.	C1	136
Morton, Wa., U.S.	C3	140
Morton, co., Ks., U.S.	E2	109
Morton, co., N.D., U.S.	C4	127
Morton Grove, Il., U.S.	h9	106
Morton Pass, Wy., U.S.	E7	143
Mortons Gap, Ky., U.S.	C2	110
Morwell, Austl.	H4	62
Moscow see Moskva, Russia	D5	26
Moscow, Id., U.S.	C2	105
Moscow, Pa., U.S.	m18	131
Moscow Mills, Mo., U.S.	C7	118
Mosel (Moselle), stm., Eur.	B10	16
Moselle, Ms., U.S.	D4	117
Moselle (Mosel), stm., Eur.	C10	16
Moses Coulee, val., Wa., U.S.	B6	140
Moses Lake, Wa., U.S.	B6	140
Moses Lake, l., Wa., U.S.	B6	140
Mosheim, Tn., U.S.	C11	135
Moshi, Tan.	D7	54
Mosinee, Wi., U.S.	D4	142
Mosjøen, Nor.	D5	10
Moskva (Moscow), Russia	D5	26
Mosqueiro, Braz.	B2	74
Mosquera, Col.	C4	70
Mosquito Creek Lake, res., Oh., U.S.	A5	128
Mosquito Lagoon, b., Fl., U.S.	D6	102
Mosquitos, Golfo de los, b., Pan.	D3	80
Moss, Nor.	G4	10
Mossaka, Congo	D3	54
Moss Bluff, La., U.S.	D2	111
Mosselbaai, S. Afr.	E3	56
Mossman, Austl.	D4	62
Mossoró, Braz.	C4	74
Moss Point, Ms., U.S.	E5	117
Most, Czech Rep.	D2	20
Mostar, Bos.	C6	18
Møsting, Kap, c., Grnld.	F32	82
Mosul see Al-Mawṣil, Iraq	C4	42
Møsvatnet, l., Nor.	G3	10
Moswansicut Pond, l., R.I., U.S.	C3	132
Mot'a, Eth.	A7	54
Motagua, stm., N.A.	B2	80
Motala, Swe.	G6	10
Motherwell, Scot., U.K.	C5	12
Motley, co., Tx., U.S.	B2	136
Motril, Spain	I5	16
Mott, N.D., U.S.	C3	127
Motueka, N.Z.	p13	63c
Motyklejka, Russia	D16	26
Mouaskar, Alg.	D4	14
Moudjéria, Maur.	C2	50
Mouila, Gabon	D2	54
Moulins, Fr.	D8	16
Moulouya, Oued, stm., Mor.	D4	48
Moulton, Al., U.S.	A2	94
Moulton, Ia., U.S.	D5	108
Moultrie, Ga., U.S.	E3	103
Moultrie, co., Il., U.S.	D5	106
Moultrie, Lake, res., S.C., U.S.	E7	133
Mounana, Gabon	D2	54
Mound, Mn., U.S.	n11	116
Mound Bayou, Ms., U.S.	B3	117
Mound City, Il., U.S.	F4	106
Mound City, Ks., U.S.	D9	109
Mound City, Mo., U.S.	A2	118
Mound City Group National Monument, Oh., U.S.	C2	128
Moundou, Chad	E8	50
Moundridge, Ks., U.S.	D6	109
Mounds, Il., U.S.	F4	106
Mounds, Ok., U.S.	B5	129
Mounds View, Mn., U.S.	m12	116
Moundsville, W.V., U.S.	B4	141
Moundville, Al., U.S.	C2	94
Mountainair, N.M., U.S.	C3	124
Mountainaire, Az., U.S.	B4	96
Mountain Brook, Al., U.S.	g7	94
Mountain City, Ga., U.S.	B3	103
Mountain City, Nv., U.S.	B6	121
Mountain City, Tn., U.S.	C12	135
Mountain Fork, stm., Ok., U.S.	C7	129
Mountain Grove, Mo., U.S.	D5	118
Mountain Home, Ar., U.S.	A3	97
Mountain Home, Id., U.S.	F3	105
Mountain Home Air Force Base, mil., Id., U.S.	F3	105
Mountain Iron, Mn., U.S.	C6	116
Mountain Lake, Mn., U.S.	G4	116
Mountain Lake Park, Md., U.S.	m12	113
Mountain Nile see Jabal, Baḥr al-, stm., Sudan	I11	48
Mountain Pine, Ar., U.S.	C2	97
Mountainside, N.J., U.S.	B4	123
Mountain View, Ar., U.S.	B3	97
Mountain View, Ca., U.S.	k8	98
Mountain View, Mo., U.S.	D6	118
Mountain View, N.M., U.S.	C3	124
Mountain View, Ok., U.S.	B3	129
Mountain View, Wy., U.S.	E3	143
Mountain Village, Ak., U.S.	C7	95
Mount Airy, Md., U.S.	B3	113
Mount Airy, N.C., U.S.	A2	126
Mount Albert, On., Can.	C5	89
Mount Angel, Or., U.S.	B4	130
Mount Arlington, N.J., U.S.	B3	123
Mount Augustus, Austl.	E2	60
Mount Ayr, Ia., U.S.	D3	108
Mount Barker, Austl.	G2	60
Mount Carmel, Il., U.S.	E6	106
Mount Carmel, Oh., U.S.	o13	128
Mount Carmel, Pa., U.S.	E9	131
Mount Carmel [-Mitchell's Brook-Saint Catherine's], Nf., Can.	E5	88
Mount Forest, On., Can.	D4	89
Mount Gambier, Austl.	H3	62
Mount Gay, W.V., U.S.	D2	141
Mount Gilead, N.C., U.S.	B3	126
Mount Gilead, Oh., U.S.	B3	128
Mount Hagen, Pap. N. Gui.	H11	32
Mount Healthy, Oh., U.S.	o12	128
Mount Holly, N.C., U.S.	B1	126
Mount Holly, N.J., U.S.	D3	123
Mount Holly Springs, Pa., U.S.	F7	131
Mount Hope, Ks., U.S.	E6	109
Mount Hope, W.V., U.S.	D3	141
Mount Hope, stm., Ct., U.S.	B7	100
Mount Hope Bay, b., U.S.	D6	132
Mount Horeb, Wi., U.S.	E4	142
Mount Ida, Ar., U.S.	C2	97
Mount Isa, Austl.	E2	62
Mount Jackson, Va., U.S.	B4	139
Mount Jewett, Pa., U.S.	C4	131
Mount Joy, Pa., U.S.	F9	131
Mount Juliet, Tn., U.S.	A5	135
Mount Kisco, N.Y., U.S.	D7	125
Mount Lebanon, Pa., U.S.	F1	131
Mount Magnet, Austl.	F2	60
Mount Morris, Il., U.S.	A4	106
Mount Morris, Mi., U.S.	E7	115
Mount Morris, N.Y., U.S.	C3	125
Mount Olive, Al., U.S.	B3	94
Mount Olive, Il., U.S.	D4	106
Mount Olive, Ms., U.S.	D4	117
Mount Olive, N.C., U.S.	B4	126
Mount Olive, Tn., U.S.	n14	135
Mount Orab, Oh., U.S.	C2	128
Mount Pearl, Nf., Can.	E5	88
Mount Penn, Pa., U.S.	F10	131
Mount Pleasant, Ia., U.S.	D6	108
Mount Pleasant, Mi., U.S.	E6	115
Mount Pleasant, N.C., U.S.	B2	126
Mount Pleasant, Pa., U.S.	F2	131
Mount Pleasant, S.C., U.S.	F8	133
Mount Pleasant, Tn., U.S.	B4	135
Mount Pleasant, Tx., U.S.	C5	136
Mount Pleasant, Ut., U.S.	D4	137
Mount Pocono, Pa., U.S.	D11	131
Mount Prospect, Il., U.S.	A6	106
Mount Pulaski, Il., U.S.	C4	106
Mountrail, co., N.D., U.S.	A3	127
Mount Rainier, Md., U.S.	f9	113
Mount Rainier National Park, Wa., U.S.	C4	140
Mount Revelstoke National Park, B.C., Can.	D8	85
Mount Riddock, Austl.	E5	60
Mount Rogers National Recreation Area, Va., U.S.	D1	139
Mount Roskill, N.Z.	o13	63c
Mount Rushmore National Memorial, hist., S.D., U.S.	D2	134
Mount Savage, Md., U.S.	k13	113
Mount Shasta, Ca., U.S.	B2	98
Mount Sterling, Il., U.S.	D3	106
Mount Sterling, Ky., U.S.	B6	110
Mount Sterling, Oh., U.S.	C2	128
Mount Uniacke, N.S., Can.	E6	87
Mount Union, Pa., U.S.	F6	131
Mount Vernon, Austl.	E2	60
Mount Vernon, Al., U.S.	D1	94
Mount Vernon, Ga., U.S.	D4	103
Mount Vernon, Ia., U.S.	C6	108
Mount Vernon, Il., U.S.	E5	106
Mount Vernon, In., U.S.	I2	107
Mount Vernon, Ky., U.S.	C5	110
Mount Vernon, Mo., U.S.	D4	118
Mount Vernon, N.Y., U.S.	h13	125
Mount Vernon, Oh., U.S.	B3	128
Mount Vernon, Tx., U.S.	C5	136
Mount Vernon, Wa., U.S.	A3	140
Mount View, R.I., U.S.	D4	132
Mount Washington, Ky., U.S.	B4	110
Mount Wolf, Pa., U.S.	F8	131
Mount Zion, Il., U.S.	D5	106
Moura, Braz.	D7	70
Moussa 'Ali, mtn., Afr.	H4	38
Moussoro, Chad	D8	50
Moutong, Indon.	C6	36
Moville, Ia., U.S.	B1	108
Moweaqua, Il., U.S.	D4	106
Mower, co., Mn., U.S.	G6	116
Moxee City, Wa., U.S.	C5	140
Moyale, Kenya	C7	54
Moyamba, S.L.	E2	50
Moyen Atlas, mts., Mor.	E3	14
Moyo, Pulau, i., Indon.	G6	36
Moyobamba, Peru	E4	70
Moyock, N.C., U.S.	A6	126
Moyu, China	B3	40
Mozambique, ctry., Afr.	B5	56
Mozambique Channel, strt., Afr.	B7	56
Mozambique Plateau	L6	64
Mozdok, Russia	B4	42
Mpala, D.R.C.	E5	54
Mpanda, Tan.	E6	54
Mpika, Zam.	A5	56
Mporokoso, Zam.	E6	54
Mpulungu, Zam.	E6	54
Mpwapwa, Tan.	E7	54
Mscislaŭ, Bela.	C11	20
M'Sila, Alg.	J9	16
Mtubatuba, S. Afr.	D5	56
Mtwara, Tan.	F8	54

Name	Map Ref.	Page

Muanda, D.R.C. E2 54
Muang Hôngsa, Laos C4 34
Muang Khammouan, Laos . C4 34
Muang Không, Laos D5 34
Muang Khôngxédôn, Laos . C5 34
Muang Ngoy, Laos B4 34
Muang Pak-Lay, Laos C4 34
Muang Pakxan, Laos C4 34
Muang Phalan, Laos C5 34
Muang Sing, Laos B4 34
Muang Thadua, Laos C4 34
Muang Vangviang, Laos . . . C4 34
Muang Xaignabouri, Laos . . C4 34
Muar, Malay. C2 36
Muaraenim, Indon. D2 36
Muarasiberut, Indon. G2 32
Mubende, Ug. C6 54
Mubi, Nig. D7 50
Muchinga Mountains, mts.,
  Zam. A5 56
Muckleshoot Indian
  Reservation, Wa., U.S. . f11 140
Mucojo, Moz. A7 56
Muconda, Ang. F4 54
Mucujê, Braz. F11 70
Mud, stm., Ky., U.S. C3 110
Mud, stm., Mn., U.S. B3 116
Mud, stm., W.V., U.S. C2 141
Mudanjiang, China C13 28
Mud Creek, stm., Ok., U.S. C4 129
Muddy Boggy Creek, stm.,
  Ok., U.S. C6 129
Muddy Creek, stm., Ut.,
  U.S. E4 137
Muddy Creek, stm., Wy.,
  U.S. C4 143
Muddy Creek, stm., Wy.,
  U.S. E5 143
Muddy Creek, stm., Wy.,
  U.S. E2 143
Muddy Creek, stm., Wy.,
  U.S. D6 143
Muddy Mountains, mts.,
  Nv., U.S. G7 121
Muddy Peak, mtn., Nv.,
  U.S. G7 121
Mudgee, Austl. G4 62
Mud Lake, l., Me., U.S. . . . A4 112
Mud Lake, l., Nv., U.S. . . . F4 121
Mueda, Moz. A6 56
Muenster, Tx., U.S. C4 136
Mufulira, Zam. A4 56
Muğla, Tur. D3 44
Muhlenberg, co., Ky., U.S. . C2 110
Mühlhausen, Ger. E12 12
Muhu, i., Est. G10 10
Muié, Ang. A3 56
Muirkirk, Md., U.S. B4 113
Muir Woods National
  Monument, Ca., U.S. . . h7 98
Muja, Russia D13 26
Mujnak, Uzb. B7 42
Mukacheve, Ukr. E7 20
Mukah, Malay. C4 36
Mukden see Shenyang,
  China C12 28
Mukilteo, Wa., U.S. B3 140
Mukinbudin, Austl. G2 60
Mukomuk, Indon. D2 36
Mukry, Turk. C9 42
Mukwonago, Wi., U.S. F5 142
Mula, Spain H6 16
Mulberry, Ar., U.S. B1 97
Mulberry, Fl., U.S. E4 102
Mulberry, In., U.S. D4 107
Mulberry, N.C., U.S. A1 126
Mulberry, stm., Ar., U.S. . . B1 97
Mulberry Fork, stm., Al.,
  U.S. B3 94
Muldraugh, Ky., U.S. C4 110
Muldrow, Ok., U.S. B7 129
Muleshoe, Tx., U.S. B1 136
Mulgrave, N.S., Can. D8 87
Mulhacén, mtn., Spain I5 16
Mulhouse, Fr. D10 16
Mull, Island of, i., Scot.,
  U.K. B3 12
Mullan, Id., U.S. B3 105
Mullan Pass, Mt., U.S. D4 119
Mullens, W.V., U.S. D3 141
Muller, Pegunungan, mts.,
  Indon. C4 36
Mullet Key, i., Fl., U.S. . . p10 102
Mullett Lake, l., Mi., U.S. . C6 115
Mullewa, Austl. F2 60
Mullica, stm., N.J., U.S. . . . D3 123
Mullins, S.C., U.S. C9 133
Mulongo, D.R.C. E5 54
Multān, Pak. D10 42
Multnomah, co., Or., U.S. . B4 130
Mulvane, Ks., U.S. E6 109
Mumbai (Bombay), India . . F2 40
Mumbwa, Zam. A4 56
Mummy Range, mts., Co.,
  U.S. A5 99
Mun, stm., Thai. C4 34
Muna, Mex. C7 78
Muna, Pulau, i., Indon. D6 36
München (Munich), Ger. . . . F12 12
Muncie, In., U.S. D7 107
Muncy, Pa., U.S. D8 131
Munday, Tx., U.S. C3 136
Mundelein, Il., U.S. A5 106
Münden, Ger. E11 12
Mundrabilla, Austl. G4 60

Munford, Al., U.S. B4 94
Munford, Tn., U.S. B2 135
Munfordville, Ky., U.S. C4 110
Mungbere, D.R.C. C5 54
Munger, India D5 40
Munhall, Pa., U.S. k14 131
Munhango, Ang. F3 54
Munich see München, Ger. F12 12
Munising, Mi., U.S. B4 115
Münster, Ger. E10 12
Munster, In., U.S. A2 107
Munster, hist. reg., Ire. . . . D2 12
Munsungan Lake, l., Me.,
  U.S. B3 112
Muntok, Indon. D3 36
Munuscong Lake, l., Mi.,
  U.S. B6 115
Muojärvi, l., Fin. D13 10
Muonio, Fin. C10 10
Muqdisho, Som. J14 48
Mur (Mura), stm., Eur. F3 20
Mura (Mur), stm., Eur. F4 20
Muradiye, Tur. C10 44
Murakami, Japan C3 31
Murana, Indon. D8 36
Muraši, Russia C8 22
Murat, stm., Tur. C9 44
Murchison, stm., Austl. . . . F1 60
Murchison Falls see
  Kabalega Falls, wtfl, Ug. C6 54
Murcia, Spain I6 16
Murderkill, stm., De., U.S. . D4 101
Murdo, S.D., U.S. D5 134
Mureş, stm., Eur. G7 20
Muret, Fr. F7 16
Murewa, Zimb. B5 56
Murfreesboro, Ar., U.S. . . . C2 97
Murfreesboro, N.C., U.S. . . A5 126
Murfreesboro, Tn., U.S. . . . B5 135
Murgab, Taj. F9 26
Murgab (Morghāb), stm.,
  Asia C8 42
Muriaé, Braz. F3 74
Müritz, l., Ger. D13 12
Murmansk, Russia C5 26
Murom, Russia D6 26
Muroran, Japan C16 28
Muroto, Japan D2 31
Murphy, Mo., U.S. g13 118
Murphy, N.C., U.S. f8 126
Murphy Island, i., S.C., U.S. E9 133
Murphysboro, Il., U.S. F4 106
Murray, Ia., U.S. C4 108
Murray, Ky., U.S. f9 110
Murray, Ut., U.S. C4 137
Murray, co., Ga., U.S. B2 103
Murray, co., Mn., U.S. F3 116
Murray, co., Ok., U.S. C4 129
Murray, stm., Austl. H3 62
Murray, Lake, l., Pap. N.
  Gui. H11 32
Murray, Lake, res., Ok., U.S. C4 129
Murray, Lake, res., S.C.,
  U.S. C5 133
Murray Bridge, Austl. H2 62
Murray Fracture Zone E24 64
Murray Head, c., P.E., Can. C7 87
Murraysburg, S. Afr. E3 56
Murrayville, Ga., U.S. B3 103
Murree, Pak. C2 40
Murrells Inlet, S.C., U.S. . . D9 133
Murrells Inlet, b., S.C., U.S. D10 133
Murrumbidgee, stm., Austl. G4 62
Murrupula, Moz. B6 56
Mursala, Pulau, i., Indon. . . C1 36
Murua Island, i., Pap. N.
  Gui. H13 32
Murud, Gunong, mtn.,
  Malay. C5 36
Murukta, Russia C12 26
Murwāra, India E4 40
Murwillumbah, Austl. F5 62
Murzuq, Libya E7 48
Murzūq, Idhān, des., Libya . B7 50
Muş, Tur. C9 44
Musa Ālī Terara see Moussa
  'Ali, mtn., Afr. H4 38
Musā'id, Libya E9 14
Musala, mtn., Bul. C9 18
Musan-ŭp, N. Kor. B1 31
Musayʽīd, Qatar F6 42
Muscat see Masqaţ, Oman . F7 38
Muscat and Oman see
  Oman, ctry., Asia G7 38
Muscatatuck, stm., In., U.S. G5 107
Muscatine, Ia., U.S. C6 108
Muscatine, co., Ia., U.S. . . . C6 108
Muscle Shoals, Al., U.S. . . . A2 94
Musclow, Mount, mtn.,
  B.C., Can. C4 85
Muscoda, Wi., U.S. E3 142
Muscogee, co., Ga., U.S. . . D2 103
Musconetcong, stm., N.J.,
  U.S. B4 123
Muscooten Bay, l., Il., U.S. C3 106
Muse, Pa., U.S. F1 131
Musgrave Harbour, Nf.,
  Can. D5 88
Musgravetown, Nf., Can. . . D5 88
Mushie, D.R.C. D3 54
Mushin, Nig. E5 50
Musi, stm., Indon. D2 36
Musicians Seamounts E22 64
Muskeg Bay, b., Mn., U.S. . B3 116

Muskeget Island, i., Ma.,
  U.S. D7 114
Muskego, Wi., U.S. F5 142
Muskego Lake, l., Wi., U.S. n11 142
Muskegon, Mi., U.S. E4 115
Muskegon, co., Mi., U.S. . . E4 115
Muskegon, stm., Mi., U.S. . E4 115
Muskegon Heights, Mi.,
  U.S. E4 115
Muskegon Lake, l., Mi., U.S. E4 115
Muskingum, co., Oh., U.S. . B4 128
Muskingum, stm., Oh., U.S. C4 128
Muskogee, Ok., U.S. B6 129
Muskogee, co., Ok., U.S. . . B6 129
Musoma, Tan. D6 54
Musquacook Lakes, l., Me.,
  U.S. B3 112
Musquodoboit Harbour,
  N.S., Can. E6 87
Mussau Island, i., Pap. N.
  Gui. G12 32
Musselshell, co., Mt., U.S. . D8 119
Musselshell, stm., Mt., U.S. D9 119
Mussende, Ang. F3 54
Mussuma, Ang. A3 56
Mustafakemalpaşa, Tur. . . . C3 44
Mustahīl, Eth. B8 54
Mustang, Ok., U.S. B4 129
Mustinka, stm., Mn., U.S. . E2 116
Muswellbrook, Austl. G5 62
Mut, Tur. D5 44
Mutare, Zimb. B5 56
Mutoraj, Russia C12 26
Mutsamudu, Com. A7 56
Mutshatsha, D.R.C. F4 54
Mutsu, Japan C16 28
Mutsu-wan, b., Japan B4 31
Mutton Mountains, mts.,
  Or., U.S. C5 130
Muxima, Ang. E2 54
Muyinga, Bdi. D6 54
Muyumba, D.R.C. E5 54
Muzaffarābād, Pak. D10 42
Muzaffargarh, Pak. D10 42
Muzaffarnagar, India D3 40
Muzaffarpur, India D5 40
Muži, Russia C8 26
Muzon, Cape, c., Ak., U.S. . n23 95
Muztag, mtn., China D5 28
Mvuma, Zimb. B5 56
Mwadui, Tan. D6 54
Mweka, D.R.C. D4 54
Mwene-Ditu, D.R.C. E4 54
Mwenezi, Zimb. C5 56
Mweru, Lake, l., Afr. E5 54
Mwinilunga, Zam. A3 56
Myakka, stm., Fl., U.S. E4 102
Myanaung, Myan. C3 34
Myanmar (Burma), ctry.,
  Asia B3 34
Myaungmya, Myan. C2 34
Myerstown, Pa., U.S. F9 131
Myingyan, Myan. B3 34
Myitkyinā, Myan. A3 34
Myittha, Myan. B3 34
Mykolaïv, Ukr. F11 20
Mymensingh, Bngl. E6 40
Mynaral, Kaz. A10 42
Mýrdalsjökull, Ice. m19 10a
Myrhorod, Ukr. E12 20
Myrtle Beach, S.C., U.S. . . D10 133
Myrtle Grove, Fl., U.S. u14 102
Myrtle Point, Or., U.S. D2 130
Mysore, India G3 40
Mysore see Karnātaka,
  prov., India G3 40
Mystic, Ct., U.S. D8 100
Mystic Lakes, l., Ma., U.S. . g11 114
Mys Vhodnoj, Russia B10 26
Mys Želanija, Russia B8 26
Myszków, Pol. D5 20
My Tho, Viet. D5 34
Mzimba, Mwi. A5 56
Mzuzu, Mwi. A5 56

N

Naalehu, Hi., U.S. D6 104
Naberežnye Čelny, Russia . D7 26
Nabeul, Tun. C7 48
Nabire, Indon. G10 32
Nabī Shu'ayb, Jabal an-,
  mtn., Yemen G4 38
Nabnasset, Ma., U.S. A5 114
Nābulus, W.B. F6 44
Nacala-a-Velha, Moz. A7 56
Naches, stm., Wa., U.S. . . . C5 140
Nachingwea, Tan. F7 54
Náchod, Czech Rep. D4 20
Nachuge, India G6 40
Nacimiento, Lake, res., Ca.,
  U.S. E3 98
Naco, Az., U.S. F6 96
Nacogdoches, Tx., U.S. . . . D5 136
Nacogdoches, co., Tx., U.S. D5 136
Nacozari de García, Mex. . . A3 78
Nadiād, India E2 40
Nador, Mor. J5 16
Nadvirna, Ukr. E8 20
Nadym, Russia C9 26
Næstved, Den. I4 10
Nafada, Nig. D7 50
Nafī, Sau. Ar. E4 42

Naga, Phil. D8 34
Nāgāland, prov., India D6 40
Nagano, Japan D15 28
Nagaoka, Japan D15 28
Nagaon, India D6 40
Nāgappattinam, India G3 40
Nagasaki, Japan E13 28
Nāgaur, India D2 40
Nagda, India E3 40
Nāgercoil, India H3 40
Nago, Japan A9 34
Nagoya, Japan D15 28
Nāgpur, India E3 40
Nagqu, China E6 28
Nags Head, N.C., U.S. B7 126
Nagykanizsa, Hung. F4 20
Naha, Japan A9 34
Nahant, Ma., U.S. g12 114
Nahāvand, Iran E13 44
Nahe, China B12 28
Nahmakanta Lake, l., Me.,
  U.S. C3 112
Nahodka, Russia E15 26
Nahunta, Ga., U.S. E5 103
Nain, Nf., Can. g9 88
Nairobi, Kenya D7 54
Naivasha, Kenya D7 54
Najafābād, Iran D6 42
Najd, hist. reg., Sau. Ar. . . E4 38
Nájera, Spain F5 16
Najin, N. Kor. C14 28
Nakano-shima, i., Japan . . I1 31
Nakhichevan see Naxçıvan,
  Azer. C11 44
Nakhon Pathom, Thai. D4 34
Nakhon Phanom, Thai. . . . C4 34
Nakhon Ratchasima, Thai. . D4 34
Nakhon Sawan, Thai. C4 34
Nakhon Si Thammarat, Thai. E3 34
Nakina, On., U.S. o18 89
Nakło nad Notecią, Pol. . . . C4 20
Naknek, Ak., U.S. D8 95
Naknek Lake, l., Ak., U.S. . D8 95
Nakonde, Zam. E6 54
Nakskov, Den. I4 10
Nakuru, Kenya D7 54
Nakusp, B.C., Can. D9 85
Nalʹčik, Russia E6 26
Nalgonda, India F3 40
Nallıhan, Tur. B4 44
Nālūt, Libya D7 48
Namak, daryāčeh-ye, l.,
  Iran D6 42
Namanga, Kenya D7 54
Namangan, Uzb. E9 26
Namanock Island, i., N.J.,
  U.S. A3 123
Namapa, Moz. A6 56
Namarrói, Moz. B6 56
Namatanai, Pap. N. Gui. . . E9 58
Nambour, Austl. F5 62
Nam Co, l., China E6 28
Nam Dinh, Viet. B5 34
Namekagon, stm., Wi., U.S. B2 142
Namekagon Lake, l., Wi.,
  U.S. B2 142
Namen see Namur, Bel. . . . E9 12
Nametil, Moz. B6 56
Namhkam, Myan. B3 34
Namib Desert, des., Nmb. . B1 56
Namibe, Ang. B1 56
Namibia, ctry., Afr. C2 56
Namīn, Iran C13 44
Namjagbarwa Feng, mtn.,
  China F7 28
Namlea, Indon. D7 36
Nam Ngum Reservoir, res.,
  Laos C4 34
Nampa, Id., U.S. F2 105
Nampula, Moz. B6 56
Namsang, Myan. B3 34
Namsos, Nor. D4 10
Namtu, Myan. B3 34
Namur, Bel. E9 12
Namutoni, Nmb. B2 56
Namwala, Zam. B4 56
Nan, Thai. C4 34
Nanaimo, B.C., Can. E5 85
Nanakuli, Hi., U.S. B3 104
Nanao, Japan D15 28
Nance, co., Ne., U.S. C7 120
Nancha, China A1 31
Nanchang, China F11 28
Nancheng, China D4 30
Nanchong, China E9 28
Nancy, Fr. C10 16
Nanda Devi, mtn., India . . . C3 40
Nānded, India F3 40
Nandurbār, India E2 40
Nandyāl, India F3 40
Nanfeng, China D4 30
Nanga-Eboko, Cam. C2 54
Nanga Parbat, mtn., Pak. . . C10 42
Nangatayap, Indon. D4 36
Nangong, China A3 30
Nanjing, China E11 28
Nankang, China D3 30
Nanking see Nanjing, China E11 28
Nanle, China B4 30
Nannine, Austl. F2 60
Nanning, China G9 28
Nannup, Austl. G2 60
Nanping, China F11 28
Nansei-shotō (Ryukyu
  Islands), is., Japan A9 34

Nansemond, stm., Va., U.S. k14 139
Nansen Basin E21 144
Nansen Cordillera E22 144
Nan Shan see Qilian Shan,
  mts., China D7 28
Nantes, Fr. D6 16
Nanticoke, On., Can. E4 89
Nanticoke, Pa., U.S. D10 131
Nanticoke, stm., U.S. D6 113
Nanton, Ab., Can. D4 84
Nantong, China E12 28
Nantucket, Ma., U.S. D7 114
Nantucket, co., Ma., U.S. . . D7 114
Nantucket Island, i., Ma.,
  U.S. D7 114
Nantucket Sound, strt., Ma.,
  U.S. C7 114
Nantulo, Moz. A6 56
Nantuxent Point, c., N.J.,
  U.S. E2 123
Nanty Glo, Pa., U.S. F4 131
Nanuet, N.Y., U.S. g12 125
Nanuque, Braz. E3 74
Nanusa, Kepulauan, is.,
  Indon. C7 36
Nanxiong, China F10 28
Nanyang, China E10 28
Nanyuki, Kenya C7 54
Nanzhao, China C3 30
Naoma, W.V., U.S. n13 141
Naomi Peak, mtn., Ut., U.S. B4 137
Napa, Ca., U.S. C2 98
Napa, co., Ca., U.S. C2 98
Napanee, On., Can. C8 89
Napatree Point, c., R.I., U.S. G1 132
Napavine, Wa., U.S. C3 140
Napè, Laos C5 34
Naperville, Il., U.S. B5 106
Napier, N.Z. o14 63c
Napier Mountains, mts.,
  Ant. C10 67
Napierville, P.Q., Can. D4 90
Naples see Napoli, Italy . . . D5 18
Naples, Fl., U.S. F5 102
Naples, Tx., U.S. C5 136
Naples, Ut., U.S. C6 137
Napo, stm., S.A. D5 70
Napoleon, N.D., U.S. C6 127
Napoleon, Oh., U.S. A1 128
Napoleonville, La., U.S. . . . E4 111
Napoli (Naples), Italy D5 18
Napoli, Golfo di, b., Italy . . D5 18
Nappanee, In., U.S. B5 107
Naqadeh, Iran D11 44
Nara, Japan E15 28
Nara, Mali C3 50
Naracoorte, Austl. H3 62
Naramata, B.C., Can. E8 85
Naranja, Fl., U.S. G6 102
Narasapur, India F4 40
Narathiwat, Thai. E4 34
Nārāyanganj, Bngl. E6 40
Narberth, Pa., U.S. p20 131
Narbonne, Fr. F8 16
Narʹjan-Mar, Russia C7 26
Narmada, stm., India E2 40
Nārnaul, India D3 40
Narodnaja, gora, hills,
  Russia C8 26
Naro-Fominsk, Russia B14 20
Narooma, Austl. H5 62
Narrabri, Austl. G4 62
Narragansett, R.I., U.S. . . . F4 132
Narragansett Bay, b., R.I.,
  U.S. E5 132
Narraguagus, stm., Me., U.S. D5 112
Narrandera, Austl. G4 62
Narrogin, Austl. G2 60
Narromine, Austl. G4 62
Narrows, Va., U.S. C2 139
Narsaq, Grnld. F30 82
Narva, Est. G13 10
Narvik, Nor. B7 10
Naryn, Kyrg. E9 26
Naryn, stm., Asia A3 40
Narynkol, Kaz. C4 28
Näsåker, Swe. E7 10
Nasca, Peru F5 70
Naselle, Wa., U.S. C2 140
Nash, Tx., U.S. C5 136
Nash, co., N.C., U.S. A4 126
Nashawena Island, i., Ma.,
  U.S. D6 114
Nāshik, India E2 40
Nash Stream, stm., N.H.,
  U.S. A4 122
Nashua, Ia., U.S. B5 108
Nashua, N.H., U.S. E4 122
Nashua, stm., U.S. E3 122
Nashville, Ar., U.S. D2 97
Nashville, Ga., U.S. E3 103
Nashville, Il., U.S. E4 106
Nashville, In., U.S. F5 107
Nashville, Mi., U.S. F5 115
Nashville, N.C., U.S. B5 126
Nashville, Tn., U.S. A5 135
Nashwauk, Mn., U.S. C5 116
Nāşir, Sudan I11 48
Nasīrābād, India D2 40
Nasīrābād, Pak. E9 42
Naskaupi, stm., Nf., Can. . . g9 88
Nassau, Bah. D9 76
Nassau, co., Fl., U.S. B5 102
Nassau, co., N.Y., U.S. E7 125
Nassau, stm., Fl., U.S. k8 102

Name	Map Ref.	Page
Nassau Island, i., Cook Is.	F13	58
Nassau Sound, b., Fl., U.S.	B5	102
Nasser, Lake, res., Afr.	F11	48
Nässjö, Swe.	H6	10
Nasukoin Mountain, mtn., Mt., U.S.	B2	119
Nata, Bots.	C4	56
Natal, Braz.	C4	74
Natalbany, La., U.S.	D5	111
Natalia, Tx., U.S.	E3	136
Natashquan, stm., Can.	h9	88
Natchaug, stm., Ct., U.S.	B7	100
Natchez, Ms., U.S.	D2	117
Natchitoches, La., U.S.	C2	111
Natchitoches, co., La., U.S.	C2	111
Natick, Ma., U.S.	B5	114
National City, Ca., U.S.	F5	98
Natitingou, Benin	D5	50
Natividade, Braz.	F10	70
Natron, Lake, l., Afr.	D7	54
Natrona, co., Wy., U.S.	D5	143
Natrona Heights, Pa., U.S.	E2	131
Natuna Besar, i., Indon.	C3	36
Natuna Besar, Kepulauan, is., Indon.	C3	36
Natuna Selatan, Kepulauan, is., Indon.	C3	36
Natural Bridge, Ut., U.S.	F3	137
Natural Bridge, Va., U.S.	C3	139
Natural Bridges National Monument, Ut., U.S.	F6	137
Naturaliste, Cape, c., Austl.	G1	60
Nau, Cap de la, c., Spain	H7	16
Naugatuck, Ct., U.S.	D3	100
Naugatuck, stm., Ct., U.S.	D3	100
Nauru, ctry., Oc.	E10	58
Naushon Island, i., Ma., U.S.	D6	114
Nautilus Park, Ct., U.S.	D7	100
Nautla, Mex.	C5	78
Nauvoo, Il., U.S.	C2	106
Navadwip, India	E5	40
Navahrudak, Bela.	C8	20
Navajo, co., Az., U.S.	B5	96
Navajo Dam, N.M., U.S.	A2	124
Navajo Indian Reservation, U.S.	A4	96
Navajo Mountain, mtn., Ut., U.S.	F5	137
Navajo National Monument, Az., U.S.	A5	96
Navajo Reservoir, res., U.S.	A2	124
Navan, On., Can.	B9	89
Navapolack, Bela.	B10	20
Navarin, mys, c., Russia	C19	26
Navarino, Isla, i., Chile	I3	69
Navarre, hist. reg., Spain	B6	14
Navarre, Oh., U.S.	B4	128
Navarro, co., Tx., U.S.	D4	136
Navasota, Tx., U.S.	D4	136
Navassa Island, i., N.A.	B4	80
Navlja, Russia	C13	20
Navoi, Uzb.	E8	26
Navojoa, Mex.	B3	78
Navsāri, India	E2	40
Nawābshāh, Pak.	E9	42
Nawiliwili Bay, b., Hi., U.S.	B2	104
Naxçıvan, Azer.	C11	44
Naxi, China	D2	30
Náxos, Grc.	F10	18
Náxos, i., Grc.	F10	18
Nayarit, state, Mex.	C3	78
Naylor, Mo., U.S.	E7	118
Nayoro, Japan	C16	28
Nazaré, Braz.	D4	74
Nazaré, Port.	H2	16
Nazareth see Nazerat, Isr.	D3	42
Nazareth, Pa., U.S.	E11	131
Nazas, Mex.	B4	78
Nazas, stm., Mex.	B4	78
Nazca Ridge	K5	66
Naze, Japan	F13	28
Naze, The see Lindesnes, c., Nor.	H2	10
Nazerat, Isr.	D3	42
Nazilli, Tur.	D3	44
Nazko, stm., B.C., Can.	C6	85
Nazran', Russia	A11	44
Nazrēt, Eth.	B7	54
Nazwá, Oman	F7	42
N'dalatando, Ang.	E2	54
Ndélé, C.A.R.	B4	54
Ndendé, Gabon	D2	54
N'Djamena, Chad	D8	50
Ndjolé, Gabon	D2	54
Ndola, Zam.	A4	56
Neagh, Lough, l., N. Ire., U.K.	C3	12
Neah Bay, Wa., U.S.	A1	140
Néa Páfos, Cyp.	E5	44
Neápolis, Grc.	F9	18
Near Islands, is., Ak., U.S.	E2	95
Nebitdag, Turk.	F7	26
Neblina, Pico da, mtn., S.A.	C6	70
Nebo, Mount, mtn., Ut., U.S.	D4	137
Nebraska, state, U.S.	C6	120
Nebraska City, Ne., U.S.	D10	120
Nechako, stm., B.C., Can.	C5	85
Neches, stm., Tx., U.S.	D5	136
Necker Island, i., Hi., U.S.	m15	104
Necochea, Arg.	F6	72
Nederland, Co., U.S.	B5	99
Nederland, Tx., U.S.	E6	136
Nêdong, China	F6	28
Nédroma, Alg.	J6	16
Nedrow, N.Y., U.S.	C4	125
Needham, Ma., U.S.	g11	114
Needle Mountain, mtn., Wy., U.S.	B3	143
Needles, Ca., U.S.	E6	98
Needville, Tx., U.S.	r14	136
Neenah, Wi., U.S.	D5	142
Neepawa, Mb., Can.	D2	86
Neffs, Oh., U.S.	B5	128
Neffsville, Pa., U.S.	F9	131
Neftçala, Azer.	C13	44
Negage, Ang.	E3	54
Negaunee, Mi., U.S.	B3	115
Negēlē, Eth.	B7	54
Negley, Oh., U.S.	B5	128
Negombo, Sri L.	H3	40
Negritos, Peru	D3	70
Negro, stm., Arg.	F4	69
Negro, stm., S.A.	D7	70
Negros, i., Phil.	E8	34
Neguac, N.B., Can.	B4	87
Nehalem, stm., Or., U.S.	A3	130
Nehbandān, Iran	D7	42
Neiges, Piton des, mtn., Reu.	g10	57a
Neijiang, China	D2	30
Neill Point, c., Wa., U.S.	f11	140
Neillsville, Wi., U.S.	D3	142
Nei Monggol Zizhiqu (Inner Mongolia), prov., China	C10	28
Neisse see Nysa, Pol.	D4	20
Neiva, Col.	C4	70
Nejd see Najd, hist. reg., Sau. Ar.	E4	38
Nek'emtē, Eth.	B7	54
Nekoosa, Wi., U.S.	D4	142
Nelidovo, Russia	C5	22
Neligh, Ne., U.S.	B7	120
Nel'kan, Russia	D15	26
Nellis Air Force Base, mil., Nv., U.S.	G6	121
Nellore, India	G4	40
Nel'ma, Russia	E15	26
Nelson, B.C., Can.	E9	85
Nelson, N.Z.	p13	63c
Nelson, Ne., U.S.	D7	120
Nelson, co., Ky., U.S.	C4	110
Nelson, co., N.D., U.S.	B7	127
Nelson, co., Va., U.S.	C4	139
Nelson, stm., Mb., Can.	A4	86
Nelson, Cape, c., Austl.	H3	62
Nelsonville, Oh., U.S.	C3	128
Nelspruit, S. Afr.	D5	56
Néma, Maur.	C3	50
Nemacolin, Pa., U.S.	G2	131
Nemadji, stm., U.S.	B1	142
Nemaha, co., Ks., U.S.	C7	109
Nemaha, co., Ne., U.S.	D10	120
Neman (Nemunas), stm., Eur.	B7	20
Nembe, Nig.	F6	50
Nemunas (Neman), stm., Eur.	B7	20
Nemuro, Japan	C17	28
Nenana, Ak., U.S.	C10	95
Nendo, i., Sol. Is.	F10	58
Neodesha, Ks., U.S.	E8	109
Neoga, Il., U.S.	D5	106
Neola, Ia., U.S.	C2	108
Neola, Ut., U.S.	C5	137
Neopit, Wi., U.S.	D5	142
Neosho, Mo., U.S.	E3	118
Neosho, co., Ks., U.S.	E8	109
Neosho, stm., Ok., U.S.	A6	129
Nepal, ctry., Asia	D4	40
Nepālgañj, Nepal	D4	40
Nepaug Reservoir, res., Ct., U.S.	B3	100
Nepean, On., Can.	h12	89
Nepewassi Lake, l., On., Can.	A4	89
Nephi, Ut., U.S.	D4	137
Nepisiguit, stm., N.B., Can.	B3	87
Nepisiguit Bay, b., N.B., Can.	B4	87
Neponset, stm., Ma., U.S.	h11	114
Neptune, N.J., U.S.	C4	123
Neptune Beach, Fl., U.S.	B5	102
Neptune City, N.J., U.S.	C4	123
Nerčinsk, Russia	A11	28
Nerčinskij Zavod, Russia	D13	26
Nerehta, Russia	C7	22
Neriquinha, Ang.	B3	56
Nescopeck, Pa., U.S.	D9	131
Neshanic, stm., N.J., U.S.	C3	123
Neshoba, co., Ms., U.S.	C4	117
Neskaupstadur, Ice.	l22	10a
Nesna, Nor.	C5	10
Nesowadnehunk, l., Me., U.S.	B3	112
Nesquehoning, Pa., U.S.	E10	131
Ness, co., Ks., U.S.	D4	109
Ness, Loch, l., Scot., U.K.	B4	12
Ness City, Ks., U.S.	D4	109
Néstos, stm., Eur.	D10	18
Netanya, Isr.	D2	42
Netcong, N.J., U.S.	B3	123
Netherlands, ctry., Eur.	D9	12
Netherlands Antilles, dep., N.A.	F11	76
Netherlands Guiana see Suriname, ctry., S.A.	C8	70
Nettie, W.V., U.S.	C4	141
Nett Lake, l., Mn., U.S.	B5	116
Nett Lake Indian Reservation, Mn., U.S.	B6	116
Nettleton, Ms., U.S.	A5	117
Neubrandenburg, Ger.	D13	12
Neuchâtel, Switz.	A1	18
Neuchâtel, Lac de, l., Switz.	A1	18
Neufchâtel-en-Bray, Fr.	C7	16
Neumarkt in der Oberpfalz, Ger.	F12	12
Neumünster, Ger.	C12	12
Neuquén, Arg.	E3	69
Neuruppin, Ger.	D13	12
Neuse, stm., N.C., U.S.	B6	126
Neustrelitz, Ger.	D13	12
Neuville, P.Q., Can.	C6	90
Nevada, Ia., U.S.	B4	108
Nevada, Mo., U.S.	D3	118
Nevada, co., Ar., U.S.	D2	97
Nevada, co., Ca., U.S.	C3	98
Nevada, state, U.S.	D5	121
Nevada, Sierra, mts., Ca., U.S.	D4	98
Nevada City, Ca., U.S.	C3	98
Nevado, Cerro, mtn., Arg.	F4	72
Nevado, Cerro, mtn., Col.	C5	70
Nevel', Russia	A10	20
Nevel'sk, Russia	E16	26
Never, Russia	D14	26
Nevers, Fr.	D8	16
Neversink, stm., N.Y., U.S.	D6	125
Nevinnomyssk, Russia	B4	42
Nevis, i., St. K./N.	B7	80
Nevis, Ben, mtn., Scot., U.K.	B4	12
Nevjansk, Russia	C11	22
Nevşehir, Tur.	C6	44
New, stm., Az., U.S.	k8	96
New, stm., N.C., U.S.	C5	126
New, stm., U.S.	C3	141
Newala, Tan.	F7	54
New Albany, In., U.S.	H6	107
New Albany, Ms., U.S.	A4	117
New Albany, Oh., U.S.	k11	128
New Amsterdam, Guy.	B8	70
Newark, Ar., U.S.	B4	97
Newark, Ca., U.S.	h8	98
Newark, De., U.S.	B3	101
Newark, Il., U.S.	B5	106
Newark, N.J., U.S.	B4	123
Newark, N.Y., U.S.	B3	125
Newark, Oh., U.S.	B3	128
Newark Bay, b., N.J., U.S.	k8	123
Newark Lake, l., Nv., U.S.	D6	121
New Athens, Il., U.S.	E4	106
New Augusta, Ms., U.S.	D4	117
Newaygo, Mi., U.S.	E5	115
Newaygo, co., Mi., U.S.	E5	115
New Baden, Il., U.S.	E4	106
New Baltimore, Mi., U.S.	F8	115
New Bedford, Ma., U.S.	C6	114
New Bedford, Pa., U.S.	D1	131
Newberg, Or., U.S.	B4	130
New Berlin, Il., U.S.	D4	106
New Berlin, Wi., U.S.	n11	142
New Bern, N.C., U.S.	B5	126
Newbern, Tn., U.S.	A2	135
Newberry, Fl., U.S.	C4	102
Newberry, Mi., U.S.	B5	115
Newberry, S.C., U.S.	C4	133
Newberry, co., S.C., U.S.	C4	133
New Bethlehem, Pa., U.S.	D3	131
New Bloomfield, Pa., U.S.	F7	131
New Boston, Mi., U.S.	p15	115
New Boston, Oh., U.S.	D3	128
New Boston, Tx., U.S.	C5	136
New Braunfels, Tx., U.S.	E3	136
New Bremen, Oh., U.S.	B1	128
New Brighton, Mn., U.S.	m12	116
New Brighton, Pa., U.S.	E1	131
New Britain, Ct., U.S.	C4	100
New Britain, i., Pap. N. Gui.	H13	32
New Brockton, Al., U.S.	D4	94
New Brunswick, N.J., U.S.	C4	123
New Brunswick, prov., Can.	B3	87
New Buffalo, Mi., U.S.	G4	115
Newburg, Wi., U.S.	E5	142
Newburgh, On., Can.	C8	89
Newburgh, In., U.S.	I3	107
Newburgh, N.Y., U.S.	D6	125
Newburgh Heights, Oh., U.S.	h9	128
Newburyport, Ma., U.S.	A6	114
New Caledonia, dep., Oc.	l9	62a
New Caledonia Basin	K19	64
New Canaan, Ct., U.S.	E2	100
New Carlisle, In., U.S.	A4	107
New Carlisle, Oh., U.S.	C1	128
Newcastle, Austl.	G5	62
Newcastle, N.B., Can.	C4	87
Newcastle, On., Can.	D6	89
Newcastle, S. Afr.	D4	56
New Castle, Al., U.S.	B3	94
New Castle, Co., U.S.	B3	99
New Castle, De., U.S.	B3	101
New Castle, In., U.S.	E7	107
New Castle, Ky., U.S.	B4	110
Newcastle, Ok., U.S.	B4	129
New Castle, Pa., U.S.	D1	131
Newcastle, Wy., U.S.	C8	143
New Castle, co., De., U.S.	B3	101
Newcastle upon Tyne, Eng., U.K.	C6	12
Newcastle Waters, Austl.	D5	60
New City, N.Y., U.S.	D6	125
Newcomerstown, Oh., U.S.	B4	128
New Concord, Oh., U.S.	C4	128
New Cumberland, Pa., U.S.	F8	131
New Cumberland, W.V., U.S.	A4	141
Newdegate, Austl.	G2	60
New Delhi, India	D3	40
Newell, Ia., U.S.	B2	108
Newell, S.D., U.S.	C2	134
Newell, W.V., U.S.	A4	141
New Ellenton, S.C., U.S.	E4	133
Newellton, La., U.S.	B4	111
New England, N.D., U.S.	C3	127
Newenham, Cape, c., Ak., U.S.	D7	95
New Fairfield, Ct., U.S.	D2	100
Newfane, N.Y., U.S.	B2	125
Newfields, N.H., U.S.	D5	122
New Florence, Mo., U.S.	C6	118
Newfound Gap, U.S.	f9	126
Newfound Lake, l., N.H., U.S.	C3	122
Newfoundland, prov., Can.	D4	88
Newfoundland, i., Nf., Can.	D3	88
Newfoundland Basin	D9	66
New Franklin, Mo., U.S.	B5	118
New Freedom, Pa., U.S.	G8	131
New Georgia Sound, strt., Sol. Is.	B6	62
New Germany, N.S., Can.	E5	87
New Glarus, Wi., U.S.	F4	142
New Guinea, i.	G11	32
New Hampshire, state, U.S.	C3	122
New Hampton, Ia., U.S.	A5	108
New Hanover, co., N.C., U.S.	C5	126
New Hanover, i., Pap. N. Gui.	G13	32
New Harbour, Nf., Can.	E5	88
New Harmony, In., U.S.	H2	107
New Hartford, Ct., U.S.	B4	100
New Hartford, Ia., U.S.	B5	108
New Haven, Ct., U.S.	D4	100
New Haven, In., U.S.	B7	107
New Haven, Ky., U.S.	C4	110
New Haven, Mi., U.S.	F8	115
New Haven, Mo., U.S.	C6	118
New Haven, W.V., U.S.	C3	141
New Haven, co., Ct., U.S.	D4	100
New Haven, stm., Vt., U.S.	C2	138
New Haven Harbor, b., Ct., U.S.	E4	100
New Hazelton, B.C., Can.	B4	85
New Hebrides see Vanuatu, ctry., Oc.	F10	58
New Hebrides, is., Vanuatu	F10	58
New Hebrides Trench	K19	64
New Holland, Ga., U.S.	B3	103
New Holland, Pa., U.S.	F9	131
New Holstein, Wi., U.S.	E5	142
New Hope, Al., U.S.	A3	94
New Hope, Ky., U.S.	C4	110
New Hope, Mn., U.S.	m12	116
New Hope, Pa., U.S.	F12	131
New Hudson, Mi., U.S.	o14	115
New Iberia, La., U.S.	D4	111
New Inlet, b., N.C., U.S.	D5	126
New Ireland, i., Pap. N. Gui.	G13	32
New Jersey, state, U.S.	C4	123
New Johnsonville, Tn., U.S.	A4	135
New Kensington, Pa., U.S.	E2	131
New Kent, co., Va., U.S.	C5	139
Newkirk, Ok., U.S.	A4	129
New Kowloon see Xinjiulong, China	E3	30
New Laguna, N.M., U.S.	B2	124
New Lake, l., N.C., U.S.	B6	126
New Lenox, Il., U.S.	B6	106
New Lexington, Oh., U.S.	C3	128
New Liberty, Ky., U.S.	B5	110
New Lisbon, Wi., U.S.	D3	142
New Liskeard, On., Can.	p20	89
Newllano, La., U.S.	C2	111
New London, Ct., U.S.	D7	100
New London, Ia., U.S.	D6	108
New London, Mn., U.S.	E4	116
New London, Mo., U.S.	B6	118
New London, N.H., U.S.	D3	122
New London, Oh., U.S.	A3	128
New London, Wi., U.S.	D5	142
New London, co., Ct., U.S.	C7	100
New London Submarine Base, mil., Ct., U.S.	D7	100
New Madison, Oh., U.S.	C1	128
New Madrid, Mo., U.S.	E8	118
New Madrid, co., Mo., U.S.	E8	118
Newman, Austl.	E2	60
Newman, Ca., U.S.	D3	98
Newman, Il., U.S.	D6	106
New Manchester, W.V., U.S.	e8	141
Newman Grove, Ne., U.S.	C8	120
Newman Lake, l., Wa., U.S.	B8	140
Newmanstown, Pa., U.S.	F9	131
Newmarket, On., Can.	C5	89
New Market, Al., U.S.	A3	94
New Market, In., U.S.	E4	107
New Market, N.H., U.S.	D5	122
New Market, Tn., U.S.	C10	135
New Market, Va., U.S.	B4	139
New Martinsville, W.V., U.S.	B4	141
New Matamoras, Oh., U.S.	C4	128
New Mexico, state, U.S.	C3	124
New Miami, Oh., U.S.	C1	128
New Milford, Ct., U.S.	C2	100
New Milford, N.J., U.S.	h8	123
New Milford, Pa., U.S.	C10	131
Newnan, Ga., U.S.	C2	103
Newnans Lake, l., Fl., U.S.	C4	102
New Norfolk, Austl.	I4	62
New Orleans, La., U.S.	E5	111
New Orleans Naval Air Station, mil., La., U.S.	k11	111
New Oxford, Pa., U.S.	G7	131
New Palestine, In., U.S.	E6	107
New Paltz, N.Y., U.S.	D6	125
New Paris, In., U.S.	B6	107
New Paris, Oh., U.S.	C1	128
New Philadelphia, Oh., U.S.	B4	128
New Philadelphia, Pa., U.S.	E9	131
New Plymouth, N.Z.	o13	63c
New Plymouth, Id., U.S.	F2	105
New Point Comfort, c., Va., U.S.	C6	139
Newport, Wales, U.K.	E5	12
Newport, Ar., U.S.	B4	97
Newport, De., U.S.	B3	101
Newport, In., U.S.	E3	107
Newport, Ky., U.S.	A5	110
Newport, Me., U.S.	D3	112
Newport, Mi., U.S.	G7	115
Newport, Mn., U.S.	n13	116
Newport, N.C., U.S.	C6	126
Newport, N.H., U.S.	D2	122
Newport, Oh., U.S.	C4	128
Newport, Or., U.S.	C2	130
Newport, Pa., U.S.	F7	131
Newport, R.I., U.S.	F5	132
Newport, Tn., U.S.	D10	135
Newport, Vt., U.S.	B4	138
Newport, Wa., U.S.	A8	140
Newport, co., R.I., U.S.	E5	132
Newport Beach, Ca., U.S.	n13	98
Newport News, Va., U.S.	D6	139
New Port Richey, Fl., U.S.	D4	102
New Prague, Mn., U.S.	F5	116
New Preston, Ct., U.S.	C2	100
New Providence, N.J., U.S.	B4	123
New Providence, i., Bah.	C9	76
Newquay, Eng., U.K.	E4	12
New Richland, Mn., U.S.	G5	116
New Richmond, P.Q., Can.	A4	87
New Richmond, Oh., U.S.	D1	128
New Richmond, Wi., U.S.	C1	142
New River Inlet, b., N.C., U.S.	C5	126
New Roads, La., U.S.	D4	111
New Rochelle, N.Y., U.S.	E7	125
New Rockford, N.D., U.S.	B6	127
Newry, N. Ire., U.K.	C3	12
New Salem, N.D., U.S.	C4	127
New Sarpy, La., U.S.	k11	111
New Schwabenland, reg., Ant.	D5	67
New Sharon, Ia., U.S.	C5	108
New Siberian Islands see Novosibirskie ostrova, is., Russia	B16	26
New Site, Al., U.S.	B4	94
New Smyrna Beach, Fl., U.S.	C6	102
New South Wales, state, Austl.	G4	62
New Straitsville, Oh., U.S.	C3	128
New Tazewell, Tn., U.S.	C10	135
Newton, Al., U.S.	D4	94
Newton, Ga., U.S.	E2	103
Newton, Ia., U.S.	C4	108
Newton, Il., U.S.	E5	106
Newton, Ks., U.S.	D6	109
Newton, Ma., U.S.	B5	114
Newton, Ms., U.S.	C4	117
Newton, N.C., U.S.	B1	126
Newton, N.J., U.S.	A3	123
Newton, Tx., U.S.	D6	136
Newton, Ut., U.S.	B4	137
Newton, co., Ar., U.S.	B2	97
Newton, co., Ga., U.S.	C3	103
Newton, co., In., U.S.	B3	107
Newton, co., Ms., U.S.	C4	117
Newton, co., Mo., U.S.	E3	118
Newton, co., Tx., U.S.	D6	136
Newton Falls, Oh., U.S.	A5	128
Newton Lake, res., Il., U.S.	E5	106
Newtown, Ct., U.S.	D2	100
Newtown, Oh., U.S.	C1	128
New Town, N.D., U.S.	B3	127
Newtown Square, Pa., U.S.	p20	131
New Ulm, Mn., U.S.	F4	116
New Vienna, Oh., U.S.	C2	128
Newville, Pa., U.S.	F7	131
New Washington, In., U.S.	G6	107
New Washington, Oh., U.S.	B3	128
New Waterford, Oh., U.S.	B5	128
New Westminster, B.C., Can.	E6	85
New Whiteland, In., U.S.	E5	107
New Wilmington, Pa., U.S.	D1	131
New Windsor, Il., U.S.	B3	106
New Windsor, Md., U.S.	A3	113
New Windsor, N.Y., U.S.	D6	125
New World Island, i., Nf., Can.	D4	88
New York, N.Y., U.S.	E7	125
New York, co., N.Y., U.S.	k13	125
New York, state, U.S.	C6	125
New York Mills, Mn., U.S.	D3	116
New Zealand, ctry., Oc.	H10	58

Name	Map Ref.	Page

Neyrīz, Iran E6 42
Neyshābūr, Iran C7 42
Nezahualcóyotl, Presa, res.,
  Mex. D6 78
Nez Perce, co., Id., U.S. . . C2 105
Nez Perce Indian
  Reservation, Id., U.S. . . . C2 105
Ngabé, Congo D3 54
Ngangala, Sudan C6 54
Ngangla Ringco, l., China . . E4 28
Ngaoundéré, Cam. B2 54
Ngeaur, i., Palau E9 32
Ngidinga, D.R.C. E3 54
Ngoring Hu, l., China E7 28
Ngouri, Chad. D8 50
Nguigmi, Niger D7 50
Nguru, Nig. D7 50
Nha Trang, Viet. D5 34
Nhill, Austl. H3 62
Nhoma, stm., Afr. B2 56
Niafounké, Mali C4 50
Niagara, Wi., U.S. C6 142
Niagara, co., N.Y., U.S. . . . B2 125
Niagara Falls, On., Can. . . . D5 89
Niagara Falls, N.Y., U.S. . . . B1 125
Niagara-on-the-Lake, On.,
  Can. D5 89
Niah, Malay. C4 36
Niakaramandougou, C. Iv. . . E3 50
Niamey, Niger D5 50
Niangara, D.R.C. C5 54
Niangua, stm., Mo., U.S. . . D5 118
Nia-Nia, D.R.C. C5 54
Niantic, Ct., U.S. D7 100
Nias, Pulau, i., Indon. C1 36
Niatupo, Pan. D4 80
Nibley, Ut., U.S. B4 137
Nicaragua, ctry., N.A. F7 76
Nicaragua, Lago de, l., Nic. . C2 80
Nicatous Lake, l., Me., U.S. . C4 112
Nice, Fr. F10 16
Niceville, Fl., U.S. u15 102
Nichinan, Japan E14 28
Nicholas, co., Ky., U.S. . . . B6 110
Nicholas, co., W.V., U.S. . . C4 141
Nicholas Channel, strt., N.A. A3 80
Nicholasville, Ky., U.S. . . . C5 110
Nicholls, Ga., U.S. E4 103
Nichols Hills, Ok., U.S. . . . B4 129
Nicholson, Ms., U.S. E4 117
Nickajack Lake, res., Tn.,
  U.S. D8 135
Nickel Centre, On., Can. . . p19 89
Nickerson, Ks., U.S. D5 109
Nicobar Islands, is., India . . H6 40
Nicolet, P.Q., Can. C5 90
Nicolet, stm., P.Q., Can. . . C5 90
Nicolet, Lake, l., Mi., U.S. . . B6 115
Nicollet, Mn., U.S. F4 116
Nicollet, co., Mn., U.S. . . . F4 116
Nicoma Park, Ok., U.S. . . . B4 129
Nicosia, Cyp. E5 44
Nicoya, Golfo de, b., C.R. . . D2 80
Nicoya, Península de, pen.,
  C.R. D2 80
Nidzica, Pol. C6 20
Niellé, C. Iv. D3 50
Nienburg, Ger. D11 12
Nieuw Amsterdam, Sur. . . . B8 70
Nieuw Nickerie, Sur. B8 70
Nigadoo, N.B., Can. B4 87
Niğde, Tur. D6 44
Niger, ctry., Afr. C6 50
Niger, stm., Afr. E6 50
Nigeria, ctry., Afr. E6 50
Nihoa, i., Hi., U.S. m15 104
Niigata, Japan D15 28
Niihama, Japan D2 31
Niihau, i., Hi., U.S. B1 104
Nijmegen, Neth. E10 12
Nikel', Russia B14 10
Nikishka, Ak., U.S. g16 95
Nikkō, Japan D15 28
Nikol'sk, Russia D8 22
Nikol'sk, Russia D6 26
Nikopol', Ukr. F13 20
Niksar, Tur. B7 44
Nīkshahr, Iran E8 42
Nikšić, Yugo. C7 18
Nila, Pulau, i., Indon. E7 36
Niland, Ca., U.S. F6 98
Nile, stm., Afr. E11 48
Niles, Il., U.S. h9 106
Niles, Mi., U.S. G4 115
Niles, Oh., U.S. A5 128
Nīmach, India E2 40
Nimba, Mount, mtn., Afr. . . E3 50
Nîmes, Fr. F9 16
Nimrod Lake, res., Ar., U.S. C2 97
Nimule, Sudan J11 48
Ninawá, hist., Iraq C4 42
Ninda, Ang. A3 56
Nine Degree Channel, strt.,
  India H2 40
Nine Mile Creek, stm., Ut.,
  U.S. D5 137
Ninemile Point, c., Mi., U.S. C6 115
Ninetyeast Ridge J11 64
Ninety Mile Beach, Austl. . . H4 62
Ninety Six, S.C., U.S. C3 133
Nineveh see Ninawá, hist.,
  Iraq C4 42
Ning'an, China B1 31
Ningbo, China F12 28
Ningcheng, China C11 28

Ningde, China D4 30
Ningdu, China F11 28
Ninghai, China D5 30
Ninghua, China D4 30
Ningi, Nig. D6 50
Ningming, China E2 30
Ningnan, China A4 34
Ningshan, China C2 30
Ningsia Hui Autonomous
  Region see Ningxia
  Huiza Zizhiqu, prov.,
  China D9 28
Ningxia Huiza Zizhiqu,
  prov., China D9 28
Ningxiang, China D3 30
Ninh Binh, Viet. B5 34
Ninigo Group, is., Pap. N.
  Gui. G11 32
Ninigret Pond, l., R.I., U.S. . G2 132
Ninilchik, Ak., U.S. C9 95
Ninnescah, stm., Ks., U.S. . E6 109
Ninohe, Japan B4 31
Niobrara, co., Wy., U.S. . . . C8 143
Niobrara, stm., U.S. B7 120
Nioki, D.R.C. D3 54
Niono, Mali D3 50
Nioro du Sahel, Mali C3 50
Niort, Fr. D6 16
Niota, Tn., U.S. D9 135
Nipigon, Lake, l., On., Can. o17 89
Nipissing, Lake, l., On.,
  Can. A5 89
Nipomo, Ca., U.S. E3 98
Nipple Mountain, mtn., Co.,
  U.S. D2 99
Niquero, Cuba A4 80
Nirmal, India F3 40
Niscemi, Italy F5 18
Niskayuna, N.Y., U.S. C7 125
Nisqually, stm., Wa., U.S. . . C3 140
Nisswa, Mn., U.S. D4 116
Nistru (Dniester) (Dnister)
  stm., Eur. F10 20
Niterói, Braz. F3 74
Nitra, Slvk. E5 20
Nitro, W.V., U.S. C3 141
Niuafo'ou, i., Tonga F13 58
Niuke, China C4 40
Niulakita, i., Tuvalu E11 58
Niverville, Mb., Can. E3 86
Niwot, Co., U.S. A5 99
Nixa, Mo., U.S. D4 118
Nixon, Nv., U.S. D2 121
Nixon, Tx., U.S. E4 136
Nizāmābād, India F3 40
Nizhyn, Ukr. D11 20
Nizip, Tur. D7 44
Nižneangarsk, Russia D12 26
Nižnee Kujto, ozero, l.,
  Russia D14 10
Nižnekamsk, Russia C9 22
Nižneudinsk, Russia D11 26
Nižnevartovsk, Russia C9 26
Nižnij Novgorod (Gor'kij),
  Russia D6 26
Nižnij Tagil, Russia D8 26
Nižnjaja Peša, Russia A8 22
Nižnjaja Tunguska, stm.,
  Russia C11 26
Njandoma, Russia C6 26
Njazidja, i., Com. A7 56
Njinjo, Tan. E7 54
Njombe, Tan. E6 54
Njuhča, Russia B8 22
Njurba, Russia C13 26
Njuvčim, Russia B9 22
Nkambe, Cam. B2 54
Nkawkaw, Ghana E4 50
Nkhata Bay, Mwi. A5 56
Nkhotakota, Mwi. A5 56
Nkongsamba, Cam. C1 54
Noākhāli, Bngl. E6 40
Noank, Ct., U.S. D8 100
Noatak, Ak., U.S. B7 95
Noatak, stm., Ak., U.S. . . . B7 95
Nobel, On., Can. B4 89
Nobeoka, Japan D2 31
Noble, Ok., U.S. B4 129
Noble, co., In., U.S. B7 107
Noble, co., Oh., U.S. C4 128
Noble, co., Ok., U.S. A4 129
Nobles, co., Mn., U.S. G3 116
Noblesville, In., U.S. D6 107
Nocatee, Fl., U.S. E5 102
Nocona, Tx., U.S. C4 136
Nodaway, co., Mo., U.S. . . A3 118
Nodaway, stm., U.S. A2 118
Noel, Mo., U.S. E3 118
Nogales, Mex. A2 78
Nogales, Az., U.S. F5 96
Nogent-le-Rotrou, Fr. C7 16
Noginsk, Russia C6 22
Nohar, India D6 40
Noirmoutier, Île de, i., Fr. . . D5 16
Nokaneng, Bots. B3 56
Nokia, Fin. F10 10
Nokomis, Fl., U.S. E4 102
Nokomis, Il., U.S. D4 106
Nokomis, Lake, res., Wi.,
  U.S. C4 142
Nokuku, Vanuatu j9 62a
Nola, C.A.R. C3 54
Nolan, co., Tx., U.S. C2 136
Nolichucky, stm., Tn., U.S. . C10 135

Nolin, stm., Ky., U.S. C3 110
Nolin Lake, res., Ky., U.S. . C3 110
Nolinsk, Russia C9 22
Nomans Land, i., Ma., U.S. . D6 114
Nome, Ak., U.S. C6 95
Nominingue, P.Q., Can. . . . C2 90
Nonesuch, stm., Me., U.S. . g7 112
Nong'an, China C13 28
Nong Khai, Thai. C4 34
Nonquit Pond, l., R.I., U.S. . E6 132
Nooksack, North Fork, stm.,
  Wa., U.S. A4 140
Nooksack, South Fork, stm.,
  Wa., U.S. A3 140
Noonkanbah, Austl. D3 60
Noorvik, Ak., U.S. B7 95
Nootka Sound, strt., B.C.,
  Can. E4 85
No Point, Point, c., Md.,
  U.S. D5 113
Noquebay, Lake, l., Wi.,
  U.S. C6 142
Nóqui, Ang. E2 54
Noranda (part of Rouyn [-
  Noranda]), P.Q., Can. . . . k11 90
Nora Springs, Ia., U.S. . . . A5 108
Norborne, Mo., U.S. B4 118
Norco, La., U.S. E5 111
Norcross, Ga., U.S. C2 103
Nordaustlandet, i., Nor. . . . A4 26
Norden, Ger. D10 12
Nordenham, Ger. D11 12
Nordenšel'da, arhipelag, is.,
  Russia B11 26
Nordfjordeid, Nor. F2 10
Nordhausen, Ger. E12 12
Nordkapp, c., Nor. A11 10
Nord-Ostsee-Kanal, Ger. . . C11 12
Nordre Strømfjord, b.,
  Grnld. E29 82
Nordvik, Russia B13 26
Norfolk, Ct., U.S. B3 100
Norfolk, Ne., U.S. B8 120
Norfolk, N.Y., U.S. f9 125
Norfolk, Va., U.S. D6 139
Norfolk, co., Ma., U.S. . . . B5 114
Norfolk Island, dep., Oc. . . G10 58
Norfolk Naval Base, mil.,
  Va., U.S. k15 139
Norfolk Naval Shipyard,
  mil., Va., U.S. k15 139
Norfolk Ridge K19 64
Norfork Dam, Ar., U.S. . . . A3 97
Norfork Lake, res., U.S. . . . A3 97
Noril'sk, Russia C10 26
Norland, Fl., U.S. s13 102
Norlina, N.C., U.S. A4 126
Normal, Il., U.S. C5 106
Norman, Ok., U.S. B4 129
Norman, co., Mn., U.S. . . . C2 116
Norman, Lake, res., N.C.,
  U.S. B2 126
Normandie, hist. reg., Fr. . . C6 16
Normandie, Collines de,
  hills, Fr. C6 16
Normandy, Mo., U.S. f13 118
Normandy see Normandie,
  hist. reg., Fr. C6 16
Normandy, Hills of see
  Normandie, Collines
  de, hills, Fr. C6 16
Norman Park, Ga., U.S. . . . E3 103
Normanton, Austl. D3 62
Norphlet, Ar., U.S. D3 97
Ñorquinco, Arg. F2 69
Norra Kvarken
  (Merenkurkku), strt.,
  Eur. E9 10
Norrbotten, hist. reg., Swe. C10 10
Nørresundby, Den. H3 10
Norridge, Il., U.S. k9 106
Norridgewock, Me., U.S. . . D3 112
Norris, S.C., U.S. B2 133
Norris, Tn., U.S. C9 135
Norris Arm, Nf., Can. D4 88
Norris City, Il., U.S. F5 106
Norris Dam, Tn., U.S. C9 135
Norris Lake, res., Tn., U.S. . C10 135
Norris Point, Nf., Can. D3 88
Norristown, Pa., U.S. F11 131
Norrköping, Swe. G7 10
Norrtälje, Swe. G8 10
Norseman, Austl. G3 60
Norsjö, Swe. D8 10
Norsk, Russia D15 26
North, S.C., U.S. D5 133
North, co., Al., U.S. B2 94
North, stm., Ia., U.S. f8 108
North, stm., Ma., U.S. h12 114
North, stm., W.V., U.S. . . . B6 141
North, Cape, c., N.S., Can. . B9 87
North Adams, Ma., U.S. . . . A1 114
North Albany, Or., U.S. . . . k11 130
Northam, Austl. G2 60
North America C5 4
North American Basin E7 66
North Amherst, Ma., U.S. . . B2 114
Northampton, Austl. F1 60
Northampton, Eng., U.K. . . D6 12
Northampton, Ma., U.S. . . . B2 114
Northampton, Pa., U.S. . . . E11 131
Northampton, co., N.C.,
  U.S. A5 126
Northampton, co., Pa., U.S. E11 131
Northampton, co., Va., U.S. C7 139

North Andaman, i., India . . G6 40
North Andover, Ma., U.S. . . A5 114
North Anna, stm., Va., U.S. B5 139
North Anson, Me., U.S. . . . D3 112
North Apollo, Pa., U.S. . . . E2 131
North Arapaho Peak, mtn.,
  Co., U.S. A5 99
North Arlington, N.J., U.S. . h8 123
North Atlanta, Ga., U.S. . . . h8 103
North Attleboro, Ma., U.S. . C5 114
North Augusta, S.C., U.S. . . D4 133
North Aurora, Il., U.S. k8 106
North Australian Basin J14 64
North Baltimore, Oh., U.S. . A2 128
North Bay, On., Can. A5 89
North Beach, Md., U.S. . . . C4 113
North Belmont, N.C., U.S. . B1 126
North Bend, Ne., U.S. C9 120
North Bend, Or., U.S. D2 130
North Bend, Wa., U.S. B4 140
North Bennington, Vt., U.S. F2 138
North Bergen, N.J., U.S. . . h8 123
North Berwick, Me., U.S. . . E2 112
North Billerica, Ma., U.S. . . A5 114
North Branch, Mi., U.S. . . . E7 115
North Branch, Mn., U.S. . . E6 116
North Branch, N.H., U.S. . . D3 122
North Branch, N.J., U.S. . . . B3 123
North Branford, Ct., U.S. . . D4 100
Northbridge, Ma., U.S. . . . B4 114
Northbrook, Il., U.S. h9 106
North Brookfield, Ma., U.S. B3 114
North Brunswick, N.J., U.S. C4 123
North Caicos, i., T./C. Is. . . A5 80
North Caldwell, N.J., U.S. . . B4 123
North Canadian, stm., Ok.,
  U.S. A5 129
North Canton, Ga., U.S. . . . B2 103
North Canton, Oh., U.S. . . . B4 128
North Cape, c., P.E., Can. . . B6 87
North Cape, c., N.Z. n13 63c
North Cape see Nordkapp,
  c., Nor. A11 10
North Cape May, N.J., U.S. F3 123
North Carolina, state, U.S. . B3 126
North Cascades National
  Park, Wa., U.S. A4 140
North Channel, strt., On.,
  Can. A2 89
North Channel, strt., U.K. . . C4 12
North Charleston, S.C., U.S. F8 133
North Chicago, Il., U.S. . . . A6 106
North Clarendon, Vt., U.S. . D3 138
Northcliffe, Austl. G2 60
North College Hill, Oh.,
  U.S. o12 128
North Conway, N.H., U.S. . . B4 122
North Corbin, Ky., U.S. . . . D5 110
North Crossett, Ar., U.S. . . D4 97
North Cyprus, ctry., Asia . . E5 44
North Dakota, state, U.S. . . B5 127
North Dartmouth, Ma., U.S. C6 114
North Eagle Butte, S.D.,
  U.S. B4 134
North East, Md., U.S. A6 113
North East, Pa., U.S. B2 131
Northeast, Cape, c., Ak.,
  U.S. C6 95
Northeast Cape Fear, stm.,
  N.C., U.S. C5 126
Northeast Harbor, Me., U.S. D4 112
North Easton, Ma., U.S. . . . B5 114
Northeast Pond, l., N.H.,
  U.S. D5 122
North Edisto, stm., S.C.,
  U.S. k11 133
North English, Ia., U.S. . . . C5 108
North English, stm., Ia., U.S. C5 108
North Enid, Ok., U.S. A4 129
Northern Cheyenne Indian
  Reservation, Mt., U.S. . . E10 119
Northern Cook Islands, is.,
  Cook Is. F13 58
Northern Donets, stm., Eur. E15 20
Northern Dvina see
  Severnaja Dvina, stm.,
  Russia C6 26
Northern Indian Lake, l.,
  Mb., Can. A3 86
Northern Ireland, prov., N.
  Ire., U.K. C3 12
Northern Mariana Islands,
  dep., Oc. C9 58
Northern Sporades see
  Vórioi Sporádhes, is.,
  Grc. E10 18
Northern Territory, ter.,
  Austl. D5 60
North Falmouth, Ma., U.S. . C6 114
Northfield, Mn., U.S. F5 116
Northfield, N.J., U.S. E3 123
Northfield, Oh., U.S. h9 128
Northfield, Vt., U.S. C3 138
Northfield Falls, Vt., U.S. . . C3 138
North Fiji Basin J20 64
North Flinders Range, mts.,
  Austl. G2 62
North Fond du Lac, Wi.,
  U.S. E5 142
Northford, Ct., U.S. D4 100
North Fork Reservoir, res.,
  Or., U.S. B4 130

North Fort Myers, Fl., U.S. . F5 102
North Fox Island, i., Mi.,
  U.S. C5 115
Northglenn, Co., U.S. B6 99
North Gower, On., Can. . . . B9 89
North Grafton, Ma., U.S. . . B4 114
North Grosvenordale, Ct.,
  U.S. B8 100
North Gulfport, Ms., U.S. . . E4 117
North Haledon, N.J., U.S. . . B4 123
North Hampton, N.H., U.S. E5 122
North Hartland Reservoir,
  res., Vt., U.S. D4 138
North Hatley, P.Q., Can. . . D6 90
North Haven, Ct., U.S. . . . D4 100
North Head, N.B., Can. . . . E3 87
North Hero Island, i., Vt.,
  U.S. B2 138
North Horn Lake, l., Tn.,
  U.S. e8 135
North Industry, Oh., U.S. . . B4 128
North Inlet, b., S.C., U.S. . . E9 133
North Island, i., N.Z. o14 63c
North Island, i., S.C., U.S. . E9 133
North Island Naval Air
  Station, mil., Ca., U.S. . . o15 98
North Islands, is., La., U.S. . E7 111
North Judson, In., U.S. . . . B4 107
North Kansas City, Mo.,
  U.S. h10 118
North Kingstown, R.I., U.S. E4 132
North Kingsville, Oh., U.S. . A5 128
North La Junta, Co., U.S. . . C7 99
Northlake, Il., U.S. k9 106
North Lakhimpur, India . . . D6 40
North Laramie, stm., Wy.,
  U.S. D7 143
North Las Vegas, Nv., U.S. G6 121
North La Veta Pass, Co.,
  U.S. D5 99
North Lewisburg, Oh., U.S. B2 128
North Liberty, Ia., U.S. . . . C6 108
North Liberty, In., U.S. . . . A5 107
North Lima, Oh., U.S. B5 128
North Little Rock, Ar., U.S. . C3 97
North Logan, Ut., U.S. . . . B4 137
North Loon Mountain, mtn.,
  Id., U.S. D3 105
North Magnetic Pole D33 144
North Mamm Peak, mtn.,
  Co., U.S. B3 99
North Manchester, In., U.S. C6 107
North Manitou Island, i.,
  Mi., U.S. C4 115
North Mankato, Mn., U.S. . F4 116
North Miami, Fl., U.S. G6 102
North Miami Beach, Fl.,
  U.S. s13 102
North Middletown, Ky.,
  U.S. B5 110
North Moose Lake, l., Mb.,
  Can. B1 86
North Mountain, mtn., Pa.,
  U.S. D9 131
North Muskegon, Mi., U.S. E4 115
North Myrtle Beach, S.C.,
  U.S. D10 133
North Naples, Fl., U.S. . . . F5 102
North New River Canal, Fl.,
  U.S. F6 102
North Ogden, Ut., U.S. . . . B4 137
North Olmsted, Oh., U.S. . . h9 128
North Ossetia see Severnaja
  Osetija, state, Russia . . . E6 26
North Palisade, mtn., Ca.,
  U.S. D4 98
North Park, Il., U.S. A4 106
North Park, val., Co., U.S. . A4 99
North Pass, strt., La., U.S. . E7 111
North Pembroke, Ma., U.S. B6 114
North Plainfield, N.J., U.S. . B4 123
North Plains, Or., U.S. B4 130
North Plains, pl., N.M., U.S. C1 124
North Platte, Ne., U.S. . . . C5 120
North Platte, stm., U.S. . . . C7 92
North Point, c., Md., U.S. . . B5 113
North Point, c., Mi., U.S. . . C7 115
North Pole E12 144
Northport, Al., U.S. B2 94
North Prairie, Wi., U.S. . . . F5 142
North Providence, R.I., U.S. C4 132
North Raccoon, stm., Ia.,
  U.S. C3 108
North Reading, Ma., U.S. . . f11 114
North Richland Hills, Tx.,
  U.S. n9 136
Northridge, Oh., U.S. C2 128
North Ridgeville, Oh., U.S. . A3 128
North Royalton, Oh., U.S. . h9 128
North Rustico, P.E., Can. . . C6 87
North Salem, N.H., U.S. . . . E4 122
North Salt Lake, Ut., U.S. . . C4 137
North Santee, stm., S.C.,
  U.S. E9 133
North Saskatchewan, stm.,
  Can. H18 82
North Schell Peak, mtn.,
  Nv., U.S. D7 121
North Scituate, Ma., U.S. . . h12 114
North Sea, Eur. D6 6
North Shore City, N.Z. o13 63c
North Shoshone Peak, mtn.,
  Nv., U.S. D4 121

Name	Map Ref.	Page

North Siberian Lowland see
Severo-Sibirskaja
nizmennost', pl., Russia **B11** 26
North Sioux City, S.D., U.S. **E9** 134
North Skunk, stm., Ia., U.S. **C5** 108
North Springfield, Vt., U.S. **E3** 138
North Springfield Reservoir,
res., Vt., U.S. **E4** 138
North Star, De., U.S. **A3** 101
North St. Paul, Mn., U.S. **m13** 116
North Stradbroke Island, i.,
Austl. **F5** 62
North Stratford, N.H., U.S. **A3** 122
North Sudbury, Ma., U.S. **g10** 114
North Swanzey, N.H., U.S. **E2** 122
North Syracuse, N.Y., U.S. **B4** 125
North Taranaki Bight, b.,
N.Z. **o13** 63c
North Tarrytown, N.Y., U.S. **D7** 125
North Terre Haute, In., U.S. **E3** 107
North Thompson, stm.,
B.C., Can. **D8** 85
North Tonawanda, N.Y.,
U.S. **B2** 125
North Troy, Vt., U.S. **B4** 138
North Tunica, Ms., U.S. **A3** 117
North Twin Lake, l., Wi.,
U.S. **B4** 142
Northumberland, Pa., U.S. **E8** 131
Northumberland, co., Pa.,
U.S. **D8** 131
Northumberland, co., Va.,
U.S. **C6** 139
Northumberland Strait, strt.,
Can. **C6** 87
North Umpqua, stm., Or.,
U.S. **D3** 130
North Uxbridge, Ma., U.S. **B4** 114
Northvale, N.J., U.S. **g9** 123
North Vancouver, B.C.,
Can. **E6** 85
North Vassalboro, Me., U.S. **D3** 112
North Vernon, In., U.S. **F6** 107
Northville, Mi., U.S. **p15** 115
North Wales, Pa., U.S. **F11** 131
North Walpole, N.H., U.S. **D2** 122
North Warren, Pa., U.S. **C3** 131
North Webster, In., U.S. **B6** 107
North West Cape, c., Austl. **E1** 60
Northwest Miramichi, stm.,
N.B., Can. **B3** 87
Northwest Pacific Basin **E18** 64
Northwest Territories, ter.,
Can. **E15** 82
North Wildwood, N.J., U.S. **E3** 123
North Wilkesboro, N.C.,
U.S. **A1** 126
North Windham, Ct., U.S. **C7** 100
North Windham, Me., U.S. **E2** 112
Northwood, Ia., U.S. **A4** 108
Northwood, N.D., U.S. **B8** 127
North Woodstock, N.H.,
U.S. **B3** 122
North York, On., Can. **D5** 89
North York, Pa., U.S. **G8** 131
Norton, N.B., Can. **D4** 87
Norton, Ks., U.S. **C4** 109
Norton, Ma., U.S. **C5** 114
Norton, Oh., U.S. **A4** 128
Norton, Va., U.S. **f9** 139
Norton, co., Ks., U.S. **C4** 109
Norton Bay, b., Ak., U.S. **C7** 95
Norton Pond, l., Vt., U.S. **B5** 138
Norton Reservoir, res., Ks.,
U.S. **C3** 109
Norton Shores, Mi., U.S. **E4** 115
Norton Sound, strt., Ak.,
U.S. **C6** 95
Nortonville, Ks., U.S. **C8** 109
Nortonville, Ky., U.S. **C2** 110
Norvegia, Cape, c., Ant. **C3** 95
Norwalk, Ca., U.S. **n12** 98
Norwalk, Ct., U.S. **E2** 100
Norwalk, Ia., U.S. **C4** 108
Norwalk, Oh., U.S. **A3** 128
Norwalk, stm., Ct., U.S. **E2** 100
Norwalk Islands, is., Ct.,
U.S. **E2** 100
Norway, Me., U.S. **D2** 112
Norway, Mi., U.S. **C3** 115
Norway, ctry., Eur. **B9** 4
Norway House, Mb., Can. **C3** 86
Norway Lake, l., Mn., U.S. **E3** 116
Norwegian Basin **C23** 144
Norwegian Sea, Eur. **I22** 10a
Norwich, Eng., U.K. **D7** 12
Norwich, Ct., U.S. **C7** 100
Norwich, N.Y., U.S. **C5** 125
Norwich, Vt., U.S. **D4** 138
Norwood, On., Can. **C7** 89
Norwood, Ma., U.S. **B5** 114
Norwood, Mn., U.S. **F5** 116
Norwood, N.C., U.S. **B2** 126
Norwood, N.J., U.S. **h9** 123
Norwood, N.Y., U.S. **f10** 125
Norwood, Oh., U.S. **o13** 128
Norwood, Pa., U.S. **p20** 131
Norwoodville, Ia., U.S. **e8** 108
Noshiro, Japan **C16** 28
Nosivka, Ukr. **D11** 20
Nossob, stm., Afr. **C2** 56
Nosy-Varika, Madag. **C8** 56
Notasulga, Al., U.S. **C4** 94
Notch Peak, mtn., Ut., U.S. **D2** 137
Noteć, stm., Pol. **C4** 20

Notodden, Nor. **G3** 10
Noto-hantō, pen., Japan **C3** 31
Notre Dame, Monts, mts.,
P.Q., Can. **k13** 90
Notre Dame Bay, b., Nf.,
Can. **D4** 88
Notre Dame de Lourdes,
Mb., Can. **E2** 86
Notre-Dame-du-Lac, P.Q.,
Can. **B9** 90
Nottawasaga Bay, b., On.,
Can. **C4** 89
Nottaway, stm., P.Q., Can. **h11** 90
Nottingham, Eng., U.K. **D6** 12
Nottoway, co., Va., U.S. **C4** 139
Nottoway, stm., Va., U.S. **D5** 139
Nouâdhibou, Maur. **B1** 50
Nouâdhibou, Râs, c., Afr. **B1** 50
Nouakchott, Maur. **C1** 50
Nouâmghâr, Maur. **C1** 50
Nouméa, N. Cal. **I9** 62a
Noupoort, S. Afr. **E3** 56
Nouveau-Brunswick see
New Brunswick, prov.,
Can. **C3** 87
Nouvelle-Calédonie, i., N.
Cal. **I9** 62a
Nova Caipemba, Ang. **E2** 54
Nova Friburgo, Braz. **F3** 74
Nova Iguaçu, Braz. **F3** 74
Novaja Kazanka, Kaz. **E8** 22
Novaja Sibir', ostrov, i.,
Russia **B17** 26
Novaja Zemlja, is., Russia **B7** 26
Nova Kakhovka, Ukr. **F12** 20
Nova Lima, Braz. **F3** 74
Nova Lisboa see Huambo,
Ang. **F3** 54
Nova Mambone, Moz. **C6** 56
Novara, Italy **B2** 18
Novato, Ca., U.S. **C2** 98
Nova Scotia, prov., Can. **D6** 87
Nova Venécia, Braz. **E3** 74
Novaya Zemlya see Novaja
Zemlja, is., Russia **B7** 26
Nova Zagora, Bul. **C11** 18
Nové Zámky, Slvk. **E5** 20
Novgorod, Russia **D5** 26
Novhorod-Sivers'kyi, Ukr. **D12** 20
Novi, Mi., U.S. **p15** 115
Novikovo, Russia **A4** 31
Novi Ligure, Italy **B2** 18
Novi Pazar, Bul. **C11** 18
Novi Pazar, Yugo. **C8** 18
Novi Sad, Yugo. **B7** 18
Novo Aripuanã, Braz. **E7** 70
Novoazovs'k, Ukr. **F15** 20
Novočerkassk, Russia **E7** 22
Novodvinsk, Russia **B7** 22
Novo Hamburgo, Braz. **D7** 72
Novohrad-Volyns'kyi, Ukr. **D9** 20
Novokazalinsk, Kaz. **E8** 26
Novokujbyševsk, Russia **D8** 22
Novokuzneck, Russia **D10** 26
Novomihajlovskij, Russia **G15** 20
Novomoskovsk, Russia **D5** 26
Novomoskovs'k, Ukr. **E13** 20
Novomyrhorod, Ukr. **E11** 20
Novorossijsk, Russia **E5** 26
Novošahtinsk, Russia **F15** 20
Novosergievka, Russia **D9** 22
Novosibirsk, Russia **D10** 26
Novosibirskie ostrova, is.,
Russia **B16** 26
Novotroick, Russia **D10** 22
Novotroickoe, Russia **B10** 42
Novotroïts'ke, Ukr. **F13** 20
Novoukraïnka, Ukr. **E11** 20
Novouzensk, Russia **D8** 22
Novovjatsk, Russia **C8** 22
Novovolyns'k, Ukr. **D8** 20
Novozybkov, Russia **C11** 20
Novyi Buh, Ukr. **F12** 20
Novyj Oskol, Russia **D14** 20
Novyj Port, Russia **C9** 26
Novyj Uzen', Kaz. **E7** 26
Nowa Ruda, Pol. **D4** 20
Nowata, Ok., U.S. **A6** 129
Nowata, co., Ok., U.S. **A6** 129
Nowood, stm., Wy., U.S. **B5** 143
Nowra, Austl. **G5** 62
Nowshāk, mtn., Asia **B2** 40
Nowy Dwór Mazowiecki,
Pol. **C6** 20
Nowy Sącz, Pol. **E6** 20

Nueces, stm., Tx., U.S. **E3** 136
Nueltin Lake, l., Can. **F20** 82
Nueva Antioquia, Col. **D6** 80
Nueva Gerona, Cuba **A3** 80
Nueva Imperial, Chile **E2** 69
Nueva Italia de Ruiz, Mex. **D4** 78
Nueva Rosita, Mex. **B4** 78
Nueve de Julio, Arg. **F5** 72
Nuevitas, Cuba **A4** 80
Nuevo, Cayo, i., Mex. **C6** 78
Nuevo, Golfo, b., Arg. **F4** 69
Nuevo Casas Grandes, Mex. **A3** 78
Nuevo Laredo, Mex. **B5** 78
Nuevo León, state, Mex. **B5** 78
Nui, atoll, Tuvalu **E11** 58
Nukuʻalofa, Tonga **G12** 58
Nukus, Uzb. **E7** 26
Nulato, Ak., U.S. **C8** 95
Nulhegan, stm., Vt., U.S. **B5** 138
Nullagine, Austl. **E3** 60
Nullarbor, Austl. **G5** 60
Nullarbor Plain, pl., Austl. **G4** 60
Numan, Nig. **E7** 50
Numancia, hist., Spain **G5** 16
Numazu, Japan **D3** 31
Nunivak Island, i., Ak., U.S. **D6** 95
Nunjiang, China **B13** 28
Nuoro, Italy **D2** 18
Nuremberg, Pa., U.S. **E9** 131
Nurmes, Fin. **E13** 10
Nürnberg, Ger. **F12** 12
Nusaybin, Tur. **D9** 44
Nu Shan, mts., China **F7** 28
Nushki, Pak. **E9** 42
Nutley, N.J., U.S. **B4** 123
Nutter Fort, W.V., U.S. **k10** 141
Nutting Lake, Ma., U.S. **f10** 114
Nuuanu Pali, Hi., U.S. **g10** 104
Nuuk see Godthåb, Grnld. **F29** 82
Nyabing, Austl. **G2** 60
Nyack, N.Y., U.S. **D7** 125
Nyaingêntanglha Shan, mts.,
China **E6** 28
Nyakanazi, Tan. **D6** 54
Nyala, Sudan **H10** 48
Nyamlell, Sudan **B5** 54
Nyanza-Lac, Bdi. **D5** 54
Nyasa, Lake (Malaŵi, Lake),
l., Afr. **F6** 54
Nyasaland see Malawi, ctry.,
Afr. **A5** 56
Nyaunglebin, Myan. **C3** 34
Nyborg, Den. **I4** 10
Nybro, Swe. **H6** 10
Nyda, Russia **C9** 26
Nye, co., Nv., U.S. **E5** 121
Nyeri, Kenya **D7** 54
Nyimba, Zam. **A5** 56
Nyingchi, China **D6** 40
Nyíregyháza, Hung. **F6** 20
Nykøbing, Den. **I4** 10
Nyköping, Swe. **G7** 10
Nylstroom, S. Afr. **C4** 56
Nynäshamn, Swe. **G7** 10
Nyngan, Austl. **G4** 62
Nyš, Russia **D16** 26
Nysa, Pol. **D4** 20
Nyssa, Or., U.S. **D9** 130
Nyunzu, D.R.C. **E5** 54
Nzébéla, Gui. **E3** 50
Nzérékoré, Gui. **E3** 50
N'zeto, Ang. **E2** 54
Nzwani, i., Com. **A7** 56

O

Oahe, Lake, res., U.S. **B7** 92
Oahe Dam, S.D., U.S. **C5** 134
Oahu, i., Hi., U.S. **B4** 104
Oak Bay, B.C., Can. **h12** 85
Oak Bluffs, Ma., U.S. **D6** 114
Oak Creek, Co., U.S. **A4** 99
Oak Creek, Wi., U.S. **n12** 142
Oakdale, Ca., U.S. **D3** 98
Oakdale, Ga., U.S. **h8** 103
Oakdale, La., U.S. **D3** 111
Oakdale, Pa., U.S. **k13** 131
Oakes, N.D., U.S. **C7** 127
Oakfield, N.Y., U.S. **B2** 125
Oakfield, Wi., U.S. **E5** 142
Oak Forest, Il., U.S. **k9** 106
Oak Grove, Ky., U.S. **D2** 110
Oak Grove, La., U.S. **B4** 111
Oak Grove, Or., U.S. **B4** 130
Oak Harbor, Oh., U.S. **A2** 128
Oak Harbor, Wa., U.S. **A3** 140
Oak Hill, Mi., U.S. **D4** 115
Oak Hill, Oh., U.S. **D3** 128
Oak Hill, W.V., U.S. **D3** 141
Oak Hill, mtn., Ma., U.S. **f9** 114
Oakhurst, Ok., U.S. **A5** 129
Oak Island, i., Wi., U.S. **B3** 142
Oak Lake, l., Mb., Can. **E1** 86
Oakland, Ca., U.S. **D2** 98
Oakland, Ia., U.S. **C2** 108
Oakland, Il., U.S. **D5** 106
Oakland, Md., U.S. **m12** 113
Oakland, Me., U.S. **D3** 112
Oakland, Ne., U.S. **C9** 120
Oakland, N.J., U.S. **A4** 123
Oakland, Ok., U.S. **C5** 129
Oakland, R.I., U.S. **B2** 132
Oakland, co., Mi., U.S. **F7** 115
Oakland City, In., U.S. **H3** 107

Oakland Park, Fl., U.S. **r13** 102
Oak Lawn, Il., U.S. **B6** 106
Oaklawn, Ks., U.S. **g12** 109
Oakley, Id., U.S. **G5** 105
Oakley, Ks., U.S. **C3** 109
Oakman, Al., U.S. **B2** 94
Oakmont, Pa., U.S. **E2** 131
Oak Mountain, mtn., Ga.,
U.S. **D2** 103
Oak Orchard, De., U.S. **F5** 101
Oak Park, Il., U.S. **B6** 106
Oak Park, Mi., U.S. **p15** 115
Oak Ridge, N.C., U.S. **A3** 126
Oakridge, Or., U.S. **D4** 130
Oak Ridge, Tn., U.S. **C9** 135
Oak Ridge Reservoir, res.,
N.J., U.S. **A3** 123
Oakton, Va., U.S. **g12** 139
Oaktown, In., U.S. **G3** 107
Oak Valley, N.J., U.S. **D2** 123
Oakville, On., Can. **D5** 89
Oakville, Ct., U.S. **C3** 100
Oakville, Mo., U.S. **g13** 118
Oakwood, Ga., U.S. **B3** 103
Oakwood, Il., U.S. **C6** 106
Oakwood, Oh., U.S. **C1** 128
Oamaru, N.Z. **q13** 63c
Oaxaca, state, Mex. **D5** 78
Oaxaca de Juárez, Mex. **D5** 78
Ob', stm., Russia **B9** 26
Oban, Scot., U.K. **B4** 12
Ob Bay see Obskaja guba,
b., Russia **C9** 26
Obed, stm., Tn., U.S. **C9** 135
Oberlin, Ks., U.S. **C3** 109
Oberlin, La., U.S. **D3** 111
Oberlin, Oh., U.S. **A3** 128
Obetz, Oh., U.S. **C3** 128
Obi, Kepulauan, is., Indon. **D7** 36
Obi, Pulau, i., Indon. **D7** 36
Obi, Selat, strt., Indon. **D7** 36
Óbidos, Braz. **D8** 70
Obihiro, Japan **C16** 28
Obion, Tn., U.S. **A2** 135
Obion, co., Tn., U.S. **A2** 135
Obion, stm., Tn., U.S. **A2** 135
Oblong, Il., U.S. **D6** 106
Obluče, Russia **B14** 28
Obninsk, Russia **B14** 20
Obo, C.A.R. **B5** 54
Obojan', Russia **D14** 20
O'Brien, co., Ia., U.S. **A2** 108
Obščij syrt, mts., Eur. **D9** 22
Observation Peak, mtn.,
Ca., U.S. **B3** 98
Obskaja guba, b., Russia **C9** 26
Obuasi, Ghana **E4** 50
Obudu, Nig. **E6** 50
Ocala, Fl., U.S. **C4** 102
Ocaña, Col. **B5** 70
Ocaña, Spain **H5** 16
Occidental, Cordillera, mts.,
Col. **E4** 80
Occidental, Cordillera, mts.,
Peru **E4** 70
Ocean, co., N.J., U.S. **D4** 123
Oceana, W.V., U.S. **D3** 141
Oceana, co., Mi., U.S. **E4** 115
Oceana Naval Air Station,
mil., Va., U.S. **k15** 139
Ocean Bluff, Ma., U.S. **B6** 114
Ocean City, Fl., U.S. **u15** 102
Ocean City, Md., U.S. **D7** 113
Ocean City, N.J., U.S. **E3** 123
Ocean Grove, Ma., U.S. **C5** 114
Ocean Island see Banaba, i.,
Kir. **E10** 58
Ocean Park, Wa., U.S. **C1** 140
Oceanport, N.J., U.S. **C4** 123
Oceanside, Ca., U.S. **F5** 98
Ocean Springs, Ms., U.S. **E5** 117
Ocean [Township], N.J.,
U.S. **C4** 123
Ocean View, De., U.S. **F5** 101
Ocheda Lake, l., Mn., U.S. **G3** 116
Ocheyedan, stm., Ia., U.S. **A2** 108
Ochiltree, co., Tx., U.S. **A2** 136
Ochlockonee, stm., Fl., U.S. **B2** 102
Ochoco Lake, res., Or., U.S. **C6** 130
Ocilla, Ga., U.S. **E3** 103
Ockelbo, Swe. **F7** 10
Ocmulgee, stm., Ga., U.S. **D3** 103
Ocoa, Bahía de, b., Dom.
Rep. **B5** 80
Ocoee, Fl., U.S. **D5** 102
Ocoee, Lake, res., Tn., U.S. **D9** 135
Oconee, co., Ga., U.S. **C3** 103
Oconee, co., S.C., U.S. **B1** 133
Oconee, stm., Ga., U.S. **D3** 103
Oconee, Lake, res., Ga.,
U.S. **C3** 103
Oconomowoc, Wi., U.S. **E5** 142
Oconto, Wi., U.S. **D6** 142
Oconto, co., Wi., U.S. **D5** 142
Oconto, stm., Wi., U.S. **D5** 142
Oconto Falls, Wi., U.S. **D5** 142
Ocosingo, Mex. **D6** 78
Ocotal, Nic. **C2** 80
Ocotlán, Mex. **C4** 78

October Revolution Island
see Oktjabr'skoj
Revoljucii, ostrov, i.,
Russia **B11** 26
Octoraro Creek, stm., U.S. **A5** 113
Ocumare del Tuy, Ven. **C6** 80
Oda, Ghana **E4** 50
Oda, Jabal, mtn., Sudan **F12** 48
Odebolt, Ia., U.S. **B2** 108
Odell, Il., U.S. **B5** 106
Odell, Or., U.S. **B5** 130
Odell Lake, l., Or., U.S. **E5** 130
Odem, Tx., U.S. **F4** 136
Odemira, Port. **I2** 16
Ödemiş, Tur. **C2** 44
Odendaalsrus, S. Afr. **D4** 56
Odense, Den. **I4** 10
Odenton, Md., U.S. **B4** 113
Odenville, Al., U.S. **B3** 94
Oder, stm., Eur. **C3** 20
Odesa, Ukr. **F11** 20
Odessa, Ont., Can. **C8** 89
Odessa see Odesa, Ukr. **F11** 20
Odessa, De., U.S. **C3** 101
Odessa, Mo., U.S. **C4** 118
Odessa, Tx., U.S. **D1** 136
Odessa, Wa., U.S. **B7** 140
Odienné, C. Iv. **E3** 50
Odin, Il., U.S. **E4** 106
Odon, In., U.S. **G4** 107
O'Donnell, Tx., U.S. **C2** 136
Odorheiu Secuiesc, Rom. **F8** 20
Oeiras, Braz. **C3** 74
Oelwein, Ia., U.S. **B6** 108
Oenpelli, Austl. **C5** 60
Of, Tur. **B9** 44
O'Fallon, Il., U.S. **E4** 106
O'Fallon, Mo., U.S. **f12** 118
Ofanto, stm., Italy **D5** 18
Offa, Nig. **E5** 50
Offenburg, Ger. **F10** 12
Offutt Air Force Base, mil.,
Ne., U.S. **g3** 120
Ofotfjorden, b., Nor. **B7** 10
Ogaden, reg., Afr. **I14** 48
Ogallala, Ne., U.S. **C4** 120
Ogasawara-guntō, is., Japan **F16** 64
Ogbomosho, Nig. **E5** 50
Ogden, Ia., U.S. **B3** 108
Ogden, Ks., U.S. **C7** 109
Ogden, Ut., U.S. **B4** 137
Ogden, Mount, mtn., N.A. **k23** 95
Ogdensburg, N.J., U.S. **A3** 123
Ogdensburg, N.Y., U.S. **f9** 125
Ogeechee, stm., Ga., U.S. **D5** 103
Ogemaw, co., Mi., U.S. **D6** 115
Ogle, co., Il., U.S. **A4** 106
Oglesby, Il., U.S. **B4** 106
Oglethorpe, Ga., U.S. **D2** 103
Oglethorpe, co., Ga., U.S. **C3** 103
Oglethorpe, Mount, mtn.,
Ga., U.S. **B2** 103
Ogoja, Nig. **E6** 50
Ogooué, stm., Afr. **D2** 54
Ogre, Lat. **H11** 10
Ogunquit, Me., U.S. **E2** 112
Ogurdžaly, ostrov, i., Turk. **C6** 42
Oha, Russia **D16** 26
Ohanet, Alg. **E6** 48
Ohatchee, Al., U.S. **B3** 94
Ohio, co., In., U.S. **G7** 107
Ohio, co., Ky., U.S. **C3** 110
Ohio, co., W.V., U.S. **A4** 141
Ohio, state, U.S. **B3** 128
Ohio, stm., U.S. **D10** 92
Ohio Brush Creek, stm.,
Oh., U.S. **D2** 128
Ohio City, Oh., U.S. **B1** 128
Ohio Peak, mtn., Co., U.S. **C3** 99
Ohioville, Pa., U.S. **E1** 131
Ohoopee, stm., Ga., U.S. **D4** 103
Ohotsk, Russia **D16** 26
Ohrid, Mac. **D8** 18
Ohrid, Lake, l., Eur. **C8** 14
Oiapoque, Braz. **C9** 70
Oiapoque (Oyapok), stm.,
S.A. **C9** 70
Oil City, La., U.S. **B2** 111
Oil City, Pa., U.S. **D2** 131
Oil Creek, stm., Pa., U.S. **C2** 131
Oildale, Ca., U.S. **E4** 98
Oil Springs, On., Can. **E2** 89
Oilton, Ok., U.S. **A5** 129
Oise, stm., Eur. **C8** 16
Ōita, Japan **E14** 28
Ojai, Ca., U.S. **E4** 98
Ojinaga, Mex. **B4** 78
Ojmjakon, Russia **D16** 26
Ojocaliente, Mex. **C4** 78
Ojos del Salado, Cerro see
Ojos del Salado,
Nevado, mtn., S.A. **D4** 72
Ojos del Salado, Nevado,
mtn., S.A. **D4** 72
Oka, stm., Russia **D6** 26
Okaba, Indon. **H10** 32
Okahandja, Nmb. **C2** 56
Okaloosa, co., Fl., U.S. **u15** 102
Okamanpeedan Lake, l.,
U.S. **A3** 108
Okanagan Falls, B.C., Can. **E8** 85
Okanagan Lake, l., B.C.,
Can. **D8** 85
Okanagan Landing, B.C.,
Can. **D8** 85

Name	Map Ref.	Page
Okanogan, Wa., U.S.	A6	140
Okanogan, co., Wa., U.S.	A5	140
Okāra, Pak.	D10	42
Okarche, Ok., U.S.	B4	129
Okatibee Reservoir, res., Ms., U.S.	C5	117
Okaukuejo, Nmb.	B2	56
Okavango (Cubango), stm., Afr.	B3	56
Okavango Delta, Bots.	B3	56
Okawville, Il., U.S.	E4	106
Okaya, Japan	C3	31
Okayama, Japan	E14	28
Okazaki, Japan	D3	31
Okeechobee, Fl., U.S.	E6	102
Okeechobee, co., Fl., U.S.	E6	102
Okeechobee, Lake, l., Fl., U.S.	F6	102
Okeene, Ok., U.S.	A3	129
Okefenokee Swamp, sw., U.S.	F4	103
Okemah, Ok., U.S.	B5	129
Okene, Nig.	E6	50
Okfuskee, co., Ok., U.S.	B5	129
Okhotsk see Ohotsk, Russia	D16	26
Okhotsk, Sea of, Asia	D16	26
Okhotsk Basin	B7	144
Okhtyrka, Ukr.	D13	20
Okinawa, Japan	g6	31a
Okinawa-jima, i., Japan	A9	34
Okinawa-shotō, is., Japan	g6	31a
Okino-Erabu-shima, i., Japan	A9	34
Okino-Tori-shima, i., Japan	G15	28
Oki-shotō, is., Japan	D14	28
Okitipupa, Nig.	E5	50
Oklahoma, co., Ok., U.S.	B4	129
Oklahoma, state, U.S.	B4	129
Oklahoma City, Ok., U.S.	B4	129
Oklawaha, Fl., U.S.	C5	102
Oklawaha, stm., Fl., U.S.	C5	102
Oklawaha, Lake, res., Fl., U.S.	C5	102
Okmulgee, Ok., U.S.	B6	129
Okmulgee, co., Ok., U.S.	B5	129
Okoboji, Ia., U.S.	A2	108
Okobojo Creek, stm., S.D., U.S.	C5	134
Okolona, Ky., U.S.	g11	110
Okolona, Ms., U.S.	B5	117
Okondja, Gabon	D2	54
Okotoks, Ab., Can.	D4	84
Oktibbeha, co., Ms., U.S.	B5	117
Oktjabr'sk, Russia	E7	26
Oktjabr'skij, Russia	D9	22
Oktjabr'skoe, Russia	B12	22
Oktjabr'skoj Revoljucii, ostrov, i., Russia	B11	26
Oktwin, Myan.	C3	34
Okushiri-tō, i., Japan	C15	28
Ola, Ar., U.S.	B2	97
Ólafsfjörður, Ice.	k19	10a
Olancha Peak, mtn., Ca., U.S.	D4	98
Olanchito, Hond.	B2	80
Öland, i., Swe.	H7	10
Olanta, S.C., U.S.	D8	133
Olathe, Co., U.S.	C3	99
Olathe, Ks., U.S.	D9	109
Olavarría, Arg.	F5	72
Olbia, Italy	D2	18
Olcott, N.Y., U.S.	B2	125
Old Bahama Channel, strt., N.A.	A4	80
Old Bridge, N.J., U.S.	C4	123
Old Castile see Castilla la Vieja, hist. reg., Spain	G5	16
Oldenburg, Ger.	D11	12
Oldenburg, In., U.S.	F7	107
Oldenburg in Holstein, Ger.	C12	12
Old Faithful Geyser, Wy., U.S.	B2	143
Old Forge, Pa., U.S.	D10	131
Old Fort, N.C., U.S.	f10	126
Oldham, co., Ky., U.S.	B4	110
Oldham, co., Tx., U.S.	B1	136
Old Harbor, Ak., U.S.	D9	95
Old Hickory Lake, res., Tn., U.S.	A5	135
Oldman, stm., Ab., Can.	E4	84
Old Man of the Mountain, N.H., U.S.	B3	122
Oldmans Creek, stm., N.J., U.S.	D2	123
Old Orchard Beach, Me., U.S.	E2	112
Old Perlican, Nf., Can.	D5	88
Old Point Comfort, c., Va., U.S.	h15	139
Old Rhodes Key, i., Fl., U.S.	G6	102
Old River Lake, l., Ar., U.S.	k10	97
Olds, Ab., Can.	D3	84
Old Saybrook, Ct., U.S.	D6	100
Oldsmar, Fl., U.S.	o10	102
Old Tampa Bay, b., Fl., U.S.	p10	102
Old Tappan, N.J., U.S.	g9	123
Old Tate, Bots.	C4	56
Old Topsail Inlet, b., N.C., U.S.	C5	126
Old Town, Me., U.S.	D4	112
Old Wives Lake, l., Sk., Can.	G2	91
Olean, N.Y., U.S.	C2	125
O'Leary, P.E., Can.	C5	87
Olëkma, stm., Russia	C14	26
Olekminsk, Russia	C14	26
Oleksandriia, Ukr.	E12	20
Olenegorsk, Russia	B15	10
Olenëk, Russia	C13	26
Olenëk, stm., Russia	B13	26
Olenëkskij zaliv, b., Russia	B14	26
Olentangy, stm., Oh., U.S.	B3	128
Oléron, Île d', i., Fr.	E6	16
Olevsk, Ukr.	D9	20
Ol'ga, Russia	E15	26
Olga, Mount, mtn., Austl.	F5	60
Ölgiy, Mong.	B6	28
Olhão, Port.	I3	16
Olifants (Elefantes), stm., Afr.	C4	56
Olifants, stm., Nmb.	C2	56
Olifantshoek, S. Afr.	D3	56
Ólimbos, mtn., Cyp.	E5	44
Ólimbos, Óros, mtn., Grc.	D9	18
Olin, Ia., U.S.	B6	108
Olinda, Braz.	C5	74
Olive Branch, Ms., U.S.	A4	117
Olive Hill, Ky., U.S.	B6	110
Olivehurst, Ca., U.S.	C3	98
Oliveira, Braz.	D7	74
Oliver, B.C., Can.	E8	85
Oliver, Pa., U.S.	G2	131
Oliver, co., N.D., U.S.	B4	127
Oliver Dam, U.S.	C5	94
Oliver Springs, Tn., U.S.	C9	135
Olivet, Mi., U.S.	F6	115
Olivia, Mn., U.S.	F4	116
Oljutorskij, mys, c., Russia	D19	26
Olla, La., U.S.	C3	111
Ollagüe, Chile	B3	69
Olmito, Tx., U.S.	F4	136
Olmos, Peru	A2	70
Olmos Park, Tx., U.S.	k7	136
Olmsted, co., Mn., U.S.	G6	116
Olmsted Falls, Oh., U.S.	h9	128
Olney, Il., U.S.	E5	106
Olney, Md., U.S.	B3	113
Olney, Tx., U.S.	C3	136
Olomouc, Czech Rep.	E4	20
Olonec, Russia	B5	22
Olongapo, Phil.	D8	34
Olot, Spain	F8	16
Olovjannaja, Russia	A11	28
Olsztyn, Pol.	C6	20
Oltenița, Rom.	G9	20
Olton, Tx., U.S.	B1	136
Oltu, Tur.	B10	44
Olustee, Ok., U.S.	C2	129
Olympia, Wa., U.S.	B3	140
Olympic Mountains, mts., Wa., U.S.	B2	140
Olympic National Park, Wa., U.S.	B2	140
Olympus see Ólimbos, mtn., Cyp.	E5	44
Olympus, Mount see Ólimbos, Óros, mtn., Grc.	D9	18
Olympus, Mount, mtn., Wa., U.S.	B2	140
Olyphant, Pa., U.S.	D10	131
Omagh, N. Ire., U.K.	C3	12
Omaha, Ne., U.S.	C10	120
Omaha Indian Reservation, Ne., U.S.	B9	120
Omak, Wa., U.S.	A6	140
Omak Lake, l., Wa., U.S.	A6	140
Oman, ctry., Asia	G7	38
Oman, Gulf of, b., Asia	F7	42
Omar, W.V., U.S.	D3	94
Omarama, N.Z.	p12	63c
Omaruru, Nmb.	C2	56
Omatako, stm., Nmb.	B2	56
Ombai, Selat, strt., Indon.	E7	36
Omboué, Gabon	D1	54
Omčak, Russia	C16	26
Omdurman see Umm Durmān, Sudan	G11	48
Omega, Ga., U.S.	E3	103
Omemee, On., Can.	C6	89
Omerville, P.Q., Can.	D5	90
Ometepe, Isla de, i., Nic.	C2	80
Ometepec, Mex.	D5	78
Omineca, stm., B.C., Can.	B5	85
Omineca Mountains, mts., B.C., Can.	A4	85
Ōmiya, Japan	C3	31
Ommaney, Cape, c., Ak., U.S.	D12	95
Omolon, stm., Russia	C17	26
Ompompanoosuc, stm., Vt., U.S.	D4	138
Omro, Wi., U.S.	D5	142
Omsk, Russia	D9	26
Omsukčan, Russia	C17	26
Ōmuda (Ōmuta), Japan	E14	28
Ōmura, Japan	D1	31
Ōmuta (Ōmuda), Japan	E14	28
Omutninsk, Russia	C9	22
Onaga, Ks., U.S.	C7	109
Onalaska, Wa., U.S.	C3	140
Onalaska, Wi., U.S.	E2	142
Onamia, Mn., U.S.	D5	116
Onancock, Va., U.S.	C7	139
Onarga, Il., U.S.	C6	106
Onawa, Ia., U.S.	B1	108
Onawa, Lake, l., Me., U.S.	C3	112
Onaway, Mi., U.S.	C6	115
Ondangwa, Nmb.	B2	56
Ondjiva, Ang.	B2	56
Ondo, Nig.	E5	50
Öndörhaan, Mong.	B10	28
Oneco, Fl., U.S.	E4	102
Onega, Russia	C5	26
Onega, stm., Russia	B6	22
Onega, Lake see Onežskoe ozero, l., Russia	C5	26
Onega Bay see Onežskaja guba, b., Russia	B6	22
One Hundred Fifty Mile House, B.C., Can.	C7	85
One Hundred Mile House, B.C., Can.	D7	85
Oneida, Ky., U.S.	C6	110
Oneida, N.Y., U.S.	B5	125
Oneida, Oh., U.S.	C1	128
Oneida, Tn., U.S.	C9	135
Oneida, co., Id., U.S.	G6	105
Oneida, co., N.Y., U.S.	B5	125
Oneida, co., Wi., U.S.	C4	142
Oneida Lake, l., N.Y., U.S.	B5	125
O'Neill, Ne., U.S.	B7	120
Onekotan, ostrov, i., Russia	E17	26
Oneonta, Al., U.S.	B3	94
Oneonta, N.Y., U.S.	C5	125
Onești, Rom.	F9	20
Onežskaja guba, b., Russia	B6	22
Onežskoe ozero, l., Russia	C5	26
Ongole, India	F4	40
Onida, S.D., U.S.	C5	134
Onitsha, Nig.	E6	50
Onondaga, co., N.Y., U.S.	C4	125
Onondaga Indian Reservation, N.Y., U.S.	C4	125
Onota Lake, l., Ma., U.S.	B1	114
Onoway, Ab., Can.	C3	84
Onseepkans, S. Afr.	D2	56
Onset, Ma., U.S.	C6	114
Onslow, Austl.	E1	60
Onslow, co., N.C., U.S.	C5	126
Onslow Bay, b., N.C., U.S.	C5	126
Onsted, Mi., U.S.	F6	115
Ontario, Ca., U.S.	E5	98
Ontario, Oh., U.S.	B3	128
Ontario, Or., U.S.	C10	130
Ontario, co., N.Y., U.S.	C3	125
Ontario, prov., Can.	C6	89
Ontario, Lake, l., N.A.	C12	92
Ontinyent, Spain	H6	16
Ontonagon, Mi., U.S.	m12	115
Ontonagon, co., Mi., U.S.	m12	115
Ontonagon Indian Reservation, Mi., U.S.	B1	115
Oodnadatta, Austl.	F2	62
Ooldea, Austl.	G5	60
Oolitic, In., U.S.	G4	107
Oologah, Ok., U.S.	A6	129
Oologah Lake, res., Ok., U.S.	A6	129
Ooltewah, Tn., U.S.	D8	135
Oostburg, Wi., U.S.	E6	142
Oostende, Bel.	E8	12
Ootsa Lake, l., B.C., Can.	C4	85
Opala, D.R.C.	D4	54
Opa-Locka, Fl., U.S.	s13	102
Opava, Czech Rep.	E4	20
Opelika, Al., U.S.	C4	94
Opelousas, La., U.S.	D3	111
Opequon Creek, stm., W.V., U.S.	B6	141
Opobo, Nig.	F6	50
Opočka, Russia	H13	10
Opole, Pol.	D4	20
Opotiki, N.Z.	o14	63c
Opp, Al., U.S.	D3	94
Oppdal, Nor.	E3	10
Oppelo, Ar., U.S.	B3	97
Opportunity, Wa., U.S.	B8	140
Optima Reservoir, res., Ok., U.S.	e9	129
Opuwo, Nmb.	B1	56
Oquawka, Il., U.S.	C3	106
Oracle, Az., U.S.	E5	96
Oradea, Rom.	F6	20
Oradell, N.J., U.S.	h8	123
Oradell Reservoir, res., N.J., U.S.	h9	123
Öræfajökull, Ice.	I20	10a
Orai, India	D3	40
Oraibi, Az., U.S.	B5	96
Oran see Wahran, Alg.	C4	48
Oran, Mo., U.S.	D8	118
Oran, Sebkha d', l., Alg.	J6	16
Orange, Austl.	G4	62
Orange, Fr.	E9	16
Orange, Ca., U.S.	n13	98
Orange, Ct., U.S.	D3	100
Orange, Ma., U.S.	A3	114
Orange, N.J., U.S.	B4	123
Orange, Tx., U.S.	D6	136
Orange, Va., U.S.	B4	139
Orange, co., Ca., U.S.	F5	98
Orange, co., Fl., U.S.	D5	102
Orange, co., In., U.S.	G4	107
Orange, co., N.C., U.S.	A3	126
Orange, co., N.Y., U.S.	D6	125
Orange, co., Tx., U.S.	D6	136
Orange, co., Va., U.S.	B4	139
Orange, co., Vt., U.S.	D3	138
Orange (Oranje), stm., Afr.	D2	56
Orange, Cabo, c., Braz.	C9	70
Orange Beach, Al., U.S.	E2	94
Orangeburg, S.C., U.S.	E6	133
Orangeburg, co., S.C., U.S.	E6	133
Orange City, Fl., U.S.	D5	102
Orange City, Ia., U.S.	B1	108
Orange Grove, Ms., U.S.	E5	117
Orange Grove, Tx., U.S.	F4	136
Orange Lake, l., Fl., U.S.	C4	102
Orange Park, Fl., U.S.	B5	102
Orangeville, On., Can.	D4	89
Orangeville, Ut., U.S.	D4	137
Orange Walk, Belize	B2	80
Oranienburg, Ger.	D13	12
Oranje see Orange, stm., Afr.	D2	56
Oranjemund, Nmb.	D2	56
Oranjestad, Aruba	C6	80
Orbetello, Italy	C3	18
Orbost, Austl.	H4	62
Orcas Island, i., Wa., U.S.	A3	140
Orchard City, Co., U.S.	C3	99
Orchard Homes, Mt., U.S.	D2	119
Orchard Park, N.Y., U.S.	C2	125
Orchards, Wa., U.S.	D3	140
Orchard Valley, Wy., U.S.	E8	143
Orcutt, Ca., U.S.	E3	98
Ord, Ne., U.S.	C7	120
Ord, Mount, mtn., Austl.	D4	60
Ordu, Tur.	B7	44
Ordway, Co., U.S.	C7	99
Ordzhonikidze see Vladikavkaz, Russia	I6	26
Ordzhonikidze see Yenakiieve, Ukr.	E15	20
Ordzhonikidze, Ukr.	F13	20
Ordžonikidzeabad, Taj.	C9	42
Oreana, Il., U.S.	D5	106
Örebro, Swe.	G6	10
Oregon, Il., U.S.	A4	106
Oregon, Mo., U.S.	B2	118
Oregon, Oh., U.S.	A2	128
Oregon, Wi., U.S.	F4	142
Oregon, co., Mo., U.S.	E6	118
Oregon, state, U.S.	C6	130
Oregon Caves National Monument, Or., U.S.	E2	130
Oregon City, Or., U.S.	B4	130
Oregon Inlet, b., N.C., U.S.	B7	126
Orehovo-Zuevo, Russia	C6	22
Orel, Russia	D5	26
Orem, Ut., U.S.	C4	137
Ore Mountains see Erzgebirge, mts., Eur.	E9	8
Orenburg, Russia	D7	26
Orense, Arg.	F6	72
Orestiás, Grc.	D11	18
Orfanoú, Kólpos, b., Grc.	D9	18
Orfordville, Wi., U.S.	F4	142
Organ Mountains, mts., N.M., U.S.	E3	124
Organ Pipe Cactus National Monument, Az., U.S.	E3	96
Orgūn, Afg.	D9	42
Orhei, Mol.	F10	20
Orhon, stm., Mong.	A9	28
Oriental, N.C., U.S.	B6	126
Oriental, Cordillera, mts., Col.	D5	80
Oriental, Cordillera, mts., Peru	F5	70
Orikhiv, Ukr.	F13	20
Oriximiná, Braz.	D8	70
Oriola, Spain	H6	16
Orinoco, stm., S.A.	B6	70
Orion, Il., U.S.	B3	106
Orissa, prov., India	E4	40
Oristano, Italy	E2	18
Oristano, Golfo di, b., Italy	E2	18
Orivesi, Fin.	F11	10
Orizaba, Mex.	D5	78
Orkney, S. Afr.	D4	56
Orkney Islands, is., U.K.	A5	12
Orland, Ca., U.S.	C2	98
Orlando, Fl., U.S.	D5	102
Orland Park, Il., U.S.	k9	106
Orléanais, hist. reg., Fr.	C7	16
Orléans, Fr.	D7	16
Orleans, Ma., U.S.	C7	114
Orleans, Vt., U.S.	B4	138
Orleans, co., La., U.S.	E6	111
Orleans, co., N.Y., U.S.	B2	125
Orleans, co., Vt., U.S.	B4	138
Orléans, Île d', i., P.Q., Can.	C6	90
Orlik, Russia	A7	28
Orman Dam, S.D., U.S.	C2	134
Ormāra, Pak.	E8	42
Ormoc, Phil.	D8	34
Ormond Beach, Fl., U.S.	C5	102
Ormstown, P.Q., Can.	D3	90
Örnsköldsvik, Swe.	E8	10
Orocué, Col.	C5	70
Orofino, Id., U.S.	C2	105
Oromocto, N.B., Can.	D3	87
Oromocto Lake, l., N.B., Can.	D2	87
Oron, Nig.	F6	50
Orono, Me., U.S.	D4	112
Oronoco, Mn., U.S.	F6	116
Oroquieta, Phil.	E8	34
Orosei, Golfo di, b., Italy	D3	18
Oroville, Ca., U.S.	C3	98
Oroville, Wa., U.S.	A6	140
Oroville, Lake, res., Ca., U.S.	C3	98
Orrick, Mo., U.S.	B3	118
Orrville, Oh., U.S.	B4	128
Orša, Bela.	B11	20
Orsk, Russia	D7	26
Ortaca, Tur.	D3	44
Ortegal, Cabo, c., Spain	F3	16
Orting, Wa., U.S.	B3	140
Ortiz, Mex.	B2	78
Ortonville, Mi., U.S.	F7	115
Ortonville, Mn., U.S.	E2	116
Orto-Tokoj, Kyrg.	A3	40
Orūmīyeh, Iran	C5	42
Orūmīyeh, Daryācheh-ye, l., Iran	C5	42
Oruro, Bol.	B4	72
Orwell, Oh., U.S.	A5	128
Orwigsburg, Pa., U.S.	E9	131
Oš, Kyrg.	E9	26
Osa, Península de, pen., C.R.	D3	80
Osage, Ia., U.S.	A5	108
Osage, Wy., U.S.	C8	143
Osage, co., Ks., U.S.	D8	109
Osage, co., Mo., U.S.	C6	118
Osage, co., Ok., U.S.	A5	129
Osage, stm., Mo., U.S.	C3	118
Osage Beach, Mo., U.S.	C5	118
Osage City, Ks., U.S.	D8	109
Ōsaka, Japan	E15	28
Osakis, Mn., U.S.	E3	116
Osakis, Lake, l., Mn., U.S.	E3	116
Osawatomie, Ks., U.S.	D9	109
Osborne, Ks., U.S.	C5	109
Osborne, co., Ks., U.S.	C5	109
Osburn, Id., U.S.	B3	105
Osceola, Ar., U.S.	B6	97
Osceola, Ia., U.S.	C4	108
Osceola, In., U.S.	A5	107
Osceola, Mo., U.S.	C4	118
Osceola, Ne., U.S.	C8	120
Osceola, Wi., U.S.	C1	142
Osceola, co., Fl., U.S.	E5	102
Osceola, co., Ia., U.S.	A2	108
Osceola, co., Mi., U.S.	E5	115
Osceola Mills, Pa., U.S.	E5	131
Oscoda, Mi., U.S.	D7	115
Oscoda, co., Mi., U.S.	D6	115
Oscura Mountains, mts., N.M., U.S.	D3	124
Osgood, In., U.S.	F7	107
Oshawa, On., Can.	D6	89
Ō-shima, i., Japan	D3	31
Oshkosh, Ne., U.S.	C3	120
Oshkosh, Wi., U.S.	D5	142
Oshnovīyeh, Iran	D11	44
Oshogbo, Nig.	E5	50
Oshtorīnān, Iran	E13	44
Oshwe, D.R.C.	D3	54
Osijek, Cro.	B7	18
Oskaloosa, Ia., U.S.	C5	108
Oskaloosa, Ks., U.S.	C8	109
Oskarshamn, Swe.	H7	10
Oskū, Iran	D12	44
Oslo, Nor.	G4	10
Oslofjorden, b., Nor.	G4	10
Osmānābād, India	F3	40
Osmancık, Tur.	B6	44
Osmaniye, Tur.	D7	44
Osmond, Ne., U.S.	B8	120
Osnabrück, Ger.	D11	12
Osorno, Chile	F2	69
Osoyoos, B.C., Can.	E8	85
Osoyoos Lake, l., Wa., U.S.	A6	140
Osprey, Fl., U.S.	E4	102
Ossa, Mount, mtn., Austl.	I4	62
Ossabaw Island, i., Ga., U.S.	E5	103
Osseo, Mn., U.S.	m12	116
Osseo, Wi., U.S.	D2	142
Ossian, Ia., U.S.	A6	108
Ossian, In., U.S.	C7	107
Ossining, N.Y., U.S.	D7	125
Ossipee, stm., U.S.	C5	122
Ossipee Lake, l., N.H., U.S.	C4	122
Ossora, Russia	D18	26
Ostaškov, Russia	C5	22
Östersund, Swe.	E6	10
Osterville, Ma., U.S.	C7	114
Ostfriesische Inseln, is., Ger.	D10	12
Ostrava, Czech Rep.	E5	20
Ostróda, Pol.	C5	20
Ostrogožsk, Russia	D15	20
Ostroh, Ukr.	D9	20
Ostrołęka, Pol.	C6	20
Ostrov, Russia	H13	10
Ostrowiec Świętokrzyski, Pol.	D6	20
Ostrów Mazowiecka, Pol.	C6	20
Ostrów Wielkopolski, Pol.	D4	20
Ostuni, Italy	D6	18
Ōsumi-shotō, is., Japan	E14	28
Osuna, Spain	I4	16
Oswegatchie, stm., N.Y., U.S.	f9	125
Oswego, Il., U.S.	B5	106
Oswego, Ks., U.S.	E8	109
Oswego, N.Y., U.S.	B4	125
Oswego, co., N.Y., U.S.	B4	125
Oswego, stm., N.J., U.S.	D4	123
Oswego, stm., N.Y., U.S.	B4	125
Otanmäki, Fin.	D12	10
Otaru, Japan	C16	28
Otava, Russia	F12	10
Otavi, Nmb.	B2	56
Oteen, N.C., U.S.	f10	126
Otero, co., Co., U.S.	D7	99

Name	Map Ref.	Page

Otero, co., N.M., U.S. **E3** 124
Othello, Wa., U.S. **C6** 140
Otis Orchards, Wa., U.S. . . **g14** 140
Otis Reservoir, res., Ma.,
  U.S. **B1** 114
Otisville, Mi., U.S. **E7** 115
Otjikondo, Nmb. **B2** 56
Otjiwarongo, Nmb. **C2** 56
Otoe, co., Ne., U.S. **D9** 120
Otra, stm., Nor. **G2** 10
Otradnyj, Russia **D9** 22
Ótranto, Italy **D7** 18
Ótranto, Strait of, strt., Eur. **C7** 14
Otsego, Mi., U.S. **F5** 115
Otsego, co., Mi., U.S. **C6** 115
Otsego, co., N.Y., U.S. . . . **C5** 125
Otsego Lake, l., N.Y., U.S. **C6** 125
Ōtsu, Japan 31
Ottauquechee, stm., Vt.,
  U.S. **D4** 138
Ottawa, On., Can. **B9** 89
Ottawa, Il., U.S. **B5** 106
Ottawa, Ks., U.S. **D8** 109
Ottawa, Oh., U.S. **A1** 128
Ottawa, co., Ks., U.S. **C6** 109
Ottawa, co., Mi., U.S. **F4** 115
Ottawa, co., Oh., U.S. . . . **A2** 128
Ottawa, co., Ok., U.S. . . . **A7** 129
Ottawa, stm., Can. **I24** 82
Ottawa, stm., Oh., U.S. . . . **e6** 128
Ottawa Hills, Oh., U.S. . . . **e6** 128
Ottenby, Swe. **H7** 10
Otterbein, In., U.S. **D3** 107
Otter Brook, stm., N.H.,
  U.S. **E2** 122
Otter Brook Lake, res.,
  N.H., U.S. **E2** 122
Otter Creek, stm., Ut., U.S. **E4** 137
Otter Creek, stm., Vt., U.S. **C2** 138
Otter Creek Reservoir, res.,
  Ut., U.S. **E4** 137
Otter Islands, is., S.C., U.S. **m11** 133
Otter Tail, co., Mn., U.S. . . **D3** 116
Otter Tail, stm., Mn., U.S. . **D2** 116
Otter Tail Lake, l., Mn., U.S. **D3** 116
Otterville, On., Can. **E4** 89
Ottumwa, Ia., U.S. **C5** 108
Otway, Cape, c., Austl. . . . **H3** 62
Otwock, Pol. **C6** 20
Ouachita, co., La., U.S. . . . **D3** 97
Ouachita, co., La., U.S. . . . **B3** 111
Ouachita, Lake, res., Ar.,
  U.S. **C2** 97
Ouachita Mountains, mts.,
  U.S. **E9** 92
Ouadda, C.A.R. **B4** 54
Ouagadougou, Burkina . . . **D4** 50
Ouahigouya, Burkina **D4** 50
Ouahran see Wahran, Alg. . **C4** 50
Oualâta, Maur. **C3** 50
Ouallam, Niger **D5** 50
Ouallene, Alg. **F5** 48
Ouanda Djallé, C.A.R. **B4** 54
Ouangolodougou, C. Iv. . . **E3** 50
Ouarâne, reg., Maur. **B2** 50
Ouarzazate, Mor. **D3** 48
Oubangui (Ubangi), stm.,
  Afr. **D3** 54
Oudtshoorn, S. Afr. **E3** 56
Oued Rhiou, Alg. **J7** 16
Oued-Zem, Mor. **E2** 14
Ouellé, C. Iv. **E4** 50
Ouémé, stm., Benin **E5** 50
Ouessant, Île d', i., Fr. . . . **C4** 16
Ouesso, Congo **C3** 54
Ouezzane, Mor. **D3** 48
Ouham, stm., Afr. **B3** 54
Ouidah, Benin **E5** 50
Oujda, Mor. **D4** 48
Oulu, Fin. **D11** 10
Oulujärvi, l., Fin. **D12** 10
Oulujoki, stm., Fin. **D12** 10
Oum-Chalouba, Chad **G9** 48
Oumé, C. Iv. **E3** 50
Ounianga Kébir, Chad **G9** 48
Ouray, Co., U.S. **C3** 99
Ouray, co., Co., U.S. **C3** 99
Ouray, Mount, mtn., Co.,
  U.S. **C4** 99
Ourense, Spain **F3** 16
Ouricuri, Braz. **C3** 74
Ourinhos, Braz. **F2** 74
Ouro Preto, Braz. **F3** 74
Outagamie, co., Wi., U.S. . **D5** 142
Outardes Quatre, Réservoir,
  res., P.Q., Can. **h13** 90
Outer Hebrides, is., Scot.,
  U.K. **B3** 12
Outer Island, i., Wi., U.S. . **A3** 142
Outer Santa Barbara
  Passage, strt., Ca., U.S. **F4** 98
Outjo, Nmb. **C2** 56
Outpost Mountain, mtn.,
  Ak., U.S. **B9** 95
Outremont, P.Q., Can. . . . **p19** 90
Ouvéa, i., N. Cal. **l9** 62a
Ouyen, Austl. **H3** 62
Ovalle, Chile **D2** 69
Overbrook, Ks., U.S. **D8** 109
Overgaard, Az., U.S. **C5** 96
Overland, Mo., U.S. **f13** 118
Overland Park, Ks., U.S. . . **m16** 109
Overlea, Md., U.S. **B4** 113
Overton, Nv., U.S. **G7** 121
Overton, Tx., U.S. **C5** 136

Overton, co., Tn., U.S. **C8** 135
Ovett, Ms., U.S. **D4** 117
Ovid, Mi., U.S. **E6** 115
Oviedo, Spain **F4** 16
Ovoot, Mong. **B10** 28
Ovruch, Ukr. **D10** 20
Owando, Congo **D3** 54
Owasco Lake, l., N.Y., U.S. **C4** 125
Owasso, Ok., U.S. **A6** 129
Owatonna, Mn., U.S. **F5** 116
Owego, N.Y., U.S. **C4** 125
Owen, Wi., U.S. **D3** 142
Owen, co., In., U.S. **F4** 107
Owen, co., Ky., U.S. **B5** 110
Owen, Lake, l., Wi., U.S. . . **B2** 142
Owen, Mount, mtn., Co.,
  U.S. **C3** 99
Owendo, Gabon **C1** 54
Owens, stm., Ca., U.S. . . . **D4** 98
Owensboro, Ky., U.S. **C2** 110
Owens Cross Roads, Al.,
  U.S. **A3** 94
Owens Lake, l., Ca., U.S. . . **D5** 98
Owen Sound, On., Can. . . . **C4** 89
Owen Sound, b., On., Can. **C4** 89
Owen Stanley Range, mts.,
  Pap. N. Gui. **H12** 32
Owensville, In., U.S. **H2** 107
Owensville, Mo., U.S. **C6** 118
Owensville, Oh., U.S. **C1** 128
Owenton, Ky., U.S. **B5** 110
Owerri, Nig. **E6** 50
Owings Mills, Md., U.S. . . . **B4** 113
Owingsville, Ky., U.S. **B6** 110
Owl Creek, stm., Wy., U.S. **C4** 143
Owl Creek Mountains, mts.,
  Wy., U.S. **C4** 143
Owo, Nig. **E6** 50
Owosso, Mi., U.S. **E6** 115
Owsley, co., Ky., U.S. **C6** 110
Owyhee, Nv., U.S. **B5** 121
Owyhee, co., Id., U.S. **G2** 105
Owyhee, stm., U.S. **E9** 130
Owyhee, Lake, res., Or.,
  U.S. **D9** 130
Owyhee Dam, Or., U.S. . . . **D9** 130
Owyhee Mountains, mts.,
  U.S. **G2** 105
Oxbow Dam, U.S. **E2** 105
Oxelösund, Swe. **G7** 10
Oxford, N.S., Can. **D6** 87
Oxford, Eng., U.K. **E6** 12
Oxford, Al., U.S. **B4** 94
Oxford, Ct., U.S. **D3** 100
Oxford, Ga., U.S. **C3** 103
Oxford, Ia., U.S. **C6** 108
Oxford, In., U.S. **C3** 107
Oxford, Ks., U.S. **E6** 109
Oxford, Ma., U.S. **B4** 114
Oxford, Md., U.S. **C5** 113
Oxford, Me., U.S. **D2** 112
Oxford, Mi., U.S. **F7** 115
Oxford, Ms., U.S. **A4** 117
Oxford, N.C., U.S. **A4** 126
Oxford, Ne., U.S. **D6** 120
Oxford, N.Y., U.S. **C5** 125
Oxford, Oh., U.S. **C1** 128
Oxford, Pa., U.S. **G10** 131
Oxford, co., Me., U.S. **D2** 112
Oxford Lake, l., Mb., Can. . **B4** 86
Oxford Peak, mtn., Id., U.S. **G6** 105
Oxnard, Ca., U.S. **E4** 98
Oxon Hill, Md., U.S. **f9** 113
Oxus see Amu Darya, stm.,
  Asia **B8** 42
Oyama, B.C., Can. **D8** 85
Oyapok (Oiapoque), stm.,
  S.A. **C9** 70
Oyem, Gabon **C2** 54
Oyen, Ab., Can. **D5** 84
Oyo, Nig. **E5** 50
Oyster Bay, N.Y., U.S. **E7** 125
Oyster Keys, is., Fl., U.S. . **G6** 102
Ozamis, Phil. **E8** 34
Ozark, Al., U.S. **D4** 94
Ozark, Ar., U.S. **B2** 97
Ozark, Mo., U.S. **D4** 118
Ozark, co., Mo., U.S. **E5** 118
Ozark Plateau, plat., U.S. . **D9** 92
Ozark Reservoir, res., Ar.,
  U.S. **B1** 97
Ozarks, Lake of the, res.,
  Mo., U.S. **C5** 118
Ozaukee, co., Wi., U.S. . . . **E6** 142
Ózd, Hung. **E6** 20
Ozernovskij, Russia **D17** 26
Ozërnyj, Russia **D11** 22
Ozette Lake, l., Wa., U.S. . **A1** 140
Ozieri, Italy **D2** 18
Ozinki, Russia **D8** 22
Ozona, Fl., U.S. **o10** 102
Ozona, Tx., U.S. **D2** 136
Ozurgeti, Geor. **B10** 44

P

Paarl, S. Afr. **E2** 56
Paauilo, Hi., U.S. **C6** 104
Pabianice, Pol. **D5** 20
Pābna, Bngl. **E5** 40
Pacajus, Braz. **B4** 74
Pacasmayo, Peru **E4** 70
Pace, Fl., U.S. **u14** 102
Pachacamac, hist., Peru . . **A2** 72
Pachaug Pond, l., Ct., U.S. **C8** 100

Pachino, Italy **F5** 18
Pachuca de Soto, Mex. . . . **C5** 78
Pacific, Mo., U.S. **C7** 118
Pacific, Wa., U.S. **f11** 140
Pacific, co., Wa., U.S. **C2** 140
Pacifica, Ca., U.S. **h8** 98
Pacific-Antarctic Ridge . . **O22** 64
Pacific Beach, Wa., U.S. . . **B1** 140
Pacific City, Or., U.S. **B3** 130
Pacific Creek, stm., Wy.,
  U.S. **D3** 143
Pacific Grove, Ca., U.S. . . **D3** 98
Pacific Ocean **E20** 64
Pacific Palisades, Hi., U.S. **g10** 104
Pacific Ranges, mts., B.C.,
  Can. **D4** 85
Pacific Rim National Park,
  B.C., Can. **E5** 85
Pack Monadnock Mountain,
  mtn., N.H., U.S. **E3** 122
Packwood, Wa., U.S. **C4** 140
Pacolet, S.C., U.S. **B4** 133
Pacolet, stm., S.C., U.S. . . **A4** 133
Pacolet Mills, S.C., U.S. . . **B4** 133
Pactola Reservoir, res., S.D.,
  U.S. **C2** 134
Padang, Indon. **D2** 36
Padangpanjang, Indon. . . . **D2** 36
Padangsidempuan, Indon. . **C1** 36
Paddock Lake, Wi., U.S. . . **n11** 142
Paden City, W.V., U.S. . . . **B4** 141
Paderborn, Ger. **E11** 12
Padma see Ganges, stm.,
  Asia **D5** 40
Pádova, Italy **B3** 18
Padrauna, India **D4** 40
Padre Island, i., Tx., U.S. . **F4** 136
Padre Island National
  Seashore, Tx., U.S. . . . **F4** 136
Padua see Pádova, Italy . . **B3** 18
Paducah, Ky., U.S. **e9** 110
Paducah, Tx., U.S. **B2** 136
Paektu, Mount, mtn., Asia **C13** 28
Paektu-san see Paektu,
  Mount, mtn., Asia **C13** 28
Paestum, hist., Italy **D5** 18
Pafúri, Moz. **C5** 56
Pag, Otok, i., Cro. **B5** 18
Pagadian, Phil. **E8** 34
Pagai Selatan, Pulau, i.,
  Indon. **D2** 36
Pagai Utara, Pulau, i.,
  Indon. **D2** 36
Pagalu see Annobón, i., Eq.
  Gui. **C1** 52
Pagan, i., N. Mar. Is. **C12** 32
Pagasitikós Kólpos, b., Grc. **E9** 18
Page, Az., U.S. **A4** 96
Page, W.V., U.S. **C3** 141
Page, co., Ia., U.S. **D2** 108
Page, co., Va., U.S. **B4** 139
Pageland, S.C., U.S. **B7** 133
Pagoda Peak, mtn., Co.,
  U.S. **A3** 99
Pago Pago, Am. Sam. . . **F12** 58
Pagosa Springs, Co., U.S. . **D3** 99
Paguate, N.M., U.S. **B2** 124
Pahala, Hi., U.S. **D6** 104
Pahang, stm., Malay. **C2** 36
Pahoa, Hi., U.S. **D7** 104
Pahokee, Fl., U.S. **F6** 102
Pahrump, Nv., U.S. **G6** 121
Pahute Mesa, mtn., Nv.,
  U.S. **F5** 121
Paia, Hi., U.S. **C5** 104
Paide, Est. **G11** 10
Päijänne, l., Fin. **F11** 10
Pailolo Channel, strt., Hi.,
  U.S. **B5** 104
Painan, Indon. **D2** 36
Paincourtville, La., U.S. . . . **k9** 111
Painesville, Oh., U.S. **A4** 128
Paint, stm., Mi., U.S. **B2** 115
Paint Creek, stm., Oh., U.S. **C2** 128
Paint Creek, stm., W.V.,
  U.S. **m13** 141
Paint Creek, North Fork,
  stm., Oh., U.S. **C2** 128
Paint Creek Lake, res., Oh.,
  U.S. **C2** 128
Painted Desert, des., Az.,
  U.S. **B4** 96
Painted Post, N.Y., U.S. . . **C3** 125
Painted Rock Reservoir,
  res., Az., U.S. **D3** 96
Paintsville, Ky., U.S. **C7** 110
Paisley, On., Can. **C3** 89
Pajala, Swe. **C10** 10
Pakaraima Mountains, mts.,
  S.A. **E9** 70
Pakistan, ctry., Asia **E9** 42
Pakistan, East see
  Bangladesh, ctry., Asia . **B2** 34
Pakokku, Myan. **B3** 34
Pakowki Lake, l., Ab., Can. **E5** 84
Pak Phanang, Thai. **E4** 34
Paks, Hung. **F5** 20
Pakxé, Laos **C5** 34
Pala, Chad **E7** 50
Palacios, Tx., U.S. **E4** 136
Palana, Russia **D17** 26
Palangkaraya, Indon. **D4** 36
Palani, India **G3** 40
Pālanpur, India **E2** 40
Palaoa Point, c., Hi., U.S. . **C4** 104

Palapye, Bots. **C4** 56
Palatine, Il., U.S. **A5** 106
Palatka, Fl., U.S. **C5** 102
Palau, ctry., Oc. **F10** 32
Palau Islands, is., Palau . . **E9** 32
Palaw, Myan. **D3** 34
Palawan, i., Phil. **E7** 34
Palawan Passage, strt., Phil. **E7** 34
Pālayankottai, India **H3** 40
Paldiski, Est. **G11** 10
Palembang, Indon. **D2** 36
Palencia, Spain **F4** 16
Palenque, hist., Mex. **D6** 78
Palermo, Italy **E4** 18
Palestine, Ar., U.S. **C5** 97
Palestine, Il., U.S. **D6** 106
Palestine, Tx., U.S. **D5** 136
Palestine, hist. reg., Asia . **G6** 44
Palestine, Lake, res., Tx.,
  U.S. **C5** 136
Paletwa, Myan. **B2** 34
Pālghāt, India **G3** 40
Pāli, India **D2** 40
Palikea, mtn., Hi., U.S. . . . **g9** 104
Palisade, Co., U.S. **B2** 99
Palisades Park, N.J., U.S. . **h8** 123
Palisades Reservoir, res.,
  U.S. **F7** 105
Pālitāna, India **E2** 40
Palk Strait, strt., Asia **H3** 40
Palliser, Cape, c., N.Z. . . **p14** 63c
Palma, Moz. **A7** 56
Palma del Río, Spain **I4** 16
Palma de Mallorca, Spain . **H8** 16
Palmares, Braz. **C4** 74
Palma Soriano, Cuba **A4** 80
Palm Bay, Fl., U.S. **D6** 102
Palm Beach, Fl., U.S. **F6** 102
Palm Beach, co., Fl., U.S. . **F6** 102
Palmdale, Ca., U.S. **E4** 98
Palmeira das Missões, Braz. **D7** 72
Palmeira dos Índios, Braz. **C4** 74
Palmer, Ak., U.S. **C10** 95
Palmer, Ma., U.S. **B3** 114
Palmer, Mi., U.S. **B3** 115
Palmer, Ms., U.S. **D4** 117
Palmer, Ne., U.S. **C7** 120
Palmer, Tn., U.S. **D8** 135
Palmer, Tx., U.S. **n10** 136
Palmer Land, reg., Ant. . . **D34** 67
Palmerston, On., Can. . . . **D4** 89
Palmerston, atoll, Cook Is. **F13** 58
Palmerston North, N.Z. . . **p14** 63c
Palmerton, Pa., U.S. **E10** 131
Palmetto, Fl., U.S. **E4** 102
Palmetto, Ga., U.S. **C2** 103
Palm Harbor, Fl., U.S. . . **o10** 102
Palmi, Italy **E5** 18
Palmira, Col. **C4** 70
Palms, Isle of, i., S.C., U.S. **F8** 133
Palm Springs, Ca., U.S. . . **F5** 98
Palmyra see Tudmur, Syria **E8** 44
Palmyra, In., U.S. **H5** 107
Palmyra, Mo., U.S. **B6** 118
Palmyra, N.J., U.S. **C2** 123
Palmyra, N.Y., U.S. **B3** 125
Palmyra, Pa., U.S. **F8** 131
Palmyra, Wi., U.S. **F5** 142
Palmyra, hist., Syria **E8** 44
Palo Alto, Ca., U.S. **D2** 98
Palo Alto, co., Ia., U.S. . . . **A3** 108
Paloich, Sudan **H11** 48
Palomar Mountain, mtn.,
  Ca., U.S. **F5** 98
Palomas Mountains, mts.,
  Az., U.S. **D2** 96
Palo Pinto, co., Tx., U.S. . **C3** 136
Palopo, Indon. **D6** 36
Palo Santo, Arg. **D6** 72
Palos Park, Il., U.S. **k9** 106
Palos Verdes Estates, Ca.,
  U.S. **n12** 98
Palourde, Lake, l., La., U.S. **k9** 111
Palouse, Wa., U.S. **C8** 140
Palouse, stm., Wa., U.S. . . **C7** 140
Palu, Indon. **D5** 36
Palu, Tur. **C8** 44
Pamekasan, Indon. **E4** 36
Pamiers, Fr. **F7** 16
Pamir, mts., Asia **B2** 40
Pamlico, co., N.C., U.S. . . **B6** 126
Pamlico, stm., N.C., U.S. . **B6** 126
Pamlico Sound, strt., N.C.,
  U.S. **B6** 126
Pampa, Tx., U.S. **B2** 136
Pampa, reg., Arg. **F5** 72
Pampa del Infierno, Arg. . . **D5** 72
Pampas, Peru **A3** 72
Pamplico, S.C., U.S. . . . • . **D8** 133
Pamplona, Col. **B5** 70
Pamplona, Spain **F6** 16
Pamunkey, stm., Va., U.S. . **C5** 139
Pana, Il., U.S. **D4** 106
Panaca, Nv., U.S. **F7** 121
Panache, Lake, l., On., Can. **A3** 89
Panaji, India **F2** 40
Panamá, Pan. **D4** 80
Panama, Ok., U.S. **B7** 129
Panama, ctry., N.A. **I11** 75
Panamá, Bahía de, b., Pan. **D4** 80
Panamá, Canal de, Pan. . . **D4** 80
Panamá, Golfo de, b., Pan. **D4** 80

Panama, Gulf of see
  Panamá, Golfo de, b.,
  Pan. **D4** 80
Panamá, Istmo de, Pan. . . **D4** 80
Panama Basin **H30** 64
Panama Canal see Panamá,
  Canal de, Pan. **D4** 80
Panama City see Panamá,
  Pan. **D4** 80
Panama City, Fl., U.S. . . **u16** 102
Panama City Beach, Fl., U.S. **u16** 102
Panamint Range, mts., Ca.,
  U.S. **D5** 98
Panay, i., Phil. **D8** 34
Pancake Range, mts., Nv.,
  U.S. **E6** 121
Pančevo, Yugo. **B8** 18
Pandharpur, India **F3** 40
Pandora, Oh., U.S. **B2** 128
Panfilov, Kaz. **E9** 26
Pangala, Congo **D2** 54
Pangani, Tan. **E7** 54
Pangburn, Ar., U.S. **B4** 97
Pangi, D.R.C. **D5** 54
Pangkajene, Indon. **D5** 36
Pangkalanbuun, Indon. . . . **D4** 36
Pangkalpinang, Indon. . . . **D3** 36
Pango Aluquem, Ang. **E2** 54
Panguitch, Ut., U.S. **F3** 137
Pangutaran Group, is., Phil. **E7** 34
Panhandle, Tx., U.S. **B2** 136
Paniau, mtn., Hi., U.S. . . . **B1** 104
Panié, Mont, mtn., N. Cal. . **l8** 62a
Panīpāt, India **D3** 40
Panj see Amu Darya, stm.,
  Asia **B8** 42
Panjang, Indon. **E3** 36
Panjgūr, Pak. **E8** 42
Pankshin, Nig. **E6** 50
Panna, India **E4** 40
Pannawonica, Austl. **E2** 60
Panola, co., Ms., U.S. **A3** 117
Panola, co., Tx., U.S. **C5** 136
Panora, Ia., U.S. **C3** 108
Pantar, Pulau, i., Indon. . . **E6** 36
Pantelleria, Isola di, i., Italy **F3** 18
Pánuco, Mex. **C5** 78
Pánuco, stm., Mex. **C5** 78
Panxian, China **F8** 28
Panyam, Nig. **E6** 50
Panyu, China **B6** 34
Paola, Italy **E5** 18
Paola, Ks., U.S. **D9** 109
Paoli, In., U.S. **G5** 107
Paoli, Pa., U.S. **o20** 131
Paonia, Co., U.S. **C3** 99
Pápa, Hung. **F4** 20
Papagayo, Golfo de, b.,
  C.R. **C2** 80
Papago Indian Reservation,
  Az., U.S. **E3** 96
Papaikou, Hi., U.S. **D6** 104
Papantla de Olarte, Mex. . **C5** 78
Papawai Point, c., Hi., U.S. **C5** 104
Papeete, Fr. Poly. **F15** 58
Papenburg, Ger. **D10** 12
Paphos see Néa Páfos, Cyp. **E5** 44
Papigochic, stm., Mex. . . . **B3** 78
Papillion, Ne., U.S. **C9** 120
Papineauville, P.Q., Can. . **D2** 90
Paposo, Chile **C3** 72
Papua, Gulf of, b., Pap. N.
  Gui. **H11** 32
Papua New Guinea, ctry.,
  Oc. **H11** 32
Papun, Myan. **C3** 34
Pará see Belém, Braz. **B2** 74
Pará, state, Braz. **E9** 70
Parabel', Russia **D10** 26
Paraburdoo, Austl. **E2** 60
Paracatu, Braz. **E2** 74
Paracel Islands (Xisha
  Qundao), is., China . . . **C6** 34
Parachute, Co., U.S. **B2** 99
Paraćin, Yugo. **C8** 18
Paracuru, Braz. **B4** 74
Paradis, La., U.S. **k11** 111
Paradise, Ca., U.S. **C3** 98
Paradise, Nv., U.S. **G6** 121
Paradise, stm., Nf., Can. . . **B3** 88
Paradise Hills, N.M., U.S. . **B3** 124
Paradise Valley, Az., U.S. . **k9** 96
Paradise Valley, Nv., U.S. . **B4** 121
Pāradwīp, India **E5** 40
Paragould, Ar., U.S. **A5** 97
Paraguá (Paraguay), stm.,
  S.A. **B6** 72
Paraguaná, Península de,
  pen., Ven. **C6** 80
Paraguay, ctry., S.A. **C6** 72
Paraguay (Paraguai), stm.,
  S.A. **C6** 72
Paraíba, state, Braz. **C4** 74
Paraíba do Sul, stm., Braz. **F3** 74
Parakou, Benin **E5** 50
Paramaribo, Sur. **B8** 70
Paramirim, Braz. **F11** 70
Paramount, Md., U.S. **A2** 113
Paramus, N.J., U.S. **h8** 123
Paramušir, ostrov, i., Russia **D17** 26
Paraná, Arg. **E5** 72
Paraná, Braz. **F10** 70
Paraná, state, Braz. **C7** 72
Paraná, stm., Braz. **F5** 68
Paraná, stm., S.A. **E6** 72

Name	Map Ref.	Page
Paranaguá, Braz.	D8	72
Paranaíba, Braz.	E2	74
Paranapanema, stm., Braz.	C7	72
Paranavaí, Braz.	C7	72
Parang, Phil.	E8	34
Parangaba, Braz.	B4	74
Paranhos, Braz.	C6	72
Paray-le-Monial, Fr.	D9	16
Pārbati, stm., India	D3	40
Parbhani, India	F3	40
Parchment, Mi., U.S.	F5	115
Pardeeville, Wi., U.S.	E4	142
Pardo, stm., Braz.	F2	74
Pardubice, Czech Rep.	E3	20
Parecis, Braz.	A6	72
Parecis, Chapada dos, mts., Braz.	A6	72
Paren', Russia	C18	26
Parepare, Indon.	D5	36
Paria, stm., U.S.	A4	96
Paria, Gulf of, b.	C7	80
Pariaman, Indon.	D2	36
Parigi, Indon.	D6	36
Parika, Guy.	B8	70
Paris, On., Can.	D4	89
Paris, Fr.	C8	16
Paris, Ar., U.S.	B2	97
Paris, Il., U.S.	D6	106
Paris, Ky., U.S.	B5	110
Paris, Mo., U.S.	B5	118
Paris, Tn., U.S.	A3	135
Paris, Tx., U.S.	C5	136
Paris Peak, mtn., Id., U.S.	G7	105
Parita, Bahía de, b., Pan.	D3	80
Park, co., Co., U.S.	B5	99
Park, co., Mt., U.S.	E6	119
Park, co., Wy., U.S.	B3	143
Park, stm., N.D., U.S.	A8	127
Park City, Ks., U.S.	g12	109
Park City, Ut., U.S.	C4	137
Parkdale, P.E., Can.	C6	87
Parke, co., In., U.S.	E3	107
Parker, Az., U.S.	C1	96
Parker, Co., U.S.	B6	99
Parker, Fl., U.S.	u16	102
Parker, S.D., U.S.	D8	134
Parker, co., Tx., U.S.	C4	136
Parker City, In., U.S.	D7	107
Parker Dam, U.S.	C1	96
Parkersburg, Ia., U.S.	B5	108
Parkersburg, W.V., U.S.	B3	141
Parkers Prairie, Mn., U.S.	D3	116
Parkes, Austl.	G4	62
Parkesburg, Pa., U.S.	G10	131
Park Falls, Wi., U.S.	C3	142
Park Forest, Il., U.S.	B6	106
Park Hall, Md., U.S.	D5	113
Parkhill, On., Can.	D3	89
Park Hills, Ky., U.S.	h13	110
Parkin, Ar., U.S.	B5	97
Parkland, Wa., U.S.	f11	140
Park Layne, Oh., U.S.	C1	128
Park Range, mts., Co., U.S.	A4	99
Park Rapids, Mn., U.S.	D3	116
Park Ridge, Il., U.S.	B6	106
Park Ridge, N.J., U.S.	g8	123
Park River, N.D., U.S.	A8	127
Parkrose, Or., U.S.	B4	130
Parksley, Va., U.S.	C7	139
Parkston, S.D., U.S.	D8	134
Parksville, B.C., Can.	E5	85
Parkville, Md., U.S.	B4	113
Parkville, Mo., U.S.	B3	118
Parkwater, Wa., U.S.	g14	140
Parkwood, N.C., U.S.	B4	126
Parlãkimidi, India	F4	40
Parle, Lac qui, l., Mn., U.S.	E3	116
Parlier, Ca., U.S.	D4	98
Parma, Italy	B3	18
Parma, Id., U.S.	F2	105
Parma, Mi., U.S.	F6	115
Parma, Mo., U.S.	E8	118
Parma, Oh., U.S.	A4	128
Parmachenee Lake, l., Me., U.S.	C2	112
Parma Heights, Oh., U.S.	h9	128
Parmer, co., Tx., U.S.	B1	136
Parnaguá, Braz.	F11	70
Parnaíba, Braz.	B3	74
Parnaíba, stm., Braz.	B3	74
Parnassós, mtn., Grc.	E9	18
Pärnu, Est.	G11	10
Paro, Bhu.	D5	40
Paromaj, Russia	D16	26
Parowan, Ut., U.S.	F3	137
Par Pond, res., S.C., U.S.	D5	133
Parral, Chile	F3	72
Parramatta, Austl.	G5	62
Parramore Island, i., Va., U.S.	C7	139
Parras de la Fuente, Mex.	B4	78
Parrish, Al., U.S.	B2	94
Parrsboro, N.S., Can.	D5	87
Parry, Mount, mtn., B.C., Can.	C3	85
Parry Sound, On., Can.	B4	89
Parshall, N.D., U.S.	B3	127
Parsons, Ks., U.S.	E8	109
Parsons, Tn., U.S.	B3	135
Parsons, W.V., U.S.	B5	141
Parsonsburg, Md., U.S.	D7	113
Parthenay, Fr.	D6	16
Partille, Swe.	H5	10
Partizansk, Russia	B2	31
Partridge Point, c., Nf., Can.	C3	88
Paru, stm., Braz.	D9	70
Paru de Oeste, stm., Braz.	C8	70
Pārvatīpuram, India	F4	40
Paryang, China	C4	40
Parys, S. Afr.	D4	56
Pasadena, Nf., Can.	D3	88
Pasadena, Ca., U.S.	E4	98
Pasadena, Md., U.S.	B4	113
Pasadena, Tx., U.S.	r14	136
Pascagoula, Ms., U.S.	E5	117
Pascagoula, stm., Ms., U.S.	E5	117
Pascagoula Bay, b., Ms., U.S.	f8	117
Paşcani, Rom.	F9	20
Pasco, Wa., U.S.	C6	140
Pasco, co., Fl., U.S.	D4	102
Pascoag, R.I., U.S.	B2	132
Pascoag Reservoir, res., R.I., U.S.	B2	132
Pascua, Isla de (Easter Island), i., Chile	K28	64
Pasinler, Tur.	B9	44
Pasir Mas, Malay.	B2	36
Pasni, Pak.	E8	42
Paso de los Libres, Arg.	D6	72
Paso de los Toros, Ur.	E6	72
Paso Robles, Ca., U.S.	E3	98
Pasque Island, i., Ma., U.S.	D6	114
Pasquotank, co., N.C., U.S.	A6	126
Passaic, N.J., U.S.	B4	123
Passaic, co., N.J., U.S.	A4	123
Passaic, stm., N.J., U.S.	h8	123
Passamaquoddy Bay, b., Me., U.S.	C6	112
Passau, Ger.	F13	12
Pass Christian, Ms., U.S.	E4	117
Passero, Capo, c., Italy	F5	18
Passo Fundo, Braz.	D7	72
Passos, Braz.	F2	74
Passumpsic, stm., Vt., U.S.	C4	138
Pastavy, Bela.	B9	20
Pastaza, stm., S.A.	D4	70
Pasto, Col.	C4	70
Pastora Peak, mtn., Az., U.S.	A6	96
Pasuruan, Indon.	E4	36
Pasvalys, Lith.	H11	10
Patadkal, hist., India	F3	40
Patagonia, Az., U.S.	F5	96
Patagonia, reg., Arg.	F3	69
Pātan, India	E2	40
Patapsco, stm., Md., U.S.	B4	113
Pataskala, Oh., U.S.	C3	128
Patchet Brook Reservoir, res., R.I., U.S.	E6	132
Patchogue, N.Y., U.S.	n15	125
Pategi, Nig.	E6	50
Pate Island, i., Kenya	D8	54
Paterna, Spain	H6	16
Paternò, Italy	F5	18
Paterson, N.J., U.S.	B4	123
Pathānkot, India	C3	40
Pathein, Myan.	C2	34
Pathfinder Reservoir, res., Wy., U.S.	D6	143
Patiāla, India	C3	40
Patience Island, i., R.I., U.S.	D5	132
Patman, Lake, res., Tx., U.S.	C5	136
Patna, India	D5	40
Patnos, Tur.	C10	44
Pato Branco, Braz.	D7	72
Patoka, In., U.S.	H2	107
Patoka, stm., In., U.S.	H2	107
Patoka Lake, res., In., U.S.	H4	107
Patos, Braz.	E11	74
Patos, Lagoa dos, b., Braz.	E7	72
Patos de Minas, Braz.	E2	74
Patquía, Arg.	D4	72
Pátrai, Grc.	E8	18
Patraïkós Kólpos, b., Grc.	E8	18
Patrick, co., Va., U.S.	D2	139
Patrick Air Force Base, mil., Fl., U.S.	D6	102
Patrocínio, Braz.	E2	74
Pattani, Thai.	E4	34
Patten, Me., U.S.	C4	112
Patterson, Ga., U.S.	E4	103
Patterson, La., U.S.	E4	111
Patterson Creek, stm., W.V., U.S.	B5	141
Patton, Pa., U.S.	E4	131
Patuãkhāli, Bngl.	E6	40
Patuca, stm., Hond.	B3	80
Patuxent, stm., Md., U.S.	D4	113
Patuxent Naval Air Test Center, mil., Md., U.S.	D5	113
Pátzcuaro, Mex.	H8	78
Pau, Fr.	F6	16
Paul, Id., U.S.	G5	105
Paulding, Oh., U.S.	A1	128
Paulding, co., Ga., U.S.	C2	103
Paulding, co., Oh., U.S.	A1	128
Paulina, La., U.S.	h10	111
Paulina Mountains, mts., Or., U.S.	D5	130
Paulina Peak, mtn., Or., U.S.	E5	130
Paulins Kill, stm., N.J., U.S.	A3	123
Paulistana, Braz.	E11	70
Paullina, Ia., U.S.	B2	108
Paulo Afonso, Braz.	C4	74
Paulsboro, N.J., U.S.	D2	123
Paul Stream, stm., Vt., U.S.	B5	138
Pauls Valley, Ok., U.S.	C4	129
Paungde, Myan.	C3	34
Pāveh, Iran	E12	44
Pavia, Italy	B2	18
Pavilion Key, i., Fl., U.S.	G5	102
Pāvilosta, Lat.	H9	10
Pavlodar, Kaz.	D9	26
Pavlof Volcano, vol., Ak., U.S.	D7	95
Pavlohrad, Ukr.	E13	20
Pavlovo, Russia	C7	22
Pavo, Ga., U.S.	F3	103
Pawcatuck, Ct., U.S.	D8	100
Pawcatuck, stm., R.I., U.S.	G1	132
Paw Creek, N.C., U.S.	B2	126
Pawhuska, Ok., U.S.	A5	129
Pawling, N.Y., U.S.	D7	125
Pawnee, Il., U.S.	D4	106
Pawnee, Ok., U.S.	A5	129
Pawnee, co., Ks., U.S.	D4	109
Pawnee, co., Ne., U.S.	D9	120
Pawnee, co., Ok., U.S.	A5	129
Pawnee, stm., Ks., U.S.	D3	109
Pawnee City, Ne., U.S.	D9	120
Pawpaw, Il., U.S.	B5	106
Paw Paw, Mi., U.S.	F5	115
Paw Paw, stm., Mi., U.S.	F4	115
Pawpaw Creek, stm., W.V., U.S.	h10	141
Pawtuckaway Pond, l., N.H., U.S.	D4	122
Pawtucket, R.I., U.S.	C4	132
Pawtuxet, stm., R.I., U.S.	C4	132
Paxton, Il., U.S.	C5	106
Paxton, Ma., U.S.	B4	114
Payakumbuh, Indon.	D2	36
Payeti, Indon.	E6	36
Payette, Id., U.S.	E2	105
Payette, co., Id., U.S.	E2	105
Payette, North Fork, stm., Id., U.S.	E2	105
Payette, South Fork, stm., Id., U.S.	E3	105
Payette Lake, res., Id., U.S.	E3	105
Payne, Oh., U.S.	A1	128
Payne, co., Ok., U.S.	A4	129
Payne, Lac, l., Can.	G25	82
Paynes Find, Austl.	F2	60
Paynesville, Mn., U.S.	E4	116
Paysandú, Ur.	E6	72
Payson, Az., U.S.	C4	96
Payson, Il., U.S.	D2	106
Payson, Ut., U.S.	C4	137
Pazar, Tur.	B9	44
Pazarcık, Tur.	D7	44
Pazardžik, Bul.	C10	18
Paz de Río, Col.	D5	80
Pea, stm., Al., U.S.	D3	94
Peabody, Ks., U.S.	D6	109
Peabody, Ma., U.S.	A6	114
Peabody, stm., N.H., U.S.	B4	122
Peace, stm., Can.	D8	75
Peace, stm., Fl., U.S.	E5	102
Peace Dale, R.I., U.S.	F3	132
Peace River, Ab., Can.	A2	84
Peach, co., Ga., U.S.	D3	103
Peacham Pond, res., Vt., U.S.	C4	138
Peach Point, c., Ma., U.S.	f12	114
Peach Springs, Az., U.S.	B2	96
Peak Hill, Austl.	F2	60
Peaks Island, i., Me., U.S.	g7	112
Peale, Mount, mtn., Ut., U.S.	E6	137
Pea Patch Island, i., De., U.S.	B3	101
Pea Ridge, Ar., U.S.	A1	97
Pea Ridge National Military Park, Ar., U.S.	A1	97
Pearisburg, Va., U.S.	C2	139
Pearl, Ms., U.S.	C3	117
Pearl, stm., U.S.	D3	117
Pearland, Tx., U.S.	r14	136
Pearl and Hermes Reef, rf., Hi., U.S.	k12	104
Pearl City, Hi., U.S.	B4	104
Pearl Harbor, b., Hi., U.S.	B3	104
Pearl Harbor Naval Station, mil., Hi., U.S.	g10	104
Pearlington, Ms., U.S.	E4	117
Pearl River, La., U.S.	D6	111
Pearl River, N.Y., U.S.	g12	125
Pearl River, co., Ms., U.S.	E4	117
Pearsall, Tx., U.S.	E3	136
Pearsoll Peak, mtn., Or., U.S.	E3	130
Pearson, Ga., U.S.	E4	103
Peary Land, reg., Grnld.	B32	82
Pease, stm., Tx., U.S.	B3	136
Pebane, Moz.	B6	56
Peć, Yugo.	C8	18
Pecatonica, Il., U.S.	A4	106
Pecatonica, stm., U.S.	A4	106
Pecatonica, East Branch, stm., Wi., U.S.	F4	142
Pečenga, Russia	C5	26
Pechora see Pečora, stm., Russia	C7	26
Pechora Bay see Pečorskaja guba, b., Russia	A9	22
Peckerwood Lake, res., Ar., U.S.	C4	97
Pečora, Russia	C7	26
Pečora, stm., Russia	C7	26
Pečorskaja guba, b., Russia	A9	22
Pečorskoe more, Russia	C7	26
Pecos, N.M., U.S.	B4	124
Pecos, Tx., U.S.	D1	136
Pecos, co., Tx., U.S.	D1	136
Pecos, stm., U.S.	E7	92
Pecos National Monument, N.M., U.S.	B4	124
Pécs, Hung.	F5	20
Peculiar, Mo., U.S.	C3	118
Peddocks Island, i., Ma., U.S.	g12	114
Pedernales, Ven.	D7	80
Pedra Azul, Braz.	E3	74
Pedreiras, Braz.	B3	74
Pedro Afonso, Braz.	E10	70
Pedro II, Braz.	B3	74
Pedro Juan Caballero, Para.	C6	72
Peebles, Oh., U.S.	D2	128
Peekskill, N.Y., U.S.	D7	125
Pegasus Bay, b., N.Z.	p13	63c
Pegram, Tn., U.S.	A4	135
Pehuajó, Arg.	F5	72
Peikang, Tai.	E5	30
Peipus, Lake, l., Eur.	G12	10
Peixian, China	C4	30
Pekalongan, Indon.	E3	36
Pekanbaru, Indon.	C2	36
Pekin, Il., U.S.	C4	106
Pekin, In., U.S.	G5	107
Peking see Beijing, China	D11	28
Pelagie, Isole, is., Italy	G4	18
Pelahatchie, Ms., U.S.	C4	117
Pelee, Island, i., On., Can.	F2	89
Peleng, Pulau, i., Indon.	D6	36
Pelham, On., Can.	D5	89
Pelham, Al., U.S.	B3	94
Pelham, Ga., U.S.	E2	103
Pelham, N.H., U.S.	E4	122
Pelham Manor, N.Y., U.S.	h13	125
Pelican Bay, b., Mb., Can.	C1	86
Pelican Lake, l., Mb., Can.	C1	86
Pelican Lake, l., Mn., U.S.	E5	116
Pelican Lake, l., Mn., U.S.	B6	116
Pelican Lake, l., Mn., U.S.	D3	116
Pelican Lake, l., Mn., U.S.	D4	116
Pelican Lake, l., Wi., U.S.	C4	142
Pelican Mountain, mtn., Ab., Can.	B4	84
Pelican Rapids, Mn., U.S.	D2	116
Pella, Ia., U.S.	C5	108
Pell City, Al., U.S.	B3	94
Pell Lake, Wi., U.S.	n11	142
Pello, Fin.	C11	10
Peloponnesus see Pelopónnisos, pen., Grc.	F8	18
Pelopónnisos, pen., Grc.	F8	18
Pelotas, Braz.	E7	72
Pelton, Lake, l., La., U.S.	E5	111
Pemadumcook Lake, l., Me., U.S.	C3	112
Pematangsiantar, Indon.	C1	36
Pemba, Moz.	A7	56
Pemba, i., Tan.	E7	54
Pemberton, Austl.	G2	60
Pemberville, Oh., U.S.	A2	128
Pembina, N.D., U.S.	A8	127
Pembina, co., N.D., U.S.	A8	127
Pembina, stm., Ab., Can.	C3	84
Pembroke, On., Can.	B7	89
Pembroke, Wales, U.K.	E4	12
Pembroke, Ga., U.S.	D5	103
Pembroke, Ky., U.S.	D2	110
Pembroke, Ma., U.S.	B6	114
Pembroke, N.C., U.S.	C3	126
Pembroke, Va., U.S.	C2	139
Pembroke Pines, Fl., U.S.	r13	102
Pemigewasset, stm., N.H., U.S.	C3	122
Pemiscot, co., Mo., U.S.	E8	118
Penang see George Town, Malay.	B2	36
Peñaranda de Bracamonte, Spain	G4	16
Pen Argyl, Pa., U.S.	E11	131
Peñarroya-Pueblonuevo, Spain	H4	16
Penas, Golfo de, b., Chile	G1	69
Penasco, N.M., U.S.	A4	124
Peñasco, Rio, stm., N.M., U.S.	E4	124
Penbrook, Pa., U.S.	F8	131
Pendembu, S.L.	E2	50
Pendembu, S.L.	E2	50
Pender, Ne., U.S.	B9	120
Pender, co., N.C., U.S.	C4	126
Pendleton, In., U.S.	E6	107
Pendleton, Or., U.S.	B8	130
Pendleton, S.C., U.S.	B2	133
Pendleton, co., Ky., U.S.	B5	110
Pendleton, co., W.V., U.S.	C5	141
Pend Oreille, co., Wa., U.S.	A8	140
Pend Oreille, Lake, l., Id., U.S.	A2	105
Pend Oreille, Mount, mtn., Id., U.S.	A2	105
Penedo, Braz.	D4	74
Penetanguishene, On., Can.	C5	89
Penglai, China	D12	28
Pengshui, China	F9	28
Pengxian, China	C1	30
Penhold, Ab., Can.	C4	84
Peniche, Port.	H2	16
Penida, Nusa, i., Indon.	E5	36
Pennant Point, c., N.S., Can.	E6	87
Pennask Mountain, mtn., B.C., Can.	E7	85
Pennell, Mount, mtn., Ut., U.S.	F5	137
Penneru, stm., India	G3	40
Penn Hills, Pa., U.S.	k14	131
Pennington, co., Mn., U.S.	B2	116
Pennington, co., S.D., U.S.	D2	134
Pennington Gap, Va., U.S.	f8	139
Pennsauken, N.J., U.S.	D2	123
Pennsboro, W.V., U.S.	B4	141
Pennsburg, Pa., U.S.	F11	131
Penns Grove, N.J., U.S.	D2	123
Pennsville, N.J., U.S.	D1	123
Pennsylvania, state, U.S.	E7	131
Pennville, In., U.S.	D7	107
Penn Yan, N.Y., U.S.	C3	125
Penobscot, co., Me., U.S.	C4	112
Penobscot, stm., Me., U.S.	C4	112
Penobscot Bay, b., Me., U.S.	D3	112
Penobscot Lake, l., Me., U.S.	C2	112
Penong, Austl.	G5	60
Penonomé, Pan.	D3	80
Penrhyn, atoll, Cook Is.	E14	58
Penrith, Austl.	G5	62
Penrith, Eng., U.K.	C5	12
Pensacola, Fl., U.S.	u14	102
Pensacola Bay, b., Fl., U.S.	u14	102
Pensacola Dam, Ok., U.S.	A6	129
Pensacola Mountains, mts., Ant.	E36	67
Pentagon Mountain, mtn., Mt., U.S.	C3	119
Pentecost Island see Pentecôte, i., Vanuatu	k9	62a
Pentecôte, i., Vanuatu	k9	62a
Penticton, B.C., Can.	E8	85
Pentland Firth, strt., Scot., U.K.	A5	12
Pentwater, Mi., U.S.	E4	115
Penza, Russia	D6	26
Penzance, Eng., U.K.	E4	12
Penžinskaja guba, b., Russia	C18	26
Peonan Point, c., Mb., Can.	D2	86
Peoria, Az., U.S.	D3	96
Peoria, Il., U.S.	C4	106
Peoria, co., Il., U.S.	C4	106
Peoria Heights, Il., U.S.	C4	106
Peotone, Il., U.S.	B6	106
Pepacton Reservoir, res., N.Y., U.S.	C6	125
Pepeekeo, Hi., U.S.	D6	104
Pepin, Wi., U.S.	D1	142
Pepin, co., Wi., U.S.	D2	142
Pepin, Lake, l., U.S.	D1	142
Pepperell, Ma., U.S.	A4	114
Pequannock, N.J., U.S.	B4	123
Pequest, stm., N.J., U.S.	B2	123
Pequop Mountains, mts., Nv., U.S.	C7	121
Pequot Lakes, Mn., U.S.	D4	116
Perabumulih, Indon.	D2	36
Percival Lakes, l., Austl.	E3	60
Percy, Il., U.S.	E4	106
Perdido, Al., U.S.	D2	94
Perdido, stm., U.S.	E2	94
Perdido Bay, b., Al., U.S.	E2	94
Pereira, Col.	C4	70
Pereislav-Khmel'nyts'kyi, Ukr.	D11	20
Pere Marquette, stm., Mi., U.S.	E4	115
Pereslavl'-Zalesskij, Russia	C6	22
Pergamino, Arg.	E5	72
Pergamum, hist., Tur.	C2	44
Perham, Mn., U.S.	D3	116
Perico, Arg.	C4	72
Pericos, Mex.	B3	78
Peridot, Az., U.S.	D5	96
Périgueux, Fr.	E7	16
Perijá, Serranía de, mts., S.A.	G10	76
Perkasie, Pa., U.S.	F11	131
Perkins, Ok., U.S.	B4	129
Perkins, co., Ne., U.S.	D4	120
Perkins, co., S.D., U.S.	B3	134
Perkinston, Ms., U.S.	E4	117
Perlas, Archipiélago de las, is., Pan.	D4	80
Perlas, Laguna de b., Nic.	C3	80
Perm', Russia	D7	26
Pernambuco, state, Braz.	C4	74
Pernik, Bul.	C9	18
Perpignan, Fr.	F8	16
Perquimans, co., N.C., U.S.	A6	126
Perrine, Fl., U.S.	G6	102
Perris, Ca., U.S.	F5	98
Perro, Laguna del, l., N.M., U.S.	C4	124
Perry, Fl., U.S.	B3	102
Perry, Ga., U.S.	D3	103
Perry, Ia., U.S.	C3	108
Perry, Ks., U.S.	C8	109
Perry, Mi., U.S.	F6	115
Perry, Mo., U.S.	B6	118
Perry, N.Y., U.S.	C2	125
Perry, Oh., U.S.	A4	128
Perry, Ok., U.S.	A4	129
Perry, Ut., U.S.	B3	137
Perry, co., Al., U.S.	C2	94
Perry, co., Ar., U.S.	C3	97
Perry, co., Il., U.S.	E4	106

Name	Map Ref.	Page
Perry, co., In., U.S.	H4	107
Perry, co., Ky., U.S.	C6	110
Perry, co., Mo., U.S.	D8	118
Perry, co., Ms., U.S.	D4	117
Perry, co., Oh., U.S.	C3	128
Perry, co., Pa., U.S.	F7	131
Perry, co., Tn., U.S.	B4	135
Perry Hall, Md., U.S.	B5	113
Perry Lake, res., Ks., U.S.	C8	109
Perryman, Md., U.S.	B5	113
Perrysburg, Oh., U.S.	A2	128
Perry Stream, stm., N.H., U.S.	f7	122
Perry's Victory and International Peace Memorial, hist., Oh., U.S.	A2	128
Perryton, Tx., U.S.	A2	136
Perryville, Ar., U.S.	B3	97
Perryville, Ky., U.S.	C5	110
Perryville, Md., U.S.	A5	113
Perryville, Mo., U.S.	D8	118
Pershing, co., Nv., U.S.	C3	121
Persia see Iran, ctry., Asia	D6	42
Persian Gulf (The Gulf), b., Asia	E6	42
Person, co., N.C., U.S.	A3	126
Perth, Austl.	G2	60
Perth, On., Can.	C8	89
Perth, Scot., U.K.	B5	12
Perth Amboy, N.J., U.S.	B4	123
Perth-Andover, N.B., Can.	D10	87
Perth Basin	K13	64
Peru, Il., U.S.	B4	106
Peru, In., U.S.	C5	107
Peru, Ne., U.S.	D10	120
Peru, N.Y., U.S.	f11	125
Peru, ctry., S.A.	E4	70
Peru Basin	J5	66
Peru-Chile Trench	J6	66
Perugia, Italy	C4	18
Peruíbe, Braz.	C8	72
Pervari, Tur.	D10	44
Pervomais'k, Ukr.	E11	20
Pervoural'sk, Russia	D7	26
Pesaro, Italy	C4	18
Pescara, Italy	C5	18
Peshastin, Wa., U.S.	B5	140
Peshāwar, Pak.	D10	42
Peshtigo, Wi., U.S.	C6	142
Peshtigo, stm., Wi., U.S.	C5	142
Pesqueira, Braz.	C4	74
Pessac, Fr.	E6	16
Pëstraja Dresva, Russia	C17	26
Petaḥ Tiqwa, Isr.	F6	44
Petal, Ms., U.S.	D4	117
Petaluma, Ca., U.S.	C2	98
Petatlán, Mex.	D4	78
Petawawa, On., Can.	B7	89
Petawawa, stm., On., Can.	A6	89
Petenwell Lake, res., Wi., U.S.	D4	142
Peterborough, Austl.	G2	62
Peterborough, On., Can.	C6	89
Peterborough, Eng., U.K.	D6	12
Peterborough, N.H., U.S.	E3	122
Peterhead, Scot., U.K.	B6	12
Peter I Island, i., Ant.	C31	67
Peter Pond Lake, l., Sk., Can.	m7	91
Petersburg, Ak., U.S.	D13	95
Petersburg, Il., U.S.	C4	106
Petersburg, In., U.S.	H3	107
Petersburg, Mi., U.S.	G7	115
Petersburg, Oh., U.S.	B5	128
Petersburg, Tx., U.S.	C2	136
Petersburg, Va., U.S.	C5	139
Petersburg, W.V., U.S.	B5	141
Peters Creek, stm., W.V., U.S.	m14	141
Peterson, Al., U.S.	B2	94
Peterson Field, mil., Co., U.S.	C6	99
Petersville, Al., U.S.	A2	94
Peter the Great Bay see Petra Velikogo, zaliv, b., Russia	C14	28
Pétion-Ville, Haiti	B5	80
Petit Bois Island, i., Ms., U.S.	E5	117
Petitcodiac, N.B., Can.	D4	87
Petitcodiac, stm., N.B., Can.	C5	87
Petite Amite, stm., La., U.S.	h10	111
Petite Rivière Noire, Piton de la, mtn., Mrts.	g10	57a
Petit Jean, stm., Ar., U.S.	B2	97
Petit Lac Des Allemands, l., La., U.S.	k11	111
Petit Lake, l., La., U.S.	k12	111
Petit-Rocher, N.B., Can.	B4	87
Petitsikapau Lake, l., Nf., Can.	g8	88
Peto, Mex.	C7	78
Petoskey, Mi., U.S.	C6	115
Petra see Al-Batrā', hist., Jord.	D3	42
Petra Velikogo, zaliv, b., Russia	C14	28
Petrič, Bul.	D9	18
Petrified Forest National Park, Az., U.S.	B6	96
Petrila, Rom.	G7	20
Petrodvorec, Russia	G13	10
Petrograd see Sankt-Peterburg, Russia	D5	26
Petrolândia, Braz.	C4	74
Petroleum, co., Mt., U.S.	C8	119
Petrolia, On., Can.	E2	89
Petrolina, Braz.	C3	74
Petropavlovsk, Kaz.	D8	26
Petropavlovsk-Kamčatskij, Russia	D17	26
Petrópolis, Braz.	F3	74
Petros, Tn., U.S.	C9	135
Petroşani, Rom.	G7	20
Petrovsk, Russia	D8	22
Petrozavodsk, Russia	C5	26
Pettaquamscutt Lake Shores, R.I., U.S.	F4	132
Pettingell Peak, mtn., Co., U.S.	B5	99
Pettis, co., Mo., U.S.	C4	118
Pevek, Russia	C19	26
Pevely, Mo., U.S.	g13	118
Pewaukee, Wi., U.S.	E5	142
Pewaukee Lake, l., Wi., U.S.	m11	142
Pewee Valley, Ky., U.S.	B4	110
Pha-an, Myan.	C3	34
Phalaborwa, S. Afr.	C5	56
Phalodi, India	D2	40
Phangan, Ko, i., Thai.	E4	34
Phangnga, Thai.	E3	34
Phanom Dongrak Range, mts., Asia	D4	34
Phan Rang, Viet.	D5	34
Phan Si Pan see Fan Si Pan, mtn., Viet.	B4	34
Phan Thiet, Viet.	D5	34
Pharr, Tx., U.S.	F3	136
Phatthalung, Thai.	E4	34
Phayao, Thai.	C3	34
Phelps, Ky., U.S.	C7	110
Phelps, N.Y., U.S.	C3	125
Phelps, Wi., U.S.	B4	142
Phelps, co., Mo., U.S.	D6	118
Phelps, co., Ne., U.S.	D6	120
Phelps Lake, l., N.C., U.S.	B6	126
Phenix City, Al., U.S.	C4	94
Phetchabun, Thai.	C4	34
Phetchaburi, Thai.	D3	34
Phibun Mangsahan, Thai.	C5	34
Phichit, Thai.	C4	34
Philadelphia, Ms., U.S.	C4	117
Philadelphia, Pa., U.S.	G11	131
Philadelphia, co., Pa., U.S.	G12	131
Philadelphia Naval Shipyard, mil., Pa., U.S.	P21	131
Phil Campbell, Al., U.S.	A2	94
Philip, S.D., U.S.	C4	134
Philippeville see Skikda, Alg.	C6	48
Philippi, W.V., U.S.	B4	141
Philippi see Fílippoi, hist., Grc.	D10	18
Philippine Basin	G15	64
Philippines, ctry., Asia	C8	34
Philippine Sea	H16	24
Philippine Trench	H15	64
Philippopolis see Plovdiv, Bul.	C10	18
Philipsburg, Mt., U.S.	D3	119
Philipsburg, Pa., U.S.	E5	131
Philleo Lake, l., Wa., U.S.	h14	140
Phillips, Me., U.S.	D2	112
Phillips, Tx., U.S.	B2	136
Phillips, Wi., U.S.	C3	142
Phillips, co., Ar., U.S.	C5	97
Phillips, co., Co., U.S.	A8	99
Phillips, co., Ks., U.S.	C4	109
Phillips, co., Mt., U.S.	B8	119
Phillips Brook, stm., N.H., U.S.	A4	122
Phillipsburg, Ks., U.S.	C4	109
Phillipsburg, N.J., U.S.	B2	123
Philmont, N.Y., U.S.	C7	125
Philo, Il., U.S.	C5	106
Philomath, Or., U.S.	C3	130
Philpott Reservoir, res., Va., U.S.	D2	139
Phitsanulok, Thai.	C4	34
Phnom Penh see Phnum Pénh, Camb.	D4	34
Phnum Pénh (Phnom Penh), Camb.	D4	34
Phoenix, Az., U.S.	D3	96
Phoenix, Il., U.S.	k9	106
Phoenix, N.Y., U.S.	B4	125
Phoenix, Or., U.S.	E4	130
Phoenix Islands, is., Kir.	E12	58
Phoenixville, Pa., U.S.	F10	131
Phon, Thai.	C4	34
Phôngsali, Laos	B4	34
Phrae, Thai.	C4	34
Phra Nakhon Si Ayutthaya, Thai.	D4	34
Phuket, Thai.	E3	34
Phuket, Ko, i., Thai.	E3	34
Phumĭ Chhuk, Camb.	D4	34
Phumĭ Kâmpóng Srâlau, Camb.	D5	34
Phumĭ Kaôh Kông, Camb.	D4	34
Phu Quoc, Dao, i., Viet.	D4	34
Piacenza, Italy	B2	18
Pianosa, Isola, i., Italy	C3	18
Piatra-Neamț, Rom.	F9	20
Piatt, co., Il., U.S.	D5	106
Piauí, state, Braz.	C3	74
Piave, stm., Italy	A4	18
Pibor Post, Sudan	I11	48
Picacho, Az., U.S.	E4	96
Picardie, hist. reg., Fr.	C8	16
Picardy see Picardie, hist. reg., Fr.	C8	16
Picayune, Ms., U.S.	E4	117
Piccadilly, Nf., Can.	D2	88
Pichanal, Arg.	C5	72
Picher, Ok., U.S.	A7	129
Pichilemu, Chile	E3	72
Pickaway, co., Oh., U.S.	C2	128
Pickens, Ms., U.S.	C4	117
Pickens, S.C., U.S.	B2	133
Pickens, co., Al., U.S.	B1	94
Pickens, co., Ga., U.S.	B2	103
Pickens, co., S.C., U.S.	B2	133
Pickerel Lake, l., Wi., U.S.	C5	142
Pickering, On., Can.	D5	89
Pickerington, Oh., U.S.	C3	128
Pickett, co., Tn., U.S.	C8	135
Pickwick Lake, res., U.S.	A6	117
Pickworth Point, c., Ma., U.S.	f12	114
Pico de Orizaba, Volcán, vol., Mex.	D5	78
Pico Rivera, Ca., U.S.	n12	98
Picos, Braz.	C3	74
Picton, On., Can.	D7	89
Pictou Island, i., N.S., Can.	D7	87
Picture Butte, Ab., Can.	E4	84
Pictured Rocks National Lakeshore, Mi., U.S.	B4	115
Pidurutalagala, mtn., Sri L.	H4	40
Piedecuesta, Col.	D5	80
Piedmont, Al., U.S.	B4	94
Piedmont, Ca., U.S.	h8	98
Piedmont, Mo., U.S.	D7	118
Piedmont, Ok., U.S.	B4	129
Piedmont, S.C., U.S.	B3	133
Piedmont, W.V., U.S.	B5	141
Piedmont Lake, res., Oh., U.S.	B4	128
Piedra, stm., Co., U.S.	D3	99
Piedras Blancas, Point, c., Ca., U.S.	E3	98
Piedras Negras, Guat.	B1	80
Piedras Negras, Mex.	B4	78
Pieksämäki, Fin.	E12	10
Pielinen, l., Fin.	E13	10
Pierce, Co., U.S.	A6	99
Pierce, Id., U.S.	C3	105
Pierce, Ne., U.S.	B8	120
Pierce, co., Ga., U.S.	E4	103
Pierce, co., N.D., U.S.	A5	127
Pierce, co., Ne., U.S.	B8	120
Pierce, co., Wa., U.S.	C3	140
Pierce, co., Wi., U.S.	D1	142
Pierce, Lake, l., Fl., U.S.	E5	102
Pierce City, Mo., U.S.	E3	118
Pierceton, In., U.S.	B6	107
Pierre, S.D., U.S.	C5	134
Pierrefonds, P.Q., Can.	q19	90
Pierre Part, La., U.S.	k9	111
Pierreville, P.Q., Can.	C5	90
Pierson, Fl., U.S.	C5	102
Pierz, Mn., U.S.	E4	116
Piešťany, Slvk.	E4	20
Pietarsaari, Fin.	E10	10
Pietermaritzburg, S. Afr.	D5	56
Pietersburg, S. Afr.	C4	56
Piet Retief, S. Afr.	D5	56
Pigeon, Mi., U.S.	E7	115
Pigeon, stm., In., U.S.	A6	107
Pigeon, stm., Mn., U.S.	h10	116
Pigeon, stm., Wi., U.S.	k10	142
Pigeon, stm., U.S.	f9	126
Pigeon Cove, Ma., U.S.	A6	114
Pigeon Forge, Tn., U.S.	D10	135
Pigeon Point, c., Mn., U.S.	h10	116
Pigg, stm., Va., U.S.	D3	139
Piggott, Ar., U.S.	A5	97
Pigüé, Arg.	F5	72
Pihlajavesi, l., Fin.	F13	10
Pihtipudas, Fin.	E11	10
Pijijiapan, Mex.	D6	78
Pike, co., Al., U.S.	D4	94
Pike, co., Ar., U.S.	C2	97
Pike, co., Ga., U.S.	C2	103
Pike, co., Il., U.S.	D2	106
Pike, co., In., U.S.	H3	107
Pike, co., Ky., U.S.	C7	110
Pike, co., Mo., U.S.	B6	118
Pike, co., Ms., U.S.	D3	117
Pike, co., Oh., U.S.	C2	128
Pike, co., Pa., U.S.	D11	131
Pike, stm., Wi., U.S.	C6	142
Pike Island Dam, U.S.	f8	141
Pike Lake, Mn., U.S.	D6	116
Pikes Peak, mtn., Co., U.S.	C5	99
Pikesville, Md., U.S.	B4	113
Piketberg, S. Afr.	E2	56
Piketon, Oh., U.S.	C2	128
Pikeville, Ky., U.S.	C7	110
Pikeville, Tn., U.S.	D8	135
Piła, Pol.	C4	20
Pilcomayo, stm., S.A.	C5	72
Pīlībhīt, India	D3	40
Pillar Point, c., Ca., U.S.	k7	98
Pílos, Grc.	F8	18
Pilot Grove, Mo., U.S.	C5	118
Pilot Knob, Mo., U.S.	D7	118
Pilot Knob, mtn., Id., U.S.	D3	105
Pilot Mound, Mb., Can.	E2	86
Pilot Mountain, N.C., U.S.	A2	126
Pilot Peak, mtn., Nv., U.S.	B7	121
Pilot Peak, mtn., Nv., U.S.	E4	121
Pilot Peak, mtn., Wy., U.S.	B3	143
Pilot Point, Tx., U.S.	C4	136
Pilot Range, mts., Nv., U.S.	B7	121
Pilot Rock, Or., U.S.	B8	130
Pilot Station, Ak., U.S.	C7	95
Pilsen see Plzeň, Czech Rep.	E2	20
Pima, Az., U.S.	E6	96
Pima, co., Az., U.S.	E3	96
Pimmit Hills, Va., U.S.	g12	139
Pinal, co., Az., U.S.	E4	96
Pinaleno Mountains, mts., Az., U.S.	E5	96
Pinal Mountains, mts., Az., U.S.	D5	96
Pinang see George Town, Malay.	B2	36
Pınarbaşı, Tur.	C7	44
Pinar del Río, Cuba	A3	80
Pinardville, N.H., U.S.	E3	122
Pincher Creek, Ab., Can.	E4	84
Pinckard, Al., U.S.	D4	94
Pinckney, Mi., U.S.	F7	115
Pinckney Island, i., S.C., U.S.	G6	133
Pinckneyville, Il., U.S.	E4	106
Pinconning, Mi., U.S.	E7	115
Pindaré-Mirim, Braz.	B2	74
Píndhos Óros, mts., Grc.	E8	18
Pindus Mountains see Píndhos Óros, mts., Grc.	E8	18
Pine, Az., U.S.	C4	96
Pine, co., Mn., U.S.	D6	116
Pine, stm., Mi., U.S.	D7	115
Pine, stm., Mi., U.S.	D5	115
Pine, stm., N.H., U.S.	C4	122
Pine, stm., Wi., U.S.	C5	142
Pine, stm., Wi., U.S.	C4	142
Pine Barrens, reg., N.J., U.S.	D3	123
Pine Bluff, Ar., U.S.	C3	97
Pinebluff, N.C., U.S.	B3	126
Pine Bluffs, Wy., U.S.	E8	143
Pine Bridge, Ct., U.S.	D3	100
Pine Castle, Fl., U.S.	D5	102
Pine City, Mn., U.S.	E6	116
Pine Creek, Austl.	C5	60
Pine Creek, stm., Nv., U.S.	C5	121
Pine Creek, stm., Pa., U.S.	C6	131
Pine Creek, stm., Wa., U.S.	B8	140
Pine Creek Lake, res., Ok., U.S.	C6	129
Pinedale, Wy., U.S.	D3	143
Pine Falls, Mb., Can.	D3	86
Pine Forest Range, mts., Nv., U.S.	B3	121
Pine Grove, Pa., U.S.	E9	131
Pine Grove Mills, Pa., U.S.	E6	131
Pine Hill, N.J., U.S.	D3	123
Pine Hills, Fl., U.S.	D5	102
Pinehouse Lake, Sk., Can.	B2	91
Pinehouse Lake, l., Sk., Can.	B2	91
Pinehurst, Ma., U.S.	f11	114
Pinehurst, N.C., U.S.	B3	126
Pine Island, Mn., U.S.	F6	116
Pine Island, i., Fl., U.S.	F4	102
Pine Island Sound, strt., Fl., U.S.	F4	102
Pine Key, i., Fl., U.S.	p10	102
Pine Knot, Ky., U.S.	D5	110
Pine Lake, Ga., U.S.	h8	103
Pine Lake, l., In., U.S.	A4	107
Pine Lake, l., Wi., U.S.	C5	142
Pine Lawn, Mo., U.S.	f13	118
Pine Level, N.C., U.S.	B4	126
Pinellas, co., Fl., U.S.	D4	102
Pinellas, Point, c., Fl., U.S.	p10	102
Pinellas Park, Fl., U.S.	E4	102
Pine Mountain, Ga., U.S.	D2	103
Pine Mountain, mtn., Or., U.S.	D6	130
Pine Mountain, mtn., Wy., U.S.	E3	143
Pine Point, Me., U.S.	E2	112
Pine Prairie, La., U.S.	D3	111
Pine Ridge, S.D., U.S.	D3	134
Pine Ridge Indian Reservation, S.D., U.S.	D3	134
Pine River, Mn., U.S.	D4	116
Pines, Isle of see Juventud, Isla de la, i., Cuba	A3	80
Pines, Lake O' the, res., Tx., U.S.	C5	136
Pinesdale, Mt., U.S.	D2	119
Pinetops, N.C., U.S.	B5	126
Pinetown, S. Afr.	D5	56
Pine Valley, val., Ut., U.S.	E2	137
Pineville, Ky., U.S.	D6	110
Pineville, La., U.S.	C3	111
Pineville, N.C., U.S.	B2	126
Pineville, W.V., U.S.	D3	141
Pinewood, S.C., U.S.	D7	133
Piney Creek, stm., W.V., U.S.	n13	141
Piney Fork, stm., W.V., U.S.	h9	141
Piney Point, Md., U.S.	D4	113
Piney View, W.V., U.S.	n13	141
Pingdu, China	B4	30
Pingelly, Austl.	G2	60
Pingjiang, China	F10	28
Pingle, China	E3	30
Pingliang, China	D9	28
Pingluo, China	B2	30
Pingquan, China	C11	28
Pingtan, China	D4	30
P'ingtung, Tai.	E5	30
Pingwu, China	E8	28
Pingxiang, China	G9	28
Pingxiang, China	F10	28
Pingyang, China	D5	30
Pingyao, China	B3	30
Pingyin, China	B4	30
Pinheiro, Braz.	B2	74
Pini, Pulau, i., Indon.	C1	36
Pinjarra, Austl.	G2	60
Pinjug, Russia	B8	22
Pinnacles National Monument, Ca., U.S.	D3	98
Pinole, Ca., U.S.	h8	98
Pinopolis Dam, S.C., U.S.	E8	133
Pinos, Mount, mtn., Ca., U.S.	E4	98
Pinrang, Indon.	D5	36
Pins, Île des, i., N. Cal.	I9	62a
Pins, Pointe aux, c., On., Can.	E3	89
Pinsk, Bela.	C9	20
Pinsk Marshes see Polesye, reg., Eur.	D8	20
Pinson, Al., U.S.	f7	94
Pinta, Isla, i., Ec.	C1	70
Pinta, Sierra, mts., Az., U.S.	E2	96
Pintados, Chile	C4	72
Pintwater Range, mts., Nv., U.S.	G6	121
Pioche, Nv., U.S.	F7	121
Piombino, Italy	C3	18
Pioneer, Oh., U.S.	A1	128
Pioneer Mountains, mts., Id., U.S.	F5	105
Pioneer Mountains, mts., Mt., U.S.	E3	119
Pioner, ostrov, i., Russia	B10	26
Piotrków Trybunalski, Pol.	D5	20
Pīpār, India	D2	40
Pipe Spring National Monument, Az., U.S.	A3	96
Pipestem Creek, stm., N.D., U.S.	B6	127
Pipestone, Mn., U.S.	G2	116
Pipestone, co., Mn., U.S.	F2	116
Pipestone National Monument, Mn., U.S.	G2	116
Pipestone Pass, Mt., U.S.	E4	119
Pipmuacan, Réservoir, res., P.Q., Can.	k12	90
Piqua, Oh., U.S.	B1	128
Piracicaba, Braz.	F2	74
Piracuruca, Braz.	B3	74
Piraeus see Piraiévs, Grc.	E9	18
Piraiévs, Grc.	E9	18
Piranhas, Braz.	E1	74
Pīrān Shahr, Iran	D11	44
Pirapora, Braz.	E3	74
Pires do Rio, Braz.	E2	74
Pírgos, Grc.	F8	18
Piripiri, Braz.	B3	74
Pirot, Yugo.	C9	18
Pīr Panjāl Range, mts., Asia	E2	28
Pirtleville, Az., U.S.	F6	96
Piru, Indon.	D7	36
Pisa, Italy	C3	18
Pisagua, Chile	A2	69
Piscataqua, stm., N.H., U.S.	D5	122
Piscataquis, co., Me., U.S.	C3	112
Piscataquis, stm., Me., U.S.	C3	112
Piscataquog, stm., N.H., U.S.	D3	122
Piscataway, N.J., U.S.	B4	123
Pisco, Peru	F4	70
Piseco Lake, l., N.Y., U.S.	B6	125
Písek, Czech Rep.	E3	20
Pisgah, Al., U.S.	A4	94
Pisgah, Oh., U.S.	n13	128
Pisgah, Mount, mtn., Wy., U.S.	B8	143
Pisgah Forest, N.C., U.S.	f10	126
Pishan, China	D3	28
Pismo Beach, Ca., U.S.	E3	98
Pisticci, Italy	D6	18
Pistoia, Italy	C3	18
Pistolet Bay, b., Nf., Can.	C4	88
Pit, stm., Ca., U.S.	B3	98
Pita, Gui.	D2	50
Pitcairn, Pa., U.S.	k14	131
Pitcairn, dep., Oc.	K26	64
Piteå, Swe.	D9	10
Piteälven, stm., Swe.	C8	10
Pitești, Rom.	G8	20
Pithara, Austl.	G2	60
Pitkin, co., Co., U.S.	B4	99
Pitkjaranta, Russia	B5	22
Pitman, N.J., U.S.	D2	123
Pitt, co., N.C., U.S.	B5	126
Pitt Island, i., B.C., Can.	C3	85
Pittsboro, In., U.S.	E5	107
Pittsboro, N.C., U.S.	B3	126
Pittsburg, Ca., U.S.	g9	98
Pittsburg, Ks., U.S.	E9	109
Pittsburg, Ky., U.S.	C5	110
Pittsburg, Tx., U.S.	C5	136
Pittsburg, co., Ok., U.S.	C6	129
Pittsburgh, Pa., U.S.	F1	131
Pittsfield, Il., U.S.	D3	106
Pittsfield, Ma., U.S.	B1	114
Pittsfield, Me., U.S.	D3	112
Pittsfield, N.H., U.S.	D4	122
Pittsford, Vt., U.S.	D2	138
Pittston, Pa., U.S.	D10	131
Pittsville, Md., U.S.	D7	113
Pittsville, Wi., U.S.	D3	142
Pittsylvania, co., Va., U.S.	D3	139

Name	Map Ref.	Page
Pium, Braz.	F10	70
Piura, Peru	E3	70
Piute, co., Ut., U.S.	E3	137
Piute Peak, mtn., Ca., U.S.	E4	98
Piute Reservoir, res., Ut., U.S.	E3	137
Pivdennyi Buh, stm., Ukr.	F11	20
Pixley, Ca., U.S.	E4	98
Pjandž, stm., Asia	B1	40
Pjaozero, ozero, l., Russia	D14	10
Pjasina, stm., Russia	B10	26
Pjatigorsk, Russia	B4	42
Placentia, Nf., Can.	E5	88
Placentia Bay, b., Nf., Can.	E4	88
Placer, co., Ca., U.S.	C3	98
Placer Mountain, mtn., N.M., U.S.	k8	124
Placerville, Ca., U.S.	C3	98
Placetas, Cuba	A4	80
Placid, Lake, l., Fl., U.S.	E5	102
Placid, Lake, l., N.Y., U.S.	f11	125
Placitas, N.M., U.S.	B3	124
Plain City, Oh., U.S.	B2	128
Plain City, Ut., U.S.	B3	137
Plain Dealing, La., U.S.	B2	111
Plainfield, Ct., U.S.	C8	100
Plainfield, Il., U.S.	B5	106
Plainfield, In., U.S.	E5	107
Plainfield, N.J., U.S.	B4	123
Plainfield, Vt., U.S.	C4	138
Plainfield, Wi., U.S.	D4	142
Plains, Ga., U.S.	D2	103
Plains, Ks., U.S.	E3	109
Plains, Mt., U.S.	C2	119
Plains, Pa., U.S.	n17	131
Plains, Tx., U.S.	C1	136
Plainview, Ar., U.S.	C2	97
Plainview, Mn., U.S.	F6	116
Plainview, Ne., U.S.	B8	120
Plainview, Tx., U.S.	B2	136
Plainville, Ct., U.S.	C4	100
Plainville, Ks., U.S.	C4	109
Plainville, Ma., U.S.	B5	114
Plainwell, Mi., U.S.	F5	115
Plaistow, N.H., U.S.	E4	122
Plampang, Indon.	E5	36
Planeta Rica, Col.	D4	80
Plankinton, S.D., U.S.	D7	134
Plano, Il., U.S.	B5	106
Plano, Tx., U.S.	C4	136
Plantagenet, On., Can.	B9	89
Plantation, Fl., U.S.	r13	102
Plant City, Fl., U.S.	D4	102
Plantersville, Al., U.S.	C3	94
Plantersville, Ms., U.S.	A5	117
Plantsite, Az., U.S.	D6	96
Plantsville, Ct., U.S.	C4	100
Plaquemine, La., U.S.	D4	111
Plaquemines, co., La., U.S.	E6	111
Plasencia, Spain	G3	16
Plaster Rock, N.B., Can.	C2	87
Plata, Río de la, est., S.A.	E6	72
Plate, Île, i., Sey.	i13	57b
Plato, Col.	B5	70
Platte, S.D., U.S.	D7	134
Platte, co., Mo., U.S.	B3	118
Platte, co., Ne., U.S.	C8	120
Platte, co., Wy., U.S.	D7	143
Platte, stm., Mn., U.S.	E4	116
Platte, stm., Ne., U.S.	D6	120
Platte, stm., U.S.	B3	118
Platte City, Mo., U.S.	B3	118
Platteville, Co., U.S.	A6	99
Platteville, Wi., U.S.	F3	142
Plattsburg, Mo., U.S.	B3	118
Plattsburgh, N.Y., U.S.	f11	125
Plattsmouth, Ne., U.S.	D10	120
Plauen, Ger.	E12	12
Plavsk, Russia	C14	20
Playas Lake, l., N.M., U.S.	F2	124
Playgreen Lake, l., Mb., Can.	B2	86
Play Ku, Viet.	D5	34
Pleasant, stm., Me., U.S.	C3	112
Pleasant, Lake, res., Az., U.S.	D3	96
Pleasant Gap, Pa., U.S.	E6	131
Pleasant Garden, N.C., U.S.	B3	126
Pleasant Grove, Al., U.S.	g7	94
Pleasant Grove, Ut., U.S.	C4	137
Pleasant Hill, Ca., U.S.	h8	98
Pleasant Hill, Ia., U.S.	e8	108
Pleasant Hill, Il., U.S.	D3	106
Pleasant Hill, La., U.S.	C2	111
Pleasant Hill, Mo., U.S.	C3	118
Pleasant Hill, Oh., U.S.	B1	128
Pleasant Lake, l., A.7	A7	107
Pleasant Lake, l., Me., U.S.	C5	112
Pleasant Lake, l., N.H., U.S.	D4	122
Pleasanton, Ca., U.S.	h9	98
Pleasanton, Ks., U.S.	D9	109
Pleasanton, Tx., U.S.	E3	136
Pleasant Prairie, Wi., U.S.	n12	142
Pleasants, co., W.V., U.S.	B3	141
Pleasant Valley, Ia., U.S.	g11	108
Pleasant Valley, Mo., U.S.	h11	118
Pleasant View, Ut., U.S.	B3	137
Pleasantville, Ia., U.S.	C4	108
Pleasantville, N.J., U.S.	E3	123
Pleasantville, N.Y., U.S.	D7	125
Pleasantville, Oh., U.S.	C3	128
Pleasure Beach, Ct., U.S.	D7	100
Pleasure Ridge Park, Ky., U.S.	g11	110
Pleasureville, Ky., U.S.	B4	110
Plenty, Bay of, b., N.Z.	o14	63c
Plentywood, Mt., U.S.	B12	119
Pleseck, Russia	C6	26
Plessisville, P.Q., Can.	C6	90
Pleszew, Pol.	D4	20
Pleven, Bul.	C10	18
Pljussa, Russia	G13	10
Płock, Pol.	C5	20
Ploiești, Rom.	G9	20
Plomosa Mountains, mts., Az., U.S.	D1	96
Plonge, Lac la, l., Sk., Can.	B2	91
Płońsk, Pol.	C6	20
Plovdiv, Bul.	C10	18
Plover, Wi., U.S.	D4	142
Plover, stm., Wi., U.S.	D4	142
Plum, Pa., U.S.	k14	131
Plumas, co., Ca., U.S.	B3	98
Plum Coulee, Mb., Can.	E3	86
Plumerville, Ar., U.S.	B3	97
Plum Island, i., Ma., U.S.	A6	114
Plummer, Id., U.S.	B2	105
Plumsteadville, Pa., U.S.	F11	131
Plumtree, Zimb.	C4	56
Plungė, Lith.	I9	10
Plutarco Elías Calles, Presa, res., Mex.	B3	78
Plymouth, Monts.	B7	80
Plymouth, Eng., U.K.	E4	12
Plymouth, Ct., U.S.	C3	100
Plymouth, Fl., U.S.	D5	102
Plymouth, In., U.S.	B5	107
Plymouth, Ma., U.S.	C6	114
Plymouth, Mi., U.S.	p15	115
Plymouth, Mn., U.S.	m12	116
Plymouth, N.C., U.S.	B6	126
Plymouth, N.H., U.S.	C3	122
Plymouth, Oh., U.S.	A3	128
Plymouth, Pa., U.S.	D10	131
Plymouth, Wi., U.S.	E6	142
Plymouth, co., Ia., U.S.	B1	108
Plymouth, co., Ma., U.S.	C6	114
Plymouth Bay, b., Ma., U.S.	C6	114
Plzeň, Czech Rep.	E2	20
Pô, Burkina	D4	50
Po, stm., Italy	B3	18
Po, stm., Va., U.S.	B5	139
Pobè, Benin	E5	50
Pobeda, gora, mtn., Russia	C16	26
Pobedy, Peak, mtn., Asia	B11	42
Pocahontas, Ar., U.S.	A5	97
Pocahontas, Ia., U.S.	B3	108
Pocahontas, Il., U.S.	E4	106
Pocahontas, co., Ia., U.S.	B3	108
Pocahontas, co., W.V., U.S.	C4	141
Pocasset, Ma., U.S.	C6	114
Pocatalico, W.V., U.S.	C3	141
Pocatalico, stm., W.V., U.S.	C3	141
Pocatello, Id., U.S.	G6	105
Počep, Russia	C12	20
Počinok, Russia	B12	20
Poções, Braz.	D3	74
Pocola, Ok., U.S.	B7	129
Pocomoke, stm., Md., U.S.	D7	113
Pocomoke City, Md., U.S.	D6	113
Pocomoke Sound, strt., Md., U.S.	E6	113
Poconé, Braz.	B6	72
Pocono Mountains, hills, Pa., U.S.	E11	131
Pocono Pines, Pa., U.S.	D11	131
Poços de Caldas, Braz.	F2	74
Pocotopaug Lake, res., Ct., U.S.	C6	100
Podgorica, Yugo.	C7	18
Podkamennaja Tunguska, Russia	C10	26
Podkamennaja Tunguska, stm., Russia	C11	26
Podol'sk, Russia	C6	22
Podor, Sen.	C2	50
Podporože, Russia	B5	22
Pofadder, S. Afr.	D2	56
Poge, Cape, c., Ma., U.S.	D7	114
Pograničnyj, Russia	C14	28
P'ohang, S. Kor.	D13	28
Pohénégamook, P.Q., Can.	B8	90
Pohjanmaa, reg., Fin.	D11	10
Pohnpei, i., Micron.	D9	58
Pohue Bay, b., Hi., U.S.	E6	104
Pohvistnevo, Russia	D9	22
Poinsett, co., Ar., U.S.	B5	97
Poinsett, Cape, c., Ant.	C16	67
Poinsett, Lake, l., Fl., U.S.	D6	102
Poinsett, Lake, l., S.D., U.S.	C8	134
Point Clear, Al., U.S.	E2	94
Pointe a la Hache, La., U.S.	E6	111
Pointe-à-Pitre, Guad.	B7	80
Pointe-au-Pic, P.Q., Can.	B7	90
Pointe-Calumet, P.Q., Can.	p19	90
Pointe-Claire, P.Q., Can.	D4	90
Pointe Coupee, co., La., U.S.	D4	111
Pointe-des-Cascades, P.Q., Can.	q19	90
Point Edward, On., Can.	D2	89
Pointe-Noire, Congo	D2	54
Pointe-Verte, N.B., Can.	B4	87
Point Fortin, Trin.	C7	80
Point Hope, Ak., U.S.	B6	95
Point Imperial, mtn., Az., U.S.	A4	96
Point Judith Pond, l., R.I., U.S.	F4	132
Point Leamington, Nf., Can.	D4	88
Point Marion, Pa., U.S.	G2	131
Point Mugu Naval Air Station, mil., Ca., U.S.	E4	98
Point of Rocks, Md., U.S.	B2	113
Point Pelee National Park, On., Can.	F2	89
Point Pleasant, N.J., U.S.	C4	123
Point Pleasant, W.V., U.S.	C2	141
Point Pleasant Beach, N.J., U.S.	C4	123
Point Reyes National Seashore, Ca., U.S.	C2	98
Point Roberts, Wa., U.S.	A2	140
Poipu, Hi., U.S.	B2	104
Poison Creek, stm., Wy., U.S.	C5	143
Poisson Blanc, Lac du, res., P.Q., Can.	C2	90
Poitiers, Fr.	D7	16
Poitou, hist. reg., Fr.	D6	16
Poivre Atoll, i., Sey.	i12	57b
Pojarkovo, Russia	B13	28
Pokaran, India	D2	40
Pokegama Lake, l., Mn., U.S.	C5	116
Pokegama Lake, l., Wi., U.S.	C2	142
Pokharā, Nepal	D4	40
Pokhrā, Nepal	D4	40
Polacca, Az., U.S.	B5	96
Polack, Bela.	B10	20
Pola de Lena, Spain	F4	16
Pola de Siero, Spain	F4	16
Poland, ctry., Eur.	C5	20
Polar Bear Provincial Park, On., Can.	n18	89
Polatlı, Tur.	C5	44
Polecat Creek, stm., Ok., U.S.	B5	129
Pol-e Khomrī, Afg.	C9	42
Polesye, reg., Eur.	D8	20
Polewali, Indon.	D5	36
Policastro, Golfo di, b., Italy	E5	18
Pólis, Cyp.	E5	44
Poljarnyj, Russia	B15	10
Polk, Pa., U.S.	D2	131
Polk, co., Ar., U.S.	C1	97
Polk, co., Fl., U.S.	E5	102
Polk, co., Ga., U.S.	C1	103
Polk, co., Ia., U.S.	C4	108
Polk, co., Mn., U.S.	C2	116
Polk, co., Mo., U.S.	D4	118
Polk, co., N.C., U.S.	f10	126
Polk, co., Or., U.S.	C3	130
Polk, co., Tn., U.S.	D9	135
Polk, co., Tx., U.S.	D5	136
Polk, co., Wi., U.S.	C1	142
Polk City, Fl., U.S.	D5	102
Polk City, Ia., U.S.	C4	108
Pol'kino, Russia	B11	26
Pollāchi, India	G3	40
Pollença, Spain	H8	16
Polo, Il., U.S.	B4	106
Polohy, Ukr.	F14	20
Polonnaruwa, Sri L.	H4	40
Polonne, Ukr.	D9	20
Polson, Mt., U.S.	C2	119
Poltava, Ukr.	E13	20
Põltsamaa, Est.	C10	10
Polunočnoe, Russia	B11	22
Polynesia, is., Oc.	I23	64
Pombal, Braz.	C4	74
Pomerania, hist. reg., Eur.	C4	20
Pomeroy, In., U.S.	B3	108
Pomeroy, Oh., U.S.	C3	128
Pomeroy, Wa., U.S.	C8	140
Pomme de Terre, stm., Mn., U.S.	E3	116
Pomme de Terre, stm., Mo., U.S.	D4	118
Pomme de Terre Lake, res., Mo., U.S.	D4	118
Pomona, Ca., U.S.	E5	98
Pomona, Ks., U.S.	D8	109
Pomona Lake, res., Ks., U.S.	D7	109
Pompano Beach, Fl., U.S.	F6	102
Pompei, Italy	D5	18
Pompéu, Braz.	E2	74
Pompton Lakes, N.J., U.S.	A4	123
Ponaganset, stm., R.I., U.S.	C2	132
Ponaganset Reservoir, res., R.I., U.S.	B2	132
Ponape see Pohnpei, i., Micron.	D9	58
Ponca, Ne., U.S.	B9	120
Ponca City, Ok., U.S.	A4	129
Ponca Creek, stm., U.S.	A6	120
Ponca Indian Reservation, Ne., U.S.	B7	120
Ponce, P.R.	B6	80
Ponce de Leon Bay, b., Fl., U.S.	G5	102
Ponce de Leon Inlet, b., Fl., U.S.	C6	102
Poncha Pass, Co., U.S.	C4	99
Ponchatoula, La., U.S.	D5	111
Pond, stm., Ky., U.S.	C2	110
Pond Creek, Ok., U.S.	A3	129
Pondera, co., Mt., U.S.	B4	119
Pond Fork, stm., W.V., U.S.	D3	141
Pondicherry, India	G3	40
Pone Island, i., Md., U.S.	D5	113
Ponferrada, Spain	F3	16
Ponoj, Russia	C6	26
Ponoka, Ab., Can.	C4	84
Ponta Delgada, Port.	F7	46
Ponta Grossa, Braz.	D8	72
Pontalina, Braz.	E2	74
Ponta Porã, Braz.	H8	70
Pontarlier, Fr.	D10	16
Pontchartrain, Lake, l., La., U.S.	D5	111
Ponteix, Sk., Can.	H2	91
Ponte Nova, Braz.	F3	74
Pontevedra, Spain	F2	16
Ponte Vedra Beach, Fl., U.S.	B5	102
Pontiac, Il., U.S.	C5	106
Pontiac, Mi., U.S.	F7	115
Pontianak, Indon.	C3	36
Pontine Islands see Ponziane, Isole, is., Italy	D4	18
Pontoosuc Lake, l., Ma., U.S.	B1	114
Pontotoc, Ms., U.S.	A4	117
Pontotoc, co., Ms., U.S.	A4	117
Pontotoc, co., Ok., U.S.	C5	129
Pont-Rouge, P.Q., Can.	C6	90
Pontus Mountains see Doğu Karadeniz Dağları, mts., Tur.	B8	44
Pontypool, On., Can.	C6	89
Ponziane, Isole, is., Italy	D4	18
Poole, Eng., U.K.	E5	12
Pooler, Ga., U.S.	D5	103
Pooles Island, i., Md., U.S.	B5	113
Poolesville, Md., U.S.	B3	113
Poopó, Bol.	B4	72
Poopó, Lago, l., Bol.	B4	72
Popayán, Col.	C4	70
Pope, co., Ar., U.S.	B2	97
Pope, co., Il., U.S.	F5	106
Pope, co., Mn., U.S.	E3	116
Pope Air Force Base, mil., N.C., U.S.	B3	126
Poplar, Mt., U.S.	B11	119
Poplar, stm., Can.	C3	86
Poplar, stm., Mn., U.S.	C2	116
Poplar Bluff, Mo., U.S.	E7	118
Poplar Island, i., Md., U.S.	C5	113
Poplarville, Ms., U.S.	E4	117
Popocatépetl, Volcán, vol., Mex.	D5	78
Popokabaka, D.R.C.	E3	54
Popondetta, Pap. N. Gui.	H12	32
Popovo, Bul.	C11	18
Popple, stm., Wi., U.S.	C5	142
Poprad, Slvk.	E6	20
Poquonock, Ct., U.S.	B5	100
Poquonock Bridge, Ct., U.S.	D7	100
Poquoson, Va., U.S.	C6	139
Porangatu, Braz.	D2	74
Porbandar, India	I4	40
Porcher Island, i., B.C., Can.	C2	85
Porcupine, stm., N.A.	E11	82
Porcupine Mountains, mts., Mi., U.S.	m12	115
Pordenone, Italy	B4	18
Pori, Fin.	F9	10
Porirua, N.Z.	p13	63c
Porlamar, Ven.	A7	70
Poronajsk, Russia	E16	26
Porpoise Bay, b., Ant.	C17	67
Porsangen, b., Nor.	A11	10
Porsgrunn, Nor.	G3	10
Portachuelo, Bol.	B5	72
Port Adelaide, Austl.	G2	62
Portadown, N. Ire., U.K.	C3	12
Portage, In., U.S.	A3	107
Portage, Mi., U.S.	F5	115
Portage, Pa., U.S.	F4	131
Portage, Wi., U.S.	E4	142
Portage, co., Oh., U.S.	A4	128
Portage, co., Wi., U.S.	D4	142
Portage, stm., Oh., U.S.	B2	128
Portage Bay, b., Mb., Can.	D2	86
Portage Head, c., Wa., U.S.	A1	140
Portage Lake, l., Me., U.S.	B4	112
Portage Lakes, Oh., U.S.	A4	128
Portage la Prairie, Mb., Can.	E2	86
Portageville, Mo., U.S.	E8	118
Port Alberni, B.C., Can.	E5	85
Portales, N.M., U.S.	C6	124
Port Alfred, S. Afr.	E4	56
Port Alice, B.C., Can.	D4	85
Port Allegany, Pa., U.S.	C5	131
Port Allen, La., U.S.	D4	111
Port Angeles, Wa., U.S.	A2	140
Port Antonio, Jam.	B4	80
Port Aransas, Tx., U.S.	F4	136
Port Arthur see Lüshun, China	D12	28
Port Arthur, Tx., U.S.	E6	136
Port Augusta, Austl.	G2	62
Port-au-Prince, Haiti	B5	80
Port au Peace Peninsula, pen., Nf., Can.	D2	88
Port Austin, Mi., U.S.	D7	115
Port Barre, La., U.S.	D4	111
Port Blair, India	G6	40
Port Blandford, Nf., Can.	D4	88
Port Bolivar, Tx., U.S.	E5	136
Port Burwell, On., Can.	E4	89
Port Byron, Il., U.S.	B3	106
Port Carbon, Pa., U.S.	E9	131
Port Carling, On., Can.	B5	89
Port-Cartier-Ouest, P.Q., Can.	k13	90
Port Chalmers, N.Z.	q13	63c
Port Charlotte, Fl., U.S.	F4	102
Port Chester, N.Y., U.S.	E7	125
Port Clinton, Oh., U.S.	A3	128
Port Colborne, On., Can.	E5	89
Port Coquitlam, B.C., Can.	E6	85
Port Deposit, Md., U.S.	A5	113
Port Dickinson, N.Y., U.S.	C5	125
Port Edward, B.C., Can.	B2	85
Port Edward, S. Afr.	E5	56
Port Edwards, Wi., U.S.	D4	142
Portel, Braz.	B1	74
Port Elgin, On., Can.	C3	89
Port Elizabeth, S. Afr.	E4	56
Porter, In., U.S.	A3	107
Porter, Tx., U.S.	D5	136
Porter, co., In., U.S.	B3	107
Porter Creek, stm., W.V., U.S.	m13	141
Porterdale, Ga., U.S.	C3	103
Porterville, Ca., U.S.	D4	98
Port Ewen, N.Y., U.S.	D7	125
Port Fairy, Austl.	H3	62
Port Gamble Indian Reservation, Wa., U.S.	B3	140
Port-Gentil, Gabon	D1	54
Port Gibson, Ms., U.S.	D3	117
Port-Harcourt, Nig.	F6	50
Port Hedland, Austl.	E2	62
Port Hood, N.S., Can.	C8	87
Port Hope, On., Can.	D6	89
Port Hope Simpson, Nf., Can.	B3	88
Port Hueneme, Ca., U.S.	E4	98
Port Huron, Mi., U.S.	F8	115
Portimão, Port.	I2	16
Port Isabel, Tx., U.S.	F4	136
Port Jefferson, N.Y., U.S.	n15	125
Port Jervis, N.Y., U.S.	D6	125
Port Lairge see Waterford, Ire.	D3	12
Portland, Austl.	H3	62
Portland, Ct., U.S.	C5	100
Portland, In., U.S.	D8	107
Portland, Me., U.S.	E2	112
Portland, Mi., U.S.	F6	115
Portland, N.D., U.S.	B8	127
Portland, Or., U.S.	B4	130
Portland, Tn., U.S.	A5	135
Portland, Tx., U.S.	F4	136
Portland, Cape, c., Austl.	I4	62
Portland Inlet, b., B.C., Can.	B2	85
Port Laoise, Ire.	D3	12
Port Lavaca, Tx., U.S.	E4	136
Port Lincoln, Austl.	G2	62
Port Loko, S.L.	E2	50
Port Louis, Mrts.	f10	57a
Port Ludlow, Wa., U.S.	B3	140
Port Macquarie, Austl.	G5	62
Port Madison Indian Reservation, Wa., U.S.	B3	140
Port McNeil, B.C., Can.	D4	85
Port McNicoll, On., Can.	C5	89
Port Monmouth, N.J., U.S.	C4	123
Port Moresby, Pap. N. Gui.	H12	32
Port Morien, N.S., Can.	C10	87
Port Neches, Tx., U.S.	E6	136
Portneuf, P.Q., Can.	C6	90
Port Nolloth, S. Afr.	D2	56
Porto, Port.	G2	16
Porto Alegre, Braz.	E7	72
Porto Amboim, Ang.	F2	54
Portobelo, Pan.	D4	80
Porto de Moz, Braz.	D9	70
Porto Esperança, Braz.	G8	70
Porto Esperidião, Braz.	G8	70
Portoferraio, Italy	C3	18
Port of Spain, Trin.	C7	80
Portola, Ca., U.S.	C3	98
Porto Murtinho, Braz.	H8	70
Porto Nacional, Braz.	D2	74
Porto-Novo, Benin	E5	50
Port Orange, Fl., U.S.	C6	102
Port Orchard, Wa., U.S.	B3	140
Port Orford, Or., U.S.	E2	130
Porto Santana, Braz.	B1	74
Porto Santo, i., Port.	D1	48
Porto Seguro, Braz.	E4	74
Porto Torres, Italy	D2	18
Porto-Vecchio, Fr.	D2	18
Porto Velho, Braz.	E7	70
Portoviejo, Ec.	D3	70
Port Penn, De., U.S.	B3	101
Port Phillip Bay, b., Austl.	H3	62
Port Richey, Fl., U.S.	D4	102
Port Rowan, On., Can.	E4	89
Port Royal, S.C., U.S.	G6	133
Port Royal Island, i., S.C., U.S.	G6	133
Port Royal Sound, strt., S.C., U.S.	G6	133
Port Said see Būr Sa'īd, Egypt	E10	48
Port Saint Joe, Fl., U.S.	C1	102
Port Saint Johns, S. Afr.	E4	56
Port Saint Lucie, Fl., U.S.	E6	102
Port Salerno, Fl., U.S.	E6	102
Port Sanders, Nf., Can.	C3	88
Port Shepstone, S. Afr.	E5	56
Portsmouth, Eng., U.K.	E6	12
Portsmouth, N.H., U.S.	D5	122
Portsmouth, Oh., U.S.	D3	128
Portsmouth, R.I., U.S.	E6	132

Name	Map Ref.	Page

Portsmouth, Va., U.S. D6 139
Portsmouth Naval Shipyard, mil., Me., U.S. D5 122
Port Stanley, On., Can. . . E3 89
Port Stanley see Stanley, Falk. Is. H5 69
Port Sudan see Būr Sūdān, Sudan G12 48
Port Sulphur, La., U.S. E6 111
Port Talbot, Wales, U.K. . . E5 12
Porttipahdan tekojärvi, l., Fin. B12 10
Port Townsend, Wa., U.S. . . A3 140
Portugal, ctry., Eur. G3 16
Port Union, Nf., Can. D5 88
Port Vila, Vanuatu k9 62a
Port Washington, N.Y., U.S. h13 125
Port Washington, Wi., U.S. E6 142
Port Wentworth, Ga., U.S. . D5 103
Porum, Ok., U.S. B6 129
Porvenir, Chile H2 69
Porvoo, Fin. F11 10
Posadas, Arg. D6 72
Posen see Poznań, Pol. . . . C4 20
Posen, Il., U.S. k9 106
Poset, Russia E15 26
Posey, co., In., U.S. H2 107
Poseyville, In., U.S. H2 107
Posio, Fin. C13 10
Poso, Indon. D6 36
Posse, Braz. D2 74
Post, Tx., U.S. C2 136
Post Falls, Id., U.S. B2 105
Postmasburg, S. Afr. D3 56
Postville, Ia., U.S. A6 108
Potawatomi Indian Reservation, Ks., U.S. . . C8 109
Potchefstroom, S. Afr. D4 56
Poteau, Ok., U.S. B7 129
Poteau, stm., U.S. B7 129
Poteet, Tx., U.S. E3 136
Potenza, Italy D5 18
Potgietersrus, S. Afr. C4 56
Poth, Tx., U.S. E3 136
Potholes Reservoir, res., Wa., U.S. B6 140
Poti, Geor. A9 44
Potiskum, Nig. D7 50
Potlatch, Id., U.S. C2 105
Potomac, Md., U.S. B3 113
Potomac, stm., U.S. D4 113
Potomac Heights, Md., U.S. C3 113
Potomac Park, Md., U.S. . . k13 113
Potosí, Bol. B4 72
Potosi, Mo., U.S. D7 118
Potsdam, Ger. D13 12
Potsdam, N.Y., U.S. f10 125
Pottawatomie, co., Ks., U.S. C7 109
Pottawatomie, co., Ok., U.S. B4 129
Pottawattamie, co., Ia., U.S. C2 108
Potter, co., Pa., U.S. C6 131
Potter, co., S.D., U.S. B6 134
Potter, co., Tx., U.S. B2 136
Potter Valley, Ca., U.S. C2 98
Potts Creek, stm., U.S. C2 139
Pottstown, Pa., U.S. F10 131
Pottsville, Ar., U.S. B2 97
Pottsville, Pa., U.S. E9 131
Pouce Coupe, B.C., Can. . . B7 85
Pouch Cove, Nf., Can. E5 88
Poughkeepsie, N.Y., U.S. . . D7 125
Poulan, Ga., U.S. E3 103
Poulsbo, Wa., U.S. B3 140
Poultney, Vt., U.S. D2 138
Poultney, stm., Vt., U.S. . . . D2 138
Pound, Va., U.S. e9 139
Pound Gap, U.S. C7 110
Pouso Alegre, Braz. F2 74
Poŭthĭsăt, Camb. D4 34
Póvoa de Varzim, Port. . . . G2 16
Povungnituk, P.Q., Can. . . . f11 90
Powassan, On., Can. A5 89
Poway, Ca., U.S. F5 98
Powder, stm., Or., U.S. C9 130
Powder, stm., U.S. B6 92
Powder, Middle Fork, stm., Wy., U.S. C6 143
Powder, North Fork, stm., Wy., U.S. C6 143
Powder, South Fork, stm., Wy., U.S. C6 143
Powder River, stm., U.S. . . . E11 119
Powder River Pass, Wy., U.S. B5 143
Powder Springs, Ga., U.S. . h8 103
Powell, Oh., U.S. B2 128
Powell, Tn., U.S. m13 135
Powell, Wy., U.S. B4 143
Powell, co., Ky., U.S. C6 110
Powell, co., Mt., U.S. D4 119
Powell, stm., U.S. C10 135
Powell, Lake, res., U.S. D5 92
Powell, Lake, res., U.S. F5 137
Powell, Mount, mtn., Co., U.S. B4 99
Powell, Mount, mtn., N.M., U.S. B1 124
Powell Butte, Or., U.S. C5 130
Powell Park, reg., Co., U.S. A2 99
Powell River, B.C., Can. . . . E5 85
Powellton, W.V., U.S. C3 141
Power, co., Id., U.S. G5 105
Powers, Or., U.S. E2 130
Powerview, Mb., Can. D3 86

Poweshiek, co., Ia., U.S. . . C5 108
Powhatan, Va., U.S. C5 139
Powhatan, co., Va., U.S. . . . C5 139
Powhatan Point, Oh., U.S. . C5 128
Poxoréu, Braz. G9 70
Poyang Hu, l., China F11 28
Poyang Lake see Poyang Hu, l., China F11 28
Poygan, Lake, l., Wi., U.S. . D5 142
Poynette, Wi., U.S. E4 142
Požarevac, Yugo. B8 18
Poza Rica, Mex. C5 78
Požega, Cro. B6 18
Poznań, Pol. C4 20
Pozo Redondo Mountains, mts., Az., U.S. E3 96
Pozuelos, Ven. C7 80
Prachuap Khiri Khan, Thai. . D3 34
Prado, Braz. G12 70
Prague see Praha, Czech Rep. D3 20
Prague, Ok., U.S. B5 129
Praha (Prague), Czech Rep. D3 20
Praia, C.V. h10 50a
Prainha Nova, Braz. E7 70
Prairie, co., Ar., U.S. C4 97
Prairie, co., Mt., U.S. D11 119
Prairie, stm., Mn., U.S. C5 116
Prairie, stm., Wi., U.S. C4 142
Prairie City, Ia., U.S. C4 108
Prairie City, Or., U.S. C8 130
Prairie Creek Reservoir, res., In., U.S. D7 107
Prairie Dog Creek, stm., U.S. C3 109
Prairie du Chien, Wi., U.S. . E2 142
Prairie du Sac, Wi., U.S. . . E4 142
Prairie Grove, Ar., U.S. . . . B1 97
Prairie View, Tx., U.S. D5 136
Prairie Village, Ks., U.S. . . m16 109
Prairies, Rivière des, stm., P.Q., Can. p19 90
Praslin, i., Sey. h13 57b
Prātāpgarh, India E2 40
Pratas Island see Tungsha Tao, i., Tai. E4 30
Prater Mountain, mtn., Wy., U.S. C2 143
Prato, Italy C3 18
Pratt, Ks., U.S. E5 109
Pratt, co., Ks., U.S. E5 109
Prattville, Al., U.S. C3 94
Praya, Indon. E5 36
Preble, co., Oh., U.S. C1 128
Prečistoe, Russia B12 20
Premont, Tx., U.S. F3 136
Prentiss, Ms., U.S. D4 117
Prentiss, co., Ms., U.S. A5 117
Prenzlau, Ger. B13 12
Preparis Island, i., Myan. . . D2 34
Preparis North Channel, strt., Myan. C2 34
Preparis South Channel, strt., Myan. D2 34
Přerov, Czech Rep. E4 20
Prescott, On., Can. C9 89
Prescott, Ar., U.S. D2 97
Prescott, Az., U.S. C3 96
Prescott, Wi., U.S. D1 142
Presho, S.D., U.S. D5 134
Presidencia Roque Sáenz Peña, Arg. C4 69
Presidente Dutra, Braz. . . . E10 74
Presidente Epitácio, Braz. . . F1 74
Presidente Prudente, Braz. . F1 74
Presidential Range, mts., N.H., U.S. B4 122
Presidio, Tx., U.S. p12 136
Presidio, co., Tx., U.S. o12 136
Prešov, Slvk. E6 20
Prespa, Lake, l., Eur. D8 18
Presque Isle, Me., U.S. B5 112
Presque Isle, co., Mi., U.S. . C6 115
Prestea, Ghana E4 50
Preston, Eng., U.K. D5 12
Preston, Ia., U.S. B7 108
Preston, Id., U.S. G7 105
Preston, Mn., U.S. G6 116
Preston, co., W.V., U.S. B5 141
Preston Peak, mtn., Ca., U.S. B2 98
Prestonsburg, Ky., U.S. . . . C7 110
Presumpscot, stm., Me., U.S. g7 112
Pretoria, S. Afr. D4 56
Prettyboy Reservoir, res., Md., U.S. A4 113
Pretty Prairie, Ks., U.S. . . . E5 109
Préveza, Grc. E8 18
Prewitt Reservoir, res., Co., U.S. A7 99
Pribilof Islands, is., Ak., U.S. D5 95
Příbram, Czech Rep. E3 20
Price, Ut., U.S. D5 137
Price, co., Wi., U.S. C3 142
Price, stm., Ut., U.S. D5 137
Price Inlet, b., S.C., U.S. . . . k12 133
Prichard, Al., U.S. E1 94
Prieska, S. Afr. D3 56
Priest Lake, l., Id., U.S. . . . A2 105
Priest River, Id., U.S. A2 105
Priest Rapids Dam, Wa., U.S. C6 140
Priest Rapids Lake, res., Wa., U.S. C6 140
Priest River, Id., U.S. A2 105

Prievidza, Slvk. E5 20
Prijedor, Bos. B6 18
Prilep, Mac. D8 18
Prim, Point, c., P.E., Can. . . C5 87
Primghar, Ia., U.S. A2 108
Primorsk, Russia F13 10
Primorsko-Ahtarsk, Russia . F15 20
Primrose, R.I., U.S. B3 132
Primrose Lake, l., Can. . . . H18 82
Prince, Lake, res., Va., U.S. k14 139
Prince Albert National Park, Sk., Can. C2 91
Prince Charles Mountains, mts., Ant. D11 67
Prince Edward, co., Va., U.S. C4 139
Prince Edward Island, prov., Can. C6 87
Prince Edward Island National Park, P.E., Can. C6 87
Prince Edward Islands, is., S. Afr. N13 46
Prince Frederick, Md., U.S. C4 113
Prince George, B.C., Can. . C6 85
Prince George, co., Va., U.S. C5 139
Prince Georges, co., Md., U.S. C4 113
Prince of Wales, Cape, c., Ak., U.S. B6 95
Prince of Wales Island, i., Austl. C3 62
Prince of Wales Island, i., Ak., U.S. n23 95
Prince Olav Coast, is., Ant. C9 67
Prince Rupert, B.C., Can. . . B2 85
Princes Lakes, In., U.S. . . . F5 107
Princess Anne, Md., U.S. . . D6 113
Princess Astrid Coast, Ant. D5 67
Princess Martha Coast, Ant. D3 67
Princess Ragnhild Coast, Ant. D7 67
Princess Royal Channel, strt., B.C., Can. C3 85
Princess Royal Island, i., B.C., Can. C3 85
Princeton, B.C., Can. E7 85
Princeton, Fl., U.S. G6 102
Princeton, Ia., U.S. C7 108
Princeton, Il., U.S. B4 106
Princeton, In., U.S. H2 107
Princeton, Ky., U.S. C2 110
Princeton, Me., U.S. C5 112
Princeton, Mn., U.S. E5 116
Princeton, Mo., U.S. A4 118
Princeton, N.C., U.S. B4 126
Princeton, N.J., U.S. C3 123
Princeton, W.V., U.S. D3 141
Princeton, Wi., U.S. E4 142
Princeton, Mount, mtn., Co., U.S. C4 99
Princeville, P.Q., Can. C6 90
Princeville, Il., U.S. C4 106
Princeville, N.C., U.S. B5 126
Prince William, co., Va., U.S. B5 139
Prince William Sound, strt., Ak., U.S. g18 95
Príncipe, i., S. Tom./P. C1 54
Príncipe Channel, strt., B.C., Can. C3 85
Príncipe da Beira, Braz. . . . F7 70
Prineville, Or., U.S. C6 130
Prineville Reservoir, res., Or., U.S. C6 130
Prinzapolka, Nic. C3 80
Prior Lake, Mn., U.S. F5 116
Priozersk, Russia F14 10
Pripet (Pryp'yat') (Pripjat'), stm., Eur. C9 20
Pripet Marshes, reg., Eur. . . C10 20
Pripyat see Pripet, stm., Eur. C9 20
Priština, Yugo. C8 18
Pritchards Island, i., S.C., U.S. G6 133
Pritzwalk, Ger. B13 12
Privas, Fr. E9 16
Privolžskaja vozvyšennost', plat., Russia D6 26
Prizren, Yugo. C8 18
Probolinggo, Indon. E4 36
Proctor, Mn., U.S. D6 116
Proctor, Vt., U.S. D2 138
Proctor Lake, res., Tx., U.S. C3 136
Proctorsville, Vt., U.S. E3 138
Proddatūr, India G3 40
Progreso, Mex. C7 78
Prohladnyj, Russia F7 22
Prokopevsk, Russia D10 26
Prokuplje, Yugo. C8 18
Prome, Myan. C3 34
Promontory Mountains, mts., Ut., U.S. B3 137
Prophetstown, Il., U.S. B4 106
Propriá, Braz. F11 74
Proserpine, Austl. D9 62
Prospect, Ct., U.S. C4 100
Prospect, Oh., U.S. B2 128
Prospect, Or., U.S. E4 130
Prospect, Pa., U.S. E1 131
Prospect Hill, mtn., Or., U.S. k11 130

Prospect Park, N.J., U.S. . . B4 123
Prospect Park, Pa., U.S. . . . p20 131
Prosperidad, Phil. E9 34
Prosperity, S.C., U.S. C4 133
Prosperity, W.V., U.S. n13 141
Prosser, Wa., U.S. C6 140
Protection, Ks., U.S. E4 109
Provadija, Bul. C11 18
Providence, Ky., U.S. C2 110
Providence, R.I., U.S. C4 132
Providence, Ut., U.S. B4 137
Providence, co., R.I., U.S. . . C2 132
Providence, stm., R.I., U.S. . C5 132
Providence Point, c., R.I., U.S. D5 132
Providencia, Isla de, i., Col. C3 80
Providencija, Russia C20 26
Province Lake, l., N.H., U.S. C5 122
Provincetown, Ma., U.S. . . . B7 114
Provins, Fr. C8 16
Provo, Ut., U.S. C4 137
Provo, stm., Ut., U.S. C4 137
Provost, Ab., Can. C5 84
Prowers, co., Co., U.S. D8 99
Prudence Island, i., R.I., U.S. E5 132
Prudentópolis, Braz. D7 72
Prudenville, Mi., U.S. D6 115
Prudhoe Bay, Ak., U.S. . . . A10 95
Prudhoe Bay, b., Ak., U.S. . A10 95
Prut, stm., Eur. G10 20
Pružany, Bela. C9 20
Pryluky, Ukr. D12 20
Prymors'k, Ukr. F14 20
Pryor, Mt., U.S. E8 119
Pryor, Ok., U.S. A6 129
Pryor Mountains, mts., Mt., U.S. E8 119
Pryp'yat' (Pripet) (Pripjat'), stm., Eur. D8 20
Przasnysz, Pol. C6 20
Przemyśl, Pol. E7 20
Psël (Ps'ol), stm., Eur. D13 20
Pskov, Russia D4 26
Pskov, Lake, l., Eur. G13 10
Ps'ol (Psël), stm., Eur. D13 20
Ptolemaís, Grc. D8 18
Pucallpa, Peru E5 70
Pucheng, China F11 28
Puckaway Lake, l., Wi., U.S. E4 142
Pudož, Russia B6 22
Pudukkottai, India G3 40
Puebla, state, Mex. D5 78
Puebla de Zaragoza, Mex. . D5 78
Pueblo, Co., U.S. C6 99
Pueblo, co., Co., U.S. C6 99
Pueblo Mountain, mtn., Or., U.S. E8 130
Pueblo Mountains, mts., Or., U.S. E8 130
Pueblo Reservoir, res., Co., U.S. C6 99
Puente Genil, Spain I4 16
Pueo Point, c., Hi., U.S. . . . B1 104
Puerco, stm., U.S. C6 96
Puerco, Rio, stm., N.M., U.S. B2 124
Puerto Acosta, Bol. B4 72
Puerto Ángel, Mex. D5 78
Puerto Armuelles, Pan. D3 80
Puerto Asís, Col. C4 70
Puerto Ayacucho, Ven. B6 70
Puerto Baquerizo Moreno, Ec. D2 70
Puerto Barrios, Guat. B2 80
Puerto Bermúdez, Peru . . . F5 70
Puerto Berrío, Col. B5 70
Puerto Bolívar, Col. C5 80
Puerto Boyacá, Col. D5 80
Puerto Cabello, Ven. A6 70
Puerto Cabezas, Nic. C3 80
Puerto Carreño, Col. B6 70
Puerto Chicama, Peru E4 70
Puerto Cortés, Hond. B2 80
Puerto Cumarebo, Ven. . . . A6 70
Puerto de la Cruz, Spain . . A1 50
Puerto del Rosario, Spain . . A2 50
Puerto Deseado, Arg. G3 69
Puerto Esperanza, Arg. . . . D7 72
Puerto Guaraní, Para. C6 72
Puerto Inírida, Col. E6 80
Puerto Juárez, Mex. C7 78
Puerto la Cruz, Ven. A7 70
Puerto Leguízamo, Col. . . . D5 70
Puerto Libertad, Mex. B2 78
Puerto Limón, C.R. C3 80
Puertollano, Spain H4 16
Puerto Lobos, Arg. F3 69
Puerto Madryn, Arg. F3 69
Puerto Maldonado, Peru . . F6 70
Puerto Montt, Chile F2 69
Puerto Morazán, Nic. C2 80
Puerto Nariño, Col. D6 80
Puerto Natales, Chile H2 69
Puerto Padre, Cuba A4 80
Puerto Páez, Ven. B6 70
Puerto Peñasco, Mex. A2 78
Puerto Plata, Dom. Rep. . . . B5 80
Puerto Princesa, Phil. E7 34
Puerto Rico, Bol. F6 70
Puerto Rico, dep., N.A. B6 80
Puerto Rico Trench G7 66
Puerto San José, Guat. C1 80
Puerto San Julián, Arg. G3 69

Puerto Santa Cruz, Arg. . . . H3 69
Puerto Sastre, Para. C6 72
Puerto Suárez, Bol. B6 72
Puerto Vallarta, Mex. C3 78
Puerto Villamil, Ec. D1 70
Puerto Wilches, Col. B5 70
Puerto Ybapobó, Para. C6 72
Pugačov, Russia D8 22
Puget Sound, strt., Wa., U.S. B3 140
Puget Sound Naval Shipyard, mil., Wa., U.S. e10 140
Pugwash, N.S., Can. D6 87
Puhi, Hi., U.S. B2 104
Pukalani, Hi., U.S. C5 104
Pukaskwa National Park, On., Can. o18 89
Pukch'ŏng-ŭp, N. Kor. C13 28
Pukeashun Mountain, mtn., B.C., Can. D8 85
Pukou, China C4 30
Pula, Cro. B4 18
Pulaski, N.Y., U.S. B4 125
Pulaski, Tn., U.S. B4 135
Pulaski, Va., U.S. C2 139
Pulaski, Wi., U.S. D5 142
Pulaski, co., Ar., U.S. C3 97
Pulaski, co., Ga., U.S. D3 103
Pulaski, co., Il., U.S. F4 106
Pulaski, co., In., U.S. B4 107
Pulaski, co., Ky., U.S. C5 110
Pulaski, co., Mo., U.S. D5 118
Pulaski, co., Va., U.S. C2 139
Puławy, Pol. D7 20
Pulicat Lake, l., India G4 40
Pullman, Wa., U.S. C8 140
Pumphrey, Md., U.S. h11 113
Puná, Isla, i., Ec. D3 70
Punakha, Bhu. D5 40
Punata, Bol. B4 72
Pune, India F2 40
Pungo Lake, l., N.C., U.S. . . B6 126
Punia, D.R.C. D5 54
Punjab, prov., India C3 40
Punjab, prov., Pak. D11 42
Puno, Peru G5 70
Punta, Cerro de, mtn., P.R. . B6 80
Punta Alta, Arg. F5 72
Punta Arenas, Chile H2 69
Punta de Díaz, Chile D3 72
Punta del Este, Ur. F7 72
Punta Delgada, Arg. F4 69
Punta Gorda, Fl., U.S. F4 102
Punta Gorda, Bahía de, b., Nic. C3 80
Puntarenas, C.R. C2 80
Punto Fijo, Ven. A5 70
Punxsutawney, Pa., U.S. . . . E4 131
Puolanka, Fin. D12 10
Puqi, China F10 28
Puquio, Peru F5 70
Purcell, Ok., U.S. B4 129
Purcellville, Va., U.S. A5 139
Purdy, Mo., U.S. E4 118
Purgatoire, stm., Co., U.S. . . D7 99
Purgatoire Peak, mtn., Co., U.S. D5 99
Puri, India F5 40
Pūrnia, India D5 40
Purus (Purús), stm., S.A. . . . D7 70
Purvis, Ms., U.S. D4 117
Purwakarta, Indon. E3 36
Purwokerto, Indon. E3 36
Pusan, S. Kor. D13 28
Pushaw Lake, l., Me., U.S. . D4 112
Pushkar, India D2 40
Pushmataha, co., Ok., U.S. C6 129
Puškin, Russia G15 10
Putao, Myan. A3 34
Putaruru, N.Z. o14 63c
Putian, China D4 30
Puting, Tanjung, c., Indon. . D4 36
Putnam, Ct., U.S. B8 100
Putnam, co., Fl., U.S. C5 102
Putnam, co., Ga., U.S. C3 103
Putnam, co., Il., U.S. B4 106
Putnam, co., In., U.S. E4 107
Putnam, co., Mo., U.S. A4 118
Putnam, co., N.Y., U.S. D7 125
Putnam, co., Oh., U.S. B1 128
Putnam, co., Tn., U.S. C8 135
Putnam, co., W.V., U.S. C3 141
Putney, Ga., U.S. E2 103
Putney, Vt., U.S. F3 138
Putorana, plato, plat., Russia C11 26
Puttalam, Sri L. H3 40
Puttgarden, Ger. C12 12
Putumayo (Içá), stm., S.A. . D5 70
Putussibau, Indon. C4 36
Puukohola Heiau National Historic Site, hist., Hi., U.S. D6 104
Puula, l., Fin. F12 10
Puxico, Mo., U.S. E7 118
Puyallup, Wa., U.S. B3 140
Puyallup, stm., Wa., U.S. . . . B3 140
Puyang, China B3 30
Pweto, D.R.C. E5 54
Pyandz see Amu Darya, stm., Asia B8 42
Pyapon, Myan. C3 34
Pyhäjoki, Fin. D11 10
Pyhäselkä, l., Fin. E13 10
Pyinmana, Myan. C3 34

Name	Map Ref.	Page

Pyles Fork, stm., W.V., U.S. **h10** 141
Pymatuning Reservoir, res., U.S. **C1** 131
P'yŏngyang, N. Kor. **D13** 28
Pyramid Lake, l., Nv., U.S. **C2** 121
Pyramid Lake Indian Reservation, Nv., U.S. **D2** 121
Pyramid Mountains, mts., N.M., U.S. **E1** 124
Pyramid Peak, mtn., N.M., U.S. **E1** 124
Pyramid Peak, mtn., Wy., U.S. **C2** 143
Pyrenees, mts., Eur. **F7** 16
Pyriatyn, Ukr. **D12** 20
Pyu, Myan. **C3** 34

Q

Qaanaaq see Thule, Grnld. **C26** 82
Qacentina, Alg. **C6** 48
Qā'emshahr, Iran **C6** 42
Qā'en, Iran **D7** 42
Qaidam Pendi, China. **D6** 28
Qalāt, Afg. **D9** 42
Qal'at Bīshah, Sau. Ar. **G4** 38
Qal'at Sukkar, Iraq **G12** 44
Qal'eh-ye Now, Afg. **D8** 42
Qallābāt, Sudan **H3** 38
Qamar, Ghubbat al-, b., Yemen **G6** 38
Qamar Bay see Qamar, Ghubbat al-, b., Yemen **G6** 38
Qamdo, China **E7** 28
Qandahār, Afg. **D9** 42
Qandala, Som. **H5** 38
Qardho, Som. **I14** 38
Qareh Sū, stm., Iran **C12** 44
Qasr el-Boukhari, Alg. **J8** 48
Qasr Farāfra, Egypt **E10** 48
Qaṭanā, Syria **F7** 44
Qatar, ctry., Asia **E6** 42
Qattâra, Munkhafad el-, depr., Egypt **E10** 48
Qattara Depression see Qattâra, Munkhafad el-, depr., Egypt **E10** 48
Qazimämmäd, Azer. **B13** 44
Qazvīn, Iran **C5** 42
Qena, Egypt **E11** 48
Qeydar, Iran **D13** 44
Qianwei, China **D1** 30
Qianxi, China **D2** 30
Qianyang, China **D3** 30
Qiemo, China **D5** 28
Qigong, China **A4** 34
Qijiang, China **D2** 30
Qilian Shan, mts., China **D7** 28
Qimen, China **D4** 30
Qingdao, China **D12** 28
Qinghai, state, China **D7** 28
Qinghai Hu, l., China **D8** 28
Qingjiang, China **E11** 28
Qinglong, China **A4** 30
Qinglong, China **D2** 30
Qingshen, China **D1** 30
Qingtang, China **G10** 28
Qingyang, China **D9** 28
Qingyuan, China **E3** 30
Qing Zang Gaoyuan (Tibet, Plateau of), plat., China **E4** 28
Qinhuangdao, China **D11** 28
Qin Ling, mts., China **E9** 28
Qinxian, China **B3** 30
Qinzhou, China **E2** 30
Qionghai, China **F3** 30
Qionglai, China **E8** 28
Qiongzhong, China **H9** 28
Qiongzhou Haixia, strt., China **G9** 28
Qiqihar, China **B12** 28
Qiryat Shemona, Isr. **F6** 44
Qishn, Yemen **G6** 38
Qitai, China **C5** 28
Qiyang, China **D3** 30
Qobustan, Azer. **B13** 44
Qogir Feng see K2, mtn., Asia **B3** 40
Qom, Iran **D6** 42
Qomolangma Feng see Everest, Mount, mtn., Asia **D5** 40
Qomsheh, Iran **D6** 42
Qorveh, Iran **E12** 44
Quabbin Reservoir, res., Ma., U.S. **B3** 114
Quaddick Reservoir, res., Ct., U.S. **B8** 100
Quail Oaks, Va., U.S. **n18** 139
Quaker Hill, Ct., U.S. **D7** 100
Quakertown, Pa., U.S. **F11** 131
Qualicum Beach, B.C., Can. **E5** 85
Quanah, Tx., U.S. **B3** 136
Quang Ngai, Viet. **C5** 34
Quannapowitt, Lake, l., Ma., U.S. **f11** 114
Quantico, Va., U.S. **B5** 139
Quantico Marine Corps Air Station, mil., Va., U.S. **B5** 139
Quanzhou, China **G11** 28
Quanzhou, China **D3** 30
Quapaw, Ok., U.S. **A7** 129
Qu'Appelle, Sk., Can. **G4** 91
Qu'Appelle, stm., Can. **G4** 91
Quarryville, Pa., U.S. **G9** 131

Quartu Sant'Elena, Italy **E2** 18
Quartz Mountain, mtn., Or., U.S. **D4** 130
Quartzsite, Az., U.S. **D1** 96
Quassapaug, Lake, l., Ct., U.S. **C3** 100
Quatsino Sound, strt., B.C., Can. **D3** 85
Quay, co., N.M., U.S. **C6** 124
Quba, Azer. **B13** 44
Qūchān, Iran **C7** 42
Queanbeyan, Austl. **H4** 62
Québec, P.Q., Can. **C6** 90
Quebec, prov., Can. **C5** 90
Quechee, Vt., U.S. **D4** 138
Queen, stm., R.I., U.S. **E3** 132
Queen Annes, co., Md., U.S. **B5** 113
Queen Bess, Mount, mtn., B.C., Can. **D5** 85
Queen Charlotte Islands, is., B.C., Can. **C1** 85
Queen Charlotte Mountains, mts., B.C., Can. **C1** 85
Queen Charlotte Sound, strt., B.C., Can. **H14** 82
Queen Charlotte Strait, strt., B.C., Can. **D4** 85
Queen City, Mo., U.S. **A5** 118
Queen City, Tx., U.S. **C5** 136
Queen Creek, Az., U.S. **m9** 96
Queen Mary Coast, Ant. **C14** 67
Queen Maud Land, reg., Ant. **D4** 67
Queen Maud Mountains, mts., Ant. **E25** 67
Queens, co., N.Y., U.S. **E7** 125
Queensland, state, Austl. **E3** 62
Queenstown, Austl. **I4** 62
Queenstown, S. Afr. **E4** 56
Quela, Ang. **E3** 54
Quelimane, Moz. **B6** 56
Querétaro, Mex. **C4** 78
Querétaro, state, Mex. **C5** 78
Queshan, China **C3** 30
Quesnel, B.C., Can. **C6** 85
Quesnel, stm., B.C., Can. **C6** 85
Quesnel Lake, l., B.C., Can. **C7** 85
Questa, N.M., U.S. **A4** 124
Quetico Provincial Park, On., Can. **o17** 89
Quetta, Pak. **D9** 42
Quevedo, Ec. **D4** 70
Quezon City, Phil. **D8** 34
Quibala, Ang. **F3** 54
Quibdó, Col. **B4** 70
Quicksand Pond, l., R.I., U.S. **E6** 132
Quiculungo, Ang. **E3** 54
Quidnessett, R.I., U.S. **E4** 132
Quidnick, R.I., U.S. **D3** 132
Quidnick Reservoir, res., R.I., U.S. **D2** 132
Quila, Mex. **C3** 78
Quilcene, Wa., U.S. **B3** 140
Quileute Indian Reservation, Wa., U.S. **B1** 140
Quillota, Chile **D2** 69
Quilon, India **H3** 40
Quimaria, Ang. **E2** 54
Quimili, Arg. **D5** 72
Quimper, Fr. **D4** 16
Quimperlé, Fr. **D5** 16
Quinault, stm., Wa., U.S. **B1** 140
Quinault, Lake, l., Wa., U.S. **B2** 140
Quinault Indian Reservation, Wa., U.S. **B1** 140
Quince Mil, Peru **F5** 70
Quincy, Ca., U.S. **C3** 98
Quincy, Fl., U.S. **B2** 102
Quincy, Il., U.S. **D2** 106
Quincy, Ma., U.S. **B5** 114
Quincy, Mi., U.S. **G6** 115
Quincy, Wa., U.S. **B6** 140
Quincy Bay, b., Ma., U.S. **g12** 114
Quinebaug, Ct., U.S. **A8** 100
Quinebaug, stm., Ct., U.S. **C8** 100
Quinhagak, Ak., U.S. **D7** 95
Quinlan, Tx., U.S. **C4** 136
Quinn, stm., Nv., U.S. **B3** 121
Quinn Canyon Range, mts., Nv., U.S. **F6** 121
Quinnesec, Mi., U.S. **C3** 115
Quinnipiac, stm., Ct., U.S. **D4** 100
Quintana Roo, state, Mex. **D7** 78
Quinter, Ks., U.S. **C3** 109
Quinton, Ok., U.S. **B6** 129
Quirinópolis, Braz. **E1** 74
Quissanga, Moz. **A7** 56
Quiterajo, Moz. **A7** 56
Quitman, Ar., U.S. **B3** 97
Quitman, Ga., U.S. **F3** 103
Quitman, Ms., U.S. **C5** 117
Quitman, Tx., U.S. **C5** 136
Quitman, co., Ga., U.S. **E1** 103
Quitman, co., Ms., U.S. **A3** 117
Quito, Ec. **D4** 70
Quixadá, Braz. **B4** 74
Quixeramobim, Braz. **C4** 74
Qujing, China **F8** 28
Qumarlêb, China **E7** 28
Qunayyin, Sabkhat al-, l., Libya **E8** 14

Quonnipaug Lake, l., Ct., U.S. **D5** 100
Quonochontaug, R.I., U.S. **G2** 132
Quonochontaug Pond, l., R.I., U.S. **G2** 132
Quonset Point, c., R.I., U.S. **E4** 132
Quseir, Egypt **E11** 48
Qutdligssat, Grnld. **D29** 82
Quthing, Leso. **E4** 56
Qüxü, China **D6** 40
Quy Nhon, Viet. **D5** 34
Quzhou, China **F11** 28

R

Raab see Győr, Hung. **F4** 20
Raahe, Fin. **D11** 10
Rab, Otok, i., Cro. **B5** 18
Raba, Indon. **E5** 36
Rába, stm., Eur. **F4** 20
Rabat, Mor. **D3** 48
Rabaul, Pap. N. Gui. **G13** 32
Rabbit Creek, stm., S.D., U.S. **B3** 134
Rabbit Ears Pass, Co., U.S. **A4** 99
Rabi, i., Fiji **m11** 63b
Rābigh, Sau. Ar. **F3** 38
Râbniţa, Mol. **F10** 20
Rabun, co., Ga., U.S. **B3** 103
Rabun Bald, mtn., Ga., U.S. **B3** 103
Rabyānah, Ramlat, des., Libya **F8** 48
Raccoon Creek, stm., Oh., U.S. **D3** 128
Raccourci Island, i., La., U.S. **D4** 111
Race, Cape, c., Nf., Can. **E5** 88
Raceland, Ky., U.S. **B7** 110
Raceland, La., U.S. **E5** 111
Race Point, c., Ma., U.S. **B7** 114
Rach Gia, Viet. **E4** 34
Racine, W.V., U.S. **C3** 141
Racine, Wi., U.S. **F6** 142
Racine, co., Wi., U.S. **F5** 142
Racine Dam, U.S. **C3** 141
Rădăuţi, Rom. **F8** 20
Radcliff, Ky., U.S. **C4** 110
Radford, Va., U.S. **C2** 139
Radom, Pol. **D6** 20
Radomsko, Pol. **D5** 20
Radomyshl', Ukr. **D10** 20
Rāe Bareli, India **D4** 40
Raeford, N.C., U.S. **C3** 126
Rafaela, Arg. **E5** 72
Rafah, Gaza Str. **G6** 44
Rafhā', Sau. Ar. **E4** 38
Rafsanjān, Iran **D7** 42
Raft, stm., Id., U.S. **G5** 105
Raft River Mountains, mts., Ut., U.S. **B2** 137
Raga, Sudan **I10** 48
Ragay Gulf, b., Phil. **D8** 34
Ragged Island, i., Me., U.S. **E4** 112
Ragged Island Range, is., Bah. **D9** 76
Ragged Lake, l., Me., U.S. **C3** 112
Ragged Top Mountain, mtn., Wy., U.S. **E7** 143
Ragland, Al., U.S. **B3** 94
Ragusa, Italy **F5** 18
Rahīmyār Khān, Pak. **E10** 42
Rahway, N.J., U.S. **B4** 123
Rahway, stm., N.J., U.S. **k7** 123
Rāichūr, India **F3** 40
Raiganj, India **D5** 40
Raigarh, India **E4** 40
Railroad Valley, val., Nv., U.S. **E6** 121
Rainbow Bridge National Monument, Ut., U.S. **F5** 137
Rainbow Falls, wtfl, Tn., U.S. **D10** 135
Rainbow Flowage, res., Wi., U.S. **C4** 142
Rainbow Lake, l., Me., U.S. **C3** 112
Rainelle, W.V., U.S. **D4** 141
Rainier, Or., U.S. **A4** 130
Rainier, Wa., U.S. **C3** 140
Rainier, Mount, mtn., Wa., U.S. **C4** 140
Raohe, China **A2** 31
Rains, co., Tx., U.S. **C5** 136
Rainsville, Al., U.S. **A4** 94
Rainy Lake, l., Mn., U.S. **B5** 116
Rainy River, On., Can. **o16** 89
Raipur, India **E4** 40
Rājahmundry, India **F4** 40
Rajang, stm., Malay. **E4** 36
Rājapālaiyam, India **H3** 40
Rājasthān, prov., India **D2** 40
Rajčihinsk, Russia **E14** 26
Rāj Gangpur, India **E4** 40
Rājkot, India **E4** 40
Rāj Nāndgaon, India **E4** 40
Rājshāhi, Bngl. **E5** 40
Rakhiv, Ukr. **E8** 20
Rakvere, Est. **G12** 10
Raleigh, Ms., U.S. **C4** 117
Raleigh, N.C., U.S. **B4** 126
Raleigh, W.V., U.S. **n13** 141
Raleigh, co., W.V., U.S. **D3** 141
Raleigh Bay, b., N.C., U.S. **C6** 126
Ralls, Tx., U.S. **C2** 136
Ralls, co., Mo., U.S. **B6** 118
Ralston, Ne., U.S. **g12** 120

Ralston Valley, val., Nv., U.S. **E4** 121
Ramah, N.M., U.S. **B1** 124
Ramah Indian Reservation, N.M., U.S. **C1** 124
Ramapo, stm., N.J., U.S. **A4** 123
Ramblewood, N.J., U.S. **D3** 123
Rambouillet, Fr. **C7** 16
Ramea, Nf., Can. **E3** 88
Rāmeswaram, India **H3** 40
Rāmhormoz, Iran **D5** 42
Ramm, Jabal, mtn., Jord. **E3** 42
Râmnicu Sărat, Rom. **G9** 20
Râmnicu Vâlcea, Rom. **G8** 20
Ramona, Ca., U.S. **F5** 98
Rampart Range, mts., Co., U.S. **B5** 99
Rāmpur, India **D3** 40
Ramree Island, i., Myan. **C2** 34
Ramsay, Mi., U.S. **n12** 115
Ramsele, Swe. **E7** 10
Ramseur, N.C., U.S. **B3** 126
Ramsey, Il., U.S. **D4** 106
Ramsey, N.J., U.S. **A4** 123
Ramsey, co., Mn., U.S. **E5** 116
Ramsey, co., N.D., U.S. **A7** 127
Ramsgate, Eng., U.K. **E7** 12
Ramshorn Peak, mtn., Mt., U.S. **E5** 119
Ramshorn Peak, mtn., Wy., U.S. **C3** 143
Ramu, Kenya **C8** 54
Rāna Pratāp Sāgar, res., India **D2** 40
Rancagua, Chile **D2** 69
Ranchería Braz. **F1** 74
Rancheria Rock, mtn., Or., U.S. **C6** 130
Ranchester, Wy., U.S. **B5** 143
Rānchi, India **E5** 40
Ranchos de Taos, N.M., U.S. **A4** 124
Rancocas Creek, stm., N.J., U.S. **C3** 123
Rand, W.V., U.S. **C3** 141
Randall, co., Tx., U.S. **B2** 136
Randallstown, Md., U.S. **B4** 113
Randers, Den. **H4** 10
Randijaure, l., Swe. **C8** 10
Randle, Wa., U.S. **C4** 140
Randleman, N.C., U.S. **B3** 126
Randolph, Ma., U.S. **B5** 114
Randolph, Me., U.S. **D3** 112
Randolph, Ne., U.S. **B8** 120
Randolph, Vt., U.S. **D3** 138
Randolph, Wi., U.S. **E5** 142
Randolph, co., Al., U.S. **B4** 94
Randolph, co., Ar., U.S. **A4** 97
Randolph, co., Ga., U.S. **E2** 103
Randolph, co., Il., U.S. **E4** 106
Randolph, co., In., U.S. **D7** 107
Randolph, co., Mo., U.S. **B5** 118
Randolph, co., N.C., U.S. **B3** 126
Randolph, co., W.V., U.S. **C5** 141
Randolph Air Force Base, mil., Tx., U.S. **h7** 136
Randolph Hills, Md., U.S. **B3** 113
Random Island, i., Nf., Can. **D5** 88
Random Lake, Wi., U.S. **E6** 142
Randsfjorden, l., Nor. **F4** 10
Rāngāmāti, Bngl. **E6** 40
Rangeley, Me., U.S. **D2** 112
Rangeley Lake, l., Me., U.S. **D2** 112
Rangely, Co., U.S. **A2** 99
Ranger, Tx., U.S. **C3** 136
Ranger Lake, l., N.M., U.S. **D6** 124
Rangoon see Yangon, Myan. **C3** 34
Rangpur, Bngl. **D5** 40
Rānībennur, India **G3** 40
Rankin, Pa., U.S. **k14** 131
Rankin, co., Ms., U.S. **C4** 117
Rann of Kutch see Kutch, Rann of, reg., Asia **E1** 40
Ranohira, Madag. **C8** 56
Ranong, Thai. **E3** 34
Ransiki, Indon. **D8** 36
Ransom, co., N.D., U.S. **C8** 127
Ranson, W.V., U.S. **B7** 141
Rantauprapat, Indon. **C1** 36
Rantoul, Il., U.S. **C5** 106
Raohe, China **A2** 31
Raoul, Ga., U.S. **B3** 103
Rapallo, Italy **B2** 18
Rapid, stm., Mn., U.S. **B4** 116
Rapid City, S.D., U.S. **C2** 134
Rapides, co., La., U.S. **C3** 111
Rapid River, Mi., U.S. **C4** 115
Rapids City, Il., U.S. **B3** 106
Rappahannock, co., Va., U.S. **B4** 139
Rappahannock, stm., Va., U.S. **B5** 139
Raquette, stm., N.Y., U.S. **f10** 125
Raquette Lake, l., N.Y., U.S. **B6** 125
Raraka, atoll, Fr. Poly. **F15** 58
Raritan, N.J., U.S. **B3** 123
Raritan, stm., N.J., U.S. **C4** 123
Raritan Bay, b., N.J., U.S. **C4** 123
Rarotonga, i., Cook Is. **G14** 58
Ra's al-Khaymah, U.A.E. **E7** 42
Ras Dashen Terara, mtn., Eth. **H12** 48
Rashid, Egypt **E10** 14
Rasht, Iran **C5** 42
Rассua, ostrov, i., Russia **E17** 26

Ratangarh, India **D2** 40
Rāth, India **D3** 40
Rathbun Lake, res., Ia., U.S. **D5** 108
Rathdrum, Id., U.S. **B2** 105
Rat Islands, is., Ak., U.S. **E3** 95
Ratlām, India **E3** 40
Ratnāgiri, India **F2** 40
Ratnapura, Sri L. **H4** 40
Raton, N.M., U.S. **A5** 124
Raton Pass, N.M., U.S. **A5** 124
Rattlesnake Creek, stm., Oh., U.S. **C2** 128
Rattlesnake Creek, stm., Wa., U.S. **C6** 140
Rättvik, Swe. **F6** 10
Raub, Malay. **C2** 36
Rauch, Arg. **F6** 72
Rauma, Fin. **F9** 10
Raurkela, India **E5** 40
Ravalli, co., Mt., U.S. **D2** 119
Raven, Va., U.S. **e10** 139
Ravena, N.Y., U.S. **C7** 125
Ravenel, S.C., U.S. **k11** 133
Ravenna, Italy **B4** 18
Ravenna, Ky., U.S. **C6** 110
Ravenna, Mi., U.S. **E5** 115
Ravenna, Ne., U.S. **C7** 120
Ravenna, Oh., U.S. **A4** 128
Raven Park, reg., Co., U.S. **A2** 99
Ravensburg, Ger. **G11** 12
Ravensthorpe, Austl. **G3** 60
Ravenswood, W.V., U.S. **C3** 141
Rāvi, stm., Asia **C2** 40
Ravnina, Turk. **C8** 42
Rawaki, atoll, Kir. **E12** 58
Rāwalpindi, Pak. **D10** 42
Rawdon, P.Q., Can. **C4** 90
Rawhide Creek, stm., Wy., U.S. **D8** 143
Rawlings, Md., U.S. **k13** 113
Rawlinna, Austl. **G4** 60
Rawlins, Wy., U.S. **E5** 143
Rawlins, co., Ks., U.S. **C2** 109
Rawson, Arg. **F3** 69
Ray, N.D., U.S. **A2** 127
Ray, co., Mo., U.S. **B3** 118
Ray, Cape, c., Nf., Can. **E2** 88
Raya, Bukit, mtn., Indon. **C4** 36
Rāyachoti, India **G3** 40
Rāyadurg, India **G3** 40
Ray City, Ga., U.S. **E3** 103
Raymond, Ab., Can. **E4** 84
Raymond, Il., U.S. **D4** 106
Raymond, Mn., U.S. **E3** 116
Raymond, Ms., U.S. **C3** 117
Raymond, N.H., U.S. **D4** 122
Raymond, Wa., U.S. **C2** 140
Raymondville, Tx., U.S. **F4** 136
Raymore, Sk., Can. **F3** 91
Raymore, Mo., U.S. **C3** 118
Rayne, La., U.S. **D3** 111
Raynham, Ma., U.S. **C5** 114
Raynham Center, Ma., U.S. **C5** 114
Rayong, Thai. **D4** 34
Raytown, Mo., U.S. **h11** 118
Rayville, La., U.S. **B4** 111
Razdoľ'noe, Russia **B2** 31
Razgrad, Bul. **C11** 18
Ré, Île de, i., Fr. **D6** 16
Reader, W.V., U.S. **B4** 141
Reading, Eng., U.K. **E6** 12
Reading, Ma., U.S. **A5** 114
Reading, Mi., U.S. **G6** 115
Reading, Oh., U.S. **C1** 128
Reading, Pa., U.S. **F10** 131
Readlyn, Ia., U.S. **B5** 108
Reagan, co., Tx., U.S. **D2** 136
Real, co., Tx., U.S. **E3** 136
Real, Cordillera, mts., S.A. **G6** 70
Realicó, Arg. **E5** 72
Reamstown, Pa., U.S. **F9** 131
Rebiana Sand Sea see Rabyānah, Ramlat, des., Libya **F8** 48
Rebun-tō, i., Japan **B16** 28
Recherche, Archipelago of the, is., Austl. **G3** 60
Recife, Braz. **C5** 74
Reconquista, Arg. **D6** 72
Rector, Ar., U.S. **A5** 97
Rècyċa, Bela. **C11** 20
Red, stm., Asia **B4** 34
Red, stm., N.A. **B8** 92
Red, stm., Ky., U.S. **C6** 110
Red, stm., Tn., U.S. **A4** 135
Red, stm., U.S. **E9** 92
Red Bank, N.J., U.S. **C4** 123
Red Bank, Tn., U.S. **D8** 135
Red Bay, Al., U.S. **A1** 94
Redberry Lake, l., Sk., Can. **E2** 91
Redbird, Oh., U.S. **A4** 128
Red Bird, stm., Ky., U.S. **C6** 110
Red Bluff, Ca., U.S. **B2** 98
Red Bluff Lake, res., U.S. **o12** 136
Red Boiling Springs, Tn., U.S. **C8** 135
Red Bud, Il., U.S. **E4** 106
Red Butte, mtn., Ut., U.S. **B3** 137
Red Cedar, stm., Wi., U.S. **C2** 142
Red Cedar Lake, l., Wi., U.S. **C2** 142
Redcliff, Ab., Can. **D5** 84
Redcliffe, Austl. **F5** 62

Name	Map Ref.	Page

Redcliffe, Mount, mtn., Austl. **F3** 60
Red Cliff Indian Reservation, Wi., U.S. . **B2** 142
Red Cloud, Ne., U.S. **D7** 120
Redcloud Peak, mtn., Co., U.S. **D3** 99
Red Deer, Ab., Can. **C4** 84
Red Deer, stm., Can. **D4** 84
Red Deer, stm., Can. **E4** 91
Redding, Ca., U.S. **B2** 98
Redding, Ct., U.S. **D2** 100
Redeye, stm., Mn., U.S. . . **D3** 116
Redfield, Ar., U.S. **C3** 97
Redfield, Ia., U.S. **C3** 108
Redfield, S.D., U.S. **C7** 134
Redford, Mi., U.S. **F7** 115
Redgranite, Wi., U.S. **D4** 142
Red Hook, N.Y., U.S. **C7** 125
Red Indian Lake, l., Nf., Can. **D3** 88
Red Jacket, W.V., U.S. . . . **D2** 141
Redkey, In., U.S. **D7** 107
Redlake, Mn., U.S. **C3** 116
Red Lake, co., Mn., U.S. . . **C2** 116
Red Lake, l., Az., U.S. . . . **B1** 96
Red Lake, stm., Mn., U.S. . **C2** 116
Red Lake Falls, Mn., U.S. . **C2** 116
Red Lake Indian Reservation, Mn., U.S. **B3** 116
Redlands, Ca., U.S. **E5** 98
Red Lion, Pa., U.S. **G8** 131
Red Lodge, Mt., U.S. **E7** 119
Red Mill Pond, l., De., U.S. **E5** 101
Redmond, Or., U.S. **C5** 130
Redmond, Ut., U.S. **E4** 137
Redmond, Wa., U.S. **e11** 140
Red Mountain, mtn., Ca., U.S. **B2** 98
Red Mountain, mtn., Mt., U.S. **C4** 119
Red Mountain Pass, Co., U.S. **D3** 99
Red Oak, Ga., U.S. **h7** 103
Red Oak, Ia., U.S. **D2** 108
Red Oak, Ok., U.S. **C6** 129
Red Oak, Tx., U.S. **n10** 136
Red Oaks, La., U.S. **h9** 111
Redon, Fr. **D5** 16
Redondo, Wa., U.S. **f11** 140
Redondo Beach, Ca., U.S. **n12** 98
Redoubt Volcano, vol., Ak., U.S. **g15** 95
Red Peak, mtn., Co., U.S. . **B4** 99
Red River, co., La., U.S. . . **B2** 111
Red River, co., Tx., U.S. . . **C5** 136
Red Rock, stm., Mt., U.S. . **F4** 119
Red Rock, Lake, res., Ia., U.S. **C4** 108
Redruth, Eng., U.K. **E4** 12
Red Sea **F3** 38
Red Springs, N.C., U.S. . . **C3** 126
Red Table Mountain, mts., Co., U.S. **B4** 99
Redwater, Ab., Can. **C4** 84
Redwater, stm., Mt., U.S. . **C11** 119
Red Willow, co., Ne., U.S. **D5** 120
Redwillow, stm., Can. . . . **B7** 85
Red Wing, Mn., U.S. **F6** 116
Redwood, co., Mn., U.S. . **F3** 116
Redwood, stm., Mn., U.S. . **F3** 116
Redwood City, Ca., U.S. . . **D2** 98
Redwood Falls, Mn., U.S. . **F3** 116
Redwood National Park, Ca., U.S. **B2** 98
Redwood Valley, Ca., U.S. **C2** 98
Ree, Lough, l., Ire. **D2** 12
Reed City, Mi., U.S. **E5** 115
Reedley, Ca., U.S. **D4** 98
Reedsburg, Wi., U.S. **E3** 142
Reeds Peak, mtn., N.M., U.S. **D2** 124
Reedsport, Or., U.S. **D2** 130
Reedsville, Pa., U.S. **E6** 131
Reedsville, Wi., U.S. **D6** 142
Reedy, stm., S.C., U.S. . . . **C3** 133
Reedy Lake, l., Fl., U.S. . . **E5** 102
Reefton, N.Z. **p13** 63c
Reelfoot Lake, l., Tn., U.S. **A2** 135
Reese, Mi., U.S. **E7** 115
Reese, stm., Nv., U.S. . . . **C4** 121
Reese Air Force Base, mil., Tx., U.S. **C1** 136
Reeves, co., Tx., U.S. . . . **o13** 136
Reform, Al., U.S. **B1** 94
Refugio, Tx., U.S. **E4** 136
Refugio, co., Tx., U.S. . . . **E4** 136
Regensburg, Ger. **F12** 12
Reggâne, Alg. **E4** 48
Reggio di Calabria, Italy . . **E5** 18
Reggio nell'Emilia, Italy . . **B3** 18
Reghin, Rom. **F8** 20
Regina, Sk., Can. **G3** 91
Régina, Fr. Gu. **C9** 70
Regina Beach, Sk., Can. . . **G3** 91
Registro, Braz. **C8** 72
Regozero, Russia **D14** 10
Rehoboth, Nmb. **C2** 56
Rehoboth Bay, b., De., U.S. **F5** 101
Rehoboth Beach, De., U.S. **F5** 101
Reid, Mount, mtn., Ak., U.S. **n24** 95
Reidland, Ky., U.S. **e9** 110
Reidsville, Ga., U.S. **D4** 103
Reidsville, N.C., U.S. **A3** 126
Reigate, Eng., U.K. **E6** 12

Reims, Fr. **C9** 16
Reinbeck, Ia., U.S. **B5** 108
Reindeer Island, i., Mb., Can. **C3** 86
Reindeer Lake, l., Can. . . . **G19** 82
Reisterstown, Md., U.S. . . **B4** 113
Reliance, Wy., U.S. **E3** 143
Remada, Tun. **D7** 48
Remanso, Braz. **C3** 74
Rembang, Indon. **E4** 36
Remington, In., U.S. **C3** 107
Remiremont, Fr. **C10** 16
Remmel Dam, Ar., U.S. . . **g8** 97
Remsen, Ia., U.S. **B2** 108
Rena, Nor. **F4** 10
Rend Lake, res., Il., U.S. . . **E5** 106
Rendsburg, Ger. **C11** 12
Renforth, N.B., Can. **D4** 87
Renfrew, On., Can. **B8** 89
Rengat, Indon. **D2** 36
Rengo, Chile **E3** 72
Reng Tläng, mtn., Asia . . **B2** 34
Rennes, Fr. **C6** 16
Reno, Nv., U.S. **D2** 121
Reno, co., Ks., U.S. **E5** 109
Reno, Lake, l., Mn., U.S. . **E3** 116
Reno Hill, mtn., Wy., U.S. **D6** 143
Renovo, Pa., U.S. **D6** 131
Renqiu, China **B4** 30
Rensselaer, In., U.S. **C3** 107
Rensselaer, N.Y., U.S. . . . **C7** 125
Rensselaer, co., N.Y., U.S. **C7** 125
Renton, Wa., U.S. **B3** 140
Renville, Mn., U.S. **F3** 116
Renville, co., Mn., U.S. . . **F4** 116
Renville, co., N.D., U.S. . . **A4** 127
Reo, Indon. **E6** 36
Repentigny, P.Q., Can. . . . **D4** 90
Repetek, Turk. **C8** 42
Republic, Mi., U.S. **B3** 115
Republic, Mo., U.S. **D4** 118
Republic, Pa., U.S. **G2** 131
Republic, Wa., U.S. **A7** 140
Republic, co., Ks., U.S. . . **C6** 109
Republican, stm., U.S. . . . **C8** 92
Republican, stm., U.S. . . . **C6** 109
Republic of Korea see Korea, South, ctry., Asia **D10** 28
Reşadiye, Tur. **B7** 44
Reserve, La., U.S. **h10** 111
Resistencia, Arg. **D6** 72
Reşiţa, Rom. **G6** 20
Resolute, N.T., Can. **D20** 82
Resolution Island, i., N.Z. **q12** 63c
Reston, Mb., Can. **E1** 86
Reston, Va., U.S. **B5** 139
Réthimnon, Grc. **G10** 18
Réunion, dep., Afr. **g10** 57a
Reus, Spain **G7** 16
Reutlingen, Ger. **F11** 12
Revelo, Ky., U.S. **D5** 110
Revelstoke, B.C., Can. . . . **D8** 85
Revelstoke, Lake, res., B.C., Can. **D8** 85
Reventazón, Peru **E3** 70
Revere, La., U.S. **h11** 114
Revillagigedo, Islas, is., Mex. **D2** 78
Revillagigedo Island, i., Ak., U.S. **n24** 95
Revin, Fr. **C9** 16
Rewa, India **E4** 40
Rex, Ga., U.S. **h8** 103
Rexburg, Id., U.S. **F7** 105
Rexton, N.B., Can. **C5** 87
Rey, Isla del, i., Pan. **D4** 80
Reyes, Point, c., Ca., U.S. **C2** 98
Reyhanlı, Tur. **D7** 44
Reykjanes Ridge **B26** 144
Reykjavík, Ice. **I18** 10a
Reynolds, Ga., U.S. **D2** 103
Reynolds, co., Mo., U.S. . **D6** 118
Reynoldsburg, Oh., U.S. . **C3** 128
Reynoldsville, Pa., U.S. . . **D4** 131
Reynosa, Mex. **B5** 78
Rezé, Fr. **D6** 16
Rēzekne, Lat. **H12** 10
Rhaetian Alps, mts., Eur. . **A2** 18
Rhea, co., Tn., U.S. **D9** 135
Rheims see Reims, Fr. . . . **C9** 16
Rheine, Ger. **D10** 12
Rhine (Rhein), stm., Eur. . **A5** 14
Rhinebeck, N.Y., U.S. . . . **D7** 125
Rhinelander, Wi., U.S. . . . **C4** 142
Rhir, Cap, c., Mor. **D2** 48
Rho, Italy **B2** 18
Rhode Island, state, U.S. . **D3** 132
Rhode Island, i., R.I., U.S. **E5** 132
Rhode Island Sound, strt., U.S. **F5** 132
Rhodes see Ródhos, i., Grc. **G12** 18
Rhodesia see Zimbabwe, ctry., Afr. **B4** 56
Rhodes Peak, mtn., Id., U.S. **C4** 105
Rhodes' Tomb, hist., Zimb. **C4** 56
Rhodope Mountains, mts., Eur. **D10** 18
Rhône, stm., Eur. **E9** 16
Riachão do Jacuípe, Braz. **D4** 74
Rialto, Ca., U.S. **m14** 98
Riau, Kepulauan, is., Indon. **C2** 36
Riaza, Spain **G5** 16
Ribáuè, Moz. **A6** 56
Ribe, Den. **I3** 10
Ribeira do Pombal, Braz. . **D4** 74
Ribeira Grande, C.V. **g9** 50a

Ribeirão, Braz. **C4** 74
Ribeirão Preto, Braz. **F2** 74
Riberalta, Bol. **F6** 70
Rib Lake, Wi., U.S. **C3** 142
Riccione, Italy **B4** 18
Rice, Mn., U.S. **E4** 116
Rice, co., Ks., U.S. **D5** 109
Rice, co., Mn., U.S. **F5** 116
Riceboro, Ga., U.S. **E5** 103
Rice Lake, Wi., U.S. **C2** 142
Rice Lake, l., On., Can. . . **C6** 89
Rice Lake, l., Mn., U.S. . . **D5** 116
Riceville, Ia., U.S. **A5** 108
Rich, co., Ut., U.S. **B4** 137
Rich, Cape, c., On., Can. . **C4** 89
Richards Bay, S. Afr. **D5** 56
Richardson, Tx., U.S. . . . **n10** 136
Richardson, co., Ne., U.S. **D10** 120
Richardson Lakes, l., Me., U.S. **D2** 112
Richard Toll, Sen. **C1** 50
Richardton, N.D., U.S. . . . **C3** 127
Rich Creek, Va., U.S. **C2** 139
Riche, Pointe, c., Nf., Can. **C3** 88
Richfield, Mn., U.S. **F5** 116
Richfield, Ut., U.S. **E3** 137
Richford, Vt., U.S. **B3** 138
Rich Hill, Mo., U.S. **C3** 118
Richibucto, N.B., Can. . . . **C5** 87
Richland, Ga., U.S. **D2** 103
Richland, Mo., U.S. **D5** 118
Richland, Wa., U.S. **C6** 140
Richland, co., Il., U.S. . . . **E5** 106
Richland, co., La., U.S. . . **B4** 111
Richland, co., Mt., U.S. . **C12** 119
Richland, co., N.D., U.S. . **C8** 127
Richland, co., Oh., U.S. . . **B3** 128
Richland, co., S.C., U.S. . **D6** 133
Richland, co., Wi., U.S. . . **E3** 142
Richland Balsam, mtn., N.C., U.S. **f10** 126
Richland Center, Wi., U.S. **E3** 142
Richland Creek, stm., Tn., U.S. **B5** 135
Richlands, N.C., U.S. **C5** 126
Richlands, Va., U.S. **e10** 139
Richlandtown, Pa., U.S. . **F11** 131
Richmond, Austl. **E3** 62
Richmond, B.C., Can. . . . **E6** 85
Richmond, P.Q., Can. . . . **D5** 90
Richmond, N.Z. **p13** 63c
Richmond, Ca., U.S. **D2** 98
Richmond, Il., U.S. **A5** 106
Richmond, In., U.S. **E8** 107
Richmond, Ky., U.S. **C5** 110
Richmond, Me., U.S. **D3** 112
Richmond, Mi., U.S. **F8** 115
Richmond, Mn., U.S. **E4** 116
Richmond, Mo., U.S. **B4** 118
Richmond, Tx., U.S. **E5** 136
Richmond, Ut., U.S. **B4** 137
Richmond, Va., U.S. **C5** 139
Richmond, Vt., U.S. **C3** 138
Richmond, co., Ga., U.S. . **C4** 103
Richmond, co., N.C., U.S. **B3** 126
Richmond, co., N.Y., U.S. **E6** 125
Richmond, co., Va., U.S. . **C6** 139
Richmond Heights, Fl., U.S. **s13** 102
Richmond Heights, Mo., U.S. **f13** 118
Richmond Hill, On., Can. . **D5** 89
Richmond Hill, Ga., U.S. . **E5** 103
Richmond National Battlefield Park, Va., U.S. **n18** 139
Rich Square, N.C., U.S. . . **A5** 126
Richthofen, Mount, mtn., Co., U.S. **A5** 99
Richton, Ms., U.S. **D5** 117
Richwood, Oh., U.S. **B2** 128
Richwood, W.V., U.S. . . . **C4** 141
Rickman, Tn., U.S. **C8** 135
Riddle, Or., U.S. **E3** 130
Riddle Mountain, mtn., Or., U.S. **D8** 130
Rideau, stm., On., Can. . . **B9** 89
Ridgecrest, Ca., U.S. **E5** 98
Ridge Farm, Il., U.S. **D6** 106
Ridgefield, Ct., U.S. **D2** 100
Ridgefield, N.J., U.S. **h8** 123
Ridgefield, Wa., U.S. **D3** 140
Ridgefield Park, N.J., U.S. **B4** 123
Ridgeland, Ms., U.S. **C3** 117
Ridgeland, S.C., U.S. **G6** 133
Ridgeley, W.V., U.S. **B6** 141
Ridgely, Md., U.S. **C6** 113
Ridgely, Tn., U.S. **A2** 135
Ridge Spring, S.C., U.S. . . **D4** 133
Ridgetop, Tn., U.S. **A5** 135
Ridgetown, On., Can. . . . **E3** 89
Ridgeview, W.V., U.S. . . . **C3** 141
Ridgeville, In., U.S. **D7** 107
Ridgeville, S.C., U.S. **E7** 133
Ridgeway, Va., U.S. **D3** 139
Ridgewood, N.J., U.S. . . . **B4** 123
Ridgway, Il., U.S. **F5** 106
Ridgway, Pa., U.S. **D4** 131
Riding Mountain National Park, Mb., Can. **D1** 86
Ridley Park, Pa., U.S. . . . **p20** 131
Riesa, Ger. **E13** 12
Rieti, Italy **C4** 18
Rif, mts., Mor. **E3** 14
Riffe Lake, res., Wa., U.S. **C3** 140
Rifle, Co., U.S. **B3** 99

Rifle, stm., Mi., U.S. **D6** 115
Rift Valley, val., Afr. **C6** 54
Rīga, Lat. **H11** 10
Riga, Gulf of, b., Eur. . . **G10** 10
Rigaud, P.Q., Can. **D3** 90
Rigby, Id., U.S. **F7** 105
Rīgestān, reg., Afg. **D9** 42
Rigo, Pap. N. Gui. **H12** 32
Riihimäki, Fin. **F11** 10
Riiser-Larsen Peninsula, pen., Ant. **C8** 67
Rijeka, Cro. **B5** 18
Riley, Ks., U.S. **C7** 109
Riley, co., Ks., U.S. **C7** 109
Riley, Mount, mtn., N.M., U.S. **F2** 124
Rimbey, Ab., Can. **C3** 84
Rimersburg, Pa., U.S. . . . **D3** 131
Rimini, Italy **B4** 18
Rimouski, P.Q., Can. **A9** 90
Rimouski, stm., P.Q., Can. **A9** 90
Rimouski-Est, P.Q., Can. . **A9** 90
Rimrock Lake, res., Wa., U.S. **C4** 140
Rinca, Pulau, i., Indon. . . **E5** 36
Rincon, Ga., U.S. **D5** 103
Rincón del Bonete, Lago Artificial de, res., Ur. . **E6** 72
Rincón de Romos, Mex. . . **C4** 78
Rincon Mountains, mts., Az., U.S. **E5** 96
Ringdove, Vanuatu **k9** 62a
Ringgold, Ga., U.S. **B1** 103
Ringgold, La., U.S. **B2** 111
Ringgold, co., Ia., U.S. . . **D3** 108
Ringim, Nig. **D6** 50
Ringkøbing, Den. **H3** 10
Ringkøbing Fjord, b., Den. **I3** 10
Ringling, Ok., U.S. **C4** 129
Ringwood, N.J., U.S. **A4** 123
Ringvassøya, i., Nor. **B8** 10
Rinjani, Gunung, vol., Indon. **E5** 36
Rio, Fl., U.S. **E6** 102
Rio, Wi., U.S. **E4** 142
Rio Arriba, co., N.M., U.S. **A2** 124
Riobamba, Ec. **D4** 70
Rio Blanco, co., Co., U.S. **B2** 99
Rio Branco, Braz. **E6** 70
Río Claro, Braz. **F2** 74
Rio Claro, Braz. **E4** 69
Río Cuarto, Arg. **E5** 72
Rio de Janeiro, Braz. **F3** 74
Rio de Janeiro, state, Braz. **F3** 74
Rio Dell, Ca., U.S. **B1** 98
Río Gallegos, Arg. **H3** 69
Río Grande, Arg. **H3** 69
Río Grande, Braz. **E7** 72
Rio Grande, Mex. **C4** 78
Rio Grande, Oh., U.S. . . . **D3** 128
Rio Grande, co., Co., U.S. **D4** 99
Rio Grande (Bravo), stm., N.A. **F7** 92
Rio Grande City, Tx., U.S. **F3** 136
Rio Grande do Norte, state, Braz. **E12** 70
Rio Grande do Sul, state, Braz. **D7** 72
Rio Grande Reservoir, res., Co., U.S. **D3** 99
Ríohacha, Col. **A5** 70
Río Hato, Pan. **D3** 80
Rio Hondo, Tx., U.S. **F4** 136
Rio Largo, Braz. **C4** 74
Riom, Fr. **E8** 16
Río Mayo, Arg. **G2** 69
Ríonegro, Col. **D5** 80
Rio Negro, Pantanal do, sw., Braz. **G8** 70
Rio Rancho, N.M., U.S. . . **B3** 124
Rio Real, Braz. **D4** 74
Ríosucio, Col. **D4** 80
Rio Tercero, Arg. **E5** 72
Rio Tinto, Braz. **C4** 74
Rio Verde, Braz. **E1** 74
Ríoverde, Mex. **C5** 78
Rio Verde de Mato Grosso, Braz. **B7** 72
Rio Vista, Ca., U.S. **C3** 98
Ripley, Ms., U.S. **A5** 117
Ripley, Oh., U.S. **D2** 128
Ripley, Tn., U.S. **B2** 135
Ripley, W.V., U.S. **C3** 141
Ripley, co., In., U.S. **F7** 107
Ripley, co., Mo., U.S. . . . **E7** 118
Ripon, Eng., U.K. **C6** 12
Ripon, Wi., U.S. **E5** 142
Rippowam, stm., Ct., U.S. **E1** 100
Ririe Lake, res., Id., U.S. . **F7** 105
Rishiri-tō, i., Japan **B16** 28
Rishon LeZiyyon, Isr. . . . **G6** 44
Rising Sun, De., U.S. **D3** 101
Rising Sun, In., U.S. **G8** 107
Rising Sun, Md., U.S. . . . **A5** 113
Rison, Ar., U.S. **D3** 97
Ristijärvi, Fin. **D13** 10
Ritchie, co., W.V., U.S. . . **B3** 141
Ritter, Mount, mtn., Ca., U.S. **D4** 98
Rittman, Oh., U.S. **B4** 128
Ritzville, Wa., U.S. **B7** 140
Riva del Garda, Italy **B3** 18
Rivanna, stm., Va., U.S. . **C4** 139
Rivas, Nic. **C2** 80

Rivera, Ur. **E6** 72
Riverbank, Ca., U.S. **D3** 98
River Bourgeois, N.S., Can. **D9** 87
River Cess, Lib. **E3** 50
Riverdale, Ca., U.S. **D4** 98
Riverdale, Il., U.S. **k9** 106
Riverdale, Md., U.S. **C4** 113
River Edge, N.J., U.S. . . . **h8** 123
River Falls, Al., U.S. **D3** 94
River Falls, Wi., U.S. **D1** 142
River Forest, Il., U.S. **k9** 106
River Grove, Il., U.S. **k9** 106
Riverhead, N.Y., U.S. . . **n16** 125
River Hebert, N.S., Can. . **D5** 87
River Heights, Ut., U.S. . . **B4** 137
River Hills, Wi., U.S. . . . **m12** 142
River Pines, Ma., U.S. . . **f10** 114
River Ridge, La., U.S. . . **k11** 111
River Road, Or., U.S. . . . **C3** 130
River Rouge, Mi., U.S. . . **p15** 115
Rivers, Mb., Can. **D1** 86
Riversdale, S. Afr. **E3** 56
Riverside, Al., U.S. **B3** 94
Riverside, Ca., U.S. **F5** 98
Riverside, Ia., U.S. **C6** 108
Riverside, Il., U.S. **k9** 106
Riverside, N.J., U.S. **C3** 123
Riverside, Pa., U.S. **E8** 131
Riverside, co., Ca., U.S. . . **F5** 98
Riverside Reservoir, res., Co., U.S. **A6** 99
Riverton, Mb., Can. **D3** 86
Riverton, N.Z. **q12** 63c
Riverton, Il., U.S. **D4** 106
Riverton, Ks., U.S. **E9** 109
Riverton, N.J., U.S. **C3** 123
Riverton, Ut., U.S. **C4** 137
Riverton, Vt., U.S. **C3** 138
Riverton, Wy., U.S. **C4** 143
Riverton Heights, Wa., U.S. **f11** 140
River Vale, N.J., U.S. **h8** 123
Riverview, Fl., U.S. **p11** 102
Riverview, Mi., U.S. **p15** 115
Rivesville, W.V., U.S. . . . **B4** 141
Riviera Beach, Fl., U.S. . . **F6** 102
Riviera Beach, Md., U.S. . **B4** 113
Rivière-du-Loup, P.Q., Can. **B8** 90
Rivière-Verte, N.B., Can. . **B1** 87
Rivne, Ukr. **D9** 20
Rivoli, Italy **B1** 18
Riyadh see Ar-Riyāḍ, Sau. Ar. **F5** 38
Rizhao, China **D11** 28
Rjazan', Russia **D6** 26
Rjažsk, Russia **C16** 20
Rjukan, Nor. **G3** 10
Roachdale, In., U.S. **E4** 107
Road Town, Br. Vir. Is. . . **B7** 80
Roane, co., Tn., U.S. **D9** 135
Roane, co., W.V., U.S. . . **C3** 141
Roan Mountain, Tn., U.S. **C11** 135
Roanne, Fr. **D8** 16
Roanoke, Al., U.S. **B4** 94
Roanoke, In., U.S. **C7** 107
Roanoke, La., U.S. **D3** 111
Roanoke, Tx., U.S. **m9** 136
Roanoke, Va., U.S. **C3** 139
Roanoke, co., Va., U.S. . . **C2** 139
Roanoke see Staunton, stm., U.S. **D12** 92
Roanoke, stm., U.S. **A5** 126
Roanoke Island, i., N.C., U.S. **B7** 126
Roanoke Rapids, N.C., U.S. **A5** 126
Roanoke Rapids Lake, res., U.S. **A5** 126
Roaring Fork, stm., Co., U.S. **C4** 99
Roaring Spring, Pa., U.S. . **F5** 131
Roatán, Isla de, i., Hond. . **B2** 80
Robbins, Il., U.S. **k9** 106
Robbins, N.C., U.S. **B3** 126
Robbinsdale, Mn., U.S. . **m12** 116
Robbinsville, N.C., U.S. . . **f9** 126
Robe, Austl. **H2** 62
Robersonville, N.C., U.S. . **B5** 126
Roberta, Ga., U.S. **D2** 103
Robert Lee, Tx., U.S. **D2** 136
Roberts, Wi., U.S. **C1** 142
Roberts, co., S.D., U.S. . . **B8** 134
Roberts, co., Tx., U.S. . . . **B2** 136
Roberts, Point, c., Wa., U.S. **A2** 140
Robert's Arm, Nf., Can. . . **D4** 88
Roberts Creek Mountain, mtn., Nv., U.S. **D5** 121
Robertsdale, Al., U.S. . . . **E2** 94
Robert S. Kerr Reservoir, res., Ok., U.S. **B6** 129
Roberts Mountain, mtn., Ak., U.S. **C6** 95
Roberts Mountain, mtn., Wy., U.S. **D3** 143
Robertson, co., Ky., U.S. . **B5** 110
Robertson, co., Tn., U.S. . **A5** 135
Robertson, co., Tx., U.S. . **D4** 136
Robertsonville, P.Q., Can. **C6** 90
Roberts Port, Lib. **E2** 50
Robertville, N.B., Can. . . **B4** 87
Roberval, P.Q., Can. **A5** 90
Robeson, co., N.C., U.S. . **C3** 126
Robins, Ia., U.S. **B6** 108
Robinson, Il., U.S. **D6** 106
Róbinson Crusoe, Isla, i., Chile **E2** 72

Name	Map Ref.	Page
Robinson Fork, stm., W.V., U.S.	k9	141
Robinson Fork, stm., W.V., U.S.	m14	141
Robinvale, Austl.	G3	62
Roblin, Mb., Can.	D1	86
Roboré, Bol.	B6	72
Robson, Mount, mtn., B.C., Can.	C8	85
Robstown, Tx., U.S.	F4	136
Roca Partida, Isla, i., Mex.	D2	78
Rocha, Ur.	E7	72
Rochefort, Fr.	E6	16
Rochelle, Ga., U.S.	E3	103
Rochelle, Il., U.S.	B4	106
Rochelle Park, N.J., U.S.	h8	123
Rochester, Il., U.S.	D4	106
Rochester, In., U.S.	B5	107
Rochester, Mi., U.S.	F7	115
Rochester, Mn., U.S.	F6	116
Rochester, N.H., U.S.	D5	122
Rochester, N.Y., U.S.	B3	125
Rochester, Pa., U.S.	E1	131
Rochester, Vt., U.S.	D3	138
Rochester, Wa., U.S.	C2	140
Rochester, Wi., U.S.	n11	142
Rock, co., Mn., U.S.	G2	116
Rock, co., Ne., U.S.	B6	120
Rock, co., Wi., U.S.	F4	142
Rock, stm., U.S.	B3	106
Rock, stm., U.S.	A1	108
Rockall, i., Scot., U.K.	D3	6
Rockall Rise	B24	144
Rockaway, N.J., U.S.	B3	123
Rockaway, Or., U.S.	B3	130
Rockbridge, co., Va., U.S.	C3	139
Rockcastle, co., Ky., U.S.	C5	110
Rockcastle, stm., Ky., U.S.	C5	110
Rockcliffe Park, On., Can.	h12	89
Rock Creek, Mn., U.S.	E6	116
Rock Creek, stm., Nv., U.S.	C5	121
Rock Creek, stm., Or., U.S.	B6	130
Rock Creek, stm., Wa., U.S.	B8	140
Rock Creek, stm., Wa., U.S.	D5	140
Rock Creek, stm., Wy., U.S.	E6	143
Rock Creek, stm., U.S.	B3	143
Rock Creek, stm., U.S.	h14	140
Rock Creek Butte, mtn., Or., U.S.	C8	130
Rockdale, Il., U.S.	B5	106
Rockdale, Md., U.S.	B4	113
Rockdale, Tx., U.S.	D4	136
Rockdale, co., Ga., U.S.	C3	103
Rockefeller Plateau, plat., Ant.	E27	67
Rockfall, Ct., U.S.	C5	100
Rockford, Ia., U.S.	A5	108
Rockford, Il., U.S.	A4	106
Rockford, Mi., U.S.	E5	115
Rockford, Mn., U.S.	E5	116
Rockford, Oh., U.S.	B1	128
Rockford, Tn., U.S.	D10	135
Rock Hall, Md., U.S.	B5	113
Rockhampton, Austl.	E5	62
Rockhampton Downs, Austl.	D6	60
Rock Hill, S.C., U.S.	B5	133
Rockingham, Austl.	G2	60
Rockingham, N.C., U.S.	C3	126
Rockingham, co., N.C., U.S.	A3	126
Rockingham, co., N.H., U.S.	D4	122
Rockingham, co., Va., U.S.	B4	139
Rock Island, P.Q., Can.	D5	90
Rock Island, Il., U.S.	B3	106
Rock Island, co., Il., U.S.	B3	106
Rock Island, i., Fl., U.S.	C3	102
Rock Island, i., Wi., U.S.	C7	142
Rock Lake, i., Wa., U.S.	B8	140
Rockland, On., Can.	B9	89
Rockland, Ma., U.S.	B6	114
Rockland, Me., U.S.	D3	112
Rockland, co., N.Y., U.S.	D6	125
Rockledge, Fl., U.S.	D6	102
Rockledge, Pa., U.S.	o20	131
Rocklin, Ca., U.S.	C3	98
Rockmart, Ga., U.S.	B1	103
Rock Mountain, mtn., Co., U.S.	D3	99
Rockport, In., U.S.	I3	107
Rockport, Ma., U.S.	A6	114
Rockport, Me., U.S.	D3	112
Rock Port, Mo., U.S.	A2	118
Rockport, Tx., U.S.	F4	136
Rock Rapids, Ia., U.S.	A1	108
Rock River, Wy., U.S.	E7	143
Rocksprings, Tx., U.S.	D2	136
Rock Springs, Wy., U.S.	E3	143
Rockstone, Guy.	B8	70
Rockton, Il., U.S.	A4	106
Rock Valley, Ia., U.S.	A1	108
Rockville, In., U.S.	E3	107
Rockville, Md., U.S.	B3	113
Rockville Centre, N.Y., U.S.	n15	125
Rockwall, Tx., U.S.	C4	136
Rockwall, co., Tx., U.S.	C4	136
Rockwell, Ia., U.S.	B4	108
Rockwell, N.C., U.S.	B2	126
Rockwell City, Ia., U.S.	B3	108
Rockwell Park, N.C., U.S.	B2	126
Rockwood, Mi., U.S.	F7	115
Rockwood, Pa., U.S.	G3	131
Rockwood, Tn., U.S.	D9	135
Rocky, stm., N.C., U.S.	B2	126
Rocky, stm., S.C., U.S.	C2	133
Rocky, East Branch, stm., Oh., U.S.	h9	128
Rocky, West Branch, stm., Oh., U.S.	h9	128
Rocky Boys Indian Reservation, Mt., U.S.	B7	119
Rocky Ford, Co., U.S.	C7	99
Rocky Fork Lake, l., Oh., U.S.	C2	128
Rocky Harbour, Nf., Can.	D3	88
Rocky Hill, Ct., U.S.	C5	100
Rocky Lake, l., Me., U.S.	D5	112
Rocky Mount, N.C., U.S.	B5	126
Rocky Mount, Va., U.S.	D3	139
Rocky Mountain, mtn., Mt., U.S.	C4	119
Rocky Mountain House, Ab., Can.	C3	84
Rocky Mountain National Park, Co., U.S.	A5	99
Rocky Mountains, mts., N.A.	B5	92
Rocky Ripple, In., U.S.	k10	107
Rocky River, Oh., U.S.	A4	128
Rocky Top, mtn., Or., U.S.	C4	130
Roddickton, Nf., Can.	C3	88
Rodeo, Arg.	E4	72
Roderfield, W.V., U.S.	D3	141
Rodez, Fr.	E8	16
Ródhos, Grc.	F12	18
Ródhos (Rhodes), i., Grc.	G12	18
Rodney, On., Can.	E3	89
Rodney, Cape, c., Ak., U.S.	C6	95
Rodney Village, De., U.S.	D3	101
Rodrigues, i., Mrts.	F12	52
Roebourne, Austl.	E2	60
Roebuck, S.C., U.S.	B4	133
Roeland Park, Ks., U.S.	k16	109
Roeselare, Bel.	E8	12
Roff, Ok., U.S.	C5	129
Roger Mills, co., Ok., U.S.	B2	129
Rogers, Ar., U.S.	A1	97
Rogers, Mn., U.S.	E5	116
Rogers, Tx., U.S.	D4	136
Rogers, co., Ok., U.S.	A6	129
Rogers, Mount, mtn., Va., U.S.	f10	139
Rogers City, Mi., U.S.	C7	115
Rogers Lake, res., Ct., U.S.	D6	100
Rogers Pass, Mt., U.S.	C4	119
Rogersville, N.B., Can.	C4	87
Rogersville, Al., U.S.	A2	94
Rogersville, Mo., U.S.	D4	118
Rogersville, Tn., U.S.	C10	135
Rogue, stm., Or., U.S.	E2	130
Rogue River, Or., U.S.	E2	130
Rohri, Pak.	E9	42
Rohtak, India	D3	40
Roi Et, Thai.	C4	34
Rokan, stm., Indon.	C2	36
Roland, Ia., U.S.	B4	108
Roland, Ok., U.S.	B7	129
Roland, Lake, res., Md., U.S.	g11	113
Rolette, N.D., U.S.	A6	127
Rolette, co., N.D., U.S.	A6	127
Rolfe, Ia., U.S.	B3	108
Rolla, Mo., U.S.	D6	118
Rolla, N.D., U.S.	A6	127
Rollingbay, Wa., U.S.	e10	140
Rolling Fork, Ms., U.S.	C3	117
Rolling Fork, stm., Ar., U.S.	C1	97
Rolling Fork, stm., Ky., U.S.	C4	110
Rolling Meadows, Il., U.S.	h8	106
Rollingstone, Mn., U.S.	F7	116
Rollinsford, N.H., U.S.	D5	122
Rolvsøya, i., Nor.	A10	10
Roma, Austl.	F4	62
Roma (Rome), Italy	D4	18
Roma, Tx., U.S.	F3	136
Romain, Cape, c., S.C., U.S.	F9	133
Roman, Rom.	F9	20
Romanche Gap	I12	66
Romang, Pulau, i., Indon.	E7	36
Romania, ctry., Eur.	F8	20
Roman Nose Mountain, mtn., Or., U.S.	D3	130
Romano, Cape, c., Fl., U.S.	G5	102
Romano, Cayo, i., Cuba	A4	80
Romans-sur-Isère, Fr.	E9	16
Romanzof, Cape, c., Ak., U.S.	C6	95
Romanzof Mountains, mts., Ak., U.S.	B11	95
Rome see Roma, Italy	D4	18
Rome, Ga., U.S.	B1	103
Rome, Il., U.S.	C4	106
Rome, N.Y., U.S.	B5	125
Rome City, In., U.S.	B7	107
Romeo, Mi., U.S.	F7	115
Romeoville, Il., U.S.	k8	106
Romney, W.V., U.S.	B6	141
Romny, Ukr.	D12	20
Romorantin-Lanthenay, Fr.	D7	16
Romulus, Mi., U.S.	p15	115
Ronan, Mt., U.S.	C2	119
Roncador, Serra do, plat., Braz.	D1	74
Ronceverte, W.V., U.S.	D4	141
Ronda, Spain	I4	16
Rondônia, state, Braz.	F7	70
Rondonópolis, Braz.	G9	70
Rong'an, China	D2	30
Rongcheng, China	B5	30
Ronge, Lac la, l., Sk., Can.	B3	91
Rongelap, atoll, Marsh. Is.	C10	58
Rongjiang, China	D2	30
Rongxian, China	E3	30
Rønne, Den.	I6	10
Ronneby, Swe.	H6	10
Ronne Ice Shelf, Ant.	D34	67
Roodhouse, Il., U.S.	D3	106
Rooks, co., Ks., U.S.	C4	109
Roosevelt, Ut., U.S.	C5	137
Roosevelt, co., Mt., U.S.	B11	119
Roosevelt, co., N.M., U.S.	C6	124
Roosevelt, stm., Braz.	E7	70
Roosevelt Island, i., Ant.	D24	67
Roosevelt Park, Mi., U.S.	E4	115
Root, stm., Mn., U.S.	G7	116
Root, stm., Wi., U.S.	n12	142
Roper, N.C., U.S.	B6	126
Roper Valley, Austl.	C5	60
Ropi, Fin.	B9	10
Roraima, state, Braz.	C7	70
Roraima, Mount, mtn., S.A.	B7	70
Røros, Nor.	E4	10
Rosamond, Ca., U.S.	E4	98
Rosario, Arg.	E5	72
Rosário, Braz.	B3	74
Rosario, Mex.	C3	78
Rosario, Para.	C6	72
Rosario de la Frontera, Arg.	D5	72
Rosário do Sul, Braz.	E6	72
Rosário Oeste, Braz.	F8	70
Roscoe, Il., U.S.	A5	106
Roscoe, Tx., U.S.	C2	136
Roscommon, Ire.	D2	12
Roscommon, Mi., U.S.	D6	115
Roscommon, co., Mi., U.S.	D6	115
Rose, Mount, mtn., Nv., U.S.	D2	121
Roseau, Dom.	B7	80
Roseau, Mn., U.S.	B3	116
Roseau, co., Mn., U.S.	B3	116
Roseau, South Fork, stm., Mn., U.S.	B3	116
Rose-Blanche [-Harbour le Cou], Nf., Can.	E2	88
Roseboro, N.C., U.S.	C4	126
Rosebud, S.D., U.S.	D5	134
Rosebud, Tx., U.S.	D4	136
Rosebud, co., Mt., U.S.	D10	119
Rosebud Indian Reservation, S.D., U.S.	D5	134
Roseburg, Or., U.S.	D3	130
Rosedale, In., U.S.	E3	107
Rosedale, Md., U.S.	g11	113
Rosedale, Ms., U.S.	B2	117
Rose Hill, Ks., U.S.	E6	109
Rose Hill, N.C., U.S.	C4	126
Rose Hill, Va., U.S.	f8	139
Roseland, Fl., U.S.	E6	102
Roseland, In., U.S.	A5	107
Roseland, La., U.S.	D5	111
Roseland, Oh., U.S.	B4	128
Roselle, Il., U.S.	k8	106
Roselle, N.J., U.S.	k7	123
Roselle Park, N.J., U.S.	k7	123
Rosemère, P.Q., Can.	p19	90
Rosemount, Mn., U.S.	F5	116
Rosenberg, Tx., U.S.	E5	136
Rosendale, Wi., U.S.	E5	142
Rosenheim, Ger.	G13	12
Rose Peak, mtn., Az., U.S.	D6	96
Rosepine, La., U.S.	D2	111
Rose Point, c., B.C., Can.	B2	85
Roseto, Pa., U.S.	E11	131
Rosetta see Rashid, Egypt	E10	14
Roseville, Ca., U.S.	C3	98
Roseville, Il., U.S.	C3	106
Roseville, Mi., U.S.	o16	115
Roseville, Mn., U.S.	m12	116
Roseville, Oh., U.S.	C3	128
Rosewood Heights, Il., U.S.	E3	106
Rosiclare, Il., U.S.	F5	106
Roşiori de Vede, Rom.	G8	20
Roskilde, Den.	I5	10
Roslavl', Russia	C12	20
Roslyn, Wa., U.S.	B4	140
Roslyn Heights, N.Y., U.S.	h13	125
Ross, Oh., U.S.	C1	128
Ross, co., Oh., U.S.	C2	128
Rossano, Italy	E6	18
Ross Barnett Reservoir, res., Ms., U.S.	C3	117
Rossburn, Mb., Can.	D1	86
Ross Dam, Wa., U.S.	A4	140
Rossford, Oh., U.S.	A2	128
Ross Ice Shelf, Ant.	E23	67
Rossignol, Lake, l., N.S., Can.	E4	87
Ross Island, i., Ant.	D22	67
Ross Island, i., Mb., Can.	B3	86
Ross Lake National Recreation Area, Wa., U.S.	A5	140
Rossland, B.C., Can.	E9	85
Rosso, Maur.	C1	50
Rossoš', Russia	D15	20
Ross Sea, Ant.	D24	67
Røssvatnet, l., Nor.	D5	10
Rossville, Ga., U.S.	B1	103
Rossville, Il., U.S.	C6	106
Rossville, In., U.S.	D4	107
Rossville, Ks., U.S.	C8	109
Roštaki, Taj.	C10	42
Rostock, Ger.	D12	12
Rostov, Russia	C6	22
Rostov-na-Donu, Russia	E6	26
Roswell, Ga., U.S.	B2	103
Roswell, N.M., U.S.	D5	124
Rota, i., N. Mar. Is.	D12	32
Rotan, Tx., U.S.	C2	136
Rothesay, N.B., Can.	D4	87
Rothschild, Wi., U.S.	D4	142
Rothsville, Pa., U.S.	F9	131
Roti, Pulau, i., Indon.	F6	36
Rotorua, N.Z.	o14	63c
Rotterdam, Neth.	E9	12
Rotterdam, N.Y., U.S.	C6	125
Roubaix, Fr.	B8	16
Rouen, Fr.	C7	16
Rouge, stm., P.Q., Can.	D3	90
Rough, stm., Ky., U.S.	C3	110
Rough River Lake, res., Ky., U.S.	C3	110
Rouiba, Alg.	I8	16
Roulette, Pa., U.S.	C5	131
Round Island, i., Ms., U.S.	g8	117
Round Lake, Il., U.S.	h8	106
Round Lake Beach, Il., U.S.	h8	106
Round Mountain, Nv., U.S.	E4	121
Round Rock, Tx., U.S.	D4	136
Roundup, Mt., U.S.	D8	119
Round Valley Indian Reservation, Ca., U.S.	C2	98
Round Valley Reservoir, res., N.J., U.S.	B3	123
Rouses Point, N.Y., U.S.	f11	125
Routt, co., Co., U.S.	A3	99
Rouyn [-Noranda], P.Q., Can.	k11	90
Rouzerville, Pa., U.S.	G6	131
Rovaniemi, Fin.	C11	10
Rovereto, Italy	B3	18
Rovigo, Italy	B3	18
Rovuma (Ruvuma), stm., Afr.	F8	54
Rowan, co., Ky., U.S.	B6	110
Rowan, co., N.C., U.S.	B2	126
Rowland, N.C., U.S.	C3	126
Rowlesburg, W.V., U.S.	B5	141
Roxas, Phil.	D8	34
Roxboro, N.C., U.S.	A4	126
Roxburgh, N.Z.	q12	63c
Roxton Falls, P.Q., Can.	D5	90
Roxton Pond, P.Q., Can.	D5	90
Roy, Ut., U.S.	B3	137
Royal, stm., Me., U.S.	g7	112
Royal Center, In., U.S.	C4	107
Royale, Isle, i., Mi., U.S.	h9	115
Royal Gorge, val., Co., U.S.	C5	99
Royal Oak, Mi., U.S.	F7	115
Royal Pines, N.C., U.S.	f10	126
Royalton, Il., U.S.	F4	106
Royalton, Mn., U.S.	E4	116
Royan, Fr.	E6	16
Royersford, Pa., U.S.	F10	131
Royerton, In., U.S.	D7	107
Royse City, Tx., U.S.	C4	136
Royston, B.C., Can.	E5	85
Royston, Ga., U.S.	B3	103
Rtiščevo, Russia	D7	22
Ruacana Falls, wtfl, Afr.	B1	56
Ruapehu, Mount, vol., N.Z.	o14	63c
Rubcovsk, Russia	D10	26
Rubidoux, Ca., U.S.	n14	98
Rubondo Island, i., Tan.	D6	54
Ruby Dome, mtn., Nv., U.S.	C6	121
Ruby Lake, l., Nv., U.S.	C6	121
Ruby Mountains, mts., Nv., U.S.	C6	121
Ruby Range, mts., Co., U.S.	C3	99
Ruby Range, mts., Mt., U.S.	E4	119
Rūdbār, Afg.	D8	42
Rudnja, Russia	B11	20
Rudnyj, Russia	D8	26
Rudolf, Lake (Turkana, Lake), l., Afr.	C7	54
Rudyard, Mi., U.S.	B6	115
Rufiji, stm., Tan.	E7	54
Rufino, Arg.	E5	72
Rufisque, Sen.	D1	50
Rufus Woods Lake, res., Wa., U.S.	A6	140
Rugby, N.D., U.S.	A6	127
Rügen, i., Ger.	C13	12
Ruhengeri, Rw.	D5	54
Rui'an, China	F12	28
Ruidoso, N.M., U.S.	D4	124
Ruidoso Downs, N.M., U.S.	D4	124
Ruijin, China	F11	28
Ruiz, Mex.	C3	78
Ruki, stm., D.R.C.	D3	54
Rukwa, Lake, l., Tan.	E6	54
Ruleville, Ms., U.S.	B3	117
Rum, stm., Mn., U.S.	D5	116
Ruma, Yugo.	B7	18
Rumbek, Sudan	I10	48
Rum Cay, i., Bah.	D10	76
Rum Creek, stm., W.V., U.S.	n12	141
Rumford, Me., U.S.	D2	112
Rum Jungle, Austl.	C5	60
Rumoi, Japan	C16	28
Rumphi, Mwi.	A5	56
Rumson, N.J., U.S.	C4	123
Rumstick Point, c., R.I., U.S.	D5	132
Runan, China	E10	28
Rundu, Nmb.	B2	56
Runge, Tx., U.S.	E4	136
Rungwa, Tan.	E6	54
Runnels, co., Tx., U.S.	D3	136
Runnemede, N.J., U.S.	D2	123
Ruoqiang, China	D5	28
Rupat, Pulau, i., Indon.	C2	36
Rupert, Id., U.S.	G5	105
Rupert, W.V., U.S.	D4	141
Rupert, Rivière de, stm., P.Q., Can.	h11	90
Rural Hall, N.C., U.S.	A2	126
Rural Retreat, Va., U.S.	D1	139
Rurrenabaque, Bol.	A4	72
Rusagonis, N.B., Can.	D3	87
Rusape, Zimb.	B5	56
Ruse, Bul.	C11	18
Rush, co., In., U.S.	E6	107
Rush, co., Ks., U.S.	D4	109
Rush, stm., Mn., U.S.	F4	116
Rush, stm., Wi., U.S.	D1	142
Rush City, Mn., U.S.	E6	116
Rush Creek, stm., Oh., U.S.	B2	128
Rush Creek, stm., Ok., U.S.	C4	129
Rushford, Mn., U.S.	G7	116
Rush Lake, l., Mn., U.S.	D3	116
Rush Lake, l., Mn., U.S.	E5	116
Rush Lake, l., Wi., U.S.	E5	142
Rushmere, Va., U.S.	h14	139
Rush Springs, Ok., U.S.	C4	129
Rushville, Il., U.S.	C3	106
Rushville, In., U.S.	E7	107
Rushville, Ne., U.S.	B3	120
Rusk, Tx., U.S.	D5	136
Rusk, co., Tx., U.S.	C5	136
Rusk, co., Wi., U.S.	C2	142
Ruskin, Fl., U.S.	E4	102
Russas, Braz.	B4	74
Russell, Mb., Can.	D1	86
Russell, On., Can.	B9	89
Russell, Ks., U.S.	D5	109
Russell, Ky., U.S.	B7	110
Russell, Pa., U.S.	C3	131
Russell, co., Al., U.S.	C4	94
Russell, co., Ks., U.S.	D5	109
Russell, co., Ky., U.S.	D4	110
Russell, co., Va., U.S.	f9	139
Russell, Mount, mtn., Ak., U.S.	f16	95
Russell Cave National Monument, Al., U.S.	A4	94
Russell Fork, stm., U.S.	C7	110
Russell Springs, Ky., U.S.	C4	110
Russellville, Al., U.S.	A2	94
Russellville, Ar., U.S.	B2	97
Russellville, Ky., U.S.	D3	110
Russellville, Mo., U.S.	C5	118
Russellville, Tn., U.S.	C10	135
Russia, ctry., Eur.	C11	26
Russian, stm., Ca., U.S.	C2	98
Russiaville, In., U.S.	D5	107
Russkaja Gavan', Russia	B8	26
Rustavi, Geor.	B11	44
Rustburg, Va., U.S.	C3	139
Rustenburg, S. Afr.	D4	56
Ruston, La., U.S.	B3	111
Ruston, Wa., U.S.	B3	140
Rutana, Bdi.	D6	54
Ruteng, Indon.	E6	36
Ruth, Nv., U.S.	D6	121
Rutherford, N.J., U.S.	B4	123
Rutherford, Tn., U.S.	A3	135
Rutherford, co., N.C., U.S.	B1	126
Rutherford, co., Tn., U.S.	B5	135
Rutherfordton, N.C., U.S.	B1	126
Ruthven, Ia., U.S.	A3	108
Rutland, Ma., U.S.	B4	114
Rutland, Vt., U.S.	D3	138
Rutland, co., Vt., U.S.	D2	138
Rutledge, Ga., U.S.	C3	103
Rutledge, Tn., U.S.	C10	135
Rutog, China	C3	40
Rutshuru, D.R.C.	D5	54
Ruvuma (Rovuma), stm., Afr.	F8	54
Ruy Barbosa, Braz.	D3	74
Ruzaevka, Russia	D7	22
Rwanda, ctry., Afr.	D5	54
Ryan, Ok., U.S.	C4	129
Ryan Peak, mtn., Id., U.S.	F4	105
Rybače, Kaz.	E10	26
Rybačij, poluostrov, pen., Russia	B15	10
Rybinsk, Russia	D5	26
Rybinskoe vodohranilišče, res., Russia	D5	26
Rybinsk Reservoir see Rybinskoe vodohranilišče, res., Russia	D5	26
Rybnik, Pol.	D5	20
Rycroft, Ab., Can.	B1	84
Rye, N.H., U.S.	D5	122
Rye, N.Y., U.S.	h13	125
Rye Beach, N.H., U.S.	E5	122
Rye Patch Dam, Nv., U.S.	C3	121
Rye Patch Reservoir, res., Nv., U.S.	C3	121
Ryl's, Russia	D13	20
Ryukyu Islands see Nansei-shotō, is., Japan	A9	34
Ryukyu Trench	F15	64
Rzeszów, Pol.	D7	20
Ržev, Russia	D5	26

S

Name	Map Ref.	Page
Saarbrücken, Ger.	F10	12
Saaremaa, i., Est.	G10	10
Saarijärvi, Fin.	E11	10

Name	Map Ref.	Page

Saarlouis, Ger. **F10** 12
Saatlı, Azer. **C13** 44
Saba, i., Neth. Ant. **B7** 80
Šabac, Yugo. **B7** 18
Sabadell, Spain **G8** 16
Sabah, hist. reg., Malay. . . . **B5** 36
Sabana, Archipiélago de, is., Cuba **A3** 80
Sabanalarga, Col. **C5** 80
Sabattus, Me., U.S. **D2** 112
Şāberī, Hāmūn-e, l., Asia . . **D8** 42
Sabetha, Ks., U.S. **C8** 109
Sabhā, Libya **E7** 48
Sabi (Save), stm., Afr. **B5** 56
Sabillasville, Md., U.S. **A3** 113
Sabina, Oh., U.S. **C2** 128
Sabinal, Tx., U.S. **E3** 136
Sabinal, Cayo, i., Cuba **A4** 80
Sabinas, Mex. **B4** 78
Sabinas Hidalgo, Mex. **B4** 78
Sabine, co., La., U.S. **C2** 111
Sabine, co., Tx., U.S. **D6** 136
Sabine, stm., U.S. **E9** 92
Sabine, stm., Mo., U.S. **D6** 136
Sabine Lake, l., U.S. **E2** 111
Sabine Pass, strt., U.S. **E2** 111
Sabirabad, Azer. **B13** 44
Sable, Cape, c., Fl., U.S. . . . **G5** 102
Sable Island, i., N.S., Can. . **F10** 87
Sabrina Coast, Ant. **C16** 67
Sabula, Ia., U.S. **B7** 108
Şabyā, Sau. Ar. **G4** 38
Sabzevār, Iran **C7** 42
Sac, co., Ia., U.S. **B2** 108
Sac, stm., Mo., U.S. **D4** 118
Sacajawea, Lake, res., Wa., U.S. **C7** 140
Sacajawea Peak, mtn., Or., U.S. **B9** 130
Sacandaga Lake, l., N.Y., U.S. **B6** 125
Sac and Fox Indian Reservation, Ia., U.S. . . **C5** 108
Sacaton, Az., U.S. **D4** 96
Sac City, Ia., U.S. **B2** 108
Săcele, Rom. **G8** 20
Sachse, Tx., U.S. **n10** 136
Sachsen, hist. reg., Ger. . . . **E13** 12
Sachuest Point, c., R.I., U.S. **F6** 132
Sackville, N.B., Can. **D5** 87
Saco, Me., U.S. **E2** 112
Saco, stm., U.S. **E2** 112
Saco, East Branch, stm., N.H., U.S. **B4** 122
Sacramento, Ca., U.S. **C3** 98
Sacramento, co., Ca., U.S. . . **C3** 98
Sacramento, stm., Ca., U.S. **C3** 98
Sacramento, stm., N.M., U.S. **E4** 124
Sacramento Mountains, mts., N.M., U.S. **E4** 124
Sacramento Valley, val., Ca., U.S. **C2** 98
Sacré-Coeur-Saguenay, P.Q., Can. **A8** 90
Sacred Heart, Mn., U.S. . . . **F3** 116
Şa'dah, Yemen **G4** 38
Saddle, stm., N.J., U.S. **h8** 123
Saddleback Mountain, mtn., Az., U.S. **k8** 96
Saddle Brook, N.J., U.S. . . . **h8** 123
Saddlebunch Keys, is., Fl., U.S. **H5** 102
Saddle Mountain, mtn., Or., U.S. **B3** 130
Saddle Mountains, mts., Wa., U.S. **C5** 140
Saddle River, N.J., U.S. **A4** 123
Sa Dec, Viet. **D5** 34
Sado, i., Japan **D15** 28
Sado-kaikyō, strt., Japan . . **C3** 31
Šadrinsk, Russia **D8** 26
Saegertown, Pa., U.S. **C1** 131
Safāga, Egypt **E11** 48
Safety Harbor, Fl., U.S. . . . **E4** 102
Säffle, Swe. **G5** 10
Safford, Az., U.S. **E6** 96
Safi, Mor. **D3** 48
Safonovo, Russia **B12** 20
Safonovo, Russia **A8** 22
Safranbolu, Tur. **B5** 44
Saga, China **F5** 28
Saga, Japan **D2** 31
Sagadahoc, co., Me., U.S. . . **E3** 112
Sagaing, Myan. **B3** 34
Sagamore Hills, Oh., U.S. . . **h9** 128
Saganaga Lake, l., Mn., U.S. **B7** 116
Sāgar, India **E3** 40
Sagarmāthā see Everest, Mount, mtn., Asia . . . **D5** 40
Sagay, Phil. **D8** 34
Sag Harbor, N.Y., U.S. **m16** 125
Saginaw, Mi., U.S. **E7** 115
Saginaw, Tx., U.S. **n9** 136
Saginaw, co., Mi., U.S. **E6** 115
Saginaw Bay, b., Mi., U.S. . **E7** 115
Sagiz, Kaz. **E10** 22
Saglek Bay, b., Nf., Can. . . . **f9** 88
Šagonar, Russia **A6** 28
Saguache, co., Co., U.S. . . . **C4** 99
Sagua de Tánamo, Cuba . . **A4** 80
Sagua la Grande, Cuba . . . **A3** 80
Saguaro Lake, res., Az., U.S. **k10** 96

Saguaro National Monument (Tucson Mountain Section), Az., U.S. **E4** 96
Saguaro National Monument, Az., U.S. . . **E5** 96
Saguenay, stm., P.Q., Can. . **A7** 90
Sagunt, Spain **H6** 16
Sahagún, Col. **D4** 80
Sahalin, ostrov, i., Russia . . **D16** 26
Sahara, des., Afr. **F6** 48
Sahāranpur, India **D3** 40
Sahel see Sudan, reg., Afr. . **H8** 48
Sāhīwāl, Pak. **D10** 42
Sāhīwāl, Pak. **D10** 42
Şahneh, Iran **E12** 44
Şahrisabz, Uzb. **F8** 26
Šahty, Russia **E5** 26
Sahuaripa, Mex. **B3** 78
Sahuarita, Az., U.S. **F5** 96
Šahunja, Russia **C8** 22
Sa Huynh, Viet. **D5** 34
Saibai Island, i., Austl. . . . **B3** 62
Saïda, Alg. **E4** 14
Saidpur, Bngl. **D5** 40
Saidu, Pak. **D10** 42
Saigon see Thanh Pho Ho Chi Minh, Viet. **D5** 34
Saiki, Japan **D2** 31
Šaim, Russia **B11** 22
Saimaa, l., Fin. **F13** 10
Şā'īn Dezh, Iran **D12** 44
Saint Adolphe, Mb., Can. . . **E3** 86
Sainte-Agathe, P.Q., Can. . . **C6** 90
Sainte-Agathe-des-Monts, P.Q., Can. **C3** 90
Saint-Aimé (Massueville), P.Q., Can. **D5** 90
Saint-Alban, P.Q., Can. . . . **C5** 90
Saint Alban's, Nf., Can. . . . **E4** 88
Saint Albans, Vt., U.S. **B2** 138
Saint Albans, W.V., U.S. . . . **C3** 141
Saint Albans Bay, b., Vt., U.S. **B2** 138
Saint Albert, Ab., Can. **C4** 84
Saint-Amand-Montrond, Fr. **D8** 16
Saint-Ambroise, P.Q., Can. . **A6** 90
Saint-André-Avellin, P.Q., Can. **D2** 90
Saint-André-Est, P.Q., Can. . **D3** 90
Saint Andrew Bay, b., Fl., U.S. **u16** 102
Saint Andrews, N.B., Can. . . **D2** 87
Saint Andrews, Scot., U.K. . **B5** 12
Saint Andrews, S.C., U.S. . . **C5** 133
Saint Andrews, S.C., U.S. . . **F7** 133
Saint Anne, Il., U.S. **B6** 106
Sainte-Anne-de-Beaupré, P.Q., Can. **B7** 90
Sainte-Anne [-de-Bellevue], P.Q., Can. **q19** 90
Sainte Anne-de-Madawaska, N.B., Can. **B1** 87
Sainte Anne-des-Chênes, Mb., Can. **E3** 86
Saint-Anselme, P.Q., Can. . . **C7** 90
Saint Ansgar, Ia., U.S. **A5** 108
Saint Anthony, Nf., Can. . . . **C4** 88
Saint Anthony, Id., U.S. . . . **F7** 105
Saint Antoine, N.B., Can. . . **C5** 87
Saint-Apollinaire, P.Q., Can. **C6** 90
Saint Arnaud, Austl. **H3** 62
Saint Arthur, N.B., Can. . . . **B3** 87
Saint-Aubert, P.Q., Can. . . . **B7** 90
Saint Augustin, stm., Can. . **C2** 88
Saint Augustine, Fl., U.S. . . **C5** 102
Saint-Austell, Eng., U.K. . . . **E4** 12
Saint-Avold, Fr. **C10** 16
Saint Basile, N.B., Can. . . . **B1** 87
Saint-Basile [-Sud], P.Q., Can. **C6** 90
Saint-Bernard, P.Q., Can. . . **C6** 90
Saint Bernard, Al., U.S. . . . **A3** 94
Saint Bernard, La., U.S. . . . **E6** 111
Saint Bernard, Oh., U.S. . . . **o13** 128
Saint Bernard, co., La., U.S. **E6** 111
Saint Bernice, In., U.S. . . . **E2** 107
Saint Bride, Mount, mtn., Ab., Can. **D3** 84
Saint Bride's, Nf., Can. **E4** 88
Saint-Brieuc, Fr. **C5** 16
Saint-Bruno, P.Q., Can. . . . **A6** 90
Saint-Casimir, P.Q., Can. . . **C5** 90
Saint Catharines, On., Can. **D5** 89
Saint Catherine, Lake, l., Vt., U.S. **E2** 138
Saint Catherines Island, i., Ga., U.S. **E5** 103
Saint-Célestin (Annaville), P.Q., Can. **C5** 90
Saint-Césaire, P.Q., Can. . . **D4** 90
Saint-Chamond, Fr. **E9** 16
Saint-Charles, P.Q., Can. . . **C7** 90
Saint Charles, Il., U.S. **B5** 106
Saint Charles, Mi., U.S. . . . **E6** 115
Saint Charles, Mn., U.S. . . . **G6** 116
Saint Charles, Mo., U.S. . . . **C7** 118
Saint Charles, co., La., U.S. **E5** 111
Saint Charles, co., Mo., U.S. **C7** 118
Saint Christopher (Saint Kitts), i., St. K./N. . . . **B7** 80
Saint Christopher and Nevis see Saint Kitts and Nevis, ctry., N.A. **E12** 76

Saint-Chrysostome, P.Q., Can. **D4** 90
Saint Clair, Mi., U.S. **F8** 115
Saint Clair, Mn., U.S. **F5** 116
Saint Clair, Mo., U.S. **C6** 118
Saint Clair, Pa., U.S. **E9** 131
Saint Clair, co., Al., U.S. . . . **B3** 94
Saint Clair, co., Il., U.S. . . . **E3** 106
Saint Clair, co., Mi., U.S. . . **F8** 115
Saint Clair, co., Mo., U.S. . . **C4** 118
Saint Clair Shores, Mi., U.S. **p16** 115
Saint Clairsville, Oh., U.S. . . **B5** 128
Saint Claude, Mb., Can. . . . **E2** 86
Saint Cloud, Fl., U.S. **D5** 102
Saint Cloud, Mn., U.S. **E4** 116
Saint-Coeur-de-Marie, P.Q., Can. **A6** 90
Saint-Constant, P.Q., Can. . **q19** 90
Sainte-Croix, P.Q., Can. . . . **C6** 90
Saint Croix, co., Wi., U.S. . . **C1** 142
Saint Croix, i., V.I.U.S. **B7** 80
Saint Croix, co., Wi., U.S. . . **C1** 142
Saint Croix, stm., U.S. **C1** 142
Saint Croix, Lake, l., U.S. . . **D1** 142
Saint Croix Falls, Wi., U.S. . **C1** 142
Saint Croix Stream, stm., Me., U.S. **B4** 112
Saint-Damase, P.Q., Can. . . **D4** 90
Saint David, Az., U.S. **F5** 96
Saint-David-de-l'Auberivière, P.Q., Can. **n17** 90
Saint-Denis, P.Q., Can. **D4** 90
Saint-Denis, Reu. **g10** 57a
Saint-Dié, Fr. **C10** 16
Saint-Dizier, Fr. **C9** 16
Saint-Dominique, P.Q., Can. **D5** 90
Saint Edward, Ne., U.S. . . . **C8** 120
Saint Eleanor's, P.E., Can. . . **C6** 87
Saint Elias, Cape, c., Ak., U.S. **D11** 95
Saint Elias, Mount, mtn., N.A. **F11** 82
Saint-Élie, Fr. Gu. **C9** 70
Saint Elmo, Al., U.S. **E1** 94
Saint Elmo, Il., U.S. **D5** 106
Saint-Éphrem [-de-Tring], P.Q., Can. **C7** 90
Saint-Étienne, Fr. **E9** 16
Saint-Eustache, P.Q., Can. . **D4** 90
Saint-Félicien, P.Q., Can. . . **A5** 90
Saint-Félix-de-Valois, P.Q., Can. **C4** 90
Saint-Ferdinand (Bernierville), P.Q., Can. **C6** 90
Saint-Ferréol [-les-Neiges], P.Q., Can. **B7** 90
Saint-Flavien, P.Q., Can. . . **C6** 90
Sainte-Foy, P.Q., Can. **n17** 90
Saint Francis, Ks., U.S. **C2** 109
Saint Francis, Mn., U.S. . . . **E5** 116
Saint Francis, S.D., U.S. . . . **D5** 134
Saint Francis, Wi., U.S. . . . **n12** 142
Saint Francis, co., Ar., U.S. . **B5** 97
Saint Francis, stm., U.S. . . . **A5** 97
Saint Francis, Cape, c., Nf., Can. **E5** 88
Saint Francis, Cape, c., S. Afr. **E3** 56
Saint Francisville, Il., U.S. . . **E6** 106
Saint Francisville, La., U.S. . **D4** 111
Saint Francois, co., Mo., U.S. **D7** 118
Saint-François, stm., P.Q., Can. **D5** 90
Saint-François, Lac, l., P.Q., Can. **D6** 90
Saint Francois Mountains, hills, Mo., U.S. **D7** 118
Saint Froid Lake, l., Me., U.S. **B4** 112
Saint-Fulgence, P.Q., Can. . **A7** 90
Saint-Gabriel, P.Q., Can. . . **C4** 90
Saint-Gaudens, Fr. **F7** 16
Saint-Gédéon, P.Q., Can. . . **D7** 90
Sainte Genevieve, Mo., U.S. **D7** 118
Sainte Genevieve, co., Mo., U.S. **D7** 118
Saint George, Austl. **F4** 62
Saint George, N.B., Can. . . . **D3** 87
Saint George, On., Can. . . . **D4** 89
Saint George, S.C., U.S. . . . **E6** 133
Saint George, Ut., U.S. **F2** 137
Saint George, Cape, c., Nf., Can. **D2** 88
Saint George, Cape, c., Fl., U.S. **C1** 102
Saint George Island, i., Ak., U.S. **D6** 95
Saint George Island, i., Fl., U.S. **C2** 102
Saint George's, Nf., Can. . . **D2** 88
Saint-Georges, P.Q., Can. . . **C5** 90
Saint-Georges, Fr. Gu. **C9** 70
Saint Georges, Gren. **C7** 80
Saint Georges, De., U.S. . . . **B3** 101
Saint George's Bay, b., Nf., Can. **D2** 88
Saint Georges Bay, b., N.S., Can. **D8** 87
Saint George's Channel, strt., Eur. **B3** 16
Saint-Georges-Ouest (part of Ville-Saint-Georges), P.Q., Can. **C7** 90

Saint-Gervais, P.Q., Can. . . **C7** 90
Saint-Gilles, P.Q., Can. . . . **C6** 90
Saint Gotthard Pass see San Gottardo, Passo del, Switz. **A2** 18
Saint-Grégoire (Larochelle), P.Q., Can. **C5** 90
Saint-Guillaume-d'Upton, P.Q., Can. **D5** 90
Saint Helen, Lake, l., Mi., U.S. **D6** 115
Saint Helena, Ca., U.S. **C2** 98
Saint Helena, co., La., U.S. . **D5** 111
Saint Helena, dep., Afr. . . . **K9** 46
Saint Helena Island, i., S.C., U.S. **G6** 133
Saint Helena Sound, strt., S.C., U.S. **G7** 133
Saint Helens, Or., U.S. **B4** 130
Saint Helens, Mount, vol., Wa., U.S. **C3** 140
Saint Helier, Jersey **F5** 12
Saint Henry, Oh., U.S. **B1** 128
Saint-Honoré, P.Q., Can. . . **D7** 90
Saint-Hubert, P.Q., Can. . . **q20** 90
Saint-Hubert-de-Témiscouata, P.Q., Can. **B8** 90
Saint-Hyacinthe, P.Q., Can. **D5** 90
Saint Ignace, Mi., U.S. **C6** 115
Saint Ignatius, Mt., U.S. . . . **C2** 119
Saint Isidore de Prescott, On., Can. **B10** 89
Saint Jacobs, On., Can. . . . **D4** 89
Saint Jacques, N.B., Can. . . **B1** 87
Saint-Jacques, P.Q., Can. . . **D4** 90
Saint James, Mn., U.S. **G4** 116
Saint James, Mo., U.S. **D6** 118
Saint James, co., La., U.S. . . **D5** 111
Saint James, Cape, c., Ak., U.S. **D2** 85
Saint James City, Fl., U.S. . . **F4** 102
Saint-Jean, stm., P.Q., Can. **A7** 90
Saint-Jean, Lac, l., P.Q., Can. **A5** 90
Saint Jean Baptiste, Mb., Can. **E3** 86
Saint-Jean-Chrysostome, P.Q., Can. **o17** 90
Saint-Jean-d'Angély, Fr. . . . **E6** 16
Saint-Jean-sur-Richelieu, P.Q., Can. **D4** 90
Saint-Jérôme, P.Q., Can. . . **D3** 90
Saint Jo, Tx., U.S. **C4** 136
Saint-Joachim, P.Q., Can. . . **B7** 90
Saint Joe, stm., Id., U.S. . . . **B3** 105
Saint John, N.B., Can. **D3** 87
Saint John, In., U.S. **B3** 107
Saint John, Ks., U.S. **E5** 109
Saint John, i., V.I.U.S. **B7** 80
Saint John, stm., N.A. **B14** 92
Saint John, Cape, c., Nf., Can. **D4** 88
Saint John Bay, b., Nf., Can. **C3** 88
Saint John's, Antig. **B7** 80
Saint John's, Nf., Can. **E5** 88
Saint Johns, Az., U.S. **C6** 96
Saint Johns, Mi., U.S. **F6** 115
Saint Johns, co., Fl., U.S. . . **C5** 102
Saint Johns, stm., Fl., U.S. . **B5** 102
Saint Johnsbury, Vt., U.S. . . **C4** 138
Saint Johnsville, N.Y., U.S. . **B6** 125
Saint John the Baptist, co., La., U.S. **D5** 111
Saint Jones, stm., De., U.S. . **D4** 101
Saint Joseph, N.B., Can. . . . **D5** 87
Saint Joseph, Il., U.S. **C5** 106
Saint Joseph, La., U.S. **C4** 111
Saint Joseph, Mi., U.S. **F4** 115
Saint Joseph, Mn., U.S. . . . **E4** 116
Saint Joseph, Mo., U.S. . . . **B3** 118
Saint Joseph, Tn., U.S. **B4** 135
Saint Joseph, co., In., U.S. . **A5** 107
Saint Joseph, co., Mi., U.S. **G5** 115
Saint-Joseph, stm., U.S. . . . **F5** 115
Saint-Joseph, Lac, l., P.Q., Can. **n16** 90
Saint Joseph, Lake, l., On., Can. **o17** 89
Saint Joseph Bay, b., Fl., U.S. **C1** 102
Saint-Joseph-de-Beauce, P.Q., Can. **C7** 90
Saint Joseph Point, c., Fl., U.S. **v16** 102
Saint Joseph Sound, strt., Fl., U.S. **o10** 102
Saint-Jovite, P.Q., Can. . . . **C3** 90
Saint-Junien, Fr. **E7** 16
Saint Kilda, i., Scot., U.K. . . **B2** 12
Saint Kitts see Saint Christopher, i., St. K./N. **B7** 80
Saint Kitts and Nevis, ctry., N.A. **E12** 76
Saint-Lambert, P.Q., Can. . . **p19** 90
Saint Landry, co., La., U.S. . **D3** 111
Saint-Laurent, P.Q., Can. . . **p19** 90
Saint-Laurent du Maroni, Fr. Gu. **B9** 70
Saint Lawrence, Nf., Can. . . **E4** 88
Saint Lawrence, stm., N.Y., U.S. **A5** 125
Saint Lawrence, stm., N.A. . **B14** 92

Saint Lawrence, Cape, c., N.S., Can. **B9** 87
Saint Lawrence, Gulf of, b., Can. **I27** 82
Saint Lawrence Island, i., Ak., U.S. **C5** 95
Saint Lawrence Islands National Park, On., Can. **C9** 89
Saint Léonard, N.B., Can. . . **B2** 87
Saint-Léonard [-d'Aston], P.Q., Can. **C5** 90
Saint-Liboire, P.Q., Can. . . **D5** 90
Saint-Lô, Fr. **C6** 16
Saint-Louis, Sen. **C1** 50
Saint Louis, Mi., U.S. **E6** 115
Saint Louis, Mo., U.S. **C7** 118
Saint Louis, co., Mn., U.S. . **C6** 116
Saint Louis, co., Mo., U.S. . **C7** 118
Saint-Louis, stm., U.S. **D6** 116
Saint-Louis, Lac, l., P.Q., Can. **q19** 90
Saint Louis Bay, b., Ms., U.S. **f7** 117
Saint-Louis-de-Gonzague, P.Q., Can. **D3** 90
Saint-Louis-de-Kent, N.B., Can. **C5** 87
Saint-Louis-du-Ha! Ha!, P.Q., Can. **B8** 90
Saint Louis Park, Mn., U.S. **n12** 116
Saint-Luc, P.Q., Can. **D4** 90
Saint Lucia, ctry., N.A. **F12** 76
Saint Lucia, lake, l., S. Afr. . **D5** 56
Saint Lucia Channel, strt., N.A. **C7** 80
Saint Lucie, co., Fl., U.S. . . . **E6** 102
Saint Lucie Canal, Fl., U.S. . **F6** 102
Saint Lucie Inlet, b., Fl., U.S. **E6** 102
Sainte-Madeleine, P.Q., Can. **D4** 90
Saint Magnus Bay, b., Scot., U.K. **h19** 12a
Saint Malo, Mb., Can. **E3** 86
Saint-Malo, Fr. **C5** 16
Saint-Malo, Golfe de, b., Fr. **C5** 16
Saint-Marc, Haiti **B5** 80
Saint-Marc [-des-Carrières], P.Q., Can. **C5** 90
Saint Margaret Bay, b., Nf., Can. **C3** 88
Sainte-Marguerite, stm., P.Q., Can. **A7** 90
Sainte-Marie, P.Q., Can. . . **C6** 90
Sainte Marie, Nosy, i., Madag. **B8** 56
Saint Maries, Id., U.S. **B2** 105
Sainte-Marthe, P.Q., Can. . **D3** 90
Saint Martin, co., La., U.S. . **D4** 111
Saint-Martin, i., N.A. **B7** 80
Saint Martin, Lake, l., Mb., Can. **D2** 86
Saint Martin Island, i., Mi., U.S. **C4** 115
Saint Martinville, La., U.S. . **D4** 111
Saint Mary, co., La., U.S. . . **E4** 111
Saint Mary-of-the-Woods, In., U.S. **E3** 107
Saint Mary Peak, mtn., Austl. **G2** 62
Saint Marys, Austl. **I4** 62
Saint Mary's, Nf., Can. **E5** 88
Saint Mary's, On., Can. . . . **D3** 89
Saint Marys, Ak., U.S. **C7** 95
Saint Marys, Ga., U.S. **F5** 103
Saint Marys, In., U.S. **A5** 107
Saint Marys, Ks., U.S. **C7** 109
Saint Marys, Oh., U.S. **B1** 128
Saint Marys, Pa., U.S. **D4** 131
Saint Marys, W.V., U.S. . . . **B3** 141
Saint Marys, co., Md., U.S. . **D4** 113
Saint Marys, stm., N.S., Can. **D8** 87
Saint Marys, stm., Md., U.S. **D5** 113
Saint Marys, stm., U.S. . . . **F5** 103
Saint Marys, stm., U.S. . . . **C8** 107
Saint Mary's, Cape, c., Nf., Can. **E4** 88
Saint Mary's Bay, b., Nf., Can. **E5** 88
Saint Marys Bay, b., N.S., Can. **E3** 87
Saint Marys City, Md., U.S. **D5** 113
Saint Matthew Island, i., Ak., U.S. **C5** 95
Saint Matthews, Ky., U.S. . . **B4** 110
Saint Matthews, S.C., U.S. . **D6** 133
Saint-Maurice, stm., P.Q., Can. **C5** 90
Saint Michael, Mn., U.S. . . **E5** 116
Saint Michaels, Md., U.S. . . **C5** 113
Saint-Michel [-de-Bellechasse], P.Q., Can. **C7** 90
Saint-Nazaire, Fr. **D5** 16
Saint-Nicolas, P.Q., Can. . . **o17** 90
Saint-Odilon, P.Q., Can. . . . **C7** 90
Saint-Omer, Fr. **B8** 16
Saint-Ours, P.Q., Can. **D4** 90
Saint-Pacôme, P.Q., Can. . . **B8** 90
Saint-Pamphile, P.Q., Can. . **C8** 90
Saint Paris, Oh., U.S. **B2** 128
Saint-Pascal, P.Q., Can. . . . **B8** 90
Saint Paul, Ab., Can. **B5** 84
Saint-Paul, Reu. **g10** 57a
Saint Paul, Ak., U.S. **D5** 95

Name	Map Ref.	Page
Saint Paul, In., U.S.	F6	107
Saint Paul, Ks., U.S.	E8	109
Saint Paul, Mn., U.S.	F5	116
Saint Paul, Mo., U.S.	f12	118
Saint Paul, Ne., U.S.	C7	120
Saint Paul, Va., U.S.	f9	139
Saint Paul Island, i., Ak., U.S.	D5	95
Saint Paul Park, Mn., U.S.	n12	116
Saint Pauls, N.C., U.S.	C4	126
Sainte-Perpétue-de-L'Islet, P.Q., Can.	B8	90
Saint Peter, Mn., U.S.	F5	116
Saint Peter Port, Guernsey	F5	12
Saint Peters, N.S., Can.	D9	87
Saint Peters, Mo., U.S.	C7	118
Saint Petersburg see Sankt-Peterburg, Russia	D5	26
Saint Petersburg, Fl., U.S.	E4	102
Saint Petersburg Beach, Fl., U.S.	p10	102
Saint Phillips Island, i., S.C., U.S.	G6	133
Saint-Pie, P.Q., Can.	D5	90
Saint-Pierre, Reu.	g10	57a
Saint-Pierre, St. P./M.	E3	88
Saint-Pierre, i., Sey.	i12	57b
Saint-Pierre, Lac, l., P.Q., Can.	C5	90
Saint Pierre and Miquelon, dep., N.A.	I28	82
Saint Pierre-Jolys, Mb., Can.	E3	86
Saint-Prime, P.Q., Can.	A5	90
Saint Quentin, N.B., Can.	B2	87
Saint-Quentin, Fr.	C8	16
Saint-Raphaël, P.Q., Can.	C7	90
Saint-Raphaël, Fr.	F10	16
Saint-Raymond, P.Q., Can.	C6	90
Saint-Rédempteur, P.Q., Can.	o17	90
Saint Regis, Mt., U.S.	C1	119
Saint Regis, West Branch, stm., N.Y., U.S.	f10	125
Saint-Rémi, P.Q., Can.	D4	90
Saint-Romuald, P.Q., Can.	C6	90
Saint Rose, La., U.S.	k11	111
Sainte Rose du Lac, Mb., Can.	D2	86
Saintes, Fr.	E6	16
Saint Sauveur, N.B., Can.	B4	87
Saint-Sauveur-des-Monts, P.Q., Can.	D3	90
Saint-Siméon, P.Q., Can.	B8	90
Saint Simons Island, Ga., U.S.	E5	103
Saint Simons Island, i., Ga., U.S.	E5	103
Saint Stephen, N.B., Can.	D2	87
Saint Stephen, S.C., U.S.	E8	133
Saint Tammany, co., La., U.S.	D5	111
Sainte-Thècle, P.Q., Can.	C5	90
Sainte-Thérèse, P.Q., Can.	D4	90
Saint Thomas, On., Can.	E3	89
Saint Thomas, i., V.I.U.S.	B6	80
Saint Timothée, P.Q., Can.	q18	90
Saint-Tite, P.Q., Can.	C5	90
Saint-Tropez, Fr.	F10	16
Sainte-Véronique, P.Q., Can.	C3	90
Saint-Victor, P.Q., Can.	C7	90
Saint Vincent, i., St. Vin.	C7	80
Saint Vincent and the Grenadines, ctry., N.A.	F12	76
Saint Vincent Island, i., Fl., U.S.	C1	102
Saint Vincent Passage, strt., N.A.	C7	80
Saint Vincent's [-Saint Stephens-Peter's River], Nf., U.S.	E5	88
Saint Walburg, Sk., Can.	D1	91
Saint-Zacharie, P.Q., Can.	C7	90
Saipan, i., N. Mar. Is.	C12	32
Sajama, Nevado, mtn., Bol.	B4	72
Sakakawea, Lake, res., N.D., U.S.	B3	127
Sakania, D.R.C.	F5	54
Sakarya, Tur.	B4	44
Sakarya, stm., Tur.	B4	44
Sakata, Japan	D15	28
Sakété, Benin	E5	50
Sakha see Jakutija, state, Russia	C14	26
Sakhalin see Sahalin, ostrov, i., Russia	D16	26
Sakon Nakhon, Thai.	C4	34
Sakonnet, stm., R.I., U.S.	E6	132
Sakonnet Point, c., R.I., U.S.	F6	132
Sakrivier, S. Afr.	E3	56
Saky, Ukr.	G12	20
Sal, i., C.V.	g10	50a
Sal, Point, c., Ca., U.S.	E3	98
Sala, Swe.	G7	10
Salaberry-de-Valleyfield, P.Q., Can.	D3	90
Salacgrīva, Lat.	H11	10
Salada, Laguna, l., Mex.	A1	78
Saladillo, Ar.	F6	72
Salado, stm., Arg.	F4	72
Salado, stm., Arg.	F6	72
Salado, stm., Arg.	D5	72
Salado, stm., Mex.	B5	78
Salado, Río, stm., N.M., U.S.	C2	124
Salaga, Ghana	E4	50
Salal, Chad	D8	50
Şalālah, Oman	G6	38
Salamanca, Mex.	C4	78
Salamanca, Spain	G4	16
Salamanca, N.Y., U.S.	C2	125
Salamís, i., Grc.	F9	18
Salamis, hist., N. Cyp.	E5	44
Salamīyah, Syria	E7	44
Salamonie, stm., In., U.S.	C6	107
Salamonie Lake, res., In., U.S.	C6	107
Salavat, Russia	D7	26
Salawati, i., Indon.	D8	36
Sala y Gómez, Isla, i., Chile	K28	64
Sala y Gomez Ridge	K28	64
Saldanha, S. Afr.	E2	56
Saldus, Lat.	H10	10
Sale, Austl.	H4	62
Salé, Mor.	E2	14
Sale Creek, Tn., U.S.	D8	135
Salehard, Russia	C8	26
Salem, India	G3	40
Salem, Ar., U.S.	A4	97
Salem, Il., U.S.	E5	106
Salem, In., U.S.	G5	107
Salem, Ky., U.S.	e9	110
Salem, Ma., U.S.	A6	114
Salem, Mo., U.S.	D6	118
Salem, N.H., U.S.	E4	122
Salem, N.J., U.S.	D2	123
Salem, Oh., U.S.	B5	128
Salem, Or., U.S.	C4	130
Salem, S.D., U.S.	D8	134
Salem, Ut., U.S.	C4	137
Salem, Va., U.S.	C2	139
Salem, W.V., U.S.	B4	141
Salem, Wi., U.S.	n11	142
Salem, co., N.J., U.S.	D2	123
Salem, stm., N.J., U.S.	D2	123
Salem, Lake, l., Vt., U.S.	B4	138
Salerno, Italy	D5	18
Salerno, Golfo di, b., Italy	D5	18
Salgótarján, Hung.	E5	20
Salgueiro, Braz.	C4	74
Salida, Co., U.S.	C5	99
Salihli, Tur.	C3	44
Salihorsk, Bela.	C9	20
Salima, Mwi.	A5	56
Salina, Ks., U.S.	D6	109
Salina, Ok., U.S.	A6	129
Salina, Ut., U.S.	E4	137
Salina Cruz, Mex.	D5	78
Salinas, Braz.	E3	74
Salinas, Ec.	D3	70
Salinas, Ca., U.S.	D3	98
Salinas, stm., N.A.	B1	80
Salinas, stm., Ca., U.S.	D3	98
Salinas de Hidalgo, Mex.	C4	78
Salinas Peak, mtn., N.M., U.S.	D3	124
Salinas Pueblo Missions National Monument, N.M., U.S.	C3	124
Saline, Mi., U.S.	F7	115
Saline, co., Ar., U.S.	C3	97
Saline, co., Il., U.S.	F5	106
Saline, co., Ks., U.S.	D6	109
Saline, co., Mo., U.S.	B4	118
Saline, co., Ne., U.S.	D8	120
Saline, stm., Ar., U.S.	C1	97
Saline, stm., Ar., U.S.	D4	97
Saline, stm., Ks., U.S.	C3	109
Saline, North Fork, stm., Il., U.S.	F5	106
Saline Lake, l., La., U.S.	C3	111
Salineville, Oh., U.S.	B5	128
Salinópolis, Braz.	B2	74
Salisbury, Austl.	G2	62
Salisbury, N.B., Can.	C4	87
Salisbury, Ct., U.S.	B2	100
Salisbury, Ma., U.S.	A6	114
Salisbury, Md., U.S.	D6	113
Salisbury, Mo., U.S.	B5	118
Salisbury, N.C., U.S.	B2	126
Salisbury see Harare, Zimb.	B5	56
Salish Mountains, mts., Mt., U.S.	B2	119
Salkehatchie, stm., S.C., U.S.	E5	133
Salla, Fin.	C13	10
Sallisaw, Ok., U.S.	B7	129
Salluit, P.Q., Can.	f11	90
Salmās, Iran	C11	44
Salmo, B.C., Can.	E9	85
Salmon, Id., U.S.	D5	105
Salmon, stm., N.B., Can.	C4	87
Salmon, stm., Id., U.S.	D3	105
Salmon Creek, Wa., U.S.	D3	140
Salmon Creek Reservoir, res., Id., U.S.	G4	105
Salmon Falls, stm., U.S.	D5	122
Salmon Falls Creek, stm., U.S.	G4	105
Salmon Mountains, mts., Ca., U.S.	B2	98
Salmon Point, c., On., Can.	D7	89
Salmon River Mountains, mts., Id., U.S.	E3	105
Salmon River Reservoir, res., N.Y., U.S.	B5	125
Salo, Fin.	F10	10
Salò, Italy	B3	18
Salome, Az., U.S.	D2	96
Salon-de-Provence, Fr.	F9	16
Salonika see Thessaloníki, Grc.	D9	18
Salonika, Gulf of see Thermaïkós Kólpos, b., Grc.	D9	18
Salonta, Rom.	F6	20
Sal'sk, Russia	E7	22
Salt, stm., Az., U.S.	D4	96
Salt, stm., Ky., U.S.	C4	110
Salt, stm., Mo., U.S.	B6	118
Salta, Arg.	A4	72
Salt Creek, stm., N.M., U.S.	D5	124
Salt Creek, stm., Oh., U.S.	C3	128
Salt Creek, stm., Wy., U.S.	C6	143
Salter Path, N.C., U.S.	C6	126
Salt Fork Lake, res., Oh., U.S.	B4	128
Saltillo, Mex.	B4	78
Saltillo, Ms., U.S.	A5	117
Salt Lake, co., Ut., U.S.	C3	137
Salt Lake, l., Hi., U.S.	g10	104
Salt Lake, l., N.M., U.S.	E6	124
Salt Lake City, Ut., U.S.	C4	137
Salto, Ur.	E6	72
Salton Sea, l., Ca., U.S.	F5	98
Saltonstall, Lake, l., Ct., U.S.	D4	100
Salt Point, c., Ca., U.S.	C2	98
Salt River Indian Reservation, Az., U.S.	k9	96
Salt River Range, mts., Wy., U.S.	D2	143
Saltsburg, Pa., U.S.	F3	131
Salt Springs, Fl., U.S.	C5	102
Saltville, Va., U.S.	f10	139
Salt Wells Creek, stm., Wy., U.S.	E4	143
Saluda, S.C., U.S.	C4	133
Saluda, co., S.C., U.S.	C4	133
Saluda, stm., S.C., U.S.	C4	133
Saluda Dam, S.C., U.S.	C5	133
Salūm, Egypt	D10	48
Sālūr, India	F4	40
Salvador, Braz.	D4	74
Salvador, El see El Salvador, ctry., N.A.	C2	80
Salvador, Lake, l., La., U.S.	E5	111
Salween, stm., Asia	G7	28
Salyan, Azer.	C13	44
Salyān, Nepal	D4	40
Salyersville, Ky., U.S.	C6	110
Salzburg, Aus.	G13	12
Salzgitter, Ger.	D12	12
Samah, Libya	F7	14
Samālūt, Egypt	F10	14
Samana Cay, i., Bah.	A5	80
Samandağ, Tur.	D6	44
Samar, i., Phil.	D9	34
Samara (Kujbyšev), Russia	D7	26
Samarai, Pap. N. Gui.	I13	32
Samarinda, Indon.	D5	36
Samarkand, Uzb.	F8	26
Sāmarrā', Iraq	D4	42
Samar Sea, Phil.	D8	34
Şamaxi, Azer.	B13	44
Samba Caju, Ang.	E3	54
Sambalpur, India	E4	40
Sambas, Indon.	C3	36
Sambava, Madag.	A9	56
Sambhal, India	D3	40
Sāmbhar, India	D3	40
Sambir, Ukr.	E7	20
Samboja, Indon.	D5	36
Samborombón, Bahía, b., Arg.	F6	72
Samch'ŏk, S. Kor.	D13	28
Same, Tan.	D7	54
Samfya, Zam.	A4	56
Şämkir, Azer.	B11	44
Sammamish, Lake, l., Wa., U.S.	e11	140
Samoa, ctry., Oc.	F11	58
Samoa Islands, is., Oc.	F12	58
Samoded, Russia	B7	22
Sámos, i., Grc.	F11	18
Samoset, Fl., U.S.	q10	102
Samothrace see Samothráki, i., Grc.	D10	18
Samothráki, i., Grc.	D10	18
Sampit, Indon.	D4	36
Sampit, stm., S.C., U.S.	E9	133
Sampit, Teluk, b., Indon.	D4	36
Sampson, co., N.C., U.S.	B4	126
Sam Rayburn Reservoir, res., Tx., U.S.	D5	136
Samsang, China	C4	40
Samson, Al., U.S.	D3	94
Sam Son, Viet.	C5	34
Samsun, Tur.	A4	44
Samtredia, Geor.	A10	44
Samuels, Id., U.S.	A2	105
Samui, Ko, i., Thai.	E4	34
Samur, stm., Asia	B13	44
Samut Prakan, Thai.	D4	34
Samut Songkhram, Thai.	D4	34
San, Mali	D4	50
Şan'ā', Yemen	G4	38
Sanaba, Burkina	D4	50
Sanaga, stm., Cam.	C2	54
San Agustin, Cape, c., Phil.	E9	34
San Agustin, Plains of, pl., N.M., U.S.	C2	124
Sanak Islands, is., Ak., U.S.	E7	95
San Ambrosio, Isla, i., Chile	H7	2
Sanana, Pulau, i., Indon.	D7	36
Sanandaj, Iran	C5	42
San Andreas, Ca., U.S.	C3	98
San Andrés, Col.	A3	70
San Andres, Isla de, i., Col.	A3	70
San Andres Mountains, mts., N.M., U.S.	E3	124
San Andres Peak, mtn., N.M., U.S.	E3	124
San Andrés Tuxtla, Mex.	D5	78
San Angelo, Tx., U.S.	D2	136
San Anselmo, Ca., U.S.	h7	98
San Antonio, Chile	E3	72
San Antonio, Tx., U.S.	E3	136
San Antonio, Cabo, c., Arg.	F6	72
San Antonio, Cabo de, c., Cuba	A2	80
San Antonio Bay, b., Tx., U.S.	E4	136
San Antonio de los Baños, Cuba	A3	80
San Antonio Mountain, mtn., N.M., U.S.	A3	124
San Antonio Oeste, Arg.	F4	69
San Augustine, Tx., U.S.	D5	136
San Augustine, co., Tx., U.S.	D5	136
San Benedetto del Tronto, Italy	C4	18
San Benedicto, Isla, i., Mex.	D2	78
San Benito, Guat.	B2	80
San Benito, Tx., U.S.	F4	136
San Benito, co., Ca., U.S.	D3	98
San Benito Mountain, mtn., Ca., U.S.	D3	98
San Bernardino, Ca., U.S.	E5	98
San Bernardino, co., Ca., U.S.	E5	98
San Blas, Cape, c., Fl., U.S.	v16	102
San Borja, Bol.	A4	72
Sanborn, Ia., U.S.	A2	108
Sanborn, co., S.D., U.S.	D7	134
Sanbornville, N.H., U.S.	C4	122
San Bruno, Ca., U.S.	D2	98
San Carlos, Arg.	D4	72
San Carlos, Chile	E2	69
San Carlos, Phil.	D8	34
San Carlos, Phil.	C8	34
San Carlos, Az., U.S.	D5	96
San Carlos, Ca., U.S.	k8	98
San Carlos, Ven.	D6	80
San Carlos de Bariloche, Arg.	F2	69
San Carlos de Bolívar, Arg.	F5	72
San Carlos del Zulia, Ven.	B5	70
San Carlos de Río Negro, Ven.	C6	70
San Carlos Indian Reservation, Az., U.S.	D5	96
San Carlos Lake, res., Az., U.S.	D5	96
Sánchez, Dom. Rep.	B6	80
San Clemente, Ca., U.S.	F5	98
San Clemente Island, i., Ca., U.S.	F4	98
San Cristóbal, Arg.	E5	72
San Cristóbal, Dom. Rep.	B5	80
San Cristóbal, Ven.	B5	70
San Cristóbal, Isla, i., Ec.	D2	70
San Cristóbal de las Casas, Mex.	D6	78
Sancti Spíritus, Cuba	A4	80
Sancy, Puy de, mtn., Fr.	E8	16
Sandakan, Malay.	B5	36
Sandaré, Mali	D2	50
Sand Creek, stm., Wy., U.S.	C7	143
Sandefjord, Nor.	G4	10
Sanders, Az., U.S.	B6	96
Sanders, co., Mt., U.S.	C1	119
Sanderson, Tx., U.S.	D1	136
Sandersville, Ga., U.S.	D4	103
Sandersville, Ms., U.S.	D4	117
Sand Hill, Ma., U.S.	h13	114
Sand Hill, stm., Mn., U.S.	C2	116
Sandia Crest, mtn., N.M., U.S.	k8	124
Sandia Indian Reservation, N.M., U.S.	k7	124
Sandia Mountains, mts., N.M., U.S.	k8	124
San Diego, Ca., U.S.	F5	98
San Diego, Tx., U.S.	F3	136
San Diego, co., Ca., U.S.	F5	98
San Diego, stm., Ca., U.S.	o15	98
San Diego, Cabo, c., Arg.	H3	69
San Diego Naval Station, mil., Ca., U.S.	o15	98
San Diego Naval Training Center, mil., Ca., U.S.	o15	98
Sand Island, i., Hi., U.S.	g10	104
Sand Island, i., Wi., U.S.	B3	142
Sand Key, i., Fl., U.S.	E4	102
Sandlick Creek, stm., W.V., U.S.	n13	141
Sandnes, Nor.	G1	10
Sandoa, D.R.C.	E4	54
Sandoval, Il., U.S.	E4	106
Sandoval, co., N.M., U.S.	B2	124
Sandoway, Myan.	C2	34
Sand Point, Ak., U.S.	D7	95
Sandpoint, Id., U.S.	A2	105
Sands Key, i., Fl., U.S.	s3	102
Sand Springs, Ok., U.S.	A5	129
Sandston, Va., U.S.	m18	139
Sandstone, Austl.	F2	60
Sandstone, Mn., U.S.	D6	116
Sandusky, Mi., U.S.	E8	115
Sandusky, Oh., U.S.	A3	128
Sandusky, co., Oh., U.S.	A2	128
Sandusky, stm., Oh., U.S.	A2	128
Sandvika, Nor.	G4	10
Sandviken, Swe.	F7	10
Sandwich, Il., U.S.	B5	106
Sandwich, Ma., U.S.	C7	114
Sandwich Bay, b., Nf., Can.	B3	88
Sandy, Or., U.S.	B4	130
Sandy, Ut., U.S.	C4	137
Sandy, stm., Me., U.S.	D2	112
Sandy Cape, c., Austl.	E5	62
Sandy Creek, stm., Oh., U.S.	B4	128
Sandy Creek, stm., Ok., U.S.	C2	129
Sandy Hook, Ct., U.S.	D2	100
Sandy Hook, spit, N.J., U.S.	C5	123
Sandy Island, i., S.C., U.S.	D9	133
Sandykači, Turk.	F8	26
Sandy Lake, l., Nf., Can.	D3	88
Sandy Lake, l., On., Can.	n16	89
Sandy Neck, pen., Ma., U.S.	C7	114
Sandy Point, c., R.I., U.S.	h7	132
Sandy Springs, Ga., U.S.	h8	103
Sandy Springs, S.C., U.S.	B2	133
Sandyville, Md., U.S.	A4	113
San Felipe, Chile	E3	72
San Felipe, Col.	C6	70
San Felipe, Mex.	A2	78
San Felipe, Ven.	A6	70
San Felipe Indian Reservation, N.M., U.S.	k8	124
San Felipe Pueblo, N.M., U.S.	B3	124
San Fernando, Chile	D2	69
San Fernando, Mex.	C5	78
San Fernando, Phil.	C8	34
San Fernando, Phil.	C8	34
San Fernando, Spain	I3	16
San Fernando, Trin.	C7	80
San Fernando, Ca., U.S.	m12	98
San Fernando de Apure, Ven.	B6	70
San Fernando de Atabapo, Ven.	C6	70
San Fernando del Valle de Catamarca, Arg.	D4	72
Sanford, Co., U.S.	D5	99
Sanford, Fl., U.S.	D5	102
Sanford, Me., U.S.	E2	112
Sanford, Mi., U.S.	E6	115
Sanford, N.C., U.S.	B3	126
Sanford, Mount, mtn., Ak., U.S.	C11	95
San Francisco, Arg.	E5	72
San Francisco, Ca., U.S.	D2	98
San Francisco, co., Ca., U.S.	D2	98
San Francisco, stm., U.S.	D6	96
San Francisco Bay, b., Ca., U.S.	h8	98
San Francisco del Oro, Mex.	B3	78
San Francisco del Rincón, Mex.	C4	78
San Francisco de Macorís, Dom. Rep.	B5	80
San Gabriel Mountains, mts., Ca., U.S.	m12	98
Sangamner, India	F2	40
Sangamon, co., Il., U.S.	D4	106
Sangamon, stm., Il., U.S.	C3	106
Sangar, Russia	C14	26
Sange, D.R.C.	E5	54
Sanger, Ca., U.S.	D4	98
Sanger, Tx., U.S.	C4	136
Sanggau, Indon.	C4	36
Sangha, stm., Afr.	D3	54
Sangihe, Kepulauan, is., Indon.	C7	36
Sangihe, Pulau, i., Indon.	C7	36
San Gil, Col.	D5	80
San Giovanni in Fiore, Italy	E6	18
Sangiyn Dalay, Mong.	C9	28
Sānglī, India	F2	40
Sangmélima, Cam.	C2	54
San Gorgonio Mountain, mtn., Ca., U.S.	E5	98
San Gottardo, Passo del, Switz.	A2	18
Sanibel, Fl., U.S.	F4	102
Sanibel Island, i., Fl., U.S.	F4	102
San Ignacio, Mex.	B2	78
San Ignacio, Para.	D6	72
San Ignacio de Moxo, Bol.	A4	72
San Ignacio de Velasco, Bol.	G7	70
Sanilac, co., Mi., U.S.	E8	115
San Isidro, Arg.	E6	72
San Jacinto, Col.	D4	80
San Jacinto, co., Tx., U.S.	D5	136
San Jacinto, stm., Tx., U.S.	r14	136
San Javier, Bol.	B5	72
San Joaquín, Bol.	F7	70
San Joaquin, co., Ca., U.S.	D3	98
San Joaquin, stm., Ca., U.S.	D3	98
San Joaquin Valley, val., Ca., U.S.	D3	98
San Jorge, Arg.	E5	72
San Jorge, Golfo de, b., Arg.	G3	69
San José, C.R.	D3	80
San José, Ca., U.S.	D3	98
San José, Isla, i., Mex.	C2	78
San José de Chiquitos, Bol.	B5	72
San José de Guanipa, Ven.	D7	80
San José de Jáchal, Arg.	E4	72
San José de las Lajas, Cuba	A3	80

Name	Map Ref.	Page

San José del Cabo, Mex. . . . C3 78
San José del Guaviare, Col. . C5 70
San Jose Island, i., Tx., U.S. E4 136
San Juan, Arg. E4 72
San Juan, P.R. B6 80
San Juan, Tx., U.S. F3 136
San Juan, co., Co., U.S. . . . D3 99
San Juan, co., N.M., U.S. . . A1 124
San Juan, co., Ut., U.S. . . . F5 137
San Juan, co., Wa., U.S. . . . A2 140
San Juan, stm., N.A. F8 76
San Juan Bautista, Para. . . . D6 72
San Juan Capistrano, Ca.,
  U.S. F5 98
San Juan de Colón, Ven. . . . D5 80
San Juan de la Maguana,
  Dom. Rep. B5 80
San Juan del Norte, Nic. . . . C3 80
San Juan de los Morros,
  Ven. D6 80
San Juan del Sur, Nic. C2 80
San Juan Island, i., Wa.,
  U.S. A2 140
San Juan Mountains, mts.,
  Co., U.S. D3 99
San Justo, Arg. E5 72
Sankt Gallen, Switz. A2 18
Sankt-Peterburg (Saint
  Petersburg), Russia . . . D5 26
Sankt Pölten, Aus. F14 12
Sankuru, stm., D.R.C. D4 54
San Lázaro, Cabo, c., Mex. . C2 78
San Leandro, Ca., U.S. h8 98
Şanlıurfa, Tur. D8 44
San Lorenzo, Arg. E5 72
San Lorenzo, Bol. C5 72
San Lorenzo, Ec. C4 70
San Lorenzo, Cabo, c., Ec. . D3 70
Sanlúcar de Barrameda,
  Spain I3 16
San Lucas, Bol. C4 72
San Lucas, Mex. C3 78
San Lucas, Cabo, c., Mex. . . C3 78
San Luis, Arg. E4 72
San Luis, Guat. B2 80
San Luis, Az., U.S. E1 96
San Luis, Co., U.S. D5 99
San Luis, Point, c., Ca., U.S. E3 98
San Luis Obispo, Ca., U.S. . E3 98
San Luis Obispo, co., Ca.,
  U.S. E3 98
San Luis Pass, strt., Tx., U.S. r14 136
San Luis Peak, mtn., Co.,
  U.S. D4 99
San Luis Potosí, Mex. C4 78
San Luis Potosí, state, Mex. C4 78
San Luis Río Colorado, Mex. A2
San Luis Valley, val., Co.,
  U.S. D4 99
San Manuel, Az., U.S. E5 96
San Marcos, Tx., U.S. E4 136
San Marcos, stm., Tx., U.S. . h8 136
San Marino, Ca., U.S. m12 98
San Marino, ctry., Eur. C4 18
San Martín, Arg. E4 72
San Martín, Col. E5 80
San Martín, Lago, l., S.A. . . G2 69
San Martín de los Andes,
  Arg. F2 69
San Mateo, Ca., U.S. D2 98
San Mateo, co., Ca., U.S. . . D2 98
San Mateo Mountains, mts.,
  N.M., U.S. B2 124
San Mateo Mountains, mts.,
  N.M., U.S. D2 124
San Matías, Golfo, b., Arg. . F4 69
Sanmenxia, China E10 28
San Miguel, El Sal. C2 80
San Miguel, co., N.M., U.S. B5 124
San Miguel, stm., Co., U.S. . C2 99
San Miguel, Golfo de, b.,
  Pan. D4 80
San Miguel de Tucumán,
  Arg. D4 72
San Miguel Island, i., Ca.,
  U.S. E3 98
San Miguel Mountains, mts.,
  Co., U.S. D2 99
Sanming, China D4 30
Sannär, Sudan H11 48
San Nicolás, Peru B2 72
San Nicolás de los Arroyos,
  Arg. E5 72
San Nicolás de los Garza,
  Mex. B4 78
San Nicolas Island, i., Ca.,
  U.S. F4 98
Sânnicolau Mare, Rom. . . . F6 20
Sannikova, proliv, strt.,
  Russia B15 26
Sanok, Pol. E7 20
San Pablo, Phil. D8 34
San Pablo Bay, b., Ca., U.S. g8 98
San Patricio, co., Tx., U.S. . E4 136
San Pedro, Arg. C5 72
San Pedro, Arg. E6 72
San-Pédro, C. Iv. F3 50
San Pedro, stm., N.A. A2 78
San Pedro, stm., Az., U.S. . . E5 96
San Pedro Bay, b., Ca., U.S. n12 98
San Pedro de las Colonias,
  Mex. B4 78
San Pedro de Macorís,
  Dom. Rep. B6 80

San Pedro de Ycuamandiyú,
  Para. C6 72
San Pedro Peaks, mts.,
  N.M., U.S. A3 124
San Pedro Sula, Hond. B2 80
Sanpete, co., Ut., U.S. D4 137
San Pietro, Isola di, i., Italy . E2 18
Sanpoil, stm., Wa., U.S. . . . A7 140
San Quintín, Cabo, c., Mex. A1 78
San Rafael, Arg. E4 72
San Rafael, Ca., U.S. D2 98
San Rafael, N.M., U.S. B2 124
San Rafael, Ven. C5 80
San Rafael, stm., Ut., U.S. . . D5 137
San Rafael Knob, mtn., Ut.,
  U.S. E5 137
San Rafael Mountains, mts.,
  Ca., U.S. E4 98
San Ramon, Ca., U.S. h9 98
San Ramón de la Nueva
  Orán, Arg. C5 72
San Remo, Italy C1 18
San Roque, Punta, c., Mex. B2 78
San Saba, Tx., U.S. D3 136
San Saba, co., Tx., U.S. . . . D3 136
San Salvador, El Sal. C2 80
San Salvador, i., Bah. D10 76
San Salvador de Jujuy, Arg. C4 72
Sansanné-Mango, Togo . . . D5 50
San Sebastián see Donostia,
  Spain F6 16
San Severo, Italy D5 18
San Simon, stm., Az., U.S. . E6 96
Santa Ana, Bol. A4 72
Santa Ana, El Sal. C1 80
Santa Ana, Mex. A2 78
Santa Ana, Ca., U.S. F5 98
Santa Ana, stm., Ca., U.S. . . n13 98
Santa Ana Indian
  Reservation, N.M., U.S. h7 124
Santa Ana Mountains, mts.,
  Ca., U.S. n13 98
Santa Anna, Tx., U.S. D3 136
Santa Bárbara, Hond. B2 80
Santa Bárbara, Mex. B3 78
Santa Barbara, Ca., U.S. . . . E4 98
Santa Bárbara, Ven. D5 80
Santa Barbara, co., Ca., U.S. E3 98
Santa Barbara Channel, strt.,
  Ca., U.S. E3 98
Santa Barbara Island, i., Ca.,
  U.S. F4 98
Santa Catalina, Gulf of, b.,
  Ca., U.S. F5 98
Santa Catalina Island, i., Ca.,
  U.S. F4 98
Santa Catalina Mountains,
  mts., Az., U.S. E5 96
Santa Catarina, state, Braz. . D7 72
Santa Catarina, Ilha de, i.,
  Braz. D8 72
Santa Clara, Cuba A3 80
Santa Clara, Ca., U.S. D2 98
Santa Clara, Ut., U.S. F2 137
Santa Clara, co., Ca., U.S. . D3 98
Santa Clara, stm., Ca., U.S. . E4 98
Santa Claus, In., U.S. H4 107
Santa Cruz, Phil. D8 34
Santa Cruz, Ca., U.S. D2 98
Santa Cruz, N.M., U.S. B3 124
Santa Cruz, co., Az., U.S. . . F5 96
Santa Cruz, co., Ca., U.S. . . D2 98
Santa Cruz, stm., Az., U.S. . E4 96
Santa Cruz, Isla, i., Ec. D1 70
Santa Cruz de la Palma,
  Spain A1 50
Santa Cruz de la Sierra, Bol. B5 72
Santa Cruz del Quiché,
  Guat. B1 80
Santa Cruz del Sur, Cuba . . A4 80
Santa Cruz de Tenerife,
  Spain A1 50
Santa Cruz do Sul, Braz. . . D7 72
Santa Cruz Island, i., Ca.,
  U.S. F4 98
Santa Cruz Islands, is., Sol.
  Is. F10 58
Santa Elena, Arg. E6 72
Santa Fe, Arg. E5 72
Santa Fe, N.M., U.S. B4 124
Santa Fe, Tx., U.S. r14 136
Santa Fe, co., N.M., U.S. . . B3 124
Santa Fe, stm., N.M., U.S. . h8 124
Santa Fe Baldy, mtn., N.M.,
  U.S. A4 124
Santa Fé do Sul, Braz. F1 74
Santa Filomena, Braz. E10 70
Santa Helena, Braz. B2 74
Santa Helena de Goiás,
  Braz. E1 74
Santai, China E9 28
Santa Inés, Isla, i., Chile . . . H2 69
Santa Isabel, Arg. F4 72
Santa Isabel, i., Sol. Is. B6 62
Santa Isabel see Malabo, Eq.
  Gui. C1 54
Santa Lucia Range, mts.,
  Ca., U.S. E3 98
Santa Magdalena, Isla, i.,
  Mex. B2 78
Santa Margarita, Ca., U.S. . . E3 98
Santa Margarita, Isla, i.,
  Mex. C2 78
Santa Maria, Braz. D7 72
Santa Maria, Ca., U.S. E3 98

Santa Maria, i., Vanuatu . . . j9 62a
Santa Maria, stm., Az., U.S. . C2 96
Santa Maria, Cabo de, c.,
  Ang. A1 56
Santa María, Isla, i., Ec. . . . D1 70
Santa Maria Mountains,
  mts., Az., U.S. C3 96
Santa Marta, Col. A5 70
Santa Monica, Ca., U.S. . . . m12 98
Santana, Braz. D3 74
Santana do Livramento,
  Braz. E6 72
Santander, Phil. E8 34
Santander, Spain F5 16
Santanilla, Islas, is., Hond. . B3 80
Sant'Antioco, Italy E2 18
Sant'Antioco, Isola di, i.,
  Italy E2 18
Sant Antoni de Portmany,
  Spain H7 16
Santa Paula, Ca., U.S. E4 98
Santaquin, Ut., U.S. D4 137
Santarém, Braz. D9 70
Santarém, Port. H2 16
Santa Rita, Hond. B2 80
Santa Rita, Ven. C5 80
Santa Rosa, Arg. F5 72
Santa Rosa, Braz. D7 72
Santa Rosa, Ec. D4 70
Santa Rosa, Ca., U.S. C2 98
Santa Rosa, N.M., U.S. . . . C5 124
Santa Rosa, Ven. D6 80
Santa Rosa, co., Fl., U.S. . . u14 102
Santa Rosa de Copán,
  Hond. C2 80
Santa Rosa Island, i., Ca.,
  U.S. F3 98
Santa Rosa Island, i., Fl.,
  U.S. u14 102
Santa Rosalía, Mex. B2 78
Santa Rosa Range, mts.,
  Nv., U.S. B4 121
Šantarske ostrova, is.,
  Russia D15 26
Santa Sylvina, Arg. D5 72
Santa Vitória do Palmar,
  Braz. E7 72
Santa Ynez, Ca., U.S. E3 98
Santee, Ca., U.S. o16 98
Santee, stm., S.C., U.S. E8 133
Santee Dam, S.C., U.S. E7 133
Santee Indian Reservation,
  Ne., U.S. B8 120
Sant Feliu de Guíxols, Spain G8 16
Santiago, Braz. D7 72
Santiago, Chile D2 69
Santiago, Mex. C3 78
Santiago, Pan. D3 80
Santiago, i., C.V. h10 50a
Santiago, Isla, i., Ec. D1 70
Santiago de Compostela,
  Spain F2 16
Santiago de Cuba, Cuba . . B4 80
Santiago del Estero, Arg. . . D5 72
Santiago de los Caballeros,
  Dom. Rep. B5 80
Santiago Ixcuintla, Mex. . . C3 78
Santiago Jamiltepec, Mex. . D5 78
Santiago Papasquiaro, Mex. B3 78
Santiago Peak, mtn., Ca.,
  U.S. n13 98
Santiago Reservoir, res., Ca.,
  U.S. n13 98
Santiam Pass, Or., U.S. . . . C4 130
Sant Jordi, Golf de, b.,
  Spain G7 16
Santo Amaro, Braz. D4 74
Santo André, Braz. F2 74
Santo Ângelo, Braz. D7 72
Santo Antão, i., C.V. g10 50a
Santo Antônio, S. Tom./P. . C1 54
Santo Antônio de Jesus,
  Braz. D4 74
Santo Antônio do Içá, Braz. D6 70
Santo Domingo, Dom. Rep. B6 80
Santo Domingo see
  Hispaniola, i., N.A. . . . A5 80
Santo Domingo Indian
  Reservation, N.M., U.S. h8 124
Santo Domingo Pueblo,
  N.M., U.S. B3 124
Santorini see Thíra, i., Grc. F10 18
Santos, Braz. F2 74
Santos Dumont, Braz. F3 74
Santo Tomé de Guayana
  see Ciudad Guayana,
  Ven. B7 70
San Valentín, Monte, mtn.,
  Chile G2 69
San Vicente, El Sal. C2 80
San Vicente de Cañete,
  Peru F4 70
San Vicente del Caguán,
  Col. C5 70
San Vicente Reservoir, res.,
  Ca., U.S. o16 98
San Xavier Indian
  Reservation, Az., U.S. . E4 96
Sanya, China H9 28
Sanyuan, China E9 28
Sanza Pombo, Ang. E3 54
São Bento, Braz. B3 74
São Borja, Braz. D6 72
São Carlos, Braz. F2 74
São Domingos, Braz. A8 72

São Domingos, Gui.-B. D1 50
São Francisco, Braz. E3 74
São Francisco, stm., Braz. . . C4 74
São Francisco do Sul, Braz. D8 72
São Gabriel, Braz. E7 72
Sao Hill, Tan. E7 54
São João da Barra, Braz. . . . F3 74
São João da Boa Vista, Braz. F2 74
São João da Madeira, Port. . G2 16
São João Del Rei, Braz. . . . F3 74
São João do Araguaia, Braz. E10 70
São Jorge, i., Port. F7 46
São José, Braz. D8 72
São José do Rio Preto, Braz. F2 74
São José dos Campos, Braz. F2 74
São Leopoldo, Braz. D7 72
São Lourenço, Pantanal de,
  sw., Braz. G8 70
São Lourenço do Sul, Braz. E7 72
São Luís, Braz. B3 74
São Luís Gonzaga, Braz. . . D7 72
São Manuel, stm., Braz. . . . E8 70
São Mateus, Braz. E4 74
São Miguel, i., Port. F7 46
São Miguel do Araguaia,
  Braz. D1 74
São Nicolau, i., C.V. g10 50a
São Paulo, Braz. F2 74
São Paulo, state, Braz. C7 72
São Paulo de Olivença,
  Braz. D6 70
São Raimundo Nonato,
  Braz. C3 74
São Roque, Cabo de, c.,
  Braz. C4 74
São Sebastião, Braz. F2 74
São Sebastião, Ilha de, i.,
  Braz. F2 74
São Sebastião do Paraíso,
  Braz. F2 74
São Simão, Represa de, res.,
  Braz. B7 72
São Tomé, S. Tom./P. C1 54
São Tomé, i., S. Tom./P. . . . C1 54
São Tomé, Cabo de, c.,
  Braz. F3 74
Sao Tome and Principe,
  ctry., Afr. C1 54
São Vicente, Braz. F2 74
São Vicente, i., C.V. g9 50a
São Vicente, Cabo de, c.,
  Port. I2 16
Sapé, Braz. C4 74
Sapele, Nig. E6 50
Sapelo Island, i., Ga., U.S. . E5 103
Sapitwa, mtn., Mwi. B6 56
Sappa Creek, stm., U.S. . . . E5 120
Sapphire Mountains, mts.,
  Mt., U.S. D3 119
Sappington, Mo., U.S. f13 118
Sapporo, Japan C16 28
Sapulpa, Ok., U.S. B5 129
Sapwe, D.R.C. F5 54
Saqqez, Iran C5 42
Sarāb, Iran C5 42
Saraburi, Thai. D4 34
Saragossa see Zaragoza,
  Spain G6 16
Sarajevo, Bos. C7 18
Sarakhs, Iran C8 42
Saraktaš, Russia D10 22
Saraland, Al., U.S. E1 94
Saranac, Mi., U.S. F5 115
Saranac, stm., N.Y., U.S. . . . F11 125
Saranac Lake, N.Y., U.S. . . . f10 125
Saranac Lakes, l., N.Y., U.S. f10 125
Sarandë, Alb. E8 18
Sārangarh, India E4 40
Saranpaul', Russia B11 22
Saransk, Russia D6 26
Sarapul, Russia D7 26
Sarasota, Fl., U.S. E4 102
Sarasota, co., Fl., U.S. E4 102
Sarasota Bay, b., Fl., U.S. . . E4 102
Saratoga, Ca., U.S. k8 98
Saratoga, co., N.Y., U.S. . . . D5 136
Saratoga, Wy., U.S. E6 143
Saratoga, co., N.Y., U.S. . . . B7 125
Saratoga Lake, l., N.Y., U.S. C7 125
Saratoga National Historical
  Park, N.Y., U.S. B7 125
Saratoga Springs, N.Y., U.S. B7 125
Saratov, Russia D6 26
Saratov Reservoir see
  Saratovskoe
  vodohranilišče, res.,
  Russia D8 22
Saratovskoe vodohranilišče,
  res., Russia D8 22
Saravan, Laos C5 34
Sarawak, hist. reg., Malay. . C4 36
Saray, Tur. B2 44
Saraya, Gui. D2 50
Sarayköy, Tur. D3 44
Sarcoxie, Mo., U.S. D3 118
Sardārshahr, India D2 40
Sar Dasht, Iran D11 44
Sardegna (Sardinia), i., Italy D2 18
Sardinia see Sardegna, i.,
  Italy D2 18
Sardis, Ga., U.S. D5 103
Sardis, Ms., U.S. A4 117
Sardis Lake, res., Ms., U.S. . A4 117

Sarek, mtn., Swe. C7 10
Sar-e Pol, Afg. C9 42
Sarepta, La., U.S. B2 111
Sargent, Ga., U.S. C2 103
Sargent, Ne., U.S. C6 120
Sargent, co., N.D., U.S. . . . C8 127
Sargodha, Pak. D10 42
Sarh, Chad B3 54
Sārī, Iran C6 42
Sarigan, i., N. Mar. Is. C12 32
Sarıkamış, Tur. B10 44
Sarıkaya, Tur. C6 44
Sarikei, Malay. C4 36
Sarīr, Libya F8 14
Sariwŏn, N. Kor. D13 28
Sarıyar Barajı, res., Tur. . . . C4 44
Şarja, Russia D6 26
Şarkikaraağaç, Tur. C4 44
Şarkışla, Tur. C7 44
Şarköy, Tur. B2 44
Sarmi, Indon. G10 32
Särna, Swe. F5 10
Sarnia, On., Can. E2 89
Sarny, Ukr. D9 20
Saronic Gulf see Saronikós
  Kólpos, b., Grc. F9 18
Saronikós Kólpos, b., Grc. . F9 18
Saros Körfezi, b., Tur. B2 44
Sarreguemines, Fr. C10 16
Sartell, Mn., U.S. E4 116
Sartène, Fr. D2 18
Şărur, Azer. C11 44
Sarus see Seyhan, stm., Tur. D6 44
Saryg-Sep, Russia D11 26
Sarykamyšskoe ozero, l.,
  Asia B7 42
Saryozek, Kaz. E9 26
Sarysu, stm., Kaz. E8 26
Sary-Taš, Kyrg. B2 40
Sasabeneh, Eth. B8 54
Sāsarām, India E4 40
Sasebo, Japan D1 31
Saskatchewan, prov., Can. . C3 91
Saskatchewan, stm., Can. . . H19 82
Saskylah, Russia B13 26
Sasovo, Russia B16 20
Sassafras, stm., Md., U.S. . . B5 113
Sassafras Mountain, mtn.,
  U.S. A2 133
Sassandra, C. Iv. E3 50
Sassandra, stm., C. Iv. E3 50
Sassari, Italy D2 18
Sassnitz, Ger. C13 12
Satah Mountain, mtn., B.C.,
  Can. C5 85
Sata-misaki, c., Japan D2 31
Satanta, Ks., U.S. E3 109
Sātāra, India F2 40
Säter, Swe. F6 10
Satilla, stm., Ga., U.S. E5 103
Satka, Russia D10 22
Satluj see Sutlej, stm., Asia . D2 40
Satna, India E4 40
Sátoraljaújhely, Hung. E6 20
Sātpura Range, mts., India . E3 40
Satsuma, Al., U.S. E1 94
Satu Mare, Rom. F7 20
Satun, Thai. E3 34
Satus Creek, stm., Wa., U.S. C5 140
Sauceda Mountains, mts.,
  Az., U.S. E3 96
Saudárkrókur, Ice. I19 10a
Saudi Arabia, ctry., Asia . . . F4 38
Saufley Field Naval Air
  Station, mil., Fl., U.S. . . u14 102
Saugatuck, Mi., U.S. F4 115
Saugatuck, stm., Ct., U.S. . . D2 100
Saugatucket, stm., R.I., U.S. F4 132
Saugatuck Reservoir, res.,
  Ct., U.S. D2 100
Saugerties, N.Y., U.S. C7 125
Saugus, Ma., U.S. B5 114
Saugus, stm., Ma., U.S. . . . g11 114
Sauk, co., Wi., U.S. E4 142
Sauk, stm., Mn., U.S. E4 116
Sauk, stm., Wa., U.S. A4 140
Sauk Centre, Mn., U.S. . . . E4 116
Sauk City, Wi., U.S. E4 142
Sauk Rapids, Mn., U.S. . . . E4 116
Saukville, Wi., U.S. E6 142
Saül, Fr. Gu. C9 70
Saulnierville, N.S., Can. . . . E3 87
Sault-au-Mouton, P.Q., Can. A8 90
Sault Sainte Marie, On.,
  Can. p18 89
Sault Sainte Marie, Mi., U.S. B6 115
Saumarez Reef, rf., Austl. . . E5 62
Saumlaki, Indon. E8 36
Saumur, Fr. D6 16
Saunders, co., Ne., U.S. . . . C9 120
Saunderstown, R.I., U.S. . . . E4 132
Saurimo, Ang. E4 54
Sausalito, Ca., U.S. D2 98
Sava, stm., Eur. G5 20
Savage, Md., U.S. B4 113
Savage, stm., Md., U.S. . . . k12 113
Savage River Reservoir, res.,
  Md., U.S. k12 113
Savaiʻi, i., Samoa F12 58
Savalou, Benin E5 50
Savanna, Il., U.S. A3 106
Savanna, Ok., U.S. C6 129
Savannah, Ga., U.S. D5 103
Savannah, Mo., U.S. B3 118

Name	Map Ref.	Page

Savannah, Tn., U.S. **B3** 135
Savannah, stm., U.S. **E11** 92
Savannah, stm., U.S. **F5** 133
Savannah River Plant, sci.,
S.C., U.S. **E4** 133
Savannakhét, Laos **C4** 34
Savanna Lake, l., Md., U.S. . **D6** 113
Savanna-la-Mar, Jam. **B4** 80
Savaştepe, Tur. **C2** 44
Savè, Benin **E5** 50
Save (Sabi), stm., Afr. **C5** 56
Sāveh, Iran **C6** 42
Savelugu, Ghana **E4** 50
Saverne, Fr. **C10** 16
Saville Dam, Ct., U.S. **B4** 100
Savitaipale, Fin. **F12** 10
Savona, Italy **B2** 18
Savonlinna, Fin. **F13** 10
Savoonga, Ak., U.S. **C5** 95
Savoy, Il., U.S. **C5** 106
Savu Sea see Sawu, Laut,
Indon. **E6** 36
Sawāi Mādhopur, India . . . **D3** 40
Sawākin, Sudan **G12** 48
Sawankhalok, Thai. **C3** 34
Sawatch Range, mts., Co.,
U.S. **B4** 99
Sawdā', Jabal as-, hills,
Libya **F7** 14
Sawdā', Qurnat as-, mtn.,
Leb. **E7** 44
Sawnee Mountain, mtn.,
Ga., U.S. **B2** 103
Sawtooth Mountains, mts.,
Id., U.S. **F4** 105
Sawtooth National
Recreation Area, Id.,
U.S. **E3** 105
Sawu, Laut (Savu Sea),
Indon. **E6** 36
Sawu, Pulau, i., Indon. **F6** 36
Sawyer, co., Wi., U.S. **C2** 142
Sawyerville, P.Q., Can. **D6** 90
Saxonburg, Pa., U.S. **E2** 131
Saxtons, stm., Vt., U.S. **E3** 138
Saxtons River, Vt., U.S. . . . **E3** 138
Sayan Mountains, mts., Asia **D11** 26
Saybrook, Il., U.S. **C5** 106
Saybrook Manor, Ct., U.S. . **D6** 100
Şaydā, Leb. **F6** 44
Saydel, Ia., U.S. **e8** 108
Sayhūt, Yemen **G6** 38
Saylac, Som. **H4** 38
Saylesville, R.I., U.S. **B4** 132
Saylorsburg, Pa., U.S. **E11** 131
Saylorville, Ia., U.S. **e8** 108
Saylorville Lake, res., Ia.,
U.S. **C4** 108
Saynshand, Mong. **C10** 28
Sayre, Al., U.S. **B3** 94
Sayre, Ok., U.S. **B2** 129
Sayre, Pa., U.S. **C8** 131
Sayreville, N.J., U.S. **C4** 123
Sayula, Mex. **D4** 78
Sayville, N.Y., U.S. **n15** 125
Saywūn, Yemen **G5** 38
Sba, Alg. **F3** 14
Scalp Level, Pa., U.S. **F4** 131
Scanlon, Mn., U.S. **D6** 116
Scapegoat Mountain, mtn.,
Mt., U.S. **C3** 119
Scappoose, Or., U.S. **B4** 130
Scarborough, On., Can. **m15** 89
Scarborough, Trin. **C7** 80
Scarborough, Eng., U.K. . . . **C6** 12
Scarborough, Me., U.S. **E2** 112
Scarbro, W.V., U.S. **n13** 141
Scarsdale, N.Y., U.S. **h13** 125
Ščekino, Russia **C14** 20
Ščerbakovo, Russia **C18** 26
Schaefferstown, Pa., U.S. . . **F9** 131
Schaller, Ia., U.S. **B2** 108
Schaumburg, Il., U.S. **h8** 106
Schell Creek Range, mts.,
Nv., U.S. **D7** 121
Schenectady, N.Y., U.S. **C7** 125
Schenectady, co., N.Y., U.S. **C6** 125
Schererville, In., U.S. **B3** 107
Schertz, Tx., U.S. **h7** 136
Schiller Park, Il., U.S. **k9** 106
Schio, Italy **B3** 18
Schleicher, co., Tx., U.S. . . . **D2** 136
Schleswig, Ger. **C11** 12
Schleswig, Ia., U.S. **B2** 108
Schley, co., Ga., U.S. **D2** 103
Schofield, Wi., U.S. **D4** 142
Schofield Barracks, mil., Hi.,
U.S. **g9** 104
Schoharie, co., N.Y., U.S. . . **C6** 125
Schoharie Creek, stm., N.Y.,
U.S. **C6** 125
Schoodic Lake, l., Me., U.S. **C4** 112
Schoolcraft, Mi., U.S. **F5** 115
Schoolcraft, co., Mi., U.S. . . **B4** 115
Schroon Lake, l., N.Y., U.S. **B7** 125
Schulenburg, Tx., U.S. **E4** 136
Schulter, Ok., U.S. **B6** 129
Schurz, Nv., U.S. **E3** 121
Schuyler, Ne., U.S. **C8** 120
Schuyler, co., Il., U.S. **C3** 106
Schuyler, co., Mo., U.S. . . . **A5** 118
Schuyler, co., N.Y., U.S. . . . **C4** 125
Schuylkill, co., Pa., U.S. . . . **E9** 131
Schuylkill, stm., Pa., U.S. . . **F10** 131
Schuylkill Haven, Pa., U.S. . **E9** 131

Schwaben, hist. reg., Ger. . . **F11** 12
Schwarzwald (Black Forest),
mts., Ger. **F11** 12
Schwedt, Ger. **D14** 12
Schwerin, Ger. **D12** 12
Schwyz, Switz. **A2** 18
Sciacca, Italy **F4** 18
Science Hill, Ky., U.S. **C5** 110
Ščigry, Russia **D14** 20
Scilly, Isles of, is., Eng., U.K.**F3** 12
Scio, Or., U.S. **C4** 130
Scioto, co., Oh., U.S. **D3** 128
Scioto, stm., Oh., U.S. **B2** 128
Scituate, Ma., U.S. **B6** 114
Scituate Reservoir, res., R.I.,
U.S. **C3** 132
Scobey, Mt., U.S. **B11** 119
Scofield Reservoir, res., Ut.,
U.S. **D4** 137
Scotch Plains, N.J., U.S. . . . **B4** 123
Scotia, Ca., U.S. **B1** 98
Scotia, N.Y., U.S. **C7** 125
Scotia Ridge **N8** 66
Scotia Sea **B36** 67
Scotland, On., Can. **D4** 89
Scotland, S.D., U.S. **D8** 134
Scotland, prov., U.K. **B5** 12
Scotland, co., Mo., U.S. . . . **A5** 118
Scotland, co., N.C., U.S. . . . **C3** 126
Scotland Neck, N.C., U.S. . . **A5** 126
Scotlandville, La., U.S. **D4** 111
Scotrun, Pa., U.S. **D11** 131
Scotstown, P.Q., Can. **D6** 90
Scott, La., U.S. **D3** 111
Scott, co., Ar., U.S. **C1** 97
Scott, co., Ia., U.S. **C7** 108
Scott, co., Il., U.S. **D3** 106
Scott, co., In., U.S. **G6** 107
Scott, co., Ks., U.S. **D3** 109
Scott, co., Ky., U.S. **B5** 110
Scott, co., Mn., U.S. **F5** 116
Scott, co., Mo., U.S. **D8** 118
Scott, co., Ms., U.S. **C4** 117
Scott, co., Tn., U.S. **C9** 135
Scott, co., Va., U.S. **f9** 139
Scott, Cape, c., B.C., Can. . . **D3** 85
Scott, Mount, mtn., Or.,
U.S. **E4** 130
Scott Air Force Base, mil.,
Il., U.S. **E4** 106
Scott City, Ks., U.S. **D3** 109
Scott City, Mo., U.S. **D8** 118
Scottdale, Ga., U.S. **h8** 103
Scottdale, Pa., U.S. **F2** 131
Scott Mountain, mtn., Id.,
U.S. **E3** 105
Scott Peak, mtn., Id., U.S. . **E6** 105
Scott Reef, rf., Austl. **C3** 60
Scott Reservoir, res., N.C.,
U.S. **A1** 126
Scottsbluff, Ne., U.S. **C2** 120
Scotts Bluff, co., Ne., U.S. . **C2** 120
Scotts Bluff National
Monument, Ne., U.S. . . **C2** 120
Scottsboro, Al., U.S. **A3** 94
Scottsburg, In., U.S. **G6** 107
Scottsdale, Az., U.S. **D4** 96
Scottsville, Ky., U.S. **D3** 110
Scottsville, N.Y., U.S. **B3** 125
Scottville, Mi., U.S. **E4** 115
Scraggly Lake, l., Me., U.S. . **B4** 112
Scranton, Ks., U.S. **D8** 109
Scranton, Pa., U.S. **D10** 131
Scranton, S.C., U.S. **D8** 133
Screven, Ga., U.S. **E4** 103
Screven, co., Ga., U.S. **D5** 103
Scribner, Ne., U.S. **C9** 120
Ščučinsk, Kaz. **D8** 26
Scugog, Lake, l., On., Can. . **C6** 89
Scurry, co., Tx., U.S. **C2** 136
Scutari see Shkodër, Alb. . . **C7** 18
Scutari, Lake, l., Eur. **C7** 18
Scyros see Skíros, i., Grc. . . **E10** 18
Seaboard, N.C., U.S. **A5** 126
Seabreeze, De., U.S. **F5** 101
Seabrook, N.H., U.S. **E5** 122
Seabrook, Tx., U.S. **r14** 136
Seabrook Island, i., S.C.,
U.S. **F7** 133
Seadrift, Tx., U.S. **E4** 136
Seaford, De., U.S. **F3** 101
Seaford, Va., U.S. **h15** 139
Seaforth, On., Can. **D3** 89
Seagoville, Tx., U.S. **n10** 136
Seagraves, Tx., U.S. **C1** 136
Sea Islands, is., U.S. **E11** 92
Sea Isle City, N.J., U.S. **E3** 123
Seal Cove, Nf., Can. **D3** 88
Seal Point, c., P.E., Can. . . . **C5** 87
Seal Rock, Or., U.S. **C2** 130
Sealy, Tx., U.S. **E4** 136
Seaman, Oh., U.S. **D2** 128
Seaman Range, mts., Nv.,
U.S. **F6** 121
Searchlight, Nv., U.S. **H7** 121
Searcy, Ar., U.S. **B4** 97
Searcy, co., Ar., U.S. **B3** 97
Searles Lake, l., Ca., U.S. . . **E5** 98
Searsport, Me., U.S. **D4** 112
Seaside, Or., U.S. **B3** 130
Seat Pleasant, Md., U.S. . . . **C4** 113
Seattle, Wa., U.S. **B3** 140
Seattle-Tacoma International
Airport, Wa., U.S. **f11** 140
Seaview, Wa., U.S. **C1** 140

Sebago Lake, Me., U.S. **E2** 112
Šebalino, Russia **D10** 26
Sebangka, Pulau, i., Indon. . **C2** 36
Sebastian, Fl., U.S. **E6** 102
Sebastian, co., Ar., U.S. . . . **B1** 97
Sebastian, Cape, c., Or.,
U.S. **E2** 130
Sebastian Inlet, b., Fl., U.S. **E6** 102
Sebastián Vizcaíno, Bahía,
b., Mex. **B2** 78
Sebasticook Lake, l., Me.,
U.S. **D3** 112
Sebec Lake, l., Me., U.S. . . **C3** 112
Sebeka, Mn., U.S. **D3** 116
Šebekino, Russia **D14** 20
Sebeş, Rom. **G7** 20
Sebewaing, Mi., U.S. **E7** 115
Şebinkarahisar, Tur. **B8** 44
Seboeis, stm., Me., U.S. . . . **B4** 112
Seboeis Lake, l., Me., U.S. . **C4** 112
Seboomook Lake, l., Me.,
U.S. **C3** 112
Sebree, Ky., U.S. **C2** 110
Sebring, Fl., U.S. **E5** 102
Sebring, Oh., U.S. **B4** 128
Secaucus, N.J., U.S. **h8** 123
Sechelt, B.C., Can. **E6** 85
Sechura, Bahía de, b., Peru **E3** 70
Second Lake, l., N.H., U.S. . **f7** 122
Second Mesa, Az., U.S. . . . **B5** 96
Secret Lake, l., R.I., U.S. . . **E4** 132
Section, Al., U.S. **A4** 94
Security, Co., U.S. **C6** 99
Seda, China **E8** 28
Sedalia, Mo., U.S. **C4** 118
Sedan, Fr. **C9** 16
Sedan, Ks., U.S. **E7** 109
Sedgewick, Ab., Can. **C5** 84
Sedgewick, Mount, mtn.,
N.M., U.S. **B1** 124
Sedgwick, Ks., U.S. **E6** 109
Sedgwick, co., Co., U.S. . . . **A8** 99
Sedgwick, co., Ks., U.S. . . . **E6** 109
Sédhiou, Sen. **D1** 50
Sedley, Va., U.S. **D6** 139
Sedona, Az., U.S. **C4** 96
Sedro Woolley, Wa., U.S. . . **A3** 140
Seekonk, Ma., U.S. **C5** 114
Seekonk, stm., R.I., U.S. . . . **C4** 132
Seeley, Ca., U.S. **F6** 98
Seeley Lake, Mt., U.S. **C3** 119
Seelyville, In., U.S. **F3** 107
Şefaatli, Tur. **C6** 44
Sefadu, S.L. **E2** 50
Seferihisar, Tur. **C2** 44
Segamat, Malay. **C2** 36
Segesta, hist., Italy **F4** 18
Segeža, Russia **C5** 26
Ségou, Mali **D3** 50
Segovia, Spain **G4** 16
Seguam Island, i., Ak., U.S. **E5** 95
Seguam Pass, strt., Ak., U.S. **E5** 95
Séguédine, Niger **B7** 50
Séguéla, C. Iv. **E4** 50
Seguin, Tx., U.S. **E4** 136
Segura, stm., Spain **I6** 16
Seiling, Ok., U.S. **A3** 129
Seinäjoki, Fin. **E10** 10
Seine, stm., Fr. **C7** 16
Seine, Baie de la, b., Fr. . . . **C6** 16
Sejm, stm., Eur. **D12** 20
Sejmčan, Russia **C17** 26
Şeki, Azer. **B12** 44
Sekiu, Wa., U.S. **A1** 140
Sekondi-Takoradi, Ghana . . **F4** 50
Selah, Wa., U.S. **C5** 140
Selaru, Pulau, i., Indon. . . . **E8** 36
Selatan, Tanjung, c., Indon. **D4** 36
Selawik, Ak., U.S. **B7** 95
Selawik Lake, l., Ak., U.S. . . **B7** 95
Selayar, Pulau, i., Indon. . . . **E6** 36
Selby, S.D., U.S. **B5** 134
Selbyville, De., U.S. **G5** 101
Selçuk, Tur. **D2** 44
Seldovia, Ak., U.S. **D9** 95
Selebi-Phikwe, Bots. **C4** 56
Selenge, D.R.C. **D3** 54
Selenge, stm., Asia **E12** 26
Sélibabi, Maur. **C2** 50
Seligman, Az., U.S. **B3** 96
Šelihova, zaliv, b., Russia . . **C17** 26
Selinsgrove, Pa., U.S. **E8** 131
Seljord, Nor. **G3** 10
Selkirk, Mb., Can. **D3** 86
Sellersburg, In., U.S. **H6** 107
Sellersville, Pa., U.S. **F11** 131
Sells, Az., U.S. **F4** 96
Selma, Al., U.S. **C2** 94
Selma, Ca., U.S. **D4** 98
Selma, In., U.S. **D7** 107
Selma, N.C., U.S. **B4** 126
Selmer, Tn., U.S. **B3** 135
Selvagens, Ilhas, is., Port. . . **D1** 48
Selvas, for., Braz. **E6** 70
Selway, stm., Id., U.S. **C3** 105
Selwyn Lake, l., Can. **G15** 82
Selwyn Mountains, mts.,
Can. **F13** 82
Selwyn Range, mts., Austl. . **E3** 62
Semara, W. Sah. **A2** 50
Semarang, Indon. **E4** 36
Semananjung Malaysia, hist.
reg., Malay. **C2** 36
Semenivka, Ukr. **C12** 20
Semenov, Russia **C7** 22

Semey see Semipalatinsk,
Kaz. **D10** 26
Semiluki, Russia **D15** 20
Seminoe Mountains, mts.,
Wy., U.S. **D6** 143
Seminoe Reservoir, res.,
Wy., U.S. **D6** 143
Seminole, Ok., U.S. **B5** 129
Seminole, Tx., U.S. **C1** 136
Seminole, co., Fl., U.S. **D5** 102
Seminole, co., Ga., U.S. . . . **F2** 103
Seminole, co., Ok., U.S. . . . **B5** 129
Seminole, Lake, res., Fl., U.S. **F2** 103
Semipalatinsk, Kaz. **D10** 26
Semisopochnoi Island, i.,
Ak., U.S. **E3** 95
Semitau, Indon. **C4** 36
Semmes, Al., U.S. **E1** 94
Semnān, Iran **C6** 42
Senachwine Lake, l., Il., U.S.**B4** 106
Senador Pompeu, Braz. . . . **C4** 74
Senaki, Geor. **A10** 44
Sena Madureira, Braz. **E6** 70
Senanga, Zam. **B3** 56
Senath, Mo., U.S. **E7** 118
Senatobia, Ms., U.S. **A4** 117
Sendai, Japan **D16** 28
Sendelingsdrif, Nmb. **D2** 56
Seneca, Il., U.S. **B5** 106
Seneca, Ks., U.S. **C7** 109
Seneca, Mo., U.S. **E3** 118
Seneca, Pa., U.S. **D2** 131
Seneca, S.C., U.S. **B2** 133
Seneca, co., N.Y., U.S. **C4** 125
Seneca, co., Oh., U.S. **A2** 128
Seneca Falls, N.Y., U.S. **C4** 125
Seneca Lake, l., N.Y., U.S. . . **C4** 125
Senecaville Lake, res., Oh.,
U.S. **C4** 128
Sénégal, stm., Afr. **C2** 50
Senegal, ctry., Afr. **D1** 50
Senekal, S. Afr. **D4** 56
Senftenberg, Ger. **E13** 12
Senhor do Bonfim, Braz. . . . **D3** 74
Senica, Slvk. **E4** 20
Senigallia, Italy **C4** 18
Senja, i., Nor. **B7** 10
Šenkursk, Russia **B7** 22
Senneterre, P.Q., Can. **k11** 90
Senoia, Ga., U.S. **C2** 103
Senqu see Orange, stm.,
Afr. **D2** 56
Sens, Fr. **C8** 16
Senta, Yugo. **B8** 18
Sentinel, Ok., U.S. **B2** 129
Seoni, India **E3** 40
Seoul see Sŏul, S. Kor. **D13** 28
Sepanjang, Pulau, i., Indon. **E5** 36
Sepik, stm., Pap. N. Gui. . . . **G11** 32
Sept-Îles (Seven Islands),
P.Q., Can. **h13** 90
Sepulga, stm., Al., U.S. **D3** 94
Sequatchie, co., Tn., U.S. . . **D8** 135
Sequatchie, stm., Tn., U.S. . **D8** 135
Sequim, Wa., U.S. **A2** 140
Sequoia National Park, Ca.,
U.S. **D4** 98
Sequoyah, co., Ok., U.S. . . . **B7** 129
Şerabad, Uzb. **C9** 42
Serafimovič, Russia **E7** 22
Serang, Indon. **E3** 36
Serasan, Pulau, i., Indon. . . **C3** 36
Serasan, Selat, strt., Indon. **C3** 36
Serbia see Srbija, prov.,
Yugo. **B8** 18
Serdobsk, Russia **D7** 22
Sered', Slvk. **E4** 20
Şereflikoçhisar, Tur. **C5** 44
Seremban, Malay. **C2** 36
Serengeti Plain, pl., Tan. . . . **D6** 54
Serenje, Zam. **A5** 56
Sergač, Russia **C8** 22
Sergeant Bluff, Ia., U.S. . . . **B1** 108
Sergeevka, Russia **B2** 31
Sergeja Kirova, ostrova, is.,
Russia **B10** 26
Sergiev Posad, Russia **D5** 26
Serginskij, Russia **C8** 26
Sergipe, state, Braz. **D4** 74
Seria, Bru. **C4** 36
Serian, Malay. **C4** 36
Sérifos, i., Grc. **F10** 18
Serik, Tur. **D4** 44
Šerlovaja Gora, Russia **A11** 28
Serov, Russia **D8** 26
Serowe, Bots. **C4** 56
Serpa, Port. **I3** 16
Serpiente, Boca de la, strt. . **B7** 80
Serpuhov, Russia **B14** 20
Serra do Navio, Braz. **C9** 70
Sérrai, Grc. **D9** 18
Serra Talhada, Braz. **C4** 74
Serrezuela, Arg. **E4** 72
Serrinha, Braz. **D4** 74
Sertânia, Braz. **D4** 74
Sêrxü, China **E7** 28
Sese Islands, is., Ug. **D6** 54
Sesfontein, Nmb. **B1** 56
Sesheke, Zam. **B3** 56
Sesser, Il., U.S. **E4** 106
Sestroreck, Russia **F13** 10
Sète, Fr. **F8** 16

Sete Lagoas, Braz. **E3** 74
Seth, W.V., U.S. **C3** 141
Sétif, Alg. **C6** 48
Seto-naikai, Japan **E14** 28
Setté Cama, Gabon **D1** 54
Setúbal, Port. **H2** 16
Setúbal, Baía de, b., Port. . . **H2** 16
Seul, Lac, l., On., Can. **o16** 89
Seul Choix Point, c., Mi.,
U.S. **C5** 115
Sevan, Arm. **B11** 44
Sevana Lich, l., Arm. **B11** 44
Sevastopol', Ukr. **G12** 20
Seven Devils Lake, res., Ar.,
U.S. **D4** 97
Seven Devils Mountains,
mts., Id., U.S. **D2** 105
Seven Hills, Oh., U.S. **h9** 128
Seven Mile Beach, N.J., U.S.**E3** 123
Severn, Md., U.S. **B4** 113
Severn, stm., On., Can. **n17** 89
Severn, stm., U.K. **D5** 12
Severnaja Dvina, stm.,
Russia **C6** 26
Severnaja Osetija, state,
Russia **E6** 26
Severnaja Sos'va, stm.,
Russia **B11** 22
Severnaja Zemlja, is., Russia **B12** 26
Severna Park, Md., U.S. . . . **B4** 113
Severn River, b., Md., U.S. . **B4** 113
Severnye uvaly, hills, Russia **D6** 26
Severodvinsk, Russia **C5** 26
Severo-Enisejskij, Russia . . . **C11** 26
Severomorsk, Russia **B15** 10
Severo-Sibirskaja
nizmennost', pl., Russia **B11** 26
Severoural'sk, Russia **B11** 22
Sevier, co., Ar., U.S. **D1** 97
Sevier, co., Tn., U.S. **D10** 135
Sevier, co., Ut., U.S. **E4** 137
Sevier, stm., Ut., U.S. **D3** 137
Sevier Bridge Reservoir,
res., Ut., U.S. **D4** 137
Sevier Lake, l., Ut., U.S. . . . **E2** 137
Sevierville, Tn., U.S. **D10** 135
Sevilla, Col. **E4** 80
Sevilla (Seville), Spain **I4** 16
Seville see Sevilla, Spain . . . **I4** 16
Seville, Oh., U.S. **A4** 128
Sewanee, Tn., U.S. **D8** 135
Seward, Ak., U.S. **C10** 95
Seward, Ne., U.S. **D8** 120
Seward, co., Ks., U.S. **E3** 109
Seward, co., Ne., U.S. **D8** 120
Seward Peninsula, pen., Ak.,
U.S. **B7** 95
Sewickley, Pa., U.S. **E1** 131
Sexsmith, Ab., Can. **B1** 84
Seychelles, ctry., Afr. **i12** 57b
Seychelles, is., Afr. **h13** 57b
Seydişehir, Tur. **D4** 44
Seydisfjördur, Ice. **l21** 10a
Seyhan, stm., Tur. **D6** 44
Seyhan Baraji, res., Tur. . . . **D6** 44
Seymour, Austl. **H4** 62
Seymour, Ct., U.S. **D3** 100
Seymour, Ia., U.S. **D4** 108
Seymour, In., U.S. **G6** 107
Seymour, Mo., U.S. **D5** 118
Seymour, Tx., U.S. **C3** 136
Seymour, Wi., U.S. **D5** 142
Seymour Inlet, b., B.C.,
Can. **D4** 85
Seymour Johnson Air Force
Base, mil., N.C., U.S. . . . **B5** 126
Seymour Lake, l., Vt., U.S. . **B4** 138
Seymourville, La., U.S. **h9** 111
Sfântu Gheorghe, Rom. . . . **G8** 20
Sfax, Tun. **D7** 48
's-Gravenhage (The Hague),
Neth. **D8** 12
Shaanxi, state, China **D9** 28
Shabbona, Il., U.S. **B5** 106
Shabeelle (Shebelē Wenz,
Wabē), stm., Afr. **G8** 54
Shabunda, D.R.C. **D5** 54
Shache, China **D3** 28
Shackelford, co., Tx., U.S. . . **C3** 136
Shackleton Ice Shelf, Ant. . **C14** 67
Shackleton Range, mts.,
Ant. **E2** 67
Shadehill Dam, S.D., U.S. . . **B3** 134
Shadehill Reservoir, res.,
S.D., U.S. **B3** 134
Shadow Mountain National
Recreation Area, Co.,
U.S. **A4** 99
Shady Cove, Or., U.S. **E4** 130
Shady Side, Md., U.S. **C4** 113
Shadyside, Oh., U.S. **C5** 128
Shady Spring, W.V., U.S. . . . **D3** 141
Shafer, Lake, l., In., U.S. . . . **C4** 107
Shafer Butte, mtn., Id., U.S. **F2** 105
Shafter, Ca., U.S. **E4** 98
Shaftsbury, Vt., U.S. **E2** 138
Shag Rocks, rock, S. Geor. . **H8** 69
Shah Alam, Malay. **C2** 36
Shahdol, India **E4** 40
Shāhjahānpur, India **D3** 40
Shāhpura, India **D2** 40
Shahr-e Kord, Iran **D6** 42
Shahr-e Rey, Iran **C6** 42
Shājāpur, India **E3** 40
Shakawe, Bots. **B3** 56

Name	Map Ref.	Page

Shaker Heights, Oh., U.S. — A4 128
Shaki, Nig. — E5 50
Shakopee, Mn., U.S. — F5 116
Shallotte, N.C., U.S. — D4 126
Shallotte Inlet, b., N.C., U.S. — D4 126
Shallowater, Tx., U.S. — C2 136
Shām, Jabal ash-, mtn., Oman — F7 38
Shambe, Sudan — B6 54
Shambu, Eth. — B7 54
Shamokin, Pa., U.S. — E8 131
Shamokin Dam, Pa., U.S. — E8 131
Shamrock, Tx., U.S. — B2 136
Shamva, Zimb. — B5 56
Shandī, Sudan — G11 48
Shandong, state, China — D11 28
Shandong Bandao, pen., China — D12 28
Shangcai, China — C3 30
Shangcheng, China — C4 30
Shangchuan Dao, i., China — A3 30
Shangdu, China — A3 30
Shanghai, China — E12 28
Shanghang, China — D4 30
Shangqiu, China — E11 28
Shangrao, China — F11 28
Shangxian, China — E10 28
Shangzhi, China — B13 28
Shanhaiguan, China — A4 30
Shannock, R.I., U.S. — F2 132
Shannon, Ga., U.S. — B1 103
Shannon, Il., U.S. — A4 106
Shannon, Ms., U.S. — A5 117
Shannon, co., Ms., U.S. — D6 118
Shannon, co., S.D., U.S. — D3 134
Shannon, stm., Ire. — D2 12
Shannon, Lake, l., Wa., U.S. — A4 140
Shannontown, S.C., U.S. — D7 133
Shantou, China — G11 28
Shantung Peninsula see Shandong Bandao, pen., China — D12 28
Shanxi, state, China — D10 28
Shanxian, China — C4 30
Shanyin, China — B3 30
Shaoguan, China — G10 28
Shaowu, China — F11 28
Shaoxing, China — E12 28
Shaoyang, China — F10 28
Shaqrā', Sau. Ar. — E5 38
Shaqrā', Yemen — H5 38
Shara, gora, mtn., Asia — A10 44
Shark Bay, b., Austl. — F1 60
Sharkey, co., Ms., U.S. — C3 117
Shark Point, c., Fl., U.S. — H5 102
Sharm El Sheikh, Egypt — E11 48
Sharon, Ct., U.S. — B2 100
Sharon, Ma., U.S. — B5 114
Sharon, Pa., U.S. — D1 131
Sharon, Tn., U.S. — A3 135
Sharon, Wi., U.S. — F5 142
Sharon Hill, Pa., U.S. — p20 131
Sharon Park, Oh., U.S. — n12 128
Sharon Springs, Ks., U.S. — D2 109
Sharonville, Oh., U.S. — n13 128
Sharp, co., Ar., U.S. — A4 97
Sharpe, Lake, res., S.D., U.S. — C6 134
Sharpes, Fl., U.S. — D6 102
Sharpley, De., U.S. — h7 101
Sharpsburg, Md., U.S. — B2 113
Sharpsburg, N.C., U.S. — B5 126
Sharpsburg, Pa., U.S. — k14 131
Sharpsville, In., U.S. — D5 107
Sharpsville, Pa., U.S. — D1 131
Sharptown, Md., U.S. — C6 113
Shashe, stm., Afr. — C4 56
Shashemenē, Eth. — B7 54
Shashi, China — E10 28
Shasta, co., Ca., U.S. — B3 98
Shasta, Mount, vol., Ca., U.S. — B2 98
Shasta Lake, l., Ca., U.S. — B2 98
Shattuck, Ok., U.S. — A2 129
Shaw, Ms., U.S. — B3 117
Shaw Air Force Base, mil., S.C., U.S. — D7 133
Shawano, Wi., U.S. — D5 142
Shawano, co., Wi., U.S. — D5 142
Shawano Lake, l., Wi., U.S. — D5 142
Shawinigan, P.Q., Can. — C5 90
Shawinigan-Sud, P.Q., Can. — C5 90
Shawnee, Ks., U.S. — k16 109
Shawnee, Ok., U.S. — B5 129
Shawnee, co., Ks., U.S. — D8 109
Shawneetown, Il., U.S. — F5 106
Shawsheen, stm., Ma., U.S. — f11 114
Shay Gap, Austl. — E3 60
Shaykh, Jabal ash- see Hermon, Mount, mtn., Asia — F6 44
Shaykh Sa'd, Iraq — F12 44
Shaykh 'Uthmān, Yemen — H5 38
Shebelē Wenz, Wabē (Shabeelle), stm., Afr. — B8 54
Sheberghān, Afg. — C9 42
Sheboygan, Wi., U.S. — E6 142
Sheboygan, co., Wi., U.S. — E6 142
Sheboygan, stm., Wi., U.S. — k10 142
Sheboygan Falls, Wi., U.S. — E6 142
Shediac, N.B., Can. — C5 87
Sheenjek, stm., Ak., U.S. — B11 95
Sheep Mountain, mtn., Az., U.S. — E1 96

Sheep Mountain, mtn., Wy., U.S. — B5 143
Sheep Mountain, mtn., Wy., U.S. — C2 143
Sheep Peak, mtn., Nv., U.S. — G6 121
Sheep Range, mts., Nv., U.S. — G6 121
Sheet Harbour, N.S., Can. — E7 87
Sheffield, Eng., U.K. — D6 12
Sheffield, Al., U.S. — A2 94
Sheffield, Ia., U.S. — B4 108
Sheffield, Il., U.S. — B4 106
Sheffield, Pa., U.S. — C3 131
Sheffield Lake, Oh., U.S. — A3 128
Shehong, China — C2 30
Sheila, N.B., Can. — B5 87
Shekhūpura, Pak. — D10 42
Shelagyote Peak, mtn., B.C., Can. — B4 85
Shelbiana, Ky., U.S. — C7 110
Shelbina, Mo., U.S. — B5 118
Shelburn, In., U.S. — F3 107
Shelburne, On., Can. — C4 89
Shelburne Falls, Ma., U.S. — A2 114
Shelburne Pond, l., Vt., U.S. — C2 138
Shelby, Al., U.S. — B3 94
Shelby, Ia., U.S. — C2 108
Shelby, In., U.S. — B3 107
Shelby, Mi., U.S. — E4 115
Shelby, Ms., U.S. — B3 117
Shelby, Mt., U.S. — B5 119
Shelby, N.C., U.S. — B1 126
Shelby, Oh., U.S. — B3 128
Shelby, co., Al., U.S. — B3 94
Shelby, co., Ia., U.S. — C2 108
Shelby, co., Il., U.S. — D5 106
Shelby, co., In., U.S. — E6 107
Shelby, co., Ky., U.S. — B4 110
Shelby, co., Mo., U.S. — B5 118
Shelby, co., Oh., U.S. — B1 128
Shelby, co., Tn., U.S. — B2 135
Shelby, co., Tx., U.S. — D5 136
Shelbyville, Il., U.S. — D5 106
Shelbyville, In., U.S. — F6 107
Shelbyville, Ky., U.S. — B4 110
Shelbyville, Tn., U.S. — B5 135
Shelbyville, Lake, res., Il., U.S. — D5 106
Sheldon, Ia., U.S. — A2 108
Sheldon, Il., U.S. — C6 106
Sheldon, Tx., U.S. — r14 136
Shelekhov, Gulf of see Šelihova, zaliv, b., Russia — C17 26
Shelikof Strait, strt., Ak., U.S. — D9 95
Shell Creek, stm., Wy. — B5 143
Shell Creek, stm., U.S. — A2 99
Shelley, Id., U.S. — F6 105
Shellharbour, Austl. — G5 62
Shell Lake, Wi., U.S. — C2 142
Shell Lake, l., Mn., U.S. — D3 116
Shell Lake, l., Wi., U.S. — C2 142
Shellman, Ga., U.S. — E2 103
Shell Rock, Ia., U.S. — B5 108
Shell Rock, stm., Ia., U.S. — B5 108
Shellsburg, Ia., U.S. — B6 108
Shelly Mountain, mtn., Id., U.S. — F5 105
Shelter Island, N.Y., U.S. — m16 125
Shelton, Ct., U.S. — D3 100
Shelton, Ne., U.S. — D7 120
Shelton, Wa., U.S. — B2 140
Shemya Air Force Base, mil., Ak., U.S. — E2 95
Shenandoah, Ia., U.S. — D2 108
Shenandoah, Pa., U.S. — E9 131
Shenandoah, Va., U.S. — B4 139
Shenandoah, co., Va., U.S. — B4 139
Shenandoah, stm., U.S. — A5 139
Shenandoah, North Fork, stm., Va., U.S. — B4 139
Shenandoah, South Fork, stm., Va., U.S. — B4 139
Shenandoah Mountain, mtn., U.S. — B3 139
Shenandoah National Park, Va., U.S. — B4 139
Shenango River Lake, res., U.S. — D1 131
Shendam, Nig. — E6 50
Shenipsit Lake, l., Ct., U.S. — B6 100
Shenmu, China — B3 30
Shenqiu, China — C4 30
Shenxian, China — B4 30
Shenyang, China — C12 28
Shenzhen, China — E3 30
Shepaug, stm., Ct., U.S. — C2 100
Shepaug Dam, Ct., U.S. — D2 100
Shepaug Reservoir, res., Ct., U.S. — C2 100
Shepetivka, Ukr. — D9 20
Shepherd, Mi., U.S. — E6 115
Shepherd, Tx., U.S. — D5 136
Shepherdstown, W.V., U.S. — B7 141
Shepherdsville, Ky., U.S. — C4 110
Sheppard Air Force Base, mil., Tx., U.S. — C3 136
Shepparton, Austl. — H4 62
Sherborn, Ma., U.S. — h10 114
Sherbro Island, i., S.L. — E2 50
Sherbrooke, P.Q., Can. — D6 90
Sherburn, Mn., U.S. — G4 116
Sherburne, co., Mn., U.S. — E5 116

Sheridan, Ar., U.S. — C3 97
Sheridan, Il., U.S. — B5 106
Sheridan, In., U.S. — D5 107
Sheridan, Mi., U.S. — E5 115
Sheridan, Mt., U.S. — E4 119
Sheridan, Or., U.S. — B3 130
Sheridan, Wy., U.S. — B6 143
Sheridan, co., Ks., U.S. — C3 109
Sheridan, co., Mt., U.S. — B12 119
Sheridan, co., N.D., U.S. — B5 127
Sheridan, co., Ne., U.S. — B3 120
Sheridan, co., Wy., U.S. — B5 143
Sheridan, Mount, mtn., Wy., U.S. — B2 143
Sherman, Tx., U.S. — C4 136
Sherman, co., Ks., U.S. — C2 109
Sherman, co., Ne., U.S. — C6 120
Sherman, co., Or., U.S. — B6 130
Sherman, co., Tx., U.S. — A2 136
Sherman Reservoir, res., Ne., U.S. — C7 120
Sherpur, Bngl. — D6 40
Sherrill, N.Y., U.S. — B5 125
Sherwood, P.E., Can. — C6 87
Sherwood, Ar., U.S. — C3 97
Sherwood, Or., U.S. — h12 130
Sherwood, Wi., U.S. — h9 142
Sherwood Manor, Ct., U.S. — A5 100
Sherwood Park, De., U.S. — i7 101
Shetek, Lake, l., Mn., U.S. — G3 116
Shetland Islands, is., Scot., U.K. — h19 12a
Shetucket, stm., Ct., U.S. — C7 100
Sheyenne, N.D., U.S. — B6 127
Sheyenne, stm., N.D., U.S. — C8 127
Sheyenne Lake, res., N.D., U.S. — B5 127
Shiawassee, co., Mi., U.S. — F6 115
Shibām, Yemen — G5 38
Shicheng, China — A7 34
Shickshinny, Pa., U.S. — D9 131
Shidao, China — D12 28
Shiguaigou, China — A3 30
Shijiazhuang, China — D10 28
Shikārpur, Pak. — E9 42
Shikoku, i., Japan — E14 28
Shilabo, Eth. — B8 54
Shiliguri, India — D5 40
Shillington, Pa., U.S. — F10 131
Shillong, India — D6 40
Shiloh National Military Park, Tn., U.S. — B3 135
Shimla, India — C3 40
Shimoga, India — G3 40
Shimonoseki, Japan — E14 28
Shīndand, Afg. — D8 42
Shiner, Tx., U.S. — E4 136
Shinglehouse, Pa., U.S. — C5 131
Shingū, Japan — E15 28
Shinnston, W.V., U.S. — B4 141
Shinyanga, Tan. — D6 54
Shiocton, Wi., U.S. — D5 142
Shiono-misaki, c., Japan — D3 31
Shiping, China — B4 34
Ship Island, i., Ms., U.S. — E5 117
Ship Island Pass, strt., Ms., U.S. — g7 117
Shippegan, N.B., Can. — B5 87
Shippensburg, Pa., U.S. — F6 131
Shiprock, N.M., U.S. — A1 124
Ship Rock, mtn., N.M., U.S. — A1 124
Shīrāz, Iran — E6 42
Shiretoko-misaki, c., Japan — B5 31
Shirley, In., U.S. — E6 107
Shirley, Ma., U.S. — A4 114
Shirley Mountains, mts., Wy., U.S. — D6 143
Shīrvān, Iran — C7 42
Shishaldin Volcano, vol., Ak., U.S. — E7 95
Shishmaref, Ak., U.S. — B6 95
Shithāthah, Iraq — F10 44
Shively, Ky., U.S. — B4 110
Shivpuri, India — D3 40
Shizuoka, Japan — C3 31
Shkodër, Alb. — C7 18
Shoal Creek, stm., U.S. — B4 135
Shoal Harbour, Nf., Can. — D4 88
Shoal Lake, Mb., Can. — D1 86
Shoals, In., U.S. — G4 107
Shoals, Isles of, is., Me., U.S. — E2 112
Shoalwater, Cape, c., Wa., U.S. — C1 140
Shoemakersville, Pa., U.S. — F10 131
Shongopovi, Az., U.S. — B5 96
Shonto, Az., U.S. — A5 96
Shoreham, Mi., U.S. — F4 115
Shores Acres, R.I., U.S. — E4 132
Shoreview, Mn., U.S. — m12 116
Shorewood, Il., U.S. — k8 106
Shorewood, Mn., U.S. — n11 116
Shorewood, Wi., U.S. — E6 142
Short Beach, Ct., U.S. — D4 100
Shoshone, Id., U.S. — G4 105
Shoshone, co., Id., U.S. — B2 105
Shoshone, stm., Wy., U.S. — B4 143
Shoshone Falls, wtfl, Id., U.S. — G4 105
Shoshone Lake, l., Wy., U.S. — B2 143
Shoshone Mountains, mts., Nv., U.S. — E4 121
Shoshone Peak, mtn., Nv., U.S. — G5 121

Shoshone Range, mts., Nv., U.S. — C5 121
Shoshong, Bots. — C4 56
Shoshoni, Wy., U.S. — C4 143
Shostka, Ukr. — D12 20
Shouchang, China — D4 30
Shouguang, China — B4 30
Shoup, Id., U.S. — D4 105
Shouxian, China — C4 30
Show Low, Az., U.S. — C5 96
Shreve, Oh., U.S. — B3 128
Shreveport, La., U.S. — B2 111
Shrewsbury, Eng., U.K. — D5 12
Shrewsbury, Ma., U.S. — B4 114
Shrewsbury, N.J., U.S. — C4 123
Shrewsbury, Pa., U.S. — G8 131
Shuangcheng, China — B13 28
Shuangjiang, China — B3 34
Shuangliao, China — C12 28
Shuangyashan, China — B14 28
Shubenacadie, N.S., Can. — D6 87
Shubrâ El-Kheima, Egypt — E10 14
Shuksan, Mount, mtn., Wa., U.S. — A4 140
Shule, China — B3 40
Shullsburg, Wi., U.S. — F3 142
Shumagin Islands, is., Ak., U.S. — E7 95
Shunde, China — B6 34
Shungnak, Ak., U.S. — B8 95
Shurugwi, Zimb. — B5 56
Shūsh, Iran — F13 44
Shūshtar, Iran — D5 42
Shuswap Lake, l., B.C., Can. — D8 85
Shuyang, China — C4 30
Shwebo, Myan. — B3 34
Shwenyaung, Myan. — B3 34
Shyok, stm., Asia — C3 40
Siālkot, Pak. — D10 42
Siam see Thailand, ctry., Asia — C4 34
Siam, Gulf of see Thailand, Gulf of, b., Asia — D4 34
Sian see Xi'an, China — E9 28
Šiargao Island, i., Phil. — D8 34
Siau, Pulau, i., Indon. — C7 36
Šiašikotan, ostrov, i., Russia — E17 26
Sibaj, Russia — D10 22
Šibenik, Cro. — C5 18
Siberia see Sibir', reg., Russia — C12 26
Siberut, Pulau, i., Indon. — D1 36
Sibi, Pak. — E9 42
Sibir' (Siberia), reg., Russia — C12 26
Sibircevo, Russia — B6 31
Sibirjakova, ostrov, i., Russia — B9 26
Sibiti, Congo — D2 54
Sibiu, Rom. — G8 20
Sibley, Ia., U.S. — A2 108
Sibley, La., U.S. — B2 111
Sibley, co., Mn., U.S. — F4 116
Sibolga, Indon. — C1 36
Sibsāgar, India — D6 40
Sibu, Malay. — C4 36
Sibuguey Bay, b., Phil. — E8 34
Sibut, C.A.R. — B3 54
Sibutu Island, i., Phil. — F7 34
Sibuyan Island, i., Phil. — D8 34
Sibuyan Sea, Phil. — D8 34
Sicamous, B.C., Can. — D8 85
Sichuan, prov., China — E8 28
Sicilia (Sicily), i., Italy — F4 18
Sicily see Sicilia, i., Italy — F4 18
Sicily, Strait of, strt. — F3 18
Sico Tinto, stm., Hond. — B2 80
Sicuani, Peru — F5 70
Siddipet, India — F3 40
Sidéradougou, Burkina — D4 50
Siderno, Italy — E6 18
Sidhi, India — E4 40
Sîdi Barrâni, Egypt — D10 48
Sidi bel Abbès, Alg. — C4 48
Sidi-Ifni, Mor. — E2 48
Sidley, Mount, mtn., Ant. — D28 67
Sidney, B.C., Can. — E6 85
Sidney, Ia., U.S. — D2 108
Sidney, Il., U.S. — C5 106
Sidney, Mt., U.S. — C12 119
Sidney, Ne., U.S. — C3 120
Sidney, N.Y., U.S. — C5 125
Sidney, Oh., U.S. — B1 128
Sidney Lanier, Lake, res., Ga., U.S. — B2 103
Sidon see Şaydā, Leb. — F6 44
Sidra, Gulf of see Surt, Khalīj, b., Libya — D8 48
Sidrolândia, Braz. — C6 72
Siedlce, Pol. — C7 20
Siegen, Ger. — E11 12
Siena, Italy — C3 18
Sieradz, Pol. — D5 20
Sierpc, Pol. — C5 20
Sierra, co., Ca., U.S. — C3 98
Sierra, co., N.M., U.S. — D2 124
Sierra Blanca Peak, mtn., N.M., U.S. — D4 124
Sierra Estrella, mts., Az., U.S. — m8 96
Sierra Gorda, Chile — C4 72
Sierra Leone, ctry., Afr. — E2 50
Sierra Madre, stm. — m12 98
Sierra Nevada see Nevada, Sierra, mts., Ca., U.S. — D4 98
Sierra Vista, Az., U.S. — F5 96
Siesta Key, i., Fl., U.S. — E4 102

Sieverodonets'k, Ukr. — E15 20
Sífnos, i., Grc. — F10 18
Sig, Alg. — J6 16
Sighetu Marmaţiei, Rom. — F7 20
Sighişoara, Rom. — F8 20
Siglan, Russia — D17 26
Siglufjördur, Ice. — k19 10a
Signal Mountain, Tn., U.S. — D8 135
Signal Peak, mtn., Az., U.S. — D1 96
Signal Peak, mtn., Ut., U.S. — F2 137
Sigourney, Ia., U.S. — C5 108
Siguatepeque, Hond. — C2 80
Siguiri, Gui. — D3 50
Sigulda, Lat. — H11 10
Siguri Falls, wtfl, Tan. — E7 54
Sihanoukville see Kâmpóng Saôm, Camb. — D4 34
Sihote-Alin', mts., Russia — E15 26
Siirt, Tur. — D9 44
Síkar, India — D3 40
Sikasso, Mali — D3 50
Sikeston, Mo., U.S. — E8 118
Sikiá, Grc. — D9 18
Sikiang see Xi, stm., China — G10 28
Sikkim, prov., India — D5 40
Šikotan, ostrov, i., Russia — E16 26
Siktjah, Russia — B14 26
Silao, Mex. — C4 78
Silchar, India — E6 40
Siler City, N.C., U.S. — B3 126
Silesia, hist. reg., Eur. — D4 20
Siletz, Or., U.S. — C3 130
Silghāt, India — D6 40
Silhouette, i., Sey. — h13 57b
Silifke, Tur. — D5 44
Siling Co, l., China — E5 28
Silistra, Bul. — B11 18
Silivri, Tur. — B3 44
Siljan, l., Swe. — F6 10
Šilka, Russia — D13 26
Šilka, stm., Russia — D13 26
Silkeborg, Den. — H3 10
Sillery, P.Q., Can. — n17 90
Sillustani, hist., Peru — B3 72
Silovo, Russia — B16 20
Silsbee, Tx., U.S. — D5 136
Şilt, Co., U.S. — B3 99
Šilutė, Lith. — I9 10
Silvan, Tur. — C9 44
Silvassa, India — E2 40
Silver Bay, Mn., U.S. — C7 116
Silver Bow, co., Mt., U.S. — E4 119
Silver City, N.M., U.S. — E1 124
Silver City, Nv., U.S. — D2 121
Silver Creek, Ne., U.S. — C8 120
Silver Creek, N.Y., U.S. — C1 125
Silver Creek, stm., Or., U.S. — D7 130
Silverdale, Wa., U.S. — B3 140
Silver Grove, Ky., U.S. — h14 110
Silver Hill, Md., U.S. — f9 113
Silver Lake, Ks., U.S. — C8 109
Silver Lake, Ma., U.S. — f11 114
Silver Lake, Mn., U.S. — F4 116
Silver Lake, Wi., U.S. — F5 142
Silver Lake, l., De., U.S. — D3 101
Silver Lake, l., Ia., U.S. — A3 108
Silver Lake, l., Me., U.S. — C3 112
Silver Lake, l., N.H., U.S. — C4 122
Silver Lake, l., N.H., U.S. — E2 122
Silver Lake, l., Or., U.S. — D7 130
Silver Lake, l., Wa., U.S. — g13 140
Silverpeak, Nv., U.S. — F4 121
Silver Peak Range, mts., Nv., U.S. — F4 121
Silver Spring, Md., U.S. — C3 113
Silver Springs, Nv., U.S. — D2 121
Silver Star Mountain, mtn., Wa., U.S. — A5 140
Silverthrone Mountain, mtn., B.C., Can. — D4 85
Silvertip Mountain, mtn., Mt., U.S. — C3 119
Silverton, Co., U.S. — D3 99
Silverton, Id., U.S. — B3 105
Silverton, N.J., U.S. — C4 123
Silverton, Oh., U.S. — o13 128
Silverton, Or., U.S. — C4 130
Silvies, stm., Or., U.S. — D7 130
Silview, De., U.S. — B3 101
Silvis, Il., U.S. — B3 106
Šimanovsk, Russia — D14 26
Simao, China — G8 28
Simav, stm., Tur. — C3 44
Simba, D.R.C. — C4 54
Simcoe, On., Can. — E4 89
Simcoe, Lake, l., On., Can. — C5 89
Simeulue, Palau, i., Indon. — C1 36
Simferopol', Ukr. — G13 20
Simití, Col. — B5 70
Simi Valley, Ca., U.S. — E4 98
Simmesport, La., U.S. — D4 111
Simms Stream, stm., N.H., U.S. — g7 122
Simonette, stm., Ab., Can. — B1 84
Simpson, Pa., U.S. — C11 131
Simpson, co., Ky., U.S. — D3 110
Simpson, co., Ms., U.S. — D4 117
Simpson Creek, stm., W.V., U.S. — k10 141
Simpson Desert, des., Austl. — E6 60
Simpsonville, Ky., U.S. — B4 110
Simpsonville, S.C., U.S. — B3 133

Name	Map Ref.	Page
Simsboro, La., U.S.	B3	111
Simsbury, Ct., U.S.	B4	100
Simušir, ostrov, i., Russia	E17	26
Sinabang, Indon.	C1	36
Sinai, pen., Egypt	E11	48
Sinai Peninsula see Sinai, pen., Egypt	E11	48
Sinaloa, state, Mex.	B3	78
Sīnāwin, Libya	D7	48
Sincelejo, Col.	B4	70
Sinclair, Wy., U.S.	E5	143
Sindangbarang, Indon.	E3	36
Sindara, Gabon	D2	54
Sindor, Russia	B9	22
Sinfra, C. Iv.	E3	50
Singalamwe, Nmb.	B3	56
Singapore, Sing.	C2	36
Singapore, ctry., Asia	C2	36
Singaraja, Indon.	H6	32
Singen, Ger.	G11	12
Singida, Tan.	D6	54
Singkaling Hkāmti, Myan.	A3	34
Singkang, Indon.	D6	36
Singkawang, Indon.	C3	36
Singkep, Pulau, i., Indon.	D2	36
Singleton, Austl.	G5	62
Sinjai, Indon.	E6	36
Sinjār, Iraq	D9	44
Sinkāt, Sudan	G12	48
Sinkiang see Xinjiang Uygur Zizhiqu, prov., China	C5	28
Sinnemahoning Creek, stm., Pa., U.S.	D5	131
Sinop, Tur.	A6	44
Sinskoe, Russia	C14	26
Sintang, Indon.	C4	36
Sint Helenabaai, b., S. Afr.	E2	56
Sinton, Tx., U.S.	E4	136
Siocon, Phil.	E8	34
Siófok, Hung.	F5	20
Sion, Switz.	A1	18
Sioux, co., Ia., U.S.	A1	108
Sioux, co., N.D., U.S.	C4	127
Sioux, co., Ne., U.S.	B2	120
Sioux Center, Ia., U.S.	A1	108
Sioux City, Ia., U.S.	B1	108
Sioux Falls, S.D., U.S.	D9	134
Sioux Lookout, On., Can.	o17	89
Sioux Rapids, Ia., U.S.	B2	108
Sipalay, Phil.	E8	34
Siping, China	C12	28
Sipiwesk Lake, l., Mb., Can.	B3	86
Siple, Mount, mtn., Ant.	D28	67
Sipsey, stm., Al., U.S.	B2	94
Sipsey Fork, stm., Al., U.S.	A2	94
Sipura, Pulau, i., Indon.	D1	36
Siquijor Island, i., Phil.	E8	34
Si Racha, Thai.	D4	34
Siracusa, Italy	F5	18
Sirājganj, Bngl.	E5	40
Sir Douglas, Mount, mtn., Can.	D3	84
Sir Edward Pellew Group, is., Austl.	D6	60
Siren, Wi., U.S.	C1	142
Siret, stm., Eur.	G9	20
Sīrjān, Iran	E7	42
Şırnak, Tur.	D10	44
Sirohi, India	E2	40
Sironj, India	E3	40
Síros, i., Grc.	F10	18
Sirsa, India	D3	40
Sir Sandford, Mount, mtn., B.C., Can.	D9	85
Sirte, Gulf of see Surt, Khalīj, b., Libya	D8	48
Sir Wilfrid Laurier, Mount, mtn., B.C., Can.	C8	85
Sisaba, mtn., Tan.	E5	54
Sisak, Cro.	B6	18
Si Sa Ket, Thai.	C4	34
Sishen, S. Afr.	D3	56
Sisian, Arm.	C12	44
Siskiyou, co., Ca., U.S.	B2	98
Siskiyou Mountains, mts., U.S.	F3	130
Siskiyou Pass, Or., U.S.	E4	130
Sisŏphŏn, Camb.	D4	34
Sisseton, S.D., U.S.	B8	134
Sisseton Indian Reservation, U.S.	B8	134
Sissiboo, stm., N.S., Can.	E4	87
Sisson Branch Reservoir, res., N.B., Can.	B2	87
Sissonville, W.V., U.S.	C3	141
Sistersville, W.V., U.S.	B4	141
Sītāpur, India	D4	40
Sitasjaure, l., Eur.	C7	10
Sitka, Ak., U.S.	D12	95
Sitka National Historical Park, Ak., U.S.	m22	95
Sitka Sound, strt., Ak., U.S.	m22	95
Sittoung, stm., Myan.	C3	34
Sittwe, Myan.	B2	34
Sivas, Tur.	C7	44
Sivers'kyi Donets' see Northern Donets, stm., Eur.	E14	20
Sivrihisar, Tur.	C4	44
Siwa, Egypt	E10	48
Sixian, China	C4	30
Sixth Cataract, wtfl, Sudan	G11	48
Siyäzän, Azer.	B13	44
Siziwang Qi, China	A3	30
Sjælland, i., Den.	I4	10
Skadovs'k, Ukr.	F12	20
Skærbæk, Den.	I3	10
Skagen, Den.	H4	10
Skagerrak, strt., Eur.	B11	12
Skagit, co., Wa., U.S.	A4	140
Skagway, Ak., U.S.	D12	95
Skamania, co., Wa., U.S.	D3	140
Skanderborg, Den.	H3	10
Skåne, hist. reg., Swe.	I5	10
Skaneateles, N.Y., U.S.	C4	125
Skaneateles Lake, l., N.Y., U.S.	C4	125
Skärdu, Pak.	C11	42
Skarżysko-Kamienna, Pol.	D6	20
Skaudvilė, Lith.	I10	10
Skaw, The see Grenen, c., Den.	H4	10
Skegness, Eng., U.K.	D7	12
Skeleton Lake, l., On., Can.	B5	89
Skellefteå, Swe.	D9	10
Skellefteälven, stm., Swe.	D8	10
Ski, Nor.	G4	10
Skiatook, Ok., U.S.	A5	129
Skiatook Reservoir, res., Ok., U.S.	A5	129
Skien, Nor.	G3	10
Skierniewice, Pol.	D6	20
Skihist Mountain, mtn., B.C., Can.	D7	85
Skikda, Alg.	C6	48
Skillet Fork, stm., Il., U.S.	E5	106
Skive, Den.	H3	10
Sklad, Russia	B14	26
Skokie, Il., U.S.	A6	106
Skokomish Indian Reservation, Wa., U.S.	B2	140
Skópelos, i., Grc.	E9	18
Skopin, Russia	C15	20
Skopje, Mac.	C8	18
Skövde, Swe.	G5	10
Skowhegan, Me., U.S.	D3	112
Skull Valley, val., Ut., U.S.	C3	137
Skull Valley Indian Reservation, Ut., U.S.	C3	137
Skuna, stm., Ms., U.S.	B4	117
Skunk, stm., Ia., U.S.	D6	108
Skvyra, Ukr.	E10	20
Skwentna, stm., Ak., U.S.	g15	95
Skye, Island of, i., Scot., U.K.	B3	12
Skykomish, stm., Wa., U.S.	B4	140
Skyland, N.C., U.S.	f10	126
Skyland, Nv., U.S.	D2	121
Skyline, Al., U.S.	A3	94
Slagnäs, Swe.	D8	10
Slamet, Gunung, vol., Indon.	E3	36
Slancy, Russia	G13	10
Slater, Ia., U.S.	C4	108
Slater, Mo., U.S.	B4	118
Slater, S.C., U.S.	A3	133
Slatersville, R.I., U.S.	A3	132
Slatersville Reservoir, res., R.I., U.S.	B3	132
Slatina, Rom.	G8	20
Slatington, Pa., U.S.	E10	131
Slaton, Tx., U.S.	C2	136
Slaughter, La., U.S.	D4	111
Slautnoe, Russia	C18	26
Slave, stm., Can.	F17	82
Slave Lake, Ab., Can.	B3	84
Slavgorod, Russia	D9	26
Slavjanka, Russia	B2	31
Slavjansk-na-Kubani, Russia	G15	20
Slavonia see Slavonija, hist. reg., Cro.	B6	18
Slavonija, hist. reg., Cro.	B6	18
Slavonski Brod, Cro.	B6	18
Slavuta, Ukr.	D9	20
Sławno, Pol.	B4	20
Slayton, Mn., U.S.	G3	116
Sleeping Bear Dunes National Lakeshore, Mi., U.S.	D4	115
Sleeping Bear Point, c., Mi., U.S.	D4	115
Sleepy Eye, Mn., U.S.	F4	116
Slickville, Pa., U.S.	F2	131
Slidell, La., U.S.	D6	111
Sliderock Mountain, mtn., Mt., U.S.	D3	119
Sligo, Ire.	C2	12
Slinger, Wi., U.S.	E5	142
Slippery Rock, Pa., U.S.	D1	131
Sliven, Bul.	C11	18
Sljudjanka, Russia	D12	26
Sloan, Ia., U.S.	B1	108
Sloan, N.Y., U.S.	C2	125
Slobodskoj, Russia	D7	26
Slobozia, Mol.	F10	20
Slobozia, Rom.	G9	20
Slocomb, Al., U.S.	D4	94
Slonim, Bela.	C8	20
Slope, co., N.D., U.S.	C2	127
Slough, Eng., U.K.	E6	12
Slovakia, ctry., Eur.	E6	20
Slovenia, ctry., Eur.	A5	18
Slov'ians'k, Ukr.	E14	20
Sluch, stm., Ukr.	D9	20
Sluck, Bela.	C9	20
Słupsk, Pol.	B4	20
Smackover, Ar., U.S.	D3	97
Småland, hist. reg., Swe.	H6	10
Small Point, c., Me., U.S.	g8	112
Smallwood Reservoir, res., Nf., Can.	g8	88
Smarhon', Bela.	B9	20
Smederevo, Yugo.	B8	18
Smethport, Pa., U.S.	C5	131
Smidovič, Russia	B14	28
Smila, Ukr.	E11	20
Smith, co., Ks., U.S.	C5	109
Smith, co., Ms., U.S.	C4	117
Smith, co., Tn., U.S.	A5	135
Smith, co., Tx., U.S.	C5	136
Smith, stm., Mt., U.S.	D5	119
Smith, stm., U.S.	D3	139
Smith and Sayles Reservoir, res., R.I., U.S.	B2	132
Smith Bay, b., Ak., U.S.	A9	95
Smith Canyon, val., Co., U.S.	D7	99
Smith Center, Ks., U.S.	C5	109
Smithers, B.C., Can.	B4	85
Smithers, W.V., U.S.	C3	141
Smithfield, N.C., U.S.	B4	126
Smithfield, Pa., U.S.	G2	131
Smithfield, Ut., U.S.	B4	137
Smithfield, Va., U.S.	D6	139
Smith Island, i., Va., U.S.	C7	139
Smith Island, i., U.S.	D5	113
Smith Mountain Lake, res., Va., U.S.	C3	139
Smith Peak, mtn., Id., U.S.	A2	105
Smith Point, c., Ma., U.S.	D7	114
Smith Point, c., Va., U.S.	C6	139
Smiths, Al., U.S.	C4	94
Smithsburg, Md., U.S.	A2	113
Smiths Falls, On., Can.	C8	89
Smiths Grove, Ky., U.S.	C3	110
Smithton, Austl.	I4	62
Smithton, Il., U.S.	E4	106
Smithtown, N.Y., U.S.	n15	125
Smithville, Mo., U.S.	B3	118
Smithville, Ms., U.S.	A5	117
Smithville, Oh., U.S.	B4	128
Smithville, Tn., U.S.	D8	135
Smithville, Tx., U.S.	D4	136
Smithville Lake, res., Mo., U.S.	B3	118
Smoke Creek Desert, des., Nv., U.S.	C2	121
Smokey, Cape, c., N.S., Can.	C9	87
Smokey Dome, mtn., Id., U.S.	F4	105
Smoky, stm., Ab., Can.	B1	84
Smoky Hill, stm., U.S.	D5	109
Smoky Lake, Ab., Can.	B4	84
Smoky Mountains, mts., Id., U.S.	F4	105
Smøla, i., Nor.	E6	10
Smolensk, Russia	D5	26
Smoljan, Bul.	D10	18
Smooth Rock Falls, On., Can.	o19	89
Smoothstone Lake, l., Sk., Can.	C2	91
Smyrna see İzmir, Tur.	C2	44
Smyrna, De., U.S.	C3	101
Smyrna, Ga., U.S.	C2	103
Smyrna, Tn., U.S.	B5	135
Smyrna, stm., De., U.S.	C3	101
Smyth, co., Va., U.S.	f10	139
Snake, stm., Mn., U.S.	B1	116
Snake, stm., Ne., U.S.	B4	120
Snake, stm., U.S.	C4	92
Snake, stm., U.S.	D5	116
Snake Range, mts., Nv., U.S.	E7	121
Snake River Plain, pl., Id., U.S.	F2	105
Snake River Range, mts., U.S.	C3	143
Sneads, Fl., U.S.	B2	102
Sneedville, Tn., U.S.	C10	135
Snihurivka, Ukr.	F12	20
Snipe Keys, is., Fl., U.S.	H5	102
Snøhetta, mtn., Nor.	E3	10
Snohomish, Wa., U.S.	B3	140
Snohomish, co., Wa., U.S.	A4	140
Snoqualmie, Wa., U.S.	B4	140
Snoqualmie, stm., Wa., U.S.	B4	140
Snoqualmie Pass, Wa., U.S.	B4	140
Snøtinden, mtn., Nor.	C5	10
Snowbank Lake, l., Mn., U.S.	B7	116
Snowdon, mtn., Wales, U.K.	D4	12
Snowdrift see Łutselk'e, N.T., Can.	F17	82
Snowflake, Az., U.S.	C5	96
Snow Hill, Md., U.S.	D7	113
Snow Hill, N.C., U.S.	B5	126
Snowking Mountain, mtn., Wa., U.S.	A4	140
Snow Lake, Mb., Can.	B1	86
Snowmass Mountain, mtn., Co., U.S.	B3	99
Snow Peak, mtn., Wa., U.S.	A7	140
Snowshoe Lake, l., Me., U.S.	B4	112
Snowshoe Peak, mtn., Mt., U.S.	B1	119
Snow Water Lake, l., Nv., U.S.	C7	121
Snowy Mountains, mts., Austl.	H4	62
Snowyside Peak, mtn., Id., U.S.	F4	105
Snyder, Ok., U.S.	C3	129
Snyder, Tx., U.S.	C2	136
Snyder, co., Pa., U.S.	E7	131
Soacha, Col.	E5	80
Soalala, Madag.	B8	56
Soap Lake, Wa., U.S.	B6	140
Sobradinho, Represa de, res., Braz.	D3	74
Sobral, Braz.	B3	74
Socastee, S.C., U.S.	D9	133
Soči, Russia	E5	26
Social Circle, Ga., U.S.	C3	103
Société, Archipel de la (Society Islands), is., Fr. Poly.	F14	58
Society Hill, S.C., U.S.	B8	133
Society Islands see Société, Archipel de la, is., Fr. Poly.	F14	58
Socorro, Col.	B5	70
Socorro, N.M., U.S.	C3	124
Socorro, co., N.M., U.S.	D2	124
Socorro, Isla, i., Mex.	D2	78
Socotra see Suquṭrā, i., Yemen	H6	38
Soc Trang, Viet.	E5	34
Sodankylä, Fin.	C12	10
Soda Springs, Id., U.S.	G7	105
Soddy-Daisy, Tn., U.S.	D8	135
Söderköping, Swe.	G7	10
Södertälje, Swe.	G7	10
Sodo, Eth.	B7	54
Sodus, N.Y., U.S.	B3	125
Soe, Indon.	E6	36
Sofala, Moz.	C5	56
Sofia see Sofija, Bul.	C9	18
Sofija, Bul.	C9	18
Sogamoso, Col.	D5	80
Sognefjorden, b., Nor.	F1	10
Sog Xian, China	E6	28
Soissons, Fr.	C8	16
Sojat, India	D2	40
Šojna, Russia	A7	22
Söke, Tur.	D2	44
Sokodé, Togo	E5	50
Sokol, Russia	C7	22
Sokol, Russia	B14	26
Sokółka, Pol.	C7	20
Sokolo, Mali	D3	50
Sokoto, Nig.	D6	50
Sokoto, stm., Nig.	D5	50
Solai, Kenya	C7	54
Solana, Fl., U.S.	F5	102
Solano, Phil.	C8	34
Solano, co., Ca., U.S.	C3	98
Solāpur, India	F3	40
Soldier, stm., Ia., U.S.	C2	108
Soldier Key, i., Fl., U.S.	s3	102
Soldotna, Ak., U.S.	g16	95
Soledad, Col.	A5	70
Soledad, Ca., U.S.	D3	98
Soledad Díez Gutiérrez, Mex.	C4	78
Solikamsk, Russia	D7	26
Sol'-Ileck, Russia	D10	22
Solimões see Amazon, stm., S.A.	D6	70
Sollefteå, Swe.	E7	10
Sóller, Spain	H8	16
Šologoncy, Russia	C13	26
Solomon, Ks., U.S.	D6	109
Solomon, stm., Ks., U.S.	C4	109
Solomon Basin	I18	64
Solomon Islands, ctry., Oc.	B6	62
Solomon Islands, is., Oc.	B5	62
Solomon Sea, Oc.	A9	62
Solomons, Md., U.S.	D5	113
Solon, China	B12	28
Solon, Ia., U.S.	C6	108
Solon, Oh., U.S.	A4	128
Solothurn, Switz.	A1	18
Solov'evsk, Russia	A11	28
Solvay, N.Y., U.S.	B4	125
Solway Firth, b., U.K.	C5	12
Solwezi, Zam.	A4	56
Soma, Tur.	C2	44
Somabhula, Zimb.	B4	56
Somalia, ctry., Afr.	I14	46
Somali Basin	H8	64
Sombor, Yugo.	B7	18
Sombrerete, Mex.	C4	78
Sombrero Channel, strt., India	H6	40
Somerdale, N.J., U.S.	D2	123
Somers, Ct., U.S.	B6	100
Somers, Mt., U.S.	B2	119
Somerset, Ky., U.S.	C5	110
Somerset, Ma., U.S.	C5	114
Somerset, Mb., Can.	E2	86
Somerset, N.J., U.S.	B3	123
Somerset, Oh., U.S.	C3	128
Somerset, Pa., U.S.	F3	131
Somerset, Tx., U.S.	k7	136
Somerset, Wi., U.S.	C1	142
Somerset, co., Md., U.S.	D6	113
Somerset, co., Me., U.S.	C2	112
Somerset, co., N.J., U.S.	B3	123
Somerset, co., Pa., U.S.	G3	131
Somerset, co., Eng., U.K.	E4	56
Somerset Reservoir, res., Vt., U.S.	E3	138
Somers Point, N.J., U.S.	E3	123
Somersville, Ct., U.S.	B6	100
Somersworth, N.H., U.S.	D5	122
Somerton, Az., U.S.	E1	96
Somervell, co., Tx., U.S.	C4	136
Somerville, Ma., U.S.	B5	114
Somerville, N.J., U.S.	B3	123
Somerville, Tn., U.S.	B2	135
Somerville, Tx., U.S.	D4	136
Somerville Lake, res., Tx., U.S.	D4	136
Somonauk, Il., U.S.	B5	106
Son, stm., India	E4	40
Sønderborg, Den.	I3	10
Søndre Strømfjord, Grnld.	E29	82
Søndre Strømfjord, b., Grnld.	E29	82
Sondrio, Italy	A2	18
Sonepur, India	E4	40
Song, Nig.	E7	50
Song Cau, Viet.	D5	34
Songea, Tan.	F7	54
Songhua, stm., China	B14	28
Songhua Hu, res., China	C13	28
Songkhla, Thai.	E4	34
Songnim, N. Kor.	D13	28
Songololo, D.R.C.	E2	54
Songpan, China	C1	30
Sonid Youqi, China	C10	28
Sonīpat, India	D3	40
Sonkël', ozero, l., Kyrg.	A3	40
Son La, Viet.	B4	34
Sonmiāni Bay, b., Pak.	E9	42
Sonneberg, Ger.	E12	12
Sonoma, Ca., U.S.	C2	98
Sonoma, co., Ca., U.S.	C2	98
Sonoma Peak, mtn., Nv., U.S.	C4	121
Sonoma Range, mts., Nv., U.S.	C4	121
Sonora, Ca., U.S.	D3	98
Sonora, Tx., U.S.	D2	136
Sonora, state, Mex.	B2	78
Sonora, stm., Mex.	B2	78
Sonoran Desert, des., N.A.	E5	92
Sonoyta, Mex.	A2	78
Sonqor, Iran	E12	44
Sonsón, Col.	D4	80
Sonsonate, El Sal.	C1	80
Sonsorol Islands, is., Palau	E9	32
Son Tay, Viet.	B5	34
Sonthofen, Ger.	G12	12
Soochow see Suzhou, China	E12	28
Soperton, Ga., U.S.	D4	103
Sophia, W.V., U.S.	D3	141
Sopot, Pol.	B5	20
Sopron, Hung.	F4	20
Sopur, India	C2	40
Sorel, P.Q., Can.	C4	90
Sorgun, Tur.	C6	44
Soria, Spain	G5	16
Soroca, Mol.	E10	20
Sorocaba, Braz.	F2	74
Soročinsk, Russia	D9	22
Sorong, Indon.	D8	36
Soroti, Ug.	C6	54
Sørøya, i., Nor.	A10	10
Sorrento, La., U.S.	D5	111
Sør Rondane Mountains, mts., Ant.	D7	67
Sorsele, Swe.	D7	10
Sorsogon, Phil.	D8	34
Sort, Spain	F7	16
Sortavala, Russia	F14	10
Sosnogorsk, Russia	B9	22
Sosnovka, Russia	A7	22
Sosnovo-Ozërskoe, Russia	A10	28
Sosnowiec, Pol.	D5	20
Sos'va, Russia	B11	22
Sotouboua, Togo	E5	50
Soubré, C. Iv.	E3	50
Soucook, stm., N.H., U.S.	D4	122
Soudan, Mn., U.S.	C6	116
Souderton, Pa., U.S.	F11	131
Souhegan, stm., N.H., U.S.	E3	122
Sŏul (Seoul), S. Kor.	D13	28
Souq Ahras, Alg.	F1	18
Sources, Mont-aux-, mtn., Afr.	D4	56
Soure, Braz.	B2	74
Souris, Mb., Can.	E1	86
Souris, P.E., Can.	C7	87
Souris, stm., N.A.	B7	92
Sousa, Braz.	C4	74
Sousse, Tun.	C7	48
South, stm., Ia., U.S.	C4	108
South, stm., N.C., U.S.	C4	126
South Acton, Ma., U.S.	g10	114
South Africa, ctry., Afr.	E3	56
South Amboy, N.J., U.S.	C4	123
South America	G9	4
South Amherst, Ma., U.S.	B2	114
South Amherst, Oh., U.S.	A3	128
Southampton, On., Can.	C3	89
Southampton, Eng., U.K.	E6	12
Southampton, N.Y., U.S.	n16	125
Southampton, i., Nu., Can.	D15	82
South Andaman, i., India	G6	40
South Anna, stm., Va., U.S.	C5	139
South Australia, state, Austl.	F5	60
South Australian Basin	L16	64
Southaven, Ms., U.S.	A3	117
South Bald Mountain, mtn., Co., U.S.	A5	99
South Baldy, mtn., N.M., U.S.	D2	124

Name	Map Ref.	Page

South Barre, Vt., U.S. **C3** 138
South Bay, Fl., U.S. **F6** 102
South Beloit, Il., U.S. **A4** 106
South Bend, In., U.S. **A5** 107
South Bend, Wa., U.S. **C2** 140
South Berwick, Me., U.S. . . **B4** 112
South Bloomfield, Oh., U.S. **C3** 128
South Boston, Va., U.S. . . . **D4** 139
South Bound Brook, N.J.,
   U.S. **B3** 123
South Branch Lake, l., Me.,
   U.S. **C4** 112
Southbridge, Ma., U.S. . . . **B3** 114
South Bristol, Me., U.S. . . . **E3** 112
South Britain, Ct., U.S. . . . **D3** 100
South Broadway, Wa., U.S. . **C5** 140
South Burlington, Vt., U.S. . **C2** 138
Southbury, Ct., U.S. **D3** 100
South Carolina, state, U.S. . **D6** 133
South Charleston, Oh., U.S. **C2** 128
South Charleston, W.V.,
   U.S. **C3** 141
South Chicago Heights, Il.,
   U.S. **m9** 106
South China Basin **G14** 64
South China Sea, Asia **G13** 32
South Coffeyville, Ok., U.S. **A6** 129
South Congaree, S.C., U.S. . **D5** 133
South Connellsville, Pa.,
   U.S. **G2** 131
South Dakota, state, U.S. . . **C5** 134
South Dartmouth, Ma., U.S. **C6** 114
South Daytona, Fl., U.S. . . . **C5** 102
South Deerfield, Ma., U.S. . **B2** 114
South Dennis, Ma., U.S. . . . **C7** 114
South Duxbury, Ma., U.S. . . **B6** 114
South East Cape, c., Austl. . **I4** 62
Southeast Cape, c., Ak.,
   U.S. **C6** 95
Southeast Indian Ridge . . . **M13** 64
South Easton, Ma., U.S. . . . **B5** 114
Southeast Pacific Basin . . . **O25** 64
Southeast Pass, strt., La.,
   U.S. **E7** 111
South East Point, c., Austl. . **H4** 62
Southeast Point, c., R.I.,
   U.S. **h7** 132
South Elgin, Il., U.S. **B5** 106
Southend-on-Sea, Eng., U.K. **E7** 12
South Range, Mi., U.S. **A2** 115
Southern Alps, mts., N.Z. . . **p13** 63c
Southern Cook Islands, is.,
   Cook Is. **F13** 58
Southern Cross, Austl. **G2** 60
Southern Indian Lake, l.,
   Mb., Can. **f8** 86
Southern Ocean **J19** 4
Southern Pines, N.C., U.S. . **B3** 126
Southern Ute Indian
   Reservation, Co., U.S. . **D2** 99
South Euclid, Oh., U.S. . . . **g9** 128
Southey, Sk., Can. **G3** 91
South Fabius, stm., Mo.,
   U.S. **A5** 118
South Fallsburg, N.Y., U.S. . **D6** 125
Southfield, Mi., U.S. **o15** 115
South Fiji Basin **K20** 64
South Fork, Pa., U.S. **F4** 131
South Fox Island, i., Mi.,
   U.S. **C5** 115
South Fulton, Tn., U.S. **A3** 135
South Gastonia, N.C., U.S. . **B1** 126
South Gate, Ca., U.S. **n12** 98
Southgate, Ky., U.S. **h14** 110
Southgate, Mi., U.S. **p15** 115
South Georgia, i., S. Geor. . **H9** 69
South Glastonbury, Ct., U.S. **C5** 100
South Glens Falls, N.Y., U.S. **B7** 125
South Grafton, Ma., U.S. . . **B4** 114
South Grand, stm., Mo.,
   U.S. **C3** 118
South Hadley, Ma., U.S. . . . **B2** 114
South Hadley Falls, Ma.,
   U.S. **B2** 114
South Hamilton, Ma., U.S. . **A6** 114
South Haven, In., U.S. **A3** 107
South Haven, Mi., U.S. **F4** 115
South Hero Island, i., Vt.,
   U.S. **B2** 138
South Hill, Va., U.S. **D4** 139
South Hingham, Ma., U.S. . **h12** 114
South Holland, Il., U.S. . . . **k9** 106
South Holston Lake, res.,
   U.S. **A9** 135
South Honshu Ridge **E16** 64
South Hooksett, N.H., U.S. . **D4** 122
South Hopkinton, R.I., U.S. **F1** 132
South Houston, Tx., U.S. . . **r14** 136
South Hutchinson, Ks., U.S. **f11** 109
South Indian Basin **N12** 64
South Indian Lake, Mb.,
   Can. **A2** 86
Southington, Ct., U.S. **C4** 100
South International Falls,
   Mn., U.S. **B5** 116
South Island, i., N.Z. **I10** 58
South Island, i., S.C., U.S. . **E9** 133
South Jacksonville, Il., U.S. **D3** 106
South Jordan, Ut., U.S. . . . **C3** 137
South Kenosha, Wi., U.S. . . **F6** 142
South Korea see Korea,
   South, ctry., Asia **D10** 28
South Lake Tahoe, Ca., U.S. **E4** 98
South Lancaster, Ma., U.S. . **B4** 114
South Lebanon, Oh., U.S. . . **C1** 128
South Lyon, Mi., U.S. **F7** 115

South Magnetic Pole **C18** 67
South Manitou Island, i.,
   Mi., U.S. **C4** 115
South Marsh Island, i., Md.,
   U.S. **D5** 113
South Miami, Fl., U.S. **G6** 102
South Miami Heights, Fl.,
   U.S. **s13** 102
South Mills, N.C., U.S. **A6** 126
South Milwaukee, Wi., U.S. **F6** 142
Southmont, N.C., U.S. **B2** 126
South Moose Lake, l., Mb.,
   Can. **C1** 86
South Mountain, mtn., Id.,
   U.S. **G2** 105
South Mountain, mtn.,
   N.M., U.S. **k8** 124
South Mountains, mts., Az.,
   U.S. **m8** 96
South Mountains, mts.,
   N.C., U.S. **B1** 126
South New River Canal, Fl.,
   U.S. **r3** 102
South Ogden, Ut., U.S. . . . **B4** 137
Southold, N.Y., U.S. **m16** 125
South Orange, N.J., U.S. . . **B4** 123
South Orkney Islands, is.,
   Ant. **C36** 67
South Paris, Me., U.S. **D2** 112
South Park, val., Co., U.S. . **B5** 99
South Pass, Wy., U.S. **D4** 143
South Pass, strt., La., U.S. . **F6** 111
South Patrick Shores, Fl.,
   U.S. **D6** 102
South Pekin, Il., U.S. **C4** 106
South Pittsburg, Tn., U.S. . . **D8** 135
South Plainfield, N.J., U.S. . **B4** 123
South Platte, stm., U.S. . . . **C7** 92
South Point, c., Mi., U.S. . . **D7** 115
South Pole **E35** 67
Southport (Gold Coast),
   Austl. **F5** 62
Southport, Fl., U.S. **u16** 102
Southport, In., U.S. **E5** 107
Southport, N.C., U.S. **D4** 126
Southport, N.Y., U.S. **C4** 125
South Portland, Me., U.S. . . **E2** 112
South Portsmouth, Ky., U.S. **B6** 110
South River, On., Can. **B5** 89
South River, N.J., U.S. **C4** 123
South River, b., Md., U.S. . . **C4** 113
South Royalton, Vt., U.S. . . **D3** 138
South Saint Paul, Mn., U.S. **n12** 116
South Sandwich Islands, is.,
   S. Geor. **B2** 67
South Sandwich Trench . . . **N11** 66
South San Francisco, Ca.,
   U.S. **h8** 98
South Shetland Islands, is.,
   Ant. **B35** 67
Southside, Al., U.S. **B3** 94
Southside Place, Tx., U.S. . **r14** 136
South Sioux City, Ne., U.S. **B9** 120
South Skunk, stm., Ia., U.S. **C4** 108
South Streator, Il., U.S. . . . **B5** 106
South Taranaki Bight, b.,
   N.Z. **o13** 63c
South Tasman Rise **M17** 64
South Toms River, N.J., U.S. **D4** 123
South Torrington, Wy., U.S. **D8** 143
South Tucson, Az., U.S. . . . **E5** 96
South Venice, Fl., U.S. **E4** 102
South Ventana Cone, vol.,
   Ca., U.S. **D3** 98
South Waverly, Pa., U.S. . . **C8** 131
South Wellfleet, Ma., U.S. . **C8** 114
South Wellington, B.C.,
   Can. **f12** 85
South Wenatchee, Wa.,
   U.S. **B5** 140
South West Africa see
   Namibia, ctry., Afr. . . . **C2** 56
South West Cape, c., N.Z. . **q12** 63c
Southwest Channel, strt.,
   Fl., U.S. **E4** 102
South West City, Mo., U.S. **E3** 118
Southwest Harbor, Me.,
   U.S. **D4** 112
Southwest Head, c., N.B.,
   Can. **E3** 87
Southwest Indian Ridge . . . **L8** 64
Southwest Miramichi, stm.,
   N.B., Can. **C3** 87
Southwest Pacific Basin . . . **L23** 64
Southwest Pass, strt., La.,
   U.S. **E3** 111
Southwest Pass, strt., La.,
   U.S. **F6** 111
Southwest Point, c., R.I.,
   U.S. **h7** 132
South Weymouth Naval Air
   Station, mil., Ma., U.S. **h12** 114
South Whitley, In., U.S. . . . **B6** 107
South Williamson, Ky., U.S. **C7** 110
South Williamsport, Pa.,
   U.S. **D7** 131
South Windham, Ct., U.S. . . **C7** 100
South Windham, Me., U.S. . **E2** 112
South Windsor, Ct., U.S. . . **B5** 100
Southwood Acres, Ct., U.S. **A5** 100
South Woodstock, Ct., U.S. **B8** 100
South Yarmouth, Ma., U.S. . **C7** 114
South Zanesville, Oh., U.S. **C3** 128
Sovetsk, Russia **I9** 10

Sovetsk, Russia **C8** 22
Sovetskaja Gavan', Russia . **E16** 26
Soviets'kyi, Ukr. **G13** 20
Soyo, Ang. **E2** 54
Sozh, stm., Eur. **C11** 20
Spain, ctry., Eur. **H5** 16
Spalding, co., Ga., U.S. . . . **C2** 103
Spanaway, Wa., U.S. **B3** 140
Spangler, Pa., U.S. **E4** 131
Spaniard's Bay, Nf., Can. . . **E5** 88
Spanish Fork, Ut., U.S. . . . **C4** 137
Spanish Fort, Al., U.S. **E2** 94
Spanish Lake, Mo., U.S. . . **f13** 118
Spanish Peak, mtn., Or.,
   U.S. **C7** 130
Spanish Sahara see Western
   Sahara, dep., Afr. **B2** 50
Spanish Town, Jam. **B4** 80
Sparks, Ga., U.S. **E3** 103
Sparks, Nv., U.S. **D2** 121
Sparta, Ga., U.S. **C4** 103
Sparta, Il., U.S. **E4** 106
Sparta, Mi., U.S. **E5** 115
Sparta, Mo., U.S. **D4** 118
Sparta, N.C., U.S. **A1** 126
Sparta (Lake Mohawk), N.J.,
   U.S. **A3** 123
Sparta, Tn., U.S. **D8** 135
Sparta, Wi., U.S. **E3** 142
Spartanburg, S.C., U.S. . . . **B4** 133
Spartanburg, co., S.C., U.S. **B3** 133
Spárti, Grc. **F9** 18
Spartivento, Capo, c., Italy **E2** 18
Sparwood, B.C., Can. **E10** 85
Spavinaw Creek, stm., Ok.,
   U.S. **A7** 129
Spear, Cape, c., Nf., Can. . **E5** 88
Spearfish, S.D., U.S. **C2** 134
Spearman, Tx., U.S. **A2** 136
Spearville, Ks., U.S. **E4** 109
Speed, In., U.S. **H6** 107
Speedway, In., U.S. **E5** 107
Speke Gulf, b., Tan. **D6** 54
Spence Bay see Taloyoak,
   N.T., Can. **E21** 82
Spencer, Ia., U.S. **A2** 108
Spencer, In., U.S. **F4** 107
Spencer, Ma., U.S. **B4** 114
Spencer, N.C., U.S. **B2** 126
Spencer, Tn., U.S. **D8** 135
Spencer, W.V., U.S. **C3** 141
Spencer, Wi., U.S. **D3** 142
Spencer, co., In., U.S. **H4** 107
Spencer, co., Ky., U.S. . . . **B4** 110
Spencer, Cape, c., Austl. . . **F4** 91
Spencer, Cape, c., Ak., U.S. **k21** 95
Spencer Gulf, b., Austl. . . . **G2** 62
Spencer Lake, l., Me., U.S. **C2** 112
Spencerport, N.Y., U.S. . . . **B3** 125
Spencerville, Md., U.S. . . . **B4** 113
Spencerville, Oh., U.S. . . . **B1** 128
Sperry, Ok., U.S. **A6** 129
Spesutie Island, i., Md., U.S. **B5** 113
Speyer, Ger. **F11** 12
Spezia see La Spezia, Italy **B2** 18
Spiceland, In., U.S. **E7** 107
Spicer, Mn., U.S. **E4** 116
Spider Lake, l., Wi., U.S. . . **B2** 142
Spindale, N.C., U.S. **B1** 126
Spink, co., S.D., U.S. **C7** 134
Spirit Lake, Ia., U.S. **A2** 108
Spirit Lake, l., Id., U.S. . . . **A2** 105
Spirit Lake, l., Ia., U.S. . . . **A2** 108
Spirit Lake, l., Wa., U.S. . . **C3** 140
Spirit River, Ab., Can. **B1** 84
Spirit River Flowage, res.,
   Wi., U.S. **C4** 142
Spiro, Ok., U.S. **B7** 129
Spišská Nová Ves, Slvk. . . . **E6** 20
Spitsbergen, i., Nor. **B3** 26
Spittal an der Drau, Aus. . . **G13** 12
Split, Cro. **C6** 18
Split, Cape, c., N.S., Can. . **D5** 87
Split Lake, l., Mb., Can. . . . **A4** 86
Split Rock Creek, stm., U.S. **G2** 116
Spofford Lake, l., N.H., U.S. **E2** 122
Spokane, Wa., U.S. **B8** 140
Spokane, co., Wa., U.S. . . **B8** 140
Spokane, stm., U.S. **B8** 140
Spokane, Mount, mtn., Wa.,
   U.S. **B8** 140
Spokane Indian Reservation,
   Wa., U.S. **B8** 140
Spoleto, Italy **C4** 18
Spoon, stm., Il., U.S. **C3** 106
Spooner, Wi., U.S. **C2** 142
Spooner Lake, l., Wi., U.S. **C2** 142
Spornoe, Russia **C17** 26
Spotswood, N.J., U.S. **C4** 123
Spotsylvania, co., Va., U.S. **B5** 139
Sprague, W.V., U.S. **n13** 141
Sprague, stm., Or., U.S. . . **E5** 130
Sprague Lake, l., Wa., U.S. **B7** 140
Spratly Islands, is., Asia . . **E6** 34
Spring Arbor, Mi., U.S. . . . **F6** 115
Spring Bay, b., Ut., U.S. . . **B3** 137
Springbok, S. Afr. **D2** 56
Springboro, Oh., U.S. **C1** 128
Spring Brook, stm., Pa., U.S. **n18** 131
Sretensk, Russia **D13** 26
Sri Jayawardenepura, Sri L. **H4** 40
Srīkākulam, India **F4** 40
Sri Kālahasti, India **G3** 40

Spring Creek, stm., N.D.,
   U.S. **B3** 127
Spring Creek, stm., Nv.,
   U.S. **C4** 121
Spring Creek, stm., U.S. . . **D4** 120
Springdale, Nf., Can. **D3** 88
Springdale, Ar., U.S. **A1** 97
Springdale, Oh., U.S. **n13** 128
Springdale, Pa., U.S. **E2** 131
Springdale, S.C., U.S. **D5** 133
Springer, N.M., U.S. **A5** 124
Springerville, Az., U.S. . . . **C6** 96
Springfield, Co., U.S. **D8** 99
Springfield, Fl., U.S. **u16** 102
Springfield, Ga., U.S. **D5** 103
Springfield, Il., U.S. **D4** 106
Springfield, Ky., U.S. **C4** 110
Springfield, Ma., U.S. **B2** 114
Springfield, Mn., U.S. **F4** 116
Springfield, Mo., U.S. **D4** 118
Springfield, Ne., U.S. **C9** 120
Springfield, N.J., U.S. **B4** 123
Springfield, Oh., U.S. **C2** 128
Springfield, Or., U.S. **C4** 130
Springfield, Pa., U.S. **p20** 131
Springfield, S.D., U.S. **E8** 134
Springfield, Tn., U.S. **A5** 135
Springfield, Va., U.S. **g12** 139
Springfield, Vt., U.S. **E4** 138
Springfield, Lake, res., Il.,
   U.S. **D4** 106
Springfontein, S. Afr. **E4** 56
Spring Garden, Guy. **B8** 70
Spring Glen, Ut., U.S. **D5** 137
Spring Green, Wi., U.S. . . . **E3** 142
Spring Grove, Il., U.S. **h8** 106
Spring Grove, Pa., U.S. . . . **G8** 131
Spring Hill, Fl., U.S. **D4** 102
Spring Hill, Ks., U.S. **D9** 109
Springhill, La., U.S. **A2** 111
Spring Hill, Tn., U.S. **B5** 135
Spring Hope, N.C., U.S. . . . **B4** 126
Spring Island, i., S.C., U.S. **G6** 133
Spring Lake, Mi., U.S. **E4** 115
Spring Lake, N.C., U.S. . . . **B4** 126
Spring Lake, N.J., U.S. . . . **C4** 123
Spring Lake, l., Me., U.S. . **C2** 112
Spring Lake, res., U.S. . . . **B3** 106
Spring Lake Heights, N.J.,
   U.S. **C4** 123
Spring Mountains, mts., Nv.,
   U.S. **G6** 121
Springport, Mi., U.S. **F6** 115
Springs, S. Afr. **D4** 56
Springside, Sk., Can. **F4** 91
Springsure, Austl. **E4** 62
Springvale, Me., U.S. **E2** 112
Spring Valley, Ca., U.S. . . . **o16** 98
Spring Valley, Il., U.S. **B4** 106
Spring Valley, Mn., U.S. . . . **G6** 116
Spring Valley, N.Y., U.S. . . **g12** 125
Spring Valley, Wi., U.S. . . . **D1** 142
Springville, Al., U.S. **B3** 94
Springville, Ia., U.S. **B6** 108
Springville, N.Y., U.S. **C2** 125
Springville, Ut., U.S. **C4** 137
Spruce Fork, stm., W.V.,
   U.S. **m12** 141
Spruce Grove, Ab., Can. . . **C4** 84
Spruce Knob, mtn., W.V.,
   U.S. **C6** 141
Spruce Knob-Seneca Rocks
   National Recreation
   Area, W.V., U.S. **C5** 141
Spruce Mountain, mtn., Az.,
   U.S. **C3** 96
Spruce Mountain, mtn., Nv.,
   U.S. **C7** 121
Spruce Pine, N.C., U.S. . . . **f10** 126
Spruce Run Reservoir, res.,
   N.J., U.S. **B3** 123
Spur, Tx., U.S. **C2** 136
Spurr, Mount, mtn., Ak.,
   U.S. **g15** 95
Squam Lake, l., N.H., U.S. . **C4** 122
Squapan Lake, l., Me., U.S. **B4** 112
Square Lake, l., Me., U.S. . **A4** 112
Squatec, P.Q., Can. **B9** 90
Squaw Cap Mountain, mtn.,
   N.B., Can. **B3** 87
Squaw Hill, mtn., Wy., U.S. **E7** 143
Squaw Peak, mtn., Mt., U.S. **C2** 119
Squibnocket Point, c., Ma.,
   U.S. **D6** 114
Squillace, Golfo di, b., Italy **E6** 18
Squire, W.V., U.S. **D3** 141
Srbija (Serbia), prov., Yugo. **B8** 18
Srbobran, Yugo. **B7** 18
Sredinnyj hrebet, mts.,
   Russia **D17** 26
Srednee Kujto, ozero, l.,
   Russia **D14** 10
Srednekolymsk, Russia . . . **C17** 26
Srednerusskaja
   vozvyšennost', plat.,
   Russia **D5** 26
Srednesibirskoe ploskogor'e,
   plat., Russia **C12** 26
Šrem, Pol. **C4** 20
Sremska Mitrovica, Yugo. . **B7** 18
Spring City, Pa., U.S. **F10** 131
Spring City, Tn., U.S. **D9** 135
Spring City, Ut., U.S. **D4** 137

Sri Lanka, ctry., Asia **H4** 40
Srīnagar, India **C2** 40
Stack Reservoir, res., R.I.,
   U.S. **C3** 132
Stade, Ger. **D11** 12
Stafford, Eng., U.K. **D5** 12
Stafford, Ks., U.S. **E5** 109
Stafford, Va., U.S. **B5** 139
Stafford, co., Ks., U.S. . . . **D5** 109
Stafford, co., Va., U.S. . . . **B5** 139
Stafford Pond, l., R.I., U.S. **D6** 132
Stafford Springs, Ct., U.S. . **B6** 100
Staked Plain see Estacado,
   Llano, pl., U.S. **E7** 92
Stakhanov, Ukr. **E15** 20
Stalin see Varna, Bul. **C11** 18
Stalingrad see Volgograd,
   Russia **E6** 26
Stalinogorsk see
   Novomoskovsk, Russia **D5** 26
Stalinsk see Novokuzneck,
   Russia **D10** 26
Stalowa Wola, Pol. **D7** 20
Stambaugh, Mi., U.S. **B2** 115
Stamford, Ct., U.S. **E1** 100
Stamford, Tx., U.S. **C3** 136
Stamford, Vt., U.S. **F2** 138
Stamford, Lake, res., Tx.,
   U.S. **C3** 136
Stamping Ground, Ky., U.S. **B5** 110
Stampriet, Nmb. **C2** 56
Stamps, Ar., U.S. **D2** 97
Stanaford, W.V., U.S. **D3** 141
Stanberry, Mo., U.S. **A3** 118
Standerton, S. Afr. **D4** 56
Standing Rock Indian
   Reservation, U.S. **B4** 134
Standish, Mi., U.S. **E7** 115
Stanfield, Az., U.S. **E3** 96
Stanfield, Or., U.S. **B7** 130
Stanford, Ky., U.S. **C5** 110
Stanhope, N.J., U.S. **B3** 123
Stanislaus, co., Ca., U.S. . . **D3** 98
Stanley, Falk. Is. **H5** 69
Stanley, N.C., U.S. **B1** 126
Stanley, N.D., U.S. **A3** 127
Stanley, Va., U.S. **B4** 139
Stanley, Wi., U.S. **D3** 142
Stanley, co., S.D., U.S. . . . **C5** 134
Stanley Falls, wtfl, D.R.C. . **C5** 54
Stanley Reservoir, res., India **G3** 40
Stanleytown, Va., U.S. **D3** 139
Stanleyville, N.C., U.S. . . . **A2** 126
Stanly, co., N.C., U.S. **B2** 126
Stanovoe nagor'e, mts.,
   Russia **D13** 26
Stanovoj hrebet, mts.,
   Russia **D14** 26
Stanovoy Mountains see
   Stanovoe nagor'e, mts.,
   Russia **D13** 26
Stanstead, P.Q., Can. **D5** 90
Stanthorpe, Austl. **F5** 62
Stanton, Ia., U.S. **D2** 108
Stanton, Ky., U.S. **C6** 110
Stanton, Mi., U.S. **E5** 115
Stanton, Ne., U.S. **C8** 120
Stanton, Tx., U.S. **C2** 136
Stanton, co., Ks., U.S. . . . **E2** 109
Stanton, co., Ne., U.S. . . . **C8** 120
Stantonsburg, N.C., U.S. . . **B5** 126
Stanwood, Ia., U.S. **C6** 108
Stanwood, Wa., U.S. **A3** 140
Staples, Mn., U.S. **D4** 116
Stapleton, Al., U.S. **E2** 94
Star, Id., U.S. **F2** 105
Star, N.C., U.S. **B3** 126
Staraja Russa, Russia **C5** 22
Stara Planina (Balkan
   Mountains), mts., Eur. . **C9** 18
Stara Zagora, Bul. **C10** 18
Starbuck, Mn., U.S. **E3** 116
Starbuck, i., Kir. **E14** 58
Star City, Ar., U.S. **D4** 97
Star City, W.V., U.S. **B5** 141
Stargard Szczeciński, Pol. . **C3** 20
Stargo, Az., U.S. **D6** 96
Stark, co., Il., U.S. **B4** 106
Stark, co., N.D., U.S. **C3** 127
Stark, co., Oh., U.S. **B4** 128
Starke, Fl., U.S. **C4** 102
Starke, co., In., U.S. **B4** 107
Starks, La., U.S. **D2** 111
Starkville, Ms., U.S. **B5** 117
Star Lake, l., Mn., U.S. . . . **D3** 116
Startex, S.C., U.S. **B3** 133
Staryj Oskol, Russia **D5** 26
State Center, Ia., U.S. **B4** 108
State College, Pa., U.S. . . . **E6** 131
Stateline, Nv., U.S. **E2** 121
State Line, Pa., U.S. **G6** 131
Staten Island see Estados,
   Isla de los, i., Arg. **H4** 69
Staten Island, i., N.Y., U.S. **k12** 125
Statenville, Ga., U.S. **F4** 103
Statesboro, Ga., U.S. **D5** 103
Statesville, N.C., U.S. **B2** 126
Statham, Ga., U.S. **C3** 103
Statue of Liberty National
   Monument, N.J., U.S. . . **k8** 123

Name	Map Ref.	Page
Staunton, Il., U.S.	D4	106
Staunton, Va., U.S.	B3	139
Staunton, stm., U.S.	D12	92
Stavanger, Nor.	G1	10
Stavropol see Toljatti, Russia	D6	26
Stavropol', Russia	E6	26
Stawell, Austl.	H3	62
Stayner, On., Can.	C4	89
Stayton, Or., U.S.	C4	130
Steamboat, Nv., U.S.	D2	121
Steamboat Mountain, mtn., Mt., U.S.	C4	119
Steamboat Mountain, mtn., Wy., U.S.	E4	143
Steamboat Springs, Co., U.S.	A4	99
Stearns, Ky., U.S.	D5	110
Stearns, co., Mn., U.S.	E4	116
Stearns Brook, stm., N.H., U.S.	A4	122
Stebbins, Ak., U.S.	C7	95
Steele, Al., U.S.	B3	94
Steele, Mo., U.S.	E8	118
Steele, N.D., U.S.	C6	127
Steele, co., Mn., U.S.	F5	116
Steele, co., N.D., U.S.	B8	127
Steele, Mount, mtn., Wy., U.S.	E6	143
Steeleville, Il., U.S.	E4	106
Steelton, Pa., U.S.	F8	131
Steelville, Mo., U.S.	D6	118
Steens Mountain, mts., Or., U.S.	E8	130
Stefanie, Lake, l., Afr.	C7	54
Steger, Il., U.S.	B6	106
Steilacoom, Wa., U.S.	f10	140
Steinbach, Mb., Can.	E3	86
Steinhatchee, stm., Fl., U.S.	C3	102
Steinkjer, Nor.	E4	10
Steinkopf, S. Afr.	D2	56
Stellenbosch, S. Afr.	E2	56
Stendal, Ger.	D12	12
Stepanakert see Xankändi, Azer.	C12	44
Stephen, Mn., U.S.	B2	116
Stephens, Ar., U.S.	D2	97
Stephens, co., Ga., U.S.	B3	103
Stephens, co., Ok., U.S.	C4	129
Stephens, co., Tx., U.S.	C3	136
Stephens City, Va., U.S.	A4	139
Stephens Lake, res., Mb., Can.	A4	86
Stephenson, Mi., U.S.	C3	115
Stephenson, co., Il., U.S.	A4	106
Stephens Passage, strt., Ak., U.S.	m23	95
Stephenville, Nf., Can.	D2	88
Stephenville, Tx., U.S.	C3	136
Stephenville Crossing, Nf., Can.	D2	88
Sterkstroom, S. Afr.	E4	56
Sterling, Ak., U.S.	g16	95
Sterling, Co., U.S.	A7	99
Sterling, Il., U.S.	B4	106
Sterling, Ks., U.S.	D5	109
Sterling, Ok., U.S.	C3	129
Sterling, Va., U.S.	A5	139
Sterling, co., Tx., U.S.	D2	136
Sterling City, Tx., U.S.	D2	136
Sterling Heights, Mi., U.S.	o15	115
Sterling Reservoir, res., Co., U.S.	A7	99
Sterlington, La., U.S.	B3	111
Sterlitamak, Russia	D7	26
Stettler, Ab., Can.	C4	84
Steuben, co., In., U.S.	A7	107
Steuben, co., N.Y., U.S.	C3	125
Steubenville, Oh., U.S.	B5	128
Stevens, co., Ks., U.S.	E2	109
Stevens, co., Mn., U.S.	E2	116
Stevens, co., Wa., U.S.	A7	140
Stevens Creek Dam, U.S.	C4	103
Stevenson, Al., U.S.	A4	94
Stevenson, Ct., U.S.	D3	100
Stevenson, Wa., U.S.	D4	140
Stevenson Lake, l., Mb., Can.	C4	86
Stevens Pass, Wa., U.S.	B4	140
Stevens Peak, mtn., Id., U.S.	B3	105
Stevens Point, Wi., U.S.	D4	142
Stevensville, Md., U.S.	C5	113
Stevensville, Mi., U.S.	F4	115
Stevensville, Mt., U.S.	D2	119
Stewart, co., Ga., U.S.	D2	103
Stewart, co., Tn., U.S.	A4	135
Stewart Island, i., N.Z.	q12	63c
Stewart Mountain, mtn., Az., U.S.	k9	96
Stewartstown, Pa., U.S.	G8	131
Stewartsville, Mo., U.S.	B3	118
Stewartville, Mn., U.S.	G6	116
Stewiacke, N.S., Can.	D6	87
Steyr, Aus.	F14	12
Stigler, Ok., U.S.	B6	129
Stikine, stm., Ak., U.S.	D13	95
Still, stm., Ct., U.S.	B3	100
Stillaguamish, North Fork, stm., Wa., U.S.	A4	140
Stillaguamish, South Fork, stm., Wa., U.S.	A4	140
Stillhouse Hollow Lake, res., Tx., U.S.	D4	136
Stillman Valley, Il., U.S.	A4	106
Stillmore, Ga., U.S.	D4	103
Stillwater, Mn., U.S.	E6	116
Stillwater, Ok., U.S.	A4	129
Stillwater, co., Mt., U.S.	E7	119
Stillwater Range, mts., Nv., U.S.	D3	121
Stillwater Reservoir, res., N.Y., U.S.	B5	125
Stillwater Reservoir, res., R.I., U.S.	B3	132
Stilwell, Ok., U.S.	B7	129
Stimson, Mount, mtn., Mt., U.S.	B3	119
Stine Mountain, mtn., Mt., U.S.	E3	119
Stinking Lake, l., N.M., U.S.	A3	124
Stinnett, Tx., U.S.	B2	136
Štip, Mac.	D9	18
Stirling, Austl.	G2	60
Stirling, Austl.	E5	60
Stirling, Ab., Can.	E4	84
Stirling, On., Can.	C7	89
Stockbridge, Ga., U.S.	C2	103
Stockbridge, Mi., U.S.	F6	115
Stockbridge-Munsee Indian Reservation, Wi., U.S.	D5	142
Stockdale, Tx., U.S.	E4	136
Stockholm, Swe.	G8	10
Stockton, Ca., U.S.	D3	98
Stockton, Il., U.S.	A3	106
Stockton, Ks., U.S.	C4	109
Stockton, Md., U.S.	D7	113
Stockton, Mo., U.S.	D4	118
Stockton Island, i., Wi., U.S.	B3	142
Stockton Lake, res., Mo., U.S.	D4	118
Stoddard, Wi., U.S.	E2	142
Stoddard, co., Mo., U.S.	E8	118
Stœng Trêng, Camb.	D5	34
Stoke-on-Trent, Eng., U.K.	D5	12
Stokes, co., N.C., U.S.	A2	126
Stokesdale, N.C., U.S.	A3	126
Stolbovoj, ostrov, i., Russia	B15	26
Stolin, Bela.	D9	20
Stollings, W.V., U.S.	n12	141
Stone, co., Ar., U.S.	B3	97
Stone, co., Mo., U.S.	E4	118
Stone, co., Ms., U.S.	E4	117
Stoneboro, Pa., U.S.	D1	131
Stone Corral Lake, l., Or., U.S.	E7	130
Stoneham, Ma., U.S.	g11	114
Stonehaven, Scot., U.K.	E5	12
Stonehenge, hist., Eng., U.K.	E6	12
Stone Mountain, Ga., U.S.	C2	103
Stone Mountain, mtn., Ga., U.S.	C2	103
Stones River National Battlefield, hist., Tn., U.S.	B4	135
Stoneville, N.C., U.S.	A3	126
Stonewall, Mb., Can.	D3	86
Stonewall, La., U.S.	B2	111
Stonewall, Ms., U.S.	C5	117
Stonewall, co., Tx., U.S.	C2	136
Stonewood, W.V., U.S.	k10	141
Stoney Creek, On., Can.	D5	89
Stonington, Ct., U.S.	D8	100
Stonington, Il., U.S.	D4	106
Stonington, Me., U.S.	D4	112
Stono, stm., S.C., U.S.	k11	133
Stono Inlet, b., S.C., U.S.	F8	133
Stony Brook, N.Y., U.S.	n15	125
Stony Brook, stm., N.J., U.S.	C3	123
Stony Creek, stm., Va., U.S.	C5	139
Stony Island, i., N.Y., U.S.	B4	125
Stony Plain, Ab., Can.	C3	84
Stony Point, N.C., U.S.	B1	126
Storavan, l., Swe.	D8	10
Storebælt, strt., Den.	I4	10
Storey, co., Nv., U.S.	D2	121
Storlien, Swe.	E6	10
Storm Bay, b., Austl.	I4	62
Storm Lake, Ia., U.S.	B2	108
Storm Lake, l., Ia., U.S.	B2	108
Storm Mountain, mtn., Ak., U.S.	h16	95
Stornoway, Scot., U.K.	A3	12
Storrs, Ct., U.S.	B7	100
Storsjön, l., Swe.	E6	10
Storslett, Nor.	B9	10
Storuman, Swe.	D7	10
Storuman, l., Swe.	D7	10
Story, Wy., U.S.	B6	143
Story, co., Ia., U.S.	B4	108
Story City, Ia., U.S.	B4	108
Stoubcy, Bela.	C9	20
Stoughton, Sk., Can.	H4	91
Stoughton, Ma., U.S.	B5	114
Stoughton, Wi., U.S.	F4	142
Stover, Mo., U.S.	C5	118
Stow, Oh., U.S.	A4	128
Stow Creek, stm., N.J., U.S.	E2	123
Stowe, Pa., U.S.	F10	131
Stowe, Vt., U.S.	C3	138
Stoyoma Mountain, mtn., B.C., U.S.	E7	85
Strabane, Pa., U.S.	F1	131
Strafford, Mo., U.S.	D4	118
Strafford, co., N.H., U.S.	D4	122
Straffordville, On., Can.	E4	89
Strakonice, Czech Rep.	E2	12
Stralsund, Ger.	C13	12
Strand, S. Afr.	E2	56
Stranraer, Scot., U.K.	C4	12
Strasbourg, Fr.	C10	16
Strasburg, Co., U.S.	B6	99
Strasburg, Oh., U.S.	B4	128
Strasburg, Pa., U.S.	G9	131
Strasburg, Va., U.S.	B4	139
Stratford, On., Can.	D3	89
Stratford, N.Z.	o13	63c
Stratford, Ct., U.S.	E3	100
Stratford, Ia., U.S.	B4	108
Stratford, N.J., U.S.	D2	123
Stratford, Ok., U.S.	C5	129
Stratford, Tx., U.S.	A1	136
Stratford, Wi., U.S.	D3	142
Stratford Point, c., Ct., U.S.	E3	100
Stratham, N.H., U.S.	D5	122
Strathmore, Ab., Can.	D4	84
Strathmore, Ca., U.S.	D4	98
Strathroy, On., Can.	E3	89
Stratton, Co., U.S.	B8	99
Straubing, Ger.	F13	12
Strawberry, stm., Ar., U.S.	A4	97
Strawberry, stm., Ut., U.S.	C5	137
Strawberry Mountain, mtn., Or., U.S.	C8	130
Strawberry Point, Ia., U.S.	B6	108
Strawberry Point, c., Ma., U.S.	B6	114
Strawberry Range, mts., Or., U.S.	C8	130
Strawberry Reservoir, res., Ut., U.S.	C4	137
Streaky Bay, b., Austl.	G5	60
Streator, Il., U.S.	B5	106
Strelka-Čunja, Russia	C12	26
Strimón (Struma), stm., Eur.	D9	18
Strimon, Gulf of see Orfanoú, Kólpos, b., Grc.	D9	18
Stromsburg, Ne., U.S.	C8	120
Strömsund, Swe.	E6	10
Strong, Ar., U.S.	D3	97
Strong, Me., U.S.	D2	112
Strong, stm., Ms., U.S.	C4	117
Strong City, Ks., U.S.	D7	109
Stronghurst, Il., U.S.	C3	106
Strongsville, Oh., U.S.	A4	128
Stroud, Ok., U.S.	B5	129
Stroudsburg, Pa., U.S.	E11	131
Stroudwater, stm., Me., U.S.	g7	112
Strum, Wi., U.S.	D2	142
Struma (Strimón), stm., Eur.	D9	18
Strumica, Mac.	D9	18
Struthers, Oh., U.S.	A5	128
Strydenburg, S. Afr.	D3	56
Stryi, Ukr.	E7	20
Stryker, Oh., U.S.	A1	128
Stuart, Fl., U.S.	E6	102
Stuart, Ia., U.S.	C3	108
Stuart, Ne., U.S.	B6	120
Stuart, Va., U.S.	D2	139
Stuart, Mount, mtn., Wa., U.S.	B5	140
Stuart Lake, l., B.C., Can.	B5	85
Stuarts Draft, Va., U.S.	B3	139
Stull, stm., Can.	B5	86
Stump Lake, l., N.D., U.S.	B7	127
Stump Pond, res., R.I., U.S.	D2	132
Stupino, Russia	B15	20
Sturbridge, Ma., U.S.	B3	114
Sturgeon, Mo., U.S.	B5	118
Sturgeon, stm., Mi., U.S.	B4	115
Sturgeon Bay, Wi., U.S.	D6	142
Sturgeon Bay, b., Mb., Can.	C3	86
Sturgeon Falls, On., Can.	A5	89
Sturgeon Lake, l., On., Can.	C6	89
Sturgis, Sk., Can.	F4	91
Sturgis, Ky., U.S.	e10	110
Sturgis, Mi., U.S.	G5	115
Sturgis, S.D., U.S.	C2	134
Sturtevant, Wi., U.S.	F6	142
Sturt Stony Desert, des., Austl.	F3	62
Stutsman, co., N.D., U.S.	B6	127
Stutterheim, S. Afr.	E4	56
Stuttgart, Ger.	F11	12
Stuttgart, Ar., U.S.	C4	97
Styr, stm., Eur.	D8	20
Šu, Kaz.	E9	26
Suaita, Col.	D5	80
Šubarkuduk, Kaz.	I10	22
Sûbât, stm., Sudan	I11	48
Subei, China	B7	40
Sublette, Ks., U.S.	E3	109
Sublette, co., Wy., U.S.	D2	143
Sublett Range, mts., Id., U.S.	G6	105
Sublimity, Or., U.S.	C4	130
Subotica, Yugo.	A7	18
Sucarnoochee, stm., Al., U.S.	C1	94
Succasunna, N.J., U.S.	B3	123
Suceava, Rom.	F9	20
Sucre, Bol.	B4	72
Sud, Canal du, strt., Haiti	B5	80
Sudan, ctry., Afr.	H10	48
Sudan, reg., Afr.	H8	48
Sudbury, On., Can.	A4	89
Sudbury, Ma., U.S.	B5	114
Sudbury, stm., Ma., U.S.	B5	114
Sudbury Center, Ma., U.S.	g10	114
Sudbury Reservoir, res., Ma., U.S.	g10	114
Suez see El-Suweis, Egypt	E11	48
Suez, Gulf of see Suweis, Khalîg el-, b., Egypt	F10	14
Suez Canal see Suweis, Qanâ el-, Egypt	E10	14
Suffern, N.Y., U.S.	D6	125
Suffield, Ct., U.S.	B5	100
Suffolk, Va., U.S.	D6	139
Suffolk, co., Ma., U.S.	B5	114
Suffolk, co., N.Y., U.S.	n15	125
Sugar, stm., N.H., U.S.	D2	122
Sugar, stm., Wi., U.S.	F4	142
Sugar City, Id., U.S.	F7	105
Sugar Creek, Mo., U.S.	h11	118
Sugarcreek, Pa., U.S.	D2	131
Sugar Creek, stm., Oh., U.S.	C2	128
Sugar Creek, stm., Pa., U.S.	C8	131
Sugar Grove, Va., U.S.	D1	139
Sugar Hill, Ga., U.S.	B2	103
Sugar Island, i., Mi., U.S.	B6	115
Sugar Land, Tx., U.S.	E5	136
Sugar Loaf, c., Tx., U.S.	C3	139
Sugarloaf Mountain, mtn., Mt., U.S.	C4	119
Sugar Notch, Pa., U.S.	n17	131
Suggi Lake, l., Sk., Can.	C4	91
Suğla Gölü, l., Tur.	D5	44
Suhag, Egypt	E11	48
Suhana, Russia	C13	26
Suhār, Oman	F7	38
Sühbaatar, Mong.	A9	28
Suhl, Ger.	E12	12
Suhona, stm., Russia	C6	26
Suiattle, stm., Wa., U.S.	A4	140
Suichang, China	D4	30
Suichuan, China	D3	30
Suide, China	D10	28
Suijiang, China	D1	30
Suining, China	E9	28
Suining, China	C4	30
Suitland, Md., U.S.	C4	113
Suixi, China	C4	30
Suiyang, China	B2	31
Suizhong, China	C12	28
Suizhou, China	E10	28
Sukabumi, Indon.	E3	36
Sukadana, Indon.	D3	36
Sukaraja, Indon.	D4	36
Sukarnapura see Jayapura, Indon.	G11	32
Sukhothai, Thai.	C3	34
Sukkertoppen, Grnld.	E29	82
Sukkozero, Russia	B5	22
Sukkur, Pak.	E9	42
Sukses, Nmb.	C2	56
Sukumo, Japan	D2	31
Sula, Kepulauan, is., Indon.	D7	36
Sulaimān Range, mts., Pak.	E9	42
Sulawesi (Celebes), i., Indon.	D6	36
Sulawesi, Laut see Celebes Sea, Asia	C6	36
Sulechów, Pol.	C3	20
Sullana, Peru	D3	70
Sulligent, Al., U.S.	B1	94
Sullivan, Il., U.S.	D5	106
Sullivan, In., U.S.	F3	107
Sullivan, Mo., U.S.	C6	118
Sullivan, co., In., U.S.	F3	107
Sullivan, co., Mo., U.S.	A4	118
Sullivan, co., N.H., U.S.	D2	122
Sullivan, co., N.Y., U.S.	D6	125
Sullivan, co., Pa., U.S.	D9	131
Sullivan, co., Tn., U.S.	C11	135
Sullivan Lake, l., Ab., Can.	D5	84
Sullivans Island, S.C., U.S.	k12	133
Sully, Ia., U.S.	C5	108
Sully, co., S.D., U.S.	C5	134
Sulmona, Italy	C4	18
Sulphur, La., U.S.	D2	111
Sulphur, Ok., U.S.	C5	129
Sulphur, stm., U.S.	C5	97
Sulphur Spring Range, mts., Nv., U.S.	C5	121
Sulphur Springs, Tx., U.S.	C5	136
Sultan, Wa., U.S.	B4	140
Sultānpur, India	D4	40
Sulu Archipelago, is., Phil.	F7	34
Sulūq, Libya	D9	48
Sulu Sea, Asia	E7	34
Sumas, Wa., U.S.	A3	140
Sumatera (Sumatra), i., Indon.	C2	36
Sumatra see Sumatera, i., Indon.	C2	36
Sumba, i., Indon.	F5	36
Sumba, Selat, strt., Indon.	E6	36
Sumbawa, i., Indon.	E5	36
Sumbawa Besar, Indon.	E5	36
Sumbawanga, Tan.	E6	54
Sumbe, Ang.	F2	54
Sumedang, Indon.	E3	36
Šumen, Bul.	C11	18
Sumenep, Indon.	E4	36
Šumerlja, Russia	C8	22
Šumiha, Russia	C11	22
Sumisu-jima, i., Japan	E16	28
Sumiton, Al., U.S.	B2	94
Summerfield, N.C., U.S.	A3	126
Summerford, Nf., Can.	D4	88
Summer Island, i., Mi., U.S.	C4	115
Summer Lake, l., Or., U.S.	E6	130
Summerland, B.C., Can.	E8	85
Summers, co., W.V., U.S.	D4	141
Summerside, P.E., Can.	C6	87
Summersville, W.V., U.S.	C4	141
Summersville Lake, res., W.V., U.S.	C4	141
Summerton, S.C., U.S.	D7	133
Summertown, Tn., U.S.	B4	135
Summerville, Ga., U.S.	B1	103
Summerville, S.C., U.S.	E7	133
Summit, Il., U.S.	k9	106
Summit, Ms., U.S.	D3	117
Summit, N.J., U.S.	B4	123
Summit, Wa., U.S.	h11	140
Summit, co., Co., U.S.	B4	99
Summit, co., Oh., U.S.	A4	128
Summit, co., Ut., U.S.	C5	137
Summit Hill, Pa., U.S.	E10	131
Summit Lake, l., Ia., U.S.	C3	108
Summit Lake Indian Reservation, Nv., U.S.	B2	121
Summit Mountain, mtn., Nv., U.S.	D5	121
Summit Peak, mtn., Co., U.S.	D4	99
Summitville, In., U.S.	D6	107
Sumner, Ia., U.S.	B5	108
Sumner, Il., U.S.	E6	106
Sumner, Wa., U.S.	B3	140
Sumner, co., Ks., U.S.	E6	109
Sumner, co., Tn., U.S.	A5	135
Sumner Dam, N.M., U.S.	C5	124
Sumner Strait, strt., Ak., U.S.	m23	95
Šumperk, Czech Rep.	E4	20
Sumqayıt, Azer.	B13	44
Sumrall, Ms., U.S.	D4	117
Šumšu, ostrov, i., Russia	D17	26
Sumter, S.C., U.S.	D7	133
Sumter, co., Al., U.S.	C1	94
Sumter, co., Fl., U.S.	D4	102
Sumter, co., Ga., U.S.	D2	103
Sumter, co., S.C., U.S.	D7	133
Sumy, Ukr.	D13	20
Sumzom, China	D7	40
Sun, stm., Mt., U.S.	C4	119
Sunapee, N.H., U.S.	D2	122
Sunapee Lake, l., N.H., U.S.	D2	122
Sunbright, Tn., U.S.	C9	135
Sunbury, Oh., U.S.	B3	128
Sunbury, Pa., U.S.	E8	131
Sunchales, Arg.	E5	72
Suncho Corral, Arg.	D5	72
Sun City, Az., U.S.	k8	96
Suncook, N.H., U.S.	D4	122
Suncook, stm., N.H., U.S.	D4	122
Suncook Lakes, l., N.H., U.S.	D4	122
Sunda, Selat, strt., Indon.	E3	36
Sundance, Wy., U.S.	B8	143
Sundance Mountain, mtn., Wy., U.S.	B8	143
Sundarbans, reg., Asia	B1	34
Sunda Shelf	H13	64
Sunda Strait see Sunda, Selat, strt., Indon.	E3	36
Sunderland, On., Can.	C5	89
Sunderland, Eng., U.K.	C6	12
Sundown, Austl.	F5	60
Sundown, Tx., U.S.	C1	136
Sundre, Ab., Can.	D3	84
Sundridge, On., Can.	B5	89
Sundsvall, Swe.	E7	10
Sunflower, Ms., U.S.	B3	117
Sunflower, co., Ms., U.S.	B3	117
Sunflower, Mount, mtn., Ks., U.S.	C2	109
Sungaidareh, Indon.	D2	36
Sungai Kolok, Thai.	E4	34
Sungai Petani, Malay.	B2	36
Sungari see Songhua, stm., China	B14	28
Sungari Reservoir see Songhua Hu, res., China	C13	28
Sungurlu, Tur.	B6	44
Sunland Park, N.M., U.S.	F3	124
Sunlight Creek, stm., Wy., U.S.	B3	143
Sunman, In., U.S.	F7	107
Sunne, Swe.	G5	10
Sunnyside, Nf., Can.	E5	88
Sunnyside, Wa., U.S.	C5	140
Sunnyvale, Ca., U.S.	k8	98
Sun Prairie, Wi., U.S.	E4	142
Sunray, Tx., U.S.	A2	136
Sunset, La., U.S.	D3	111
Sunset, Ut., U.S.	B4	137
Sunset Beach, Hi., U.S.	f9	104
Sunset Crater National Monument, Az., U.S.	B4	96
Sunset Lake, l., Vt., U.S.	D2	138
Sunshine, Austl.	H3	62
Suntar, Russia	C13	26
Suntar-Hajata, hrebet, mts., Russia	C16	26
Suntaug Lake, l., Ma., U.S.	f11	114
Sun Valley, Id., U.S.	F4	105
Sun Valley, Nv., U.S.	D2	121
Sunyani, Ghana	E4	50
Suojarvi, Russia	B5	22
Suomussalmi, Fin.	D13	10
Superior, Az., U.S.	D4	96
Superior, Mt., U.S.	C2	119
Superior, Ne., U.S.	D7	120
Superior, Wi., U.S.	B1	142
Superior, Wy., U.S.	E4	143
Superior, Lake, l., N.A.	B10	92
Superstition Mountains, mts., Az., U.S.	m10	96
Suphan Buri, Thai.	D4	34

Name	Map Ref.	Page
Suquamish, Wa., U.S.	B3	140
Suqutrā, i., Yemen	H6	38
Şūr, Leb.	F6	44
Şūr, Oman	F7	38
Sur, Point, c., Ca., U.S.	D3	98
Sura, stm., Russia	E15	6
Surabaya, Indon.	E4	36
Surakarta, Indon.	E4	36
Sūrat, India	E2	40
Sūratgarh, India	D2	40
Surat Thani, Thai.	E3	34
Surendranagar, India	E2	40
Surfside, Fl., U.S.	s13	102
Surfside Beach, S.C., U.S.	D10	133
Surgoinsville, Tn., U.S.	C11	135
Surgut, Russia	C9	26
Surigao, Phil.	E9	34
Surigao Strait, strt., Phil.	E9	34
Surin, Thai.	D4	34
Suriname, ctry., S.A.	C8	70
Surprise, Az., U.S.	k8	96
Surrey, N.D., U.S.	A4	127
Surry, co., N.C., U.S.	A2	126
Surry, co., Va., U.S.	C6	139
Surry Mountain Lake, res., N.H., U.S.	D2	122
Surt, Libya	D8	48
Surt, Khalīj, b., Libya	D8	48
Sürüç, Tur.	D8	44
Surulangun, Indon.	D2	36
Šuryškary, Russia	A12	22
Süsangerd, Iran	G13	44
Susanville, Ca., U.S.	B3	98
Suşehri, Tur.	B8	44
Susitna, stm., Ak., U.S.	C10	95
Susquehanna, Pa., U.S.	C10	131
Susquehanna, co., Pa., U.S.	C10	131
Susquehanna, stm., U.S.	A5	113
Susquehanna, West Branch, stm., Pa., U.S.	D5	131
Sussex, N.B., Can.	D4	87
Sussex, N.J., U.S.	A3	123
Sussex, Wi., U.S.	m11	142
Sussex, co., De., U.S.	F4	101
Sussex, co., N.J., U.S.	A3	123
Sussex, co., Va., U.S.	D5	139
Susuman, Russia	C16	26
Susurluk, Tur.	C3	44
Sutherland, S. Afr.	E3	56
Sutherland, Ia., U.S.	B2	108
Sutherland, Ne., U.S.	C4	120
Sutherlin, Or., U.S.	D3	130
Sutlej (Satluj), stm., Asia	D2	40
Sutter, co., Ca., U.S.	C3	98
Sutter Creek, Ca., U.S.	C3	98
Sutton, P.Q., Can.	D5	90
Sutton, Ne., U.S.	D8	120
Sutton, W.V., U.S.	C4	141
Sutton, co., Tx., U.S.	D2	136
Sutton Lake, res., W.V., U.S.	C4	141
Sutwik Island, i., Ak., U.S.	D8	95
Süüj, Mong.	B8	28
Suur Munamägi, hill, Est.	H12	10
Suva, Fiji	F11	58
Suwałki, Pol.	B7	20
Suwanee, Ga., U.S.	B2	103
Suwannee, co., Fl., U.S.	B3	102
Suwannee, stm., U.S.	C4	102
Suwannee Sound, strt., Fl., U.S.	C3	102
Suwanose-jima, i., Japan	F14	28
Suwarrow, atoll, Cook Is.	F13	58
Suweis, Khalīg el- (Suez, Gulf of), b., Egypt	F10	14
Suweis, Qanâ el- (Suez Canal), Egypt	E10	14
Suwŏn, S. Kor.	D13	28
Suzak, Kaz.	B9	42
Suzhou, China	E12	28
Suzhou, China	E11	28
Svalbard, dep., Nor.	D20	144
Svaliava, Ukr.	E7	20
Svappavaara, Swe.	C9	10
Svatove, Ukr.	E15	20
Svay Riĕng, Camb.	D5	34
Sveg, Swe.	E6	10
Švenčionéliai, Lith.	I11	10
Svendborg, Den.	I4	10
Svensen, Or., U.S.	A3	130
Sverdlovsk see Ekaterinburg, Russia	D8	22
Sverdrup, ostrov, i., Russia	B9	26
Svetlahorsk, Bela.	C10	20
Svetlaja, Russia	E15	26
Svetlograd, Russia	A4	42
Svetlyj, Russia	D11	22
Svetlyj, Russia	D13	26
Svetogorsk, Russia	F13	10
Svirsk, Russia	A8	28
Svištov, Bul.	C10	18
Svitavy, Czech Rep.	E4	20
Svjatoj Nos, mys, c., Russia	A7	22
Svjatoj Nos, mys, c., Russia	B15	26
Svobodnyj, Russia	D14	26
Svolvær, Nor.	B6	10
Swabia see Schwaben, hist. reg., Ger.	F11	12
Swain, co., N.C., U.S.	f9	126
Swain Reefs, rf., Austl.	E5	62
Swainsboro, Ga., U.S.	D4	103
Swakopmund, Nmb.	C1	56
Swampscott, Ma., U.S.	B6	114
Swan, stm., Can.	C1	86
Swan Creek, stm., Oh., U.S.	e6	128
Swan Falls, wtfl, Id., U.S.	F2	105
Swan Hill, Austl.	H3	62
Swan Hills, Ab., Can.	B3	84
Swan Islands see Santanilla, Islas, is., Hond.	B3	80
Swan Lake, l., Mb., Can.	C1	86
Swan Lake, l., Me., U.S.	D4	112
Swan Lake, l., Ne., U.S.	C3	120
Swannanoa, N.C., U.S.	f10	126
Swan Peak, mtn., Mt., U.S.	C3	119
Swan Range, mts., Mt., U.S.	C3	119
Swan River, Mb., Can.	C1	86
Swansboro, N.C., U.S.	C5	126
Swansea, Wales, U.K.	E4	12
Swansea, Il., U.S.	E4	106
Swanson Lake, res., Ne., U.S.	D4	120
Swanton, Oh., U.S.	A2	128
Swanton, Vt., U.S.	B2	138
Swanzey Center, N.H., U.S.	E2	122
Swarthmore, Pa., U.S.	p20	131
Swartswood Lake, l., N.J., U.S.	A3	123
Swartz Creek, Mi., U.S.	F7	115
Swayzee, In., U.S.	C6	107
Swaziland, ctry., Afr.	D5	56
Swea City, Ia., U.S.	A3	108
Sweden, ctry., Eur.	E7	10
Swedru, Ghana	E4	50
Sweeny, Tx., U.S.	r14	136
Sweet Grass, co., Mt., U.S.	E7	119
Sweet Home, Or., U.S.	C4	130
Sweetser, In., U.S.	C6	107
Sweet Springs, Mo., U.S.	C4	118
Sweetwater, Tn., U.S.	D9	135
Sweetwater, Tx., U.S.	C2	136
Sweetwater, co., Wy., U.S.	E3	143
Sweetwater, stm., Wy., U.S.	D4	143
Sweetwater Creek, Fl., U.S.	p10	102
Sweetwater Creek, stm., Ok., U.S.	B1	129
Swellendam, S. Afr.	E3	56
Swepsonville, N.C., U.S.	A3	126
Świdwin, Pol.	C3	20
Świebodzin, Pol.	C3	20
Świecie, Pol.	C5	20
Swift, co., Mn., U.S.	E3	116
Swift, stm., N.H., U.S.	B4	122
Swift Creek, stm., N.C., U.S.	B5	126
Swift Creek, stm., Va., U.S.	n17	139
Swift Diamond, stm., N.H., U.S.	g7	122
Swifton, Ar., U.S.	B4	97
Swift Reservoir, res., Wa., U.S.	C3	140
Swindon, Eng., U.K.	E6	12
Swinomish Indian Reservation, Wa., U.S.	A3	140
Świnoujście, Pol.	C3	20
Swisher, Ia., U.S.	C6	108
Swisher, co., Tx., U.S.	B2	136
Swissvale, Pa., U.S.	k14	131
Switzer, W.V., U.S.	D3	141
Switzerland, Fl., U.S.	m8	102
Switzerland, co., In., U.S.	G7	107
Switzerland, ctry., Eur.	A2	18
Swoyerville, Pa., U.S.	D10	131
Syalah, Russia	C14	26
Sycamore, Al., U.S.	B3	94
Sycamore, Il., U.S.	B5	106
Sycamore, Oh., U.S.	B2	128
Sycamore Creek, stm., W.V., U.S.	m13	141
Sydenham, On., Can.	C8	89
Sydney, Austl.	G5	62
Sykesville, Md., U.S.	B4	113
Sykesville, Pa., U.S.	D4	131
Syktyvkar, Russia	C7	26
Sylacauga, Al., U.S.	B3	94
Sylhet, Bngl.	E6	40
Sylt, i., Ger.	C11	12
Sylva, N.C., U.S.	f9	126
Sylvania, Al., U.S.	A4	94
Sylvania, Ga., U.S.	D5	103
Sylvania, Oh., U.S.	A2	128
Sylvan Lake, Ab., Can.	C3	84
Sylvan Lake, Mi., U.S.	o15	115
Sylvan Lake, l., In., U.S.	B7	107
Sylvan Pass, Wy., U.S.	B2	143
Sylvester, Ga., U.S.	E3	103
Sym, Russia	C10	26
Šymkent, Kaz.	E8	26
Symmes Creek, stm., Oh., U.S.	D3	128
Symsonia, Ky., U.S.	f9	110
Syracuse, In., U.S.	B6	107
Syracuse, Ks., U.S.	E2	109
Syracuse, Ne., U.S.	D9	120
Syracuse, N.Y., U.S.	B4	125
Syracuse, Ut., U.S.	B3	137
Syrdarja, Uzb.	B9	42
Syr Darya (Syrdar'ja), stm., Asia	B9	42
Syria, ctry., Asia	E8	44
Syriam, Myan.	C3	34
Syrian Desert, des., Asia	F8	44
Syros see Ermoúpolis, Grc.	F10	18
Sysladobsis Lake, l., Me., U.S.	C4	112
Syvash, zatoka, strt., Ukr.	F13	20
Syzran', Russia	D6	26
Szamotuły, Pol.	C4	20
Szczecin, Pol.	C3	20
Szczecinek, Pol.	C4	20
Szczytno, Pol.	C6	20
Szechwan see Sichuan, prov., China	E8	28
Szeged, Hung.	F6	20
Székesfehérvár, Hung.	F5	20
Szekszárd, Hung.	F5	20
Szentes, Hung.	F6	20
Szolnok, Hung.	F6	20
Szombathely, Hung.	F4	20

T

Name	Map Ref.	Page
Tabar Islands, is., Pap. N. Gui.	G13	32
Tabarka, Tun.	F2	18
Tabasco, state, Mex.	D6	78
Tabayin, Myan.	B3	34
Tabbys Peak, mtn., Ut., U.S.	C3	137
Tabelbala, Alg.	E4	48
Taber, Ab., Can.	E4	84
Tablas Island, i., Phil.	D8	34
Table Head, c., Nf., Can.	B4	88
Table Mountain, mtn., Az., U.S.	E5	96
Table Rock Lake, res., U.S.	E4	118
Table Top, mtn., Az., U.S.	E3	96
Tábor, Czech Rep.	E3	20
Tabor, Russia	B17	26
Tabor, Ia., U.S.	D2	108
Tabor City, N.C., U.S.	C4	126
Tabora, Tan.	D6	54
Tabou, C. Iv.	F3	50
Tabrīz, Iran	C5	42
Tabūk, Sau. Ar.	E3	38
Tabuleiro do Norte, Braz.	C4	74
Täby, Swe.	G8	10
Tacloban, Phil.	D9	34
Tacna, Peru	G5	70
Tacoma, Wa., U.S.	B3	140
Taconic Range, mts., U.S.	A1	114
Tacuarembó, Ur.	E6	72
Tacurong, Phil.	E8	34
Tademaït, Plateau du, plat., Alg.	E5	48
Tadjemout, Alg.	A5	50
Tadoussac, P.Q., Can.	A8	90
T'aebaek-sanmaek, mts., Asia	D13	28
Taegu, S. Kor.	D13	28
Taejŏn, S. Kor.	D13	28
Tafalla, Spain	F6	16
Tafo, Ghana	E4	50
Taft, Ca., U.S.	E4	98
Taft, Tx., U.S.	F4	136
Taganrog, Russia	F15	20
Tagânt, reg., Maur.	C2	50
Tagaytay, Phil.	D8	34
Tagbilaran, Phil.	E8	34
Taguke, China	E4	28
Tagum, Phil.	E9	34
Tagus, stm., Eur.	H2	16
Tahan, Gunong, mtn., Malay.	C2	36
Tahat, mtn., Alg.	F6	48
Tahiataš, Uzb.	B7	42
Tahifet, Alg.	B6	50
Tahiti, i., Fr. Poly.	F15	58
Tahlequah, Ok., U.S.	B7	129
Tahoe, Lake, l., U.S.	D3	92
Tahoe, Lake, l., U.S.	E1	121
Tahoe City, Ca., U.S.	C3	98
Tahoka, Tx., U.S.	C2	136
Taholah, Wa., U.S.	B1	140
Tahoua, Niger	D6	50
Tahquamenon, stm., Mi., U.S.	B5	115
Tahsis, B.C., Can.	E4	85
Tahta, Egypt	F10	14
Tahta-Bazar, Turk.	C8	42
Tahtakupyr, Uzb.	B8	42
Tahtsa Peak, mtn., B.C., Can.	C4	85
Tahulandang, Pulau, i., Indon.	C7	36
Tahuna, Indon.	C7	36
Tai'an, China	D11	28
Taibai Shan, mtn., China	C2	30
Taibus Qi, China	A4	30
T'aichung, Tai.	E5	30
Taigu, China	B3	30
Taihang Shan, mts., China	B3	30
Taihape, N.Z.	o14	63c
Taihe, China	D3	30
Taihu, China	C4	30
Tai Hu, l., China	E11	28
Taikang, China	C4	30
Tailai, China	B12	28
Tai Lake see Tai Hu, l., China	E11	28
Taimba, Russia	C11	26
T'ainan, Tai.	E5	30
Taínaron, Ákra, c., Grc.	F9	18
Taínaron, Cape see Taínaron, Ákra, c., Grc.	F9	18
T'aipei, Tai.	D5	30
Taiping, Malay.	C2	36
Taisha, Japan	D3	31
Taishan, China	E3	30
Taishun, China	F11	28
Taitao, Península de, pen., Chile	G1	69
T'aitung, Tai.	E5	30
Taivalkoski, Fin.	D13	10
Taiwan, ctry., Asia	B8	34
Taiwan Strait, strt., Asia	E4	30
Taiyuan, China	D10	28
Taizhou, China	C4	30
Ta'izz, Yemen	H4	38
Tajikistan, ctry., Asia	B2	40
Tāj Mahal, hist., India	D3	40
Tajmyr, ozero, l., Russia	B12	26
Tajmyr, poluostrov, pen., Russia	B12	26
Tajšet, Russia	D11	26
Tak, Thai.	C3	34
Takāb, Iran	D12	44
Takalar, Indon.	E5	36
Takamatsu, Japan	E14	28
Takaoka, Japan	C3	31
Takasaki, Japan	C3	31
Takatsuki, Japan	D3	31
Takêv, Camb.	D4	34
Takhli, Thai.	C4	34
Takikawa, Japan	B4	31
Takla Lake, l., B.C., Can.	B5	85
Taklimakan Shamo, des., China	D4	28
Takoma Park, Md., U.S.	f8	113
Taku Glacier, Ak., U.S.	k22	95
Takum, Nig.	E7	50
Takutea, i., Cook Is.	F14	58
Talak, reg., Niger	C6	50
Talara, Peru	D3	70
Talas, Kyrg.	E9	26
Talasea, Pap. N. Gui.	H13	32
Talata Mafara, Nig.	D6	50
Talaud, Kepulauan, is., Indon.	C7	36
Talavera de la Reina, Spain	H4	16
Talawdī, Sudan	A6	54
Talbot, co., Ga., U.S.	D2	103
Talbot, co., Md., U.S.	C5	113
Talbot Island, i., Fl., U.S.	B5	102
Talbot Lake, l., Mb., Can.	B2	86
Talbotton, Ga., U.S.	D2	103
Talca, Chile	E2	69
Talcahuano, Chile	E2	69
Taldykorgan, Kaz.	E9	26
Talent, Or., U.S.	E4	130
Talgar, Kaz.	B11	42
Taliabu, Pulau, i., Indon.	D6	36
Taliaferro, co., Ga., U.S.	C4	103
Talihina, Ok., U.S.	C6	129
Talish Mountains see Ţavālesh, Kūhhā-ye, mts., Asia	D13	44
Taliwang, Indon.	E5	36
Talkeetna, Ak., U.S.	C10	95
Talkeetna Mountains, mts., Ak., U.S.	f17	95
Talladega, Al., U.S.	B3	94
Talladega, co., Al., U.S.	C4	94
Tall 'Afar, Iraq	D10	44
Tallahassee, Fl., U.S.	B2	102
Tallahatchie, co., Ms., U.S.	B3	117
Tallahatchie, stm., Ms., U.S.	B3	117
Tallangatta, Austl.	H4	62
Tallapoosa, Ga., U.S.	C1	103
Tallapoosa, co., Al., U.S.	C4	94
Tallapoosa, stm., Al., U.S.	C3	94
Tallassee, Al., U.S.	C4	94
Talleyville, De., U.S.	A3	101
Tallinn, Est.	G11	10
Tall Kūjik, Syria	D9	44
Tallmadge, Oh., U.S.	A4	128
Tallulah, La., U.S.	B4	111
Tal'nyj, Ukr.	E11	20
Talok, Indon.	C5	36
Tāloqān, Afg.	C9	42
Taloyoak, N.T., Can.	E21	82
Talquin, Lake, res., Fl., U.S.	B2	102
Talsi, Lat.	H10	10
Taltal, Chile	C2	69
Talu, Indon.	C1	36
Taluk, Indon.	D2	36
Tama, Ia., U.S.	C5	108
Tama, co., Ia., U.S.	B5	108
Tamale, Ghana	E4	50
Tamalpais, Mount, mtn., Ca., U.S.	h7	98
Tamaqua, Pa., U.S.	E10	131
Tamaroa, Il., U.S.	E4	106
Tamaulipas, state, Mex.	C5	78
Tamazulapan del Progreso, Mex.	D5	78
Tamazunchale, Mex.	C5	78
Tambacounda, Sen.	D2	50
Tambej, Russia	B9	26
Tambelan, Kepulauan, is., indon.	C3	36
Tamberías, Arg.	E4	72
Tambohorano, Madag.	B7	56
Tambora, Gunung, vol., Indon.	E5	36
Tambov, Russia	D6	26
Tambura, Sudan	I10	48
Tâmchekket, Maur.	C2	50
Tame, Col.	B5	70
Tamel Aike, Arg.	G2	69
Tamenghest, Alg.	F6	48
Tamiahua, Mex.	C5	78
Tamiahua, Laguna de, l., Mex.	C5	78
Tamiami Canal, Fl., U.S.	G6	102
Tamil Nādu, prov., India	G3	40
Tam Ky, Viet.	C5	34
Tampa, Fl., U.S.	E4	102
Tampa Bay, b., Fl., U.S.	E4	102
Tampere, Fin.	F10	10
Tampico, Mex.	C5	78
Tampico, Il., U.S.	B4	106
Tam Quan, Viet.	D5	34
Tamsagbulag, Mong.	B11	28
Tamu, Myan.	B2	34
Tamworth, Austl.	G5	62
Tana (Teno), stm., Eur.	B12	10
Tana, stm., Kenya	D7	54
Tanabe, Japan	D3	31
Tanafjorden, Nor.	A13	10
Tanaga Island, i., Ak., U.S.	E4	95
Tanahbala, Pulau, i., Indon.	D1	36
Tanahjampea, Pulau, i., Indon.	E5	36
Tanahmasa, Pulau, i., Indon.	D1	36
Tanahmerah, Indon.	H11	32
Tanami Desert, des., Austl.	D4	60
Tanana, Ak., U.S.	B9	95
Tanana, stm., Ak., U.S.	C10	95
Tananarive see Antananarivo, Madag.	B8	56
Tanch'ŏn-ŭp, N. Kor.	C13	28
Tandag, Phil.	E9	34
Ţăndărei, Rom.	G9	20
Tandil, Arg.	F6	72
Tanega-shima, i., Japan	E14	28
Taney, co., Mo., U.S.	E4	118
Taneycomo, Lake, res., Mo., U.S.	E4	118
Taneytown, Md., U.S.	A3	113
Tanezrouft, des., Afr.	E4	50
Tanga, Tan.	E7	54
Tanganyika see Tanzania, ctry., Afr.	E6	54
Tanganyika, Lake, l., Afr.	E5	54
Tanger, Mor.	C3	48
Tanggula Shan, mts., China	E5	28
Tanghe, China	C3	30
Tangier Island, i., Va., U.S.	C7	139
Tangier Sound, strt., Md., U.S.	D6	113
Tangipahoa, co., La., U.S.	D5	111
Tangipahoa, stm., La., U.S.	D5	111
Tangmai, China	C7	40
Tangra Yumco, l., China	C5	40
Tangshan, China	D11	28
Tangyin, China	B3	30
Tangyuan, China	A1	31
Tanhoj, Russia	A9	28
Tanimbar, Kepulauan, is., Indon.	E8	36
Tanjungbalai, Indon.	C1	36
Tanjungkarang-Telukbetung, Indon.	E3	36
Tanjungpandan, Indon.	D3	36
Tanjungpinang, Indon.	C2	36
Tanjungredep, Indon.	C5	36
Tānk, Pak.	D10	42
Tanna, i., Vanuatu	k9	62a
Tännäs, Swe.	E5	10
Tanner, Al., U.S.	A3	94
Tannu-Ola Mountains, mts., Asia	A6	28
Tanout, Niger	C6	50
Tanta, Egypt	D11	48
Tan-Tan, Mor.	A2	50
Tantoyuca, Mex.	C5	78
Tanzania, ctry., Afr.	E6	54
Taormina, Italy	F5	18
Taos, Mo., U.S.	C5	118
Taos, N.M., U.S.	A4	124
Taos, co., N.M., U.S.	A4	124
Taos Pueblo, N.M., U.S.	A4	124
Taoudenni, Mali	B4	50
Taounate, Mor.	E3	14
Taourirt, Mor.	E3	14
Tapa, Est.	G11	10
Tapachula, Mex.	E6	78
Tapajós, stm., Braz.	D8	70
Tapaktuan, Indon.	C1	36
Taphan Hin, Thai.	C4	34
Tāpi, stm., India	E2	40
Tappahannock, Va., U.S.	C6	139
Tappan, N.Y., U.S.	g13	125
Tappan, Lake, res., N.J., U.S.	g9	123
Tappan, Lake, res., Oh., U.S.	B4	128
Tapul Group, is., Phil.	E8	34
Tapurucuara, Braz.	D6	70
Taqāţu' Hayyā, Sudan	G12	48
Taquari Novo, stm., Braz.	G8	70
Tar, stm., N.C., U.S.	B5	126
Tara, On., Can.	C3	89
Tara, Russia	D9	26
Tarabuco, Bol.	B5	72
Ţarābulus (Tripoli), Leb.	E6	44
Ţarābulus (Tripoli), Libya	D7	48
Ţarābulus (Tripolitania), hist. reg., Libya	E7	14
Tarakan, Indon.	C5	36
Taranaki, Mount (Egmont, Mount), vol., N.Z.	o13	63c
Tarancón, Spain	G5	16
Taranto, Italy	D6	18
Taranto, Golfo di, b., Italy	D6	18
Taranto, Gulf of see Taranto, Golfo di, b., Italy	D6	18
Tarapoto, Peru	E4	70
Taraquá, Braz.	C6	70
Tarat, Alg.	A6	50
Tarata, Bol.	B4	72
Tarauacá, Braz.	E5	70
Tarawa, atoll, Kir.	D11	58
Tarazona, Spain	G6	16

Name	Map Ref.	Page
Tarbagatay Range, mts., Asia	B4	28
Tarbes, Fr.	F7	16
Tarboro, N.C., U.S.	B5	126
Tarbū, Libya	E8	48
Tarcoola, Austl.	G5	60
Tardoki-Jani, gora, mtn., Russia	B15	28
Taree, Austl.	G5	62
Tareja, Russia	B11	26
Tarentum, Pa., U.S.	E2	131
Tarfaya, Mor.	E2	48
Targhee Pass, U.S.	E7	105
Târgovişte, Bul.	C11	18
Târgovişte, Rom.	G8	20
Târgu Jiu, Rom.	G7	20
Târgu Mureş, Rom.	F8	20
Târgu-Neamţ, Rom.	F9	20
Târgu Ocna, Rom.	F9	20
Tarifa, Spain	I4	16
Tariffville, Ct., U.S.	B4	100
Tarija, Bol.	C5	72
Tarim, stm., China	C4	28
Tarim Pendi, China	D4	28
Tarīn Kowt, Afg.	D9	42
Tarkastad, S. Afr.	E4	56
Tarkio, Mo., U.S.	A2	118
Tarko-Sale, Russia	C9	26
Tarkwa, Ghana	E4	50
Tarma, Peru	F4	70
Tarn, stm., Fr.	F7	16
Tärnaby, Swe.	D6	10
Târnăveni, Rom.	F8	20
Tarnobrzeg, Pol.	D6	20
Tarnów, Pol.	E6	20
Tarpey, Ca., U.S.	D4	98
Tarpon, Lake, l., Fl., U.S.	o10	102
Tarpon Springs, Fl., U.S.	D4	102
Tarquinia, Italy	C3	18
Tarragona, Spain	G7	16
Tarrant, Al., U.S.	B3	94
Tarrant, co., Tx., U.S.	C4	136
Tarryall Mountains, mts., Co., U.S.	B5	99
Tarrytown, N.Y., U.S.	D7	125
Tarsus, Tur.	D6	44
Tartagal, Arg.	C5	72
Tärtär, Azer.	B12	44
Tartu, Est.	G12	10
Ţarţūs, Syria	E6	44
Tarutung, Indon.	C1	36
Tasāwah, Libya	A7	48
Tasbuget, Kaz.	B9	42
Taseko Mountain, mtn., B.C., Can.	D6	85
Ţashk, Daryācheh-ye, l., Iran	E6	42
Tashkent see Taškent, Uzb.	E8	26
Taškent, Uzb.	E8	26
Taškepri, Turk.	C8	42
Taşköprü, Tur.	B6	44
Tasman Basin	M18	64
Tasman Bay, b., N.Z.	p13	63c
Tasmania, state, Austl.	I4	62
Tasmania, i., Austl.	I3	62
Tasman Sea, Oc.	L18	64
Taşova, Tur.	B7	44
Tasso, Tn., U.S.	D9	135
Taštagol, Russia	D10	26
Tata, Hung.	F5	20
Tatarbunary, Ukr.	G10	20
Tatarija, state, Russia	D6	26
Tatarsk, Russia	D9	26
Tatarskij proliv, strt., Russia	E16	26
Tatarstan see Tatarija, state, Russia	D6	26
Tatar Strait see Tatarskij proliv, strt., Russia	E16	26
Tate, Ga., U.S.	B2	103
Tate, co., Ms., U.S.	A4	117
Tateville, Ky., U.S.	D5	110
Tatnam, Cape, c., Mb., Can.	f9	86
Tatta, Pak.	F9	42
Tattnall, co., Ga., U.S.	D4	103
Tatum, N.M., U.S.	D6	124
Tatvan, Tur.	C10	44
Tauá, Braz.	C3	74
Taučik, Kaz.	B6	42
Taujskaja guba, b., Russia	D17	26
Taum Sauk Mountain, mtn., Mo., U.S.	D6	118
Taunggyi, Myan.	B3	34
Taungup, Myan.	C2	34
Taunton, Eng., U.K.	E5	12
Taunton, Ma., U.S.	C5	114
Taunton, stm., Ma., U.S.	C5	114
Taupo, N.Z.	o14	63c
Taupo, Lake, l., N.Z.	o14	63c
Tauranga, N.Z.	o14	63c
Taureau, Réservoir, res., P.Q., Can.	C4	90
Taurus Mountains see Toros Dağları, mts., Tur.	D5	44
Ţavālesh, Kūhhā-ye, mts., Asia	D13	44
Tavares, Fl., U.S.	D5	102
Tavas, Tur.	D3	44
Tavda, Russia	D8	26
Tavda, stm., Russia	D8	26
Tavernier, Fl., U.S.	G6	102
Taveuni, i., Fiji	m11	63b
Tavşanlı, Tur.	C3	44
Tawakoni, Lake, res., Tx., U.S.	C4	136
Tawas City, Mi., U.S.	D7	115
Tawas Lake, l., Mi., U.S.	D7	115
Tawau, Malay.	C5	36
Tawitawi Group, is., Phil.	E8	34
Tawkar, Sudan	G12	48
Taxco de Alarcón, Mex.	D5	78
Taxkorgan Tajik Zizhixian, China	B3	40
Taylor, B.C., Can.	A7	85
Taylor, Ar., U.S.	D2	97
Taylor, Az., U.S.	C5	96
Taylor, Mi., U.S.	p15	115
Taylor, Pa., U.S.	D10	131
Taylor, Tx., U.S.	D4	136
Taylor, co., Fl., U.S.	B3	102
Taylor, co., Ga., U.S.	D2	103
Taylor, co., Ia., U.S.	D3	108
Taylor, co., Ky., U.S.	C4	110
Taylor, co., Tx., U.S.	C3	136
Taylor, co., W.V., U.S.	B4	141
Taylor, co., Wi., U.S.	C3	142
Taylor, stm., Co., U.S.	C4	99
Taylor, Mount, mtn., N.M., U.S.	B2	124
Taylor Mill, Ky., U.S.	k14	110
Taylor Mountain, mtn., Id., U.S.	E4	105
Taylor Park Reservoir, res., Co., U.S.	C4	99
Taylors, S.C., U.S.	B3	133
Taylors Falls, Mn., U.S.	E6	116
Taylors Island, i., Md., U.S.	D5	113
Taylorsville, In., U.S.	F6	107
Taylorsville, Ky., U.S.	B4	110
Taylorsville, Ms., U.S.	D4	117
Taylorsville, N.C., U.S.	B1	126
Taylorville, Il., U.S.	D4	106
Taymā', Sau. Ar.	E3	38
Taymyr Peninsula see Tajmyr, poluostrov, pen., Russia	B12	26
Tay Ninh, Viet.	D5	34
Taytay, Phil.	D7	34
Taz, stm., Russia	D9	26
Taza, Mor.	E3	14
Tazewell, Tn., U.S.	C10	135
Tazewell, Va., U.S.	e10	139
Tazewell, co., Il., U.S.	C4	106
Tazewell, co., Va., U.S.	e10	139
Tazovskij, Russia	C9	26
Tbessa, Alg.	C6	48
Tbilisi, Geor.	B11	44
Tchaourou, Benin	E5	50
Tchefuncta, stm., La., U.S.	D5	111
Tchibanga, Gabon	D2	54
Tchula, Ms., U.S.	B3	117
Tczew, Pol.	B5	20
Tea, S.D., U.S.	D9	134
Teague, Tx., U.S.	D4	136
Teakean Butte, mtn., Id., U.S.	C2	105
Teaneck, N.J., U.S.	h8	123
Teapa, Mex.	D6	78
Teaticket, Ma., U.S.	C6	114
Te Awamutu, N.Z.	o14	63c
Tebingtinggi, Indon.	C1	36
Tebingtinggi, Pulau, i., Indon.	C2	36
Téboursouk, Tun.	F2	18
Techlé, W. Sah.	B2	50
Tecka, Arg.	F2	69
Tecomán, Mex.	D4	78
Tecpan de Galeana, Mex.	D4	78
Tecuala, Mex.	C7	78
Tecuci, Rom.	C9	20
Tecumseh, On., Can.	E2	89
Tecumseh, Ks., U.S.	k14	109
Tecumseh, Mi., U.S.	G7	115
Tecumseh, Ne., U.S.	D9	120
Tecumseh, Ok., U.S.	B5	129
Tedžen, Turk.	F8	26
Teeli, Russia	D10	26
Teeswater, On., Can.	C3	89
Tefé, Braz.	D7	70
Tegal, Indon.	E3	36
Tégama, reg., Niger	C6	50
Tegucigalpa, Hond.	C2	80
Tehachapi, Ca., U.S.	E4	98
Tehachapi Mountains, mts., Ca., U.S.	E4	98
Tehama, co., Ca., U.S.	B2	98
Tehrān, Iran	C6	42
Tehuacán, Mex.	D5	78
Tehuantepec, Golfo de, b., Mex.	D6	78
Tehuantepec, Istmo de, Mex.	D6	78
Teide, Pico del, mtn., Spain	A1	50
Teixeira Pinto, Gui.-B.	D1	50
Tejo see Tagus, stm., Eur.	H3	16
Tekamah, Ne., U.S.	C9	120
Tekax, Mex.	C7	78
Tekeli, Kaz.	I12	28
Tekes, China	A4	40
Tekirdağ, Tur.	B2	44
Tekoa, Wa., U.S.	B8	140
Tekonsha, Mi., U.S.	F5	115
Telavi, Geor.	B11	44
Tel Aviv-Yafo, Isr.	D2	42
Teleckoe, ozero, l., Russia	A5	28
Telêmaco Borba, Braz.	C7	72
Telemark, prov., Nor.	G3	10
Telén, Arg.	F4	72
Telescope Peak, mtn., Ca., U.S.	D5	98
Telfair, co., Ga., U.S.	E4	103
Telford, Eng., U.K.	D5	12
Telford, Pa., U.S.	F11	131
Télimélé, Gui.	D2	50
Telkwa, B.C., Can.	B4	85
Tell City, In., U.S.	I4	107
Teller, co., Co., U.S.	C5	99
Tellicherry, India	G3	40
Tellico Plains, Tn., U.S.	D9	135
Telluride, Co., U.S.	D3	99
Telos Lake, l., Me., U.S.	B3	112
Telsen, Arg.	F3	69
Telukbatang, Indon.	D3	36
Teluk Intan, Malay.	C2	36
Tema, Ghana	E5	50
Temax, Mex.	C7	78
Tembilahan, Indon.	D2	36
Temecula, Ca., U.S.	F5	98
Teminaabuan, Indon.	D8	36
Temir, Kaz.	E10	22
Temirtau, Kaz.	E9	26
Témiscouata, Lac, l., P.Q., Can.	B9	90
Te-Moak Indian Reservation, Nv., U.S.	C6	121
Temora, Austl.	G4	62
Temosachic, Mex.	B3	78
Tempe, Az., U.S.	D4	96
Temperance, Mi., U.S.	G7	115
Temperance, stm., Mn., U.S.	C8	116
Temple, Ga., U.S.	C1	103
Temple, Ok., U.S.	C3	129
Temple, Pa., U.S.	F10	131
Temple, Tx., U.S.	D4	136
Temple Terrace, Fl., U.S.	o11	102
Temrjuk, Russia	G14	20
Temuco, Chile	E2	69
Tenafly, N.J., U.S.	B5	123
Tenaha, Tx., U.S.	D5	136
Tena Kourou, mtn., Burkina	D3	50
Tenāli, India	F4	40
Tenasserim, Myan.	D3	34
Tendaho, Eth.	H13	48
Ten Degree Channel, strt., India	H6	40
Ténéré, des., Niger	C6	50
Tenerife, i., Spain	A1	50
Tengchong, China	G7	28
Tenggara, Nusa (Lesser Sunda Islands), is., Indon.	E5	36
Tengiz, ozero, l., Kaz.	D8	26
Tengréla, C. Iv.	D3	50
Tengxian, China	B4	30
Tengxian, China	E3	30
Tenino, Wa., U.S.	C3	140
Tenke, D.R.C.	F5	54
Tenkeli, Russia	C16	26
Tenkiller Ferry Lake, res., Ok., U.S.	B6	129
Tenkodogo, Burkina	D4	50
Tenmile, stm., U.S.	B5	132
Tenmile Creek, stm., W.V., U.S.	k10	141
Tenmile Lake, l., Mn., U.S.	D3	116
Tennant Creek, Austl.	D5	60
Tennessee, state, U.S.	B5	135
Tennessee, stm., U.S.	B3	135
Tennessee Pass, Co., U.S.	B4	99
Tennessee Ridge, Tn., U.S.	A4	135
Tennille, Ga., U.S.	D4	103
Teno (Tana), stm., Eur.	B12	10
Tenosique, Mex.	D6	78
Tensas, co., La., U.S.	B4	111
Tensas, stm., La., U.S.	B4	111
Tensaw, stm., Al., U.S.	E2	94
Ten Sleep, Wy., U.S.	B5	143
Tenterfield, Austl.	F5	62
Ten Thousand Islands, is., Fl., U.S.	G5	102
Teófilo Otoni, Braz.	E3	74
Tepa, Indon.	E7	36
Tepehuanes, Mex.	B3	78
Tepic, Mex.	C4	78
Téra, Niger	D5	50
Teramo, Italy	C4	18
Terceira, i., Port.	F7	46
Terek, Russia	A11	44
Terek, stm., Russia	B5	42
Teresina, Braz.	C3	74
Tergüün Bogd uul, mtn., Mong.	C8	28
Termas de Río Hondo, Arg.	D5	72
Terme, Tur.	B7	44
Termez, Uzb.	F2	42
Términos, Laguna de, b., Mex.	D6	78
Ternej, Russia	A3	31
Terneuzen, Neth.	E8	12
Terni, Italy	C4	18
Ternopil', Ukr.	E8	20
Terpenija, mys, c., Russia	E16	26
Terra Alta, W.V., U.S.	B5	141
Terrace, B.C., Can.	B3	85
Terracina, Italy	D4	18
Terra Nova National Park, Nf., Can.	D4	88
Terrassa, Spain	G8	16
Terrebonne, P.Q., Can.	D4	90
Terrebonne, Or., U.S.	C5	130
Terrebonne, co., La., U.S.	E5	111
Terrebonne Bay, b., La., U.S.	E5	111
Terre Haute, In., U.S.	F3	107
Terre Hill, Pa., U.S.	F9	131
Terrell, Tx., U.S.	C4	136
Terrell, co., Ga., U.S.	E2	103
Terrell, co., Tx., U.S.	D1	136
Terrell Hills, Tx., U.S.	k7	136
Terrenceville, Nf., Can.	E4	88
Terry, Ms., U.S.	C3	117
Terry, Mt., U.S.	D11	119
Terry, co., Tx., U.S.	C1	136
Terrytown, Ne., U.S.	C2	120
Terryville, Ct., U.S.	C3	100
Teruel, Spain	G6	16
Teseney, Erit.	G12	48
Teshekpuk Lake, l., Ak., U.S.	A9	95
Teshio, Japan	B4	31
Tessalit, Mali	B5	50
Tessaoua, Niger	D6	50
Tesuque, N.M., U.S.	B4	124
Tete, Moz.	B5	56
Teteriv, stm., Ukr.	D10	20
Tetovo, Mac.	C8	18
Tetouan, Mor.	C3	48
Teulon, Mb., Can.	D3	86
Teutopolis, Il., U.S.	D5	106
Tevere, stm., Italy	C4	18
Teverya, Isr.	D3	42
Tewksbury, Ma., U.S.	A5	114
Texada Island, i., B.C., Can.	E5	85
Texarkana, Ar., U.S.	D1	97
Texarkana, Tx., U.S.	C5	136
Texas, co., Mo., U.S.	D5	118
Texas, co., Ok., U.S.	e9	129
Texas, state, U.S.	D3	136
Texas City, Tx., U.S.	E5	136
Texel, i., Neth.	D9	12
Texhoma, Ok., U.S.	e9	129
Texico, N.M., U.S.	C6	124
Texoma, Lake, res., U.S.	D5	129
Teziutlán, Mex.	D5	78
Tezpur, India	D6	40
Thabana-Ntlenyana, mtn., Leso.	D4	56
Thabazimbi, S. Afr.	C4	56
Thai Binh, Viet.	B5	34
Thailand, ctry., Asia	C4	34
Thailand, Gulf of, b., Asia	D4	34
Thai Nguyen, Viet.	B5	34
Thames, N.Z.	o14	63c
Thames, stm., On., Can.	E3	89
Thames, stm., Eng., U.K.	E7	12
Thames, stm., Ct., U.S.	D7	100
Thamesville, On., Can.	E3	89
Thāna, India	F2	40
Thanh Hoa, Viet.	C5	34
Thanh Pho Ho Chi Minh (Saigon), Viet.	D5	34
Thanjāvūr, India	G3	40
Tharād, India	E2	40
Thar Desert (Great Indian Desert), des., Asia	D2	40
Tharrawaddy, Myan.	C3	34
Tharros, hist., Italy	E2	18
Tharthār, Buhayrat ath-, res., Iraq	E10	44
Thásos, Grc.	D10	18
Thásos, i., Grc.	D10	18
Thatcher, Az., U.S.	E6	96
Thaton, Myan.	C3	34
Thayer, Mo., U.S.	E6	118
Thayer, co., Ne., U.S.	D8	120
Thayetmyo, Myan.	C3	34
Thayne, Wy., U.S.	D1	143
Thazi, Myan.	B3	34
Thealka, Ky., U.S.	C7	110
The Barrens, plat., Tn., U.S.	B5	135
Thebes see Thívai, Grc.	E9	18
The Dalles, Or., U.S.	B5	130
The Dells, val., Wi., U.S.	E4	142
Thedford, On., Can.	D3	89
The Everglades, sw., Fl., U.S.	G6	102
The Flat Tops, mts., Co., U.S.	B3	99
The Flume, wtfl, N.H., U.S.	B3	122
The Graves, is., Ma., U.S.	g12	114
The Hague see 's-Gravenhage, Neth.	D8	12
The Heads, c., Or., U.S.	E2	130
The Little Minch see Little Minch, The, strt., Scot., U.K.	B3	12
The Minch, strt., Scot., U.K.	A4	12
The Narrows, strt., Wa., U.S.	f10	140
Theodore, Al., U.S.	E1	94
Theodore Roosevelt Lake, res., Az., U.S.	D4	96
Theodore Roosevelt National Park (North Unit), N.D., U.S.	B2	127
Theodore Roosevelt National Park (South Unit), N.D., U.S.	C2	127
The Pas, Mb., Can.	C1	86
The Plains, Oh., U.S.	C3	128
Theresa, Wi., U.S.	E5	142
Thermaïkós Kólpos, b., Grc.	D9	18
Thermopílai, hist., Grc.	E9	18
Thermopolis, Wy., U.S.	C4	143
Thermopylae see Thermopílai, hist., Grc.	E9	18
The Rockies, mts., Wa., U.S.	C3	140
Thessalía, hist. reg., Grc.	E9	18
Thessalon, On., Can.	p19	89
Thessaloníki (Salonika), Grc.	D9	18
Thessaly see Thessalía, hist. reg., Grc.	E9	18
Thetford Mines, P.Q., Can.	C6	90
The Thimbles, is., Ct., U.S.	E5	100
The Valley, Anguilla	B7	80
The Village, Ok., U.S.	B4	129
The Wash, b., Eng., U.K.	D7	12
Thibodaux, La., U.S.	E5	111
Thief, stm., Mn., U.S.	B2	116
Thief Lake, l., Mn., U.S.	B3	116
Thief River Falls, Mn., U.S.	B2	116
Thielsen, Mount, mtn., Or., U.S.	D4	130
Thiensville, Wi., U.S.	E6	142
Thiès, Sen.	D1	50
Thika, Kenya	D7	54
Thimphu, Bhu.	D5	40
Thingvellir, Ice.	I18	10a
Thio, N. Cal.	I9	62a
Thionville, Fr.	C10	16
Thíra, i., Grc.	F10	18
Third Cataract, wtfl, Sudan	G11	48
Third Lake, l., N.H., U.S.	f7	122
Thisted, Den.	H3	10
Thistilfjördur, b., Ice.	k21	10a
Thívai, Grc.	E9	18
Thjórsá, stm., Ice.	m18	10a
Thomas, Ok., U.S.	B3	129
Thomas, co., Ga., U.S.	F3	103
Thomas, co., Ks., U.S.	C2	109
Thomas, co., Ne., U.S.	C5	120
Thomasboro, Il., U.S.	C5	106
Thomaston, Ct., U.S.	C3	100
Thomaston, Ga., U.S.	D2	103
Thomaston, Me., U.S.	D3	112
Thomaston Reservoir, res., Ct., U.S.	C3	100
Thomasville, Al., U.S.	D2	94
Thomasville, Ga., U.S.	F3	103
Thomasville, N.C., U.S.	B2	126
Thompson, Mb., Can.	B3	86
Thompson, Ct., U.S.	B8	100
Thompson, N.D., U.S.	B8	127
Thompson, stm., U.S.	A4	118
Thompson Falls, Mt., U.S.	C1	119
Thompson Island, i., Ma., U.S.	g11	114
Thompson Lake, l., Me., U.S.	D2	112
Thompson Peak, mtn., Ca., U.S.	B2	98
Thompson Peak, mtn., N.M., U.S.	h9	124
Thompson Reservoir, res., Or., U.S.	E5	130
Thomson, Ga., U.S.	C4	103
Thongwa, Myan.	C3	34
Thonon-les-Bains, Fr.	D10	16
Thonotosassa, Fl., U.S.	D4	102
Thonze, Myan.	C3	34
Thorburn, N.S., Can.	D7	87
Thoreau, N.M., U.S.	B1	124
Thornbury, On., Can.	C4	89
Thorndale, Tx., U.S.	D4	136
Thornton, On., Can.	C5	89
Thorntown, In., U.S.	D4	107
Thorold, On., Can.	D5	89
Thorp, Wi., U.S.	D3	142
Thorsby, Al., U.S.	C3	94
Thorshavn see Tórshavn, Far. Is.	n23	10b
Thórshöfn, Ice.	k21	10a
Thouars, Fr.	D6	16
Thousand Islands, is., N.Y., U.S.	A4	125
Thousand Lake Mountain, mtn., Ut., U.S.	E4	137
Thousand Springs Creek, stm., U.S.	B7	121
Thrace, hist. reg., Eur.	D11	18
Thrakikón Pélagos, Grc.	D10	18
Three Fingered Jack, mtn., Or., U.S.	C5	130
Three Forks, Mt., U.S.	E5	119
Three Hills, Ab., Can.	D4	84
Three Hummock Island, i., Austl.	I4	62
Three Kings Islands, is., N.Z.	n13	63c
Three Lakes, Wi., U.S.	C4	142
Three Mile Plains, N.S., Can.	E5	87
Three Oaks, Mi., U.S.	G4	115
Three Pagodas Pass, Asia	C3	34
Three Points, Cape, c., Ghana	F4	50
Three Rivers, Ma., U.S.	B3	114
Three Rivers, Mi., U.S.	G5	115
Three Rivers, Tx., U.S.	E3	136
Three Sisters, mtn., Or., U.S.	C5	130
Three Springs, Austl.	F2	60
Throckmorton, co., Tx., U.S.	C3	136
Throop, Pa., U.S.	m18	131
Thule (Qaanaaq), Grnld.	C26	82
Thun, Switz.	A1	18
Thunder Bay, On., Can.	o17	89
Thunder Bay, b., Mi., U.S.	D7	115

Name	Map Ref.	Page

Thunder Bay, stm., Mi., U.S. **D6** 115
Thunderbird, Lake, res., Ok., U.S. **B4** 129
Thunderbolt, Ga., U.S. **D5** 103
Thunder Butte Creek, stm., S.D., U.S. **B3** 134
Thurmont, Md., U.S. **A3** 113
Thurso, P.Q., Can. **D2** 90
Thurso, Scot., U.K. **A5** 12
Thurston, co., Ne., U.S. **B9** 120
Thurston, co., Wa., U.S. **C2** 140
Thy, reg., Den. **H3** 10
Thyolo, Mwi. **B6** 56
Tianchang, China **C4** 30
Tiandong, China **E2** 30
Tianguá, Braz. **B3** 74
Tianjin, China **D11** 28
Tianjun, China **D7** 28
Tianlin, China **E2** 30
Tianmen, China **E10** 28
Tianshui, China **E9** 28
Tiantai, China **F12** 28
Tianyang, China **E2** 30
Tianzhu, China **D8** 28
Tiassalé, C. Iv. **E4** 50
Tibasti, Sarīr, des., Libya **B8** 50
Tibati, Cam. **B2** 54
Tiber see Tevere, stm., Italy **C4** 18
Tiberias see Teverya, Isr. **D3** 42
Tibesti, mts., Afr. **B8** 50
Tibet see Xizang Zizhiqu, prov., China **E5** 28
Tibet, Plateau of see Qing Zang Gaoyuan, plat., China **E4** 28
Tiburón, Isla, i., Mex. **B2** 78
Tice, Fl., U.S. **F5** 102
Tîchît, Maur. **C3** 50
Tickfaw, stm., La., U.S. **C5** 111
Ticonderoga, N.Y., U.S. **B7** 125
Ticul, Mex. **C7** 78
Tidaholm, Swe. **G5** 10
Tide Head, N.B., Can. **B3** 87
Tidjikja, Maur. **C2** 50
Tiébissou, C. Iv. **E3** 50
Tieli, China **A1** 31
Tieling, China **C12** 28
Tien Shan, mts., Asia **C3** 28
Tientsin see Tianjin, China **D11** 28
Tierp, Swe. **F7** 10
Tierra Amarilla, N.M., U.S. **A3** 124
Tierra Blanca, Mex. **D5** 78
Tierra de Campos, reg., Spain **F4** 16
Tierra del Fuego, i., S.A. **H3** 69
Tietê, stm., Braz. **F1** 74
Tieton, Wa., U.S. **C5** 140
Tieton, stm., Wa., U.S. **C4** 140
Tieton Dam, Wa., U.S. **C4** 140
Tiffany Mountain, mtn., Wa., U.S. **A6** 140
Tiffin, Oh., U.S. **A2** 128
Tiffin, stm., Oh., U.S. **A1** 128
Tift, co., Ga., U.S. **E3** 103
Tifton, Ga., U.S. **E3** 103
Tigard, Or., U.S. **h12** 130
Tigerton, Wi., U.S. **D4** 142
Tighina, Mol. **F10** 20
Tignall, Ga., U.S. **C4** 103
Tignish, P.E., Can. **C5** 87
Tigris (Dicle) (Dijlah), stm., Asia **D5** 42
Tiguentourine, Alg. **F5** 14
Tihert, Alg. **D4** 14
Tihoreck, Russia **E6** 26
Tihvin, Russia **C5** 22
Tijuana, Mex. **A1** 78
Tikal, hist., Guat. **B2** 80
Tīkamgarh, India **E3** 40
Tikrīt, Iraq **D4** 42
Tikšeozero, ozero, l., Russia **C15** 22
Tiksi, Russia **B14** 26
Tilburg, Neth. **E9** 12
Tilbury, On., Can. **E2** 89
Tilden, Il., U.S. **E4** 106
Tilden, Ne., U.S. **B8** 120
Tilghman, Md., U.S. **C5** 113
Tilghman Island, i., Md., U.S. **C5** 113
Tilimsen, Alg. **D4** 48
Tillabéri, Niger **D5** 50
Tillamook, Or., U.S. **B3** 130
Tillamook, co., Or., U.S. **B3** 130
Tillanchãng Dwīp, i., India **H6** 40
Tillery, Lake, res., N.C., U.S. **B2** 126
Tillman, co., Ok., U.S. **C2** 129
Tillmans Corner, Al., U.S. **E1** 94
Tillsonburg, On., Can. **E4** 89
Tílos, i., Grc. **F11** 18
Tilton, Il., U.S. **C6** 106
Tilton, N.H., U.S. **D3** 122
Tiltonsville, Oh., U.S. **B5** 128
Timanskij krjaž, hills, Russia **C7** 26
Timaru, N.Z. **p13** 63c
Timaševsk, Russia **G15** 20
Timbalier Island, i., La., U.S. **E5** 111
Timbaúba, Braz. **C4** 74
Timbedgha, Maur. **C3** 50
Timberlake, Va., U.S. **C3** 139
Timberville, Va., U.S. **B4** 139
Timbuktu see Tombouctou, Mali **C4** 50
Timimoun, Alg. **E5** 48
Timirist, Râs, c., Maur. **C1** 50

Timişoara, Rom. **G6** 20
Timmins, On., Can. **o19** 89
Timmonsville, S.C., U.S. **C8** 133
Timms Hill, hill, Wi., U.S. **C3** 142
Timon, Braz. **C3** 74
Timor, i., Indon. **E7** 36
Timor Sea **F6** 58
Timošino, Russia **B6** 22
Timpanogos Cave National Monument, Ut., U.S. **C4** 137
Timşer, Russia **B9** 22
Tims Ford Lake, res., Tn., U.S. **B5** 135
Tinaca Point, c., Phil. **E9** 34
Tinaquillo, Ven. **C6** 80
Tindouf, Alg. **E3** 48
Tinghert, Ḥamādat, plat., Afr. **E7** 48
Tingmerkpuk Mountain, mtn., Ak., U.S. **B7** 95
Tingo María, Peru **E4** 70
Tingsryd, Swe. **H6** 10
Tinian, i., N. Mar. Is. **D12** 32
Tinker Air Force Base, mil., Ok., U.S. **B4** 129
Tinley Park, Il., U.S. **k9** 106
Tinniswood, Mount, mtn., B.C., Can. **D6** 85
Tinogasta, Arg. **D4** 72
Tínos, i., Grc. **F10** 18
Tinsukia, India **D7** 40
Tintina, Arg. **D5** 72
Tinton Falls, N.J., U.S. **C4** 123
Tioga, La., U.S. **C3** 111
Tioga, N.D., U.S. **A3** 127
Tioga, co., N.Y., U.S. **C4** 125
Tioga, co., Pa., U.S. **C7** 131
Tioga, stm., Pa., U.S. **B7** 131
Tiogue Lake, res., R.I., U.S. **D3** 132
Tioman, Pulau, i., Malay. **C2** 36
Tionesta Creek, stm., Pa., U.S. **C3** 131
Tionesta Lake, res., Pa., U.S. **D3** 131
Tioughnioga, stm., N.Y., U.S. **C4** 125
Tipitapa, Nic. **C2** 80
Tippah, co., Ms., U.S. **A5** 117
Tippah, stm., Ms., U.S. **A4** 117
Tipp City, Oh., U.S. **C1** 128
Tippecanoe, co., In., U.S. **D4** 107
Tippecanoe, stm., In., U.S. **C4** 107
Tipperary, Austl. **C5** 60
Tipton, Ca., U.S. **D4** 98
Tipton, Ia., U.S. **C6** 108
Tipton, In., U.S. **D5** 107
Tipton, Mo., U.S. **C5** 118
Tipton, Ok., U.S. **C2** 129
Tipton, co., In., U.S. **D5** 107
Tipton, co., Tn., U.S. **B2** 135
Tipton, Mount, mtn., Az., U.S. **B1** 96
Tiptonville, Tn., U.S. **A2** 135
Tirana see Tiranë, Alb. **D7** 18
Tiranë, Alb. **D7** 18
Tiraspol, Mol. **F10** 20
Tire, Tur. **C2** 44
Tirebolu, Tur. **B8** 44
Tiree, i., Scot., U.K. **B3** 12
Tírnavos, Grc. **E9** 18
Tiruchchirāppalli, India **G3** 40
Tirunelveli, India **H3** 40
Tirupati, India **G3** 40
Tiruppur, India **G3** 40
Tiruvannāmalai, India **G3** 40
Tirūvottiyūr, India **G4** 40
Tisa (Tisza) (Tysa), stm., Eur. **G6** 20
Tishomingo, Ok., U.S. **C5** 129
Tishomingo, co., Ms., U.S. **A5** 117
Tiskilwa, Il., U.S. **B4** 106
Tissemsilt, Alg. **J7** 16
Tīsta, stm., Asia **A1** 34
Tisza (Tisa) (Tysa), stm., Eur. **F6** 20
Titicaca, Lake, l., S.A. **E4** 68
Titilāgarh, India **E4** 40
Titograd see Podgorica, Yugo. **C7** 18
Titonka, Ia., U.S. **A3** 108
Titov Veles, Mac. **D8** 18
Titran, Nor. **E3** 10
Titule, D.R.C. **C5** 54
Titus, co., Tx., U.S. **C5** 136
Titusville, Fl., U.S. **D6** 102
Titusville, Pa., U.S. **C2** 131
Tivaouane, Sen. **C1** 50
Tiverton, On., Can. **C3** 89
Tiverton, R.I., U.S. **D6** 132
Tizimín, Mex. **C7** 78
Tizi-Ouzou, Alg. **C5** 48
Tjeggelvas, l., Swe. **C7** 10
Tjukalinsk, Russia **D9** 26
Tjul'gan, Russia **D10** 22
Tjumen', Russia **D8** 26
Tkibuli, Geor. **A10** 44
Tkvarčeli, Geor. **A9** 44
Tlahualilo de Zaragoza, Mex. **B4** 78
Tlalnepantla, Mex. **D5** 78
Tlaquepaque, Mex. **C4** 78
Tlaxcala, state, Mex. **D5** 78
Tlaxcala de Xicohténcatl, Mex. **D5** 78
Tmassah, Libya **A8** 50
Toamasina, Madag. **B8** 56
Toano, Va., U.S. **C6** 139

Toano Range, mts., Nv., U.S. **C7** 121
Toast, N.C., U.S. **A2** 126
Toba, Danau, l., Indon. **C1** 36
Tobacco Root Mountains, mts., Mt., U.S. **E5** 119
Tobago, i., Trin. **C7** 80
Toba Inlet, b., B.C., Can. **D5** 85
Toba Kākar Range, mts., Pak. **D9** 42
Tobejuba, Isla, i., Ven. **D7** 80
Tobin, Mount, mtn., Nv., U.S. **C4** 121
Tobin Lake, l., Sk., Can. **D4** 91
Tobin Range, mts., Nv., U.S. **C4** 121
Tobique, stm., N.B., Can. **B2** 87
Tobol, Kaz. **D11** 22
Tobol, stm., Asia **D8** 26
Tobol'sk, Russia **D8** 26
Tobyhanna, Pa., U.S. **D11** 131
Tocantínia, Braz. **E10** 70
Tocantinópolis, Braz. **C2** 74
Tocantins, state, Braz. **D2** 74
Tocantins, stm., Braz. **B2** 74
Toccoa, Ga., U.S. **B3** 103
Toccoa, stm., Ga., U.S. **B2** 103
Toccoa Falls, Ga., U.S. **B3** 103
Tocopilla, Chile **B2** 69
Todd, co., Ky., U.S. **D2** 110
Todd, co., Mn., U.S. **D4** 116
Todd, co., S.D., U.S. **D5** 134
Tofield, Ab., Can. **C4** 84
Tofino, B.C., Can. **E5** 85
Togiak, Ak., U.S. **D7** 95
Togian, Kepulauan, is., Indon. **D6** 36
Togo, ctry., Afr. **E5** 50
Togtoh, China **A3** 30
Togwotee Pass, Wy., U.S. **C2** 143
Tohakum Peak, mtn., Nv., U.S. **C2** 121
Tohatchi, N.M., U.S. **B1** 124
Tohopekaliga, Lake, l., Fl., U.S. **D5** 102
Toiyabe Range, mts., Nv., U.S. **D4** 121
Tok, Ak., U.S. **C11** 95
Tōkamachi, Japan **C3** 31
Tokat, Tur. **B7** 44
Tokelau, dep., Oc. **E12** 58
Tokmak, Kyrg. **A3** 40
Tokmak, Ukr. **F13** 20
Tokoroa, N.Z. **o14** 63c
Tokuno-shima, i., Japan **A9** 34
Tokushima, Japan **D2** 31
Tōkyō, Japan **D16** 28
Tōlañaro, Madag. **D8** 56
Topeka, Ks., U.S. **C8** 109
Toledo, Braz. **C7** 72
Toledo, Spain **H4** 16
Toledo, Ia., U.S. **B5** 108
Toledo, Il., U.S. **D5** 106
Toledo, Oh., U.S. **A2** 128
Toledo, Or., U.S. **C3** 130
Toledo Bend Reservoir, res., U.S. **E9** 92
Toledo Bend Reservoir, res., U.S. **C2** 111
Toler, Ky., U.S. **C7** 110
Toliara, Madag. **C7** 56
Tolima, Nevado del, vol., Col. **C4** 70
Tolitoli, Indon. **C6** 36
Toljatti, Russia **D6** 26
Tolland, Ct., U.S. **B6** 100
Tolland, co., Ct., U.S. **B6** 100
Tollesboro, Ky., U.S. **B6** 110
Tolleson, Az., U.S. **m8** 96
Tolo, D.R.C. **D3** 54
Tolo, Gulf of see Tolo, Teluk, b., Indon. **D6** 36
Tolo, Teluk, b., Indon. **D6** 36
Tolono, Il., U.S. **D5** 106
Tolstoj, mys, c., Russia **D17** 26
Tolt Reservoir, res., Wa., U.S. **B4** 140
Tolú, Col. **C4** 80
Toluca, Il., U.S. **B4** 106
Toluca de Lerdo, Mex. **D5** 78
Tomah, Wi., U.S. **E3** 142
Tomahawk, Wi., U.S. **C4** 142
Tomahawk Lake, l., Wi., U.S. **C4** 142
Tomakomai, Japan **C16** 28
Tomaszów Lubelski, Pol. **D7** 20
Tomaszów Mazowiecki, Pol. **D6** 20
Tomball, Tx., U.S. **D5** 136
Tombe, Sudan **B6** 54
Tombigbee, stm., U.S. **D1** 94
Tombouctou, Mali **C4** 50
Tombstone, Az., U.S. **F5** 96
Tombua, Ang. **B1** 56
Tomé, Chile **F3** 72
Tomé-Açu, Braz. **B2** 74
Tomelloso, Spain **H5** 16
Tom Green, co., Tx., U.S. **D2** 136
Tomini, Indon. **C6** 36
Tomini, Gulf of see Tomini, Teluk, b., Indon. **D6** 36
Tomini, Teluk, b., Indon. **D6** 36
Tom Nevers Head, c., Ma. **D8** 114
Tomo, stm., Col. **B6** 70

Tompkins, co., N.Y., U.S. **C4** 125
Tompkinsville, Ky., U.S. **D4** 110
Tom Price, Austl. **E2** 60
Tomptokan, Russia **D15** 26
Toms, stm., N.J., U.S. **C4** 123
Tomsk, Russia **D10** 26
Toms River, N.J., U.S. **D4** 123
Tonalá, Mex. **D6** 78
Tonasket, Wa., U.S. **A6** 140
Tonawanda Indian Reservation, N.Y., U.S. **B2** 125
Tondano, Indon. **C6** 36
Tonekābon, Iran **C6** 42
Tonga, ctry., Oc. **F12** 58
Tonganoxie, Ks., U.S. **C8** 109
Tonga Ridge **J21** 64
Tongatapu, i., Tonga **G12** 58
Tonga Trench **K21** 64
Tongcheng, China **E11** 28
Tongchuan, China **D9** 28
Tongguan, China **E10** 28
Tonghai, China **G8** 28
Tonghua, China **C13** 28
Tongjiang, China **C2** 30
Tongjiang, China **A2** 31
Tongjosŏn-man, b., N. Kor. **D13** 28
Tongliao, China **C12** 28
Tongoy, Chile **D2** 69
Tongren, China **F9** 28
Tongren, China **B1** 30
Tongsa Dzong, Bhu. **D6** 40
Tongtian, stm., China **E7** 28
Tongue, stm., Mt., U.S. **E10** 119
Tongue, stm., Tx., U.S. **p13** 136
Tongxian, China **D11** 28
Tongyu, China **C12** 28
Tongzi, China **F9** 28
Tonk, India **D3** 40
Tonkawa, Ok., U.S. **A4** 129
Tonkin, Gulf of, b., Asia **B5** 34
Tônlé Sab, Bœng, l., Camb. **D4** 34
Tonle Sap see Tônlé Sab, Bœng, l., Camb. **D4** 34
Tonopah, Nv., U.S. **E4** 121
Tønsberg, Nor. **G4** 10
Tonstad, Nor. **G2** 10
Tonto National Monument, Az., U.S. **D4** 96
Tonto Natural Bridge, Az., U.S. **C4** 96
Tooele, Ut., U.S. **C3** 137
Tooele, co., Ut., U.S. **C2** 137
Toole, co., Mt., U.S. **B5** 119
Toombs, co., Ga., U.S. **D4** 103
Toomsboro, Ga., U.S. **D3** 103
Toora-Hem, Russia **D11** 26
Toowoomba, Austl. **F5** 62
Topeka, Al., U.S. **A6** 107
Topeka, Ks., U.S. **C8** 109
Topock, Az., U.S. **C1** 96
Topol'čany, Slvk. **E5** 20
Topolobampo, Mex. **B3** 78
Topozero, ozero, l., Russia **D14** 22
Toppenish, Wa., U.S. **C5** 140
Topsail, Ma., U.S. **A6** 114
Topsham, Me., U.S. **E3** 112
Top Springs, Austl. **D5** 60
Topton, Pa., U.S. **F10** 131
Toquima Range, mts., Nv., U.S. **E5** 121
Tor, Eth. **B6** 54
Torbalı, Tur. **C2** 44
Torbat-e Ḥeydarīyeh, Iran **C7** 42
Torbat-e Jām, Iran **C8** 42
Torbay, Nf., Can. **E5** 88
Torbay see Torquay, Eng., U.K. **E5** 12
Torbert, Mount, mtn., Ak., U.S. **g15** 95
Torch Lake, l., Mi., U.S. **D5** 115
Tordesillas, Spain **G4** 16
Töre, Swe. **D10** 10
Torez, Ukr. **E15** 20
Torino (Turin), Italy **B1** 18
Torit, Sudan **J11** 48
Tornälven (Tornionjoki), stm., Eur. **C9** 10
Torneträsk, l., Swe. **B8** 10
Torngat Mountains, mts., Can. **f8** 88
Tornio, Fin. **D11** 10
Tornionjoki (Torneälven), stm., Eur. **C10** 10
Tornquist, Arg. **F5** 72
Toro, Spain **G4** 16
Toronto, On., Can. **D5** 89
Toronto, Oh., U.S. **B5** 128
Toronto Lake, res., Ks., U.S. **E7** 109
Toro Peak, mtn., Ca., U.S. **F5** 98
Tororo, Ug. **C6** 54
Toros Dağları, mts., Tur. **D5** 44
Torquay, Eng., U.K. **E5** 12
Torrance, Ca., U.S. **n12** 98
Torrance, co., N.M., U.S. **C3** 124
Torrelavega, Spain **F4** 16
Torremolinos, Spain **I4** 16
Torrens, Lake, l., Austl. **G2** 62
Torrent, Spain **H6** 16
Torreón, Mex. **B4** 78
Torres, Îles, is., Vanuatu **j9** 62a
Torres Strait, strt., Oc. **B3** 62
Torres Vedras, Port. **H2** 16
Torrington, Ct., U.S. **B3** 100
Torrington, Wy., U.S. **D8** 143
Tórshavn, Far. Is. **n23** 10b

Tórtolas, Cerro las, mtn., S.A. **D4** 72
Tortosa, Spain **G7** 16
Tortue, Île de la, i., Haiti **A5** 80
Toruń, Pol. **C5** 20
Toržok, Russia **C5** 22
Tostado, Arg. **D5** 72
Tōstamaa, Est. **G10** 10
Tosya, Tur. **B5** 44
Totagatic, stm., Wi., U.S. **B2** 142
Totana, Spain **I6** 16
Toteng, Bots. **C3** 56
Tot'ma, Russia **B7** 22
Totowa, N.J., U.S. **B4** 123
Totson Mountain, mtn., Ak., U.S. **C8** 95
Tottenham (part of Alliston Beeton Tecumseth and Tottenham), On., Can. **C5** 89
Tottori, Japan **C2** 31
Touba, C. Iv. **E3** 50
Toubkal, Jebel, mtn., Mor. **D3** 48
Touchet, stm., Wa., U.S. **C7** 140
Toudao see Songhua, stm., China **B14** 28
Touggourt, Alg. **D6** 48
Touisset, Ma., U.S. **C5** 114
Toul, Fr. **C9** 16
Touliu, Tai. **E5** 30
Toulon, Fr. **F9** 16
Toulon, Il., U.S. **B4** 106
Toulouse, Fr. **F7** 16
Toumodi, C. Iv. **E3** 50
Toungoo, Myan. **C3** 34
Touraine, hist. reg., Fr. **D7** 16
Tournai, Bel. **E8** 12
Tours, Fr. **D7** 16
Toussaint Creek, stm., Oh., U.S. **f7** 128
Toussidé, Pic, vol., Chad **B8** 50
Toutle, North Fork, stm., Wa., U.S. **C3** 140
Touwsrivier, S. Afr. **E3** 56
Tovarkovskij, Russia **C15** 20
Tovuz, Azer. **B11** 44
Towanda, Il., U.S. **C5** 106
Towanda, Ks., U.S. **E7** 109
Towanda, Pa., U.S. **C9** 131
Towanda Creek, stm., Pa., U.S. **C8** 131
Tower City, Pa., U.S. **E8** 131
Town Creek, Al., U.S. **A2** 94
Towner, N.D., U.S. **A5** 127
Towner, co., N.D., U.S. **A6** 127
Towns, co., Ga., U.S. **B3** 103
Townsend, De., U.S. **C3** 101
Townsend, Mt., U.S. **D5** 119
Townshend Reservoir, res., Vt., U.S. **E3** 138
Townsville, Austl. **D4** 62
Towson, Md., U.S. **B4** 113
Towuti, Danau, l., Indon. **D6** 36
Toyama, Japan **C3** 31
Toyohashi, Japan **D3** 31
Toyota, Japan **C3** 31
Tozeur, Tun. **D6** 48
Trabzon, Tur. **B8** 44
Tracadie, N.B., Can. **B5** 87
Tracy, N.B., Can. **D3** 87
Tracy, P.Q., Can. **C4** 90
Tracy, Ca., U.S. **D3** 98
Tracy, Mn., U.S. **F3** 116
Tracy City, Tn., U.S. **D8** 135
Tracyton, Wa., U.S. **e10** 140
Tradewater, stm., Ky., U.S. **C2** 110
Traer, Ia., U.S. **B5** 108
Trafford, Pa., U.S. **k14** 131
Trafford, Lake, l., Fl., U.S. **F5** 102
Trail, B.C., Can. **E9** 85
Trail Creek, In., U.S. **A4** 107
Traill, co., N.D., U.S. **B8** 127
Trail Ridge, mtn., U.S. **F4** 103
Tralee, Ire. **D2** 12
Tranås, Swe. **G6** 10
Trancas, Arg. **D4** 72
Trang, Thai. **E3** 34
Trangan, Pulau, i., Indon. **E8** 36
Trani, Italy **D6** 18
Transantarctic Mountains, mts., Ant. **E32** 67
Transkei, hist. reg., S. Afr. **E4** 56
Transylvania, co., N.C., U.S. **f10** 126
Transylvania, hist. reg., Rom. **F7** 20
Transylvanian Alps see Carpaţii Meridionali, mts., Rom. **G7** 20
Trapani, Italy **E4** 18
Trappe, Md., U.S. **C5** 113
Trapper Peak, mtn., Mt., U.S. **E2** 119
Traralgon, Austl. **H4** 62
Trârza, reg., Maur. **C1** 50
Trasimeno, Lago, l., Italy **E3** 18
Travelers Rest, S.C., U.S. **B3** 133
Traverse, co., Mn., U.S. **E2** 116
Traverse, Lake, l., U.S. **B9** 134
Traverse City, Mi., U.S. **D5** 115
Tra Vinh, Viet. **E5** 34
Travis, co., Tx., U.S. **D4** 136
Travis Air Force Base, mil., Ca., U.S. **C2** 98
Travnik, Bos. **B6** 18
Tray Mountain, mtn., Ga., U.S. **B3** 103

Name	Map Ref.	Page
Trayning, Austl.	G2	60
Treasure, co., Mt., U.S.	D9	119
Treasure Island Naval Station, mil., Ca., U.S.	h8	98
Třebíč, Czech Rep.	E3	20
Trebišov, Slvk.	E6	20
Trego, co., Ks., U.S.	D4	109
Treherne, Mb., Can.	E2	86
Treinta y Tres, Ur.	E7	72
Trelew, Arg.	F3	69
Trelleborg, Swe.	I5	10
Tremblant, Mont, mtn., P.Q., Can.	C3	90
Tremont, Il., U.S.	C4	106
Tremont, Pa., U.S.	E9	131
Tremonton, Ut., U.S.	B3	137
Tremp, Spain	F7	16
Trempealeau, Wi., U.S.	D2	142
Trempealeau, co., Wi., U.S.	D2	142
Trempealeau, stm., Wi., U.S.	D2	142
Trenche, stm., P.Q., Can.	B5	90
Trenčín, Slvk.	E5	20
Trenque Lauquen, Arg.	F5	72
Trent, stm., Eng., U.K.	D6	12
Trent, stm., N.C., U.S.	B5	126
Trente et un Milles, Lac des, l., P.Q., Can.	C2	90
Trento, Italy	A3	18
Trenton, On., Can.	C7	89
Trenton, Fl., U.S.	C4	102
Trenton, Ga., U.S.	B1	103
Trenton, Il., U.S.	E4	106
Trenton, Mi., U.S.	F7	115
Trenton, Mo., U.S.	A4	118
Trenton, Ne., U.S.	D4	120
Trenton, N.J., U.S.	C3	123
Trenton, Oh., U.S.	C1	128
Trenton, Tn., U.S.	B3	135
Trepassey, Nf., Can.	E5	88
Trepassey Bay, b., Nf., Can.	E5	88
Tres Arroyos, Arg.	F5	72
Tresckow, Pa., U.S.	E10	131
Três Corações, Braz.	F2	74
Tres Esquinas, Col.	C4	70
Três Lagoas, Braz.	F1	74
Tres Marías, Islas, is., Mex.	C3	78
Três Marias, Represa de, res., Braz.	E2	74
Tres Puntas, Cabo, c., Arg.	G3	69
Três Rios, Braz.	F3	74
Tres Zapotes, hist., Mex.	D5	78
Treutlen, co., Ga., U.S.	D4	103
Treviso, Italy	B4	18
Trevor, Wi., U.S.	n11	142
Trevorton, Pa., U.S.	E8	131
Treynor, Ia., U.S.	C2	108
Trezevant, Tn., U.S.	A3	135
Triadelphia, W.V., U.S.	A4	141
Triadelphia Reservoir, res., Md., U.S.	B3	113
Triangle, Va., U.S.	B5	139
Tribune, Ks., U.S.	D2	109
Tricase, Italy	E7	18
Trichinopoly see Tiruchchirāppalli, India	G3	40
Trichūr, India	G3	40
Tri City, Or., U.S.	E3	130
Trident Peak, mtn., Nv., U.S.	B3	121
Trier, Ger.	F10	12
Trieste, Italy	B4	18
Trigg, co., Ky., U.S.	D2	110
Triglav, mtn., Slvn.	A4	18
Trigo Mountains, mts., Az., U.S.	D1	96
Tríkala, Grc.	E8	18
Trikora, Puncak, mtn., Indon.	G10	32
Tri Lakes, In., U.S.	B7	107
Trimble, Tn., U.S.	A2	135
Trimble, co., Ky., U.S.	B4	110
Trimont, Mn., U.S.	G4	116
Trincomalee, Sri L.	H4	40
Tring Jonction, P.Q., Can.	C6	90
Trinidad, Bol.	A5	72
Trinidad, Col.	B5	70
Trinidad, Cuba	A3	80
Trinidad, Co., U.S.	D6	99
Trinidad, Tx., U.S.	C4	136
Trinidad, Ur.	E6	72
Trinidad, i., Trin.	C7	80
Trinidad and Tobago, ctry., N.A.	F12	76
Trinidad Head, c., Ca., U.S.	B1	98
Trinity, Al., U.S.	A2	94
Trinity, Tx., U.S.	D5	136
Trinity, co., Ca., U.S.	B2	98
Trinity, co., Tx., U.S.	D5	136
Trinity, stm., Ca., U.S.	B2	98
Trinity, stm., Tx., U.S.	D5	136
Trinity Bay, b., Nf., Can.	D5	88
Trinity Islands, is., Ak., U.S.	D9	95
Trinity Mountain, mtn., Id., U.S.	F3	105
Trinity Mountains, mts., Ca., U.S.	B2	98
Trinity Peak, mtn., Nv., U.S.	C3	121
Trinity Range, mts., Nv., U.S.	C3	121
Trion, Ga., U.S.	B1	103
Tripoli see Țarābulus, Leb.	E6	44
Tripoli see Țarābulus, Libya	D7	48
Tripoli, Ia., U.S.	B5	108
Trípolis, Grc.	F9	18

Name	Map Ref.	Page
Tripolitania see Țarābulus, hist. reg., Libya	E7	14
Tripp, S.D., U.S.	D8	134
Tripp, co., S.D., U.S.	D6	134
Tripura, prov., India	E6	40
Tristan da Cunha Group, is., St. Hel.	M8	46
Triumph, La., U.S.	E6	111
Trivandrum, India	H3	40
Trnava, Slvk.	E4	20
Trochu, Ab., Can.	D4	84
Troick, Russia	D8	26
Troicko-Pečorsk, Russia	B10	22
Trois-Pistoles, P.Q., Can.	A8	90
Trois-Rivières, P.Q., Can.	C5	90
Trois-Rivières-Ouest, P.Q., Can.	C5	90
Troïts'ke, Ukr.	F11	20
Trollhättan, Swe.	G5	10
Tromsø, Nor.	B8	10
Trona, Ca., U.S.	E5	98
Tronador, Monte, mtn., S.A.	F2	69
Trondheim, Nor.	E4	10
Trondheimsfjorden, b., Nor.	E4	10
Trophy Mountain, mtn., B.C., Can.	D8	85
Trotwood, Oh., U.S.	C1	128
Troup, co., Ga., U.S.	C1	103
Trousdale, co., Tn., U.S.	A5	135
Trout, stm., Fl., U.S.	m8	102
Trout, stm., Vt., U.S.	B3	138
Trout Creek, On., Can.	B5	89
Trout Creek Pass, Co., U.S.	C5	99
Trout Lake, Wa., U.S.	D4	140
Trout Lake, l., On., Can.	o16	89
Trout Lake, l., Mn., U.S.	B6	116
Trout Lake, l., Wi., U.S.	B4	142
Troutman, N.C., U.S.	B2	126
Trout Peak, mtn., Wy., U.S.	B3	143
Trout River, Nf., Can.	D2	88
Troy, Al., U.S.	D4	94
Troy, Id., U.S.	C2	105
Troy, Il., U.S.	E4	106
Troy, Ks., U.S.	C8	109
Troy, Mi., U.S.	o15	115
Troy, Mo., U.S.	C7	118
Troy, Mt., U.S.	B1	119
Troy, N.C., U.S.	B3	126
Troy, N.H., U.S.	E2	122
Troy, N.Y., U.S.	C7	125
Troy, Oh., U.S.	B1	128
Troy, Pa., U.S.	C8	131
Troy, Tn., U.S.	A2	135
Troy see Truva, hist., Tur.	C2	44
Troyes, Fr.	C8	16
Troy Peak, mtn., Nv., U.S.	E6	121
Trubčevsk, Russia	C12	20
Truchas Peak, mtn., N.M., U.S.	B4	124
Trucial States see United Arab Emirates, ctry., Asia	F6	42
Truckee, Ca., U.S.	C3	98
Truckee, stm., U.S.	D2	121
Trujillo, Hond.	B2	80
Trujillo, Peru	E4	70
Trujillo, Spain	H4	16
Trujillo, Ven.	B5	70
Truk Islands see Chuuk Islands, is., Micron.	D9	58
Truman, Mn., U.S.	G4	116
Trumann, Ar., U.S.	B5	97
Trumansburg, N.Y., U.S.	C4	125
Trumbull, Ct., U.S.	E3	100
Trumbull, co., Oh., U.S.	A5	128
Trumbull, Mount, mtn., Az., U.S.	A2	96
Trussville, Al., U.S.	B3	94
Trustom Pond, l., R.I., U.S.	G3	132
Truth or Consequences (Hot Springs), N.M., U.S.	D2	124
Truva (Troy), hist., Tur.	C2	44
Tryon, N.C., U.S.	f10	126
Trzcianka, Pol.	C4	20
Tsaidam Basin see Qaidam Pendi, China	D6	28
Tsala Apopka Lake, l., Fl., U.S.	D4	102
Tsaratanana, Madag.	B8	56
Tsaratanana, mts., Madag.	A8	56
Tsau, Bots.	C3	56
Tsavo, Kenya	D7	54
Tschida, Lake, res., N.D., U.S.	C4	127
Tselinograd see Akmola, Kaz.	D9	26
Tses, Nmb.	D2	56
Tsévié, Togo	E5	50
Tshabong, Bots.	D3	56
Tshane, Bots.	C3	56
Tshela, D.R.C.	E2	54
Tshikapa, D.R.C.	E4	54
Tshofa, D.R.C.	E5	54
Tshumbe (Chiumbe), stm., Afr.	E4	54
Tsimlyansk Reservoir see Cimljanskoe vodohranilišče, res., Russia	E7	22
Tsintsabis, Nmb.	B2	56
Tsiombe, Madag.	D8	56
Tsiroanomandidy, Madag.	B8	56
Tsu, Japan	D3	31
Tsugaru-kaikyō, strt., Japan	C16	28

Name	Map Ref.	Page
Tsumeb, Nmb.	B2	56
Tsuruoka, Japan	D15	28
Tsushima, is., Japan	D1	31
Tsuyama, Japan	C2	31
Tswaane, Bots.	C3	56
Tual, Indon.	E6	36
Tualatin, stm., Or., U.S.	h11	130
Tuamotu, Îles, is., Fr. Poly.	F15	58
Tuamotu Ridge	J24	64
Tuangku, Pulau, i., Indon.	C1	36
Tuapse, Russia	E5	26
Tuba City, Az., U.S.	A4	96
Tuban, Indon.	E4	36
Tubarão, Braz.	D8	72
Tübingen, Ger.	F11	12
Țubruq, Libya	D9	48
Tubuai, i., Fr. Poly.	G15	58
Tucacas, Ven.	A6	70
Tucannon, stm., Wa., U.S.	C8	140
Tucano, Braz.	D4	74
Tuckahoe, N.Y., U.S.	h13	125
Tuckahoe, stm., N.J., U.S.	E3	123
Tuckanarra, Austl.	F2	60
Tucker, Ga., U.S.	h8	103
Tucker, co., W.V., U.S.	B5	141
Tucker Island, i., N.J., U.S.	E4	123
Tuckerman, Ar., U.S.	B4	97
Tuckernuck Island, i., Ma., U.S.	D7	114
Tuckerton, N.J., U.S.	D4	123
Tucson, Az., U.S.	E5	96
Tucumcari, N.M., U.S.	B6	124
Tucumcari Mountain, mtn., N.M., U.S.	B6	124
Tucupita, Ven.	B7	70
Tucuruí, Braz.	B2	74
Tucuruí, Represa de, res., Braz.	B2	74
Tudela, Spain	F6	16
Tudmur, Syria	E8	44
Tugaloo Lake, res., U.S.	B1	133
Tugela, stm., S. Afr.	D5	56
Tug Fork, stm., U.S.	C2	141
Tuguegarao City, Phil.	C8	34
Tugur, Russia	D15	26
Tujmazy, Russia	D9	22
Tukangbesi, Kepulauan, is., Indon.	E6	36
Țūkrah, Libya	E8	14
Tukums, Lat.	H10	10
Tukuyu, Tan.	E6	54
Tukwila, Wa., U.S.	f11	140
Tula, Mex.	C5	78
Tula, Russia	D5	26
Tulalip Indian Reservation, Wa., U.S.	A3	140
Tulancingo, Mex.	C5	78
Tulare, Ca., U.S.	D4	98
Tulare, co., Ca., U.S.	D4	98
Tulare Lake, l., Ca., U.S.	D4	98
Tularosa, N.M., U.S.	D3	124
Tularosa Mountains, mts., N.M., U.S.	D1	124
Tularosa Valley, val., N.M., U.S.	E3	124
Tulbagh, S. Afr.	E2	56
Tulcán, Ec.	C4	70
Tulcea, Rom.	G10	20
Tul'chyn, Ukr.	E10	20
Tule River Indian Reservation, Ca., U.S.	E4	98
Tule Valley, val., Ut., U.S.	D2	137
Tuli, Zimb.	C4	56
Tulia, Tx., U.S.	B2	136
Tullahoma, Tn., U.S.	B5	135
Tulle, Fr.	E7	16
Tully, Austl.	D4	62
Tulsa, Ok., U.S.	A6	129
Tulsa, co., Ok., U.S.	B6	129
Tuluá, Col.	E4	80
Tulun, Russia	D12	26
Tulungagung, Indon.	E4	36
Tumacacori National Monument, Az., U.S.	F4	96
Tumaco, Col.	C4	70
Tuman-gang (Tumen), stm., Asia	B1	31
Tumanovo, Russia	B13	20
Tumbarumba, Austl.	H4	62
Tumbes, Peru	D3	70
Tumble Mountain, mtn., Mt., U.S.	E7	119
Tumbler Ridge, B.C., Can.	B7	85
Tumen, China	C13	28
Tumen (Tuman-gang), stm., Asia	B1	31
Tumeremo, Ven.	B7	70
Tumkūr, India	G3	40
Tumuc-Humac Mountains, mts., S.A.	C8	70
Tumut, Austl.	H4	62
Tumwater, Wa., U.S.	B3	140
Tunceli, Tur.	C8	44
Tunduru, Tan.	F7	54
Tunga, Nig.	E6	50
Tungabhadra, stm., India	F3	40
Tungabhadra Reservoir, res., India	F3	40
Tungkang, Tai.	E5	30
Tungsha Tao (Pratas Island), i., Tai.	E4	30
Tuni, India	F4	40
Tunica, Ms., U.S.	A3	117
Tunica, co., Ms., U.S.	A3	117

Name	Map Ref.	Page
Tunis, Tun.	C7	48
Tunis, Golfe de, b., Tun.	F3	18
Tunis, Gulf of see Tunis, Golfe de, b., Tun.	F3	18
Tunisia, ctry., Afr.	D7	48
Tunja, Col.	B5	70
Tunkhannock, Pa., U.S.	C10	131
Tunk Lake, l., Me., U.S.	D4	112
Tunp Range, mts., Wy., U.S.	D2	143
Tunnel Hill, Ga., U.S.	B1	103
Tunp Range, mts., Wy., U.S.	D2	143
Tununak, Ak., U.S.	C6	95
Tunuyán, Arg.	E4	72
Tunxi, China	D4	30
Tuolumne, Ca., U.S.	D3	98
Tuolumne, co., Ca., U.S.	C4	98
Tuolumne, stm., Ca., U.S.	D3	98
Tupã, Braz.	F1	74
Tupaciguara, Braz.	E2	74
Tupelo, Ms., U.S.	A5	117
Tupiza, Bol.	C4	72
Tupper Lake, N.Y., U.S.	A6	125
Tupper Lake, l., N.Y., U.S.	A6	125
Tura, India	D6	40
Tura, Russia	C11	26
Tura, stm., Russia	D18	6
Turan, Russia	A6	28
Turan Lowland, pl., Asia	B7	42
Țurayf, Sau. Ar.	G8	44
Turbat, Pak.	E8	42
Turbeville, S.C., U.S.	D7	133
Turbo, Col.	B4	70
Turda, Rom.	F7	20
Turgaj, Kaz.	E8	26
Turgaj, stm., Kaz.	E8	26
Turgajskaja ložbina, reg., Kaz.	D8	26
Turgutlu, Tur.	C2	44
Turhal, Tur.	B7	44
Turia, stm., Spain	H6	16
Turin see Torino, Italy	B1	18
Turinsk, Russia	C11	22
Turkana, Lake see Rudolf, Lake, l., Afr.	C7	54
Turkestan, Kaz.	E8	26
Turkey, ctry., Asia	C3	38
Turkey, stm., Ia., U.S.	B6	108
Turkey Creek, stm., Ok., U.S.	A3	129
Turkey Point, c., Md., U.S.	B5	113
Turkish Republic of Northern Cyprus see North Cyprus, ctry., Asia	C2	44
Turkmenbaši, Turk.	E7	26
Turkmenistan, ctry., Asia	C7	42
Türkoğlu, Tur.	D7	44
Turks and Caicos Islands, dep., N.A.	D10	76
Turks Islands, is., T./C. Is.	A5	80
Turku (Åbo), Fin.	F10	10
Turley, Ok., U.S.	A6	129
Turlock, Ca., U.S.	D3	98
Turnbull, Mount, mtn., Az., U.S.	D5	96
Turneffe Islands, is., Belize	B2	80
Turner, Or., U.S.	C4	130
Turner, co., Ga., U.S.	E3	103
Turner, co., S.D., U.S.	D8	134
Turners Falls, Ma., U.S.	A2	114
Turner Valley, Ab., Can.	D3	84
Turnor Lake, l., Sk., Can.	m7	91
Turnu Măgurele, Rom.	H8	20
Turpan, China	C5	28
Turpan Pendi, depr., China	C5	28
Turquino, Pico, mtn., Cuba	B0	80
Turrell, Ar., U.S.	B5	97
Turret Peak, mtn., Az., U.S.	C4	96
Turtle Creek, Pa., U.S.	k14	131
Turtle Flambeau Flowage, res., Wi., U.S.	B3	142
Turtle Lake, N.D., U.S.	B5	127
Turtle Lake, Wi., U.S.	C1	142
Turtle Lake, l., Sk., Can.	D1	91
Turtle Mountain Indian Reservation, N.D., U.S.	A6	127
Turuhansk, Russia	C10	26
Tuscaloosa, Al., U.S.	B2	94
Tuscaloosa, co., Al., U.S.	B2	94
Tuscarawas, co., Oh., U.S.	B4	128
Tuscarawas, stm., Oh., U.S.	B4	128
Tuscarora Indian Reservation, N.Y., U.S.	B2	125
Tuscarora Mountain, mtn., Pa., U.S.	F6	131
Tuscarora Mountains, mts., Nv., U.S.	B5	121
Tuscola, Il., U.S.	D5	106
Tuscola, co., Mi., U.S.	E7	115
Tuscumbia, Al., U.S.	A2	94
Tuskegee, Al., U.S.	C4	94
Tusket, stm., N.S., Can.	E4	87
Tustumena Lake, l., Ak., U.S.	g16	95
Tutak, Tur.	C10	44
Tuticorin, India	H3	40
Tutrakan, Bul.	B11	18
Tuttle, Ok., U.S.	B4	129
Tuttle Creek Lake, res., Ks., U.S.	C7	109
Tuttlingen, Ger.	F11	12
Tutuila, i., Am. Sam.	F12	58
Tutupaca, Volcán, vol., Peru	G5	70
Tututalak Mountain, mtn., Ak., U.S.	B7	95
Tutwiler, Ms., U.S.	A3	117

Name	Map Ref.	Page
Tuva, state, Russia	D11	26
Tuvalu, ctry., Oc.	E11	58
Țuwayq, Jabal, mts., Sau. Ar.	F5	38
Tuxedo, N.C., U.S.	f10	126
Tuxedo Park, De., U.S.	i7	101
Tuxpan, Mex.	C3	78
Tuxpan de Rodríguez Cano, Mex.	C5	78
Tuxtepec, Mex.	D5	78
Tuxtla Gutiérrez, Mex.	D6	78
Tuyen Quang, Viet.	B5	34
Tuy Hoa, Viet.	D5	34
Tūysarkān, Iran	E13	44
Tuz, Iraq	E11	44
Tuz Gölü, l., Tur.	C5	44
Tuzigoot National Monument, Az., U.S.	C4	96
Tuzla, Bos.	B7	18
Tver', Russia	D5	26
Tweed, On., Can.	C7	89
Tweedsmuir Provincial Park, B.C., Can.	C4	85
Tweedy Mountain, mtn., Mt., U.S.	E4	119
Twelvepole Creek, stm., W.V., U.S.	C2	141
Twentymile Creek, stm., W.V., U.S.	C3	141
Twentynine Palms, Ca., U.S.	E5	98
Twentynine Palms Marine Corps Base, mil., Ca., U.S.	E5	98
Twiggs, co., Ga., U.S.	D3	103
Twillingate, Nf., Can.	D4	88
Twin Buttes, mtn., Or., U.S.	C4	130
Twin Buttes Reservoir, res., Tx., U.S.	D2	136
Twin City, Ga., U.S.	D4	103
Twin Creek, stm., Oh., U.S.	C1	128
Twin Falls, Id., U.S.	G4	105
Twin Falls, co., Id., U.S.	G4	105
Twin Knolls, Az., U.S.	m9	96
Twin Lakes, Ga., U.S.	F3	103
Twin Lakes, Wi., U.S.	F5	142
Twin Lakes, l., Ct., U.S.	A2	100
Twin Lakes, l., Ia., U.S.	B3	108
Twin Lakes, l., Me., U.S.	C4	112
Twin Mountains, mtn., Wy., U.S.	E7	143
Twin Peaks, mts., Id., U.S.	E4	105
Twin Rivers, N.J., U.S.	C4	123
Twinsburg, Oh., U.S.	A4	128
Twin Valley, Mn., U.S.	C2	116
Twisp, Wa., U.S.	A5	140
Two Harbors, Mn., U.S.	C7	116
Two Hills, Ab., Can.	C5	84
Two Mile Beach, N.J., U.S.	F3	123
Two Rivers, Wi., U.S.	D6	142
Two Rivers, North Branch, stm., Mn., U.S.	B2	116
Two Rivers, South Branch, stm., Mn., U.S.	B2	116
Tybee Island, Ga., U.S.	D6	103
Tygart Lake, res., W.V., U.S.	B5	141
Tygart River, Falls of the, wtfl, W.V., U.S.	k10	141
Tygart Valley, stm., W.V., U.S.	B4	141
Tyger, stm., S.C., U.S.	B4	133
Tyler, Mn., U.S.	F2	116
Tyler, Tx., U.S.	C5	136
Tyler, co., Tx., U.S.	D5	136
Tyler, co., W.V., U.S.	B4	141
Tyler, Lake, res., Tx., U.S.	C5	136
Tyler Branch, stm., Vt., U.S.	B3	138
Tyler Heights, W.V., U.S.	C3	141
Tylertown, Ms., U.S.	D3	117
Tymochtee Creek, stm., Oh., U.S.	B2	128
Tynda, Russia	D14	26
Tyndall, S.D., U.S.	E8	134
Tyndall Air Force Base, mil., Fl., U.S.	u16	102
Tyne, stm., Eng., U.K.	C5	12
Tyonek, Ak., U.S.	C9	95
Tyre see Şūr, Leb.	F6	44
Tyrifjorden, l., Nor.	F3	10
Tyrma, Russia	A14	28
Tyrone, N.M., U.S.	E1	124
Tyrone, Ok., U.S.	e9	129
Tyrone, Pa., U.S.	E5	131
Tyronza, Ar., U.S.	B5	97
Tyrrell, co., N.C., U.S.	B6	126
Tyrrhenian Sea, Eur.	D3	18
Tysa (Tisza), stm., Eur.	E7	20
Tysnesøya, i., Nor.	G1	10
Tzaneen, S. Afr.	C5	56

U

Name	Map Ref.	Page
Uaupés (Vaupés), stm., S.A.	C6	70
Ubá, Braz.	F3	74
Ubangi (Oubangui), stm., Afr.	D3	54
Ubatã, Braz.	D4	74
Ube, Japan	E14	28
Úbeda, Spain	I5	16
Uberaba, Braz.	E2	74
Uberlândia, Braz.	E2	74
Ubly, Mi., U.S.	E8	115
Ubon Ratchathani, Thai.	C4	34
Ubrique, Spain	I4	16
Ubundu, D.R.C.	D5	54
Učaly, Russia	D10	22

Name	Map Ref.	Page
Učami, Russia	C11	26
Ucar, Azer.	B12	44
Uchiura-wan, b., Japan	C16	28
Uchiza, Peru	E4	70
Učkuduk, Uzb.	B8	42
Ucluelet, B.C., Can.	E5	85
Ucon, Id., U.S.	F7	105
Udagamandalam, India	G3	40
Udaipur, India	E2	40
Udall, Ks., U.S.	E6	109
Uddevalla, Swe.	G4	10
Uddjaure, l., Swe.	D7	10
Udgīr, India	F3	40
Udine, Italy	A4	18
Udmurtia see Udmurtija, state, Russia	D7	26
Udmurtija, state, Russia	D7	26
Udon Thani, Thai.	C4	34
Udupi, India	G2	40
Ueda, Japan	C13	31
Uedinenija, ostrov, i., Russia	B10	26
Uele, stm., D.R.C.	C4	54
Uelʹkalʹ, Russia	C19	26
Uelzen, Ger.	D12	12
Ufa, Russia	D7	26
Uganda, ctry., Afr.	C6	54
Ugarit, hist., Syria	E6	44
Ugashik Lakes, l., Ak., U.S.	D8	95
Uglegorsk, Russia	E16	26
Uglič, Russia	C6	22
Uherské Hradiště, Czech Rep.	E4	20
Uhrichsville, Oh., U.S.	B4	128
Uhta, Russia	C7	26
Uíge, Ang.	E3	54
Uil, Kaz.	E9	22
Uinta, co., Wy., U.S.	E2	143
Uinta, stm., Ut., U.S.	C5	137
Uintah, co., Ut., U.S.	D6	137
Uintah and Ouray Indian Reservation, Ut., U.S.	C5	137
Uinta Mountains, mts., Ut., U.S.	C5	137
Uitenhage, S. Afr.	E4	56
Uivak, Cape, c., Nf., Can.	f9	88
Ujar, Russia	D11	26
Ujelang, atoll, Marsh. Is.	D10	58
Ujiji, Tan.	D5	54
Ujjain, India	E3	40
Ujungpandang, Indon.	E5	36
Uka, Russia	D18	26
Ukara Island, i., Tan.	D6	54
Ukerewe Island, i., Tan.	D6	54
Ukiah, Ca., U.S.	C2	98
Ukyr, Russia	B9	28
Ulaanbaatar (Ulan Bator), Mong.	B9	28
Ulaangom, Mong.	B6	28
Ulaan-Uul, Mong.	C10	28
Ulak Island, i., Ak., U.S.	E4	95
Ulan Bator see Ulaanbaatar, Mong.	B9	28
Ulan-Ude, Russia	D12	26
Ulan Ul Hu, l., China	C6	40
Ulchin, S. Kor.	C1	31
Ulcinj, Yugo.	D7	18
Ulhāsnagar, India	F2	40
Uliastay, Mong.	B7	28
Ulja, Russia	D16	26
Uljanovsk, Russia	D6	26
Ullŭng-do, i., S. Kor.	C2	31
Ulm, Ger.	F11	12
Ulónguè, Moz.	A5	56
Ulsan, S. Kor.	C1	31
Ulster, co., N.Y., U.S.	D6	125
Ulster, hist. reg., Eur.	C3	12
Ulu, Indon.	C7	36
Ulu, Russia	C14	26
Ulúa, stm., Hond.	B2	80
Ulubat Gölü, l., Tur.	B3	44
Ulundi, S. Afr.	D5	56
Ulungur Hu, l., China	B5	28
Uluru (Ayers Rock), mtn., Austl.	F5	60
Ulverstone, Austl.	I4	62
Ulysses, Ks., U.S.	E2	109
Umán, Mex.	C7	78
Uman, Ukr.	E11	20
Umanak, Grnld.	D29	82
Umarkot, Pak.	E9	42
Umatilla, Fl., U.S.	D5	102
Umatilla, Or., U.S.	B7	130
Umatilla, co., Or., U.S.	B8	130
Umatilla, stm., Or., U.S.	B7	130
Umatilla Indian Reservation, Or., U.S.	B8	130
Umba, Russia	A5	22
Umbagog Lake, l., U.S.	A4	122
Umboi Island, i., Pap. N. Gui.	H12	32
Umcolcus Lake, l., Me., U.S.	B4	112
Umeå, Swe.	E9	10
Umeälven, stm., Swe.	D9	10
Umm al-ʿAbīd, Libya	A8	50
Umm Durmān, Sudan	G11	48
Umm Lajj, Sau. Ar.	E3	42
Umnak Island, i., Ak., U.S.	E6	95
Umpqua, stm., Or., U.S.	D3	130
Umsaskis Lake, l., Me., U.S.	B3	112
Umtata, S. Afr.	E4	56
Umuarama, Braz.	H9	70
Umzinto, S. Afr.	E5	56
Unadilla, Ga., U.S.	D3	103
Unadilla, stm., N.Y., U.S.	C5	125
Unaí, Braz.	E2	74
Unalakleet, Ak., U.S.	C7	95
Unalaska Island, i., Ak., U.S.	E6	95
ʿUnayzah, Sau. Ar.	E4	38
ʿUnayzah, Jabal, mtn., Asia	F8	44
Uncasville, Ct., U.S.	D7	100
Uncompahgre, stm., Co., U.S.	C3	99
Uncompahgre Mountains, mts., Co., U.S.	C3	99
Uncompahgre Peak, mtn., Co., U.S.	C3	99
Underwood, Al., U.S.	B3	94
Underwood, N.D., U.S.	B4	127
Uneča, Russia	C12	20
Ungava, Péninsule d', pen., P.Q., Can.	g12	90
Ungava Bay, b., Can.	G26	82
Ungava Peninsula see Ungava, Péninsule d', pen., P.Q., Can.	F25	82
União, Braz.	B3	74
Uniãoda Vitória, Braz.	D7	72
União dos Palmares, Braz.	C4	74
Unicoi, Tn., U.S.	C11	135
Unicoi, co., Tn., U.S.	C11	135
Unicoi Mountains, mts., U.S.	D9	135
Unimak Island, i., Ak., U.S.	D7	95
Unimak Pass, strt., Ak., U.S.	E6	95
Unión, Arg.	F4	72
Union, Ky., U.S.	k13	110
Union, Mo., U.S.	C6	118
Union, Ms., U.S.	C4	117
Union, Or., U.S.	B9	130
Union, S.C., U.S.	B4	133
Union, Wa., U.S.	B2	140
Union, co., Ar., U.S.	D3	97
Union, co., Fl., U.S.	B4	102
Union, co., Ga., U.S.	B2	103
Union, co., Ia., U.S.	C3	108
Union, co., Il., U.S.	F4	106
Union, co., In., U.S.	E8	107
Union, co., Ky., U.S.	C2	110
Union, co., La., U.S.	B3	111
Union, co., Ms., U.S.	A4	117
Union, co., N.C., U.S.	B2	126
Union, co., N.J., U.S.	B4	123
Union, co., N.M., U.S.	A6	124
Union, co., Oh., U.S.	B2	128
Union, co., Or., U.S.	B8	130
Union, co., Pa., U.S.	E7	131
Union, co., S.C., U.S.	B4	133
Union, co., S.D., U.S.	E9	134
Union, co., Tn., U.S.	C10	135
Union, West Branch, stm., Me., U.S.	D4	112
Union Beach, N.J., U.S.	C4	123
Union Bridge, Md., U.S.	A3	113
Union City, Ca., U.S.	h8	98
Union City, Ca., U.S.	C2	103
Union City, In., U.S.	D8	107
Union City, Mi., U.S.	F5	115
Union City, N.J., U.S.	h8	123
Union City, Oh., U.S.	B1	128
Union City, Pa., U.S.	C2	131
Union City, Tn., U.S.	A2	135
Union Flat Creek, stm., Wa., U.S.	C8	140
Union Gap, Wa., U.S.	C5	140
Union Grove, Wi., U.S.	F5	142
Union Lake, l., N.J., U.S.	E2	123
Union Pier, Mi., U.S.	G4	115
Union Point, Ga., U.S.	C3	103
Union Springs, Al., U.S.	C4	94
Uniontown, Al., U.S.	C2	94
Uniontown, Ky., U.S.	C2	110
Uniontown, Oh., U.S.	B4	128
Uniontown, Pa., U.S.	G2	131
Union Village, R.I., U.S.	B3	132
Union Village Reservoir, res., Vt., U.S.	D4	138
Unionville, Ct., U.S.	B4	100
Unionville, Mo., U.S.	A4	118
United Arab Emirates, ctry., Asia	F6	42
United Arab Republic see Egypt, ctry., Afr.	E10	48
United Kingdom, ctry., Eur.	C6	12
United Nations Headquarters, N.Y., U.S.	h12	125
United States, ctry., N.A.	D6	92
United States Air Force Academy, mil., Co., U.S.	B6	99
United States Military Academy, mil., N.Y., U.S.	C6	125
United States Naval Academy, mil., Md., U.S.	C4	113
Unity Reservoir, res., Or., U.S.	C8	130
University City, Mo., U.S.	C7	118
University Heights, Ia., U.S.	C6	108
University Heights, Oh., U.S.	h9	128
University Park, Ia., U.S.	C5	108
University Park, N.M., U.S.	E3	124
University Park, Tx., U.S.	n10	136
University Place, Wa., U.S.	f10	140
Unnão, India	D4	40
Unuli Horog, China	B6	40
Ünye, Tur.	B7	44
Unža, stm., Russia	C7	22
Upata, Ven.	B7	70
Upernavik, Grnld.	D28	82
Upington, S. Afr.	D3	56
Upland, Ca., U.S.	m13	98
Upland, In., U.S.	D7	107
Upolu, i., Samoa	F12	58
Upolu Point, c., Hi., U.S.	C6	104
Upper Ammonoosuc, stm., N.H., U.S.	A4	122
Upper Arlington, Oh., U.S.	B2	128
Upper Arrow Lake, res., B.C., Can.	D9	85
Upperco, Md., U.S.	A4	113
Upper Darby, Pa., U.S.	G11	131
Upper Greenwood Lake, N.J., U.S.	A4	123
Upper Humber, stm., Nf., Can.	D3	88
Upper Hutt, N.Z.	p14	63c
Upper Iowa, stm., Ia., U.S.	A5	108
Upper Island Cove, Nf., Can.	E5	88
Upper Klamath Lake, l., Or., U.S.	E4	130
Upper Marlboro, Md., U.S.	C4	113
Upper New York Bay, b., U.S.	k8	123
Upper Red Lake, l., Mn., U.S.	B4	116
Upper Saddle River, N.J., U.S.	A4	123
Upper Sandusky, Oh., U.S.	B2	128
Upper Sheila [Haut Sheila], N.B., Can.	B5	87
Upper Volta see Burkina Faso, ctry., Afr.	D4	50
Uppland, hist. reg., Swe.	F7	10
Uppsala, Swe.	G7	10
Upright, Cape, c., Ak., U.S.	C5	95
Upshur, co., Tx., U.S.	C5	136
Upshur, co., W.V., U.S.	C4	141
Upson, co., Ga., U.S.	D2	103
Upton, P.Q., Can.	D5	90
Upton, Ky., U.S.	C4	110
Upton, Ma., U.S.	B4	114
Upton, Wy., U.S.	B8	143
Upton, co., Tx., U.S.	D2	136
Uraj, Russia	B12	22
Urakawa, Japan	B4	31
Ural, stm.	E9	22
Ural Mountains see Uralʹskie gory, mts., Russia	D7	26
Uralʹsk, Kaz.	D7	26
Uralʹskie gory (Ural Mountains), mts., Russia	D7	26
Urania, La., U.S.	C3	111
Ura-Tjube, Taj.	C9	42
Urbana, Il., U.S.	C5	106
Urbana, Oh., U.S.	B2	128
Urbancrest, Oh., U.S.	m10	128
Urbandale, Ia., U.S.	C4	108
Urbino, Italy	C4	18
Ures, Mex.	B2	78
Urfa see Şanlıurfa, Tur.	D8	44
Urgenč, Uzb.	E8	26
Ürgüp, Tur.	C6	44
Uribia, Col.	A5	70
Urjung-Haja, Russia	B13	26
Urjupinsk, Russia	D7	22
Urla, Tur.	C2	44
Urmia see Orūmīyeh, Iran	C5	42
Urmia, Lake see Orūmīyeh, Daryācheh-ye, l., Iran	C5	42
Uromi, Nig.	E6	50
Uroševac, Yugo.	C8	18
Urrao, Col.	D4	70
Uruapan del Progreso, Mex.	D4	78
Uruguai (Uruguay), stm., S.A.	E6	72
Uruguaiana, Braz.	D6	72
Uruguay, ctry., S.A.	E6	72
Uruguay (Uruguai), stm., S.A.	D6	72
Ürümqi, China	C5	28
Urundi see Burundi, ctry., Afr.	D5	54
Urup, ostrov, i., Russia	E17	26
Urziceni, Rom.	G9	20
Uržum, Russia	C8	22
Usa, Japan	D2	31
Uşak, Tur.	C3	44
Usakos, Nmb.	C2	56
Usborne, Mount, mtn., Falk. Is.	H5	69
Usedom, i., Eur.	B3	20
Ushuaia, Arg.	H3	69
Usinsk, Russia	C7	26
Usman', Russia	C15	20
Usoke, Tan.	C6	54
Usole-Sibirskoe, Russia	D12	26
Usquepaug, R.I., U.S.	F3	132
Ussuri (Wusuli), stm., Asia	E15	26
Ussurijsk, Russia	E15	26
Ustʹ-Barguzin, Russia	D12	26
Ustʹ-Belaja, Russia	C19	26
Ustʹ-Čaun, Russia	C19	26
Ustʹ-Cilʹma, Russia	A9	22
Ustʹ-Ilimsk, Russia	D12	26
Ústí nad Labem, Czech Rep.	D3	20
Ustinov see Iževsk, Russia	D7	26
Ustka, Pol.	B4	20
Ustʹ-Kamčatsk, Russia	D18	26
Ustʹ-Kamenogorsk, Kaz.	E10	26
Ustʹ-Koksa, Russia	A5	28
Ustʹ-Kujda, Russia	C15	26
Ustʹ-Kut, Russia	D12	26
Ustʹ-Lyža, Russia	A10	22
Ustʹ-Maja, Russia	C15	26
Ustʹ-Manʹja, Russia	B11	22
Ustʹ-Nera, Russia	C16	26
Ustʹ-Njukža, Russia	D14	26
Ustʹ-Tym, Russia	D10	26
Ust-Urt Plateau, plat., Asia	B7	42
Usu, China	C4	28
Usulután, El Sal.	C2	80
Usumacinta, stm., N.A.	D6	78
Ušumun, Russia	A13	28
Utah, co., Ut., U.S.	C4	137
Utah, state, U.S.	D4	137
Utah Lake, l., Ut., U.S.	C4	137
Ute Creek, stm., N.M., U.S.	A6	124
Ute Mountain Indian Reservation, U.S.	D2	99
Utena, Lith.	I11	10
Ute Reservoir, res., N.M., U.S.	B6	124
Utete, Tan.	E7	54
Uthai Thani, Thai.	C4	34
Utiariti, Braz.	F8	70
Utica, Il., U.S.	B5	106
Utica, Mi., U.S.	F7	115
Utica, Ms., U.S.	C3	117
Utica, Ne., U.S.	D8	120
Utica, N.Y., U.S.	B5	125
Utica, Oh., U.S.	B3	128
Utiel, Spain	H6	16
Utikuma Lake, l., Ab., Can.	B3	84
Utila, Isla de, i., Hond.	B2	80
Utopia, Austl.	E5	60
Utrecht, Neth.	D9	12
Utrecht, S. Afr.	D5	56
Utrera, Spain	I4	16
Utsunomiya, Japan	D16	28
Uttaradit, Thai.	C4	34
Uttar Pradesh, prov., India	D3	40
Uusikaupunki, Fin.	F9	10
Uvalde, Tx., U.S.	E3	136
Uvalde, co., Tx., U.S.	E3	136
Uvarovo, Russia	D7	22
Uvinza, Tan.	E6	54
Uvira, D.R.C.	D5	54
Uvs Lake, l., Asia	A6	28
Uwajima, Japan	E14	28
Uwayl, Sudan	B5	54
Uxbridge, Ma., U.S.	B4	114
Uyo, Nig.	E6	50
Uyuni, Bol.	C4	72
Uyuni, Salar de, pl., Bol.	C4	72
Uzbekistan, ctry., Asia	C8	42
Uzhhorod, Ukr.	E7	20
Uzlovaja, Russia	C15	20
Uzunköprü, Tur.	B2	44
Užur, Russia	D11	26

V

Name	Map Ref.	Page
Vaal, stm., S. Afr.	D4	56
Vaaldam, res., S. Afr.	D4	56
Vaasa, Fin.	E9	10
Vác, Hung.	F5	20
Vaca Key, i., Fl., U.S.	H5	102
Vacaria, Braz.	D7	72
Vacaville, Ca., U.S.	C3	98
Vache, Île à, i., Haiti	E5	80
Vacherie, La., U.S.	h10	111
Vadodara, India	E2	40
Vadsø, Nor.	A13	10
Vaduz, Liech.	G11	12
Vaga, stm., Russia	B7	22
Vah, stm., Russia	C9	26
Váh, stm., Slvk.	E4	20
Vaiden, Ms., U.S.	B4	117
Vail, Co., U.S.	B4	99
Vajgač, ostrov, i., Russia	B7	26
Vākhān, hist. reg., Afg.	C10	42
Val-Béliard, P.Q., Can.	n17	90
Valcourt, P.Q., Can.	D5	90
Valdai Hills see Valdajskaja vozvyšennost', hills, Russia	C5	22
Valdaj, Russia	C5	22
Valdajskaja vozvyšennost', hills, Russia	C5	22
Valday see Valdaj, Russia	C5	22
Valdemarsvik, Swe.	G7	10
Valdepeñas, Spain	H5	16
Valders, Wi., U.S.	D6	142
Valdés, Península, pen., Arg.	E4	69
Valdez, N.C., U.S.	B1	126
Valdez, Ak., U.S.	C10	95
Valdivia, Chile	E2	69
Val-d'Or, P.Q., Can.	k11	90
Valdosta, Ga., U.S.	F3	103
Vale, Or., U.S.	D9	130
Valemount, B.C., Can.	C8	85
Valença, Braz.	D4	74
Valença do Piauí, Braz.	C3	74
Valence, Fr.	E9	16
València, Spain	H6	16
Valencia, Az., U.S.	m7	96
Valencia, Ven.	B6	70
Valencia, co., N.M., U.S.	C3	124
València, Golf de, b., Spain	H7	16
Valencia de Alcántara, Spain	H3	16
Valencia Heights, S.C., U.S.	D6	133
Valenciennes, Fr.	B8	16
Valentine, Ne., U.S.	B5	120
Valera, Ven.	B5	70
Valga, Est.	H12	10
Valhalla, N.Y., U.S.	D7	125
Valhermoso Springs, Al., U.S.	A3	94
Valjevo, Yugo.	B7	18
Valkeakoski, Fin.	F11	10
Valladolid, Mex.	C7	78
Valladolid, Spain	G4	16
Vallecito Reservoir, res., Co., U.S.	D3	99
Valle de la Pascua, Ven.	B6	70
Valledupar, Col.	A5	70
Vallée-Jonction, P.Q., Can.	C7	90
Vallegrande, Bol.	B5	72
Valle Hermoso, Mex.	B5	78
Vallejo, Ca., U.S.	C2	98
Vallenar, Chile	C2	69
Valletta, Malta	G5	18
Valley, Ne., U.S.	C9	120
Valley, co., Id., U.S.	E3	105
Valley, co., Mt., U.S.	B10	119
Valley, co., Ne., U.S.	C6	120
Valley, stm., Mb., Can.	D1	86
Valley Center, Ks., U.S.	E6	109
Valley City, N.D., U.S.	C8	127
Valley Cottage, N.Y., U.S.	g13	125
Valley East, On., Can.	p19	89
Valley Falls, Ks., U.S.	C8	109
Valley Falls, R.I., U.S.	B4	132
Valley Forge, Pa., U.S.	o20	131
Valley Mills, Tx., U.S.	D4	136
Valley Park, Mo., U.S.	f12	118
Valley Springs, S.D., U.S.	D9	134
Valley Station, Ky., U.S.	g11	110
Valley Stream, N.Y., U.S.	n15	125
Valleyview, Ab., Can.	B2	84
Valley View, Pa., U.S.	E8	131
Valliant, Ok., U.S.	D6	129
Valls, Spain	G7	16
Vallscreek, W.V., U.S.	D3	141
Valmeyer, Il., U.S.	E3	106
Valmiera, Lat.	H11	10
Valona see Vlorë, Alb.	D7	18
Vālpārai, India	G3	40
Valparaíso, Chile	D2	69
Valparaiso, Fl., U.S.	u15	102
Valparaiso, In., U.S.	B3	107
Vals, Tanjung, c., Indon.	H10	32
Valsbaai, b., S. Afr.	E2	56
Valtimo, Fin.	E13	10
Valujki, Russia	D15	20
Val Verde, Ut., U.S.	C4	137
Val Verde, co., Tx., U.S.	E2	136
Valverde del Camino, Spain	I3	16
Van, Tur.	C10	44
Van, Tx., U.S.	C5	136
Van, W.V., U.S.	n12	141
Vanadzor, Arm.	B11	44
Van Alstyne, Tx., U.S.	C4	136
Vanavara, Russia	C12	26
Van Buren, Ar., U.S.	B1	97
Van Buren, In., U.S.	C6	107
Van Buren, Me., U.S.	A5	112
Van Buren, Mo., U.S.	E6	118
Van Buren, co., Ar., U.S.	B3	97
Van Buren, co., Ia., U.S.	D6	108
Van Buren, co., Mi., U.S.	F4	115
Van Buren, co., Tn., U.S.	D8	135
Vanč, Taj.	C10	42
Vance, co., N.C., U.S.	A4	126
Vance Air Force Base, mil., Ok., U.S.	A3	129
Vanceboro, N.C., U.S.	B5	126
Vanceburg, Ky., U.S.	B6	110
Vancleave, Ms., U.S.	E5	117
Vancouver, B.C., Can.	E6	85
Vancouver, Wa., U.S.	D3	140
Vancouver Island, i., B.C., Can.	E4	85
Vancouver Island Ranges, mts., B.C., Can.	D4	85
Vandalia, Il., U.S.	E4	106
Vandalia, Mo., U.S.	B6	118
Vandenberg Air Force Base, mil., Ca., U.S.	E3	98
Vander, N.C., U.S.	B4	126
Vanderbilt Peak, mtn., N.M., U.S.	E1	124
Vanderburgh, co., In., U.S.	H2	107
Vandergrift, Pa., U.S.	E2	131
Vanderhoof, B.C., Can.	C5	85
Vanderlin Island, i., Austl.	D2	62
Van Diemen Gulf, b., Austl.	C5	60
Vänern, l., Swe.	G5	10
Vänersborg, Swe.	G5	10
Vangaindrano, Madag.	C8	56
Van Gölü, l., Tur.	C10	44
Van Horn, Tx., U.S.	o12	136
Van Horne, Ia., U.S.	B5	108
Vanier, On., Can.	h12	89
Vanimo, Pap. N. Gui.	G11	32
Vanino, Russia	B16	28
Vankarem, Russia	C20	26
Vankleek Hill, On., Can.	B10	89
Van Lear, Ky., U.S.	C7	110
Van Meter, Ia., U.S.	C4	108
Vännäs, Swe.	E8	10
Vannes, Fr.	D5	16

Name	Map Ref.	Page
Van Rees, Pegunungan, mts., Indon.	G10	32
Vanrhynsdorp, S. Afr.	E2	56
Vansant, Va., U.S.	e9	139
Vanua Lava, i., Vanuatu	j9	62a
Vanua Levu, i., Fiji	F11	58
Vanuatu, ctry., Oc.	F10	58
Van Vleck, Tx., U.S.	r14	136
Van Wert, Oh., U.S.	B1	128
Van Wert, co., Oh., U.S.	B1	128
Vanwyksvlei, S. Afr.	E3	56
Van Zandt, co., Tx., U.S.	C5	136
Vārānasi (Benares), India	D4	40
Varangerfjorden, b., Nor.	A13	10
Varaždin, Cro.	A6	18
Varberg, Swe.	H5	10
Vardaman, Ms., U.S.	B4	117
Vardar (Axiós), stm., Eur.	D9	18
Varde, Den.	I3	10
Vardø, Nor.	A14	10
Varennes, P.Q., Can.	D4	90
Varese, Italy	B2	18
Varginha, Braz.	F2	74
Varina, Va., U.S.	C5	139
Varkaus, Fin.	E12	10
Värmland, hist. reg., Swe.	G5	10
Varna, Bul.	C11	18
Varna, Russia	D11	22
Värnamo, Swe.	H6	10
Varnville, S.C., U.S.	F5	133
Varto, Tur.	C9	44
Várzea Grande, Braz.	B6	72
Vashon, Point, c., Wa., U.S.	e11	140
Vashon Island, i., Wa., U.S.	f11	140
Vaslui, Rom.	F9	20
Vass, N.C., U.S.	B3	126
Vassar, Mi., U.S.	E7	115
Vastenjaure, l., Swe.	C7	10
Västerås, Swe.	G7	10
Västerbotten, hist. reg., Swe.	D8	10
Västerdalälven, stm., Swe.	F5	10
Västervik, Swe.	H7	10
Vasto, Italy	C5	18
Vasylivka, Ukr.	F13	20
Vasyl'kiv, Ukr.	D11	20
Vatican City, ctry., Eur.	D4	18
Vatnajökull, Ice.	l20	10a
Vatomandry, Madag.	B8	56
Vatra Dornei, Rom.	F8	20
Vättern, l., Swe.	G6	10
Vaudreuil, P.Q., Can.	D3	90
Vaughan, On., Can.	D5	89
Vaughn, Mt., U.S.	C5	119
Vaughn, N.M., U.S.	C4	124
Vaukavysk, Bela.	—	—
Vaupés (Uaupés), stm., S.A.	C5	70
Vauxhall, Ab., Can.	D4	84
Vava'u, i., Tonga	F12	58
Vavoua, C. Iv.	E3	50
Vavuniya, Sri L.	H4	40
Växjö, Swe.	H6	10
Vaygach Island see Vajgač, ostrov, i., Russia	B7	26
Važgort, Russia	B8	22
Veazie, Me., U.S.	D4	112
Veedersburg, In., U.S.	D3	107
Veendam, Neth.	D10	12
Vega, i., Nor.	D4	10
Vegreville, Ab., Can.	C4	84
Veinticinco de Mayo, Arg.	F5	72
Vejle, Den.	I3	10
Vélez-Málaga, Spain	I4	16
Velika Morava, stm., Yugo.	B8	18
Velikie Luki, Russia	D5	26
Velikij Ustjug, Russia	C6	26
Vélingara, Sen.	D2	50
Velletri, Italy	D4	18
Vellore, India	G3	40
Velma, Ok., U.S.	C4	129
Vel'sk, Russia	C6	26
Velva, N.D., U.S.	A5	127
Venado Tuerto, Arg.	E5	72
Venango, co., Pa., U.S.	D2	131
Vendôme, Fr.	D7	16
Veneta, Or., U.S.	C3	130
Venézia (Venice), Italy	B4	18
Venezuela, ctry., S.A.	B6	70
Venezuela, Golfo de, b., S.A.	A5	70
Venezuela, Gulf of see Venezuela, Golfo de, b., S.A.	A5	70
Venezuelan Basin	G7	66
Veniaminof, Mount, mtn., Ak., U.S.	D8	95
Venice see Venézia, Italy	B4	18
Venice, Fl., U.S.	E4	102
Venice, Il., U.S.	E3	106
Venice, Gulf of, b., Eur.	B4	18
Venta, stm., Eur.	H10	10
Ventimiglia, Italy	C1	18
Ventnor City, N.J., U.S.	E4	123
Ventspils, Lat.	H9	10
Ventura (San Buenaventura), Ca., U.S.	E4	98
Ventura, co., Ca., U.S.	E4	98
Vera, Arg.	D5	72
Vera, Spain	I6	16
Veracruz, Mex.	D5	78
Veracruz, state, Mex.	D5	78
Verāval, India	E2	40
Verbania, Italy	B2	18
Vercelli, Italy	B2	18
Verchères, P.Q., Can.	D4	90

Verda, Ky., U.S.	D6	110
Verde, stm., Az., U.S.	C4	96
Verden, Ger.	D11	12
Verdi, Nv., U.S.	D2	121
Verdigre, Ne., U.S.	B7	120
Verdigris, Ok., U.S.	A6	129
Verdigris, stm., U.S.	A6	129
Verdun, P.Q., Can.	q19	90
Verdun-sur-Meuse, Fr.	C9	16
Vereeniging, S. Afr.	D4	56
Vereščagino, Russia	C10	26
Vergennes, Vt., U.S.	C2	138
Verhneimbatsk, Russia	C10	26
Verhnemulomskoe vodohranilišče, res., Russia	B14	10
Verhnetulomskij, Russia	B14	10
Verhneural'sk, Russia	D10	22
Verhnij Baskunčak, Russia	E8	22
Verhnij Ufalej, Russia	C11	22
Verhnjaja Amga, Russia	D14	26
Verhnjaja Inta, Russia	A11	22
Verhnjaja Salda, Russia	C11	22
Verhojansk, Russia	C15	26
Verhojanskij hrebet, mts., Russia	C14	26
Verhoture, Russia	C11	22
Verkhoyansk see Verhojansk, Russia	C15	26
Vermilion, Ab., Can.	C5	84
Vermilion, Oh., U.S.	A3	128
Vermilion, co., Il., U.S.	C6	106
Vermilion, co., La., U.S.	E3	111
Vermilion, stm., Ab., Can.	C5	84
Vermilion, stm., Il., U.S.	C5	106
Vermilion, stm., La., U.S.	E3	111
Vermilion, stm., Mn., U.S.	B6	116
Vermilion, stm., Oh., U.S.	A3	128
Vermilion Bay, b., La., U.S.	E3	111
Vermilion Lake, l., Mn., U.S.	C6	116
Vermilion Pass, Can.	D2	84
Vermillion, S.D., U.S.	E9	134
Vermillion, co., S.D., U.S.	E2	107
Vermillion, East Fork, stm., S.D., U.S.	D8	134
Vermillion, stm., P.Q., Can.	B4	90
Vermont, Il., U.S.	C3	106
Vermont, state, U.S.	D3	138
Vermontville, Mi., U.S.	F5	115
Vernal, Ut., U.S.	C6	137
Vernon, B.C., Can.	D8	85
Vernon, Al., U.S.	B1	94
Vernon, Tx., U.S.	B3	136
Vernon, co., La., U.S.	C2	111
Vernon, co., Mo., U.S.	D3	118
Vernon, co., Wi., U.S.	E3	142
Vernon Hills, Il., U.S.	h9	106
Vernonia, Or., U.S.	B3	130
Vero Beach, Fl., U.S.	E6	102
Véroia, Grc.	D9	18
Verona, On., Can.	C8	89
Verona, Italy	B3	18
Verona, Ms., U.S.	A5	117
Verona, N.J., U.S.	B4	123
Verona, Pa., U.S.	k14	131
Verona, Wi., U.S.	E4	142
Verret, Lake, l., La., U.S.	E4	111
Versailles, Fr.	C8	16
Versailles, In., U.S.	F7	107
Versailles, Ky., U.S.	B5	110
Versailles, Mo., U.S.	C5	118
Versailles, Oh., U.S.	B1	128
Vert, Cap, c., Sen.	D1	50
Vertientes, Cuba	A4	80
Vesele, Ukr.	F13	20
Vešenskaja, Russia	F15	8
Vesoul, Fr.	D10	16
Vestal, N.Y., U.S.	C4	125
Vestavia Hills, Al., U.S.	g7	94
Vesterålen, is., Nor.	B6	10
Vestfjorden, b., Nor.	C5	10
Vestmannaeyjar, Ice.	m18	10a
Vesuvio, vol., Italy	D5	18
Vesuvius see Vesuvio, vol., Italy	D5	18
Veszprém, Hung.	F4	20
Vetlanda, Swe.	H6	10
Vetluga, Russia	C8	22
Vetluga, stm., Russia	C8	22
Vevay, In., U.S.	G7	107
Vezirköprü, Tur.	B6	44
Viacha, Bol.	B4	72
Vian, Ok., U.S.	B7	129
Viana, Braz.	B2	74
Viana do Castelo, Port.	G2	16
Viangchan (Vientiane), Laos	C4	34
Viangphoukha, Laos	B4	34
Viareggio, Italy	C5	18
Viborg, Den.	H3	10
Viborg, S.D., U.S.	D8	134
Vibo Valentia, Italy	E5	18
Viburnum, Mo., U.S.	D6	118
Vic, Spain	G8	16
Vicebsk, Bela.	B11	20
Vicente, Point, c., Ca., U.S.	n12	98
Vicente Guerrero, Presa, res., Mex.	C5	78
Vicenza, Italy	B3	18
Vichada, stm., Col.	C5	70
Vichy, Fr.	D8	16
Vici, Ok., U.S.	A2	129
Vicksburg, Mi., U.S.	F5	115
Vicksburg, Ms., U.S.	C3	117

Vicksburg National Military Park, Ms., U.S.	C3	117
Victor, Ia., U.S.	C5	108
Victor, N.Y., U.S.	C3	125
Victoria see Limbe, Cam.	C1	54
Victoria, B.C., Can.	E6	85
Victoria, Nf., Can.	E5	88
Victoria, Chile	E2	69
Victoria see Xianggang, China	E3	30
Victoria, Gui.	D2	50
Victoria, Sey.	h13	57b
Victoria, Ks., U.S.	D4	109
Victoria, Tx., U.S.	E4	136
Victoria, state, Austl.	H3	62
Victoria, co., Tx., U.S.	E4	136
Victoria, stm., Austl.	D5	60
Victoria, Lake, l., Afr.	D6	54
Victoria, Mount, mtn., Pap. N. Gui.	H12	32
Victoria Falls, wtfl, Afr.	B4	56
Victoria Harbour, On., Can.	C5	89
Victoria Island, i., N.T., Can.	D17	82
Victoria Lake, res., Nf., Can.	D3	88
Victoria Land, reg., Ant.	D21	67
Victoria Nile, stm., Ug.	C6	54
Victoria Peak, mtn., Belize	B2	80
Victoria River Downs, Austl.	D5	60
Victorias, Phil.	D8	34
Victoriaville, P.Q., Can.	C6	90
Victoria West, S. Afr.	E3	56
Victorville, Ca., U.S.	E5	98
Vicuña Mackenna, Arg.	E5	72
Vidalia, Ga., U.S.	D4	103
Vidalia, La., U.S.	C4	111
Vidin, Bul.	C9	18
Vidisha, India	E3	40
Vidor, Tx., U.S.	D5	136
Viedma, Arg.	F4	69
Viedma, Lago, l., Arg.	G2	69
Vienna see Wien, Aus.	F15	12
Vienna, Ga., U.S.	D3	103
Vienna, Il., U.S.	F5	106
Vienna, Mo., U.S.	C6	118
Vienna, Va., U.S.	B5	139
Vienna, W.V., U.S.	B3	141
Vienne, Fr.	E9	16
Vienne, stm., Fr.	D7	16
Vientiane see Viangchan, Laos	C4	34
Vieques, Isla de, i., P.R.	B6	80
Vierwaldstätter See, l., Switz.	A2	18
Vierzon, Fr.	D8	16
Vieste, Italy	D6	18
Vietnam, ctry., Asia	C5	34
Viet Tri, Viet.	B5	34
Vieux Desert, Lac, l., Wi., U.S.	B4	142
Vigan, Phil.	C8	34
Vigo, Spain	F2	16
Vigo, co., In., U.S.	F3	107
Vijayawāda, India	F4	40
Vike, Arm.	C11	44
Viking, Ab., Can.	C5	84
Vikna, Nor.	D4	10
Vikna, i., Nor.	D4	10
Vikramasingapuram, India	H3	40
Vila de Sena, Moz.	B6	56
Vila do Ibo, Moz.	A7	56
Vila Fontes, Moz.	B6	56
Vila Gamito, Moz.	A5	56
Vilagarcía de Arousa, Spain	F2	16
Vilanandro, Tanjona, c., Madag.	B7	56
Vilankulo, Moz.	C6	56
Vilanova i la Geltrú, Spain	G7	16
Vila Real, Port.	G3	16
Vilas, co., Wi., U.S.	B4	142
Vila Velha, Braz.	F3	74
Vilejka, Bela.	B9	20
Vilhelmina, Swe.	D7	10
Vilhena, Braz.	F7	70
Viljandi, Est.	G11	10
Viljuj, stm., Russia	C14	26
Viljujsk, Russia	C14	26
Vil'kickogo, proliv, strt., Russia	B11	26
Villa Ángela, Arg.	D5	72
Villa Bella, Bol.	F6	70
Villacañas, Spain	H5	16
Villacarrillo, Spain	H5	16
Villach, Aus.	G13	12
Villa Dolores, Arg.	E4	72
Villa Grove, Il., U.S.	D5	106
Villaguay, Arg.	E6	72
Villahermosa, Mex.	D6	78
Villaldama, Mex.	D4	78
Villalonga, Arg.	E4	69
Villa María, Arg.	E5	72
Villa Mercedes, Arg.	E4	72
Villa Montes, Bol.	C5	72
Villanueva de la Serena, Spain	H4	16
Villa Ocampo, Arg.	D6	72
Villa Ojo de Agua, Arg.	D5	72
Villa Park, Il., U.S.	k8	106
Villa Rica, Ga., U.S.	C2	103
Villarrica, Chile	E2	69
Villarrica, Para.	D6	72
Villarrobledo, Spain	H5	16
Villas, N.J., U.S.	E3	123
Villa Unión, Mex.	C3	78
Villa Valeria, Arg.	E4	72
Villavicencio, Col.	C5	70

Villefranche-sur-Saône, Fr.	E9	16
Villena, Spain	H6	16
Villeneuve-sur-Lot, Fr.	E7	16
Ville Platte, La., U.S.	D3	111
Ville Saint-Georges, P.Q., Can.	C7	90
Villeurbanne, Fr.	E9	16
Villisca, Ia., U.S.	D3	108
Vilnius, Lith.	I11	10
Vilonia, Ar., U.S.	B3	97
Vimmerby, Swe.	H6	10
Viña del Mar, Chile	D2	69
Vinalhaven, Me., U.S.	D4	112
Vinalhaven Island, i., Me., U.S.	D4	112
Vinarós, Spain	G7	16
Vincennes, In., U.S.	G2	107
Vincennes Bay, b., Ant.	C15	67
Vincent, Al., U.S.	B3	94
Vindhya Range, mts., India	E3	40
Vine Brook, stm., Ma., U.S.	g11	114
Vine Grove, Ky., U.S.	C4	110
Vineland, N.J., U.S.	E2	123
Vineyard Haven, Ma., U.S.	D6	114
Vineyard Sound, strt., Ma., U.S.	D6	114
Vinh, Viet.	C5	34
Vinh Long, Viet.	D5	34
Vinita, Ok., U.S.	A6	129
Vinkovci, Cro.	B7	18
Vinson Massif, mtn., Ant.	D32	67
Vinton, Ia., U.S.	B5	108
Vinton, La., U.S.	D2	111
Vinton, Va., U.S.	C3	139
Vinton, co., Oh., U.S.	C3	128
Viola, Il., U.S.	B3	106
Violet, La., U.S.	k12	111
Viramgām, India	E2	40
Virandozero, Russia	C14	8
Viranşehir, Tur.	D8	44
Virden, Mb., Can.	E1	86
Virden, Il., U.S.	D4	106
Vire, Fr.	C6	16
Virgin, stm., U.S.	G8	121
Virgin Gorda, i., Br. Vir. Is.	B7	80
Virginia, S. Afr.	D4	56
Virginia, Al., U.S.	g6	94
Virginia, Il., U.S.	D3	106
Virginia, Mn., U.S.	C6	116
Virginia, state, U.S.	C4	139
Virginia Beach, Va., U.S.	D7	139
Virginia City, Nv., U.S.	D2	121
Virginia Peak, mtn., Nv., U.S.	D2	121
Virgin Islands, dep., N.A.	B7	80
Virgin Islands, is., N.A.	E11	76
Viroqua, Wi., U.S.	E3	142
Virovitica, Cro.	B6	18
Virrat, Fin.	E10	10
Virtsu, Est.	G10	10
Visalia, Ca., U.S.	D4	98
Visayan Sea, Phil.	D8	34
Visby, Swe.	H8	10
Viscount Melville Sound, strt., N.T., Can.	D17	82
Viseu, Port.	G3	16
Vishākhapatnam, India	F4	40
Vista, Ca., U.S.	F5	98
Vistula see Wisła, stm., Pol.	C5	20
Vitarte, Peru	F4	70
Viterbo, Italy	C3	18
Viti Levu, i., Fiji	F11	58
Vitim, Russia	D13	26
Vitim, stm., Russia	D13	26
Vitória, Braz.	F3	74
Vitoria see Gasteiz, Spain	F5	16
Vitória da Conquista, Braz.	D3	74
Vitré, Fr.	C6	16
Vitry-le-François, Fr.	C9	16
Vittoria, Italy	F5	18
Vittorio Veneto, Italy	B4	18
Vivian, La., U.S.	B2	111
Vize, ostrov, i., Russia	B9	26
Vizianagaram, India	F4	40
Vizinga, Russia	B9	22
Vjatka, stm., Russia	D7	26
Vjatskie Poljany, Russia	C9	22
Vjazemskij, Russia	B14	28
Vjaz'ma, Russia	B13	20
Vladikavkaz, Russia	E6	26
Vladikavkaz see Ordzhonikidze, Ukr.	F13	20
Vladimir, Russia	D6	26
Vladivostok, Russia	E15	26
Vlissingen, Neth.	E8	12
Vlorë, Alb.	D7	18
Vogel Peak see Dimlang, mtn., Nig.	E7	50
Vohimena, Tanjona, c., Madag.	D8	56
Voi, Kenya	D7	54
Voinjama, Lib.	E3	50
Voj-Vož, Russia	B9	22
Volcano, Hi., U.S.	D6	104
Volcano Islands see Kazan-rettō, is., Japan	F17	64
Volga, S.D., U.S.	C9	134
Volga, stm., Russia	E6	26
Volga-Baltic Canal see Volgo-Baltijskij kanal, Russia	B6	22

Volga Plateau see Privolžskaja vozvyšennost', plat., Russia	D6	26
Volgo-Baltijskij kanal, Russia	B6	22
Volgodonsk, Russia	E6	26
Volgograd, Russia	E6	26
Volgograd Reservoir see Volgogradskoe vodohranilišče, res., Russia	D8	22
Volgogradskoe vodohranilišče, res., Russia	D8	22
Volhov, Russia	D12	6
Volksrust, S. Afr.	D4	56
Volnovakha, Ukr.	F14	20
Vološanka, Russia	B11	26
Volodarskoe, Kaz.	G8	26
Volodymyr-Volyns'kyi, Ukr.	D8	20
Vologda, Russia	D6	26
Vólos, Grc.	E9	18
Volos, Gulf of see Pagasitikós Kólpos, b., Grc.	E9	18
Volosovo, Russia	G13	10
Vol'sk, Russia	D6	26
Volta, stm., Ghana	E5	50
Volta Lake, res., Ghana	E5	50
Volta Redonda, Braz.	F3	74
Volterra, Italy	C3	18
Volusia, co., Fl., U.S.	C5	102
Volžsk, Russia	C8	22
Volžskij, Russia	E6	26
Vondrozo, Madag.	C8	56
Von Frank Mountain, mtn., Ak., U.S.	C9	95
Vonore, Tn., U.S.	D9	135
Vordingborg, Den.	I4	10
Vórioi Sporádhes, is., Grc.	E10	18
Vórios Evvoïkós Kólpos, b., Grc.	E9	18
Vorkuta, Russia	C8	26
Vormsi, i., Est.	G10	10
Voronež, Russia	D5	26
Voroshilovsk see Alchevs'k, Ukr.	E15	20
Vorpommern, hist. reg., Ger.	D13	12
Võrtsjärv, l., Est.	G12	10
Võru, Est.	H12	10
Vosges, mts., Fr.	C10	16
Voss, Nor.	F2	10
Vostočno-Sibirskoe more, Russia	B17	26
Vostočnyj Sajan, mts., Russia	D11	26
Vostok, i., Kir.	F14	58
Votkinsk, Russia	D7	26
Votuporanga, Braz.	F2	74
Voyageurs National Park, Mn., U.S.	B5	116
Vožega, Russia	B7	22
Voznesens'k, Ukr.	F11	20
Vis, Otok, i., Cro.	C6	18
Vranje, Yugo.	C8	18
Vrede, S. Afr.	D4	56
Vršac, Yugo.	B8	18
Vryburg, S. Afr.	D3	56
Vryheid, S. Afr.	D5	56
Vsevidof, Mount, mtn., Ak., U.S.	E6	95
Vukovar, Cro.	B7	18
Vulcan, Ab., Can.	D4	84
Vyborg, Russia	C4	26
Vyčegda, stm., Russia	C6	26
Vym', stm., Russia	B9	22
Vyšnij Voločok, Russia	C5	22
Vytegra, Russia	B6	22

W

Wa, Ghana	D4	50
Waajid, Som.	C8	54
Waal, stm., Eur.	E9	12
Waawaa, Puu, mtn., Hi., U.S.	D6	104
Wabag, Pap. N. Gui.	H11	32
Wabana (Bell Island), Nf., Can.	E5	88
Wabasca, Ab., Can.	B4	84
Wabasca, stm., Ab., Can.	f1	84
Wabash, In., U.S.	C6	107
Wabash, co., In., U.S.	C6	107
Wabash, stm., U.S.	D10	92
Wabash, stm., U.S.	H2	107
Wabasha, Mn., U.S.	F6	116
Wabasha, co., Mn., U.S.	F6	116
Wabasso, Fl., U.S.	E6	102
Wabasso, Mn., U.S.	F3	116
Wabaunsee, co., Ks., U.S.	D7	109
Wabeno, Wi., U.S.	C5	142
Wabowden, Mb., Can.	B2	86
Wabush, Nf., Can.	h8	88
Waccamaw, stm., U.S.	D9	133
Waccamaw, Lake, l., N.C., U.S.	C4	126
Waccasassa Bay, b., Fl., U.S.	C4	102
Wachusett Mountain, mtn., Ma., U.S.	B4	114
Wachusett Reservoir, res., Ma., U.S.	B4	114
Waco, Tx., U.S.	D4	136

Name	Map Ref.	Page

Waco Lake, res., Tx., U.S. D4   136
Waconda Lake, res., Ks.,
  U.S. C5   109
Waconia, Mn., U.S. F5   116
Waddān, Libya E8   48
Waddenzee, strt., Neth. . . . D9   12
Waddi Chappal, Afr. B2   54
Waddington, Mount, mtn.,
  B.C., Can. D5   85
Wadena, Mn., U.S. D3   116
Wadena, co., Mn., U.S. D4   116
Wadesboro, N.C., U.S. C2   126
Wadley, Ga., U.S. D4   103
Wad Madanī, Sudan H11   48
Wadmalaw Island, i., S.C.,
  U.S. F7   133
Wadsworth, Il., U.S. h9   106
Wadsworth, Nv., U.S. D2   121
Wadsworth, Oh., U.S. A4   128
Wafangdian, China B5   30
Wagadugu see
  Ouagadougou, Burkina   D4   50
Wagener, S.C., U.S. D5   133
Wagga Wagga, Austl. H4   62
Wagin, Austl. G2   60
Wagner, S.D., U.S. D7   134
Wagoner, Ok., U.S. B6   129
Wagoner, co., Ok., U.S. . . . B6   129
Wagontire Mountain, mtn.,
  Or., U.S. D7   130
Waha, Libya E9   48
Wahai, Indon. D7   36
Wāh Cantonment, Pak. D10   42
Wahiawa, Hi., U.S. B3   104
Wahiawa Reservoir, res.,
  Hi., U.S. g9   104
Wahkiakum, co., Wa., U.S.   C2   140
Wahoo, Ne., U.S. C9   120
Wahpeton, N.D., U.S. C9   127
Wahran, Alg. A4   48
Wahweap Creek, stm., Ut.,
  U.S. F4   137
Waialua, Hi., U.S. B3   104
Waialua Bay, b., Hi., U.S. . . B3   104
Waianae, Hi., U.S. B3   104
Waianae Range, mts., Hi.,
  U.S. f9   104
Waidhofen an der Ybbs,
  Aus. G14   12
Waigeo, Pulau, i., Indon. . . . C8   36
Waikabubak, Indon. E5   36
Waikapu, Hi., U.S. C5   104
Waikato, stm., N.Z. o14   63c
Waikiki Beach, Hi., U.S. . . g10   104
Wailua, Hi., U.S. A2   104
Wailuku, Hi., U.S. C5   104
Waimanalo, Hi., U.S. B4   104
Waimanalo Bay, b., Hi.,
  U.S. g11   104
Waimate, N.Z. p13   63c
Waimea, Hi., U.S. B2   104
Waimea, Hi., U.S. f9   104
Wainganga, stm., India E3   40
Waingapu, Indon. E6   36
Wainwright, Ab., Can. C5   84
Wainwright, Ak., U.S. A8   95
Waipahu, Hi., U.S. B3   104
Waipara, N.Z. p13   63c
Waipio Acres, Hi., U.S. g9   104
Waipio Peninsula, pen., Hi.,
  U.S. g10   104
Wairoa, N.Z. o14   63c
Waitara, N.Z. o13   63c
Waitemata, N.Z. o13   63c
Waite Park, Mn., U.S. E4   116
Waits, stm., Vt., U.S. C4   138
Waitsburg, Wa., U.S. C7   140
Wajir, Kenya C8   54
Waka, D.R.C. C4   54
Waka, Eth. B7   54
Wakarusa, In., U.S. A5   107
Wakarusa, stm., Ks., U.S. . . D8   109
Wakasa-wan, b., Japan C3   31
Wakatomika Creek, stm.,
  Oh., U.S. B3   128
Wakayama, Japan E15   28
Wake, co., N.C., U.S. B4   126
WaKeeney, Ks., U.S. C4   109
Wakefield, P.Q., Can. D2   90
Wakefield, Ks., U.S. C6   109
Wakefield, Ma., U.S. B5   114
Wakefield, Mi., U.S. n12   115
Wakefield, Ne., U.S. B9   120
Wakefield, R.I., U.S. F3   132
Wakefield, Va., U.S. D6   139
Wake Forest, N.C., U.S. . . . B4   126
Wake Island, dep., Oc. . . . C10   58
Wakema, Myan. C3   34
Wakeman, Oh., U.S. A3   128
Wakkanai, Japan B16   28
Waku Kungo, Ang. F3   54
Wakulla, co., Fl., U.S. B2   102
Walachia, hist. reg., Rom. . . G8   20
Walbridge, Oh., U.S. e6   128
Wałbrzych, Pol. D4   20
Walcott, Ia., U.S. C7   108
Walcott, Lake, res., Id., U.S. G5   105
Wałcz, Pol. C4   20
Walden, On., Can. A3   89
Walden, Co., U.S. A4   99
Walden, N.Y., U.S. D6   125
Waldenburg see Wałbrzych,
  Pol. D4   20

Walden Ridge, mtn., Tn.,
  U.S. D8   135
Waldheim, Sk., Can. E2   91
Waldo, Ar., U.S. D2   97
Waldo, co., Me., U.S. D3   112
Waldoboro, Me., U.S. D3   112
Waldo Lake, l., Ma., U.S. . . h11   114
Waldo Lake, l., Or., U.S. . . . D4   130
Waldport, Or., U.S. C2   130
Waldron, Ar., U.S. C1   97
Waldron, In., U.S. F6   107
Waldwick, N.J., U.S. A4   123
Wales, prov., U.K. E4   12
Waleska, Ga., U.S. B2   103
Walgett, Austl. G4   62
Walgreen Coast, Ant. D30   67
Walhalla, N.D., U.S. A8   127
Walhalla, S.C., U.S. B1   133
Walhonding, stm., Oh., U.S. B3   128
Walikale, D.R.C. D5   54
Walker, Ia., U.S. B6   108
Walker, La., U.S. g10   111
Walker, Mi., U.S. E5   115
Walker, Mn., U.S. C4   116
Walker, co., Al., U.S. B2   94
Walker, co., Ga., U.S. B1   103
Walker, co., Tx., U.S. D5   136
Walker, stm., Nv., U.S. D3   121
Walker Lake, l., Nv., U.S. . . E3   121
Walker River Indian
  Reservation, Nv., U.S. . . D3   121
Walkersville, Md., U.S. B3   113
Walkerton, On., Can. C3   89
Walkerton, In., U.S. B5   107
Walkertown, N.C., U.S. A2   126
Walkerville, Mt., U.S. D4   119
Wall, S.D., U.S. D3   134
Wallace, Id., U.S. B3   105
Wallace, N.C., U.S. C4   126
Wallace, co., Ks., U.S. D2   109
Wallaceburg, On., Can. . . . E2   89
Wallace Lake, res., La., U.S. B2   111
Walla Walla, Wa., U.S. C7   140
Walla Walla, co., Wa., U.S.   C7   140
Walla Walla, stm., Wa., U.S. C7   140
Walled Lake, Mi., U.S. o15   115
Wallen, In., U.S. B7   107
Wallenpaupack, Lake, l.,
  Pa., U.S. D11   131
Waller, Tx., U.S. q14   136
Waller, co., Tx., U.S. E4   136
Wallingford, Ct., U.S. D4   100
Wallingford, Vt., U.S. E3   138
Wallington, N.J., U.S. h8   123
Wallis, Îles, is., Wal./F. . . . F12   58
Wallis and Futuna, dep.,
  Oc. F12   58
Wallkill, N.Y., U.S. D6   125
Wallkill, stm., N.Y., U.S. . . . D6   125
Wall Lake, Ia., U.S. B2   108
Wall Lake, l., Ia., U.S. B4   108
Walloomsac, stm., U.S. . . . F2   138
Walloon Lake, l., Mi., U.S.   C6   115
Wallowa, Or., U.S. B9   130
Wallowa, co., Or., U.S. B9   130
Wallowa Mountains, mts.,
  Or., U.S. B9   130
Wallula, Lake, res., U.S. . . . C7   140
Wallum Lake, l., U.S. A1   132
Walnut, Ia., U.S. C2   108
Walnut, Il., U.S. B4   106
Walnut, stm., Ks., U.S. E6   109
Walnut Canyon National
  Monument, Az., U.S. . . . B4   96
Walnut Cove, N.C., U.S. . . . A2   126
Walnut Creek, Ca., U.S. . . . h8   98
Walnut Creek, stm., Ks.,
  U.S. D4   109
Walnut Grove, Al., U.S. . . . A3   94
Walnut Grove, Mn., U.S. . . . F3   116
Walnutport, Pa., U.S. E10   131
Walnut Ridge, Ar., U.S. . . . A5   97
Walpole, Austl. H2   60
Walpole, Ma., U.S. B5   114
Walpole, N.H., U.S. D2   122
Walsall, Eng., U.K. D6   12
Walsenburg, Co., U.S. D6   99
Walsh, Co., U.S. D8   99
Walsh, co., N.D., U.S. A8   127
Walterboro, S.C., U.S. F6   133
Walter F. George Dam, U.S. D4   94
Walter F. George Lake, res.,
  U.S. D4   94
Walters, Ok., U.S. C3   129
Walthall, co., Ms., U.S. . . . D3   117
Waltham, Ma., U.S. B5   114
Walthill, Ne., U.S. B9   120
Walthourville, Ga., U.S. . . . E5   103
Walton, In., U.S. C5   107
Walton, Ky., U.S. B5   110
Walton, N.Y., U.S. C5   125
Walton, co., Fl., U.S. u15   102
Walton, co., Ga., U.S. C3   103
Walvis Bay, Nmb. C1   56
Walvis Bay, b., Nmb. C1   56
Walvis Ridge K14   66
Walworth, Wi., U.S. F5   142
Walworth, co., S.D., U.S. . . B5   134
Walworth, co., Wi., U.S. . . . F5   142
Wamac, Il., U.S. E4   106
Wamba, D.R.C. C5   54
Wamba, Nig. E6   50
Wamba, stm., Afr. E3   54
Wamego, Ks., U.S. C7   109
Wamesit, Ma., U.S. A5   114

Wamsutter, Wy., U.S. E5   143
Wanaka, N.Z. p12   63c
Wanamingo, Mn., U.S. F6   116
Wanapum Dam, Wa., U.S.   C6   140
Wanapum Lake, res., Wa.,
  U.S. B6   140
Wanaque, N.J., U.S. A4   123
Wanaque Reservoir, res.,
  N.J., U.S. A4   123
Wanatah, In., U.S. B4   107
Wanchese, N.C., U.S. B7   126
Wando, stm., S.C., U.S. . . . F8   133
Wando Woods, S.C., U.S. . . k11   133
Wanfoxia, China A7   40
Wangaratta, Austl. H4   62
Wangiwangi, Pulau, i.,
  Indon. E6   36
Wangqing, China B1   31
Wanigela, Pap. N. Gui. . . . H12   32
Wanneroo, Austl. G2   60
Wanning, China F3   30
Wanxian, China E9   28
Wanyuan, China C2   30
Wanzai, China D3   30
Wapakoneta, Oh., U.S. B1   128
Wapato, Wa., U.S. C5   140
Wapawekka Lake, l., Sk.,
  Can. C3   91
Wapello, Ia., U.S. C6   108
Wapello, co., Ia., U.S. C5   108
Wapiti, stm., Can. B1   84
Wappapello, Lake, res.,
  Mo., U.S. D7   118
Wappingers Falls, N.Y., U.S. D7   125
Wapsipinicon, stm., Ia., U.S.B6   108
War, W.V., U.S. D3   141
Waramaug, Lake, l., Ct.,
  U.S. C2   100
Warangal, India F3   40
Ward, Ar., U.S. B4   97
Ward, co., N.D., U.S. A4   127
Ward, co., Tx., U.S. D1   136
Warden, Wa., U.S. C6   140
Wardha, India E3   40
Ward Mountain, mtn., Mt.,
  U.S. D2   119
Ware, Ma., U.S. B3   114
Ware, co., Ga., U.S. E4   103
Ware, stm., Ma., U.S. B3   114
War Eagle Mountain, mtn.,
  Id., U.S. G2   105
Wareham, Ma., U.S. C6   114
Warehouse Point, Ct., U.S. B5   100
Waren, Indon. G10   32
Ware Shoals, S.C., U.S. . . . C3   133
Warfield, B.C., Can. E9   85
Wargla, Alg. D6   48
Warialda, Austl. F5   62
Warin Chamrap, Thai. C4   34
Warmbad, Nmb. D2   56
Warmbad, S. Afr. C4   56
Warminster, Pa., U.S. F11   131
Warm Springs Indian
  Reservation, Or., U.S. . . C5   130
Warm Springs Reservoir,
  res., Or., U.S. D8   130
Warner, N.H., U.S. D3   122
Warner, Ok., U.S. B6   129
Warner, stm., N.H., U.S. . . . D3   122
Warner Mountains, mts.,
  Ca., U.S. B3   98
Warner Peak, mtn., Or.,
  U.S. E7   130
Warner Robins, Ga., U.S. . . D3   103
Warracknabeal, Austl. H3   62
Warr Acres, Ok., U.S. B4   129
Warragul, Austl. H4   62
Warren, Ar., U.S. D3   97
Warren, Il., U.S. A4   106
Warren, In., U.S. C7   107
Warren, Ma., U.S. B3   114
Warren, Mi., U.S. F7   115
Warren, Mn., U.S. B2   116
Warren, Oh., U.S. A5   128
Warren, Or., U.S. B4   130
Warren, Pa., U.S. C3   131
Warren, R.I., U.S. D5   132
Warren, Vt., U.S. C3   138
Warren, co., Ga., U.S. C4   103
Warren, co., Ia., U.S. C4   108
Warren, co., Il., U.S. C3   106
Warren, co., In., U.S. D3   107
Warren, co., Ky., U.S. C3   110
Warren, co., Mo., U.S. C6   118
Warren, co., Ms., U.S. C3   117
Warren, co., N.C., U.S. A4   126
Warren, co., N.J., U.S. B3   123
Warren, co., N.Y., U.S. B7   125
Warren, co., Oh., U.S. C1   128
Warren, co., Pa., U.S. C3   131
Warren, co., Tn., U.S. D8   135
Warren, co., Va., U.S. B4   139
Warren, stm., U.S. D5   132
Warren Park, In., U.S. k10   107
Warren Peaks, mts., Wy.,
  U.S. B8   143
Warrensburg, Il., U.S. D4   106
Warrensburg, Mo., U.S. . . . C4   118
Warrensburg, N.Y., U.S. . . . B7   125
Warrensville Heights, Oh.,
  U.S. h9   128
Warrenton, S. Afr. D3   56
Warrenton, Ga., U.S. C4   103
Warrenton, Mo., U.S. C6   118

Warrenton, N.C., U.S. A4   126
Warrenton, Or., U.S. A3   130
Warrenton, Va., U.S. B5   139
Warrenville, Il., U.S. k8   106
Warrenville, S.C., U.S. D4   133
Warri, Nig. E6   50
Warrick, co., In., U.S. H3   107
Warrington, Fl., U.S. u14   102
Warrior, Al., U.S. B3   94
Warrior Lake, res., Al., U.S. C2   94
Warrnambool, Austl. H3   62
Warroad, Mn., U.S. B3   116
Warsaw see Warszawa, Pol. C6   20
Warsaw, Il., U.S. C2   106
Warsaw, In., U.S. B6   107
Warsaw, Ky., U.S. B5   110
Warsaw, Mo., U.S. C4   118
Warsaw, N.C., U.S. B4   126
Warsaw, N.Y., U.S. C2   125
Warsaw, Va., U.S. C6   139
Warszawa (Warsaw), Pol. . . C6   20
Wartburg, Tn., U.S. C9   135
Warwick, Austl. F5   62
Warwick, P.Q., Can. D6   90
Warwick, Md., U.S. B6   113
Warwick, N.Y., U.S. D6   125
Warwick, R.I., U.S. D4   132
Wasaga Beach, On., Can. . . C4   89
Wasatch, co., Ut., U.S. C4   137
Wasco, Ca., U.S. E4   98
Wasco, co., Or., U.S. B5   130
Waseca, Mn., U.S. F5   116
Waseca, co., Mn., U.S. F5   116
Washakie, co., Wy., U.S. . . . C5   143
Washakie Needles, mts.,
  Wy., U.S. C3   143
Washburn, Il., U.S. B5   108
Washburn, Il., U.S. C4   106
Washburn, Me., U.S. B4   112
Washburn, N.D., U.S. B5   127
Washburn, Wi., U.S. B3   142
Washburn, co., Wi., U.S. . . . C2   142
Washburn, Mount, mtn.,
  Wy., U.S. B2   143
Washim, India E3   40
Washington, D.C., U.S. C3   113
Washington, Ga., U.S. C4   103
Washington, Ia., U.S. C6   108
Washington, Il., U.S. C4   106
Washington, In., U.S. G3   107
Washington, Ks., U.S. C6   109
Washington, Ky., U.S. B6   110
Washington, La., U.S. D3   111
Washington, Mo., U.S. C6   118
Washington, Ms., U.S. D2   117
Washington, N.C., U.S. B5   126
Washington, N.J., U.S. B3   123
Washington, Pa., U.S. F1   131
Washington, Ut., U.S. F2   137
Washington, co., Al., U.S. . . D1   94
Washington, co., Ar., U.S. . . A1   97
Washington, co., Co., U.S. . . B7   99
Washington, co., Fl., U.S. . . u16   102
Washington, co., Ga., U.S. . . C4   103
Washington, co., Ia., U.S. . . C6   108
Washington, co., Id., U.S. . . E2   105
Washington, co., Il., U.S. . . . E4   106
Washington, co., In., U.S. . . G5   107
Washington, co., Ks., U.S. . . C6   109
Washington, co., Ky., U.S. . . C4   110
Washington, co., La., U.S. . . D5   111
Washington, co., Md., U.S. . . A2   113
Washington, co., Me., U.S. . . D5   112
Washington, co., Mn., U.S. . . E6   116
Washington, co., Mo., U.S. . . D7   118
Washington, co., Ms., U.S. . . B3   117
Washington, co., N.C., U.S. . B6   126
Washington, co., Ne., U.S. . . C9   120
Washington, co., N.Y., U.S. . B7   125
Washington, co., Oh., U.S. . . C4   128
Washington, co., Ok., U.S. . . A6   129
Washington, co., Or., U.S. . . B3   130
Washington, co., Pa., U.S. . . F1   131
Washington, co., R.I., U.S. . . E2   132
Washington, co., Tn., U.S. . C11   135
Washington, co., Tx., U.S. . . D4   136
Washington, co., Ut., U.S. . . F2   137
Washington, co., Va., U.S. . . f9   139
Washington, co., Vt., U.S. . . C3   138
Washington, co., Wi., U.S. . . E5   142
Washington, Lake, l., Fl.,
  U.S. D6   102
Washington, Lake, l., Mn.,
  U.S. E4   116
Washington, Lake, l., Ms.,
  U.S. B3   117
Washington, Lake, l., Wa.,
  U.S. e11   140
Washington, Mount, mtn.,
  N.H., U.S. B4   122
Washington Court House,
  Oh., U.S. C2   128
Washington Island, i., Wi.,
  U.S. C7   142
Washington Park, Il., U.S. . E3   106
Washington Terrace, Ut.,
  U.S. B4   137
Washita, co., Ok., U.S. B2   129
Washita, stm., Ok., U.S. . . . C4   129
Washoe, co., Nv., U.S. C2   121
Washoe City, Nv., U.S. D2   121
Washougal, Wa., U.S. D3   140
Washow Bay, b., Mb., Can. D3   86
Washtenaw, co., Mi., U.S. . . F7   115

Wasilla, Ak., U.S. C10   95
Wasior, Indon. D8   36
Waskom, Tx., U.S. C5   136
Waspam, Nic. C3   80
Wasque Point, c., Ma., U.S. D7   114
Wassookeag, Lake, l., Me.,
  U.S. C3   112
Wassuk Range, mts., Nv.,
  U.S. E3   121
Wataga, Il., U.S. B3   106
Watampone, Indon. D6   36
Watansopeng, Indon. D5   36
Watauga, co., N.C., U.S. . . A1   126
Watauga, stm., Tn., U.S. . . C12   135
Watauga Lake, res., Tn.,
  U.S. C12   135
Watchaug Pond, l., R.I.,
  U.S. F2   132
Watch Hill Point, c., R.I.,
  U.S. G1   132
Watchung, N.J., U.S. B4   123
Waterbury, Ct., U.S. C3   100
Waterbury, Vt., U.S. C3   138
Waterbury Center, Vt., U.S. C3   138
Waterbury Reservoir, res.,
  Vt., U.S. C3   138
Wateree, stm., S.C., U.S. . . D6   133
Wateree Lake, res., S.C.,
  U.S. C6   133
Waterford, Ire. D3   12
Waterford, Ct., U.S. D7   100
Waterford, N.Y., U.S. C7   125
Waterford, Pa., U.S. C2   131
Waterford, Wi., U.S. F5   142
Waterhen Lake, l., Mb.,
  Can. C2   86
Waterloo, Bel. E9   12
Waterloo, On., Can. D4   89
Waterloo, P.Q., Can. D5   90
Waterloo, Ia., U.S. B5   108
Waterloo, Il., U.S. E3   106
Waterloo, In., U.S. B7   107
Waterloo, N.Y., U.S. C4   125
Waterloo, Wi., U.S. E5   142
Waterman, Il., U.S. B5   106
Waterman Reservoir, res.,
  R.I., U.S. B3   132
Waterproof, La., U.S. C4   111
Watersmeet, Mi., U.S. n12   115
Waterton Lakes National
  Park, Ab., Can. E3   84
Watertown, Ct., U.S. C3   100
Watertown, Ma., U.S. g11   114
Watertown, N.Y., U.S. B5   125
Watertown, S.D., U.S. C8   134
Watertown, Tn., U.S. A5   135
Watertown, Wi., U.S. E5   142
Water Valley, Ms., U.S. A4   117
Waterville, Ks., U.S. C7   109
Waterville, Me., U.S. D3   112
Waterville, Mn., U.S. F5   116
Waterville, N.Y., U.S. C5   125
Waterville, Oh., U.S. A2   128
Waterville, Wa., U.S. B5   140
Watervliet, Mi., U.S. F4   115
Watervliet, N.Y., U.S. C7   125
Watford, On., Can. E3   89
Watford City, N.D., U.S. . . . B2   127
Wathena, Ks., U.S. C9   109
Watheroo, Austl. G2   60
Watkins, Mn., U.S. E4   116
Watkins Glen, N.Y., U.S. . . . C4   125
Watkinsville, Ga., U.S. C3   103
Watling Island see San
  Salvador, i., Bah. D10   76
Watonga, Ok., U.S. B3   129
Watonwan, co., Mn., U.S. . . F4   116
Watonwan, stm., Mn., U.S. G4   116
Watsa, D.R.C. C5   54
Watseka, Il., U.S. C6   106
Watsontown, Pa., U.S. D8   131
Watsonville, Ca., U.S. D3   98
Watts Bar Dam, Tn., U.S. . . D9   135
Watts Bar Lake, res., Tn.,
  U.S. D9   135
Wattsville, S.C., U.S. B4   133
Watubela, Kepulauan, is.,
  Indon. D8   36
Waubaushene, On., Can. . . C5   89
Waubay, S.D., U.S. B8   134
Waubay Lake, l., S.D., U.S. B8   134
Wauchope, Austl. E5   60
Wauchula, Fl., U.S. E5   102
Wauconda, Il., U.S. h8   106
Waugh Mountain, mtn., Id.,
  U.S. D4   105
Waukee, Ia., U.S. C4   108
Waukegan, Il., U.S. A6   106
Waukesha, Wi., U.S. F5   142
Waukesha, co., Wi., U.S. . . . E5   142
Waukewan, Lake, l., N.H.,
  U.S. C3   122
Waukomis, Ok., U.S. A4   129
Waukon, Ia., U.S. A6   108
Waunakee, Wi., U.S. E4   142
Wauneta, Ne., U.S. D4   120
Waungumbaug Lake, l., Ct.,
  U.S. B6   100
Waupaca, Wi., U.S. D4   142
Waupaca, co., Wi., U.S. . . . D5   142
Waupun, Wi., U.S. E5   142
Wauregan, Ct., U.S. C8   100
Waurika, Ok., U.S. C4   129
Waurika Lake, res., Ok.,
  U.S. C3   129

Name	Map Ref.	Page

Wausau, Wi., U.S. **D4** 142
Wausau, Lake, res., Wi., U.S. **D4** 142
Wauseon, Oh., U.S. **A1** 128
Wautoma, Wi., U.S. **D4** 142
Wauwatosa, Wi., U.S. . . **m12** 142
Wave Hill, Austl. **D5** 60
Waushara, co., Wi., U.S. . . **D4** 142
Wauseon, Oh., U.S. **A1** 128
Wautoma, Wi., U.S. **D4** 142
Wauwatosa, Wi., U.S. . . **m12** 142
Wave Hill, Austl. **D5** 60
Waveland, Ms., U.S. **E4** 117
Waverley, N.S., Can. **E6** 87
Waverly, Ia., U.S. **B5** 108
Waverly, Il., U.S. **D4** 106
Waverly, Ks., U.S. **D8** 109
Waverly, Mn., U.S. **E5** 116
Waverly, Mo., U.S. **B4** 118
Waverly, Ne., U.S. **D9** 120
Waverly, N.Y., U.S. **C4** 125
Waverly, Oh., U.S. **C3** 128
Waverly, Tn., U.S. **A4** 135
Waverly, Va., U.S. **C5** 139
Waverly, W.V., U.S. **B3** 141
Waverly Hall, Ga., U.S. . . **D2** 103
Wāw, Sudan **I10** 48
Wāw al-Kabīr, Libya **E8** 48
Wawanesa, Mb., Can. . . . **E2** 86
Wawasee, Lake, l., In., U.S. **B6** 107
Wawayanda Lake, l., N.J., U.S. **A4** 123
Wawota, Sk., Can. **H4** 91
Waxahachie, Tx., U.S. . . . **C4** 136
Waxhaw, N.C., U.S. **C2** 126
Waycross, Ga., U.S. **E4** 103
Wayland, Ia., U.S. **C6** 108
Wayland, Ma., U.S. **g10** 114
Wayland, Mi., U.S. **F5** 115
Wayland, N.Y., U.S. **C3** 125
Waylyn, S.C., U.S. **k12** 133
Waymart, Pa., U.S. **C11** 131
Wayne, Mi., U.S. **p15** 115
Wayne, Ne., U.S. **B8** 120
Wayne, N.J., U.S. **B4** 123
Wayne, W.V., U.S. **C2** 141
Wayne, co., Ga., U.S. . . . **E5** 103
Wayne, co., Ia., U.S. **D4** 108
Wayne, co., In., U.S. **E7** 107
Wayne, co., Ky., U.S. **D5** 110
Wayne, co., Mi., U.S. **F7** 115
Wayne, co., Mo., U.S. . . . **D7** 118
Wayne, co., Ms., U.S. . . . **D5** 117
Wayne, co., N.C., U.S. . . . **B4** 126
Wayne, co., Ne., U.S. **B8** 120
Wayne, co., N.Y., U.S. . . . **B3** 125
Wayne, co., Oh., U.S. . . . **B4** 128
Wayne, co., Pa., U.S. . . . **C11** 131
Wayne, co., Tn., U.S. **B4** 135
Wayne, co., Ut., U.S. **E4** 137
Wayne, co., W.V., U.S. . . . **C2** 141
Wayne City, Il., U.S. **E5** 106
Waynesboro, Ga., U.S. . . . **C4** 103
Waynesboro, Ms., U.S. . . . **D5** 117
Waynesboro, Pa., U.S. . . . **G6** 131
Waynesboro, Tn., U.S. . . . **B4** 135
Waynesboro, Va., U.S. . . . **B4** 139
Waynesburg, Oh., U.S. . . . **B4** 128
Waynesburg, Pa., U.S. . . . **G1** 131
Waynesville, Mo., U.S. . . . **D5** 118
Waynesville, N.C., U.S. . . **f10** 126
Waynesville, Oh., U.S. . . . **C1** 128
Waynetown, In., U.S. **D3** 107
Waynewood, Va., U.S. . . **g12** 139
Waynoka, Ok., U.S. **A3** 129
Wayzata, Mn., U.S. **n11** 116
Waza, Cam. **D7** 50
We, Pulau, i., Indon. **B1** 36
Weakley, co., Tn., U.S. . . . **A3** 135
Weatherford, Ok., U.S. . . . **B3** 129
Weatherford, Tx., U.S. . . . **C4** 136
Weatherly, Pa., U.S. **E10** 131
Weatogue, Ct., U.S. **B4** 100
Weaver, Al., U.S. **B4** 94
Weaver Mountains, mts., Az., U.S. **C3** 96
Weaverville, Ca., U.S. . . . **B2** 98
Weaverville, N.C., U.S. . . **f10** 126
Webb, Al., U.S. **D4** 94
Webb, Ms., U.S. **B3** 117
Webb, co., Tx., U.S. **F3** 136
Webb City, Mo., U.S. **D3** 118
Webbers Falls, Ok., U.S. . . **B6** 129
Webberville, Mi., U.S. . . . **F6** 115
Webb Lake, l., Me., U.S. . . **D2** 112
Weber, co., Ut., U.S. **B4** 137
Weber City, Va., U.S. **f9** 139
Webster, Ma., U.S. **B4** 114
Webster, N.Y., U.S. **B3** 125
Webster, Pa., U.S. **F2** 131
Webster, S.D., U.S. **B8** 134
Webster, co., Ga., U.S. . . . **D2** 103
Webster, co., Ia., U.S. . . . **B3** 108
Webster, co., Ky., U.S. . . . **C2** 110
Webster, co., La., U.S. . . . **B2** 111
Webster, co., Mo., U.S. . . . **D5** 118
Webster, co., Ms., U.S. . . . **B4** 117
Webster, co., Ne., U.S. . . . **D7** 120
Webster, co., W.V., U.S. . . **C4** 141
Webster City, Ia., U.S. . . . **B4** 108
Webster Groves, Mo., U.S. **f13** 118
Webster Reservoir, res., Ks., U.S. **C4** 109
Webster Springs, W.V., U.S. **C4** 141
Websterville, Vt., U.S. . . . **C4** 138
Weda, Indon. **C7** 36
Weddell Sea, Ant. **C1** 67
Wedgeport, N.S., Can. . . . **F4** 87

Wedgewood, Mo., U.S. . . **f13** 118
Wedowee, Al., U.S. **B4** 94
Weed, Ca., U.S. **B2** 98
Weed Heights, Nv., U.S. . . **E2** 121
Weedon, P.Q., Can. **D6** 90
Weedsport, N.Y., U.S. . . . **B4** 125
Weedville, Pa., U.S. **D5** 131
Weehawken, N.J., U.S. . . **h8** 123
Weeksbury, Ky., U.S. **C7** 110
Weeping Water, Ne., U.S. . **D9** 120
Weichang, China **A4** 30
Weiden in der Oberpfalz, Ger. **F12** 12
Weifang, China **D11** 28
Weihai, China **D12** 28
Weimar, Ger. **E12** 12
Weimar, Tx., U.S. **E4** 136
Weinan, China **E9** 28
Weiner, Ar., U.S. **B5** 97
Weippe, Id., U.S. **C3** 105
Weir, Ks., U.S. **E9** 109
Weir, Lake, l., Fl., U.S. . . . **C5** 102
Weirsdale, Fl., U.S. **D5** 102
Weirton, W.V., U.S. **A4** 141
Weiser, Id., U.S. **E2** 105
Weiser, stm., Id., U.S. . . . **E2** 105
Weishan Hu, l., China . . . **B4** 30
Weissenburg in Bayern, Ger. **F12** 12
Weissenfels, Ger. **E12** 12
Weiss Lake, res., U.S. . . . **A4** 94
Weixi, China **A3** 34
Weixian, China **B4** 30
Wejherowo, Pol. **B5** 20
Welbourn Hill, Austl. **F5** 60
Welch, W.V., U.S. **D3** 141
Welcome, Mn., U.S. **G4** 116
Welcome, S.C., U.S. **B3** 133
Weld, co., Co., U.S. **A6** 99
Weldon, N.C., U.S. **A5** 126
Weldon Spring, Mo., U.S. . **f12** 118
Weleetka, Ok., U.S. **B5** 129
Welk'īṭē, Eth. **B7** 54
Welkom, S. Afr. **D4** 56
Welland, On., Can. **E5** 89
Wellesley, On., Can. **D4** 89
Wellesley, Ma., U.S. **B5** 114
Wellesley Islands, is., Austl. **D2** 62
Wellford, S.C., U.S. **B3** 133
Wellington, Austl. **G4** 62
Wellington, On., Can. . . . **D7** 89
Wellington, N.Z. **I11** 58
Wellington, Co., U.S. **A5** 99
Wellington, Ks., U.S. **E6** 109
Wellington, Mo., U.S. . . . **B4** 118
Wellington, Nv., U.S. **E2** 121
Wellington, Oh., U.S. . . . **A3** 128
Wellington, Tx., U.S. **B2** 136
Wellington, Ut., U.S. **D5** 137
Wellington, Isla, i., Chile . . **G2** 69
Wellman, Ia., U.S. **C6** 108
Wells, Me., U.S. **E2** 112
Wells, Mn., U.S. **G5** 116
Wells, Nv., U.S. **B7** 121
Wellman, Ia., U.S. **C6** 108
Wells, co., In., U.S. **C7** 107
Wells, co., N.D., U.S. **B6** 127
Wells, stm., Vt., U.S. **C4** 138
Wellsboro, Pa., U.S. **C7** 131
Wellsburg, Ia., U.S. **B5** 108
Wellsburg, W.V., U.S. . . . **A4** 141
Wellston, Oh., U.S. **C3** 128
Wellston, Ok., U.S. **B4** 129
Wellsville, Ks., U.S. **D8** 109
Wellsville, Mo., U.S. **B6** 118
Wellsville, N.Y., U.S. **C3** 125
Wellsville, Oh., U.S. **B5** 128
Wellsville, Ut., U.S. **B4** 137
Wellton, Az., U.S. **E1** 96
Wels, Aus. **F13** 12
Welsh, La., U.S. **D3** 111
Wembley, Ab., Can. **B1** 84
Wenatchee, Wa., U.S. . . . **B5** 140
Wenatchee, stm., Wa., U.S. **B5** 140
Wenatchee Lake, l., Wa., U.S. **B5** 140
Wenatchee Mountains, mts., Wa., U.S. **B5** 140
Wenchang, China **F3** 30
Wenchi, Ghana **E4** 50
Wendell, Id., U.S. **G4** 105
Wendell, N.C., U.S. **B4** 126
Wendeng, China **B5** 30
Wendover, Ut., U.S. **C1** 137
Wengyuan, China **E3** 30
Wenham, Ma., U.S. **A6** 114
Wenham Lake, l., Ma., U.S. **f12** 114
Wenling, China **D5** 30
Wenshan, China **G8** 28
Wenshang, China **B4** 30
Wensu, China **A4** 40
Wentworth, Austl. **G3** 62
Wentworth, Lake, l., N.H., U.S. **C4** 122
Wentzville, Mo., U.S. . . . **C7** 118
Wenzhou, China **F12** 28
Weohyakapka, Lake, l., Fl., U.S. **E5** 102
Werda, Bots. **D3** 56
Weri, Indon. **D8** 36
Werribee, Austl. **H3** 62
Wesel, Ger. **E10** 12
Weser, stm., Ger. **D11** 12
Weslaco, Tx., U.S. **F4** 136
Wesleyville, Nf., Can. **D5** 88

Wesleyville, Pa., U.S. **B2** 131
Wessel, Cape, c., Austl. . . **C6** 60
Wessel Islands, is., Austl. . . **C6** 60
Wesserunsett Lake, l., Me., U.S. **D3** 112
Wessington Springs, S.D., U.S. **C7** 134
Wesson, Ms., U.S. **D3** 117
West, Tx., U.S. **D4** 136
West, stm., Ct., U.S. **D5** 100
West, stm., Ma., U.S. . . . **h9** 114
West, stm., Vt., U.S. **E3** 138
West Acton, Ma., U.S. . . **g10** 114
West Alexandria, Oh., U.S. **C1** 128
West Allis, Wi., U.S. **m11** 142
West Alton, Mo., U.S. . . . **f13** 118
West Andover, Ma., U.S. . **A5** 114
West Antarctica, reg., Ant. **E29** 67
West Baden Springs, In., U.S. **G4** 107
West Baton Rouge, co., La., U.S. **D4** 111
West Bay, b., Fl., U.S. . . . **u16** 102
West Bay, b., N.C., U.S. . . **B6** 126
West Bay, b., Tx., U.S. . . . **r15** 136
West Bend, Ia., U.S. **B3** 108
West Bend, Wi., U.S. **E5** 142
West Bengal, prov., India . **E5** 40
West Berlin, N.J., U.S. . . . **D3** 123
West Billerica, Ma., U.S. . **f10** 114
West Blocton, Al., U.S. . . . **B2** 94
Westborough, Ma., U.S. . . **B4** 114
West Bountiful, Ut., U.S. . **C4** 137
West Boylston, Ma., U.S. . **B4** 114
West Branch, Ia., U.S. . . . **C6** 108
West Branch, Mi., U.S. . . . **D6** 115
West Branch Reservoir, res., Ct., U.S. **B3** 100
West Bridgewater, Ma., U.S. **B5** 114
Westbrook, Ct., U.S. **D6** 100
Westbrook, Me., U.S. . . . **E2** 112
Westbrook, Mn., U.S. . . . **F3** 116
West Burlington, Ia., U.S. . **D6** 108
West Butte, mtn., Mt., U.S. **B5** 119
Westby, Wi., U.S. **E3** 142
West Cache Creek, stm., Ok., U.S. **C3** 129
West Caldwell, N.J., U.S. . **B4** 123
West Canada Creek, stm., N.Y., U.S. **B6** 125
West Cape Howe, c., Austl. **H2** 60
West Caroline Basin **H16** 64
West Carroll, co., La., U.S. **B4** 111
West Carrollton, Oh., U.S. **C1** 128
West Carthage, N.Y., U.S. . **B5** 125
Westchester, Il., U.S. **k9** 106
West Chester, Pa., U.S. . . **G10** 131
Westchester, co., N.Y., U.S. **D7** 125
West Chicago, Il., U.S. . . . **k8** 106
West College Corner, In., U.S. **E8** 107
West Columbia, S.C., U.S. **D5** 133
West Columbia, Tx., U.S. . **E5** 136
West Concord, Ma., U.S. . **B5** 114
West Concord, Mn., U.S. . **F6** 116
West Concord, N.C., U.S. . **B2** 126
Westconnaug Reservoir, res., R.I., U.S. **C2** 132
West Cote Blanche Bay, b., La., U.S. **E4** 111
West Covina, Ca., U.S. . . **m13** 98
West Crossett, Ar., U.S. . . **D4** 97
West Cumberland, Me., U.S. **E2** 112
West Dennis, Ma., U.S. . . **C7** 114
West Des Moines, Ia., U.S. **C4** 108
West Elk Mountains, mts., Co., U.S. **C3** 99
West Elk Peak, mtn., Co., U.S. **C3** 99
Westerly, R.I., U.S. **F1** 132
Western Australia, state, Austl. **E2** 60
Western Desert, des., Egypt **F9** 14
Western Dvina (Zapadnaja Dvina), stm., Eur. **C4** 22
Western Ghāts, mts., India **F2** 40
Westernport, Md., U.S. . . **m12** 113
Western Sahara, dep., Afr. **B2** 50
Western Samoa see Samoa, ctry., Oc. **F12** 58
Western Sayans see Zapadnyj Sajan, mts., Russia **D11** 26
Western Springs, Il., U.S. . **k9** 106
Westerville, Oh., U.S. **B3** 128
West European Basin **D11** 66
West Falkland, i., Falk. Is. . **H4** 69
West Falmouth, Ma., U.S. **C6** 114
West Fargo, N.D., U.S. . . . **C9** 127
West Feliciana, co., La., U.S. **D4** 111
Westfield, N.B., Can. **D3** 87
Westfield, In., U.S. **D5** 107
Westfield, Ma., U.S. **B2** 114
Westfield, N.J., U.S. **B4** 123
Westfield, N.Y., U.S. **C1** 125
Westfield, Pa., U.S. **C6** 131
Westfield, Wi., U.S. **E4** 142
Westfield, stm., Ma., U.S. . **B2** 114
West Fork, Ar., U.S. **B1** 97
West Fork, stm., W.V., U.S. **B4** 141
Wessel Frankfort, Il., U.S. . **F5** 106
West Salem, Il., U.S. **E5** 106
West Salem, Oh., U.S. . . . **B3** 128

West Friendship, Md., U.S. **B4** 113
Westgate, Fl., U.S. **F6** 102
West Grand Lake, l., Me., U.S. **C5** 112
West Grove, Pa., U.S. . . . **G10** 131
West Hanover, Ma., U.S. . **h12** 114
West Hartford, Ct., U.S. . . **B4** 100
West Haven, Ct., U.S. . . . **D4** 100
West Hazleton, Pa., U.S. . **E9** 131
West Helena, Ar., U.S. . . . **C5** 97
West Hill Reservoir, res., Ma., U.S. **B4** 114
Westhope, N.D., U.S. . . . **A4** 127
West Ice Shelf, Ant. **C13** 67
West Indies, is. **D11** 76
West Island, i., Ma., U.S. . **C6** 114
West Jefferson, N.C., U.S. . **A1** 126
West Jefferson, Oh., U.S. . **C2** 128
West Jordan, Ut., U.S. . . . **C3** 137
West Kingston, R.I., U.S. . **F3** 132
West Lafayette, In., U.S. . . **D4** 107
West Lafayette, Oh., U.S. . **B4** 128
Westlake, La., U.S. **D2** 111
Westlake, Oh., U.S. **h9** 128
West Lake, l., Me., U.S. . . **C4** 112
West Laramie, Wy., U.S. . . **E7** 143
West Lawn, Pa., U.S. . . . **F10** 131
West Lebanon, In., U.S. . . **D3** 107
West Liberty, Ia., U.S. . . . **C6** 108
West Liberty, Ky., U.S. . . . **C6** 110
West Liberty, Oh., U.S. . . . **B2** 128
West Liberty, W.V., U.S. . . **f8** 141
West Linn, Or., U.S. **B4** 130
West Long Branch, N.J., U.S. **C4** 123
West Lorne, On., Can. . . . **E3** 89
West Marion, N.C., U.S. . **f10** 126
West Medway, Ma., U.S. . **B5** 114
West Memphis, Ar., U.S. . **B5** 97
West Miami, Fl., U.S. . . . **s13** 102
West Middlesex, Pa., U.S. . **D1** 131
West Mifflin, Pa., U.S. . . . **F2** 131
West Milton, Oh., U.S. . . . **C1** 128
West Milwaukee, Wi., U.S. **m12** 142
Westminster, Ca., U.S. . . **n12** 98
Westminster, Co., U.S. . . . **B5** 99
Westminster, Md., U.S. . . **A4** 113
Westminster, S.C., U.S. . . **B1** 133
West Monroe, La., U.S. . . **B3** 111
Westmont, Il., U.S. **k9** 106
Westmont, N.J., U.S. **D2** 123
Westmont, Pa., U.S. **F4** 131
Westmoreland, Tn., U.S. . **A5** 135
Westmoreland, co., Pa., U.S. **F2** 131
Westmoreland, co., Va., U.S. **B6** 139
Westmorland, Ca., U.S. . . **F6** 98
West Musquash Lake, l., Me., U.S. **C5** 112
West Mystic, Ct., U.S. . . . **D8** 100
West Newton, Pa., U.S. . . **F2** 131
West New York, N.J., U.S. **h8** 123
West Nicholson, Zimb. . . . **C4** 56
West Nishnabotna, stm., Ia., U.S. **C2** 108
West Norriton, Pa., U.S. . **o20** 131
Weston, Ct., U.S. **E2** 100
Weston, Ma., U.S. **g10** 114
Weston, Mo., U.S. **B3** 118
Weston, Oh., U.S. **A2** 128
Weston, Or., U.S. **B8** 130
Weston, W.V., U.S. **B4** 141
Weston, co., Wy., U.S. . . . **C8** 143
Weston-super-Mare, Eng., U.K. **E5** 12
West Orange, N.J., U.S. . . **B4** 123
Westover, Md., U.S. **D6** 113
Westover, W.V., U.S. **B5** 141
Westover Air Force Base, mil., Ma., U.S. **B2** 114
West Palm Beach, Fl., U.S. **F6** 102
West Pawlet, Vt., U.S. . . . **E2** 138
West Pearl, stm., La., U.S. **D6** 111
West Pelzer, S.C., U.S. . . . **B3** 133
West Pensacola, Fl., U.S. . **u14** 102
West Peoria, Il., U.S. **C4** 106
West Pittsburg, Pa., U.S. . **E1** 131
West Pittston, Pa., U.S. . **m17** 131
West Plains, Mo., U.S. . . . **E6** 118
West Point, Ca., U.S. **C3** 98
West Point, Ga., U.S. **D1** 103
West Point, Ia., U.S. **D6** 108
West Point, Ky., U.S. **C4** 110
West Point, Ms., U.S. **B5** 117
West Point, Ne., U.S. **C9** 120
West Point, N.Y., U.S. . . . **D7** 125
West Point, Va., U.S. **C6** 139
West Point, mtn., Ak., U.S. **C11** 95
West Point Lake, res., U.S. **C1** 103
Westport, On., Can. **C8** 89
Westport, Ct., U.S. **E2** 100
Westport, In., U.S. **F6** 107
Westport, Wa., U.S. **C1** 140
West Portsmouth, Oh., U.S. **D2** 128
West Quoddy Head, c., Me., U.S. **D6** 112
West Reading, Pa., U.S. . **F10** 131
West Rutland, Vt., U.S. . . **D2** 138
West Saint Paul, Mn., U.S. **n12** 116
West Salem, Il., U.S. **E5** 106
West Salem, Oh., U.S. . . . **B3** 128

West Salem, Wi., U.S. . . . **E2** 142
West Scarborough, Me., U.S. **E2** 112
West Seneca, N.Y., U.S. . . **C2** 125
West Siberian Lowland see Zapadno-Sibirskaja ravnina, pl., Russia . . . **C9** 26
West Simsbury, Ct., U.S. . **B4** 100
West Slope, Or., U.S. . . . **g12** 130
West Spanish Peak, mtn., Co., U.S. **D6** 99
West Springfield, Ma., U.S. **B2** 114
West Springfield, Va., U.S. **g12** 139
West Swanzey, N.H., U.S. . **E2** 122
West Terre Haute, In., U.S. **F3** 107
West Thompson Lake, res., Ct., U.S. **B8** 100
West Union, Ia., U.S. **B6** 108
West Union, Oh., U.S. . . . **D2** 128
West Union, W.V., U.S. . . **B4** 141
West Unity, Oh., U.S. **A1** 128
West University Place, Tx., U.S. **r14** 136
West Valley City, Ut., U.S. . **C4** 137
West Vancouver, B.C., Can. **f12** 85
West Van Lear, Ky., U.S. . **C7** 110
West View, Pa., U.S. . . . **h13** 131
Westville, Il., U.S. **C6** 106
Westville, In., U.S. **A4** 107
Westville, N.H., U.S. **E4** 122
Westville, N.J., U.S. **D2** 123
Westville, Ok., U.S. **A7** 129
Westville Lake, res., Ma., U.S. **B3** 114
West Virginia, state, U.S. . **C4** 141
West Walker, stm., U.S. . . **E2** 121
West Wareham, Ma., U.S. **C6** 114
West Warwick, R.I., U.S. . . **D3** 132
Westwego, La., U.S. . . . **k11** 111
Westwood, Ca., U.S. **B3** 98
Westwood, Ks., U.S. . . . **k16** 109
Westwood, Ky., U.S. **B7** 110
Westwood, Ma., U.S. . . . **B5** 114
Westwood, N.J., U.S. **B4** 123
Westwood Lakes, Fl., U.S. **s13** 102
West Wyalong, Austl. . . . **G4** 62
West Wyoming, Pa., U.S. **n17** 131
West Yarmouth, Ma., U.S. **C7** 114
West Yellowstone, Mt., U.S. **F5** 119
West York, Pa., U.S. **G8** 131
Wetar, Pulau, i., Indon. . . **E7** 36
Wetar, Selat, strt., Indon. . **E7** 36
Wetaskiwin, Ab., Can. . . . **C4** 84
Wete, Tan. **D7** 54
Wethersfield, Ct., U.S. . . . **C5** 100
Wet Mountains, mts., Co., U.S. **C5** 99
Wetumka, Ok., U.S. **B5** 129
Wetumpka, Al., U.S. **C3** 94
Wetzel, co., W.V., U.S. . . . **B4** 141
Wetzlar, Ger. **E11** 12
Wewahitchka, Fl., U.S. . . . **B1** 102
Wewak, Pap. N. Gui. . . . **G11** 32
Wewoka, Ok., U.S. **B5** 129
Wexford, Ire. **D3** 12
Wexford, co., Mi., U.S. . . . **D5** 115
Weyauwega, Wi., U.S. . . . **D5** 142
Weymouth, Eng., U.K. . . . **E5** 12
Weymouth, Ma., U.S. . . . **B6** 114
Whakatane, N.Z. **o14** 63c
Whaleysville, Md., U.S. . . **D7** 113
Whangarei, N.Z. **o13** 63c
Wharton, N.J., U.S. **B3** 123
Wharton, Tx., U.S. **E4** 136
Wharton, co., Tx., U.S. . . **E4** 136
Wharton Basin **J13** 64
What Cheer, Ia., U.S. . . . **C5** 108
Whatcom, co., Wa., U.S. . **A4** 140
Whatcom, Lake, l., Wa., U.S. **A3** 140
Wheatfield, In., U.S. **B3** 107
Wheatland, Ca., U.S. **C3** 98
Wheatland, Ia., U.S. **C7** 108
Wheatland, Wy., U.S. . . . **D8** 143
Wheatland, co., Mt., U.S. . **D7** 119
Wheatland Reservoir, res., Wy., U.S. **E7** 143
Wheatley, On., Can. **E2** 89
Wheaton, Il., U.S. **B5** 106
Wheaton, Md., U.S. **B3** 113
Wheaton, Mn., U.S. **E2** 116
Wheaton, Mo., U.S. **E3** 118
Wheat Ridge, Co., U.S. . . **B5** 99
Wheelbarrow Peak, mtn., Nv., U.S. **F5** 121
Wheeler, Ms., U.S. **A5** 117
Wheeler, Tx., U.S. **B2** 136
Wheeler, co., Ga., U.S. . . **D4** 103
Wheeler, co., Ne., U.S. . . **C7** 120
Wheeler, co., Or., U.S. . . . **C6** 130
Wheeler, co., Tx., U.S. . . . **B2** 136
Wheeler Air Force Base, mil., Hi., U.S. **g9** 104
Wheeler Lake, res., Al., U.S. **A2** 94
Wheeler Peak, mtn., Ca., U.S. **C4** 98
Wheeler Peak, mtn., N.M., U.S. **A4** 124
Wheeler Peak, mtn., Nv., U.S. **E7** 121
Wheelersburg, Oh., U.S. . **D3** 128
Wheeling, Il., U.S. **h9** 106
Wheeling, W.V., U.S. **A4** 141
Wheeling Creek, stm., W.V., U.S. **f8** 141

Name	Map Ref.	Page

Wheelwright, Ky., U.S. **C7** 110
Whetstone, stm., U.S. **E2** 116
Whidbey Island, i., Wa., U.S. **A3** 140
Whidbey Island Naval Air Station, mil., Wa., U.S. **A3** 140
Whigham, Ga., U.S. **F2** 103
Whiskey Peak, mtn., Wy., U.S. **D5** 143
Whiskeytown-Shasta-Trinity National Recreation Area, Ca., U.S. **B2** 98
Whistler, B.C., Can. **D6** 85
Whitacres, Ct., U.S. **A5** 100
Whitakers, N.C., U.S. **A5** 126
Whitbourne, Nf., Can. . . . **E5** 88
Whitby, On., Can. **D6** 89
Whitchurch-Stouffville, On., Can. **D5** 89
White, co., Ar., U.S. **B4** 97
White, co., Ga., U.S. **B3** 103
White, co., Il., U.S. **E5** 106
White, co., In., U.S. **C4** 107
White, co., Tn., U.S. **D8** 135
White, stm., Az., U.S. **D5** 96
White, stm., In., U.S. **H2** 107
White, stm., Mi., U.S. **E4** 115
White, stm., Nv., U.S. **E6** 121
White, stm., Tx., U.S. **C2** 136
White, stm., Vt., U.S. **D4** 138
White, stm., Wa., U.S. **B5** 140
White, stm., Wa., U.S. **B4** 140
White, stm., U.S. **C4** 97
White, stm., U.S. **D5** 134
White, stm., U.S. **C7** 137
White Bay, b., Nf., Can. . . . **D3** 88
White Bear, stm., Nf., Can. . **E3** 88
White Bear Lake, Mn., U.S. **E5** 116
White Bluff, Tn., U.S. **A4** 135
White Butte, mtn., N.D., U.S. **C2** 127
White Castle, La., U.S. . . . **D4** 111
White Center, Wa., U.S. . . . **e11** 140
White City, Or., U.S. **E4** 130
White Clay Creek, stm., U.S. **A3** 120
White Cliffs, Austl. **F3** 60
White Cliffs, Austl. **G3** 62
White Cloud, Mi., U.S. **E5** 115
Whitecourt, Ab., Can. **B3** 84
White Creek, stm., U.S. . . **E2** 138
Whiteday, stm., W.V., U.S. **h10** 141
White Deer, Tx., U.S. **B2** 136
White Earth Indian Reservation, Mn., U.S. **C3** 116
White Earth Lake, l., Mn., U.S. **C3** 116
Whiteface, stm., Mn., U.S. **C6** 116
Whiteface Mountain, mtn., N.Y., U.S. **f11** 125
Whitefield, N.H., U.S. **B3** 122
Whitefish, Mt., U.S. **B2** 119
Whitefish Bay, Wi., U.S. . . **m12** 142
Whitefish Bay, b., Mi., U.S. **B6** 115
Whitefish Lake, l., Mn., U.S. **D4** 116
Whitefish Range, mts., Mt., U.S. **B2** 119
Whiteford, Md., U.S. **A5** 113
White Hall, Al., U.S. **C3** 94
White Hall, Ar., U.S. **C3** 97
White Hall, Il., U.S. **D3** 106
Whitehall, Mi., U.S. **E4** 115
Whitehall, Mt., U.S. **E4** 119
Whitehall, N.Y., U.S. **B7** 125
Whitehall, Oh., U.S. **m11** 128
Whitehall, Wi., U.S. **D2** 142
Whitehall Reservoir, res., Ma., U.S. **h9** 114
Whitehaven, Eng., U.K. . . . **C5** 12
White Haven, Pa., U.S. . . **D10** 131
Whitehorn, Point, c., Wa., U.S. **A3** 140
Whitehorse, Yk., Can. . . . **F13** 82
White Horse, N.J., U.S. . . . **C3** 123
Whitehouse, Oh., U.S. . . . **A2** 128
White House, Tn., U.S. . . . **A5** 135
White Island Shores, Ma., U.S. **C6** 114
White Knob Mountains, mts., Id., U.S. **F5** 105
White Lake, l., La., U.S. . . . **E3** 111
Whiteman Air Force Base, mil., Mo., U.S. **C4** 118
White Mesa Natural Bridge, Az., U.S. **A4** 96
White Mountain Peak, mtn., Ca., U.S. **D4** 98
White Mountains, mts., N.H., U.S. **B3** 122
White Mountains, mts., U.S. **D4** 98
Whitemouth, stm., Mb., Can. **E4** 86
Whitemouth Lake, l., Mb., Can. **E4** 86
White Nile see Abyad, Al-Baḥr al-, stm., Sudan . **H11** 48
White Oak, Oh., U.S. . . . **o12** 128
White Oak Creek, stm., Oh., U.S. **D2** 128
Whiteoak Creek, stm., Tn., U.S. **A4** 135
White Oak Lake, res., Ar., U.S. **D2** 97
White Pigeon, Mi., U.S. . . . **G5** 115
White Pine, Mi., U.S. . . . **m12** 115

White Pine, Tn., U.S. **C10** 135
White Pine, co., Nv., U.S. . . **D6** 121
White Plains, Md., U.S. . . . **C4** 113
White Plains, N.Y., U.S. . . . **D7** 125
Whiteriver, Az., U.S. **D6** 96
White River Junction, Vt., U.S. **D4** 138
White Rock, B.C., Can. . . . **E6** 85
White Russia see Belarus, ctry., Eur. **C9** 20
White Salmon, Wa., U.S. . . **D4** 140
White Salmon, stm., Wa., U.S. **D4** 140
White Sands Missile Range, mil., N.M., U.S. **E3** 124
White Sands National Monument, N.M., U.S. **E3** 124
Whitesboro, N.Y., U.S. . . . **B5** 125
Whitesboro, Tx., U.S. **C4** 136
Whitesburg, Ga., U.S. **C2** 103
Whitesburg, Ky., U.S. **C7** 110
Whites Creek, stm., Tn., U.S. **g10** 135
White Sea see Beloe more, Russia **C5** 26
Whiteside, co., Il., U.S. . . . **B3** 106
White Sulphur Springs, Mt., U.S. **D6** 119
White Sulphur Springs, W.V., U.S. **D4** 141
Whitesville, Ky., U.S. **C3** 110
White Swan, Wa., U.S. . . . **C5** 140
White Tank Mountains, mts., Az., U.S. **k7** 96
Whiteville, N.C., U.S. **C4** 126
Whiteville, Tn., U.S. **B2** 135
White Volta, stm., Afr. **E4** 50
Whitewater, Ks., U.S. **E6** 109
Whitewater, Wi., U.S. **F5** 142
Whitewater, stm., Ks., U.S. **E6** 109
Whitewater, stm., U.S. **F7** 107
Whitewater Baldy, mtn., N.M., U.S. **D1** 124
Whitewater Bay, b., Fl., U.S. **G6** 102
Whitewood, S.D., U.S. **C2** 134
Whitewright, Tx., U.S. **C4** 136
Whitfield, co., Ga., U.S. . . . **B2** 103
Whitfield Estates, Fl., U.S. **q10** 102
Whiting, Ia., U.S. **B1** 108
Whiting, In., U.S. **A3** 107
Whiting, Wi., U.S. **D4** 142
Whiting Field Naval Air Station, mil., Fl., U.S. **u14** 102
Whitinsville, Ma., U.S. **B4** 114
Whitley, co., In., U.S. **B6** 107
Whitley, co., Ky., U.S. **D5** 110
Whitley City, Ky., U.S. **D5** 110
Whitman, Ma., U.S. **B6** 114
Whitman, W.V., U.S. **D2** 141
Whitman, co., Wa., U.S. . . . **B8** 140
Whitman Square, N.J., U.S. **D2** 123
Whitmire, S.C., U.S. **B4** 133
Whitmore Lake, Mi., U.S. . **p14** 115
Whitmore Mountains, mts., Ant. **E31** 67
Whitmore Village, Hi., U.S. **f9** 104
Whitney, S.C., U.S. **B4** 133
Whitney, Tx., U.S. **D4** 136
Whitney, Lake, res., Tx., U.S. **D4** 136
Whitney, Mount, mtn., Ca., U.S. **D4** 98
Whitney Point Lake, res., N.Y., U.S. **C5** 125
Whitsunday Island, i., Austl. **E4** 62
Whittier, Ak., U.S. **C10** 95
Whittier, Ca., U.S. **F4** 98
Whitwell, Tn., U.S. **D8** 135
Whyalla, Austl. **G2** 62
Wiarton, On., Can. **C3** 89
Wibaux, Mt., U.S. **D12** 119
Wibaux, co., Mt., U.S. . . **D12** 119
Wichita, Ks., U.S. **E6** 109
Wichita, co., Ks., U.S. **D2** 109
Wichita, co., Tx., U.S. **B3** 136
Wichita Falls, Tx., U.S. . . . **C3** 136
Wichita Mountains, mts., Ok., U.S. **C3** 129
Wick, Scot., U.K. **A5** 12
Wickenburg, Az., U.S. **D3** 96
Wickham, Austl. **E2** 60
Wickham, Cape, c., Austl. **H3** 62
Wickiup Reservoir, res., Or., U.S. **E5** 130
Wickliffe, Ky., U.S. **f8** 110
Wickliffe, Oh., U.S. **A4** 128
Wicklow, Ire. **D3** 12
Wicomico, co., Md., U.S. . . **D6** 113
Wicomico, stm., Md., U.S. . **D6** 113
Wiconisco, Pa., U.S. **E8** 131
Widefield, Co., U.S. **C6** 99
Widgiemooltha, Austl. **G3** 60
Wieluń, Pol. **D5** 20
Wien, Aus. **F15** 12
Wiener Neustadt, Aus. . . **G15** 12
Wieprz, stm., Pol. **D7** 20
Wiesbaden, Ger. **E11** 12
Wiggins, Ms., U.S. **E4** 117
Wiggins Peak, mtn., Wy., U.S. **C3** 143
Wight, Isle of, i., Eng., U.K. **E6** 12
Wikwemikong, On., Can. **B3** 89
Wilbarger, co., Tx., U.S. . . . **B3** 136
Wilber, Ne., U.S. **D9** 120
Wilberforce, Oh., U.S. **C2** 128

Wilbraham, Ma., U.S. **B3** 114
Wilbur, Wa., U.S. **B7** 140
Wilburton, Ok., U.S. **C6** 129
Wilcannia, Austl. **G3** 62
Wilcox, Pa., U.S. **C4** 131
Wilcox, co., Al., U.S. **D2** 94
Wilcox, co., Ga., U.S. **E3** 103
Wild, stm., U.S. **B4** 122
Wild Ammonoosuc, stm., N.H., U.S. **B3** 122
Wild Branch, stm., Vt., U.S. **B4** 138
Wilder, Id., U.S. **F2** 105
Wilder, Vt., U.S. **D4** 138
Wilder Dam, stm., U.S. . . . **C2** 122
Wildhorse Creek, stm., Ok., U.S. **C4** 129
Wild Horse Reservoir, res., Nv., U.S. **B6** 121
Wild Rice, stm., Mn., U.S. . **C2** 116
Wild Rice, stm., N.D., U.S. **C8** 127
Wildwood, Fl., U.S. **D4** 102
Wildwood, N.J., U.S. **F3** 123
Wildwood Crest, N.J., U.S. **F3** 123
Wilhelm, Mount, mtn., Pap. N. Gui. **H12** 32
Wilhelmina Peak see Trikora, Puncak, mtn., Indon. **G10** 32
Wilhelmshaven, Ger. **D10** 12
Wilkes, co., Ga., U.S. **C4** 103
Wilkes, co., N.C., U.S. **A1** 126
Wilkes-Barre, Pa., U.S. . . **D10** 131
Wilkesboro, N.C., U.S. **A1** 126
Wilkes Land, reg., Ant. . . . **D16** 67
Wilkin, co., Mn., U.S. **D2** 116
Wilkinsburg, Pa., U.S. **F2** 131
Wilkinson, W.V., U.S. **D3** 141
Wilkinson, co., Ga., U.S. . . **D3** 103
Wilkinson, co., Ms., U.S. . . **D2** 117
Will, co., Il., U.S. **B6** 106
Willacoochee, Ga., U.S. . . . **E3** 103
Willacy, co., Tx., U.S. **F4** 136
Willamette, stm., Or., U.S. **C3** 130
Willamette Pass, Or., U.S. **D4** 130
Willamina, Or., U.S. **B3** 130
Willapa Bay, b., Wa., U.S. **C1** 140
Willard, Mo., U.S. **D4** 118
Willard, Oh., U.S. **A3** 128
Willard, Ut., U.S. **B3** 137
Willard Bay, b., Ut., U.S. . . **B3** 137
Willards, Md., U.S. **D7** 113
Willard Stream, stm., Vt., U.S. **B5** 138
Willcox, Az., U.S. **E6** 96
Willcox Playa, l., Az., U.S. **E5** 96
Willemstad, Neth. Ant. . . . **C6** 80
William Bill Dannelly Reservoir, res., Al., U.S. **C2** 94
Williams, Az., U.S. **B3** 96
Williams, Ca., U.S. **C2** 98
Williams, co., N.D., U.S. . . **A2** 127
Williams, co., Oh., U.S. . . . **A1** 128
Williams, stm., Vt., U.S. . . . **E3** 138
Williams, stm., W.V., U.S. . **C4** 141
Williams Bay, Wi., U.S. . . . **F5** 142
Williamsburg, Ia., U.S. . . . **C5** 108
Williamsburg, In., U.S. . . . **E8** 107
Williamsburg, Ky., U.S. . . . **D5** 110
Williamsburg, Oh., U.S. . . . **C1** 128
Williamsburg, Pa., U.S. . . . **F5** 131
Williamsburg, Va., U.S. . . . **C6** 139
Williamsburg, co., S.C., U.S. **D8** 133
Williams Fork, stm., Co., U.S. **A3** 99
Williams Lake, B.C., Can. . . **C6** 85
Williamson, N.Y., U.S. **B3** 125
Williamson, W.V., U.S. . . . **D2** 141
Williamson, co., Il., U.S. . . **F4** 106
Williamson, co., Tn., U.S. . . **B5** 135
Williamson, co., Tx., U.S. . . **D4** 136
Williamsport, In., U.S. **D3** 107
Williamsport, Md., U.S. . . . **A2** 113
Williamsport, Pa., U.S. . . . **D7** 131
Williamston, Mi., U.S. **F6** 115
Williamston, N.C., U.S. . . . **B5** 126
Williamston, S.C., U.S. . . . **B3** 133
Williamstown, Ky., U.S. . . . **B5** 110
Williamstown, Ma., U.S. . . **A1** 114
Williamstown, N.J., U.S. . . **D3** 123
Williamstown, Pa., U.S. . . . **E8** 131
Williamstown, Vt., U.S. . . . **C4** 138
Williamstown, W.V., U.S. . **B3** 141
Williamsville, Il., U.S. **D4** 106
Williamsville, N.Y., U.S. . . **C2** 125
Willimantic, Ct., U.S. **C7** 100
Willimantic, stm., Ct., U.S. **B6** 100
Willimantic Reservoir, res., Ct., U.S. **C7** 100
Willingboro, N.J., U.S. . . . **C3** 123
Willis, Tx., U.S. **D5** 136
Willis Group, is., Austl. . . . **D5** 62
Williston, S. Afr. **E3** 56
Williston, Fl., U.S. **C4** 102
Williston, N.D., U.S. **A2** 127
Williston, S.C., U.S. **E5** 133
Williston Lake, res., B.C., Can. **B6** 85
Willits, Ca., U.S. **C2** 98
Willmar, Mn., U.S. **E3** 116
Willoughby, Oh., U.S. **A4** 128
Willoughby, Lake, l., Vt., U.S. **B4** 138
Willoughby Hills, Oh., U.S. **A4** 128
Willow, Ak., U.S. **g17** 95

Willow Creek, stm., Nv., U.S. **E5** 121
Willow Creek, stm., Ut., U.S. **D6** 137
Willow Creek, stm., Wy., U.S. **C6** 143
Willow Grove Naval Air Station, mil., Pa., U.S. **F11** 131
Willowick, Oh., U.S. **A4** 128
Willowmore, S. Afr. **E3** 56
Willow Reservoir, res., Wi., U.S. **C3** 142
Willow Run, De., U.S. **i7** 101
Willow Run, Mi., U.S. . . . **p14** 115
Willows, Ca., U.S. **C2** 98
Willow Springs, Il., U.S. . . **k9** 106
Willow Springs, Mo., U.S. **E6** 118
Wilmar, Ar., U.S. **D4** 97
Wilmerding, Pa., U.S. . . . **k14** 131
Wilmette, Il., U.S. **A6** 106
Wilmington, De., U.S. **B3** 101
Wilmington, Il., U.S. **B5** 106
Wilmington, Ma., U.S. **A5** 114
Wilmington, N.C., U.S. . . . **C5** 126
Wilmington, Oh., U.S. **C2** 128
Wilmington, Vt., U.S. **F3** 138
Wilmington Manor, De., U.S. **i7** 101
Wilmore, Ky., U.S. **C5** 110
Wilmot, Ar., U.S. **D4** 97
Wilson, Ar., U.S. **B5** 97
Wilson, Ks., U.S. **D5** 109
Wilson, La., U.S. **D4** 111
Wilson, N.C., U.S. **B5** 126
Wilson, Ok., U.S. **C4** 129
Wilson, Pa., U.S. **E11** 131
Wilson, Wy., U.S. **C2** 143
Wilson, co., Ks., U.S. **E8** 109
Wilson, co., N.C., U.S. **B5** 126
Wilson, co., Tn., U.S. **A5** 135
Wilson, co., Tx., U.S. **E3** 136
Wilson, Mount, mtn., Az., U.S. **B1** 96
Wilson, Mount, mtn., Ca., U.S. **m12** 98
Wilson, Mount, mtn., Co., U.S. **D2** 99
Wilson, Mount, mtn., Nv., U.S. **E7** 121
Wilson, Mount, mtn., Or., U.S. **B5** 130
Wilson Creek, stm., Wa., U.S. **B5** 140
Wilson Creek, stm., Wa., U.S. **B6** 140
Wilson Lake, res., Al., U.S. **A2** 94
Wilson Lake, res., Ks., U.S. **D4** 109
Wilsons Beach, N.B., Can. . **E3** 87
Wilsons Promontory, pen., Austl. **H4** 62
Wilsonville, Al., U.S. **B3** 94
Wilsonville, Or., U.S. **h12** 130
Wilton, Al., U.S. **B3** 94
Wilton, Ct., U.S. **E2** 100
Wilton, Ia., U.S. **C6** 108
Wilton, Me., U.S. **D2** 112
Wilton, N.D., U.S. **B5** 127
Wilton, N.H., U.S. **E3** 122
Wiluna, Austl. **F3** 60
Wimauma, Fl., U.S. **E4** 102
Wimico, Lake, l., Fl., U.S. . . **C1** 102
Winamac, In., U.S. **B4** 107
Winburg, S. Afr. **D4** 56
Wincheck Pond, l., R.I., U.S. **E1** 132
Winchendon, Ma., U.S. . . . **A3** 114
Winchester, On., Can. **B9** 89
Winchester, Eng., U.K. . . . **E6** 12
Winchester, Il., U.S. **D3** 106
Winchester, In., U.S. **D8** 107
Winchester, Ks., U.S. . . . **k15** 109
Winchester, Ky., U.S. **C5** 110
Winchester, Ma., U.S. . . . **g11** 114
Winchester, N.H., U.S. . . . **E2** 122
Winchester, Nv., U.S. **G6** 121
Winchester, Oh., U.S. **D2** 128
Winchester, Tn., U.S. **B5** 135
Winchester, Va., U.S. **A4** 139
Winchester Bay, Or., U.S. **D2** 130
Wind, stm., Wa., U.S. **D4** 140
Wind, stm., Wy., U.S. **C4** 143
Windber, Pa., U.S. **F4** 131
Wind Cave National Park, S.D., U.S. **D2** 134
Winder, Ga., U.S. **C3** 103
Windfall, In., U.S. **D6** 107
Windgap, Pa., U.S. **E11** 131
Windham, Ct., U.S. **C7** 100
Windham, co., Ct., U.S. . . . **B7** 100
Windham, co., Vt., U.S. . . . **F3** 138
Windhoek, Nmb. **C2** 56
Wind Lake, Wi., U.S. **F5** 142
Wind Lake, l., Wi., U.S. . . **n11** 142
Windmill Point, c., Va., U.S. **C6** 139
Windom, Mn., U.S. **G3** 116
Windom Peak, mtn., Co., U.S. **D3** 99
Window Rock, Az., U.S. . . . **B6** 96
Wind Point, Wi., U.S. . . . **n12** 142
Wind River Indian Reservation, Wy., U.S. **C4** 143
Wind River Peak, mtn., Wy., U.S. **D3** 143

Wind River Range, mts., Wy., U.S. **C3** 143
Windsor (part of Grand Falls-Windsor), Nf., Can. **D4** 88
Windsor, On., Can. **E1** 89
Windsor, P.Q., Can. **D5** 90
Windsor, Co., U.S. **A6** 99
Windsor, Ct., U.S. **B5** 100
Windsor, Il., U.S. **D5** 106
Windsor, Mo., U.S. **C4** 118
Windsor, N.C., U.S. **A6** 126
Windsor, Pa., U.S. **G8** 131
Windsor, Va., U.S. **D6** 139
Windsor, Vt., U.S. **E4** 138
Windsor, co., Vt., U.S. **D3** 138
Windsor Heights, Ia., U.S. . **e8** 108
Windsor Locks, Ct., U.S. . . **B5** 100
Windward Islands, is., N.A. **F12** 76
Windward Passage, strt., N.A. **E10** 76
Windy Hill, S.C., U.S. **C8** 133
Windy Peak, mtn., Wa., U.S. **A6** 140
Winefred Lake, l., Ab., Can. **B5** 84
Winfield, Al., U.S. **B2** 94
Winfield, Ia., U.S. **C6** 108
Winfield, Ks., U.S. **E7** 109
Winfield, Mo., U.S. **C7** 118
Winfield, W.V., U.S. **C3** 141
Wing, stm., Mn., U.S. **D3** 116
Wingate, N.C., U.S. **C2** 126
Wingham, On., Can. **D3** 89
Winifrede, W.V., U.S. . . . **m12** 141
Winisk, stm., On., Can. . . **n18** 89
Wink, Tx., U.S. **D1** 136
Winkelman, Az., U.S. **E5** 96
Winkler, Mb., Can. **E3** 86
Winkler, co., Tx., U.S. **D1** 136
Winlock, Wa., U.S. **C3** 140
Winn, co., La., U.S. **C3** 111
Winneba, Ghana **E4** 50
Winnebago, Il., U.S. **A4** 106
Winnebago, Mn., U.S. **G4** 116
Winnebago, Ne., U.S. **B9** 120
Winnebago, Wi., U.S. **h8** 142
Winnebago, co., Ia., U.S. . . **A4** 108
Winnebago, co., Il., U.S. . . **A4** 106
Winnebago, co., Wi., U.S. . **D5** 142
Winnebago, stm., Ia., U.S. . **A4** 108
Winnebago, Lake, l., Wi., U.S. **E5** 142
Winnebago Indian Reservation, Ne., U.S. **B9** 120
Winneconne, Wi., U.S. . . . **D5** 142
Winnemucca, Nv., U.S. . . . **C4** 121
Winnemucca Lake, l., Nv., U.S. **C2** 121
Winner, S.D., U.S. **D6** 134
Winneshiek, co., Ia., U.S. . . **A6** 108
Winnetka, Il., U.S. **A6** 106
Winnfield, La., U.S. **C3** 111
Winnibigoshish, Lake, l., Mn., U.S. **C4** 116
Winnipeg, Mb., Can. **E3** 86
Winnipeg, stm., Can. **D4** 86
Winnipeg, Lake, l., Mb., Can. **C3** 86
Winnipeg Beach, Mb., Can. **D3** 86
Winnipegosis, Mb., Can. . . **D2** 86
Winnipegosis, Lake, l., Mb., Can. **C2** 86
Winnipesaukee, Lake, l., N.H., U.S. **C4** 122
Winnisquam, N.H., U.S. . . **C3** 122
Winnisquam Lake, l., N.H., U.S. **C3** 122
Winnsboro, La., U.S. **B4** 111
Winnsboro, S.C., U.S. **C5** 133
Winnsboro, Tx., U.S. **C5** 136
Winnsboro Mills, S.C., U.S. **C5** 133
Winona, Mn., U.S. **F7** 116
Winona, Mo., U.S. **D6** 118
Winona, Ms., U.S. **B4** 117
Winona, co., Mn., U.S. . . . **F7** 116
Winona Lake, In., U.S. . . . **B6** 107
Winona Lake, l., Vt., U.S. . . **C2** 138
Winooski, Vt., U.S. **C2** 138
Winooski, stm., Vt., U.S. . . **C3** 138
Winslow, Az., U.S. **C5** 96
Winslow, In., U.S. **H3** 107
Winslow, Me., U.S. **D3** 112
Winsted, Ct., U.S. **B3** 100
Winsted, Mn., U.S. **F4** 116
Winston, Fl., U.S. **D4** 102
Winston, Or., U.S. **D3** 130
Winston, co., Al., U.S. **A2** 94
Winston, co., Ms., U.S. . . . **B4** 117
Winston-Salem, N.C., U.S. **A2** 126
Winter Garden, Fl., U.S. . . **D5** 102
Winter Harbor, Me., U.S. . . **D4** 112
Winter Haven, Fl., U.S. . . . **D5** 102
Winter Park, Fl., U.S. **D5** 102
Winter Park, N.C., U.S. . . . **C5** 126
Winterport, Me., U.S. **D4** 112
Winter Ridge, mtn., Or., U.S. **E6** 130
Winters, Ca., U.S. **C2** 98
Winters, Tx., U.S. **D3** 136
Winterset, Ia., U.S. **C4** 108
Wintersville, Oh., U.S. **B5** 128
Winterthur, Switz. **G11** 12
Winterton, Nf., Can. **E5** 88
Winterville, Ga., U.S. **C3** 103
Winterville, N.C., U.S. **B5** 126

Name	Map Ref.	Page
Winthrop, Ia., U.S.	B6	108
Winthrop, Ma., U.S.	B6	114
Winthrop, Me., U.S.	D3	112
Winthrop, Mn., U.S.	F4	116
Winthrop, Lake, l., Ma., U.S.	h10	114
Winthrop Harbor, Il., U.S.	A6	106
Wintinna, Austl.	F5	60
Winton, Austl.	E3	62
Winton, N.Z.	q12	63c
Winton, N.C., U.S.	A6	126
Winton Lake, res., Oh., U.S.	o12	129
Winyah Bay, b., S.C., U.S.	E9	133
Wirt, co., W.V., U.S.	B3	141
Wiscasset, Me., U.S.	D3	112
Wisconsin, state, U.S.	D4	142
Wisconsin, stm., Wi., U.S.	E3	142
Wisconsin, Lake, res., Wi., U.S.	E4	142
Wisconsin Dells, Wi., U.S.	E4	142
Wisconsin Rapids, Wi., U.S.	D4	142
Wise, Va., U.S.	f9	139
Wise, co., Tx., U.S.	C4	136
Wise, co., Va., U.S.	e9	139
Wishek, N.D., U.S.	C6	127
Wishram, Wa., U.S.	D4	140
Wisła, stm., Pol.	C5	20
Wismar, Ger.	D12	12
Wisner, La., U.S.	C4	111
Wisner, Ne., U.S.	C9	120
Wissota, Lake, res., Wi., U.S.	D2	142
Wister, Ok., U.S.	C7	129
Wister Lake, res., Ok., U.S.	C7	129
Witbank, S. Afr.	D4	56
Withamsville, Oh., U.S.	C1	128
Witherspoon, Mount, mtn., Ak., U.S.	g18	95
Withlacoochee, stm., Fl., U.S.	C4	102
Withlacoochee, stm., U.S.	B3	102
Witless Bay, Nf., Can.	E5	88
Witt, Il., U.S.	D4	106
Wittenberg, Wi., U.S.	D4	142
Wittenberge, Ger.	D12	12
Wittenoom, Austl.	E2	60
Wittlich, Ger.	E10	12
Wittman, Md., U.S.	C5	113
Wittmann, Az., U.S.	D3	96
Witu Islands, is., Pap. N. Gui.	G12	32
Wixom, Mi., U.S.	o14	115
Wixom Lake, res., Mi., U.S.	E6	115
Włocławek, Pol.	C5	20
Woburn, Ma., U.S.	B5	114
Wodonga, Austl.	H4	62
Wokam, Pulau, i., Indon.	H9	32
Wolcott, Ct., U.S.	C4	100
Wolcott, In., U.S.	C3	107
Wolcottville, In., U.S.	A7	107
Woleai, atoll, Micron.	D8	58
Wolf, stm., Ms., U.S.	E4	117
Wolf, stm., Tn., U.S.	e9	135
Wolf, stm., Wi., U.S.	C5	142
Wolf, Volcán, vol., Ec.	C1	70
Wolf Creek, Or., U.S.	E3	130
Wolf Creek, stm., W.V., U.S.	m13	141
Wolf Creek, stm., U.S.	A2	129
Wolf Creek Pass, Co., U.S.	D3	99
Wolfe, co., Ky., U.S.	C6	110
Wolfeboro, N.H., U.S.	C4	122
Wolfeboro Falls, N.H., U.S.	C4	122
Wolfe City, Tx., U.S.	C4	136
Wolfen, Ger.	E13	12
Wolf Lake, Mi., U.S.	E4	115
Wolf Lake, l., Il., U.S.	k9	106
Wolf Mountain, mtn., Ak., U.S.	B9	95
Wolf Point, Mt., U.S.	B11	119
Wolfsberg, Aus.	G14	12
Wolfsburg, Ger.	D12	12
Wolf Swamp, sw., N.C., U.S.	C5	126
Wollaston, Islas, is., Chile	I3	69
Wollaston Lake, l., Sk., Can.	m8	91
Wollongong, Austl.	G5	62
Wolmaransstad, S. Afr.	D4	56
Wolverhampton, Eng., U.K.	D5	12
Woman Lake, l., Mn., U.S.	D4	116
Womelsdorf, Pa., U.S.	F9	131
Wonder Lake, Il., U.S.	A5	106
Wondinong, Austl.	F2	60
Wonewoc, Wi., U.S.	E3	142
Wŏnsan, N. Kor.	D13	28
Wonthaggi, Austl.	H4	62
Wood, co., Oh., U.S.	A2	128
Wood, co., Tx., U.S.	C5	136
Wood, co., W.V., U.S.	B3	141
Wood, co., Wi., U.S.	D3	142
Wood, stm., Sk., Can.	H2	91
Wood, stm., R.I., U.S.	F2	132
Wood, stm., Wy., U.S.	C3	143
Wood, Mount, mtn., Mt., U.S.	E7	119
Woodall Mountain, mtn., Ms., U.S.	A5	117
Woodbine, Ga., U.S.	F5	103
Woodbine, Ia., U.S.	C2	108
Woodbine, Ky., U.S.	D5	110
Woodbine, N.J., U.S.	E3	123
Woodbridge, Ct., U.S.	D3	100
Woodbridge, Va., U.S.	B5	139
Woodbridge [Township], N.J., U.S.	B4	123
Woodburn, In., U.S.	B8	107
Woodburn, Or., U.S.	B4	130
Woodbury, Ct., U.S.	C3	100
Woodbury, Ga., U.S.	D2	103
Woodbury, Mn., U.S.	F6	116
Woodbury, N.J., U.S.	D2	123
Woodbury, Tn., U.S.	B5	135
Woodbury, co., Ia., U.S.	B1	108
Woodcliff Lake, N.J., U.S.	g8	123
Woodcliff Lake, l., N.J., U.S.	g8	123
Wood Dale, Il., U.S.	k9	106
Wood End, spit, Ma., U.S.	B7	114
Woodfield, S.C., U.S.	C6	133
Woodford, co., Il., U.S.	C4	106
Woodford, co., Ky., U.S.	B5	110
Woodhull, Il., U.S.	B3	106
Woodlake, Ca., U.S.	D4	98
Woodland, Ca., U.S.	C3	98
Woodland, Me., U.S.	C5	112
Woodland, N.C., U.S.	A5	126
Woodland, Wa., U.S.	D3	140
Woodland Acres, Co., U.S.	D6	99
Woodland Park, Co., U.S.	C5	99
Woodlawn, Ky., U.S.	e9	110
Woodlawn, Md., U.S.	g10	113
Woodlawn, Oh., U.S.	n13	128
Woodlawn, Va., U.S.	D2	139
Woodmont, Ct., U.S.	E4	100
Woodmoor, Md., U.S.	B4	113
Woodridge, Il., U.S.	k8	106
Wood-Ridge, N.J., U.S.	h8	123
Wood River, Il., U.S.	E3	106
Wood River, Ne., U.S.	D7	120
Woodroffe, Mount, mtn., Austl.	F5	60
Woodruff, S.C., U.S.	B3	133
Woodruff, Wi., U.S.	C4	142
Woodruff, co., Ar., U.S.	B4	97
Woods, co., Ok., U.S.	A3	129
Woods, Lake, res., Tn., U.S.	B5	135
Woods, Lake of the, l., N.A.	B9	92
Woodsboro, Tx., U.S.	E4	136
Woods Cross, Ut., U.S.	C4	137
Woodsfield, Oh., U.S.	C4	128
Woods Hole, Ma., U.S.	C6	114
Woodson, Ar., U.S.	C3	97
Woodson, co., Ks., U.S.	E8	109
Woodstock, N.B., Can.	C2	87
Woodstock, On., Can.	D4	89
Woodstock, Ga., U.S.	B2	103
Woodstock, Il., U.S.	A5	106
Woodstock, Md., U.S.	B4	113
Woodstock, N.Y., U.S.	C6	125
Woodstock, Va., U.S.	B4	139
Woodstock, Vt., U.S.	D3	138
Woodstown, N.J., U.S.	D2	123
Woodsville, N.H., U.S.	B2	122
Woodville, Fl., U.S.	B2	102
Woodville, Ms., U.S.	D2	117
Woodville, Oh., U.S.	A2	128
Woodville, Tx., U.S.	D5	136
Woodville, Wi., U.S.	D1	142
Woodward, Ia., U.S.	C4	108
Woodward, Ok., U.S.	A2	129
Woodward, co., Ok., U.S.	A2	129
Woodworth, La., U.S.	C3	111
Woolmarket, Ms., U.S.	E5	117
Woolrich, Pa., U.S.	D7	131
Woolsey Peak, mtn., Az., U.S.	D3	96
Woomera, Austl.	G2	62
Woonsocket, R.I., U.S.	A3	132
Woonsocket, S.D., U.S.	C7	134
Woonsocket Reservoir Number Three, res., R.I., U.S.	B3	132
Wooster, Oh., U.S.	B4	128
Worcester, S. Afr.	E2	56
Worcester, Eng., U.K.	D5	12
Worcester, Ma., U.S.	B4	114
Worcester, co., Ma., U.S.	A3	114
Worcester, co., Md., U.S.	D7	113
Worden, Il., U.S.	E4	106
Worden Pond, l., R.I., U.S.	F3	132
Worland, Wy., U.S.	B5	143
Worms, Ger.	F11	12
Worth, Il., U.S.	k9	106
Worth, co., Ga., U.S.	E3	103
Worth, co., Ia., U.S.	A4	108
Worth, co., Mo., U.S.	A3	118
Worthing, Eng., U.K.	E6	12
Worthington, In., U.S.	F4	107
Worthington, Ky., U.S.	B7	110
Worthington, Mn., U.S.	G3	116
Worthington, Oh., U.S.	B2	128
Worthington Peak, mtn., Nv., U.S.	F6	121
Wosu, Indon.	D6	36
Wour, Chad	B8	50
Wowoni, Pulau, i., Indon.	D6	36
Woy Woy, Austl.	G5	62
Wrangel Island see Vrangelja, ostrov, i., Russia	B20	26
Wrangell, Ak., U.S.	D13	95
Wrangell, Cape, c., Ak., U.S.	E2	95
Wrangell, Mount, mtn., Ak., U.S.	f19	95
Wrangell Island, i., Ak., U.S.	m24	95
Wrangell Mountains, mts., Ak., U.S.	C11	95
Wrangell-Saint Elias National Park, Ak., U.S.	C11	95
Wrath, Cape, c., Scot., U.K.	A4	12
Wray, Co., U.S.	A8	99
Wrens, Ga., U.S.	C4	103
Wrentham, Ma., U.S.	B5	114
Wrexham, Wales, U.K.	D5	12
Wright, co., Ia., U.S.	B4	108
Wright, co., Mn., U.S.	E4	116
Wright, co., Mo., U.S.	D5	118
Wright, Mount, mtn., Mt., U.S.	C4	119
Wright City, Mo., U.S.	C8	118
Wright City, Ok., U.S.	C6	129
Wright Patman Lake, res., Tx., U.S.	A6	78
Wright-Patterson Air Force Base, mil., Oh., U.S.	C1	128
Wrightson, Mount, mtn., Az., U.S.	F5	96
Wrightstown, N.J., U.S.	C3	123
Wrightstown, Wi., U.S.	D5	142
Wrightsville, Ar., U.S.	C3	97
Wrightsville, Ga., U.S.	D4	103
Wrightsville, Pa., U.S.	F8	131
Wrightsville Beach, N.C., U.S.	C5	126
Wrightsville Reservoir, res., Vt., U.S.	C3	138
Wrocław, Pol.	D4	20
Wu, stm., China	F9	28
Wuchuan, China	E3	30
Wuchuan, China	A3	30
Wuda, China	B2	30
Wudaoliang, China	D6	28
Wudi, China	B4	30
Wuding, China	A4	34
Wudu, China	E8	28
Wugang, China	F10	28
Wuhai, China	D9	28
Wuhan, China	E10	28
Wuhe, China	C4	30
Wuhu, China	E11	28
Wüjang, China	E3	28
Wukari, Nig.	E6	50
Wuliang Shan, mts., China	G8	28
Wuming, China	B5	34
Wupatki National Monument, Az., U.S.	B4	96
Wuppertal, Ger.	E10	12
Wuqi, China	B2	30
Wuqing, China	B4	30
Wurno, Nig.	D6	50
Würzburg, Ger.	F12	12
Wushan, China	C2	30
Wushenqi, China	D9	28
Wusuli (Ussuri), stm., Asia	E15	26
Wutai Shan, mtn., China	D10	28
Wutongqiao, China	F8	28
Wuvulu Island, i., Pap. N. Gui.	G11	32
Wuwei, China	D8	28
Wuwei, China	C4	30
Wuxi, China	E12	28
Wuyi Shan, mts., China	F11	28
Wuyuan, China	C9	28
Wuzhi Shan, mtn., China	H9	28
Wuzhong, China	D9	28
Wuzhou, China	G10	28
Wyaconda, stm., Mo., U.S.	A6	118
Wyandot, co., Oh., U.S.	B2	128
Wyandotte, Mi., U.S.	F7	115
Wyandotte, co., Ks., U.S.	C9	109
Wyanet, Il., U.S.	B4	106
Wye, stm., U.K.	D5	12
Wylie, Lake, res., U.S.	A5	133
Wyman Lake, res., Me., U.S.	C3	112
Wymore, Ne., U.S.	D9	120
Wyndham, Austl.	D4	60
Wynndel, B.C., Can.	E9	85
Wynne, Ar., U.S.	B5	97
Wynnewood, Ok., U.S.	C4	129
Wynoochee, stm., Wa., U.S.	B2	140
Wyoming, On., Can.	E2	89
Wyoming, De., U.S.	D3	101
Wyoming, Ia., U.S.	B6	108
Wyoming, Il., U.S.	B4	106
Wyoming, Mi., U.S.	F5	115
Wyoming, Mn., U.S.	E6	116
Wyoming, Oh., U.S.	o13	128
Wyoming, Pa., U.S.	n17	131
Wyoming, R.I., U.S.	E2	132
Wyoming, co., N.Y., U.S.	C2	125
Wyoming, co., Pa., U.S.	D9	131
Wyoming, co., W.V., U.S.	D3	141
Wyoming, state, U.S.	C5	143
Wyoming Peak, mtn., Wy., U.S.	D2	143
Wyoming Range, mts., Wy., U.S.	D2	143
Wyomissing, Pa., U.S.	F10	131
Wyong, Austl.	G5	62
Wysocking Bay, b., N.C., U.S.	B7	126
Wythe, co., Va., U.S.	D1	139
Wytheville, Va., U.S.	D1	139
Xaafuun, Raas, c., Som.	H15	48
Xaçmaz, Azer.	B13	44
Xaidulla, China	D3	28
Xainza, China	E5	28
Xai-Xai, Moz.	D5	56
Xalapa, Mex.	D5	78
Xam Nua, Laos	B4	34
Xá-Muteba, Ang.	E3	54
Xangongo, Ang.	B2	56
Xankändi, Azer.	C12	44
Xánthi, Grc.	D10	18
Xanxerê, Braz.	D7	72
Xapuri, Braz.	F6	70
Xàtiva, Spain	H6	16
Xau, Lake, pl., Bots.	C3	56
Xenia, Oh., U.S.	C2	128
Xi, stm., China	G10	28
Xiachuan Dao, i., China	E3	30
Xiamen, China	G11	28
Xi'an, China	E9	28
Xianfeng, China	D2	30
Xiangfan, China	E10	28
Xianggang (Hong Kong), China	E3	30
Xiangkhoang, Laos	C4	34
Xiangride, China	D7	28
Xiangtan, China	F10	28
Xianju, China	D5	30
Xianning, China	D3	30
Xianyang, China	C2	30
Xianyou, China	F11	28
Xiaogan, China	E10	28
Xiao Hinggan Ling, mts., China	A1	31
Xiaojin, China	C1	30
Xiapu, China	F12	28
Xiayi, China	C4	30
Xichang, China	F8	28
Xigazê, China	F5	28
Ximiao, China	C8	28
Xin'anjiang Shuiku, res., China	D4	30
Xinavane, Moz.	C5	56
Xincai, China	C4	30
Xing'an, China	F10	28
Xingcheng, China	A5	30
Xinghe, China	A3	30
Xingren, China	D2	30
Xingtai, China	D10	28
Xingu, stm., Braz.	D9	70
Xingxian, China	B3	30
Xingyi, China	F8	28
Xinhua, China	D3	30
Xining, China	D8	28
Xinji, China	B4	30
Xinjiang Uygur Zizhiqu (Sinkiang), prov., China	C5	28
Xinjin, China	C1	30
Xinjin, China	B5	30
Xinjiulong (New Kowloon), China	E3	30
Xinning, China	D3	30
Xinwen, China	B4	30
Xinxian, China	B3	30
Xinxiang, China	D10	28
Xinyang, China	E10	28
Xique-Xique, Braz.	D3	74
Xisha Qundao (Paracel Islands), is., China	C6	34
Xiushan, China	D2	30
Xiushui, China	D3	30
Xixiang, China	C2	30
Xizang Zizhiqu (Tibet), prov., China	E5	28
Xuancheng, China	E11	28
Xuanhan, China	C2	30
Xuanhua, China	A4	30
Xuanwei, China	D1	30
Xuchang, China	E10	28
Xupu, China	D3	30
Xuwen, China	G10	28
Xuyong, China	F9	28
Xuzhou, China	E11	28
Yaan, China	E8	28
Yablonovy Range see Jablonovyj hrebet, mts., Russia	D13	26
Yabrīn, Sau. Ar.	F5	42
Yacolt, Wa., U.S.	D3	140
Yacuiba, Bol.	C5	72
Yādgīr, India	F3	40
Yadkin, co., N.C., U.S.	A2	126
Yadkin, stm., N.C., U.S.	B2	126
Yadkinville, N.C., U.S.	A2	126
Yadong, China	A1	34
Yafran, Libya	E6	14
Yagoua, Cam.	A3	54
Yagradagzê Shan, mtn., China	D7	28
Yahyalı, Tur.	C6	44
Yainax Butte, mtn., Or., U.S.	E5	130
Yakima, Wa., U.S.	C5	140
Yakima, co., Wa., U.S.	C4	140
Yakima, stm., Wa., U.S.	C6	140
Yakima Indian Reservation, Wa., U.S.	C5	140
Yako, Burkina	D4	50
Yakobi Island, i., Ak., U.S.	m21	95
Yakoma, D.R.C.	C4	54
Yakumo, Japan	B3	31
Yaku-shima, i., Japan	E14	28
Yakutat, Ak., U.S.	D12	95
Yakutat Bay, b., Ak., U.S.	D11	95
Yakutia see Jakutija, state, Russia	C14	26
Yakutsk see Jakutsk, Russia	C14	26
Yakymivka, Ukr.	F13	20
Yala, Thai.	E4	34
Yale, Mi., U.S.	E8	115
Yale, Ok., U.S.	A5	129
Yale, Mount, mtn., Co., U.S.	C5	99
Yale Lake, res., Wa., U.S.	D3	140
Yalgoo, Austl.	F2	60
Yalinga, C.A.R.	B4	54
Yalobusha, co., Ms., U.S.	A4	117
Yalobusha, stm., Ms., U.S.	B4	117
Yalong, stm., China	E7	28
Yalova, Tur.	B3	44
Yalta, Ukr.	G13	20
Yalu, stm., Asia	C13	28
Yalvaç, Tur.	C4	44
Yamachiche, P.Q., Can.	C5	90
Yamagata, Japan	D16	28
Yamaguchi, Japan	D2	31
Yamal Peninsula see Jamal, poluostrov, pen., Russia	B8	26
Yambio, Sudan	J10	48
Yamdena, Pulau, i., Indon.	E8	36
Yamethin, Myan.	B3	34
Yamhill, Or., U.S.	h11	130
Yamhill, co., Or., U.S.	B3	130
Yamoussoukro, C. Iv.	E3	50
Yampa, stm., Co., U.S.	A2	99
Yampil', Ukr.	E10	20
Yamsay Mountain, mtn., Or., U.S.	E5	130
Yamuna, stm., India	D4	40
Yamunānagar, India	C3	40
Yamzho Yumco, l., China	F6	28
Yana see Jana, stm., Russia	C15	26
Yanam, India	F4	40
Yan'an, China	D9	28
Yanbu' al-Baḥr, Sau. Ar.	F3	38
Yancey, co., N.C., U.S.	f10	126
Yanceyville, N.C., U.S.	A3	126
Yancheng, China	E12	28
Yanchi, China	D9	28
Yanfolila, Mali	D3	50
Yangambi, D.R.C.	C4	54
Yangchun, China	E3	30
Yanggao, China	A3	30
Yangjiang, China	G10	28
Yangliuqing, China	B4	30
Yangon (Rangoon), Myan.	C3	34
Yangquan, China	D10	28
Yangshan, China	E3	30
Yangshuo, China	E3	30
Yangtze see Chang, stm., China	E9	28
Yangxian, China	C2	30
Yangxin, China	D4	30
Yangzhou, China	E11	28
Yanji, China	C13	28
Yankton, S.D., U.S.	E8	134
Yankton, co., S.D., U.S.	D8	134
Yanqi, China	C5	28
Yantai, China	D12	28
Yantic, stm., Ct., U.S.	C7	100
Yanting, China	C2	30
Yanyuan, China	A4	34
Yanzhou, China	B4	30
Yaoundé, Cam.	C2	54
Yap, i., Micron.	E10	32
Yapen, Pulau, i., Indon.	G10	32
Yaqui, stm., Mex.	B3	78
Yardley, Pa., U.S.	F12	131
Yardville, N.J., U.S.	C3	123
Yarīm, Yemen	H4	38
Yarkand see Shache, China	D3	28
Yarkand see Yarkant, stm., China	B3	40
Yarkant, stm., China	B3	40
Yarloop, Austl.	G2	60
Yarmouth, Me., U.S.	E2	112
Yarnell, Az., U.S.	C3	96
Yaroslavl' see Jaroslavl', Russia	D6	26
Yarumal, Col.	B4	70
Yass, Austl.	G4	62
Yatağan, Tur.	D3	44
Yaté, N. Cal.	I9	62a
Yates, co., N.Y., U.S.	C3	125
Yates Center, Ks., U.S.	E8	109
Yates City, Il., U.S.	C3	106
Yatsushiro, Japan	E14	28
Yatta Plateau, plat., Kenya	D7	54
Yavapai, co., Az., U.S.	C3	96
Yavari (Javari), stm., S.A.	D5	70
Yavatmāl, India	E3	40
Yaví, Cerro, mtn., Ven.	B6	70
Yawgoog Pond, l., R.I., U.S.	E1	132
Yazd, Iran	D6	42
Yazoo, co., Ms., U.S.	C3	117
Yazoo, stm., Ms., U.S.	C3	117
Yazoo City, Ms., U.S.	C3	117
Ye, Myan.	C3	34
Yeadon, Pa., U.S.	p21	131
Yeagertown, Pa., U.S.	E6	131
Yecheng, China	D3	28
Yecla, Spain	H6	16
Yeeda, Austl.	D3	60
Yei, Sudan	C6	54
Yélimané, Mali	C2	50
Yell, co., Ar., U.S.	B2	97
Yellow see Huang, stm., China	D11	28
Yellow, stm., In., U.S.	B4	107
Yellow, stm., Wi., U.S.	C3	142

Name	Map Ref.	Page

Yellow, stm., Wi., U.S. **D3** 142
Yellow, stm., U.S. **u15** 102
Yellow Creek, stm., Tn.,
U.S. **A4** 135
Yellowhead Pass, Can. **C1** 84
Yellowjacket Mountains,
mts., Id., U.S. **D4** 105
Yellowknife, N.T., Can. . . . **F17** 82
Yellow Lake, l., Wi., U.S. . . **C1** 142
Yellow Medicine, co., Mn.,
U.S. **F2** 116
Yellow Sea, Asia **D12** 28
Yellow Springs, Oh., U.S. . . **C2** 128
Yellowstone, co., Mt., U.S. . **B3** 40
Yellowstone, stm., U.S. . . **D10** 119
Yellowstone Lake, l., Wy.,
U.S. **B2** 143
Yellowstone National Park,
co., Mt., U.S. **E6** 119
Yellowstone National Park,
U.S. **B2** 143
Yellville, Ar., U.S. **A3** 97
Yelm, Wa., U.S. **C3** 140
Yemassee, S.C., U.S. **F6** 133
Yemen, ctry., Asia **G5** 38
Yenagoa, Nig. **F6** 50
Yenakiieve, Ukr. **E15** 20
Yenangyaung, Myan. **B2** 34
Yen Bai, Viet. **B4** 34
Yendéré, Burkina **D4** 50
Yendi, Ghana **E4** 50
Yengisar, China **D3** 28
Yenice, stm., Tur. **B5** 44
Yenişehir, Tur. **B3** 44
Yenisey see Enisej, stm.,
Russia **C10** 26
Yentna, stm., Ak., U.S. . . . **f16** 95
Yerevan, Arm. **B11** 44
Yerington, Nv., U.S. **E2** 121
Yerington Indian
Reservation, Nv., U.S. . **D2** 121
Yerköy, Tur. **C6** 44
Yermo, Ca., U.S. **E5** 98
Yerupaja, Nevado, mtn.,
Peru **F4** 70
Yerushalayim, Isr. **D3** 42
Yeşilhisar, Tur. **C6** 44
Yetti, reg., Afr. **A3** 50
Yeu, Île d', i., Fr. **D5** 16
Yevpatoriia, Ukr. **G12** 20
Ygatimí, Para. **C6** 72
Yi'an, China **B13** 28
Yibin, China **F8** 28
Yichang, China **E10** 28
Yichuan, China **B3** 30
Yichun, China **B13** 28
Yichun, China **D3** 30
Yidu, China **B4** 30
Yidu, China **C3** 30
Yilan, China **B13** 28
Yıldızeli, Tur. **C7** 44
Yiliang, China **G8** 28
Yinchuan, China **D9** 28
Yingde, China **E3** 30
Yingkou, China **C12** 28
Yingtan, China **F11** 28
Yining, China **C4** 28
Yinmabin, Myan. **B2** 34
Yirga 'Alem, Eth. **B7** 54
Yirol, Sudan **B6** 54
Yishan, China **E2** 30
Yitulihe, China **A12** 28
Yiyang, China **F10** 28
Yiyang, China **D4** 30
Yizhang, China **D3** 30
Yli-Kitka, l., Fin. **C13** 10
Yoakum, Tx., U.S. **E4** 136
Yoakum, co., Tx., U.S. . . . **C1** 136
Yockanookany, stm., Ms.,
U.S. **C4** 117
Yocona, stm., Ms., U.S. . . . **A4** 117
Yogyakarta, Indon. **E4** 36
Yoho National Park, B.C.,
Can. **D9** 85
Yokadouma, Cam. **C2** 54
Yoko, Cam. **B2** 54
Yokohama, Japan **D15** 28
Yokosuka, Japan **C3** 31
Yokote, Japan **C4** 31
Yola, Nig. **E7** 50
Yolo, co., Ca., U.S. **C2** 98
Yom, stm., Thai. **C3** 34
Yomba Indian Reservation,
Nv., U.S. **D4** 121
Yonago, Japan **D14** 28
Yoncalla, Or., U.S. **D3** 130
Yonezawa, Japan **C3** 31
Yong'an, China **F11** 28

Yongchang, China **B1** 30
Yongchuan, China **D2** 30
Yongding, China **E4** 30
Yongfeng, China **A7** 34
Yongkang, China **D5** 30
Yongping, China **A3** 34
Yongren, China **F8** 28
Yongshan, China **F8** 28
Yongxiu, China **D4** 30
Yongzhou, China **F10** 28
Yonkers, N.Y., U.S. **E7** 125
Yonne, stm., Fr. **C8** 16
Yopal, Col. **D5** 80
Yopurga, China **B3** 40
York, Austl. **G2** 60
York, On., Can. **D5** 89
York, Eng., U.K. **C6** 12
York, Al., U.S. **C1** 94
York, Me., U.S. **E2** 112
York, Ne., U.S. **D8** 120
York, Pa., U.S. **G8** 131
York, S.C., U.S. **B5** 133
York, co., Me., U.S. **E2** 112
York, co., Ne., U.S. **D8** 120
York, co., Pa., U.S. **G8** 131
York, co., S.C., U.S. **A5** 133
York, co., Va., U.S. **C6** 139
York, stm., On., Can. **B7** 89
York, stm., Va., U.S. **C6** 139
York, Cape, c., Austl. **C3** 62
York, Kap, c., Grnld. **C26** 82
York Beach, Me., U.S. **E2** 112
Yorke Peninsula, pen.,
Austl. **G2** 62
York Harbor, Me., U.S. . . . **E2** 112
Yorklyn, De., U.S. **A3** 101
Yorktown, In., U.S. **D7** 107
Yorktown, Tx., U.S. **E4** 136
Yorktown, Va., U.S. **C6** 139
Yorktown Manor, R.I., U.S. **E4** 132
Yorkville, Il., U.S. **B5** 106
Yorkville, N.Y., U.S. **B5** 125
Yorkville, Oh., U.S. **B5** 128
Yoro, Hond. **B2** 80
Yoron-jima, i., Japan **g6** 31a
Yosemite National Park,
Ca., U.S. **D4** 98
Yos Sudarso, Pulau, i.,
Indon. **H10** 32
Yotaú, Bol. **B5** 72
You, stm., China **G9** 28
Youbou, B.C., Can. **g11** 85
Youghiogheny, stm., U.S. . . **F2** 131
Youghiogheny River Lake,
res., U.S. **G3** 131
Young, Austl. **G4** 62
Young, Az., U.S. **C5** 96
Young, co., Tx., U.S. **C3** 136
Young Harris, Ga., U.S. . . . **B3** 103
Youngs, Lake, l., Wa., U.S. **f11** 140
Youngstown, N.Y., U.S. . . . **B1** 125
Youngstown, Oh., U.S. . . . **A5** 128
Youngsville, La., U.S. **D3** 111
Youngsville, Pa., U.S. **C3** 131
Youngtown, Az., U.S. **k8** 96
Youngwood, Pa., U.S. **F2** 131
Youxian, China **D3** 30
Youyang, China **F9** 28
Yozgat, Tur. **C6** 44
Ypacaraí, Para. **D6** 72
Ypsilanti, Mi., U.S. **F7** 115
Yreka, Ca., U.S. **B2** 98
Ystad, Swe. **I5** 10
Yuanling, China **F10** 28
Yuanmou, China **F8** 28
Yuba, co., Ca., U.S. **C3** 98
Yuba, stm., Ca., U.S. **C3** 98
Yuba City, Ca., U.S. **C3** 98
Yūbari, Japan **C16** 28
Yucatán, state, Mex. **C7** 78
Yucatan Channel, strt., N.A. **A2** 80
Yucatan Peninsula, pen.,
N.A. **B2** 80
Yucca Lake, l., Nv., U.S. . . **F5** 121
Yucca Mountain, mtn., Nv.,
U.S. **G5** 121
Yucheng, China **B4** 30
Yudu, China **D4** 30
Yueqing, China **D5** 30
Yuexi, China **A4** 34
Yueyang, China **F10** 28
Yugoslavia, ctry., Eur. **C8** 18
Yukon, Ok., U.S. **B4** 129
Yukon, ter., Can. **F12** 82
Yukon, stm., N.A. **F7** 82
Yulee, Fl., U.S. **B5** 102
Yulin, China **D9** 28
Yulin, China **G10** 28

Yuma, Az., U.S. **E1** 96
Yuma, Co., U.S. **A8** 99
Yuma, co., Az., U.S. **E1** 96
Yuma, co., Co., U.S. **A8** 99
Yuma Marine Corps Air
Station, mil., Az., U.S. . **E1** 96
Yumbi, D.R.C. **D3** 54
Yumbo, Col. **E4** 80
Yumen, China **D7** 28
Yuncheng, China **D10** 28
Yunnan, state, China **G8** 28
Yunxian, China **E10** 28
Yunxiao, China **E4** 30
Yunyang, China **C2** 30
Yurimaguas, Peru **E4** 70
Yuruá see Juruá, stm., S.A. **E6** 70
Yushan, China **D4** 30
Yü Shan, mtn., Tai. **E5** 30
Yushu, China **E7** 28
Yutan, Ne., U.S. **C9** 120
Yutian, China **D4** 28
Yuyao, China **C5** 30
Yvetot, Fr. **C7** 16

Z

Žabasak, Kaz. **D11** 22
Zabīd, Yemen **H4** 38
Zābol, Iran **D8** 42
Zacapa, Guat. **B2** 80
Zacapu, Mex. **D4** 78
Zacatecas, Mex. **C4** 78
Zacatecas, state, Mex. . . . **C4** 78
Zachary, La., U.S. **D4** 111
Zadar, Cro. **B5** 18
Zadoi, China **C7** 40
Zadonsk, Russia **C15** 20
Zafer Burnu, c., N. Cyp. . . . **E6** 44
Zafra, Spain **H3** 16
Zagazig, Egypt **E10** 14
Zagora, Mor. **E2** 14
Zagreb, Cro. **B5** 18
Zāgros, Kūhhā-ye (Zagros
Mountains), mts., Iran . **D6** 42
Zagros Mountains see
Zāgros, Kūhhā-ye, mts.,
Iran **D6** 42
Zāhedān, Iran **E8** 42
Zahīrābād, India **F3** 40
Zaḥlah, Leb. **F6** 44
Zaire see Congo,
Democratic Republic of
the, ctry., Afr. **D4** 54
Zaïre see Congo, stm., Afr. **D2** 54
Zaječar, Yugo. **C9** 18
Zajsan, Kaz. **E10** 26
Zajsan, ozero, l., Kaz. . . . **E10** 26
Zakamensk, Russia **D12** 26
Zakho, Iraq **D10** 44
Zákinthos, Grc. **F8** 18
Zákinthos, i., Grc. **F8** 18
Zakopane, Pol. **E6** 20
Zakouma, Chad **A3** 54
Zalaegerszeg, Hung. **F4** 20
Zalău, Rom. **F7** 20
Zalishchyky, Ukr. **E8** 20
Zamanti, stm., Tur. **D6** 44
Zambeze (Zambezi), stm.,
Afr. **A3** 56
Zambezi, Zam. **A3** 56
Zambezi (Zambeze), stm.,
Afr. **B5** 56
Zambia, ctry., Afr. **E5** 52
Zamboanga, Phil. **E8** 34
Zamboanga Peninsula, pen.,
Phil. **E8** 34
Zambrów, Pol. **C7** 20
Zâmbuè, Moz. **B5** 56
Žambyl, Kaz. **E9** 26
Zamora, Spain **G4** 16
Zamora de Hidalgo, Mex. . **D4** 78
Zamość, Pol. **D7** 20
Zanaga, Congo **D2** 54
Žanatas, Kaz. **B9** 42
Zanesville, Oh., U.S. **C4** 128
Zanjān, Iran **C5** 42
Zante see Zákinthos, i., Grc. **F8** 18
Zanthus, Austl. **G3** 60
Zanzibar, Tan. **E7** 54
Zanzibar, i., Tan. **E7** 54
Zanzibar Channel, strt., Tan. **E7** 54
Zaozhuang, China **C4** 30
Zapadno-Sibirskaja ravnina,
pl., Russia **C9** 26
Zapadnyj Sajan, mts., Russia **D11** 26
Zapala, Arg. **E2** 69

Zapata, Tx., U.S. **F3** 136
Zapata, co., Tx., U.S. **F3** 136
Zapopan, Mex. **C4** 78
Zaporizhzhia, Ukr. **F13** 20
Zaqatala, Azer. **B12** 44
Zara, Tur. **C7** 44
Zaragoza, Spain **G6** 16
Zarajsk, Russia **B15** 20
Zaranj, Afg. **D8** 42
Zarasai, Lith. **I12** 10
Zárate, Arg. **E6** 72
Zarembo Island, i., Ak., U.S. **m23** 95
Zarghūn Shahr, Afg. **D9** 42
Zaria, Nig. **D6** 50
Žarkamys, Kaz. **E10** 22
Žarma, Kaz. **B4** 28
Žary, Pol. **D3** 20
Zāskār Mountains, mts.,
Asia **C3** 40
Zavala, co., Tx., U.S. **E3** 136
Zave, Zimb. **B5** 56
Zavitinsk, Russia **A13** 28
Zawiercie, Pol. **D5** 20
Zāwiyat Masūs, Libya **E8** 14
Zaysan, Lake see Zajsan,
ozero, l., Kaz. **E10** 26
Zdolbuniv, Ukr. **D9** 20
Zduńska Wola, Pol. **D5** 20
Zearing, Ia., U.S. **B4** 108
Zebulon, Ga., U.S. **C2** 103
Zebulon, N.C., U.S. **B4** 126
Zeehan, Austl. **I4** 62
Zeeland, Mi., U.S. **F5** 115
Zeerust, S. Afr. **D4** 56
Zeigler, Il., U.S. **F4** 106
Zeja, Russia **D14** 26
Zeja, stm., Russia **D14** 26
Zejskoe vodohranilišče, res.,
Russia **D14** 26
Zelenogorsk, Russia **F13** 10
Zelenokumsk, Russia **B4** 42
Železnodorožnyj, Russia . . **B9** 22
Železnogorsk, Russia **C13** 20
Železnogorsk-Ilimskij, Russia **D12** 26
Zelienople, Pa., U.S. **E1** 131
Zell am See, Aus. **G13** 12
Zémio, C.A.R. **B5** 54
Zenica, Bos. **B6** 18
Zenith, Wa., U.S. **f11** 140
Zenobia Peak, mtn., Co.,
U.S. **A2** 99
Zenza do Itombe, Ang. . . . **E2** 54
Zephyr Cove, Nv., U.S. . . . **E2** 121
Zephyrhills, Fl., U.S. **D4** 102
Žerdevka, Russia **D7** 22
Zestafoni, Geor. **A10** 44
Zeya see Zeja, stm., Russia **D14** 26
Zeya Reservoir see Zejskoe
vodohranilišče, res.,
Russia **D14** 26
Žezkazgan, Kaz. **E8** 26
Zgierz, Pol. **D5** 20
Zhangjiakou, China **C10** 28
Zhangping, China **F11** 28
Zhangpu, China **E4** 30
Zhangye, China **D8** 28
Zhangzhou, China **G11** 28
Zhanhua, China **B4** 30
Zhanjiang, China **G10** 28
Zhao'an, China **G11** 28
Zhaojue, China **D1** 30
Zhaoqing, China **G10** 28
Zhaotong, China **F8** 28
Zhashkiv, Ukr. **E11** 20
Zhaxigang, China **E3** 28
Zhdanov see Mariupol',
Ukr. **F14** 20
Zhejiang, state, China . . . **F11** 28
Zhenghe, China **D4** 30
Zhenglan Qi, China **A4** 30
Zhengzhou, China **D10** 28
Zhenjiang, China **C4** 30
Zhenning, China **D2** 30
Zhenping, China **E10** 28
Zhenxiong, China **D1** 30
Zhenyuan, China **F9** 28
Zhidoi, China **C6** 40
Zhijiang, China **D2** 30
Zhmerynka, Ukr. **E10** 20
Zhob, Pak. **D9** 42
Zhob, stm., Pak. **D9** 42
Zhongba, China **E4** 28
Zhongdian, China **F7** 28
Zhongning, China **D9** 28
Zhongshan, China **B6** 34

Zhongwei, China **B2** 30
Zhongxian, China **C2** 30
Zhongxiang, China **E10** 28
Zhoushan Qundao, is.,
China **E12** 28
Zhovtneve, Ukr. **F12** 20
Zhuanghe, China **B5** 30
Zhucheng, China **B4** 30
Zhumadian, China **C3** 30
Zhuolu, China **A4** 30
Zhuozhou, China **D11** 28
Zhushan, China **E10** 28
Zhuzhou, China **F10** 28
Zhytomyr, Ukr. **D10** 20
Zia Indian Reservation,
N.M., U.S. **h7** 124
Zibo, China **D11** 28
Ziebach, co., S.D., U.S. . . **C4** 134
Zielona Góra, Pol. **D3** 20
Žigalovo, Russia **D12** 26
Žigansk, Russia **C14** 26
Zigong, China **F8** 28
Ziguinchor, Sen. **D1** 50
Zihuatanejo, Mex. **D4** 78
Zile, Tur. **B6** 44
Žilina, Slvk. **E5** 20
Zillah, Libya **I8** 48
Zillah, Wa., U.S. **C5** 140
Zilwaukee, Mi., U.S. **E7** 115
Zima, Russia **D12** 26
Zimbabwe, ctry., Afr. **B4** 56
Zimi, S.L. **H2** 50
Zimmerman, Mn., U.S. . . . **E5** 116
Zinder, Niger **D6** 50
Zion, Il., U.S. **A6** 106
Zion National Park, Ut.,
U.S. **F3** 137
Zion Reservoir, res., Az.,
U.S. **C6** 96
Zionsville, In., U.S. **E5** 107
Zipaquirá, Col. **D5** 80
Zirkel, Mount, mtn., Co.,
U.S. **A4** 99
Zitong, China **C2** 30
Zittau, Ger. **E14** 12
Zitundo, Moz. **D5** 56
Ziway Hāyk', l., Eth. **B7** 54
Ziyun, China **D2** 30
Zlatoust, Russia **D7** 26
Zlītan, Libya **D7** 48
Žlobin, Bela. **C11** 20
Złotów, Pol. **C4** 20
Zmeinogorsk, Russia **A4** 28
Znam'ianka, Ukr. **E12** 20
Znojmo, Czech Rep. **E4** 20
Žodzina, Bela. **B10** 20
Zolfo Springs, Fl., U.S. . . . **E5** 102
Zomba, Mwi. **B6** 56
Zonguldak, Tur. **B4** 44
Zouar, Chad **B8** 50
Zouérat, Maur. **B2** 50
Zrenjanin, Yugo. **B8** 18
Žuantobe, Kaz. **B9** 42
Zug, Switz. **A2** 18
Zugdidi, Geor. **A9** 44
Zugspitze, mtn., Eur. . . . **G12** 12
Žukovka, Russia **C12** 20
Zumbo, Moz. **B5** 56
Zumbro, stm., Mn., U.S. . . **F6** 116
Zumbrota, Mn., U.S. **F6** 116
Zuni (Zuni Pueblo), N.M.,
U.S. **B1** 124
Zuni, stm., U.S. **C6** 96
Zuni Indian Reservation,
N.M., U.S. **B1** 124
Zuni Mountains, mts., N.M.,
U.S. **B1** 124
Zunyi, China **F9** 28
Zūrābād, Iran **C11** 44
Zurich, On., Can. **D3** 89
Zürich, Switz. **A2** 18
Zurich, Lake see Zürichsee,
l., Switz. **A2** 18
Zürichsee, l., Switz. **A2** 18
Zuru, Nig. **D6** 50
Zuwārah, Libya **E6** 14
Zvishavane, Zimb. **C4** 56
Zvolen, Slvk. **E5** 20
Zwedru, Lib. **E3** 50
Zwickau, Ger. **E13** 12
Zwolle, La., U.S. **C2** 111
Zwolle, Neth. **D10** 12
Żyrardów, Pol. **C6** 20
Žyrjanka, Russia **C17** 26
Zyrjanovsk, Kaz. **E10** 26
Żywiec, Pol. **E5** 20